해커스토익 READING

KB086760

200% 활용법

토익 한 번에 끝내는 해커스만의 학습자료

TIP 해커스 토익 교재에 수록된 QR코드로 더 빠르게 연결하고 편리하게 공부해보세요!

무료 온라인 실전모의고사 이용 방법

방법 해커스토익(Hackers.co.kr) 접속 ▶ 상단 메뉴의 [교재/무료MP3] 클릭 → [토익] 클릭 ▶ 해커스 토익 READING 교재 클릭 ▶ [온라인 모의고사] 클릭하여 이용하기

무료 문법&어휘 인강 이용 방법

방법1 해커스토익(Hackers.co.kr) 접속 ▶ 상단 메뉴의 [교재/무료MP3] 클릭 → [토익] 클릭 ▶ 해커스 토익 READING 교재 클릭 ▶ [무료강의] 클릭하여 이용하기

방법2 해커스토익 어플 다운로드 및 실행 ▶ 상단의 [교재/MP3] 클릭 ▶ 본 교재의 [무료강의] 클릭하여 보기

동영상강의 바로 듣기 ▶

무료 단어암기 MP3 이용 방법

방법 해커스인강(HackersIngang.com) 접속 ▶ 상단 메뉴의 [MP3/자료 → 무료 MP3/자료] 클릭 ▶ 본 교재의 [단어암기 MP3] 이용하기

MP3/자료 바로 가기 ▶

무료 진단고사 해설강의 이용 방법

방법 해커스인강(HackersIngang.com) 접속 ▶ 상단 메뉴의 [무료강의] 클릭 ▶ 상단의 [진단고사 해설강의] 클릭하여 보기

진단고사 해설강의 바로 듣기 ▶

토익 READING 최신 출제 경향 한눈에 보기

토익 READING 최신 출제 경향을 분석한 결과, 정답을 선택하기 까다로운 문제들이 출제되며, 지문의 내용을 신속하고 정확하게 파악해야 하는 등 다소 어려운 문제들이 출제되고 있다.

《해커스 토익 READING》은 이러한 경향을 반영하여, 까다로운 문법/어휘 포인트에 대한 상세한 설명을 제공하고, 지문의 내용을 신속하게 파악하여 문제의 정답을 정확히 골라낼 수 있는 전략과 풍부한 실전 문제를 수록하고 있다.

최신 출제 경향 요약

1. 까다롭게 출제되는 Part 5&6 문법/어휘 문제
2. 지문의 문맥을 정확히 파악해야 하는 Part 6
3. 지문의 내용을 신속하고 정확하게 파악해야 하는 Part 7

Part 5&6 최신 출제 경향

1. 까다롭게 출제되는 Part 5&6 문법/어휘 문제

문법

<가정법 도치>, <부정대명사/부정형용사>, <명사절 접속사>와 같은 까다로운 문법 포인트가 출제되고 있다.

가정법 도치 p.98, 토익실전문제 1번	Had the materials ------- on time, the company might have fulfilled the customer's request for a rush order. (A) order　　　(B) ordered　　　(C) been ordered　　　(D) were ordered
부정대명사/ 부정형용사 p.145, 토익실전문제 3번	The project approval committee received 40 proposals, ------- of which were related to the transmission of electricity to rural areas. (A) most　　　(B) the most　　　(C) any　　　(D) almost
명사절 접속사 p.211, 토익실전문제 3번	The committee will have a discussion about ------- to allocate funds for an online marketing campaign. (A) if　　　(B) that　　　(C) whether　　　(D) which

어휘

비슷한 의미를 가진 어휘들의 쓰임을 정확히 구별해야 정답을 고를 수 있는 문제가 출제되고 있다.

비슷한 의미를 가진 두 단어의 쓰임을 구별해야 하는 문제 p.322, Hackers Test 8번	The goal of the new public relations campaign is the ------- of the company's reputation. (A) increment　　　(B) comparison　　　(C) disruption　　　(D) enhancement

---

《해커스 토익 READING》으로 토익 Part 5&6 완벽 대비!

1) 까다로운 문법 포인트 설명 수록!
   [참고] 가정법 도치(p.98), 부정대명사/부정형용사(p.144-145), 명사절 접속사(p.210-213)

2) 의미가 비슷하지만 쓰임이 다른 어휘 리스트 및 예문 수록!
   [참고] 유사의미 핵심 단어 리스트(p.313-315, 319-321 등)

2. 지문의 문맥을 정확히 파악해야 하는 Part 6

Part 6에서는 빈칸이 있는 문장뿐만 아니라 빈칸 문장의 주변 또는 지문 전체 문맥까지 파악해야 정답을 고를 수 있는 문제가 출제되고 있다.

| 주로 출제되는 빈칸 문장 주변 또는 지문 전체 문맥까지 파악해야 하는 문제 유형 |

1) 빈칸이 있는 문장과 앞뒤 문장의 관계를 파악하여 알맞은 **접속부사**를 고르는 문제
2) 지문 앞부분의 내용을 바탕으로 빈칸에 들어갈 알맞은 **대명사**를 고르는 문제
3) 지문 전체의 문맥을 파악하여 알맞은 **시제**를 고르는 문제
4) 지문 전체의 문맥을 파악하여 알맞은 **어휘**를 고르는 문제
5) 지문 전체의 문맥을 파악하여 흐름상 빈칸에 들어갈 알맞은 **문장**을 고르는 문제

| 빈칸 문장 주변 또는 지문 전체 문맥까지 파악해야 하는 문제 평균 출제 비율 |

| 빈칸 문장 내에 정답의 단서가 있는 문법·어휘 문제 (5문제) | 빈칸 문장 주변 또는 지문 전체 문맥까지 파악해야 하는 문법·어휘 문제 (7문제) | 빈칸 문장 주변 또는 지문 전체 문맥까지 파악해야 하는 문장 고르기 문제 (4문제) |

문맥 파악 문제 (전체 16 문제 중 평균 11문제)

《해커스 토익 READING》으로 토익 Part 6 완벽 대비!

1) 다양한 의미의 접속부사와 접속부사 역할을 하는 어구 리스트 및 문제 수록!
   [참고] 접속부사(p.163)

2) 지문 앞부분의 내용에 맞는 대명사 고르기에 대한 설명 및 문제 수록!
   [참고] 명사-대명사 일치(p.146)

3) 문맥에 알맞은 시제를 고르는 문맥 파악 문제 수록!
   [참고] 시제 문제(p.139 Hackers Test 19번, p.207 Hackers Test 20번 등)

4) 문맥에 알맞은 어휘를 고르는 문맥 파악 문제 수록!
   [참고] 문맥 파악 어휘 문제(p.291 Hackers Test 14번, p.303 Hackers Test 11번 등)

5) 지문의 흐름상 빈칸에 들어갈 알맞은 단어/문장 고르기에 대한 설명 및 문제 수록!
   [참고] 단어 고르기(p.334-339), 문장 고르기(p.340-345)

3. 지문의 내용을 신속하고 정확하게 파악해야 하는 Part 7

Part 7에서는 지문의 특정 세부 내용에 대해 묻는 문제와 문맥을 파악해야 풀 수 있는 문제의 출제 비중이 높아짐에 따라 지문의 내용을 신속하고 정확하게 파악하는 것이 요구된다.

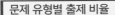
문제 유형별 출제 비율

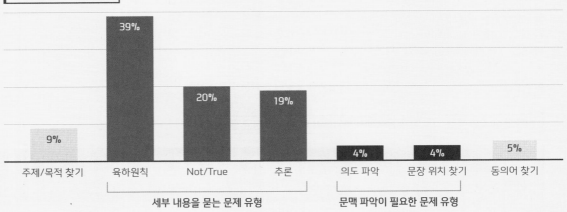

| 주제/목적 찾기 | 육하원칙 | Not/True | 추론 | 의도 파악 | 문장 위치 찾기 | 동의어 찾기 |
| 9% | 39% | 20% | 19% | 4% | 4% | 5% |

세부 내용을 묻는 문제 유형 / 문맥 파악이 필요한 문제 유형

세부 내용을 묻는 문제

지문의 특정 세부 내용을 찾아 질문에 알맞은 정답을 고르는 **육하원칙 문제**, 지문의 세부 내용과 보기 4개를 대조하여 옳은 것 또는 틀린 것을 골라내는 **Not/True 문제**, 그리고 지문의 세부 내용을 바탕으로 새로운 사실을 추론해야 하는 **추론 문제**가 많이 출제되고 있다.

육하원칙 문제	What should Mr. Jones give the client by Friday? Mr. Jones는 무엇을 금요일까지 의뢰인에게 주어야 하는가?
Not/True 문제	What is indicated about reservations? 예약에 대해 언급된 것은? What is NOT mentioned in the article? 기사에서 언급되지 않은 것은?
추론 문제	What is suggested about Carrington Shipping Agency? Carrington 운송사에 대해 암시되는 것은? What will most likely happen on October 9? 10월 9일에 무엇이 일어날 것 같은가?

화자가 언급한 인용구가 문맥상 어떤 의도인지를 묻는 **의도 파악 문제**와, 지문의 흐름상 주어진 문장이 들어가기에 가장 알맞은 위치를 고르는 **문장 위치 찾기 문제**가 출제된다.

의도 파악 문제	At 14:01, what does Ms. Hillard mean when she writes, "Just go ahead"? 14시 01분에, Ms. Hillard가 "Just go ahead"라고 썼을 때, 그녀가 의도한 것은?
문장 위치 찾기 문제	In which of the positions marked [1], [2], [3], and [4] does the following sentence best belong? "In addition, they will be invited to members-only functions." [1], [2], [3], [4]로 표시된 위치 중, 다음 문장이 들어갈 곳으로 가장 적절한 것은? "또한, 그들은 회원제 행사에 초대받게 될 것이다."

지문의 문맥과 세부 내용을 정확히 파악해야 하는 문제

(p.388, Hackers Test 1-4번 중 3, 4번)

We received your order of a rectangular Edgewood-series dining table with four matching chairs in light oak. However, we are sorry to say that the size you ordered is sold out at all our locations and will not be restocked by our supplier until the end of the month. — [1] —. We have given your order the highest priority and can ship it to you as soon as we receive it. — [2] —. If you need a table sooner, we would like to suggest the same model in a slightly larger size. It is also rectangular but measures 1.1 by 1.3 meters. — [3] —. Or you can check out other designs available that are in your preferred size. We hope to receive your reply as soon as possible so that we know how to proceed with your order. — [4] —.

Our deepest apologies for any inconvenience. Do let me know if you have any questions.

03. What is NOT an option that Ms. Lewis offers?

(A) Getting a larger size
(B) Paying a rush fee
(C) Viewing other available products
(D) Waiting for an item to be in stock

04. In which of the positions marked [1], [2], [3], and [4] does the following sentence best belong?

"To help you decide, we have attached a catalog so that you can compare each of the two table sizes."

(A) [1]
(B) [2]
(C) [3]
(D) [4]

《해커스 토익 READING》으로 토익 Part 7 완벽 대비!

1) 세부 내용 관련 문제의 정답을 정확하게 골라내는 전략과 풍부한 실전 문제 수록!
   [참고] 육하원칙 문제(p.360-365), Not/True 문제(p.366-371), 추론 문제(p.372-377)

2) 문맥을 신속하게 파악하여 문제의 정답을 골라내는 전략과 풍부한 실전 문제 수록!
   [참고] 의도 파악 문제(p.378-383), 문장 위치 찾기 문제(p.384-389)

해커스토익에서 제공하는
토익 정복에 필요한
특별한 혜택!

01
무료 동영상강의 제공
(Hackers.co.kr)

《해커스 토익 READING》
교재 학습자를 위한 무료
동영상강의 제공!

02
온라인 실전모의고사
무료 제공
(Hackers.co.kr)

실전 감각을 키워주는 온라인
실전모의고사 무료 제공!

03
토익 적중 예상특강
(Hackers.co.kr)

해커스어학원에서 실제로
강의하시는 선생님들의 이번 달
토익 적중 예상특강 제공!

04
진단고사 무료 해설강의
(HackersIngang.com)

《해커스 토익 READING》
교재에 수록된 진단고사의
해설강의 무료 제공!

05
무료 단어암기 MP3 제공
(HackersIngang.com)

단어암기 MP3로 언제, 어디서든
효과적인 단어 학습 가능!

06
토익 성공수기 및
무료 학습자료
(Hackers.co.kr)

성공적인 토익 학습방법부터
다양한 무료 학습자료까지
풍부한 정보 제공!

토익 리딩의 기본서 · 최신개정판

해커스 토익

최신기출경향
완벽 반영

READING RC

해커스 어학연구소

토익은 역시 해커스입니다.

<해커스 토익>의 목적은 '토익을 통한 올바른 영어공부'입니다.

토익 시험은 영어 실력을 재는 잣대로서 졸업과 취업 등 점차 많은 곳에서 이를 요구하고 있으며, 많은 토익 학습자들이 토익 공부에 소중한 시간과 노력을 투자하고 있습니다. <해커스 토익>은 토익 학습자들에게 단순한 토익 공부가 아닌 '토익 공부와 함께 세계를 살아가는 도구로서의 영어공부'의 방향을 제시하고자 하는 마음에서 시작되었습니다.

이번에도 학습자들이 영어 실력을 향상하고 토익 고득점을 달성하는 데 도움을 주고자 하는 마음으로 《해커스 토익 READING》(최신개정판)을 출간하게 되었습니다.

토익 최신 출제 경향이 반영된 최고의 대비서, <해커스 토익>
《해커스 토익 READING》은 토익 최신 출제 경향이 완벽하게 반영되었습니다. 특히, 오랜 시간 토익을 연구해온 해커스만의 문제 풀이 전략이 제시되어 있으며, 토익 최신 출제 경향이 완벽 반영된 실전 문제들이 풍부하게 수록되어 있어 토익 리딩에 완벽하게 대비할 수 있습니다.

기본부터 실전까지 한 권으로 학습할 수 있는 <해커스 토익>
최신 출제 경향을 적극 반영한 실전 문제와 더불어 《해커스 토익 READING》만의 장점은 기본부터 실전까지 한 권으로 학습할 수 있는 구성입니다. 토익 문제 유형을 철저하게 분석하여 정리해 놓은 이론서이자 충분한 양의 문제를 수록한 실전 문제집으로, 학습자가 가장 효율적으로 학습할 수 있도록 구성하였습니다. 이러한 구성은 기본을 다지려는 수험생과 실전 감각과 점수를 높이려는 수험생 모두에게 도움을 줄 수 있을 것입니다.

다양한 학습자료와 학습자들 간의 교류, <해커스 토익>
마지막으로, 《해커스 토익 READING》과 함께 토익 학습을 더욱 재미있고 수준 높게 만들어 줄 해커스토익 사이트(Hackers.co.kr)는 이미 최고의 영어학습 사이트로 자리매김하여, '사귐과 연대를 통한 함께함의 커뮤니티'를 꿈꾸는 해커스 철학을 십분 나타내고 있습니다.

공부가 단순히 나 혼자 사는 연습이 아니라, 서로의 도움을 통해 더 나은 사회, 그리고 건전한 경쟁과 협력이 공존하는 참사회를 꿈꾸는 것이 바로 해커스의 정신입니다. 해커스의 열정과 정신이 그대로 담긴 해커스 토익책이 토익 점수 획득이라는 단기 목표에만 그치지 않고, 한 사람 한 사람의 마음 속 깊은 곳에 건전한 철학을 심어주어 더욱더 살기 좋은 사회를 함께 실현하는 데 이바지하였으면 합니다.

David Cho

CONTENTS

최신 출제 경향을 파악하고, 문제 풀이 전략을 익힌다!

토익 READING 최신 출제 경향 한눈에 보기

Part 5 & 6 최신 출제 경향

1. 까다롭게 출제되는 Part 5&6 문법/어휘 문제

문법

<가정법 도치>, <부정대명사/부정형용사>, <명사절 접속사>와 같은 까다로운 문법 포인트가 출제되고 있다.

가정법 도치 p.98, 토익실전문제 1번	Had the materials ------- on time, the company might have fulfilled the customer's request for a rush order. (A) order (B) ordered (C) been ordered (D) were ordered
부정대명사/	The project approval committee received 40 proposals, ------- of which were

최근 토익 시험에 출제되는 문제 유형과 경향을 철저히 분석하여 알기 쉽도록 정리하였으며, 《해커스 토익 READING》 교재 내에서 중점적으로 학습할 수 있는 페이지를 제시하였습니다. 이를 통해 토익 시험의 **최신 출제 경향을 파악**하는 것은 물론, **전략적인 학습 또한 가능**합니다.

파트별 문제 풀이 방법

Part 7 예제 – Triple Passages

Questions 1 refer to the following **e-mail, form, and notice.**

To: Misty Cabrera <msmisty427@mailfix.com>
From: Customer Service <cs@boulderoutdoor.com>
Subject: **RE: Order no. 102R398NF9**
Date: August 28

Dear Ms. Cabrera,

I am writing in reference to your inquiry about returning the above order. We'd be happy to provide you with a refund or exchange.

Should you decide to **process the return on our Web site,** I am obligated to tell you that **credit card refunds may take up to two weeks to process,** whereas store credit will be issued within 24 hours.

Sincerely,

Theodore Wood
Customer service representative
Boulder Outdoor

1. 지문 유형이 e-mail(이메일), form(양식), notice(공고)이고 제목이 각각 RE: Order no. 102R398NF9, ONLINE RETURN FORM, Return Policy for Online Purchases이므로, 이메일에서는 주문에 관련한 답변이 안내되고, 양식에서는 온라인 주문의 환불에 대한 내용이 이어지고, 공고에서는 온라인 구매의 환불 정책에 관한 내용이 공지될 것임을 예측한다.

3. 이메일에서 Ms. Cabrera가 웹사이트에서 환불을 처리하기로 결정했다면 상점 포인트는 24시간 이내로 발행될 수 있는 반면, 신용카드 환불을 처리하는 데 2주 정도까지 걸릴 수도 있다는 단서를 확인할 수 있다. 하지만 Ms. Cabrera가 어떠한 방법으로 환불받는지가 언급되지 않았으므로, 두 번째 지문인 양식에서 Ms. Cabrera가 상점 포인트를 통해 환불받는다는 두 번째 단서를 확인한다. 환불이 처리될 때, 상점 포인트는 24시간

Grammar/Vocabulary/Reading 모든 파트의 **최신 출제 경향 분석 자료와 대비 전략**을 함께 제시하였습니다. 《해커스 토익 READING》 교재 내 수록된 이론 설명, 문제에도 최신 출제 경향을 완벽하게 반영하여 **효과적으로 실전에 대비**할 수 있습니다.

기본기와 실전 감각을 동시에 쌓는다!

토익 필수 개념 다지기

Grammar 영역에서는 시험에 출제되는 핵심 문법 사항을 정리하여, 문법 문제 및 토익 시험에 꼭 **필요한 필수 문법 사항을 확실하게 학습**할 수 있도록 하였습니다.

토익 출제 유형 및 전략

Vocabulary와 Reading 영역의 출제 유형을 철저히 분석하였으며, **제시된 문제 풀이 전략과 예시를 함께 적용하여 문제를 풀어보는 연습**을 할 수 있습니다.

Hackers Practice / Hackers Test

Hackers Practice에서는 실제 시험에 출제될 만한 문장들로 배운 내용을 간단히 확인할 수 있으며, Hackers Test에서는 실전 유형과 동일한 문제를 수록하여 체계적인 학습이 가능합니다.

실전모의고사 4회분

토익 시험 전, 마무리 단계에서 **자신의 실력을 정확하게 점검**하고, **실전 감각을 키울 수 있도록** 하였습니다.

*교재에 2회분을 수록하였고, 해커스토익(Hackers. co.kr)에서 온라인 실전모의고사 2회분을 추가로 제공합니다.

토익 점수, <해커스 토익>으로 확실하게 잡는다!

상세한 해설로 한 문제를 풀어도 제대로 푼다!

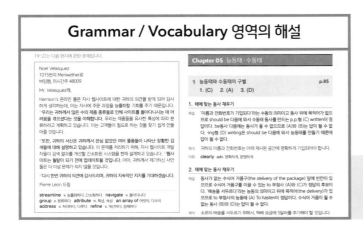

교재 내 수록된 모든 문제에 대해 쉽게 이해하고, 관련 내용을 확실하게 학습할 수 있도록 **꼼꼼하고 상세한 해설**을 제공하였습니다.

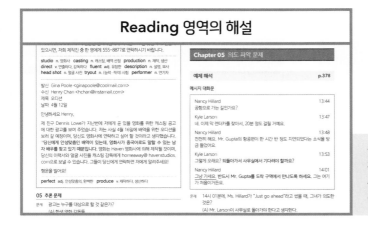

실제 문제를 푸는 순서와 문제 풀이 전략을 적용한 해설로, 해설을 읽는 것만으로도 문제 풀이 방법과 전략 적용 노하우를 자연스럽게 익힐 수 있도록 하였습니다.

*해설집은 **책 속의 책**으로 제공하여 보다 편리하게 학습할 수 있습니다.

해커스의 노하우가 담긴 학습자료를 적극 활용한다!

해설강의

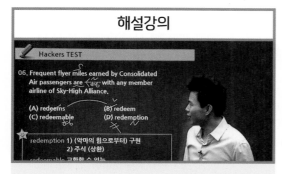

실전 문제 중 실제 시험에서 오답률이 높은 문제와 유사한 문제들에 대한 **해설강의**를 무료로 제공합니다. QR코드를 이용해 어려운 문제들에 대한 해설강의를 보며 학습할 수 있습니다.

토익 RC 필수 어휘(별책) & 단어암기 MP3

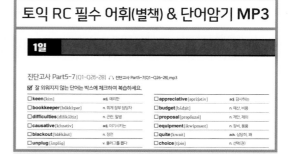

각 챕터별로 핵심 어휘를 30일 동안 학습할 수 있도록 구성하였습니다. 해커스인강(HackersIngang.com)에서 제공하는 **무료 단어암기 MP3**로 이동할 때나 자투리 시간에도 편리하게 단어를 암기할 수 있습니다.

온라인 실전모의고사 2회분

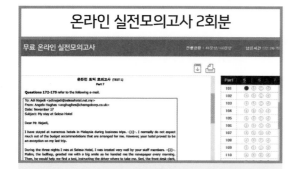

《해커스 토익 READING》 교재로 공부하는 학습자들이 혼자서도 효과적으로 공부하고 토익 실전 감각을 향상시킬 수 있도록 해커스토익(Hackers.co.kr)에서 **온라인 실전모의고사 2회분**을 제공합니다.

무료 동영상강의

보다 깊이 있는 학습이 가능하도록 해커스토익(Hackers.co.kr)에서 **무료 동영상강의**를 제공합니다. 또한 무료로 제공하는 매일 토익 문제 풀이와 토익 적중 예상 특강, 영어뉴스 청취 등 방대한 영어 학습자료로 영어 실력 향상이 가능합니다.

토익 소개

토익이란 무엇인가?

TOEIC은 Test Of English for International Communication의 약자로 영어가 모국어가 아닌 사람들을 대상으로 언어 본래의 기능인 '커뮤니케이션' 능력에 중점을 두고 일상생활 또는 국제 업무 등에 필요한 실용영어 능력을 평가하는 시험이다. 토익은 일상 생활 및 비즈니스 현장에서 필요로 하는 내용을 평가하기 위해 개발되었고 다음과 같은 실용적인 주제들을 주로 다룬다.

- 협력 개발: 연구, 제품 개발
- 재무 회계: 대출, 투자, 세금, 회계, 은행 업무
- 일반 업무: 계약, 협상, 마케팅, 판매
- 기술 영역: 전기, 공업 기술, 컴퓨터, 실험실
- 사무 영역: 회의, 서류 업무
- 물품 구입: 쇼핑, 물건 주문, 대금 지불

- 식사: 레스토랑, 회식, 만찬
- 문화: 극장, 스포츠, 피크닉
- 건강: 의료 보험, 병원 진료, 치과
- 제조: 생산 조립 라인, 공장 경영
- 직원: 채용, 은퇴, 급여, 진급, 고용 기회
- 주택: 부동산, 이사, 기업 부지

토익 시험의 구성

구성		내용	문항수	시간	배점
Listening Test	Part 1	사진 묘사	**6문항** (1번-6번)	45분	495점
	Part 2	질의 응답	**25문항** (7번-31번)		
	Part 3	짧은 대화	**39문항, 13지문** (32번-70번)		
	Part 4	짧은 담화	**30문항, 10지문** (71번-100번)		
Reading Test	Part 5	단문 빈칸 채우기 (문법/어휘)	**30문항** (101번-130번)	75분	495점
	Part 6	장문 빈칸 채우기 (문법/어휘/문장 고르기)	**16문항, 4지문** (131번-146번)		
	Part 7	지문 독해	**54문항, 15지문** (147번-200번)		
		– 단일 지문 (Single Passage)	– 29문항, 10지문 (147번-175번)		
		– 이중 지문 (Double Passages)	– 10문항, 2지문 (176번-185번)		
		– 삼중 지문 (Triple Passages)	– 15문항, 3지문 (186번-200번)		
Total	**7 Parts**		200문항	120분	990점

토익, 접수부터 성적 확인까지!

1. 토익 접수

- 접수 기간을 TOEIC위원회 인터넷 사이트(www.toeic.co.kr) 혹은 공식 애플리케이션에서 확인한다.
- 추가시험은 연중 상시로 시행되니 인터넷으로 확인하고 접수한다.
- 접수 시, jpg형식의 사진 파일이 필요하므로 미리 준비해 둔다.

2. 시험 당일 준비물

| 신분증 | 연필&지우개 | 시계 | 수험번호를 적어 둔 메모 | 오답노트&토익 RC 필수 어휘 |

* 시험 당일 신분증이 없으면 시험에 응시할 수 없으므로, 반드시 ETS에서 요구하는 신분증(주민등록증, 운전면허증, 공무원증 등)을 지참해야 한다.
ETS에서 인정하는 신분증 종류는 TOEIC위원회 인터넷 사이트(www.toeic.co.kr)에서 확인 가능하다.

3. 시험 진행 순서

정기시험/추가시험(오전)	추가시험(오후)	진행
AM 09:30 – 09:45	PM 2:30 – 2:45	답안지 작성 오리엔테이션
AM 09:45 – 09:50	PM 2:45 – 2:50	쉬는 시간
AM 09:50 – 10:10	PM 2:50 – 3:10	신분 확인 및 문제지 배부
AM 10:10 – 10:55	PM 3:10 – 3:55	듣기 평가(Listening Test)
AM 10:55 – 12:10	PM 3:55 – 5:10	독해 평가(Reading Test)

* 추가시험은 토요일 오전 또는 오후에 시행되므로 이 사항도 꼼꼼히 확인한다.
* 당일 진행 순서에 대해 더 자세한 내용은 해커스토익 사이트(Hackers.co.kr)에서 확인할 수 있다.

4. 성적 확인

- 시험일로부터 약 10일 이후 TOEIC위원회 인터넷 사이트(www.toeic.co.kr) 혹은 공식 애플리케이션에서 확인한다.
  (성적 발표 기간은 회차마다 상이함)
- 시험 접수 시, 우편 수령과 온라인 출력 중 성적 수령 방법을 선택할 수 있다.
  *온라인 출력은 성적 발표 즉시 발급 가능하나, 우편 수령은 약 7일가량의 발송 기간이 소요된다.

파트별 문제 유형

Part 5 단문 빈칸 채우기 (30문제)

- 한 문장의 빈칸에 알맞은 어휘나 문법 사항을 4개의 보기 중에서 고르는 유형
- 권장 소요 시간: 11분 (문제당 풀이 시간: 20초~22초)

문법

101. The store gave Ms. Weathers a ------- refund for her purchase as the item she returned had already been used.

(A) partial   (B) partially

(C) partiality   (D) part

해설 형용사 자리 채우기
빈칸이 명사 앞에 있으므로 형용사 자리를 채우는 유형이다. 명사(refund)를 꾸며줄 수 있는 형용사 (A) partial이 정답이다.

어휘

102. Although it is generally uninhabitable, seven nations currently ------- territory in Antarctica.

(A) fix   (B) run

(C) hold   (D) watch

해설 동사 어휘 고르기
모든 보기가 뜻이 다른 동사로 되어 있으므로 문맥에 맞는 동사를 고르는 유형이다. 빈칸을 포함한 구절인 '영토를 ___하다'라는 문맥에 가장 어울리는 단어는 동사 (C) hold(차지하다)이다.

Part 6 장문 빈칸 채우기 (16문제)

- 한 지문 내의 4개 빈칸에 알맞은 문법 사항이나 어휘, 문장을 고르는 유형. 총 4개의 지문 출제.
- 권장 소요 시간: 8분 (문제당 풀이 시간: 25초~30초)

Questions 131-134 refer to the following article.

In a press statement released last week, Wittington Studios said ------- for its newest film will begin on
131.
April 17 in Michigan. ------- tax incentives offered to film companies by the state, the studio has
132.
decided not to make the movie at its facilities in Hollywood, California. According to industry experts,

------- studios are more worried about finances today than they were in the past. In an effort to reduce
133.
the total cost of producing a film, studios are turning to Michigan and other states that offer tax

incentives. -------. By filming in these locations, producers have more funds to create a better film.
134.

어휘 **131.** (A) procedure   (B) production
            (C) promotion   (D) previews

문법 **132.** (A) Because of   (B) Even though
            (C) Despite   (D) On behalf of

문법 **133.** (A) much   (B) almost
            (C) many   (D) every

문장 고르기 **134.** (A) California is offering tax breaks to television and film producers.
(B) State laws strictly prohibit tax lures for the entertainment industry.
(C) Some states even offer filmmakers up to 25 percent in tax credits.
(D) Michigan does not permit visiting filmmakers to film in their state.

해설

131. 명사 어휘 고르기 주변 문맥 파악
모든 보기가 뜻이 다른 명사로 되어 있으므로 문맥에 맞는 명사를 고르는 유형이다. 빈칸을 포함한 구절이 '미시간에서 최신 영화 ___이/가 시작될 것이다'라는 문맥인데, 다음 문장에서 스튜디오가 할리우드에서 영화를 만들지 않기로 결정했다고 하고 있으므로 명사 (B) production이 정답이다.

132. 전치사 채우기
빈칸 뒤에 명사구(tax incentives)가 왔으므로 전치사 자리를 채우는 유형이다. 문맥상 스튜디오가 할리우드에서 영화를 만들지 않기로 결정한 이유가 나와야 한다. 따라서 '감세 혜택 때문에'라는 의미를 만드는 전치사 (A) Because of(~ 때문에)가 정답이다.

133. 명사에 맞는 수량 표현 채우기
모든 보기가 수량과 관계된 표현이므로 빈칸 뒤의 명사 형태에 맞는 표현을 고르는 유형이다. 복수 명사(studios) 앞에 빈칸이 있으므로 복수 명사 앞에 쓰는 수량 표현인 (C) many가 정답이다.

134. 문장 고르기
빈칸의 주변 문맥이나 전체 문맥을 파악하여 빈칸에 들어갈 알맞은 문장을 고르는 유형이다. 앞부분에서 영화사들이 비용 절감을 위해 감세 혜택을 제공하는 주를 선호한다고 했고, 뒤 문장 'By filming in these locations, producers have more funds to create a better film.'에서 이런 지역들에서 촬영함으로써 제작자들이 더 나은 영화 창작을 위한 많은 자금을 가지게 된다고 했으므로 빈칸에는 어떤 주들은 영화사에 최대 25퍼센트의 감세 혜택을 제공한다는 내용이 들어가야 함을 알 수 있다. 따라서 (C) Some states even offer filmmakers up to 25 percent in tax credits가 정답이다.

파트별 문제 유형

Part 7 지문을 읽고 문제 풀기 (54문제)

■ 지문을 읽고 지문과 관련된 질문들에 대해 가장 적절한 보기를 정답으로 고르는 유형
■ 구성: Single Passage에서 29문제, Double Passages에서 10문제, Triple Passages에서 15문제가 출제

| Single Passage | 29문제

Questions 147-150 refer to the following advertisement.

Tudor Towers: The New Home for Business

Located in the heart of London's business district, Tudor Towers is the ideal location for your business!

We provide single or multiple room units to suit your needs, and each comes with a private parking space and a state-of-the-art security system. — [1] —. This 24-story building was designed by renowned architect Denver Hanks and is a beautiful addition to the city's skyline. Just minutes from a bus stop and tube station, Tudor Towers is perfectly situated for commuters. A coffee and snack bar are located on the first floor, and the Tower's management anticipates that all available retail units will be occupied in the near future. — [2] —.

Units are currently available for monthly rent, long-term lease, or sale. Custodial fees are between $60 and $200 per month, based on the size of units. — [3] —.

For a virtual tour of Tudor Towers, go to www.tudortowers.co.uk. Or you can stop by our showroom, between 10 A.M. and 7 P.M. Monday through Saturday, at 590 Bates Street to check out model units in person. — [4] —. Our helpful associates will provide you with all the details you may require and can answer any questions you may have. Or you can simply call us at 555-9975 during the same business hours for live assistance from one of our representatives.

---

147. What is being advertised?
(A) A real estate agency
(B) Residential units
(C) Office space
(D) A historical site

148. What is suggested about Tudor Towers?
(A) It is a landmark structure.
(B) It has some empty retail spaces.
(C) It only has units for lease.
(D) It is located outside the city.

149. What is NOT mentioned as a way businesses can learn more about the facilities?
(A) Visiting an online site
(B) Dropping by an establishment
(C) Telephoning an associate
(D) Reading an informational brochure

150. In which of the positions marked [1], [2], [3], and [4] does the following sentence best belong?

"Management uses these funds for trash removal, building cleaning and upkeep, and landscaping work."

(A) [1]
(B) [2]
(C) [3]
(D) [4]

해설

147. 주제/목적 찾기 문제
광고의 주제를 묻는 문제이다. 'Tudor Towers is the ideal location for your business'(1문단 1번째 줄)에서 Tudor Towers가 귀하의 사업을 위한 이상적인 장소라고 한 후, 건물의 장점에 대해 언급하고 있으므로 (C) Office space가 정답이다.

148. 추론 문제
Tudor Towers에 대해 암시되는 것을 묻는 문제이다. 'the Tower's management anticipates that all available retail units will be occupied in the near future'(2문단 5번째 줄)에서 이용 가능한 모든 소매 상점이 가까운 미래에 사용될 것을 예상한다고 했으므로 현재 비어 있는 소매점 공간이 있다는 사실을 추론할 수 있다. 따라서 (B) It has some empty retail spaces가 정답이다.

149. Not/True 문제
질문의 핵심 어구인 a way businesses can learn more about the facilities와 관련된 내용을 지문에서 찾아 보기와 대조하는 Not/True 문제이다. (A)는 'For a virtual tour of Tudor Towers, go to www.tudortowers.co.uk.'(4문단 1번째 줄)에서 Tudor Towers에 대한 가상 견학을 원하면 www.tudortowers.co.uk 로 가라고 했으므로 지문의 내용과 일치한다. (B)는 'Or you can stop by our showroom ~ to check out model units in person.'(4문단 1번째 줄)에서 직접 견본 아파트를 확인하기 위해서는 전시실에 들를 수 있다고 했으므로 지문의 내용과 일치한다. (C)는 'Or you can simply call us ~ for live assistance'(4문단 4번째 줄)에서 실시간 도움을 받으려면 간단하게 전화할 수 있다고 했으므로 지문의 내용과 일치한다. (D)는 지문에 언급되지 않은 내용이다. 따라서 (D) Reading an informational brochure가 정답이다.

150. 문장 위치 찾기 문제
지문의 흐름상 주어진 문장이 들어가기에 가장 적절한 곳을 고르는 문제이다. Management uses these funds for trash removal, building cleaning and upkeep, and landscaping work에서 관리진이 이 자금을 쓰레기 제거, 건물 청소와 유지, 그리고 조경 작업에 사용한다고 했으므로 주어진 문장 앞에 자금과 관련된 내용이 있을 것임을 예상할 수 있다. [3]의 앞 문장인 'Custodial fees are between $60 and $200 per month, based on the size of units.'에서 가구 크기에 기반하여 관리 비용이 월 60달러와 200달러 사이라고 했으므로, [3]에 주어진 문장이 들어가면 관리 비용에 대한 세부 정보와 용도를 설명하는 자연스러운 문맥이 된다는 것을 알 수 있다. 따라서 (C) [3]이 정답이다.

Double Passages | 10문제

Questions 176-180 refer to the following e-mails.

To: Danielle Rider <d_rider@mollysdepartmentstore.com>
From: Joel Brown <j_brown@mollysdepartmentstore.com>
Date: September 26
Subject: Inventory Timetable

Starting next week, we will be conducting our annual store-wide inventory. The work will be taking place during business hours, so all staff should be prepared. The head of accounting, Michelle Sanders, will be in charge of the process as usual, and has come up with the following timetable:

> Toys, October 1, 9 A.M.-3 P.M.
> Clothing, October 2, 10 A.M.-4 P.M.
> Furniture, October 3, 9 A.M.-3 P.M.
> Hardware, October 4, 7 A.M.-1 P.M.

If you have any concerns regarding the timetable, let me know immediately. Thank you.

To: Joel Brown <j_brown@mollysdepartmentstore.com>
From: Danielle Rider <d_rider@mollysdepartmentstore.com>
Date: September 26
Subject: Inventory Schedule

I was hoping you could move the inventory for my department to a later time. My entire staff will be busy arranging displays of new merchandise on our scheduled day. The items will get here in the morning at 9 A.M., and I expect the work to last for about two hours. Would it be possible to start the inventory two hours later than scheduled? It's just that we are under an urgent deadline.

Please let me know as soon as possible.

Danielle Rider
Toy Section Supervisor

176. What is the purpose of the first e-mail?
(A) To postpone a management meeting
(B) To announce a section reorganization
(C) To give details about an upcoming procedure
(D) To update the monthly shift schedule

177. What does the first e-mail indicate about the inventory?
(A) It will not happen during store operating hours.
(B) The organizer will be different than before.
(C) It is an event that takes place every year.
(D) The store outsources the work to another firm.

178. The word "entire" in paragraph 1, line 1 of the second e-mail is closest in meaning to
(A) final
(B) whole
(C) ideal
(D) part

179. When does Ms. Rider want to have the inventory conducted in her department?
(A) At 7:00 A.M.
(B) At 9:00 A.M.
(C) At 10:00 A.M.
(D) At 11:00 A.M.

180. Why did Ms. Rider request a different timetable for her department?
(A) They have a pressing task to complete.
(B) They will be having a month-long sale.
(C) They need to cover the shifts of the employees on leave.
(D) They will be preparing for a product launch.

해설

176. 주제/목적 찾기 문제
첫 번째 이메일의 목적을 묻는 문제이다. 첫 번째 이메일의 'Starting next week, we will be conducting our annual store-wide inventory.'(1문단 1번째 줄)에서 다음 주부터, 연례 점포 전체 재고 조사를 실시할 것이라고 한 후, 자세한 일정에 대해 알려주고 있으므로 (C) To give details about an upcoming procedure가 정답이다.

177. Not/True 문제
첫 번째 이메일에서 재고 조사에 대해 언급한 것을 묻는 문제이다. (C)는 첫번째 이메일의 'we will be conducting our annual store-wide inventory'(1문단 1번째 줄)에서 연례 점포 전체 재고 조사를 실시할 것이라고 했으므로 (C) It is an event that takes place every year가 정답이다.

178. 동의어 찾기 문제
entire의 동의어를 묻는 문제이다. entire를 포함하고 있는 문장 'My entire staff will be busy arranging displays of new merchandise on our scheduled day.'에서 entire가 '전체의'라는 뜻으로 사용되었다. 따라서 '전체의'라는 뜻을 가진 (B) whole이 정답이다.

179. 육하원칙 문제 연계
두 지문의 내용을 종합해서 풀어야 하는 연계 문제이다. 두 번째 이메일에서 장난감 구역 관리자인 Ms. Rider가 재고 조사를 예정된 것보다 두 시간 늦게 시작하는 것이 가능할지 묻고 있고, 첫 번째 이메일의 장난감 구역 재고 조사 시간이 오전 9시로 나와 있으므로 Ms. Rider가 그녀의 부서 재고 조사를 하고 싶어하는 시간은 오전 11시임을 알 수 있다. 따라서 (D) At 11:00 A.M.이 정답이다.

180. 육하원칙 문제
Ms. Rider가 왜(Why) 그녀의 부서를 위해 다른 일정표를 요청했는지를 묻는 문제이다. Ms. Rider가 쓴 두 번째 이메일에서 직원 전체가 새로운 상품을 전시하느라 바쁠 것이며, 마감 시간이 촉박하여 다른 일정표를 요청한 것임을 알 수 있다. 따라서 (A) They have a pressing task to complete가 정답이다.

Triple Passages | 15문제

Questions 186-190 refer to the following memo, e-mail, and order form.

MEMO
To: Public relations staff
From: Paul Archer, Public Relations
Subject: Company anniversary

Goldstein Company's twentieth year in business falls on January 27. To commemorate it, we will be offering product promotions and issuing a press release to major newspapers. We'll also be holding a dinner for the entire company and some valued clientele. Our department will be responsible for planning and organizing all of this. You've been divided into three teams, each of which has been assigned to a project. Please check the list on our Web site to see what team you're on, and meet with your leaders for specific assignments. Let's make this anniversary a really great one!

To: Thomas Neely <t.neely@uptowncatering.com>
From: Lesley Crawford <l.crawford@goldstein.com>
Subject: Inquiry
Attachment: Order Form

Dear Mr. Neely,

I represent Goldstein Company. My supervisor recommended I contact you as he was pleased with your services during an investors' event last year. We are holding a 20th anniversary dinner on January 27 and would like you to provide the food. I made an inquiry on the order form I've attached, but I'd also like to know if your company decorates the room and sets everything up. Please notify me as soon as possible at 555-9387. I will have to get some staff to volunteer to help if you're unable to do so.

Lesley Crawford

Uptown Catering
Arlington, VA 22203

EVENT: Anniversary Dinner   **Date:** January 10

Customer: Goldstein Company   **Event Date:** 6 to 10 P.M., January 27
Contact: Lesley Crawford   **Location:** Company headquarters
Telephone: 555-2410   **Menu:** Course A and vegetarian options
                                         Number of Guests: 120

Customer Notes: Do you offer wine service throughout the meal, or must we provide our own?

---

186. According to the memo, what is NOT a task mentioned by Paul Archer?
(A) Preparing special product offers
(B) Arranging a company-wide dinner
(C) Forming a provisional team
(D) Having an official statement published

187. What does Ms. Crawford inquire about?
(A) The vacancy of an event venue
(B) The availability of items to decorate a location
(C) The cost of hiring wait staff
(D) The number of place settings needed

188. What is indicated about the anniversary dinner?
(A) It will last for approximately three hours.
(B) It will be held at Goldstein Company's main offices.
(C) It will be attended by local news reporters.
(D) It will not require table service by waiters.

189. What is true about Ms. Crawford?
(A) She is a supervisor at Goldstein Company.
(B) She is in charge of organizing a press event.
(C) She works for the public relations department.
(D) She attended a meal for investors the previous year.

190. What is indicated about Goldstein Company?
(A) It will feature an open bar at a dinner.
(B) It requires its staff to decorate a venue.
(C) It employs fewer than 120 people.
(D) It specializes in event planning.

해설

186. Not/True 문제
첫 번째 지문인 회람에서 Paul Archer에 의해 언급되지 않은 업무를 묻는 문제이다. (A)는 기념 행사가 있는 주 내내 상품 홍보가 가능할 것이라고 했고, (B)는 회사 전체를 위해 만찬을 개최할 것이라고 했고, (D)는 보도 자료를 발행할 것이라고 했으므로 모두 지문의 내용과 일치한다. (C)는 지문에 언급되지 않은 내용이다. 따라서 (C) Forming a provisional team이 정답이다.

187. 육하원칙 문제
Ms. Crawford가 무엇(What)에 대해 문의하는지를 묻는 문제이다. 두 번째 지문인 Ms. Crawford가 쓴 이메일의 'I'd also like to know if your company decorates the room'(4번째 줄)에서 음식 제공 업체가 행사장을 장식해 주는지를 묻고 있으므로 (B) The availability of items to decorate a location이 정답이다.

188. 추론 문제
기념 만찬 행사에 대해 암시되는 것을 묻는 문제이다. 세 번째 지문인 주문 양식의 'EVENT: Anniversary Dinner, Customer: Goldstein Company(양식 왼쪽 열 1, 2번째 줄), Location: Company headquarters'(양식 오른쪽 열 2번째 줄)에서 Goldstein사의 기념 만찬 행사가 회사 본사에서 열릴 것임을 추론할 수 있으므로 (B) It will be held at Goldstein Company's main offices가 정답이다.

189. Not/True 문제 연계
두 지문의 내용을 종합해서 풀어야 하는 연계 문제이다. 두 번째 지문인 Ms. Crawford가 쓴 이메일에서 Ms. Crawford가 기념 행사를 위한 음식 제공 서비스를 이용하고 싶다고 하며 회사를 대표하여 연락한다고 했고, 첫 번째 지문인 회람에서 홍보부가 기념 행사의 모든 기획과 준비를 맡을 것이라고 했으므로 Ms. Crawford는 홍보부에서 근무함을 알 수 있다. 따라서 (C) She works for the public relations department가 정답이다.

190. 추론 문제 연계
두 지문의 내용을 종합해서 풀어야 하는 연계 문제이다. 첫 번째 지문인 회람에서 회사 전체와 중요한 고객들을 위해 만찬을 개최할 것이라고 했고, 세 번째 지문인 주문 양식에서 기념 행사의 손님 수가 120명이라고 했으므로 사원들의 수는 120명보다 적다는 사실을 추론할 수 있다. 따라서 (C) It employs fewer than 120 people이 정답이다.

학습 성향별 맞춤 공부 방법

*학습 플랜은 24페이지와 25페이지에 수록되어 있습니다.

개별학습 혼자서 공부할 때 가장 집중이 잘 된다!

1. 나만의 학습 플랜을 세운다!

'수준별 맞춤 학습 방법(p.22)'을 통해 학습 플랜을 선택하고, 학습 플랜에 맞는 목표와 학습 일정을 꼼꼼히 적는다.

2. 파트별 유형을 익히고 실전 문제를 푼다!

학습 플랜에 따라, 각 파트의 유형과 핵심 전략을 익히고, 예제와 Hackers Practice에서 적용해 본다. 학습 내용을 바탕으로 Hackers Test를 실전처럼 풀면서 실전 감각을 키운다.

3. 토익 RC 필수 어휘(별책)로 마무리한다!

그날 학습 분량을 마친 후, 토익 RC 필수 어휘(별책)로 어휘 능력을 탄탄히 한다.

* 해커스토익 사이트(Hackers.co.kr)의 『교재/무료MP3』 → 『교재 Q&A』에서 궁금한 사항을 질문할 수 있습니다.

스터디학습 다른 사람과 함께 공부할 때 더 열심히 한다!

1. 개별 예습으로 스터디를 준비한다!

스터디원들끼리 정한 학습 플랜의 진도에 따라 개별적으로 각 파트의 유형과 핵심 전략, Hackers Practice를 예습한다. 그날 학습할 토익 RC 필수 어휘(별책)의 단어도 미리 외운다.

2. 토론학습으로 완벽하게 이해한다!

스터디는 단어 암기 미니 테스트로 시작한다. Hackers Test를 다같이 실전처럼 풀어본 후, 틀렸거나 잘 모르는 문제는 토론을 통해 완벽하게 이해한다.

3. 토익 RC 필수 어휘(별책)로 개별 복습한다!

스터디가 끝난 후, 토익 RC 필수 어휘(별책)로 개별 복습한다.

* 해커스토익 사이트(Hackers.co.kr)의 『해티즌/제2외국어』 → 『스터디모집 게시판』에서 스터디를 결성할 수 있고, 『교재/무료MP3』 → 『교재 Q&A』에서 궁금한 사항을 질문할 수 있습니다.

동영상학습　원하는 시간, 원하는 장소에서 강의를 듣고 싶다!

1. 동영상강의 학습 플랜을 세운다!
해커스인강 사이트(HackersIngang.com)에서 『샘플강의보기』를 통해 강의를 미리 둘러보고, 『스터디플랜』을 통해 자신의 학습 플랜을 세운다.

2. 마이클래스에서 집중해서 강의를 듣는다!
스터디플랜에 따라 오늘 공부해야 할 강의를 집중해서 듣고, 『마이클래스』 메뉴의 단어장과 메모장을 활용한다.

3. 『선생님께 질문하기』를 적극 활용한다!
강의를 듣다가 모르는 부분이 있거나 질문할 것이 생기면 『선생님께 질문하기』를 이용하여 확실히 이해하도록 한다.

학원학습　선생님의 강의를 직접 들을 때 가장 효과적이다!

1. 100% 출석을 목표로 한다!
자신의 스케줄에 맞는 수업을 등록하고, 개강일부터 종강일까지 100% 출석을 목표로 빠짐없이 수업에 참여한다. 스터디가 진행되는 수업의 경우, 스터디도 반드시 참여한다.

2. 예습과 복습을 철저히 한다!
수업 전에 미리 그날 배울 표현, 단어 등을 훑어본다. 수업이 끝난 후, 토익 RC 필수 어휘(별책), 오답노트를 통해 스스로 복습한다.

3. 수업자료들을 적극 활용한다!
학원 진도에 맞춰 수업을 듣고, 선생님이 나눠 주는 학습자료를 적극 활용한다.

* 해커스토익 사이트(Hackers.co.kr)의 『교재/무료MP3』 → 『교재 Q&A』에서 궁금한 사항을 질문할 수 있습니다.
* 해커스어학원 수강생은 해커스어학원 사이트(Hackers.ac)의 『반별게시판』에서 선생님이 올려 주는 학습자료를 다운받을 수 있습니다.

수준별 맞춤 학습 방법

*27페이지의 진단고사를 본 후, 본인이 맞은 개수에 해당하는 레벨의 학습방법을 참고하시면 됩니다.
*학습 플랜은 24페이지와 25페이지에 수록되어 있습니다.

Level 1 | 진단고사 22개 미만

나는야 초보! 그러나 해커스와 함께라면 초보 탈출은 문제 없다!

추천 플랜 | 학습 플랜 A

학습 방법 | 문법과 어휘의 기초를 쌓자!

1. 학습 플랜에 따라 챕터별로 각 페이지의 설명 및 예문을 꼼꼼하게 읽고 정리합니다.
2. 시간이 걸리더라도 토익실전문제, Hackers Practice, Hackers Test에 실린 문제들을 앞에서 배운 문법, 어휘, 독해 포인트를 기억하여 푸는 연습을 합니다.
3. 해설집으로 문법포인트와 어휘를 포함한 문제 풀이 방법을 정리합니다. 특히, 토익 RC 필수 어휘(별책)에 정리된 어휘는 모두 외운다는 각오로 학습합니다.

Level 2 | 진단고사 23~35개

이제 점수 좀 올려볼까? 중수로 발돋움 한다!

추천 플랜 | 학습 플랜 A

학습 방법 | 문제 풀이 방법을 꼼꼼히 익히자!

1. 학습 플랜에 따라 챕터별로 각 페이지의 설명 및 예문을 꼼꼼하게 읽습니다.
2. 토익실전문제, Hackers Practice, Hackers Test에 실린 문제들을 앞에서 배운 문제 풀이 방법을 적용시켜 푸는 연습을 합니다.
3. 틀린 문제는 반드시 해설을 통해 어느 부분에서 잘못 풀었는지를 확인하고, 다시 한번 풀어보도록 합니다. 토익 RC 필수 어휘(별책)로 모르는 단어를 학습합니다.

Level 3 | 진단고사 36~45개

어중간한 점수대는 이제 그만! 토익의 고수가 되고 싶다!

추천 플랜 | 학습 플랜 B

학습 방법 | 실전감각을 최대한으로 끌어올리자!

1. 학습 플랜에 따라 챕터별로 각 페이지에서 모르는 부분을 반드시 따로 정리합니다.
2. 시간을 정해놓고 토익실전문제, Hackers Practice, Hackers Test에 실린 문제들을 풀되, 헷갈리거나 어려운 문제들을 따로 표시해가면서 풉니다.
3. 해설을 통해 틀린 문제 및 표시해 둔 문제들의 문법, 어휘 포인트를 꼼꼼히 확인하고, 토익 RC 필수 어휘(별책)로 모르는 단어를 확실하게 외웁니다.

Level 4 | 진단고사 46~50개

해커스 토익과 함께 만점으로 토익을 졸업한다!

추천 플랜 | 학습 플랜 B

학습 방법 | 틀린 문제 위주로 유형별 문제 풀이 전략을 마스터하자!

1. 학습 플랜에 따라 각 페이지의 포인트를 훑으며 모르는 부분을 확실하게 정리합니다.
2. 토익실전문제, Hackers Practice, Hackers Test에 실린 문제들을 빠르게 풀되, 한번에 풀리지 않거나 헷갈리는 문제들은 따로 표시를 해둡니다.
3. 해설을 통해 틀린 문제 및 표시해 둔 문제들을 다시 한번 확인하고, 토익 RC 필수 어휘(별책)로 모르는 단어를 확실하게 정리합니다.

해커스 학습 플랜

학습 플랜 A   Grammar + Vocabulary → Reading

		1st Day	2nd Day	3rd Day	4th Day	5th Day	6th Day	7th Day
1st week	Grammar	진단(Part 5&6) (p.28~31)	Ch 1 (p.48~55)	Ch 2 (p.56~65)	Ch 3 (p.68~75)	Ch 4 (p.76~83)	Ch 5 (p.84~91)	Ch 6 (p.92~101)
	Vocabulary	Ch 1 (p.240~244)	Ch 1 (p.245~249)	Ch 2 (p.250~254)	Ch 2 (p.255~259)	Ch 3 (p.260~264)	Ch 3 (p.265~269)	Ch 4 (p.270~273)
2nd week	Grammar	Ch 7 (p.104~111)	Ch 8 (p.112~119)	Ch 9 (p.120~127)	Ch 10 (p.130~139)	Ch 11 (p.140~149)	Ch 12 (p.150~157)	Ch 13 (p.158~169)
	Vocabulary	Ch 4 (p.274~277)	Ch 5 (p.280~285)	Ch 6 (p.286~291)	Ch 7 (p.292~297)	Ch 8 (p.298~303)	Ch 9 (p.304~309)	Ch 10 (p.312~314)
3rd week	Grammar	Ch 14 (p.170~181)	Ch 15-16 (p.184~197)	Ch 17 (p.198~207)	Ch 18 (p.208~217)	Ch 19 (p.220~227)	Ch 20 (p.228~233)	실전1·2 (Part 5&6) (p.516~522) (p.544~550)
	Vocabulary	Ch 10 (p.315~317)	Ch 11 (p.318~320)	Ch 11 (p.321~323)	Ch 12 (p.324~326)	Ch 12 (p.327~329)	Section 1 복습	Section 2-3 복습
4th week	Reading	진단(Part 7) (p.32~41) Ch 1-2(Part 6) (p.334~345) Ch 1-2(Part 7) (p.354~365)	Ch 3-6 (p.366~389)	Ch 7-10 (p.390~425)	Ch 11-14 (p.426~457)	Ch 15-17 (p.458~487)	Ch 18-20 (p.488~513)	실전1·2 (Part 7) (p.523~543) (p.551~571)

* 2주 동안에 단기로 책을 완성하고 싶으시면 이틀 분량을 하루 동안에 학습하면 됩니다.

* 8주 동안 완성을 원할 경우 위의 표에서 하루 분량을 이틀에 걸쳐서 학습하면 됩니다.

* 매일의 학습을 완료한 후 토익 RC 필수 어휘(별책)에 정리된 단어들을 복습합니다.

학습 플랜 B Grammar + Vocabulary + Reading

1st week

	1st Day	2nd Day	3rd Day	4th Day	5th Day	6th Day	7th Day
Grammar		Ch 1 (p.48~55)	Ch 2 (p.56~65)	Section 1 복습	Ch 3 (p.68~75)	Ch 4 (p.76~83)	Ch 5 (p.84~91)
Vocabulary	진단 (p.28~41)	Ch 1 (p.240~244)	Ch 1 (p.245~249)	Ch 2 (p.250~253)	Ch 2 (p.254~256)	Ch 2 (p.257~259)	Ch 3 (p.260~264)
Reading		Ch 1-2(Part 6) (p.334~345)	Ch 1(Part 7) (p.354~359)	Ch 2 (p.360~365)	Ch 3 (p.366~371)	Ch 4 (p.372~377)	Ch 5 (p.378~383)

2nd week

	1st Day	2nd Day	3rd Day	4th Day	5th Day	6th Day	7th Day
Grammar	Ch 6 (p.92~101)	Section 2 복습	Ch 7 (p.104~111)	Ch 8 (p.112~119)	Ch 9 (p.120~127)	Section 3 복습	Ch 10 (p.130~139)
Vocabulary	Ch 3 (p.265~269)	Ch 4 (p.270~273)	Ch 4 (p.274~277)	Section 1 복습	Ch 5 (p.280~285)	Ch 6 (p.286~291)	Ch 7 (p.292~297)
Reading	Ch 6 (p.384~389)	Ch 7 (p.390~399)	Section 1 복습	Ch 8 (p.402~409)	Ch 9 (p.410~417)	Ch 10 (p.418~425)	Ch 11 (p.426~433)

3rd week

	1st Day	2nd Day	3rd Day	4th Day	5th Day	6th Day	7th Day
Grammar	Ch 11 (p.140~149)	Ch 12 (p.150~157)	Ch 13 (p.158~169)	Ch 14 (p.170~181)	Section 4 복습	Ch 15-16 (p.184~197)	Ch 17 (p.198~207)
Vocabulary	Ch 8 (p.298~303)	Ch 9 (p.304~309)	Section 2 복습	Ch 10 (p.312~314)	Ch 10 (p.315~317)	Ch 11 (p.318~320)	Ch 11 (p.321~323)
Reading	Ch 12 (p.434~441)	Ch 13 (p.442~449)	Ch 14 (p.450~457)	Ch 15 (p.458~465)	Section 2 복습	Ch 16 (p.468~477)	Ch 17 (p.478~487)

4th week

	1st Day	2nd Day	3rd Day	4th Day	5th Day	6th Day	7th Day
Grammar	Ch 18 (p.208~217)	Section 5 복습	Ch 19-20 (p.220~233)	Section 6 복습			
Vocabulary	Ch 12 (p.324~326)	Ch 12 (p.327~329)	Section 3 복습	Section 1-3 복습	실전 1 (p.516~543)	실전 2 (p.544~571)	실전 1·2 오답확인
Reading	Ch 18 (p.488~497)	Ch 19 (p.498~505)	Ch 20 (p.506~513)	Section 3 복습			

* 2주 동안에 단기로 책을 완성하고 싶으시면 이틀 분량을 하루 동안에 학습하면 됩니다.
* 8주 동안 완성을 원할 경우 위의 표에서 하루 분량을 이틀에 걸쳐서 학습하면 됩니다.
* 매일의 학습을 완료한 후 토익 RC 필수 어휘(별책)에 정리된 단어들을 복습합니다.

Hackers TOEIC Reading

진단고사

★ 실제 토익 리딩 시험과 유사한 진단고사를 통해 본인의 실력을 평가해 보고, 본인에게 맞는 학습 방법(p.22~23)으로 본 교재를 학습합니다.

★ 진단고사 무료 해설강의(HackersIngang.com)를 활용하여 틀렸거나 잘 이해되지 않는 문제를 복습합니다.

* 교재 p.573에 수록된 Answer sheet를 활용하여 실제 시험처럼 풀어 보세요.

🕐 제한 시간 35분

READING TEST

In this section, you must demonstrate your ability to read and comprehend English. You will be given a variety of texts and asked to answer questions about these texts. This section is divided into three parts and will take 35 minutes to complete.

PART 5

Directions: In each question, you will be asked to review a statement that is missing a word or phrase. Four answer choices will be provided for each statement. Select the best answer and mark the corresponding letter (A), (B), (C), or (D) on your textbook.

01 With ------- keen sense of detail, Mr. Watson was able to provide comprehensive data analysis for the research project.

(A) him
(B) his
(C) he
(D) himself

02 Attending the quarterly seminar on customer service was ------- for the staff members of Moon River Hotel.

(A) help
(B) helpful
(C) helpfully
(D) helpfulness

03 As the cost of getting the printer ------- was nearly the same as its original price, management chose to purchase a new model.

(A) affirmed
(B) repaired
(C) identified
(D) recognized

04 The structural plan for Sunrise Property's 50-story office tower has ------- been reviewed by Mr. Collins, the project director.

(A) already
(B) by chance
(C) enough
(D) yet

05 Carmoan Industries currently needs two experienced bookkeepers to work in ------- accounting department.

(A) its
(B) them
(C) whom
(D) theirs

06 Attendees may ------- their complimentary tickets to the movie premiere of *Cornerstone* by visiting any World Pass outlet or picking them up at the box office.

(A) charge
(B) claim
(C) give
(D) refund

07 Technical problems with the audio-visual system at the venue ------- difficulties for the organizers of the career seminar.

(A) have caused
(B) are caused
(C) causative
(D) causing

08 The computers used by the graphics team have been ------- with new ones that are capable of running the latest photo-editing software.

(A) inspected
(B) rejected
(C) replaced
(D) purchased

09 During a blackout, residents of ------- areas should unplug all appliances to reduce the risk of power surges when the electricity has been restored.

(A) affect
(B) affectively
(C) affected
(D) affection

10 Last Friday, the city council ------- accepted a proposal to construct a new community athletics center in the Maple Ridge area.

(A) intermittently
(B) formally
(C) customarily
(D) externally

11 Never has the customer service department ------- as many complaints as it did last month when it was announced that items purchased while on sale could not be returned.

(A) receipts
(B) to receive
(C) receiving
(D) received

12 The consumer reviews of products currently available on the market in *Public Pulse* are ------- more reliable than those provided by similar publications.

(A) marginal
(B) marginalize
(C) marginalization
(D) marginally

13 The final payment for the fabric and sewing supplies cannot be released ------- the missing orders are delivered to the warehouse.

(A) through
(B) until
(C) toward
(D) beyond

14 The markets in the Trastevere area of Rome are popular due to their ------- to several famous landmarks and historic sites.

(A) immediacy
(B) availability
(C) proximity
(D) vacancy

15 Because the effects of the proposed changes to the tax law were not confirmed, the government demanded that further studies -------.

(A) to conduct
(B) be conducted
(C) conduction
(D) conducting

GO ON TO THE NEXT PAGE

PART 6

Directions: In this part, you will be asked to read four English texts. Each text is missing a word, phrase, or sentence. Select the answer choice that correctly completes the text and mark the corresponding letter (A), (B), (C), or (D) on your textbook.

Questions 16-19 refer to the following memo.

To: All staff members
From: Building Administration Office
Date: November 27
Subject: Elevator Maintenance Work

The building administration office is scheduled to conduct a regular ------- of the passenger elevator that services the building's even-numbered floors in a few days. That elevator will be unavailable starting December 3. Therefore, building occupants who ------- take this elevator are requested to use the one that serves all floors. Since our technicians will be checking electrical wiring as well as key parts of the lifting device, it will be ------- for at least three days. Please note that it may be necessary to keep the elevator closed for longer if a part needs to be replaced or repair is required. -------. We understand that this will be an inconvenience, but the safety of our tenants is our utmost priority.

Nevertheless, be assured that we will do everything we can to restore regular operations as quickly as possible. Your patience and understanding regarding this matter are greatly appreciated.

Thank you.

16 (A) consideration
    (B) experiment
    (C) inspection
    (D) demonstration

17 (A) normal
    (B) normalize
    (C) normality
    (D) normally

18 (A) impossible
    (B) undisclosed
    (C) inaccessible
    (D) undetermined

19 (A) Report to the maintenance crew once repairs are complete.
    (B) It is mandatory for tenants to vacate their apartments at this time.
    (C) We will send another notice if we need more time.
    (D) All of the building's elevators will be examined simultaneously.

Questions 20-23 refer to the following e-mail.

To: Jeanne Parton <careers@writemoves.com>
From: Carson Diaz <cdiaz@mailpal.com>
Date: September 2
Subject: Job opportunity

Dear Ms. Parton,

I would like to express my interest in the Spanish translator position that is ------- posted on the WriteMoves Web site. I have a master's degree from Monterey University's Department of Translation and Interpretation, ------- is renowned for its innovative program.

I spent four years as a technical writer for a software company in Dallas called NoroSoft. During my time in this position, I translated manuals from English into Spanish. -------. Prior to this, I interned at the Ministry of Foreign Affairs assisting Spanish-speaking dignitaries. -------, I interpreted anything that was said to them at special events. Having had both of these past experiences, I am equally skilled at written translation and oral interpretation.

If you have any questions, please do not hesitate to contact me.

Sincerely,

Carson Diaz

20 (A) immediately
(B) previously
(C) abruptly
(D) currently

21 (A) where
(B) which
(C) when
(D) whom

22 (A) I am very appreciative of your invitation for an interview.
(B) I have attached one of them so you can view my work.
(C) I was unable to contact one of the references you listed.
(D) I understand that the position is only a temporary one.

23 (A) Even so
(B) Instead of
(C) Regardless
(D) In particular

GO ON TO THE NEXT PAGE

PART 7

Directions: In this part, you will be asked to read several texts, such as advertisements, articles, instant messages, or examples of business correspondence. Each text is followed by several questions. Select the best answer and mark the corresponding letter (A), (B), (C), or (D) on your textbook.

Questions 24-25 refer to the following online chat.

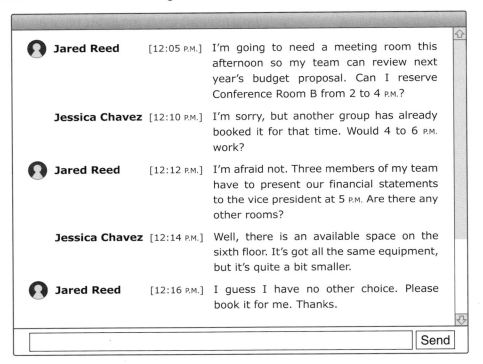

Jared Reed [12:05 P.M.] I'm going to need a meeting room this afternoon so my team can review next year's budget proposal. Can I reserve Conference Room B from 2 to 4 P.M.?

Jessica Chavez [12:10 P.M.] I'm sorry, but another group has already booked it for that time. Would 4 to 6 P.M. work?

Jared Reed [12:12 P.M.] I'm afraid not. Three members of my team have to present our financial statements to the vice president at 5 P.M. Are there any other rooms?

Jessica Chavez [12:14 P.M.] Well, there is an available space on the sixth floor. It's got all the same equipment, but it's quite a bit smaller.

Jared Reed [12:16 P.M.] I guess I have no other choice. Please book it for me. Thanks.

24 What is suggested about Mr. Reed?

(A) He had a meeting this morning.
(B) He recently hired a new team member.
(C) He will visit Ms. Chavez today.
(D) He works in the finance department.

25 At 12:16 P.M., what does Mr. Reed mean when he writes, "I guess I have no other choice"?

(A) He plans to visit a space without a reservation.
(B) He will not have access to presentation equipment.
(C) He has decided to use a less spacious room.
(D) He will have to change a meeting time.

Lose that extra weight with Vibrastep!

Vibrastep provides the same benefits that you can get from working out at the gym for an hour. This state-of-the-art machine made by Athletrex, a well-known manufacturer of exercise machines, delivers therapeutic vibrations throughout the body while the user stands over a vibrating metal plate. Prior to its release on the market, the machine was used in clinics and hospitals, and its benefits have been verified by doctors.

Vibration exercise works by causing muscle contractions. It aids not only in burning fat and cellulite but also in improving blood circulation and metabolism. Other advantages include:
• Skin toning and tightening
• Elevated serotonin levels to enhance your mood and overall well-being
• An increase in muscle strength of up to 50 percent in less than a month
• Improved bone density, which prevents osteoporosis
• A boost in the production of collagen

For only 15 minutes a day, seven days a week, you can lose weight effectively! Contact us at 1-800-555-4880 to make your order. Our product comes with a two-year warranty and is not available in stores. Order one today!

26 For whom is the advertisement most likely intended?

(A) Proprietors of sports facilities
(B) Experts working in the medical industry
(C) People wanting to improve their health
(D) Retailers of sporting goods

27 What is suggested about Vibrastep?

(A) Its cost is equivalent to a gym membership.
(B) It can be purchased over the phone only.
(C) Its use requires the supervision of a doctor.
(D) It can be found in many sports facilities.

28 What is NOT a benefit of using the Vibrastep?

(A) Greater stamina for sports activities
(B) Strengthening of muscles
(C) Loss of excess weight
(D) Improved skin condition

GO ON TO THE NEXT PAGE

Questions 29-31 refer to the following press release.

Pacific Film
707 Sycamore Street
San Jose, CA 95131
Phone: (408) 555-2552 to 2560
Fax: (408) 555-2565
www.pacificfilm.com

Contact: Janina Compton
Phone: (408) 555-2556
E-mail: jcompton@pacificfilm.com

Pacific Film to Make Improvements in January

SAN JOSE, CA, December 4 - This week, a representative from Pacific Film revealed that the company would be undertaking a series of changes in its organization at the beginning of next year.

In January, Pacific Film will be implementing new strategies to keep pace with its rivals. One of these includes increasing investments in research and development of products such as cameras, memory cards, and other devices used in digital photography. Another is the establishment of regional offices and manufacturing plants in China and Vietnam in order to cut down on operational and production costs.

"Over the years, many companies have emerged to challenge Pacific Film in the world of digital photography. Therefore, we must take steps to ensure that Pacific Film products remain competitive," said CEO Anthony Villman.

A multinational company based in the United States, Pacific Film was among the first to introduce digital photography products to the market 10 years ago.

29 Why was the press release written?

(A) To announce the establishment of a film studio
(B) To provide information on a line of new products
(C) To give details on a company's planned activities
(D) To describe an upcoming movie production

30 What is indicated about Pacific Film?

(A) It is relocating its main office to another city.
(B) It is aiming to improve a line of goods.
(C) It opened production plants in Asia.
(D) It has a new chief executive officer.

31 What is mentioned about the company's digital photography products?

(A) They are Pacific Film's best-selling items.
(B) They are more expensive compared to other brands.
(C) They have recently experienced a rise in sales.
(D) They were first launched on the market a decade ago.

Questions 32-35 refer to the following letter.

Cater Source
1602 Hampstead Street
Las Vegas, NV 89101
Phone: (702) 555-7596 / Fax: (702) 555-7600
www.catersource.com

August 27

Giada Durand
Le Cuisine Francois
952 Oakway Lane
Los Angeles, CA 90017

Dear Ms. Durand,

We at Cater Source appreciate your interest. To reiterate what I told you over the phone, we offer a wide selection of contemporary and traditional dinnerware made of porcelain, glass, and plastic in either a glazed or matte finish. In addition, our items come in a variety of patterns with matching serving accessories designed to meet the demands of most restaurant operations.

For your reference, I have sent you a complete product catalog. Once you are ready to order, just fill out the order form and mail it back to us. For faster processing, you may also go to our Web site and place your order there. Discounts are available to clients who order items in bulk. All our products include a six-month warranty in addition to any manufacturers' warranties.

If you have any further questions, you may e-mail me at awilson@catersource.com.

Yours Truly,

Anthony Wilson
Marketing Representative
Cater Source

---

32 What is the main purpose of the letter?

(A) To confirm an order of supplies
(B) To provide details about a restaurant event
(C) To ask for information about products
(D) To address a potential customer's questions

33 What is mentioned about Cater Source's products?

(A) They are available in several retail outlets.
(B) They are made of a variety of different materials.
(C) They are only sold to dining establishments.
(D) They are guaranteed for a period of one year.

34 The word "place" in paragraph 2, line 3, is closest in meaning to

(A) set
(B) locate
(C) submit
(D) rate

35 What did Mr. Wilson send to Ms. Durand?

(A) A warranty card
(B) A sample of merchandise
(C) A billing statement
(D) A listing of products

GO ON TO THE NEXT PAGE

Questions 36-40 refer to the following letters.

April 12

Lorraine Amici
Client Relations
Pacific Waterworks

Ms. Amici,

I bought a water pump from your store and had it installed in my home last Friday. On Monday, I observed that the machine would switch on and off at very short intervals, which prompted me to call your hotline for assistance. I was pleased to receive help within 24 hours. However, I was dissatisfied with the service of the repair crew that came to my house on Tuesday.

After finding out that the pump was defective, I thought they would replace it with a new one. Instead, they only changed some components on the machine. As I expected, the problem occurred again the following day.

Your substandard product has inconvenienced my family long enough, so I demand that you replace the entire unit immediately. If you do not address this matter within three days, I will ask for a full refund because of the damage.

I have enclosed the copies of my official receipt and warranty card for your reference.

Benito Garcia

Pacific Waterworks
1016 West Jackson Boulevard, Chicago, IL 60607
www.pacificwater.com
555-6392

April 14

Benito Garcia
6035 St. Lawrence Avenue
Chicago, IL 60637

Dear Mr. Garcia,

On behalf of Pacific Waterworks management, I would like to express our sincerest regrets for the troubles that have been caused. I have sent some of our staff to personally deliver this letter along with a new water pump, which they will install today.

In addition, I want to thank you for bringing the problem to our attention. Appropriate measures are currently being taken to prevent such an incident from happening again. Please allow us to make it up to you with a $100 gift certificate enclosed with this letter. You may use the certificate the next time you buy any product from Pacific Waterworks.

Thank you for your consideration.

Respectfully yours,

Lorraine Amici
Client Relations Officer
Pacific Waterworks

36 Why did the client send a letter?

(A) To provide special delivery instructions
(B) To seek help with completing an order
(C) To ask for an exchange of equipment
(D) To confirm the status of a delayed shipment

37 In the first letter, the word "address" in paragraph 3, line 2, is closest in meaning to

(A) direct
(B) send
(C) mark
(D) resolve

38 What is suggested about Pacific Waterworks?

(A) It charges customers for house calls.
(B) It provides quick responses to service requests.
(C) It imports spare parts from other countries.
(D) It has an affiliation with a construction firm.

39 How did Pacific Waterworks respond to Mr. Garcia's concerns?

(A) By sending a formal apology from its president
(B) By extending the warranty of a machine
(C) By granting the initial request in his complaint
(D) By depositing a refund to his bank account

40 What is indicated about Mr. Garcia?

(A) He is a regular customer of Pacific Waterworks.
(B) He would like to get his warranty extended.
(C) He can save money on a purchase in the future.
(D) He has experienced similar problems before.

GO ON TO THE NEXT PAGE

Questions 41-45 refer to the following letter, schedule of events, and e-mail.

Chicago Publishers Association
355-345 Lawson Street
Chicago, IL 60615
cgott@cpubassoc.org

October 17

Claude Hutchins
3301 Bellevue Offices
Seattle, WA 98101

Dear Mr. Hutchins,

It is our pleasure to inform you that the Chicago Publishers Association has chosen you as the recipient of the Children's Book of The Year award. Your book *Digging for Treasure* has topped the country's best-seller lists for a year now and is praised by critics and readers alike.

The awards ceremony will be held at the Alexandria Hotel in Chicago. Enclosed is a tentative schedule for you to review. We truly hope you will be present to receive the award, and we kindly ask that you inform us of whether you can attend by October 20 at the latest.

Sincerely yours,

Cecilia Gott
Director

Chicago Publishers Association
November 15

Book of the Year Awards
Alexandria Hotel Ballroom

Program

7:00 P.M. - 7:15 P.M.	**Welcoming remarks**
7:15 P.M. - 8:30 P.M.	**Awards Ceremony**

7:15 P.M. - 7:30 P.M.	Literary Novel of the Year
7:30 P.M. - 7:45 P.M.	Poetry Book of the Year
7:45 P.M. - 8:00 P.M.	Children's Book of the Year
8:00 P.M. - 8:15 P.M.	Short Story Anthology of the Year
8:15 P.M. - 8:30 P.M.	Nonfiction Book of the Year

8:30 P.M. - 8:45 P.M.	**Closing remarks**

NOTE: Award recipients will read excerpts from their winning books during the ceremony.

Dinner and drinks will be served at the start of the ceremony. Live music will be played after the closing remarks.

From:	Robert Magee <rmagee@smail.com>
To:	Cecilia Gott <cgott@cpubassoc.org>
Subject:	Regrets
Date:	October 19

Dear Ms. Gott,

I am writing on behalf of Julia Conde, who is currently in London. Her factual account of the global economic crisis became a best-seller here in the United Kingdom as well, so she is very much in demand and has been on a book tour throughout the country. Ms. Conde would like to express her sincere gratitude and appreciation for being accorded such a prestigious award, but she will be unable to make it to the ceremony. After the United Kingdom, she will be traveling for other engagements in Europe for the rest of October. Then, she will be making a few appearances in Asia in November. It is a busy time as you can imagine and Ms. Conde would like to get some rest for the remainder of the year before starting research on her next book in January.

Ms. Conde has asked me to convey her best wishes to the Chicago Publishers Association and to once again express her gratitude for such an honor.

Best regards,

Robert Magee

---

41 What is the main purpose of the letter?

(A) To congratulate a writer on his new work
(B) To invite the recipient to watch a performance
(C) To notify an author that he was selected for an award
(D) To request a copy of a best-selling book

42 What does Ms. Gott indicate about the schedule?

(A) It will be posted at an event venue.
(B) It should be kept confidential.
(C) It needs to be approved by the Alexandria Hotel.
(D) It is subject to further revision.

43 At what time will Mr. Hutchins be asked to speak at a ceremony?

(A) At 7:30 P.M.
(B) At 7:45 P.M.
(C) At 8:00 P.M.
(D) At 8:15 P.M.

44 According to Mr. Magee, what is included in Ms. Conde's plans for the rest of the year?

(A) Participating in a televised interview
(B) Conducting initial research for a future book
(C) Taking some time off from a hectic schedule
(D) Traveling to parts of Asia while on a holiday

45 For which award was Ms. Conde most likely chosen?

(A) Literary Novel of the Year
(B) Poetry Book of the Year
(C) Short Story Anthology of the Year
(D) Nonfiction Book of the Year

GO ON TO THE NEXT PAGE

Questions 46-50 refer to the following advertisement, order form, and letter.

Baldwin's Uniform Services:
For all your customized clothing needs

Look no further than Baldwin's for your uniform and customized clothing needs! Baldwin's can create T-shirts, polo shirts, and jackets with company names or logos. We also tailor trousers, skirts, and dresses to fit the needs of your establishment. Whether you run a restaurant, hotel, or other service business, our friendly staff will work with you to select the ideal styles, colors, and fabrics. Browse through our catalog of designs, or let us customize uniforms for you! Our prices start at $10 for a basic printed T-shirt with your company's logo and increase depending on fabric choice and complexity of design. Discounts apply for bulk purchases. Drop by our shop at 112 Gambit Lane in downtown Carlton City and check out everything we have to offer!

BALDWIN'S UNIFORM SERVICES

CUSTOMIZATION ORDER FORM: 4903948	DATE: April 9
NAME: Jerod Walton	COMPANY: Dade Security Bank
ADDRESS: 498 Gambit Lane, Carlton City WY, 74898	PHONE: 555-4938
	E-MAIL: J-Walt@dadesecuritybank.com

Please provide the following details:

GARMENT TYPE	T-shirts
NUMBER OF EACH SIZE WANTED	30 extra-large, 120 large, 150 medium, 80 small
COLOR	Light blue
INSTRUCTIONS	I would like basic printed T-shirts with the bank's logo printed in the center of the front side, in red.

Once an order has been submitted, Baldwin's Uniform Services will provide initial samples within four business days. Additional samples or changes to the original request will incur a $25 surcharge. If the client finds the garment satisfactory, a deposit of 50 percent of the full order price is required, with the remainder due within two days of the delivery date.

TO	Susanna Baldwin <susanna@baldwinsuniforms.com>
FROM	Jerod Walton <J-Walt@dadesecuritybank.com>
SUBJECT	Customized sample
DATE	April 13

Dear Ms. Baldwin,

Thanks for sending over the sample of the customized T-shirts you're making for us. I'm very pleased with the quality and color of the printing. However, I think the color of the shirt doesn't match the color of the logo as well as I thought it would. Could I see how it would look on a black or gray shirt? As this is quite a large order, I just want to ensure that everything is perfect. Please reply to this e-mail to let me know if you could do that for me. Once I've found a suitable color, I will provide you with the deposit by credit card, and you can proceed with the work.

Thanks!

Jerod Walton

46 What is being advertised?

(A) A uniform cleaning service
(B) A clothing supplier for businesses
(C) A chain of fashion boutiques
(D) A graphic design company

47 What is NOT included on the order form?

(A) The contact information of a customer
(B) The cost of each item purchased
(C) The number of products required
(D) The specific instructions for an order

48 What is indicated about Dade Security Bank?

(A) It is giving away T-shirts at an event.
(B) It is located on the same street as Baldwin's.
(C) It does not require staff to wear business attire.
(D) It is planning to have its logo redesigned.

49 What is suggested about Mr. Walton's order?

(A) It will come in five different sizes.
(B) It must be delivered in four days' time.
(C) It will be subject to an added cost.
(D) It must be partially paid by April 13.

50 Why most likely would Ms. Baldwin reply to the e-mail?

(A) To provide bank details for a wire transfer
(B) To inform a client of sizes currently available
(C) To confirm customer's satisfaction with a logo design
(D) To respond to a request for sample merchandise

• 채점 후 p.22를 보고 본인의 맞은 개수에 해당하는 학습 방법을 참고하세요.
• 진단고사 무료 해설강의가 해커스 동영상강의 포털 해커스인강 사이트 (HackersIngang.com)에서 제공됩니다.

해커스 스타강사의 ▶
무료 해설강의 바로 보기
(1~50번 문제)

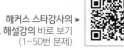

Hackers
TOEIC
Reading

GRAMMAR
PART 5,6

GRAMMAR Part 5,6

1. 토익 문법의 특징

토익 문법은 모두 비즈니스 상황과 관련된 문장에서 출제된다.

토익의 문법은 주로 회사 업무와 같은 비즈니스 상황에서의 영어 활용 능력을 측정하는 것이 목적이므로, 비즈니스 상황에서 실제로 사용되는 문장 내에서의 문법 사항들이 주로 출제된다. 따라서 이러한 상황에서 쓰이는 관련 주제, 어휘, 상황들에 익숙해지는 것이 중요하다.

토익 문법에서는 주로 출제되는 특정 유형이 있다.

토익의 문법에서는 비즈니스 상황에서 자주 사용되는 기본적인 문법 사항에 대한 지식을 측정하기 위하여 특정 유형의 문법이 반복되어 출제된다. 따라서 토익에서 자주 출제되는 문법의 세부 유형들을 알아 두는 것이 매우 중요하다.

2. 토익 문법 문제 유형

토익에 나오는 문법 문제는 크게 문장패턴, 동사구, 준동사구, 품사, 접속사와 절, 특수 구문으로 유형을 나눌 수 있다. 해커스 토익 Grammar에서는 이러한 문제 유형을 Section으로 구성하여 세부적인 문법 사항 및 전략을 제공하고 있다.

문장패턴	주어, 동사, 목적어, 보어, 수식어 자리에 들어갈 알맞은 단어를 채우는 문제 유형이다. 문장패턴 유형 문제의 대부분은 아래에 제시된 다른 유형으로도 분류될 수 있다.
동사구	동사 자리에 주어와의 수일치, 태, 시제 등과 관련하여 동사형태를 채우는 문제 유형이다.
준동사구	준동사로 분류되는 to 부정사, 동명사, 분사의 형태 및 역할, 의미상의 주어, 관련 표현을 묻는 문제 유형이다.
품사	명사, 대명사, 형용사, 부사, 전치사와 같은 품사의 역할과 관련된 다양한 표현을 묻는 문제 유형이다.
접속사와 절	알맞은 등위접속사와 상관접속사를 채우거나 관계절, 부사절, 명사절의 형태 및 쓰임에 대해서 묻는 문제 유형이다.
특수 구문	비교 구문의 알맞은 표현을 채우는 문제, 병치 구문을 완성하는 문제, 그리고 도치 구문의 올바른 형태를 묻는 문제 유형이다.

3. 토익 문법 문제 유형별 출제 비율

토익 문법 문제의 출제 비율을 그래프로 나타내면 아래와 같다.

*문장패턴 유형은 다른 유형으로 세분화되는 문제를 제외한 나머지만 그래프에 포함하였다.

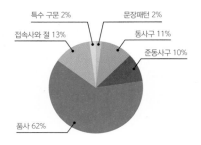

특수 구문 2%
문장패턴 2%
접속사와 절 13%
동사구 11%
준동사구 10%
품사 62%

4. 토익 문법 문제 풀이 방법

1. 보기를 보고 문법 문제임을 확인한다.

문법 문제 보기는 대체로 동일 어근을 갖는 단어들로 구성되거나 문법 범주가 유사한 단어들로 구성되어 있다. 예를 들어 품사 문제 유형 중 명사, 형용사, 부사 자리 채우기와 같은 유형의 보기는 동일한 어근을 가진 다른 품사의 단어들(ex - information, inform, informative, informatively)로 제시되고, 준동사 문제 유형의 보기는 주로 여러 형태의 준동사와 동사(ex - give, to give, giving, given)로 제시되므로 이를 통해 문법 문제임을 확인할 수 있다.

2. 문장의 구조나 해석을 통해 정답을 선택한다.

· 빈칸 주변이나 문장의 전체적인 구조를 통해 빈칸에 필요한 문법적 요소를 확인한 후 정답을 선택한다.
· 문법적 요소의 확인만으로 정답을 선택할 수 없는 경우, 해석을 통해 문맥에 알맞은 보기를 정답으로 선택한다.
· Part 6의 경우 빈칸이 있는 문장 외에 주변 문장과의 문맥을 파악하여 정답을 선택해야 하는 경우도 있다.

※ Part 6에서 문맥을 파악하여 정답을 선택해야 하는 문맥 파악 문제에 관해서는 Reading-Part 6(p.331)에서 자세히 다룬다.

Part 5 예제

Any experienced **baristas ------- might be interested in working at Highland Coffee** can apply through our Web site.
(A) who (B) where   (C) when   (D) which

> 1. 보기가 유사한 문법 범주에 포함되는 단어들, 즉 관계대명사와 관계부사로 구성되어 있으므로 문법 문제라는 것을 확인할 수 있다.

> 2. 빈칸 뒤의 절(might ~ Highland Coffee)에 주어가 없으므로, 주격 관계대명사 (A)와 (D)가 정답의 후보이다. 선행사(baristas)가 사람이므로 사람 관계대명사인 (A) who가 정답이다.

Part 6 예제

To: All managers

Please note that, due to unexpected problems, the March 1 opening of Fulton Industries' new office in Boston has been delayed. We are working to resolve these problems and **will ------- open** in the last week of May instead. Please ensure that your respective staff members are informed. Thank you.

(A) hope   **(B) hopefully**   (C) hoped   (D) hopeful

> 2. 빈칸이 조동사와 동사 사이에 있으므로 부사 자리라는 것을 알 수 있다. 따라서 정답은 부사 (B) hopefully이다.

> 1. 보기가 동일한 어근을 가진 다른 품사의 단어들로 제시되어 있으므로 문법 문제라는 것을 확인할 수 있다.

SECTION 1
문장패턴

CHAPTER 01 주어·동사

토익, 이렇게 나온다!
주어·동사 관련 문제는 평균 7~8문제 정도 꾸준히 출제된다. 주어 자리에 명사를 채우는 문제와 알맞은 동사 형태를 채우는 문제가 주로 출제된다.

토익 필수 개념 다지기

01 동사는 문장에서 말하고 있는 동작이나 상태를, 주어는 그 동작이나 상태의 주체(누가/무엇이)를 가리키는 말이다.

John cooked dinner. John은 저녁 식사를 요리했다.

이 문장에서 묘사하고 있는 동작인 'cooked(요리했다)'가 바로 이 문장의 동사이다. 그리고 'cooked'한 주체, 즉 누가 요리했는지의 '누가'에 해당하는 John이 바로 이 문장의 주어이다.

02 모든 문장에는 주어와 동사가 반드시 있어야 한다.

John dinner. (×) John 저녁 식사
cooked dinner. (×) 요리했다 저녁 식사

위의 두 문장은 틀리다. 첫 번째 문장은 묘사하고 있는 동작을 가리키는 말(동사)이 없어서 문장 성립이 안 되고 두 번째 문장은 동작(cooked)의 주체(주어)가 없어서 문장이 말이 안 된다. 즉 모든 문장이 성립하기 위해서는 주어와 동사가 반드시 있어야 한다.

03 절 [주어 + 동사]과 절 [주어 + 동사] 사이에는 반드시 접속사가 있어야 한다.

<u>Beth reads</u> <u>she goes to sleep.</u> (×) Beth는 독서한다 그녀는 잠든다.
절1 [주어1 동사1] 절2 [주어2 동사2]

절1 [주어1 동사1]과 절2 [주어2 동사2]가 중간에 아무런 접속사 없이 이렇게 나란히 올 수 없다.
다시 말해 절(주어 + 동사)과 절(주어 + 동사)은 접속사로 연결되어야 한다.

<u>Beth reads</u> **before** <u>she goes to sleep.</u> (○) Beth는 잠들기 전에 독서한다.
절1 [주어1 동사1] 접속사 절2 [주어2 동사2]

01 주어가 될 수 있는 것은 명사 역할을 하는 것들이다.

명사구	**The sales manager** led a training session for new staff. 그 영업부장은 신입 사원들을 위한 교육을 이끌었다.
대명사	**We** are attending a conference this weekend. 우리는 이번 주말에 회의에 참석할 것이다.
동명사구	**Running a business** is difficult. 회사를 경영하는 것은 어렵다.
to 부정사구	**To complete the report by Friday** is my goal. 보고서를 금요일까지 완성하는 것이 나의 목표이다.
명사절	**What Bob plans to discuss at the meeting** is unclear. Bob이 회의에서 논의하려고 계획한 것이 무엇인지 분명하지 않다.

▶ 밑줄 친 부분은 주어의 핵심이 되는 부분으로, 토익에서는 이 부분에 대해 묻는다.

고득점 포인트 to 부정사가 주어 자리에 오는 경우는 많지 않다. to 부정사는 주로 가짜 주어 it에 대한 진짜 주어로 쓰인다.

02 동사, 형용사 등은 문장의 주어 자리에 올 수 없다.

The film's exciting (~~conclude~~, **conclusion**) was praised by critics. 그 영화의 흥미진진한 결말은 비평가들에 의해 찬사 받았다.
▶ 동사(conclude)가 아닌 명사(conclusion)가 주어 자리에 와야 한다.

The economic (~~stable~~, **stability**) of the country is in doubt. 그 나라의 경제적 안정성이 의심스럽다.
▶ 형용사(stable)가 아닌 명사(stability)가 주어 자리에 와야 한다.

고득점 포인트

❶ 형용사처럼 보이지만 품사가 명사인 단어들을 주의해야 한다.

applicant 몡지원자	delivery 몡배달	denial 몡부인, 부정	proposal 몡제안
complaint 몡불만	arrival 몡도착	disposal 몡처리, 처분	withdrawal 몡인출
referral 몡추천, 소개			

❷ 동사나 형용사로 많이 사용되지만 명사로도 사용되는 단어들을 주의해야 한다.

prospect 몡전망 통조사하다	respect 몡존경 통존경하다	request 몡요청 통요청하다	review 몡검토 통검토하다
help 몡도움 통돕다	charge 몡요금 통청구하다	raise 몡인상 통올리다	check 몡수표, 저지 통점검하다, 저지하다
deal 몡거래 통취급하다	leave 몡휴가 통떠나다	effect 몡영향, 효과 통초래하다	increase 몡증가 통증가하다(증가시키다)
offer 몡제공 통제공하다	pay 몡급료 통지불하다	control 몡통제 통통제하다	interest 몡이자, 흥미 통흥미를 갖게 하다
objective 몡목적 톙객관적인	respondent 몡응답자 톙응하는	alternative 몡대안 톙대안의	representative 몡대표자 톙대표하는, 대리의
normal 몡표준, 평균 톙보통의	individual 몡개인 톙개인적인	potential 몡가능성 톙잠재하는	original 몡원본 톙원래의, 독창적인

03 주어는 동사와 수일치되어야 한다.

The (~~outlooks~~, **outlook**) for higher revenues in the second quarter is positive.
이사분기에 더 높은 수익에 대한 전망은 긍정적이다.
▶ 단수 동사(is)가 왔으므로 복수 주어(outlooks)가 아닌 단수 주어(outlook)를 써야 한다.

토익실전문제

출제 포인트 주어 자리 채우기
주어로 명사구를 채우는 것이 가장 많이 출제된다.

1. The building manager notified the tenants that the ------- of the lobby would be postponed for a week.

(A) renovation   (B) renovate
(C) renovated   (D) renovator

2. Archaeological ------- in a study published in the *Journal of Science* are generating excitement among scientists doing research on the Greek relics.

(A) finding   (B) findable
(C) findings   (D) found

3. The new ------- that is going up on Williams Street will accommodate hundreds of commercial enterprises.

(A) structural   (B) structurally
(C) structured   (D) structure

정답·해설·해석 p.12

01 it은 to 부정사구, that절 같은 긴 주어를 대신해서 쓰인다. 이때, it을 '가주어', 긴 주어를 '진주어'라고 한다.

It is important to monitor the customers' feedback carefully. 고객들의 의견을 신중하게 검토하는 것은 중요하다.
가주어 　　　　　　　　　 진주어(to 부정사구)

It is expected that Ms. Bennet will be promoted in this month. Ms. Bennet이 이번 달에 승진될 것이라고 예상된다.
가주어 　　　　　　　 진주어(that절)

고득점 포인트

❶ it은 명사, 전치사구 등을 강조할 때 that과 함께 쓰여, 'it – that 강조구문'을 만든다.
　It was Susan **that** damaged my car. 내 차를 훼손한 사람은 바로 Susan이었다.
　　　 강조되는 내용
　It is at my parents' home **that** I hope to spend the holidays. 내가 휴일을 보내기를 희망하는 곳은 바로 내 부모님 댁이다.
　　　　강조되는 내용

❷ 강조되는 것이 사람명사일 경우 that대신 who(m)를, 사물명사일 경우 which를 쓸 수도 있다.
　It was Garth who paid the bill. 청구서를 지불한 사람은 바로 Garth였다.
　It is the bookshelf which I want to buy for my sister. 내가 내 여동생에게 사주고 싶은 것은 바로 그 책장이다.

02 there는 '~이 있다'를 나타내기 위해 쓰이며, 'there + 동사(be, remain, …) + 진짜 주어(명사구)' 형태를 이룬다.

There are many cars in the parking lot. 주차장에는 많은 차들이 있다.
가짜 주어　　 진짜 주어(명사구)

There remain a few questions about the upcoming conference. 곧 있을 회의에 대해 몇 가지 질문들이 남아 있다.
가짜 주어　　　 진짜 주어(명사구)

고득점 포인트

[there + 동사 + 진짜 주어] 구문의 진짜 주어 자리에 동사는 올 수 없다.
The receptionist will confirm that there are reserved(→ reservations). 그 접수원은 예약이 있는지를 확인해 줄 것이다.

03 가짜 주어 it과 there 자리에 다른 단어는 올 수 없다.

(~~That~~, **It**) is unbelievable that Mr. Evans organized the workshop by himself.
Mr. Evans가 홀로 워크숍을 준비했다는 것은 믿기 어렵다.
▶ 가짜 주어 It 자리에 다른 단어는 올 수 없다.

(~~Any~~, **There**) is no additional charge to access the event. 행사에 참석하기 위한 추가 요금은 없다.
▶ 가짜 주어 There 자리에 다른 단어는 올 수 없다.

고득점 포인트

동사가 '~이다/~하다'로 해석되면 it, '~이 있다'로 해석되면 there를 쓴다.
When you are planning a trip, there(→ it) is a good idea to compare prices. 여행을 계획할 때, 가격을 비교하는 것은 좋은 생각이다.
It(→ There) is a brochure at the information desk. 안내 데스크에 안내 책자가 있다.

토익실전문제

출제 포인트 가짜 주어, 진짜 주어 자리 채우기
가짜 주어(it이나 there)와 진짜 주어(to 부정사/that절이나 명사구)를 채우는 문제가 출제된다.

1. The publisher prints corrections on the second page of the magazine when there are ------- in previous issues.

　(A) mistaking 　　　　　(B) mistake
　(C) mistakes 　　　　　 (D) mistaken

2. It is mandatory to ------- a driver's license before operating a vehicle on a public road.

　(A) obtain 　　　　　　(B) obtaining
　(C) obtainment 　　　　(D) obtained

3. ------- remain significant challenges for the fledgling business as it tries to gain a foothold in a highly competitive market.

　(A) Any 　　　　　　　(B) There
　(C) These 　　　　　　 (D) That

정답·해설·해석 p.12

토익 공식 3 동사 자리에 올 수 있는 것 : '(조동사 +) 동사'

01 문장의 동사가 될 수 있는 것은 '(조동사 +) 동사'이다.

The manager **oversees** more than 50 workers. 그 관리자는 50명 이상의 근로자들을 감독한다.
The manager **can oversee** more than 50 workers. 그 관리자는 50명 이상의 근로자들을 감독할 수 있다.

02 '동사원형 + -ing'나 'to + 동사원형'과 같은 형태는 문장의 동사가 되지 못한다.

The manager **overseeing/to oversee** more than 50 workers. (×)
▶ overseeing이나 to oversee는 동사처럼 보이지만 동사가 아니다. 이와 같이 동사처럼 보이는 overseeing(동명사, 분사), to oversee(부정사)를 '준동사'라고 한다.

※ 준동사에 관해서는 Section 3(p.103)에서 자세히 다룬다.

03 명사나 형용사 등은 문장의 동사 자리에 올 수 없다.

Bill (**adjustment**, **adjusted**) the project's deadline. Bill은 프로젝트 마감일을 조정했다.
▶ 명사(adjustment)가 아닌 동사(adjusted)가 문장의 동사 자리에 와야 한다.

Nelson Company (**short**, **shortens**) its production time by using robots. Nelson사는 로봇을 사용하여 생산 시간을 단축한다.
▶ 형용사(short)가 아닌 동사(shortens)가 문장의 동사 자리에 와야 한다.

고득점 포인트 주로 명사나 형용사로 쓰이지만 동사로도 사용되어 혼동을 일으키는 단어들이 있으므로 주의해야 한다.

function 명기능 통기능하다	question 명질문 통질문하다	name 명이름 통명명하다, 임명하다	document 명서류 통문서에 기록하다
finance 명재정 통자금을 공급하다	cost 명비용 통비용이 들다	experience 명경험 통경험하다	access 명입장, 접근 통들어가다, 접근하다
process 명과정, 공정 통처리하다	purchase 명구입 통구입하다	place 명장소 통두다	transfer 명이동 통이동하다, 옮기다
contact 명접촉 통연락하다	demand 명요청, 수요 통요구하다	feature 명특징 통특징으로 삼다	schedule 명스케줄 통예정에 넣다
deposit 명보증금 통예금하다	complete 형완전한 통완성하다	secure 형안전한 통지키다	correct 형정확한 통고치다

04 동사는 수, 태, 시제가 맞아야 한다.

The chairperson (**review**, **reviews**) his notes before each meeting. 그 회장은 각 회의 전에 그의 메모를 검토한다.
▶ 주어가 단수(chairperson)이므로 복수 동사(review)가 아닌 단수 동사(reviews)가 와야 한다.

The inspection (**conducted**, **was conducted**) by a representative from the health department.
그 검사는 보건부 직원에 의해 실시되었다.
▶ 주어인 The inspection이 a representative에 의해 실시되었다는 수동의 의미이므로 수동태 동사 was conducted가 와야 한다.

Denise (**makes**, **made**) the reservation two days ago. Denise는 이틀 전에 예약을 했다.
▶ 과거를 나타내는 표현(two days ago)이 있으므로 동사로는 과거 시제 made가 와야 한다.

※ 주어와의 수일치, 능동태·수동태, 시제에 관해서는 각각 Chapter 04(p.76), Chapter 05(p.84), Chapter 06(p.92)에서 자세히 다룬다.

토익실전문제

출제 포인트 동사 자리 채우기
동사 자리에 올 수 없는 준동사나 다른 품사(명사, 형용사 등)를 제외하고 동사를 채우거나, 수, 태, 시제가 맞는 동사를 채우는 문제가 주로 출제된다.

1. The value of the dollar ------- yesterday against the Japanese yen after it was announced that American imports had risen.

   (A) soaring (B) to soar
   (C) soarer (D) soared

2. An announcement about the new sanitation regulations ------- in the restaurant's kitchen.

   (A) were posted (B) have posted
   (C) to post (D) will be posted

3. Salaried employees ------- a 10 percent increase in wages last year as an incentive to raise production levels.

   (A) acquirement (B) to acquire
   (C) acquired (D) acquiring

정답·해설·해석 p.12

01 명령문은 주어 없이 동사원형으로 시작된다.

Place the application form on top of the pile. 그 신청서를 쌓아 올린 더미 맨 위에 놓아 주십시오.

Please **complete** this survey and sign at the bottom. 이 설문지를 작성하시고 하단에 서명해 주십시오.

고득점 포인트   명령문은 주어 you가 생략되어 있는 문장으로, 공손함을 나타내는 표현인 please를 명령문의 동사 앞에 자주 쓴다.

02 When절/If절 + 명령문 : ~할 때/~한다면, ~해라

When applying for a visa, **verify** that all the necessary documents are present.
비자를 신청할 때, 모든 필요한 서류들이 있는지 확인하십시오.

If you would like to fly first class, **contact** your travel agent. 일등석에 타기를 원하신다면, 여행사 직원에게 연락하십시오.

▶ 토익에서는 바로 명령문으로 시작되는 문장보다 if절이나 when절 뒤에 나오는 명령문의 동사를 묻는 경우가 많다.
  명령문 앞에 드물게 whatever절 등이 나오기도 한다.

03 명령문의 동사 자리에, 원형이 아닌 동사나 준동사, 명사 등은 오지 못한다.

Please (~~has~~, **have**) a seat. 자리에 앉아 주십시오.
▶ 동사원형을 제외한 동사(3인칭 단수형, 과거형 등)는 명령문의 동사 자리에 올 수 없다.

Whenever you need dietary supplements, (~~visiting~~, **visit**) Health Stop for the finest products in the region.
건강 보조 식품이 필요할 때는 언제든지, 지역 내 가장 좋은 제품들이 있는 Health Stop에 방문해 주십시오.
▶ 준동사인 '동사원형 + ing'(동명사, 분사)는 명령문의 동사 자리에 올 수 없다.

When operating machinery, (~~follower~~, **follow**) the safety rules. 기계를 작동할 때는, 안전 규칙을 따르십시오.
▶ 명사나 형용사는 명령문의 동사 자리에 올 수 없다.

토익실전문제

출제 포인트   명령문의 동사 자리 채우기
When절이나 If절 뒤에 나오는 명령문의 첫 자리에 동사원형을 채우는 문제
가 주로 출제된다.

1. When making a presentation, ------- discussing matters already known to the audience.

   (A) to avoid   (B) avoids
   (C) avoiding   (D) avoid

2. For your family's financial security, ------- on North Star Insurance Corporation to provide compensation in the event of a medical emergency.

   (A) relies   (B) rely
   (C) relied   (D) relying

3. If the strategy fails to meet the team's objectives, ------- the plan in order to determine what its shortcomings are.

   (A) evaluating   (B) to evaluate
   (C) evaluate   (D) evaluation

정답·해설·해석 p.12

둘 중 맞는 형태를 고르세요.

01 The accounting team ------- over the weekend to complete the annual report.
ⓐ working   ⓑ worked

02 ------- remains one more training session to be conducted before staff can start using the new program.
ⓐ It   ⓑ There

03 The restaurant's main course menu ------- according to the season.
ⓐ vary   ⓑ varies

04 ------- the time spent at meetings will increase productivity in the office.
ⓐ Reduce   ⓑ Reducing

05 The audience at the convention ------- doctors and other medical personnel.
ⓐ comprises   ⓑ comprisal

06 ------- is important to instruct the new workers on the company's code of conduct.
ⓐ It   ⓑ That

07 Next quarter's budget proposal should ------- to the director's office by this coming Friday.
ⓐ send   ⓑ be sent

틀린 곳이 있으면 바르게 고치세요.

08 Efficient is critical when carrying out work assignments at Hoovers Company.

09 When Mr. Miller finishes writing the memorandum yesterday, he examined it carefully for errors.

10 If you are uncertain of meeting a deadline, requests an extension from your manager.

11 The brochure designed by Mr. Clark is being edited by a department head.

12 There is known that 40 percent of American households do not have broadband Internet access.

13 At the meeting last night, the coordinator evaluation the project.

14 The data's omit from the research paper shows that it was unimportant.

정답·해석 p.13

무료 해설 ▶
바로 보기

맞은 문제 개수: / 14
틀린 문제에 해당하는 토익 공식을 다시 한번 학습하세요.

Chapter 01 주어·동사 | 53

🕐 제한 시간 12분

Part 5

01 The final ------- for regional sales manager submitted by the hiring committee include three candidates already working within the company.

(A) selects
(B) select
(C) selections
(D) selectable

02 The unemployment rate ------- people who have been out of a job for over nine months.

(A) exclude
(B) excluding
(C) excludes
(D) exclusion

03 Mr. Jenson called the courier to complain that an important ------- did not arrive on schedule.

(A) documented
(B) document
(C) documenting
(D) documentation

04 The lipstick samples ------- back to the manufacturer when it was discovered that a number of the products' cases were damaged.

(A) were sent
(B) were sending
(C) sent
(D) being sent

05 Consumer spending ------- significantly during the past three months, resulting in a nationwide economic recovery.

(A) rise
(B) will rise
(C) has risen
(D) rising

06 Renters planning on renovating their apartments must make certain that the changes they make ------- to the relevant clauses of their lease contracts.

(A) adherable
(B) adhering
(C) adherence
(D) adhere

07 The governor will provide additional funding to the Department of Transportation, as ------- of additional state highways is a priority.

(A) construct
(B) construction
(C) to construct
(D) constructible

08 By the end of the first quarter, operating expenses ------- the company's estimates by over 10 percent.

(A) surpassing
(B) had surpassed
(C) was surpassed
(D) to surpass

09 A special ------- was formed by the government to look into the financial activity of the development firm to determine if it was obeying all tax policies.

(A) commissioner
(B) commissioned
(C) commission
(D) commissioning

10 When sending a requested sample to buyers, ------- them that the package is on its way.

(A) information
(B) inform
(C) informs
(D) informing

11 Sartek Incorporated's recent ------- of Telstar Limited will allow it to dominate the mobile communications market.

(A) acquire
(B) acquisition
(C) acquirable
(D) acquired

12 The committee carefully ------- the consultant's recommendations before changing the vacation policy in the employee manual.

(A) studied
(B) studying
(C) study
(D) was studied

13 Katherine Bryant ------- Purcell Firm 40 years ago, making her one of the longest-serving employees since the organization was first established.

(A) entering
(B) enter
(C) entered
(D) enters

14 The ------- of the agreement forced Ms. Zhang to negotiate a new contract with the owner of the raw materials supplier.

(A) terminate
(B) termination
(C) terminating
(D) terminated

15 The manager ------- that the expenses claimed by the sales team are invalid and will not be reimbursed.

(A) have affirmed   (B) affirms
(C) to affirm   (D) affirming

16 Over half of the survey respondents ------- the city's garbage collection fees to be too high.

(A) consider   (B) considers
(C) is considering   (D) has considered

17 ------- is vital that employees change e-mail passwords periodically to prevent unauthorized access to their accounts.

(A) What   (B) This
(C) That   (D) It

18 The applicant has relevant work experience, but his academic ------- do not meet the requirements specified for the position.

(A) qualify   (B) to qualify
(C) qualified   (D) qualifications

Part 6

Questions 19-22 refer to the following e-mail.

Date: April 10
To: Steve Vickers
From: Susan White
Subject: Possible Workshops

Hi Steve,

I just got back from a marketing conference in Denver and was thinking about organizing a workshop for my team based on the information I received at the event. The ------- would be to update staff on
₁₉
current broadcast advertising trends.

I think the information could be very useful to the team as they are developing new television commercials. I ------- we hold two sessions, one on Monday, May 9 and another on Thursday, May
₂₀
12, as there will be a lot of material to cover.

Just to give you an idea, advertising on Internet-connected television is something we definitely need to -------. To reach a larger audience, we require a better understanding of how to appeal to viewers
₂₁
who may not watch much traditional television. -------.
₂₂

Please let me know what you think, and if you'd like me to go ahead and schedule the workshops.

---

19 (A) objected   (B) objective
(C) objection   (D) objectionable

20 (A) suggestion   (B) suggesting
(C) suggest   (D) suggestive

21 (A) dispute   (B) limit
(C) explore   (D) terminate

22 (A) The commercials we are working on should be released in a week.
(B) This is crucial as our clients hope to advertise in innovative ways.
(C) Having two sessions as you suggested seems unnecessary.
(D) The team should tell us this week if they can attend.

목적어·보어·수식어

토익, 이렇게 나온다!
목적어·보어·수식어 관련 문제는 평균 11~12문제 정도 꾸준히 출제된다. 목적어 자리에 명사를 채우는 문제와 보어 자리에 분사를 채우는 문제, 수식어 거품 자리에 전치사나 부사절을 이끄는 것을 채우는 문제가 자주 출제된다.

토익 필수 개념 다지기

01 목적어는 동사의 대상을 나타내며, 목적어를 꼭 필요로 하는 타동사 뒤에 반드시 나와야 맞는 문장이 된다.

John likes **movies**. John은 영화를 좋아한다.

여기서 동사 likes의 대상인 movies가 바로 이 문장의 목적어이다. 만약 목적어 movies가 없으면 '무엇을 좋아하는지'를 알 수 없어 의미가 완전해지지 않으므로 틀린 문장이 된다.

John likes. (×) John은 좋아한다.

02 보어는 주어나 목적어를 보충해 주며, 보어를 꼭 필요로 하는 동사 뒤에 반드시 나와야 맞는 문장이 된다.

She is **a doctor**. 그녀는 의사이다.
The student finds history **interesting**. 그 학생은 역사가 재미있다고 생각한다.

여기서 a doctor는 주어 She를 보충하는 주격 보어, interesting은 목적어 history를 보충하는 목적격 보어이다.
만약 이 보어들이 없다면 She가 '누구인지', history가 '어떠한지'를 알 수 없어 의미가 완전해지지 않으므로 틀린 문장이 된다.

She is. (×) 그녀는 ~이다.
The student finds history. (×) 그 학생은 역사를 ~이라고 생각한다.

03 수식어는 문장의 필수성분(주어, 동사, 목적어/보어)에 의미를 더해 주는 역할을 하며, 문장에 없어도 되는 부가적인 성분이다.

Bill is sitting **on a chair**. Bill이 의자에 앉아 있다.
　필수성분　　　　수식어

주어와 동사 Bill is sitting은 문장에 없어서는 안 될 필수적인 부분이다. on a chair는 필수성분으로 된 문장(Bill이 앉아 있다)에 '장소'(의자에)에 대한 추가 정보를 더해 주고 있다. 수식어 on a chair가 없어도 문장은 성립되므로 '수식어 거품'이라고 부르기도 한다.

토익 공식 1 목적어 자리에 올 수 있는 것 : 명사 역할을 하는 것

01 목적어가 될 수 있는 것은 명사 역할을 하는 것들이다.

명사구	Peter has **sufficient money** to buy an apartment. Peter는 아파트 한 채를 사기에 충분한 돈이 있다.
대명사	We cannot meet **them** this afternoon. 우리는 오늘 오후에 그들을 만날 수 없다.
동명사구	Steve prefers **exercising in the morning**. Steve는 오전에 운동하는 것을 선호한다.
to 부정사구	I hope **to finish** the report soon. 나는 곧 보고서를 마무리하고 싶다.
명사절	Ms. Lee confirms **that the numbers are inaccurate**. Ms. Lee는 숫자들이 부정확하다는 것이 사실임을 확인해 준다.

▶ 밑줄 친 부분은 목적어의 핵심이 되는 부분으로, 토익에서는 이 부분에 대해 묻는다.

02 동사, 형용사 등은 목적어 자리에 올 수 없다.

The policy provides (~~insure~~, **insurance**) for damage caused by natural disasters.
그 보험 증서는 자연재해에 의해 초래된 피해에 대한 보험금을 제공한다.

▶ 동사(insure)가 아닌 명사(insurance)가 목적어 자리에 와야 한다.

The accountant calculated the (~~expensive~~, **expense**) of expanding the store.
그 회계사는 상점을 확장하는 것에 대한 비용을 계산했다.

▶ 형용사(expensive)가 아닌 명사(expense)가 목적어 자리에 와야 한다.

토익실전문제

출제 포인트 목적어 자리 채우기
목적어로 명사구를 채우는 것이 답으로 가장 많이 출제된다.

1. Reliance Travel Agency paid much ------- to complaints that flights booked for clients had been canceled at the last minute by the airline.

(A) attend   (B) attention
(C) attentive   (D) attends

2. In response to the company's financial difficulties, the finance manager was asked to implement a ------- on limiting operating costs.

(A) regulatory   (B) regulatively
(C) regulation   (D) regulate

3. The researcher will analyze the recent ------- in wireless technology before making suggestions to the new design of the laptop.

(A) develop   (B) develops
(C) developmental   (D) developments

정답·해설·해석 **p.15**

GRAMMAR Part 5,6   Ch 02 목적어·보어·수식어   Hackers TOEIC Reading

01 목적격 보어가 있는 문장에서, to 부정사구나 that절이 목적어일 경우 뒤로 보내고 그 자리에 가목적어 it을 사용한다.

I thought ~~to understand the lecture difficult~~. 나는 그 강의를 이해하는 것이 어렵다고 생각했다.
　　　　　　it difficult to understand the lecture

▶ 문장의 진목적어인 to 부정사구(to understand the lecture)가 문장 뒤로 가고, 그 자리에 가목적어 it이 와야 한다.

The faculty found ~~that the new professor had two doctoral degrees impressive~~.
　　　　　　　　it impressive that the new professor had two doctoral degrees
교수단은 신임 교수가 두 개의 박사 학위를 가진 것을 인상 깊게 여겼다.

▶ 문장의 진목적어인 that절(that the new professor had two doctoral degrees)이 문장 뒤로 가고, 그 자리에 가목적어 it이 와야 한다.

> **고득점 포인트**
> 단, 목적어가 to 부정사구나 that 명사절이 아닌 '명사(구)'일 때는, 가목적어 it을 쓰지 않는다.
> The manual made it easy the installation of the software program. (×)
> The manual made the installation of the software program easy. (○) 설명서는 그 소프트웨어 프로그램의 설치를 쉽게 했다.

02 가목적어 it이 쓰이는 대표적인 구문 「make it possible」

The machinery will make **it** possible **to increase productivity**. 그 기계는 생산성을 증가시키는 것을 가능하게 할 것이다.

▶ make it possible 구문에서 진목적어인 to 부정사구(to increase productivity)와 가목적어 it은 반드시 함께 나와야 한다.

Revisions to the contract will make **it** possible (**negotiate**, **to negotiate**) interest rates.
계약에 대한 수정은 금리를 협상하는 것을 가능하게 할 것이다.

▶ make it possible 구문에서 진목적어 자리에는 동사(negotiate)가 올 수 없으며 대신 to 부정사(to negotiate)가 와야 한다.

> **고득점 포인트**
> make it possible 구문에서 possible 대신 easy, difficult, necessary와 같은 형용사가 쓰이기도 하며, 그 구문의 의미는 '주어가 ~하는 것을 쉽게/어렵게/필요하게 하다'이다.
> The Internet makes it easy to find information about job openings. 인터넷은 채용 정보를 찾는 것을 쉽게 해준다.
> Our busy schedules made it difficult to arrange a meeting. 우리의 바쁜 일정은 회의를 준비하는 것을 어렵게 했다.

토익실전문제

출제 포인트 진목적어 자리 채우기
진목적어 자리에 to 부정사구나 that절을 채우는 문제가 주로 출제된다.

1. The proposed budget increases would make it possible ------- added support to each sector of the company.

(A) give　　　　　　(B) gave
(C) to give　　　　　(D) in giving

2. Local civic groups find it unreasonable ------- the local government would make a proposition to establish a landfill next to a residential area.

(A) which　　　　　(B) about
(C) that　　　　　　(D) what

3. Warehouse workers must make it a point ------- with all safety regulations in order to reduce the potential for accidents.

(A) comply　　　　　(B) to comply
(C) of complying　　(D) complied

정답·해설·해석 p.15

보어 자리에 올 수 있는 것 : 명사 또는 형용사

01 보어가 될 수 있는 것은 명사 또는 형용사 역할을 하는 것들이다.

• 명사 역할을 하는 것들

명사구	Previous work experience is **a great asset** for job seekers. 이전의 근무 경력은 구직자들에게 큰 자산이다.
동명사구	Mike's hobby is **collecting sports souvenirs**. Mike의 취미는 스포츠 기념품을 수집하는 것이다.
to 부정사구	The important thing is **to remember your seat number**. 중요한 것은 너의 좌석 번호를 기억하는 것이다.
명사절	The problem is **that the job candidates are equally talented**. 문제는 입사 지원자들이 동등하게 재능이 있다는 것이다.

• 형용사 역할을 하는 것들

형용사	The instructor's directions are **understandable**. 그 강사의 지시 사항은 이해하기 쉽다.
분사	John considers my lecture notes **disorganized**. John은 내 강의 노트가 엉터리라고 생각한다.

▶ 밑줄 친 부분은 보어의 핵심이 되는 부분으로, 토익에서는 이 부분에 대해 묻는다.

02 보어 자리에 동사, 부사는 올 수 없다.

Students were (**appreciate**, **appreciative**) of the mentoring program. 학생들은 멘토링 프로그램에 대해 고마워했다.
▶ 동사(appreciate)가 아닌 형용사(appreciative)가 보어 자리에 와야 한다.

Outstanding special effects made the movie (**entertainingly**, **entertaining**). 뛰어난 특수 효과가 그 영화를 재미있게 만들었다.
▶ 부사(entertainingly)가 아닌 형용사 역할을 하는 분사(entertaining)가 보어 자리에 와야 한다.

03 주격 보어를 갖는 동사, 목적격 보어를 갖는 동사

주격 보어를 갖는 동사 (연결동사)	be ~이다/되다	become ~이 되다	get ~이 되다	seem ~인 것 같다	remain 여전히 ~이다
	turn ~이 되다	taste ~한 맛이 나다	feel ~처럼 느끼다	look ~처럼 보이다	sound ~하게 들리다
목적격 보어를 갖는 동사	make ~을 ~으로 만들다	keep ~을 ~하게 유지하다	find ~이 ~함을 알게 되다	consider ~을 ~라고 여기다	call ~을 ~이라고 부르다

Edward <u>became</u> **a certified pharmacist**. Edward는 공인된 약사가 되었다.
Ms. Bellini <u>considers</u> cooking **an enjoyable activity**. Ms. Bellini는 요리를 즐거운 활동으로 여긴다.

토익실전문제

출제 포인트 보어 자리 채우기
주격 보어 자리를 채우는 문제가 주로 출제된다.

2. Everyone felt that it was a huge ------- that Brian Mann did not receive the Employee of the Year Award because he deserved it.

(A) oversee   (B) oversaw
(C) overseeing   (D) oversight

1. Frank McKenzie was particularly ------- in the firm's recent decision to expand into the Hong Kong financial market.

(A) influences   (B) influential
(C) influencing   (D) influenced

3. Attendees enjoyed all the presentations during the seminar, and everyone agreed that Mr. Simm's talk was especially -------.

(A) instructive   (B) instructed
(C) instruct   (D) instructing

정답·해설·해석 p.16

01 보어가 주어나 목적어와 동격 관계를 이루면 보어 자리에 명사가 온다.

My father is **an architect**. 내 아버지는 건축가이다.
Following her first year of employment, Janelle became **the director** of her department.
입사 1년 후에, Janelle은 그녀 부서의 부장이 되었다.

▶ 주어(My father/Janelle)가 주격 보어(an architect/the director)와 동격 관계를 이루므로 명사가 보어 자리에 온다.

The professor called his student **a genius**. 그 교수는 그의 학생을 천재라고 불렀다.
The French consider snails **a delicacy**. 프랑스인들은 달팽이를 별미로 여긴다.

▶ 목적어(his student/snails)가 목적격 보어(a genius/a delicacy)와 동격 관계를 이루므로 명사가 보어 자리에 온다.

02 보어가 주어나 목적어를 설명해 주면 보어 자리에 형용사가 온다.

The show was **hilarious**. 그 쇼는 매우 유쾌했다.
They seemed **apprehensive** about the deadline. 그들은 마감일에 대해 걱정하는 것처럼 보였다.

▶ 주격 보어(hilarious/apprehensive)가 주어(The show/They)를 설명해 주고 있으므로, 형용사가 보어 자리에 온다.

The traffic jam made me **impatient**. 교통 체증은 나를 짜증나게 했다.
The bank keeps its depositors **informed** about investment opportunities.
그 은행은 예금자들에게 투자 기회에 대해 계속 알려 준다.

▶ 목적격 보어(impatient/informed)가 목적어(me/its depositors)를 설명해 주고 있으므로, 형용사가 보어 자리에 온다.

> **고득점 포인트** 가짜 주어(it)-진짜 주어(to 부정사나 that절)의 보어 자리
>
> It is my recommendation for all team members to attend the seminar. 모든 팀원들이 세미나에 참석하는 것이 나의 권고사항이다.
> It is recommendable for all team members to attend the seminar. 모든 팀원들이 세미나에 참석하는 것은 권할 만하다.
>
> → 보어 자리에 명사(recommendation)가 오든 형용사(recommendable)가 오든 모두 맞는 문장이다. 단, 이 경우 명사(recommendation)가 소유격(my) 없이 혼자 오면 틀린 문장이 된다는 것에 주의해야 한다.
>
> It is a wonder that the book sold many copies. 그 책이 많이 팔렸다는 것은 경탄할 만한 일이다.
> It is wonderful that the book sold many copies. 그 책이 많이 팔렸다는 것은 경탄할 만하다.
>
> → 보어 자리에 명사(wonder)가 오든 형용사(wonderful)가 오든 모두 맞는 문장이다. 단, 이 경우 명사(wonder)가 관사(a) 없이 혼자 오면 틀린 문장이 된다.

토익실전문제

출제 포인트 보어 자리 채우기
주격 보어 자리에 명사와 형용사 중 알맞은 것을 선택해서 채우는 문제가 주로 출제된다.

1. Management was ------- in renegotiating the terms of the labor agreement with the union last month.

   (A) successful (B) success
   (C) successor (D) successfully

2. Because the price offered by the supplier was -------, the company agreed to increase its purchase order.

   (A) reason (B) reasonable
   (C) reasonably (D) reasoned

3. It is ------- for investors to check a company's performance before purchasing any shares.

   (A) sense (B) sensible
   (C) sensed (D) sensor

정답·해설·해석 p.16

토익 공식 5 수식어 거품

01 수식어 거품이 될 수 있는 것

전치사구   **At the conference**, we attended some lectures. 회의에서, 우리는 몇몇 강연에 참석했다.

to 부정사구   I came here **to see you**. 나는 너를 보러 여기에 왔다.

분사(구문)   The bag **left in the lobby** belongs to Ms. Lopez. 로비에 남겨진 가방은 Ms. Lopez의 것이다.

관계절   I have a colleague **who works extremely hard**. 나는 매우 열심히 일하는 동료가 있다.

부사절   **When the concert ended**, all of the audience applauded. 콘서트가 끝났을 때, 모든 청중은 박수를 쳤다.

▶ 밑줄 친 부분은 수식어 거품의 핵심이 되는 부분으로, 토익에서는 이 부분에 대해 묻는다.

※ 전치사구는 Chapter 14(p.170), to 부정사구는 Chapter 07(p.104), 분사(구문)는 Chapter 09(p.120), 관계절은 Chapter 16(p.190), 그리고 부사절은 Chapter 17(p.198)에서 자세히 다룬다.

02 수식어 거품이 오는 자리

● + 주어 + 동사   [Despite the economic slowdown], the company will proceed with the expansion.
      수식어 거품(전치사구)   주어   동사
경기 침체에도 불구하고, 그 회사는 확장을 계속 진행할 것이다.

주어 + ● + 동사   The people [waiting in line] are becoming impatient.
      주어   수식어 거품(분사)   동사
줄을 서서 기다리고 있는 사람들은 조바심을 내고 있다.

주어 + 동사 ~ + ●   Peter offered to give me a ride [even though he was very busy].
      주어   동사   목적어   수식어 거품(부사절)
Peter는 매우 바빴음에도 불구하고 나를 데려다 주겠다고 제안했다.

03 수식어 거품 파악하기 순서

• 문장의 동사 찾기 ⇨ 문장의 주어 찾기 ⇨ 수식어 거품에 [ ] 표시

Candidates [applying for the job] must take an entrance exam. 그 직무에 지원한 후보자들은 입사 시험을 치러야만 한다.
   2) 주어   3) 수식어 거품   1) 동사

▶ 문장에서 동사(must take)를 찾은 후 주어(Candidates)를 찾는다. 그리고 나서 수식어 거품을 파악한다.

토익실전문제

출제 포인트 수식어 거품 채우기

분사(구문)나 부사절 수식어 거품을 채우는 문제가 주로 출제된다.

1. ------- the new supervisor is mild-mannered and soft-spoken, he is very strict about employee punctuality.

(A) Nearly   (B) Then
(C) Unless   (D) While

2. The membership rates ------- are charged by Southtown Book Club will be raised to match those of its major competitors.

(A) theirs   (B) that
(C) them   (D) this

3. The suspect didn't respond to a police summons, ------- that he would present himself only when accompanied by a lawyer.

(A) insisting   (B) be insisted
(C) insist   (D) insists

정답·해설·해석 p.16

01 수식어 거품구는 주어, 동사가 없는 '구'의 형태로, 전치사구, to 부정사구, 분사(구문)가 이에 속한다.

전치사구 **Because of a lack of interest**, the lecture series was cancelled.
관심이 부족했기 때문에, 그 강연 시리즈는 취소되었다.

to 부정사구 The advertising team came up with an idea **to increase revenue**.
광고팀은 수익을 증가시킬 수 있는 아이디어를 내놓았다.

분사(구문) Guests **invited to the museum** may view all of the private exhibits.
박물관으로 초대받은 손님들은 모든 개인 소유 전시품들을 관람할 수 있다.

▶ 밑줄 친 부분인 전치사(Because of), to 부정사(to increase), 분사(invited)가 수식어 거품구를 이끌며, 토익에서는 이 부분을 묻는다.

02 수식어 거품절은 주어, 동사가 있는 '절'의 형태로, 관계절, 부사절이 이에 속한다.

관계절 The tour group will be staying in a hotel **which was built in 1890**.
그 여행 단체는 1890년에 지어진 호텔에 머무르게 될 것이다.

부사절 Reimbursement will not be provided **until expense reports are filed**.
경비 보고서가 제출될 때까지 상환은 제공되지 않을 것이다.

▶ 밑줄 친 부분인 관계사(which), 부사절 접속사(until)가 수식어 거품절을 이끌며, 토익에서는 이 부분을 묻는다.

03 수식어 거품구를 이끄는 것과 수식어 거품절을 이끄는 것 구분하기

• 수식어 거품 안에 동사가 없으면 ⇨ 수식어 거품구를 이끄는 전치사, to 부정사, 분사가 와야 한다.
• 수식어 거품 안에 동사가 있으면 ⇨ 수식어 거품절을 이끄는 관계사, 부사절 접속사가 와야 한다.

She left **without a word to anyone**. 그녀는 어느 누구에게도 말없이 떠났다.
▶ 수식어 거품(without a word to anyone) 안에 동사가 없으므로 전치사(without)가 와야 한다.

Unless he is late for work, Serge never takes a taxi. 회사에 늦지 않는 한, Serge는 절대로 택시를 타지 않는다.
▶ 수식어 거품(Unless he is late for work) 안에 동사(is)가 있으므로 부사절 접속사(Unless)가 와야 한다.

토익실전문제

출제 포인트 수식어 거품을 이끄는 것 채우기
수식어 거품구를 이끄는 전치사와 수식어 거품절을 이끄는 접속사를 구별하는 문제가 주로 출제된다.

1. ------ this is only Ms. Planter's third week with the company, she has quickly become a standout in the marketing division.

(A) Although (B) In spite of
(C) Nevertheless (D) However

2. The breakdown of a major piece of machinery ------ production forced the owner to announce a temporary plant shutdown.

(A) since (B) during
(C) while (D) except

3. ------ the problems Team B is experiencing, the manager decided that it would be best to give them a little more time to write their project assessment report.

(A) In case (B) After
(C) Moreover (D) Because of

정답·해설·해석 p.17

HACKERS PRACTICE 토익 고득점을 위한 필수 연습

수식어를 찾아 [ ] 표시하세요.

01 The customer who purchased the printer wants a refund.

02 The company announced the transfer of several staff from the main office.

03 While Erica set the table for dinner, Donald made a salad.

둘 중 맞는 형태를 고르세요.

04 The airline made passengers ------- by providing seats with lots of legroom.
ⓐ comfortable   ⓑ comfortably

05 James presented the proposal ------- he wasn't sure of its feasibility.
ⓐ even though   ⓑ despite

06 The spectators showed ------- at the unexpected victory of the local basketball team.
ⓐ surprising   ⓑ surprise

07 Jose is looking for an apartment ------- is located near his office.
ⓐ and   ⓑ which

08 Wendy requested that her secretary keep her ------- about itinerary changes.
ⓐ update   ⓑ updated

09 Employee evaluations will be conducted ------- October.
ⓐ during   ⓑ while

10 Only visitors who have received written ------- can tour the plant.
ⓐ permission   ⓑ permitted

틀린 곳이 있으면 바르게 고치세요.

11 High production costs made it necessary raise the prices of the products.

12 Many people consider the CEO's achievement admiration.

13 The assembly line will be functional as soon as the equipment is installed.

14 When applying for a business loan, you need submit your bank account information.

정답·해설 p.17

무료 해설 ▶
바로 보기

맞은 문제 개수: / 14
틀린 문제에 해당하는 토익 공식을 다시 한번 학습하세요.

🕐 제한 시간 12분

Part 5

01 The city council will not grant ------- for construction in cases where damage to the environment will be particularly severe.
(A) approve
(B) approval
(C) approved
(D) approvable

02 Most recruiters admit that it is a ------- for candidates to have a strong background in at least one foreign language.
(A) benefit
(B) benefited
(C) beneficial
(D) beneficially

03 Cerda Electronics Limited keeps its employees ------- by administering regular performance evaluations and providing annual bonuses.
(A) production
(B) produce
(C) productively
(D) productive

04 All products in the catalog are available in our online store, ------- clients to shop from the convenience of their homes.
(A) enables
(B) enable
(C) will enable
(D) enabling

05 John Carlyle's ------- to make the sales presentation a success was appreciated by his coworkers.
(A) determined
(B) determinedly
(C) determination
(D) determine

06 Frequent flyer miles earned by Consolidated Air passengers are ------- with any member airline of Sky-High Alliance.
(A) redeems
(B) redeem
(C) redeemable
(D) redemption

07 The expertise that enabled Steve Holden to start a successful investment firm was gained ------- three decades of working at a multinational bank.
(A) regarding
(B) but
(C) when
(D) through

08 Although jury duty is mandatory for citizens of the United States, an individual may request an ------- for medical reasons.
(A) exemptible
(B) exemption
(C) exempt
(D) exempted

09 Lyle Stevens, whose paintings are currently on exhibit at the Parkinson Art Center, has given ------- to struggling young artists.
(A) motivate
(B) motivating
(C) motivated
(D) motivation

10 Several experts on climate change met ------- practical options for creating new and affordable sources of energy.
(A) to discuss
(B) discuss
(C) discusser
(D) discussion

11 It is ------- that with the glut of digital products coming into the market, the electronics industry is entering a challenging phase.
(A) clears
(B) clearly
(C) clearest
(D) clear

12 Please check with Mr. Davidson before the marketing presentation begins this afternoon ------- he requires additional documents.
(A) in case
(B) although
(C) in spite of
(D) furthermore

13 Every Friday, Mr. Kelly ------- the travel expenses of the sales team to ensure that all reimbursement requests are legitimate.
(A) reviews
(B) reviewing
(C) are reviewed
(D) to review

14 ------- worries that the government will be unable to control the budget deficit, it is expected that national spending will reach an all-time high.
(A) Nonetheless
(B) Despite
(C) After
(D) However

15 An outstanding tenor and a captivating plot made last night's opera at the Metropolitan Concert Hall very -------.

(A) moving
(B) movable
(C) movingly
(D) movement

16 Companies are decreasing the amount of fuel they use ------- increased prices for energy sources have begun to cut into their profits.

(A) except
(B) as
(C) until
(D) at

17 The executives consider it best ------- a feasibility study, as investors regard the venture as risky.

(A) conduct
(B) to conduct
(C) by conducting
(D) conducted

18 The studio is expected to produce a sequel to its summer blockbuster ------- it can negotiate an agreement with the director and leading actor.

(A) that
(B) for
(C) if
(D) while

Part 6

Questions 19-22 refer to the following article.

A research team led by Hae-Eun Kang, a professor of business management at Renwood University, has just released a report on the nation's small businesses. According to the report, small businesses have been growing at a remarkable pace. Over 100,000 new jobs ------- by the growth of start-ups in the last two quarters. Furthermore, new companies are 20 percent more likely to survive their first year of operation than they were five years ago. -------.

However, Professor Kang warns that there are inherent risks involved with starting a small business and that caution should continue to be exercised. "Local markets are -------, and entrepreneurs need to set themselves apart by offering new and original products to consumers. Being ------- in this way will provide small business owners with a greater chance of long-term success," she said.

19 (A) creation
(B) to create
(C) have been created
(D) being created

20 (A) It is unsurprising that such businesses are able to get these types of loans.
(B) The unemployment rate varies significantly from region to region.
(C) There is reason to believe that new policies are creating this downturn.
(D) This has led many people to consider going into business.

21 (A) competitor
(B) competitive
(C) competition
(D) competitively

22 (A) innovative
(B) elaborate
(C) arbitrary
(D) generous

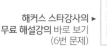

해커스 스타강사의 ▶
무료 해설강의 바로 보기
(6번 문제)

GRAMMAR Part 5,6   Ch 02 목적어·보어·수식어   Hackers TOEIC Reading

Hackers TOEIC Reading

SECTION 2
동사구

동사의 형태와 종류

토익, 이렇게 나온다!

동사의 형태와 종류 관련 문제는 출제 비율은 높지 않지만, 토익 문제의 문장에서 사용되므로 그 개념을 반드시 알고 있어야 한다. 조동사 다음에 동사원형을 채우는 문제가 주로 출제된다.

토익 필수 개념 다지기

01 동사는 다섯 가지 형태를 가지고 있다.

① 기본형(동사원형)
I **work** for an airline. 나는 항공사에서 일한다.

② 3인칭 단수 현재형(동사원형 + s)
He **likes** to play basketball. 그는 농구하는 것을 좋아한다.

③ 과거형(동사원형 + ed / 불규칙 변화)
Mr. Murray **called** his son yesterday. Mr. Murray는 어제 그의 아들에게 전화했다.
Erin **gave** him a birthday present. Erin은 그에게 생일 선물을 주었다.

④ 현재분사형(동사원형 + ing)
Janice is **running** home now. Janice는 지금 집으로 달려가고 있다.

⑤ 과거분사형(동사원형 + ed / 불규칙 변화)
The package was **delivered** by the courier. 그 소포는 택배 회사에 의해 배달되었다.
He had **spent** too much money on clothes. 그는 옷에 너무 많은 돈을 소비했다.

→ 과거분사형(past participle)은 약자로 p.p.라고 표기한다.

02 동사에는 목적어를 필요로 하지 않는 자동사와 목적어가 필요한 타동사가 있다. 자동사는 1·2형식 문장을, 타동사는 3·4·5형식 문장을 만든다.

① 1형식(주어 + 자동사)
Jason **laughed**. Jason이 웃었다.

② 2형식(주어 + 자동사 + 보어)
Erik **is tall**. Erik은 키가 크다.

③ 3형식(주어 + 타동사 + 목적어)
Martha **enjoys shopping**. Martha는 쇼핑하는 것을 즐긴다.

④ 4형식(주어 + 타동사 + 간접 목적어 + 직접 목적어)
Harold **wrote his mother a letter**. Harold는 그의 어머니에게 편지를 썼다.

⑤ 5형식(주어 + 타동사 + 목적어 + 목적격 보어)
She **made everyone happy**. 그녀는 모든 사람들을 행복하게 만들었다.

1 조동사 + 동사원형

01 조동사(will/would, may/might, can/could, must, should) 다음에는 반드시 동사원형이 와야 한다.

Anne <u>will</u> (~~to answer~~, **answer**) the phone. Anne은 전화를 받을 것이다.
▶ 조동사(will) 다음에는 to 부정사(to answer)가 올 수 없고 동사원형(answer)이 와야 한다.

Robert <u>can</u> (~~finishing~~, **finish**) the marketing report by Monday. Robert는 월요일까지 마케팅 보고서를 끝낼 수 있다.
▶ 조동사(can) 다음에는 -ing형(finishing)이 올 수 없고 동사원형(finish)이 와야 한다.

Campers <u>should</u> (**removal**, **remove**) all trash from the site before leaving.
야영객들은 떠나기 전에 현장의 모든 쓰레기를 치워야 한다.
▶ 조동사(should) 다음에는 명사(removal)가 올 수 없고 동사원형(remove)이 와야 한다.

He <u>will</u> (**buys**, **buy**) a new car. 그는 새 차를 살 것이다.
▶ 조동사(will) 다음에는 3인칭 단수형 동사(buys)가 올 수 없고 동사원형(buy)이 와야 한다.

고득점 포인트

❶ 조동사와 동사원형 사이에 not이나 부사가 올 경우, 동사원형 자리에 다른 형태를 쓰지 않도록 주의한다.
The board of directors <u>must not</u> hastily <u>selects</u>(→ select) a new CEO. 이사회는 새로운 최고 경영자를 성급하게 선발해서는 안 된다.

❷ 다음과 같이 조동사처럼 쓰이는 표현들 뒤에도 동사원형을 쓴다.

ought to ~해야 한다	had better ~하는 게 좋다	would like to ~하고 싶다	used to ~했었다, ~하곤 했다
have to ~해야 한다	be able to ~할 수 있다	be going to ~할 것이다	

I used to <u>live</u> in Baltimore. 나는 볼티모어에서 살았었다.
Sandra is able to <u>speak</u> German fluently. Sandra는 독일어를 유창하게 말할 수 있다.

02 부정문이나 도치 구문을 만드는 조동사(do/does/did) 다음에도 반드시 동사원형이 와야 한다.

The train <u>did not</u> (**left**, **leave**) until 2 P.M. 기차는 오후 2시까지 떠나지 않았다.
▶ 부정문을 만드는 조동사(did) 다음에는 과거형 동사(left)가 올 수 없고 동사원형(leave)이 와야 한다.

Never <u>did</u> he (**agreed**, **agree**) to the moving plan. 그는 이사 계획에 결코 동의하지 않았다.
▶ 도치 구문을 만드는 조동사(did) 다음에는 과거형 동사(agreed)가 올 수 없고 동사원형(agree)이 와야 한다.

토익실전문제

출제 포인트 조동사 다음에 동사원형 채우기
조동사 바로 뒤에 동사원형을 채우는 문제가 주로 출제된다.

1. The corporation's plan to overhaul the employee benefits program will ------- because it has the full support of management.
   (A) processor   (B) proceed
   (C) proceeds   (D) to proceed

2. To achieve a favorable outcome in today's competitive environment, companies should ------- a solid business plan.
   (A) to create   (B) creating
   (C) create   (D) creates

3. The computer technician could not ------- the files from the hard drive because they had been damaged by the virus.
   (A) retrieval   (B) retrieve
   (C) retrieving   (D) retrieved

정답·해설·해석 p.19

진행형(be + -ing) / 수동형(be + p.p.) / 완료형(have + p.p.)

01 -ing와 p.p.는 be동사, have동사와 결합하여 진행형(be + -ing), 수동형(be + p.p.), 완료형(have + p.p.)을 만든다.

진행형   She **is waiting** for her grandmother. 그녀는 그녀의 할머니를 기다리는 중이다.

수동형   Supplies **were transported** to the office. 비품들이 사무실로 운송되었다.

완료형   I **have seen** *A Man of Many Wishes*. 나는 *A Man of Many Wishes*를 본 적이 있다.

> **고득점**
> **포인트**   조동사(may, must, can …) 다음에 be동사는 am, is, are, was, were가 아닌 원형 be를 그대로 쓴다.
>
> Brad may <u>is</u>(→ be) working late tomorrow. Brad는 내일 늦게까지 근무할지도 모른다.
> Supplies must <u>are</u>(→ be) transported to the office. 비품들은 사무실로 운송되어야 한다.

02 be동사와 have동사 다음에는 동사원형이 올 수 없다.

My parents <u>are</u> (**play**, **playing**) golf this afternoon. 나의 부모님은 오늘 오후에 골프를 칠 것이다.

▶ be동사 다음에는 동사원형(play)이 올 수 없으므로 -ing형(playing)이 와서 진행형 문장을 만들어야 한다.

The forms must <u>be</u> (**distribute**, **distributed**) by Tuesday. 신청 용지들은 화요일까지 배부되어야 한다.

▶ be동사 다음에는 동사원형(distribute)이 올 수 없으므로 p.p.형(distributed)이 와서 수동형 문장을 만들어야 한다.

We <u>have</u> (**taste**, **tasted**) the new Italian dish. 우리는 새로운 이탈리아 음식을 먹어 보았다.

▶ 조동사인 have동사 다음에는 동사원형(taste)이 올 수 없으므로 p.p.형(tasted)이 와서 완료형 문장을 만들어야 한다.

> **고득점**
> **포인트**   '가지다, 먹다'를 뜻하는 have는 조동사가 아니라 일반동사이다.
>
> The library <u>has</u> an extensive encyclopedia section. 그 도서관은 아주 넓은 백과사전 구역을 가지고 있다.

토익실전문제

출제 포인트 'be동사 + -ing/p.p.' 또는 'have동사 + p.p.' 채우기
be동사나 have동사 뒤에 p.p.를 채우는 문제가 주로 출제된다.

1. A project analyst should be able to spot any potential problems in a strategic plan before it is -------.

   (A) implement   (B) implementation
   (C) implementing   (D) implemented

2. Senator Owens has publicly ------- the president's decision to provide additional subsidies to the electronics industry.

   (A) commendable   (B) commended
   (C) commendation   (D) commend

3. The recent population density graph shows that young rural residents have been ------- to the major cities to get college educations and jobs.

   (A) move   (B) mover
   (C) moved   (D) moving

정답·해설·해석 p.20

토익 공식 3 혼동하기 쉬운 자동사와 타동사, 3형식과 4형식 동사

01 자동사가 목적어를 갖기 위해서는 꼭 전치사가 있어야 하지만, 타동사는 전치사 없이 목적어를 바로 가져야 한다.

의미	자동사 + 전치사 + 목적어	타동사 + 목적어
말하다	**speak to** a group 단체에게 말하다 **talk to** your customer 당신의 고객에게 말을 걸다 **talk about** the problem 문제에 대해 이야기하다 **account for** your absence 당신의 불참에 대해 설명하다	**mention** his absence 그의 결근을 언급하다 **discuss** the issue 사안에 대해 토론하다 **instruct** me to hire a lawyer 나에게 변호사를 고용하라고 지시하다 **explain** the contract 약정을 설명하다 **address** him 그에게 말을 하다
답하다	**reply to** letters 편지에 답장하다 **react to** the updated version 최신판에 반응하다 **respond to** a question 질문에 대답하다	**answer** the question 질문에 대답하다
동의/반대 하다	**agree with(to, on)** the sales policy 판매 정책에 동의하다 **object to** the plan 계획에 반대하다 **consent to** a suggestion 제안에 동의하다	**approve** the request 요청을 승낙하다 **oppose** the new system 새로운 시스템에 반대하다
기타	**participate in** the workshop 워크숍에 참가하다 **arrive at** the airport 공항에 도착하다 **wait for** the new product 신제품을 기다리다	**attend** a seminar 세미나에 참석하다 **reach** the destination 목적지에 도착하다 **await** the release 출시를 기다리다

The director was requested to (**explain**, **account**) for the unexpected decrease in sales.
그 이사는 예상치 못한 매출의 감소에 대해 설명하도록 요구되었다.
▶ 목적어(the unexpected decrease) 앞에 전치사(for)가 있으므로, 전치사 없이 목적어를 바로 가져야 하는 타동사(explain)가 아닌 자동사(account)를 써야 한다.

02 목적어(that절)를 하나만 가지는 3형식 동사와, 목적어를 2개 가지는 4형식 동사를 구별해서 써야 한다.

3형식 동사 + 목적어(that절)	4형식 동사 + 목적어1(~에게) + 목적어2(that절)
say / mention / announce (to me) that 말하다 **suggest / propose / recommend** (to me) that 제안하다 **explain / describe** (to me) that 설명하다	**tell / inform / notify** me that 말하다 **assure / convince** me that 확신시키다

The consultant (**said**, **told**) the owner that operating costs were too high.
컨설턴트는 운영비가 너무 높다고 소유주에게 말했다.
▶ 목적어가 2개(the owner와 that operating costs were too high)이므로 3형식 동사(said)가 아닌 4형식 동사(told)를 써야 한다.

토익실전문제

출제 포인트 쓰임에 맞는 동사 채우기
4개의 동사 보기들 중 가장 쓰임이 적절한 동사를 채우는 문제가 출제된다.

1. The chief of security ------- to all staff that precautions should be taken to ensure no information is leaked to the press.

(A) informed
(B) convinced
(C) notified
(D) mentioned

2. The council ------- the director that continued support of the Baker Project might result in financial loss.

(A) advised
(B) explained
(C) described
(D) proposed

3. The stockbroker ------- the investors about a safe investment plan that would secure their financial future.

(A) gave
(B) told
(C) recommended
(D) suggested

정답·해설·해석 p.20

01 주절에 제안·요청·의무를 나타내는 동사/형용사/명사가 나오면, 종속절에는 동사원형이 와야 한다.

동사	suggest 제안하다	propose 제안하다	recommend 추천하다	request 요청하다	ask 요청하다
	require 요구하다	demand 요구하다	insist 주장하다	command 명령하다	order 명령하다
형용사	imperative 필수적인	essential 필수적인	necessary 필요한	important 중요한	
명사	advice 충고				

The airline requests that all baggage (**is kept**, **be kept**) in the overhead compartments.
그 항공사는 모든 수하물이 머리 위 짐칸에 보관되기를 요청한다.
▶ 주절에 요청을 나타내는 동사(requests)가 왔으므로, 종속절의 동사로는 원형(be kept)이 와야 한다.

It is essential that the process (**is completed**, **be completed**) in a timely fashion.
그 과정이 시기적절하게 마쳐져야 한다는 것은 필수적이다.
▶ 주절에 의무를 나타내는 형용사(essential)가 왔으므로, 종속절의 동사로는 원형(be completed)이 와야 한다.

My advice is that he (**accepts**, **accept**) the terms of his contract.
내 충고는 그가 계약서의 조항들을 수락해야 한다는 것이다.
▶ 주절에 제안을 나타내는 명사(advice)가 왔으므로, 종속절의 동사로는 원형(accept)이 와야 한다.

고득점 포인트 위의 동사/형용사/명사가 주절에 쓰였더라도, 제안·요청·의무를 의미하지 않는다면 that절에 동사원형을 쓸 수 없다.
The article suggests that advertising create(→ creates) higher consumer demand.
그 기사는 광고가 더 높은 고객 수요를 창출한다는 것을 시사한다.
→ 이 문장의 suggests는 '제안하다'가 아니라, '시사하다', '암시하다'를 의미하기 때문에, that절에 동사원형을 쓸 수 없다.

토익실전문제

출제 포인트 제안·요청·의무의 주절을 뒤따르는 that절에 '동사원형' 채우기
제안·요청·의무를 나타내는 동사가 나올 때 that절에 동사원형을 채우는 문제가 주로 출제된다.

1. The university suggests that students ------- their textbooks at least two weeks prior to the start of classes.

(A) orders   (B) ordering
(C) ordered   (D) order

2. The customer requested that the operating system ------- restored to the previous version because of its incompatibilities with other programs.

(A) is   (B) be
(C) have   (D) has

3. Due to the urgency of the matter, it is important that Mr. Lambert ------- headquarters this week to discuss the need for an additional funding.

(A) is visiting   (B) will visit
(C) visit   (D) visited

정답·해설·해석 p.20

둘 중 맞는 형태를 고르세요.

01 Dr. Jensen will clearly ------- his recent research study.
    ⓐ explain   ⓑ explanation

02 It is important that every guest ------- a visitors' badge at all times.
    ⓐ wear   ⓑ wears

03 The senator was invited to ------- to members of congress about the new tax legislation.
    ⓐ discuss   ⓑ speak

04 Never did he ------- his dream to become a professional athlete.
    ⓐ abandon   ⓑ abandons

05 The gas station attendant asked if we would like to ------- the engine checked regularly.
    ⓐ have   ⓑ had

06 Local residents ------- plans for the new highway, as it would destroy the natural habitat.
    ⓐ object   ⓑ oppose

07 The travel agent forgot to ------- to me that there was a stopover in Tokyo.
    ⓐ notify   ⓑ mention

틀린 곳을 바르게 고치세요.

08 I had better called your boss and let her know that you are sick.

09 Eric has agree to help out with product research.

10 The company requests that the employees will write progress reports at the end of every month.

11 The marathon will be sponsor by several local companies.

12 Seldom does Fairfield Supermarket provides refunds for purchases.

13 Helen is study the relation between global warming and environmental pollution.

14 It is essential that we to remain aware of our competitors' activities.

정답·해석 p.20

무료 해설 ▶
바로 보기

맞은 문제 개수: / 14
틀린 문제에 해당하는 토익 공식을 다시 한번 학습하세요.

🕐 제한 시간 12분

Part 5

01 All registration paperwork should ------- within two days if applicants do not wish to forfeit their reservations.

(A) be submitting
(B) be submitted
(C) to submit
(D) have submitted

02 Although Steve Pearson used to ------- as a statistical analyst for a private corporation, he is now a financial consultant for the government.

(A) has worked
(B) worked
(C) work
(D) working

03 The human resources head thinks it is imperative that employees ------- regularly to increase their value in the increasingly competitive market.

(A) instructed
(B) instruct
(C) be instructed
(D) instruction

04 Until recently, the Family Entertainment Arcade located in the mall ------- not generating the revenue its owners expected.

(A) is
(B) was
(C) to be
(D) be

05 Financial advisers suggest that setting aside cash for emergencies ------- it easier for a first-time investor to recover from losses.

(A) makes
(B) be made
(C) make
(D) making

06 Because the positions need to be filled immediately, applications must ------- no later than March 21.

(A) postmark
(B) postmarked
(C) postmarking
(D) be postmarked

07 The supervisor insists that notification ------- at least one month in advance if a project deadline cannot be met.

(A) provides
(B) providing
(C) be provided
(D) to provide

08 A series of earthquakes has caused ------- to residential and commercial areas of several major cities in Southeast Asia.

(A) damaged
(B) damageable
(C) damage
(D) to damage

09 During the presentation, the marketing manager will ------- about the need to target consumers from key demographic groups with new products.

(A) object
(B) mention
(C) talk
(D) discuss

10 Because this year marks the company's fiftieth anniversary, Maguire Incorporated will ------- the occasion with a massive party.

(A) celebration
(B) celebrate
(C) celebrated
(D) celebrates

11 The director did not ------- with the idea to expand into the cosmetics sector, as he felt the competition was too intense.

(A) concurring
(B) concurred
(C) concur
(D) to concur

12 The inspector recommends that the factory's waste disposal equipment ------- to lessen the risk of environmental damage.

(A) upgrade
(B) upgrading
(C) be upgraded
(D) are upgraded

13 A test was given to the applicants to eliminate those who do not ------- the basic knowledge requirements for the job.

(A) satisfy
(B) satisfying
(C) be satisfied
(D) to satisfy

14 The final report should ------- on the more recent findings rather than on the data collected a few months ago.

(A) base
(B) based
(C) be based
(D) to base

15 ------- the sudden collapse of the firm, hundreds of people found themselves without jobs.

(A) As
(B) While
(C) However
(D) Because of

16 To avoid incurring a budget deficit, the finance team ------- expenses that it considered inessential.

(A) trim
(B) trimming
(C) trimmed
(D) was trimmed

17 An administrative assistant ------- assembly participants that the venue had been changed to one closer to the bus depot.

(A) described
(B) informed
(C) suggested
(D) recommended

18 Because many employees have vacations scheduled in August, the editor has ------- that the deadline for the photography book be extended to October.

(A) request
(B) requesting
(C) requested
(D) be requested

Part 6

Questions 19-22 refer to the following article.

New Organic Fertilizers for Agriculture

Since the early twentieth century, many domestic farms have been using inorganic fertilizers as they readily dissolve in soil and are quickly absorbed by plants. However, it was eventually discovered that the faster absorption rate negatively affects plant growth and soil quality. Now, Green Agri-Company is introducing a new organic compost called GreenGrowth, which can ------- plants from absorbing nutrients too quickly.
                                                      19

To test the effectiveness of GreenGrowth, a farmer in West Virginia has ------- the product for several
                                                                              20
months on small plots of vegetables on his farm. In a report published by the company, the farmer stated that crop yields increased. This was because the fertilizer was ------- for the soil and allowed
                                                                              21
the plants to take in the nutrients slowly, enabling them to retain both nutritive elements and water. Furthermore, the fertility of the soil improved significantly, creating an ideal environment for crop growth. -------.
              22
GreenGrowth is now available at agricultural product retailers.

19 (A) prevent
(B) to prevent
(C) preventing
(D) prevented

20 (A) utilize
(B) utility
(C) utilizing
(D) utilized

21 (A) notable
(B) suitable
(C) essential
(D) relevant

22 (A) GreenGrowth requires further testing before being approved for distribution.
(B) Researchers do not yet know why GreenGrowth works so well.
(C) More detailed results can be accessed through the company's Web site.
(D) The deterioration of soil quality caused by GreenGrowth is a minor concern.

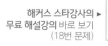
해커스 스타강사의 ▶
무료 해설강의 바로 보기
(18번 문제)

CHAPTER 04

주어와의 수일치

토익, 이렇게 나온다!
주어와의 수일치 관련 문제는 출제 비율이 높지 않지만, 모든 문장 구조 파악의 기본이므로 반드시 알고 있어야 한다. 주어의 수와 일치하는 동사를 채우는 문제가 가장 많이 출제된다.

토익 필수 개념 다지기

01 동사는 주어와 그 수가 일치해야 한다.

A boy sings. 소년이 노래한다.
주어(단수) 동사(단수)

Boys sing. 소년들이 노래한다.
주어(복수) 동사(복수)

첫 번째 문장의 주어인 A boy는 단수이고 두 번째 문장의 주어인 Boys는 복수이다.
주어가 단수인 첫 번째 문장에는 단수 동사인 sings, 주어가 복수인 두 번째 문장에는 복수 동사인 sing을 써야 한다. 이처럼 동사는 주어와 반드시 수일치가 되어야 한다.

02 단수 동사는 동사의 기본형에 -(e)s를 붙이고 복수 동사는 동사의 기본형을 그대로 쓴다.

기본형	단수동사	복수동사
visit	visits	visit
watch	watches	watch
do	does	do

The child **does** homework after dinner every night. 그 아이는 매일 밤 저녁 식사 후에 숙제를 한다.
The children **do** homework after dinner every night. 그 아이들은 매일 밤 저녁 식사 후에 숙제를 한다.

이러한 단수 동사와 복수 동사의 구별은 현재형일 때만 해당되며 과거형의 경우는 단수/복수 같은 형태를 취한다.

The doctor **recommended** that Jill exercise more often.
The doctors **recommended** that Jill exercise more often.
의사는(들은) Jill이 좀 더 자주 운동할 것을 추천했다.

단, be동사의 경우는 과거형의 경우에도 단/복수의 구별이 있다.

기본형		단수동사	복수동사
be	(현재)	am/is	are
	(과거)	was	were

01 단수 주어 뒤에는 단수 동사를, 복수 주어 뒤에는 복수 동사를 쓴다.

The door **opens** automatically. 그 문은 자동으로 열린다.

▶ 주어(The door)가 단수이므로 단수 동사(opens)가 와야 한다.

The apartment units **have** an air conditioner, stove, and refrigerator.
그 아파트는 에어컨, 가스레인지, 그리고 냉장고를 갖추고 있다.

▶ 주어(The apartment units)가 복수이므로 복수 동사(have)가 와야 한다.

고득점 포인트

❶ 단수 주어가 되는 것은 단수 가산 명사와 불가산 명사이고, 복수 주어가 되는 것은 복수 가산 명사이다. 다음의 명사들이 토익에 주로 출제된다.

단수 가산 명사	a client, a manager, a visitor, a supplier, an employee, an increase ...
불가산 명사	information, equipment, furniture, access, advice, permission ...
복수 가산 명사	representatives, plans, people, goods, funds, savings, belongings, standards, instructions, regulations ...

❷ -s로 끝나 복수 명사로 보이더라도 단수로 취급되는 다음과 같은 명사들은 수일치에 주의해야 한다.

학문 이름	economics 경제학, statistics 통계학, mathematics 수학, electronics 전자공학 ...
고유 명사	World Satellite Atlas, the United States, Times ...
기타 명사	news, woods, measles ...

02 동명사구/명사절 주어는 단수 주어로 취급하여 단수 동사를 쓴다.

Reading a book **makes** me feel sleepy. 책을 읽는 것은 나를 졸리게 만든다.

▶ 동명사구 주어(Reading a book)는 단수 주어로 취급하여 단수 동사(makes)를 써야 한다.

What he appreciates **is** the excellent customer service. 그가 높이 평가하는 것은 훌륭한 고객 서비스이다.

▶ 명사절 주어(What he appreciates)는 단수 주어로 취급하여 단수 동사(is)를 써야 한다.

03 주어와 동사 사이에 있는 수식어 거품은 동사의 수 결정에 아무런 영향을 주지 않는다.

The facilities [at the health center] (~~includes~~, include) a spa. 그 의료 센터의 시설은 온천을 포함한다.

▶ 동사(include) 바로 앞에 있는 수식어 거품(at the health center) 속의 health center를 주어로 혼동하여 단수 동사를 쓰는 일이 없도록 주의해야 한다.

The contract [signed by Cox Associates] (specify, **specifies**) the cost of the services.
Cox Associates사에 의해 서명된 계약서는 서비스 비용을 명시한다.

▶ 동사(specifies) 바로 앞에 있는 수식어 거품(signed by Cox Associates) 속의 Cox Associates를 복수 주어로 혼동하여 복수 동사를 쓰는 일이 없도록 주의해야 한다.

토익실전문제

출제 포인트 주어(동사)와 수일치하는 동사(주어) 채우기

주어와 동사 사이의 수식어 거품을 지우고 주어의 수와 일치하는 동사를 채우는 문제가 주로 출제된다.
동사의 수에 일치하는 주어를 채우는 문제도 가끔 출제된다.

1. The recent meeting between the two companies ------- that a deal is near.

(A) suggest   (B) suggests
(C) was suggested   (D) suggesting

2. Management has come to realize that its ------- to implement the new accounting system next month needs to be reconsidered.

(A) decision   (B) decisive
(C) decisions   (D) decided

3. The government's program to reduce tuition fees ------- students who are struggling to pay for their education.

(A) aid   (B) aids
(C) aiding   (D) was aided

정답·해설·해석 p.23

01 단수 취급되는 수량 표현에는 단수 동사를, 복수 취급되는 수량 표현에는 복수 동사를 쓴다.

단수 취급되는 수량 표현	복수 취급되는 수량 표현
one (+ 명사), each (+ 명사), every + 명사 the number of + 복수 명사 ~의 수 somebody, someone, something anybody, anyone, anything everybody, everyone, everything nobody, no one, nothing	many/several/few/both + (of the) + 복수 명사 a number of + 복수 명사 많은 수의 ~ a couple/variety of + 복수 명사

One of the technicians **has completed** his maintenance work. 기술자들 중 한 명이 정비 작업을 끝마쳤다.
Every participant at the meeting **looks** prepared. 그 회의의 모든 참가자는 준비된 것처럼 보인다.
Many students **study** in foreign countries. 많은 학생들이 외국에서 공부한다.
Many of the local museums **offer** discounts to the elderly. 많은 지역 박물관들이 고령자에게 할인을 제공한다.
A variety of pastries **are** available at the dessert counter. 다양한 빵과자들은 디저트 판매대에서 구할 수 있다.

고득점 포인트 many, several, few, both와 같은 단어 자체가 주어로 쓰여도 복수 취급한다는 것에 주의한다.
Many **expect** oil prices to increase next month. 많은 사람은 다음 달에 유가가 상승할 것이라고 예상한다.

02 부분이나 전체를 나타내는 표현이 주어로 쓰이면 of 뒤의 명사에 동사를 수일치시킨다.

all, most, any, some, half, a lot (lots) part, the rest, the bulk, percent, 분수	+ of +	단수/불가산 명사 + 단수 동사 복수 명사 + 복수 동사

Half of our workforce **takes** the subway to the office. 자사 직원의 절반은 사무실까지 지하철을 탄다.
▶ half of 뒤의 명사가 단수 명사(our workforce)이므로, 단수 동사(takes)를 쓴다.

Half of the people in this room **are** medical doctors. 이 방에 있는 사람들의 절반은 의학 박사들이다.
▶ half of 뒤의 명사가 복수 명사(the people)이므로, 복수 동사(are)를 쓴다.

※ 수량 표현·부분/전체 표현과의 수일치는 특히 형용사와 함께 학습해 두어야 하며, 형용사에 관해서는 Section 4 품사의 Chapter 12(p.150)에서 자세히 다룬다.

토익실전문제

출제 포인트 주어(수량 표현·부분/전체 표현)와 수일치하는 동사 채우기
주어에 사용된 수량 표현이나, 부분/전체 표현과 수일치하는 동사를 채우는 문제가 주로 출제된다.

1. A large number of refund requests ------- when purchased items are recalled because of safety issues or defects.

   (A) occur
   (B) occurs
   (C) is occurred
   (D) are occurred

2. Every employee ------- to consider what his or her prospects are for career advancement and personal growth.

   (A) have needed
   (B) needs
   (C) needing
   (D) to need

3. All of the consultants' suggestions about the company's position regarding the upcoming merger ------- into consideration by the CEO.

   (A) is taking
   (B) was taken
   (C) will take
   (D) have been taken

정답·해설·해석 p.23

01 접속사 and로 연결된 주어는 복수 동사를 쓴다.

The lawyer <u>and</u> his legal assistant **are** preparing the documents for the hearing.
변호사와 그의 법무 보조원은 청문회를 위한 서류들을 준비하고 있다.

▶ 단수 명사 The lawyer와 his legal assistant가 접속사 and로 연결되어 있으므로, 복수 동사(are)를 쓴다.

고득점
포인트

❶ 'Both A and B'의 경우도 복수 동사를 쓴다.

Both the database and the timetable <u>have</u> to be updated. 데이터베이스와 일정표 모두 갱신되어야 한다.

❷ 두 사항을 연결하는 의미가 있는 in addition to ~, along with ~, together with ~(~에 더하여, ~와 함께)는 동사의 수에 영향을 주지 않는 수식어 거품이다.

The editor, [along with several writers], <u>are</u>(→ is) working on a special report about the elections.
그 편집장은 몇몇 기자들과 함께 선거에 관한 특별 보도를 작업하고 있다.

→ 수식어 거품(along with several writers)은 동사의 수에 영향을 주지 않으므로 문장의 주어인 단수 명사(The editor)에 맞추어 단수 동사(is)가 와야 한다.

02 접속사 or로 연결된 주어(A or B)의 수일치는 B에 시킨다.

Two vans <u>or</u> a bus **is** needed to take the children to the zoo.
두 대의 승합차 또는 한 대의 버스가 아이들을 동물원으로 데려가는 데 필요하다.

▶ 복수 명사(Two vans)와 단수 명사(a bus)가 접속사 or로 연결되어 있으므로, or 뒤에 오는 명사(a bus)에 맞추어 단수 동사(is)를 쓴다.

고득점
포인트

B에 동사의 수를 일치시키는 다른 구문들은 아래와 같다.

Either A or B	A나 B 둘 중 하나
Neither A nor B	A나 B 둘 중 어느 것도 아닌
Not A but B	A가 아니고 B인
Not only A but (also) B	A뿐만 아니라 B도
B as well as A	A뿐만 아니라 B도

토익실전문제

출제 포인트 주어(접속사로 연결된 주어)와 수일치하는 동사 채우기
접속사 and나 or로 연결된 주어와 수일치하는 동사를 채우는 문제가 주로 출제된다.

1. Mr. Burns and his secretary of the firm's Arlington branch ------- to the weekend gathering.

(A) is coming   (B) are coming
(C) comes   (D) has come

2. The chef's assistant and I ------- a special menu for this evening's wine tasting event, which will be attended by some top food critics.

(A) am preparing   (B) prepares
(C) are preparing   (D) has prepared

3. The federal government, along with leading industrial companies, ------- to create more jobs for skilled workers.

(A) is pushing   (B) are pushing
(C) pushing   (D) have been pushed

정답·해설·해석 p.23

01 주격 관계절의 동사는 선행사와 수일치한다.

> 단수 선행사
> 복수 선행사 + 주격 관계사(who, which, that) + 단수 동사
> 복수 동사

Management prefers a consultant who is knowledgeable about unions.
경영진은 노동조합에 대해 아는 것이 많은 자문 위원을 선호한다.

▶ 선행사(a consultant)가 단수이므로 주격 관계절에는 단수 동사(is)를 쓴다.

Applicants who don't speak two languages have a disadvantage over other job seekers.
두 개 언어를 구사하지 못하는 지원자들은 다른 구직자들보다 불리하다.

▶ 선행사(Applicants)가 복수이므로 주격 관계절에는 복수 동사(don't speak)를 쓴다.

> **고득점 포인트** 관계절의 동사는 관계절의 주어 또는 선행사와 수, 태가 맞아야 한다.
> **The visitors are sitting in a room whose walls is(→ are) painted white.** 방문객들은 벽이 흰색으로 페인트칠 된 방에 앉아 있다.
> → 관계절의 주어(whose walls)가 복수이므로, 동사로 복수 동사(are)를 써야 한다.
> **The investors toured the plant, which established(→ was established) ten years ago.**
> 투자자들은 공장을 견학했는데, 그 공장은 10년 전에 설립되었다.
> → 관계절의 선행사(the plant)와 동사(establish)가 수동 관계이므로, 수동태(was established)를 써야 한다.

02 선행사 뒤에 있는 수식어 거품 속의 명사를 선행사와 혼동해서는 안 된다.

Payments [for electricity usage] that (is, are) received late will be reflected in the next month's bill.
늦게 접수된 전기 사용 대금은 다음 달 명세서에 반영될 것이다.

▶ 선행사(Payments)가 복수이므로 주격 관계절에는 복수 동사(are)를 쓴다. 관계사(that) 바로 앞에 있는 수식어 거품(for electricity usage) 속의 단수 명사(usage)를 선행사로 혼동하여 관계절의 동사를 단수 동사(is)로 쓰는 일이 없도록 주의해야 한다.

An article [on vitamin supplements], which (were, was) printed in newspapers, was inaccurate.
신문에 게재된 비타민 보조제에 대한 기사는 부정확했다.

▶ 선행사(An article)가 단수이므로 주격 관계절에는 단수 동사(was)를 쓴다. 관계사(which) 바로 앞에 있는 수식어 거품(on vitamin supplements) 속의 복수 명사(supplements)를 선행사로 혼동하여 관계절의 동사를 복수 동사(were)로 쓰는 일이 없도록 주의해야 한다.

토익실전문제

출제 포인트 주어(선행사)와 수일치하는 동사(주격 관계절의 동사) 채우기

선행사의 수와 일치하는 동사를 고른 후 그 중 태에 맞는 동사를 선택하여 채우는 문제가 주로 출제된다.

1. Files that ------- at the main office have been relocated to a new archive in an effort to consolidate all records.

   (A) were stored   (B) have stored
   (C) was stored   (D) stores

2. Each year, the manufacturer sends representatives to the technology conferences that ------- by universities throughout the country.

   (A) hosted   (B) are hosted
   (C) are hosting   (D) was hosted

3. The number of users who ------- support has increased since the company released the latest version of its software.

   (A) require   (B) requires
   (C) is required   (D) are required

정답·해설·해석 p.24

HACKERS PRACTICE 토익 고득점을 위한 필수 연습

둘 중 맞는 형태를 고르세요.

01 Details regarding the upcoming company picnic ------- e-mailed to all employees.
ⓐ was　　　　ⓑ were

02 Attendees of the conference who ------- making presentations are asked to provide their contact information to the organizers.
ⓐ is　　　　ⓑ are

03 ------- feel that the company's budget plan is unreasonable.
ⓐ Many　　　　ⓑ Much

04 All documents in the archive ------- converted to electronic format.
ⓐ was　　　　ⓑ were

05 The speakers introduced at the start of the symposium ------- experts in online advertising.
ⓐ is　　　　ⓑ are

06 Internet ------- in the city have started charging higher fees.
ⓐ café　　　　ⓑ cafés

07 The movie director, together with the crew members, ------- going to retake a scene.
ⓐ is　　　　ⓑ are

틀린 곳이 있으면 바르게 고치세요.

08 A rare diamond and a large sapphire is on display till the end of the week.

09 Half of the coffee shops in the area opens until midnight.

10 Some contributors write for the magazine only once a month.

11 The news report that the highway will be closed until further notice.

12 The passengers with a first-class ticket is allowed to use the express line when checking in.

13 Current data is essential when conducting a financial analysis.

14 Boosting sales through promotional offers are a tactic commonly used by entrepreneurs.

정답·해석 p.24

무료 해설 ▶
바로 보기

맞은 문제 개수:　　/ 14
틀린 문제에 해당하는 토익 공식을 다시 한번 학습하세요.

⏱ 제한 시간 12분

Part 5

01 All ------- for information about upcoming products are handled by the public relations department.

(A) request
(B) requesting
(C) to request
(D) requests

02 The Price-Rite and Herald chain stores are popular with the public because ------- offer quality goods at affordable prices.

(A) each
(B) us
(C) both
(D) either

03 *American Social Trends*, a documentary that explores the relationship between individualism and capitalism, ------- in August.

(A) broadcast
(B) to broadcast
(C) will be broadcast
(D) have been broadcast

04 Questions ------- the recent changes in employee benefits and eligibility should be addressed to Mr. Henderson in the personnel department.

(A) concerning
(B) concern
(C) concerned
(D) concerns

05 The proposed layout for the office ------- two months ago, but the decision to install additional workstations will result in changes.

(A) to approve
(B) approve
(C) was approved
(D) is approved

06 Salespeople who ------- their interactions with customers on a case-by-case basis are more effective than those who stick to the same approach with everyone.

(A) handle
(B) handles
(C) are handled
(D) handling

07 The flu epidemic will probably ------- an increased demand for over-the-counter medications.

(A) generates
(B) generated
(C) to generate
(D) generate

08 The growing middle class in India ------- as a promising market for many multinational corporations.

(A) is viewed
(B) has viewed
(C) view
(D) viewing

09 The purchase button for some of the products on the shopping Web site ------- temporarily, making it impossible to add these items to a shopping cart.

(A) is disappeared
(B) disappearing
(C) has disappeared
(D) have disappeared

10 The government's proposed plan to expand the region's infrastructure by constructing a new power plant and reservoir ------- shape over the last two months.

(A) to take
(B) taking
(C) has taken
(D) take

11 Applying an incentive system in the workplace ------- employees to improve their performance.

(A) motivation
(B) motivates
(C) motivating
(D) motivate

12 A scholarship is offered to anyone who ------- a 4.0 grade point average during his or her first two years of study.

(A) maintaining
(B) maintain
(C) maintenance
(D) maintains

13 Participants were informed that the fees for the two-day educational event ------- reference materials, lodging, and meals.

(A) include
(B) to include
(C) is included
(D) has included

14 Before purchasing the property in Miami, Jeff Damon made an appointment with an investment trust company that ------- advice on real estate development.

(A) to provide
(B) provides
(C) was provided
(D) have provided

15 Signing bonuses equivalent to one month's salary are being offered to ------- who accept a two-year employment contract.

(A) recruit (B) recruiter
(C) recruits (D) recruitment

16 The regulations listed on the first page of the employee handbook ------- the code of conduct workers are expected to adhere to.

(A) describe (B) describing
(C) is describing (D) to be described

17 If the economy of China continues to expand at its current rate, many ------- that its GDP will surpass that of the United States within six years.

(A) estimating (B) to estimate
(C) estimate (D) has estimated

18 The number of individuals being hired by the company this summer for temporary jobs ------- to exceed 50.

(A) is expected (B) are expecting
(C) expects (D) expecting

Part 6

Questions 19-22 refer to the following letter.

Noel Velasquez
1015 Meriwether Drive
Birmingham, MI 48009

Dear Mr. Velasquez,

Harrison's Online Mall appreciates receiving your feedback on our Web site, as it gives us the opportunity to streamline the process for making orders. We ------- that you had some difficulty navigating the site because of the large number of product categories. We are planning to group products according to similar attributes. This will make it easier for customers to find what they need.

In addition, your letter describes lengthy searches that ------- in an array of items that you were not interested in. To address this problem, our Web site developers are currently designing a simplified system that will refine search results. -------. Hopefully, the issues you raised will no longer be a concern.

Once again, we are grateful to you for your -------, and we look forward to your continued support.

Sincerely yours,
Pierre Leon

19 (A) understand (B) understanding
(C) to understand (D) understandable

20 (A) has resulted (B) results
(C) result (D) were resulted

21 (A) Shoppers will be informed of upcoming sales.
(B) The number of product categories will be increased to add more variety.
(C) You will be notified when the items you ordered are in stock.
(D) The Web site will be updated before the end of the month.

22 (A) work (B) comments
(C) orders (D) requests

해커스 스타강사의 ▶
무료 해설강의 바로 보기
(2번 문제)

CHAPTER 05 능동태·수동태

토익, 이렇게 나온다!
능동태·수동태 관련 문제는 평균 1문제 정도 출제되며 최대 4문제까지 출제된다. 태에 알맞은 동사를 채우는 문제가 가장 많이 출제된다.

토익 필수 개념 다지기

01 능동태는 '주어가 ~하다'라는 의미로 주어가 행위의 주체가 되며, 수동태는 '주어가 ~되다, 당하다'라는 의미로 주어가 행위의 대상이 된다. 수동태 동사의 기본 형태는 'be + p.p.'이다.

능동태   Daniel **prepared** this dish.
수동태   This dish **was prepared** by Daniel.

첫 번째 문장은 'Daniel이 이 요리를 준비했다'라는 능동의 의미를 가지므로 능동태를 쓴다.
반면에 두 번째 문장은 '이 요리는 Daniel에 의해 준비되었다'라는 수동의 의미를 가지므로 수동태를 쓴다.

형태	기본형	진행형	완료형
능동태	동사의 현재/과거/미래형	be + -ing	have + p.p.
수동태	be + p.p.	be being + p.p.	have been + p.p.

02 능동태 문장의 목적어가 문장의 주어 자리로 오면서 수동태 문장이 형성된다.

능동태   <u>Patrick</u> **designed** <u>the Web site</u>. Patrick이 그 웹사이트를 디자인했다.
            주어   능동태 동사   목적어

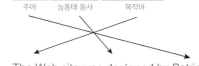

수동태   <u>The Web site</u> **was designed** by Patrick. 그 웹사이트는 Patrick에 의해 디자인되었다.
            주어   수동태 동사   by + 행위의 주체

03 능동태 문장의 목적어가 수동태 문장의 주어가 되므로, 반드시 목적어를 가지는 타동사만 수동태가 될 수 있고, 자동사는 수동태가 될 수 없다.

A celebrity **was appeared** at the charity event. (×)
A celebrity **appeared** at the charity event. (○) 한 유명 인사가 자선 행사에 나타났다.

자동사(appear)는 목적어를 가지지 못하므로 수동태가 될 수 없다.

토익에는 자동사가 수동태 문장으로 나온 오류를 찾는 문제가 자주 나온다.

토익에 자주 나오는 자동사: take place(개최되다, 일어나다), rise(오르다), occur/happen(발생하다), consist(구성되다), arrive(도착하다), emerge(나타나다), exist(존재하다), function(작동하다), depart(출발하다), become(~이 되다), stay(머무르다, ~한 상태를 유지하다), seem(~해 보이다), remain(~인 채로 남다)

토익 공식 1 능동태와 수동태의 구별

01 능동태에서 반드시 목적어를 가지는 타동사의 경우, 수동태에서는 목적어를 가지지 않는다.

My mother (**is played**, **plays**) the piano. 내 어머니는 피아노를 연주하신다.

▶ 능동태에서 반드시 목적어를 가지는 타동사(play) 뒤에 목적어(the piano)가 있으므로, 능동태 동사(plays)를 써야 한다.

A billing statement will (**provide**, **be provided**). 요금 청구서가 제공될 것이다.

▶ 능동태에서 반드시 목적어를 가지는 타동사(provide) 뒤에 목적어가 없으므로, 수동태 동사(be provided)를 써야 한다.

02 to 부정사의 동사와 관계절 동사의 능동태/수동태 구별도 목적어 여부에 따라 결정한다.

Employees are required (**to be submitted**, **to submit**) tax forms at the end of every year.
직원들은 매년 말에 납세 신고서를 제출하도록 요구된다.

▶ 능동태에서 반드시 목적어를 가지는 타동사(submit) 뒤에 목적어(tax forms)가 있으므로, to 부정사의 능동태(to submit)를 써야 한다.

The research findings are going (**to present**, **to be presented**) by Mr. Barnes.
연구 결과들은 Mr. Barnes에 의해 공개될 것이다.

▶ 능동태에서 반드시 목적어를 가지는 타동사(present) 뒤에 목적어가 없으므로, to 부정사의 수동태(to be presented)를 써야 한다.

A famous author who (**is written**, **writes**) children's fairy tales is giving a reading today.
아동용 동화책을 집필하는 유명 작가가 오늘 낭독할 것이다.

▶ 능동태에서 반드시 목적어를 가지는 타동사(write) 뒤에 목적어(children's fairy tales)가 있으므로, 능동태 동사(writes)를 써야 한다.

I received the products that (**indicate**, **are indicated**) on the shipping order.
나는 선적 주문서에 명시된 상품들을 받았다.

▶ 능동태에서 반드시 목적어를 가지는 타동사(indicate) 뒤에 목적어가 없으므로, 수동태 동사(are indicated)를 써야 한다.

토익실전문제

출제 포인트 태에 맞는 동사 채우기
태에 맞는 동사의 전체와 일부를 채우는 문제가 고루 출제된다.

1. Your name and telephone number should be ------- clearly in the space provided below.

(A) wrote
(B) write
(C) written
(D) writing

2. ------- the delivery of the package, you will need to add five dollars to the courier fee.

(A) To hasten
(B) Hastens
(C) To be hastened
(D) Will hasten

3. All newly hired employees are required to fill out the personal information form, a copy of which ------- to the contract.

(A) attach
(B) attachment
(C) is attaching
(D) is attached

정답·해설·해석 p.26

01 목적어를 두 개 가지는 4형식 동사가 수동태가 될 때는, 목적어 중 한 개가 수동태 동사 뒤에 남는다.

능동태	William gave Joan a book. William은 Joan에게 책을 주었다.
간접 목적어가 주어로 간 수동태	<u>Joan</u> was given **a book**. Joan은 책을 받았다.
직접 목적어가 주어로 간 수동태	<u>A book</u> was given **to Joan**. 책이 Joan에게 주어졌다.

▶ 간접 목적어(Joan)가 주어로 가서 수동태가 될 경우에는 직접 목적어(a book)가 수동태 동사(was given) 뒤에 그대로 남아 수동태 동사가 목적어를 가진 것처럼 보이므로 주의한다. 직접 목적어(a book)가 주어로 가서 수동태가 될 경우에는 수동태 동사(was given) 뒤에 '전치사 + 간접 목적어(to Joan)'가 온다.

고득점 포인트 일반적인 4형식 동사들(give, send, grant, show, offer, bring, permit, assign, award)의 직접 목적어가 주어 자리로 가서 수동태가 될 경우, 수동태 동사 뒤에 '전치사 to + 간접 목적어'가 온다. 그러나, buy, make, get, find, build, save와 같은 4형식 동사는 전치사 to 대신 for를 쓴다.
An exhibit hall was built to(→ for) local artists. 전시회장은 지역 예술가들을 위해 설립되었다.

02 목적어와 목적격 보어를 가지는 5형식 동사가 수동태가 될 때는, 목적격 보어가 수동태 동사 뒤에 남는다.

• 목적격 보어가 '명사구'인 5형식 동사의 수동태

능동태	Mr. Edwards considers the project a success. Mr. Edwards는 그 프로젝트를 성공으로 여긴다.
수동태	The project is considered **a success**. 그 프로젝트는 성공으로 여겨진다.

▶ 목적어(the project)가 주어 자리로 가서 수동태가 될 때, 명사구 목적격 보어(a success)가 수동태 동사(is considered) 뒤에 그대로 온다. 이것을 수동태 동사가 목적어를 가진 것으로 잘못 보아 틀린 문장이라 생각하지 않도록 주의해야 한다.

• 목적격 보어가 'to 부정사구'인 5형식 동사의 수동태

능동태	The passenger asked the taxi driver to slow down. 그 승객은 택시 운전사에게 속도를 늦춰줄 것을 부탁했다.
수동태	The taxi driver was asked **to slow down**. 택시 운전사는 속도를 늦춰줄 것을 부탁받았다.

▶ 목적어(the taxi driver)가 주어 자리로 가서 수동태가 될 때, to 부정사구 목적격 보어(to slow down)가 수동태 동사(was asked) 뒤에 그대로 온다.

고득점 포인트 ❶ 명사구를 목적격 보어로 취하는 5형식 동사는 consider(여기다, 간주하다), call(부르다), elect(선출하다), name(임명하다) 등이 있고, to 부정사구를 목적격 보어로 취하는 5형식 동사는 advise/urge(충고하다), ask/invite(요청하다), allow/permit(허락하다), instruct/direct(지시하다), encourage/inspire(격려하다, 북돋우다), tell(말하다), expect(기대하다), remind(상기시키다), require(요구하다) 등이 있다.

❷ consider가 3형식 동사로 쓰인 경우와 5형식 동사로 쓰인 경우를 혼동하지 않도록 주의해야 한다.
The committee is <u>considered</u>(→ is considering) delaying the event. 위원회는 행사를 연기할 것을 고려하고 있다.
→ 이 문장에서 consider는 '고려하다'라는 의미의 3형식 동사로 뒤에 목적어(delaying the event)가 왔으므로, 능동태 동사(is considering)가 나와야 한다.

토익실전문제

출제 포인트 태에 맞는 동사 채우기
목적어나 목적격 보어로 사용되는 명사 앞에 4형식, 5형식 동사의 수동태를 완성하는 문제가 출제된다.

1. The manager has suggested that the promising candidate ------- a better salary and benefits package.

(A) offered (B) offer
(C) be offered (D) has offered

2. Though somewhat new at making presentations, Paul ------- the best public speaker in the department.

(A) considers (B) to consider
(C) is considering (D) is considered

3. The research team ------- to make backup files of all their work to prevent loss of valuable data.

(A) reminded (B) was reminded
(C) will remind (D) was reminding

정답·해설·해석 p.26

01 감정을 나타내는 타동사의 경우에는, 주어가 감정의 원인이면 능동태, 주어가 감정을 느끼면 수동태를 쓴다.

재미·만족	interest 흥미를 일으키다	excite 흥분시키다	amuse 즐겁게 하다	please 기쁘게 하다
	fascinate 매료시키다	encourage 용기를 주다	satisfy 만족시키다	thrill 흥분시키다
낙담·불만족	disappoint 실망시키다	discourage 낙담시키다	dissatisfy 불만을 느끼게 하다	depress 낙담시키다
	tire 피곤하게 하다	trouble 걱정시키다	frustrate 실망시키다	
당황·충격	bewilder 당황하게 하다	shock 충격을 주다	surprise 놀라게 하다	

The high profits (~~were pleased~~, **pleased**) both CEO and the investors.
높은 수익은 최고 경영자와 투자자들 모두를 기쁘게 했다.
▶ 주어(The high profits)가 기쁨을 주는 원인이므로, 수동태 동사(were pleased)가 아닌 능동태 동사(pleased)를 쓴다.

Mike (~~was pleasing~~, **was pleased**) to learn that he had been promoted. Mike는 그가 승진했다는 것을 알게 되어 기뻤다.
▶ 주어(Mike)가 기쁨을 느끼므로, 능동태 동사(was pleasing)가 아닌 수동태 동사(was pleased)를 쓴다.

The proposal (~~was dissatisfied~~, **dissatisfied**) the director because it didn't fulfill her request.
그 제안서는 요구를 충족하지 않았기 때문에 이사를 불만스럽게 했다.
▶ 주어(The proposal)가 불만스럽게 하는 원인이므로, 수동태 동사(was dissatisfied)가 아닌 능동태 동사(dissatisfied)를 쓴다.

The workers (**dissatisfy**, **are dissatisfied**) with management's handling of the situation.
노동자들은 경영진의 상황 대처 방식에 불만을 느낀다.
▶ 주어(The workers)가 불만을 느끼므로, 능동태 동사(dissatisfy)가 아닌 수동태 동사(are dissatisfied)를 쓴다.

The barking dog (~~was surprised~~, **surprised**) my sister. 짖고 있는 개가 내 여동생을 놀라게 했다.
▶ 주어(The barking dog)가 놀라게 하는 원인이므로, 수동태 동사(was surprised)가 아닌 능동태 동사(surprised)를 쓴다.

My sister (**surprised**, **was surprised**) by the barking dog. 내 여동생은 짖고 있는 개에 놀랐다.
▶ 주어(My sister)가 놀람을 느끼므로, 능동태 동사(surprised)가 아닌 수동태 동사(was surprised)를 쓴다.

토익실전문제

출제 포인트 | 태에 맞는 동사 채우기
동사 자리 전체가 아니라, be동사 다음에 -ing형 또는 p.p.형만을 묻는 문제
가 주로 출제된다.

1. Young entrepreneurs who set up venture companies should not be ------- if sales are slow at first.

   (A) to disappoint   (B) disappointed
   (C) disappointing   (D) disappointment

2. When he took up cooking, Jerry Porter was ------- to learn how easy it was to make inexpensive, great tasting meals.

   (A) fascinate   (B) fascinating
   (C) being fascinated   (D) fascinated

3. The manager ------- her staff with news of an upcoming bonus in an effort to reach the company's goals before the end of the quarter.

   (A) encourage   (B) was encouraged
   (C) encouraging   (D) encouraged

정답·해설·해석 p.27

01 수동태 동사 + 전치사

be amused at ~을 즐거워하다	be surprised at ~에 놀라다	be worried about ~을 걱정하다
be pleased with ~을 기뻐하다	be alarmed at ~에 놀라다	be concerned about/over ~을 걱정하다
be delighted with ~을 기뻐하다	be astonished at ~에 놀라다	be bored with ~을 지루해하다
be satisfied with ~에 만족하다	be frightened at ~에 놀라다	be tired of ~에 싫증나다
be gratified with ~에 만족하다	be shocked at ~에 충격을 받다	be convinced of ~을 확신하다
be disappointed at ~에 실망하다	be interested in ~에 관심이 있다	
be involved in ~에 관여하다	be absorbed in ~에 열중하다	be equipped with ~을 갖추고 있다
be engaged in ~에 종사하다	be indulged in ~에 빠지다	be covered with ~으로 덮이다
be associated with ~와 관련되다	be devoted to ~에 헌신하다	be crowded with ~으로 붐비다
be related to ~와 관련되어 있다	be dedicated to ~에 헌신하다, 전념하다	be based on ~에 근거하다
be divided into ~로 나뉘다	be exposed to ~에 노출되다	be credited with ~으로 명성을 얻다
be finished with ~이 끝나다		

The office space **is equipped with** conference rooms and a staff lounge.
그 사무실 공간은 회의실과 직원 휴게실을 갖추고 있다.

Consumer demand **is** strongly **related to** production rates.
소비자 수요는 생산율과 강하게 관련되어 있다.

02 수동태 동사 + to 부정사

be asked to ~하라고 요청받다	be required to ~하도록 요구받다	be allowed to ~하도록 허가받다
be requested to ~하도록 요청받다	be urged to ~하라고 요구받다	be permitted to ~하도록 허가받다
be told to ~하라는 말을 듣다	be advised to ~하라고 충고받다	be prepared to ~할 준비가 되다
be reminded to ~하라는 말을 듣다	be warned to ~하도록 경고받다	be supposed to ~하기로 되어 있다
be encouraged to ~하라고 권고받다	be intended to ~을 위한 목적이다	be scheduled to ~할 예정이다
be invited to ~할 것을 요청받다	be expected to ~할 것으로 기대되다	be projected to ~할 것이라 예상되다

All guests **are required to** check in at the front desk.
모든 투숙객들은 안내 데스크에서 숙박 수속을 하도록 요구받는다.

Staff members **are reminded to** file leave requests at least two weeks in advance.
직원들은 휴가 신청서를 최소한 2주 전에 제출하라는 말을 듣는다.

토익실전문제

출제 포인트 태에 맞는 동사 채우기
태에 맞는 동사를 채우는 문제 외에도, 5형식 수동태 동사 뒤에 to 부정사를 채우는 문제가 출제된다.

1. The accounting team ------- to providing accurate billing statements and resolving all customer inquiries within 24 hours.

   (A) is dedicating   (B) is dedicated
   (C) dedicates   (D) dedication

2. Coretek's sales associates are asked ------- in a customer relations workshop, which will be held on June 14 at 2 P.M.

   (A) participation   (B) to participate
   (C) participate   (D) participated

3. Members of the board were truly ------- with the positive consumer response to the company's new advertising campaign.

   (A) delight   (B) delighting
   (C) delighted   (D) delightedly

정답·해설·해석 p.27

둘 중 맞는 형태를 고르세요.

01 Bill ------- that he needed another assistant to finish the project before November.
  ⓐ stated   ⓑ was stated

02 Flights ------- to arrive on schedule in spite of the poor weather.
  ⓐ expected   ⓑ are expected

03 The shop owner ------- the customer's demand for a complete refund.
  ⓐ accepted   ⓑ was accepted

04 Dr. Menkin was ------- by the inadequate facilities at the clinic.
  ⓐ frustrating   ⓑ frustrated

05 A local film company ------- a documentary on the music industry.
  ⓐ has produced   ⓑ has been produced

06 The movers ------- the furniture to the company's new headquarters.
  ⓐ will transport   ⓑ will be transported

07 Joshua was ------- to learn that he was being transferred to the Paris branch.
  ⓐ exciting   ⓑ excited

틀린 곳이 있으면 바르게 고치세요.

08 The price of an apartment is closely relating to its location.

09 Due to strong winds, passengers will be experiencing turbulence during the flight.

10 Additional training for new staff has suggested by the consultant.

11 The vehicle designed for people in suburban areas who have to commute long distances.

12 Laboratory staff members are advised wearing protective eyewear and gloves at all times.

13 A promotion awarded to Ms. King because of her excellent managerial skills.

14 The organization is devoted to providing educational opportunities to underprivileged children.

정답·해석 p.27

무료 해설 ▶
바로 보기

맞은 문제 개수: / 14
틀린 문제에 해당하는 토익 공식을 다시 한번 학습하세요.

🕐 제한 시간 12분

Part 5

01 A substantial sum of money has just been ------- from the firm's bank account to pay for the construction of the new research facility.

(A) withdrew
(B) withdrawal
(C) withdrawn
(D) withdraw

02 Federal law stipulates that all companies ------- to provide their staff a minimum of 10 days paid vacation annually.

(A) requirement
(B) require
(C) are required
(D) are requiring

03 The campaigns that ------- to the broadcasting division have been scrapped because they were not effective.

(A) have assigned
(B) were assigned
(C) assigned
(D) assigns

04 The policy change announced by Mr. Stuart last Friday is meant to ------- the reimbursement process for employee travel expenses.

(A) simplified
(B) be simplified
(C) simplification
(D) simplify

05 First class seats ------- with Internet connections, global telephones, and fax machines for the convenience of Ray-Air's passengers.

(A) equipped
(B) equipment
(C) are equipped
(D) are equipping

06 Morgan Corporation is ------- to report that the company will be giving stock options to all employees.

(A) please
(B) pleased
(C) pleasurable
(D) pleasing

07 Until the trade and finance commission approves the revised policy on investments, the agency will be ------- current regulations for all start-up businesses.

(A) enforcement
(B) enforcer
(C) enforced
(D) enforcing

08 Visitors to the manufacturing facility are to be escorted ------- the floor manager, who will give them a tour of the factory.

(A) with
(B) from
(C) by
(D) into

09 Senator Jordan of California will be ------- a statement to the media this afternoon about the proposed changes to the tax code.

(A) release
(B) releases
(C) to release
(D) releasing

10 In order to facilitate planning for the fiscal year, several pertinent reports will ------- to all those in attendance at the workshop.

(A) send
(B) be sent
(C) be sending
(D) have sent

11 The receipt for the shipment from the supplier ------- all relevant taxes, customs fees, and international delivery charges.

(A) lists
(B) to list
(C) have listed
(D) listing

12 The introduction of specially trained conflict resolution advisors ------- to reduce tension between management and employees in the company.

(A) expecting
(B) is expected
(C) has expected
(D) will be expecting

13 If the director ------- that the top candidate was still a consultant for Master Lines Incorporated, he would have given the others greater priority.

(A) inform
(B) informing
(C) had informed
(D) had been informed

14 ------- the plant's production output, an inspection will be conducted to identify inefficiencies in the work process.

(A) To be maximized
(B) To maximize
(C) Will maximize
(D) Maximized

15 The winners of the logo contest are ------- to be at the dinner this evening, which will begin at 8 P.M. in the Lawrence Convention Center's main dining room.

(A) plan
(B) plans
(C) planning
(D) planned

16 Seminar participants who wish to stay near the venue are ------- to book their hotel rooms early.

(A) advice
(B) advisory
(C) advising
(D) advised

17 Once the structural renovations begin, tenants cannot ------- the lobby until they receive notice from the building's management.

(A) entrant
(B) entrance
(C) enter
(D) be entered

18 The use of the company credit card for personal expenses ------- and will result in immediate disciplinary action.

(A) prohibit
(B) to prohibit
(C) is prohibited
(D) has prohibited

Part 6

Questions 19-22 refer to the following memo.

To: All Carver Media staff
From: Jean Dubois, Human resources department
Subject: Recycling
Date: December 12

We are starting a recycling program in order to reduce the amount of trash we create. -------. Please make sure to put any recyclable items in the appropriate bin. They are all clearly labeled, so glass, tin, plastic, and paper should not ------- together. It is ------- to rinse out any containers that have food in them. This is because the recycling will only be collected once each week, and we'd like to keep the office as clean as possible. Batteries, which sometimes ------- harmful chemicals, should be left in the cardboard box by the photocopier machine. Thank you for your cooperation in this matter.

19 (A) There have been some complaints about the lack of space.
(B) Residents will no longer have to pay for waste collection.
(C) Volunteers may be needed to help come up with a solution.
(D) Four separate containers have been added to the break room.

20 (A) place
(B) placing
(C) be placed
(D) have placed

21 (A) difficult
(B) essential
(C) unnecessary
(D) various

22 (A) leak
(B) leaks
(C) leaking
(D) to leak

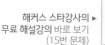

시제와 가정법

토익, 이렇게 나온다!
시제와 가정법 관련 문제는 평균 1~2문제 정도 꾸준히 출제되며 최대 3문제까지 출제된다. 문맥에 알맞은 시제의 동사를 채우는 문제와 시간 표현과 일치하는 시제의 동사를 채우는 문제가 주로 출제된다.

토익 필수 개념 다지기

01 **동사는 각각 다른 형태로 시간을 표현하는데, 이것을 동사의 시제라고 한다. 동사의 시제에는 단순, 진행, 완료 시제가 있다.**

단순 시제 : 특정 시간의 동작이나 상태를 나타내며, '동사 (+ s)', '동사 + ed', 'will + 동사'의 형태를 취한다.

현재	He **works** at the factory each day. 그는 매일 그 공장에서 일한다.
과거	He **worked** at the factory two years ago. 그는 2년 전에 그 공장에서 일했다.
미래	He **will work** at the factory next month. 그는 다음 달에 그 공장에서 일할 것이다.

진행 시제 : 한 시점에 동작이 계속 '진행'되고 있는 것을 나타내며 'be + -ing' 형태를 취한다.

현재진행	George **is dancing**. George는 춤추고 있다.
과거진행	George **was dancing**. George는 춤추고 있었다.
미래진행	George **will be dancing** at the festival. George는 축제에서 춤추고 있을 것이다.

완료 시제 : 특정한 어떤 기준 시점에서 그 이전에 일어난 일이나 그 기준 시점까지의 기간 동안 동작이나 상태가 계속되는 것을 나타내며 'have + p.p.' 형태를 취한다.

현재완료	Ellen **has left**. Ellen은 떠나고 없다.
과거완료	Ellen **had already left**. Ellen은 이미 떠나고 없었다.
미래완료	Ellen **will have left** by then. Ellen은 그때쯤엔 이미 떠나고 없을 것이다.

02 **가정법 문장은 현재나 과거의 반대 상황을 가정하여 표현한다. 대개 if로 시작되며, 특별한 시제를 사용한다.**

If I **were** tall, I **would play** basketball. 내가 키가 크다면, 농구를 할 텐데.

현재 키가 크지 않은 사람이 자신이 키가 크다면 농구를 할 것이라고 가정하는 문장이다. '현재'의 반대 상황을 가정하기 위해, if절에 '과거 시제(were)'를 쓰고, 주절에서 '조동사의 과거형 + 동사원형(would play)'을 쓴다.

If I **had been** tall, I **would have played** basketball in high school.
내가 키가 컸다면, 고등학교 때 농구를 했을 텐데.

과거에 키가 크지 않았던 사람이 그 당시 자신이 키가 컸다면 농구를 했을 것이라고 가정하는 문장이다. '과거'의 반대 상황을 가정하기 위해, if절에서 '과거완료 시제(had been)'를 쓰고, 주절에서 '조동사의 과거형 + have p.p.(would have played)'를 쓴다.

* 가정법 문장은 if로 시작하는 조건절과 구별해야 한다. 어떤 일을 실제의 사실로 받아들이고 말하는 조건절은 특별한 시제가 아니라 일반적으로 사용하는 시제(현재 표현에 현재 시제, 과거 표현에 과거 시제)를 쓴다.

  If you **require** changes to your itinerary, please notify a travel agent.
  여행 일정 변경이 필요하시다면, 여행사 직원에게 알려 주시기 바랍니다.

토익 공식
1 현재 / 과거 / 미래

01 현재 시제는 현재의 상태나 반복되는 동작, 일반적인 사실을 표현한다.

The travel package **includes** first class hotel accommodations. 그 여행 패키지는 일급 호텔 숙박 시설을 포함한다.
▶ 여행 패키지의 현재의 구성 상태를 나타내기 위해서는 현재 시제(includes)를 쓴다.

Robert usually **takes** the subway to commute to the office. Robert는 사무실로 통근하기 위해 보통 지하철을 탄다.
▶ 반복적으로 지하철을 타는 행동을 나타내기 위해서는 현재 시제(takes)를 쓴다.

Exercising on a regular basis **improves** a person's health. 정기적으로 운동하는 것은 사람의 건강을 향상시킨다.
▶ 정기적인 운동의 효과라는 일반적인 사실을 나타내기 위해서는 현재 시제(improves)를 쓴다.

02 과거 시제는 이미 끝난 과거의 동작이나 상태를 표현한다.

I **shipped** the requested sample products to the buyer two days ago. 나는 요청받은 견본 제품을 구매자에게 이틀 전에 보냈다.
▶ 제품을 보낸 것은 이미 이틀 전에 일어난 일이므로, 과거 시제(shipped)를 쓴다.

03 미래 시제는 미래의 상황에 대한 추측이나 의지를 표현한다.

I **will do** my best to win the tennis competition. 나는 테니스 경기에서 이기기 위해 최선을 다할 것이다.
▶ 테니스 경기에서 이기겠다는 의지를 표현하기 위해 미래 시제(will do)를 쓴다.

고득점
포인트
❶ 현재진행형(be동사 + -ing)과 'be going to + 동사원형'의 형태도 예정된 일이나 곧 일어나려고 하는 일을 표현하여 미래를 나타낸다.
We are having lunch with Dan on Wednesday. 우리는 수요일에 Dan과 함께 점심을 먹을 것이다.
Brenda is going to visit her sister in Boston tomorrow. Brenda는 내일 보스턴에 있는 그녀의 여동생을 방문할 것이다.
❷ 현재 시제도 가까운 미래를 나타내는 부사(구)와 함께 쓰여 미래에 확실히 일어나도록 예정되어 있는 일을 나타낼 수 있다.
Minos Apparel's annual charity event begins two weeks from now. Minos Apparel사의 연례 자선 행사가 앞으로 2주 후에 시작할 것이다.

04 시간이나 조건을 나타내는 종속절에서는, 미래 시제 대신 현재 시제를 쓴다.

When the writer (**will finish**, **finishes**) the first draft, it will be reviewed immediately by the editor.
작가가 1차 초안을 끝마칠 때, 그것은 편집자에 의해 즉시 검토될 것이다.
▶ when으로 시작되는 시간절에서, 미래를 나타내기 위해 미래 시제(will finish)가 아닌 현재 시제(finishes)를 써야 한다.

If the proposal (**will be**, **is**) approved, the publisher will send you a timetable.
그 제안이 승인되면, 출판사가 귀하에게 일정표를 보낼 것입니다.
▶ if로 시작되는 조건절에서, 미래를 나타내기 위해 미래 시제(will be)가 아닌 현재 시제(is)를 써야 한다.

고득점
포인트
❶ 시간, 조건 종속절을 이끄는 접속사에는 when, before, after, as soon as, once, if, unless, by the time 등이 있다.
❷ 시간, 조건을 나타내는 종속절과 함께 쓰인 주절에는 미래 시제 대신 현재 시제를 쓰지 않고 그대로 미래 시제를 쓴다.
When the writer finishes the first draft, it is reviewed(→will be reviewed) immediately by the editor.
→ 시간을 나타내는 종속절인 when절은 미래 시제(will finish) 대신 현재 시제(finishes)를 쓰지만, 함께 쓰인 주절에는 현재 시제(is reviewed)가 아닌 미래 시제(will be reviewed)를 써야 한다.

토익실전문제

출제 포인트 올바른 시제의 동사 채우기
주절의 시제가 미래일 때 if절이나 when절에 현재 시제의 동사를 채우는 문제가 자주 출제된다.

1. Steve Malkin, who ------- a philanthropic organization after retiring, is visiting Sub-Saharan Africa to determine how he can help its youth.

(A) establishing   (B) establishment
(C) establishes   (D) established

2. Mr. Sanders ------- on a business trip to Tokyo until the end of this week, so he will not be able to complete the sales report as scheduled.

(A) would have been   (B) will be
(C) will have been   (D) was being

3. If Ms. Lee ------- the office renovations to be finished ahead of time, she will authorize the hiring of additional workers.

(A) will require   (B) requires
(C) will have required   (D) would require

정답·해설·해석 p.29

01 현재진행 시제(am/is/are + -ing)는 현재 시점에 진행되고 있는 일을 표현한다.

She **is talking** on the phone at the moment. 그녀는 지금 전화 통화를 하고 있다.

▶ 현재 시점(at the moment)에 전화 통화를 하고 있다는 것을 표현하기 위해 현재진행 시제(is talking)를 쓴다.

Food Delight Magazine **is** currently **accepting** applications for the chief editor position.
*Food Delight*지는 현재 편집장 자리에 대한 지원서를 받고 있다.

▶ 현재 시점(currently)에 지원서를 받고 있다는 것을 표현하기 위해 현재진행 시제(is accepting)를 쓴다.

고득점 포인트
❶ 반복적으로 일어나는 행동을 나타내기 위해서는 현재진행 시제가 아닌 현재 시제를 쓴다.
Mr. Clark is usually giving(→usually gives) us time off in the afternoon. Mr. Clark는 보통 오후에 우리에게 휴식 시간을 준다.
→ 반복적으로 휴식 시간을 주는 행동을 나타내고 있으므로 현재진행 시제(is usually giving)가 아닌 현재 시제(usually gives)를 써야 한다.

❷ 바로 지금 일어나고 있는 행동을 나타내기 위해서는 현재 시제가 아닌 현재진행 시제를 쓴다.
The baby sleeps(→is sleeping) on the bed. 아기가 침대 위에서 잠자고 있다.
→ 바로 지금 일어나는 행동을 나타내고 있으므로 현재 시제(sleeps)가 아닌 현재진행 시제(is sleeping)를 써야 한다.

02 과거진행 시제(was/were + -ing)는 특정한 과거 시점에 진행되고 있던 일을 표현한다.

I **was watching** TV at 8 o'clock last night. 나는 어젯밤 8시에 TV를 시청하고 있었다.

▶ 특정 과거 시점(at 8 o'clock last night)에 TV를 시청하고 있었다는 것을 표현하기 위해 과거진행 시제(was watching)를 쓴다.

03 미래진행 시제(will be + -ing)는 특정한 미래 시점에 진행되고 있을 일을 표현한다.

By this time next Monday, we **will be traveling** to Paris! 다음 주 월요일 이때쯤이면, 우리는 파리로 여행을 가고 있을 거야!

▶ 특정 미래 시점(By this time next Monday)에 파리로 여행을 가고 있을 것을 표현하기 위해 미래진행 시제(will be traveling)를 쓴다.

04 진행 시제로 쓸 수 없는 동사

| 감정 동사 | surprise 놀라게 하다 | shock 충격을 주다 | hate 미워하다 | prefer 선호하다 | want 원하다 | believe 이해하다 |
| 상태 동사 | include 포함하다 | need 필요로 하다 | be ~이다 | know 알다 | exist 존재하다 | consist 이루어져 있다 |

I (**am preferring**, **prefer**) to relax in a quiet room alone. 나는 조용한 방에서 혼자 휴식을 취하는 것을 선호한다.

▶ 감정 동사는 진행 시제(am preferring)로 쓸 수 없으므로 단순 시제인 현재 시제(prefer)를 써야 한다.

A delivery person (**is being**, **is**) in the building's lobby. 배달부는 건물 로비에 있다.

▶ 상태 동사는 진행 시제(is being)로 쓸 수 없으므로 단순 시제인 현재 시제(is)를 써야 한다.

토익실전문제

출제 포인트 올바른 시제의 동사 채우기
감정 동사나 상태 동사의 경우, 진행형 보기를 제외하고 알맞은 시제를 선택하는 문제가 주로 출제된다.

1. Representatives of Kamata Heavy Industries ------ with shareholders at 4:00 P.M. next Wednesday to address concerns regarding the proposed merger with KLX Limited.

   (A) had met   (B) met
   (C) will be meeting   (D) is meeting

2. Gentech Incorporated's recently constructed research facilities ------ of state-of-the-art biology and chemistry laboratories, as well as a medical-testing center.

   (A) are consisting   (B) consist
   (C) consists   (D) has consisted

3. No one was more ------ than the company president to discover that a few of his most trusted employees had resigned and taken jobs with a competitor.

   (A) surprising   (B) surprise
   (C) surprised   (D) being surprised

정답·해설·해석 p.30

현재완료 / 과거완료 / 미래완료

01 현재완료 시제(has/have + p.p.)는 과거에 시작된 일이 현재까지 계속되거나 방금 완료된 일, 과거의 경험, 그리고 과거에 발생한 일이 현재까지 영향을 미치는 것을 표현한다.

GDX Technologies **has provided** innovative products for a decade now.
GDX Technologies사는 현재까지 10년 동안 혁신적인 상품들을 제공해 왔다.

▶ 과거 10년 전 시작하여 현재까지 계속 상품을 제공하고 있으므로 현재완료 시제(has provided)를 쓴다.

I **have** just **asked** the shipping department to process your order. 귀하의 주문을 처리해 달라고 배송부에 방금 요청했습니다.

▶ 배송부에 요청하는 것이 방금 완료되었으므로 현재완료 시제(have asked)를 쓴다.

Jerry **has** never **eaten** Thai food. Jerry는 태국 음식을 먹어본 적이 없다.

▶ 과거에 태국 음식을 먹어 본 경험을 나타내므로 현재완료 시제(has eaten)를 쓴다.

The assistant **has lost** the document. 그 비서는 서류를 분실했다.

▶ 과거에 서류를 분실해 현재 서류를 가지고 있지 않은 상태를 나타내므로 현재완료 시제(has lost)를 쓴다.

고득점 포인트
❶ 완료 시제 문장이 계속을 의미할 때는 for나 since, 완료를 의미할 때는 already나 just, 경험을 의미할 때는 ever, never, yet과 함께 쓰인다.

❷ 현재완료와 현재완료진행 둘 다 과거부터 현재까지 계속되는 일을 나타낼 수 있지만, 현재완료진행에는 현재 그 동작이 진행되고 있다는 의미가 더해진다.

Over the past few days, heavy snow <u>has fallen</u> continuously. 지난 며칠 동안, 많은 양의 눈이 계속해서 내려왔다.
Heavy snow <u>has been falling</u> recently. 최근 많은 양의 눈이 내려오고 있다.

02 과거완료 시제(had + p.p.)는 과거의 특정 시점 이전에 발생한 일을 표현한다.

When I arrived at the station, the train **had** already **left**. 내가 역에 도착했을 때, 기차는 이미 떠나 있었다.

▶ 과거의 특정 시점(역에 도착한 시점) 이전에, 이미 기차가 떠났다는 사실을 표현하기 위해 과거완료 시제(had left)를 쓴다.

The TV show **had** already **ended** by the time I **turned on** the TV. 내가 TV를 틀었을 때, TV쇼는 이미 끝나 있었다.

▶ 과거의 특정 시점(TV를 튼 시점) 이전에, 이미 TV쇼가 끝나 있었다는 사실을 표현하기 위해 과거완료 시제(had ended)를 쓴다.

03 미래완료 시제(will have + p.p.)는 미래 특정 시점 이전에 발생한 동작이 미래의 그 시점에 완료될 것임을 표현한다.

Jim **will have lived** in this house for 10 years by next month. Jim은 다음 달이면 이 집에서 10년 동안 살아온 것이 된다.

▶ 이전부터 이 집에서 살아왔던 사실이 특정 미래 시점(by next month)에 10년이 되는 것을 표현하기 위해 미래완료 시제(will have lived)를 쓴다.

Eleanor **will have worked** at Trine Bank for 15 years next year. Eleanor는 내년이면 Trine 은행에서 15년 동안 일해온 것이 된다.

▶ 이전부터 Trine 은행에서 일해왔던 사실이 특정 미래 시점(next year)에 15년이 되는 것을 표현하기 위해 미래완료 시제(will have worked)를 쓴다.

토익실전문제

출제 포인트 올바른 시제의 동사 채우기
현재완료 시제가 주로 출제된다.

1. For several months, the car industry ------- many investors because automotive products now make up 15 percent of the country's exports.

(A) interest   (B) has interested
(C) interesting   (D) had interested

2. By exercising at the gym during her lunch break, Linda was able to relieve the work-related stress that ------- caused by a busy morning.

(A) were   (B) would
(C) has been   (D) had been

3. By next month, $38 million ------- spent on the research into the relationship between the use of fossil fuels and climate change.

(A) has been   (B) is
(C) were being   (D) will have been

정답·해설·해석 p.30

01 과거, 현재, 현재완료, 미래 시제와 함께 자주 쓰이는 표현들이 있다.

과거	현재	현재완료	미래·미래완료
yesterday recently 시간 표현 + ago last + 시간 표현 in + 과거	usually often each month(year) generally	since + 과거 in the last(past) ~ over the last(past) recently	tomorrow next + 시간 표현 by / until + 미래 * 단, until은 미래완료와 함께 쓰이지 않는다. as of + 미래 by the time + 주어 + 현재 동사 when + 주어 + 현재 동사

He (**has begun**, **began**) going to the health club <u>last week</u>. 그는 지난주에 헬스클럽에 다니기 시작했다.

▶ 과거 시간 표현(last week)이 있으므로 현재완료 시제(has begun)가 아닌 과거 시제(began)를 써야 한다.

Doris (**rented**, **has rented**) that flat <u>since</u> she came to L.A. Doris는 로스앤젤레스에 온 이래로 그 아파트를 임대해 왔다.

▶ 종속절이 'since + 과거'이므로, 주절 동사는 과거 시제(rented)가 아닌 현재완료 시제(has rented)를 써야 한다.

He (**has relocated**, **will have relocated**) to Dallas <u>by the time</u> the branch opens.
그 지점이 문을 열 때쯤 그는 댈러스로 이전해 있을 것이다.

▶ 미래 시점을 나타내는 'by the time + 주어 + 현재 동사'가 왔으므로 현재완료 시제(has relocated)가 아닌 미래완료 시제(will have relocated)를 써야 한다.

고득점 포인트 과거 시점을 나타내는 표현인 'by the time + 주어 + 과거'가 올 경우, 주절에는 과거완료 시제를 써야 한다.

He departed(→had departed) for the conference by the time it was canceled. 회의가 취소되었을 때쯤 그는 회의하러 출발했었다.

→ by the time 뒤에 과거 시제(was canceled)가 왔으므로 주절에는 과거 시제(departed)가 아닌 과거완료 시제(had departed)를 써야 한다.

02 주절이 과거 시제일 경우, 종속절에는 과거나 과거완료가 온다.

Mr. Fisher informed us that the trainees' orientation (~~is conducted~~, **was conducted**) yesterday.
Mr. Fisher는 우리에게 수습 직원 오리엔테이션이 어제 실시되었다고 알려주었다.

▶ 주절이 과거 시제(informed)이고 종속절 역시 과거의 일을 언급하므로, 종속절에는 현재 시제(is conducted)가 아닌 과거 시제(was conducted)를 써야 한다.

고득점 포인트 주절이 과거 시제이더라도, 문장이 언급되고 있는 현재 시점까지 종속절의 동작이나 상태가 계속될 경우에는 현재(완료) 시제가 올 수 있다. 그리고 문장이 언급되고 있는 현재 시점 이후에 예정된 일이라면 미래 시제가 올 수 있다.

She stated that the team has developed methods to measure pollution. 그녀는 그 팀이 오염을 측정하는 방법을 개발해 왔다고 말했다.

→ 주절이 과거 시제(stated)이더라도, 이 문장이 언급되고 있는 현재 시점에도 오염을 측정할 수 있는 방법들에 대한 개발이 지속되고 있다고 여겨진다면 현재완료 시제(has developed)가 쓰일 수 있다.

The agent told his clients that property prices <u>will drop</u> next year. 그 중개인은 고객들에게 부동산 가격이 내년에 하락할 것이라고 말했다.

→ 주절이 과거 시제(told)이더라도, 이 문장이 언급되고 있는 현재 시점 이후(next year)에 가격이 떨어질 예정이라면 미래 시제(will drop)가 쓰일 수 있다.

토익실전문제

출제 포인트 시간 표현과 일치하는 시제의 동사 채우기

시간 표현과 일치하는 과거 시제나 현재완료 시제의 동사를 채우는 문제가 가장 많이 출제된다.

1. Television viewership ------- slightly since the advent of the information age and the invention of the personal computer.

(A) drop (B) will drop
(C) has dropped (D) dropping

2. Last week, a newspaper columnist ------- an article that triggered an investigation into the university's admissions practices.

(A) writes (B) has written
(C) wrote (D) have written

3. Management was notified that the arrival of the shipment sent to the Paris office ------- because of a problem with customs.

(A) being delayed (B) would be delayed
(C) have been delayed (D) have delayed

정답·해설·해석 p.30

토익 공식 5 : 가정법 미래 / 과거 / 과거완료

01 가정법 미래/과거/과거완료 문장에서, if절과 주절의 시제는 짝을 이룬다.

미래	If + 주어 + should + 동사원형, 주어 + will(can, may, should) + 동사원형	가능성이 희박한 미래 가정
과거	If + 주어 + 과거동사(be동사의 경우 were), 주어 + would(could, might, should) + 동사원형	현재의 반대를 가정
과거완료	If + 주어 + had p.p., 주어 + would(could, might, should) have p.p.	과거의 반대를 가정

If it **should snow** tomorrow, I **will stay** indoors.
혹시라도 내일 눈이 온다면, 집에 머무를 것이다. ⇨ 내일 눈이 올 가능성이 거의 없다.

If that television **were** cheaper, I **would buy** it today.
그 텔레비전이 더 저렴하다면, 오늘 그것을 살 텐데. ⇨ 텔레비전 값이 더 싸지 않기 때문에 그것을 사지 못한다.

If someone **had offered** me a ride, I **might have gone** to the concert.
누군가 내게 태워 준다고 했다면, 나는 콘서트에 갔을 텐데. ⇨ 누군가 태워 주지 않았기 때문에 나는 콘서트에 가지 못했다.

02 혼합가정법에서는 if절과 주절의 시제가 다르다.

If 주어 had p.p., 주어 would 동사원형	"만약 ~했었다면, (지금) ~할 텐데"
가정법 과거완료　　　　가정법 과거	

→ If절에는 과거의 반대를 나타내는 '가정법 과거완료'를 썼고, 주절에는 현재의 반대를 나타내는 '가정법 과거'를 썼다.

If I **had accepted** the team leader position last year, I **would be** a manager now.
작년에 팀장 자리를 받아들였었다면, 나는 지금 부장일 텐데. ⇨ 작년에 팀장 자리를 받아들이지 않아서 지금 부장이 아니다.

▶ If절에는 과거 사실의 반대를 나타내는 가정법 과거완료(had accepted)를 썼지만, 주절에는 현재 사실의 반대를 나타내는 가정법 과거(would be)를 썼다.

> **고득점 포인트** 혼합가정법 문장에는 주로 주절에 현재 시제를 나타내는 단서(now, today)가 나온다.
>
> If I had defrosted the steaks earlier, dinner would be ready by now.
> 내가 스테이크를 더 일찍 해동시켰다면, 지금쯤 저녁 식사가 준비되었을 텐데.
>
> → If절에 가정법 과거완료를 썼더라도 주절에 now가 있는 것으로 보아 현재를 가정한 문장임을 알 수 있으므로 가정법 과거를 쓴다.

토익실전문제

출제 포인트 : 가정법 동사 채우기
주절에 가정법 동사를 채우는 문제가 주로 출제된다.
가정법 과거완료의 동사를 채우는 문제가 가장 많이 출제된다.

1. If measures had not been taken to curtail shipping expenses, the added costs would ------- by the customers.

(A) assume (B) have been assumed
(C) had been assumed (D) be assuming

2. If personal income taxes had been reduced, the national economy ------- much more quickly.

(A) improved
(B) has improved
(C) would have improved
(D) has been improved

3. If the technician had come this morning, the air conditioner ------- working now.

(A) would be (B) would have been
(C) will be (D) will have been

정답·해설·해석 p.30

01 가정법 문장에서는 if가 생략될 수 있으며, 이때 주어와 조동사의 자리가 바뀌는 도치가 일어난다.

미래	If + 주어 + should + 동사원형, 주어 + will(can, may, should) + 동사원형
	⇨ **Should** + 주어 + 동사원형, 주어 + will(can, may, should) + 동사원형
과거	If + 주어 + 과거동사(be동사의 경우 were), 주어 + would(could, might, should) + 동사원형
	⇨ **Were** + 주어 + 명사, 형용사 등, 주어 + would(could, might, should) + 동사원형
과거완료	If + 주어 + had p.p., 주어 + would(could, might, should) have p.p.
	⇨ **Had** + 주어 + **p.p.**, 주어 + would(could, might, should) have p.p.

If Mr. Harley **should** <u>agree</u> to the terms, we can sign the contract today.
혹시라도 Mr. Harley가 조건에 동의한다면, 우리는 오늘 계약을 체결할 수 있을 것이다.
⇨ **Should** Mr. Harley <u>agree</u> to the terms, we can sign the contract today.

If Valerie **were** not so <u>tired</u>, she would join us for dinner.
Valerie가 너무 피곤하지 않다면, 우리와 저녁 식사를 함께 할 텐데.
⇨ **Were** Valerie not so <u>tired</u>, she would join us for dinner.

If I **had** completed my master's degree, I would have gotten a better job.
내가 석사 과정을 마쳤었다면, 더 좋은 직업을 가졌을 텐데.
⇨ **Had** I <u>completed</u> my master's degree, I would have gotten a better job.

02 If절 대신 'without + 명사'가 와서 가정법 문장을 만들 수 있다.

가정법 과거	주어 would 동사원형 + 'without + 명사' (= if it were not for + 명사) ~이 없다면 ~할 것이다
가정법 과거완료	주어 would have p.p. + 'without + 명사' (= if it had not been for + 명사) ~이 없었다면 ~했을 것이다

I **couldn't finish** this assignment <u>without my coworker's help</u>. 동료의 도움이 없다면 나는 이 일을 끝낼 수 없을 것이다.
I **could** never **have finished** this assignment <u>without my coworker's help</u>.
동료의 도움이 없었다면 나는 이 일을 끝낼 수 없었을 것이다.

고득점 포인트　if절 대신 otherwise를 쓰기도 한다.
She made a reservation; otherwise(= If she had not made a reservation), she wouldn't have gotten a table.
그녀는 예약을 했다. 그렇지 않았다면, 그녀는 자리를 얻지 못했을 것이다.

토익실전문제

출제 포인트　가정법 동사 채우기
should를 채우는 문제, p.p.를 채우는 문제 등, 가정법 동사의 일부를 채우는 문제가 출제된다.

1. Had the materials ------- on time, the company might have fulfilled the customer's request for a rush order.

   (A) order　　　　　　(B) ordered
   (C) been ordered　　(D) were ordered

2. Had the team submitted the report on schedule, the manager ------- to postpone the meeting of the board of directors.

   (A) did not have　　　(B) would not be had
   (C) does not have　　(D) would not have had

3. ------- your loan application be denied, the financial institution will refund the cost of processing the application.

   (A) Had　　　(B) Did
   (C) Might　　(D) Should

정답·해설·해석 p.31

HACKERS PRACTICE 토익 고득점을 위한 필수 연습

둘 중 적절한 것을 고르세요.

01 When Mr. Ryes ------- his rental unit, he noticed that the tenant had remodeled the kitchen.
ⓐ inspects   ⓑ inspected

02 The technician discovered that a virus ------- several computers.
ⓐ had infected   ⓑ infects

03 If it had not been for the translator, we would not ------- the client.
ⓐ understand   ⓑ have understood

04 The market survey ------- useful when we select places to launch our new product line.
ⓐ was   ⓑ will be

05 Without the efforts of conservationists, the park ------- have been turned into a residential area.
ⓐ will   ⓑ would

06 If economists ------- that loan interest rates will increase, we should seek other sources of funding.
ⓐ think   ⓑ had thought

07 If that store ------- less, customers would be more inclined to shop there.
ⓐ charged   ⓑ has charged

08 As soon as the merchandise -------, the shipping personnel will load it into the truck.
ⓐ is packed   ⓑ will be packed

09 Had my house been bigger, I would ------- that sofa.
ⓐ buy   ⓑ have bought

10 The personnel department ------- to design a training program that will increase staff efficiency.
ⓐ wants   ⓑ is wanting

적절한 표현을 고르세요.

11 Sabre-Tech will have upgraded its plant (since/by the time) its new printers are ready for production.

12 If I had left home a bit earlier, I would (be/have been) at the airport now.

13 Maria, who once worked for a top restaurant, is preparing meals for an embassy (two years ago/at the moment).

14 Private dentists (once/usually) charge $60 for a tooth extraction.

정답·해설 p.31

무료 해설 ▶
바로 보기

맞은 문제 개수: / 14
틀린 문제에 해당하는 토익 공식을 다시 한번 학습하세요.

🕐 제한 시간 12분

Part 5

01 The employees in the accounting division were delighted to find out that their co-worker Sam Warner ------- to assistant manager.

(A) had promoted
(B) will have been promoted
(C) had been promoted
(D) promoted

02 Mayor Keating ------- Veronica Moore to serve as director of the newly formed transportation task force last week.

(A) designate
(B) is designating
(C) has designated
(D) designated

03 The company ------- the account had it not been for the support of the very talented copywriters in the advertising division.

(A) did not win
(B) will not have won
(C) would not win
(D) would not have won

04 Once the team members ------- the research report, they will send copies of it to all board members.

(A) will revise
(B) would revise
(C) revise
(D) will have revised

05 The report would not have been completed ------- the continued efforts of Bio-Data's dedicated and thorough research team.

(A) so as
(B) as to
(C) in that
(D) without

06 The two accounting firms ------- the terms of the merger and will likely release the details of the agreement to the media next Monday.

(A) negotiates
(B) negotiating
(C) are negotiating
(D) were negotiated

07 ------- a new promotion was launched by the advertising department a month ago, the company's market share has not increased.

(A) In spite of
(B) Ever
(C) Although
(D) Furthermore

08 The supervisor commented that the manual could ------- better had the company hired an editor to go over the material before it was printed.

(A) arranged
(B) be arranged
(C) have arranged
(D) have been arranged

09 If you ------- difficulties when completing the customs declaration form, contact a flight attendant for assistance.

(A) had encountered
(B) encounter
(C) were encountered
(D) encountering

10 Recently, those in supervisory positions ------- in more classes on positive leadership and employee motivation.

(A) had registered
(B) are to be registering
(C) have been registering
(D) will have been registering

11 Ms. Ross ------- next year's marketing plan to expand the customer base in overseas markets last Friday.

(A) submits
(B) submitted
(C) is submitting
(D) will submit

12 By the time the two new large printers are installed, demand for the popular publication ------- twofold.

(A) has increased
(B) had increased
(C) been increased
(D) will have increased

13 If the plans ------- confirmed on schedule, Gilbert & Sons would be conducting the feasibility study for the Safeway Water Project already.

(A) will be
(B) are being
(C) had been
(D) have been

14 Unless the meeting with our clients ends late, we ------- to the office right before 5 P.M.

(A) returned
(B) returning
(C) will return
(D) have returned

15 The price of gold ------- at $1,300 per ounce over the past week, yet most financial experts agree that it is likely to rise due to a lack of investor confidence in the stock market.

(A) is stabilizing   (B) will have stabilized
(C) will be stabilizing   (D) has stabilized

16 The administrative consultant suggests that clients ------- business contract revisions after they have been approved by management.

(A) signed   (B) signing
(C) sign   (D) to sign

17 If Cargill Sportswear's advertisement campaign were more effective, the company ------- a larger market share.

(A) would gain   (B) gain
(C) have gained   (D) will gain

18 International luxury hotel chain Mirage Hotels & Resorts Inc. ------- more than 600 hotels and resorts over the last 25 years.

(A) establishes   (B) had established
(C) has established   (D) will establish

Part 6

Questions 19-22 refer to the following e-mail.

TO: Morgan Clark <mclark@mproj.com>
FROM: Lisa Ross <lisross@envirofirst.org>
SUBJECT: Information on staffing

Dear Mr. Clark,

We ------- your proposal regarding the water management project in Hampton, Ohio two weeks
   19
ago. After reading it, our funding organization determined that the undertaking is feasible and advantageous to the intended beneficiaries. However, the proposal does not include a full description of staffing requirements. May we ask you to supply us with ------- information on this point?
        20

Other than that, we are pleased with the proposal and think that its objectives are in line with our aims. Our representative James Gray, whom you spoke with previously about the project, ------- you
     21
regarding the staffing details within the next two weeks. The committee would like to see your revised proposal as soon as possible. -------. You can be assured of our full support. Thank you.
   22

Lisa Ross

19 (A) receive   (B) received
    (C) were received   (D) will receive

20 (A) early   (B) preceding
    (C) recent   (D) additional

21 (A) contacted   (B) contacts
    (C) will contact   (D) contacting

22 (A) The restoration work on the Hampton dam is currently underway.
    (B) Should the board grant final approval, we will notify you immediately.
    (C) Technical issues have prevented us from reviewing your proposal.
    (D) Qualifications for the managerial position are listed below.

해커스 스타강사의 ▶
무료 해설강의 바로 보기
(8번 문제)

SECTION 3
준동사구

to 부정사

토익, 이렇게 나온다!

to 부정사 관련 문제는 평균 1문제 정도 출제된다. 목적을 의미하는 부사 역할의 to 부정사를 채우는 문제가 가장 많이 출제 된다.

토익 필수 개념 다지기

01 to 부정사(to + 동사원형)는 동사로부터 나왔지만, 문장 내에서 동사 역할이 아니라 명사, 형용사, 부사 역할을 한다.

I **to play** tennis. (×)
I want **to buy** a car. (○)   나는 자동차를 사기를 원한다.
I have nothing **to do** today. (○)   나는 오늘 할 일이 없다.
I exercise **to stay** healthy. (○)   나는 건강을 유지하기 위해 운동한다.

위 문장들에서 보여지듯이 to play는 동사 역할을 하지 못하고, to buy는 동사 want의 목적어로 명사 역할을, to do는 명사 nothing을 꾸며 주는 형용사 역할을 한다. 그리고 to stay는 동사 exercise의 목적을 나타내는 부사 역할을 한다. 이처럼 동사원형에 to가 붙어 문장 내에서 다양한 품사로 사용되는 to 부정사는 품사가 정해져 있지 않다는 의미로 '부정사'라고 불린다.

02 to 부정사는 문장에서 동사의 역할을 할 수는 없지만 여전히 동사의 성질을 가지고 있어, 동사처럼 목적어 또는 보어를 가질 수 있고, 부사의 꾸밈을 받을 수 있다.

We need **to buy tickets**.   우리는 티켓을 살 필요가 있다.
Joe wants **to become a singer**.   Joe는 가수가 되기를 원한다.
She tries **to drive carefully**.   그녀는 조심스럽게 운전하려고 노력한다.

위 문장들이 보여주듯이 to buy는 목적어 tickets를 갖고, to become은 보어 a singer를 갖는다. 그리고 to drive는 부사 carefully의 꾸밈을 받는다. 이와 같은 [to 부정사 + 목적어/보어/부사]의 형태를 'to 부정사구'라고 한다.

01 to 부정사는 명사, 형용사, 부사 역할을 한다.

• 명사처럼 주어, 목적어, 보어 자리에 온다.

주어	**To learn a second language** is very rewarding. 제2언어를 배우는 것은 매우 보람 있다.
목적어	Mr. Lee wants **to renegotiate the contract**. Mr. Lee는 계약을 재협상하기를 원한다.
주격 보어	The team's objective is **to design a better product**. 그 팀의 목표는 더 나은 제품을 만드는 것이다.
목적격 보어	The manager asked his employees **to research** market trends. 그 관리자는 그의 직원들에게 시장 경향을 조사해 달라고 요청했다.

• 형용사처럼 명사를 뒤에서 꾸며 준다.

명사 수식	I have some news **to report**. 나는 알릴 소식이 있다.

• 부사처럼 목적, 이유, 결과 등을 나타낸다.

목적	I will send our order earlier **to secure sufficient raw materials**. 나는 충분한 원자재를 확보하기 위해 우리 주문을 더 빨리 보낼 것이다.
이유	I am delighted **to introduce** the new branch manager. 새 지점장을 소개하게 되어 기쁘다.
결과	Philip woke up only **to realize** he was late for work. Philip은 잠에서 깨어 회사에 늦었다는 것을 깨달았을 뿐이다.

▶ 밑줄 친 부분은 to 부정사구의 핵심이 되는 부분으로, 토익에서는 이 부분에 대해 묻는다.

고득점 포인트

❶ to 부정사는 진주어와 진목적어 자리에도 올 수 있다.
  It is necessary to follow the security procedures. 보안 절차를 따르는 것이 필요하다.
  The company considers it important to maintain client confidentiality. 그 회사는 고객 기밀을 지키는 것을 중요하게 여긴다.

❷ to 부정사가 '목적'을 나타낼 때는, to 대신 in order to, so as to를 쓸 수 있다.
  Janet visited a government office in order to renew her passport. Janet은 그녀의 여권을 갱신하기 위해 관공서를 방문했다.

❸ 사람의 행동 목적(~하기 위해서)을 나타낼 때는 '전치사 for + -ing'를 쓰지 못하고 to 부정사만 쓸 수 있다.
  For attracting customers(→To attract customers), the clerks distributed flyers.
  고객들을 끌어들이기 위해, 점원들은 전단지를 배포했다.
  → 고객을 끌어들이려는 목적을 나타내므로 to 부정사를 써야 하며, for -ing는 쓰지 못한다.

02 동사는 to 부정사 자리에 올 수 없다.

Lisa needs (~~listen~~, **to listen**) to the instructions more carefully. Lisa는 지시를 좀 더 주의 깊게 들을 필요가 있다.
▶ 동사(needs)의 목적어가 되기 위해서는 동사(listen)가 올 수 없고 명사 역할을 하는 to 부정사(to listen)가 와야 한다.

The intern has several projects (~~complete~~, **to complete**) before the end of the month.
그 인턴 사원은 이달 말까지 끝마쳐야 할 몇 개의 프로젝트가 있다.
▶ 명사(projects)를 꾸미기 위해서는 동사(complete)가 올 수 없고 형용사 역할을 하는 to 부정사(to complete)가 와야 한다.

토익실전문제

출제 포인트 to 부정사 채우기
부사 역할을 하는 to 부정사를 채우는 문제가 가장 많이 출제된다.

1. The firm temporarily closed one of its smallest offices ------- operating costs.
   (A) will decrease   (B) decreases
   (C) have decreased   (D) to decrease

2. The purpose of the museum catalog is ------- detailed information on artwork currently being displayed in the gallery.
   (A) supply   (B) supplied
   (C) supplies   (D) to supply

3. The Dogwood Company is pleased ------- that customers can now purchase gardening equipment directly from its Web site.
   (A) to report   (B) report
   (C) reported   (D) be reporting

정답·해설·해석 p.33

01 to 부정사는 'to + 동사원형'의 형태를 가진다.

Call this number (**to confirmation**, ~~to confirming~~, **to confirm**) your reservation.
예약을 확정하기 위해 이 번호로 전화하십시오.
▶ to 부정사에서는 to 다음에 명사형이나 동명사가 올 수 없고 항상 동사원형이 와야 한다.

02 to 부정사(to + 동사원형)의 수동형은 to be p.p., 진행형은 to be -ing, 완료형은 to have p.p.이다.

She wants **to be known** for her accomplishments. 그녀는 그녀의 성과로 알려지기를 원한다.
▶ 그녀가 알고 싶은 것이 아니라 알려지고 싶은 것임을 나타내기 위해서, to 부정사의 수동형(to be known)을 쓴다.

The building owner seemed **to be fixing** the lock on the front door this morning.
그 빌딩 소유주는 오늘 오전에 정문 잠금장치를 고치고 있는 것처럼 보였다.
▶ 고치는 동작이 진행되고 있었음을 나타내기 위해서 to 부정사의 진행형(to be fixing)을 쓴다.

It is great **to have met** you at the convention. 총회에서 만나 뵙게 되어 반갑습니다.
▶ 총회에서 만난(meet) 시점이 반가운 감정을 느끼기(is great) 이전 시점이므로, to 부정사의 완료형(to have met)을 쓴다.

> **고득점 포인트** need, deserve, require 다음의 수동형 to 부정사(to be p.p.)는 -ing와 바꾸어 쓸 수 있다.
> The dishes need <u>to be washed</u>. = The dishes need <u>washing</u>. 그릇들은 설거지 되어야 한다.

03 to 부정사의 의미상 주어가 필요할 경우, to 앞에 'for + 명사' 또는 'for + 대명사의 목적격'을 쓴다.

The manager's objective was <u>for staff</u> **to improve** their skills. 그 관리자의 목표는 직원들이 그들의 기술을 향상시키는 것이었다.
▶ to 부정사구의 의미상 주어는 to 앞에 'for + 명사'(for staff)로 쓴다.

<u>For us</u> **to increase** sales, we must make new advertisements. 매출을 올리기 위해서, 우리는 새로운 광고를 만들어야 한다.
▶ to 부정사구의 의미상 주어는 to 앞에 'for + 대명사의 목적격'(For us)으로 쓴다.

토익실전문제

출제 포인트 to 부정사의 to 또는 동사원형, in order to 채우기
to 부정사의 형태를 완성하기 위해 to나 동사원형을 채우는 문제가 주로 출제된다.

1. Mr. Cummings, who is leading the new project, would like all the team members to convene ------- brainstorm ideas about marketing strategies.

   (A) for (B) to
   (C) as (D) with

2. With the establishment of the new branch in Argentina, the company expects to ------- a larger customer base in Latin America.

   (A) secure (B) securing
   (C) secured (D) have secured

3. The landlord will shut off the heating system in the entire building ------- determine why some floors are not being properly heated.

   (A) only if (B) such that
   (C) in order to (D) in case of

정답·해설·해석 p.34

토익 공식
3 to 부정사를 취하는 동사, 명사, 형용사

01 to 부정사를 취하는 동사

동사 + 목적어(to 부정사)					
원하다	want to	need to	wish to	hope to	desire to	expect to
계획하다	plan to	aim to	decide to			
제안/약속/거절하다	offer to	ask to	promise to	agree to	refuse to	
기타	fail to	serve to	pretend to	afford to	manage to	prefer to
	tend to	hesitate to	strive to			

동사 + 목적어 + 보어(to 부정사)					
원하다	want 목 to	need 목 to	expect 목 to	invite 목 to	
~하게 부추기다	encourage 목 to	persuade 목 to	convince 목 to	cause 목 to	ask 목 to
~하게 강요하다	force 목 to	compel 목 to	get 목 to	tell 목 to	require 목 to
~하게 허락하다	allow 목 to	permit 목 to	enable 목 to	forbid 목 to ~을 금하다	
~하라고 알려 주다	remind 목 to	warn 목 to	advise 목 to		

동사 + 보어(to 부정사)		
remain to 아직 ~해야 하다	seem to ~인 것 같다	appear to ~인 것처럼 보이다

Management wants **to reorganize** the publicity department. 경영진은 홍보부를 재편성하기를 원한다.
Their commitment to quality enabled the manufacturer **to achieve** its sales goal.
품질에 대한 그들의 전념은 그 제조사가 판매 목표를 달성할 수 있게 했다.
This photocopier appears **to be broken**. 이 복사기는 고장난 것처럼 보인다.

02 to 부정사를 취하는 명사

ability to ~하는 능력	authority to ~할 권한	capacity to ~할 능력	chance to ~할 기회	claim to ~하다는 주장
decision to ~하겠다는 결정	effort to ~하려는 노력	need to ~할 필요	opportunity to ~할 기회	plan to ~하려는 계획
readiness to ~할 의향	right to ~할 권리	time to ~할 시간	way to ~할 방법	wish to ~하려는 바람

Mr. Keith did not have a chance **to arrange** lodging for his trip. Mr. Keith는 그의 여행을 위한 숙박을 마련할 기회가 없었다.

03 to 부정사를 취하는 형용사

가능	be able to ~할 수 있다 be ready to ~할 준비가 되어 있다 be willing to 기꺼이 ~하다 be likely to ~할 것 같다
열망	be eager to 몹시 ~하고 싶다 be anxious to 몹시 ~하고 싶다
감정	be pleased to ~하는 것을 기쁘게 생각하다 be delighted to ~을 기쁘게 생각하다
판단	be easy to ~하기 쉽다 be difficult to ~하기 어렵다 be good to ~ 유익하다/알맞다 be dangerous to ~하기 위험하다

The legal team is ready **to review** the revised contract. 법률팀은 수정된 계약서를 검토할 준비가 되어 있다.

토익실전문제

출제 포인트 to 부정사 채우기
특정 동사 뒤에 to 부정사를 채우는 문제가 가장 많이 출제된다.

1. Having failed ------- a consensus, the manager asked that the decision be postponed.

(A) reaching   (B) reached
(C) reach   (D) to reach

2. The external auditor, who was hired by the finance director, has been given the right ------- the company's accounting records during inspection.

(A) examine   (B) be examined
(C) to examine   (D) examining

3. The CEO believes that the team should be able ------- the research project before the deadline if new staff are hired.

(A) complete   (B) completing
(C) completes   (D) to complete

정답·해설·해석 p.34

01 사역동사(make, let, have) + 목적어 + 원형 부정사

Mr. Wellington let Marco ~~to~~ change the schedule. Mr. Wellington은 Marco가 일정을 변경하도록 해주었다.

▶ 사역동사 let의 목적격 보어로 to 부정사가 아닌 원형 부정사가 와야 하므로 to는 생략되어야 한다.

고득점 포인트

❶ '목적어가 목적격 보어 되다'라고 수동으로 해석되면 목적격 보어로 원형 부정사가 아닌 p.p.를 써야 한다.

I will have my house paint(→painted). 나는 집이 페인트칠 되도록 할 것이다. (나는 집 페인트칠을 맡길 것이다.)

→ '내 집이 칠해지다'라고 수동으로 해석되기 때문에, 원형 부정사(paint) 대신 p.p.(painted)를 써야 한다.

❷ get은 '~하게 하다'라는 사역의 의미를 가지고 있긴 하지만, 목적격 보어로 원형 부정사가 아닌 to 부정사를 갖는다.

We got Amy send(→to send) the invitations. 우리는 Amy가 초대장을 보내게 했다.
Ms. Bates got the brochure (to be) designed by Matt Lee. Ms. Bates는 Matt Lee가 안내 책자를 디자인하게 했다.

→ '목적어가 목적격 보어 되다'라고 수동으로 해석되면 동사 get(got) 역시 목적격 보어로 p.p.(designed)를 갖는다. 이때 p.p.는 to be p.p.에서 to be가 생략된 형태이다.

02 준 사역동사 help (+ 목적어) + 원형 부정사/to 부정사

I helped Andrea **(to) finish** the research. 나는 Andrea가 연구 조사를 끝마치도록 도와주었다.

▶ 준 사역동사 help, 목적어 Andrea 다음에 목적격 보어로 원형 부정사(finish)와 to 부정사(to finish)가 모두 올 수 있다.

Regular exercise helps **(to) relieve** work-related stress. 규칙적인 운동은 업무 관련 스트레스 푸는 것을 도와준다.

▶ 준 사역동사 help 다음에 목적어가 생략되고 목적격 보어로 원형 부정사(relieve)와 to 부정사(to relieve)가 모두 올 수 있다.

03 지각동사(hear, see, watch, notice) + 목적어 + 원형 부정사/현재분사

I watched him **park** the vehicle. 나는 그가 차를 주차한 것을 지켜보았다.
I watched him **parking** the vehicle. 나는 그가 차를 주차하고 있는 것을 지켜보았다.

▶ 지각동사 watch(watched)의 목적격 보어로는 원형 부정사와 현재분사가 모두 올 수 있다. 현재분사의 경우, 동작의 진행을 강조한다.

고득점 포인트

'목적어가 목적격 보어 되다'라고 수동으로 해석되면 목적격 보어로 원형 부정사나 현재분사가 아닌 p.p.를 써야 한다.

Jack saw his memo post(→posted). Jack은 그의 회람이 게시된 것을 보았다.

토익실전문제

출제 포인트 원형 부정사 채우기
사역동사의 목적격 보어로 원형 부정사를 채우는 문제가 주로 출제된다.

1. Attending conferences related to their fields can help ------- people's professional networks.

(A) wide
(B) widen
(C) wider
(D) widely

2. The director of the human resources department said she will have her secretary ------- the applicant about the change to the interview schedule.

(A) notify
(B) notifying
(C) notified
(D) be notifying

3. Managers are asked to let their employees ------- early every Wednesday to participate in the company's volunteer program.

(A) leave
(B) to leaving
(C) left
(D) leaving

정답·해설·해석 p.34

HACKERS PRACTICE 토익 고득점을 위한 필수 연습

둘 중 맞는 형태를 고르세요.

01 The manager will be happy ------- a raise for her remarkable accomplishment.
ⓐ receive   ⓑ to receive

02 It is vital to ------- regular updates for every software program.
ⓐ distribute   ⓑ distribution

03 The requirement ------- a reference may be waived for certain applicants.
ⓐ provide   ⓑ to provide

04 Ms. MacGregor let her concern for the staff ------- her decision regarding the deadline.
ⓐ to affect   ⓑ affect

05 Additional funding from the university is needed for the biology department's research -------.
ⓐ to continue   ⓑ continue

06 Mr. Wilkins decided to have his vehicle ------- by a certified mechanic.
ⓐ inspect   ⓑ inspected

07 Professor Davis forbids his students ------- cell phones during examinations.
ⓐ using   ⓑ to use

틀린 곳이 있으면 바르게 고치세요.

08 A customer has the right requesting a refund if a product is defective or damaged.

09 Patricia hopes to complete the illustrations for the book by November 8.

10 The CEO must provide authorization for the accounting team finish the transaction.

11 Mr. Williams will have his flight reschedule by his secretary.

12 As the equipment is inexpensive, management should be willing approve its purchase.

13 Because the air-conditioner was broken, Ms. Jones got a staff member to call a technician.

14 The manufacturer must develop methods improve the efficiency of its Seattle plant.

정답·해석 p.34

무료 해설 ▶
바로 보기

맞은 문제 개수: / 14
틀린 문제에 해당하는 토익 공식을 다시 한번 학습하세요.

🕐 제한 시간 12분

Part 5

01 Mr. Coulter designated a room for records storage in order ------- the loss or damage of important documents.

(A) to prevent
(B) to be prevented
(C) prevented
(D) prevention

02 Businesses that need ------- copies of previously filed tax returns should submit a request form to the taxation office.

(A) obtain
(B) to obtain
(C) obtaining
(D) obtainment

03 Ms. Collins believes that it is necessary for the company ------- innovative products because of increased competition in the market.

(A) develop
(B) development
(C) to develop
(D) developed

04 Only the executive officer and the finance manager have the authority ------- approve major changes to the monthly budget.

(A) for
(B) with
(C) to
(D) as

05 The tutoring sessions arranged by the math department for tomorrow night will help the students ------- for the upcoming examinations.

(A) would prepare
(B) prepare
(C) will prepare
(D) prepared

06 Customers who require additional information ------- a suitable notebook model should consult the product description section of the company's homepage.

(A) select
(B) to select
(C) selected
(D) be selected

07 Customer complaints show that there may be a need for Net Manage ------- its present quality assurance and monitoring systems.

(A) improve
(B) to improve
(C) improving
(D) improved

08 As a still-life photographer, Mr. Bryant aims to ------- a particular mood when he creates a collection of pictures.

(A) express
(B) expressed
(C) expressing
(D) have expressed

09 The growing popularity of Pitman Works' products in Asia was a significant ------- with regard to the company's recent expansion.

(A) to consider
(B) considered
(C) consideration
(D) considerable

10 Ms. Evans promised to ------- the regional director weekly on the progress of the negotiations with the supplier.

(A) updated
(B) update
(C) updating
(D) having updated

11 It is mandatory ------- factory employees to sign out the tools they use and return them at the end of the workday.

(A) for
(B) further
(C) because
(D) these

12 The union has agreed to work with company officials for the purpose of developing ways ------- increased cooperation between management and employees.

(A) promote
(B) of promote
(C) to promote
(D) promoting

13 To ensure that shoppers are satisfied ------- the store's service, customer representatives are trained regularly.

(A) by
(B) to
(C) with
(D) for

14 With the prices of natural gas and other petroleum products increasing, utility companies are now asking people ------- fuel consumption.

(A) reducing
(B) reduced
(C) to reduce
(D) for reducing

15 Until a complete inspection of the equipment ------, no changes will be made to the factory's safety regulations.

(A) performs
(B) is performed
(C) is performing
(D) will be performed

16 Whether the public will react well to the new formula for the soft drink remains ------ seen.

(A) to be
(B) be
(C) had been
(D) been

17 The assistant reminded the congressperson ------ the president of the trade forum regarding her upcoming presentation.

(A) call
(B) calling
(C) called
(D) to call

18 Several new cashiers and salespeople were hired ------ with the influx of customers during the long holiday season.

(A) to cope
(B) coping
(C) to be coping
(D) to be coped

Part 6

Questions 19-22 refer to the following letter.

Edward Mitchell
1505 Main Street
Fairfax, VA 20151

Dear Mr. Mitchell,

After conducting a comprehensive review, we have decided to ------ sponsoring your organization.
We have read through the annual summary you provided and are ------ that your efforts to provide
accurate information about global warming are meeting with success. Therefore, the Sanford Institute
has chosen to extend your funding for an additional year. ------. We sincerely hope that the extra
support will enable you to achieve even more positive results.

I encourage you ------ the enclosed grant agreement and return it by courier service before this
Friday. Thank you and keep up the good work.

Sincerely,
Scott Hernandez

19 (A) question
(B) prohibit
(C) continue
(D) begin

20 (A) convince
(B) convinced
(C) convincing
(D) convincingly

21 (A) Your generous sponsorship of our association is greatly appreciated.
(B) We need more details about your programs in order to resolve the matter.
(C) We are also pleased to say that it will be increased by 15 percent.
(D) There is only so much that we can do for your organization.

22 (A) signing
(B) signed
(C) signs
(D) to sign

CHAPTER
08

동명사

토익, 이렇게 나온다!

동명사 관련 문제는 출제 비율이 높지 않지만, 토익 문제의 문장에서 사용되므로 그 개념을 반드시 알고 있어야 한다. 동명사와 명사를 구별하여 채우는 문제와 전치사의 목적어 자리를 채우는 문제가 주로 출제된다.

토익 필수 개념 다지기

01 동명사(동사 + ing)는 동사로부터 나왔다. 그러나 동명사는 문장 내에서 동사 역할이 아니라 명사 역할을 한다.

He **practicing** the cello every day. (×)
She hates **practicing** the cello. (○) 그녀는 첼로 연습하는 것을 싫어한다.

위 문장들에서 보여지듯이 practicing은 동사 역할을 하지 못하고, 동사 hate의 목적어로 명사 역할을 한다.

02 동명사는 동사의 성질을 여전히 가지고 있어, 동사처럼 목적어 또는 보어를 가질 수 있고, 부사의 수식을 받을 수 있다.

We love **watching movies**.   우리는 영화 보는 것을 좋아한다.
Becoming a lawyer requires much effort.   변호사가 되는 것은 많은 노력을 필요로 한다.
Exercising regularly is recommended by doctors. 규칙적으로 운동하는 것은 의사들에 의해 추천된다.

위 문장들에서 보여지듯이 watching은 목적어 movies를 갖고, Becoming은 보어 a lawyer를 갖는다. 그리고 Exercising은 부사 regularly의 수식을 받는다. 이와 같은 [동명사 + 목적어/보어/부사]의 형태를 '동명사구'라고 한다.

토익 공식 1 동명사의 역할, 형태, 의미상 주어

01 동명사는 명사 역할을 하여 주어, 목적어, 보어 자리에 온다.

주어 자리   **Leasing additional office space** will enable the company to hire more staff.
추가적인 사무실 공간을 임대하는 것은 회사가 더 많은 직원을 채용하는 것을 가능하게 할 것이다.

동사의 목적어 자리   He likes **reading novels**. 그는 소설을 읽는 것을 좋아한다.

전치사의 목적어 자리   The documentary aims at **promoting alternative energy sources**.
그 다큐멘터리는 대체 에너지원을 홍보하는 것을 목표로 삼는다.

보어 자리   John's hobby is **listening to music**. John의 취미는 음악을 듣는 것이다.

▶ 밑줄 친 부분은 동명사의 핵심이 되는 부분으로, 토익에서는 이 부분에 대해 묻는다.

02 동사는 동명사 자리에 올 수 없다.

Sarah is studying about (**work**, **working**) with animals in her zoology course.
Sarah는 동물학 수업에서 동물들을 다루는 것에 대해 공부하고 있다.

▶ 전치사(about)의 목적어로 동사(work)가 올 수 없고, 명사 역할을 하는 동명사(working)가 와야 한다.

03 동명사(동사 + ing)의 수동형은 being p.p., 완료형은 having p.p.이다.

My kids really like **being given** gifts. 나의 아이들은 선물을 받는 것을 정말 좋아한다.

▶ 아이들이 주는 것이 아니라 주어진다(받는다)는 수동을 나타내기 위해서 동명사의 수동형(being given)을 쓴다.

She admitted **having cheated**. 그녀는 속임수를 썼던 것을 인정했다.

▶ 속임수를 쓴(cheat) 시점이 인정하기(admit) 이전 시점이므로, 동명사의 완료형(having cheated)을 쓴다.

04 동명사의 의미상 주어가 필요할 경우, 동명사 앞에 명사(대명사)의 소유격을 쓴다.

I don't enjoy <u>Kevin's</u> **singing**. 나는 Kevin이 노래하는 것을 즐거워 하지 않는다.

▶ 동명사의 의미상 주어는 동명사 앞에 명사의 소유격(Kevin's)으로 쓴다.

<u>Her</u> **attending** the conference was confirmed. 그녀가 회의에 참석하는 것이 확정되었다.

▶ 동명사의 의미상 주어는 동명사 앞에 대명사의 소유격(Her)으로 쓴다.

토익실전문제

출제 포인트 동명사 채우기
전치사의 목적어, 동사의 목적어 자리에 동명사를 채우는 문제가 가장 많이 출제된다.

1. ------- regular donations to local charities not only helps others but also provides significant tax advantages.

(A) Make   (B) Makes
(C) Making   (D) Made

2. Department heads distributed a memo reminding employees to refrain from ------- friends online during office hours.

(A) to contact   (B) contacting
(C) contacts   (D) contact

3. Photographers capture clear images, regardless of lighting conditions, by ------- the settings of their cameras.

(A) adjust   (B) adjusting
(C) adjusted   (D) adjusts

정답·해설·해석 p.37

토익 공식 2 동명사를 목적어로 갖는 동사

01 동명사를 목적어로 갖는 동사들이 있다.

즐기다	enjoy -ing ~을 즐기다		
제안·고려	suggest -ing ~을 제안하다	recommend -ing ~을 추천하다	consider -ing ~을 고려하다
중지·연기	finish -ing ~을 끝내다 give up -ing ~을 포기하다	quit -ing ~을 그만두다 postpone -ing ~을 연기하다	discontinue -ing ~을 중지하다
부정적 의미	dislike -ing ~을 싫어하다 avoid -ing ~을 피하다	deny -ing ~을 부인하다	mind -ing ~을 꺼리다

My manager will consider (~~to give~~, **giving**) me a week's vacation. 나의 관리자는 내게 일주일간의 휴가를 주는 것을 고려할 것이다.

▶ consider의 목적어로는 to 부정사(to give)가 아닌 동명사(giving)가 와야 한다.

02 동명사와 to 부정사를 모두 목적어로 갖는 동사들이 있다.

• 동명사가 목적어일 때와 to 부정사가 목적어일 때 문장의 의미 변화가 없는 동사들

like ~을 좋아하다	love ~을 사랑하다	prefer ~을 선호하다	hate ~을 싫어하다
start ~을 시작하다	begin ~을 시작하다	continue ~을 계속하다	intend ~을 의도하다
attempt ~을 시도하다	propose ~을 제안하다, 계획하다		

Jane has just begun (~~learned~~, **learning**, **to learn**) to drive. Jane은 이제 막 운전하는 것을 배우기 시작했다.

▶ 동사 begin은 뒤에 동명사(learning)와 to 부정사(to learn)를 모두 목적어로 취하며, 의미 차이는 없다.

• 동명사가 목적어일 때와 to 부정사가 목적어일 때 문장의 의미 변화가 있는 동사들

동사	+ 동명사 (과거 의미)	+ to 부정사 (미래 또는 목적의 의미)
remember forget regret	~한 것을 기억하다 ~한 것을 잊다 ~한 것을 후회하다	~할 것을 기억하다 ~할 것을 잊다 ~하게 되어 유감스럽다

Lisa remembered **buying** / **to buy** a spare tire. Lisa는 스페어타이어를 산 것을 / 사야 한다는 것을 기억했다.

▶ 동사 remember의 목적어가 동명사(buying)일 때는 과거 의미를, to 부정사(to buy)일 때는 미래 의미를 나타낸다.

Jim forgot **locking** / **to lock** the door. Jim은 문을 잠근 것을 / 잠가야 하는 것을 잊었다.

▶ 동사 forget의 목적어가 동명사(locking)일 때는 과거 의미를, to 부정사(to lock)일 때는 미래 의미를 나타낸다.

고득점 포인트 advise, allow, permit, forbid와 같은 동사들은 '동사 + 동명사' 또는 '동사 + 목적어 + to 부정사' 형태를 갖는다.
The museum does not permit eating / people to eat on the premises. 박물관은 관내에서 음식을 먹는 것을 허용하지 않는다.

토익실전문제

출제 포인트 동명사와 to 부정사 구별하여 채우기
동사의 목적어 자리에 to 부정사와 구별하여 동명사를 채우는 문제가 주로 출제된다.
문장의 의미에 따라 동명사와 to 부정사를 구별하여 채우는 문제가 가끔 출제된다.

1. Last year, the Department of Linguistics at the University of Ohio began ------- advanced courses in Arabic.

(A) offer
(B) offered
(C) offering
(D) has offered

2. It would be wise of the directors to consider ------- with the human resources department before they hire any new staff.

(A) consult
(B) consulted
(C) to consult
(D) consulting

3. Users should not forget ------- which version of the software is installed when requesting technical assistance.

(A) specifying
(B) specify
(C) to specify
(D) specified

정답·해설·해석 p.37

토익 공식 3 동명사 vs. 명사

01 동명사는 목적어를 가질 수 있지만 명사는 목적어를 가질 수 없다.

The corporation failed in (**establishment**, **establishing**) a branch office in Russia.
그 기업은 러시아에 지사를 설립하는 데 실패했다.

▶ 명사(establishment)는 목적어(a branch office)를 가질 수 없으므로, 동명사(establishing)가 와야 한다.

고득점 포인트　❶ 동명사나 명사 자리 뒤에 목적어가 없는 경우에는, 동명사보다 명사가 와야 한다.

　　Ms. Verne confirmed her departing(→departure) with the travel agent. Ms. Verne은 여행사 직원과 출발편을 확인했다.

　　❷ 다음과 같은 -ing 형태의 명사를 동명사로 혼동하지 않도록 주의해야 한다.

beginning 발단, 개시	belongings 소지품	broadcasting 방송	findings 발견(물), 연구 결과	gathering 모임
lodging 숙박, 하숙	meeting 회의	opening 결원, 공석	shipping 선박, 선적	training 훈련

02 동명사 앞에는 부정관사가 올 수 없지만, 명사(가산 명사 단수) 앞에는 부정관사가 올 수 있다.

Farmers noticed a significant (**decreasing**, **decrease**) in the size of their crops this year.
농장주들은 올해 수확량 규모의 현저한 감소를 알아챘다.

▶ 동명사(decreasing) 앞에는 부정관사 a가 올 수 없으므로, 명사(decrease)가 와야 한다.

03 명사와 의미가 다른 명사화된 동명사가 있는 경우에는, 의미에 맞는 것을 쓴다.

advertising 광고업 – advertisement 광고	opening 개장/빈자리/공석 – open 야외	funding 자금 지원/자금 조달 – fund 자금
housing 주택/주택 공급 – house 집	mailing 우송 – mail 우편물	marketing 마케팅 – market 시장
planning 계획 수립 – plan 계획	processing 처리/절차/가공 – process 과정/공정	seating 좌석 배치 – seat 좌석
spending 지출/소비 – spend 지출(액)/비용	staffing 직원 배치 – staff 직원	cleaning 청소 – clean 손질

To ensure speedy (**process**, **processing**) of orders, make sure to provide accurate billing information.
주문의 빠른 처리를 보장하기 위해서, 반드시 정확한 청구서 정보를 제공하시오.

▶ '빠른 처리'라는 의미가 되어야 하므로 process(과정/공정)가 아닌 processing(처리)을 써야 한다.

It is difficult in today's economic climate for a new business to enter the (**marketing**, **market**).
오늘날의 경제 풍토에서 신규 사업체가 시장에 진입하는 것은 어렵다.

▶ '시장에 진입하다'라는 의미가 되어야 하므로 marketing(마케팅)이 아닌 market(시장)을 써야 한다.

At the request of the client, Ms. White submitted another (**planning**, **plan**) for the marketing campaign.
고객의 요청으로, Ms. White는 마케팅 캠페인을 위한 또 다른 계획을 제출했다.

▶ '마케팅 캠페인을 위한 또 다른 계획을 제출하다'라는 의미가 되어야 하므로 planning(계획 수립)이 아닌 plan(계획)을 써야 한다.

토익실전문제

출제 포인트 동명사와 명사 구별하여 채우기
전치사의 목적어 자리에 동명사를 명사와 구별하여 채우는 문제가 주로 출제된다.

1. By ------- the amount of paperwork, Stamford Company is able to more efficiently accomplish routine tasks.

(A) limit　　　　(B) limited
(C) limiting　　 (D) limitation

2. The owner of the retail chain used a recently published ------- on consumer behavior to determine the layout of his stores.

(A) study　　　 (B) to study
(C) studying　　(D) studied

3. The team met for three hours to discuss strategies for ------- the distribution needs of small-to-medium-sized businesses.

(A) satisfaction　(B) to satisfy
(C) satisfying　　(D) satisfied

정답·해설·해석 p.37

01 동명사구 관용 표현

go -ing ~하러 가다	be busy (in) -ing ~하느라 바쁘다
on -ing ~하자마자	be worth -ing ~할 가치가 있다
It's no use -ing ~해도 소용없다	keep (on) -ing 계속 ~하다
spend + 시간/돈 + -ing 시간/돈을 ~하는 데 쓰다	feel like -ing ~하고 싶다
have difficulty(trouble, a problem) (in) -ing ~하는 데 어려움을 겪다	cannot help -ing ~하지 않을 수 없다

He **is busy editing** the article. 그는 기사를 편집하느라 바쁘다.
Mr. Wentworth **has difficulty seeing** without his glasses. Mr. Wentworth는 안경 없이 보는 데 어려움을 겪는다.

02 전치사 to + 동명사

contribute to -ing ~에 공헌하다	be committed to -ing ~에 전념하다
look forward to -ing ~하기를 고대하다	be dedicated to -ing ~에 헌신적이다
object to -ing ~에 반대하다, ~에 이의를 제기하다	be devoted to -ing ~에 헌신적이다
lead to -ing ~의 원인이 되다	be used to -ing ~에 익숙하다

Solartech **is dedicated to developing** clean and renewable energy sources.
Solartech사는 청정하며 재생 가능한 에너지원을 개발하는 데 헌신적이다.

The film director **is committed to making** the best movie he can.
그 영화감독은 그가 만들 수 있는 최고의 영화를 만드는 데 전념한다.

고득점 포인트

❶ 두 개 이상의 '전치사 to + 동명사'가 접속사로 연결된 경우, 전치사 to 다음에는 반드시 동명사가 나와야 한다.
I am looking forward to meeting you at the conference and to discuss(→to discussing) this further.
저는 귀하와 학회에서 만나서 이에 대해 더 논의하기를 기대하고 있습니다.
→ '전치사 to + 동명사'(to meeting, to discussing)가 and로 연결되어 있는 경우이므로, to discuss를 쓰지 않도록 주의해야 한다.

❷ 전치사 to 다음에는 명사가 올 수도 있다.
We are looking forward to the jazz concert tomorrow night. 우리는 내일 밤의 재즈 콘서트를 기대하고 있다.
→ to가 전치사이므로 다음에 명사(the jazz concert)가 왔다.

토익실전문제

출제 포인트 **동명사 채우기**
전치사 to 뒤에 동사원형이 아닌 동명사를 채우는 문제가 주로 출제된다.

1. Mr. Gray looks forward to ------- a lot about investment opportunities with Gen-Ex Corporation, which has shown significant growth.

 (A) learn (B) learning
 (C) have learned (D) be learned

2. The overseas branches have had much difficulty in ------- their operations to conform to the new accounting system.

 (A) modify (B) modifies
 (C) modified (D) modifying

3. Although the employees are satisfied with the workshop program, they object to ------- an hour each way to get to the training center and back.

 (A) travel (B) travels
 (C) traveled (D) traveling

정답·해설·해석 p.38

둘 중 맞는 형태를 고르세요.

01 Daniel is used to ------- with a large team of people.
ⓐ cooperate   ⓑ cooperating

02 Melanie forgot ------- me when she arrived at the train station, so I didn't come to pick her up.
ⓐ to call   ⓑ calling

03 Be careful to use appropriate ------- when writing up the contract.
ⓐ word   ⓑ wording

04 You have to keep ------- along this street to reach the bus terminal.
ⓐ walking   ⓑ to walk

05 Watching educational programs has been proven to expand a child's -------.
ⓐ knowledge   ⓑ knowing

06 The project contributed to ------- environmental awareness.
ⓐ raise   ⓑ raising

07 The employees cannot help ------- whether the firm will provide bonuses this year.
ⓐ to wonder   ⓑ wondering

틀린 곳이 있으면 바르게 고치세요.

08 One of Dr. Prasad's responsibilities is examine patients.

09 Mr. Roberts would like us to enlarge his office by removing this wall.

10 The cost of drive a car will increase if the price of gas goes up.

11 Tina avoids to eat sugar because she's on a diet.

12 Although she's great at designing clothes, she's bad at choose what fabrics to use.

13 The diner preferred to have a salad rather than a heavy meal.

14 Her impressive volunteering record proves that Jessica is dedicated to help others in need.

정답·해석 p.38

무료 해설 ▶
바로 보기

맞은 문제 개수: / 14
틀린 문제에 해당하는 토익 공식을 다시 한번 학습하세요.

GRAMMAR Part 5,6

Ch 08 동명사

Hackers TOEIC Reading

HACKERS TEST

토익 만점을 위한 실전 문제 정복

🕐 제한 시간 12분

Part 5

01 Too much stress and a lack of rest can contribute to a person having problems ------- at work.

(A) concentrate
(B) concentrates
(C) concentrated
(D) concentrating

02 Despite ------- more employees for the factory, the production manager still believes the facility is understaffed.

(A) having hired
(B) have hired
(C) hired
(D) were hired

03 In order to focus on the mobile communications market, ASD Technologies will discontinue ------- its line of personal computers.

(A) produced
(B) producing
(C) produce
(D) to produce

04 Northfield Books is committed to ------- affordable, high-quality textbooks in a wide range of subject areas.

(A) publication
(B) publishing
(C) publishes
(D) published

05 ANX Corporation sent a letter to shareholders disclosing its intention of ------- a competing business.

(A) obtained
(B) obtainment
(C) obtain
(D) obtaining

06 The factory supervisor ------- equipment and machinery from a second-hand dealer who sells slightly used items at bargain prices.

(A) to acquire
(B) acquire
(C) acquiring
(D) acquires

07 Express Parcel is considering ------- a change to its fee structure that would increase the cost of international deliveries by 7 percent.

(A) implement
(B) implementing
(C) to implement
(D) implemented

08 Online shopping sites continue to ------- shoppers by providing quality products, low prices, and quick delivery.

(A) impressive
(B) impress
(C) impressing
(D) impression

09 The recent cuts in budget appropriations were aimed at ------- the organization's year-end deficit.

(A) resolve
(B) resolved
(C) resolving
(D) resolution

10 Managers from both companies are trying to reach a mutually beneficial ------- by settling the remaining differences regarding the contract terms.

(A) to agree
(B) agreed
(C) agreeing
(D) agreement

11 Mr. Warren would rather go ------- on his own than with a lot of people in a tour group, as he likes to set his own schedule.

(A) traveling
(B) to travel
(C) for traveling
(D) to traveling

12 ------- business expenditures carefully each month enables corporations to identify and eliminate unnecessary expenses.

(A) Review
(B) Reviews
(C) Reviewed
(D) Reviewing

13 Members can visit the reception desk for additional details on ------- a discounted rate on their gym membership renewal.

(A) to receive
(B) receiving
(C) received
(D) receipt

14 The release of the company's latest line of cameras ------- with a massive marketing campaign that starts next week.

(A) will coincide
(B) is coincided
(C) will be coincided
(D) coinciding

15 The town does not permit ------- a vehicle in this area between 1 A.M. and 4 A.M. on Sunday when street cleaning is being conducted.

(A) leave
(B) to leave
(C) leaving
(D) left

16 ------- a high score on the bar exam, Tom Byers spent most of his waking moments reading reference materials at the library.

(A) For earning
(B) To earn
(C) By earning
(D) On earning

17 The head of the biology department enjoys ------- with other faculty members to discuss recent developments in the field of genetics.

(A) meet
(B) met
(C) meeting
(D) to meet

18 The ban on offshore oil drilling has been crucial in ------- the various aquatic species that inhabit the coastal ecosystem.

(A) protect
(B) protecting
(C) protected
(D) protection

Part 6

Questions 19-22 refer to the following e-mail.

From: tharris@comdev.com
To: ebryant@comdev.com
Subject: News on Thai Branch

I arrived back at headquarters yesterday after visiting the new Bangkok office. -------. Apparently, their objective is to facilitate communication between local staff and our dispatched managers.

-------, the office is still encountering issues with communication. I believe the problem involves not only language but also cultural differences in work style.

I'd like to suggest ------- our training program to include sessions that cover relevant differences in Thai and Western business culture. These sessions will contribute to improved relations between local and international employees.

I have ------- a report with information about the program as well as a few additional ideas I'd like to run by you. I am interested in hearing what you think, so please go through my comments and send me a reply. If you find my suggestions appropriate, I will contact the training staff. I am confident that a revised curriculum will bring about the needed changes.

19 (A) Fiscal austerity is about to be imposed soon in the branch.
(B) Employees have established good relations with customers there.
(C) Its location has become easier to access than before.
(D) The branch has been running Thai and English courses.

20 (A) Otherwise
(B) Consequently
(C) Furthermore
(D) Nevertheless

21 (A) adapt
(B) adapting
(C) to adapt
(D) adapted

22 (A) attachment
(B) attached
(C) attach
(D) been attached

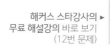

해커스 스타강사의 ▶
무료 해설강의 바로 보기
(12번 문제)

CHAPTER 09

분사

토익, 이렇게 나온다!
분사 관련 문제는 평균 1~2문제 정도 출제되며 최대 4문제까지 출제된다. 명사를 수식하는 자리에 현재분사와 과거분사를 구별하여 채우는 문제가 가장 많이 출제된다.

토익 필수 개념 다지기

01 분사(동사 + ing, 동사 + ed)는 동사에서 나왔지만 문장 내에서 동사 역할이 아니라 형용사 역할을 한다.

Joe **broken** arm. (×)
Joe can't type because of his **broken** arm. (○) Joe는 그의 부러진 팔 때문에 타자를 칠 수 없다.
The flower vase **broken** in pieces belonged to my grandmother. (○)
산산조각으로 부서진 꽃병은 내 할머니의 것이었다.

위 문장들에서 보여지듯이 분사 broken은 동사 역할을 하지 못하고, 명사 arm을 앞에서 꾸며 주거나, 명사구 The flower vase를 뒤에서 꾸며 주는 형용사 역할을 한다.

02 분사는 동사의 성질을 여전히 가지고 있어, 동사처럼 목적어 또는 보어를 가질 수 있고, 부사의 수식을 받을 수 있다.

There were many pedestrians **crossing the street**. 그 길을 건너는 보행자들이 많았다.
The furniture **delivered yesterday** is very comfortable. 어제 배달된 가구는 매우 안락하다.

위 문장들에서 보여지듯이 crossing은 목적어 the street를 갖고 delivered는 부사 yesterday의 수식을 받는다.

단, 분사가 명사를 앞에서 수식하는 경우에는, 분사와 명사 사이에 부사나 목적어/보어가 올 수 없다.

The **delivered** <u>yesterday</u> **furniture** is very comfortable. (×)

토익 공식 1 분사의 역할

01 분사는 형용사 역할을 한다.

• 형용사처럼 명사 앞이나 뒤에서 명사를 꾸민다.

명사 앞 수식   To meet **increasing** demand, ten new workers were hired for the plant.
증가하는 수요를 충족시키기 위해, 공장에 10명의 신입 근로자들이 고용되었다.

명사 뒤 수식   The staff members (who were) **expected to attend** didn't turn up.
참석할 것으로 예상되었던 직원들이 나타나지 않았다.

▶ 밑줄 친 부분은 분사의 핵심이 되는 부분으로, 토익에서는 이 부분에 대해 묻는다.

• 형용사처럼 주격 보어나 목적격 보어로 쓰인다.

주격 보어   The painting looks **fascinating**. 그 그림은 흥미로워 보인다.

목적격 보어   The workshop activities keep the participants **occupied**. 그 워크숍 활동들은 참가자들을 계속 바쁘게 한다.

고득점 포인트   분사는 목적어나 전치사구를 동반하지 않고 단독으로 쓰일 경우, 주로 명사 앞에서 명사를 꾸미지만 people questioned, people interviewed, people concerned와 같은 표현에서는 예외적으로 분사가 단독으로 명사를 뒤에서 꾸민다.

The <u>people interviewed</u> had different responses. 면접을 본 사람들은 여러 가지 반응을 보였다.

02 동사는 분사 자리에 올 수 없다.

There were some (**wait**, **waiting**) passengers at the bus stop. 버스 정류장에 기다리고 있는 승객들이 몇 명 있었다.

▶ 동사(wait)는 명사(passengers)를 꾸밀 수 없으므로, 형용사 역할을 하는 분사(waiting)가 와야 한다.

Most employees (**transfer**, **transferred**) overseas learn foreign languages quickly.
해외로 파견되는 대부분의 직원들은 외국어를 빨리 배운다.

▶ 동사(transfer)는 명사(employee)를 꾸밀 수 없으므로, 형용사 역할을 하는 분사(transferred)가 와야 한다.

토익실전문제

출제 포인트 분사 채우기
명사를 수식하는 자리에 분사를 채우는 문제가 주로 출제된다.

1. To solve the ------- unemployment problem, the government will give small loans to start-up companies in the region.

(A) exist   (B) exists
(C) existence   (D) existing

2. An e-mail newsletter ------- by the Psychology Network helps subscribers stay informed about new studies on depression.

(A) transmits   (B) transmitted
(C) are transmitted   (D) will transmit

3. Hotel guests keep their valuables ------- by utilizing the electronic safes included in all rooms.

(A) protect   (B) protects
(C) protected   (D) protection

정답·해설·해석 p.40

01 분사구문은 시간, 이유, 조건, 연속 동작 등을 나타내는 부사절 역할을 한다.

시간   **Having passed the job interview**, I told my friends the good news.
      = After I had passed the job interview
      구직 면접에 합격한 후에, 나는 그 좋은 소식을 친구들에게 말했다.

이유   **Arriving late**, Mr. Barth apologized before beginning the presentation.
      = Because he arrived late
      늦게 도착했기 때문에, Mr. Barth는 발표를 시작하기 전에 사과했다.

조건   **Distributed widely**, the flyer will attract more customers.
      = If it is distributed widely
      널리 배포된다면, 그 전단은 더 많은 고객들을 끌 것이다.

연속 동작   The company representative provided free samples, **including items from a new product line**.
                                              = and he included items from a new product line
        그 회사 직원은 무료 샘플을 제공했고, 신상품 라인의 품목들을 포함시켰다.

▶ 밑줄 친 부분은 분사구문의 핵심이 되는 부분으로, 토익에서는 이 부분에 대해 묻는다.

고득점 포인트   분사구문의 뜻을 분명하게 해주기 위해 부사절 접속사가 분사구문 앞에 올 수도 있다.
<u>Before</u> signing the contract, make sure that you fully understand it. 계약서에 서명하기 전에, 반드시 계약서를 충분히 이해하도록 하십시오.
The staff may request an allowance <u>when</u> doing field work. 직원들은 현장 작업을 할 때 수당을 청구할 수 있다.

02 동사나 명사는 분사구문 자리에 올 수 없다.

(**Delight**, **Delighted**) by the sudden surge in sales, the manager gave bonuses to his employees.
매출의 갑작스런 증가에 매우 기뻤기 때문에, 그 관리자는 직원들에게 상여금을 주었다.

▶ 분사구문 자리에 동사 Delight가 올 수 없으므로 Delighted를 써야 한다.

When (**collaboration**, **collaborating**) on an urgent project, staff must work together efficiently.
긴급한 프로젝트에 대해 공동으로 일할 때, 직원들은 함께 효율적으로 일해야 한다.

▶ 부사절 접속사(When) 뒤 분사구문 자리에 명사 collaboration이 올 수 없으므로 collaborating을 써야 한다.

03 동시에 일어나는 상황을 나타낼 때, 'with + 목적어 + 분사구문'을 쓴다.

Mr. Townsend arrived **with his umbrella dripping** water onto the floor.
Mr. Townsend는 그의 우산에서 바닥에 물을 떨어뜨리며 도착했다.

토익실전문제

출제 포인트 (부사절 접속사 +) 분사구문 채우기
부사절 접속사(unless, when, while, whenever, once 등) 다음에 분사를
채우는 문제가 주로 출제된다.

1. ------- terminated her rental contract at Lee Gardens,
Ms. Pascual was able to move to a more convenient
location.

  (A) Had   (B) Having
  (C) Have   (D) Will have

2. Although -------, the manuscript will not be published
until the editor is certain that the final draft is error
free.

  (A) completed   (B) completes
  (C) are completed   (D) have completed

3. After hastily ------- complaints that the kitchen tool
was defective, Kitchen Works Company issued an
immediate recall.

  (A) verify   (B) verifies
  (C) verifying   (D) are verified

정답·해설·해석 p.40

3 현재분사 vs. 과거분사

01 분사가 명사를 수식하는 경우, 수식받는 명사와 분사가 능동 관계면 현재분사, 수동 관계면 과거분사를 쓴다.

The marketing manager studied a paper **detailing** a strategy for product distribution.
마케팅 부장은 제품 유통 전략을 상세히 열거한 서류를 검토했다.

▶ 수식받는 명사(a paper)와 분사가 '서류가 ~을 상세히 열거하다'라는 의미의 능동 관계이므로 현재분사(detailing)를 쓴다.

Entry-level workers are satisfied with the wage **offered** at Millers Manufacturing.
신입 사원들은 Millers 제조 회사에서 제공되는 임금에 만족한다.

▶ 수식받는 명사(the wage)와 분사가 '임금이 제공되다'라는 의미의 수동 관계이므로 과거분사(offered)를 쓴다.

고득점 포인트 분사가 감정을 나타내는 경우, 수식받는 명사가 감정의 원인이면 현재분사, 감정을 느끼는 주체이면 과거분사를 쓴다.

A series of interesting seminars on business ventures was attended by many people.
벤처 기업들에 관한 일련의 흥미로운 세미나에 많은 사람들이 참석했다.

→ 수식받는 명사(seminars)가 흥미를 주는 원인이므로 현재분사(interesting)를 써야 한다.

An agent contacted a client interested in purchasing a building. 중개인은 건물을 구입하는 것에 관심이 있는 고객에게 연락했다.

→ 수식받는 명사(a client)가 흥미를 느끼는 주체이므로 과거분사(interested)를 써야 한다.

02 분사가 주격 보어이거나 목적격 보어인 경우, 주어와 보어 또는 목적어와 보어가 능동 관계면 현재분사, 수동 관계면 과거분사를 쓴다.

The sport seems **exciting**. 그 스포츠 경기는 흥미로운 것 같다.

▶ 주어(The sport)와 보어의 관계가 '스포츠 경기가 흥미를 주다'라는 의미의 능동 관계이므로 현재분사(exciting)를 쓴다.

Please keep your staff **notified** about the upcoming event. 귀하의 직원들이 다가오는 행사에 대해 계속 통보받도록 해주십시오.

▶ 목적어(your staff)와 보어의 관계가 '직원들이 통보받다'라는 의미의 수동 관계이므로 과거분사(notified)를 쓴다.

03 분사구문의 경우, 주절의 주어와 분사구문이 능동 관계면 현재분사, 수동 관계면 과거분사를 쓴다.

Visitors to the museum should check the regulations before **entering** the exhibit rooms.
박물관 방문객들은 전시실에 입장하기 전에 규정들을 확인해야 한다.

▶ 주절의 주어(Visitors)와 분사구문이 '방문객들이 입장하다'라는 의미의 능동 관계이므로 현재분사(entering)를 쓴다.

Surrounded by reporters, the senator announced his resignation.
기자들에게 둘러싸인 채, 그 상원 의원은 사임을 발표했다.

▶ 주절의 주어(the senator)와 분사구문이 '상원 의원이 둘러싸이다'라는 의미의 수동 관계이므로 과거분사(Surrounded)를 쓴다.

토익실전문제

출제 포인트 현재분사와 과거분사 구별하여 채우기
명사를 수식하는 자리에 현재분사와 과거분사를 구별하여 채우는 문제가 주로 출제된다.

1. The attachment sent to the regional manager contains the information ------- to the sales report by the accounting team.
   (A) addition
   (B) adds
   (C) added
   (D) adding

2. Customers are more likely to show interest in purchasing a product when the voiceover in an advertisement sounds -------.
   (A) appeal
   (B) appeals
   (C) appealing
   (D) appealed

3. ------- in the downtown area, the tourism center provides information on local landmarks, as well as assistance with travel and accommodation arrangements.
   (A) Situating
   (B) Situated
   (C) Situate
   (D) Situation

정답·해설·해석 p.40

01 현재분사 + 명사

in her **opening remarks**	그녀의 개회사 인사말에서
the maintenance of **existing equipment**	기존 설비의 보수 관리
a claim for the **missing luggage**	분실된 수하물에 대한 보상 청구
make a **lasting impression** on the audience	청중들에게 오래 지속되는 인상을 남기다
leading research center	일류 연구 센터
The **presiding officer** will introduce the keynote speaker.	의장이 기조 연설자를 소개할 것이다.
a **promising recruit**	유망한 신입 사원
a **challenging project**	힘든 프로젝트
an **outstanding painter**	뛰어난 화가
remaining work	남아 있는 일
a **departing employee**	(회사를) 떠나는 직원
improving skills	향상되고 있는 기량
cf) improved skills	향상된 기량

Crew Machinery, a (**led**, **leading**) maker of industrial vehicles, opened its factory 50 years ago.
일류 공업용 차량 제조 회사인 Crew Machinery사는 50년 전에 공장을 열었다.
▶ '일류의'를 의미하는 분사로는 과거분사 led가 아니라 현재분사 leading을 써야 한다.

02 과거분사 + 명사

선호, 자격	the **preferred means** of communication	선호되는 통신 수단
	revise the **proposed plan**	제출된 계획을 수정하다
	hire an **experienced (qualified, skilled) applicant**	경력 있는 (적격인, 숙련된) 지원자를 고용하다
	an **accomplished (distinguished) writer**	뛰어난 (우수한) 작가
표시, 기재	**designated smoking area**	지정된 흡연 구역
	the **reserved space** for the disabled	장애인을 위해 지정된 구역
	refer to the **detailed information**	상세한 정보를 참고하다
	receive **written consent**	서면 동의를 받다
	one-year **limited warranty**	1년 동안의 제한된 품질 보증서
	limited items	한정 품목
구입, 제조	recently **purchased office desks**	최근 구매된 사무실 책상
	a growing market for **customized products**	성장하는 주문 제작 제품 시장
	inspect **finished products** for defects	결함이 있는지 완제품을 점검하다
	the high quality of the **handcrafted goods**	수제품의 뛰어난 품질
기타	**repeated absences** from work	반복되는 결근
	request an explanation of the **attached document**	첨부된 서류에 대한 설명을 요청하다
	responsible for the **damaged items**	손상된 물건에 대해 책임이 있는

The talk show will feature several (**experiencing**, **experienced**) writers from Asia.
그 토크쇼는 아시아 출신의 몇몇 경력 있는 작가들을 특집으로 다룰 것이다.
▶ '경력 있는'을 의미하는 분사로는 현재분사 experiencing이 아니라 과거분사 experienced를 써야 한다.

토익실전문제

출제 포인트 현재분사와 과거분사 구별하여 채우기
분사를 포함하는 관용 표현에서 현재분사와 과거분사를 구별하여 채우는
문제가 주로 출제된다.

1. Although cork is the ------- means to cap wine bottles, metal screw caps have become increasingly popular with manufacturers.

    (A) preferred
    (B) preferring
    (C) preference
    (D) prefers

2. The government policy specifies that all ------- applicants must receive equal consideration for open civil service positions.

    (A) experiencing
    (B) experiences
    (C) experienced
    (D) experiential

3. Ireland's Blue Deer Furniture is world-renowned for the originality and overall quality of its ------- dressers.

    (A) handcraft
    (B) handcrafts
    (C) handcrafted
    (D) handcrafting

정답·해설·해석 p.41

둘 중 맞는 형태를 고르세요.

01 Shoppers are encouraged to use a credit card when ------- products online.
ⓐ purchased   ⓑ purchasing

02 We must make a ------- impression on our clients to maintain long-term relations with them.
ⓐ lasting   ⓑ lasted

03 The railway station attendant told the passengers to board the train by the time ------- on the ticket.
ⓐ indicating   ⓑ indicated

04 Jane received a notice from the building manager ------- her to pay her rent.
ⓐ reminding   ⓑ reminds

05 Several phone calls came in for the banker, ------- him from finishing the task at hand.
ⓐ prevention   ⓑ preventing

06 Customers ------- with the service are asked to contact a service representative.
ⓐ dissatisfying   ⓑ dissatisfied

07 Be sure to keep your antivirus program ------- to avoid infecting the office's network system.
ⓐ updated   ⓑ updating

틀린 곳이 있으면 바르게 고치세요.

08 Please give your receipts to the staff handled expense reimbursements.

09 The proposed plan was acceptable to all members of the committee.

10 Knew nothing about the project, Maureen asked her coworker to bring her up-to-date.

11 The bank will send the client a revise statement of transactions.

12 Every night before leaving, the janitor makes sure all the lights are turned off.

13 She spent several minutes reading the memo issuing by the manager.

14 Many promised applicants applied for our company's interview.

정답·해석 p.41

무료 해설 ▶
바로 보기

맞은 문제 개수: / 14
틀린 문제에 해당하는 토익 공식을 다시 한번 학습하세요.

🕐 제한 시간 12분

Part 5

01 The hotel provides personal service with careful attention to detail, ------- that guests have a relaxing and comfortable stay.

(A) be guaranteed   (B) guarantee
(C) guarantees   (D) guaranteeing

02 The user manual should be in the package ------- to your office.

(A) deliver   (B) delivered
(C) delivering   (D) delivers

03 The CEO is looking forward to meeting with branch representatives and to ------- any issues that have arisen in the past quarter.

(A) resolve   (B) resolving
(C) have resolved   (D) be resolving

04 The department heads convened to discuss how to get the employees ------- to complete tasks in a timely manner.

(A) motivation   (B) motivate
(C) motivated   (D) motivating

05 Net Connect furnishes its clients with ------- networking solutions, ranging from file and printer sharing to schedule and calendar synchronization.

(A) specialize   (B) specializes
(C) specialized   (D) specializing

06 Although Rebecca Lewis has worked at the company for only three months, she has already proved that she can cope when ------- with stressful situations.

(A) confront   (B) confronting
(C) confronts   (D) confronted

07 Many viewers found the director's latest movie ------- even though some critics maintain that the plot is unimaginative.

(A) inspire   (B) inspiration
(C) inspiring   (D) inspired

08 Many of the tax breaks ------- to strengthen the domestic steel industry will be canceled once the new administration takes office.

(A) provide   (B) provided
(C) providing   (D) provision

09 Although the product's patent negotiations were -------, both companies are pleased with the final contract terms.

(A) exhaust   (B) exhausted
(C) exhausting   (D) exhaustion

10 Customers who are unable to install the image editing software should contact the technical support hotline after ------- the manual.

(A) consult   (B) consults
(C) consultation   (D) consulting

11 The bank will conduct an information seminar next week for clients ------- to open registered retirement savings accounts.

(A) planned   (B) planning
(C) plan   (D) will plan

12 The symposium's ------- event is the Peace Ball, where delegates can meet members of the community.

(A) conclude   (B) conclusion
(C) concluding   (D) concluded

13 Employees ------- transfer to an overseas branch must meet the requirements for relocation.

(A) request   (B) will request
(C) been requested   (D) requesting

14 As publishers produce more digitally formatted textbooks, university bookstores are expected to experience ------- sales.

(A) reduce   (B) to reduce
(C) reduces   (D) reduced

15 Mr. Morris and I ------- the section of the report written by Ms. Wood because her conclusion was based on outdated information.

(A) deleting   (B) am deleting
(C) was deleted   (D) are deleting

16 Staff should use the recently ------- reference materials to expand their knowledge of communications software.

(A) ordered   (B) ordering
(C) orders   (D) order

17 The stadium was packed with a large number of people waiting to see the famous rock band -------.

(A) perform   (B) performed
(C) to perform   (D) are performing

18 The institute has initiated a policy offering cash incentives to supervisors ------- to increase employee productivity.

(A) are trying   (B) try
(C) trying   (D) will try

Part 6

Questions 19-22 refer to the following letter.

Dear Mr. Colby,

We appreciate your interest in the HomeShield System, an all-in-one package ------- home protection.
                                                                                              19

The HomeShield System includes motion and smoke detectors, fire sprinklers, and an alarm system monitored by BYT security personnel. The security system can be ------- remotely using the
                                                                                           20
HomeShield application for mobile devices. The app allows you to manage system components and ensure that they are functioning properly. This is a big advantage whenever your family spends time away from home and you need to check on your residence.

If you are interested in having a representative ------- your home, please call us at 555-6835 and
                                                       21
tell us about your security needs. Or, send us an e-mail at inquiries@bytsolutions.com. -------.
                                                                                            22
Appointments can be arranged any time after that.

Remember, your safety is in good hands with BYT Solutions. We look forward to hearing from you.

Sincerely yours,
Marilou Eaglin, BYT Solutions

19 (A) has provided   (B) provided
    (C) provide   (D) providing

20 (A) turned on   (B) operated
    (C) updated   (D) closed down

21 (A) visited   (B) visit
    (C) will visit   (D) is visiting

22 (A) Homeowners will never need to worry about their heating systems ever again.
    (B) The security system for your home was configured according to your needs.
    (C) We will provide you with an installation estimate by the next day.
    (D) The package has recently been updated to include motion detectors.

정답·해설·해석 p.41 / [별책] 토익 RC 필수 어휘 p.12

해커스 스타강사의 ▶
무료 해설강의 바로 보기
(13번 문제)

Hackers TOEIC Reading

SECTION 4
품사

명사

토익, 이렇게 나온다!

명사 관련 문제는 평균 3~4문제 정도 꾸준히 출제되며 최대 5문제까지 출제된다. 주어나 목적어 자리에 명사를 채우는 문제가 가장 많이 출제되며, 사람명사와 사물/추상명사를 구별하여 채우는 문제도 자주 출제된다.

토익 필수 개념 다지기

01 명사는 사람이나 사물, 추상적인 개념 등을 모두 가리키는 단어이다.

teacher   cat   coffee   rain   math   dream   Korea

02 명사는 셀 수 있는 명사(가산 명사)와 셀 수 없는 명사(불가산 명사)로 나뉜다.

가산 명사
- 사람/사물을 가리키는 일반적인 명사   manager, typist, ticket, letter ...
- 집합을 가리키는 명사   family, people, police, team, committee ...

불가산 명사
- 특정한 사람/사물의 이름   Tom, Seoul, Hong Kong, Mars ...
- 개념/상태/동작 등을 나타내는 명사   history, information, news, equipment ...
- 물질을 가리키는 명사   paper, water, wood, glass, oil ...

03 명사는 명사의 의미를 한정해 주는 한정사와 주로 함께 쓰이며, 한정사에는 관사, 수량 형용사, 소유격, 지시형용사 등이 있다.

① 관사

Let's see **a movie** on Saturday. 토요일에 영화 한 편 보자.

The movie I watched yesterday was funny. 내가 어제 본 영화는 재미있었다.

'부정관사 + 명사'인 'a + movie'는 특별히 정해지지 않은 영화 한 편을 의미하고, '정관사 + 명사'인 'The + movie'는 서로가 알고 있는 그 영화 한 편을 의미한다. 이처럼 부정관사(a, an)는 정해지지 않은 명사 앞에 쓰이고, 정관사(the)는 이미 정해진 명사 앞에 쓰인다.

② 수량 형용사

Some movies are unsuitable for children. 몇몇 영화들은 아이들에게 부적합하다.

③ 소유격/지시형용사

The **director's movie** has been praised by critics. 그 감독의 영화는 평론가들의 찬사를 받아 왔다.

I have already seen **this movie**. 나는 이미 이 영화를 봤다.

01 명사는 문장 내에서 주어, 목적어, 보어 자리에 온다.

주어 자리	Production **costs** are currently on the rise. 생산 비용은 현재 오름세에 있다.
타동사의 목적어 자리	The city will be constructing **railways** in suburban areas.
	그 도시는 교외 지역에 철로를 건설할 것이다.
전치사의 목적어 자리	Bills were forwarded to **customers** last month. 청구서가 지난달에 고객들에게 전송되었다.
보어 자리	The pollution created by nearby factories is a **danger** to local wildlife.
	인근 공장에 의해 발생되는 오염은 현지 야생 생물에게 위협 요소이다.
	It was an incredible **relief** that an agreement was finally reached.
	합의에 드디어 도달했다는 것은 굉장한 위안이었다.

고득점 포인트 명사는 준동사의 목적어 자리에도 온다.
Meena is attempting to finish her report before Friday. Meena는 금요일 전까지 보고서를 끝내려고 시도하고 있다.

02 명사는 다음의 품사 앞이나 뒤에 주로 붙어 나온다.

관사 + 명사 + 전치사	the **scent** of the perfume 그 향수의 향기
형용사/분사 + 명사	provide a lot of helpful **advice** 많은 도움이 되는 조언을 제공하다
소유격 + (형용사 +) 명사	will express my **gratitude** 감사를 표할 것이다
	Ms. Drake's first **novel** was more successful than the sequel.
	Ms. Drake의 첫 번째 소설은 속편보다 더 성공적이었다.
명사 + 명사 [복합명사]	check the **contact information** 연락처를 확인하다

03 명사 자리에 동사, 형용사 등은 올 수 없다.

Tax benefits can be used to promote (~~invest~~, **investment**) in small businesses.
세금 혜택은 소기업에 대한 투자를 촉진하기 위해 사용될 수 있다.
▶ to 부정사 to promote의 목적어 자리이므로 동사(invest)가 아닌 명사(investment)가 와야 한다.

They generally have plenty of data concerning their (~~industrial~~, **industry**).
그들은 일반적으로 그들이 속한 산업에 관련된 많은 자료를 갖고 있다.
▶ 전치사 concerning의 목적어 자리이므로 형용사(industrial)가 아닌 명사(industry)가 와야 한다.

토익실전문제

출제 포인트 명사 자리 채우기
타동사나 전치사의 목적어 자리에 명사를 채우는 문제가 주로 출제된다.

1. The owner followed the ------- of the marketing consultant and developed an advertising campaign for her business.

   (A) advised   (B) advise
   (C) advisable   (D) advice

2. The feasibility study, which was postponed a few months ago, is expected to resume in time for the project committee's -------.

   (A) assessed   (B) assessment
   (C) assessable   (D) assesses

3. Healthcare services and prescription medicines for the elderly are provided at great ------- to the government.

   (A) expensed   (B) expensive
   (C) expensively   (D) expense

정답·해설·해석 p.44

GRAMMAR Part 5,6   Ch 10 명사   Hackers TOEIC Reading

01 가산 명사는 반드시 앞에 관사가 오거나 복수형으로 쓰인다.

I bought (**jacket**, **a jacket**, **jackets**) with fur trim at the department store. 나는 백화점에서 털 장식이 있는 재킷을 구입했다.

▶ jacket은 가산 명사이므로 관사도 없고 복수형도 아니면 틀리다. 반드시 관사를 붙인 형태(a jacket)나 복수형(jackets)으로 써야 한다.

고득점 포인트

❶ 가산 명사에는 셀 수 있는 명사 하나를 표현한 단수 명사와 셀 수 있는 명사 두 개 이상을 표현한 복수 명사가 있다.
단수 명사 앞에는 부정관사가 오고 복수 명사에는 -(e)s를 붙인다.

Passengers may purchase <u>a ticket</u> from the kiosk. 승객들은 간이 매점에서 승차권을 구입할 수 있다.
<u>Products</u> are displayed in the window. 상품들이 창가에 진열되어 있다.

❷ 셀 수 없는 것처럼 보이지만, 가산 명사에 포함되는 명사들이 있다.

a discount 할인	a price 가격	a purpose 목적	a refund 환불	a relation 관계
an approach 접근법	a statement 진술	a workplace 일터	a source 근원, 출처	a result 결과
a compliment 찬사	a request 요청, 부탁	belongings 소지품	measures 수단, 대책	savings 저축
standards 표준, 기준	funds 기금			

02 불가산 명사는 앞에 부정관사 a/an이 올 수 없고 복수형으로 쓰일 수도 없다.

I need (**a cash**, **cashes**, **cash**) for my trip. 나는 여행을 위해 현금이 필요하다.

▶ cash는 불가산 명사이므로, 부정관사가 올 수도 없고, 복수형으로 쓰일 수도 없다.

고득점 포인트

셀 수 있는 것처럼 보이지만, 불가산 명사에 포함되는 명사들이 있다.

access 접근, 출입, 이용	advice 조언, 충고	baggage 수하물	equipment 기구, 장비	information 정보
luggage 수하물	machinery 기계류	news 뉴스	stationery 문구류	consent 동의

03 의미가 비슷하여 혼동하기 쉬운 가산 명사와 불가산 명사

가산 명사 – 불가산 명사	가산 명사 – 불가산 명사
an account 계좌 – accounting 회계(학)	a lender 대여자 – lending 대여
an advertisement 광고 – advertising 광고(업)	a letter 편지 – mail 우편(물)
clothes 옷 – clothing 의류	a permit 허가서 – permission 허가
a fund 기금, 자금 – funding 자금 지원	a process 과정 / procedures 순서, 절차 – processing 처리, 절차, 가공
furnishings 가구, 커튼, 카펫류 – furniture 가구	a seat 좌석 – seating 좌석 (배열)
goods 상품 – merchandise 상품	a ticket 티켓 – ticketing 발권

고득점 포인트

가산 명사로 쓰일 때와 불가산 명사로 쓰일 때 의미가 다른 명사들이 있다.

customs 관세, 세관 – custom 관습   manners 풍습, 예의범절 – manner 방법, 방식   savings 저금, 저축 – saving 절약

토익실전문제

출제 포인트 가산/불가산 명사, 단수/복수 명사 구별하여 채우기

가산 명사인지 불가산 명사인지 구별한 후, 관사 유무에 따라 단수/복수 명사를 구별하여 채우는 문제가 주로 출제된다.

1. According to the survey results, respondents expect a better ------- of living as technology advances and their wages increase.

   (A) standard   (B) standardizing
   (C) standards   (D) standardized

2. A report by a major civic organization recommends significant ------- to the government's immigration policies.

   (A) change   (B) changes
   (C) changing   (D) changed

3. Mr. Williams became aware of the open publicist job at J-Stone Industries through an ------- posted in a leading business journal.

   (A) advertise   (B) advertisable
   (C) advertising   (D) advertisement

정답·해설·해석 p.44

01 부정관사 a/an은 단수 가산 명사 앞에만 오며, 복수 가산 명사나 불가산 명사 앞에는 올 수 없다.

He attended **a** community <u>event</u>. 그는 한 지역 행사에 참석했다.
Several factors contributed to ~~a~~ rising transportation <u>costs</u>. 몇몇 요인들이 교통비 증가의 원인이 되었다.
The sports drink provides ~~an~~ extra <u>energy</u>. 그 스포츠 음료는 여분의 에너지를 공급한다.

▶ 부정관사 a/an은 복수인 가산 명사 costs 앞에도, 불가산 명사인 energy 앞에도 올 수 없다.

고득점 포인트 : 스펠링에 상관없이, 부정관사 바로 다음에 오는 단어가 자음 발음으로 시작되면 a를, 모음 발음으로 시작되면 an을 쓴다.

a discount   a university   an effort   an hour

02 정관사 the는 가산 명사 단·복수와 불가산 명사 모두의 앞에 올 수 있다.

Helen bought **the** <u>hat</u> that she tried on yesterday. Helen은 어제 써 본 그 모자를 구입했다.
I read **the** <u>novels</u> of John Pearson. 나는 John Pearson의 소설들을 읽었다.
Contact Henry to confirm **the** <u>information</u>. 그 정보를 확인하려면 Henry에게 연락하세요.

03 가산 명사·불가산 명사 앞에 오는 수량 형용사

가산 명사 앞			불가산 명사 앞	가산 · 불가산 명사 모두의 앞	
단수 명사	복수 명사				
one 하나의 each 각각의	(a) few 몇 개의	fewer 더 적은	(a) little 적은	no 어떤 ~도 ~ 아니다	all 모든
every 모든	many 많은	several 몇몇의	less 더 적은	more 더 많은	most 대부분의
	both 둘 다의	various 여러, 많은	much 많은	some 몇몇의, 어떤	any 어떤

The applicant has <u>several</u> impressive (**skill**, **skills**) listed on her résumé.
그 지원자는 이력서에 기재된 몇 가지 인상적인 능력들을 가지고 있다.

▶ 복수 명사와 함께 쓰이는 수량 형용사(several) 뒤에는 단수 명사(skill)가 아니라 복수 명사(skills)가 와야 한다.

고득점 포인트 : 단, all, more, most는 가산 명사와 쓰일 때 복수 명사 앞에 온다.

Most <u>resident</u>(→residents) agree with the new city legislation, but some remain skeptical.
대부분의 주민들은 새로운 시 법률 제정에 동의하지만, 몇몇 주민들은 여전히 회의적이다.

토익실전문제

출제 포인트 명사(한정사)에 맞는 한정사(명사) 채우기
한정사를 보고 명사를 채우는 문제가 주로 출제된다.

1. ------- merchandise returned to the store after purchase must be checked for damage and functionality before being put back on the shelf.

   (A) An   (B) That is
   (C) Any   (D) In case

2. The company issued a formal statement to notify employees of several plant ------- throughout the country.

   (A) to close   (B) close
   (C) closing   (D) closures

3. Each probationary ------- must undergo six months' instruction before advancing to a full-time accountant position.

   (A) training   (B) trainees
   (C) trainee   (D) trained

정답·해설·해석 p.44

01 사람/사물/추상명사는 모두 명사 자리에 올 수 있다. 그러나 이 중, 문장 안에서 자연스러운 의미를 만드는 명사가 와야 한다.

accountant 회계사 - account 계좌, 계산 - accounting 회계
applicant 지원자 - application 지원, 신청서 - appliance 기구, 장치
attendant 참석자, 안내원 - attendance 출석 - attendee 출석자
consultant 상담자 - consultation 상담 - consultancy 컨설팅사
employer 고용인 - employee 피고용인 - employment 고용
facilitator 조력자, 협력자 - facility 시설 - facilitation 편리화
journalist 기자 - journal 잡지, 학술지 - journalism 언론(학)
occupant 입주자 - occupancy 점유 - occupation 직업
producer 생산자 - production 생산 - product 생산품
receptionist 접수원 - reception 접대, 수령 - receptacle 그릇, 용기
recruiter 신입을 모집하는 사람 - recruit 신입 사원 - recruitment 채용
analyst 분석가 - analysis 분석
architect 건축가 - architecture 건축(술)
assembler 조립공 - assembly 조립
assistant 조수 - assistance 원조, 보조
authority 권위자 - authorization 권한 부여
beneficiary 수익자 - benefit 이익
committee 위원(회) - commitment 위탁, 헌신
consumer 고객 - consumption 소비
contributor 공헌자 - contribution 공헌
coordinator 진행자, 조정자 - coordination 합동, 조화
correspondent 통신원 - correspondence 일치, 대응
distributor 분배자, 판매자 - distribution 분배, 배포

donor 기증자 - donation 기증
editor 편집자 - edition (발행)판
engineer 기술자 - engineering 공학
enthusiast 팬, 열성적인 사람 - enthusiasm 열의, 열광
founder 설립자 - foundation 설립, 재단
inspector 검사자 - inspection 검사, 정밀 조사
instructor 가르치는 사람 - instruction 교육
investor 투자자 - investment 투자
licensor 검열관 - license 면허, 자격증
manager 관리자, 경영자 - management 경영, (집합적) 경영진
manufacturer 제조업자 - manufacture 제조업
negotiator 협상가 - negotiation 교섭, 협상
operator (기계 등의) 운전자, 기사 - operation 작동, 영업, 경영
owner 소유자 - ownership 소유권
participant 참가자 - participation 참여
performer 연주자 - performance 연주, 실적, 성과
presenter 발표자, 진행자 - presentation 발표, 소개, 제출
relative 친척 - relation 관계
representative 직원, 대표자 - representation 대표
resident 거주자 - residence 거주
subscriber 구독자 - subscription 구독, 가입
supervisor 감독자 - supervision 감독
technician 기술자 - technology 과학 기술

An (**architecture**, **architect**) designed the firm's new headquarters in Bangkok.
한 건축가가 방콕에 있는 그 회사의 새로운 본사를 디자인했다.

▶ '건축가가 디자인했다'는 의미가 되어야 하므로, '건축'이라는 의미의 추상명사(architecture)가 아닌, '건축가'라는 의미의 사람명사(architect)가 와야 한다.

The (**founder**, **foundation**) of a community center will improve the residents' quality of life.
지역 문화 회관의 설립은 주민들의 삶의 질을 향상시킬 것이다.

▶ '지역 문화 회관의 설립'이라는 의미가 되어야 하므로, '설립자'라는 의미의 사람명사(founder)가 아닌, '설립'이라는 의미의 추상명사(foundation)가 와야 한다.

토익실전문제

출제 포인트 사람명사, 사물/추상명사 구별하여 채우기

주어나 목적어 자리에 문장의 의미에 알맞게 사람명사 또는 사물/추상명사 중 하나를 선택하여 채우는 문제가 주로 출제된다.

2. Good research skills and attention to detail are necessary qualities for working in the field of -------.

(A) journalistic
(B) journalist
(C) journalism
(D) journal

1. Most workers are seeking regular ------- because they prefer the financial security of a permanent position.

(A) employs
(B) employee
(C) employing
(D) employment

3. Manufacturers frequently hire psychologists as ------- to obtain their insights in designing toys for children of different ages.

(A) consult
(B) consultants
(C) consultancy
(D) consultations

정답·해설·해석 p.44

01 복합 명사는 '명사 + 명사'로 되어 있다. 이때, 앞의 명사 자리에 형용사나 분사, 또는 동사는 올 수 없다.

account number 계좌 번호	expansion project 확장 계획	reception desk 접수처
application fee 신청비	expiration date 만기일	reference letter 추천서
application form 신청서	feasibility study 예비 조사, 타당성 조사	registration form 등록 양식, 신청서
arrival date 도착일	growth rate 성장률	research program 연구 프로그램
assembly line 조립 라인	housing department 주택 개발부	retail sales 소매 판매
attendance record 출근(출석) 기록	interest rate 금리, 이율	retirement celebration 퇴직 기념 축하연
communication skill 의사소통 능력	investment advice 투자 조언	retirement luncheon 퇴직 기념 오찬
conference room 회의장	keynote speaker 기조 연설자	return policy 환불 정책
confidentiality policy 보안 정책	living expenses 생활비	safety inspection 안전 검사
confirmation number 예약확인 번호	occupancy rate 점유율	safety regulations 안전 규정
customer satisfaction 고객 만족	performance appraisals/evaluations 업무수행평가	sales representative 외판원
enrollment form 등록 양식	planning stage 기획 단계	security card 보안 카드
exchange rate 환율	product description 제품 설명서	service desk 안내 데스크
exercise equipment 운동 기구	quality requirement 품질 요구사항	travel arrangement 여행(출장) 준비

Excellent (~~communicated~~, **communication**) skills are required for the position. 훌륭한 의사소통 능력이 그 직위에 필요하다.

02 복합 명사를 복수형으로 만들 때는 뒤의 명사에 -(e)s를 붙인다.

research program → research program**s**
job opening → job opening**s**

> **고득점 포인트** 복합 명사(명사 + 명사)에서 앞의 명사에는 -(e)s가 붙을 수 없다. 그러나 예외적으로 [명사s + 명사]의 형태를 가지는 복합 명사가 있다.
>
> customs office 세관　public relations department 홍보부　electronics company 전자 회사　earnings growth 수익 성장
> savings account/bank/plan 예금 계좌/은행/상품　sales division/promotion 판매 부서/촉진　human resources department 인사부

03 [숫자 + 단위명사 + 명사]에서 단위명사에는 -s가 붙지 못한다.

six **hundreds** students (×) → six **hundred** students (○) 600명의 학생들
a four-**years**-old girl (×) → a four-**year**-old girl (○) 네 살짜리 소녀

> **고득점 포인트** thousand, hundred, year 등의 명사가 다른 명사를 수식하지 않을 경우에는 -s가 붙어야 한다.
>
> hundred(→hundreds) of students
> She is four year(→years) old.
> → 여기서 years는 old를 수식하는 것이 아니다. old는 four years를 뒤에서 꾸며 주는 형용사이다.

토익실전문제

출제 포인트 다른 명사를 수식하는 명사 채우기
명사 앞에 형용사나 분사가 아닌 다른 명사를 채워 복합 명사를 완성하는 문제가 주로 출제된다.

1. The ------- program was funded by a government agency and carried out by capable scientists at the university's engineering facility.

   (A) researching (B) researched
   (C) research (D) researches

2. The ------- equipment featured in the advertisement is guaranteed to help people achieve greater muscle tone in just a few weeks.

   (A) exercise (B) exercises
   (C) exercising (D) exercised

3. The retailer filed a complaint with the supplier claiming that the ------- dates on the facial creams she ordered had already passed.

   (A) expired (B) expire
   (C) expiration (D) expires

정답·해설·해석 p.45

01 형태는 비슷하지만 의미가 달라 혼동을 주는 명사들을 주의해야 한다.

closing 폐쇄, 밀폐	close 끝, 종결	the **closing** of offices 사무실의 폐쇄
coverage (취재, 보상, 적용) 범위	cover 표지 covering 덮개	long-term insurance **coverage** 장기 보험 보상 범위
competition 경쟁	competence 능력	win a **competition** 경쟁에서 이기다
entry 참가 등록 entrant 참가자	entrance 입장, 입구	submit **entries** online 온라인으로 참가 등록하다
identification 신분증명	identity 정체성	display a form of **identification** 신분증명서를 보여주다
interests 이익	interest 관심	the **interests** of the students 학생들의 이익 have **interest** in European history 유럽 역사에 관심을 갖다
likelihood 가능성	likeness 유사성	the **likelihood** of traffic congestion 교통 정체의 가능성
objective 목표 object 목표, 물체	objectivity 객관성 objection 반대	Our **objective** is to raise awareness. 우리의 목표는 인지도를 높이는 것이다.
percent 퍼센트	percentage 비율	20 **percent** off on all purchases 모든 구매에 대한 20퍼센트 할인 low **percentage** of the population 인구의 낮은 비율 * percent는 숫자와 함께, percentage는 그 이외의 경우에 쓴다.
permit 허가증	permission 허가	request a business **permit** 사업 허가증을 요청하다
procedure 절차	proceedings 의사록	medical examination **procedures** 건강 진단 절차
productivity 생산성	product 생산품 produce 농산물 production 생산량, 생산	find ways to improve **productivity** 생산성을 향상시킬 방법을 찾다 **Production** is at an all-time low. 생산량이 사상 최저치이다.
professionalism 전문성	profession 직업 professional 전문가	demonstrate **professionalism** in the workplace 직장에서 전문성을 발휘하다
remainder 나머지	remains 유물	over the **remainder** of this month 이번 달의 나머지 기간 동안
responsibility 책임	responsiveness 반응	give additional **responsibility** 추가적인 책임을 부여하다
sense 감각	sensation 감동, 흥분	have a **sense** of humor 유머 감각이 있다
utilization 활용, 이용	utility 공익 설비(전기, 가스 등)	the **utilization** of innovative ideas 획기적인 생각의 활용

→ 맨 왼쪽에 제시된 단어들이 답으로 자주 나온다.

Giorgio was assigned the (**responsiveness**, **responsibility**) of contacting the guest speakers.
Giorgio는 초청 연사들에게 연락하는 책임을 배정받았다.

▶ '책임을 배정받다'라는 의미가 되어야 하므로 responsiveness(반응)가 아닌 responsibility(책임)를 써야 한다.

토익실전문제

출제 포인트 의미 구별하여 명사 채우기
주어나 목적어 자리에 형태는 비슷하지만 의미가 다른 두 명사를 구별하여
채우는 문제가 출제된다.

1. A panel of published authors will review all ------
submitted by the May 12 deadline to determine the
winner of this year's Young Writer Award.

    (A) enters (B) entries
    (C) entered (D) entrance

2. Visitors are not allowed to leave their cars in the lot
behind the building without first obtaining a parking
------ from the attendant.

    (A) permit (B) permission
    (C) permitting (D) to permit

3. Having good financial ------ can help one to create
a retirement plan that provides for a comfortable
lifestyle over the long term.

    (A) to sense (B) sensor
    (C) sensation (D) sense

정답·해설·해석 p.45

HACKERS PRACTICE 토익 고득점을 위한 필수 연습

둘 중 맞는 형태를 고르세요.

01 Staff at Portside Hospital are known for their ------- to serving patients to the best of their abilities.
ⓐ dedicate   ⓑ dedication

02 It is the ------- of hotel guests to make sure their valuables are kept in a safe location.
ⓐ responsibility   ⓑ responsiveness

03 The film's ------- timetable was modified to accommodate the lead actress's other commitments.
ⓐ productivity   ⓑ production

04 Due to the ------- that the hurricane will cause flooding, residents of coastal areas are advised to evacuate.
ⓐ likeness   ⓑ likelihood

05 The ------- of women wearing trousers came about in the early 1900s.
ⓐ trend   ⓑ trendy

06 The bank's consultants provide ------- advice to clients interested in purchasing mutual funds.
ⓐ investing   ⓑ investment

07 Marshall is in charge of checking and filing ------- records for the marketing department.
ⓐ attendance   ⓑ attending

틀린 곳이 있으면 바르게 고치세요.

08 The sales director went to the train station to await the arrive of an important client.

09 Every applicants was given an official receipt for fees paid.

10 A workshop on the developer of economic relations between the EU and Japan took place in Tokyo.

11 The general manager handles the supervisor of all employees.

12 Because Mr. Lee is a frequent business traveling, he was allowed to enter the exclusive airport lounge.

13 Although his occupancy was teaching, he also dabbled in stock trading.

14 The Power Health Club urges people to discover the beneficiaries of organized fitness activities.

정답·해석 p.45

무료 해설 ▶
바로 보기

맞은 문제 개수: / 14
틀린 문제에 해당하는 토익 공식을 다시 한번 학습하세요.

🕐 제한 시간 12분

Part 5

01 Denise Samson reviewed her completed ------- to ensure that there were no errors before handing it to the human resources director.

(A) applying   (B) applied
(C) applicant   (D) application

02 The administrative supervisor will consider the ------- of his assistant's contract in light of her inability to get along with other workers.

(A) terminate   (B) terminating
(C) terminated   (D) termination

03 The report indicated that the firm's average annual earnings ------- was much higher than analysts had estimated.

(A) grows   (B) growing
(C) growth   (D) grew

04 The ------- of the new bookcase was more difficult than expected.

(A) assembles   (B) assembly
(C) assembler   (D) assembled

05 Management was impressed with the increase in ------- achieved by the workers at the company's factory in San Jose.

(A) product   (B) productivity
(C) productive   (D) produce

06 A copy of the ------- text must be reviewed by the managing editor for inaccuracies prior to the publication of the book.

(A) revised   (B) revision
(C) revising   (D) revise

07 The pension scheme that was recently established by the government has attracted fewer ------- than originally expected.

(A) registers   (B) registered
(C) registration   (D) registrants

08 The CEO said that there was no ------- but to drop the expansion plans until the company could raise enough capital.

(A) alternate   (B) alternative
(C) alternation   (D) alternatively

09 According to city officials, Oklahoma City's improvement project will require the ------- of several roads and bridges for up to six months.

(A) close   (B) closely
(C) closed   (D) closing

10 ------- numbers of former customers will be maintained in the database for six months as part of the company's new policy.

(A) Account   (B) Accounts
(C) Accounting   (D) Accountable

11 Mr. Barrett will collect the ------- from last month's customer survey and prepare a detailed report.

(A) result   (B) results
(C) to result   (D) resulted

12 The operator will not set the machinery in ------- until all necessary raw materials are in place.

(A) moving   (B) moved
(C) move   (D) motion

13 In an effort to ensure ------- in the workplace, the government has established laws on the maintenance of equipment and the use and storage of hazardous substances.

(A) safe   (B) safely
(C) saved   (D) safety

14 Demands for modifications to the new healthcare coverage program ------- dramatically, resulting in strikes at several major hospitals.

(A) was risen   (B) has risen
(C) rose   (D) rising

15 Out of ------- for the wishes of the university's founder, academically-gifted students from poor families are provided with full scholarships.

(A) respect
(B) respecting
(C) respectable
(D) respected

16 If the ------- attached to the form do not meet the size requirements, the Department of Foreign Affairs will be unable to issue a passport.

(A) photographs
(B) photography
(C) photographers
(D) photographic

17 The state of Florida is popular with ------- because it has warm weather for most of the year.

(A) retires
(B) retiree
(C) retirees
(D) retired

18 Payment via credit card or online bank transfer must be sent to the ------- within two days to ensure that the product will be shipped on the date requested.

(A) sell
(B) sold
(C) seller
(D) selling

Part 6

Questions 19-22 refer to the following memo.

To: All branch managers
From: Jane Dawson, Regional Manager – Southeast Asia
Date: June 7

As discussed during our meeting in Singapore last month, GLE Inc. is implementing a new incentive program for sales personnel. All branches ------- it on July 1.
                                                                                19

-------. Staff members will be given a 5 percent bonus for any sale they make totaling $500 or more.
20
Furthermore, to help employees stay motivated, the salesperson with the best annual record will be rewarded the ------- amount of a month's salary every December.
                              21

We believe that this program will improve employee ------- and lead to increased profits for the
                                                     22
company. Please discuss the incentive system with your staff members before it goes into effect, and let me know if you have any questions. As always, thank you for all your hard work.

19 (A) adopting
(B) would have adopted
(C) will adopt
(D) adopted

20 (A) It will involve providing commissions on big transactions.
(B) Similar programs have cost the company too much money.
(C) Our sales representatives receive regular training.
(D) We have yet to determine the minimum sales amount.

21 (A) remaining
(B) equivalent
(C) accessible
(D) refundable

22 (A) satisfactorily
(B) satisfaction
(C) satisfying
(D) satisfactory

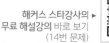
해커스 스타강사의 ▶
무료 해설강의 바로 보기
(14번 문제)

GRAMMAR Part 5,6 Ch 10 명사 Hackers TOEIC Reading

CHAPTER 11

대명사

토익, 이렇게 나온다!

대명사 관련 문제는 평균 2~3문제 정도 꾸준히 출제되며 최대 5문제까지 출제된다. 격에 맞는 인칭대명사를 채우는 문제와 부정대명사를 채우는 문제가 주로 출제된다.

토익 필수 개념 다지기

01 동일한 명사가 반복되어 쓰이는 것을 막기 위해 명사 대신 쓰는 것이 대명사이다. 따라서 대명사는 명사처럼 문장에서 주어, 목적어, 보어의 역할을 한다.

I met Sandra at a restaurant, and <u>Sandra</u> paid for dinner.
→ I met Sandra at a restaurant, and **she** paid for dinner.
나는 레스토랑에서 Sandra를 만났고, 그녀는 저녁값을 냈다.

she는 앞에 나온 명사(Sandra)가 반복되어 쓰이는 것을 막기 위해 대신하여 쓴 대명사로, 절에서 주어로 쓰이고 있다.

02 대명사는 그 쓰임에 따라 인칭대명사, 재귀대명사, 지시대명사, 부정대명사로 분류한다.

① 인칭대명사(I, you, she, he, they 등)는 사람이나 사물을 대신할 때 쓰인다.

Dan went to the embassy as **he** had to renew **his** passport. (he, his = Dan)
Dan은 그의 여권을 갱신해야 했기 때문에 대사관에 갔다.

② 재귀대명사(himself, herself, themselves 등)는 인칭대명사에 -self(-selves)를 붙여 '~ 자신'이라는 뜻을 가지며 인칭대명사 바로 그 자신을 나타낸다.

단수	myself	yourself	himself, herself, itself
복수	ourselves	yourselves	themselves

Sally leaves notes for **herself** on the refrigerator. (herself = Sally)
Sally는 냉장고에 자신을 위한 쪽지를 남긴다.

③ 지시대명사(this/these, that/those 등)는 '이것(들)', '저것(들)'이라는 뜻을 가지고 특정 사람이나 사물을 가리키는 역할을 한다. 이것은 또한 명사 앞에서 '이-', '저-'와 같은 의미의 지시형용사로 쓰이기도 한다.

This is my favorite science-fiction novel. ('This'가 지시대명사)
이것은 내가 가장 좋아하는 공상 과학 소설이다.

I have never been to **this** restaurant before. ('this'가 지시형용사)
나는 이전에 이 식당에 와본 적이 없다.

④ 부정대명사(some, any 등)는 막연한 사물이나 사람, 수량을 나타낼 때 쓰인다. 이것 또한 명사 앞에서 '어떤 ~', '몇몇의 ~' 등을 의미하는 부정형용사로 쓰이기도 한다.

Some of the employees were late today. ('Some'이 부정대명사) 오늘 직원들 중 몇몇이 늦었다.
Some employees were late today. ('Some'이 부정형용사) 오늘 몇몇 직원들이 늦었다.

01 인칭대명사의 종류

인칭	수/성		주격	소유격	목적격	소유대명사
1 인칭	단 수		I	my	me	mine
	복 수		we	our	us	ours
2 인칭	단/복수		you	your	you	yours
3 인칭	단 수	남 성	he	his	him	his
		여 성	she	her	her	hers
		사 물	it	its	it	-
	복 수		they	their	them	theirs

02 주격은 주어 자리에 쓴다.

She will host the party if **we** help with the preparations. 우리가 준비를 돕는다면 그녀는 파티를 주최할 것이다.

03 소유격은 형용사처럼 명사 앞에 쓰며 '~의'로 해석된다.

Students select classes based on **their** interests. 학생들은 그들의 흥미에 근거하여 수업들을 선택한다.

> **고득점 포인트** 소유격 앞에는 a/an/the와 같은 관사를 쓸 수 없으므로 a my client가 아니라 소유대명사를 써서 a client of mine으로 써야 한다.

04 목적격은 타동사의 목적어, 전치사의 목적어 자리에 쓴다.

The real estate agent <u>advised</u> **them** to reject the offer. 부동산 중개인은 그 제안을 거절하라고 그들에게 조언했다.
My grandfather lives <u>with</u> **me**. 내 할아버지께서는 나와 함께 사신다.

> **고득점 포인트** 전치사만 보고 바로 목적격을 쓰지 않도록 주의해야 한다.
> I am concerned about <u>me</u>(→my) friend. 나는 내 친구가 걱정된다.
> → 뒤에 명사 friend가 있으므로 소유격 my가 와야 한다.

05 소유대명사는 '소유격 + 명사'를 대신한 것으로 '~의 것'으로 해석되며 주어·목적어·보어 자리에 쓴다. 이때 소유대명사 뒤에는 절대 명사가 나올 수 없다.

<u>My major</u> is physics while (~~hers major~~, **hers**) is art. 내 전공은 물리학인데 그녀의 것은 미술이다.

토익실전문제

출제 포인트 격에 맞는 인칭대명사 채우기
주격, 소유격, 목적격 인칭대명사를 채우는 문제가 모두 고루 출제된다.

1. When the trade negotiators arrived at the airport, ------- were picked up and brought to a local hotel.

    (A) them (B) theirs
    (C) themselves (D) they

2. After revising ------- report, Ms. Seaward met with the regional manager to go over the changes.

    (A) she (B) her
    (C) hers (D) herself

3. Customers who experience problems using the Web site may reach ------- by sending an e-mail or calling a service representative.

    (A) we (B) us
    (C) our (D) ours

정답·해설·해석 p.48

01 목적어가 주어와 같은 사람/사물을 지칭할 때 목적어 자리에 재귀대명사를 쓴다. 이때 재귀대명사는 생략할 수 없다.

Bill always treats **himself** to a coffee in the morning. (Bill = himself) Bill은 아침에 항상 커피를 즐긴다.

▶ 목적어 자리에 재귀대명사 himself를 썼으므로 Bill이 바로 Bill 자신에게 커피를 대접한다는 의미이다. 이 경우 himself는 생략할 수 없다.

cf) Bill always treats **him** to a coffee in the morning. (Bill≠him) Bill은 아침에 항상 그에게 커피를 대접한다.

▶ 목적어 자리에 목적격 him을 쓰게 되면 Bill 자신이 아닌 다른 남자에게 대접한다는 의미이다.

02 주어나 목적어를 강조하기 위해서 강조하고자 하는 말 바로 뒤나, 문장 맨 뒤에 재귀대명사를 쓴다.
이때 재귀대명사는 생략할 수 있다.

The president **himself** announced the new economic reform policy. 대통령이 직접 새 경제 개혁 정책을 발표했다.
Ms. Hill reviewed the article **herself** prior to publication. Ms. Hill은 발행에 앞서 직접 그 기사를 검토했다.
The apartment **itself** is fine, but it is in a bad location. 아파트 그 자체는 괜찮지만, 좋지 않은 위치에 있다.

고득점 포인트 명령문에는 주어 you가 생략되어 있으므로, 주어가 표시되어 있지 않더라도 yourself를 쓴다.
Don't install the software oneself(→yourself). 소프트웨어를 직접 설치하지 마십시오.

03 재귀대명사 관련 관용 표현

by oneself(=alone, on one's own) 홀로, 혼자 힘으로   for oneself 혼자 힘으로   of itself 저절로   in itself 자체로, 본질적으로

Mr. Eaton should be able to complete the report **by himself**. Mr. Eaton은 그 보고서를 혼자 작성할 수 있어야 한다.
You must decide **for yourself**. 당신은 혼자 힘으로 결정을 내려야 한다.

토익실전문제

출제 포인트 재귀대명사 채우기
by oneself와 for oneself 등의 관용 표현을 완성하는 문제가 주로 출제된다.

1. As I was unavailable to give the presentation to the client ------, I asked Mr. Perez to go over the product information with her.

(A) me   (B) myself
(C) mine   (D) my

2. Chad Reyes's total sales for this year topped everyone else's in the sales department, so the manager offered ------- a substantial bonus.

(A) him   (B) he
(C) his   (D) himself

3. Ms. Cole visited the construction site by ------- to check up on the progress of the warehouse being built.

(A) her   (B) she
(C) herself   (D) hers

정답·해설·해석 p.48

01 지시대명사 that/those는 앞에 나온 명사를 대신해서 사용한다.

Jim's résumé is more impressive than **that** [of the other applicant]. Jim의 이력서는 다른 지원자의 이력서보다 더 인상적이다.
The mountains in the Himalayas are much larger than **those** [in the Alps]. 히말라야의 산은 알프스의 산보다 훨씬 더 크다.
The least expensive beef products in the supermarket are **those** [imported from Australia].
그 슈퍼켓에서 가장 저렴한 소고기 제품은 호주에서 수입된 제품이다.

▶ 이때 that과 those 뒤에는 반드시 수식어(전치사구, 관계절, 분사)가 온다.

고득점 포인트
❶ that은 사람명사를 대신하지 못한다.
This salesclerk is more helpful than that(→the one) I dealt with yesterday. 이 점원은 어제 내가 상대했던 점원보다 더 도움이 된다.
cf) These salesclerks are more helpful than those I dealt with yesterday.

❷ that/those 자리에 this/these는 올 수 없다.
Jim's résumé is more impressive than this(→that) of the other applicant.
Coleridge and Associate's fees are higher than these(→those) of other law firms.
Coleridge and Associate사의 수수료는 다른 법률 회사들의 수수료보다 높다.

02 those는 '~한 사람들'이란 의미로도 쓰인다.

Those [who submitted an entry on time] are eligible to win a substantial cash prize.
출품작을 제때에 제출한 사람들은 상당한 상금을 받을 자격이 있다.

Those [stranded in the airport due to the storm] will receive complimentary meals.
태풍 때문에 공항에서 꼼짝 못하게 된 사람들은 무료 식사를 받을 것이다.

▶ 이 경우 those는 앞에 오는 명사를 대신하는 것이 아니라 막연히 '~한 사람들'이란 의미로 쓰이고 있다. 이때도 역시 those 뒤에 반드시 수식어(관계절, 분사, 전치사구)가 온다.

고득점 포인트
those 자리에 they나 them을 쓸 수 없다. (they나 them 뒤에는 수식어가 나올 수 없다.)
They(→Those) stranded in the airport due to the storm will receive complimentary meals.

03 this/that과 these/those는 명사 앞에서 지시형용사로 쓰여 '이-', '저-'의 의미를 갖는다.

This seminar has been canceled. 이 세미나는 취소되었다.
Those mountains are popular hiking areas. 저 산들은 인기 있는 등산 지역이다.

고득점 포인트
지시형용사 those는 '저-'라는 의미를 갖지 않고 마치 'the'처럼 쓰이기도 한다.
Those buildings(=The buildings) that were damaged by the earthquake will be repaired within six weeks.
지진으로 피해 입은 그 건물들은 6주 이내에 수리될 것이다.
Those athletes(=The athletes) who trained hard are likely to win medals. 열심히 훈련했던 그 선수들이 메달을 딸 것 같다.

토익실전문제

출제 포인트 that/those 채우기
of 전치사구 앞 또는 분사 앞에 지시대명사 that/those를 채우는 문제가
주로 출제된다.

1. The laboratory facilities at New York College are comparable to ------- of other major universities in the region.
   (A) this
   (B) them
   (C) that
   (D) those

2. For ------- hoping to participate in this year's marathon, an application form has been made available online to facilitate quick and easy registration.
   (A) those
   (B) whom
   (C) ones
   (D) they

3. Food prices in general rose last year, with the cost of meat nearly doubling, and ------- of vegetables increasing by almost 15 percent.
   (A) this
   (B) that
   (C) these
   (D) those

정답·해설·해석 p.48

01 one은 정해지지 않은 단수 가산 명사를 대신한다.

My sweater didn't fit, so I purchased a bigger **one**. 내 스웨터가 맞지 않아서, 나는 더 큰 스웨터를 구입했다.

▶ one 앞에는 반드시 one이 대신하는 명사가 와야 한다.

고득점 포인트 one의 복수형은 ones로, 정해지지 않은 복수 가산 명사를 대신한다.
My gloves didn't fit, so I purchased bigger ones. 내 장갑이 맞지 않아서, 나는 더 큰 장갑을 구입했다.

02 another는 '이미 언급한 것 이외의 또 다른 하나'라는 의미로 쓰인다.

One of the visitors is in the living room. **Another visitor** is in the kitchen. (**Another** is in the kitchen.)
손님들 중 한 명이 거실에 있다. 또 다른 한 명의 손님은 부엌에 있다.

▶ another가 형용사로 쓰일 때 뒤에는 반드시 단수 가산 명사가 나와야 한다. 그리고 another 앞에는 the를 붙여 쓸 수 없다.

03 other/others는 '이미 언급한 것 이외의 것들 중 몇몇'이라는 의미로 쓰인다.

One of the visitors is in the living room. **Other visitors** are in the kitchen. (**Others** are in the kitchen.)
손님들 중 한 명이 거실에 있다. 다른 손님들은 부엌에 있다.

▶ other는 형용사로만 쓰이며 뒤에 복수 가산 명사가 오고 others는 대명사로만 쓰인다.

고득점 포인트 other 뒤에는 불가산 명사도 올 수 있다.
We can get other information from the Web site. 우리는 웹사이트에서 다른 정보를 얻을 수 있다.

04 the other(s)는 '정해진 것 중 남은 것 전부'를 의미한다.

John has four friends. Three are here. **The other friend** is at home. (**The other** is at home.)
John은 네 명의 친구들이 있다. 세 명은 여기에 있다. 나머지 한 명의 친구는 집에 있다.

John has four friends. One is here. **The other friends** are at home. (**The others** are at home.)
John은 네 명의 친구들이 있다. 한 명은 여기에 있다. 나머지 친구들은 집에 있다.

▶ 남아 있는 것이 하나일 때는 'the other + 단수 명사' 또는 the other로 쓰고, 남아 있는 것이 2개 이상일 경우 'the other + 복수 명사' 또는 the others로 쓴다.

고득점 포인트 '서로'를 의미하는 관용 표현으로 each other, one another가 자주 쓰인다.
Business partners should make an effort to earn each other's trust. 사업 파트너들은 서로의 신뢰를 얻기 위해 노력해야 한다.
Pedestrians on the busy street frequently bump into one another. 바쁜 거리에서 보행자들은 서로 자주 부딪친다.

토익실전문제

출제 포인트 부정대명사/형용사 채우기
부정대명사 another/other/others를 의미와 쓰임에 맞게 구별하여 채우는 문제가 주로 출제된다.

1. Demand for XTD Design's products is so high that the company will launch one line of clothing in January and ------- in April.

(A) each one   (B) one another
(C) other   (D) another

2. Several suppliers agreed to the company's request for discounts, but ------- were unwilling to reduce their products' prices.

(A) other   (B) others
(C) one   (D) both

3. During the orientation for new employees, it was discovered that two of the workers already knew each -------.

(A) one another   (B) other
(C) the other   (D) ones

정답·해설·해석 p.48

01 some은 '몇몇(의), 약간(의)'이라는 의미의 대명사와 형용사로 주로 긍정문에 쓰고, any는 '몇몇(의), 조금(의)'이라는 의미의 대명사와 형용사로 주로 부정문, 의문문, 조건문에 쓴다.

Some of the computers need to be repaired. 컴퓨터들 중 몇 대는 수리될 필요가 있다.

Carl met **some** coworkers at a restaurant. Carl은 몇몇 동료들을 식당에서 만났다.

Some milk was spilled on the counter. 약간의 우유가 조리대 위에 엎질러져 있었다.

The airline staff couldn't find **any** of my luggage. 항공사 직원들은 내 수하물 중 어느 것도 찾을 수 없었다.

Do you have **any** questions about the presentation? 발표에 대해 질문이 조금이라도 있습니까?

If there are **any** problems, please notify the front desk staff. 조금이라도 문제가 있는 경우, 안내 데스크 직원에게 알려주시기 바랍니다.

> **고득점 포인트**
>
> ❶ 권유나 요청을 나타내는 의문문일 경우에 some을 쓴다.
>
> Would you like <u>some</u> coffee? (권유) 커피 좀 드시겠어요? / Can I have <u>some</u> water? (요청) 물 좀 마실 수 있을까요?
>
> ❷ any가 긍정문에 쓰이면 '어떤 ~라도'라는 의미를 갖게 된다.
>
> <u>Any</u> questions will be answered at the end of the presentation. [=If there are any questions]
> 어떤 질문이라도 발표가 끝날 때 답변될 것입니다.
>
> <u>Anyone</u> interested in local history can attend the lecture. 지역 역사에 관심 있는 사람은 누구라도 강의에 참석할 수 있다.
>
> ❸ something, somebody, someone은 some처럼 긍정문에 쓰고, anything, anybody, anyone은 any처럼 부정문, 의문문, 조건문에 쓴다.
>
> There's <u>somebody</u> at the door. 문에 누군가가 있다. / I don't want <u>anything</u> to eat. 아무것도 먹고 싶지 않다.

02 no는 형용사로 뒤에 반드시 명사가 와야 하고, none은 대명사로 혼자 명사 자리에 온다.

As I had **no** money, I paid with my credit card. 나는 현금이 없었기 때문에, 신용카드로 계산했다.

Those files have all been deleted. **None** of them are left. 그 파일들은 모두 삭제되었다. 아무것도 남은 것이 없다.

None of the hotel's rooms were available. 호텔 객실 중 아무것도 이용할 수 없었다.

> **고득점 포인트**
>
> ❶ no one은 'of+사람'의 수식을 받을 수 없지만, not은 a/an이나 one을 앞에서 강조할 수 있다.
>
> No(→Not) one of the guests arrived on time. 손님들 중 아무도 제때 도착하지 않았다.
>
> ❷ nothing은 not anything과 같은 말로, 부정문에 사용되는 anything은 nothing 자리에 올 수 없다.
>
> There is anything(→nothing) I can do about the situation. 그 상황에 대해 내가 할 수 있는 것은 아무것도 없다.

03 most는 '대부분(의)'이라는 의미의 대명사와 형용사로 쓰이고, almost는 '거의'라는 의미의 부사로 쓰인다.

Most of the schools are closed because of weather conditions. 기상 상태 때문에 학교들 대부분이 문을 닫았다.

Most schools are closed because of weather conditions. 기상 상태 때문에 대부분의 학교들이 문을 닫았다.

Almost all the schools are closed because of weather conditions. 기상 상태 때문에 거의 모든 학교들이 문을 닫았다.

토익실전문제

출제 포인트 부정대명사/형용사 채우기

부정대명사로 사용되는 some/any/most를 채우는 문제가 주로 출제된다.

1. ------- of the members of the publishing department are relieved that the deadline for the layout project has been extended.

   (A) No (B) One
   (C) Some (D) Any

2. Having lived in Rome for nearly ten years, Mr. Spencer considers himself ------- of an expert on Italian cuisine.

   (A) something (B) anywhere
   (C) anything (D) somewhere

3. The project approval committee received 40 proposals, ------- of which were related to the transmission of electricity to rural areas.

   (A) most (B) the most
   (C) any (D) almost

정답·해설·해석 p.49

01 대명사는 명사와 수일치되어야 한다. 즉 단수 명사는 단수 대명사로, 복수 명사는 복수 대명사로 받아야 한다.

	단수	복수
인칭대명사	he/his/him, she/her/her, it/its/it	they/their/them
재귀대명사	himself, herself, itself	themselves
지시대명사	this, that	these, those

Politicians should consider the social implications of (~~its~~, **their**) decisions.
정치인들은 그들의 결정이 갖는 사회적 의미를 고려해야 한다.

Mr. Stevens and a few of the tenants attempted to repair the damaged window (~~himself~~, **themselves**).
Mr. Stevens와 세입자들 중 몇몇은 파손된 창문을 직접 수리하려고 시도했다.

Mr. Thompson's office is larger than (~~those~~, **that**) of Mr. O'Neil. Mr. Thompson의 사무실은 Mr. O'Neil의 사무실보다 크다.

고득점 포인트 명사 앞에서 형용사처럼 쓰이는 경우 역시 뒤에 오는 명사와 수일치되어야 하므로 this/that + 단수 명사, these/those + 복수 명사를 쓴다.

these(→this) very well organized summary 이 아주 잘 정리된 요약   this(→these) areas 이 지역들

02 대명사는 명사와 성/인칭이 일치되어야 한다.

Mr. Grady felt so stressed from work that (~~it~~, **he**) decided to take a vacation.
Mr. Grady는 일로부터 스트레스를 너무 많이 받았기 때문에 휴가를 가기로 결정했다.

Ms. Porter and (~~his~~, **her**) son spent the day playing together in the park.
Ms. Porter와 그녀의 아들은 공원에서 함께 놀면서 하루를 보냈다.

Littleton Magazine featured an interview with author George Collins on (~~his~~, **its**) Web site.
Littleton 잡지사는 자사 웹사이트에 작가 George Collins와의 인터뷰를 대서특필했다.

Green Valley College is famous for (~~your~~, **its**) state-of-the-art computer science program.
Green Valley 대학은 최신 컴퓨터 공학 과정으로 유명하다.

토익실전문제

출제 포인트 명사와 수/인칭 일치된 대명사 채우기
명사와 수일치하는 대명사를 선택하여 채우는 문제가 주로 출제된다.

1. The author's latest novel was popular with the general public, and ------- also received praise from several important critics.

(A) they   (B) she
(C) it   (D) we

2. Ms. Davidson called the hotel to double-check whether the room ------- reserved could accommodate four people.

(A) she   (B) that
(C) they   (D) he

3. Ms. Lee instructed the finance committee to submit ------- budget recommendations to the head of accounting for review.

(A) its   (B) his
(C) her   (D) theirs

정답·해설·해석 p.49

둘 중 맞는 형태를 고르세요.

01 All employees are required to submit progress reports to ------- direct supervisors every week.
ⓐ them　　　　　　ⓑ their

02 Jamaica is a popular tourist destination because its beaches are nicer than ------- of nearby countries.
ⓐ that　　　　　　ⓑ those

03 To receive an advance on your wages, you must file ------- request before the end of the month.
ⓐ your　　　　　　ⓑ yours

04 Team leaders must obtain authorization from the manager to assign ------- employee to a project.
ⓐ another　　　　　ⓑ other

05 Jack decided to go to the movie by ------- because all of his friends were busy on the weekend.
ⓐ him　　　　　　ⓑ himself

06 Mr. Edwards believes ------- to be the most suitable candidate for the operations director job.
ⓐ her　　　　　　ⓑ hers

07 ------- documents that were sent by courier this morning should arrive at the Dallas office tomorrow.
ⓐ That　　　　　　ⓑ Those

틀린 곳이 있으면 바르게 고치세요.

08 The tourists went to the information desk, but there wasn't someone there to assist them.

09 The issue is that city workers refuse to reconsider its demand for a 6 percent salary increase.

10 Sunrise Resort offers delicious meals and has our own swimming pool.

11 Even though *Forrest Hills* was not successful at the box office, most film reviewers consider them a masterpiece.

12 Students must register for its classes for the fall semester no later than August 3.

13 We are committed to providing its customers with quality products and excellent service.

14 Ms. Jenson contacted the members of the tour group to notify themselves that the travel itinerary had been changed.

정답·해석 p.49

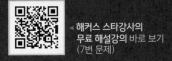
🕐 제한 시간 12분

Part 5

01 Mr. Harrington suggested that Drake Industries may have decided to open several manufacturing plants in Europe to expand ------- production capacity.

(A) its
(B) it
(C) his
(D) he

02 One employee at the company prefers working during fixed hours, while ------- appreciates the flexible working hours system recently installed by the manager.

(A) no
(B) other
(C) neither
(D) another

03 The marketing department has finished its budget for next year, but we in the public relations department haven't completed ------- yet.

(A) us
(B) our
(C) ourselves
(D) ours

04 Mr. Eisenhower was offered a number of positions at the company, ------- of which were exactly what he was looking for.

(A) little
(B) none
(C) much
(D) every

05 The CEO emphasized that the GED Motor Company could not let its current patent dispute with a competitor ------- its reputation with the public.

(A) damage
(B) damaged
(C) to damage
(D) damaging

06 Famous people sometimes make good use of ------- celebrity status by launching product lines.

(A) they
(B) their
(C) them
(D) themselves

07 The assistant accounting manager has not been given ------- authority to release the documents the client is requesting.

(A) other
(B) some
(C) no
(D) any

08 It is the company's policy that the director ------- must abstain from any political involvement while carrying out her official duties.

(A) hers
(B) herself
(C) she
(D) her

09 Employees working on an incentive-based contract are more efficient than ------- who receive a fixed wage or salary.

(A) such
(B) that
(C) those
(D) anyone

10 ------- a single file has been recovered since the office computer server crashed, but fortunately most employees had made backup copies of their work.

(A) No
(B) Any
(C) None
(D) Not

11 One associate remained in the main office with the visiting executives while ------- hurried to gather the printed reports and documents.

(A) other
(B) the other
(C) each other
(D) one another

12 ------- the Web site designers had two or three years of experience in graphic design before working for Windermere Studios.

(A) Most
(B) Most of
(C) Almost
(D) Some

13 Companies which donate a certain portion of ------- earnings to charitable organizations often develop a positive public image.

(A) its
(B) their
(C) it
(D) them

14 The financial consultant recommended a salary freeze to reduce costs, but ------- suggestion was rejected by the board of directors.

(A) that
(B) those
(C) they
(D) its

15 If any employee wishes to take more than one day off, a superior will have to be ------- at least one week in advance.

(A) inform   (B) information
(C) informing   (D) informed

16 The two companies agreed to reveal research findings only to -------, and not to publicly release the results or involve a third party.

(A) another   (B) the other
(C) ones   (D) each other

17 ------- determined to qualify for managerial positions at the firm must make an effort to develop leadership skills.

(A) They   (B) That
(C) Those   (D) No one

18 The finance expert received the proposals and will now read through ------- before determining which one will best suit the company's interests.

(A) it   (B) them
(C) theirs   (D) ours

Part 6

Questions 19-22 refer to the following letter.

November 4
Eileen Rivera
213 West 35th Street, Suite 1301
New York, NY 10001

Dear Ms. Rivera,

We received your draft and would like to thank you for your interest in having our firm publish it. We ------- your creativity and talent and are very excited about working with you.
　　　19

Prior to the actual publication, however, an overall review of your source materials -------. In this
　　20
regard, may we ask you to provide us with a list of the references used in your writing? This

procedure is mandatory in order to prevent any plagiarism issues. -------. Please note that the reason
　　　　　　　　　　　　　　　　　　　　　　　　　　　　　　　　　21
we ask this of you has nothing to do with your work specifically. This is something we ask of all

writers whose work we publish. We look forward to hearing from -------.
　　　　　　　　　　　　　　　　　　　　　　　　　　　　22

Sincerely yours,
Bill Patterson, Director of Publishing

---

19 (A) appreciate   (B) assure
   (C) address   (D) anticipate

20 (A) will be held   (B) is held
   (C) has been held   (D) was held

21 (A) It is unfortunate that we are unable to accept your work.
   (B) We hope you understand and will comply with our request.
   (C) Your document has been forwarded as requested.
   (D) The company is looking for unpublished writers.

22 (A) them   (B) her
   (C) him   (D) you

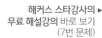

해커스 스타강사의 ▶
무료 해설강의 바로 보기
(7번 문제)

정답·해설·해석 p.49 / [별책] 토익 RC 필수 어휘 p.14

CHAPTER

12

형용사

토익, 이렇게 나온다!

형용사 관련 문제는 평균 2~3문제 정도 꾸준히 출제되며 최대 5문제까지 출제된다. 명사를 수식하는 자리에 형용사를 채우는 문제가 가장 많이 출제되며, 가산/불가산 명사 앞에 알맞은 수량 표현을 채우는 문제도 가끔 출제된다.

토익 필수 개념 다지기

01 형용사는 명사의 성질이나 상태를 한정하거나 설명해 준다.

I like **short** hair. 나는 짧은 머리를 좋아한다.
This book is **very old**. 이 책은 매우 낡았다.

첫 문장은 여러 종류의 머리 스타일 중에서 짧은 머리를 좋아한다는 의미로, short라는 형용사가 명사 hair의 종류를 한정해 주고 있다. 이와 조금 다르게, 두 번째 문장의 old는 명사 book의 상태를 설명해 주고 있다.

02 형용사는 대개 -able, -al, -ible, -ic, -tive, -ous, -ful, -y로 끝난다.

advisable	formal	responsible	specific
effective	previous	successful	heavy

-ly로 끝나는 형용사도 있으며, 이 형용사를 부사로 혼동하지 않도록 해야 한다.

lively 활기 있는   costly 값비싼   deadly 치명적인   friendly 친절한

-ing(현재분사) 또는 -ed(과거분사)로 끝나는 분사가 형용사로 굳어져 쓰이기도 한다.

challenging 어려운	demanding 힘든	promising 유망한	leading 선두에 있는
complicated 복잡한	dedicated 전념하는	detailed 상세한	qualified 자격 있는

01 형용사는 명사를 수식하는 자리에 온다.

- (관사) + (부사) + 형용사 + 명사

Travelers will receive the **final** confirmation for their trip on Monday.
여행자들은 월요일에 여행에 대한 최종 확인을 받을 것이다.

The surprisingly **suspenseful** film has proven popular with moviegoers.
그 놀랄 만큼 긴장감 넘치는 영화는 영화 팬들에게 인기 있음이 입증되었다.

- 형용사 + 복합 명사(명사 + 명사)

John was praised for his **incredible** job performance during the advertising campaign.
John은 광고 캠페인 동안 굉장한 업무 성과로 칭찬받았다.

- 명사 + 형용사

The bank makes every effort **possible** to ensure the safety of the cashiers.
그 은행은 출납원들의 안전을 보장하기 위해 가능한 모든 노력을 기울인다.

> **고득점 포인트** 주로 -able/-ible로 끝나는 형용사(available, possible 등)들이 명사를 뒤에서 수식한다.
> The apartments available in New York City are incredibly expensive. 뉴욕시의 입주 가능한 아파트들은 엄청나게 비싸다.

02 형용사는 보어 자리에 온다.

주격 보어 자리   It is **necessary** to be **imaginative** when writing children's literature.
아동 문학을 쓸 때 상상력이 풍부한 것은 필수적이다.

목적격 보어 자리   Natural fibers make clothes **comfortable**. 천연 섬유는 의복을 편하게 만들어 준다.

03 형용사 자리에 부사나 명사는 올 수 없다.

People can become overweight because of a (~~poorly~~, **poor**) diet. 사람들은 나쁜 식습관 때문에 과체중이 될 수 있다.

▶ 명사(diet)를 꾸며 주기 위해서는 부사(poorly)가 아닌 형용사(poor)가 와야 한다.

An advertisement was posted for a (~~qualification~~, **qualified**) safety inspector.
자격을 갖춘 안전 검사관을 구하는 광고가 게시되었다.

▶ 복합 명사(safety inspector)를 꾸며 주기 위해서는 명사(qualification)가 아닌 형용사(qualified)가 와야 한다.

토익실전문제

출제 포인트 형용사 자리 채우기
명사를 수식하는 자리와 주격 보어 자리에 형용사를 채우는 문제가 주로 출제된다.

1. Commercial banks are advised to take ------- action to deal with the serious currency shortfall.

(A) directness   (B) direction
(C) directly   (D) direct

2. The ------- installation instructions in the manual make it simple to set up the machine for use.

(A) easy   (B) eased
(C) easily   (D) easing

3. Workers in general are much less ------- during the day if they haven't had sufficient sleep.

(A) productive   (B) production
(C) productively   (D) productiveness

정답·해설·해석 p.51

01 가산 명사·불가산 명사 앞에 오는 수량 표현

가산 명사 앞			불가산 명사 앞	가산·불가산 명사 모두의 앞
단수 명사	**복수 명사**			
a/an 하나의	one of ~ 중 하나	each of ~의 각각	(a) little 적은	no 어떤 ~도 ~ 아니다 · all 모든
each 각각의	(a) few 몇 개의	fewer 더 적은	less 더 적은	more 더 많은 · most 대부분의
one 하나의	both 둘 다의	many 많은	much 많은	some 몇몇의, 어떤 · any 어떤
every 모든	several 여러 개의	numerous 많은	a great deal of 많은	lots of 많은 · a lot of 많은
another 또 다른	various 다양한	a variety of 다양한	a large amount of 많은	plenty of 많은 · other 다른
a single 하나의	a couple of 몇몇의	a number of 많은		a wealth of 수많은, 풍부한
	a majority of 대부분의	a (wide) range of 다양한		

(Much, Many) <u>students</u> live in dormitories on campus. 많은 학생들이 교내에 있는 기숙사에 산다.
▶ students는 가산 명사이므로, 불가산 명사 앞에 오는 수량 표현(Much)이 아니라 가산 명사 앞에 오는 수량 표현(Many)이 와야 한다.

Customers were provided with **(few, little)** <u>assistance</u> by the clerk. 고객들은 그 점원에게 거의 도움을 받지 못했다.
▶ assistance는 불가산 명사이므로, 가산 명사 앞에 오는 수량 표현(few)이 아니라 불가산 명사 앞에 오는 수량 표현(little)이 와야 한다.

고득점 포인트

❶ 단, all, more, most, lots of, a lot of, plenty of, other, a wealth of는 가산 명사와 쓰일 때 복수 명사 앞에만 올 수 있다.
All ticket(→tickets) are nonrefundable. 모든 티켓은 환불되지 않습니다.

❷ another와 every는 'few/숫자 + 복수 명사' 앞에도 올 수 있다. 이때 뒤에 온 'few/숫자 + 복수 명사'는 한 단위로 취급되며, another는 '(~만큼) 더', every는 매 (~만큼)마다'라는 의미이다.
Ms. Choi was informed that she could upgrade to business class for another <u>100 dollars</u>.
Ms. Choi는 100달러를 더 내면 비즈니스석으로 업그레이드할 수 있음을 알게 되었다.

02 수량 표현과 명사 사이에 of the가 와서 한정된 명사의 부분이나 전체를 나타내는 경우, of와 the는 하나라도 빠질 수 없다.

one/two	each	all	both	none
many	much	most		several + of the + 명사
some	any	(a) few		(a) little

Some **(of, the, of the)** equipment in the factory is very out-of-date. 공장에 있는 장비 중 일부는 매우 낡았다.
▶ 수량 표현(Some)과 명사(equipment) 사이에는 of나 the 중 하나만은 올 수 없고, of와 the가 모두 와야 한다.

고득점 포인트

❶ 예외적으로 all과 both는 of 없이 쓰일 수 있다.
All (of) the employees planning to work overtime must notify their supervisors in advance.
초과 근무를 계획하는 모든 직원들은 미리 그들의 관리자에게 알려야 한다.

❷ 명사 앞의 the 대신에 소유격이 올 수 있다.
All of <u>our</u> instructors have master's degrees. 우리 강사들 모두는 석사 학위를 가지고 있다.

❸ many는 'of the + 명사' 없이 쓰일 수 있다. 이때 many는 부정대명사이며 '다수(의 사람)'라는 의미이다.
<u>Many</u> did not attend the meeting due to the stormy weather. 다수의 사람들이 험한 날씨 때문에 회의에 참석하지 않았다.

토익실전문제

출제 포인트 명사에 맞는 수량 표현 채우기
가산 명사 앞이나 불가산 명사 앞에 알맞은 수량 표현을 구별하여 채우는 문제가 출제된다.

1. ------- order that comes to the shipping department is processed with the utmost care and attention.

   (A) Many　　　　　(B) Some
   (C) Every　　　　　(D) More

2. Rumors that the new government regulations would create instability in the financial market resulted in ------- anxiety among investors.

   (A) much　　　　　(B) many
   (C) mostly　　　　(D) almost

3. Customers who have used Ceylon Cosmetics' new hand cream give it rave reviews because of the product's ------- benefits.

   (A) each　　　　　(B) a lot
   (C) many　　　　　(D) some of

정답·해설·해석 p.52

01 형태가 비슷하지만 의미가 달라 혼동을 주는 형용사들을 주의해야 한다.

acceptable 받아들일만한, 만족스러운 – accepting 흔쾌히 받아들이는	informed 정통한, 알고 있는, 정보에 입각한 – informative 유익한
admirable 칭찬할만한, 훌륭한 – admiring 감탄하는	managerial 경영의 – manageable 관리할 수 있는
appreciative 감사하는, 감사의 – appreciable 상당한	persuasive 설득력 있는 – persuaded 확신하고 있는
argumentative 논쟁적인, 논쟁을 좋아하는 – arguable 논박할 수 있는	practical 실제적인, 현실적인 – practicing 활동하고 있는, 개업 중인
beneficial 유익한 – beneficent 인정 많은	probable 유망한, 확실한 – probabilistic 가능성에 근거한
careful 세심한, 조심스러운 – caring 보살피는	profitable 유리한, 이익이 있는 – proficient 능숙한
considerable 상당한, 중요한 – considerate 사려 깊은	prospective 장래의 – prosperous 번영하는
comparable 필적할 만한 – comparative 비교의	reliable 믿을 수 있는 – reliant 의지하는
comprehensible 이해할 수 있는 – comprehensive 포괄/종합적인	respectable 존경할 만한 – respective 각자의
dependent ~에 좌우되는, 의존적인 – dependable 믿을 수 있는	responsible 책임이 있는, 믿을 수 있는 – responsive 민감하게 반응하는
economic 경제의 – economical 경제적인, 절약하는	seasonal 계절적인 – seasoned 경험이 많은
exhaustive 철저한, 완전한 – exhausted 기진맥진한, 탈진한	successful 성공한, 성공의 – successive 연속의, 상속의
favorable 호의적인 – favorite 가장 좋아하는	understanding 이해심 있는 – understandable 이해할 만한
impressive 인상적인 – impressed 감명받은	

Professor William received a gift from his (~~appreciable~~, **appreciative**) students.
William 교수는 그에게 감사하는 학생들로부터 선물을 받았다.
▶ '감사하는 학생들'이라는 의미이므로, appreciable(상당한)이 아닌 appreciative가 와야 한다.

It is vital to keep staff (~~informative~~, **informed**) about any scheduling changes.
어떤 일정 변경에 대해서든 직원들이 계속 알고 있도록 하는 것은 필수적이다.
▶ '알고 있는'이라는 의미이므로, informative(유익한)가 아닌 informed가 와야 한다.

Coworkers should avoid being (~~arguable~~, **argumentative**) when they disagree with each other.
함께 일하는 직원들은 서로 의견이 다를 때 논쟁적이지 않도록 해야 한다.
▶ '논쟁적인'이라는 의미이므로, arguable(논박할 수 있는)이 아닌 argumentative가 와야 한다.

(~~Caring~~, **Careful**) packing of items is essential in order to prevent product damage.
제품 손상을 방지하기 위해 물품의 세심한 포장은 필수적이다.
▶ '세심한 포장'이라는 의미이므로, Caring(보살피는)이 아닌 Careful이 와야 한다.

(~~Manageable~~, **Managerial**) experience is a requirement for the marketing director position.
경영 경험은 마케팅 부장직의 필수 요건이다.
▶ '경영 경험'이라는 의미이므로, Manageable(관리할 수 있는)이 아닌 Managerial이 와야 한다.

토익실전문제

출제 포인트 형용사 자리 채우기, 문맥에 어울리는 형용사 채우기
형용사 자리에 올 수 없는 품사(명사, 부사)를 제외한 후, 혼동을 주는 형용사를 의미적으로 구별하여 채우는 문제가 출제된다.

1. Prior to the start of the project, Mr. Hanks exerted ------- effort to determine the feasibility of the construction plan.

   (A) considers   (B) considerate
   (C) considerable   (D) considerably

2. The cost of a product remains ------- upon the price of the raw materials used during the manufacturing process.

   (A) dependable   (B) depends
   (C) dependent   (D) dependably

3. Stunned by the ------- performance of the violinist, the music critic was at a loss for words when he sat down to write a review of the show.

   (A) impresses   (B) impressed
   (C) impression   (D) impressive

정답·해설·해석 p.52

01 형용사는 be동사 다음에 와서 다음과 같은 관용 표현으로 쓰인다.

표현	예문
be about to do 막 ~하려고 하다	Passengers are asked to go to Gate 23 as the flight **is about to** depart. <small>비행편이 막 출발하려고 하므로 탑승객들은 23번 탑승구로 갈 것이 요구된다.</small>
be likely to do = be apt to do = be liable to + 명사/to do ~할 것 같다	The birth rate **is likely to** increase once the new family policy is implemented. <small>새로운 가족 정책이 시행되면 출산율이 상승할 것 같다.</small>
be available to do ~할 수 있다	The technician said he **was available to** repair the copier tomorrow morning. <small>그 기술자는 복사기를 내일 오전에 수리할 수 있다고 말했다.</small>
be available for ~이 가능하다	I **am** generally **available for** consultations on weekday mornings. <small>저는 보통 주중 오전에 상담이 가능합니다.</small>
be aware of = be conscious of = be cognizant of ~을 알고 있다	Drivers need to **be aware of** the icy conditions on Highway 9. <small>운전자들은 9번 고속도로의 빙판 상황을 알고 있어야 합니다.</small>
be capable of -ing ~할 능력이 있다	Mr. Ryan **is capable of** leading a team of staff members. <small>Mr. Ryan은 팀을 이끌 능력이 있다.</small>
be comparable to + 명사 ~에 필적하다	Job vacancy statistics for this year **are comparable to** rates recorded over the past two years. <small>올해의 일자리 통계는 지난 2년 동안의 비율에 필적한다. (비율과 엇비슷하다)</small>
be consistent with ~와 일치되다	The construction plans need to **be consistent with** government building regulations. <small>건설 계획은 정부의 건축 규정과 일치되어야 한다.</small>
be eligible for/to do ~할 자격이 있다	Only full-time staff **are eligible for** the 25 percent employee discount. <small>정규직 근로자만이 25퍼센트 직원 할인을 받을 자격이 있다.</small>
be responsible for ~에 책임이 있다	Tom Colton **was responsible for** distributing the flyers. <small>Tom Colton은 전단지를 배포하는 것에 책임이 있었다.</small>
be skilled in/at ~에 능력이 있다	Applicants who **are skilled in** copyediting are preferred for the job. <small>교정 작업에 능력이 있는 지원자가 그 일에 선호된다.</small>
be subject to + 명사 ~되다/되기 쉽다	The itinerary may **be subject to** change. <small>여행 일정표는 변경될 수 있다.</small>
cf) be subjective to + 명사 ~에 따라 다르다/주관적이다	cf) Success **is subjective to** the individual. <small>성공은 개인에 따라 다르다.</small>
be willing to do 기꺼이 ~하다	Rachel **is willing to** contact companies concerning corporate sponsorship. <small>Rachel은 기업 후원에 관한 것이라면 기꺼이 회사들과 연락한다.</small>
be bound to 틀림없이 ~할 것이다	Real estate prices **are bound to** rise. <small>부동산 가격이 틀림없이 오를 것이다.</small>

토익실전문제

출제 포인트 형용사 관용 표현 채우기
혼동을 주는 두 형용사를 구별하여 관용 표현을 완성하는 문제가 주로 출제된다.

1. Given the recent trends in stocks and bonds, the market is ------- to drop by 2 percent over the next quarter.

   (A) like   (B) alike
   (C) likely   (D) likelihood

2. Unless the proof of age requirement is satisfied, application for membership to the online shopping club is ------- to rejection.

   (A) subject   (B) subjectively
   (C) subjective   (D) subjecting

3. Citizens are not ------- to receive a government pension until they have reached the mandatory retirement age.

   (A) eligibility   (B) eligibleness
   (C) eligible   (D) eligibly

정답·해설·해석 p.52

HACKERS PRACTICE 토익 고득점을 위한 필수 연습

둘 중 맞는 형태를 고르세요.

01 The pilot turned the seatbelt sign on, so the passengers returned to their ------- seats.
ⓐ respective   ⓑ respectable

02 David Williams didn't get good grades at Brookstone College for five ------- semesters.
ⓐ successful   ⓑ successive

03 Mr. Walton reads the newspaper ------- day while having breakfast.
ⓐ every   ⓑ several

04 In general, this year's gross output is ------- to that of the previous three years.
ⓐ comparative   ⓑ comparable

05 The agent asked for the ------- schedule for Mr. Kang's upcoming business trip.
ⓐ revised   ⓑ revision

06 Because there is so ------- traffic during rush hour, commuters are often on the road for hours.
ⓐ many   ⓑ much

07 It was incredibly ------- of the director to give the workers extra vacation time this holiday season.
ⓐ considerable   ⓑ considerate

틀린 곳이 있으면 바르게 고치세요.

08 The economical recession has affected public spending.

09 The government asked contractors to bid for the construction of a newly stadium for the Olympics.

10 Please be awareness of the policy that our hotel does not accept debit cards.

11 According to the reporter, Ogden Bank is like to expand its operations next quarter.

12 Difference issues were discussed during the last board meeting.

13 Dr. Menkin is an understandable physician who treats his patients with care and concern.

14 The goal of the chamber of commerce is to give assistance to regionally businesses.

정답·해석 p.52

무료 해설 ▶
바로 보기

맞은 문제 개수: / 14
틀린 문제에 해당하는 토익 공식을 다시 한번 학습하세요.

해커스 스타강사의
무료 해설강의 바로 보기
(14번 문제)

🕐 제한 시간 12분

Part 5

01 Mr. Jefferson is considered a good negotiator because he offers ------- solutions in a way that people find appealing.

(A) innovates
(B) innovator
(C) innovative
(D) innovation

02 Coleridge Limited has called in a number of competent ------- consultants to ask their opinions about the proposed merger.

(A) legalize
(B) legal
(C) legalized
(D) legally

03 Brokers must provide clients with information that is completely ------- so that they are able to make wise investment decisions.

(A) reliability
(B) reliable
(C) reliant
(D) relied

04 Until the marketing director receives ------- details about a product, he is unwilling to make any recommendations about an advertising strategy.

(A) mostly
(B) a lot
(C) quite
(D) more

05 Before the technician updates the software on all office computers, the office ------- will notify staff of the schedule via e-mail.

(A) supervision
(B) supervise
(C) supervising
(D) supervisor

06 The conference organizers sent a letter stating that attendees are ------- for arranging their own accommodations.

(A) responsibly
(B) responsible
(C) responsibility
(D) responsive

07 The creation of the award-winning logo design was the result of a ------- effort by several members of the graphics team.

(A) collect
(B) collects
(C) collective
(D) collecting

08 The employees were ------- with the instructions given by a Ministry of Health representative during an inspection of the factory's facilities.

(A) comply
(B) compliant
(C) complies
(D) compliancy

09 The survey demonstrates that ------- small business owners are dissatisfied with the government's efforts to reform the tax code.

(A) the most
(B) almost
(C) most of
(D) most

10 James Davis stated in the interview that writing his critically acclaimed novel was a demanding ------- process that lasted for over three years.

(A) creative
(B) created
(C) creates
(D) creatively

11 The manufacturer's most recent line of luggage is ------- to people who travel often for business, as it was created with their needs in mind.

(A) attracted
(B) attractive
(C) attraction
(D) attractively

12 The new social networking service allows registered users to post content on a ------- Web site that can be viewed by friends and family.

(A) personalize
(B) personally
(C) personalized
(D) personalization

13 Although the ------- reason for the company's declining market share has not been determined, it is likely that increased competition is a factor.

(A) specific
(B) specifics
(C) specified
(D) specifically

14 Every method ------- will be considered in the company's attempt to increase its share of the women's apparel market.

(A) availability
(B) available
(C) availabilities
(D) availably

15 The ------- design of the new laptop appeals to many consumers, as it includes a larger screen and a more powerful processor.

(A) improve   (B) improving
(C) improved   (D) improvement

16 Taking the annual inventory should be ------- trouble than it was last year because management has come up with a detailed plan.

(A) fewer   (B) least
(C) few   (D) less

17 ------- report, written by Ms. Sanders, includes a thorough comparison of the financial performance of each of the company's overseas branches.

(A) This   (B) Who
(C) These   (D) Whom

18 At the party, a number of Jack's newspaper colleagues congratulated him on winning an award for a very ------- story about the effects of global warming.

(A) succeed   (B) successive
(C) succeeded   (D) successful

Part 6

Questions 19-22 refer to the following e-mail.

To: Janet Burke
From: Pat Summers, Human resources department administrator

Dear Ms. Burke,

We would like to inform you that your request to transfer to our overseas branch in Berlin, Germany has been -------. We plan to visit the German embassy by June 4 to apply for your work visa, so you must submit the documents ------- in the attached file as soon as possible.

Prior to your relocation, you will need to complete an intensive course in the German language as well as a program on cross-cultural coping skills. Afterward, you will attend orientation training at the Berlin branch. -------. We have every confidence that these sessions will prove very helpful.

While you are undergoing training, you will stay ------- in your current position as public relations assistant until we find a replacement, which should be within three or four weeks.

If you have any questions about your new appointment, please get in touch with me.

Sincerely,
Pat Summers

19 (A) received   (B) added
(C) declined   (D) approved

20 (A) specifies   (B) specifying
(C) specified   (D) are specified

21 (A) Please submit the curriculum you designed before the course starts.
(B) These programs should familiarize you with your new surroundings.
(C) You should train the person replacing you.
(D) We are certain you have fully adapted to the branch.

22 (A) action   (B) acted
(C) active   (D) activity

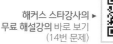
해커스 스타강사의 ▶
무료 해설강의 바로 보기
(14번 문제)

CHAPTER 13

부사

토익, 이렇게 나온다!

부사 관련 문제는 평균 4문제 정도 꾸준히 출제되며 최대 6문제까지 출제된다. 동사나 준동사를 수식하는 자리에 부사를 채우는 문제가 가장 많이 출제되며, 문맥에 알맞은 접속부사를 채우는 문제도 자주 출제된다.

토익 필수 개념 다지기

01 부사는 명사를 제외한 나머지 품사들, 즉 형용사, 부사, 동사 및 준동사(to 부정사, 동명사, 분사)를 꾸며 주거나, 구, 절, 문장 전체를 꾸며 주는 역할을 한다.

형용사 수식   The musical was **really** interesting. 그 뮤지컬은 정말 재미있었다.

다른 부사 수식   He finished his work **very** quickly. 그는 그의 일을 매우 빨리 끝냈다.

동사 수식   Kyle **cautiously** crossed the busy street. Kyle은 번잡한 거리를 조심스럽게 건넜다.

to 부정사 수식   Employees are expected to arrive **promptly** at 9:00 A.M.
                 직원들은 오전 9시에 시간을 엄수하여 도착할 것으로 기대된다.

동명사 수식   Talking **loudly** is not permitted in the library. 시끄럽게 떠드는 것은 도서관 내에서 허용되지 않는다.

분사 수식   The **brightly** painted house is mine. 선명하게 페인트칠 된 집이 내 집이다.

구 수식   I exercise **early** in the morning. 나는 아침 일찍 운동한다.

절 수식   I finished the interview **just** before the meeting started.
                 나는 회의가 시작되기 직전에 면접을 끝마쳤다.

문장 전체 수식   **Frequently**, I eat lunch at my desk. 종종, 나는 내 책상에서 점심을 먹는다.

02 부사는 주로 '형용사 + ly'의 형태를 가진다.

calmly, completely, entirely, heavily, temporarily와 같이 대개의 부사는 -ly로 끝난다.
그러나 ahead, just, only, still, well과 같이 -ly로 끝나지 않는 형태의 부사도 있다.

costly, elderly, friendly, silly, ugly, worldly와 같이 -ly로 끝나는 형용사들을 부사로 혼동하지 않도록 주의해야 한다.

Mary gave me a **costly** present. Mary는 나에게 값비싼 선물을 주었다.

토익 공식 1 부사 자리

01 부사가 동사를 수식하는 경우는 [(준)동사 + 목적어] 앞이나 뒤, [조동사 + -ing/p.p.] 사이 또는 그 뒤에 온다.

- 부사는 [(준)동사 + 목적어] 앞이나 뒤에 오며, (준)동사와 목적어 사이에는 오지 못한다.
  Ms. Newton **politely** asked her supervisor for an opinion. Ms. Newton은 그녀의 관리자에게 의견을 정중히 요청했다.
  The company managers want to increase ~~significantly~~ revenue **significantly**.
  그 회사의 관리자들은 수입을 많이 늘리고 싶어 한다.

- 진행, 수동, 완료형 동사의 경우, 부사는 [조동사 + -ing/p.p.] 사이 또는 그 뒤에 온다.
  Mr. Edwards is **still** deliberating about the brochure layout. Mr. Edwards는 안내 책자 지면 배치에 대해 여전히 심사숙고 중이다.
  The new security system has been **thoroughly** tested. 새 보안 시스템은 철저히 검사되었다.
  Ms. Pearson is seeing clients **frequently** these days. Ms. Pearson은 요즘 고객들을 자주 만나고 있다.

02 부사가 동사 이외의 것을 수식하는 경우는 수식받는 것 앞에 온다.

The CEO needs a **meticulously** researched report on labor costs.
그 최고 경영자는 노동 비용에 대해 꼼꼼하게 조사된 보고서가 필요하다.
This is the most **recently** acquired data on consumer trends. 이것은 가장 최근에 입수된 소비 경향 관련 자료이다.
He finished his work **extremely** quickly. 그는 일을 매우 빠르게 끝마쳤다.
The updated software is available **only** in North America. 그 최신 소프트웨어는 오직 북미에서만 구할 수 있다.

> **고득점 포인트** 형용사 역할을 하는 '수 표현'을 앞에서 수식할 수 있는 것도 형용사가 아닌 부사이다.
> Rough(→Roughly) 200 biologists will attend the genetics conference. 대략 200명의 생물학자들이 유전학 학회에 참석할 것이다.

03 부사 자리에 형용사는 올 수 없다.

The election was reported (**different**, **differently**) by each newspaper. 선거는 각 신문에 의해 다르게 보도되었다.
▶ 동사(was reported)를 수식하기 위해서는 형용사(different)가 아닌, 부사(differently)가 와야 한다.

Mark built the new porch (**complete**, **completely**) on his own. Mark는 새 현관을 순전히 혼자 힘으로 만들었다.
▶ 구(on his own)를 수식하기 위해서는 형용사(complete)가 아닌, 부사(completely)가 와야 한다.

> **고득점 포인트**
> ❶ '형용사 + 명사' 앞에 부사가 아닌 형용사가 오기도 하며, 이때, 형용사는 명사를 수식한다. '형용사 + 명사' 앞에 형용사 혹은 부사를 쓸지는 문맥에 따라 결정된다.
> The severe tropical storm caused extensive damage to the city. 극심한 열대 폭풍은 그 도시에 막대한 피해를 초래했다.
> The doctor provided medical treatment to the severely injured man. 그 의사는 심각하게 다친 남자에게 의학적 치료를 제공했다.
>
> ❷ 원급 구문에서 as ~ as 사이에 형용사 혹은 부사가 올 것인지는 as ~ as −를 지우고 선택한다.
> The room was as warmly as a sauna.(×) → The room was warmly(→warm). 그 방은 사우나처럼 따뜻했다.
> I greeted her as warm as possible.(×) → I greeted her warm(→warmly). 나는 그녀를 가능한 한 따뜻하게 맞이했다.

토익실전문제

출제 포인트 부사 자리 채우기
동사나 준동사를 수식하는 자리에 부사를 넣는 문제가 주로 출제된다.

1. A surveyor's inspection shows that the building may be ------- unsound due to the use of substandard materials during construction.

   (A) structurally   (B) structure
   (C) structured   (D) structural

2. Recent advances in telecommunications have made it possible for mobile phone owners to ------- access a wide range of digital media content.

   (A) free   (B) freer
   (C) freest   (D) freely

3. Mr. Ling was hired ------- after being interviewed for the managerial position at the Boston branch of Inglewood Financial.

   (A) short   (B) shorter
   (C) shortly   (D) shorten

정답·해설·해석 p.55

01 형태가 비슷하지만 의미가 다른 부사들을 주의해야 한다.

부 사	예 문
hard 열심히, 힘들게	Students who study **hard** tend to receive high scores on tests. 열심히 공부하는 학생들은 시험에서 높은 점수를 받는 경향이 있다.
hardly 거의 ~않다	I have **hardly** enough money to pay the bill. 나는 요금을 내기에 거의 충분하지 않은 돈을 갖고 있다.
high (높이·목표) 높게	The plane soared **high** into the sky. 그 비행기는 하늘 높이 날아올랐다.
highly (위상·평가·금액) 높게/매우	Mr. Jones thinks **highly** of his personal assistant. Mr. Jones는 그의 개인 비서를 높게 평가한다. Eating fresh fruits and vegetables is a diet **highly** recommended by all doctors. 신선한 과일과 야채를 먹는 것은 모든 의사들에 의해 매우 추천되는 식이 요법이다.
great 잘	The CEO thought that Janice did **great** on her first sales presentation. 그 최고 경영자는 Janice가 그녀의 첫 제품 소개를 잘했다고 생각했다.
greatly 매우	Ms. Lopez was **greatly** impressed by the dishes served at the wedding. Ms. Lopez는 결혼식에서 제공된 요리들에 매우 감명받았다.
late 늦게	Passengers were annoyed that the shuttle bus departed **late** from the airport. 탑승객들은 셔틀버스가 공항에서 늦게 출발한 것에 화가 났다.
lately 최근에	Due to her hectic work schedule, Shannon hasn't taken a vacation **lately**. 몹시 바쁜 업무 일정 때문에, Shannon은 최근에 휴가를 갖지 못해 왔다.
most 가장 많이/매우	The cost of the office renovations worries Mr. Park **most**. 사무실 수리 비용이 Mr. Park을 가장 많이 걱정하게 한다.
mostly 대체로/주로	Greg is **mostly** satisfied with his job, although he wants a pay raise. Greg은 임금 인상을 원하지만, 대체로 그의 직업에 만족한다.
near 가까이	The company's 15th anniversary is coming **near**. 그 회사의 15주년 창립 기념일이 가까이 다가오고 있다.
nearly 거의(= almost)	The game was **nearly** over when a player was injured. 한 선수가 다쳤을 때 경기는 거의 종료되었다.

고득점 포인트 한 단어가 형용사와 부사의 의미를 모두 가지는 경우도 있다.

early 웹 이른, 조기의 뷔 일찍	late 웹 늦은 뷔 늦게	hard 웹 힘든, 단단한 뷔 열심히, 힘들게	high 웹 높은 뷔 높게
long 웹 오랜 뷔 오래	fast 웹 빠른 뷔 빨리	far 웹 먼 뷔 멀리	near 웹 가까운 뷔 가까이
daily 웹 매일(의) 뷔 매일	weekly 웹 매주(의) 뷔 매주	monthly 웹 매달(의) 뷔 매달	yearly 웹 매년(의) 뷔 매년
enough 웹 충분한, 필요한 만큼의 뷔 충분히, 필요한 만큼	likely 웹 ~할 것 같은 뷔 아마		

형용사 　 Mr. Crosby has been criticizing the company making <u>early</u> decisions on downsizing.
　　　　　Mr. Crosby는 인원 삭감에 대해 이른 결정을 내린 그 회사를 비난해 왔다.

부사 　　 The technician came to the office <u>early</u> to work on the wireless Internet connection.
　　　　　그 기술자는 무선 인터넷 연결을 작업하기 위해 사무실에 일찍 왔다.

토익실전문제

출제 포인트 의미에 맞는 부사 채우기
형태가 비슷하지만 의미가 다른 부사를 구별하여 채우는 문제가 주로 출제
된다.

1. The manager sent a memo commending those
who met the deadline and admonishing those who
submitted their reports one or two days -------.

(A) lately 　　　　　　(B) lateness
(C) latest 　　　　　　 (D) late

2. Prices of basic commodities such as rice and corn
have risen ------- 13 percent since January.

(A) nearly 　　　　　　(B) near
(C) neared 　　　　　　(D) nearer

3. The musicians practice ------- in order to make it a
point to be thoroughly familiar with the musical pieces
they are playing before a performance.

(A) hardly 　　　　　　(B) harden
(C) hard 　　　　　　　(D) hardening

정답·해설·해석 p.55

부사 선택 1 : 시간 부사 already/still/yet, ever/ago/once

01 already/still/yet

• already는 '이미, 벌써'(긍정문)라는 뜻으로 쓰인다.
  The director has **already** approved the new logo design. 그 이사는 새로운 로고 디자인을 이미 승인했다.

• still은 '아직, 여전히'(긍정문, 부정문, 의문문)라는 뜻으로 쓰인다.
  Senator Bedford is **still** considering whether to run for reelection.
  Bedford 상원 의원은 재선에 출마할지 여부를 아직 고려 중이다.

• yet은 '아직'(부정문), '이미, 벌써'(의문문)라는 뜻으로 예상하고 있는 일이 일어났는지를 물을 때 쓰인다.
  Has the schedule been posted **yet**? 일정이 이미 게시되었습니까?

> **고득점 포인트**
>
> ❶ 부정문에서 still과 yet은 모두 '아직'을 의미하지만, still이 not 앞에 오는 반면 yet은 not 뒤에 온다.
>   The title of the book is <u>still</u> <u>not</u> decided. 그 책의 제목은 아직 정해지지 않았다.
>   The blueprints haven't been submitted <u>yet</u>. 그 청사진은 아직 제출되지 않았다.
>
> ❷ have yet to + 동사원형: 아직 ~하지 못했다
>   The students <u>have yet to</u> turn in their term papers. 학생들은 학기말 과제물을 아직 제출하지 못했다.
>
> ❸ finally(마침내, 결국)는 오랫동안 기다리던 일이 일어났을 때 쓰인다.
>   Softek has <u>finally</u> released an English version of its video game. Softek사는 마침내 그들의 비디오 게임의 영어 버전을 출시했다.
>
> ❹ soon(곧)은 얼마 지나지 않아 일이 일어날 예정이거나 일어났을 때 쓰인다.
>   The committee's recommendations will be announced <u>soon</u> to the employees.
>   위원회의 권고 사항이 직원들에게 곧 발표될 것이다.

02 ever/ago/once(이전에)

• ever는 막연한 과거의 시점을 나타낼 때 쓰이며, 부정문이나 의문문에 온다.
  Kevin rarely **ever** participated in extracurricular activities at school. Kevin은 학교에서 과외 활동에 거의 참여하지 않았다.

• ago는 시간 바로 다음에 와서, 현재를 기준으로 그 시간 이전에 일어난 일을 나타낸다.
  The manufacturing facility was inspected just <u>a month</u> **ago**. 그 제조 시설은 바로 한 달 전에 점검받았다.

• once는 막연한 과거의 시점을 나타낼 때 쓰이며, 형용사를 수식하기도 한다.
  Ms. Young **once** attended Western State University. Ms. Young은 한때 Western 주립 대학교에 다녔다.
  A **once** <u>popular</u> restaurant operates in the building's basement. 한때 인기 있었던 식당은 그 건물 지하에서 영업한다.

토익실전문제

출제 포인트 시간 부사 채우기
문맥에 알맞은 시간 부사를 구별하여 채우는 문제가 가장 많이 출제된다.

1. The traffic was so heavy that by the time we arrived at the theater, the award-winning play had ------- begun.

   (A) yet   (B) already
   (C) never   (D) then

2. Although infrastructure contracts should be awarded through open bids, the administration has not ------- devised a policy that would allow for it.

   (A) yet   (B) still
   (C) never   (D) already

3. Union leaders have been negotiating with management representatives ever since most of the company's workers went on strike about two days -------.

   (A) still   (B) once
   (C) ago   (D) even

정답·해설·해석 p.55

01 빈도를 나타내는 부사는 '얼마나 자주' 일이 발생하는가를 표현하며, 보통 일반동사의 앞 또는 조동사나 be동사의 뒤에 온다.

always 항상	almost 거의	often 자주	frequently 종종	usually 보통
once 한 번	sometimes 때때로	hardly/rarely/seldom/scarcely/barely 거의 ~않다		
never 결코 ~않다				

My sister **often** goes to the gym. 내 여동생은 체육관에 자주 간다.
The room is so noisy that I can **hardly** concentrate on my work. 그 방은 너무 시끄러워서 내가 일에 거의 집중할 수 없다.
Jenny is **usually** punctual. Jenny는 보통 시간을 잘 지킨다.
The film festival takes place **once** a year. 이 영화제는 1년에 한 번씩 개최된다.

고득점 포인트

❶ hardly ever : 좀처럼 ~않다, 쉽사리 ~않다.
He <u>hardly ever</u> speaks. 그는 좀처럼 이야기하지 않는다.

❷ usually나 often은 문장 맨 앞에나 뒤에도 올 수 있지만, always는 문장 앞에나 뒤에 올 수 없다.
<u>Always</u>(→Usually), this restaurant offers affordable lunch specials. 보통, 이 음식점은 알맞은 가격의 점심 특선을 제공한다.
He visits his mother <u>always</u>(→often). 그는 그의 어머니를 자주 방문한다.

❸ 빈도 부사 자리에 시간 부사를 쓰지 않도록 주의해야 한다.
Employees of the firm are <u>ever</u>(→usually) provided with a bonus at the end of the year.
그 회사의 직원들은 연말에 보통 보너스를 받는다.

❹ barely는 '가까스로 ~하다'를 의미하기도 한다.
We had <u>barely</u> finished eating when the waiter announced that the restaurant would close soon.
웨이터가 식당이 곧 문을 닫을 것이라고 알렸을 때 우리는 가까스로 식사를 마쳤다.

02 hardly/rarely/seldom/scarcely/barely(거의 ~않다)는 부정의 의미를 담고 있으며, 일반동사의 앞 또는 조동사나 be동사의 뒤에 온다.

Tom **barely** finished his assignment by the deadline. Tom은 그의 과제를 마감일까지 거의 끝마치지 못했다.
We could **hardly** see the performance from our seats in the back row.
뒷줄에 있는 우리 자리에서는 공연을 거의 볼 수 없었다.

고득점 포인트

❶ 이러한 부정 부사들이 강조를 위해 문장 맨 앞으로 나오면 주어-동사 도치가 일어난다.
<u>Seldom</u> have sales at the store been as high as they were during the last holiday season.
그 상점의 매출이 지난 휴가철만큼 높았던 적은 거의 없었다.

❷ 이러한 부정 부사들은 이미 부정의 뜻을 담고 있어, not과 같은 또 다른 부정어와 함께 올 수 없다.
Bill rarely <u>never</u>(→ever) does overtime. Bill은 초과 근무를 거의 하지 않는다.
→ rarely는 이미 부정의 뜻을 담고 있어 never와 함께 쓸 수 없으므로 never는 삭제되거나 ever로 바뀌어야 한다.

토익실전문제

출제 포인트 빈도 부사 채우기
문맥에 알맞은 빈도 부사를 구별하여 채우는 문제가 주로 출제된다.

1. At Calvin's Outlet Store, evaluations of team leaders are ------- done at the end of every quarter.

(A) almost (B) well
(C) constantly (D) usually

2. The research staff writes project status reports ------- to provide updates to managers and directors.

(A) soon (B) often
(C) shortly (D) yet

3. ------- has Mr. Conrad seen such an eager and enthusiastic recruit with so much experience in software design.

(A) Ever (B) Although
(C) Rarely (D) Even

정답·해설·해석 p.56

토익 공식 5 : 부사 선택 3 : 접속부사 besides, therefore, however, otherwise

01 접속부사는 앞뒤 절의 의미를 연결해 주는 부사이다.

additionally 게다가	besides 게다가	moreover 더욱이	furthermore 더욱이
previously 이전에, 미리	then 그러고 나서, 그때	afterwards 그 후에	accordingly 그러므로, 그에 따라서
therefore/thus 그러므로	hence 그러므로	consequently 결과적으로	however 그러나
nevertheless 그럼에도 불구하고	nonetheless 그럼에도 불구하고	otherwise 그렇지 않으면	instead 대신에
meantime 그동안	meanwhile 그동안	fortunately 다행스럽게도	

Having forgotten his passport, Mr. Harris was **consequently** unable to board his flight to Rome.
여권을 갖고 오는 것을 잊었기 때문에, Mr. Harris는 결과적으로 로마행 비행기에 탑승할 수 없었다.

Look over the tour package descriptions and **then** make a selection. 패키지 여행 설명서를 훑어보고 나서 선택을 하십시오.

> **고득점 포인트** otherwise가 일반 부사로 사용되어 동사, 형용사, 부사를 꾸밀 때에는 '그렇지 않게, 달리' 또는 '다른 점에서'라는 뜻으로 사용된다.
>
> Ms. Fields believes that the marketing campaign was effective, but the survey indicates otherwise.
> Ms. Fields는 마케팅 캠페인이 효과적이었다고 생각하지만, 조사는 그렇지 않게 보여준다.
>
> The lead actor's performance was the only disappointment in an otherwise excellent film.
> 그 주연 배우의 연기는 다른 점에서 훌륭했던 영화에서 유일한 실망거리였다.

02 접속부사는 부사이기 때문에 혼자서는 두 개의 절을 연결할 수 없고, 접속사 역할을 하는 세미콜론(;)과 함께 와야 한다.

It's too far from here **besides** I don't want to go there. (×)
It's too far from here; **besides** I don't want to go there. (○) 여기서 너무 먼 데다가 나는 그곳에 가고 싶지 않다.

▶ 접속부사(besides)가 두 개의 절을 연결하기 위해서는 세미콜론(;)을 접속부사 앞에 써야 한다.

03 접속부사는 콤마와 함께 문장의 맨 앞에 위치하여 두 개의 문장을 의미적으로 연결한다. 이때, 접속부사 자리에 부사절 접속사는 올 수 없다.

Jack tried to cut down on his spending. (**Although**, **However**), he still ran short of money.
Jack은 소비를 줄이려고 노력했다. 그러나, 여전히 돈이 부족했다.

▶ 콤마와 함께 문장의 맨 앞에서 두 개의 문장을 의미적으로 연결하기 위해서는 부사절 접속사(Although)가 아닌 접속부사(However)가 와야 한다.

> **고득점 포인트**
>
> ❶ then이 일반 부사로 사용되어 '그렇다면, 그러면'을 의미하는 경우는 if절 뒤에 나올 수 있다.
>
> If he had wanted a better hotel room, then he should have asked for one. 그가 더 나은 호텔 객실을 원했었다면, 그것을 요청했어야 했다.
>
> ❷ 다음과 같이 두 단어 이상으로 이루어진 부사구가 문장 맨 앞에 위치하여 접속부사처럼 앞뒤 절의 의미를 연결할 수도 있다.
>
> Mr. Sheldon won the Best Employee Award this year. In addition, he achieved the highest sales in his department.
> Mr. Sheldon은 올해 최고의 직원상을 수상했다. 게다가, 그는 가장 높은 매출액을 달성하였다.

in addition 게다가	in fact 실제로, 사실은	as a matter of fact 사실은	after all 결국에는
as a result 결과적으로	for this reason 이런 이유 때문에	in particular 특히	even so 그렇기는 하지만
if so 만일 그렇다면	in the meantime 그동안에	at the same time 동시에	after that 그 후
since then 그 이후, 그때부터	to that end 그 목적을 달하기 위하여	in response 이에 대응하여	by comparison 그에 비해서
on the contrary 그와는 반대로	in contrast 그와는 대조적으로	in this way 이렇게 하면	for example 예를 들어

토익실전문제

출제 포인트 접속부사 채우기
문맥에 알맞은 접속부사를 구별하여 채우는 문제가 주로 출제된다.

1. Suggestions made by staff are always accepted by management; -------, most suggestions are usually not acted upon until after the board meetings are held.

(A) hence
(B) else
(C) instead
(D) however

2. Unless ------- stated, the contact information in this database is up-to-date as of June 30.

(A) meanwhile
(B) otherwise
(C) also
(D) however

3. Please check the recipient's name printed on the billing statement and ------- make your payment via credit card or online transfer.

(A) moreover
(B) then
(C) although
(D) whereas

정답·해설·해석 p.56

01 just/right(바로)는 before나 after를 앞에서 강조한다.

Please have my car ready **just(=right)** before I have to leave. 내가 떠나기 직전에 내 차를 준비해 주십시오.

> 고득점 포인트
> ❶ just enough: 겨우 충족될 만큼, 간신히
> Sarah had just enough money to buy herself dinner. Sarah는 겨우 저녁을 살 만큼의 돈만 있었다.
>
> ❷ just는 동사를 꾸며 '막, 방금'을 의미하기도 한다.
> DFX Systems just released its newest MP3 player. DFX Systems사는 자사의 최신 MP3 플레이어를 막 공개했다.

02 only/just(오직, 단지)는 전치사구나 명사구 등을 강조한다.

Employees may wear casual attire **only** on Fridays. 직원들은 오직 금요일에만 편한 복장을 입을 수 있다.
There will be **just** a brief delay while we test the equipment. 우리가 장비를 점검할 동안 단지 잠깐의 지연만 있을 것이다.

03 well(훨씬)은 전치사구를 강조한다.

The final cost of the renovations was **well** under the original estimate. 수리의 최종 비용은 원래의 추정치에 훨씬 못 미쳤다.

> 고득점 포인트
> well은 good의 부사로 사용되어 '잘, 훌륭하게'를 의미하기도 한다.
> Lucy did her presentation well. Lucy는 발표를 잘했다.

04 even(~조차도, ~까지도)은 단어나 구를 앞에서 강조한다.

Even my mother felt that the drama was too sentimental. 내 어머니조차도 그 드라마가 너무 감상적이라고 느꼈다.
The hotel will **even** arrange transportation to and from the airport. 그 호텔은 공항을 오가는 교통편까지도 마련해 줄 것이다.

▶ even이 '조동사 + 일반동사'를 강조할 때는 조동사와 일반동사 사이에 온다.

05 quite(굉장한)는 'a/an + 명사'를 앞에서 강조한다.

The singer's nightly concert was **quite** an accomplishment. 그 가수의 밤 콘서트는 굉장한 성취였다.

> 고득점 포인트
> ❶ not quite: 완전히 ~은 아니다.
> Mr. Vernon is not quite able to accept the situation. Mr. Vernon은 그 상황을 완전히 받아들일 수는 없다.
>
> ❷ quite가 동사, 형용사, 부사 등을 꾸밀 때는 '상당히, 매우, 꽤'를 의미한다.
> The speed of the hybrid car was quite surprising. 그 하이브리드 자동차의 속도는 상당히 놀라웠다.

06 nearly(거의)/almost(거의)/just(꼭)는 원급을, much/even/still/far/a lot/by far(훨씬)는 비교급을,
by far/quite/very(단연코)는 최상급을 강조한다.

This resort is **just** as luxurious as the one further up the beach. 이 리조트는 꼭 해변 더 위쪽에 있는 리조트만큼 호화롭다.
Aron's proposal was **much** better than Steve's. Aron의 제안은 Steve의 제안보다 훨씬 더 좋았다.
Seron is **by far** the largest steel producer in the country. Seron사는 그 나라에서 단연코 가장 큰 제철 생산 회사이다.

토익실전문제

출제 포인트 강조 부사 채우기
강조 부사를 문맥과 쓰임에 따라 구별하여 채우는 문제가 주로 출제된다.

1. This business visa allows the passport holder to travel within the country ------- for the period indicated.

   (A) also
   (B) only
   (C) even
   (D) however

2. Parmalac sold its ImClone stocks at a price that was ------- below the market value at the time of sale.

   (A) very
   (B) so
   (C) well
   (D) such

3. The company decided that a ------- more aggressive approach to advertising was needed to pull ahead of the competition.

   (A) just
   (B) very
   (C) much
   (D) quite

정답·해설·해석 p.56

01 so는 '매우'를 의미하는 부사이므로 형용사/부사를 수식한다.

The subway was **so** crowded this morning that I could hardly move.
오늘 아침 지하철이 매우 붐벼서 나는 거의 움직일 수 없었다.

Devin was very happy to find a jacket that fit him **so** well. Devin은 매우 잘 맞는 재킷을 찾아서 무척 기뻤다.

고득점
포인트

❶ such도 '매우'를 의미하지만, 부사인 so와는 달리 such는 형용사이므로 명사를 수식한다.

Wharton Laboratories is world-renowned because it develops <u>such</u> innovative products.
Wharton 연구소는 매우 혁신적인 제품들을 개발하기 때문에 세계적으로 유명하다.

❷ such가 단수 명사를 수식할 때에는, such 다음에 a/an이 온다.

Gary is pleased to have hired <u>such</u> a skilled carpenter to renovate his living room.
Gary는 자신의 거실을 개조하기 위해 매우 숙련된 목수를 고용하게 되어 만족한다.

02 very(매우)는 so와 의미는 같지만, so와 달리 뒤에 that절과 함께 쓰일 수 없다.

The directions in the manual are **very** easy to understand. 설명서에 있는 사용법이 매우 이해하기 쉽다.

The project was (**very**, **so**) costly that the board of directors was forced to authorize additional funding.
그 프로젝트에 매우 많은 비용이 들어 이사회는 추가 자금을 승인할 수밖에 없었다.

03 too(너무)는 so/such/very와 달리, '너무 ~하다'라는 부정적인 의미를 갖는다.

The receptionist was **too** busy to go for lunch. 그 접수원은 너무 바빠서 점심 식사를 하러 나갈 수 없었다.

▶ '접수원이 너무 바빠서 점심 식사를 하러 나갈 수 없었다'는 부정적인 의미를 갖는다.

cf) The restaurant was **very** busy, but we found a table. 식당이 매우 붐볐지만, 우리는 자리를 잡을 수 있었다.

▶ '식당이 붐볐지만 자리가 있었다'는 의미로, 부정적인 의미가 아니다.

고득점
포인트

❶ too + 형용사/부사 + to 부정사 (너무나 ~해서 ~할 수 없다)

The salary is <u>too low</u> for Mr. Anderson <u>to accept</u> the position. 봉급이 너무 낮아서 Mr. Anderson은 그 직책을 수락할 수 없다.

→ too와 to 부정사 사이에, to 부정사의 의미상 주어로 'for + 목적격'을 넣을 수 있다.

❷ too much/many + 명사 (너무나 많은 ~) (=far too much/many)

I have had <u>too much coffee</u> to go to sleep right now. 나는 너무나 많은 커피를 마셔서 지금 당장 잠자리에 들 수 없다.

❸ much too + 형용사/부사 (너무나 ~한/~하게) (=far too)

The competition is <u>much too fierce</u> for new companies to enter the market.
경쟁은 신생 회사들이 시장에 진입하기에 너무 치열하다.

토익실전문제

출제 포인트 so/such/very/too 구별하여 채우기
so/such/very/too를 문맥과 쓰임에 따라 구별하여 채우는 문제가 출제된다.

1. The city's cultural exposition is ------- a sizable event that several committees are required to plan the festivities.

(A) so (B) far
(C) such (D) too

2. It was surprising that the director was ------- satisfied with the results considering the job was done in a rush.

(A) too (B) enough
(C) even (D) very

3. If the proposed rate increase is approved, taxes in the region will be ------- burdensome for the smaller businesses to handle.

(A) much too (B) such
(C) so (D) not quite

정답·해설·해석 p.56

01 also/too/as well/either(또한)

- also는 문장 처음이나 중간에 오며, 문장 끝에는 올 수 없다.
  The firm has offices in New York, Vancouver, and **also** London. 그 회사는 뉴욕, 밴쿠버, 그리고 또한 런던에도 사무실이 있다.
  Professors must publish academic articles and **also** teach classes.
  교수들은 학술 논문을 발표해야 하며 또한 수업도 해야 한다.

- too와 as well은 문장 끝에 온다.
  The accounting manager will attend the conference **too**. 회계부장 또한 회의에 참석할 것이다.
  Jenna would like to visit Beijing this summer **as well**. Jenna는 이번 여름 또한 베이징을 방문하길 원한다.

- either는 부정문을 언급한 후, 또 다른 부정문을 덧붙일 때 쓰인다.
  Steven won't be working on Saturday; Sarah won't be working **either**.
  Steven은 토요일에 일하지 않을 것이며, Sarah 또한 일하지 않을 것이다.

02 later(이후에)/thereafter(그 이후에)/since(그 이래로)

- later는 시간 표현 바로 다음에 와서 '그 시간 이후에'를 의미한다.
  City council approved the construction project six weeks **later**. 시 의회는 6주 후에 건설 프로젝트를 승인했다.
  Why don't we talk this over **later**? 나중에 이것에 대해 다시 얘기하는 것이 어떨까요?
  ▶ later가 시간 표현 없이 오면 '지금 이후에(after now)'를 의미한다.

- thereafter는 '그 이후에(after that)'를 의미한다.
  Sally left and her package was delivered shortly (**later**, **thereafter**). Sally는 떠났고 그녀의 짐은 그 이후에 바로 배달되었다.
  ▶ later는 시간 표현 없이 쓰일 때 '지금 이후에'를 의미하므로, 이 문장의 '그때 이후에'라는 의미와는 맞지 않는다.

- since는 '그 이래로'를 의미한다.
  Fiona finished university and has **since** been employed by a publishing company.
  Fiona는 대학을 마쳤고 그 이래로 출판사에 고용되어 있었다.

03 forward(앞을 향해서)/ahead(앞에), backward(뒤를 향해서)/behind(뒤에)

- '방향'을 가리킬 때는 forward/backward를, '상태'를 가리킬 때는 ahead/behind를 쓴다.
  The repairman leaned (**ahead**, **forward**) to examine the machine. 그 수리공은 기계를 검사하기 위해 앞쪽으로 몸을 숙였다.
  ▶ 앞을 향해서 몸을 숙인다는 '방향'을 나타내므로 forward를 써야 한다.

  In the months (**forward**, **ahead**), employees will have to work extra hours.
  앞으로 몇 달간, 직원들은 초과 근무를 해야 할 것이다.
  ▶ 앞에 여러 달이 남아 있는 '상태'를 나타내므로 ahead를 써야 한다.

토익실전문제

출제 포인트 부사 채우기
비슷한 의미의 부사를 구별하여 채우는 문제가 출제된다.

1. Ms. Peters thinks that the designs are marvelous, but she ------- needs to see what they would look like in a display window.

   (A) thereafter   (B) either
   (C) also   (D) as well

2. The plane will take off at 3:15 P.M., and a light snack will be served to the passengers shortly -------.

   (A) later   (B) thereafter
   (C) already   (D) suddenly

3. The executives considered Ms. Bernal's appointment as the company's CEO a great step ------- because of her expertise.

   (A) ahead   (B) forward
   (C) toward   (D) behind

정답·해설·해석 p.57

둘 중 맞는 형태를 고르세요.

01 The board has not ------- chosen a location for the convention center the company plans to construct.
　ⓐ still　　　　　ⓑ yet

02 The equipment needed for the laboratory is ------- pricey that management has postponed the purchase.
　ⓐ so　　　　　ⓑ such

03 They prepared ------- food, believing that many people would be attending.
　ⓐ much too　　　ⓑ too much

04 Please cancel the hotel reservation by the end of the day; -------, we will have to pay a 25 percent cancellation fee.
　ⓐ otherwise　　　ⓑ however

05 The employees were ------- satisfied with the commission system proposed by the manager.
　ⓐ such　　　　　ⓑ very

06 Online Solutions offers its clients network management, Web site design, and ------- search engine optimization services.
　ⓐ also　　　　　ⓑ as well

07 ------- before his scheduled speech, Mr. Richards was told that he had an urgent telephone call from the office.
　ⓐ Ever　　　　　ⓑ Right

틀린 곳이 있으면 바르게 고치세요.

08 Always, I have a sandwich for lunch when my work schedule is full.

09 Ciko Cosmetics was able to great increase sales by implementing new marketing strategy.

10 The CEO demands that the dress code policy be strictly enforced in all branches.

11 Hiring additional workers resulted in the production capacity of the factory being expanded significance.

12 The accountant hardly never approves reimbursement for travel expenses.

13 The researchers must determine exactly what caused the problems with the prototype.

14 The latest reports indicate that consumer spending rose slight during the last quarter.

정답·해석 p.57

무료 해설 ▶
바로 보기

맞은 문제 개수:　　/ 14
틀린 문제에 해당하는 토익 공식을 다시 한번 학습하세요.

🕐 제한 시간 12분

Part 5

01 Officials spent a whole year ------- investigating the causes of the plane crash.

(A) extent
(B) extensive
(C) extensively
(D) extending

02 The new Perfect Presenter is the most ------- recommended office software on the market today.

(A) high
(B) height
(C) highly
(D) highest

03 The drafting programs available at our firm are ------- too advanced for the trainees to use.

(A) well
(B) quite
(C) pretty
(D) far

04 Staying at a guest house is cheaper than checking into a first-class hotel, and its amenities are ------- as comfortable.

(A) as well
(B) even
(C) just
(D) much

05 Once the power outage problem on the second floor is resolved, the electric service in the entire building will be restored as ------- as possible.

(A) prompt
(B) promptly
(C) prompted
(D) promptness

06 Mr. Richards is known to be a very dedicated worker who is never late and ------- ever misses a day of work.

(A) quite
(B) just
(C) nearly
(D) hardly

07 Although the restaurant is new, it has already been praised by *Food Review* and all of ------- restaurant rating services.

(A) other
(B) the other
(C) one another
(D) others

08 Consumer views are becoming a ------- more important factor in determining the way a product is presented and packaged.

(A) progress
(B) progressing
(C) progressive
(D) progressively

09 Pendleton Enterprises cannot always guarantee that everything in the catalog is in stock at its authorized outlets, so please call ------- to make sure.

(A) ahead
(B) once
(C) whether
(D) advance

10 A number of large investment projects have ------- sprung up in rural areas where agriculture is the main industry.

(A) latest
(B) late
(C) later
(D) lately

11 To register for your online account, proceed to the Web site ------- and click on the sign-up button.

(A) immediately
(B) immediate
(C) immediateness
(D) immediacy

12 Synco-Vac needs to boost productivity, and the company has ------- agreed to base wage increases on annual profits.

(A) therefore
(B) however
(C) although
(D) in contrast

13 To prevent the skin from drying out on cold days, the moisturizer may be used as ------- as required.

(A) closely
(B) often
(C) far
(D) hardly

14 Ms. Jones asked the staff to submit their research even though they had not ------- finished making the analysis.

(A) quite
(B) more
(C) already
(D) only

15 Had the information collection work been divided ------- among the researchers, the survey of the respondents would be completed by now.

(A) equal
(B) equally
(C) equality
(D) equalize

16 -------, none of the people who left negative comments about the product had actually bought one.

(A) Interest
(B) Interested
(C) Interesting
(D) Interestingly

17 ------- serving as a member of the board of Giltmore Corporation, Mr. Bennett also works as a consultant for several smaller enterprises.

(A) Else
(B) Due
(C) As good as
(D) Besides

18 The nutrient content of food products sold in supermarkets should be summarized much more ------- to help people understand what's on the label.

(A) simple
(B) simply
(C) simplest
(D) simplicity

Part 6

Questions 19-22 refer to the following letter.

Marsha Berger

Tyrrell Manufacturing

Dear Ms. Berger,

-------. As our company is currently undergoing restructuring, it is impossible for me to leave New
$\quad$ 19
York. Please be assured that we are eager ------- your proposal to incorporate your products into our
$\quad$ 20
own line of merchandise.

To make up for my absence, I would like to invite you to a breakfast meeting at the Tilton Hotel on

July 7. -------, if you are unable to meet with me on that day, I will also be free on the evening of
$\quad$ 21
July 8. Please let me know which day would be more convenient. I'd like to discuss your ideas with

you ------- so that I can present them to our board of directors on July 10. We have been seeking
$\quad$ 22
cooperative endeavors with other producers for some time now. So, your proposal will be of great

interest to management.

I believe that both our companies are headed in the same direction, and a joint venture would be

mutually beneficial. I look forward to the opportunity to meet with you this week.

Justin White

Garnet Distribution

19 (A) This is to notify you that the proposal was eventually turned down.
(B) I am writing to inform you that I will be unable to attend the conference.
(C) This is to ensure that what we agreed on will proceed as scheduled.
(D) I am writing to ask you at which location you would like to meet.

20 (A) developing
(B) develop
(C) to develop
(D) development

21 (A) However
(B) Furthermore
(C) Besides
(D) While

22 (A) soon
(B) since
(C) still
(D) often

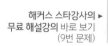
해커스 스타강사의 ▶
무료 해설강의 바로 보기
(9번 문제)

CHAPTER 14 전치사

토익, 이렇게 나온다!

전치사 관련 문제는 평균 4~5문제 정도 꾸준히 출제되며 최대 8문제까지 출제된다. 문맥에 알맞은 전치사를 채우는 문제가 가장 많이 출제되며, 전치사가 포함된 숙어 표현을 완성하는 문제도 가끔 출제된다.

토익 필수 개념 다지기

01 전치사는 명사 앞에 와서 장소, 시간, 이유 등을 나타낸다.

I bought fresh vegetables **at** <u>the market</u>. 나는 시장에서 신선한 야채를 샀다.
Many people go to ski resorts **in** <u>the winter</u>. 많은 사람들은 겨울에 스키장에 간다.
Jane's school is closed today **because of** <u>the severe storm</u>.
심한 폭풍우 때문에 Jane의 학교는 오늘 휴교한다.

여기서 at은 장소를, in은 시간을, because of는 이유를 나타내는 전치사이다. 전치사는 명사 이외에도 대명사, 동명사, 명사절과 같이 '명사 역할을 하는 것'들을 목적어로 취할 수 있으며, [전치사 + 전치사의 목적어]를 '전치사구'라고 한다.

He reserved a hotel room **for** <u>us</u>. [전치사 + 대명사]
그는 우리를 위해 호텔 객실을 예약했다.
I am going to work late tonight **instead of** <u>working</u> this weekend. [전치사 + 동명사]
나는 이번 주말에 일하는 대신 오늘 저녁 늦게까지 일하겠다.
Jonathan gives his business card **to** <u>whomever he meets</u>. [전치사 + 명사절]
Jonathan은 그가 만나는 모든 사람들에게 명함을 준다.

02 전치사구는 문장에서 명사를 꾸미는 형용사나 동사를 꾸미는 부사 역할을 한다.

<u>The picture **on the wall**</u> is beautiful. 벽에 걸려 있는 그림은 아름답다.

I <u>exercise **in the evening**</u>. 나는 저녁에 운동한다.

전치사구 on the wall은 명사 The picture를 꾸미는 형용사 역할을 하고, in the evening은 동사 exercise를 꾸미는 부사 역할을 한다.

01 시간 전치사 in/at/on

전치사	쓰 임	예	
in	월·연도 계절·세기 ~(시간) 후에·아침/오후/저녁	**in** August 8월에 **in** winter 겨울에 **in** three days 3일 후에	**in** 2008 2008년에 **in** the 21st century 21세기에 **in** the morning/afternoon/evening 아침/오후/저녁에
at	시각·시점	**at** 7 o'clock 7시에 **at** the beginning/end of the month 월초에/월말에	**at** noon/night/midnight 정오/밤/자정에
on	날짜·요일·특정일	**on** August 15 8월 15일에	**on** Friday 금요일에 **on** Christmas Day 크리스마스 날에

02 장소 전치사 in/at/on

전치사	쓰 임	예	
in	큰 공간 내 장소	**in** the world/country 세계/국가에서	**in** the city/room/town 도시/방/마을에서
at	지점·번지	**at** the intersection 교차로에서 **at** the station 역에서	**at** the bus stop 버스 정류장에서 **at** Franklin Street Franklin가에서
on	표면 위·일직선 상의 지점	**on** the table 테이블에 **on** the first floor(level) 1층에	**on** the Han River 한강에 **on** the wall 벽에

> **고득점 포인트** 같은 장소명이라도, 그 장소의 안을 의미할 때는 in을, 장소 자체를 의미할 때는 at을 사용한다.
> I was <u>in</u> the shop when he came in. 그가 들어왔을 때 나는 상점 안에 있었다.
> I stopped <u>at</u> the shop on the way home. 나는 집에 가는 길에 상점에 들렀다.

03 in/at/on 숙어 표현

전치사	표　　현		
in	**in** advance 미리, 사전에 **in** time 때 맞추어, 이르게 **in** place 제자리에, 적소에	**in** effect 효력을 발휘하여 **in** particular 특히 **in** writing 서면으로	**in** one's absence ~의 부재 시에 **in** a timely manner 시기적절하게 **in** the foreseeable future 가까운 미래에
at	**at** once 즉시, 동시에 **at** times 때때로 **at** least 적어도 **at** all times 항상 **at** the latest 늦어도	**at** regular intervals 규칙적으로 **at** a good pace 상당한 속도로 **at** high speed 급속히 **at** a low price 낮은 가격으로 **at** 60 miles an hour 한 시간에 60마일로	**at** the rate of ~의 비율로, ~의 속도로 **at** the age of ~의 나이로 **at** a charge of ~의 비용 부담으로 **at** one's expense ~의 비용으로 **at** your earliest convenience 가급적 빨리
on	**on** time 정시에 **on** a regular basis 규칙적으로 **on** call 대기 중인	**on**/**upon** arrival 도착하는 즉시 **on**/**upon** request 요청 시에 **on** vacation 휴가 중인	**on** the waiting list 대기자 명단에 **on** the recommendation of ~의 추천으로

토익실전문제

출제 포인트 in/at/on 구별하여 채우기
시각 앞에 at을, 장소 앞에 in을 채우는 문제가 가장 많이 출제된다.
in/at/on이 포함된 숙어 표현을 완성하는 문제도 출제된다.

1. The interview with the real estate agent is scheduled for tomorrow afternoon ------- 4 o'clock.

(A) on
(B) at
(C) in
(D) of

2. If the new low-fat potato chip becomes a hot seller in Springfield, it will be test-marketed ------- several other urban centers across the US.

(A) on
(B) in
(C) against
(D) to

3. All of the drilling machines are ------- place and ready to begin oil extraction at the direction of the chief executive.

(A) to
(B) on
(C) in
(D) by

정답·해설·해석 p.59

01 시점을 나타내는 전치사

since ~ 이래로	from ~부터	+	시점 표현 (3 o'clock, July, Friday morning 등)
until/by ~까지	before/prior to ~ 전에		

The construction work will be finished **before** January. 건설 공사는 1월 전에 끝날 것이다.

고득점 포인트

❶ until은 '상황, 상태가 계속될 때까지'를, by는 '행동이 발생할 때까지'를 의미한다.

The library will be open until 7 o'clock. 도서관은 7시까지 문을 열 것이다. → 도서관이 문을 열고 있는 상태가 7시까지 계속된다.

You should hand in the form by 7 o'clock. 너는 7시까지 그 양식을 제출해야 한다. → 7시 이전까지 양식을 제출하는 행동이 끝난다.

❷ 시점을 나타내는 전치사가 들어가는 숙어 표현

two weeks from now 지금부터 2주 후에　　three weeks prior to the date 그날로부터 3주 전에　　from 5 o'clock onward(s) 5시 이후

02 기간을 나타내는 전치사

for/during ~ 동안		
over/through/throughout ~ 동안, ~ 내내	+	기간 표현 (three years, a decade, holiday, process 등)
within ~ 이내에		

I have been working at this plant **for** six years. 나는 이 공장에서 6년 동안 일해 왔다.

Mr. Majors led participants **through** the registration process. Mr. Majors는 등록 과정 내내 참가자들을 인솔했다.

고득점 포인트

❶ for는 숫자를 포함한 기간 표현 앞에 와서 '얼마나 오랫동안 지속되는지'를, during은 명사 앞에 와서 '언제 일어나는지'를 나타낸다. 단, during 다음에 한정사(the, 소유격)가 나오면 숫자 기간 표현이 올 수 있다.

The reporter interviewed Ms. Kim for nearly two hours. 그 기자는 거의 2시간 동안 Ms. Kim을 인터뷰했다.

Most resorts in the area are busiest during summer. 이 지역 대부분의 리조트들은 여름 동안 가장 바쁘다.

The instructor tried to get to know everyone during the first fifteen minutes. 그 강사는 처음 15분 동안 모든 사람을 알기 위해 노력했다.

❷ in 다음에도 기간 표현이 올 수 있는데, 이때 in은 일반적으로 '~ 후에, ~가 지나서'를 의미한다. 단, 서수(first, second 등), 최상급이 쓰인 문장이나 부정문에서 'in + 기간 표현'이 쓰이면 '~ 만에, ~ 동안'을 의미한다.

Your request for membership will be approved in two days. 귀하의 회원 신청은 이틀 후에 승인될 것이다.

The sales figures have gone up for the first time in five years. 매출이 5년 만에 처음으로 올랐다.

03 시점을 나타내는 전치사와 기간을 나타내는 전치사의 구별

I will have this done (**within**, by) the end of next week. 나는 다음 주 말까지 이것을 완료할 것이다.

▶ 전치사 within 다음에는 시점을 나타내는 표현(the end of next week)이 올 수 없으므로, by가 와야 한다.

I have studied economics (**since**, for) three years. 나는 3년 동안 경제학을 공부해 왔다.

▶ 전치사 since 다음에는 기간을 나타내는 표현(three years)이 올 수 없으므로, for가 와야 한다.

토익실전문제

출제 포인트 시점/기간 전치사 구별하여 채우기

시점(until/by), 기간(for/during)을 나타내는 전치사들을 서로 구별하여 채우는 문제가 출제된다.

1. As the CEO had to leave for Europe unexpectedly to deal with a management problem at the Moscow branch, the company dinner was postponed to two weeks ------- today.

(A) until　　　　　(B) before
(C) from　　　　　(D) for

2. The rental deposit must be transferred to the landlord's bank account at least 15 days ------- the moving-in date.

(A) by　　　　　　(B) until
(C) prior to　　　　(D) due to

3. The warranty form must be mailed to the company ------- one month of the receipt of your product in order for the parts and service guarantee to be valid.

(A) from　　　　　(B) within
(C) until　　　　　(D) since

정답·해설·해석 p.59

01 위치를 나타내는 전치사

전치사	예 문
above/over ~ 위에	He lifted his hands **above/over** his head. 그는 머리 위로 두 손을 들어 올렸다.
below/under ~ 아래에	Extra paper is kept **below/under** the photocopier. 여분의 용지는 복사기 아래에 보관된다.
beside/next to ~ 옆에	She took the seat **beside/next to** the podium. 그녀는 연단 옆에 앉았다.
behind ~ 뒤에	There is an alleyway **behind** the supermarket. 그 슈퍼마켓 뒤에 골목이 있다. * behind는 물리적 의미 외에 '~보다 뒤떨어져'라는 뜻으로도 사용된다.
between/among ~ 사이에	There is a table **between** the sofa and the TV. 소파와 텔레비전 사이에 탁자가 하나 있다. The performance took place **between** 5 and 6 o'clock. 공연은 5시와 6시 사이에 열렸다. The celebrity was standing **among** her fans. 그 유명 인사는 그녀의 팬들 사이에 서 있었다.
near ~ 가까이	We'd prefer to live **near** a park. 우리는 공원 가까이에 사는 것을 선호한다.
within ~ 내에	The manager spoke about policy changes **within** the firm. 그 관리자는 회사 내 정책 변경에 관해 말했다. That noise seems to be coming from **within** the building. 저 소리는 건물 내에서부터 나오는 것 같다.
outside ~ 밖에	The car is parked **outside** the clinic. 그 자동차는 병원 밖에 주차되어 있다.
around ~ 주위에	Many tourists like to walk **around** the lake. 많은 관광객들은 호수 주위를 걷는 것을 좋아한다.
past ~을 지나	The post office is just **past** the subway station. 우체국은 지하철역을 지나 바로 있다.
opposite ~ 건너편에, ~ 맞은편에	The bank is **opposite** the supermarket. 은행은 슈퍼마켓 건너편에 있다.

고득점 포인트

❶ between은 '둘 사이'에 쓰여서, 위치와 시간의 '사이' 모두를 의미하고, among은 '셋 이상의 사물/사람 사이'에 쓴다.

❷ above/over와 below/under는 각각 '~ 이상'과 '~ 이하'를 의미하기도 한다.
He spent <u>over</u> $200 to repair his car. 그는 그의 차를 수리하는 데 200달러 이상 썼다.
My phone bill was <u>under</u> $40. 내 전화 요금은 40달러 이하였다.

❸ around는 수사 앞에 쓰여 '대략, ~쯤'을 의미하기도 한다.

02 위치 전치사 숙어 표현

전치사	표 현	
above	**above** one's expectations 기대 이상인	
over	have the edge/advantage **over** ~보다 유리하다	
under	**under** new management 새 경영진하에서	**under** investigation 조사 중인
	under new policy 새로운 정책하에서	**under** review 검토 중인
	under close supervision 엄격한 감독하에서	**under** consideration 고려 중인
	under current contract 현 계약하에서	**under** discussion 토론 중인
	under control 통제하에 있는	**under** construction 공사 중인
	under pressure 압력 받고 있는	**under** way 진행 중인
between	a difference/gap **between** A and B A와 B의 차이	
within	**within** walking distance of ~에서 걸어갈 수 있는 곳에	**within** the limit 범위 내에서
around	**around** the world 전 세계에	**around** the corner 길 모퉁이를 돌아, 위기를 넘겨, 임박하여

토익실전문제

출제 포인트 **전치사 채우기**

위치를 나타내는 전치사들을 서로 구별하여 채우거나 숙어 표현을 완성하는 문제가 출제된다.

1. A recent study mentions that prescription drug use has steadily increased ------- people aged 45 years and above over the past two decades.

(A) among   (B) within
(C) between   (D) around

2. The annex to the office building on Lester Avenue will be ------- construction until April.

(A) in   (B) by
(C) on   (D) under

3. Last summer's heavy precipitation levels caused sales of beachwear to fall 20 percent ------- normal.

(A) after   (B) below
(C) behind   (D) around

정답·해설·해석 p.60

GRAMMAR Part 5,6   Ch 14 전치사   Hackers TOEIC Reading

01 방향을 나타내는 전치사

전치사	예문
from ~에서, ~로부터	You can pick up a brochure **from** the front desk. 안내 데스크에서 소책자를 가져가실 수 있습니다.
to ~로, ~ 쪽으로	A schedule of events will be sent **to** your e-mail. 행사 일정표가 이메일로 전송될 것이다.
across ~을 가로질러 ~의 전역에 걸쳐	We walked **across** the ice. 우리는 얼음 표면을 가로질러 걸었다. Bramton Co.'s products are delivered free of charge **across** Britain. Bramton사의 제품들은 영국 전역에 무료로 배송됩니다.
through ~을 통과하여 along ~을 따라서	Some passengers exited **through** the back of the plane. 일부 승객들은 비행기 뒤편을 통과하여 나갔다. They often walk **along** the river. 그들은 강을 따라서 자주 걷는다.
for ~을 향해 toward(s) ~ 쪽으로(막연한 방향) (경향·결과가) ~을 향하여	I bought a plane ticket **for** New York. 나는 뉴욕으로 향하는 비행기 표를 샀다. She ran **toward** me. 그녀는 내 쪽으로 뛰어왔다. Our company strives **toward** creating a cleaner environment. 우리 회사는 더 깨끗한 환경 조성을 향하여 노력한다.
into ~ 안으로 out of ~ 밖으로	Students rushed **into** the classroom. 학생들은 강의실 안으로 뛰어 들어갔다. My mother took the dishes **out of** the cupboard. 어머니께서는 찬장 밖으로 그릇들을 꺼내셨다.

고득점 포인트

❶ along with는 '~와 함께'라는 의미의 전치사로 사용된다.
I had an omelet for breakfast <u>along with</u> a cup of coffee. 나는 아침으로 커피 한 잔과 함께 오믈렛을 먹었다.

❷ out of는 '~ 중에'라는 의미의 전치사로도 사용된다.
<u>Out of</u> 30 contestants, the judges chose 10. 30명의 참가자 중에, 심사위원들은 10명을 선발했다.

02 방향 전치사 숙어 표현

전치사	표현		
from	**from** one's view point ~의 관점으로 보면 * in terms of도 '~의 관점에서'라는 뜻의 전치사 표현이다.		
to	**to** the relief of ~가 안심하도록 **to** the point 적절한	**to** a great extent 상당한 정도까지 **to** one's satisfaction ~가 만족스럽도록	**to** my knowledge 내가 알기로는 **to** your heart's content 네가 만족할 정도로
along across	**along** the shore 해변을 따라 **across** the street 길 건너편에	**along** the side of ~의 측면을 따라 **across** from the post office 우체국 맞은편에	**across** the nation 전국에, 전역에 걸쳐
out of	**out of** date 시대에 뒤진, 구식인 **out of** room 공간이 부족한 **out of** season 제철이 아닌 **out of** paper 종이가 다 떨어진	**out of** reach 손이 닿지 않는, 힘이 미치지 않는 **out of** print 절판된 **out of** control 통제할 수 없는	**out of** order 고장 난 **out of** stock 재고가 떨어진 **out of** town 시내에 없는, 다른 곳으로 떠난

토익실전문제

출제 포인트 전치사 채우기

방향을 나타내는 전치사들을 서로 구별하여 채우거나 숙어 표현을 완성하는 문제가 출제된다.

1. Subscribers to the online newsletter were informed that their names would be removed ------- the mailing list if they did not reply to the e-mail requesting renewal of subscription.

(A) into   (B) from
(C) across   (D) with

2. The new highway, which will run ------- the mountains, is expected to cause irreversible damage to wildlife and the ecosystem.

(A) through   (B) during
(C) out   (D) against

3. Because the broken light fixture was hanging ------- reach, the technician asked for a stepladder.

(A) instead of   (B) out of
(C) because of   (D) without

정답·해설·해석 p.60

01 이유, 양보, 목적을 나타내는 전치사

전치사	의미	예 문
because of due to owing to on account of	~ 때문에	Traffic was terrible **because of** an accident. 사고 때문에 교통 체증이 극심했다. **Due to** the rain, the event was postponed to next Monday. 비 때문에, 그 행사는 다음 월요일로 연기되었다. * thanks to는 '~ 덕분에', as a result of는 '~의 결과로'를 의미하는 이유의 전치사이다.
despite in spite of with all notwithstanding	~에도 불구하고	**Despite** his busy schedule, Bill made it to the meeting on time. 바쁜 일정에도 불구하고, Bill은 정시에 회의에 도착했다.
for	~을 위해서	The corporation is holding an awards ceremony **for** its staff. 그 회사는 직원들을 위해 시상식을 개최할 것이다.

고득점 포인트 전치사 for가 포함된 표현
for your convenience 여러분의 편의를 위해　　for future use 추후 사용하기 위해　　for safety reasons 안전상의 이유로
for further information 더 많은 정보를 위해　　articles for sale 판매용 물건　　money for supplies 물품 구입비
a coupon for every $100 매 100달러에 대한 쿠폰

02 제외, 부가를 나타내는 전치사

전치사	의미	예 문
except (for) excepting apart from aside from outside	~을 제외하고는, ~ 외에는	I cleaned all the rooms **except (for)** the bathroom. 나는 욕실을 제외한 모든 방을 청소했다. **Apart from** credit cards, no other payment methods are accepted. 신용카드를 제외하고, 다른 결제 수단은 받지 않습니다. Deliveries cannot be made **outside** of business hours. 배달은 영업 시간 외에는 되지 않는다.
barring without but for	~이 없(었)다면	We will probably finish the report today, **barring** any unexpected problems. 예기치 않은 문제들만 없다면, 우리는 아마도 오늘 보고서를 완성할 것이다. I would have failed the exam **but for** your help. 네 도움이 없었다면 나는 시험에서 낙제했을 것이다.
instead of	~ 대신에	Use graphics **instead of** words. 글자 대신 그림을 사용하시오.
in addition to besides apart from plus	~에 더해서	**In addition to** his smartphone, Oscar will bring a laptop on the business trip. 스마트폰에 더해서, Oscar는 출장 갈 때 휴대용 컴퓨터를 가져갈 것이다. **Besides** a hot lunch, the airline also served snacks on the flight. 따뜻한 점심에 더해서, 그 항공사는 운행 중에 간식도 제공했다. New customers receive a coupon **plus** a gift. 신규 고객들은 선물에 더해서 쿠폰을 받는다.

고득점 포인트 except 다음에 [접속사 + 절(주어 + 동사)]이 오는 경우에는, for를 쓰지 못한다.
I haven't heard a thing about the trip, except for that(→ except that) it was put off.
그 여행이 연기되었다는 것을 제외하고는, 나는 그 여행에 대해 어떤 것도 듣지 못했다.
→ except 다음에 오는 접속사로 that이 가장 자주 오지만, when, where, what, while도 올 수 있다.

토익실전문제

출제 포인트 전치사 채우기
이유, 양보, 목적을 나타내는 전치사들을 구별하여 채우는 문제가 주로 출제된다.
due to와 in spite of(despite)를 구별하여 채우는 문제가 가장 많이 출제된다.

1. The company announced that it will host a special ceremony ------- Kyle Wood in recognition of his outstanding sales record.

(A) through (B) for
(C) over (D) among

2. The manager said that ------- any changes, the proposal would be presented at a special meeting of sustainable development organizations.

(A) instead of (B) barring
(C) if (D) although

3. Western Steel's stock price rose significantly over the past year ------- the overall decline in the profitability of the steel industry.

(A) in spite of (B) except
(C) even though (D) apart from

정답·해설·해석 p.60

01 A of B

쓰임	예
의미상 A가 동사, B가 주어인 경우	the launch **of** the new shop 새 상점의 개점 (⇐ 새 상점이 개점하다) departure **of** the ship 배의 출발 (⇐ 배가 출발하다) decision **of** the manager 관리자의 결정 (⇐ 관리자가 결정하다)
의미상 A가 동사, B가 목적어인 경우	unveiling **of** the new car model 새 자동차 모델의 발표 (⇐ 새 자동차 모델을 발표하다) the advertising **of** luxury goods 명품의 광고 (⇐ 명품을 광고하다) the renovation **of** the building 건물의 수리 (⇐ 건물을 수리하다) the construction **of** a hospital wing 병원 병동의 건축 (⇐ 병원 병동을 건축하다)
A와 B가 동격인 경우	a chance **of** rain tomorrow 내일 비가 올 확률 (⇐ 확률 = 내일 비가 오는 것) the idea **of** online promotion 온라인 홍보에 대한 생각 (⇐ 생각 = 온라인으로 홍보하는 것) a refund **of** $100 100달러의 환불액 (⇐ 환불액 = 100달러)
A가 B의 부분, 소속인 경우	this part **of** the state 그 주의 이 지역 (⇐ 그 주에 속한 이 지역) the top **of** the tower 그 탑의 꼭대기 (⇐ 그 탑에 속한 꼭대기 부분) the animals **of** the zoo 그 동물원의 동물들 (⇐ 그 동물원에 속한 동물들)

02 '~에 관하여'라는 의미로 쓰이는 전치사

about	on/upon	over
as to	as for	
concerning	regarding	
with/in regard to	with respect to	with/in reference to

The customer brought up a problem **concerning** her recent purchase.
그 고객은 그녀의 최근 구매에 관하여 문제를 제기했다.

Please read through the revised regulations **on** employee office wear.
직원 사무 복장에 관하여 수정된 규정들을 꼼꼼히 읽어 주시기 바랍니다.

토익실전문제

출제 포인트 전치사 채우기
문맥에 알맞게 '~에 관하여'라는 뜻의 전치사를 채우는 문제가 출제된다.

1. The independent audit of the company is expected to be concluded by the end ------- this month.

   (A) in (B) at
   (C) of (D) on

2. Dr. Wilson will attend the workshop to moderate a panel discussion ------- ethical issues related to new medical technology.

   (A) by (B) to
   (C) on (D) with

3. A dispute ------- workers' salaries has caused union members employed at the factory to go on strike.

   (A) over (B) beyond
   (C) of (D) along

정답·해설·해석 p.60

01 기타 전치사

전치사	의미	예 문
by through throughout	~에 의해 ~함으로써 ~을 통해서 ~ 전역에, 도처에 ~ 전반에 걸친	Get a full schedule of updates **by** visiting our Web site. 저희 웹사이트를 방문함으로써 모든 업데이트 일정을 얻으십시오. Wisdom is gained **through** experience. 지혜는 경험을 통해서 얻어진다. There are more than 70 hotels **throughout** the city of Winnipeg. 위니펙시 전역에 70개가 넘는 호텔이 있다.
with without	~와 함께 ~을 가지고 ~ 없이	I go on a business trip **with** my assistant at all times. 나는 항상 나의 조수와 함께 출장을 간다. The Internet allows people to make purchases **without** leaving their homes. 인터넷은 사람들에게 집을 떠나지 않고 물건을 살 수 있도록 해준다.
as	~로서	Tim had worked **as** a section supervisor at the Ministry of Education. Tim은 교육부에서 부서장으로 일했다.
like unlike	~처럼 ~와 달리	**Like** coffee, tea contains a lot of caffeine. 커피처럼, 차도 많은 카페인을 함유하고 있다. This cereal, **unlike** other similar products, contains no added sugar. 이 시리얼은 다른 유사 제품들과 달리, 설탕 첨가물을 함유하고 있지 않다.
against	~에 반대하여 ~에 기대어	Local residents have demonstrated **against** city expansion plans. 지역 주민들은 도시 확장 계획에 반대하는 시위 운동을 해왔다.
beyond	~보다 뛰어난 ~ 이상으로	Its functions go **beyond** what is necessary for an MP3 player. 그것의 기능은 MP3 플레이어에 필요한 기능보다 뛰어나다.
following	~에 이어	**Following** the screening, the director will answer questions from the audience. 영화 상영에 이어, 그 감독은 관객들의 질문에 답할 것이다.
amid	~한 가운데	**Amid** the growing unemployment rate, corporations are being encouraged to hire more people. 실업률이 상승하는 가운데, 기업들은 더 많은 사람들을 고용하도록 권장되고 있다.

02 기타 전치사 숙어 표현

전치사	표 현	
by through	**by** telephone/fax/mail 전화/팩스/우편으로 **by** land 육로로 **through** the use of ~의 사용을 통해서	**by** cash/check/credit card 현금/수표/신용카드로 **by** law 법에 의해 **through** cooperation 협력을 통해
with without	**with** no doubt 의심할 바 없이 **with** the aim of ~을 목적으로 **with** regularity 규칙대로	**with** no exception 예외 없이 **with** emphasis 강조하여 **without** approval 승인 없이
against	**against** the law 불법인, 법에 저촉되는	act **against** one's will ~의 의지에 반하여 행동하다
beyond	**beyond** repair 수리가 불가능한	**beyond** one's capacity ~의 능력 밖인

토익실전문제

출제 포인트 전치사 채우기

문맥에 맞게 전치사를 채우거나 숙어 표현을 완성하는 문제가 출제된다.

1. The government suggests that all businesses keep copies of their financial statements ------- evidence of tax compliance.

(A) as   (B) by
(C) like   (D) through

2. Companies can save money on airfare ------- video conference calls, which allow for international meetings without leaving the office.

(A) under   (B) through
(C) into   (D) within

3. All employees expressed contentment with their salaries and hours, ------- the exception of those in shipping who requested a pay increase.

(A) like   (B) following
(C) on   (D) with

정답·해설·해석 p.61

01 '동사 + 전치사' 표현

advertise on ~에 광고하다	depend/rely/count on(upon) ~에 의존하다	direct A to B A를 B로 보내다, A에게 B로 가는 길을 알려주다
account for ~을 설명하다	consist of ~로 구성되다	extract/obtain A from B B에서 A를 얻다
register for ~에 등록하다	keep track of ~을 계속 알고 있다	limit A to B A를 B 내로 제한하다
wait for ~을 기다리다	contribute to ~에 기여하다	praise A for B B에 대해 A를 칭찬하다
add to ~을 더하다	associate A with B A를 B에 관련시켜 생각하다	supply/provide A with B A에게 B를 공급하다
coincide with ~와 동시에 일어나다	congratulate A on B A에게 B를 축하하다	return A to B A를 B로 돌려보내다
comply with ~을 따르다	credit A to B A를 B의 공으로 돌리다	transfer A to B A를 B로 옮기다

Tenants are required to **comply with** building regulations. 세입자들은 건물 규정을 따르도록 요구된다.
Most people **associate** that brand **with** reliability. 대부분의 사람들은 그 브랜드를 신뢰도에 관련시켜 생각한다.

02 '형용사 + 전치사' 표현

responsible for ~에 책임이 있는	equivalent to ~와 동일한	comparable with ~와 비교되는	aware of ~을 알고 있는
eligible for ~에 대한 자격이 있는	comparable to ~에 필적하는	familiar with ~에 익숙한	capable of ~을 할 수 있는
grateful for ~에 감사하는	identical to ~와 동일한	consistent with ~와 일관된	conscious of ~을 인식하고 있는
appropriate for ~에 적합한	similar to ~와 비슷한	absent from ~에 불참한	open to ~에 열려 있는

The company's new logo was **similar to** that of a competitor. 그 회사의 새로운 로고는 경쟁사의 로고와 비슷했다.

03 '명사 + 전치사' 표현

access to ~에의 접근, 출입	respect for ~에 대한 존경	an advocate for(of) ~의 옹호자
a cause/reason for ~의 원인/이유	a solution to ~에 대한 해결책	a lack of ~의 부족
a demand for ~에 대한 요구	concern over(about) ~에 대한 걱정	a dispute over ~에 대한 논쟁
permission from ~로부터의 허가	a problem with ~의 문제	a comment on ~에 대한 언급
a discount on ~에 대한 할인	a question about(concerning/regarding) ~에 대한 질문	
an effect(impact/influence) on ~에 대한 영향	a decrease/an increase/a rise/a drop in ~의 감소/증가/상승/하락	

The purchase of the property was delayed because of **a lack of** capital. 자금 부족 때문에 그 건물의 구매가 연기되었다.

04 두 단어 이상으로 이루어진 전치사

ahead of + 시간/장소 ~보다 빨리, ~ 앞에	as of + 시간 ~부터, ~부로	at the request of ~의 요청으로
in place of ~을 대신하여	contrary to ~와 반대로	in excess of ~을 초과하여
in preparation for ~에 대비하여	regardless of ~에 상관없이	in exchange for ~의 대신으로
in respect of ~에 관해서는	by means of ~의 수단으로	in honor of ~에게 경의를 표하여
in response to ~에 응하여	in celebration of ~을 축하하여	in keeping with ~와 어울려
in violation of ~을 위반하여	in charge of ~을 책임지고 있는	in light of ~을 고려하여
in favor of ~에 찬성하여	in compliance with ~을 준수하여	in observance of ~을 준수하여, ~을 기념하여
in terms of ~에 관해서는	in the process of ~의 과정에서	on behalf of ~을 대신하여

I will be traveling to Berlin **in place of** my boss. 나는 상사를 대신해서 베를린으로 출장 갈 것이다.

토익실전문제

출제 포인트 전치사 채우기
특정 동사, 형용사, 명사와 함께 쓰인 전치사 표현을 완성하는 문제가 출제된다.

1. Management has decided to transfer certain responsibilities formerly held by the administrative division ------- the accounting department.

(A) on (B) for
(C) to (D) of

2. Mr. Han is an advocate ------- effective early education through home- and school-based programs.

(A) to (B) by
(C) of (D) over

3. ------- complaints from guests about long waits, the hotel is adding two more elevators.

(A) In addition to (B) In response to
(C) In exchange of (D) On behalf of

정답·해설·해석 p.61

둘 중 맞는 형태를 고르세요.

01 The country has suffered from little investment ------- the past decade as a result of political instability.
ⓐ over　　　　ⓑ until

02 ------- rising costs of raw materials, import prices went up by 16 percent in August.
ⓐ Due to　　　　ⓑ Except for

03 In recent years, private investors have become increasingly attracted to this area ------- the city.
ⓐ among　　　　ⓑ of

04 Requests for assistance via e-mail or live Internet support are only processed ------- business hours.
ⓐ from　　　　ⓑ during

05 ------- a looming fiscal crisis, the country's economy has bounced back from a slump.
ⓐ Despite　　　　ⓑ For

06 Workshops are offered ------- the year on a variety of job search skills including résumé writing.
ⓐ before　　　　ⓑ throughout

07 ------- the acquisition costs, the manager anticipated additional expenses for operation and restructuring.
ⓐ Aside from　　　　ⓑ Thereafter

틀린 곳이 있으면 바르게 고치세요.

08 A recent report said the inflation rate could reach 4 percent on the beginning of next quarter.

09 Green Garden is the most popular vegan restaurant on the city.

10 Guests can leave their personal items at the hotel's front desk for safekeeping.

11 At terms of conduct, staff are expected to treat each other with respect.

12 In observance for Labor Day, all US exchanges will not be open on September 6.

13 Passengers are reminded that boarding passes must be retained to connecting flights.

14 The financial firm is below investigation for tax evasion, but most corporate lawyers agree that no laws were broken.

정답·해석 p.61

무료 해설 ▶
바로 보기

맞은 문제 개수: 　 / 14
틀린 문제에 해당하는 토익 공식을 다시 한번 학습하세요.

🕐 제한 시간 12분

Part 5

01 The firm's anniversary party will be held ------- August 26, so attendees must make a note of this date.

(A) in
(B) by
(C) on
(D) to

02 The innovative Web site allows tourists to search for and find locations of interest ------- easy traveling distance of their hotels.

(A) across
(B) within
(C) for
(D) along

03 Companies that wish to participate in the Boston Technology Exhibition should submit their applications ------- November 5.

(A) in
(B) to
(C) by
(D) until

04 Ms. Turner asked us to use the original design for the product display ------- the one submitted by the marketing team.

(A) although
(B) instead of
(C) despite
(D) when

05 The workshop teaches managers and employees how to dispute someone else's ideas ------- causing offense.

(A) except
(B) without
(C) whereas
(D) otherwise

06 The supervisor wants all of the items shipped by the end of the week, ------- of the cost.

(A) regardless
(B) regardful
(C) regarding
(D) regarded

07 The director's latest work was filmed ------- in New Zealand, although a few of the scenes were shot in Los Angeles and New York.

(A) prime
(B) primed
(C) primarily
(D) primary

08 Several staff members were required to use the workstations in the conference room ------- a lack of space in the main office.

(A) except for
(B) thanks to
(C) aside from
(D) because of

09 Due to funding constraints, BCN Limited will not accept applications for transfers to overseas branches ------- early next year.

(A) by
(B) when
(C) until
(D) through

10 Furniture appraisers are able to tell the difference ------- a genuine antique and a reproduction.

(A) upon
(B) about
(C) during
(D) between

11 The Field Gallery will host an event on July 3 to congratulate David Young ------- his nomination for the National Art Award.

(A) with
(B) of
(C) on
(D) along

12 ------- the last ten years, professional and business services have comprised 38 percent of the total job growth in the Washington region.

(A) In
(B) On
(C) Since
(D) While

13 As always, Gray Consulting looks ------- to assisting its customers with their legal needs.

(A) down
(B) out
(C) forward
(D) on

14 The agency's payroll office is located ------- the corner of Faribault and 23rd Street, across from the Trade Commission Center.

(A) at
(B) for
(C) under
(D) over

15 Wageworks Corporation is planning to replace nearly half of its computer equipment with updated devices ------- the next couple of days.

(A) on
(B) by
(C) from
(D) over

16 Many people are concerned about the high costs associated ------- homeownership, such as maintenance fees and property taxes.

(A) to
(B) on
(C) with
(D) for

17 *Teen* magazine is offering a special promotion, which entitles ------- to gift certificates at top clothing boutiques.

(A) subscribe
(B) subscribing
(C) subscribers
(D) subscription

18 The manager hopes to increase production ------- introducing bonuses for all employees who meet the output quota.

(A) by
(B) from
(C) over
(D) regarding

Part 6

Questions 19-22 refer to the following article.

Orashi Air Launches New Route

September 9—Nigeria's Orashi Air is one of West Africa's fastest-growing airlines. ------- the last decade, it has made a name for itself by offering world-class service on its frequent flights to Ghana, Chad, and Cameroon. -------.
                                                              19
                                              20

Orashi will begin by establishing a direct flight from Abuja to Paris. This is in response to a growing trend toward European travel. ------- this route, there are plans to initiate flight services to London in the near future.
                                                21

To facilitate the expansion, Orashi Air is set to purchase two new AeroJet 540-XW planes, which are more fuel efficient and have the ------- to seat 350 passengers.
                                        22

---

19 (A) Throughout
(B) Before
(C) Along
(D) Between

20 (A) This has drastically affected the visa application process.
(B) As a result, airports need tighter security measures.
(C) Now, the company hopes to expand by starting its first European route.
(D) The cost of fuel has a direct impact on the airline industry's ticket prices.

21 (A) Instead of
(B) In addition to
(C) As long as
(D) In preparation for

22 (A) quantity
(B) reservation
(C) capacity
(D) principle

해커스 스타강사의 ▶
무료 해설강의 바로 보기
(3번 문제)

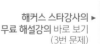

Hackers TOEIC Reading

SECTION 5
접속사와 절

등위접속사와 상관접속사

토익, 이렇게 나온다!

등위접속사와 상관접속사 관련 문제는 평균 1문제 정도 출제된다. 문맥에 알맞은 등위접속사를 채우는 문제가 가장 많이 출제되며, 상관접속사의 짝을 채우는 문제도 가끔 출제된다.

토익 필수 개념 다지기

01 등위접속사는 단어와 단어, 구와 구, 절과 절을 대등하게 연결해 주는 역할을 한다.

Students **and** teachers attended the commencement.
학생들과 교사들은 졸업식에 참석했다.

My parents are growing vegetables **and** raising animals in the countryside.
내 부모님은 시골에서 채소를 재배하고 가축을 사육하고 있다.

The power went out, **so** I left the office early. 전기가 나갔고, 그래서 나는 사무실을 일찍 떠났다.

이때, 등위접속사로 연결된 구나 절에서 서로 중복된 단어는 생략될 수 있다.

A copy editor's job is to find **(errors) and (to)** correct errors in a manuscript.
교열 담당자의 일은 원고에서 오류를 발견하고 수정하는 것이다.

He went to the department store and **(he)** bought a new wallet.
그는 백화점에 갔고 새 지갑을 샀다.

02 상관접속사는 두 단어가 서로 짝을 이루어 함께 쓰이는 접속사로, 단어와 단어, 구와 구, 절과 절을 대등하게 연결해 주는 역할을 한다.

The gallery displays **both** paintings **and** sculptures.
그 미술관은 그림과 조각품 모두 전시한다.

Payments can be made **either** with cash **or** by credit card.
결제는 현금으로 또는 신용카드로 할 수 있다.

Neither who they are **nor** what they do is known at this point.
현재로서는 그들이 누구인지도, 그들이 무엇을 하는지도 알려져 있지 않다.

토익 공식 1 등위접속사

01 등위접속사의 종류

and 그리고	or 또는	but 그러나	yet 그러나	so 그래서	for 왜냐하면

Students need to be diligent **and** responsible. 학생들은 성실하고 책임감이 있어야 한다.
John usually spends his free time reading **or** exercising. John은 보통 독서를 하거나 또는 운동을 하며 여가 시간을 보낸다.
We must clean the house, **for** my parents are visiting this evening.
우리는 집을 청소해야 하는데, 왜냐하면 부모님이 오늘 저녁에 방문하실 예정이기 때문이다.

고득점 포인트

❶ 단, so와 for는 오직 절과 절을 연결할 수 있으며, 단어나 구는 연결하지 못한다.

We all stayed late at the office, for the deadline was approaching. (○)
우리는 모두 늦게까지 사무실에 남았는데, 왜냐하면 마감일이 다가오고 있었기 때문이다.
My apartment is warm so comfortable. (×) 내 아파트는 따뜻하고 편안하다.

❷ 등위접속사 자리에 접속부사(however, therefore, instead)나 일반부사(also)는 올 수 없다.

Joseph believed that the company was profitable, therefore(→so) he bought some stocks.
Joseph은 그 회사가 수익성이 있다고 믿었고, 그래서 주식을 조금 샀다.

❸ and so(그래서), and yet(그런데도), and then(그리고 나서)은 등위접속사에 부사가 합쳐져 더욱 분명하게 의미를 전달한다.

I dislike large cities and yet I live in Los Angeles. 나는 대도시를 싫어하는데도 로스앤젤레스에 산다.

02 등위접속사는 문맥에 맞는 것을 선택해야 한다.

I ordered a wooden bed (**but**, **and**) a soft mattress. 나는 나무로 된 침대와 푹신한 매트리스를 주문했다.
▶ '나무로 된 침대와 푹신한 매트리스를 주문했다'는 문맥이 되어야 하므로, but이 아니라 and를 써야 한다.

James wants to travel to Italy, (**so**, **but**, **yet**) Sarah insists on going to Mexico.
James는 이탈리아로 여행 가고 싶지만, Sarah는 멕시코로 가는 것을 고집한다.
▶ James가 여행가고 싶은 장소와 Sarah가 가고 싶은 장소가 다르다는 문맥이므로, so가 아니라 but이나 yet을 써야 한다.

03 주어가 and로 연결되면 복수 동사를 쓰고, or로 연결되면 마지막 주어에 수를 일치시킨다.

Ms. Jenkins **and** her client <u>are</u> meeting for lunch. Ms. Jenkins와 그녀의 고객은 점심을 먹기 위해 만날 것이다.
▶ 주어(Ms. Jenkins, her client)가 and로 연결되었으므로 복수 동사(are)를 써야 한다.

I think that the department heads **or** the CEO <u>is</u> going to make the announcement.
나는 부서장들 또는 최고 경영자가 발표할 것이라 생각한다.
▶ or로 연결된 마지막 주어(the CEO)가 단수이므로 단수 동사(is)를 써야 한다.

토익실전문제

출제 포인트 등위접속사 채우기
문맥에 알맞은 등위접속사를 구별하여 채우는 문제가 주로 출제된다.

1. The corporation's portfolio of clients consisted of customers from 13 American states ------- 25 countries.

   (A) nor (B) and
   (C) by (D) both

2. Ms. Lee found the marketing firm's advertising proposal intriguing, ------- she was uncertain that it would be effective for her company.

   (A) or (B) but
   (C) following (D) meanwhile

3. Sky Tower ------- the Erickson Building is going to house the new regional office of Jacob and Associates.

   (A) yet (B) and
   (C) neither (D) or

정답·해설·해석 p.63

01 상관접속사의 종류

both A and B A와 B 모두	either A or B A 또는 B 중 하나
neither A nor B A도 B도 아닌	not A but B = B but not A = (only) B, not A A가 아닌 B
not only A but (also) B = B as well as A A뿐 아니라 B도	

The monument is situated **not** in the middle of the park, **but** next to the main entrance.
그 기념비는 공원의 한가운데가 아닌, 정문 옆에 위치해 있다.

Brad **not only** drove us to the airport, **but also** helped us with our luggage.
Brad는 우리를 공항으로 운전해서 데려다 주었을 뿐만 아니라, 수하물 옮기는 것도 도와주었다.

02 상관접속사는 맞는 짝끼리 쓰여야 한다.

Your jacket is either in your room (**and**, **or**) on the coat rack next to the bookshelf.
당신의 재킷은 당신 방에 있거나 또는 책장 옆의 코트 걸이에 있습니다.
▶ 상관접속사 either의 맞는 짝은 and가 아니고 or이다.

Sarah (**either**, **neither**) plays a musical instrument nor sings. Sarah는 악기를 연주하지도 노래를 부르지도 않는다.
▶ 상관접속사 nor의 맞는 짝은 either가 아니고 neither이다.

03 상관접속사로 연결된 주어와 동사의 수일치에 주의한다.

B에 일치시키는 경우	not A but B	either A or B	neither A nor B	not only A but also B
항상 복수 동사를 쓰는 경우	both A and B			

Either French fries **or** baked potato is served with the entree. 감자 튀김 또는 구운 감자가 메인 요리와 함께 제공된다.
▶ Either A or B에서는 B에 동사를 일치시키므로, B인 단수 명사 baked potato에 일치시켜 단수 동사 is를 쓴다.

Both Brazil **and** Venezuela are located in South America. 브라질과 베네수엘라 모두 남아메리카 대륙에 위치해 있다.
▶ Both A and B 뒤에는 항상 복수 동사를 쓰므로 복수 동사 are을 써야 한다.

토익실전문제

출제 포인트 상관접속사 채우기
상관접속사의 짝을 채우는 문제가 주로 출제된다.

1. Customers may purchase a copy of Ben Rand's newest novel either by visiting a bookstore ------- by ordering it online.

    (A) or   (B) nor
    (C) plus   (D) besides

2. An allowance for sales representatives in the field is given for transportation and hotel expenses, but ------- for entertainment or personal needs.

    (A) other   (B) nor
    (C) so   (D) not

3. The director complained that the report submitted by the supervisor was ------- incomplete but was also badly written.

    (A) only   (B) not
    (C) not only   (D) either

정답·해설·해석 p.64

HACKERS PRACTICE 토익 고득점을 위한 필수 연습

둘 중 맞는 형태를 고르세요.

01 Janet bought ------- wrapped several presents for her child's birthday party.
    ⓐ but   ⓑ and

02 He tried to enter the building, ------- the security guard had locked the front door.
    ⓐ but   ⓑ however

03 Retailers should offer discounts ------- provide additional services to attract consumers.
    ⓐ or   ⓑ nor

04 I have seen that movie several times, ------- I still enjoy watching it.
    ⓐ and yet   ⓑ therefore

05 Greg requested vacation leave in January, ------- he wanted to go skiing with his friends.
    ⓐ instead   ⓑ for

06 The observatory by the harbor ------- the traditional market downtown are the city's major tourist attractions.
    ⓐ so   ⓑ and

07 My car would not start this morning, ------- I had to call a tow truck.
    ⓐ and so   ⓑ also

밑줄 친 부분을 바르게 고치세요.

08 The recent healthcare legislation benefits <u>not only</u> doctors and patients.

09 It is recommended that you purchase a used vehicle <u>neither</u> online, but rather from a certified dealer.

10 The promotional spa package not only includes an hour-long massage <u>and</u> also a manicure.

11 <u>Both</u> Mr. Porter or Ms. Hale will present the research findings to the board.

12 Sandy is neither eating <u>or</u> drinking tonight because she has surgery tomorrow morning.

13 The dinner set offered by Jays Restaurant includes both appetizer <u>yet</u> dessert.

14 The damaged monitor can be either returned for a refund <u>also</u> exchanged for another unit.

정답·해석 p.64

무료 해설 ▶
바로 보기

맞은 문제 개수: / 14
틀린 문제에 해당하는 토익 공식을 다시 한번 학습하세요.

해커스 스타강사의
무료 해설강의 바로 보기
(10번 문제)

🕐 제한 시간 12분

Part 5

01 The Maxwell Byrd Company prides itself on having established a modern ------- efficient operational infrastructure that is unmatched in the industry.

(A) both
(B) so
(C) and
(D) then

02 Athletes who wish to participate in the New York Marathon should visit ------- the event's headquarters or Web site to submit a registration form.

(A) neither
(B) so
(C) both
(D) either

03 To prevent electricity outages in areas where the power supply is not stable, use major appliances early in the morning ------- late in the evening.

(A) and
(B) nor
(C) but
(D) or

04 If customers place an order ------- do not receive it within seven business days, they may contact the shipping department to make an inquiry.

(A) but
(B) also
(C) then
(D) still

05 All the workers were told to submit their tax documents to the accountant by Friday, ------- many of them missed the deadline.

(A) yet
(B) by
(C) so
(D) both

06 The new interior of the office has both improved employee morale ------- increased overall work efficiency.

(A) but
(B) so
(C) for
(D) and

07 The chief executive is trying to decide whether to assign an individual ------- an entire team to evaluate last week's event.

(A) and
(B) but
(C) or
(D) nor

08 More effective advertising that not only grabs a consumer's attention ------- also stimulates interest in the product is needed.

(A) or
(B) but
(C) and
(D) therefore

09 Promotions will be considered on the basis of candidates' prior experience ------- their level of dedication and loyalty.

(A) although
(B) furthermore
(C) as well as
(D) in addition

10 Participation in ------- support of the organization's charity benefit will help pay for the construction of shelters for underprivileged members of society.

(A) and
(B) so
(C) while
(D) therefore

11 Mr. Carrington's severance package has been processed by the head office, ------- not by the accounting department.

(A) besides
(B) nor
(C) but
(D) if

12 At the end of Sarah's first month of employment, the company evaluated ------- her daily accomplishments and her total output.

(A) neither
(B) both
(C) plus
(D) so

13 Copies of the annual financial report ------- to the heads of the human resources and strategic planning departments.

(A) send
(B) have sent
(C) have been sent
(D) are sending

14 The abundance of free user-generated media online has had a ------- effect on the business model of entertainment industries.

(A) last
(B) lasted
(C) lastly
(D) lasting

15 The company wishes to reassure all staff that its financial situation is stable, and that it is considering ------- layoffs nor pay reductions.

(A) and   (B) either
(C) any   (D) neither

16 Albom Limited will be refinanced ------- to save on long-term interest rates and to ensure a solid credit rating.

(A) all   (B) both
(C) as well   (D) not only

17 Applicants for the paralegal position can either mail their documents to the firm's business address ------- send them by e-mail.

(A) or   (B) then
(C) nor   (D) also

18 Those interested in business investment opportunities will be provided with ------- and relevant information to help them make an appropriate decision.

(A) comprehension   (B) comprehensive
(C) comprehensiveness (D) comprehensively

Part 6

Questions 19-22 refer to the following article.

New Horizon to Enter San Diego Telecom Market

New Horizon Telecom, the nation's fastest growing Internet and cellular service provider is happy to ------- that it is expanding into San Diego.
    19

The company requested that consulting firm DataVision conduct a survey early this year, and results showed significant demand for ------- New Horizon Telecom's high-speed Internet and quality phone
    20
services. Moreover, the lackluster service offered by competing telecommunications firms NationTel and Dash Wireless indicates the potential for thousands of customers to switch over to New Horizon. CEO Desmond Chang says the move makes perfect economic sense for the company. -------, Chang
    21
expects New Horizon to see around 50 million dollars in additional annual revenues.

The service should be up and running in San Diego before the end of the year. -------. Updates will be
    22
posted on the company's Web site as more information is disclosed.

---

19 (A) request   (B) support
    (C) announce   (D) certify

20 (A) not only   (B) with
    (C) as well as   (D) both

21 (A) On the other hand (B) In contrast
    (C) Specifically   (D) Regardless

22 (A) NationTel and Dash Wireless reached a similar agreement.
    (B) The added income will help the company make a decision.
    (C) Employees at regional offices perform better than those at headquarters.
    (D) However, a definite timetable has yet to be finalized.

관계절

토익, 이렇게 나온다!

관계절 관련 문제는 평균 1문제 정도 출제된다. 선행사에 알맞은 관계대명사를 선택하거나, 관계대명사의 격을
구별하여 채우는 문제가 가장 많이 출제된다.

토익 필수 개념 다지기

01 관계절은 문장 내에서 절 앞의 명사를 꾸며 주는 형용사 역할을 하는 수식어 거품이다.

The person **who sat next to me** was loud. 내 옆에 앉은 사람은 시끄러웠다.
I found a gym **where I can take aerobics classes**. 나는 에어로빅 수업을 들을 수 있는 체육관을 찾았다.

who sat next to me와 where I can take aerobics classes는 각각 절 앞에 있는 명사 The person과 a gym을 꾸미
는 형용사 역할을 하는 수식어 거품으로 문장에 없어도 문장은 성립된다. 이러한 형용사절을 관계절이라 부르고, 관계절의
수식을 받는 명사를 '선행사'라고 부른다.

02 관계절은 앞의 명사의 의미를 한정해 주는 한정적 용법과, 앞의 명사에 대해 부가 설명을 해주는 계속적 용법으로 쓰인다.

한정적 용법   Jake has a brother **who is a chef**.   Jake는 요리사인 형이 한 명 있다.
      → 관계절(who is a chef)이 명사(a brother)의 직업을 한정해 준다.
계속적 용법   Jake has a brother, **who is a chef**.   Jake는 형이 한 명 있는데, 그는 요리사이다.
      → 관계절(who is a chef)이 명사(a brother)에 대해 부가적인 설명을 해준다.

두 문장의 의미가 같아 보이지만, 첫 번째 문장의 경우 Jake에게 요리사가 아닌 다른 직업을 가진 형이 더 있을 수 있는 반
면, 두 번째 문장의 경우 Jake에게 형은 단 한 명뿐이다.

계속적 용법의 경우, 관계절이 앞 문장 전체에 대해 부가 설명을 할 수도 있다.
Wade finished his assignment early, **which** impressed his supervisor.
Wade는 그에게 할당된 일을 빨리 끝냈는데, 그 사실은 그의 상관에게 깊은 인상을 주었다.

03 관계절은 '관계대명사 + (주어) + 동사'/'관계부사 + 주어 + 동사'로 이루어진다.

Ms. Perez met with the consultant, **who provided advice on reducing costs**.
Ms. Perez는 컨설턴트를 만났는데, 그는 비용을 절감하는 것에 대한 조언을 제공해 주었다.
→ 선행사 consultant는 '관계대명사(who) + 동사(provided)'로 이루어진 관계절의 수식을 받고 있다. 여기서 관계대명
   사 who는 '접속사 + 대명사(and he/she)'의 역할을 한다.

The airport has a lounge **where passengers can relax**.
그 공항은 탑승객들이 휴식을 취할 수 있는 휴게실이 있다.
→ 선행사 lounge는 '관계부사(where) + 주어(passengers) + 동사(can relax)'로 이루어진 관계절의 수식을 받고 있다.
   여기서 관계부사 where는 '접속사 + 부사(and there)'의 역할을 한다.

관계대명사에는 who, whom, whose, which, that이 있고, 관계부사에는 when, where, why, how가 있다.

01 관계절은 수식어 거품 자리인, 주어와 동사 사이나 문장의 끝에 온다.

The students **whom Ms. Henderson taught** were from Japan. Ms. Henderson이 가르쳤던 학생들은 일본 출신이었다.
I didn't get a copy of the report **which was handed out yesterday**. 나는 어제 배부된 보고서 사본을 받지 못했다.

> 고득점 포인트 단, 관계절은 부사절과는 달리 필수성분 앞의 수식어 거품 자리에는 올 수 없다.
> Which is available from May, the new service will cost $25 per month. (×)
> The new service, which is available from May, will cost $25 per month. (○)
> 신규 서비스는 5월부터 이용 가능한데, 그 서비스는 한 달에 25달러일 것이다.

02 관계절을 이끄는 관계대명사나 관계부사 자리에 대명사나 부사는 올 수 없다.

Feel free to take the brochures, (**those**, **which**) are located at reception.
마음대로 안내 책자를 가져가시기 바라며, 안내 책자는 접수처에 있습니다.
▶ the brochures를 수식하기 위한 관계절을 이끄는 자리이므로 대명사(those)가 아닌 관계대명사(which)가 와야 한다.

I often shop at the market (**there**, **where**) farmers sell fresh produce.
나는 종종 농부들이 신선한 농산물을 판매하는 시장에서 장을 본다.
▶ the market을 수식하기 위한 관계절을 이끄는 자리이므로 부사(there)가 아닌 관계부사(where)가 와야 한다.

03 관계절의 동사 자리에 동사가 아닌 형태(준동사, 명사, 부사)는 올 수 없다.

The university will contact those who (**passing**, **pass**) the entrance exam.
그 대학은 입학 시험에 합격한 사람들에게 연락할 것이다.
▶ 관계절(who ~ exam)의 동사 자리에는 준동사(passing)가 올 수 없고 동사(pass)가 와야 한다.

> 고득점 포인트 관계절의 동사 자리에는 관계절 앞의 명사와 수, 태가 맞는 동사가 들어가야 한다.
> The company is in need of an accountant who have(→has) certification.
> 그 회사는 자격증을 가지고 있는 회계사를 필요로 하고 있다.
> → 관계절 앞의 명사(an accountant)가 단수이므로, 관계절에는 단수 동사(has)를 써야 한다.
> We received two tickets for a jazz concert, which recommended(→was recommended) by a colleague.
> 우리는 재즈 음악회 티켓 두 장을 받았는데, 그 음악회는 한 동료에 의해 추천된 것이었다.
> → 관계절 앞의 명사(a jazz concert)가 추천이 되는 것이므로, 관계절에는 수동태 동사(was recommended)를 써야 한다.

토익실전문제

출제 포인트 관계사 자리 채우기
수식어 거품절을 이끌 수 없는 명사절 접속사나 대명사를 제외하고 알맞은
관계사를 선택하여 채우는 문제가 출제된다.

출제 포인트 관계절 내 동사 채우기
관계절의 동사 자리에 올 수 없는 품사(준동사, 명사, 부사, 대명사)를 제외하
고 수, 태에 맞는 동사를 선택하여 채우는 문제가 출제된다.

1. The discounts ------ are available on the company's
Web site are only valid for a limited period of time.

(A) them   (B) those
(C) that   (D) this

2. Recently, the director released a list of engineers who
------ to lead the bridge project.

(A) have selected
(B) will be selecting
(C) have been selected
(D) selected

3. Dietary supplements ------ are produced from
synthetic materials are generally safe, but consumers
should consult a physician before using them.

(A) whatever   (B) what
(C) whichever   (D) which

정답·해설·해석 p.66

01 선행사가 사람이면 who(m), 사물이면 which를 쓴다.

Ms. Harris wants to hire <u>an assistant</u> (**which**, **who**) is well organized. Ms. Harris는 체계적인 비서를 고용하고 싶어 한다.

▶ 선행사가 사람(an assistant)이므로 which가 아닌 who를 써야 한다.

The invitations (~~who~~, **which**) were left with Ms. Rawson need to be sent out.
Ms. Rawson에게 남겨진 초대장들은 발송되어야 한다.

▶ 선행사가 사물(The invitations)이므로 who가 아닌 which를 써야 한다.

고득점 포인트 that은 선행사의 종류에 상관없이 주격이나 목적격 관계대명사로 쓰인다. 단, 콤마(,) 바로 뒤나 전치사 바로 뒤에는 that을 쓸 수 없다.
The chef, <u>that</u>(→who) is from India, decided to open a restaurant. 그 요리사는 인도 출신인데, 그는 식당을 열기로 결정했다.
The person <u>with that</u>(→with whom) I had an appointment is a potential client. 나와 만날 약속이 있었던 사람은 잠재적인 고객이다.

02 관계대명사에는 주격, 목적격, 소유격이 있다.

선행사 \ 격	주격	목적격	소유격
사람	who	whom, who	whose
사물·동물	which	which	whose, of which
사람·사물·동물	that	that	–

I haven't met the woman **who** is speaking at the podium. 나는 연단에서 연설하고 있는 여자를 만난 적이 없다.
The train **which** is at platform 9 is heading for Vienna. 9번 승강장에 있는 열차는 빈으로 향할 것이다.

▶ 주격 관계대명사(who/which)는 관계절 안에서 주어 역할을 한다. 따라서 주격 관계대명사(who, which) 바로 뒤에 동사(is)가 왔다.

The man (**whom/who**) I introduced to you is my boss. 내가 당신에게 소개한 남자는 내 상사이다.
Eva accepted the promotion (**which**) her supervisor offered. Eva는 그녀의 관리자가 제안했던 승진을 수락했다.

▶ 목적격 관계대명사(whom/which)는 관계절 안에서 목적어 역할을 하므로 목적격 관계대명사(whom, which) 바로 뒤에 '주어 + 동사'가 왔다. 목적격 관계대명사는 생략할 수 있고, whom 대신 who를 쓰기도 한다.

I visited my friend, **whose** apartment is nearby. 나는 친구를 방문했는데, 그의 아파트는 가까운 곳에 있다.
The reporter is working on an article, the subject **of which** is the upcoming election.
기자는 기사를 쓰고 있는데, 그 기사의 주제는 곧 있을 선거이다.

▶ 소유격 관계대명사(whose)는 관계절 안에서 '~의'를 의미하며 명사(apartment)를 꾸며 주는 소유격 역할을 한다. 사람/사물 선행사 모두에 whose를 쓸 수 있으며, 사물 선행사(an article)의 경우에는 whose 대신 of which를 쓸 수 있다.

고득점 포인트 관계대명사와 관계절의 동사 사이에 삽입절(we believe, he thought 등)이 오기도 한다. 여기서 삽입절은 생략 가능하며, 알맞은 관계대명사의 격을 고를 때에는 삽입절을 지우고 선택하도록 한다.
Cole is the artist <u>whom</u> we believe was selected to paint the mural. (×)
→ Cole is the artist <u>whom</u>(→who) was selected to paint the mural. Cole은 벽화를 그리는 데 선정되었던 화가이다.

토익실전문제

출제 포인트 관계대명사 채우기
선행사가 사람인지 사물인지와, 관계대명사의 격을 모두 구별해야 풀 수 있는 문제가 주로 출제된다.

1. A contract ------- has not yet been confirmed by the management will have no legal standing even if its terms have been agreed to by an employee.

(A) who
(B) which
(C) whom
(D) of which

2. Genex-Co is a company ------- president is committed to expanding into the lucrative European and Asian markets.

(A) who
(B) whoever
(C) whom
(D) whose

3. Job candidates ------- are currently employed must include their date of availability on the application form.

(A) who
(B) which
(C) whom
(D) whose

정답·해설·해석 p.66

토익 공식 3 | 전치사 + 관계대명사 / 수량 표현 + 관계대명사 / 관계대명사의 생략

01 | 전치사 + 관계대명사

- 앞 문장과의 공통명사가 뒷 문장에서 전치사의 목적어일 때 [전치사 + 관계대명사] 형태가 된다.

  I interviewed a woman. + I had previously met **with** her. 나는 한 여자를 인터뷰했다. + 나는 이전에 그녀를 만난 적이 있었다.

  → I interviewed a woman **whom** I had previously met **with** ____. 나는 이전에 만난 적이 있었던 여자를 인터뷰했다.

  → I interviewed a woman **with whom** I had previously met ____.

- [전치사 + 관계대명사]의 전치사는 선행사 또는 관계절 내의 동사에 따라 결정된다.

  I played in a soccer game **during which** I scored three goals. (⇦ during the soccer game)
  나는 세 골을 넣었던 축구 게임에서 뛰었다.

  This is the software program **about which** Mr. Lawson talked at the meeting. (⇦ talk about)
  이것이 Mr. Lawson이 회의에서 이야기했던 소프트웨어 프로그램이다.

- [전치사 + 관계대명사] 뒤에는 완전한 절이 온다.

  I will call the client **to whom** the package was delivered. 나는 소포가 배송된 고객에게 전화할 것이다.

> **고득점 포인트** 전치사 뒤 목적격 관계대명사 자리에 who와 that은 올 수 없다.

02 | 수량 표현 + 관계대명사

one/each all/both	some/any several	many/much/most half/the rest	+ of + 관계대명사(whom / which / whose+명사)

The class has 20 students. + **All** of the students are boys. 그 반에는 20명의 학생이 있다. + 학생들 모두가 남학생이다.

→ The class has 20 students, **and all of them** are boys.

→ The class has 20 students, **all of whom** are boys. 그 반에는 20명의 학생이 있는데, 그들 모두는 남학생이다.

03 | 관계대명사의 생략

- '주격 관계대명사 + be동사' 생략

  The location (which was) **selected** for the construction is downtown. 건설 공사를 위해 선정된 장소는 도심지이다.

  I need to speak with the person (who is) **responsible** for reservations. 나는 예약을 담당하는 사람과 이야기해야 한다.

  The parking lot (which is) **near our office** has been closed temporarily. 우리 사무실 근처의 주차장은 일시적으로 폐쇄되었다.

  ▶ '주격 관계대명사 + be동사(which was, who is, which is)'는 생략될 수 있으며, 그 뒤의 분사(selected), 형용사(responsible), 전치사구(near our office) 등이 남게 된다.

- 목적격 관계대명사 생략

  Laura Secord is the woman (whom/who) **I called** yesterday. Laura Secord는 내가 어제 전화했던 여자이다.

  This is the form (which) **you must fill out** for a membership. 이것은 당신이 회원권을 위해 가입해야 하는 양식입니다.

  ▶ 목적격 관계대명사(whom/who, which)는 생략될 수 있으며, 그 뒤의 '주어 + 동사(I called, you must fill out)'가 남게 된다.

토익실전문제

> **출제 포인트** '전치사 + 관계대명사' 채우기
> 전치사 뒤에 관계대명사를 채우거나, 전치사와 관계대명사 모두를 채우는 문제가 주로 출제된다.

> **출제 포인트** '수량 표현 + 관계대명사' 채우기
> 수량 표현 뒤에 관계대명사를 채우는 문제가 주로 출제된다.

> **출제 포인트** 관계대명사의 생략 시 뒤에 오는 형태 채우기
> 관계대명사와 be동사의 생략 뒤에 형용사나 분사를 채우는 문제가 주로 출제된다.

1. The inclusion of CDs and other supplemental materials is a method by ------- textbook publishers increase the educational value of their products.

   (A) whoever   (B) who
   (C) which   (D) what

2. A lot of automotive manufacturers participated in the exhibition, some of ------- took advantage of the opportunity to introduce next year's models.

   (A) who   (B) whom
   (C) they   (D) that

3. Of the three applicants ------- for appointment to a managerial position, two have experience working at an overseas branch.

   (A) suitability   (B) suitable
   (C) suitably   (D) suitableness

정답·해설·해석 p.66

01 선행사의 종류에 따라 각각 다른 관계부사가 쓰인다.

선행사	관계부사
시간 [day, year, time]	when
이유 [the reason]	why
장소 [place, building]	where
방법 [the way]	how (the way와 how는 함께 쓸 수 없으므로 the way 또는 how만 써야 한다.)

Friday is <u>the final day</u> **when** discounts are offered. 금요일은 할인이 제공되는 마지막 날이다.
<u>The apartment</u> **where** I live has a gym and swimming pool. 내가 사는 아파트는 체육관과 수영장을 가지고 있다.
Olivia didn't give me <u>a reason</u> **why** she changed the terms of the contract.
Olivia는 그녀가 계약 조건들을 변경한 이유를 내게 알려주지 않았다.
It is important to find out **the way/how** the equipment works before using it.
사용하기 전에 장비가 어떻게 작동하는지 알아내는 것이 중요하다.

02 관계부사는 '전치사 + 관계사'로 바꾸어 쓸 수 있다.

The building **where(=in which)** the employees work is safe and secure.
직원들이 일하는 건물은 안전하고 보안이 철저하다.

The date **when(=on which)** I started this job was February 28.
내가 이 일을 시작했던 날짜는 2월 28일이었다.

03 관계부사 다음에는 완전한 절이 오고, 관계대명사 다음에는 주어나 목적어가 빠진 불완전한 절이 온다.

There was <u>a time</u> **when** this restaurant served hundreds of customers each day.
이 식당이 매일 수백명의 고객들을 대접하던 시기가 있었다.
▶ 관계부사(when) 다음에는 주어와 목적어가 모두 갖춰진 완전한 절이 온다.

That is <u>the woman</u> **who** complained about her order. 저 사람이 주문에 대해 항의했던 그 여자이다.
▶ 관계대명사(who) 다음에는 주어나 목적어가 빠진 불완전한 절이 온다.

토익실전문제

출제 포인트 관계대명사와 관계부사 구별하여 채우기
관계부사와 비교하여 관계대명사를 채우는 문제가 주로 출제된다.

1. Staff members ------- would like to visit the food and beverages trade fair this week must obtain permission from their supervisors.

   (A) who (B) when
   (C) which (D) whose

2. The new shuttle service, ------- has been operating since last year, serves all of the city's main shopping districts.

   (A) who (B) which
   (C) what (D) where

3. Ms. Torres applied for a job at the hospital ------- she did volunteer work while attending university.

   (A) which (B) how
   (C) who (D) where

정답·해설·해석 p.67

둘 중 맞는 형태를 고르세요.

01 Susan can speak several languages, ------- is an asset when working with foreign clients.
ⓐ which   ⓑ they

02 Passengers ------- are standing in line need to have their travel documents ready.
ⓐ which   ⓑ who

03 All writers ------- proposals are chosen will be given extra vacation days as a reward.
ⓐ whose   ⓑ that

04 Mr. Ing installed security lights ------- automatically switch on when someone enters the room.
ⓐ those   ⓑ that

05 Customers ------- would like to apply for a store membership may stop by the information desk.
ⓐ who   ⓑ they

06 The printer model comes with an offer of six free ink cartridges, ------- is available for a limited time only.
ⓐ which   ⓑ who

07 People ------- identification numbers are on the waiting list must call again tomorrow.
ⓐ whom   ⓑ whose

틀린 곳이 있으면 바르게 고치세요.

08 On your desk is the project timetable where will be discussed at the meeting tomorrow.

09 The number of entertainment programs that is targeted at young adults has steadily increased.

10 The upcoming workshop is the first in a series that the department having organized.

11 The changing climate is an issue when has created a lot of concern amongst environmentalists.

12 The stairway, that leads to the second floor, is being rebuilt.

13 I purchased a new suit and a tie at the department store, both of them were on sale.

14 The bakery where Jake works is popular for its cakes.

정답·해석 p.67

무료 해설 ▶
바로 보기

맞은 문제 개수: / 14
틀린 문제에 해당하는 토익 공식을 다시 한번 학습하세요.

🕐 제한 시간 12분

Part 5

01 The supervisor implemented a dress code policy, ------- she believes will result in a more professional work environment.
(A) which
(B) that
(C) what
(D) who

02 A ceremony will be held in recognition of all ------- had important roles in the launch of the company's latest product.
(A) who
(B) whose
(C) these
(D) those

03 Boundless Air hired eight certified pilots, all of ------- were trained at the same institute in Manhattan.
(A) what
(B) whom
(C) they
(D) them

04 At a meeting yesterday, staff studied the most recently proposed financial plan, ------- the CEO believes will help pull the corporation out of debt.
(A) while
(B) when
(C) which
(D) that

05 The government's latest expansion of its education support program has provided students with types of tuition assistance ------- were formerly unavailable.
(A) what
(B) these
(C) that
(D) there

06 To avoid communication problems, employees assigned to work overseas are required to study the language of the country in ------- they will reside.
(A) which
(B) that
(C) whom
(D) who

07 In an attempt to improve relations with his subordinates and better understand their abilities, the boss will talk with ------- himself.
(A) anyone
(B) everyone
(C) neither one
(D) no one

08 Attached to this letter is a pre-addressed, stamped envelope ------- to place your application for membership to our club.
(A) for whom
(B) in which
(C) what
(D) wherever

09 There have been some problems with the printer, ------- it is taking the marketing department longer to produce the advertising posters than expected.
(A) that
(B) moreover
(C) so
(D) therefore

10 The information packet that ------- to participants outlines the topics that will be discussed at the workshop.
(A) mails
(B) have been mailed
(C) mail
(D) was mailed

11 A budget overrun of 3.2 billion Yen has been reported by Tekeda Construction this quarter, most of ------- is accounted for by the oil refinery project.
(A) several
(B) which
(C) both
(D) whose

12 After ------- of the planned increase in the federal minimum wage, Howser Electronics raised the prices of its software to offset any possible future losses.
(A) inform
(B) been informed
(C) being informed
(D) will inform

13 The Mother Nature Garden Show, ------- annually demonstrates the newest technology in horticulture, draws over 5,000 attendees during its week-long run.
(A) when
(B) which
(C) where
(D) whose

14 Terra Enterprises announced its intention to hire a qualified operations manager ------- has strong problem-solving skills.
(A) she
(B) if
(C) who
(D) because

15 Of all the advisors ------- with the governor's reelection campaign, Mr. McKenzie is the most knowledgeable on economic issues.

(A) associates
(B) association
(C) associating
(D) associated

16 A dinner will take place next Friday to honor Richard Perkins, ------- has been a valued employee of this bank for over 30 years.

(A) who
(B) which
(C) whose
(D) of which

17 Neo International has advertised a position for a personnel director whose professional goals ------- with the company's long-term plans.

(A) compatible
(B) compatibility
(C) are compatible
(D) has compatibility

18 An employee ------- performance during a specified period is satisfactory may receive a raise based on current pay standards.

(A) who
(B) whom
(C) whose
(D) which

Part 6

Questions 19-22 refer to the following e-mail.

From: murphy@harebuilders.com
To: williams@houston.com
Date: May 22
Subject: Arena Blueprints

Dear Mr. Williams,

Our engineers reviewed the plans for the new arena our firm -------. In preparation for construction,
19
they compared measurements of the site with our blueprints and discovered that there are some

-------. Regardless of how this happened, we have to take corrective action.
20
Therefore, you will need to draw up new plans ------- the right measurements. Unless the blueprints
21
are fixed, we cannot begin work on the project. -------. Our client will object to any postponement
22
considering that a single day can lead to thousands of dollars in additional expenses. So, I would
appreciate it if you could update the blueprints immediately.

Terry Murphy, Hare Builders

19 (A) had built
(B) built
(C) is building
(D) was building

20 (A) discrepancies
(B) statistics
(C) diagrams
(D) patterns

21 (A) has displayed
(B) that displayed
(C) that display
(D) and are displaying

22 (A) Let me specify exactly what my engineers said.
(B) It could result in costly delays for everyone involved.
(C) You can request a postponement if you need more time.
(D) We are not certain how the errors were made.

GRAMMAR Part 5,6

Ch 16 관계절   Hackers TOEIC Reading

CHAPTER 17 부사절

토익, 이렇게 나온다!
부사절 관련 문제는 평균 2문제 정도 꾸준히 출제되며 최대 4문제까지 출제된다. 문맥에 알맞은 부사절 접속사를 채우는 문제가 가장 많이 출제된다.

토익 필수 개념 다지기

01 부사절은 문장 내에서 시간이나 조건 등을 나타내는 부사 역할을 하는 수식어 거품이다.

Please call me **before you leave**. 당신이 떠나기 전에 전화해 주세요.
If you eat that, you will get sick. 그것을 먹는다면, 당신은 아플 것이다.

부사절 before you leave와 If you eat that은 문장에서 시간과 조건을 나타내는 부사 역할을 하는 수식어 거품으로 문장에 없어도 문장은 성립된다.

02 부사절은 '부사절 접속사 + 주어 + 동사'로 이루어진다.

<u>Once</u> **you finish the work**, let me know. 그 업무를 끝마치는 대로, 제게 알려 주세요.

부사절은 '부사절 접속사(Once) + 주어(you) + 동사(finish)'로 이루어진다.

단, 부사절의 동사가 be동사일 경우 [주어 + be동사]는 생략될 수 있다. 따라서 부사절 접속사 뒤에 주어와 be동사 없이 바로 형용사나 전치사구가 올 수 있다.

I can loan you some money <u>if **(it is)** necessary</u>. [부사절 접속사 + 형용사]
필요하다면 나는 당신에게 약간의 돈을 빌려줄 수 있다.

<u>When **(you are)** in business</u>, it's important to understand marketing strategies. [부사절 접속사 + 전치사구]
사업을 할 때는, 마케팅 전략을 이해하는 것이 중요하다.

부사절 접속사로는 when, if, although, because, whatever 등이 있다.

토익 공식 1 부사절의 자리와 쓰임

01 부사절은 수식어 거품 자리, 특히 필수성분 앞이나 필수성분 뒤에 온다.

If you can't meet today, we can get together tomorrow. 당신이 오늘 만날 수 없다면, 우리는 내일 모일 수 있습니다.
You can fill out this form **while you are waiting to see the doctor**.
의사에게 진료받기 위해 기다리고 계시는 동안 이 양식을 작성하실 수 있습니다.

02 부사절은 문장에서 부사 역할을 하며, 문장에서 명사를 뒤에서 꾸며 주는 형용사 역할을 하는 관계절과 구별된다.

부사절   I started looking for a house **when I accepted the job in Berlin**.
나는 베를린에 있는 일자리를 수락했을 때 집을 구하기 시작했다.

관계절   The Olton Hotel is a venue **where we held the event**. Olton 호텔은 우리가 그 행사를 주최했던 장소이다.

▶ 여기서 부사절은 시간을 나타내는 부사 역할을 하지만, 관계절은 명사(a venue)를 꾸며 주는 형용사 역할을 한다.

03 부사절 접속사는 절 앞에 오는 것이 원칙이지만, 어떤 부사절 접속사는 분사구문(-ing, p.p.) 앞에 오기도 한다.

After checking in, the passengers headed to immigration. 탑승 수속을 한 후에, 탑승객들은 출입국 심사대로 향했다.
The machine continually runs **unless** switched off. 그 기계는 꺼지지 않으면 계속해서 작동한다.

▶ 여기서 부사절 접속사(After/unless)가 분사구문(checking ~/switched ~) 앞에 와 있다.

고득점 포인트

❶ 분사구문 앞에 쓰인 부사절 접속사 대신 전치사를 쓰지 않도록 주의해야 한다.
The machine continually runs without(→unless) switched off.

❷ 분사구문 앞에 자주 오는 부사절 접속사

when ~할 때	before ~ 전에	after ~한 이후에	since ~한 이래로	while ~하는 동안
whenever ~할 때마다	unless ~이 아니라면	until ~할 때까지	once 일단 ~하면, ~하는 대로	

❸ 부사절 접속사 before/after/since 뒤에 과거분사가 포함된 분사구문이 올 경우, p.p.가 아닌 'being + p.p.' 형태가 온다.
After laid off(→ being laid off) from the firm, he started running his own business.
회사에서 정리 해고를 당한 이후에, 그는 자신의 사업을 운영하기 시작했다.

Since established(→ being established), the company has become a leader in the industry.
설립된 이후에, 그 회사는 업계의 선두가 되었다.

토익실전문제

출제 포인트 부사절 접속사 자리 채우기
수식어 거품절을 이끌 수 없는 전치사를 제외하고, 알맞은 부사절 접속사를 채우는 문제가 주로 출제된다.

1. ------- the marketing head relocates to Singapore, there will be an open position at the main office.

(A) Therefore　　(B) Wherever
(C) If　　(D) That

2. ------- the minimum wage has increased in some countries over the past few years, it is still below poverty level in many nations.

(A) However　　(B) That
(C) Whereas　　(D) Despite

3. Customers who hear music on an open telephone line ------- placed on hold are less likely to hang up.

(A) from　　(B) unless
(C) ahead　　(D) while

정답·해설·해석 p.70

01 시간을 나타내는 부사절 접속사

접속사	예 문
until ~할 때까지 before ~하기 전에	Visitors are not permitted entry **until** they have signed in. 방문객들은 서명할 때까지 입장이 허락되지 않는다. We bought tickets **before** they sold out. 우리는 매진되기 전에 티켓을 구매했다.
when ~할 때 as ~할 때, ~함에 따라 while ~하는 동안 even as 마침 ~할 때	**When** the winner was announced, the audience applauded. 우승자가 발표되었을 때, 청중은 박수를 쳤다. **While** driving to work, I listened to the news on the radio. 직장까지 운전하는 동안, 나는 라디오로 뉴스를 들었다. → 특정한 시점에 발생하는 사건에는 when을 쓰지만, 두 동작이나 상태가 동시에 오래 지속되는 경우에는 while을 쓴다.
since ~한 이래로 after ~한 이후에	I haven't been to an amusement park **since** I was a child. 나는 어린아이였던 이래로 놀이공원에 가본 적이 없다. People asked Ms. Lee questions **after** she finished her speech. Ms. Lee가 연설을 마친 이후에 사람들은 그녀에게 질문했다.
once 일단 ~하면, ~하는 대로 as soon as ~하자마자 (= immediately after)	We will ship your order **once** we receive payment. 우리는 대금을 받는 대로 귀하의 주문품을 발송할 것입니다. The students ran out of the classroom **as soon as** the bell rang. 종이 울리자마자 학생들은 교실에서 뛰어나갔다.

고득점 포인트

❶ as와 since는 '~이기 때문에', while은 '~한 반면에'를 의미하는 부사절 접속사로 쓰이기도 한다.

Sue requested maternity leave <u>since</u> she was about to have a baby. Sue는 곧 아기를 낳을 예정이었기 때문에 출산 휴가를 요청했다.
Many passengers selected the fish option, <u>while</u> others chose the beef.
다른 탑승객들이 소고기 요리를 택한 반면에, 많은 탑승객들은 생선 요리를 선택했다.

❷ 하나의 수식어 거품절 앞에 부사절 접속사가 2개 연속해서 올 수 없지만, 예외적으로 until after는 가능하다.

Please remain seated <u>until after</u> the seatbelt light has been switched off.
좌석 벨트 표시등이 꺼진 이후까지 계속 자리에 앉아 계시기 바랍니다.

02 시간을 나타내는 부사절 접속사 다음에는, 미래를 나타내기 위해서 현재 시제를 쓴다.

I need to complete my article <u>before</u> the editor (~~will leave~~, **leaves**) today.
나는 오늘 편집장이 퇴근하기 전에 기사를 완성해야 한다.

▶ 시간을 나타내는 부사절 접속사(before) 다음에는 미래를 나타내기 위해 현재 시제를 써야 하므로 will leave 대신 leaves가 와야 한다.

고득점 포인트

단, since 다음에는 과거 시제가 자주 오며, 이 경우 주절에는 현재완료 시제가 온다.

My parents <u>have lived</u> in this house <u>since</u> they <u>got</u> married. 내 부모님은 결혼하신 이래로 이 집에서 살아오셨다.

토익실전문제

출제 포인트 부사절 접속사 채우기

문맥에 알맞은 시간을 나타내는 부사절 접속사를 채우는 문제가 주로 출제된다.

1. ------ all of the appropriate paperwork has been filed, you will be officially registered as an accountant at Royers Financial Firm.

   (A) Whether   (B) Once
   (C) As if   (D) Yet

2. The author has received several interview requests ------ a positive book review was published in a major newspaper last Wednesday.

   (A) through   (B) unless
   (C) besides   (D) since

3. Patrons who arrive more than 20 minutes ------ the opera begins should wait in the lobby until the doors to the main hall are opened.

   (A) before   (B) when
   (C) during   (D) since

정답·해설·해석 p.70

토익 공식 3 부사절 접속사 2 : 조건, 양보

01 조건을 나타내는 부사절 접속사

접속사	예 문
if 만약 ~라면 assuming (that) 만약 ~라면	**If** you need to make an appointment, please call the receptionist. 만약 약속을 정하시려면, 접수원에게 전화하시기 바랍니다. **Assuming that** everyone is free, the board will gather on Monday. 만약 모두가 한가하다면, 이사회는 월요일에 모일 것이다.
unless 만약 ~이 아니라면 (= if ~ not)	Let's order some lunch, **unless** you've eaten already. 만약 이미 식사한 것이 아니라면, 점심을 주문하자.
as long as, providing (that) provided (that), on condition that only if 오직 ~하는 경우에만	You can borrow my laptop **as long as** you return it by noon. 당신은 정오까지 내 노트북 컴퓨터를 돌려주는 경우에만 그것을 빌릴 수 있다. Refunds are available **only if** items are returned within seven days. 물품이 7일 이내에 반환되는 경우에만 환불이 가능하다.
in case (that), in the event (that) ~에 대비하여 (~의 경우)	An indoor venue for the event has been arranged **in case** the weather is poor. 날씨가 궂을 경우에 대비하여 그 행사를 위한 실내 장소가 마련되었다. Exit the building immediately **in the event that** the fire alarm rings. 화재경보기가 울릴 경우 즉시 건물을 빠져나가시오. → in case (that)와 in the event (that)는 앞으로 일어날 상황에 대처할 일을 계획하고 있을 때 쓰는 표현이다.

고득점 포인트

❶ as long as는 '~하는 동안, ~만큼 오래'를 의미하는 시간의 부사절 접속사로 쓰이기도 한다.
Please hold on to a strap <u>as long as</u> the bus is in motion. 버스가 움직이는 동안 손잡이를 잡으시오.

❷ 조건을 나타내는 부사절 접속사 다음에는, 미래를 나타내기 위해서 현재 시제를 쓴다.
I will meet you at the hotel if we <u>will get(→get)</u> separated. 우리가 따로 떨어지게 된다면 나는 호텔에서 당신을 만날 것이다.

❸ if와 whether는 명사절 접속사와 부사절 접속사 모두로 쓰일 수 있다. 명사절 접속사로 쓰일 때는 의미가 같지만, 부사절 접속사로 쓰일 때는 뜻이 다르다는 점을 주의해야 한다. 명사절 접속사에 관해서는 Chapter 18(p.208)에서 자세히 다룬다.
명사절   if=whether ~인지 아닌지   I couldn't tell if(=whether) he was happy or not. 나는 그가 만족했는지 아닌지 알 수 없었다.
부사절   if 만약 ~라면   If you need extra help, give me a call. 추가적인 도움이 필요하면, 전화해 주세요.
     whether ~이든 아니든   Whether you accept it or not, my decision is final. 당신이 받아들이든 아니든, 내 결정은 최종적이다.

02 양보를 나타내는 부사절 접속사

접속사	예 문
although, though, even if even though 비록 ~이지만	**Although** the shipment arrived on time, several items were broken. 선적물은 제때 도착했지만, 몇몇 물품들이 부서졌다.
whereas, while ~한 반면에	This hotel is cheap, **whereas** others in this area are expensive. 이 지역의 다른 호텔들은 비싼 반면에 이 호텔은 저렴하다.

토익실전문제

출제 포인트   부사절 접속사 채우기

문맥에 알맞은 조건이나 양보를 나타내는 부사절 접속사를 구별하여 채우는 문제가 출제된다.
although를 because와 구별하여 채우는 문제가 자주 출제된다.

1. The value of the dollar will continue to drop ------- the government intervenes to halt the downswing.

(A) unless   (B) whether
(C) except   (D) or

2. After giving an exceptional interview, Perry James got the job he applied for, ------- he won't begin work until next month.

(A) if   (B) so
(C) although   (D) because

3. Customers may contact the service hotline ------- their computers are unable to access the Internet using the router.

(A) unless   (B) although
(C) whether   (D) if

정답·해설·해석 p.70

01 이유, 목적, 결과를 나타내는 부사절 접속사

접속사	예 문
because, as, since ~이기 때문에	Bring a sweater with you **since** the lecture hall is chilly. 강의실이 춥기 때문에 스웨터를 가져오세요.
now that ~이니까	**Now that** you understand our work schedule, let's discuss our pay scale. 당신이 우리의 업무 일정을 이해했으니까, 급여 체계를 논의합시다.
in that ~라는 점에서	This vehicle is better **in that** it can seat more people. 더 많은 사람들을 수용할 수 있다는 점에서 이 차량이 더 낫다.
so that, in order that ~할 수 있도록	Passwords are required **so that** information won't be accessed by unauthorized people. 승인되지 않은 사람들에 의해 정보가 접근될 수 없도록 비밀번호가 필요하다.
so/such ~ that - 매우 ~해서 -하다	I was **so** bored of living in the country **that** I moved to Seattle. 나는 시골에서 사는 것이 매우 지루해서 시애틀로 이사 갔다. It was **such** an interesting movie **that** I watched it twice. 매우 흥미로운 영화여서 나는 그것을 두 번이나 봤다.

02 except that/but that(~을 제외하고는)

Ms. Demian's screenplay is perfect **except that** it needs a better title.
더 나은 제목이 필요하다는 것을 제외하고는 Ms. Demian의 시나리오는 완벽하다.

03 as if/as though/(just) as(마치 ~처럼)

The readers spoke of the novel **as though** its characters were real people.
독자들은 등장인물들이 마치 실재 인물들인 것처럼 그 소설에 대해 말했다.

04 given that/considering (that)(~을 고려했을 때, ~을 고려하여)

It is great how quickly the product is selling, **considering** it was released just a week ago.
단 일주일 전에 출시되었다는 것을 고려하면, 그 제품이 얼마나 빠르게 판매되고 있는지는 대단하다.

토익실전문제

출제 포인트 부사절 접속사 채우기

이유를 나타내는 부사절에 because나 since를 채우는 문제가 가장 많이 출제된다.

1. A conference call involving all the company's senior managers has been organized ------- they can discuss problems including customer dissatisfaction.

   (A) in order   (B) so that
   (C) because   (D) only

2. A number of staff were late coming to the office ------- the East-bound A-train got stuck on the tracks.

   (A) although   (B) because
   (C) that   (D) until

3. ------- that wheat exports have declined significantly over the past year, farmers are likely to appeal to the government for assistance.

   (A) Considering   (B) So
   (C) In case   (D) Unless

정답·해설·해석 p.71

토익 공식 5 부사절 접속사 4 : 복합관계부사 whenever, wherever, however

01 복합관계부사가 이끄는 부사절은 문장 내에서 부사 역할을 한다.

> **whenever** 언제 ~하든 상관없이 (=at any time when), 언제 ~하더라도 (=no matter when)
> **wherever** 어디로/어디에 ~하든 상관없이 (=at any place where), 어디로/어디에서 ~하더라도 (=no matter where)
> **however** 어떻게 ~할지라도 (=by whatever means), 아무리 ~하더라도 (=no matter how)

I saw someone I knew **wherever(=at any place where)** I went during the trade fair.
나는 무역 박람회 동안 어디로 가든지 내가 아는 누군가를 봤다.

Guests can help themselves to refreshments **whenever(=no matter when)** they wish.
손님들은 원할 때는 언제라도 다과를 먹을 수 있다.

However(=No matter how) carefully I plan my trips, there's always something I forget.
내가 아무리 신중하게 여행을 계획하더라도, 항상 잊어버리는 무언가가 있다.

▶ however가 no matter how의 뜻일 경우에는 'however + 형용사/부사 + 주어 + 동사'의 형태로 쓰인다.

고득점 포인트

❶ however는 [however + 형용사/부사 + 주어 + 동사]의 형태로 자주 쓰인다.
  However often I've been in London, I still find the city amazing. 내가 아무리 자주 런던에 가 봤어도, 나는 여전히 그 도시가 놀랍다.

❷ however가 포함된 표현들
  Visit <u>however</u> often you can. 당신이 할 수 있는 한 자주 방문해라.   <u>however</u> hard I try 내가 아무리 열심히 노력하더라도
  <u>however</u> much it costs 그것이 아무리 비싸더라도   <u>however</u> well I perform 내가 아무리 잘 해내더라도

❸ however는 접속부사로도 자주 쓰인다.
  This restaurant has a great lunch menu; <u>however</u>, prices are high. 이 식당은 훌륭한 점심 메뉴가 있지만, 가격이 비싸다.

02 복합관계대명사 whoever, whatever, whichever도 부사절을 이끌 수 있다.

> **whoever** 누가 ~하더라도 (=no matter who)
> **whatever** 무엇이/무엇을 ~하더라도 (=no matter what)
> **whichever** 어느 것이/어느 것을 ~하더라도 (=no matter which)

Whoever(= No matter who) is at the door, ask them to come back later.
현관에 누가 있더라도, 나중에 다시 오라고 요청해 주세요.

cf) **Whatever** you want to order is okay with us. 당신이 주문하고 싶은 것이 무엇이든 우리는 괜찮습니다.

▶ 여기서 Whatever는 문장에서 주어 역할을 하는 명사절을 이끌고 있다. 복합관계대명사에 관해서는 Chapter 18의 토익 공식 5 명사절 접속사 4 (p.213)에서 자세히 다룬다.

토익실전문제

출제 포인트 복합관계부사 채우기
문맥에 알맞은 복합관계부사를 선택하여 채우는 문제가 주로 출제된다.

1. Grayson Automotive asks clients to fill out a service evaluation form ------- they have a vehicle serviced.

   (A) whichever   (B) whoever
   (C) whenever   (D) whatever

2. ------- much Mr. Taylor's employer is paying him, Carson Agency has offered to double his salary if he accepts their job proposal.

   (A) Whatever   (B) However
   (C) Whichever   (D) Wherever

3. Highly-advanced new technology allows safe and speedy transactions over the Internet from ------- a customer is located.

   (A) whichever   (B) however
   (C) wherever   (D) whatever

정답·해설·해석 p.71

01 혼동되는 부사절 접속사와 전치사

의미	부사절 접속사	전치사
시간	when ~할 때 while ~하는 동안 by the time, until ~할 때까지 after ~한 후에, before ~ 전에 once ~하는 대로, as soon as ~하자마자 since ~한 이래로	in, at ~에 during ~ 동안 by, until ~까지 following, after ~ 후에, before, prior to ~ 전에 on(upon) -ing ~하자마자 since ~ 이래로
조건	unless 만약 ~이 아니라면 in case (that), in the event (that) ~한 경우에, ~에 대비하여	without ~이 없다면, ~없이 in case of, in the event of ~의 경우에
양보	although, even though 비록 ~이지만, while ~한 반면에	despite, in spite of ~에도 불구하고
이유	because, as, since ~이기 때문에	because of, due to ~ 때문에
목적	so that ~ can -, in order that ~ can - ~할 수 있도록	so as to, in order to + 동사원형 ~하기 위해서
제외	except that, but that ~을 제외하고는	except (for), but (for) ~을 제외하고는
기타	given that, considering (that) ~을 고려했을 때 whether ~에 상관없이 as if, as though 마치 ~처럼 as ~처럼	given, considering ~을 고려했을 때 regardless of ~에 상관없이 like ~처럼 as ~로서(자격)

02 부사절 접속사는 '절' 앞에, 전치사는 '구' 앞에 온다.

The appointment was canceled **because** Mr. Stanley had an emergency.
Mr. Stanley에게 응급 상황이 생겼기 때문에 그 약속은 취소되었다.

The appointment was canceled **because of** an unexpected emergency.
예상치 못한 응급 상황 때문에 그 약속은 취소되었다.

▶ '절(주어 + 동사)' 앞에는 부사절 접속사 because를 써야 하고, '구' 앞에는 전치사 because of를 써야 한다.

> **고득점 포인트**
> 접속부사는 절을 이끌 수 없으므로, 부사절 접속사 대신 쓰일 수 없다.
> We may encounter financial difficulty <u>otherwise</u>(→unless) we can find a cheaper supplier.
> 더 저렴한 공급자를 찾지 못하면, 우리는 재정난에 직면할 수도 있다.

토익실전문제

출제 포인트 부사절 접속사 자리 채우기
부사절 접속사를 동일한 의미를 갖는 전치사와 구별하여 채우는 문제가 주로 출제된다.

1. The documents will be delivered by courier ------- a completed request form is submitted online or via fax machine.
   (A) once   (B) just
   (C) upon   (D) still

2. Gold prices have stabilized ------- oil prices have risen sharply due to a production shortage in the Middle East.
   (A) during   (B) in addition
   (C) while   (D) meantime

3. ------- the company's line of merchandise has remained unchanged over the past several years, it is still popular with consumers all over the country.
   (A) Despite   (B) Nevertheless
   (C) Then   (D) Although

정답·해설·해석 p.71

HACKERS PRACTICE 토익 고득점을 위한 필수 연습

둘 중 맞는 형태를 고르세요.

01 ------- I forgot my wallet, I didn't have any ID card.
ⓐ As ⓑ For

02 ------- the shoes cost more than I had budgeted, I got them anyway.
ⓐ Because ⓑ Although

03 I can't start the project ------- marketing research is done.
ⓐ until ⓑ while

04 ------- the restaurant is crowded, people wait in line for hours to get a table.
ⓐ Whenever ⓑ However

05 Please provide the address of an e-mail account with unlimited storage ------- we send large files.
ⓐ therefore ⓑ in case

06 The new bus terminal will begin operations in May ------- the construction is completed.
ⓐ so ⓑ if

07 I bought a color printer ------- I can print my own brochures.
ⓐ so that ⓑ furthermore

틀린 곳이 있으면 바르게 고치세요.

08 I made the reservations even I wasn't sure how many people were coming.

09 Despite the show didn't have great ratings, the network renewed it.

10 Total profit rose by 200 percent during Mr. Jameson was the president of the company.

11 The head accountant should refer to the company's yearly expense report from drawing up a new budget plan.

12 The hostess will mail out the invitations as soon they arrive from the printing shop.

13 I rescheduled the launch while the media campaign wasn't ready.

14 Not even a manager can leave work early without notification unless when he is sick.

정답·해석 p.71

무료 해설 ▶
바로 보기

맞은 문제 개수: / 14
틀린 문제에 해당하는 토익 공식을 다시 한번 학습하세요.

🕐 제한 시간 12분

Part 5

01 Everyone must identify themselves to front desk personnel ------- they are entering for a short time.

(A) regarding   (B) whether
(C) in spite of   (D) even if

02 The new sedans produced by Ventress provide drivers with all the comforts of a modern vehicle ------- saving them money on fuel consumption.

(A) while   (B) for
(C) after   (D) since

03 At Pemberton Textile Company, quarterly bonuses are awarded ------- the sales goals are met.

(A) as to   (B) in case
(C) rather than   (D) provided that

04 The manager of the convention hall has contacted several security firms ------- approval to upgrade the alarm system was given.

(A) until   (B) because of
(C) in case of   (D) since

05 Please tell the person in charge to notify the researcher ------- the survey participants have completed the assessment forms.

(A) when   (B) which
(C) who   (D) whatever

06 The club is so exclusive that applicants will not be granted membership ------- recommended by a current member.

(A) except for   (B) or else
(C) but   (D) unless

07 The policy on employee benefits was revised by management ------- the current package was considered to be too expansive.

(A) even if   (B) rather than
(C) because   (D) anyway

08 Experts are correct ------- that the country's economy is growing faster than those of other nations.

(A) in   (B) for
(C) upon   (D) so

09 The executive will accept the job ------- all of his conditions are met.

(A) up to   (B) overall
(C) only if   (D) but that

10 ------- deciding whether to purchase an apartment, it is necessary to calculate the cost of property taxes and maintenance.

(A) Whatever   (B) Whomever
(C) Whichever   (D) Whenever

11 *The National Review* became the best-selling newspaper in the country ------- hiring several notable journalists from other publications.

(A) unless   (B) at
(C) after   (D) over

12 Members of the legal team are being asked to work extra hours ------- the contract negotiations are complete.

(A) whether   (B) until
(C) through   (D) upon

13 Managers may use the corporate credit card only to pay for meals and accommodations during business trips, but ------- to purchase personal items.

(A) already   (B) nor
(C) not   (D) yet

14 This color copier will reproduce images and text with remarkable clarity ------- the machine parts are checked and cared for regularly.

(A) furthermore   (B) in case
(C) although   (D) as long as

15 An account for TikTak's streaming music service cannot be accessed or reactivated ------- deleted by the registered user.

(A) then   (B) once
(C) after   (D) later

16 ------- the bank approves his application for a small business loan, Gary intends to open his shop by the end of the year.

(A) Providing   (B) Nevertheless
(C) Regardless   (D) Until

17 Included in this month's issue is a coupon for a discounted one-year subscription ------- readers can introduce the magazine to their friends.

(A) in case   (B) so that
(C) in addition to   (D) so as

18 ------- the amount of raw materials needed, Addison Manufacturing will explore other means to obtain the supplies they require.

(A) Consider   (B) Considered
(C) Considering   (D) Consideration

Part 6

Questions 19-22 refer to the following e-mail.

Date: August 9
From: jdemers@starwaysfurniture.com
To: bkent@filconsulting.com
Subject: Job Placement Assistance

Dear Mr. Kent,

The ------- expansion of our manufacturing plant in California has made it possible for Starways Furniture to increase the production capacity and manpower at this facility. We plan to close our factories in Wisconsin and Kansas, and all furniture production ------- to the Los Angeles factory on September 1.

We have asked the workers at these two factories to relocate, but some have rejected the proposal. Therefore, we have decided to offer them job placement assistance, ------- a resignation agreement is signed.

To expedite job placement, we would like your company to provide these employees with employment training workshops. -------. The Wisconsin and Kansas plants will close over the next two weeks. Can we meet on Monday to discuss this?

Josie Demers

19 (A) adjacent   (B) modern
(C) nearest   (D) recent

20 (A) was being shifted   (B) has shifted
(C) will be shifted   (D) shifted

21 (A) during   (B) since
(C) provided   (D) for

22 (A) Having been newly hired, they may need comprehensive orientation.
(B) They have found the sessions helpful for their careers.
(C) The California factory is well-equipped to handle our needs.
(D) The trainings should take place as soon as possible.

정답·해설·해석 p.72 / [별책] 토익 RC 필수 어휘 p.20

해커스 스타강사의 ▶
무료 해설강의 바로 보기
(3번 문제)

GRAMMAR Part 5,6 Ch 17 부사절 Hackers TOEIC Reading

명사절

토익, 이렇게 나온다!

명사절 관련 문제는 출제 비율이 높지 않지만, 출제될 경우 오답률이 높으므로 반드시 학습해두어야 한다. 문맥에 알맞은 명사절 접속사를 채우는 문제가 가장 많이 출제된다.

토익 필수 개념 다지기

01 명사절은 문장 내에서 주어, 목적어, 보어의 역할을 하는 필수성분이다.

What he bought was a new briefcase. 그가 산 것은 새 서류 가방이었다.
I believe **that she forgot the appointment**. 나는 그녀가 약속을 잊었다고 생각한다.
Our concern is **whether we can finish the work on time**.
우리의 걱정은 우리가 그 작업을 제때 끝낼 수 있는지의 여부이다.

명사절 What he bought는 문장의 주어, that she forgot the appointment는 believe의 목적어, whether we can finish the work on time은 보어 역할을 하는 필수성분이다.

02 명사절은 '명사절 접속사 + 주어 + 동사'로 이루어진다.

We can't tell **whether the client was pleased or not**. 우리는 그 고객이 만족했는지 아닌지 알 수 없다.
What makes him tired is working long hours. 그를 피곤하게 하는 것은 장시간 일하는 것이다.

첫 번째 문장의 목적어는 '명사절 접속사(whether) + 주어(the client) + 동사(was)'로 이루어진 명사절이다.
두 번째 문장의 주어는 '명사절 접속사(what) + 동사(makes)'로 이루어진 명사절이다.

명사절 접속사에는 that, if/whether, 의문사(who, what, which, when, where, how, why), 복합관계대명사 (whoever, whatever, whichever) 등이 있다.

토익 공식 1

명사절의 자리와 쓰임

01 명사절은 명사처럼 주어, 목적어, 보어 자리에 온다.

주어	**Whether I need to go on the trip or not** hasn't been decided. 내가 그 여행을 가야 하는지 아닌지는 결정되지 않았다.
동사의 목적어	Marsha mentioned **that she would be late**. Marsha는 늦을 것이라고 말했다.
전치사의 목적어	The documentary was about **how pollution affects water supply**. 그 다큐멘터리는 어떻게 오염이 수도 공급에 영향을 미치는가에 대한 것이었다.
보어	The issue is **who will be held responsible for the mistake**. 쟁점은 누가 그 실수에 대한 책임을 지게 될 것인가이다.

고득점 포인트 that 명사절은 4형식 동사의 직접 목적어 자리에 오기도 한다.

The agent informed Carly that her reservations had been confirmed. 그 직원은 Carly에게 예약이 확인되었음을 알려주었다.

→ 4형식 동사인 informed의 간접 목적어는 Carly이고, 직접 목적어는 that절이다.

02 명사절 접속사 자리에 전치사나 대명사는 올 수 없다.

The administrative manager agrees (**on**, **that**) we need more salesclerks for the holiday season.
그 관리부장은 휴가 시즌에 더 많은 점원들이 필요하다는 데 동의한다.

▶ 전치사(on)는 절(we need more salesclerks ~)을 이끌 수 없으므로 접속사가 와야 한다. 그리고 동사(agrees)의 목적어가 될 수 있는 명사절이 와야 하므로 명사절 접속사(that)가 와야 한다.

The technician explained (**it**, **that**) the software was updated weekly.
그 기술자는 소프트웨어가 매주 업데이트되었다고 설명했다.

▶ 대명사(it)는 절(the software was updated ~)을 이끌 수 없으므로 접속사가 와야 한다. 그리고 동사(explained)의 목적어가 될 수 있는 명사절이 와야 하므로 명사절 접속사(that)가 와야 한다.

03 명사절은 문장에서 명사 역할을 하며, 문장에서 명사를 뒤에서 꾸며 주는 형용사 역할을 하는 관계절과 구별된다.

명사절	Aaron said **that the woman will be our new manager**. Aaron은 그 여자가 우리의 새 관리자가 될 것이라고 말했다.
관계절	I've met the woman **who will be our new manager**. 나는 우리의 새 관리자가 될 여자를 만난 적이 있다.

▶ 여기서 명사절은 동사(said)의 목적어 자리에 와서 명사 역할을 하지만, 관계절은 명사(the woman)를 뒤에서 꾸며 주는 형용사 역할을 한다.

04 명사절은 문장에서 부사 역할을 하는 부사절과 구별된다.

명사절	I recommend **that you take an earlier flight**. 나는 당신이 더 이른 항공편을 이용하는 것을 권한다.
부사절	Sarah can pick you up at the airport **if you take an earlier flight**. 당신이 더 이른 항공편을 이용한다면 Sarah가 공항으로 당신을 마중 나갈 수 있다.

▶ 여기서 명사절은 동사(recommend)의 목적어 자리에 와서 명사 역할을 하지만, 부사절은 조건을 나타내는 부사 역할을 한다.

토익실전문제

출제 포인트 명사절 접속사 채우기
동사의 목적어로 사용된 명사절의 처음에 명사절 접속사를 채우는 문제가 주로 출제된다.

1. The company's press relations officer confirmed ------- Selectric Incorporated would no longer be manufacturing pagers.

   (A) about   (B) of
   (C) that   (D) it

2. United Plastics Limited indicated ------- the past year saw a 10 percent decline in international sales.

   (A) about   (B) this
   (C) on   (D) that

3. Staff are asked to submit their picks for employee of the month to assist management in determining ------- will be given the award.

   (A) those   (B) them
   (C) who   (D) while

정답·해설·해석 p.74

01 that이 이끄는 명사절은 문장에서 주어, 동사의 목적어, 보어, 동격절로 쓰인다.

주어	**That she got a promotion** was a shock to everyone. 그녀가 승진한 것은 모두에게 충격이었다.
동사의 목적어	We understand **that she didn't have enough time**. 우리는 그녀에게 충분한 시간이 없었다는 것을 이해한다.
보어	The benefit of this plan is **that it costs less money**. 이 계획의 이점은 더 적은 돈이 든다는 것이다.
동격절	The idea **that other galaxies exist** is accepted today. [The idea = other galaxies exist]
	또 다른 은하계들이 존재한다는 생각은 오늘날 받아들여진다.

고득점 포인트

❶ that절은 전치사의 목적어로는 쓰일 수 없다.
We did not know about that(→that) the products had defects. 우리는 제품에 결함이 있었다는 것을 몰랐다.

❷ '말하다, 보고하다, 생각하다, 알다' 등을 의미하는 동사의 목적어로 쓰인 that절의 that은 생략될 수 있다.
그러나 주어나 동격으로 쓰인 that절의 that은 생략될 수 없다.
We understand (that) she didn't have enough time.
She got a promotion(→That she got a promotion) was a shock to everyone.

02 that절을 취하는 형용사

be aware that ~을 알고 있다	be glad/happy that ~해서 기쁘다	be sure that ~을 확신하다
be sorry that ~해서 유감이다	be convinced that ~을 확신하다	be afraid that 미안하지만 ~이다

Beverley **is aware that** the conference is for this afternoon. Beverley는 회의가 오늘 오후에 있다는 것을 알고 있다.
I **am sure that** I left my wallet on the desk. 나는 내가 지갑을 책상 위에 두고 온 것을 확신한다.

03 동격절을 취하는 명사

fact that ~라는 사실	statement that ~라는 언급	opinion that ~라는 의견	truth that ~라는 사실
news that ~라는 소식	report that ~라는 보도, 소문	idea that ~라는 의견, 생각	(re)assurance that ~라는 확신
rumor that ~라는 소문	claim that ~라는 주장	confirmation that ~라는 확인	

The press release announced **the news that** the bank would be expanding.
보도 자료는 그 은행이 확장할 것이라는 소식을 알렸다.

Residents were surprised by **the report that** the mayor would resign sooner than expected.
주민들은 그 시장이 예상보다 빨리 사임할 것이라는 보도에 놀랐다.

토익실전문제

출제 포인트 that 채우기
명사절과 동격절의 처음에 that을 채우는 문제가 주로 출제된다.

1. ------- the holiday is only going to last three days is a disappointment to the entire staff.

(A) That (B) Because
(C) Although (D) So

2. Mr. Forster was convinced ------- his decision to sell his stock had been correct when the company announced record losses the next day.

(A) whom (B) that
(C) within (D) but

3. During the meeting with investors, the managing director refuted the rumor ------- the company was in financial trouble.

(A) only (B) that
(C) when (D) what

정답·해설·해석 p.74

01 if나 whether (or not)가 이끄는 명사절은 '~인지 아닌지'를 의미하며, 문장에서 주어, 보어, 목적어로 쓰인다.

주어	**Whether you attend** is up to you. 당신이 참석하는지 아닌지는 당신에게 달려 있다.
보어	The customer's query is **whether the machinery will arrive on time**.
	그 고객의 문의 사항은 기계가 제때 도착할지 아닐지 하는 것이다.
동사의 목적어	We will see **if there are any tickets left**. 우리는 남은 티켓들이 있는지 볼 것이다.
전치사의 목적어	I don't know the answer to **whether or not Jason is right for the job**.
	나는 Jason이 그 일에 적합한지 아닌지에 대한 답을 모른다.

고득점 포인트

❶ whether절은 '~에 상관없이'를 의미하는 부사절로 쓰이기도 한다.

   Whether we like it or not, we all have to pay taxes. 우리가 좋아하든 아니든 상관없이, 우리는 모두 세금을 납부해야 한다.

❷ '(만약) ~라면'을 의미하는 if절은 명사절이 아닌, 조건을 나타내는 부사절이므로 if 대신 whether를 쓸 수 없다.

   I can send you a schedule whether(→if) you want. 당신이 원한다면 내가 일정표를 보내줄 수 있다.

   → '당신이 원한다면'이라는 조건을 의미하는 부사절이므로 whether가 아닌 if를 써야 한다.

02 whether는 'whether A or B', 'whether or not'으로 자주 쓰인다.

Harry didn't say **whether** he would leave **or** wait for the group. Harry는 떠날 것인지 그 무리를 기다릴 것인지 말하지 않았다.

Sara is not sure (**if**, **whether**) or not she'll apply for the relocation. Sara는 배치 전환을 지원할 것인지 아닌지 확신하지 못한다.

▶ if or not은 쓸 수 없는 표현이므로 if가 아닌 whether가 와야 한다.

03 if절은 주어 자리에도, 전치사 다음에도 올 수 없다.

(**If**, **Whether**) I work this weekend has yet to be decided. 내가 이번 주말에 일하는지 아닌지는 아직 정해지지 않았다.

▶ if절(If I work this weekend)은 주어 자리에 올 수 없으므로 if가 아닌 whether가 와야 한다.

He's uncertain about (**if**, **whether**) the boss will like his proposition.

그는 상사가 그의 제안을 좋아할지 아닐지에 대해 확신이 없다.

▶ if절(if the boss will like his proposition)은 전치사 다음에 올 수 없으므로 if가 아닌 whether가 와야 한다.

토익실전문제

출제 포인트   if나 whether 채우기

명사절 접속사 if나 whether를 채우는 문제가 자주 출제된다.

1. The human resources head wants to know ------- the in-house trainers are willing to conduct supplementary leadership seminars in the evenings.

(A) if (B) whereas
(C) however (D) while

2. Chambers Tech is still considering whether ------- to install the latest version of the operating system on its office computers.

(A) nor (B) or not
(C) but (D) yet

3. The committee will have a discussion about ------- to allocate funds for an online marketing campaign.

(A) if (B) that
(C) whether (D) which

정답·해설·해석 p.75

01 who, whom, whose, what, which는 의문대명사로 명사절을 이끌며, 그 자체가 명사절의 주어, 목적어, 보어 역할을 하므로, 의문대명사 뒤에 주어, 목적어 또는 보어가 없는 불완전한 절이 온다.

We found out **who** sent the message. 우리는 누가 그 메시지를 보냈는지 알아냈다.
What she mentioned was interesting. 그녀가 언급한 것은 흥미로웠다.
I can't decide **which** is best. 어떤 것이 최선인지 결정할 수 없다.
The board has not announced **who** the new CEO will be. 이사회는 새로운 최고 경영자가 되는 것이 누구일지 발표하지 않았다.

02 whose, what, which는 의문형용사로 뒤에 나온 명사를 꾸미면서 명사절을 이끌며, '의문형용사 + 명사'가 명사절의 주어, 목적어, 보어 역할을 하므로, 그 뒤에 주어, 목적어 또는 보어가 없는 불완전한 절이 온다.

I wasn't told **whose plan** it was. 그것이 누구의 계획이었는지 듣지 못했다.
What price you paid is irrelevant. 당신이 무슨 가격을 냈는지는 무관하다.
The talk will be about **which consumers** we should target. 그 논의는 우리가 어떤 소비자들을 겨냥해야 하는지에 대해서일 것이다.

03 when, where, how, why는 의문부사로 명사절을 이끌기 때문에, 의문부사 뒤에는 빠지는 것이 없는 완벽한 절이 온다.

I will notify you **when** the repairs will be finished. 수리가 언제 끝날지 알려 드리겠습니다.
Where you live should be indicated on the form. 당신이 사는 곳이 어디인지 양식에 명시되어야 합니다.
The researcher needs to figure out **how** he can complete the survey on time.
그 연구원은 설문 조사를 어떻게 제때 완료할 수 있을지 생각해 내야 한다.
The client was curious **why** nobody met him at the airport. 그 고객은 공항에서 왜 아무도 그를 마중하지 않았는지 궁금해 했다.

> **고득점 포인트** how는 형용사나 부사를 꾸며 주기도 하며, '얼마나 ~한'의 의미가 된다.
> The driver told us how much a trip to the hotel would cost. 그 운전사는 우리에게 호텔까지의 이동에 얼마나 많은 비용이 들 것인지 말해 주었다.
> Do you know how often the trains to Frankfurt depart? 당신은 프랑크푸르트행 기차가 얼마나 자주 출발하는지 알고 있습니까?

04 '의문사 + to 부정사'는 명사절 자리에 오며 '의문사 + 주어 + should + 동사'로 바꿀 수 있다.

I can't choose **what to read(=what I should read)** first. 나는 어떤 것을 먼저 읽어야 할지 고르지 못하겠다.
Helen wasn't informed **when to begin(=when she should begin)** the project.
Helen은 그 기획을 언제 시작해야 하는지 통지받지 않았다.

> **고득점 포인트** to 부정사 앞의 의문사 자리에 whether가 올 수도 있다.
> Leslie Ross hasn't made up her mind whether to go on the trip to Africa. Leslie Ross는 아프리카 여행을 갈지 말지를 결정하지 못했다.

토익실전문제

출제 포인트 의문사 채우기
동사의 목적어로 사용된 명사절의 처음에 의문사를 구별하여 채우는 문제가
주로 출제된다.

1. The manager wants to know ------- prepared the employee profiles for the company Web site, as he finds them detailed and well written.

(A) why   (B) that
(C) which   (D) who

2. To make preparations for the event, the caterer asked ------- many people would be present at the dinner.

(A) about   (B) concerning
(C) how   (D) what

3. Mr. Albertson will consult the company's lawyer, as she would know ------- to do about the legal problem.

(A) what   (B) that
(C) why   (D) when

정답·해설·해석 p.75

5 명사절 접속사 4 : 복합관계대명사 who(m)ever, whatever, whichever

01 복합관계대명사가 이끄는 명사절은 문장에서 주어와 목적어로 쓰이며, 이때 복합관계대명사는 '대명사 + 관계대명사'의 역할을 한다.

whoever (=anyone who) 누구든 간에	whomever (=anyone whom) 누구든 간에 (whoever의 목적격)
whatever (=anything that) 무엇이든 간에	whichever (=anything that, anyone who) 어느 것이든 간에, 어느 사람이든 간에

주어   **Whoever(=Anyone who) painted the picture** is a terrific artist. 그 그림을 그렸던 사람이 누구든 간에 훌륭한 예술가이다.

목적어   Please take **whatever(=anything that) you need**. 필요한 것은 무엇이든 가져가세요.

고득점 포인트

❶ 복합관계대명사가 이끄는 절은 명사절이 아니라 부사절로 쓰이기도 한다.
   Whatever you do, you should always do your best. 당신이 무엇을 하든지, 항상 최선을 다해야 한다.

❷ 대명사는 절을 이끌 수 없으므로 복합관계대명사(대명사 + 관계대명사) 대신 쓰일 수 없다.
   Anyone(→Whoever) painted the picture is a terrific artist.

❸ 복합관계대명사가 명사절 내에서 주어이면 주격, 목적어이면 목적격을 사용한다. 단, 목적격 whomever는 whoever로 대신할 수 있다.
   Applicants can submit the forms to whomever/whoever they find at the front desk.
   지원자들은 안내 데스크에서 찾을 수 있는 누구에게든 그 양식을 제출할 수 있다.

❹ whatever와 whichever는 뒤에 나오는 명사를 꾸미면서 복합관계형용사로도 쓰일 수 있다.
   Whichever model I wanted was sold out. 내가 원했던 모델이 어느 것이든 간에 품절이었다.

02 복합관계대명사는 그 자체가 명사절의 주어나 목적어 역할을 하므로, 그 뒤에 주어나 목적어가 없는 불완전한 절이 온다.

Whoever files a complaint will be contacted by a service representative.
항의를 제기하는 사람이 누구든 서비스 담당 직원과 연락하게 될 것이다.

Please select **whichever** color you prefer. 당신이 선호하는 어떤 색이든 고르세요.

03 복합관계사를 쓸지 의문사를 쓸지는 문맥에 따라 결정된다.

(~~Who~~, **Whoever**) is chosen for the award will receive $1,000. 그 상에 누가 선정되든지 간에 1,000달러를 받게 될 것이다.
▶ '누가 선정되든지 간에'라는 의미가 되어야 하므로, 의문대명사(who)가 아닌 복합관계대명사(whoever)가 와야 한다.

(~~Whoever~~, **Who**) will play that character hasn't been disclosed yet. 누가 그 배역을 연기할지 아직 밝혀지지 않았다.
▶ '누가 연기할지'라는 의미가 되어야 하므로, 복합관계대명사(whoever)가 아닌 의문대명사(who)가 와야 한다.

We can go to (~~which~~, **whichever**) conference room is free. 우리는 비어 있는 어느 회의실이든 갈 수 있다.
▶ '어느 회의실이든'이라는 의미가 되어야 하므로, 의문형용사(which)가 아닌 복합관계형용사(whichever)가 와야 한다.

Ben figured out (~~whichever~~, **which**) parking space was his. Ben은 어느 주차 공간이 그의 것인지 알아냈다.
▶ '어느 주차 공간'이라는 의미가 되어야 하므로, 복합관계형용사(whichever)가 아닌 의문형용사(which)가 와야 한다.

토익실전문제

출제 포인트 복합관계대명사 채우기
문맥에 알맞은 복합관계대명사를 채우는 문제가 출제된다.

출제 포인트 복합관계대명사/복합관계형용사와 의문사 구별하여 채우기
복합관계대명사/복합관계형용사(whoever, whichever)를 의문사와 구별하여 채우는 문제가 주로 출제된다.

1. ------- is discussed at the board meeting is confidential and should not be divulged to other staff for any reason.

(A) Whichever   (B) Whatever
(C) Whenever   (D) However

2. The supervisor reminded the workers that ------- needs a certificate of employment for personal reasons should ask Ms. Simon for assistance.

(A) who   (B) whenever
(C) whoever   (D) whomever

3. ------- team of sales representatives has sold the highest number of units will receive the Team of the Month Award.

(A) Which   (B) Some
(C) Whichever   (D) This

정답·해설·해석 p.75

01 what절은 명사절로만 사용되지만, that절은 명사절, 형용사절(관계절), 부사절로 모두 사용된다.

It is easy to see **what is best for the firm**. 기업을 위한 최선이 무엇인지 아는 것은 쉽다.

▶ 동사(see)의 목적어 자리에 온 what절은 명사 역할을 하는 명사절이다.

We were told **that there were no seats available**. 우리는 이용 가능한 좌석이 없다는 말을 들었다.

▶ 동사(were told)의 목적어 자리에 온 that절은 명사 역할을 하는 명사절이다.

Sophie gave me a suggestion **that may help us**. Sophie는 우리에게 도움이 될 수 있는 조언을 내게 해 주었다.

▶ 명사(suggestion)를 뒤에서 꾸미는 that절은 형용사 역할을 하는 형용사절(관계절)이다.

The cake was so delicious **that I had a second piece**. 그 케이크가 너무 맛있어서 나는 두 번째 조각을 먹었다.

▶ so/such 뒤에 오는 that절은 문장 내에서 부사 역할을 하는 부사절이다.

02 what절과 that절이 명사절로 쓰일 때, what 다음에는 불완전한 절이 오지만, that 다음에는 완전한 절이 온다.

The professor wants to figure out (~~that~~, **what**) ~~⚡~~ motivates students to learn.

그 교수는 무엇이 학생들에게 학습 동기를 부여하는지 알아내고 싶어 한다.

▶ 명사절이 주어가 빠진 불완전한 절이므로, 완전한 절을 이끄는 that이 아닌, 불완전한 절을 이끄는 what이 와야 한다.

(~~What~~, **That**) she had entered the wrong building was apparent. 그녀가 다른 빌딩에 들어갔었던 것이 분명했다.

▶ 명사절이 주어와 목적어가 모두 갖춰진 완전한 절이므로, 불완전한 절을 이끄는 what이 아닌 완전한 절을 이끄는 that이 와야 한다.

토익실전문제

출제 포인트 **what과 that 구별하여 채우기**

명사절에서 what과 that을 구별하여 채우는 문제가 주로 출제된다.

1. In the hotel industry, well-trained and experienced staff can quickly determine ------- guests need.

(A) how (B) that
(C) what (D) if

2. The staff understands ------- the company funds for corporate activities cannot be disbursed without prior approval from a director.

(A) they (B) this
(C) what (D) that

3. New computer programs have made it so easy to organize information ------- even a beginner can create impressive charts from any data.

(A) that (B) there
(C) what (D) where

정답·해설·해석 p.75

HACKERS PRACTICE 토익 고득점을 위한 필수 연습

둘 중 맞는 형태를 고르세요.

01 I am sure ------- Hank will take over operations at the Houston branch.
ⓐ that   ⓑ what

02 It is unclear ------- of the two proposals the owner will choose.
ⓐ whose   ⓑ which

03 Residents are afraid ------- suburban growth will result in the careless use of valuable land.
ⓐ that   ⓑ what

04 The reporter asked Ms. Lee about her background rather than ------- she has any current projects.
ⓐ if   ⓑ whether

05 ------- would like to apply for the position of field manager should send a résumé to the main office.
ⓐ Who   ⓑ Whoever

06 Sarah is having a hard time choosing ------- to pack for her trip to South America next week.
ⓐ when   ⓑ what

07 The CEO confirmed the report ------- the company was expanding into the semiconductor market.
ⓐ that   ⓑ which

명사절을 찾아 그 역할을 구별하세요.

08 Suppliers will have to decide when the moment is right to make a change.

09 How the offices will be assigned is the administrator's responsibility.

10 The students were worried about what questions would appear on the test.

11 Long lines at the cashier are what customers have been complaining about.

12 The foundation was established with the idea that good education should be available to all youths.

13 The manager didn't explain why the staff were being trained again.

14 The problem is that many people dislike telemarketing.

정답·해석 p.76

무료 해설 ▶
바로 보기

맞은 문제 개수: / 14
틀린 문제에 해당하는 토익 공식을 다시 한번 학습하세요.

🕐 제한 시간 12분

Part 5

01 The survey reveals ------- brands consumers admire the most.

(A) as (B) why
(C) that (D) which

02 The marketing director wants to know ------- the final revisions will be made to the contract.

(A) on (B) about
(C) which (D) when

03 At 6 o'clock, ------- club members joining the special dinner at the beach should meet at the entrance of the Lakeside Center.

(A) all (B) somewhat
(C) when (D) whichever

04 Participants of the linguistics convention were assured that ------- reports they needed could be provided if requested in advance.

(A) this (B) every
(C) whose (D) whichever

05 Mr. Turner had to go back to the office to get the documents ------- he inadvertently left on his desk.

(A) what (B) whichever
(C) those (D) that

06 International orders are generally shipped on the day payment is made ------- require three to six weeks for delivery depending on the destination.

(A) or (B) with
(C) and (D) from

07 Whether the seminar is held this month ------- in April will be decided at this afternoon's meeting.

(A) but (B) or
(C) so (D) not

08 The foreman reminded the crew to be mindful ------- steel beams would be hoisted to the top of the structure.

(A) regarding (B) to
(C) that (D) who

09 Nurses are in charge of assisting individuals in scheduling medical tests and filling out the forms needed for -------.

(A) admittance (B) admitted
(C) admittable (D) admit

10 Next week's workshop will focus on ------- to be an effective and trustworthy leader in the corporate world.

(A) which (B) how
(C) what (D) that

11 Ms. Corning wants to know to ------- account the business expenses should be charged.

(A) its (B) their
(C) whose (D) those

12 All personnel are advised ------- they should limit their requests for office supplies, as expenditure cuts will be taking effect immediately.

(A) if (B) that
(C) still (D) yet

13 Although staff members have some control when it comes to daily activities, the supervisor determines which tasks get done by -------.

(A) who (B) whoever
(C) whom (D) whomever

14 Martin's job is so demanding ------- he takes an occasional personal day to get away from the pressures of office.

(A) that (B) there
(C) what (D) where

15 ------- exits the building last is required to set the office alarm system and lock the main entrance doors.

(A) Anyone (B) Whomever
(C) Someone (D) Whoever

16 Most of the board members share the opinion ------- the company needs to hire more staff.

(A) which (B) that
(C) why (D) what

17 The legal department will be holding a meeting about the contract this afternoon to decide ------- needs to be revised before it is signed.

(A) what (B) those
(C) whether (D) there

18 For those who have opened a new business, ------- happens during the first year is an important predictor of success.

(A) that (B) as
(C) what (D) how

Part 6

Questions 19-22 refer to the following e-mail.

To: Joe Jackson <jjack@kpwritersassociation.com>
From: Eileen Davis <eileen_d@kremshainc.com>
Subject: Annual Convention for Writers
Date: November 1

Dear Mr. Jackson,

I registered for this year's Annual Convention for Writers about a month ago as I have been to it before and thoroughly enjoyed all the lectures I attended. -------, there has been a change of plans. I will not be able to go after all. -------.

I would, therefore, like to withdraw my registration. I also wish to know ------- it is possible for me to get a refund. I think I am notifying you of my cancellation far enough in advance to qualify for one, but please let me know if this is not the case. I apologize sincerely for the -------. Best wishes for a successful event.

Sincerely,
Eileen Davis

19 (A) Besides (B) Despite
(C) Likewise (D) However

20 (A) I was unable to find a suitable speaker to replace her.
(B) A vital business meeting was called, and I must attend.
(C) I wasn't that impressed with the majority of the lectures.
(D) As a lifetime member, I am entitled to a half-price ticket.

21 (A) what (B) though
(C) whereas (D) whether

22 (A) delay (B) interruption
(C) inconvenience (D) complaint

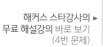

SECTION 6

특수구문

비교 구문

토익, 이렇게 나온다!
비교 구문 관련 문제는 평균 1문제 정도 출제된다. 비교급 형태를 완성하는 문제가 가장 많이 출제되며, 최상급의
형태를 완성하는 문제도 자주 출제된다.

토익 필수 개념 다지기

01 비교 구문은 둘 이상의 대상을 수량이나 성질 면에서 비교하는 구문이며, 비교 대상의 수와 비교 방법에 따라 세 가지 구문으로 나누어진다.

두 대상이 동등함을 나타내는 비교 구문은 '원급' 구문이다.
Erica is **as tall as** Melanie. Erica는 Melanie만큼 키가 크다. (Erica와 Melanie의 키는 같다.)

두 대상 중 하나가 우월함을 나타내는 비교 구문은 '비교급' 구문이다.
Erica is **taller than** Melanie. Erica는 Melanie보다 키가 더 크다.

셋 이상의 대상 중 하나가 가장 우월함을 나타내는 비교 구문은 '최상급' 구문이다.
Erica is **the tallest girl** in her class. Erica는 그녀의 학급에서 가장 키가 큰 여학생이다.

02 원급, 비교급, 최상급에서 형용사와 부사는 각각 다른 형태를 가진다.

형용사나 부사가 1음절 단어이거나, -er, -y, -ow, -some으로 끝나는 2음절 단어일 때는 다음과 같은 형태를 가진다. 이것
이 비교급, 원급, 최상급을 만드는 기본적인 형태이다.

원급(형용사나 부사의 일반 형태)	비교급(원급 + er)	최상급(원급 + est)
old	older	the oldest
clever	cleverer	the cleverest

형용사나 부사가 -able, -ful, -ous, -ive 등으로 끝나는 2음절 단어이거나, 3음절 이상의 단어일 때는 다음과 같은 형태
를 가진다.

원급(형용사나 부사의 일반 형태)	비교급(more + 원급)	최상급(the most + 원급)
useful	more useful	the most useful
important	more important	the most important

어떤 형용사와 부사는 -er/-est를 쓰지 않고 고유의 비교급/최상급 형태를 가진다.

원급	비교급	최상급
good / well	better	best
bad / badly	worse	worst
many / much	more	most
little	less	least
late	later / latter	latest / last

01 '~만큼 –한'이라는 의미로 두 대상의 동등함을 나타내는 원급 표현은 'as + 형용사/부사 + as'를 쓴다.

The kitten is **as white as** snow. 그 새끼 고양이는 눈만큼이나 하얗다.
I will send you the file **as soon as** possible. 나는 당신에게 가능한 한 빨리 파일을 전송할 것이다.

고득점 포인트
❶ '~만큼 –하지 않은'을 의미하는 경우, 'not as – as ~' 또는 'not so – as ~'로 표현한다.
The new desktop computer is <u>not as/so</u> speedy <u>as</u> the previous one. 새 데스크톱 컴퓨터는 이전 것만큼 빠르지 않다.
❷ as ~ as 사이의 형용사/부사 자리는 as ~ as –를 지우고 구별한다.
Be as <u>quietly</u> as possible during the examination.(×) → Be <u>quietly</u>(→quiet). 시험 중에는 가능한 한 조용히 해 주세요.
I walked down the stairs as <u>quiet</u> as I could.(×) → I walked down the stairs <u>quiet</u>(→quietly).
나는 가능한 한 조용히 계단을 걸어 내려갔다.

02 '~만큼 많은/적은 –'을 나타내는 원급 표현은 'as + many/much/few/little 명사 + as'를 쓴다.

I bought **as ˄ clothes** as Sam did. 나는 Sam이 산 것만큼 많은 옷을 샀다.
　　　　　many

Please provide **as ˄ evidence as** possible. 가능한 한 많은 증거를 제공해 주세요.
　　　　　　　　much

▶ 원급 표현으로 'as + 명사 + as'를 쓸 수 없으므로 반드시 명사 앞에 형용사(many/much)를 써야 한다.

03 '~와 같은 –'을 나타내는 원급 표현은 'the same (+ 명사) + as'를 쓴다.

Andrew has **the same** car **as** we do. Andrew는 우리가 가진 것과 같은 차를 가지고 있다.
Andrew's car is **the same as** ours. Andrew의 차는 우리의 것과 같다.

04 형용사나 부사의 원급을 꾸며 주는 표현으로는 nearly(거의), almost(거의), just(꼭) 등이 있다.

The replacement part is **nearly** <u>as expensive as</u> a new machine. 그 교체 부품은 거의 새 기계만큼이나 비싸다.

토익실전문제

출제 포인트 원급 표현 채우기
as와 as 사이에 형용사/부사를 채우는 문제가 주로 출제된다.
'as ~ as' 원급 표현에서 앞의 as를 채우는 문제도 출제된다.

1. In his probationary evaluation, Kevin Edwards was
   praised for working as ------- as the experienced
   employees in the department.
   (A) effectiveness　　　(B) effectively
   (C) more effective　　(D) effective

2. Studies show that laborers work twice ------- hours on
   average as skilled professionals in any field.
   (A) much　　　　　(B) more
   (C) as many　　　 (D) more than

3. For training purposes, new employees are asked to
   write up progress reports in ------- detail as possible.
   (A) as　　　　　(B) more
   (C) as much　　(D) many

정답·해설·해석 p.78

01 '~보다 -한'이라는 의미로 두 대상 중 한쪽이 우월함을 나타내는 비교급 표현은 '형용사/부사의 비교급 + than'을 쓴다.

This year's bonus is **larger than** the last one was. 올해의 상여금은 작년 것보다 더 많다.

I drove **more slowly than** usual because of the weather. 나는 날씨 때문에 평소보다 더 느리게 운전했다.

cf) The applicant I interviewed for the job was (**smarter**, **smart**). 그 일자리를 위해 내가 면접 본 지원자는 똑똑했다.

▶ 비교 대상이 없이 비교급(smarter)을 쓸 수 없으므로 원급(smart)을 써야 한다.

고득점 포인트
❶ '~보다 덜 -한'을 의미하는 경우 'less + 형용사/부사 + than'을 쓴다.
This book is less interesting than the author's other novels. 이 책은 그 작가의 다른 소설들보다 덜 흥미롭다.
❷ 비교급 구문에서 more ~ than 사이의 형용사/부사 자리는 more와 than 이하를 지우고 구별한다.
The test was more difficultly than I thought.(×) → The test was difficultly(→difficult). 그 시험은 내가 생각했던 것보다 더 어려웠다.
John works more productive than the other staff.(×) → John works productive(→productively).
John은 다른 직원들보다 더 생산적으로 일한다.

02 '~보다 많은/적은 -'을 나타내는 비교급 표현은 'more/fewer/less + 명사 + than'을 쓴다.

More orders than last month were received online. 지난달보다 많은 주문이 온라인으로 접수되었다.

03 비교급에는 the를 쓰지 않지만, 예외적으로 아래의 비교급 표현에서는 반드시 the를 써야 한다.

• the 비교급 ~, the 비교급 - (~할수록 점점 더 -하다)
The more you exercise, (**healthier**, **the healthier**) you'll be. 더 많이 운동할수록, 더 건강해질 것이다.

• the 비교급 + of the two (둘 중에 더 ~한)
Diana is (**older**, **the older**) **of the two sisters**. Diana는 두 자매 중 나이가 더 많다.

04 형용사나 부사의 비교급을 강조하는 표현으로는 much/even/still/far/a lot/by far(훨씬) 등이 있다.

How you attain success is **much** more crucial than success itself.
어떻게 성공을 이루는지가 성공 그 자체보다 훨씬 더 중요하다.

토익실전문제

출제 포인트 비교급 표현 채우기
'비교급 ~ than' 또는 'the 비교급 ~, the 비교급 -'의 형태를 완성하는 문제
가 주로 출제된다.

1. The Center for Biological Research announced that it would host a second conference on endangered species because the first one received more media interest ------- expected.

(A) and
(B) whereas
(C) if
(D) than

2. ------- the financial report is submitted to the director, the earlier it will be for him to make a decision about the next year's budget.

(A) Sooner
(B) The soonest
(C) Soon
(D) The sooner

3. The recent offer for the property in Spokane is a lot ------- than the one the developer made last week.

(A) fairest
(B) fairly
(C) fairer
(D) fair

정답·해설·해석 p.78

01 '~ 중에 가장 –한'이라는 의미로 셋 이상의 대상들 중 하나가 우월함을 나타내는 최상급 표현은 '최상급 + of ~/in ~/ that절'을 쓴다.

City Hall is **the oldest building** of all the structures. 시청은 모든 건축물들 중 가장 오래된 건물이다.
Rosita's makes **the best pizza** in town. Rosita's는 마을에서 최고의 피자를 만든다.
It is **the most interesting TV show** (that) I've ever seen. 그것은 내가 본 것 중에서 가장 재미있는 텔레비전 프로그램이다.

cf) The (**fastest**, **fast**) delivery service of the restaurant helped boost its popularity.
그 식당의 빠른 배달 서비스는 그들의 인기를 올리는 데 도움이 되었다.

▶ of ~가 '~ 중에서'라고 해석되지 않고 여러 비교 대상이 없으면 최상급(fastest)을 쓸 수 없으므로 원급(fast)을 써야 한다.

고득점
포인트
❶ '최상급 + possible/available/ever' 형태로도 쓰여 '가능한 것 중에/이용할 수 있는 것 중에/여태껏 모든 것 중에 가장 ~한'이라는 의미를 나타낼 수 있다.
The report is based on the most current data available. 이 보고서는 이용할 수 있는 가장 최신의 데이터를 기반으로 한다.
Ms. Bailey is the most rigid boss ever. Ms. Bailey는 여태껏 모든 상사 중에 가장 엄격한 상사이다.
❷ 최상급 관련 표현으로는 one of the 최상급 + 복수 명사 (가장 –한 ~ 중 하나), at least(적어도), at most(많아야), at best(기껏해야)가 있다.
India is one of the most populated countries in the world. 인도는 세계에서 가장 인구가 밀집된 나라들 중 하나이다.
This battery can last at least ten hours. 이 건전지는 적어도 10시간 동안 지속될 수 있다.

02 '최상급 + 명사' 앞에는 주로 the가 온다. 이때, the가 아닌 소유격이 올 수도 있다.

Summer Rain was **the most interesting** movie we saw during the film festival.
*Summer Rain*은 우리가 영화제 동안에 봤던 가장 재미있는 영화였다.

Mr. Sanders will sign a contract with **his most important** client today.
Mr. Sanders는 오늘 그의 가장 중요한 고객과 계약을 체결할 것이다.

고득점
포인트
'몇 번째로 가장 ~한'을 표현하기 위해서는, 서수가 최상급 앞에 온다.
Southside University is the third biggest university in the state. Southside 대학교는 그 주에서 세 번째로 큰 대학교이다.

03 형용사나 부사의 최상급을 강조하는 표현으로는 by far/quite/very(단연코) 등이 있다.

Lisa Reyes is **by far** the company's most valuable researcher. Lisa Reyes는 단연코 그 기업의 가장 소중한 연구원이다.

토익실전문제

출제 포인트 최상급 표현 채우기
'of ~/in ~'과 함께 사용되는 'the 최상급'의 형태를 완성하는 문제가 주로 출제된다.

1. The ------- capable of the workers at this plant will be transferred to a newly opened facility.
   (A) so much   (B) most
   (C) too   (D) many

2. Despite having fewer functions than most cell phones, Belmar's new model is the ------- of the hand-held devices released this year.
   (A) profits   (B) profitable
   (C) most profits   (D) most profitable

3. The Harborview Resort is the ------- building that Rising Star Incorporated has ever constructed.
   (A) larger   (B) more largely
   (C) most largely (D) largest

정답·해설·해석 p.79

01 비교급 표현

표현	예 문
more than + 명사 ~ 이상 less than + 명사 ~ 이하	There are **more than** 1 billion people in China. 중국에는 10억 명 이상의 사람들이 있다. **Less than** 10 percent of people who voted chose Lee Weathers. 투표한 사람들의 10퍼센트 이하가 Lee Weathers를 선택했다. ＊ more than이나 less than은 형용사 앞에 와서 형용사를 강조하기도 한다. The spa visit left us feeling **more than** <u>relaxed</u>. 온천 방문은 우리에게 편안함 이상을 느끼게 했다.
for a later time 나중을 위해	We decided to keep the extra brochures **for a later time**. 우리는 나중을 위해 여분의 안내 책자를 보관하기로 결정했다.
no later than 늦어도 ~까지	Passengers must arrive at the gate **no later than** 3:30 P.M. 탑승객들은 늦어도 오후 3시 30분까지 탑승구에 도착해야 한다.
no longer 더 이상 ~않다	James **no longer** goes to the gym. James는 더 이상 체육관에 가지 않는다.
no sooner ~ than – ~하자마자 ~하다	**No sooner** had Pete gone to bed **than** someone knocked on the door. Pete가 자러 가자마자 누군가가 문을 두드렸다.
other than ~ 이외에	**Other than** part-time staff, all employees must attend the meeting. 시간제 직원 이외에, 모든 직원들은 그 회의에 참석해야 한다.
rather than ~보다	I took a flight to Tampa **rather than** drive. 나는 운전해서 가기보다는 비행기를 타고 탬파에 갔다.
would rather ~ than – ~하느니 차라리 ~하다	I **would rather** eat at home **than** go to a restaurant. 나는 식당에 가느니 차라리 집에서 먹겠다.

02 원급·비교급 형태로 최상급의 의미를 만드는 표현들이 있다.

- 비교급 + than any other ~ (어떤 다른 ~보다 더 –한)
  This television is (**the cheapest**, **cheaper**) than any other model in the store.
  이 텔레비전은 그 가게에 있는 다른 어떤 모델보다 더 싸다.

  ▶ than any other ~ 앞에 최상급(the cheapest)이 아닌 비교급(cheaper) 표현을 써야 한다.

- have never/hardly/rarely been + 비교급 (더 ~해 본 적이 없다)
  My garden **has never been more beautiful** than it is now. 내 정원은 지금보다 더 아름다웠던 적이 없다.

- no other – / nothing + as 원급 as (다른 어떤 –도 ~만큼 ~하지 않다)
  no other – / nothing + 비교급 than (다른 어떤 –도 ~보다 더 ~하지 않다)
  No other person at work is **as lazy as** Nathan. 직장의 다른 어떤 누구도 Nathan만큼 게으르지 않다.
  When looking for a new home, **nothing is more critical** than location. 새집을 구할 때, 다른 어떤 것도 위치보다 더 중요하지 않다.

토익실전문제

출제 포인트 원급/비교급/최상급 표현 채우기

문맥에 알맞은 비교급 표현을 채우거나, 최상급 의미를 만드는 원급·비교급 표현을 완성하는 문제가 출제된다.

1. Professor Knight spent ------- three years studying vegetation in the Amazon Valley, which was much longer than he had planned.

   (A) within   (B) more than
   (C) after then   (D) yet

2. Mr. Clemens would rather invest now ------- wait for a better time to expand his business.

   (A) than   (B) else
   (C) whereas   (D) while

3. Garson's Steel Manufacturing states on its Web site that the A-1 steel rods are ------- than any other type it produces.

   (A) strong   (B) stronger
   (C) strongly   (D) the strongest

정답·해설·해석 p.79

HACKERS PRACTICE 토익 고득점을 위한 필수 연습

둘 중 맞는 형태를 고르세요.

01 Because of poor weather conditions, the convention will be held tomorrow rather ------- today.
ⓐ as   ⓑ than

02 The new machinery worked ------- than the previous equipment we used.
ⓐ most efficient   ⓑ more efficiently

03 Despite my busy part-time job schedule, I attended the class as ------- as I could.
ⓐ regularly   ⓑ more regularly

04 ------- had the plane taken off than the pilot announced that we were likely to experience turbulence.
ⓐ Quickly   ⓑ No sooner

05 The design of this building is ------- the most innovative of any in the city.
ⓐ by far   ⓑ far

06 Renovating the old museum will be more expensive ------- constructing a new facility.
ⓐ than   ⓑ rather

07 I think Cheryl will be ------- as organized as our previous manager.
ⓐ much   ⓑ just

틀린 곳이 있으면 바르게 고치세요.

08 The closer you get to the city, more congested traffic will be.

09 Even though I got a new job, my responsibilities are the same to my previous one.

10 Henry is the more creative person that I've ever worked with.

11 Shopping online is more conveniently than going around to different stores.

12 Our profit margin for last quarter is even higher when we'd expected.

13 Please give the students as much examples as you can so they understand everything clearly.

14 The amount of pollution in our rivers is much low than it was a decade ago.

정답·해석 p.79

무료 해설 ▶
바로 보기

맞은 문제 개수: / 14
틀린 문제에 해당하는 토익 공식을 다시 한번 학습하세요.

🕐 제한 시간 12분

Part 5

01 The company has decided that developing a customer outreach program is ------- imperative than training the sales representatives.
- (A) better
- (B) more
- (C) very
- (D) larger

02 No sooner had the company launched its music player ------- another manufacturer introduced a similar device.
- (A) such
- (B) than
- (C) whereas
- (D) so

03 Holding a meeting sometime after the project deadline would work ------- for most staff members than trying to have one this week.
- (A) better
- (B) best
- (C) so good
- (D) any good

04 In the sales division, new clerks with motivation and enthusiasm provide ------- satisfaction to customers as professional representatives.
- (A) lots of
- (B) alike
- (C) as much
- (D) many

05 It is the company's position that moving into a market with ------- government regulation will result in greater gains.
- (A) fewer
- (B) least
- (C) always
- (D) less

06 Recent changes in the regulations and procedures at the American embassy have made it more difficult to get a visa ------- a timely manner.
- (A) at
- (B) on
- (C) by
- (D) in

07 The director was pleased that his film had been released ------- public interest in the lead actor was at its greatest.
- (A) when
- (B) where
- (C) whether
- (D) how

08 According to a recent report, ------- positions are open for entry-level candidates in the fields of industrial arts and applied sciences.
- (A) lesser
- (B) fewer
- (C) kind of
- (D) much

09 Although the number of employees appointed to the project has been reduced, management hopes the work will proceed as ------- as before.
- (A) smooth
- (B) smoother
- (C) smoothly
- (D) smoothest

10 Ms. Okada is the ------- player ever to win the National Golf Tournament held every year in Sacramento.
- (A) young
- (B) younger
- (C) youngest
- (D) most young

11 The company's technicians have inspected the office computers and verified that they are ------- sufficient to meet the needs of the staff.
- (A) enough
- (B) too much
- (C) more than
- (D) such

12 Of the two government officials present at the campaign meeting, the ------- ranked one has received the most media attention.
- (A) great
- (B) many
- (C) higher
- (D) lot

13 The more ------- a piece of factory equipment is, the more skilled the operator must be to run it properly.
- (A) specialize
- (B) specialized
- (C) specializing
- (D) specialization

14 This is to remind all employees that reimbursement requests for October's expenses will no ------- be accepted after November 10.
- (A) more
- (B) less
- (C) later
- (D) longer

15 Everyone thinks the movie that won the top prize was truly the best ------- all the nominated films.

(A) of
(B) to
(C) with
(D) for

16 Requests for leave in excess of the contracted amount must be approved by the department manager ------- permitted by the team leaders.

(A) due to
(B) as if
(C) in that
(D) rather than

17 The number of commuters taking the subway has ------- been greater than it is today due to the increasing number of workers in the city.

(A) somewhat
(B) no
(C) something
(D) never

18 The departure time for the latest flight to Toronto is ------- the one scheduled to leave for San Francisco.

(A) the same as
(B) as well as
(C) together with
(D) instead of

Part 6

Questions 19-22 refer to the following e-mail.

Date: August 12
From: curtisneil@mricksupply.com
To: jtanner@mricksupply.com
Subject: Re: The new office supplies list

I apologize for the ------- in sending the list of our new office supplies to our buyers. I had intended to do
19
that right away, but I had an urgent report to complete and didn't have time to do as you requested.

Moreover, I have been unable to confirm the current addresses of ------- of the companies that have
20
bought supplies from us in the past. My assistant is now attempting to contact these companies to verify their e-mail addresses.

Once this is done, I will send the updated file of contacts to you in an e-mail. I should be able to complete the update no ------- than 5:00 this afternoon. I would appreciate if you could confirm the
21
file before the end of the workday. -------. From now on, I'll make sure to keep the customer database
22
up-to-date.

Sincerely,
Curtis Neil

19 (A) refusal
(B) delay
(C) negligence
(D) error

20 (A) much
(B) many
(C) every
(D) none

21 (A) late
(B) less late
(C) later
(D) more lately

22 (A) There will not be enough time to correct the problem.
(B) I will send the list out to the buyers right after your verification.
(C) Updating the network will take me another hour.
(D) Everyone is excited about the new office supplies.

정답·해설·해석 p.79 / [별책] 토익 RC 필수 어휘 p.22

해커스 스타강사의 ▶
무료 해설강의 바로 보기
(13번 문제)

병치·도치 구문

토익, 이렇게 나온다!
병치·도치 구문 관련 문제는 출제 비율이 높지 않지만, 토익 문제의 문장에서 사용되므로 그 개념을 반드시 알고 있어야 한다. 등위접속사의 앞뒤 병치 구문을 채우는 문제가 주로 출제된다.

토익 필수 개념 다지기

01 접속사로 연결된 항목들이 서로 같은 품사나 구조를 취해 균형을 이루고 있는 것을 병치라고 한다.

The presentation was **interesting and informative**. 그 발표는 흥미롭고 유익했다.
You may register either **at our office or on our Web site**. 저희 사무실 또는 웹사이트에서 등록하십시오.

등위접속사(and)로 연결된 첫 번째 문장의 interesting과 informative는 둘 다 형용사로 균형을 이루고 있다.
상관접속사(either ~ or)로 연결된 두 번째 문장의 at our office와 on our Web site는 둘 다 전치사구로 균형을 이루고 있다.

02 주어와 동사의 위치가 바뀌는 현상을 도치라고 하며 주로 특정한 말을 강조하고자 문장 맨 앞으로 이동시켰을 때 도치가 일어난다.

Claire was <u>never</u> happier than when she became the CEO. Claire는 최고경영자가 되었을 때보다 더 행복한 적이 없었다.

<u>Never</u> **was Claire** happier than when she became the CEO.

조동사(have/be동사 포함)가 있는 경우는 조동사가 주어 앞으로 나가지만 조동사 없이 일반동사만 있을 경우에는 do 조동사가 앞으로 나가고 그 자리에 있던 일반동사는 원형으로 바뀐다.

Guests may check in <u>only after 11 o'clock</u>. (주어 + 조동사)
→ <u>Only after 11 o'clock</u> **may guests** check in. 11시 이후에만 투숙객들은 숙박 수속을 할 수 있다.

We have been discussing <u>only recently</u> our expansion plans. (주어 + have동사)
→ <u>Only recently</u> **have we** been discussing our expansion plans.
최근에서야 우리는 확장 계획들을 논의해 왔다.

Jacob was <u>never</u> so nervous about making a speech. (주어 + be동사)
→ <u>Never</u> **was Jacob** so nervous about making a speech.
Jacob은 연설하는 것에 대해 결코 그렇게 긴장해 본 적이 없었다.

Deanna <u>rarely</u> **shops** for anything online. (주어 + 일반동사)
→ <u>Rarely</u> **does Deanna shop** for anything online. Deanna는 어떤 것이든 온라인으로는 거의 쇼핑하지 않는다.

1 병치 구문

01 병치 구문에서는 같은 품사끼리 연결되어야 한다. 즉, 명사는 명사끼리, 동사는 동사끼리, 형용사는 형용사끼리, 부사는 부사끼리 나열되어야 한다.

명사   Martina's **experience** and **qualifications** make her the perfect candidate.
        Martina의 경험과 자격 요건은 그녀를 완벽한 후보로 만든다.

동사   She will **read** and **edit** the articles for the next issue. 그녀는 다음 호를 위한 기사들을 읽고 편집할 것이다.

형용사   The hotel offers **clean** and **spacious** rooms. 그 호텔은 깨끗하고 넓은 객실들을 제공한다.

부사   Please fill out the forms **accurately** and **carefully**. 양식을 정확하고 신중하게 작성하십시오.

> **고득점 포인트** 동사의 경우 수일치, 시제 일치가 되어 있는지 확인해야 한다.
>
> Mr. Olsen operates the cash register and assist(→assists) customers at the store.
> Mr. Olsen은 상점에서 금전 등록기를 작동하고 고객들을 돕는다.
>
> Leo contacted the investors and ask(→asked) them for their mailing addresses.
> Leo는 투자자들에게 연락해서 그들의 우편 주소를 요청했다.

02 병치 구문에서는 같은 구조끼리 연결되어야 한다. 즉, 동명사구는 동명사구끼리, 부정사구는 부정사구끼리, 전치사구는 전치사구끼리, 명사절은 명사절끼리 나열되어야 한다.

동명사구   Ronaldo was praised for **helping his coworkers** and **working diligently**.
        Ronaldo는 동료를 돕는 것과 근면하게 일하는 것에 대해 칭찬받았다.

부정사구   We need **to wash the dishes** and **(to) take out the trash**.
        우리는 설거지하고 쓰레기를 밖에 내놔야 한다.

전치사구   The police officers standing **at the entrance** and **in the lobby** work for the governor.
        입구와 로비에 서 있는 경찰들은 그 주지사를 위해 일한다.

명사절   Jerry asked me **what type of paper I want** and **how much I need**.
        Jerry는 내게 어떤 종류의 종이를 원하는지 그리고 얼마나 필요로 하는지 물었다.

> **고득점 포인트** to 부정사구 병치 구문에서 두 번째에 나온 to는 생략될 수 있다.

토익실전문제

출제 포인트 병치 구문 채우기
등위접속사의 앞이나 뒤에 동일한 형태의 품사/구를 채우는 문제가 주로 출제된다.

1. For many companies, using an intermediary has proven effective and ------- when attempting to enter a foreign market.

   (A) affords   (B) affordably
   (C) affording   (D) affordable

2. Ms. Saunders books flights and ------- accommodation reservations for all staff members when they go on business trips.

   (A) make   (B) makes
   (C) to make   (D) made

3. The duties of a representative consist of ------- information about the company's products and managing the special requests of customers.

   (A) to provide   (B) providing
   (C) provided   (D) provision

정답·해설·해석 p.81

01 가정법 문장에서 if가 생략되면 도치가 일어난다.

미래	Should 주어 동사원형, 주어 will 동사원형
과거	Were 주어 ~ , 주어 would 동사원형
과거완료	Had 주어 p.p. , 주어 would have p.p.

Should clients have a problem, Ms. Harper will deal with it. (⇐ If clients should have ~)
고객들이 문제를 겪는다면, Ms. Harper가 그것을 처리할 것이다.

※ 가정법의 도치는 Chapter 06의 토익 공식 6 if 없는 가정법(p.98)에서 자세히 다루고 있다.

02 부정어(never, nor, hardly, seldom, rarely, little)가 절의 맨 앞으로 나오면 도치가 일어난다.

Never **had we** experienced such incredible success. (⇐ We had never experienced ~)
우리는 그토록 굉장한 성공을 결코 경험해 본 적이 없었다.

03 '~도 역시 그러하다/그렇지 않다'는 의미의 so, neither가 절의 맨 앞으로 나오면 도치가 일어난다.

The main store extended its business hours, and so **did all its branches**. (⇐ all its branches also did)
본점이 영업 시간을 연장했고, 모든 지점들도 역시 그렇게 했다.

Ms. Chang doesn't like the manager's proposal and neither **do I**. (⇐ I also don't like)
Ms. Chang은 관리자의 제안을 맘에 들어 하지 않으며 나도 역시 그렇지 않다.

고득점 포인트 so와 neither는 각각 긍정문과 부정문에서 앞에 나온 어구가 반복될 때 이를 대신해서 쓴다.

04 [only + 부사(구, 절)]가 문장 맨 앞으로 나오면 도치가 일어난다.

Only lately **has Cynthia shown** better work performance. (⇐ Cynthia has only lately shown ~)
최근에서야 Cynthia는 더 나은 근무 실적을 보여주었다.

고득점 포인트
❶ 도치 구문에서 주어 뒤에 오는 동사의 형태에 주의해야 한다.
   Only on weekends does Paula goes(→go) shopping. 오직 주말에만 Paula는 쇼핑하러 간다.
❷ as(~처럼)나 than(~보다) 뒤에서는 도치가 일어나기도 하고 일어나지 않기도 한다.
   Alice hopes to get her work done quickly, as do most of her colleagues. (=as most of her colleagues do)
   대부분의 동료들이 그런 것처럼, Alice도 그녀의 일이 빨리 마무리되기를 바란다.
   I read a lot more books than does my sister. (=than my sister does) 나는 내 여동생보다 훨씬 많은 책을 읽는다.
❸ 보어로 사용된 형용사, 분사가 문장 맨 앞으로 나올 경우, 도치가 일어난다.
   Enclosed is a subscription card which can be used for renewal. 동봉되어 있는 것은 기한 연장에 사용될 수 있는 구독권입니다.
   (=A subscription card which can be used for renewal is enclosed.)

토익실전문제

출제 포인트 도치 구문 채우기
if가 생략된 가정법이나 부정어 또는 only가 문장의 맨 앞에 오는 도치 구문에서 올바른 형태의 동사를 채우는 문제가 주로 출제된다.

1. Had the department store ------- that the promotional sale would not be popular with its customers, it would have canceled the event.

   (A) realize (B) realized
   (C) been realized (D) realizes

2. Seldom does Ms. Lerner's attention to detail ------- her ability to see the whole picture when making management decisions.

   (A) affected (B) to affect
   (C) affecting (D) affect

3. Only after a consensus was reached did the general manager ------- to forgo having his employees do mandatory overtime work.

   (A) decide (B) decides
   (C) decided (D) deciding

정답·해설·해석 p.82

HACKERS PRACTICE 토익 고득점을 위한 필수 연습

둘 중 맞는 형태를 고르세요.

01 The new line of luggage was developed to be ------- and easy to carry.
ⓐ strong　　　　ⓑ strength

02 ------- does this store put its products on sale, as its prices are already low.
ⓐ Ever　　　　ⓑ Seldom

03 Exercising and ------- fewer fatty foods are two of the best ways to lose extra weight.
ⓐ eating　　　　ⓑ eat

04 The waitstaff at the French restaurant will take and ------- orders to the diners.
ⓐ serving　　　　ⓑ serve

05 ------- you need to cancel an appointment, please contact our receptionist.
ⓐ Should　　　　ⓑ Whether

06 Only recently did Ms. Soper ------- that the building design was flawed.
ⓐ notice　　　　ⓑ noticed

07 The tour guide was entertaining and -------, which made the tour very enjoyable.
ⓐ intelligently　　　　ⓑ intelligent

틀린 곳이 있으면 바르게 고치세요.

08 The beverage provides stamina and energize to those involved in intense physical activity.

09 The ticket office is located on the first floor next to the main entrance.

10 Have you notified me earlier, I could have attended the meeting.

11 Both full-time workers and part-time employ will be affected by the policy change.

12 Julia regularly travels abroad and meet with foreign clients.

13 The company has an unprecedented sales record and a reputable for winning service awards.

14 This year's trade fair ran more smoothly than the one last year did.

정답·해석 p.82

무료 해설 ▶
바로 보기

맞은 문제 개수: ＿＿ / 14
틀린 문제에 해당하는 토익 공식을 다시 한번 학습하세요.

🕐 제한 시간 12분

Part 5

01 Retailers expanding into ------- and competitive markets must develop effective advertising methods to differentiate their products from those of other companies.

(A) establish
(B) established
(C) establishes
(D) establishing

02 Cullman and Sons complained to the building manager about the malfunctioning air-conditioner, ------- did many of the other tenants.

(A) as
(B) even
(C) also
(D) therefore

03 ------- boarding his flight to Dallas, Mr. Royce contacted his hotel to arrange transportation from the airport.

(A) Whereas
(B) Finally
(C) Before
(D) Next

04 Project proposals that do not provide a clear statement of purpose will not be reviewed, and ------- will those that lack a budget estimate.

(A) also
(B) however
(C) neither
(D) only

05 The museum is seeking a curator whose understanding of art history is both detailed and -------.

(A) substantially
(B) substantiality
(C) substance
(D) substantial

06 The management of personnel records is a task ------- occupies a great deal of the administrative assistant's time.

(A) what
(B) when
(C) it
(D) that

07 *Successful Leadership*, a book by Michelle Sanders, includes advice for managers on how to reward the ------- and achievements of employees.

(A) dedicate
(B) dedicated
(C) dedication
(D) dedicational

08 Had the marketing report ------- more convincingly, the investors might have considered putting their money into the electric car venture.

(A) present
(B) presented
(C) be presented
(D) been presented

09 The department store has put up a sign announcing that it will hold a one-week sale on men's ------- and casual clothing.

(A) formal
(B) formally
(C) formalizing
(D) formality

10 Companies should keep their tax records for a minimum of five years ------- the government decides to conduct an audit.

(A) therefore
(B) even if
(C) despite
(D) in case

11 ------- have motorcycle and scooter makers experienced such an increase in sales as they did during the second quarter of this year.

(A) Also
(B) Even
(C) Although
(D) Seldom

12 Mr. Desmond can contact the human resources department should ------- have any questions concerning the terms of the employment contract.

(A) he
(B) him
(C) his
(D) himself

13 Online Auction Services will not respond to questions or complaints about products sold by third-party vendors, ------- will it provide refunds for these items.

(A) or
(B) nor
(C) and
(D) yet

14 In addition to regular exercise, getting sufficient sleep and ------- a balanced diet are important elements of a healthy lifestyle.

(A) to maintain
(B) maintain
(C) maintaining
(D) maintained

15 Other architectural firms are preparing for the upcoming changes to the city's building code, and ------- are we.

(A) neither
(B) either
(C) so
(D) as

16 *The Entrepreneur's Guidebook* is the ------- compilation of information available on what to prepare when starting your own business.

(A) large
(B) largely
(C) more largely
(D) largest

17 Individual investors are increasingly using online services to acquire financial data and ------- stocks.

(A) purchase
(B) purchases
(C) have purchased
(D) purchasing

18 With the head researcher's impending resignation, an opening for a well ------- and highly experienced replacement is now being advertised.

(A) educate
(B) education
(C) educating
(D) educated

Part 6

Questions 19-22 refer to the following e-mail.

To: Janice King <jking@smail.com>
From: Geoff Greer <ggreer@altenergy.com>
Subject: Conference Presentation
Date: December 16

I received some feedback from management about the presentation ------- are planning to give at the Alternative Energy Conference. They expressed concern that the presentation does not focus on our products' features and is mostly about research findings. In order to promote our latest line of solar-powered heaters and ------- our client base, they would like us to provide more details about the items during our talk.

Therefore, I would like to meet with you to revise the presentation. ------- is a summary about the cost, functions, and specifications of the applicable products.

Please read through the included materials carefully. -------. It has the information that management wants to be the focus of the presentation. Notify me once you're done so that we can set up an appointment. I hope that we can meet this afternoon as this needs to be finished as soon as possible.

19 (A) they
(B) we
(C) you
(D) ours

20 (A) expands
(B) expanding
(C) expanded
(D) expand

21 (A) Mentioned
(B) Requested
(C) Considered
(D) Attached

22 (A) I have not been able to answer all your requests.
(B) Our research findings must be followed more closely during the revision.
(C) In particular, the last page should be reviewed in depth.
(D) Make sure to hand it in by the indicated deadline.

Hackers TOEIC Reading

VOCABULARY

VOCABULARY Part 5,6

1. 토익 어휘의 특징

토익 어휘는 비즈니스와 밀접한 표현들이 주로 출제된다.

토익의 어휘는 비즈니스 상황 중의 영어 활용 능력을 측정하는 것이 목적이므로, 이러한 상황에서 실제로 쓰임 직한 표현들이 주로 출제된다. 따라서 비즈니스 관련 주제 및 어휘를 알아 두는 것이 중요하다.

토익 어휘에서는 단순한 의미뿐만 아니라 쓰임새까지 묻는다.

토익의 어휘에서는 비즈니스 상황에 있어 어휘들을 얼마나 정확하게 구사할 수 있는가를 측정하기 위하여 비즈니스 관련 예문에서 특정 어휘의 의미뿐만 아니라 쓰임새도 함께 묻는 문제가 출제된다. 따라서 어휘의 의미와 용법을 함께 익히는 것이 중요하다.

2. 토익 어휘 출제 유형

토익에 나오는 어휘 문제는 어휘, 어구, 유사의미어로 유형을 나눌 수 있다. 해커스 토익 Vocabulary에서는 이러한 문제 유형을 Section으로 구성하여 토익에서 출제되는 어휘 리스트를 품사별로 분류하여 제공하고 있다.

어휘	동사, 명사, 형용사 또는 부사 등 동일한 품사의 네 개 단어로 이루어진 보기 중 문맥상 어울리는 의미의 단어를 골라 문장을 완성하는 문제 유형이다.
어구	형용사, 동사, 명사 관련 어구 또는 짝을 이루는 표현의 일부분을 빈칸으로 두고, 네 개의 보기 중에 하나를 골라 숙어나 짝표현을 완성하는 문제 유형이다.
유사의미어	네 개의 보기 중 두 개 이상이 비슷한 의미의 동사, 명사, 형용사 또는 부사로 구성된 경우 그 쓰임새(usage)를 기준으로 알맞은 단어를 골라 문장을 완성하는 문제 유형이다.

3. 토익 어휘 문제 유형별 출제 비율

토익 어휘의 문제 유형별 출제 비율은 첫 번째 그래프와 같다. 참고로, 토익 어휘 문제에 등장하는 품사별 출제 비율은 두 번째 그래프와 같다.

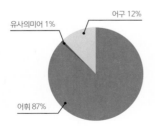

[문제 유형별 출제 비율]

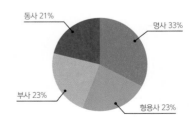

[품사별 출제 비율]

4. 토익 어휘 문제 풀이 방법

1. 보기를 보고 어휘 문제임을 확인한다.

어휘 문제는 동일 품사이면서 의미가 다른 네 개의 단어들이 보기로 제시된다. 예를 들어 형용사 어휘 문제의 보기는 의미가 다른 네 개의 형용사(ex - respective, innovative, impressive, noble)가 제시되므로 이를 통해 어휘 문제임을 확인할 수 있다.

2. 빈칸 주변의 단어와 문장의 해석을 통해 정답을 선택한다.

· 빈칸 주변의 단어가 보기 중 하나와 어구를 이루는 경우, 해당 보기를 정답으로 선택한다.
· 어구를 이루는 보기가 없을 경우 문장을 해석하여 문맥상 가장 알맞은 의미의 보기를 정답으로 선택한다. 이때, 비슷한 의미의 보기가 정답의 후보일 경우에는 각각의 쓰임새를 확인하여 알맞은 것을 정답으로 선택한다.
· Part 6의 경우 빈칸이 있는 문장뿐만 아니라 주변 문장과의 문맥이나 지문 전체의 내용을 파악하여 정답을 선택해야 하는 경우도 있다.

※ Part 6에서 문맥을 파악하여 정답을 선택해야 하는 문맥 파악 문제에 관해서는 Reading-Part 6(p.331)에서 자세히 다룬다.

Part 5 예제

When starting an office project, make sure your team members know who is ------- **for** what tasks.

(A) agreeable (B) renewable (C) comparable **(D) responsible**

1. 보기가 의미가 다른 네 개의 형용사로 구성되어 있으므로 형용사 어휘 문제이다.

2. 빈칸 주변에 어구를 이룰 만한 단어가 있는지 살펴본다. 빈칸 뒤에 전치사 for가 있으므로 이와 함께 '~에 대해 책임이 있는'의 뜻을 지닌 어구를 이루는 (D) responsible 이 정답이다.

Part 6 예제

Dear Ms. Conners,

I received your request this morning about the research being conducted here in Sydney. In answer to your query, **we have prepared a report on the ------- of the study, which you can use to check the status of our research**.

(A) awareness (B) competition **(C) progress** (D) establishment

2. 빈칸 주변에 어구를 이룰 만한 단어가 없으므로 빈칸이 있는 문장의 해석을 통해 빈칸에 필요한 의미를 확인한다. 빈칸이 있는 문장에서 보고서를 준비했으며, 이를 통해 연구의 진행 상황을 확인할 수 있다고 한 것으로 보아, 연구의 진척에 대한 보고서를 준비했음을 알 수 있다. 따라서 '진척, 진행'의 뜻을 지닌 (C) progress 가 정답이다.

1. 보기가 의미가 다른 네 개의 명사로 구성되어 있으므로 명사 어휘 문제이다.

SECTION 1

어휘

CHAPTER 01 동사

세상은 넓고 consult의 뜻은 많다.

토익이 좋아하는 consult는 'consult the manual(설명서를 참조하다)'로 쓸 때와 'consult the manager(관리자와 상담하다)'로 쓸 때 뜻이 달라진다. 문서와 함께 쓰이면 '참조하다', 사람과 함께 쓰이면 '상담하다'라고 알아두는 것이 돌아서면 잊어버리는 한글 뜻만 수십 번 보는 것보다 쉬우니 토익 동사는 같이 다니는 명사와 그 명사에 맞는 동사의 뜻을 봐두는 것이 좋다.

 토익 출제 유형 및 전략

1. 문맥에 맞는 동사를 고르는 문제로 출제된다.

2. 문장의 키워드와 접속사를 주의해서 보면 문맥을 파악하기 쉽다. 특히, 타동사의 경우 목적어와 문맥상 어울리는 단어를, 동사가 수동형인 경우는 주어와 문맥상 어울리는 단어를 정답으로 고른다.

3. Part 6에서는 빈칸이 있는 문장의 앞, 뒤 문장이나 지문 전체의 문맥을 파악하여 정답을 골라야 하는 경우도 있다.

예제

Part 5

Due to negative feedback from customers, Sycorp Wireless has opted to ------- its practice of charging high penalty fees for excessive mobile data usage.

(A) discontinue   (B) calculate   (C) isolate   (D) disturb

해설 콤마 앞의 Due to ~ customers와 Sycorp Wireless 이하의 문맥이 맞아야 한다. '고객들의 부정적인 의견 때문에, Sycorp Wireless사는 비싼 벌금을 부과하는 관행을 ＿＿＿하는 것을 선택했다'는 문맥에 맞는 동사는 (A) discontinue(중단하다)이다. (B) calculate는 '계산하다', (C) isolate는 '고립시키다', (D) disturb는 '방해하다'라는 의미이다.

해석 고객들의 부정적인 의견 때문에, Sycorp Wireless사는 과도한 모바일 데이터 사용에 대해 비싼 벌금을 부과하는 관행을 중단하는 것을 선택했다.

어휘 **feedback** n. 의견, 반응, 피드백 / **opt** v. 선택하다 / **practice** n. 관행, 관례 / **excessive** adj. 과도한, 지나친

정답 (A)

Part 6

Workers are reminded to ensure that each workstation is clean and each machine is running up to code before signing out this evening. An annual inspection will be ------- tomorrow by government-designated inspectors to make certain that our factory is operating according to federal safety standards.

(A) notified   (B) conducted   (C) defended   (D) involved

해설 주어인 An annual inspection과 어울리는 동사는 (B) conducted이다. conduct는 '(업무 등을) 실시하다'라는 뜻이고, conduct an inspection은 '검사를 실시하다'라는 뜻이다. (A)의 notify는 '(공식적으로) 알리다', (C)의 defend는 '방어하다', (D)의 involve는 '포함하다'라는 의미이다.

해석 직원들은 오늘 저녁 퇴근 전에 각 작업 장소가 청결한지와 각 장비들이 규정을 충족시키면서 작동하는지 확실하게 해야 함을 상기하기 바랍니다. 우리 공장이 연방 정부의 안전 기준에 따라 운영하고 있는지 확인하기 위해 정부가 지정한 검사관들에 의해 내일 연례 감사가 실시될 것입니다.

어휘 **ensure** v. 확실하게 하다, 보장하다 / **workstation** n. 작업 장소 / **up to code** 규정을 충족시키는 / **annual** adj. 연례의, 매년의 **inspection** n. 감사, 사찰 / **safety standard** 안전 기준

정답 (B)

핵심 단어 리스트

01 determine [ditə́:rmin]　알아내다, 밝히다

By doing a survey, the company can **determine** the best way to serve its customers.

설문 조사를 함으로써, 회사는 고객들을 응대하는 최상의 방법을 알아낼 수 있다.

출제포인트　1. '결정하다'라는 의미로도 쓰이며 이때는 decide와 의미가 같다.
　　　　　2. 逊 determination n. 결정, 결심　determined adj. 단호한

02 withdraw [wiðdrɔ́:]　빠지다, 물러나다

The tennis player was forced to **withdraw** from the tournament after injuring her knee.

그 테니스 선수는 무릎에 부상을 입은 후에 어쩔 수 없이 시합에서 빠져야 했다.

출제포인트　1. withdraw from: ~에서 빠지다, 나오다
　　　　　2. '취소하다, (예금 등을) 인출하다'라는 의미의 타동사로도 쓰인다.
　　　　　3. 逊 withdrawal n. 철수, 인출　withdrawn adj. 내성적인, 내향적인

03 anticipate [æntísəpeit]　예상하다, 기대하다

The airline **anticipates** that the snowstorm will cause some flights to be delayed.

그 항공사는 눈보라가 일부 항공편들을 지연되게 할 것이라고 예상한다.

출제포인트　1. expect와 의미가 같다.
　　　　　2. 逊 anticipated adj. 기대되는

04 monitor [mά:nitər]　관찰하다, 감시하다

The fashion design company **monitors** social media pages to help it identify new trends.

그 패션 디자인 회사는 새로운 동향을 알아보기 위해 소셜 미디어 페이지를 관찰한다.

출제포인트　'화면, 감시 장치'라는 의미의 명사로도 쓰인다.

05 analyze [ǽnəlàiz]　분석하다, 조사하다

Programmers carefully **analyzed** the computer code to learn what was causing the error.

프로그래머들은 무엇이 오류를 일으키고 있었는지를 알아내기 위해 컴퓨터 코드를 면밀하게 분석했다.

출제포인트　逊 analysis n. 분석, 분해　analyst n. 분석가
　　　　　analytic adj. 분석적인, 분해의
　　　　　analytically adv. 분석적으로, 분해적으로

06 surpass [sərpǽs]　뛰어넘다, 앞서다, 능가하다

Thanks to the marketing campaign, the company's sales **surpassed** its goal for the year.

마케팅 캠페인 덕분에, 회사의 매출은 그 해의 목표를 뛰어넘었다.

07 explore [iksplɔ́:r]　답사하다, 알아보다

Mr. Harmon **explored** different areas of the city before deciding on a place to live.

Mr. Harmon은 살 곳을 정하기 전에 도시의 여러 지역들을 답사했다.

출제포인트　1. '분석하다, 탐구하다'라는 의미로도 쓰인다.
　　　　　2. 逊 exploration n. 조사, 탐험, 탐구　explorer n. 탐험가
　　　　　exploratory adj. 탐사의, 탐구의

08 name [neim]　임명하다, 지명하다

James Wilkins, the CEO of Strand Industries, will **name** his successor at a press conference next week.

Strand Industries사의 최고경영자(CEO)인 James Wilkins는 다음 주 기자회견에서 그의 후임자를 임명할 예정이다.

출제포인트　1. appoint와 의미가 같다.
　　　　　2. name A (as) B: A를 B로 임명하다

09 redeem [ridí:m]　상품(현금)으로 교환하다

Tech Shop vouchers can be **redeemed** for products at any store branch.

Tech Shop 상품권은 어느 가게 지점에서든지 상품으로 교환될 수 있다.

출제포인트　be redeemed for A: A로 교환되다
　　　　　be redeemed with A: A를 통해 교환되다

10 excel [iksél]　뛰어나다, 잘하다

One of the requirements for the marketing manager position is that a candidate must **excel** at analyzing research.

마케팅 책임자 직책의 자격 요건들 중 하나는 지원자가 연구를 분석하는 것에 뛰어나야 한다는 것이다.

출제포인트　excel at/in A: A에 뛰어나다, A를 잘하다

11 optimize [άptəmàiz]　최적화하다, 최대한 활용하다

The software update is necessary in order to **optimize** the security system.

보안 시스템을 최적화하기 위해서는 소프트웨어 업데이트가 필수적이다.

출제포인트　逊 optimal adj. 최적의

12 differ [dífər]　다르다

WGB Technologies' new hard drive **differs** from the previous models in terms of size and weight.

WGB Technologies사의 새로운 하드 드라이브는 크기와 무게 면에서 이전 모델들과 다르다.

출제포인트　1. differ from: ~과 다르다
　　　　　2. 逊 difference n. 차이점　different adj. 다른
　　　　　differently adv. 다르게

13 conform [kənfɔ́ːrm]　　(규칙 등에) 따르다, 일치하다

The café decided to renovate its patio to **conform** to the new regulations on outdoor seating.
카페는 실외 좌석에 관한 새로운 규정에 따르기 위해 테라스를 개조하기로 결정했다.

출제포인트　conform to/with A: A에 따르다

14 resolve [rizálv]　　(문제 등을) 해결하다

The technician **resolved** the issue with the malfunctioning printer in less than 10 minutes.
기술자는 오작동하는 프린터의 문제를 10분 이내에 해결했다.

출제포인트　⑪ resolution n. 해결, 결의

15 suspend [səspénd]　　중단하다, 정지하다

Unless the patent can be acquired, the hybrid car project will have to be **suspended**.
특허가 취득될 수 없다면, 하이브리드 자동차 프로젝트는 중단되어야 할 것이다.

출제포인트　⑪ suspension n. 중단

16 resume [rizúːm]　　재개하다, 다시 시작하다

The investment seminar will **resume** after a short break.
투자 세미나는 짧은 휴식 시간 후에 재개할 것이다.

17 extend [iksténd]　　연장하다, 늘이다

Because of the heavy workload, the manager has decided to **extend** the deadline by a week.
과중한 업무량으로 인해, 관리자는 마감일을 한 주 연장하기로 결정했다.

출제포인트　1. extend an offer: 제안하다
　　　　　　　　 extend an invitation: 초대하다
　　　　　　　2. ⑪ extension n. 연장, 확장　extensive adj. 넓은

18 commence [kəméns]　　시작되다, 개시하다

The company's board meeting **commenced** with a review of last quarter's sales figures.
회사의 이사회 회의는 지난 분기의 매출액에 대한 검토부터 시작되었다.

출제포인트　initiate와 의미가 같다.

19 specify [spésəfài]　　(구체적으로) 명시하다

Customers are asked to **specify** their methods of payment at the bottom of the order form.
고객들은 주문서 하단에 지불 방법을 명시할 것이 요구된다.

출제포인트　⑪ specific adj. 명확한

20 commend [kəménd]　　칭찬하다, 추천하다

Ms. Owen's supervisor **commended** her on the detailed and informative presentation.
Ms. Owen의 감독관은 상세하고 유익한 발표에 대해 그녀를 칭찬했다.

출제포인트　commend 사람 on/for A: A에 대해 사람을 칭찬하다

21 consult [kənsált]　　상담하다, 참고하다

For any tips on the machine's maintenance, operators may **consult** the technicians.
기계의 보수 관리에 관한 어떠한 조언에 대해서라도, 기사들은 기술자들과 상담할 수 있다.

출제포인트　1. consult + 사람: ~와 상담하다
　　　　　　　2. consult + 자료: ~을 참조하다, 찾아보다

22 reserve [rizɔ́ːrv]　　예약하다, (권리·이익 등을) 보유하다

Staff attending the promotions conference must **reserve** their own hotel accommodations.
판촉 회의에 참가하는 직원들은 각자의 호텔 숙소를 예약해야 한다.

출제포인트　1. book(예약하다)을 함께 알아 두자.
　　　　　　　2. ⑪ reservation n. 예약

23 deliberate [dilíbərèit]　　심사숙고하다, 심의하다

The members of the board **deliberated** all afternoon over the merger proposition.
이사회 임원들은 오후 내내 합병안에 대해 심사숙고했다.

출제포인트　'신중한, 고의의'라는 의미의 형용사로도 쓰인다.

24 exceed [iksíːd]　　(수·양·정도를) 넘다, 초과하다

Airline policy states that carry-on baggage must not **exceed** a weight of 10 kilograms.
항공사 정책은 기내 반입 수하물이 10킬로그램의 무게를 넘지 않아야 한다는 것을 명시한다.

출제포인트　⑪ excess n. 초과　exceedingly adv. 대단히, 매우

25 address [ədrés]　　　　다루다, 제기하다

Labor union officials will **address** the recent changes to the benefits package.
노동조합 임원들은 복리 후생 제도의 최근 변화를 다룰 것이다.

출제포인트　1. address issues: 문제점들을 다루다
　　　　　　2. '주소, 연설'이라는 의미의 명사로도 쓰인다.

26 represent [rèprizént]　　　　나타내다, 의미하다

These figures **represent** a significant increase in profits, especially in the American market.
이 수치들은 특히 미국 시장에서의 상당한 수익 증가를 나타낸다.

출제포인트　⑭ representative　n. 대표, 직원

27 retain [ritéin]　　　　(계속) 유지하다, 보관하다

Federal laws require land developers to **retain** the historic features of neighborhoods.
연방법은 토지 개발자들에게 지역들의 역사적 특징을 유지할 것을 요구한다.

출제포인트　maintain과 의미가 같다.

28 hesitate [hézətèit]　　　　주저하다

If you need help, do not **hesitate** to contact one of the bank's representatives.
만약 도움이 필요하시면, 주저하지 마시고 은행 직원들 중 한 명에게 연락하세요.

출제포인트　do not hesitate to + 동사원형: 주저하지 말고 ~하다

29 waive [weiv]　　　　적용하지 않다, 포기하다

The credit card company will **waive** administrative fees for account holders spending over $10,000 annually.
그 신용카드사는 매년 1만 달러 이상 소비하는 계좌 소유자들에 대해서 관리 수수료를 적용하지 않을 것이다.

30 last [læst]　　　　오래가다, 지속하다

The ink cartridges for Tel-tech's printers don't **last** as long as those of its competitors.
Tel-tech사 프린터의 잉크 카트리지는 경쟁사들의 제품만큼 오래가지 않는다.

출제포인트　1. last for + 기간: ~ 동안 지속하다
　　　　　　2. '마지막의, 지난'이라는 의미의 형용사, '마지막으로'라는 의미의 부사로도 쓰인다.

31 relocate [rì:loukéit]　　　　(회사·주민 등이) 이전하다

Volentia announced plans to **relocate** its main office to China.
Volentia사는 본사를 중국으로 이전하려는 계획을 발표했다.

출제포인트　1. move와 의미가 같다.
　　　　　　2. ⑭ relocation　n. 이전, 재배치

32 assure [əʃúər]　　　　~라고 확실히 말하다, 보장하다

The chairperson **assured** the investors that the merger wouldn't affect the stock value.
회장은 투자자들에게 합병이 주가에 영향을 주지 않을 것임을 확실히 말했다.

출제포인트　1. assure A that절: A에게 ~을 확실히 말하다
　　　　　　2. ⑭ assurance　n. 확신, 보장

33 accommodate [əkámədèit]　　　　수용하다, 배려하다, 부응하다

The luxurious beachfront rooms can easily **accommodate** up to seven occupants.
바다가 보이는 고급스러운 방들은 사용자를 7명까지 거뜬히 수용할 수 있다.

출제포인트　1. accommodate guests: 손님들을 수용하다
　　　　　　2. accommodate increased demand: 증가한 수요에 부응하다

34 implement [ímpləmènt]　　　　시행하다, 이행하다

Sun Telecom has **implemented** an updated policy on long-distance rates.
Sun Telecom사는 장거리 통화 요금에 대한 최신 방침을 시행했다.

출제포인트　1. implement security measures: 보안 조치를 시행하다
　　　　　　2. carry out과 의미가 같다.

35 indicate [índikèit]　　　　보여주다, 나타내다

Research **indicates** that employee performance is linked to job satisfaction.
연구는 직원 성과가 직업 만족도와 관련되어 있다는 것을 보여준다.

출제포인트　1. studies indicate that절: 연구는 ~을 보여준다
　　　　　　2. ⑭ indication　n. 표시, 조짐　indicator　n. 지표

36 undergo [ʌndərgóu]　　　　겪다, 받다

Berken Corporation will **undergo** transitions in organizational structure due to recent promotions.
Berken사는 최근 승진으로 인해 조직 구조에 변화를 겪을 것이다.

출제포인트　undergo transitions: 변화를 겪다

HACKERS PRACTICE 토익 고득점을 위한 필수 연습

A와 B중 맞는 것을 고르세요.

01 **support** art education in local communities
지역 사회의 예술 교육을 ⓐ 촉진하다 ⓑ 지원하다

02 **acknowledge** that you have received the confirmation
당신이 승인받았다는 것을 ⓐ 알리다 ⓑ 부인하다

03 **appear** to need special assistance
특별한 원조가 필요 ⓐ 함을 알다 ⓑ 한 것 같이 보인다

04 **witnessed** an increase in sales
매출의 상승을 ⓐ 일으켰다 ⓑ 보였다

05 **arrange** an appointment
약속을 ⓐ 미루다 ⓑ 정하다

06 Ask a clerk at the information desk to **assist** you.
당신을 ⓐ 도와 ⓑ 깨워 달라고 안내소의 직원에게 요청하세요.

07 **cancel** a meeting
회의를 ⓐ 정하다 ⓑ 취소하다

08 **secure** financing for the project
사업을 위한 자금을 ⓐ 보내다 ⓑ 마련하다

09 The desk can be **assembled** without the use of tools.
그 책상은 도구 사용 없이 ⓐ 조립 될 ⓑ 분해 될 수 있다.

10 The new policy is **intended** to reduce air pollution.
새 정책은 공기 오염을 줄이는 것을 ⓐ 의무화한다 ⓑ 목적으로 한다.

11 The doctor chose to **operate** on Mr. Chung.
의사는 Mr. Chung을 ⓐ 입원시키기로 ⓑ 수술하기로 결정했다.

12 **utilize** a new method
새로운 방법을 ⓐ 이용하다 ⓑ 제안하다

13 I **briefed** him on the merger.
나는 그에게 합병에 대해 ⓐ 제안했다 ⓑ 간단히 설명했다.

14 **supply** replacement parts
교체 부품을 ⓐ 공급하다 ⓑ 수집하다

15 **prevent** construction accidents
건설 사고를 ⓐ 일으키다 ⓑ 예방하다

16 His skills **match** the company's requirements.
그의 기술은 그 회사의 자격 요건과 ⓐ 일치한다 ⓑ 못 미친다.

17 **encounter** opposition from the university
대학의 반대에 ⓐ 좌절하다 ⓑ 직면하다

18 A lawyer **certified** the contract.
변호사가 계약서를 ⓐ 보증했다 ⓑ 파기했다.

19 **cooperate** on a project
프로젝트에 대해 ⓐ 협력하다 ⓑ 참여하다

20 We must **strive** to meet the deadline.
우리는 마감 기한을 맞추기 위해 ⓐ 노력해야 ⓑ 시작해야 한다.

21 **reveal** the newest model
최신 모델을 ⓐ 제작하다 ⓑ 공개하다

22 **gauge** the applicants' abilities
지원자들의 능력을 ⓐ 의심하다 ⓑ 평가하다

23 Audits are regularly **scheduled**.
회계 감사가 정기적으로 ⓐ 예정되어 있다 ⓑ 논의된다.

24 **prohibit** smoking indoors
실내에서의 흡연을 ⓐ 허용하다 ⓑ 금지하다

25 Research is **proceeding** smoothly.
연구는 순조롭게 ⓐ 진행되고 ⓑ 축소되고 있다.

26 **attract** bargain hunters
저렴한 것을 찾아다니는 소비자들을 ⓐ 유인하다 ⓑ 비난하다

27 Raised funds will **benefit** local schools. 　조성된 기금은 지역 학교들에 ⓐ 도움이 될 ⓑ 통보될 것이다.

28 **expedite** the ordering process 　주문 절차를 ⓐ 상세히 설명하다 ⓑ 신속히 처리하다

29 **reject** the buyer's offer for the house 　그 집에 대한 구매자의 제의를 ⓐ 거절하다 ⓑ 수락하다

30 Mr. Hill **presided** over the council meeting. 　Mr. Hill은 의회 회의를 ⓐ 주재했다 ⓑ 재개했다.

31 need to **obtain** a license 　면허증을 ⓐ 반납해야 ⓑ 취득해야 한다

32 **release** funds 　자금을 ⓐ 풀다 ⓑ 모으다

33 **handle** the packages carefully 　소포들을 조심스럽게 ⓐ 다루다 ⓑ 포장하다

34 They will **remain** in Denver after the merger. 　그들은 합병 이후에 덴버에 ⓐ 이전할 ⓑ 남을 것이다.

35 **order** a new edition 　신판을 ⓐ 기념하다 ⓑ 주문하다

36 Organizers will meet once more to **finalize** plans. 　주최자들은 계획을 ⓐ 구성하기 ⓑ 마무리짓기 위해 한 번 더 만날 것이다.

37 **speculate** that the store would close down 　그 상점이 문을 닫을 것이라고 ⓐ 추측하다 ⓑ 확신하다

38 **enforce** the policy on absences 　결근에 관한 정책을 ⓐ 시행하다 ⓑ 발표하다

39 Traffic is being **diverted**. 　차량들이 ⓐ 전진하고 ⓑ 우회하고 있다.

40 **perceive** something is wrong 　무엇인가 잘못됨을 ⓐ 믿다 ⓑ 인지하다

41 He will **ship** the goods tomorrow. 　그는 내일 물품들을 ⓐ 수송할 ⓑ 주문할 것이다.

42 in order for the rebate to **apply** 　환불을 ⓐ 적용하기 ⓑ 진행하기 위해서는

43 **oversee** the branch in Shanghai 　상하이에 있는 지점을 ⓐ 예측하다 ⓑ 감독하다

44 **authorize** a second printing 　두 번째 인쇄를 ⓐ 허가하다 ⓑ 시작하다

45 **confirm** the booking 　예약을 ⓐ 확인하다 ⓑ 접수하다

46 **present** an official ID card 　공식 신분증을 ⓐ 발급하다 ⓑ 제시하다

47 **submit** photocopies 　복사본을 ⓐ 빌리다 ⓑ 제출하다

48 **duplicate** last year's successful event 　작년의 성공적인 행사를 ⓐ 재현하다 ⓑ 창조하다

49 **follow** the instructions 　지시를 ⓐ 발표하다 ⓑ 따르다

50 The consultant **asserts** that changes are needed. 　그 자문 위원은 변화가 필요하다고 ⓐ 단언한다 ⓑ 생각한다.

51 The discounted items are **marked** in red. 　할인된 품목은 빨간색으로 ⓐ 색칠되어 ⓑ 표시되어 있다.

52 **ensure** that the forms are signed 　양식에 서명이 되어 있는지 ⓐ 확실히 하다 ⓑ 알려주다

53 **occupy** an office on the ground floor 　1층에 있는 사무실을 ⓐ 사용하다 ⓑ 청소하다

54 **require** more details 　더 많은 세부 사항을 ⓐ 요청하다 ⓑ 검토하다

맞는 동사에 √표를 하세요.

55 The exhibition ☐ **features** ☐ **approaches** paintings by local artists. 전시는 지역 예술가들의 그림을 **특별히 포함한다.**

56 ☐ **process** ☐ **decline** the offer 제안을 거절하다

57 ☐ **cause** ☐ **launch** a decrease in demand 수요의 감소를 야기하다

58 ☐ **stray** ☐ **visit** the headquarters 본부를 방문하다

59 The board ☐ **asks** ☐ **expects** that the CEO will resign soon. 이사회는 최고 경영자가 곧 사임할 것이라고 **예상한다.**

60 ☐ **compile** ☐ **maintain** a list of suppliers 공급업체들의 목록을 수집하다

61 ☐ **promise** ☐ **use** a reliable travel agency 믿을 수 있는 여행사를 **이용하다**

62 The package ☐ **includes** ☐ **surrounds** airfare. 그 (여행) 패키지는 항공료를 포함한다.

63 The analyst ☐ **predicts** ☐ **prepares** that stock prices will rise. 분석가는 주가가 상승할 것이라고 **예측한다.**

64 ☐ **accumulate** ☐ **organize** one's thoughts 생각을 정리하다

65 ☐ **alert** ☐ **complete** the necessary documents 필요한 서류들을 완성하다

66 Mr. Gordon will ☐ **administer** ☐ **revise** tomorrow's test. Mr. Gordon은 내일 시험을 **시행할** 것이다.

67 ☐ **examine** ☐ **find** the files 파일들을 검토하다

68 ☐ **expand** ☐ **incline** service coverage 서비스 범위를 확대하다

69 The film is expected to ☐ **employ** ☐ **receive** an award. 그 영화는 상을 받을 것으로 예상된다.

70 ☐ **exhibit** ☐ **attach** paintings in an art gallery 미술관에 그림을 전시하다

71 Staff are ☐ **reminded** ☐ **remembered** that S + V. 직원들은 ~할 것이 **상기된다.**

72 Cactus plants can ☐ **tolerate** ☐ **preserve** desert climates. 선인장은 사막 기후를 견딜 수 있다.

73 ☐ **offer** ☐ **select** the dinner guests a drink 저녁 식사 손님들에게 음료를 제공하다

74 ☐ **insert** ☐ **involve** a card to pass through the secured gate 보안 장치가 있는 출입구를 통과하기 위해 카드를 **삽입하다**

정답 p.85

⏱ 제한 시간 16분

Part 5

01 Professor Wilson is ------- the essay deadline because many students have exams for other classes next week.

(A) placing
(B) supplying
(C) extending
(D) providing

02 The advertisement ------- that the company's products come with a full two-year warranty.

(A) retails
(B) specifies
(C) distributes
(D) solicits

03 Customers can ------- which product is best for them by going to the company's Web site.

(A) accept
(B) convince
(C) determine
(D) commit

04 A group of environmentalists ------- the issue of climate change, making reference to the temperature increases in Northern Canada and Russia.

(A) requested
(B) left
(C) conformed
(D) addressed

05 Turwind Air has announced that it will be ------- flights from Orlando to Vancouver because of declining passenger numbers.

(A) reflecting
(B) enclosing
(C) suspending
(D) departing

06 Because Mr. Kim needed to receive the parcel before his meeting on Monday, he inquired whether it was possible to ------- shipping.

(A) emphasize
(B) demonstrate
(C) expedite
(D) recognize

07 A number of reports ------- that providing employees with more freedom to make decisions gives them a greater sense of responsibility in the workplace.

(A) inspect
(B) interfere
(C) indicate
(D) invoke

08 When Ms. Choi ------- difficulties with the projector, she had to stop her presentation and ask for assistance.

(A) duplicated
(B) issued
(C) encountered
(D) returned

09 Residents can ------- a building permit by downloading an application from the Web site and submitting the completed form to City Hall.

(A) tear
(B) contain
(C) restore
(D) obtain

10 The CEO of Mason Electronics ------- Jack Phillips as the new head of the accounting department.

(A) named
(B) pointed
(C) founded
(D) practiced

11 Ms. Hawkins will ------- the job offer from Milestone Media because the company is not willing to provide supplementary health insurance.

(A) reject
(B) adapt
(C) convene
(D) benefit

12 The attendance at this year's conference ------- last year's number by over 3,000 people.

(A) surpassed
(B) repeated
(C) accomplished
(D) impressed

13 Westwood Travel ------- a 14 percent increase in sales once it started offering group tour packages for South America.

(A) combined
(B) commended
(C) adjusted
(D) witnessed

14 Travel expenses claimed by employees cannot ------- the amount specified in the memo from the accounting department.

(A) exist
(B) prevent
(C) delay
(D) exceed

15 Mr. Ewing phoned his supplier to ------- an order of merchandise for his new store in Manchester.

(A) contact
(B) confront
(C) confirm
(D) contend

16 For information on flight schedules, passengers should ------- displays located throughout the departure area of the terminal.

(A) browse
(B) consult
(C) pursue
(D) inform

17 The financial advisor ------- that the economic downturn would cause the price of gold to rise sharply.

(A) surveyed
(B) performed
(C) speculated
(D) characterized

18 Management ------- different kinds of accounting software before deciding which one to buy.

(A) published
(B) explored
(C) invited
(D) remarked

19 Mr. Jenkins asked his travel agent to ------- tickets for the early morning flight to Toronto next Tuesday.

(A) appoint
(B) require
(C) reserve
(D) attach

20 Ms. Anderson has ------- an office on the third floor for five years now, but she will be moving one floor up following her promotion.

(A) subscribed
(B) occupied
(C) divided
(D) associated

Part 6

Questions 21-24 refer to the following article.

Downtown Finance Center Renovations

The Downtown Finance Center is about to ------- extensive renovations, including a redesign of the
building's facade and lobby. The aim of the work is to give the Finance Center a competitive edge
in attracting high-end corporate tenants for its office space.

After completion, the building will appear ------- different due to the addition of a mirrored glass
exterior that will change color based on the time of day. Also, the upgraded seating areas in the
lobby will ------- more people than before, with special attention given to comfort and space.

What is remarkable is that the Downtown Finance Center has taken a very unconventional move
regarding the renovation. The center appointed freelance architect Janice Pana, who recently
made her debut in the architecture community after winning the Vernon Design Society's Young
Architect's Award. -------. However, the center believes that her ability will allow her to meet the
challenge.

The renovation will begin September 1 and is expected to be complete before the end of the year.

21 (A) deliberate
   (B) undergo
   (C) alleviate
   (D) retrieve

22 (A) commonly
   (B) substantially
   (C) supposedly
   (D) temporarily

23 (A) escalate
   (B) empathize
   (C) isolate
   (D) accommodate

24 (A) Many have complimented the building's
       color-changing lights.
   (B) Tenants like sitting in the lobby now that it
       has been redesigned.
   (C) Employing an individual contractor rather
       than a firm is a rare decision.
   (D) Work in the area is ongoing but will be
       completed soon.

issue의 뜻을 제대로 알아야 점수가 오르지 않는 issue가 해결된다.

토익 단어를 한 가지 뜻만 외워 놓고 시험에서 엉뚱한 답을 고르면 열심히 공부한 게 헛수고가 되고 만다. issue는 '문제'란 뜻 외에 '발행물'이란 의미가 있어서 'get free issues: 무료 발행물을 얻다'처럼 쓰이는 것을 알고 있어야 토익 시험에서 승산이 있는 법. 어휘란 용례를 알아야 제대로 쓸 수 있으니, 토익 명사를 익힐 때는 같이 다니는 동사나 형용사, 전치사가 뭔지 봐두자.

토익 출제 유형 및 전략

1. 문맥에 맞는 명사를 고르는 문제로 출제된다.

2. 접속사 및 전치사, 그리고 문장의 키워드를 주의해서 보면 문맥을 파악하기 쉽다.

3. Part 6에서는 빈칸이 있는 문장의 앞, 뒤 문장의 키워드나 지문 전체의 주제와 관련된 명사를 정답으로 골라야 하는 경우도 있다.

예제

Part 5

Having a large directory of business ------- is definitely a plus for those working in the travel industry.

(A) methods　(B) composites　(C) contacts　(D) inferences

해설　'사업상 _____의 명단을 많이 갖고 있는 것' 부분의 문맥이 맞으려면 빈칸에는 (C) contacts(연줄이 닿는 사람)가 적합하다. (business contact: 사업상 연락하는 사람) '접촉'이란 뜻으로 자주 쓰이는 contact가 3, 4차 뜻으로 출제되어 어려운 문제가 된 경우이다. (A)의 method는 '방법', (B)의 composite는 '합성물, 복합물', (D)의 inference는 '추론'이라는 의미이다.

해석　사업상 연락하는 사람들의 명단을 많이 갖고 있는 것은 여행 업계에서 일하는 사람들에게는 분명히 이점이다.

어휘　**directory** n. 명단, 전화번호부 / **plus** n. 이점

정답　(C)

Part 6

At only a fraction of the regular registration price, joining has never been easier or more advantageous. Not only will you have access to all our online services, but you will also enjoy the added ------- of full networking opportunities with Info-Mate's other member.

(A) entreaty　(B) course　(C) warranty　(D) benefit

해설　'Not only A but also B(A뿐만 아니라 B도)'의 문장 구조 내에서 'Not only ~ services' 부분과 but 이하 부분의 문맥이 맞아야 한다. '모든 온라인 서비스에 대한 이용 권한을 가지게 될 뿐만 아니라, 다른 회원들과의 많은 네트워킹 기회에 대한 추가 _____도 누리게 된다'라는 문맥에서 빈칸에 적합한 것은 (D) benefit(혜택)이다. (A) entreaty는 '간청, 애원', (B) course는 '강좌, 강의', (C) warranty는 '품질 보증서'라는 의미이다.

해석　정규 등록비의 일부만으로, 가입은 그 어느 때보다 쉽고 이롭습니다. 여러분은 우리의 모든 온라인 서비스에 대한 이용 권한을 가지게 될 뿐만 아니라, 다른 Info-Mate 회원들과의 많은 네트워킹 기회에 대한 추가 혜택도 누리게 될 것입니다.

어휘　**fraction** n. 일부, 단편 / **registration** n. 등록 / **advantageous** adj. 이로운, 유리한

정답　(D)

01 objective [əbdʒéktiv]　　목표, 목적

The **objective** of the seminar is to help participants become better managers.
세미나의 목표는 참석자들이 더 나은 관리자가 되도록 돕는 것이다.

출제포인트　1. '객관적인'이라는 의미의 형용사로도 쓰인다.
　　　　　　2. 'object: 물건, 물체'와 구별하여 알아 두자.

02 precaution [prikɔ́:ʃən]　　조심, 예방 조치

Participants must take **precautions** to avoid being injured during the race.
참가자들은 경주 중에 부상을 입는 것을 피하기 위해 조심해야 한다.

출제포인트　take precautions: 조심하다, 예방 조치를 취하다

03 output [áutput]　　생산(량)

Solar farms increased their energy **output** over the summer by 40 percent.
태양광 발전소들은 여름 동안에 에너지 생산량을 40퍼센트 정도 늘렸다.

04 dimension [diménʃən]　　치수, 크기

The decorator measured the table's **dimensions** to see if it would fit in the dining room.
그 실내 장식가는 탁자가 식당에 맞는지 확인하기 위해 탁자의 치수를 측정했다.

05 conflict [kánflikt]　　갈등, 충돌

A disagreement on the issue caused a **conflict** between the human resources and marketing departments.
그 사안에 대한 의견 불일치는 인사부와 마케팅 부서 사이의 갈등을 야기했다.

출제포인트　1. resolve conflicts: 갈등을 해결하다
　　　　　　2. a conflict between A and B: A와 B 사이의 갈등

06 influx [ínflʌks]　　쇄도, 유입

Sawyer National Park experienced an **influx** of visitors over the weekend.
Sawyer 국립공원은 주말 동안 방문객들의 쇄도를 겪었다.

출제포인트　an influx of: (사람 · 물건)의 쇄도

07 presence [prézns]　　존재(감), 영향력

The Helping Hands charitable organization has quite a big **presence** in communities across the country.
Helping Hands 자선단체는 전국의 지역사회에서 꽤 큰 존재감을 지니고 있다.

출제포인트　1. '출석, 참석'이라는 의미로도 쓰인다.
　　　　　　2. 倒 present adj. 존재하는, 현재의; n. 현재, 선물
　　　　　　3. 반의어는 absence(없음, 결핍, 결석)이다.

08 reduction [ridʌ́kʃən]　　인하, 감소

Reductions in interest rates have led to an increase in customers applying for home loans.
금리 인하는 주택 대출을 신청하는 고객들의 증가로 이어졌다.

출제포인트　倒 reduce v. 감소하다, 감소시키다

09 access [ǽkses]　　접근(권), 이용 권한, 입장

Access to the client's audio recordings is limited to the lawyers who are handling the case.
의뢰인의 음성 기록에 대한 접근권은 사건을 다루는 변호사들에게만 국한된다.

출제포인트　1. access to A: A로의 접근(권)
　　　　　　2. '~에 접근하다, 들어가다'라는 의미의 동사로 쓰일 때는 뒤에 전치사가 올 수 없다.
　　　　　　3. 倒 accessible adj. 접근 가능한　accessibility n. 접근 가능성

10 proximity [praksíməti]　　근접함, 가까움

Ajmer Hotel is popular among business travelers because of its **proximity** to the financial district.
Ajmer 호텔은 금융 지구와의 근접함 때문에 출장객들 사이에서 인기가 있다.

출제포인트　1. proximity to: ~에 근접함, ~에 가까움
　　　　　　2. in the proximity of: ~의 부근에

11 authority [əθɔ́:rəti]　　권위자, 권한

Debbie Girma is one of the top **authorities** on urban engineering.
Debbie Girma는 도시공학 분야의 최고 권위자 중 한 명이다.

출제포인트　1. 복수형(authorities)으로는 '당국'이라는 의미로도 사용된다.
　　　　　　2. 'authorization: 허가, 인가'와 구별하여 알아 두자.

12 dedication [dèdikéiʃən]　　전념, 헌신

Zhong-Tech has become the industry leader through its **dedication** to quality.
Zhong-Tech사는 품질에 대한 전념을 통해 업계 선두 주자가 되었다.

출제포인트　1. dedication to: ~에 대한 전념
　　　　　　2. 倒 dedicate v. 전념하다　dedicated adj. 전념하는, 헌신적인

13 adjustment [ədʒʌ́stmənt]　　　　조정, 수정, 적응

Legong Company had to make some **adjustments** to the plans to merge the north and south offices.

Legong사는 북부 지역과 남부 지역의 사무실들을 합병할 계획을 일부 조정해야 했다.

출제포인트　1. make adjustments to + 명사: ~을 조정하다
　　　　　2. 函 adjust v. 조정하다, 적응하다　adjustable adj. 조정할 수 있는

14 distribution [dìstrəbjúːʃən]　　　　배포, 분배, 유통

Luther will be in charge of the **distribution** of product samples at the trade fair.

Luther는 무역 박람회에서 제품 견본 배포를 담당할 것이다.

출제포인트　函 distribute v. 배포하다, 나누어 주다, 유통시키다

15 shift [ʃift]　　　　전환, 이동, 교대 근무 (시간)

The company's decision to advertise online was a major **shift** in focus.

온라인에 광고하기로 한 회사의 결정은 주안점의 중대한 전환이었다.

Nothing unusual occurred during the afternoon **shift** at the warehouse.

오후 교대 근무 시간 동안 창고에서 별다른 일이 발생하지 않았다.

16 priority [praiɔ́ːrəti]　　　　우선 사항, 우선권

The accounting firm has made it a **priority** to cultivate customer loyalty.

그 회계 법인은 고객 충성도를 돈독히 하는 것을 우선 사항으로 했다.

출제포인트　1. top priority: 최우선 사항
　　　　　2. 函 prior adj. 우선하는　prioritize v. ~에 우선순위를 매기다

17 estimate [éstəmət]　　　　견적, 추정(치), 견적서

Davies made an **estimate** that the furniture design project would cost $15,000.

Davies는 가구 디자인 프로젝트가 15,000달러의 비용이 들 것이라는 견적을 냈다.

출제포인트　1. make an estimate: 견적을 내다
　　　　　2. '견적하다, 추정하다'라는 의미의 동사로도 쓰인다.

18 recognition [rèkəgníʃən]　　　　인정, 표창, 보상

In **recognition** of Pablo Zinder's contributions to art, the city gave him its Culture Award.

Pablo Zinder의 예술에 대한 기여를 인정하여, 시는 그에게 Culture 상을 수여했다.

출제포인트　1. in recognition of: ~을 인정하여
　　　　　2. monetary recognition: 금전적인 표창

19 disclosure [disklóuʒər]　　　　공개, 폭로

The **disclosure** of financial information by companies helps investors make well-informed decisions.

기업들의 재무 정보 공개는 투자자들이 제대로 알고 내리는 결정을 할 수 있도록 돕는다.

출제포인트　函 disclose v. 공개하다, 드러내다

20 permission [pərmíʃən]　　　　허가, 허락, 승인

To examine the library's collection of rare books, **permission** is required from the chief librarian.

도서관의 희귀본 컬렉션을 살펴보기 위해서는, 도서관장의 허가가 필요하다.

출제포인트　허가 사실을 표시한 증서인 'permit(허가증)'과 구별하여 알아 두자.

21 persistence [pərsístəns]　　　　끈기, 고집

Ms. Singh's **persistence** in bringing in new clients resulted in her getting a pay raise.

새로운 고객을 끌어오려는 Ms. Singh의 끈기는 그녀가 임금 인상을 받는 결과를 낳았다.

출제포인트　函 persistent adj. 고집 센, 완고한

22 departure [dipáːrtʃər]　　　　벗어남, 출발

Featuring several ballads, Mel River's new album is a **departure** from her usual work.

몇 곡의 발라드를 특별히 포함하기 때문에, Mel River의 새 앨범은 그녀의 평소 작품에서 벗어난 것이다.

출제포인트　1. departure from ~: (늘 하던 것으로부터의) 벗어남, 일탈, (장소로부터의) 출발, 떠남
　　　　　2. 函 depart v. 출발하다, 떠나다

23 initiative [iníʃiətiv]　　　　계획, 발안, 결단력

County residents will vote on the **initiative** to ban the use of mobile phones while driving.

자치주 주민들은 운전 중 휴대 전화 사용을 금지하는 계획에 투표할 것이다.

출제포인트　1. show initiative: 결단력을 보여주다
　　　　　take initiative: 솔선해서 하다, 주도권을 잡다
　　　　　2. 函 initiate v. 시작하다, 일으키다

24 challenge [tʃǽlindʒ]　　　　과제, 문제, 도전

One **challenge** editors have is maintaining high-quality writing in spite of deadlines.

편집장들이 가진 한 가지 과제는 마감 일자에도 불구하고 고품질의 글을 유지하는 것이다.

출제포인트　'(도전이 될 일을) 요구하다'라는 의미의 동사로도 쓰인다.

25 method [méθəd]
방법, 방식

Travelers may choose from several convenient **methods** of reservation.
여행객들은 몇 가지의 편리한 예약 방법들 중에서 선택할 수 있다.

출제포인트   method of payment: 지불 방법

26 alternative [ɔ:ltə́:rnətiv]
대안

Many environmental groups promote solar energy as an **alternative** to fossil fuels.
많은 환경 보호 단체들이 화석 연료에 대한 대안으로 태양 에너지를 장려한다.

출제포인트   alternative to: ~에 대한 대안

27 shortage [ʃɔ́:rtidʒ]
부족, 결핍

Towns in northern Canada are experiencing a **shortage** of teachers and doctors.
캐나다 북부의 소도시들은 교사와 의사의 부족을 겪고 있다.

출제포인트   1. lack(부족; 부족하다)을 함께 알아두자.
      2. ⊕ short adj. 부족한, 불충분한   shortly adv. 곧

28 receipt [risí:t]
수령, 받음, 영수증

To confirm **receipt** of your purchase, please sign the shipping form on the line indicated.
구입품의 수령을 확인하기 위해, 배송 양식의 표시된 줄에 서명하세요.

출제포인트   1. upon receipt of ~: ~을 수령하는 즉시
      2. ⊕ receive v. 수령하다, 받다   recipient n. 수취인, 수령인

29 effort [éfərt]
노력

Golden Studios has made a concerted **effort** to produce films that appeal to young people.
Golden 영화사는 젊은 사람들의 관심을 끄는 영화를 제작하기 위해 협동하여 노력했다.

출제포인트   1. in an effort to + 동사원형: ~하기 위한 노력의 일환으로
      2. endeavor와 의미가 같다.
      3. ⊕ effortless adj. 힘이 들지 않는   effortlessly adv. 노력하지 않고, 쉽게

30 advantage [ædvǽntidʒ]
이점, 유리한 점

Having a broad knowledge of the computer industry is an **advantage** in this firm.
컴퓨터 산업에 대한 폭넓은 지식을 갖춘 것은 이 회사에서 이점이 된다.

출제포인트   1. 남보다 유리한 입장에 있음으로써 생기는 이점을 의미한다.
      2. 'profit: 금전상의 이익'과 'benefit: 복지와 관련된 이익'을 구별하여 알아두자.

31 profit [práfit]
수익, (금전상의) 이익, 이윤

Alasia Air's announcement of a 14 percent increase in **profits** pleased its shareholders.
수익의 14퍼센트 증가에 대한 Alasia 항공사의 발표는 주주들을 기쁘게 했다.

출제포인트   1. net profit: 순이익, 순익
       generate large profits: 많은 이익을 내다
      2. ⊕ profitable adj. 이익이 많은   profitability n. 수익성

32 issue [íʃu:]
(정기 간행물의) 호, 발행물, 문제

The interview with Velorek's CEO appeared in the last month's **issue** of *Finance & Business*.
Velorek사 최고 경영자와의 인터뷰는 *Finance & Business*지 전월호에 났다.

출제포인트   1. the next issue of a magazine: 잡지의 다음 발행호
      2. common issue: 공통적인 문제
      3. '발행하다, 발표하다'라는 의미의 동사로도 쓰인다.

33 expertise [èkspərtí:z]
전문 지식, 전문 기술

The firm's consulting team provides **expertise** in Internet broadcasting technology.
그 회사의 컨설팅 팀은 인터넷 방송 기술에 대한 전문 지식을 제공한다.

출제포인트   expertise in: ~에 대한 전문 지식

34 negotiation [nigòuʃiéiʃən]
협상, 교섭

The next stage of **negotiations** is scheduled to begin on July 7 in New York City.
협상의 다음 단계는 7월 7일에 뉴욕시에서 시작하기로 예정되어 있다.

출제포인트   1. contract negotiation: 계약 협상
      2. ⊕ negotiable adj. 협상할 여지가 있는

35 subscriber [səbskráibər]
구독자

With many **subscribers** in Asia, *Pacific Rim Affairs* is a successful politics publication.
아시아에 많은 구독자들을 두고 있는 *Pacific Rim Affairs*지는 잘 나가는 정치 간행물이다.

출제포인트   1. 신문이나 잡지를 구독하는 사람, 또는 서비스에 가입하여 서비스를 이용하는 사람을 의미한다.
      2. ⊕ subscription n. 구독(료)

36 asset [ǽset]
자산, 이점, 재산

The talented team of researchers is an **asset** to the company.
유능한 연구팀은 그 회사의 자산이다.

출제포인트   be valuable asset to: ~에 귀중한 자산이다

HACKERS PRACTICE 토익 고득점을 위한 필수 연습

A와 B중 맞는 것을 고르세요.

01 the **disposal** of waste
폐기물 ⓐ 처리 ⓑ 용기

02 a **scarcity** of jobs in rural areas
시골 지역의 일자리 ⓐ 부족 ⓑ 공급

03 a manufacturing **facility**
제조 ⓐ 공정 ⓑ 시설

04 required professional **qualifications**
필수 전문 ⓐ 이론 ⓑ 자격

05 a list of **requirements** for the loan application
대출 신청을 위한 ⓐ 증명서 ⓑ 요건 목록

06 All **contestants** must register by March 11.
모든 ⓐ 참가자들은 ⓑ 심사위원들은 3월 11일까지 등록해야 한다.

07 **Coordination** between the departments
부서 간 ⓐ 합동 ⓑ 시행

08 **feedback** from a survey
설문 조사에서 나온 ⓐ 의견 ⓑ 결정

09 The club is a **forum** for sports fans.
그 클럽은 스포츠 팬들에게 ⓐ 토론의 장 ⓑ 관심의 대상 이다.

10 evaluate the staff's **performance**
직원들의 ⓐ 성과를 ⓑ 보고서를 평가하다

11 sent a product **inquiry** in the mail
우편으로 제품 ⓐ 설명서를 ⓑ 문의를 보냈다

12 Mr. Bookman will go over the **proposals**.
Mr. Bookman은 ⓐ 회계 자료들을 ⓑ 제안서들을 검토할 것이다.

13 use a different **approach** to solve the problem
문제를 해결하기 위해 다른 ⓐ 접근법을 ⓑ 장비를 사용하다

14 voice one's **concern** about the cost of the equipment
그 장비의 비용에 대한 ⓐ 우려를 ⓑ 만족을 표하다

15 an equipment **breakdown**
장비 ⓐ 결함 ⓑ 고장

16 the car's biggest **shortcoming**
그 차량의 가장 큰 ⓐ 장점 ⓑ 결점

17 have a positive **outlook** on the company's future
회사의 미래에 대한 긍정적인 ⓐ 관점을 ⓑ 소식을 가지고 있다

18 Applicants should provide **references**.
지원자들은 ⓐ 감사 서한을 ⓑ 추천서를 제공해야 한다.

19 The CD player is under **warranty**.
그 CD 플레이어는 ⓐ 보증 기간 ⓑ 수리 중에 있다.

20 receive the board's **nomination**
위원회의 ⓐ 초대를 ⓑ 추천을 받다

21 Participants had a range of **perspectives**.
참가자들은 다양한 ⓐ 시각을 ⓑ 직업을 가졌다.

22 a **replica** of the original
원본의 ⓐ 복제품 ⓑ 출처

23 The book's **premise** is explained in the introduction.
그 책의 ⓐ 저자는 ⓑ 전제는 서문에 설명되어 있다.

24 the early **stages** of the campaign
캠페인의 초기 ⓐ 발표들 ⓑ 단계들

25 the conference room's seating **capacity**　회의실의 좌석　ⓐ 범위　ⓑ 수용력

26 The second floor will be closed for **renovation**.　2층은　ⓐ 수리를　ⓑ 대청소를　위해 폐쇄될 것이다.

27 gain good **publicity** through charity work　자선활동을 통해 좋은　ⓐ 평판을　ⓑ 수익을　얻다

28 make a **complaint** by phone　전화로　ⓐ 불만을　ⓑ 호의를　제기하다

29 opportunities for **advancement**　ⓐ 등록의　ⓑ 승진의　기회

30 Education can be viewed as the **foundation** of a career.　교육은 직업의　ⓐ 훈련으로　ⓑ 토대로　간주될 수 있다.

31 **agreement** on the issue　사안에 대한　ⓐ 만족　ⓑ 합의

32 Many **studies** indicate that S + V.　많은　ⓐ 연구들은　ⓑ 연구자들은　~라는 것을 보여 준다.

33 the **demand** for technical support staff　기술 지원직에 대한　ⓐ 수요　ⓑ 원조

34 report on the **progress** of the project　프로젝트의　ⓐ 변동　ⓑ 진척　에 대한 보고서

35 **requests** for deadline extensions　마감 일자 연장에 대한　ⓐ 요청들　ⓑ 문의들

36 rapid **transmission** of data　데이터의 빠른　ⓐ 수신　ⓑ 전송

37 The committee reviews each **entry** closely.　위원회는 각각의　ⓐ 출품작을　ⓑ 평가 기준을　면밀히 검토한다.

38 recruit **volunteers** for the campaign　캠페인을 위한　ⓐ 지원자들을　ⓑ 전문가들을　모집하다

39 Without funding, the project is in **jeopardy**.　자금 조달 없이, 그 프로젝트는　ⓐ 실패에　ⓑ 위험에　빠져 있다.

40 **specifications** including size and weight　크기와 무게를 포함한　ⓐ 견적　ⓑ 사양

41 Basic **amenities** are included in the cost.　기본　ⓐ 식사는　ⓑ 편의시설은　비용에 포함되어 있다.

42 A **variety** of factors caused the breakdown.　ⓐ 다양한　ⓑ 의외의　요인들이 고장을 야기했다.

43 traffic regulation **violations**　교통 법규　ⓐ 위반　ⓑ 준수

44 the **position** of marketing director　마케팅 부장의　ⓐ 권한　ⓑ 직위

45 develop an **expansion** plan　ⓐ 확장　ⓑ 지출　계획을 발전시키다

46 The **selection** of students surveyed was limited.　조사받는 학생들의　ⓐ 명단은　ⓑ 선발은　제한적이었다.

47 for informational **purposes** only　오직 정보 제공의　ⓐ 목적　ⓑ 수단　으로만

48 until further **notice**　추후　ⓐ 통지가　ⓑ 요청이　있을 때까지

맞는 명사에 √표를 하세요.

49 interviewed ☐ **candidates** for the job   그 직위의 **후보자들**을 인터뷰했다
                ☐ **audiences**

50 written ☐ **approval**   서면 **허가**
          ☐ **foresight**

51 after the ☐ **completion** of the landscaping   조경 **완료** 후
             ☐ **contribution**

52 sent a ☐ **reminder** through e-mail   이메일을 통해 상기시켜 주는 **메모**를 보냈다
         ☐ **parcel**

53 got a receipt for the ☐ **transaction**   **거래**의 영수증을 받았다
                   ☐ **transportation**

54 The product's ☐ **durability** must be tested.   그 제품의 **내구성**은 확인되어야 한다.
             ☐ **necessity**

55 carry out a productivity ☐ **construction**   생산성 **평가**를 수행하다
                     ☐ **evaluation**

56 ☐ **Exceptions** are rarely permitted.   **예외**는 좀처럼 허용되지 않는다.
  ☐ **Instances**

57 take notes during the ☐ **lecture**   **강의** 중에 필기하다
                  ☐ **instructor**

58 receive positive ☐ **testimonials** from customers   고객들로부터 긍정적인 **추천의 글**을 받다
                ☐ **inquiries**

59 Take ☐ **responsibility** for your actions.   당신의 행동에 대해 **책임**을 지셔야 합니다.
       ☐ **requisite**

60 The sales ☐ **proportion** helped attract new customers.   그 판매 **홍보 활동**은 신규 고객들을 끌어모으는 데 도움이 되었다.
           ☐ **promotion**

61 Plenty of room for ☐ **improvement** exists.   **개선**의 충분한 여지가 있다.
                 ☐ **establishment**

62 We apologize for the ☐ **inclination**.   **불편**에 대해 사과드립니다.
                   ☐ **inconvenience**.

63 recent international ☐ **numerals**   최근의 국제 **개발**
                 ☐ **developments**

64 a large ☐ **collection** on display   전시되어 있는 많은 **소장품**
           ☐ **connection**

65 Immigration has increased the city's cultural ☐ **diversity**.   이민은 도시의 문화적 **다양성**을 증가시켰다.
                                    ☐ **capacity**.

66 count the number of ☐ **reports**   **발생** 횟수를 세다
                 ☐ **occurrences**

67 demonstrate one's ☐ **applause**   **감사**를 표하다
               ☐ **appreciation**

68 online customer ☐ **reviews** of a new hotel   새로운 호텔에 대한 온라인 고객 **평가**
                 ☐ **requests**

정답 p.87

⏱ 제한 시간 16분

Part 5

01 Mr. Archer's ------- in pursuing a career in news reporting was finally rewarded when he was offered a news reporter position at the local TV station.

(A) adequacy
(B) persistence
(C) regularity
(D) acceptance

02 Ms. Lee has been asked to work an extra ------- this week because the company is short of staff.

(A) division
(B) system
(C) operation
(D) shift

03 The union representative attempts to resolve ------- between employees and management at the manufacturing plant.

(A) estimates
(B) conflicts
(C) announcements
(D) confirmations

04 The new executive officer possesses ------- in the areas of policy making, strategy formulation, and business acquisition.

(A) inspection
(B) purpose
(C) commission
(D) expertise

05 The environmental organization Green Planet is seeking ------- to help pick up trash in city parks this weekend.

(A) applications
(B) investors
(C) volunteers
(D) champions

06 Economists expect that rising labor costs will lead to a ------- in profits for many companies in the service sector.

(A) deliberation
(B) specification
(C) reduction
(D) precaution

07 Newspapers are changing their ------- strategies now that an increasing number of subscribers prefer to access online content.

(A) identification
(B) distribution
(C) procedure
(D) transfer

08 Making a few simple ------- to your computer monitor's settings can help protect your vision.

(A) disruptions
(B) reminders
(C) statements
(D) adjustments

09 October's ------- of *Starburst Journal* will contain a report on Carlton Electronics' manufacturing plant in Indonesia.

(A) cost
(B) issue
(C) guarantee
(D) state

10 The photography of Carlos Modano can be downloaded from his Web site by anyone who receives his -------.

(A) permission
(B) significance
(C) maintenance
(D) experience

11 The Fenwood Hotel's ------- to both the beach and a large shopping center makes it an attractive choice for many travelers.

(A) region
(B) direction
(C) benefit
(D) proximity

12 The collection of technology patents acquired through the purchase of SPS Incorporated is the greatest ------- of Telcore Industries.

(A) loss
(B) sign
(C) asset
(D) notice

13 The mayor is in support of an ------- that would increase penalties for residents who do not recycle.

(A) outreach
(B) initiative
(C) union
(D) election

14 Wagner's Online Store will process and ship a customer's order in one or two days upon ------- of payment.

(A) receipt
(B) admittance
(C) allowance
(D) occupation

15 Recent ------- in the field of genetics have provided doctors with the ability to test for a variety of hereditary health conditions.

(A) figures
(B) developments
(C) repetitions
(D) decisions

16 Buying new equipment will help the factory achieve its ------- of increasing productivity by 20 percent.

(A) contraction
(B) approval
(C) compensation
(D) objective

17 The University of Vancouver will proceed with the construction of a new dormitory to accommodate more students, despite the ------- it faces in securing funding.

(A) prelude
(B) orientation
(C) challenge
(D) contest

18 The ------- of visitors to the city during the soccer tournament made it impossible to book a hotel room.

(A) incorporation
(B) assumption
(C) allowance
(D) influx

19 The restaurant is undergoing ------- in hopes of attracting more business-class clients.

(A) formation
(B) magnification
(C) renovation
(D) premonition

20 The main ------- of Ms. Cooper's team will be to check the completed Web site for errors.

(A) suitability
(B) productivity
(C) priority
(D) satisfaction

Part 6
Questions 21-24 refer to the following memo.

From: Warran Reynolds, Public Relations Department
To: All staff

We would like to inform all employees at Burrows Design Limited that a new system will be implemented starting next month for quality -------. Strict quality regulation procedures will be introduced to guarantee that our reputation for excellence is maintained.

All employees, from design to production, will be asked to check whether our standards are being met and to maintain records of these inspections. The records will then be submitted to the departmental supervisors for -------. Meetings will be arranged to discuss the findings shortly and the managing staff will come up with feedback and recommendations based on the reports. -------. They are then expected to make corresponding changes to their work.

A special full-day introductory seminar has been scheduled for Saturday, February 19 in Conference Room 101, during which the new system will be explained in detail. It is ------- that every employee participate. Overtime will be paid accordingly.

21 (A) coverage
   (B) assurance
   (C) revenue
   (D) affiliation

22 (A) conversion
   (B) revision
   (C) evaluation
   (D) accumulation

23 (A) The findings show the need to make adjustments.
   (B) The suggestions from executives are to be sent to all employees immediately.
   (C) None of the staff will be able to attend the conference.
   (D) The quality assessment system has proven effective for years.

24 (A) decisive
   (B) applicable
   (C) resourceful
   (D) imperative

정답·해설·해석 p.87 / [별책] 토익 RC 필수 어휘 p.25

해커스 스타강사의 ▶
무료 해설강의 바로 보기
(13번 문제)

VOCABULARY Part 5,6　Ch 02 명사　Hackers TOEIC Reading

CHAPTER 03 형용사

valid의 뜻을 알면 취업의 길이 열린다.

원하는 회사에 지원하려고 하니 토익 성적표를 내라고 하는데, 이때 회사에서 요구하는 것이 'valid score(유효한 성적)'
이다. 뭔가 추상적으로 보이던 'valid'란 말에 대한 감이 오는 순간은 이렇게 valid score란 표현을 접할 때가 아닌가. 토익
형용사는 같이 쓰는 명사를 봐둬야 한다.

출제 유형 및 전략

1. 문맥에 맞는 형용사를 고르는 문제로 출제된다.

2. 접속사 및 전치사, 그리고 문장의 키워드를 주의해서 보면 문맥을 파악하기 쉽다. 특히, 명사를 수식하는 형용사로 쓰인 경우 '형용
   사 + 명사' 부분의 문맥에 어울리는 단어를, 보어 역할의 형용사로 쓰인 경우는 주어와 문맥상 어울리는 단어를 정답으로 고른다.

3. Part 6에서는 빈칸이 있는 문장의 앞, 뒤 문장에서 빈칸에 들어갈 형용사가 수식하거나 설명하는 대상에 대한 언급을 참고하여 정
   답을 골라야 하는 경우도 있다.

예제

Part 5

The cardiology team at the Asian Vascular Institute has made an ------- contribution to the treatment of heart
disease.

(A) expressive   (B) imperfect   (C) assumed   (D) impressive

해설   '심장학팀이 심장병 치료에 _____ 공헌을 해왔다'라는 문맥에 맞으려면 빈칸에는 (D) impressive(굉장한)가 적합하다. (A) expressive는 '나타
내는, 표현력이 있는', (B) imperfect는 '불완전한, 결함이 있는', (C) assumed는 '가장한, 가정한'이라는 의미이다.

해석   아시아 혈관 연구소의 심장학팀은 심장병 치료에 굉장한 공헌을 해 왔다.

어휘   **cardiology** n. 심장(병)학 / **vascular** adj. 혈관의 / **contribution** n. 공헌, 기여, 기부

정답   (D)

Part 6

Experts had predicted that prices of gas and oil would drop this fiscal quarter. However, there has been an -------
rise over the past few months, which has forced numerous companies around the globe to increase the cost of
their products.

(A) unexpected   (B) activated   (C) unrelated   (D) obligated

해설   '가격이 떨어질 것으로 예측했으나 _____ 가격 상승이 있었다'라는 문맥에서 빈칸에 가장 적절한 어휘는 (A) unexpected(예기치 못한)이다. (B)
activated는 '활성화된', (C) unrelated는 '관련 없는', (D) obligated는 '의무가 있는'을 의미한다.

해석   전문가들은 이번 회계 분기에 가스와 석유 가격이 떨어질 것으로 예측했다. 그러나, 지난 몇 달 간 예기치 못한 가격 상승이 있었고, 이는 전 세계
적으로 많은 회사들이 제품 가격을 인상하게 만들었다.

어휘   **predict** v. 예측하다 / **drop** v. 떨어지다, 하락하다 / **fiscal** adj. 회계의, 재정의 / **quarter** n. 분기, 4분의 1 / **force** v. (억지로) ~하게 만들다 /
numerous adj. 많은 / **around the globe** 전 세계적으로

정답   (A)

01 ongoing [ɑ́:ngouiŋ]　　　진행 중인, 계속하고 있는

At Friday's meeting, Mr. Tanner will talk about how the governor's new law could affect **ongoing** projects.
금요일 회의에서, Mr. Tanner는 그 총재의 새로운 법안이 진행 중인 프로젝트들에 어떻게 영향을 줄 수 있을지에 대해 이야기할 것이다.

02 acting [ǽktiŋ]　　　직무 대행의, 임시의

Ms. Coleman has asked Mr. Tyler to serve as **acting** faculty chair during her six-week absence.
Ms. Coleman은 Mr. Tyler에게 그녀의 6주간의 부재 동안에 직무 대행 학부장으로서 일해줄 것을 요청했다.

> 출제포인트　1. temporary, interim과 의미가 같다.
> 　　　　　2. '연기, 연출(법)'이라는 의미의 명사로도 쓰인다.

03 budget [bʌ́dʒit]　　　저가의, 예산이 한정된

The hotel is popular with travelers for its **budget** lodging.
그 호텔은 저가의 숙소로 여행객들에게 인기가 있다.

> 출제포인트　'예산을 세우다'라는 의미의 동사, '예산(액)'이라는 의미의 명사로도 쓰인다.

04 faulty [fɔ́:lti]　　　결함이 있는, 불완전한

The leak in the building's basement parking garage was caused by **faulty** pipes.
건물의 지하 주차장에서의 누수는 결함이 있는 배관으로 인해 야기되었다.

> 출제포인트　1. defective와 의미가 같다.
> 　　　　　2. 몡 fault n. 결함, 결점　faultless adj. 결점이 없는, 흠잡을 데 없는
> 　　　　　　 faultlessly adv. 흠 없이, 완전무결하게

05 mandatory [mǽndətɔ̀:ri]　　　의무적인

The fire alarm system must undergo **mandatory** testing each year.
화재 경보 장치는 매년 의무적인 검사를 받아야 한다.

06 immense [iméns]　　　거대한, 엄청난

Jamilog Tech's headquarters are located in an **immense** building that covers an entire city block.
Jamilog Tech사의 본사는 도시의 한 구획 전체를 차지하는 거대한 건물에 위치해 있다.

> 출제포인트　1. huge(거대한), enormous(막대한, 거대한), massive(거대한)도 함께 알아 두자.
> 　　　　　2. 몡 immensely adv. 엄청나게, 대단히

07 attentive [əténtiv]　　　주의를 기울이는

Copperfield Department Store needs to be more **attentive** to the needs of its customers.
Copperfield 백화점은 고객들의 요구에 더 주의를 기울여야 한다.

> 출제포인트　1. be attentive to: ~에 주의를 기울이다
> 　　　　　2. 몡 attention n. 주의, 주목　attentively adv. 주의하여

08 impending [impéndiŋ]　　　곧 닥칠, 임박한

The **impending** hurricane may cause nearly all the local stores to shut down for the weekend.
곧 닥칠 허리케인이 거의 모든 지역 상점들을 주말 동안 문을 닫게 할지도 모른다.

> 출제포인트　원치 않거나 나쁜 일이 곧 일어날 것이라는 의미로 많이 쓰인다.

09 compelling [kəmpéliŋ]　　　흥미진진한, 설득력 있는

Ms. Lee gave a **compelling** presentation on the future of the telecommunications industry.
Ms. Lee는 통신 산업의 미래에 관해 흥미진진한 발표를 했다.

> 출제포인트　몡 compel v. 강요하다, 강제로 ~하게 시키다

10 primary [práimeri]　　　주된, 주요한

The **primary** goal of the alumni gala will be to raise money for student scholarships.
졸업생 축제의 주된 목표는 학생 장학금을 위한 돈을 모으는 것이 될 것이다.

> 출제포인트　몡 primarily adv. 주로, 대부분

11 adequate [ǽdikwət]　　　(필요나 목적에) 충분한, 적절한

A single printer in the office is not **adequate** for the needs of 50 employees.
사무실에 있는 단 한 대의 프린터는 직원 50명의 필요에 충분하지 않다.

> 출제포인트　1. adequate for + 명사: ~에 충분한
> 　　　　　　 adequate to + 동사원형: ~하기에 충분한, 적절한
> 　　　　　2. 몡 adequately adv. 충분히, 적절히

12 thorough [θə́:rou]　　　면밀한, 철저한

A **thorough** evaluation of the housing plan was conducted before it went into effect.
주거 계획이 실시되기 전에 이에 관한 면밀한 평가가 시행되었다.

> 출제포인트　1. a thorough investigation: 철저한 조사
> 　　　　　　 a thorough review: 면밀한 검토
> 　　　　　2. 몡 thoroughly adv. 완전히, 철저히

13 excessive [iksésiv] 과도한, 지나친

The Prisa 330's **excessive** fuel consumption was mentioned in several car magazine reviews.
Prisa 330의 과도한 연료 소모는 몇몇 자동차 잡지의 평론들에서 언급되었다.

출제포인트 📖 exceed v. 초과하다, 넘다 excess n. 초과, 초과량
excessively adv. 과도하게, 매우

14 selective [siléktiv] 까다로운, 선별적인

Due to a limited budget, the buyer was **selective** about the fabrics he ordered.
제한된 예산 때문에, 구매자는 그가 주문하는 직물에 대해 까다로웠다.

출제포인트 1. selective about/in: ~에 대해 까다로운
2. 📖 select v. 선발하다, 선정하다 selection n. 선발, 선택

15 valid [vǽlid] 유효한, 정당한

As it expired on August 3, this piece of identification is no longer **valid**.
이 신분증은 8월 3일에 만료되었기 때문에, 더 이상 유효하지 않다.

출제포인트 1. be valid for 기간: ~동안 유효하다
be valid from 시점: ~부터 유효하다
2. 📖 validity n. 유효함, 타당성

16 elaborate [ilǽbərət] 공들인, 정교한

The publicity department created an **elaborate** poster for the film premiere.
홍보부는 영화 시사회를 위해 공들인 포스터를 제작했다.

출제포인트 '상세하게 설명하다, 정교하게 만들다'라는 의미의 동사로도 쓰인다.

17 appropriate [əpróupriət] 적절한, 알맞은

Before entering the construction zone, all workers have to put on the **appropriate** safety gear.
공사 구역에 출입하기 전, 모든 작업자들은 적절한 안전 장비를 착용해야 한다.

출제포인트 1. appropriate for: ~에 적절한, 어울리는
2. '충당하다, 도용하다'라는 의미의 동사로도 쓰인다.
3. 📖 appropriately adv. 적당하게, 알맞게

18 upcoming [ʌ́pkʌmiŋ] 곧 있을, 다가오는

Preparing for the **upcoming** trade fair is the marketing department's main priority this month.
곧 있을 무역 박람회를 위한 준비는 이번 달 마케팅부의 주된 우선 사항이다.

출제포인트 1. forthcoming과 의미가 같다.
2. upcoming event: 곧 있을 행사
upcoming year: 다가오는 해

19 established [istǽbliʃt] 인정받는, 확립된

Edge Homes is an **established** architecture firm with 52 years of history.
Edge Homes사는 52년의 역사를 가진 인정받는 건축 회사이다.

출제포인트 📖 establish v. 설립하다 establishment n. 설립

20 practical [prǽktikəl] 실용적인, 실제적인, 타당한

Henna's cookbook is full of **practical** ideas, like using leftover items to make omelets.
Henna의 요리책은 남은 재료들을 활용해서 오믈렛을 만드는 것과 같은 실용적인 아이디어들로 가득하다.

출제포인트 1. practical advice: 실제적인 조언
2. 비슷한 형태의 practicing(활동하고 있는)과 구별하여 알아 두자.
3. 📖 practice v. 실행하다, 실천하다 practically adv. 사실상, 거의

21 limited [límitid] 한정된, 제한된

Leavitt Furniture offers a **limited** selection of handmade items.
Leavitt Furniture사는 한정된 종류의 수제품을 제공한다.

출제포인트 a limited time: 한정된 시간
limited resources: 한정된 자원

22 detailed [díːteild] 상세한, 세부에 걸친

The seminar's instructor has given participants a **detailed** schedule of planned activities.
그 세미나의 강사는 참가자들에게 계획된 활동들에 대한 상세한 일정표를 주었다.

출제포인트 detailed descriptions: 상세한 설명

23 promising [prámisiŋ] 유망한, 촉망되는

There are **promising** signs that the corporation's stock value will rise this year.
올해 그 기업의 주가가 오를 것이라는 유망한 조짐이 있다.

출제포인트 1. a promising youth: 전도유망한 청년
2. 📖 promise v. 약속하다

24 tentative [téntətiv] 잠정적인, 임시의

The release date for the new product is still **tentative**.
신제품의 출시일은 아직 잠정적이다.

출제포인트 1. 계획이나 일정을 확정하지 않고 임시로 정해 놓은 경우에 사용한다.
2. provisional과 의미가 같다.
3. 📖 tentatively adv. 임시로

25 defective [diféktiv]   결함이 있는

The client returned several **defective** products and asked for replacements.

그 고객은 결함이 있는 몇몇 상품들을 반품했고 교환품을 요청했다.

출제포인트　1. 상품이나 기계에 결함이 있는 경우에 사용한다.
　　　　　　2. ⑪ defect n. 결점, 결함

26 exceptional [iksépʃənl]   뛰어난, 예외적인

The Alamo Convention Center has **exceptional** facilities with cutting-edge equipment.

Alamo 컨벤션 센터는 최첨단 장비를 포함하여 뛰어난 시설들을 갖추고 있다.

출제포인트　⑪ exception n. 예외　exceptionally adv. 유난히

27 affordable [əfɔ́ːrrdəbl]   가격이 알맞은

Today's personal computers are **affordable** and accessible to most people.

오늘날의 개인용 컴퓨터는 대부분의 사람들에게 가격이 알맞고 구매하기 쉽다.

출제포인트　1. 가격의 높고 낮음과 상관없이 대부분의 사람들이 구매할 수 있는 정도의 가격임을 나타낼 때 사용한다.
　　　　　　2. afford to + 동사원형: ~할 여유가 있다
　　　　　　3. ⑪ affordability n. 적당한 가격으로 구입할 수 있는 것

28 available [əvéiləbl]   이용할 수 있는, 이용 가능한

The new investment opportunities are **available** only to customers of the American First Bank.

새로운 투자 기회들은 오직 American First 은행의 고객들만 이용할 수 있습니다.

출제포인트　1. 시설, 서비스 등의 사물이 이용 가능하다는 의미로 주로 쓰인다.
　　　　　　2. A(사물) is available to B(사람): A가 B에게 이용 가능하다
　　　　　　3. ⑪ availability n. 유효성, 이용 가능성

29 consecutive [kənsékjutiv]   연속적인, 계속되는

ATLP announced that its stock value had risen for the fifth **consecutive** year.

ATLP사는 자사의 주가가 5년 연속 상승했다고 발표했다.

출제포인트　for the + 서수 + consecutive year: ~년간 연속해서

30 latest [léitist]   최신의, 최근의

Marco Textiles had to reprint their **latest** catalogs because of a few minor errors.

Marco 섬유 회사는 몇 개의 소소한 실수 때문에 그들의 최신 카탈로그를 재인쇄해야 했다.

출제포인트　up-to-date와 의미가 같다.

31 substantial [səbstǽnʃəl]   (양·크기가) 상당한

The company has used a **substantial** share of its budget for new projects.

그 회사는 새 프로젝트들을 위해 예산의 상당한 부분을 사용해 왔다.

출제포인트　1. 양이 많거나 정도가 상당함을 나타낼 때 사용한다.
　　　　　　2. ⑪ substantially adv. 상당히

32 confidential [kànfədénʃəl]   기밀의

Please remind all employees to keep **confidential** documents in a secure location.

모든 직원들에게 기밀 문서를 안전한 장소에 보관할 것을 상기시키기 바랍니다.

출제포인트　secret과 의미가 같다.

33 temporary [témpərèri]   임시의

Due to renovations, a **temporary** entrance will be open at the rear of the building.

수리로 인해, 건물 뒤쪽에 있는 임시 입구가 개방될 것입니다.

출제포인트　1. 고용이나 계획 등이 지속적이지 않고 일시적인 경우에 사용한다.
　　　　　　2. a temporary office: 임시 영업소

34 subsequent [sʌ́bsikwənt]   다음의, 그 후의

Business was slow for the first month, but sales may increase in **subsequent** months.

사업이 첫 달 동안 부진했지만, 다음 달에는 매출이 증가할 수도 있다.

출제포인트　1. successive, following과 의미가 같다.
　　　　　　2. subsequent to: ~ 후에

35 eligible [élidʒəbl]   (사람이) 자격이 있는, 적격의

Sponsors of the National Ballet are **eligible** to receive passes to performances every year.

국립 발레단의 후원자들은 매년 공연에 대한 무료 입장권을 받을 자격이 있다.

Employees are **eligible** for compensation.

직원들은 보상을 받을 자격이 있다.

출제포인트　be eligible to + 동사원형
　　　　　　be eligible for + 명사: ~할 자격이 있다

36 additional [ədíʃənl]   추가의, 부가적인

The head accountant is looking for **additional** ways to reduce operating costs.

수석 회계사는 운영비를 줄이기 위한 추가적인 방법들을 찾고 있다.

출제포인트　1. extra, supplemental과 의미가 같다.
　　　　　　2. additional charge: 추가 비용, 할증 요금
　　　　　　3. ⑪ addition n. 추가, 부가

A와 B중 맞는 것을 고르세요.

01 **conclusive** proof that the new medication works
새 약물이 효과가 있다는 ⓐ 결정적인 ⓑ 모호한 증거

02 **effective** way to reduce waste
쓰레기를 줄이기 위한 ⓐ 근본적인 ⓑ 효과적인 방법

03 an **inactive** email account
ⓐ 비활성 상태의 ⓑ 삭제된 이메일 계정

04 an **urgent** matter to attend to
처리해야 할 ⓐ 간절한 ⓑ 시급한 문제

05 Applicants must be **proficient** in French.
지원자들은 프랑스어에 ⓐ 자신 있어야 ⓑ 능숙해야 한다.

06 Be **cautious** when exiting the aircraft.
항공기에서 내릴 때 ⓐ 조심해라 ⓑ 확인해라.

07 placed an **initial** order
ⓐ 최초의 ⓑ 추가적인 주문을 했다

08 The company has a **diverse** workforce.
그 회사는 ⓐ 다양한 ⓑ 숙련된 노동력을 보유하고 있다.

09 check the Web site on a **routine** basis
웹사이트를 ⓐ 철저한 ⓑ 정기적인 기반으로 확인하다

10 take an **active** role in the organization
조직에서 ⓐ 적극적인 ⓑ 필요한 역할을 맡다

11 **accurate** figures
ⓐ 공개된 ⓑ 정확한 수치

12 offer a **vast** range of products
ⓐ 방대한 ⓑ 기발한 종류의 제품들을 제공하다

13 **perpetual** motion
ⓐ 끊임없는 ⓑ 즉각적인 운동

14 Everyone made a **concentrated** effort.
모두가 ⓐ 반복적인 ⓑ 집중적인 노력을 했다.

15 the company's **chief** source of income
그 기업의 ⓐ 주된 ⓑ 최근의 소득원

16 ensure the **efficient** operation of the machinery
기계 장치의 ⓐ 신속한 ⓑ 효율적인 운영을 보장하다

17 The garden suite is **unavailable**.
정원이 딸린 스위트룸은 ⓐ 이용할 수 없다 ⓑ 변경할 수 없다.

18 a **challenging** but rewarding task
ⓐ 어렵지만 ⓑ 바쁘지만 보람 있는 일

19 **delicate** matters involving civil rights　　　　민권이 관련된　ⓐ 심각한　ⓑ 민감한　사안

20 do **preliminary** research before creating a thesis　　논문을 작성하기 전에　ⓐ 설문　ⓑ 예비　조사를 하다

21 a **comprehensive** instruction manual　　　　ⓐ 적절한　ⓑ 종합적인　사용 설명서

22 **potential** sales of a new model　　　　새로운 모델의　ⓐ 증가한　ⓑ 잠재적인　매출액

23 achieve the **desired** results　　　　ⓐ 원하는　ⓑ 엄청난　결과를 이루다

24 The novel received **harsh** reviews.　　　　그 소설은　ⓐ 수많은　ⓑ 혹독한　비평을 받았다.

25 It is **imperative** that you go to the meeting.　　당신이 회의에 가는 것이　ⓐ 불가능합니다　ⓑ 꼭 필요합니다.

26 The entrepreneur thanked his **principal** investors.　그 사업가는 그의　ⓐ 장기적인　ⓑ 주요한　투자자들에게 감사를 표했다.

27 has a **distinguished** career　　　　ⓐ 다양한　ⓑ 뛰어난　경력을 가지고 있다

28 might be especially **beneficial**　　　　특히　ⓐ 안전할　ⓑ 유익할　것이다

29 make the facilities **accessible** to visitors　　방문자에게 시설을　ⓐ 이용할 수 있게　ⓑ 신청하게　하다

30 **Pending** orders will be processed tomorrow.　　ⓐ 미결인　ⓑ 긴급한　주문들은 내일 처리될 것이다.

31 The product contains no **hazardous** chemicals.　그 제품은　ⓐ 특수한　ⓑ 유해한　화학물질을 포함하지 않는다.

32 Buying a home is not **advisable** right now.　　지금 당장 집을 사는 것은　ⓐ 쉽지　ⓑ 바람직하지　않다.

33 It is **customary** to take off your shoes.　　신발을 벗는 것이　ⓐ 관례적이다　ⓑ 올바르다.

34 The **updated** list contains more names.　　ⓐ 최신의　ⓑ 이전의　목록은 더 많은 이름을 포함한다.

35 **artificial** ingredients　　　　ⓐ 인공적인　ⓑ 필수적인　재료들

36 **ambitious** goal of doubling annual sales　　연간 매출액 배가의　ⓐ 구체적인　ⓑ 야심찬　목표

맞는 형용사에 √표를 하세요.

37 eat at a ☐ **popular** restaurant
               ☐ **convinced**

인기 있는 식당에서 먹다

38 The museum was ☐ **worthful** the visit.
                      ☐ **worth**

그 박물관은 방문할 가치가 있었다.

39 at ☐ **shortened** prices
        ☐ **reasonable**

적당한 가격에

40 have a ☐ **damp** personality
            ☐ **confident**

자신감 있는 성격을 가지다

41 ☐ **equivalent** amount of work
    ☐ **redundant**

동등한 양의 업무

42 a lecture being held this ☐ **consequent** Monday
                               ☐ **coming**

다음 월요일에 열리는 강의

43 The hike was ☐ **outstanding**.
                  ☐ **exhausting**.

하이킹은 지치게 했다.

44 revise the publication's ☐ **existing** policies
                              ☐ **appearing**

출판물의 현재 방침을 개정하다

45 He was ☐ **apologetic** because he arrived late.
            ☐ **ingenious**

그는 늦게 도착했기 때문에 미안해 했다.

46 have a ☐ **contrary** meal
            ☐ **complimentary**

무료로 제공되는 식사를 하다

47 An ☐ **official** contract was prepared for the client.
        ☐ **overall**

공식적인 계약서가 고객을 위해 준비되었다.

48 Hard work is ☐ **crucial** to success.
                  ☐ **prosperous**

많은 노력은 성공하는 데에 중요하다.

49 This restaurant serves ☐ **subtle** Thai food.
                            ☐ **authentic**

이 식당은 정통 태국 음식을 제공한다.

정답 p.89

🕐 제한 시간 16분

Part 5

01 Without ------- funding, the redevelopment of the downtown area will be delayed for another year.

(A) multiple
(B) frustrating
(C) receptive
(D) adequate

02 ------- vehicle emissions are largely responsible for the poor air quality.

(A) Impressed
(B) Excessive
(C) Official
(D) Experienced

03 In her documentary, Tracy Hasan provides a ------- analysis of Viking culture, covering its origins and traditions.

(A) comfortable
(B) punctual
(C) thorough
(D) remaining

04 The number of goods produced by the machine in a single day is ------- to the work of 100 people.

(A) seasonal
(B) contrary
(C) equivalent
(D) established

05 The ------- plot of David Wilkin's latest film has fascinated moviegoers and earned praise from professional critics.

(A) visible
(B) durable
(C) predictable
(D) compelling

06 The earliest cars produced by the company were unpopular, but ------- ones attracted a great deal of consumer interest.

(A) previous
(B) subordinate
(C) overdue
(D) subsequent

07 Although non-members may order items from the Web site, rebates are ------- only to those who are club members.

(A) respectable
(B) noticeable
(C) sociable
(D) available

08 Mr. Bradshaw announced that the safety workshop on Saturday was ------- for all employees, with no exceptions.

(A) mandatory
(B) marginal
(C) distinct
(D) plausible

09 Although Ms. Gomez was eager to sell her home, she considered the ------- offer from the buyer to be insufficient.

(A) correct
(B) latest
(C) instant
(D) longest

10 The Tropical Island Resort includes ------- pools that feature waterslides for kids.

(A) immense
(B) mobile
(C) imaginative
(D) dense

11 An elevator was installed in the building to make all floors ------- to those in wheelchairs.

(A) extendable
(B) accomplished
(C) comprehensive
(D) accessible

12 Chang and Nobel Legal Firm provides ------- medical coverage to its part-time employees.

(A) intended
(B) restrained
(C) limited
(D) confined

13 Plans for the consultant's visit to the company are still -------, but a representative will call Mr. Lim once the arrangements are made.

(A) vigilant
(B) tentative
(C) contemporary
(D) infinite

14 For those who want to work as business analysts, experience in market research is a highly ------- attribute.

(A) beneficial
(B) repetitive
(C) superficial
(D) expensive

15 In order to visit the country, tourists must have a passport that is ------- for at least six months.

(A) ordinary
(B) local
(C) valid
(D) returning

16 Patients of the Clover Clinic can rest assured that ------- medical data will never be given to a third party.

(A) confidential
(B) accidental
(C) deliberate
(D) precise

17 Although stock options were previously offered only to management, regular office workers are now ------- to purchase shares.

(A) appropriate
(B) eligible
(C) dependable
(D) proper

18 Customers of the online bookstore are required to provide an ------- e-mail address in case one account is compromised.

(A) improvisational
(B) occasional
(C) intentional
(D) additional

19 Delivery of the items is still ------- as payment has not yet been received.

(A) pending
(B) initial
(C) dependent
(D) representative

20 Brixton Accounting Services employs a number of accounting specialists who are ------- to changes in the tax law.

(A) firm
(B) attentive
(C) unresponsive
(D) anxious

Part 6
Questions 21-24 refer to the following letter.

Carmen Anders
657 Wentworth Heights
Seattle, WA 99362

Dear Ms. Anders,

Thank you so much for your work setting up a Web site for our company. Sales have increased by an ------- rate of 28 percent in the past quarter, and most of those sales were made through the site.
21

The declining economy ------- impacted sales of our beauty products in the first few months of the
22
year, but the Web site has reversed that trend and benefited the company immensely.

We appreciate your hard work and the ------- look and design of the site. In fact, our customers
23
have given us positive feedback about the site's unique features and ingenious layout.

We are more than satisfied with the quality and results of your work and would like to inform you of our next project. We have been planning to create our recruitment page for some time now. -------.
24
Please contact me if you are interested.

We look forward to hearing from you, and many thanks again for a job well done.

Sincerely,
Mathew Lucas
CEO, Maxton Cosmetics Incorporated

---

21 (A) unprecedented
　　(B) unacceptable
　　(C) underestimated
　　(D) uncontrolled

22 (A) resentfully
　　(B) adversely
　　(C) skeptically
　　(D) contrarily

23 (A) detailed
　　(B) informative
　　(C) innovative
　　(D) diverse

24 (A) We hope that you will be able to work on this project as well.
　　(B) Online sales have suffered significantly due to the site's technical problems.
　　(C) The economic upswing has disproportionately affected cosmetics stores.
　　(D) Users think that your modifications make the site more difficult to navigate.

해커스 스타강사의 ▶
무료 해설강의 바로 보기
(13번 문제)

정답·해설·해석 p.90 / [별책] 토익 RC 필수 어휘 p.26

CHAPTER 04 부사

정답을 고른 후 다시 볼 땐 carefully!

토익에는 친숙한 부사들도 꽤 나오지만, 답을 고르기는 수월치가 않다. 'read the instructions ___: 사용 설명서를 꼼꼼히 읽다'의 빈칸에 어울리는 부사로 carefully를 골랐다가 다시 보니 exactly도 어울릴 것 같아 한참 고민하는 것이 토익에선 빈번한 일. 토익 부사는 예문을 보며 토익이 좋아하는 용례를 알아 둬야 한다. 부사가 수식하는 형용사, 동사 어구를 같이 봐두자.

토익 출제 유형 및 전략

1. 문맥에 맞는 부사를 고르는 문제로 출제된다.

2. 접속사 및 전치사, 그리고 문장의 키워드를 주의해서 보면 문맥을 파악하기 쉬우며, '부사 + 부사가 수식하는 어구' 부분만 보고도 답을 고를 수 있는 경우도 있다.

3. Part 6에서는 빈칸이 있는 문장의 앞, 뒤 문장이나 지문 전체의 문맥을 파악하여 정답을 골라야 하는 경우도 있다.

예제

Part 5

All individuals who use their credit cards frequently should ------- check their transaction history to verify that no errors have been made.

(A) periodically   (B) rarely   (C) incidentally   (D) indefinitely

해설   문맥상 '신용카드를 자주 사용하는 사람들은 거래 내역을 _____ 점검해야 한다'의 빈칸에는 (A) periodically(주기적으로)가 적합하다. (B) rarely는 '드물게', (C) incidentally는 '우연히', (D) indefinitely는 '막연히, 무기한으로'라는 의미이다.

해석   신용카드를 자주 사용하는 모든 사람들은 어떤 오류도 일어나지 않았는지 확인하기 위해 그들의 거래 내역을 주기적으로 점검해야 한다.

어휘   frequently adv. 자주 / check v. 점검하다, 확인하다 / transaction history 거래 내역 / verify v. 확인하다

정답   (A)

Part 6

In the past year, Threestar Automotive's automobile exports have increased by 12.6 percent, bringing in gross profits of around $500 million. This relatively new company has grown ------- in the five years since its inauguration. Considering the company's planned diversification into the pharmaceutical sector, the future looks bright indeed.

(A) eagerly   (B) immediately   (C) recently   (D) quickly

해설   '비교적 신생 기업인 이 회사는 5년 동안 _____ 성장해 왔다'라는 문맥에서 빈칸에 적합한 부사는 (D) quickly(빠르게)이다. (A) eagerly는 '열망하여', (B) immediately는 '즉시', (C) recently는 '최근에'를 의미한다.

해석   작년에, Threestar 자동차 회사의 자동차 수출이 12.6퍼센트 증가해 약 5억 달러의 총수익을 가져왔다. 비교적 신생 기업인 이 회사는 개업 이래 5년 동안 빠르게 성장해 왔다. 제약 분야로의 사업 다각화 계획을 고려해 보았을 때, 이 회사의 미래는 실로 밝아 보인다.

어휘   bring in (수입·이익을) 가져오다 / gross profit 총수익 / inauguration n. 개업, 취임 / diversification n. 사업 다각화 / indeed adv. 실로, 정말

정답   (D)

01 punctually [pʌ́ŋktʃuəli]
시간을 엄수하여, 정각에

Applicants are reminded to bring all of their documents and arrive **punctually** for their job interviews.

지원자들은 모든 서류를 지참하고 시간을 엄수하여 면접에 도착할 것을 주의 받았다.

출제포인트
1. on time과 의미가 같다.
2. ㈜ punctuality n. 시간 엄수, 정확함
   punctual adj. 시간을 엄수하는, 꼼꼼한

02 independently [ìndipéndəntli]
따로, 독립하여

Each component of the car's interior is produced **independently** by a different factory.

그 차 내부의 각 부품은 여러 공장에 의해 따로 생산된다.

출제포인트
1. independently of: ~과는 별개로, ~과 관계없이
2. ㈜ independence n. 독립, 자립
   independent adj. 별개의, 독립의

03 approximately [əprɑ́:ksəmətli]
대략, 거의

The staff estimates it will take **approximately** two weeks to run out of current stock.

그 직원은 현재의 재고를 소진시키는 데에 대략 2주가 걸릴 것으로 추산한다.

출제포인트
1. nearly와 의미가 같다
2. ㈜ approximate v. 어림잡다, ~와 비슷하다; adj. 대략의, 거의 정확한

04 anonymously [ənánəməsli]
익명으로

Most of the Web sites allow people to comment on articles **anonymously**.

대부분의 웹사이트들은 사람들이 기사에 대해 익명으로 의견을 남기는 것을 허용한다.

출제포인트 ㈜ anonymous adj. 익명의 anonymity n. 익명(성)

05 rapidly [rǽpidli]
급속히, 빠르게, 신속하게

The number of chimpanzees is declining **rapidly** due to habitat loss and illegal hunting.

서식지 소실과 불법 포획으로 인해 침팬지의 수가 급속히 감소하고 있다.

출제포인트
1. swiftly, quickly와 의미가 같다.
2. ㈜ rapid adj. 빠른, 신속한

06 previously [prí:viəsli]
이전에

The competent photographer Jane Harding **previously** worked with many models.

유능한 사진작가 Jane Harding은 이전에 많은 모델들과 작업했다.

출제포인트 ㈜ previous adj. 이전의

07 generally [dʒénərəli]
일반적으로, 보통, 널리

International shipping **generally** takes around one to two weeks depending on the destination.

국제 배송은 도착지에 따라서 일반적으로 1주에서 2주 정도 소요된다.

출제포인트 ㈜ general adj. 일반적인, 보통의

08 precisely [prisáisli]
정확하게, 바로

The instructor stressed the importance of proper vocabulary use for speaking **precisely**.

강사는 정확하게 말하기 위한 올바른 어휘 사용의 중요성을 강조했다.

출제포인트
1. accurately와 의미가 같다.
2. correctly(올바르게, 정확하게)도 함께 알아 두자.
3. ㈜ preciseness n. 정확성, 정밀성 precise adj. 정확한, 정밀한

09 incrementally [ínkrəmentəli]
점진적으로, 꾸준하게

Though the number of clients has risen **incrementally**, profits have increased dramatically.

고객의 수는 점진적으로 늘었지만, 이윤은 급격하게 증가했다.

출제포인트 조금씩이지만 꾸준히 변화하는 것을 나타낼 때 사용한다.

10 closely [klóusli]
면밀히, 밀접하게, 긴밀히

Jeg Phone's share price was **closely** watched by investors after the introduction of a new telecommunications law.

새로운 통신법의 도입 이후 Jeg Phone사의 주가는 투자자들에 의해 면밀히 주시되었다.

출제포인트 work closely with ~: ~와 긴밀히 협력하다

11 typically [típikəli]
일반적으로, 전형적으로

New employees are **typically** required to complete a three-week course before they are assigned to a project.

신입 사원들은 일반적으로 프로젝트에 배정되기 전에 3주 간의 과정을 이수하도록 요구된다.

출제포인트 ㈜ typical adj. 일반적인, 전형적인

12 necessarily [nèsəsérəli]
반드시, 필연적으로

Arriving early does not **necessarily** guarantee a seat at the event.

일찍 도착하는 것이 반드시 그 행사에서의 좌석을 보장해주는 것은 아니다.

출제포인트
1. not necessarily: 반드시 ~은 아닌
2. ㈜ necessary adj. 필요한, 필연적인

13 steadily [stédili] 꾸준히, 견실하게

By **steadily** expanding its business, Monsant became the largest cosmetics company in the Midwest.

꾸준히 사업을 확장함으로써, Monsant사는 중서부에서 가장 큰 화장품 회사가 되었다.

출제포인트 파 **steady** adj. 꾸준한, 한결 같은

14 regularly [régjulərli] 정기적으로

To improve their test scores, university students must **regularly** review their lecture notes.

시험 성적을 향상시키기 위해, 대학생들은 그들의 강의 노트를 정기적으로 복습해야 한다.

출제포인트 파 **regular** adj. 정기적인

15 relatively [rélətivli] 상대적으로, 비교적

Attendance at this month's job fair was **relatively** low compared to the previous one.

이번 달 취업 설명회 참석률은 이전 것과 비교하여 상대적으로 낮았다.

출제포인트 1. 동일한 종류의 다른 것들과 비교할 때 사용한다.
2. 파 **relative** adj. 상대적인

16 mutually [mjú:tʃuəli] 상호 간에, 서로

The beverage producer and the restaurant formed a **mutually** advantageous partnership.

음료 제조업체와 식당은 상호 간에 이로운 제휴를 맺었다.

출제포인트 **mutually exclusive**: 상호 배타적인

17 consistently [kənsístəntli] 일관되게, 시종일관으로

Consistently offering excellent customer service is a priority at Belleview Telecom Incorporated.

훌륭한 고객 서비스를 일관되게 제공하는 것은 Belleview 전기 통신사에서의 우선 사항이다.

출제포인트 항상 동일한 방식으로 행동하거나 동일한 성과를 이루는 등 일관된 모습을 나타내는 경우에 사용한다.

18 momentarily [mòuməntérəli] 순간적으로, 잠깐

The projector stopped working **momentarily** due to a brief power outage during the seminar.

그 프로젝터는 세미나 중에 잠깐의 정전 때문에 순간적으로 작동을 멈췄다.

19 significantly [signífikəntli] 상당히

The number of government grants for university students has **significantly** increased.

대학생들을 위한 정부 보조금의 수는 상당히 증가해 왔다.

출제포인트 1. **considerably, remarkably, fairly**와 의미가 같다.
2. 파 **significant** adj. 상당한

20 currently [kə́:rəntli] 현재

The new exhibit at the gallery is **currently** open to the public.

그 미술관에서의 새로운 전시회는 현재 대중에게 공개되어 있다.

출제포인트 1. 현재 일어나는 일이나 상태를 나타낼 때 사용한다.
2. 파 **current** adj. 현재의

21 immediately [imí:diətli] 즉시

Ms. Thompson requested that the sales projections report be sent to her **immediately**.

Ms. Thompson은 매출 예상 보고서가 그녀에게 즉시 보내지도록 요청했다.

출제포인트 1. 단독으로 쓰거나 'immediately upon -ing / immediately after + 절: ~하자마자 즉시'의 형태로 쓰인다.
2. 파 **immediate** adj. 즉시의

22 exclusively [iksklú:sivli] 독점적으로, 전적으로

A discount on Mayfair cosmetics is available **exclusively** to Beauty Store shoppers.

Mayfair사 화장품에 대한 할인은 Beauty Store 쇼핑객들만이 독점적으로 이용할 수 있다.

출제포인트 1. '오로지, 오직 ~뿐'이라는 의미로도 쓰이며 이때는 **solely**와 의미가 같다.
2. **available exclusively in** 장소: ~에서만 이용 가능한

23 occasionally [əkéiʒənəli] 때때로, 가끔

The CEO **occasionally** travels to East Asia to look for new investment opportunities.

최고 경영자는 새로운 투자 기회들을 찾기 위해 때때로 동아시아로 여행을 간다.

출제포인트 1. **sometimes**와 의미가 같다.
2. 파 **occasion** n. 때, 경우 **occasional** adj. 가끔의

24 promptly [prámptli] 즉시, 정각에

The presentation by the design team began **promptly** after lunch.

설계팀에 의한 발표는 점심 이후 즉시 시작되었다.

출제포인트 파 **prompt** adj. 즉시 ~하는, 즉각적인

A와 B중 맞는 것을 고르세요.

01 be **hardly** worth the cost　　　　비용에 비해 가치가　ⓐ 많이 있다　ⓑ 거의 없다

02 **specifically** developed for young people　　젊은 사람들을 위해　ⓐ 예정대로　ⓑ 특별히　개발되었다

03 Ms. Lee was **formerly** the CEO of Investaid.　　Ms. Lee는　ⓐ 잠재적으로　ⓑ 전에　Investaid사의 최고 경영자였다.

04 **Unfortunately**, he missed the flight.　　ⓐ 안타깝게도　ⓑ 실수로,　그는 비행기를 놓쳤다.

05 decide to **permanently** shut down the factory　　공장을　ⓐ 영구히　ⓑ 갑자기　폐쇄하기로 결정하다

06 select **randomly**　　ⓐ 올바르게　ⓑ 무작위로　선택하다

07 **briefly** talk about the impact of social media　　소셜미디어의 영향에 대해　ⓐ 간단히　ⓑ 자세히　설명하다

08 The plane was delayed **unexpectedly**.　　비행편이　ⓐ 심하게　ⓑ 예상치 못하게　지연되었다.

09 Prices declined **markedly**.　　가격들이　ⓐ 부당하게　ⓑ 현저하게　하락했다.

10 It took **nearly** a year to finish the project.　　그 프로젝트를 끝내는 데에　ⓐ 거의　ⓑ 놀랍게도　일 년이 걸렸다.

11 The shopping Web site is **routinely** updated.　　그 쇼핑 웹사이트는　ⓐ 정기적으로　ⓑ 우선적으로　갱신된다.

12 an **unusually** low profit return　　ⓐ 유별나게　ⓑ 약간　낮은 수익률

13 The wall is made **entirely** of glass.　　그 벽은　ⓐ 전부　ⓑ 일부　유리로 만들어졌다.

14 **thoroughly** examine the medical charts　　의료 기록을　ⓐ 철저하게　ⓑ 긴급하게　검토하다

15 speak **reassuringly** about the company's future　　회사의 미래에 대해　ⓐ 안심이 되게　ⓑ 부정적으로　말하다

16 Some information was **intentionally** excluded.　　몇몇 정보는　ⓐ 효과적으로　ⓑ 의도적으로　배제되었다.

17 The shop can **barely** cover its expenses.　　그 상점은　ⓐ 간신히　ⓑ 넉넉하게　지출을 충당할 수 있다.

18 Please install the air conditioner **properly**. 에어컨을 ⓐ 제대로 ⓑ 빠르게 설치해 주시기 바랍니다.

19 Some members **regretfully** declined to attend. 일부 회원들은 ⓐ 완고하게 ⓑ 유감스럽게도 참석을 거절했다.

20 be **gradually** given more responsibilities ⓐ 서서히 ⓑ 갑자기 더 많은 책임이 주어지다

21 Two workshops will be held **simultaneously**. 두 개의 워크숍은 ⓐ 즉시 ⓑ 동시에 열릴 것이다.

22 enter data **accurately** into a computer 자료를 컴퓨터에 ⓐ 과장해서 ⓑ 정확하게 입력하다

23 wait **patiently** for the flight to leave 비행기가 떠나기를 ⓐ 간절히 ⓑ 참을성 있게 기다리다

24 Six companies **collectively** dominate the industry. 여섯 개의 회사가 ⓐ 경쟁적으로 ⓑ 집단으로 그 산업을 주도한다.

25 describe the process **comprehensively** 과정을 ⓐ 포괄적으로 ⓑ 간략하게 설명하다

26 visit regional branches **periodically** for inspection 시찰을 위해 ⓐ 잠시 ⓑ 주기적으로 지사를 방문하다

27 Somebody **purposely** damaged the statue. 누군가가 ⓐ 일부러 ⓑ 남모르게 그 조각상을 손상시켰다.

28 trust the financial advisors **implicitly** 재정 고문들을 ⓐ 절대적으로 ⓑ 부분적으로 신뢰하다

29 Mr. Davis spoke **openly** about his problems. Mr. Davis는 그의 문제에 대해 ⓐ 간단히 ⓑ 숨김없이 말했다.

30 be **temporarily** unavailable ⓐ 일시적으로 ⓑ 동시에 이용할 수 없다

31 The Web site is **conveniently** organized. 그 웹사이트는 ⓐ 편리하게 ⓑ 전략적으로 구성되어 있다.

32 Additional employees will be hired **eventually**. ⓐ 아마도 ⓑ 결국 추가 사원들이 고용될 것이다.

맞는 부사에 √표를 하세요.

33 The students performed ☐ **exceptionally** well.
☐ **almost**

학생들이 매우 잘 수행하였다.

34 She ☐ **rarely** misses appointments.
☐ **extremely**

그녀는 드물게 약속을 어긴다.

35 ☐ **intensely** improved regulations
☐ **slightly**

조금 개선된 규정들

36 We are ☐ **primarily** gathering new data.
☐ **presently**

우리는 현재 새로운 데이터를 수집하고 있다.

37 He ☐ **distantly** opposed the change.
☐ **initially**

그는 처음에 그 변경을 반대했다.

38 ☐ **frequently** take public transit
☐ **arguably**

대중교통을 자주 이용하다

39 Shareholders ☐ **unanimously** voted to distribute profits.
☐ **unintentionally**

주주들은 만장일치로 수익을 분배하는 것에 투표했다.

40 feel drowsy, ☐ **hardly** in the afternoon
☐ **especially**

특히 오후에 나른하다

41 close the door ☐ **gently** on the way out
☐ **apparently**

나가는 길에 조용하게 문을 닫다

42 The workers ☐ **ever** finished the renovations.
☐ **finally**

그 노동자들은 마침내 수리를 끝냈다.

43 work out ☐ **supposedly** at the gym
☐ **regularly**

체육관에서 규칙적으로 운동하다

44 Some parts are made ☐ **elsewhere**.
☐ **everywhere**.

몇몇 부품은 다른 곳에서 제작된다.

45 For large orders, prices will be adjusted ☐ **accordingly**.
☐ **evenly**.

대량 주문에 대해서는, 가격이 그에 알맞게 조정될 것입니다.

46 The lobby was ☐ **simply** furnished.
☐ **tastefully**

그 로비는 가구가 고상하게 비치되었다.

47 a ☐ **grandly** accepted idea
☐ **widely**

널리 받아들여지는 생각

48 There is a chance of rain and ☐ **perfectly** a thunderstorm.
☐ **possibly**

비가 올 가능성이 있으며 아마도 뇌우가 올 가능성도 있다.

정답 p.92

해커스 스타강사의
무료 해설강의 바로 보기
(9번 문제)

⏱ 제한 시간 10분

Part 5

01 The air conditioner can ------- monitor the humidity level in a room.

(A) newly
(B) precisely
(C) regretfully
(D) highly

02 Bill Mathewson is ------- regarded as one of the best financial consultants for small-business owners.

(A) closely
(B) evenly
(C) generally
(D) adversely

03 Staff functions for workers in the city council department are usually held in the office lounge, but special events are ------- hosted in restaurants or hotels.

(A) early
(B) considerably
(C) remotely
(D) occasionally

04 Customer service representatives at NQ Corp. ------- respond to client inquiries within three days.

(A) overly
(B) typically
(C) greatly
(D) tightly

05 The applicants in the lobby waited ------- to be called into the office for an interview.

(A) patiently
(B) expertly
(C) cautiously
(D) jointly

06 The gift shop on Baker Street is popular with customers because it is conveniently located, and its products are ------- inexpensive.

(A) exactly
(B) narrowly
(C) relatively
(D) rarely

07 Mr. Waters ------- schedules meetings in the morning so that he can focus on other work in the afternoon.

(A) scarcely
(B) potentially
(C) explicitly
(D) purposely

08 The writing workshop was organized for inexperienced writers who haven't ------- published a book.

(A) previously
(B) eagerly
(C) shortly
(D) urgently

09 Employees should be back in the conference room by 10:00 A.M., as the meeting will resume ------- once the manager has arrived.

(A) assertively
(B) cordially
(C) promptly
(D) particularly

10 The company has ------- hired some new staff, so a gathering to introduce them will be held at the cafeteria.

(A) recently
(B) usually
(C) certainly
(D) freshly

Part 6

Questions 11-14 refer to the following notice.

Chicago Classical Music Hall
Additional Information Regarding Ticketing

This year, we have added 10 additional shows to the Classical Concert Series. Because of the overwhelming demand for tickets and the ------- seating available for each performance, people
11
interested in attending a concert are urged to make an online reservation in advance.

Tickets may be picked up at the box office any time after the reservation is made. When you reserve tickets online, you will be issued a claim number. Your ID and claim number must be presented ------- to obtain your tickets. According to our policy, only government-issued photo IDs,
12
such as driver's licenses, are acceptable. -------. You will not be able to receive your tickets without
13
a valid ID.

To show you our appreciation, we are offering a special promotion this season, so make sure you ------- your ticket. You can use it to claim a free concert T-shirt after the show.
14

For any inquiries, please call 1-500-555-1588 to speak with one of our customer representatives.

---

11 (A) limited
  (B) spacious
  (C) discreet
  (D) previous

12 (A) primarily
  (B) mutually
  (C) frequently
  (D) simultaneously

13 (A) Classical music shows continue to decline in popularity.
  (B) You will be contacted if the concert is cancelled.
  (C) Reservations are available only at the box office.
  (D) The rule is in effect to prevent others from collecting your tickets.

14 (A) commit
  (B) examine
  (C) select
  (D) retain

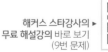

Hackers TOEIC Reading

SECTION 2

어구

CHAPTER 05

형용사 관련 어구

suitable과 for는 찰떡궁합!

떡볶이와 순대가 환상의 궁합을 자랑하듯이 영어에도 찰떡궁합을 자랑하는 '형용사와 전치사' 어구가 있다. 예를 들면 'suitable for(~에 적합한)'가 그것인데 토익에서는 suitable에 어떤 전치사를 쓰는지 등 이런 어구를 알고 있어야 풀 수 있는 문제가 출제된다. 오늘은 '형용사와 전치사' 어구에 눈도장을 찍어 두자.

출제 유형 및 전략

> **1.** 빈칸 뒤에 오는 전치사와 어구를 이루는 형용사를 고르는 문제로 출제된다.
>
> **2.** 고른 단어를 대입해서 뜻이 맞는지 재빨리 확인한 후 답으로 결정한다.

예제

Part 5

The company is looking for someone who is ------- of making important decisions in a fast-paced environment and under time constraints.

(A) inclined   (B) capable   (C) eligible   (D) responsible

해설   빈칸 앞뒤를 살펴 보았을 때, 빈칸 뒤의 전치사 of와 어울려 쓰일 수 있는 형용사는 (B) capable이다. (be capable of -ing: ~할 능력이 있다) (A) inclined는 'be inclined to do : ~하는 경향이 있다', (C) eligible은 'be eligible to do: ~할 자격이 있다', (D) responsible은 'be responsible for: ~에 책임이 있다'라는 어구로 쓰인다.

해석   회사는 빠르게 진행되는 환경에서 시간 제약 아래 중요한 결정을 내릴 능력이 있는 사람을 찾고 있다.

어휘   look for 찾다 / fast-paced adj. 빠르게 진행되는 / under time constraints 시간 제약 아래

정답   (B)

Part 6

Collingwood Industries' new factory was built in Canada because of the proximity of raw materials needed for production. Ray Davis, CEO of Collingwood, said that the new facility is ------- to keeping the costs of manufacturing low.

(A) integral   (B) comprehensive   (C) equivalent   (D) thorough

해설   빈칸 뒤의 to와 어울려 쓰이면서, '새로운 시설이 생산 비용을 낮게 유지하는 데 _____이다'의 빈칸에 와서 자연스러운 문맥을 만드는 어휘는 (A) integral이다. (be integral to: ~에 필수적이다) (B) comprehensive는 'be comprehensive of: ~을 포함하다', (C) equivalent는 'be equivalent to: ~과 동등하다', (D) thorough는 'be thorough about: ~에 철저하다'라는 어구로 쓰인다.

해석   Collingwood Industries사의 새 공장은 생산에 필요한 원자재와의 근접성 때문에 캐나다에 건설되었다. Collingwood사의 최고 경영자인 Ray Davis는 그 새로운 시설이 생산 비용을 낮게 유지하는 데 필수적이라고 말했다.

어휘   proximity n. 근접성 / raw material 원자재, 원료 / facility n. 시설, 설비

정답   (A)

01 be enthusiastic about
~에 대해 열광하다, 열중하다

The team **is enthusiastic about** its chances of winning first prize in the competition.
그 팀은 대회에서 1등 상을 받을 가능성에 대해 열광하고 있다.

출제포인트 전치사 about 대신 over를 사용하여 be enthusiastic over의 형태로 쓸 수 있다.

02 be skeptical of
~에 회의적이다, ~을 의심하다

Many scientists **are skeptical of** the report and would like to investigate the matter further.
많은 과학자들은 그 보고에 대해 회의적이고 그 문제를 더 연구하고 싶어 한다.

출제포인트 전치사 of 대신 about을 사용하여 be skeptical about의 형태로 쓸 수 있다.

03 be ideal for
~에 이상적이다

Social networking platforms **are ideal for** marketing to the younger generation.
소셜 네트워킹 플랫폼들은 젊은 세대에 대한 마케팅에 이상적이다.

04 be eligible for
~의 자격이 있다

Passengers who have the Silver Card **are eligible for** a seat upgrade on international flights.
Silver 카드를 소지한 승객들은 국제선 좌석 업그레이드의 자격이 있다.

출제포인트 be eligible for + 명사: ~의 자격이 있다
be eligible to + 동사원형: ~할 자격이 있다

05 be exempt from
~을 하지 않아도 된다, ~이 면제되다

Those participating in the conference **are exempt from** turning in travel expense receipts.
협의회에 참가하는 이들은 여행 경비 영수증을 제출하지 않아도 된다.

06 be proficient in
~에 능통하다

Ms. Schuberg **is proficient in** Spanish as well as English.
Ms. Schuberg는 영어뿐만 아니라 스페인어에도 능통하다.

출제포인트 어떤 일에 능숙하고 익숙한 것을 의미한다.

07 be devoted to
~에 헌신하다

The hospital **is devoted to** providing patients with the best quality of treatment.
그 병원은 환자들에게 최고의 치료를 제공하는 데에 헌신한다.

출제포인트 be devoted to의 to는 전치사이므로, to 다음에 동사가 아닌 명사나 -ing가 온다.

08 be encouraged to
~하도록 권장되다, 격려하다

Visitors **are encouraged to** wear protective gear during their tour of facilities.
방문객들은 시설 견학 동안 보호 장비를 착용하도록 권장된다.

09 be known to A as B
A에게 B로 알려지다

Mr. Calson **is known to** the staff **as** a highly motivated CEO.
Mr. Calson은 직원들에게 매우 의욕이 강한 최고 경영자로 알려져 있다.

출제포인트 to 다음에 사실을 알게 되는 대상이 오며, as 다음에는 신분이나 직책 등이 오는 경우가 많다.

10 be superior to
~보다 뛰어나다

Drake Hotel **was superior to** last year's venue for the annual marketing conference.
Drake 호텔은 연례 마케팅 협의회의 작년 개최지보다 뛰어났다.

출제포인트 전치사 to 다음에 비교 대상이 오며, to 자리에 than을 쓸 수 없다.

11 be likely to
~할 것 같다

The mayor currently has a 60 percent approval rating, so he **is likely to** be reelected.
그 시장은 현재 60퍼센트의 지지율을 보유하고 있으므로, 재당선이 될 것 같다.

12 be reliant on
~에 의존하다

Felicity Clothing **is** currently **reliant on** textile manufacturers based in Southeast Asia.
현재 Felicity 의류 회사는 동남아시아에 기반을 둔 섬유 제조업체들에 의존하고 있다.

출제포인트 rely on과 의미가 같다.

13 be familiar with   ~에 대해 잘 알다, 익숙하다, 친하다

The tour guides at the agency **are familiar with** the history of most major European cities.
여행사에 있는 여행 안내원들은 대부분의 주요 유럽 도시들의 역사에 대해 잘 안다.

14 be reflective of   ~을 반영하다

The analysis covered in the article **is reflective of** the latest shopping trends.
그 기사에 보도된 분석은 최신 구매 성향을 반영한다.

> **출제포인트** 전치사 of 다음에 상황을 나타내는 단어나 구가 와서 특정 상황을 반영한다는 의미로 자주 쓰인다.

15 be comparable to   ~에 필적하다, ~과 비길 만하다

The size of the city **is comparable to** that of Philadelphia.
그 도시의 크기는 필라델피아의 크기에 필적한다.

> **출제포인트** 전치사 to 다음에 비교하는 대상이 온다.

16 be responsive to   ~에 빠르게 대응하다, 반응하다

The health club staff **is responsive to** customer requests.
그 헬스클럽 직원은 고객 요청에 빠르게 대응한다.

> **출제포인트** 전치사 to 다음에 명사가 온다.

17 be compatible with   ~과 호환되다, 양립하다

The power cable provided with the computer **is compatible with** other electronic equipment.
컴퓨터와 함께 제공된 전력 케이블은 다른 전자 기기와 호환된다.

> **출제포인트** work well together와 의미가 같다.

18 be honored for   ~으로 상을 받다, 명예를 얻다

Dr. Jones will **be honored for** her research at the hospital's awards ceremony this year.
Dr. Jones는 올해 병원 시상식에서 그녀의 연구로 상을 받을 것이다.

> **출제포인트** for 다음에 상을 받거나 명예를 얻게 된 업적이 온다.

19 be uncertain about   ~에 대해 확신하지 못하다

The committee said it **is uncertain about** the results of the economic analysis.
그 위원회는 경제 분석 결과에 대해 확신하지 못한다고 말했다.

> **출제포인트** 전치사 about 대신 of를 사용하여 be uncertain of의 형태로 쓸 수 있다.

20 be concerned about/over   ~에 대해 걱정하다

The organizers **are concerned about** the seating capacity of the room.
주최자들은 그 방의 좌석 수에 대해 걱정한다.

> **출제포인트** be worried about과 의미가 같다.

21 be suitable for   ~에 적절하다, 알맞다

Most films produced by Limelight Studios **are suitable for** children of all ages.
Limelight 영화사에서 제작되는 대부분의 영화들은 모든 연령의 아이들에게 적절하다.

> **출제포인트** for 다음에는 특정한 경우나 대상, 목적이 온다.

22 be concerned with   ~과 관련되다

Mr. Bader said that the documents he sent **are concerned with** the development project.
Mr. Bader는 그가 보낸 문서들이 개발 계획과 관련된다고 말했다.

> **출제포인트** 1. 문서나 책 등의 주제가 with 다음에 오는 것과 관계가 있다는 의미이다.
> 2. '관심을 가지다'라는 의미로도 쓰인다.

23 be responsible for   ~에 대해 책임이 있다

Current road repair work **is** partly **responsible for** the traffic problems in the city center.
현 도로 보수 작업은 도심지의 교통 문제에 대해 부분적으로 책임이 있다.

> **출제포인트** be in charge of와 의미가 같다.

24 be subject to   ~의 영향을 받기 쉽다, (승인 등을) 받아야 한다

The cost of flight tickets **is subject to** current fuel prices.
항공권 가격은 현재 연료 가격의 영향을 받기 쉽다.

Sick leave applications **are subject to** company approval. 병가 신청서는 회사의 승인을 받아야 한다.

> **출제포인트** 전치사 to 다음에 명사가 온다.

맞는 것에 √표를 하세요.

01 The amount of capital **is enough** ☐ **to** / ☐ **with** start construction.
자본금의 액수는 공사를 시작하기에 **충분하다**.

02 The market **is** quite **favorable** ☐ **for** / ☐ **at** investment.
시장이 투자에 상당히 적합하다.

03 All hospital staff **are** ☐ **required** / ☐ **respected** **to** wear plastic gloves.
모든 병원 직원들은 비닐 장갑을 끼도록 요구된다.

04 suggestions that **were** ☐ **irresponsible** / ☐ **irrelevant** **to** the issue
논점과 무관했던 제안들

05 Research **is** ☐ **integral** / ☐ **equivalent** **to** the completion of the project.
연구는 프로젝트 완료에 필수적이다.

06 The restaurant **is** ☐ **evident** / ☐ **notable** **for** its desserts.
그 식당은 디저트로 유명하다.

07 **be consistent** ☐ **of** / ☐ **with** the company's code of ethics
회사의 윤리 강령과 일치하다

08 **be scheduled** ☐ **for** / ☐ **of** a presentation
발표를 하기로 예정되다

09 **be absent** ☐ **from** / ☐ **in** the training workshop
교육 워크숍에 불참하다

10 **be aware** ☐ **to** / ☐ **of** the circumstances
상황을 인식하다

11 **be** ☐ **detached** / ☐ **dedicated** **to** pursuing a banking career
은행 경력을 쌓는 데 전념하다

12 The results **were opposite** ☐ **of** / ☐ **to** what experts predicted.
결과는 전문가들이 예측했던 것과 반대였다.

13 Accountants must **be cognizant** ☐ **of** / ☐ **to** tax laws.
회계사들은 세법에 대해 알고 있어야 한다.

14 **be** ☐ **willing** / ☐ **hesitant** **to** pay in advance
기꺼이 선불로 지급하다

정답 p.94

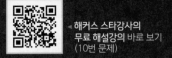
🕐 제한 시간 10분

Part 5

01 Movie fans are ------- about the film's opening and are already lining up outside theaters.

(A) potent
(B) creative
(C) enthusiastic
(D) articulate

02 When the entrepreneur checked the requirements listed on the Web site, he learned that he was ------- for a loan.

(A) economic
(B) effective
(C) eager
(D) eligible

03 The two-bedroom apartment in Star Tower is ------- for anyone working in the downtown area.

(A) known
(B) ideal
(C) simple
(D) alert

04 Though the official announcement has not been made yet, the tickets are ------- to go on sale about a month before the musical performance.

(A) likely
(B) inserted
(C) comparable
(D) increased

05 According to Cubicle Supply's Web site, shoppers who make a purchase of $500 or more are ------- from all shipping and handling charges.

(A) complimentary
(B) provided
(C) insolent
(D) exempt

06 Ms. Stein accepted the job offer as the company is ------- to let her work from home when needed.

(A) relevant
(B) relaxing
(C) willing
(D) necessary

07 The proposed change to the regulation regarding carbon emissions from factories is ------- to review by the Ministry of the Environment.

(A) compulsory
(B) subject
(C) uncovered
(D) interior

08 The library is not ------- for your personal possessions, so please do not leave your belongings unattended.

(A) dependable
(B) debatable
(C) inevitable
(D) responsible

09 The directors of Coleman Legal Services are ------- about the recent loss of several prominent clients to a competing law firm.

(A) connected
(B) considered
(C) concerned
(D) convinced

10 The Blue Ribbon Corporation is ------- to providing consistent, timely, and quality service to customers.

(A) assured
(B) concentrated
(C) offered
(D) dedicated

Part 6
Questions 11-14 refer to the following memo.

From: Richard Garfield, Vice President
To: All marketing employees
Subject: Presentation
Date: October 13

You are all aware that the company's sales have dropped this year as a result of the ongoing global slump. Those of you who are ------- with the characteristics of an economic downturn know
11
that consumers curb their spending to cope with job losses or stagnant incomes. -------.
12

After some consideration, senior management has devised several -------. These will be
13
implemented to offset decreased demand for our products. We will be scheduling a presentation that will give you a ------- overview of our plans, which mainly involve renewing our focus on
14
advertising. The date, time, and location of the presentation will be determined by tomorrow afternoon.

---

11 (A) reliant
(B) familiar
(C) consistent
(D) friendly

12 (A) With this in mind, now is the time to celebrate this accomplishment.
(B) Financial analysts have declared that the recession is over.
(C) Unsurprisingly, the recent decline in sales reflects this consumer tendency.
(D) I advise you to visit our Web site to view the latest job postings.

13 (A) measures
(B) alliances
(C) regulations
(D) standards

14 (A) extreme
(B) vulnerable
(C) detailed
(D) continuous

해커스 스타강사의 ▶
무료 해설강의 바로 보기
(10번 문제)

CHAPTER 06

동사 관련 어구 1

participate의 임자는 in!

동사 중에는 'participate in(~에 참석하다)'같이 전치사와 커플로 다니는 것들이 있는데 토익에서는 이것을 제대로 아는지 물어본다. '참석하다'라고 할 때 뒤에 in을 뻔히 보고도 participate 대신 attend를 넣으면 피오나 공주에게 슈렉 대신 호동왕자를 맺어주는 꼴이 된다. 임자를 잘못 맞어주면 몰매를 맞을 수 있으니 '동사와 전치사' 커플을 잘 기억해 두자.

출제 유형 및 전략

1. 빈칸 주변의 단어와 어구를 이루는 동사, 또는 어구 전체를 고르는 문제로 출제된다.

2. 고른 단어나 어구를 대입해서 뜻이 맞는지 재빨리 확인한 후 답으로 결정한다.

예제

Part 5

A marketing workshop was scheduled because Mr. Hong believed his team would ------- from additional training.

(A) benefit (B) generate (C) associate (D) decide

해설 '추가 교육으로부터 이익을 얻다'라는 문맥에서 빈칸 뒤의 전치사 from과 함께 쓰여 '~로부터 이익을 얻다'라는 의미의 어구를 이루는 동사 (A) benefit이 정답이다. (benefit from: ~로부터 이익을 얻다) (B) generate는 '일으키다, 초래하다'라는 의미이며, (C) associate는 '관련시켜 생각하다'라는 의미로 'associate A with B(A를 B에 관련시켜 생각하다)'로 주로 쓰인다. (D) decide는 '결정하다'라는 의미이다.

해석 마케팅 워크숍 일정이 잡혔는데 Mr. Hong은 그의 팀이 추가 교육으로부터 이익을 얻을 것이라고 생각했기 때문이다.

어휘 **additional** adj. 추가의 / **training** n. 교육, 훈련

정답 (A)

Part 6

There are a number of commonly used management techniques that can help achieve a successful outcome when dealing with difficult employees. For example, while they are speaking, you should ------- attentively to their arguments to signal that you value their opinions before raising the issues that need to be addressed.

(A) reimburse (B) dismiss (C) support (D) listen

해설 빈칸 뒤와 보기를 보면 (D) listen이 전치사 to와 어구를 이루는 것을 알 수 있다. listen을 빈칸에 넣었을 때 '그들의 주장을 주의 깊게 경청해야 한다'라는 자연스러운 의미가 되므로 문맥상으로도 (D)가 정답이다. (A) reimburse는 '변상하다', (B) dismiss는 '해산시키다, (생각 등을) 일축하다', (C) support는 '지원하다'라는 의미이며 모두 타동사이기 때문에 전치사 to가 뒤에 바로 올 수 없다. 자동사와 전치사 사이에 부사가 들어갈 수 있으므로 listen과 to 사이에 attentively가 들어간 형태도 잘 알아 두자.

해석 까다로운 직원들을 상대할 때 성공적인 결과를 얻도록 도움을 주는 일반적으로 사용되는 경영 기법들이 많이 있다. 예를 들어, 직원들이 말을 하는 동안, 다뤄져야 할 사안들을 제기하기 전에 당신이 그들의 의견을 중요시한다는 점을 알려주기 위해서 그들의 주장을 주의 깊게 경청해야 한다.

어휘 **commonly** adv. 일반적으로 / **management** n. 경영, 관리 / **outcome** n. 결과 / **deal with** ~를 상대하다 / **attentively** adv. 주의 깊게 / **value** v. 중요시하다 / **address** v. (문제·상황 등에 대해) 다루다

정답 (D)

01 equip A with B
A에 B를 장착하다, 갖추다

The manufacturer **equipped** its new line of kitchen appliances **with** energy-saving features.

그 제조업체는 새로운 주방기기 제품에 에너지 절약 기능을 장착했다.

출제포인트 1. 수동형인 'A is equipped with B: A에 B가 갖춰져 있다'로도 자주 사용된다.
2. A come equipped with B, A be outfitted with B와 의미가 같다.

02 evolve from
~에서 발달하다, 진화하다

The city **evolved from** a small, undeveloped town into a major business center in just 30 years.

그 도시는 단 30년 만에 작고 개발되지 않은 마을에서 주요한 상업 중심지로 발달했다.

03 coincide with
~과 동시에 일어나다, ~과 일치하다

The decline in the unemployment rate **coincided with** the growth of the economy.

실업률의 감소는 경제의 성장과 동시에 일어났다.

04 specialize in
~을 전문적으로 하다

Colton Enterprise **specializes in** the restoration and sale of antique or art objects.

Colton사는 골동품이나 미술품들의 복원과 판매를 전문적으로 한다.

05 conclude with
~로 마치다, ~로 끝나다

The festival will **conclude with** a speech from the city's mayor and a fireworks display.

그 축제는 시장의 연설과 불꽃놀이로 마칠 것이다.

06 prevent A from B
A가 B하는 것을 막다, 방지하다

Offering regular incentives helps **prevent** talented staff **from** leaving the company.

정기적인 장려금을 제공하는 것은 재능 있는 직원들이 회사를 떠나는 것을 막는 데 도움이 된다.

07 appeal to
~의 관심을 끌다

The office did not **appeal to** Mr. West because he wanted one with a view of the Don River.

Mr. West는 Don강의 전망이 보이는 곳을 원했기 때문에 그 사무실은 그의 관심을 끌지 못했다.

출제포인트 1. 전치사 to 다음에는 명사가 온다.
2. attract와 같은 의미이다.

08 collaborate on 사물
(사물)에 대해 협력하다

Prominent historians will **collaborate on** a textbook about South American civilizations.

저명한 사학자들은 남아메리카 문명에 관한 교과서에 대해 협력할 것이다.

출제포인트 'collaborate with 사람: ~와 협력하다'도 함께 알아 두자.

09 familiarize oneself with
~에 익숙하게 하다, ~에 정통하다

Ms. Lee **familiarized herself with** the revised contract terms prior to the client meeting.

Ms. Lee는 고객 미팅 이전에 변경된 계약 조건들에 그녀 자신이 익숙하게 했다.

출제포인트 'be acquainted with: ~에 정통하다'도 함께 알아 두자.

10 replace A with B
A를 B로 교환하다

If products are damaged during shipment, D&B Market will **replace** them **with** new items.

만약 상품들이 운송 중에 손상되면, D&B Market사는 그것들을 새 상품들로 교환해 줄 것이다.

출제포인트 replace A by B와 의미가 같다.

11 differentiate A from B
A를 B와 차별화하다, 구별하다

Veedar Motorcycles has **differentiated** its newest model **from** those of other manufacturers through its powerful engine.

Veedar Motorcycles사는 강력한 엔진을 통해 자신들의 최신형 모델을 다른 제조사의 것들과 차별화했다.

출제포인트 differentiate between A and B의 형태로 쓸 수 있다.

12 commit oneself to
~에 전념하다, ~을 떠맡다

Islands Airlines has **committed itself to** improving the level of customer satisfaction.

Islands 항공사는 고객 만족의 수준을 향상시키는 데에 전념해왔다.

출제포인트 1. 전치사 to 다음에 명사나 동명사가 온다.
2. 'commit A to B: A를 B에게 맡기다'도 함께 알아 두자.

13 be divided into
~으로 나뉘다

Attendees **were divided into** smaller groups due to the large number of workshop participants.

많은 수의 워크숍 참가자들로 인해 참석자들은 소그룹으로 나뉘었다.

> **출제포인트** 'divide A into B: A를 B로 나누다'가 수동형으로 쓰였다.

14 attribute A to B
A를 B의 덕분으로 돌리다

Analysts **attribute** the current market boom **to** an increase in individual investors.

분석가들은 현 시장의 호황을 개인 투자자들의 증가 덕분으로 돌린다.

> **출제포인트**
> 1. 수동형인 'A is attributed to B: A는 B에 기인하다'로도 자주 사용된다.
> 2. 'credit A to B, credit B with A: A를 B의 공으로 믿다'도 함께 알아 두자.

15 qualify for
~의 자격을 얻다, ~에 대한 자격을 갖추다

Applicants must possess a degree in accounting to **qualify for** a job interview.

취업 면접의 자격을 얻으려면 지원자들은 회계 분야의 학위를 갖고 있어야 한다.

> **출제포인트** 'be eligible for: ~의 자격이 있다'도 함께 알아 두자.

16 charge 대금 to A
(대금)을 A로 달아놓다, 청구하다

Customers shopping on the Web site may **charge** delivery fees **to** their accounts.

그 웹사이트에서 쇼핑을 하는 고객들은 배송비를 그들의 계좌 앞으로 달아놓을 수 있다.

> **출제포인트** 'charge 액수 for 물품: 물품 대금으로 액수를 청구하다'도 함께 알아 두자.

17 restrict A to B
A를 B로 한정하다

We **restrict** visitor parking **to** the lot adjacent to the main entrance of the facility.

우리는 방문객 주차 공간을 시설 정문에 인접한 부지로 한정합니다.

> **출제포인트**
> 1. 입장이나 예약을 특정 그룹에게로 한정할 때, 물건의 사용을 특정 장소로만 제한할 때 등에 사용한다.
> 2. A is restricted to B: A가 B로 한정되어 있다
> 3. limit A to B와 의미가 같다.

18 discourage A from B
A가 B하는 것을 그만두게 하다

The purpose of the law is to **discourage** banks **from** charging excessive interest rates.

그 법의 목적은 은행이 과도한 금리를 부과하는 것을 그만두게 하기 위함이다.

19 A is aimed at B
A는 B를 겨냥한 것이다

The new F-series luxury sedan **is aimed at** successful business executives.

새로운 F-시리즈 고급 세단은 성공한 기업체 간부들을 겨냥한 것이다.

> **출제포인트**
> 1. 제품이 특정 소비자군을 겨냥하는 경우 등에 사용한다.
> 2. 'aim: ~을 겨냥하다'가 수동형으로 쓰였다.

20 dispose of
~을 처분하다, ~을 버리다

Industrial companies must develop better ways to **dispose of** toxic waste produced by factories.

산업체들은 공장에서 생성되는 유독성 폐기물을 처분하기 위한 더 좋은 방법들을 개발해야 한다.

21 respond to
~에 응답하다, 대응하다

The client **responded** positively **to** the firm's proposal for the new advertising campaign.

그 고객은 새로운 광고 캠페인을 위한 회사의 제안에 긍정적으로 응답했다.

> **출제포인트**
> 1. 전치사 to 다음에 명사가 온다.
> 2. 'in response to: ~에 응하여', 'be responsive to: ~에 빠른 반응을 보이다', 'be unresponsive to: ~에 반응하지 않다'도 함께 알아 두자.

22 contribute to
~에 기여하다, 공헌하다

The construction of the stadium has **contributed to** the economic revitalization of the city.

경기장 건설은 그 도시의 경제 활성화에 기여했다.

23 compensate A for B
A에게 B에 대해 보상하다

The broadcasting company **compensated** Dr. Bland **for** the damage caused by the report.

그 방송국은 Dr. Bland에게 보도로 인해 야기된 피해에 대해 보상했다.

> **출제포인트** 사람에게 가해진 피해나 손실에 대해 보상하는 경우에 사용한다.

24 comply with 규칙·요구
(규칙·요구)를 준수하다, 따르다

Tenants are asked to **comply with** the building's rules and policies.

세입자들은 건물의 규칙과 방침을 준수하도록 요구된다.

> **출제포인트** 'be compliant with: ~에 부합하다'도 함께 알아 두자.

맞는 것에 √표를 하세요.

01 **credit** an increase in sales ☐ **to** / ☐ **as** him   매출 증가를 그의 공으로 믿다

02 The film **is based** ☐ **of** / ☐ **on** the story of a renowned artist.   그 영화는 한 유명 예술가의 이야기에 기반을 둔다.

03 **advertise** ☐ **to** / ☐ **on** the Internet more to reach younger consumers   젊은 소비자들에게 다가가기 위해 인터넷에 더 광고를 하다

04 The new legislation could **result** ☐ **in** / ☐ **of** a significant change.   새로운 법률 제정은 중대한 변화를 야기할 수 있다.

05 Price increases **depend** ☐ **of** / ☐ **on** the cost of gasoline.   가격 인상은 휘발유 가격에 달려 있다.

06 The compound **consists** ☐ **with** / ☐ **of** two-bedroom houses.   그 복합 주거 단지는 2개의 침실이 있는 주택들로 구성된다.

07 **engage** ☐ **in** / ☐ **to** a discussion   토론에 참여하다

08 The merger could **lead** ☐ **at** / ☐ **to** layoffs.   합병은 해고로 이어질 수 있다.

09 **compete** ☐ **along** / ☐ **for** a promotion   승진을 위해 경쟁하다

10 Lockers will **be** ☐ **assigned** / ☐ **assured** to gym members.   개인 물품 보관함이 체육관 회원들에게 배당될 것이다.

11 Employees **are** ☐ **entrusted** / ☐ **entitled** to overtime pay.   직원들은 초과 근무 수당을 받을 자격이 있다.

12 **regard** the decision ☐ **as** / ☐ **to** a mistake   그 결정을 실수로 여기다

13 Bonuses **are related** ☐ **for** / ☐ **to** performance.   보너스는 성과와 관련된다.

14 **be accompanied** ☐ **of** / ☐ **by** a cover letter   자기소개서가 동봉되다

15 **prohibit** customers ☐ **over** / ☐ **from** smo**king**   손님들이 흡연하는 것을 금지하다

16 **be involved** ☐ **at** / ☐ **in** corporate finance   기업 재무 분야에 종사하다

17 The workers **were subjected** ☐ **to** / ☐ **with** extreme heat.   노동자들은 극심한 더위에 노출되었다.

정답 p.95

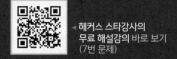
🕐 제한 시간 10분

Part 5

01 The refrigerator is ------- with a water dispenser and an automatic ice maker.

(A) assigned
(B) equipped
(C) inserted
(D) attracted

02 Occupants are only allowed to ------- of recyclables in the marked bins found at the rear of the building.

(A) dispose
(B) compose
(C) exclude
(D) abandon

03 Oakley Properties ------- in the renovation of old buildings, making them modern and convenient while retaining their unique appearance.

(A) creates
(B) researches
(C) specializes
(D) delegates

04 Since the graphic design company only made slight modifications to Radix Sportwear's logo, it is difficult to ------- it from the original version.

(A) reproduce
(B) market
(C) differentiate
(D) expand

05 The courier company, ------- to increasing demand for its services, purchased a new fleet of trucks.

(A) communicating
(B) discussing
(C) responding
(D) interviewing

06 It is library policy that admission to the archive room is ------- to professors and graduate students.

(A) enlisted
(B) restricted
(C) contradicted
(D) prevented

07 To ------- for a credit card, customers must provide evidence that they are capable of making payments in a timely fashion.

(A) propose
(B) qualify
(C) demand
(D) preserve

08 Ms. Jensen's retirement party next month ------- with the 50th anniversary of the company.

(A) associates
(B) deals
(C) coincides
(D) agrees

09 The sudden increase in sales of Superslim mobile phones is ------- to their appearance in a popular television drama series which is currently showing on NATV.

(A) permitted
(B) attributed
(C) attested
(D) allocated

10 The employees' annual bonuses are ------- on their performance and evaluations submitted by their supervisors.

(A) lifted
(B) collected
(C) related
(D) based

Part 6

Questions 11-14 refer to the following letter.

Hi-Net Cable Internet Customer Service
867 East Valley Trail NW
Great Falls, Montana 68750

To whom it may concern,

I received my billing statement from your company yesterday and noticed that it had an error. I signed up for Internet service a few weeks ago, and I was told it would cost $35 per month. However, when I got my first bill, I discovered that $50 had been ------- to my account instead. 11 As you can see on my registration form, I requested the standard service. But it seems that the customer representative ------- registered me for a high-speed connection. I called my bank to 12 cancel the automatic payment, but the money had already been sent. Please downgrade my plan immediately, and refund the difference. -------. I hope to hear back from you as soon as possible 13 and trust that this matter will be ------- shortly. 14

Sincerely,

Eleanor Briggs

---

11 (A) calculated
   (B) contributed
   (C) compensated
   (D) charged

12 (A) continually
   (B) cautiously
   (C) simultaneously
   (D) mistakenly

13 (A) Now, the service I am receiving is not as fast as I expected.
   (B) You may be eligible for the upgraded plan next month.
   (C) I apologize for the delay in paying this charge.
   (D) Or you can subtract that amount from my next bill.

14 (A) resolved
   (B) removed
   (C) reported
   (D) reduced

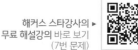

해커스 스타강사의 ▶
무료 해설강의 바로 보기
(7번 문제)

정답·해설·해석 p.95 / [별책] 토익 RC 필수 어휘 p.29

CHAPTER 07 동사 관련 어구 2

pay off를 알아야 노력이 pay off한다.

His efforts paid off. 토익 문제를 풀다가 이런 문장을 봤는데 도무지 뜻을 모르겠다. 노력이 어쨌다는 건가? pay가 쓰였으니 돈이 들었다는 것인지... pay off는 succeed, 즉 '성과를 내다'라는 뜻이다. 쉬운 succeed를 두고 왜 pay off를 쓰냐고 반문하고 싶으나 영어에서는 이런 게 허다한 일. 게다가 토익에서도 이런 것을 물어보니 오늘은 '동사 어구'를 한번 배워 볼까.

출제 유형 및 전략

1. 빈칸 주변의 단어와 어구를 이루는 동사, 또는 어구 전체를 고르는 문제로 출제된다.

2. 어구가 지닌 특유의 의미를 고려한다.

3. 고른 단어나 어구를 대입해서 뜻이 맞는지 재빨리 확인한 후 답으로 결정한다.

예제

Part 5

The tower's main elevators were ------- down for an hour this morning so that a safety inspection could be conducted.

(A) held   (B) moved   (C) dropped   (D) shut

해설　빈칸 뒤의 down과 어울려 쓰이면서, '엘리베이터는 안전 점검이 실시될 수 있도록 ＿＿＿되었다'의 빈칸에 와서 자연스러운 문맥을 만드는 어휘는 (D) shut이다. (shut down: (기계가) 정지하다, 문을 닫다) (A)의 hold는 'hold down: ~을 억제하다, 견뎌내다', (B)의 move는 'move down: 끌어내리다, 격하하다', (C)의 drop은 'drop down: 쓰러지다'라는 의미의 어구를 이룬다.

해석　그 고층 건물의 주요 엘리베이터들은 안전 점검이 실시될 수 있도록 오늘 아침 한 시간 동안 정지되었다.

어휘　**tower** n. 고층 건물, 타워 / **main** adj. 주요한, 중심이 되는 / **inspection** n. 점검, 검사

정답　(D)

Part 6

In a report written to the financial director, the consultant ------- numerous concerns she had about the company's accounting system. She provided several suggestions on how the company could solve these problems and improve its efficiency.

(A) brought up   (B) carried through   (C) looked around   (D) handed out

해설　빈칸 뒤의 concerns와 어울려 쓰이면서, '그녀가 가진 많은 우려를 ＿＿＿하다'의 빈칸에 와서 자연스러운 문맥을 만드는 어구는 (A) brought up이다. (bring up: ~을 제기하다) (B)의 carry through는 '~을 완수하다', (C)의 look around는 '둘러보다', (D)의 hand out은 '~을 나누어 주다'라는 의미이다.

해석　재무 이사 앞으로 작성된 보고서에서, 자문 위원은 회사의 회계 시스템에 대해 그녀가 가진 많은 우려를 제기하였다. 그녀는 회사가 이런 문제들을 해결하고 효율성을 높일 수 있는 방법에 대해 몇 가지 제안을 제시하였다.

어휘　**numerous** adj. 많은 / **accounting** n. 회계 / **efficiency** n. 효율성

정답　(A)

핵심 단어 리스트

01 stop by
잠시 들르다

The client plans to **stop by** the office later this week to drop off the signed contract.

그 고객은 서명된 계약서를 가져다주기 위해 이번 주 후반에 사무실에 잠시 들를 계획이다.

출제포인트 come by, drop by, swing by와 의미가 같다.

02 fall within
~에 포함되다, ~의 범위에 들어가다

Product testing **falls within** the responsibilities of the research department head.

제품 실험은 연구부장의 책무에 포함된다.

03 fill out
작성하다, ~에 기입하다

Individuals who wish to apply for a gym membership should **fill out** an application form.

체육관 회원권을 신청하기를 희망하시는 분들은 신청서를 작성하셔야 합니다.

04 turn in
제출하다

Employees planning to take extended leave should **turn in** requests two months in advance.

장기 휴가를 떠나기를 계획하는 직원들은 요청서를 두 달 전에 미리 제출해야 합니다.

출제포인트 submit과 의미가 같다.

05 pick up
~을 찾아오다, (사람 등을) 도중에서 태우다

Customers are allowed to **pick up** orders at the warehouse themselves.

고객들은 창고에서 직접 주문품을 찾아오는 것이 허용된다.

06 take in
섭취하다, 흡수하다

People trying to lose weight should carefully monitor the calories they **take in** each day.

체중을 줄이려고 노력하는 사람들은 그들이 날마다 섭취하는 칼로리를 주의 깊게 확인해야 한다.

출제포인트 take in은 이외에 '숙박시키다, 삯을 받고 맡다, 구독하다' 등 다양한 의미로도 쓰인다.

07 sign up for
~에 등록하다

Homeowners are encouraged to **sign up for** the realtors' seminar on property taxes.

주택 소유주들은 공인 부동산업자의 재산세 관련 세미나에 등록하도록 권장된다.

08 take place
진행되다, 열리다

A conference call between the Hong Kong and Singapore branches will **take place** tomorrow.

홍콩 지사와 싱가포르 지사 간의 전화 회담은 내일 진행될 것이다.

출제포인트 be held와 의미가 같다.

09 succeed in -ing
~에 성공하다

Mr. Harris **succeeded in** persuad**ing** the client to extend the deadline.

Mr. Harris는 고객이 마감 일자를 연장하도록 설득하는 데 성공했다.

10 take time off (to do)
(~하기 위해) 시간을 내다

Professor Collins **took time off** to participate in an archaeological dig in Africa.

Collins 교수는 아프리카에서의 고고학 발굴에 참여하기 위해 시간을 냈다.

출제포인트 take time off from work: 직장에서 휴가를 얻다

11 run the risk of
~의 위험을 무릅쓰다

Delco Oil **runs the risk of** missing production targets if its pipeline is not repaired soon.

Delco Oil사는 회사의 송유관이 빨리 수리되지 않을 경우에 생산 목표에 이르지 못하게 되는 위험을 무릅쓰게 된다.

출제포인트 run이 '(위험 등을) 무릅쓰다, (목숨 등을) 걸다'라는 의미로 쓰였다.

12 take over
(업무 등을) 인계받다, (가게 등을) 양도받다, 인수하다

Due to Karen Wilkins' recent promotion, Brad Messier will **take over** the shipping department.

Karen Wilkins의 최근 승진으로 인해, Brad Messier가 운송부를 인계받을 것이다.

출제포인트 over 다음에 'as + 직책/직위'가 오기도 한다.

13 call for
~을 필요로 하다, 요구하다

The recipe **calls for** two cups of cream and does not allow for substitutions.
그 요리법은 크림 2컵을 필요로 하고 대용품을 허용하지 않는다.

출제포인트 require, need와 의미가 같다.

14 check in
탑승 수속을 하다, 숙박 수속을 하다

Airline passengers should **check in** three hours before departure time.
항공기 승객들은 출발 시각 세 시간 전에 탑승 수속을 해야 한다.

출제포인트 호텔이나 공항에서 수속을 밟을 때 사용한다.

15 keep up with
~에 뒤떨어지지 않다, (유행 등)에 맞추다

Designers must **keep up with** fashion trends to make sure their clothing lines are current.
디자이너들은 그들의 의류 상품이 현재 유행하고 있음을 확실히 하기 위해서 패션 동향에 뒤떨어지지 않아야 한다.

출제포인트 형태가 비슷한 'keep up: ~을 계속하다'도 함께 구별하여 알아 두자.

16 have every intention of -ing
기꺼이 ~할 의사가 있다

The landlord **has every intention of** mak**ing** improvements to the building.
건물주는 기꺼이 건물을 개량할 의사가 있다.

출제포인트 have no intention of -ing: ~할 의사가 전혀 없다

17 keep in touch with
~와 계속 연락하다

The president of the legal firm makes an effort to **keep in touch with** his international clients.
그 법률 회사의 회장은 국제 고객들과 계속 연락하기 위해 노력한다.

출제포인트 keep 대신 stay를 사용하여 stay in touch with의 형태로 쓸 수 있다.

18 look over
(서류 등을) 검토하다

Mr. Xiung will **look over** the report tonight and provide feedback tomorrow.
Mr. Xiung은 오늘 밤 그 보고서를 검토하여 내일 의견을 줄 것이다.

출제포인트 1. 전치사 over 뒤에 검토하는 대상이 온다.
2. review와 의미가 같다.

19 keep records of
~에 대한 기록을 남기다

The customer service department **keeps** accurate **records of** complaints about products.
고객 서비스부는 상품 관련 불만들에 대한 정확한 기록을 남긴다.

출제포인트 1. record가 '기록'이라는 의미의 명사로 쓰였다.
2. sales record: 판매 기록   client record: 고객 기록

20 look into
~을 조사하다

The finance division has **looked into** the errors and corrected them.
재무부는 오류들을 조사하고 수정했다.

출제포인트 examine과 의미가 같다.

21 keep track of
~을 추적하다, ~의 정보를 알고 있다

This software allows users to easily **keep track of** inventory.
이 소프트웨어는 사용자들이 쉽게 재고를 추적할 수 있게 해 준다.

출제포인트 어떤 일에 대해 끊임없이 정보를 얻어내어 최신의 정보를 정확하게 알고 있는 상태를 나타낼 때 사용한다.

22 look upon A as B
A를 B로 고려하다, 생각하다

Ms. Murray **looks upon** Stan Rodgers **as** a candidate for a management position.
Ms. Murray는 Stan Rodgers를 관리직의 후보자로 고려한다.

출제포인트 1. 형태가 비슷한 'look up: 찾아보다'와 구별하여 알아 두자.
2. regard A as B와 의미가 같다.

23 account for
(~의 비율을) 차지하다, ~의 원인이 되다

Meetings **account for** a significant portion of the employees' time.
회의는 직원들의 근무 시간에서 상당한 부분을 차지한다.

The popularity of its competitor's products **accounts for** the company's declining profits.
경쟁사 상품의 인기는 그 회사의 하락하는 수익의 원인이 된다.

출제포인트 account for는 이외에 '처리하다'라는 의미로도 쓰인다.

24 look for
~을 찾다

The article gives advice on what to **look for** when buying a camera.
그 기사는 카메라를 구입할 때 무엇을 찾아봐야 할지에 대해 조언해 준다.

출제포인트 seek, search for와 의미가 같다.

맞는 것에 √ 표를 하세요.

01 refrain ☐ **from** / ☐ **out of** talking during the exam

시험 중에 잡담을 삼가다

02 The report **was passed** ☐ **on** / ☐ **with** to the manager.

그 보고서는 관리자에게 전달되었다.

03 take ☐ **charge** / ☐ **risks** of a team

팀을 책임지다

04 The supermarket has **run** ☐ **narrow** / ☐ **short** of fresh produce.

그 슈퍼마켓은 신선한 농산물이 다 떨어졌다.

05 take ☐ **the care** / ☐ **care** of the customer's complaint

고객 불만을 처리하다

06 The plant was ☐ **shut** / ☐ **enclosed** down for maintenance.

그 공장은 보수 관리를 위해 문을 닫았다.

07 The debate **came** ☐ **to** / ☐ **in** an end.

논쟁이 종료되었다.

08 help ☐ **set** / ☐ **distribute** up the hall for an event

행사를 위한 집회장을 준비하는 것을 돕다

09 ☐ **bring** / ☐ **hand** up the issue with Mr. Sanford

그 사안을 Mr. Sanford에게 제기하다

10 Spring sales helped **make** ☐ **out** / ☐ **up** for a slow winter.

봄 매출은 매출이 낮은 겨울을 만회하는 것을 도왔다.

11 take ☐ **advantage** / ☐ **benefit** of the special offer

특가 판매를 이용하다

12 follow ☐ **up on** / ☐ **through to** the request for an invoice

송장 요청에 대해 후속 조치하다

13 The bill **comes into** ☐ **cause** / ☐ **effect** in July.

그 법안은 7월에 시행된다.

14 The guidelines were **set** ☐ **forth** / ☐ **ahead** by the airline.

그 정책은 항공사에 의해 제시되었다.

정답 p.97

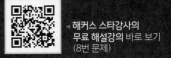
🕐 제한 시간 10분

Part 5

01 Visitors arriving at the trade fair were told to ------- out a registration form and present a business card.

(A) work
(B) leave
(C) bow
(D) fill

02 Most critics agreed that fashion designer Viola Arancia has ------- in developing a collection that is both affordable and trendy.

(A) delegated
(B) motivated
(C) revealed
(D) succeeded

03 After leaving the museum, the tour group will ------- a local marketplace for lunch.

(A) take up
(B) sit down
(C) stop by
(D) bring in

04 Mr. Lee attends seminars at the Newport Technology Society and takes online courses in order to ------- new technological trends.

(A) keep up with
(B) break away from
(C) cut down on
(D) get through with

05 Concerned that the photo developing shop would run ------- of materials, Mr. Lark sent his assistant out to buy what was needed.

(A) vast
(B) lengthy
(C) fast
(D) short

06 The customer feedback about the new smartphone model was ------- to Ms. Burnham for review.

(A) figured out
(B) passed on
(C) called off
(D) depended on

07 The orientation for new accountants will ------- next week in the main office's conference room.

(A) let in
(B) take place
(C) move around
(D) keep out

08 The speaker could not adequately answer the question as it did not ------- within his area of expertise.

(A) find
(B) ask
(C) join
(D) fall

09 Low yields of the major agricultural products in South America ------- for the latest economic instability in some of its poorest countries.

(A) account
(B) change
(C) resolve
(D) require

10 Ms. Wren will ------- the current performance director's job when he retires at the end of the month.

(A) work out
(B) bring down
(C) take over
(D) pass through

Part 6
Questions 11-14 refer to the following article.

The New Trend of Self-Investment

As bank interest rates for savings accounts continue to decline, building up a retirement fund is harder now than it was 30 years ago. Fortunately, there is a way to deal with this. Gaining an understanding of financial information is an ------- for those who are bewildered by the multiple options available.

11

Some people find investment information complicated and choose to enlist the services of an experienced broker. However, some investors have learned to rely on a variety of resources when handling their finances. They ------- online forums, business journals and periodicals to gather information for themselves. They learn how financially stable a company is and when best to make an investment instead of ------- on a middle man to do it for them. After doing their own research, investors can use their newly acquired knowledge of the market to decide where to put their capital. -------. It may sound risky, but many successful investors started out by doing research themselves.

---

11 (A) assignment
(B) obligation
(C) asset
(D) indicator

12 (A) turn in
(B) take over
(C) check in
(D) look into

13 (A) collecting
(B) depending
(C) partnering
(D) merging

14 (A) Much of the advice given on Web sites is conflicting.
(B) It is wiser to ask for a broker's advice to avoid mistakes.
(C) Even beginners can surely make better investment decisions with adequate information.
(D) Employing a broker is the only available option.

VOCABULARY Part 5,6   Ch 07 동사 관련 어구 2   Hackers TOEIC Reading

CHAPTER 08

명사 관련 어구

customer base를 알아야 사업 성공!

토익 문제를 풀다 보면 무슨 뜻인지 알기 어려운 어구가 가끔 등장하는데 그 중의 하나가 'customer base'이다. 해석하면 '고객 기초'인데 무슨 뜻인지 영 감이 안 온다. 사실 'customer base(고객층)'는 홍보나 판매의 대상이 되는 주요 고객들을 말하는데 이처럼 명사에 다른 것을 붙여서 만든 어구는 따로 익혀 두지 않고는 대응하기 버거우니 오늘은 그들과 얼굴을 터 보자.

토익 출제 유형 및 전략

1. 빈칸 주변의 단어와 어구를 이루는 명사를 고르는 문제로 출제된다.

2. 고른 단어를 대입해서 뜻이 맞는지 재빨리 확인한 후 답으로 결정한다.

예제

Part 5

The prospect of receiving a pay ------- can motivate employees to improve their performance and work to the best of their abilities.

(A) expansion   (B) hoist   (C) increase   (D) ascent

해설   빈칸 앞의 명사 pay와 함께 쓰여 '임금 인상'이라는 의미의 어구를 이루는 명사 (C) increase가 정답이다. (pay increase: 임금 인상) (A) expansion은 '확장', (B) hoist는 '들어 올리기, 승강 장치', (D) ascent는 '올라감, 오르막'이라는 의미이다.

해석   임금 인상을 받을 가능성은 직원들이 그들의 실적을 향상시키고 능력이 미치는 데까지 업무를 하도록 동기를 부여할 수 있다.

어휘   **prospect** n. 가능성, 전망 / **motivate** v. ~에게 동기를 부여하다 / **to the best of** ~이 미치는 한, ~하는 한

정답   (C)

Part 6

Today's Business Line column focuses on how to calculate your tax properly under the newly-introduced corporate tax system. It was written by Jan Delpratt, a senior executive of Merchant Associates, the nation's largest accounting firm, and a regular ------- to *The National Business Review*.

(A) leader   (B) contributor   (C) applicant   (D) accountant

해설   빈칸 뒤의 전치사 to와 어울려 쓰일 수 있는 단어는 명사 (B) contributor(기고가)이다. contributor를 빈칸에 넣었을 때 '*The National Business Review*지의 정기 기고가'라는 자연스러운 의미가 되므로 문맥상으로도 (B)가 정답이다. (A) leader는 '지도자, 대표', (C) applicant는 '지원자', (D) accountant는 '회계사'라는 의미이다.

해석   *Today's Business Line*지의 칼럼은 새로 도입된 법인세 체계하에 세금을 정확히 계산하는 방법에 대해 중점적으로 다룬다. 이 칼럼은 전국 최대의 회계 법인 Merchant Associates사의 고위 간부이자, *The National Business Review*지의 정기 기고가인 Jan Delpratt가 썼다.

어휘   **focus on** ~을 중점적으로 다루다 / **calculate** v. 계산하다 / **properly** adv. 정확히, 올바르게 / **corporate tax** 법인세 / **accounting** n. 회계

정답   (B)

핵심 단어 리스트

01 sales projection 판매 전망, 매출 예측

According to the **sales projection**, the firm is expected to make a profit this year.
판매 전망에 따르면, 그 회사는 올해에 수익을 낼 것으로 예상된다.

02 outside audit 외부 감사 (보고서)

Firms must submit to an **outside audit** of their finances if they want to become government suppliers.
기업들은 정부 공급업체가 되고자 한다면 그들의 재정에 대한 외부 감사를 받아야 한다.

03 in its/their entirety 전부, 통째로

The graphic design firm was sold **in its entirety** to the film production company.
그 그래픽 디자인 회사는 영화 제작 회사에 전부 매각되었다.

04 an assortment of 다양한

Pop Sweetie offers **an assortment of** desserts ranging from cupcakes to macaroons.
Pop Sweetie는 컵케이크부터 마카롱까지 다양한 디저트를 제공한다.

> 출제포인트 1. assortment가 '(여러가지) 모음, 종합'이라는 의미로 쓰였다.
> 2. a variety of, a (wide) range of, a wide selection of, varied, various와 의미가 같다.

05 by means of ~에 의하여, ~을 이용해서

Applicants are selected **by means of** a comprehensive evaluation of applications and interviews.
지원자들은 지원 서류와 면접의 종합적인 평가에 의하여 선발된다.

06 work shift 근무 교대

Security personnel with weekend **work shifts** should consult the schedule in the main office.
주말 근무 교대인 보안 요원은 본사에 있는 일정을 참고해야 한다.

> 출제포인트 'night shift: 야간 근무 교대'도 함께 알아 두자.

07 sales figure 판매 수치

Increased market competition resulted in lower **sales figures** last quarter for Pressman Wines.
증가된 시장 경쟁은 Pressman Wines사에 지난 분기 더 낮은 판매 수치를 야기했다.

> 출제포인트 1. figure가 '액수, 값'이라는 의미로 쓰였다.
> 2. population figure: 인구 수

08 office supplies 사무용품

Staff who run out of **office supplies** may send a request by e-mail to Mr. Rogers.
사무용품을 다 쓴 직원들은 Mr. Rogers에게 이메일로 요청을 보내면 된다.

> 출제포인트 'cleaning supplies: 청소용품'도 함께 알아 두자.

09 employee productivity 직원 생산성

Overtime pay will be raised as part of a plan to maximize **employee productivity**.
직원 생산성을 극대화하기 위한 계획의 일부로 초과 근무 수당이 인상될 것이다.

> 출제포인트 worker productivity와 의미가 같다.

10 safety inspector 안전 검사관

The **safety inspector** discovered several fire code violations at the restaurant.
안전 검사관은 그 레스토랑에서 몇 가지 소방 법규 위반 사항을 발견했다.

> 출제포인트 'housing inspector: 주택 검사관'도 함께 알아 두자.

11 time constraint 시간 제약

Due to **time constraints**, the itinerary for the tour of Taipei has to be modified slightly.
시간 제약으로 인해, 타이베이 관광 일정이 약간 수정되어야 한다.

12 contingency plan 비상 대책

Engineers worked on a **contingency plan** for the aircraft in case of an emergency landing.
기술자들은 불시착에 대비하여 항공기를 위한 비상 대책에 착수했다.

13 press release   보도 자료

According to a recent **press release**, Walton Bank will open a new branch in Hamilton.

최근 보도 자료에 의하면, Walton 은행은 해밀턴시에 신규 지점을 열 것이다.

출제포인트 'press conference: 기자 회견'도 함께 알아 두자.

14 terms of agreement   계약 조건

The **terms of agreement** state that users are prohibited from copying the software.

계약 조건은 사용자들이 소프트웨어를 복제하는 것이 금지된다고 명시한다.

출제포인트 1. terms가 '조건'이라는 의미로 사용되었다.
2. terms and conditions: (계약이나 지불 등의) 조건

15 billing statement   대금 청구서

Ms. Foster called to inquire about an error on her **billing statement** for last month.

Ms. Foster는 그녀의 지난달 대금 청구서 상의 오류에 관해 문의하기 위해 전화했다.

출제포인트 'electronic statement: 전자 청구서', 'bank statement: 은행 계좌 입출금 내역서', 'credit card statement: 신용카드 내역서'도 함께 알아 두자.

16 obligation to   ~할 의무

When applying for a loan, clients have an **obligation to** report their financial status.

대출 신청 시, 고객들은 그들의 재정 상태를 알릴 의무가 있다.

출제포인트 have no obligation to: ~할 의무가 없다

17 job opening   공석, 채용 공고

There are several **job openings** at Rewell Linens because some employees are planning to retire next month.

일부 직원들이 다음 달에 퇴직할 예정이기 때문에 Rewell Linens사에는 몇몇 공석이 있다.

18 contribution to   ~에 기부, 공헌

Mr. Molson makes frequent **contributions to** local charities and community programs.

Mr. Molson은 지역 자선 단체와 지역 사회 프로그램에 종종 기부를 한다.

19 baggage allowance   수하물 허용량

Swift Air announced that it had increased its **baggage allowance** to 22 kilograms.

Swift 항공사는 수하물 허용량을 22킬로그램까지 늘렸다고 발표했다.

출제포인트 승객 한 명당 비행기에 가지고 타거나 화물칸에 실을 수 있는 수하물의 개수 및 허용 중량을 의미한다.

20 performance appraisals   업무 수행 평가

At the end of each month, the manager conducts **performance appraisals** of staff.

매월 말에, 관리자는 직원들의 업무 수행 평가를 실시한다.

출제포인트 1. performance가 '수행, 성과'의 의미로 쓰였다.
2. appraisal은 '평가'라는 의미이며 가산 명사이므로 관사 an과 함께 쓰거나 복수형으로 써야 한다.

21 compliance with + 규칙   (규칙에) 대한 준수

The company operates in full **compliance with** current export laws.

그 회사는 현 수출법을 완전히 준수하며 운영한다.

출제포인트 'observe: (규칙 등을) 준수하다'도 함께 알아 두자.

22 confidence in   ~에 대한 신임

Management expressed **confidence in** Ms. Foster by granting her a special promotion.

경영진은 Ms. Foster의 특진을 승인함으로써 그녀에 대한 신임을 표현했다.

출제포인트 express confidence in: ~에 대한 신임을 표현하다

23 commitment to   ~에 대한 전념, 헌신

Larson Bookstores has a **commitment to** providing individualized service to customers.

Larson 서점은 개인 특성에 맞춘 서비스를 고객들에게 제공하는 데 전념한다.

출제포인트 전치사 to 다음에 명사가 온다.

24 preference for   ~에 대한 선호

Recent studies show a **preference for** booking concert tickets online.

최근 연구는 온라인으로 콘서트 입장권을 예매하는 것에 대한 선호를 보여준다.

출제포인트 preference of A to B: B보다 A를 더 선호함

맞는 것에 √표를 하세요.

01 forward a ☐ **list** / ☐ **combination** of participating universities

참가하는 대학들의 목록을 보내다

02 ☐ **lack** / ☐ **overlay** of consumer interest

소비자 관심의 부족

03 provide a ☐ **guarantee** / ☐ **partnership** of customer satisfaction

고객 만족에 대한 보장을 제공하다

04 taxes ☐ **on** / ☐ **to** luxury goods

사치품에 대한 세금

05 the written **consent** ☐ **for** / ☐ **of** the owner

문서로 된 소유주의 동의

06 place **an emphasis** ☐ **on** / ☐ **at** time management

시간 관리에 대한 강조를 하다

07 launch a ☐ **series** / ☐ **diversion** of new products

일련의 신제품을 출시하다

08 conference ☐ **participants** / ☐ **residents**

회의 참가자들

09 The election ended ☐ **in** / ☐ **with** a tie.

그 선거는 동점으로 끝났다.

10 show **regard** ☐ **for** / ☐ **at** the opinions of others

타인의 의견에 대한 배려를 보이다

11 an **advocate** ☐ **of** / ☐ **into** tax reform

세제 개혁의 옹호자

12 a **dispute** ☐ **beyond** / ☐ **over** wheat prices

밀 가격에 대한 분쟁

13 questions ☐ **concerning** / ☐ **by** shipping charges

운송비와 관련된 질문

14 an ☐ **exhibition** / ☐ **array** of products in the catalog

카탈로그에 있는 다수의 상품들

정답 p.98

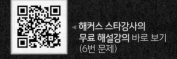
제한 시간 10분

Part 5

01 The laboratory manager will post a notice on the bulletin board each Friday if there are any changes to the work ------- for the next week.

(A) opportunity
(B) authorization
(C) statistic
(D) shift

02 Only a few questions were answered due to time ------- at the end of the workshop.

(A) constraints
(B) operations
(C) measurements
(D) units

03 The consultant advised Argento Interior managers that employee ------- could be improved by using the newest technologies.

(A) applicability
(B) quantity
(C) productivity
(D) utility

04 Employers use the Web site to post job ------- and browse the résumés of potential candidates.

(A) achievements
(B) publications
(C) openings
(D) investments

05 If the sales ------- is accurate, the company could grow its revenues by 30 percent this year.

(A) engagement
(B) recruitment
(C) commission
(D) projection

06 Thomas Engineering and Construction is under ------- to complete the new building project by next month.

(A) designation
(B) delegation
(C) obligation
(D) reservation

07 The annual sales report was printed in its ------- and distributed among the department managers.

(A) summary
(B) order
(C) facility
(D) entirety

08 Most airlines have reduced their hand baggage ------- to one item per passenger in order to ensure the comfort of everyone aboard the flight.

(A) consent
(B) allowance
(C) assessment
(D) mass

09 Dr. Rosen made a large ------- to the children's hospital, which made it possible to renovate an old pediatric wing.

(A) contribution
(B) addition
(C) concession
(D) subsidy

10 The store's continued success is primarily due to its ------- to selling only the finest quality products at reasonable prices.

(A) coordination
(B) cooperation
(C) commitment
(D) compromise

Part 6

Questions 11-14 refer to the following article.

Shop Online Safely

In recent years, online shopping has become increasingly ------- among all age groups. But with
11
more and more people making purchases with the click of a button, the incidence of cybercrime
has been rising. A ------- release made by the Department of Public Safety yesterday urged
12
online shoppers to exercise caution. Among other things, it said to always use a trusted online
retailer rather than a search engine to find items. Changing passwords frequently was also highly
recommended. -------. Furthermore, checking credit card statements ------- and reporting any
13   14
suspicious charges immediately was identified as the best way of spotting problems and resolving
them quickly. To read the full report, visit www.dps.com/tips.

---

11 (A) rare
    (B) unnecessary
    (C) popular
    (D) inconvenient

12 (A) product
    (B) press
    (C) program
    (D) preview

13 (A) Such a dependence on credit cards can
        have a long term effect on finances.
    (B) Doing so makes it more difficult for
        unauthorized people to access user
        accounts.
    (C) Additional study is needed to ensure that
        the technology can be used.
    (D) Comparing the costs of goods and services
        online has never been easier.

14 (A) hastily
    (B) flexibly
    (C) randomly
    (D) closely

해커스 스타강사의 ▶
무료 해설강의 바로 보기
(6번 문제)

CHAPTER 09 짝을 이루는 표현

hold와 conference는 단짝!

우리나라 말도 '물을 먹다'라고 하지 않고 '물을 마시다'라고 하듯이 영어도 짝이 맞는 단어끼리 함께 사용해 줘야 한다. '회의를 열다'는 'open a conference'가 아니라 'hold a conference'인 것처럼 말이다. 토익에서는 이렇게 덩어리로 외워두는 게 좋은 짝표현 관련 문제들을 물어보니, 이 장에 수록된 표현을 한 짝 한 짝 눈에 익혀 두자.

출제 유형 및 전략

1. 형용사 + 명사, 동사 + 명사, 부사 + 형용사 짝표현이 주로 출제된다.
   (예: economic forecast, seek employment, readily available)

2. 빈칸 주변의 단어와 어구를 이루는 단어를 고른다.

3. 고른 단어를 대입해서 뜻이 맞는지 재빨리 확인한 후 답으로 결정한다.

예제

Part 5

An applicant who cannot ------- an appointment with the interviewer must call to reschedule at least one day in advance.

(A) see   (B) turn   (C) bring   (D) keep

해설   빈칸 뒤의 명사 appointment와 짝표현을 이루어 '약속을 지키다'라는 의미를 나타내는 동사 (D) keep이 정답이다. (keep an appointment: 약속을 지키다) (A) see는 '보다', (B) turn은 '돌리다', (C) bring은 '가져오다, 데려오다'라는 의미이며, appointment와 짝표현을 이루지 않는다.

해석   면접관과의 약속을 지킬 수 없는 지원자는 일정을 변경하기 위해 최소한 하루 전에 미리 전화해야 한다.

어휘   **applicant** n. 지원자 / **interviewer** n. 면접관 / **reschedule** v. 일정을 변경하다 / **in advance** 미리, 사전에

정답   (D)

Part 6

Warehouse Office Products Limited is open for business between the hours of 9 A.M. and 5 P.M. Monday through Saturday. Parking is available in the lot on the corner of 7th and East Jefferson Streets in ------- spots only, so take care to ensure that you do not park in a tow-away area.

(A) designated   (B) positioned   (C) switched   (D) expected

해설   빈칸 뒤의 명사 spots와 짝표현을 이루어 '지정된 장소'라는 의미를 나타내는 과거분사 (A) designated가 정답이다. (designated spots: 지정된 장소) (B) positioned는 '배치된', (C) switched는 '교환된', (D) expected는 '예상되는'이라는 의미이다.

해석   Warehouse Office Products사는 월요일부터 토요일까지 오전 9시와 오후 5시 사이에 영업을 하고 있습니다. 주차는 7번가와 East Jefferson가의 모퉁이에 위치한 부지의 지정된 장소에서만 가능하오니, 견인 구역에 주차하지 않도록 조심해 주시기 바랍니다.

어휘   **lot** n. 부지 / **spot** n. 장소 / **take care to do** ~하도록 조심하다 / **tow-away** (주차 위반 차량의) 견인의

정답   (A)

01 rise to fame   명성을 날리다

The actor quickly **rose to fame** after only his second role in a major film.

그 배우는 고작 일류 영화에서의 두 번째 배역 후에 금방 명성을 날렸다.

<u>출제포인트</u> 편지에 무언가를 동봉할 경우 enclose를 사용한다.

---

02 frequent customer   단골 고객

The Harborview Department Store has set up a membership program to reward **frequent customers** with discounts.

Harborview 백화점은 단골 고객에게 할인을 제공할 멤버십 프로그램을 만들었다.

<u>출제포인트</u> 'regular customer: 단골 고객', 'repeat customer: 다시 찾는 고객'도 함께 알아두자.

---

03 enclosed form   동봉된 양식

Those interested in attending the lecture should return the **enclosed form** before the deadline.

강의 참석에 관심이 있으신 분들은 마감일 전에 동봉된 양식을 돌려 보내셔야 합니다.

<u>출제포인트</u> 편지에 무언가를 동봉할 경우 enclose를 사용한다.

---

04 seek employment   직업을 구하다

The company has a list of available positions on its Web site for those **seeking employment**.

그 회사는 직업을 구하는 사람들을 위해 자사 웹사이트에 지원 가능한 직책의 목록을 게재하고 있다.

<u>출제포인트</u> look for work와 의미가 같다.

---

05 pursue a career   (~로서) 일하다, 직업을 추구하다

Because of her interest in sculpture, Rachel **pursued a career** as a professional artist.

조각에 대한 흥미 때문에, Rachel은 전문 예술가로서 일했다.

<u>출제포인트</u> 'start a career: (~으로서) 일을 시작하다'도 함께 알아 두자.

---

06 renew one's subscription   구독을 갱신하다

Readers can **renew their subscriptions** to the journal by calling the toll-free number.

독자들은 수신자 부담 번호로 전화함으로써 잡지의 구독을 갱신할 수 있다.

<u>출제포인트</u> 주로 다음에 'to + 구독되는 대상'이 온다.

---

07 hold a conference   회의를 열다

The city government will **hold a conference** to share ideas for promoting local tourism.

시 정부는 지역 관광 산업을 증진시키기 위한 방안들을 공유하기 위해 회의를 열 것이다.

<u>출제포인트</u> hold가 '(회의나 의식을) 열다, 거행하다'라는 의미로 쓰였다.

---

08 investigate the feasibility   (실행) 가능성을 조사하다

They have **investigated the feasibility** of creating an energy production plant.

그들은 에너지 생산 공장을 신설하는 것의 가능성을 조사했다.

<u>출제포인트</u> investigate는 study, research와 의미가 같다.

---

09 reach an agreement   합의에 도달하다

Attorneys for both parties are in negotiation and hope to **reach an agreement** soon.

양측 변호사들은 협상 중에 있으며 곧 합의에 도달하기를 바란다.

<u>출제포인트</u> 'sign an agreement: 합의서에 서명하다'도 함께 알아 두자.

---

10 economic forecast   경제 전망, 경제 예측

The government's recent **economic forecast** shows a decline in unemployment.

정부의 최근 경제 전망은 실업률의 감소를 보여 준다.

<u>출제포인트</u> forecast가 '전망, 예측'이라는 의미로 쓰였다.

---

11 make an arrangement   준비를 하다

The event organizer has **made arrangements** for all invited speakers to stay at a nearby hotel.

행사 주최자는 모든 초청 연사들이 인근의 호텔에 머무르도록 준비를 했다.

<u>출제포인트</u> make an arrangement for + 사람: ~를 위해 준비를 하다
make an arrangement to + 동사원형: ~하기 위해 준비를 하다

---

12 deliver a presentation   발표하다

The director of marketing **delivered a** short **presentation** on product expansion plans.

마케팅부 이사가 제품 확장 계획에 관한 짧은 발표를 했다.

<u>출제포인트</u> deliver 대신 make나 give를 사용하여 'make a presentation' 또는 'give a presentation'의 형태로 쓸 수 있다.

13 gain recognition　　인정받다

The movie director has **gained recognition** around the globe as an innovative filmmaker.
그 영화 감독은 혁신적인 영화 제작자로서 전 세계적으로 인정받아 왔다.

14 moderate increase　　약간의 증가

The **moderate increase** in sales can be attributed to the popularity of our latest product line.
약간의 매출액 증가는 자사의 최신 제품 라인의 인기 덕분이다.

15 meet the demand　　수요를 충족시키다

Apel Construction is building an apartment complex to **meet the demand** for housing.
Apel 건설사는 주택 공급에 대한 수요를 충족시키기 위해 아파트 단지를 건설하고 있다.

> 출제포인트　meet이 '필요, 요구 등을 충족시키다'라는 의미로 사용되었다.

16 strictly limited　　엄격히 제한된

Access to the laboratory facilities is **strictly limited** to authorized staff.
실험 시설 출입은 허가를 받은 직원으로 엄격히 제한된다.

> 출제포인트　1. strictly는 '엄격히'라는 의미이다.
> 2. 'strictly speaking: 엄밀히 말하자면'이란 짝표현도 함께 알아 두자.

17 fulfill orders　　주문 처리를 완료하다

CIT's shipping department is responsible for **fulfilling orders** for its machinery.
CIT사의 배송부는 자사 기계의 주문 처리를 완료하는 것을 책임지고 있다.

> 출제포인트　접수된 주문에 대하여 배송까지 모든 처리를 완료함을 의미한다.

18 leave 사람/사물 unattended　　(사람/사물)을 내버려 두다

Passengers must not **leave** their personal belongings **unattended** while in the terminal.
승객들은 터미널에 있는 동안 그들의 개인 소지품을 내버려 두어서는 안 된다.

> 출제포인트　items left unattended: 내버려 둔 물건들

19 readily available　　쉽게 구할 수 있는

Applications are **readily available** at the administrative office.
신청서는 행정실에서 쉽게 구할 수 있다.

> 출제포인트　1. readily가 '쉽게(= easily)'라는 의미로 쓰였다.
> 2. available은 '구할 수 있는'이란 의미이다.

20 highly qualified　　충분히 자격을 갖춘

Ms. Dains was hired for the position, as she was the most **highly qualified** applicant.
Ms. Dains가 가장 충분히 자격을 갖춘 지원자였기 때문에 그 자리에 채용되었다.

> 출제포인트　1. highly가 '매우, 충분히'라는 의미로 쓰였다.
> 2. 'highly recommended: 적극적으로 추천되는', 'highly successful: 매우 성공한', 'highly unlikely: 가망이 없는'이란 짝표현도 함께 알아 두자.

21 work extended hours　　초과 근무를 하다, 연장 근무하다

Factory employees who **work extended hours** will receive an additional payment.
초과 근무를 하는 공장 직원들은 추가 수당을 받을 것입니다.

> 출제포인트　work overtime과 의미가 같다.

22 fiscal year　　회계 연도

The financial outlook for the next **fiscal year** is promising.
다음 회계 연도의 재정 전망은 유망하다.

> 출제포인트　1. 예산 편성, 집행 및 결산을 하기 위해 회계상으로 정해 놓은 한 해의 기간을 의미한다.
> 2. fiscal은 '회계의, 재정의'라는 의미이다.

23 standard price　　표준 가격

The **standard prices** of Color-Co's copiers are a bit higher than those of its competitors.
Color-Co사 복사기들의 표준 가격은 경쟁사들의 표준 가격보다 약간 높다.

> 출제포인트　1. 상품의 정가를 의미한다.
> 2. 'competitive price: 경쟁력 있는 가격'이라는 짝표현도 함께 알아두자.

24 do business with　　~와 거래하다

The company will mostly **do business with** subcontractors in Asia.
그 회사는 아시아 지역의 하청 업체들과 주로 거래를 할 것이다.

> 출제포인트　business가 '거래, 장사'라는 의미로 쓰였다.

맞는 것에 √표를 하세요.

01 ☐ **make** ☐ **vest** a presentation
발표를 하다

02 She **has a** ☐ **reputation** ☐ **capability** for being a skilled negotiator.
그녀는 뛰어난 협상가로서 명성이 있다.

03 **earn a** ☐ **wage** ☐ **pay**
임금을 받다

04 ☐ **suddenly** ☐ **instantly** **recognizable** brand
즉시 알아볼 수 있는 상표

05 **promotional** ☐ **offers** ☐ **judgments**
판촉용 특별 서비스

06 A **technical** ☐ **description** ☐ **subscription** of the appliance is included.
기기의 기술 설명서가 포함되어 있다.

07 **an** ☐ **invoked** ☐ **informed** **decision**
정보에 근거한 결정

08 ☐ **attract** ☐ **imprison** **one's attention**
~의 이목을 사로잡다

09 Handle the crystal **with** ☐ **extreme** ☐ **steep** **care**.
수정을 매우 주의 깊게 다루세요.

10 **be** ☐ **strategically** ☐ **cautiously** **optimistic**
조심스럽게 낙관하다

11 permit staff members to ☐ **employ** ☐ **work** **from home**
직원들이 재택근무하는 것을 허용하다

12 ☐ **Prospective** ☐ **Ultimate** **employees** will be interviewed.
채용 후보자들은 면접을 볼 것이다.

13 He **won an** ☐ **award** ☐ **allowance** for his latest novel.
그는 그의 최신 소설로 상을 받았다.

14 Use ☐ **visual** ☐ **observed** **aids** during the lecture.
강의 중에 시각 보조 교재를 이용해라.

15 **an** ☐ **inherently** ☐ **infrequently** **risky** activity
본래부터 위험한 활동

16 **meet one's** ☐ **accountability** ☐ **needs**
~의 필요를 충족시키다

17 **have** ☐ **superb** ☐ **partial** **attention to detail**
세부적인 것에 대한 큰 주의를 갖다

18 **reach one's** ☐ **large** ☐ **full** **potential**
~의 잠재력을 최대로 발휘하다

19 The company will ☐ **except** ☐ **accept** **applications** until November 1.
회사는 11월 1일까지 원서를 접수할 것이다.

20 ☐ **inquire** ☐ **raise** **awareness** of the issue
그 사안에 대한 인식을 높이다

정답 p.100

🕐 제한 시간 10분

Part 5

01 Researchers in the property development department will investigate the ------- of transforming the industrial building into residential units.

(A) sponsorship
(B) feasibility
(C) authorization
(D) prediction

02 To ------- a cable television subscription with Cable-Link, simply fill out the appropriate form on the company's Web site and submit it before your current service expires.

(A) permit
(B) renew
(C) collect
(D) validate

03 Those ------- employment with Ladlaw Real Estate must provide university transcripts and at least two reference letters, along with a copy of their résumé.

(A) hiring
(B) questioning
(C) warranting
(D) seeking

04 Virginia Hey, the plant's production manager, has decided to ------- a presentation about the practicality of the equipment upgrade.

(A) deliver
(B) proceed
(C) obtain
(D) agree

05 The administrative department requires ------- employees to undergo a probationary period lasting three months before being assigned to a permanent position.

(A) probable
(B) disgruntled
(C) prospective
(D) eventual

06 The Organization for the Protection of Animals encourages people not to ------- their pets unattended in vehicles.

(A) store
(B) leave
(C) reside
(D) put

07 Farscape Manufacturing will need to increase their production staff by 2 percent in order to ------- the orders of its customers.

(A) refine
(B) fulfill
(C) restrain
(D) notify

08 In order to determine which features should be included in its next line of products, Browder Electronics' research division will ------- a survey of its customers.

(A) conduct
(B) pursue
(C) predict
(D) mention

09 Mr. Lavington has gained significant ------- in the industry as an expert on international patent law.

(A) implication
(B) assimilation
(C) recognition
(D) perception

10 Management has requested that all store employees work ------- hours to better serve customers during the busy holiday season.

(A) partial
(B) refreshed
(C) extended
(D) former

Part 6

Questions 11-14 refer to the following advertisement.

Bargain Book Bazaar!

Novel Ideas Bookstore will be holding its annual clearance sale from 9 A.M. to 4 P.M. this Saturday, offering enormous discounts on all novels, periodicals, and travel guides. Novel Ideas Bookstore has a wide selection of bestsellers and top fiction selections, but don't stop at reading just for pleasure. You can ------- your knowledge as well. We have nonfiction books on a wide array of
                         11
topics, such as business etiquette, gourmet cooking, global cultures, and world history.

All these books and much more will be ------- available to our customers at 50 to 80 percent off
                                        12
regular prices!

As we only hold this sale once a year, discounts will be strictly limited to eight books per person.
-------. We appeal to shoppers to honor this restriction so that everyone can get a fair share of the
  13
bargains.

This event lasts seven hours, so come on down to Novel Ideas, where we guarantee that we have
the perfect book to ------- your needs!
                      14

---

11 (A) publish
    (B) broaden
    (C) emphasize
    (D) share

12 (A) improbably
    (B) eagerly
    (C) willingly
    (D) readily

13 (A) Our goods are secondhanded, but they are of high quality.
    (B) There are numerous other bookstores we are affiliated with.
    (C) Regular prices will apply to all items after the limit is passed.
    (D) Clearance items can be specially ordered for you on our Web site.

14 (A) meet
    (B) solve
    (C) inform
    (D) announce

SECTION 3

유사의미어

CHAPTER 10

유사의미 동사

Lend me some money. 돈 좀 빌려줘.

지갑을 놓고 온 날 친구에게 돈이라도 빌리려고 하면 '빌리다'라는 표현이 참 어렵다. 뜻도 생김새도 비슷한 rent와 lend 중 뭘 써야 하는지 심히 고민되어 알아보니 돈을 빌릴 때는 lend를 쓰고 rent는 차, 집 등을 임대할 때 쓴다고 한다. 이 장에는 이처럼 한글 뜻은 비슷하지만 쓰이는 상황이나 패턴이 다른 동사들을 모아 놓았으니 예문을 보며 차이를 비교해 두자.

출제 유형 및 전략

보기에 나온 동사들의 뜻이 비슷하기 때문에 정확한 쓰임의 차이를 알아야 답을 고를 수 있는 문제로 출제된다.

예제

Part 5

Some bank's ATMs can ------- as much as $30,000, but most contain less than half that amount.

(A) possess   (B) hold   (C) occupy   (D) grasp

해설   보기에 있는 동사 4개가 모두 뜻이 비슷해 보이지만 쓰임은 다르다. 문맥에 맞는 것은 (B)의 hold '(기계 등이 물건을) 담다'이다. (A) possess는 '(사람이) ~을 소유하다'(possess a work visa: 취업 비자를 소유하다), (C) occupy는 '(사람이나 사물이 장소를) 차지하다'(visitors occupied the town square: 방문객들이 도시 광장을 차지했다), (D) grasp는 '(사람이) ~을 움켜잡다'(grasp the rope: 밧줄을 움켜잡다)라는 뜻이다.

해석   몇몇 은행의 현금 자동 입출금기는 3만 달러 정도 담을 수 있지만, 대부분은 그 절반도 담지 못한다.

어휘   **ATM** 현금 자동 입출금기(Automatic Teller Machine) / **as much as** ~ 만큼 / **contain** v. 담다, 포함하다

정답   (B)

Part 6

Steel Works Incorporated has just announced plans to move their operations from Michigan to a new location near Los Angeles. The company has officially ------- staff that the current plant will be closing within six months, but jobs will be available for those prepared to relocate.

(A) explained   (B) informed   (C) expressed   (D) inquired

해설   보기에 나온 각 동사의 뜻은 비슷해 보이지만 쓰임이 다르다. 빈칸 다음에 사람(staff)이 있으므로 빈칸에는 사람을 목적어로 취하는 동사가 들어가야 한다. 따라서 'inform (사람에게) 알리다'의 과거형인 (B) informed가 정답이다. (A)의 explain '~을 설명하다'는 말하는 내용만 목적어로 올 수 있고, 듣는 사람 앞에는 꼭 to를 써야 한다. (C)의 express '~을 표현하다'는 감정, 생각 등이 목적어로 온다. (D)의 inquire는 'inquire about ~에 대해 문의하다'로 쓴다.

해석   Steel Works사는 미시간 주에서 로스앤젤레스 근처의 새 장소로 사업을 이전할 계획을 막 발표했다. 회사 측은 직원들에게 현 공장이 6개월 안에 폐쇄될 예정이지만, 이주할 준비가 된 사람들에게는 일자리가 있을 것임을 공식적으로 알렸다.

어휘   **announce** v. 발표하다 / **operation** n. 사업, 운영 / **officially** adv. 공식적으로 / **current** adj. 현재의 / **plant** n. 공장 / **relocate** v. 이주하다, 이전하다

정답   (B)

01 promote : support

promote [prəmóut]　　　　　　　　　　촉진하다, 홍보하다

The administration will provide corporations with tax incentives to **promote** economic growth.
당국은 경제 성장을 촉진하기 위해 기업들에게 세금 혜택을 제공할 것이다.

support [səpɔ́:rt]　　　　　　　　　　지지하다, 지원하다

The CEO asked the board of directors to **support** his financial restructuring plan.
최고 경영자는 이사회에게 그의 금융 구조 조정 계획을 지지해달라고 요청했다.

> **출제포인트** 1. '지지, 지원'이라는 의미의 명사로도 쓰인다.
> 2. be supportive of와 의미가 같다.
> 3. ⑩ supportive adj. 지지하는, 지원하는

03 postpone : reschedule

postpone [poustpóun]　　　　　　　연기하다, 뒤로 미루다

The launch of LDC Electronics' new monitors has been **postponed** for a week.
LDC 전자 회사의 새로운 모니터 출시는 일주일 동안 연기되었다.

> **출제포인트** delay와 의미가 같다.

reschedule [rì:skédʒu:l]　　일정을 변경하다, 다시 세우다

To **reschedule** service calls, customers must inform the office three days in advance.
서비스 방문 일정을 변경하려면, 고객들은 반드시 3일 전에 사무실에 알려야 한다.

> **출제포인트** 원래 일어나기로 되어 있던 일의 시간을 바꾸는 것을 의미한다.

02 enroll : subscribe : apply : register

enroll [inróul]　　　　　　　　등록하다, 명부에 올리다

Trainees are encouraged to **enroll** in the software training program by next Monday.
수습 직원들은 다음 주 월요일까지 소프트웨어 교육 프로그램에 등록하도록 권장된다.

> **출제포인트** enroll in: ~에 등록하다

subscribe [səbskráib]　　　　　　　　　구독하다

People who **subscribe** to *Market Trends Magazine* will receive stock tips each month.
*Market Trends*지를 구독하시는 분들은 매달 주식 정보를 받을 것입니다.

> **출제포인트** subscribe to/for: (신문·잡지 등을) 구독하다

apply [əplái]　　　　　　　　　　　　지원하다

Ms. Mannheim expects many people to **apply** for the legal assistant job at the law firm.
Ms. Mannheim은 많은 사람들이 그 법률 사무소의 법률 보조직에 지원할 것이라고 예상한다.

> **출제포인트** 1. '적용하다/적용되다', '바르다'라는 의미로도 쓰인다.
> 2. apply for: ~에 지원하다　apply to: ~에 적용되다
> 3. ⑩ applicant n. 지원자　application n. 지원서
> applicable adj. 적용되는

register [rédʒistər]　　　　　　　　　　등록하다

To **register** for an extended warranty, please complete the form included with your product.
연장된 보증서를 등록하시려면, 상품에 포함된 양식을 작성해 주십시오.

> **출제포인트** register for: ~에 등록하다

04 attend : participate in

attend [əténd]　　　　　　　　(수업·행사 등에) 참석하다

First-year students are required to **attend** the university's orientation seminar next week.
1학년 학생들은 다음 주에 대학교의 예비 교육 세미나에 참석하는 것이 요구된다.

> **출제포인트** attend 다음에 전치사 없이 바로 목적어가 온다.

participate in　　　　　　　　(수업·행사 등에) 참여하다

Individuals who **participate in** the survey will receive a gift certificate.
설문 조사에 참여하시는 분들은 상품권을 받을 것입니다.

> **출제포인트** 'participate in + 목적어'의 형태로 쓰인다. participate 다음에 in이 빠지지 않도록 유의한다.

05 advise : recommend

advise [ədváiz]　　　　　　　　　　　조언하다

The accountant **advised** the owner that filing for bankruptcy was his only option.
회계사는 그 소유주에게 파산 신청을 하는 것이 그의 유일한 선택이라고 조언했다.

> **출제포인트** advise 사람 that절: ~에게 -을 조언하다
> that절 앞에 사람 목적어가 온다.

recommend [rèkəménd]　　　　　　　　추천하다

The consultant **recommended** changes to the firm's work system in his report.
그 자문 위원은 그의 보고서에서 회사의 업무 체계의 변화를 추천했다.

> **출제포인트** recommend that절: ~을 추천하다
> that절 앞에 사람 목적어가 올 수 없다.

06 reduce : decrease : minimize

reduce [ridjúːs]　　　　　　(규모·크기·양을) 줄이다

Mr. Jeon presented management with several ideas to **reduce** expenses.

Mr. Jeon은 경영진에게 비용을 줄이기 위한 몇몇 아이디어를 제시했다.

decrease [dikríːs]　　　　　　(수량·강도를) 줄이다

The manufacturer has decided to **decrease** production of electric appliances.

그 제조업자는 전기 제품의 생산을 줄이기로 결정했다.

출제포인트　'감소'라는 의미의 명사로도 쓰인다.

minimize [mínəmàiz]　　　　　　최소화하다

You should book a direct flight to your destination to **minimize** travel time.

이동 시간을 최소화하기 위해 귀하의 목적지까지 가는 직행 항공편을 예약해야 합니다.

출제포인트　1. 반의어는 maximize(최대화하다)이다.
　　　　　2. ⓟ minimum adj. 최저의, 최소한의; n. 최저치, 최소한도

08 affect : effect

affect [əfékt]　　　　　　(사람·사물에) 영향을 미치다

The proposed security rules will **affect** all employees at the main headquarters.

제안된 보안 규정들은 본사에 있는 전 직원들에게 영향을 미칠 것이다.

effect [ifékt]　　　　　　(변화 등을) 초래하다

The company should not **effect** a change without carefully considering its consequences.

회사는 그 결과를 신중하게 고려하지 않고 변화를 초래해서는 안 된다.

출제포인트　1. '결과, 효과'라는 의미의 명사로도 쓰인다.
　　　　　2. ⓟ effective adj. 효과적인, 유효한

09 note : notice

note [nout]　　　　　　유념하다, 주목하다, 유의하다, 언급하다

The clerk told the customers to **note** that the store would be closed for two days.

점원은 고객들에게 상점이 이틀 동안 문을 닫을 것임을 유념해 달라고 말했다.

출제포인트　note + that절: ~임을 유념하다

notice [nóutis]　　　　　　알아채다, 주목하다

Ms. Riggs **noticed** the printer was broken when it began making a strange noise.

Ms. Riggs는 프린터가 이상한 소리를 내기 시작했을 때 그것이 고장 났음을 알아차렸다.

출제포인트　어떤 것을 보거나 듣고 알게 된 것을 의미한다.

07 lend : loan : borrow : rent

lend [lend]　　　　　　빌려주다, 대출하다

Shopright Program members should not **lend** their discount cards to anyone.

Shopright 프로그램 회원들은 그들의 할인 카드를 누구에게도 빌려주어서는 안 된다.

출제포인트　물건, 돈 등을 빌려주는 것을 의미한다.

loan [loun]　　　　　　대출하다, 빌려주다

The government will **loan** approximately $4 billion to struggling automakers.

정부는 어려움을 겪고 있는 자동차 제조업체들에게 약 40억 달러를 대출해 줄 것이다.

출제포인트　자금 등을 빌려주는 것을 의미한다.

borrow [bárou]　　　　　　빌리다

The city council will **borrow** funds to pay for the redevelopment of the harbor area.

시 의회는 항구 지역의 재개발 대금을 지급하기 위해 자금을 빌릴 것이다.

출제포인트　돈, 물건 등을 빌려오는 것을 의미한다.

rent [rent]　　　　　　(요금을 내고) 빌리다, (요금을 받고) 빌려주다

The firm **rented** several apartments for the overseas representatives to use.

그 회사는 해외 직원들이 사용할 몇 채의 아파트를 빌렸다.

출제포인트　차량이나 집 등을 정기적 요금을 내고 빌리거나, 요금을 받고 빌려주는 것을 의미한다.

10 demonstrate : display

demonstrate [démənstrèit]　　　　　　~을 설명하다, 보여주다, 발휘하다

The talk show host **demonstrated** different ways to dress for success.

토크쇼 진행자는 성공을 위해 옷을 입는 다양한 방법들을 설명했다.

출제포인트　1. 사용법과 같은 것들을 실험 등을 통해서 실제로 해 보인다는 의미이다.
　　　　　2. demonstrate commitment: 헌신적인 태도를 보여주다
　　　　　3. ⓟ demonstration n. 시범 설명, 증명, (감정 등의) 표시

display [displéi]　　　　　　진열하다, 전시하다

A collection of books is **displayed** on the shelf.

도서 모음집이 선반에 진열되어 있다.

출제포인트　사람들이 쉽게 볼 수 있게 물건 등을 진열한다는 의미이다.

11 notify : inform : announce : reveal

notify [nóutəfài]　　　　　　　　　통지하다

Westerland Investments **notified** its shareholders of the proposed merger.

Westerland 투자 회사는 주주들에게 제안된 합병 건에 대해 통지했다.

출제포인트 1. notify 다음에는 듣는 사람이 목적어로 온다.
　　　　　2. notify 사람 of 내용: ~에게 −에 대해 통지하다

inform [infɔ́:rm]　　　　　　　알리다, 통지하다

The manager **informed** the interns of an upcoming policy change.

부장은 인턴들에게 곧 있을 정책 변경에 대해 알렸다.

출제포인트 inform 사람 of/about 내용 : ~에게 −에 대해 알리다

announce [ənáuns]　　　　　발표하다, 알리다

Ms. Wilkins **announced** to her team that the CEO had tendered his resignation.

Ms. Wilkins는 그녀의 팀에게 최고 경영자가 사표를 제출했다는 것을 발표했다.

출제포인트 1. announce 다음에 발표하는 내용이 목적어로 오며 듣는 사람 앞에 전치사 to를 써줘야 한다.
　　　　　2. announce (to 사람) that절: (~에게) −을 발표하다
　　　　　3. unveil(발표하다, 밝히다)도 함께 알아두자.

reveal [riví:l]　　　　　　　밝히다, 누설하다

The company representative **revealed** the release date of the new mobile device to members of the press.

회사 대변인은 새로운 모바일 기기 출시 날짜를 언론에 밝혔다.

출제포인트 1. reveal 다음에 잘 알려져 있지 않던 비밀 등의 내용이 목적어로 오며 듣는 사람 앞에 전치사 to를 써줘야 한다.
　　　　　2. reveal 내용 (to 사람): (~에게) −을 밝히다

12 speak : tell : say : express

speak [spi:k]　　　　　　　　　이야기하다

Mr. Tokuyama will **speak** to the management about production cuts.

Mr. Tokuyama는 경영진에게 생산 감축에 대해 이야기할 것이다.

출제포인트 1. 듣는 사람 앞에 전치사 to를 써줘야 한다.
　　　　　2. speak to 사람 about 내용: ~에게 −에 대해 얘기하다

tell [tel]　　　　　　　　　　~에게 말하다

The supervisor will **tell** the workers about the new safety regulations this afternoon.

관리자는 오늘 오후에 근로자들에게 새로운 안전 규정에 대해 말할 것이다.

출제포인트 1. tell 다음에는 듣는 사람이 목적어로 온다. 듣는 사람 앞에 전치사를 쓰지 않는 것에 유의한다.
　　　　　2. tell 사람 that절 / tell 사람 about 내용: ~에게 −에 대해 말하다

say [sei]　　　　　　　　　　~을 말하다

The reporter **said** to the editor that the information in his article had been verified.

기자는 편집장에게 기사의 정보가 사실임이 입증되었다고 말했다.

출제포인트 1. say 다음에는 말하는 내용이 목적어로 오며 듣는 사람 앞에 전치사 to를 써줘야 한다.
　　　　　2. say (to 사람) that절: (~에게) −을 말하다

express [iksprés]　　　　(감정 · 생각을) 표현하다

The developer has **expressed** concern about purchasing the vacant lot.

그 개발업자는 공터를 매입하는 것에 대한 걱정을 표현했다.

출제포인트 express + 감정, 생각: ~을 표현하다

13 expire : invalidate

expire [ikspáiər]　　　(계약·유효 기간이) 만기가 되다

The motorist was issued a driver's license that will **expire** in four years.

그 운전자는 4년 후에 만기 될 운전 면허증을 발급받았다.

출제포인트 자동사이므로 '계약이 만기가 되다'라는 의미로 쓰일 때 능동태로 사용된다.

invalidate [invǽlədèit]　　　(계약·법을) 무효화하다

The lease was **invalidated** as the landlord did not comply with the agreement terms.

그 임대차 계약은 건물주가 계약 조건을 따르지 않았기 때문에 무효화되었다.

출제포인트 타동사이므로 '계약이 무효화되다'라는 의미로 쓰일 때 수동태로 사용된다.

14 evaluate : estimate

evaluate [ivǽljuèit]　　　　　　　평가하다

The feasibility of the acquisition has not been **evaluated** yet.

그 인수의 실행 가능성은 아직 평가되지 않았다.

estimate [éstəmèit]　　　　　　　예측하다

The total cost of the expansion project was 14 percent higher than originally **estimated**.

확장 프로젝트의 총비용은 원래 예측했던 것보다 14퍼센트 더 많이 들었다.

출제포인트 '견적, 추정'이라는 의미의 명사로도 쓰인다.

HACKERS TEST

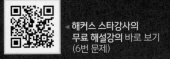

해커스 스타강사의
무료 해설강의 바로 보기
(6번 문제)

제한 시간 10분

Part 5

01 A series of government-sponsored television advertisements aims to ------- healthier food choices as a means of curbing obesity rates.

(A) support
(B) guide
(C) promote
(D) replace

02 In line with company policy, all new employees must first ------- a safety briefing before attempting to operate factory machinery.

(A) participate
(B) register
(C) attend
(D) depart

03 Unless the renegotiation for renewal succeeds, the contractual agreement will ------- at the end of July.

(A) invalidate
(B) expire
(C) violate
(D) submit

04 The contract stipulates that tenants have to ------- the landlord of any major structural changes they wish to make to their apartments.

(A) advance
(B) announce
(C) notify
(D) devise

05 Mr. Kang ------- the supervisor that one of the machines in the factory needed to be serviced.

(A) agreed
(B) told
(C) expressed
(D) directed

06 The Bank of Rhode Island has established a special program to ------- funds at low interest to those who develop local business initiatives.

(A) lend
(B) lease
(C) borrow
(D) rent

07 The potential investor will ------- the proposal to determine whether or not it is a profitable venture.

(A) coordinate
(B) evaluate
(C) estimate
(D) address

08 Customers wishing to ------- in the Central Department Store's reward program should submit an application at the information desk.

(A) enroll
(B) apply
(C) instruct
(D) interview

09 It has become quite common for young people today to ------- marriage until their later years.

(A) appoint
(B) postpone
(C) reschedule
(D) preview

10 On Saturday, a technician from the security company will visit the office to install an alarm and ------- how to activate it.

(A) expose
(B) persuade
(C) display
(D) demonstrate

Part 6

Questions 11-14 refer to the following information.

Top Researcher to Lecture on Solar Power

At the National Conference on Renewable Energy in Atlanta next month, Sunbeam Resources' top researcher, Dr. Robert Flack, will ------- about the technological advances his research facility has
                                                                    11
made in the field of solar power.

Most facilities develop solar panels using synthetic materials. However, Dr. Flack's team -------
                                                                                         12
natural materials that are affordable and easy to access. He will summarize his team's method
in a two-hour presentation. Essentially, Dr. Flack will explain why the availability of materials is a
reason for government leaders to give solar energy their full support. He will also show how solar
energy has evolved into a viable ------- to coal and other non-renewable sources of energy.
                                  13

The conference will take place at the Southern Institute of Technology from November 26 to
December 3. The presentations are repeated daily so as to allow participants to attend the
conference on a day that is convenient for them. Online registration is available until November 15.
-------. After November 15, however, enrollees can only register for the December 3 session.
  14

---

11 (A) note
   (B) speak
   (C) say
   (D) express

12 (A) studies
   (B) utilizes
   (C) secures
   (D) applies

13 (A) alternative
   (B) divergence
   (C) attribute
   (D) motivation

14 (A) Dr. Flack may not be contacted after
       Decemeber due to his research.
   (B) It was postponed to permit those who
       should be present.
   (C) The findings are confidential and cannot be
       disclosed to the public.
   (D) During the enrollment period, you may sign
       up for any day.

CHAPTER 11

유사의미 명사

change와 coin의 차이를 모르면 몸이 고생한다.

물건을 사고 거스름돈을 받아야 하는데 change(거스름돈)와 coin(동전)의 차이를 몰라 그냥 coin(동전)을 달라고 한다면? 거스름돈을 모두 동전으로 받아 양손 가득 힘들게 들고 가야 할 수도 있다. 물론 이렇게 직접 부딪쳐서 배우면 절대 까먹을 일은 없겠으나 몸이 너무 고생스러우니 이 장에 모아 놓은 뜻이 비슷한 명사들을 미리미리 익혀 두자.

출제 유형 및 전략

보기에 나온 명사들의 뜻이 비슷하기 때문에 정확한 쓰임의 차이를 알아야 답을 고를 수 있는 문제로 출제된다.

예제

Part 5

The research department's annual plan reflects the most basic ------- of the company, which is developing products that consumers need.

(A) aim (B) opinion (C) reason (D) category

해설 언뜻 보기에 네 개의 단어가 모두 답이 될 수 있을 것 같지만 문맥상 쓰임이 맞는 단어는 하나뿐이다. '회사의 기본적인 목표'라는 의미가 되어야 하므로 빈칸에는 명사 (A) aim(목표)이 정답이다. (aim of: ~의 목표) (B) opinion은 '의견', (C) reason은 '원인'(reason for: ~의 원인), (D) category는 '범주'라는 뜻이다.

해석 연구부의 연간 계획은 회사의 가장 기본적인 목표를 반영하는데, 이는 소비자들이 필요로 하는 제품들을 개발하는 것이다.

어휘 **annual** adj. 연간의 / **reflect** v. 반영하다

정답 (A)

Part 6

Now into her second year as Mayor of Detroit, Francine Menendez outlined pending improvements to the city's infrastructure. First on her list is the civic ------- of the Lakeside Precinct, which includes the conversion of an abandoned dock area into recreational parklands and the construction of a two-mile long pedestrian boardwalk with cafés and restaurants.

(A) refreshment (B) progress (C) renewal (D) structure

해설 빈칸이 있는 문장의 주변 문맥을 파악하여 정답을 고르는 문제이다. 앞 문장에서 시장이 곧 있을 개수 공사의 요점을 말했다고 했으므로 빈칸에는 이와 관련된 어휘가 필요하다. (A)와 (C) 모두 '새롭게 하다'라는 개념이어서 쓰임이 헷갈릴 수 있지만, 문맥상 빈칸에는 '재개발, 갱신'의 뜻을 가진 (C) renewal이 적합하다. (civic renewal: 도시 재개발) (A) refreshment는 '기분을 상쾌하게 함, 간식'이란 뜻이다. (B) progress는 '진보', (D) structure는 '구조'를 의미한다.

해석 디트로이트 시장으로서 현재 두 번째 해에 접어든 Francine Menendez는 곧 있을 시의 공공 기반 시설 개수 공사의 요점을 말했습니다. 그녀의 목록에 있는 첫 번째 사항은 Lakeside 구역의 도시 재개발인데, 이는 황폐한 부두 지역을 휴양 공원 지대로 개조하는 것과 카페 및 식당을 갖춘 2마일 길이의 보행자 산책로를 건설하는 것을 포함합니다.

어휘 **outline** v. ~의 요점을 말하다, 약술하다 / **pending** adj. 곧 있을, 임박한, 미결정의 / **improvement** n. 개수 공사, 개선 /
infrastructure n. 공공 기반 시설 (교통·수도·전기 따위 시설) / **civic** adj. 도시의, 시민의 / **precinct** n. (행정상의) 구역 / **conversion** n. 개조, 전환 /
abandoned adj. 황폐한, 버려진 / **dock** n. 부두 / **parkland** n. 공원 지대 / **pedestrian** n. 보행자

정답 (C)

01 proportion : size : volume

proportion [prəpɔ́:rʃən] 부분, 비율, 비

A small **proportion** of the company's profits are donated to local charities.

회사 수익의 적은 부분은 지역 자선 단체에 기부된다.

> **출제포인트** 전체에 대한 일부분의 수, 양, 크기를 나타내거나, 서로 다른 두 부분의 수나 양의 비율을 나타낸다.

size [saiz] 크기, 치수

Because of the small **size** of the auditorium, the gathering will be held at another location.

강당의 작은 크기 때문에, 모임은 다른 장소에서 열릴 것이다.

> **출제포인트** 사물의 크고 작음을 나타낸다.

volume [válju:m] 양, 용량, 용적

The human resources department has received a large **volume** of applications for the job.

인사부는 그 직무를 위한 많은 양의 지원서를 받았다.

> **출제포인트** 1. high volume of: 다량의 ~
> 2. 부피나 용량을 나타낸다.

03 enhancement : increment

enhancement [inhǽnsmənt] (가치·가격 등의) 향상, 증대, 상승

Nero Air has announced that it will be making **enhancements** to its rewards program.

Nero 항공사는 자사의 보상 프로그램을 향상시킬 것이라고 발표했다.

increment [íŋkrəmənt] (수·양의) 증가, 증대, 임금 인상

During the experiment, the substance was added to the liquid in small **increments**.

실험 중에 그 물질은 소량씩 증가되어 액체에 첨가되었다.

02 access : approach

access [ǽkses] 접근 권한, 통로

Only registered students have **access** to the university's fitness center.

오직 등록된 학생들만이 대학교 헬스클럽에 대한 접근 권한이 있다.

Access to the exhibit hall can be found on the third floor.

전시실로 이어지는 통로는 3층에서 찾을 수 있다.

> **출제포인트** 1. '접근 권한, 통로'라는 의미 둘 다 출제되며 불가산 명사이다.
> 2. have access to: ~에 대한 접근 권한이 있다, ~로 이어지는 길이 있다

approach [əpróutʃ] (문제 등에의) 접근법, 출입로

The manager tried a unique **approach** to solving communication problems.

그 관리자는 의사소통 문제들을 해결하는 것에 대한 독특한 접근법을 시도했다.

The narrow alley is a rarely used **approach** to the office building.

그 좁은 길은 사무실 건물로의 잘 사용되지 않는 출입로이다.

> **출제포인트** '(문제 등에의) 접근법'이라는 의미이다. access와 같이 '출입로'라는 의미도 가지고 있지만 approach는 가산 명사이므로 부정관사를 써줘야 하는 차이가 있다.

04 choice : option : preference

choice [tʃɔis] 선택, 선택권

Passengers are given a **choice** of beef or fish for their meals.

탑승객들은 식사로 소고기나 생선 중 선택한 것을 받게 된다.

option [ápʃən] 선택권

Customers are provided the **option** of using plastic or paper bags.

고객들에게는 비닐봉지와 종이 쇼핑백 중 선택권이 제공된다.

> **출제포인트** 여러 가지 중에 가능한 선택 사항을 의미한다.

preference [préfərəns] 선호

Attendees can state their seating **preference** when registering for the conference.

참석자들은 회의에 등록할 때 좌석 선호도를 명시할 수 있다.

05 explanation : direction

explanation [èksplənéiʃən] 설명, 해명

The supervisor gave his team an **explanation** of the new evaluation policy.

그 감독관은 그의 팀원들에게 새로운 평가 방침에 대한 설명을 전달했다.

direction [dirékʃən] 지침, 지시, 방향, 감독

Directions for the proper usage of the software are included in the manual.

소프트웨어의 올바른 사용법에 관한 지침은 설명서에 포함되어 있다.

> **출제포인트** 지침, 지시의 의미로 쓰일 때는 주로 복수형으로 쓰인다.

06 division : department : category

division [divíʒən] (회사의) 부서

The company has discussed closing the unprofitable pharmaceutical **division**.

회사는 수익을 내지 못하는 제약 부서를 폐지하는 것에 대해 논의해 왔다.

department [dipá:rtmənt] 부, 부서

Members of the personnel **department** will be attending a meeting next week.

인사부 직원들은 다음 주에 회의에 참석할 것이다.

category [kǽtəgɔ̀:ri] 종류, 부문

The Web site provides information on the different **categories** of hurricanes.

그 웹사이트는 여러 종류의 태풍에 대한 정보를 제공한다.

08 charge : fare : fee

charge [tʃɑ:rdʒ] (상품·서비스에 대한) 요금, 비용

Bank clients can ask to be notified whenever **charges** are made to their accounts.

은행 고객들은 요금이 자신들의 계좌로 청구될 때마다 통보받도록 요청할 수 있다.

출제포인트 1. additional charge: 추가 요금   shipping charge: 배송비
2. '요금 등을 청구하다'라는 의미의 동사로도 사용된다.

fare [fɛər] (교통) 요금

The driver estimated that cab **fare** to the airport would be $40.

그 운전기사는 공항까지의 택시 요금이 40달러일 것으로 예측했다.

fee [fi:] (조직·기관 등에 내는) 요금

Children under the age of eight receive a 50 percent discount on the admission **fee**.

8세 미만의 어린이는 입장료에 대해 50퍼센트의 할인을 받는다.

출제포인트 admission fee: 입장료   membership fee: 회비

10 area : site

area [ɛ́əriə] 지역

There is only one caterer in the **area** that offers vegetarian food.

그 지역에서 채식주의자를 위한 음식을 제공하는 음식 공급사는 하나뿐이다.

site [sait] (건축용) 대지

The **site** for the new park is located near the city museum.

새로운 공원을 위한 대지는 시립 박물관 근처에 위치해 있다.

출제포인트 특정 목적을 위해 사용되는 땅을 의미한다.

07 fine : tariff : expense

fine [fain] 벌금

Anyone who leaves a vehicle in a no-parking area will have to pay a **fine**.

주차 금지 지역에 차량을 두고 가는 사람은 누구든지 벌금을 내야 할 것이다.

출제포인트 penalty와 의미가 같다.

tariff [tǽrif] 관세

Tariffs are paid on luxury goods from foreign countries.

관세는 외국에서 온 사치품에 대해 납부된다.

출제포인트 세관을 통과하는 물품에 대해 부과하는 세금을 의미한다.

expense [ikspéns] 비용, 지출

The **expense** of purchasing top-of-the-line equipment is greater than expected.

최신식 장비의 구매 비용은 예상보다 훨씬 크다.

출제포인트 cost, expenditure와 의미가 같다.

09 survey : research

survey [sə́:rvei] 설문 조사

The marketing department conducted a **survey** of workshop participants.

마케팅부는 워크숍 참가자들을 대상으로 설문 조사를 실시했다.

출제포인트 1. 사람들의 설문을 통해 정보를 알아내는 표본 조사를 의미한다.
2. conduct a survey: 설문 조사를 실시하다

research [rí:sə:rtʃ] 연구, 학술 조사

The client was unhappy with the **research**, as it seemed incomplete.

의뢰인은 그 연구에 불만족스러웠는데, 이는 연구가 불충분해 보였기 때문이다.

출제포인트 특정 사실을 규명하려 노력하는 연구를 의미한다.

11 residence : venue

residence [rézədəns] 주택, 거주지

Delegates are invited to visit the official **residence** of the Prime Minister.

대표자들은 총리의 관저를 방문하도록 초대된다.

venue [vénju:] (행사·회의 등의) 회합 장소, 개최 예정지

Event coordinators selected the Greyson Exhibition Hall as the official **venue**.

행사 진행자들은 Greyson 전시장을 공식 회합 장소로 선정했다.

출제포인트 행사나 특정 활동이 이루어지는 장소를 의미한다.

12 brochure : catalog

brochure [brouʃúər]　　　　　　　소책자, 팸플릿

Guests may look at the enclosed **brochure** for information on the hotel suites.
투숙객들은 호텔 스위트룸에 관한 정보를 위해 동봉된 소책자를 볼 수 있다.

출제포인트 1. 상품이나 서비스를 사진 등과 함께 소개하는 소책자를 의미한다.
2. travel brochure: 여행 안내 책자

catalog [kǽtəlɔːg]　　　　　카탈로그, (물품·책 등의) 목록

Catalogs are sent out to consumers in October, prior to the holiday shopping season.
명절 쇼핑 시즌에 앞서, 카탈로그는 10월에 소비자들에게 발송된다.

출제포인트 1. 물품 구입 시 참고하는 상품의 목록, 혹은 박물관이나 도서관의 물품 목록을 의미한다.
2. apparel catalog: 의류 카탈로그
exhibition catalog: 전시회 카탈로그

13 description : information

description [diskrípʃən]　　　(제품 등의) 설명(서), 해설

The pamphlet contains complete **descriptions** of all services.
팸플릿은 모든 서비스에 대한 완전한 설명을 포함한다.

출제포인트 1. 서면상으로 제공되는 설명이나 해설을 의미할 때 쓰는 가산 명사이다.
2. a description of: ~에 대한 설명

information [ìnfərméiʃən]　　　　　　　　정보

For **information** on the agency's special promotions, visit its Web site.
대리점의 특별 판촉 상품에 대한 정보를 위해서, 대리점 웹사이트를 방문하십시오.

출제포인트 1. 불가산 명사이므로 부정관사 an을 쓸 수 없다.
2. information on/about: ~에 대한 정보

14 indication : show

indication [ìndikéiʃən]　　　(~을 암시하는) 징후, 표시

There are clear **indications** that the economy is beginning to turn around.
경기가 회복되기 시작하고 있음을 암시하는 확실한 징후가 있다.

출제포인트 상황이나 생각이 암시적으로 드러날 때 쓴다. that절이나 of와 함께 사용된다.

show [ʃou]　　　　　　(감정·성능 등의) 표시, 과시

In a **show** of support, the mayor endorsed the development project.
지지의 표시로써, 시장은 그 개발 프로젝트를 찬성했다.

출제포인트 1. 의도적으로 감정 등을 표시하는 경우에 쓴다.
2. a show of affection: 호의의 표시

15 view : sight

view [vjuː]　　　　　　　전망, 경관, 견해

The restaurant offers diners a **view** of the entire city thanks to its location at the top of the BW Tower.
레스토랑이 BW 타워의 맨 꼭대기에 위치한 덕분에, 그곳은 식사하는 손님들에게 도시 전체의 전망을 제공한다.

출제포인트 특정한 위치나 상황에서 볼 수 있는 것을 의미한다.

sight [sait]　　　　　　시야, 풍경, 명소

The train came into **sight** as it exited the tunnel.
기차가 터널을 빠져나오면서 시야에 들어왔다.

출제포인트 눈으로 볼 수 있는 대상이나 범위에 관해 이야기할 때 사용한다.

16 material : ingredient

material [mətíəriəl]　　　　(물건의) 재료, 물질, 자료

The fashion firm needs to purchase **material** for its upcoming collection.
그 패션 회사는 이번 신상품들을 위한 재료를 구매해야 한다.

출제포인트 promotional material 홍보 자료

ingredient [ingríːdiənt]　　　재료, (혼합물의) 성분

This beverage contains only natural **ingredients**.
이 음료수는 오직 천연 재료들만 함유하고 있습니다.

출제포인트 1. 음식의 재료, 혼합물을 이루고 있는 성분 등을 말한다.
2. the ingredients of a cake: 케이크의 재료

17 value : worth

value [vǽljuː]　　　　　(물건의) 값어치, 가격

The **value** of gold and other precious metals has recently been on the rise.
금과 그 밖의 귀금속들의 값어치가 최근 오름세에 있다.

출제포인트 물건의 가치에 상당하는 값을 의미한다.

worth [wəːrθ]　　　　　(얼마)어치, (물건의) 값어치

The winners were provided with a gift basket containing $300 **worth** of local delicacies.
우승자들은 300달러어치의 지역 별미들을 담고 있는 선물 바구니를 받았다.

출제포인트 가격 + worth of + 물건: ~어치의 물건

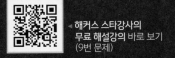
🕐 제한 시간 10분

Part 5

01 Extra luggage may be checked for an additional ------- of $50 per bag.

(A) fare
(B) toll
(C) charge
(D) estimate

02 A report in a recent issue of the business journal stated that there was an increasing ------- for online payment services among consumers.

(A) choice
(B) preference
(C) reaction
(D) promotion

03 Mr. Powell, the new consultant, has requested ------- to the company's archives to retrieve the information he needs for a feasibility study.

(A) pass
(B) access
(C) entrance
(D) approach

04 The laboratory's ------- findings show that the new line of cosmetics for Dawson Beauty Products is environmentally friendly.

(A) survey
(B) response
(C) question
(D) research

05 A significant ------- of the space in the new wing of the hospital will be used as care facilities for new mothers and infants.

(A) size
(B) content
(C) proportion
(D) number

06 At the start of the orientation, the instructor gave new staff a clear ------- of what they would learn throughout the week.

(A) direction
(B) suggestion
(C) explanation
(D) recommendation

07 Chemtech Manufacturers' catalog provides a detailed ------- of the equipment, tools and instruments used in chemical plants.

(A) information
(B) description
(C) inquiry
(D) confirmation

08 The goal of the new public relations campaign is the ------- of the company's reputation.

(A) increment
(B) comparison
(C) disruption
(D) enhancement

09 All of the hotel's guests are given a welcome packet which contains $200 ------- of coupons and vouchers for local restaurants and attractions.

(A) class
(B) value
(C) credit
(D) worth

10 Current market trends are an excellent ------- of which particular sectors are good investment opportunities.

(A) account
(B) show
(C) indication
(D) condition

Part 6

Questions 11-14 refer to the following letter.

Mark Walter

52 Southern Avenue

Great Falls, Montana 86503

Dear Mr. Walter,

I am writing to inform you that we've had ------- with the air-conditioning units in our office. I
11
contacted Coolair Corporation two weeks ago, and they sent a technician to make the necessary
repairs.

The work was done at considerable -------, as several components in each unit were damaged
12
and had to be replaced. According to the technician, the units were not properly set up by the
maintenance crew. Because the air conditioners were damaged during installation, Coolair refused
to take responsibility for the malfunction, which means that we were forced to pay for the repairs
ourselves.

I have enclosed an itemized invoice showing that the total cost of the repairs came to $785, with
$365 for ------- and $420 for labor. Our lease states that such costs are covered by the owner of the
13
building. -------. We would, therefore, appreciate it if we could be reimbursed as soon as possible for
14
the full amount.

Sincerely,

Molly Davison

---

11 (A) success
(B) issues
(C) satisfaction
(D) requests

12 (A) tariff
(B) penalty
(C) expense
(D) fine

13 (A) ingredients
(B) stationery
(C) supplements
(D) materials

14 (A) Our company believes we were
overcharged for repairs.
(B) It is appropriate for us to ask for
compensation.
(C) We have not paid for the repairs yet.
(D) The technician could not determine the
cause of the breakdown.

해커스 스타강사의 ▶
무료 해설강의 바로 보기
(9번 문제)

CHAPTER 12

유사의미 형용사 · 부사

explicitly와 markedly는 어떻게 다른가?

'명확하게 명시하다'는 영어로 'explicitly state'라고 한다. 그런데 보기에 explicitly(명확하게)와 markedly(뚜렷하게, 현저하게)가 같이 나오면 무엇을 골라야 할지 헷갈리고 만다. 사실 markedly는 '수치나 정도의 차이가 뚜렷하다'라는 뜻으로 쓴다고 하니, 뜻이 비슷한 단어는 쓰임을 정확히 익히는 사람만이 승자가 된다는 것을 잊지 말자.

토익 출제 유형 및 전략

보기에 나온 형용사, 부사들의 뜻이 비슷하기 때문에 정확한 쓰임의 차이를 알아야 답을 고를 수 있는 문제로 출제된다.

예제

Part 5

It is clearly stated in the airline's policy that ------- baggage is in no way the responsibility of the company.

(A) traumatized   (B) damaged   (C) impaired   (D) disabled

해설   보기에 있는 네 개의 단어가 모두 뜻이 비슷해 보이지만 쓰임은 다르다. baggage(짐)와 같은 사물이 손상되었을 때는 (B) damaged '(사물이) 손상된'이 적합하다. (A) traumatized는 '(정신적으로) 충격을 받은' (psychologically traumatized: 정신적으로 큰 충격을 받은), (C) impaired는 '(사람·사물의 기능이) 손상된' (visually impaired: 시각적 기능이 손상된), (D) disabled는 '장애를 가진'이란 뜻이다. (the disabled: 장애인)

해석   손상된 짐은 결코 회사 책임이 아니라는 것이 항공사 규정에 분명히 명시되어 있다.

어휘   **clearly** adv. 분명히 / **in no way** 결코 ~ 않다

정답   (B)

Part 6

Mr. Ramirez is scheduled to address the media about the merger at Wakefield Hotel at 9:00 A.M. He will have a brief meeting with Mr. Ross of Sanford Manufacturing at 10 o'clock, and then head to the airport shortly ------- for a conference in Washington, D.C.

(A) later   (B) already   (C) suddenly   (D) thereafter

해설   'later: 나중에'와 'thereafter: 그 후에'처럼 한글로만 외워두면 헷갈리는 부사들이 보기로 출제되었다. '미팅을 가진 후에 곧바로 회의를 위해 공항으로 향할 것이다'라는 문맥이므로 빈칸 앞의 shortly(곧바로)와 함께 쓰여 '그 후에'라는 뜻을 갖는 부사 (D) thereafter가 정답이다. (shortly thereafter: 그 후에 곧바로) (A) later는 말하는 시점보다 '나중에'라는 뜻이다. (two months later: 2달 후에) (B) already는 '이미, 벌써', (C) suddenly는 '갑자기'라는 의미이다.

해석   Mr. Ramirez는 오전 9시에 Wakefield 호텔에서 합병에 대해 언론 매체에 연설할 예정이다. 그는 10시에 Sanford 제조 회사의 Mr. Ross와 간단한 미팅을 가질 것이고, 그 후에 곧바로 워싱턴에서 있을 회의를 위해 공항으로 향할 것이다.

어휘   **address** v. ~에게 연설하다 / **merger** n. 합병 / **brief** adj. 간단한

정답   (D)

01 attached : connected

attached [ətǽtʃt]
첨부된, 부가적으로 붙은

The **attached** itinerary may be subject to change.

첨부된 여행 일정표는 변경의 대상이 될 수 있다.

출제포인트 1. 서류나 파일 등이 첨부되는 경우에 사용한다.
　　　　　　2. attached file: 첨부 파일

connected [kənéktid]
연결된

Greenacre Farms is **connected** to the nearest town by a narrow dirt road.

Greenacre 농장은 좁은 비포장도로를 통해 가장 가까운 마을과 연결되어 있다.

출제포인트 서로 대등한 두 개가 관계상으로 혹은 물리적으로 연결될 때 쓰인다.

02 early : previous

early [ə́ːrli]
조기의, (시간상) 이른

Early predictions indicate sales will increase.

조기 예측은 매출이 증가할 것임을 나타낸다.

출제포인트 1. 시간상 보통보다 이르다는 의미이다.
　　　　　　2. early retirement: 조기 퇴직

previous [príːviəs]
(시간상) 이전의

Previous work experience should be listed in the application.

이전 근무 경력은 지원서에 열거되어야 한다.

출제포인트 지금보다 이전에 일어난 일이나 시간을 말할 때 사용한다.

03 following : next

following [fálouiŋ]
(시간상으로) 그 다음의

An open discussion on recent development will be held during the **following** week.

최근의 개발에 대한 공개 토론이 그 다음 주 동안 열릴 것이다.

출제포인트 1. 형용사 following은 'the following + 명사'로 쓰인다.
　　　　　　2. following이 전치사일 경우에는 정관사 the를 취하지 않는다.

next [nekst]
(바로) 다음의

Next June, Tokeda Industries will begin construction of a power plant in Okinawa.

다음 6월에, Tokeda사는 오키나와에서 발전소 건설을 시작할 것이다.

출제포인트 next는 현재를 기준으로 바로 '다음의'라는 의미이며 정관사 the를 취하지 않는다.

04 likely : possible

likely [láikli]
~할 것 같은, 있음 직한

The candidate Mr. Perez interviewed yesterday is **likely** to be hired.

어제 Mr. Perez가 면접 본 후보자가 채용될 것 같다.

출제포인트 1. 어떤 일이 일어날 가능성이 높다는 의미이다.
　　　　　　2. be likely to + 동사원형: ~할 것 같다
　　　　　　3. ® likelihood n. 있음 직함, 가능성

possible [pásəbl]
가능한, 실행할 수 있는

It is **possible** that power outages will occur as a result of the hurricane.

태풍의 결과로 정전이 일어나는 것은 가능하다.

출제포인트 1. 실행 가능한 일을 말할 때 사용한다.
　　　　　　2. It is possible to + 동사원형: ~하는 것이 가능하다

05 extensive : spacious

extensive [iksténsiv]
광범위한, 폭넓은, 포괄적인

Located in the Napa Valley, Grigio Vintres produces an **extensive** variety of quality wines.

나파 밸리에 위치한, Grigio Vintres사는 광범위한 종류의 고급 와인을 생산한다.

출제포인트 1. 지식이나 품목들이 포괄적으로 많은 종류를 포함한다는 의미이다. 건물 등이 광범위한 장소에 걸쳐 위치하는 경우에도 사용한다.
　　　　　　2. ® extend v. 확장하다, 연장하다   extensively adv. 널리   extension n. 확장, 연장   extent n. 정도, 규모

spacious [spéiʃəs]
(장소가) 넓은

The firm provides each executive with a **spacious** office that overlooks the harbor.

그 회사는 각 임원에게 항구가 내려다보이는 넓은 사무실을 제공한다.

출제포인트 roomy와 의미가 같다.

06 apparent : visible

apparent [əpǽrənt]
명백한, 분명한

In spite of the **apparent** recession, sales of automobiles rose this year.

명백한 불경기임에도 불구하고, 올해의 자동차 판매량은 증가했다.

출제포인트 상황, 사실, 품질, 감정 등이 확실해졌음을 나타낼 때 사용한다.

visible [vízəbl]
눈에 보이는, 명확한

A solar eclipse will be **visible** on July 14 for people living in the Southern Hemisphere.

일식은 7월 14일에 남반구에 사는 사람들에게 보일 것이다.

출제포인트 직접적으로 보아 감지할 수 있는 사물 또는 사람을 나타낼 때 사용한다.

07 outstanding : evident

outstanding [àutstǽndiŋ]　　　뛰어난, 눈에 띄는, 미결제된

Teslak's latest cell phone model includes several **outstanding** features.

Teslak사의 최신 휴대폰 모델은 몇 가지 뛰어난 기능들을 포함한다.

> **출제포인트**　1. 사물이나 사람이 눈에 띄게 우수하다는 의미이다. 이외에 부채 등이 미결제된 경우에도 사용된다.
> 　　　　　2. outstanding account: 미결제 계좌

evident [évədənt]　　　명백한

It is **evident** that more people today get news updates online.

오늘날 더 많은 사람들이 온라인으로 최신 뉴스 정보를 얻는다는 것은 명백하다.

> **출제포인트**　사실 등이 외적으로 명백히 드러나 보일 때 사용한다.

09 unoccupied : vacant : blank

unoccupied [ʌ̀nάkjupaid]　　　비어 있는

Many of the hotel rooms are **unoccupied** during the winter.

호텔 객실들 중 다수는 겨울 동안에 비어 있다.

> **출제포인트**　1. 사람이 살지 않거나 이용하지 않아서 비어 있는 상태를 나타낸다.
> 　　　　　2. empty와 의미가 같다.

vacant [véikənt]　　　비어 있는, 사람이 없는

If there are no **vacant** spots remaining, guests may park their vehicles in the lot across the street.

남아있는 빈 자리가 없다면, 고객들은 길 건너편에 있는 부지에 주차해도 된다.

> **출제포인트**　자리·집 등이 비어 있거나, 직책·지위 따위가 공석인 경우에 주로 사용한다.

blank [blæŋk]　　　공백의, 비어 있는, 공허한

Ms. Maugham left the comment section **blank** because she had no suggestions.

Ms. Maugham은 제안 사항이 없었기 때문에 의견란을 공백으로 두었다.

> **출제포인트**　종이나 벽 등이 공백으로 있는 경우에 주로 사용한다.

10 strongly : stringently

strongly [strɔ́:ŋli]　　　강력히

The proposal to renovate the public library was **strongly** supported by local residents.

공공 도서관을 수리하자는 제안서는 지역 주민들에 의해 강력히 지지받았다.

> **출제포인트**　정도가 강력한 것을 의미한다.

stringently [stríndʒəntli]　　　엄격하게

Food additives must be **stringently** tested to ensure that they are suitable for consumption.

식품 첨가물은 섭취에 적합한지 확실히 하기 위해 엄격하게 검사되어야 한다.

> **출제포인트**　1. 법이나 규칙 등이 엄격한 것을 의미한다.
> 　　　　　2. strictly와 의미가 같다.

08 recent : current : modern : contemporary

recent [ríːsnt]　　　최근의

Noted geneticist Derek Bernier will discuss his **recent** research at the conference.

저명한 유전학자 Derek Bernier는 그의 최근 연구를 학회에서 논의할 것이다.

> **출제포인트**　1. 최근의 사건이나 시간을 말할 때, 사물이 최근 것일 때 사용한다.
> 　　　　　2. recent event: 최근의 사건
> 　　　　　　 recent address: 최근 주소
> 　　　　　3. 倒 recently　adv. 최근에

current [kə́:rənt]　　　현재의, 지금의

Duray Incorporated is planning an expansion of its **current** operations to increase productivity.

Duray사는 생산성을 증가시키기 위해 현재 사업의 확장을 계획하고 있다.

> **출제포인트**　1. 현재 일어나는 일이나 상태를 말할 때 사용한다.
> 　　　　　2. current news: 시사뉴스
> 　　　　　　 current employees: 현재 직원들
> 　　　　　3. 倒 currently adv. 현재, 일반적으로

modern [mάdərn]　　　현대의, 근대의

D-Core Technologies opened a **modern** manufacturing facility in Portland.

D-Core Technologies사는 포틀랜드에 현대식 생산 공장을 열었다.

> **출제포인트**　현재 존재하며 이전의 것과 다른 것을 의미한다.

contemporary [kəntémpərèri]　　　현대의, 당대의

The works of **contemporary** artists are displayed at the Denver Art Gallery.

현대 예술가들의 작품이 덴버 미술관에 전시되어 있다.

> **출제포인트**　현재와 관련되거나 최신의 것을 의미한다.

11 prevalent : leading

prevalent [prévələnt]　　　일반적인, 널리 퍼진

Lawsuits have become more **prevalent** in today's society.

오늘날의 사회에서 법률 소송은 더욱 일반적이게 되었다.

> **출제포인트**　현상 등이 널리 퍼져 유행한다는 의미이며 common과 의미가 같다.

leading [líːdiŋ]　　　뛰어난, 유력한

The speaker for the engineering symposium is a **leading** figure in robotic research.

공학 학술 토론회의 연설자는 로봇 연구 분야에서 뛰어난 인물이다.

> **출제포인트**　1. 사람이나 사물이 일정 분야에서 뛰어나다는 의미이다.
> 　　　　　2. leading distributor: 일류 유통 회사

12 sizable : plenty

sizable [sáizəbl]
꽤 많은, 상당한 크기의

An anonymous person has made a **sizable** donation to the hospital.

익명의 사람이 병원에 꽤 많은 기부금을 냈다.

출제포인트 '크기가 ~한'이라는 뜻으로 사용되는 sized와 구별하여 알아 둔다.

plenty [plénti]
많은, 충분한

The staff have cleaned **plenty** more rooms at the Fernando Hotel this morning.

직원들은 오늘 아침 Fernando 호텔의 더 많은 객실들을 청소했다.

출제포인트 plenty of ~: 많은 양의

13 prominently : markedly : explicitly

prominently [prámənəntli]
두드러지게, 주목을 끌게

The advertisement was **prominently** located at the entrance.

그 광고는 입구에 두드러지게 위치해 있었다.

출제포인트 어떤 사물이 두드러지게 주목을 끌 때 사용한다.

markedly [má:rkidli]
현저하게, 두드러지게

Employee morale has **markedly** improved with the introduction of the new evaluation system.

직원들의 사기는 새로운 평가 체계의 도입으로 현저하게 향상되었다.

출제포인트 1. 두드러지게 변화하거나 차이가 생기는 경우에 사용한다.
2. be markedly different: 현저하게 다르다
change markedly: 현저하게 변화하다

explicitly [iksplísitli]
명확하게, 분명히

The letter **explicitly** states the CEO's opinion regarding the property sale.

그 편지는 재산 매각에 관한 최고 경영자의 의견을 명확하게 명시하고 있다.

출제포인트 숨김없이 명확하고, 분명하게 표현하거나 보여줄 경우에 사용한다.

14 away : far

away [əwéi]
(어떤 장소에서) 떨어져, 멀리

The business center is only 500 meters **away** from the Bellevue Hotel.

상업 지구는 Bellevue 호텔에서 단지 500미터 떨어져 있다.

출제포인트 1. away 앞에 거리 단위를 사용할 수 있다.
2. 100 miles away from: ~로부터 100마일 떨어져

far [fɑːr]
(거리·공간이) 멀리

The house is set **far** back from the street to ensure privacy.

그 집은 사생활을 보장하기 위해 거리로부터 멀리 떨어져 위치해 있다.

출제포인트 far 앞에 거리 단위를 사용할 수가 없으므로 'be located 10 miles far from the airport'라고 쓰면 틀린 표현이 된다.

15 primarily : firstly

primarily [praimérəli]
주로, 근본적으로

The new laptop computers are **primarily** marketed to business users.

새 노트북 컴퓨터들은 주로 업무용 사용자들을 대상으로 시장에서 판매된다.

출제포인트 1. 근본적이고 주된 목적, 내용을 말할 때 사용한다.
2. chiefly, mainly와 의미가 같다.
3. 파 primary adj. 주요한, 첫째의

firstly [fə́:rstli]
우선, 첫째로

Firstly, the graphic artist will present a number of options for the new logo design.

우선, 그래픽 아티스트는 새로운 로고 디자인에 대해 많은 선택권을 제시할 것이다.

출제포인트 1. 여러 개를 열거할 때 사용한다.
2. in the first place와 의미가 같다.

16 continually : lastingly

continually [kəntínjuəli]
계속해서

The new manager is **continually** giving orders to the staff.

새 관리자는 직원들에게 계속해서 지시 사항을 내리고 있다.

출제포인트 어떤 일이 발생했다 멈췄다 하며 거듭해서 계속 일어날 때 사용한다.

lastingly [læstiŋli]
지속적으로

Sarah was **lastingly** affected by the motivational speaker's words.

Sarah는 동기를 부여하는 연설가의 말에 지속적으로 영향을 받았다.

출제포인트 효과 등이 오랫동안 유지되는 것을 의미한다.

17 dramatically : numerously

dramatically [drəmǽtikəli]
급격히, 극적으로

Corporate tax rates have **dramatically** declined over the past three years.

법인세율은 지난 3년 동안 급격히 감소해 왔다.

출제포인트 1. 감소/증가 동사(decrease/increase 등)와 쓰여 양의 변화를 나타낸다.
2. sharply(급격히, 격렬하게), drastically(급격히, 엄청나게)도 함께 알아 두자.

numerously [njú:mərəsli]
수없이 많이, 다수로

Governor Richards has stated **numerously** that he will not run for reelection.

주지사 Richards는 재선에 출마하지 않을 것이라고 수없이 많이 말해 왔다.

출제포인트 수나 양이 많은 것을 의미한다.

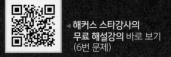
🕐 제한 시간 10분

Part 5

01 Because the candidate struggled to answer even the most basic questions, it was ------- that she lacked technological knowledge.

(A) apparent
(B) visible
(C) substantial
(D) notable

02 The position of in-house consultant was vacated when Mr. Lewis retired and continues to be -------.

(A) unoccupied
(B) disguised
(C) interrupted
(D) discarded

03 People used to carry compact disk players in their bags and backpacks, but nowadays, tiny devices for playing digital files are more -------.

(A) leading
(B) prevalent
(C) natural
(D) precedent

04 The new surveillance system allows virtually every part of the facility to be ------- monitored by security staff.

(A) everlastingly
(B) lastingly
(C) continually
(D) stirringly

05 Despite the Emperor Hotel's winter promotion, many of its rooms have remained ------- this week.

(A) resistant
(B) vacant
(C) blank
(D) ongoing

06 The security personnel ------- follow regulations on barring unauthorized people from entering the building.

(A) stringently
(B) objectively
(C) strongly
(D) evenly

07 A ------- drop in the company's stock price provided investors with an opportunity to purchase additional shares at a lower cost.

(A) stable
(B) modern
(C) recent
(D) casual

08 Jerry Mathers, the personnel director at Cleaver Financial Group, will conduct interviews for the accounting position ------- week.

(A) following
(B) next
(C) before
(D) later

09 Mr. Patrick, a freelance writer, has been writing ------- on trends in the global economy for several of financial magazines.

(A) firstly
(B) completely
(C) primarily
(D) categorically

10 Due to an unexpected illness, Tom Walton was forced to submit a letter announcing his ------- resignation.

(A) overdue
(B) early
(C) active
(D) previous

Part 6

Questions 11-14 refer to the following memo.

From: Human resources
To: All staff
Subject: New health care scheme
Date: July 6

As part of the company's efforts to provide medical support to its employees, the human resources department is pleased to ------- a new health care scheme that will be implemented from August 1.
11

After ------- consultation with employees, we have put together a comprehensive health package
12
that includes benefits that were not part of the previous insurance program, such as full optical and dental care. For more details, please refer to the new employee manual that was distributed this morning. -------. If you haven't yet received your copy, everything you need to know is available on
13
our Web site.

As the cost of the coverage will be shared by employees, a monthly salary deduction will be made automatically. We encourage you to send any ------- you might have about this to Zoe Kazan in
14
human resources. She will do her best to answer them as thoroughly as possible.

11 (A) review
(B) announce
(C) appreciate
(D) notify

12 (A) spacious
(B) preoccupied
(C) extensive
(D) hesitant

13 (A) Our corporate Web site fully explains the employee evaluation.
(B) There is information about the improved package on the last page.
(C) Be aware that the health coverage is not as inclusive as before.
(D) The deadline for prescription renewals has been extended to July 17.

14 (A) images
(B) reminders
(C) inquiries
(D) documents

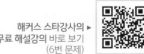

해커스 스타강사의 ▶
무료 해설강의 바로 보기
(6번 문제)

Hackers TOEIC Reading

READING

READING Part 6

1. 토익 Part 6 독해의 특징

토익 Part 6 독해는 실생활이나 비즈니스 관련 상황의 지문들이 출제된다.

토익 Part 6 독해는 실생활이나 비즈니스 상황과 관련된 지문을 제대로 이해할 수 있는가를 측정하는 것이 목적이므로, 실생활이나 비즈니스 상황에서 자주 등장할 법한 지문들이 주로 출제된다. 따라서 비즈니스 관련 주제, 어휘, 상황들에 익숙해지는 것이 중요하다.

토익 Part 6 독해는 지문 흐름에 대한 이해 능력을 측정한다.

토익 Part 6 독해는 지문의 흐름을 정확하게 파악하여 빈칸에 들어갈 알맞은 문법 사항, 어휘, 문장을 고르는 기본 독해 능력을 측정한다. 따라서 문장과 문장 간의 관계를 고려하여 지문의 전체적인 흐름을 파악하는 연습을 통해 독해 능력을 키우는 것이 매우 중요하다.

2. 토익 Part 6 독해 출제 유형

토익 Part 6에 나오는 독해 문제는 크게 빈칸이 있는 문장만 확인하여 풀 수 있는 문제와, 빈칸이 있는 문장뿐만 아니라 주변 또는 전체 문맥을 확인하여 풀 수 있는 문제로 나눌 수 있다. ≪해커스 토익 READING≫ Part 6에서는 문맥을 파악해서 풀어야 하는 문제를 단어 고르기 문제와 문장 고르기 문제로 나누어 각 CHAPTER에서 설명하고 있다.

*문맥 파악 없이 풀 수 있는 단어 고르기 문제는 Grammar-Part 5,6, Vocabulary-Part 5,6에서 학습할 수 있다.

단어 고르기   빈칸 주변 또는 전체 문맥을 파악하여 빈칸에 들어갈 알맞은 단어를 고르는 문제 유형으로, 문법 문제와 어휘 문제로 분류될 수 있다.

문장 고르기   빈칸 주변 또는 전체 문맥을 파악하여 문맥상 빈칸에 알맞은 문장을 고르는 문제이다.

3. 토익 Part 6 독해 문제 유형별 출제 비율

토익 Part 6 독해의 문제 유형별 출제 비율을 그래프로 나타내면 다음과 같다.

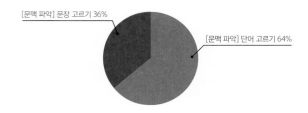

[문맥 파악] 문장 고르기 36%

[문맥 파악] 단어 고르기 64%

4. 토익 Part 6 독해 문제 풀이 방법

1. 보기를 확인하여 질문 유형을 파악한다.

· 보기를 확인하여 단어 고르기 문제인지, 문장 고르기 문제인지 파악한다.

2. 문제 유형별 전략을 적용하여 정답을 선택한다.

· 단어 고르기 문제는 문법 문제와 어휘 문제에 따라 전략이 달라진다. 문법 문제의 경우, 주로 빈칸 문장과 빈칸 주변 문장 등 주변 문맥을 확인하여 빈칸에 들어갈 알맞은 시제, 대명사, 접속부사를 고른다. 어휘 문제의 경우, 빈칸의 주변 문장에서 단서가 되는 어휘나 표현을 확인한 후, 빈칸에 들어갈 알맞은 어휘를 고른다.

· 문장 고르기 문제는 빈칸의 앞뒤 문장을 먼저 확인하여 주변 문맥을 파악하고, 필요시 전체 문맥을 파악하여 빈칸에 들어갈 알맞은 문장을 고른다.

Part 6 예제 – 단어 고르기

Auto manufacturer Lodi Motors announced that **it will be downsizing its plant** in Chicago next year by nearly 30 percent. -------, a spokesperson for the company said that **the move does not indicate any financial difficulties**, but simply that the company will be expanding its operations at other factories.

(A) Even if   **(B) However**   (C) Furthermore   (D) In fact

2. 빈칸이 문장 맨 앞에 오고, 다음에 콤마가 있는 구조를 통해 접속부사 자리임을 알 수 있다. 따라서 (B), (C), (D)가 정답의 후보이다. 빈칸의 앞 문장에서는 공장 인원을 줄인다는 내용을 언급했고, 빈칸이 있는 문장에서는 그것이 재정적인 문제를 의미하는 것은 아님을 언급했으므로 대조의 의미를 전달하는 (B) However가 정답이다.

1. 보기가 유사한 문법 범주에 포함되는 단어들, 즉 접속사와 접속부사로 구성되어 있으므로 단어 고르기 문제 중 문법 문제임을 알 수 있다.

Part 6 예제 – 문장 고르기

Dear Mr. Menaker,

Thank you for confirming your attendance at the 7th Beloit Architecture Convention. **You'll soon be receiving a personalized conference badge in the mail.** -------.

(A) I will need your name in order to verify the account.
(B) Please leave it at reception so that I can retrieve it this afternoon.
(C) Let me know if you do not receive it in the next few days.
(D) Construction permits are usually processed during regular hours.

2. 빈칸 앞 문장에서 상대방이 곧 우편으로 명찰을 보낼 것이라고 했으므로 빈칸에는 명찰 수령과 관련한 내용인 (C)가 정답이다.

1. 보기가 네 개의 문장으로 구성되어 있으므로 문장 고르기 문제이다.

문맥 파악 문제 1: 단어 고르기 문제

토익 이렇게 나온다!

단어 고르기 문제는 Part 6 지문에서 문맥상 빈칸에 들어갈 알맞은 단어를 고르는 문제로, 빈칸이 있는 문장만으로 정답을 찾을 수 없으므로 주변 문맥을 파악해야 한다. 문법 문제와 어휘 문제로 구성되며, Part 6 매회 평균 6~7문제가 출제된다.

토익 문제 풀이 전략

문제 풀이 전략

STEP 1 빈칸이 있는 문장의 내용을 파악한 후 빈칸 주변 문장에서 단서를 찾는다.

> **문법** **시제 문제**: 빈칸 주변 문장에 쓰인 동사의 시제를 확인하여 빈칸에 들어갈 동사의 시제를 예상한다. 만약 빈칸 주변 문장이나 지문 상단에 날짜가 언급되어 있다면 함께 확인하여 시간의 흐름을 파악한다.
>
> **대명사 문제**: 빈칸에서 가리키는 대상은 주로 빈칸 앞 문장에 있으므로 앞 문장에서 언급된 명사들을 확인하여 가리키는 대상을 찾는다. 이때, 빈칸에서 가리키는 대상의 수(단수/복수), 인칭 등을 중점적으로 확인한다.
>
> **접속부사 문제**: 빈칸이 있는 문장과 그 앞 문장의 의미 관계를 파악한다. 두 문장이 서로 상반되는 내용을 설명하는지, 추가적인 내용을 전달하는지, 순차적인 일을 설명하는지 등 두 문장의 의미가 어떻게 연결되는지를 파악한다.

> **어휘** 주로 빈칸의 주변 문장에 단서가 되는 어휘나 표현이 포함되어 있으므로 빈칸 주변 문장을 확인한다. 참고로, 명사 어휘 문제에서 빈칸 앞에 지시어(this/that/such 등), 정관사, 소유격이 있으면 가리키는 대상이 앞 문장에 언급되어 있으므로 빈칸 앞 문장을 우선적으로 확인한다.

STEP 2 지문의 흐름에 자연스러운 보기를 정답으로 선택한다.

예제 문법 접속부사 문제

FOR IMMEDIATE RELEASE
March 27

The latest Solaris LT-4 laptop will be released April 10. The Solaris team has used cutting-edge engineering solutions to deliver a product that features both faster processing speeds and longer-lasting battery life than the competition. Firstly, the device features the most powerful CPU and the most memory in its class. -------, the battery in this year's model can last for up to 16 hours on a single charge.

STEP 1
빈칸이 있는 문장의 내용을 파악한 후 빈칸 주변 문장에서 단서를 찾는다

(A) In addition
(B) In comparison
(C) Therefore

STEP 2
지문의 흐름에 자연스러운 보기를 정답으로 선택한다

해설 **단어 고르기 문제** 빈칸에 들어갈 알맞은 접속부사를 고르는 문제이므로 빈칸 문장과 그 앞 문장의 의미 관계를 파악한다. 앞 문장 'Firstly, the device features the most powerful CPU and the most memory in its class.'에서 우선 이 기기, 즉 최신 Solaris LT-4 노트북이 해당 종류에서 가장 강력한 중앙 처리 장치와 큰 메모리를 특징으로 한다고 한 후, 빈칸 문장 'the battery ~ can last for up to 16 hours on a single charge.'에서 배터리가 한 번 충전 시 최대 16시간까지 지속될 수 있다고 했으므로 빈칸 문장이 앞 문장에 대해 추가적인 내용을 전달하고 있음을 알 수 있다. 따라서 (A) In addition이 정답이다.

정답 (A)

지문 해석 p.107

유형 연습 지문을 읽고 빈칸에 들어갈 알맞은 것을 고르세요.

01 [문법] 시제 문제

From: Hugo Woods, Sales Director
To: Sales Staff

As many of you know, I have been discussing a deal with Hartco, currently Europe's largest cosmetics manufacturer. Their products ------- everywhere but the US. My plan is to distribute them to our clients in major US cities. To make that happen, I will need a full financial report. Please send it to my e-mail so that I can print it out before my next meeting in two weeks.

(A) are sold
(B) had been sold
(C) will be sold

02 [문법] 대명사 문제

Dear Mr. Browning,

It's my pleasure to work with you on the upcoming civic center development project. As your project manager, I will help you overcome any potential issues. Given the size of the project, we can expect a few concerns. For instance, local citizens may object to things like noise or fumes, and regulators may require additional paperwork. Steps must be taken to ensure ------- are satisfied with the project conditions. Please let me know when you are free to have a discussion.

(A) we
(B) they
(C) yours

03 [문법] 접속부사 문제

This is a reminder about the importance of cybersecurity. Please do not use the same password for different accounts. That way, you do not have to worry about losing access to multiple accounts at once. -------, one of our employees used the same password for his bank account and his e-mail. When it was stolen, he lost access to both. If you would like to receive more tips about cybersecurity, please contact the IT team. They are always ready to help.

(A) After all
(B) In effect
(C) For example

04 [어휘] 명사 어휘 문제

June 25—Due to the hot weather this summer, there will be less water available for city residents to use. The City Water Department therefore encourages all residents to use water wisely and recommends that they check their homes for any water leaks. "This measure will help reduce -------," says Water Department Chief Kyle Brenner. For more suggestions on water conservation, Mr. Brenner encourages readers to visit the department's Web site.

(A) heat
(B) waste
(C) noise

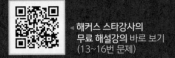
🕐 제한 시간 8분

Questions 01-04 refer to the following press release.

EI Industries Electric Vehicle Launch

EI Industries is moving in a bold, new direction. Beginning next year, the new models it introduces will ------- be electric vehicles. EI Industries CEO Ryan Yang believes it is the best way to secure the company's future.

01

The first vehicle in EI's new lineup will be the Delta SUV. -------. With its broad appeal and class-leading features, the Delta is expected to have rapidly growing sales. They may even ------- those of EI's gas-powered Gamma SUV in a few years.

02 ... **03**

The company ------- to offer parts and maintenance for gas-powered models. However, the current versions will not be updated, and EI plans to stop selling them in the near future.

04

---

01 (A) exclude
(B) excluding
(C) exclusive
(D) exclusively

02 (A) The company will be remembered for its long record of success.
(B) Sales of the Delta have been stronger than expected.
(C) The all-electric vehicle is anticipated to make a big impression.
(D) Newer models go farther on a single tank of gas.

03 (A) outperform
(B) develop
(C) assemble
(D) replace

04 (A) continued
(B) was continuing
(C) will continue
(D) had continued

Questions 05-08 refer to the following advertisement.

Sawyer and Associates

Sawyer and Associates is the Midwest region's top choice for commercial and residential architecture. For over a decade, our team has ------- buildings throughout the region.
05

Now, in addition to creating drawings and blueprints, we are expanding our business to include construction services. -------, we are seeking qualified individuals to fill crucial roles. -------.
06   07
Interested parties may apply by sending their résumé to jobs@sawyerassociates.com. Please include references and any documents ------- to past projects. Preference will be given to
08
applicants who have at least five years of relevant experience and can demonstrate an ability to meet the demands of their chosen job.

05 (A) purchased
(B) designed
(C) maintained
(D) inspected

06 (A) However
(B) Previously
(C) On the contrary
(D) For this reason

07 (A) These include skilled contractors and tradespeople.
(B) We offer clients a choice of several cost-effective solutions.
(C) The event is a wonderful opportunity for new graduates.
(D) *The Davenport Daily News* rated it the best in the area.

08 (A) relatively
(B) a relation
(C) it relates
(D) that relate

Questions 09-12 refer to the following notice.

As our loyal customers know, CT Solutions seeks to deliver every order as swiftly and as securely as possible. Our guaranteed next-day service has been the industry standard ------- we started two
09
decades ago.

Nevertheless, events are sometimes outside of our control. On these occasions, we may -------
10
to meet expectations. In the past few hours, severe blizzard conditions in the northeast have made roads slippery and visibility poor. This presents serious issues for our -------. Therefore, until
11
the weather improves and our trucks can be operated safely, we will be suspending deliveries throughout affected areas. -------. You may also check our mobile app. We sincerely apologize for
12
any inconvenience that this may cause.

09 (A) before
(B) from
(C) once
(D) since

10 (A) forget
(B) fail
(C) happen
(D) decide

11 (A) competitors
(B) technicians
(C) parcels
(D) drivers

12 (A) We apologize for the damage that occurred in transit.
(B) To learn which areas are affected, visit our Web site.
(C) Your request has been forwarded to the appropriate department.
(D) Choose another payment option if the first one is declined.

Questions 13-16 refer to the following e-mail.

To: Gabriela Novak <G_Novak@ecorp.com>
From: Eris Customer Service <customerservice@eris.com>
Date: April 25
Subject: E-Max Espresso Machine

Dear Gabriela,

Thank you for your review of the E-Max EM-70. You mentioned that the product you received was
-------. You cited an issue with the unit's grinder that prevents you from making fine grounds.
　　13

-------, some units were shipped with defective parts. To check whether your unit is one of them,
　14
please look up the manufacturing date of your EM-70. -------. If the machine was made between
　　　　　　　　　　　　　　　　　　　　　　　　　　　15
November 8 and November 15 last year, it likely has that part. In this case, we would be happy to
replace the machine with a new product at no additional cost. We can send ------- to any address
　　　　　　　　　　　　　　　　　　　　　　　　　　　　　　　　16
that you choose. Otherwise, we recommend that you bring the machine to your nearest authorized
repair center.

Yours Truly,

Ken Sebald
Customer Service Agent

---

13 (A) satisfactory
(B) complete
(C) genuine
(D) faulty

14 (A) Later
(B) Hence
(C) Unfortunately
(D) Conversely

15 (A) We proudly make all of our products here in
the United States.
(B) In fact, this can be corrected by adjusting
the knob to a higher setting.
(C) We can easily change your appointment to
a more suitable time.
(D) This is printed on the back of the machine
next to the power cord.

16 (A) it
(B) those
(C) mine
(D) theirs

정답·해설·해석 p.108 / [별책] 토익 RC 필수 어휘 p.36

해커스 스타강사의 ▶
무료 해설강의 바로 보기
(13~16번 문제)

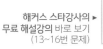

READING Part 6　Ch 01 문맥 파악 문제 1: 단어 고르기 문제　Hackers TOEIC Reading

CHAPTER 02

문맥 파악 문제 2: 문장 고르기 문제

토익 이렇게 나온다!

문장 고르기 문제는 Part 6 지문에서 문맥상 빈칸에 들어갈 알맞은 문장을 고르는 문제이다. 주로 빈칸의 앞뒤 문맥을 파악하면 알맞은 문장을 고를 수 있으며 지문 전체 문맥을 파악해야 하는 경우도 있다. Part 6 매 지문마다 각 1문제씩 총 4문제가 출제된다.

토익 문제 풀이 전략

문제 풀이 전략

STEP 1 빈칸의 주변 문맥을 파악하여 빈칸에 들어갈 내용을 예상한다.

먼저 빈칸의 바로 앞 문장과 뒤 문장을 확인하되, 주변 문맥 파악만으로는 빈칸에 들어갈 내용을 예상하기 어렵다면 지문 전체를 확인한다.

STEP 2 파악한 지문 문맥을 바탕으로 각 보기의 내용을 확인하며 빈칸에 알맞은 내용을 선택한다.
- 보기 내에 지시대명사(it, that, these 등)가 있다면 보기의 주변 문맥에 언급된 명사와 일치하는지 확인한다.
- 보기 내에 연결어(however, yet, also 등)가 있다면 빈칸의 앞뒤 문맥에 맞는 연결어인지 확인한다.

STEP 3 선택한 보기를 빈칸에 넣었을 때 지문의 흐름이 자연스러운지 확인한다.

예제 이메일

To: Susan Caldwell <scaldwell@coxfirm.com>
From: Dennis Andrews <dandrews@coxfirm.com>
Subject: Training Session

Dear Ms. Caldwell,

The administrative department has decided to use a new accounting software that was released a few months ago. This program is exceptionally easy to use and will simplify the work the accountants are doing for the administrative and finance departments. In this regard, I would like you to conduct training sessions for the entire accounting team. -------. Since we expect to begin using this software next month, these classes must be held as soon as possible.

Dennis Andrews
Administrative Department Chief

STEP 1
빈칸의 주변 문맥을 파악하여 빈칸에 들어갈 내용을 예상한다

STEP 3
선택한 보기를 빈칸에 넣었을 때 지문의 흐름이 자연스러운지 확인한다

(A) The accounting work hasn't been completed.
(B) We would like to know what you think of team members.
(C) Please make this your highest priority.

STEP 2
파악한 지문 문맥을 바탕으로 각 보기의 내용을 확인하며 빈칸에 알맞은 내용을 선택한다

해설 **문장 고르기 문제** 빈칸에 들어갈 알맞은 문장을 고르는 문제이므로 빈칸의 주변 문맥이나 전체 문맥을 파악한다. 앞 문장 'I would like you to conduct training sessions'에서 이메일의 발신자인 Dennis Andrews가 수신자인 Susan Caldwell에게 교육을 진행해주길 바란다고 한 후, 뒤 문장 'these classes must be held as soon as possible'에서 이 강좌는 가능한 한 빨리 열려야 한다고 했으므로 빈칸에는 교육을 진행하는 것이 최우선 사항으로 되어야 한다는 내용이 들어가야 함을 알 수 있다. 따라서 (C) Please make this your highest priority가 정답이다.

정답 (C)

지문 해석 p.110

유형 연습   지문을 읽고 빈칸에 들어갈 알맞은 것을 고르세요.

01 기사

March 25 - BoosTin, a beverage company based in the US, announced that its growth rate in the last quarter doubled compared to the same period last year. CEO Robert Cherish attributed this success to the company's market research. Last year, it conducted a consumer survey that revealed what people really want in their drinks. Based on the survey, BoosTin introduced new products, which led to improved customer satisfaction. -------. Cherish added, "Our experience demonstrates the importance of getting the consumer's opinion."

(A) The company now boasts much higher sales as a result.
(B) Consumers did not like the changes that the company made.
(C) The recommended changes are currently under discussion.

02 이메일

To: Gavin Dawson <gdawson@riverviewapartments.com>
From: Vern Casper <vcasper@riverviewapartments.com>

It has come to my attention that some building occupants have been leaving the fire doors open. As fire doors serve as a protective barrier, preventing flames from spreading to other floors, they must remain closed at all times. -------. Thus, I would appreciate it if you posted reminders about this in the hallways. And if you find any fire doors in need of repair, please inform me right away.

(A) We are considering removing them.
(B) Disregarding this rule can be hazardous.
(C) The doors will close automatically.

03 편지

Dear Mr. Baker,

This is a reminder regarding your quarterly health insurance premium that was due on May 1. As the payment is 30 days late, we have applied a 10 percent penalty to the original amount, bringing the total owed to $435.00. Please contact a service representative at 555-0954 or visit one of our branch offices to deal with this matter as soon as possible. -------. Otherwise, we will have no choice but to discontinue your medical coverage.

(A) The company will grant an extension if necessary.
(B) Insurance costs vary from month to month.
(C) Payment must be made by June 15 at the latest.

04 광고

At Newtown Cultural Center, we believe that everyone has the potential to tell a great story. If you're eager to develop your writing skills, visit us to enroll in a two-week workshop or a one-on-one class. -------. Whether you're a beginner wishing to brush up on grammar essentials or a seasoned author looking for feedback from a group of peers, the help we provide will be invaluable. Visit www.newtownwriting.com to see our schedule and register for an upcoming course.

(A) We are only offering beginner's fiction courses at this time.
(B) Our programs are appropriate for various levels of experience.
(C) Enrollment has been put off for another two weeks.

정답·해설·해석 p.110

🕐 제한 시간 8분

Questions 01-04 refer to the following e-mail.

From: Hattie-Mae Slocum <hattie@slocumrealty.com>
To: Peter McAllen <peter@slocumrealty.com>
Date: August 4
Subject: Sales opportunity

Dear Peter,

I read in the paper that Teva Pharmaceuticals will be opening a regional office here in Charlotte. The article said that the company will be ------- several of its executives here within six months. Once they have relocated to the new branch, I assume that most of them will be in the market for homes or, at least, temporary accommodation. -------.
01   **02**

We can contact their headquarters to let them know we ------- in corporate housing. Could you send them an e-mail ------- our firm? Please attach the brochure that features our fully furnished apartments, and make sure to emphasize that these can be moved into right away.
03   **04**

Thanks,

Hattie-Mae

01 (A) auditing
   (B) supplying
   (C) transferring
   (D) hiring

02 (A) There are several other new companies in
       the area.
   (B) The transition may be difficult for the new
       employees.
   (C) If so, it would be a great chance for us to
       make some sales.
   (D) For this reason, I'd like to discuss your most
       recent sale.

03 (A) specialize
   (B) depend
   (C) remain
   (D) speculate

04 (A) introduction
   (B) introducing
   (C) introduce
   (D) introduced

Questions 05-08 refer to the following letter.

August 22

Mary Slater
Purchasing Director
Deli Merchandising

Dear Ms. Slater,

I am a representative of Katz & Picket Frozen Food Manufacturing. For some months now, we ------- to enter the Asian market and are looking for a merchandiser. As your company distributes ₀₅ food products, we hope you will suggest ------- willing to sell what we offer. We mostly produce ₀₆ frozen vegetables, snacks, and dairy products, which have won high acclaim in the frozen food industry. Our hygienically packed edibles are superior not only in appearance and taste but also in nutrition. All of our food items are taste-tested by restaurant personnel and top caterers. -------. ₀₇

If you can schedule me in next week, I can arrange to fly in with some samples. We hope you will consider this profitable opportunity and make a deal with us. For the time being, please take a look at the brochure I have enclosed with this letter so that you can see our ------- product list. ₀₈

Sincerely,

Ross Lange
Marketing Supervisor
Katz & Picket Frozen Food Manufacturing

05 (A) planned
(B) will plan
(C) have been planning
(D) had planned

06 (A) retailers
(B) replacements
(C) commodities
(D) advertisers

07 (A) We dine only in the best restaurants.
(B) You may view their comments on our Web site.
(C) We received a positive response when we entered the Asian market.
(D) Our meeting will take place next week as planned.

08 (A) completely
(B) completing
(C) completion
(D) complete

Questions 09-12 refer to the following announcement.

Announcement: Bids for High School Gymnasium Construction

Since 1975, the students of Roosevelt High School have been using the same gymnasium for their physical education classes and sports activities. The building, however, is now old and shabby, and much of the equipment ------- to be replaced. School officials have recently approved a budget
09
to construct a new gymnasium and are asking contractors to submit bids to build it. To apply, the contractor must be ------- and have experience in the construction of school gymnasiums.
10
------- an application form to be submitted before April 15, bidders must provide a portfolio of the
11
building projects they have completed in the past five years. They must also include a list of their personnel and their résumés, as well as a description of the materials and equipment they will use to complete the project. -------. For more information, please visit our Web site.
12

09 (A) are needed
(B) needs
(C) being needed
(D) need

10 (A) realistic
(B) instructional
(C) moderate
(D) licensed

11 (A) Except for
(B) In accordance with
(C) Along with
(D) As regards

12 (A) Physical education classes are currently suspended.
(B) The project is now in the second phase of construction.
(C) Officials plan to approve the budget in the near future.
(D) Only those who meet the requirements will be contacted.

Questions 13-16 refer to the following article.

-------. The Department of Health said that those suffering from a variety of chronic ailments will
₁₃
only have to get an initial prescription from their doctors starting May 1. After that, patients will be
able to simply select a pharmacy online to fill their prescriptions. ------- the requests are submitted,
₁₄
access to them will be granted to the selected pharmacies. Patients only need to bring a valid
identification card, and a pharmacist will ------- their medication.
₁₅

Until now, many people with chronic conditions such as asthma or allergies have been forced to
visit doctors repeatedly just to get their prescriptions. Health Minister Diedre Meyer said, "Since
their medication needs are unchanging, the current procedure is actually very -------." Ms. Meyer
₁₆
hopes the new electronic prescription service will solve this problem.

13 (A) According to experts, medicine and
healthcare costs are on the rise.
(B) There is good news for patients taking
medication for persistent health conditions.
(C) It was recently announced that pharmacies
will become subject to strict legislation.
(D) A proposed insurance program may reduce
the price of prescription medications
significantly.

14 (A) While
(B) Unless
(C) Once
(D) Before

15 (A) relieve
(B) separate
(C) dispense
(D) consider

16 (A) unaffected
(B) complicated
(C) inefficient
(D) incompetent

해커스 스타강사의 ▶
무료 해설강의 바로 보기
(13~16번 문제)

Hackers TOEIC Reading

READING

PART 7

READING Part 7

1. 토익 Part 7 독해의 특징

토익 Part 7 독해는 실생활이나 비즈니스와 밀접한 지문들이 출제된다.

토익 Part 7 독해는 실생활이나 비즈니스 상황에서 영어를 제대로 활용할 수 있는가를 측정하는 것이 목적이므로, 실생활이나 비즈니스 상황에서 사용하는 다양한 편지, 이메일, 공고, 안내문 등과 같은 지문들이 주로 출제된다. 따라서 이와 같은 지문의 기본 양식과 내용들을 알아 두어야 한다.

토익 Part 7 독해는 기본적인 독해 능력을 측정한다.

토익 Part 7 독해는 실생활이나 비즈니스 상황에서 주로 사용되는 지문을 제대로 이해하여 문제를 풀 수 있는 기본 독해 능력을 측정한다. 따라서 평소 영문의 다독과 정독을 통해 독해 능력을 키우는 것이 매우 중요하다.

2. 토익 Part 7 독해 출제 유형

토익 Part 7에 나오는 독해 문제는 크게 질문 유형과 지문 유형으로 나누어 접근할 수 있다. ≪해커스 토익 READING≫ Part 7에서는 질문 유형을 Section 1, 지문 유형을 Section 2, 3에서 설명하고 있다. Section 1에서는 토익 Part 7 독해의 질문유형을 7가지로 나누어 설명하고 있으며, Section 2에서는 Single Passage에 출제되는 지문 유형을 8가지로 나누어 설명하고 있다. 마지막으로 Section 3에서는 Multiple Passages에 출제되는 연계 지문 유형을 5가지로 나누어 설명하고 있다.

질문 유형

토익 Part 7 독해에 나오는 질문 유형은 지문의 주제나 목적을 묻는 주제/목적 찾기 문제, 특정 세부 사항을 묻는 육하원칙 문제나 Not/True 문제 또는 추론 문제, 인용구의 의도를 묻는 의도 파악 문제, 주어진 문장의 알맞은 위치를 묻는 문장 위치 찾기문제, 그리고 동의어 찾기 문제로 나눌 수 있다.

지문 유형 – Single Passage

토익 Part 7 독해 Single Passage에 나오는 지문 유형은 이메일/편지, 양식 및 기타, 기사, 메시지 대화문, 광고, 공고, 회람, 안내문으로 나눌 수 있다.

지문 유형 – Multiple Passages

토익 Part 7 독해 Multiple Passages에 나오는 지문 유형은 자주 나오지 않는 회람 연계 지문과 안내문 연계 지문을 제외하고, 이메일/편지 연계 지문, 양식 연계 지문, 기사 연계 지문, 광고 연계 지문, 공고 연계 지문으로 나눌 수 있다.

3. 토익 Part 7 독해 지문 유형별 출제 비율

토익 Part 7 독해의 지문 유형별 출제 비율을 그래프로 나타내면 다음과 같다.

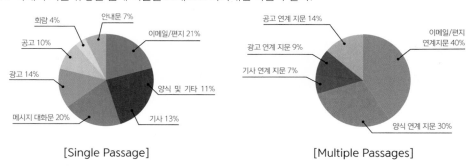

[Single Passage]　　　　　　　　　　[Multiple Passages]

4. 토익 Part 7 독해 문제 풀이 방법

1. 지문 유형과 지문의 제목을 확인하여 지문의 전반적인 내용을 예측한다.

· 각 지문 맨 위의 "Questions 문제 번호 refer to the following 지문 유형"에서 지문 유형을 확인하고, 해당 지문의 특성을 염두에 두며 문제를 풀어나간다.
· 지문의 제목은 지문 전체의 내용을 개괄적으로 보여주고 제목에서 정답의 단서가 제시되기도 하므로, 지문에 제목이 있을 경우 제목을 먼저 읽고 지문 전체의 내용을 미리 파악하도록 한다.

2. 질문을 읽고 질문 유형을 파악한다.

· 질문을 읽고 지문의 주제나 목적을 묻는 유형인지, 육하원칙, Not/True, 추론 문제 유형인지, 주어진 문장의 적절한 위치를 묻는 유형인지, 동의어 또는 인용구의 의도를 묻는 유형인지를 파악한다. Multiple Passages의 경우 어떤 지문에서 무슨 내용을 확인해야 할지도 파악한다.

3. 질문 유형별 전략을 적용하여 정답을 선택한다.

· 지문의 주제나 목적을 묻는 유형은 지문의 앞부분이나 지문 전체의 내용을 토대로 정답을 선택하고, 육하원칙, Not/True, 추론 문제 유형은 질문의 핵심 어구와 관련된 내용을 토대로 정답을 선택한다. 의도 파악 문제, 문장 위치 찾기 문제, 동의어 찾기 문제는 제시된 어휘나 문장이 언급된 절이나 관련 어구가 있는 문장 등 주변 문맥을 확인하여 정답을 선택한다. Multiple Passages의 경우 하나의 지문에서 찾은 단서가 불충분하면 나머지 지문에서 추가 단서를 찾아 두 단서를 종합하여 정답을 선택한다.
· 토익 Part 7 독해에서는 본문에 나온 어구를 질문과 보기에 그대로 사용하지 않고, 동일한 의미를 지닌 다른 어구로 바꾸어 표현하는 경우가 많은데 이를 Paraphrasing(바꾸어 표현하기)이라고 한다. Hackers Practice의 Paraphrasing 연습뿐만 아니라 해설에 정리된 Paraphrasing을 통해, Paraphrasing의 다양한 방식과, 같은 의미를 나타내는 Paraphrasing 표현들을 익혀둬야 한다.

[Paraphrasing(바꾸어 표현하기)의 종류]
– 동의어를 사용한 Paraphrasing: 지문에서 쓰인 단어를 동의어로 바꾸어 표현한 방법
  예) reorganize 재편성하다 → restructure 재구성하다
– 대체 표현을 사용한 Paraphrasing: 지문에서 쓰인 표현을 비슷한 의미의 다른 어구로 바꾸어 사용한 방법
  예) zero tolerance for defects 결함에 대해 한 치도 없는 오차 허용 → high quality standard 높은 품질 기준
– 구체적인 내용을 넓은 범주에 포함시킨 Paraphrasing: 지문에서 쓰인 어구를 그 개념을 포괄하는 넓은 범주의 어구로 바꾸어 표현한 방법
  예) e-mail address 이메일 주소 → contact information 연락 정보

Part 7 예제 - Single Passage

Question 1 refers to the following **article**.

> **Springdale Boardwalk Officially Opens to Public**
>
> **Mayor Inga Swenson officially opened the Springdale Boardwalk at a ribbon-cutting ceremony yesterday** on the waterfront. After nearly two years of construction, the boardwalk stretches 1,800 meters along the ocean and includes five restaurants, an arcade, a Ferris wheel, boat docks, a picnic area, and a gift shop for souvenirs.

1. Why was the article written?

    (A) To describe upcoming events at an entertainment venue
    (B) To announce a recently completed construction project
    (C) To give details on a newly elected city official
    (D) To promote a new government service

1. 지문 유형이 article(기사)이고 지문의 제목이 Springdale Boardwalk Officially Opens to Public이므로, Springdale 산책로가 대중에게 공식적으로 개방되는 것에 대한 기사이고 본문에서 시설에 대한 세부 내용이 이어질 것임을 예측한다.

3. 지문 앞부분에서 시장이 어제 개통식에서 Springdale 산책로를 공식적으로 개방했다고 한 후, 지문 전체에 걸쳐 완공된 산책로에 대한 설명이 이어지고 있으므로, 기사가 쓰인 이유는 최근에 완공된 산책로에 대해 알리기 위함임을 알 수 있다. 따라서 (B) To announce a recently completed construction project가 정답이며, a ribbon-cutting ceremony yesterday가 recently completed로 Paraphrasing되었다.

2. 기사가 쓰인 이유를 묻고 있으므로, 지문의 목적을 묻는 문제임을 파악한다.

Part 7 예제 - Double Passages

Question 1 refers to the following **notice** and **e-mail**.

> NOTICE: **Change in office locations**
>
> As you are aware, construction of our new office space on the third floor is complete. A moving crew will be coming in over the weekend to transfer some departments to their new locations. The following departments will be relocated:
>
> | Accounting | Room 301 |
> |---|---|
> | **Legal** | **Room 303** |
> | Marketing | Room 304 |
> | Public Relations | Room 306 |

> TO: Megan Lyle <mlyle@davenport.com>
> **FROM: Dan Kim** <dkim@davenport.com>
> DATE: April 9
> SUBJECT: **Request**
>
> Hi Megan,
>
> **My department just transferred to its new work space in Room 303.** Unfortunately, three of our employees' telephone connections aren't working. I was hoping you could send someone as soon as possible to fix the problem.
>
> Dan

1. In which department does **Dan Kim work**?

    (A) Accounting   **(B) Legal**
    (C) Marketing   (D) Public relations

1. 지문 유형이 notice(공고)와 e-mail(이메일)이고 제목이 각각 Change in office locations, Request이므로, 공고에서는 사무실 위치 변경에 대해 안내되고 이메일에서는 관련 요청에 대한 세부 내용이 이어질 것임을 예측한다.

3. 질문의 핵심 어구인 Dan Kim work와 관련하여, 이메일에서 작성자인 Dan Kim의 부서가 303호로 이동했다는 단서를 확인할 수 있다. 하지만 Dan Kim이 근무하는 부서 명칭은 언급되지 않았으므로, 첫 번째 지문인 공고에서 303호로 이동한 부서가 법무부라는 두 번째 단서를 확인한다. Dan Kim의 부서가 303호로 이동했다는 첫 번째 단서와, 303호로 이동한 부서는 법무부라는 두 번째 단서를 종합할 때, Dan Kim이 근무하는 부서가 법무부임을 알 수 있다. 따라서 (B) Legal이 정답이다.

2. Dan Kim이 어떤(which) 부서에서 일하는지를 묻고 있는 육하원칙 문제이므로 두 번째 지문인 Dan Kim이 작성한 이메일에서 관련 내용을 먼저 확인해야 함을 파악한다.

Part 7 예제 - Triple Passages

Questions 1 refer to the following **e-mail**, **form**, and **notice**.

1. 지문 유형이 e-mail(이메일), form(양식), notice(공고)이고 제목이 각각 RE: Order no. 102R398NF9, ONLINE RETURN FORM, Return Policy for Online Purchases이므로, 이메일에서는 주문에 관련한 답변이 안내되고, 양식에서는 온라인 주문의 환불에 대한 내용이 이어지고, 공고에서는 온라인 구매의 환불 정책에 관한 내용이 공지될 것임을 예측한다.

To: Misty Cabrera <msmisty427@mailfix.com>
From: Customer Service <cs@boulderoutdoor.com>
Subject: **RE: Order no. 102R398NF9**
Date: August 28

Dear Ms. Cabrera,

I am writing in reference to your inquiry about returning the above order. We'd be happy to provide you with a refund or exchange.

Should you decide to **process the return on our Web site**, I am obligated to tell you that **credit card refunds may take up to two weeks to process, whereas store credit will be issued within 24 hours**.

Sincerely,

Theodore Wood
Customer service representative
Boulder Outdoor

3. 이메일에서 Ms. Cabrera가 웹사이트에서 환불을 처리하기로 결정했다면 상점 포인트는 24시간 이내로 발행될 수 있는 반면, 신용카드 환불은 처리하는 데 2주 정도까지 걸릴 수도 있다는 단서를 확인할 수 있다. 하지만 Ms. Cabrera가 어떠한 방법으로 환불받는지가 언급되지 않았으므로, 두 번째 지문인 양식에서 Ms. Cabrera가 상점 포인트를 통해 환불받는다는 두 번째 단서를 확인한다. 환불이 처리될 때, 상점 포인트는 24시간 이내로 발행될 수 있다는 첫 번째 단서와 Ms. Cabrera가 상점 포인트를 통해 환불받는다는 두 번째 단서를 종합할 때, Ms. Cabrera의 환불이 하루 이내에 진행될 것임을 알 수 있다. 따라서 (C) She will have her refund processed within a day가 정답이다.

BOULDER OUTDOOR

ONLINE RETURN FORM
Return item: Evermore Travel Pack (red/olive) $140.00
Order number: 102R398NF9

Name: Misty Cabrera
E-mail: msmisty427@mailfix.com
Address: 6900 Wildwood Court Albuquerque, NM 87111

Payment method: *Online payment provider (Netfund)*
Refund method: *Store credit*

Return Policy for Online Purchases

· Customers must sign in to their online account and complete a form using the associated order number.
· They may choose to be refunded using the original payment method or receive the equivalent amount in the form of store credit.
· All orders returned online will incur a fee of $7 for shipping, which will be deducted from the total refund amount.

1. What is indicated about **Ms. Cabrera**?

2. 질문의 핵심 어구인 Ms. Cabrera에 대한 내용을 추론하는 문제이므로 첫 번째 지문인 Ms. Cabrera에게 쓰인 이메일에서 관련 내용을 먼저 확인해야 함을 파악한다.

(A) She is planning to shop for a gift item from an online retailer.
(B) She used a credit card to make a product purchase.
(C) She will have her refund processed within a day.
(D) She is dropping off her product at a Boulder Outdoor location.

Hackers TOEIC Reading

SECTION 1

질문 유형별 공략

CHAPTER 01 주제/목적 찾기 문제

토익 이렇게 나온다!
주제/목적 찾기 문제는 글의 주제나 목적을 정확하게 파악하고 있는지를 확인하는 문제이다. 토익의 지문은 이메일, 광고, 공고 등 정보 전달을 중심으로 하는 실용문이므로 글의 주제가 지문 앞부분에 나오고 상세 내용이 뒤에 나오는 구조를 가지고 있다. 따라서 주제/목적 찾기 문제의 경우, 지문 앞부분을 보면 대부분 정답의 단서를 찾을 수 있다. 평균 5문제가 출제된다.

토익 질문 유형 및 전략

빈출 질문 유형

글의 주제	**What** is the article **(mainly) about**? 기사는 (주로) 무엇에 대한 것인가?
	What is being **announced/advertised**? 공고되고/광고되고 있는 것은 무엇인가?
	What is **mainly discussed** (in the notice)? (공고에서) 주로 논의되는 것은 무엇인가?
글의 목적	**What** is the **(main) purpose** of the information? 안내문의 (주)목적은 무엇인가?
	What is **one purpose** of the memo? 회람의 한 가지 목적은 무엇인가?
글을 쓴 이유	**Why** was the letter **written**? 편지는 왜 쓰였는가?
	Why did Mr. Carson **write** the e-mail? Mr. Carson은 왜 이메일을 썼는가?
	Why did Ms. Kim **write** to Mr. Benet? Ms. Kim은 왜 Mr. Benet에게 글을 썼는가?

문제 풀이 전략

STEP 1 지문의 중심 내용이나 목적을 나타내는 주제 문장을 찾는다.
주제 문장은 주로 지문의 앞부분에서 찾을 수 있다. 주제 문장이 지문의 중간 또는 뒷부분에 있거나, 글 전체를 통해 주제를 파악해야 할 경우, 앞부분부터 재빨리 읽어 가면서 주제를 파악한다.

STEP 2 주제 문장을 읽고 글의 주제를 파악한다.
주제 문장을 통해, 또는 지문 전체의 내용을 요약하여 주제를 파악한다.

STEP 3 주제를 정확하게 나타낸 보기를 선택한다.
주제 문장을 paraphrasing하거나, 지문 전체의 내용을 바르게 요약한 보기를 정답으로 선택한다.

예제 광고

> **Wiggles Pet Supplies ... Everything Your Pet Needs!**
> Pet owners in Seattle want a one-stop shop for all their pet supply needs, and the newly opened Wiggles Pet Supplies on 235 Renton Avenue is just the store for them! We offer a wide selection of products for cats and dogs, including kennels, accessories, shampoos, and brushes. For this week only, all pet foods are 30 percent off the regular price. Visit us any day of the week, from 9 A.M. to 8 P.M.

STEP 1 지문의 중심 내용이나 목적을 나타내는 주제 문장을 찾는다

STEP 2 주제 문장을 읽고 글의 주제를 파악한다

Q. What is the purpose of the advertisement?
(A) To promote a recently established store
(B) To introduce a new line of pet accessories
(C) To encourage the use of veterinary services

STEP 3 주제를 정확하게 나타낸 보기를 선택한다

해설 **주제/목적 찾기 문제** 광고의 목적을 묻는 목적 찾기 문제이므로 지문의 앞부분을 주의 깊게 확인한다. 'the newly opened Wiggles Pet Supplies ~ is just the store for them'에서 이 새로 개점한 Wiggles 반려동물 용품점이 바로 그들을 위한 상점이라고 했으므로 (A) To promote a recently established store가 정답이다. 지문의 newly opened가 recently established로 바뀌어 표현되었다.

정답 (A)

지문 해석 p.114

HACKERS PRACTICE 토익 고득점을 위한 필수 연습

Paraphrasing 연습   지문의 내용과 일치하는 문장을 고르세요.

01

> Melrose Bank recently discovered that some clients who signed up for the special banking service have been paying an additional ATM fee. This ATM fee will be reimbursed to our clients' accounts next week.

(A) Customers of the bank will no longer pay any ATM fees.
(B) The bank will repay clients through their bank accounts.

02

> Protect-It plastic containers are effective at protecting anything from the elements. Ordinary storage containers cannot keep water out, but Protect-It products have patented lids and closure mechanisms that prevent moisture from entering the container.

(A) Protect-It containers can hold large amounts of water.
(B) Protect-It containers are made of water-resistant material.

03

> Capital Alliance Incorporated is looking for a CPA with a degree in accounting. The ideal candidate should have three to five years auditing and accounting experience.

(A) A university diploma is a requirement for the job.
(B) Knowledge of the newest accounting principles is required.

04

> The top two car companies are planning to trim production as the increasing cost of gasoline has caused a prolonged slump in sales of trucks and cars. Faced with an inventory pileup, Ace Motors and Townsend Cars will be cutting production by 15 percent over the next two quarters.

(A) Poor sales are causing top automobile manufacturers to cut production.
(B) Reduced production can offset increasing gas prices.

05

To make your stay at the Paradise Beach Resort a pleasant one, please pay strict attention to our rules on cleanliness. Because it is costly and difficult to remove trash and spilled liquids, guests who leave their huts dirty will forfeit the $100 key deposit for use of a hut.

(A) Visitors who lose their room key will not receive their deposit.
(B) The deposit will not be refunded if the hut is not left clean.

06

The Wells Community Center is seeking monetary donations to cover the cost of buying computers for children of low-income families in the community.

(A) Private money will be used to finance the purchase of computers.
(B) Donations of old computers are being requested.

07

Cabot Systems in Hong Kong is in the process of acquiring US-based Flexpoint, a multimedia technology company for mobile phones. Cabot Systems wants to be the dominant supplier for the mobile industry by using Flexpoint's technologies.

(A) Two companies have signed an agreement to produce mobile phones.
(B) Cabot Systems is buying out Flexpoint to gain control of the market.

08

After having a guest editor supervise *The Journal of Commerce (JOC)* for November, soon-to-retire *JOC* editor Bill Conley is now accepting applications for the editorship of *JOC*. Mr. Conley said that he is having an active hand in selecting his own replacement.

(A) *JOC*'s editor is seeking his successor.
(B) The guest editor will take over permanently.

09 이메일

I've forwarded you a copy of your travel itinerary for your business trip to Japan. Please go over the details and notify me of any needed changes. If the schedule is fine, please confirm by replying to this e-mail.

Q. Why was the e-mail written?

(A) To request confirmation of trip information
(B) To provide notice of an accommodation change
(C) To ask for a schedule for a business trip

10 기사

The National Aviation Authority (NAA) released a report yesterday which showed that the cost of domestic flights has increased by nearly 10 percent compared to last year. The report indicated that rising gas prices are only partially to blame. In reaction to negative feedback from passengers about "hidden fees" such as charges for baggage, fuel surcharges, and seat selection, many national carriers have returned to their previous pricing systems and are including such fees in their airfares. So although it appears that ticket prices have gone up, the increases may not actually have much effect on passengers.

Q. What is mainly discussed in the article?

(A) The effect of fuel costs on the airline industry
(B) The reasons for rising prices of a service
(C) The increase in passengers traveling domestically

11 편지

I heard from a colleague that your organization is looking for donations of artwork for an upcoming charity auction. I am a local artist who makes ceramic sculptures and would be happy to provide an item for the event. Please let me know where to bring the sculpture and by which date you need it. Also, could you tell me what will happen to the artwork if it isn't sold?

Q. What is one purpose of the letter?

(A) To ask about a job in a gallery
(B) To request admission to an exhibit
(C) To offer a donation for an event

12 공고

Management would like to inform all tenants of Rockport Towers that the building will be implementing a new recycling system. New containers for recyclable materials are now available in the trash area behind exit 2 on the ground floor of the building. Containers are available for glass, paper, and metal materials. There are also smaller containers provided for items such as used batteries and ink cartridges. We kindly ask that you dispose of your items appropriately. Also, please ensure that all glass and metal containers do not have any liquids left inside. Thank you for your cooperation.

Q. What is being announced?

(A) Guidelines for disposal
(B) Procedures for moving
(C) Policies for building employees

정답·해설·해석 p.114

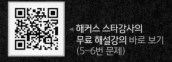
🕐 제한 시간 6분

Questions 01-04 refer to the following e-mail.

From:	Patricia Sutherland <psuth@adelaideleather.com>
To:	Timothy Cunning <timcun@zoomail.com>
Date:	March 7
Subject:	Your Order

Dear Mr. Cunning,

I received your message yesterday regarding the order of a suitcase from our Web site on February 2. You indicated that the item has not yet arrived. This is the information that I have:

Order number: 887598
Item: Lennox black patent leather carry-on suitcase model #344
Cost: $122.76 (tax included)
Shipped on: February 5
Shipped to: Timothy Cunning, 6522 Swan Lake Road, Raymont ID 99877

Please confirm that the information is correct. I contacted our delivery service provider, and they have been unable to locate the item. I deeply apologize for the inconvenience. I can offer you a full refund or send out another suitcase. Please let me know what you prefer. Also, to make up for this error, I am attaching a voucher for $30 that you may use for any future purchase.

Once again, I'd like to express my regrets for the error. We truly appreciate your patience and understanding.

Yours truly,
Patricia Sutherland
Customer Service Representative
Adelaide Leather Goods

01 Why did Ms. Sutherland write to Mr. Cunning?

(A) To provide information about a business
(B) To verify the delivery of a purchase
(C) To ask about the availability of a service
(D) To respond to his previous inquiry

02 When was Mr. Cunning's purchase sent?

(A) On February 2
(B) On February 5
(C) On March 6
(D) On March 7

03 What does Ms. Sutherland offer to do?

(A) Send a replacement for a lost item
(B) Exchange a purchase for a newer model
(C) Provide a partial refund
(D) Update a client's information

04 What did Ms. Sutherland send to Mr. Cunning?

(A) An updated invoice
(B) A credit voucher
(C) An order form
(D) A product catalog

Questions 05-06 refer to the following announcement and e-mail.

Global Geography Magazine
Now accepting submissions from freelance writers!

Global Geography Magazine is pleased to announce that it is now looking for freelance writers who are interested in the worlds of science, history, and culture. If you have an idea for an article, simply submit a proposal including the following:

- Name, address, phone number, and e-mail address
- A summary of the article you wish to write
- A sample of your writing (under 200 words)
- A list of publications you've written for (if applicable)

Our editorial team will review your proposal, and if your article is selected for publication, we offer the following pay scale:

Short article 200-500 words	$300, and a one-year subscription to *Global Geography Magazine*
Regular article 501-800 words	$500, and a one-year subscription to *Global Geography Magazine*
Feature article 801+ words	$900, and a two-year subscription to *Global Geography Magazine*
Cover story	$1,200, and a two-year subscription to *Global Geography Magazine*

Subscriptions are for 12 issues annually.

Global Geography Magazine does not accept unsolicited articles, so please contact us first. Send inquiries to submissions@globalgeography.com.

To: Christopher Gluck <chrisgluck@dmail.com>
From: Cassandra Hitchens <submissions@globalgeography.com>
Subject: Re: Submission Proposal   writercontract.word
Date: September 21

Dear Mr. Gluck,

I am pleased to inform you that your writing proposal has been approved by our editorial staff. We were very impressed with your idea, and look forward to your piece on underwater archaeology. The deadline for the article is December 1. After editing and revisions, you can expect it to be printed in our February issue.

I have attached a writer's contract to this e-mail. Please read it through, sign it, and fax it to us at (509) 555-9988 or send a scanned copy of it through e-mail.

Payment will be remitted by December 31. I will also need you to send me your necessary banking information so that the payment of $900 can be wired to your account.

Thanks for your interest, and we are eager to read your article.

Sincerely,
Cassandra Hitchens, Associate Director of Submissions

---

05 What is the announcement mainly about?

(A) A change in subscription rates
(B) A system for submissions
(C) An upcoming writing competition
(D) A launch of a new magazine

06 Why did Ms. Hitchens write the e-mail?

(A) To provide some requested bank information
(B) To ask for payment of a subscription
(C) To notify a writer about a submission
(D) To inform an author of editorial changes

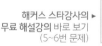

CHAPTER 02

육하원칙 문제

토익 이렇게 나온다!
육하원칙 문제는 무엇이, 언제, 어떻게, 누가 등 글의 세부 내용에 대해 제대로 파악하고 있는지를 확인하는 문제이다. 질문을 읽고 질문의 핵심 어구에 대한 단서를 지문 속에서 빨리 찾아내는 것이 중요하며, 지문의 일부만 보고도 답을 찾을 수 있기 때문에 쉽게 풀 수 있는 문제이다. 토익 리딩 Part 7에서 가장 많이 출제되는 문제 유형으로, 평균 21문제가 출제된다.

토익 질문 유형 및 전략

빈출 질문 유형

무엇이/어떤 것이 ~하는가/인가?　　**What** was Ms. King requested to do? Ms. King은 무엇을 하도록 요청되었는가?
　　　　　　　　　　　　　　　What kinds of products are sold on the Web site? 어떤 종류의 제품들이 웹사이트에서 판매되는가?

언제 ~하는가?　　　　　　　　**When** will Mr. Chapman return from his trip? Mr. Chapman은 언제 여행에서 돌아올 것인가?

어떻게/얼마나 ~하는가?　　　　**How** can Ms. Portman obtain a refund? Ms. Portman은 어떻게 환불받을 수 있는가?
　　　　　　　　　　　　　　　How much did Mr. Ryan pay for the seminar? Mr. Ryan은 세미나에 얼마를 지불했는가?

~는 누구인가?/누가 ~하는가?　　**Who** is Lee Perry? Lee Perry는 누구인가?
　　　　　　　　　　　　　　　Who will be meeting the clients at the airport? 누가 공항에서 고객들을 만날 것인가?

왜 ~하는가?　　　　　　　　　**Why** did Ms. Bailey cancel her subscription? Ms. Bailey는 왜 구독을 취소했는가?

어디서 ~하는가?　　　　　　　**Where** should visitors park their cars? 방문객들은 그들의 차를 어디에 주차해야 하는가?

문제 풀이 전략

STEP 1 질문을 읽고 의문사와 핵심 어구를 확인한다.

STEP 2 지문에서 질문의 핵심 어구와 관련된 내용을 찾는다.
　　　　　질문의 핵심 어구를 그대로 언급하거나 paraphrasing한 부분의 주변에서 정답의 단서를 찾는다. Double/Triple passages의 경우, 다른 지문에서 정답의 단서를 찾아야 할 수도 있다.

STEP 3 정답의 단서를 그대로 언급하거나 paraphrasing한 보기를 선택한다.

예제　이메일

To	Agatha Williams <a_williams@ffm.com>
From	Richard Jones <r_jones@ffm.com>

I have confirmed the target date for the launch of Perk-to-Go bottled coffee. According to the client, the launch will take place on August 27. I have to submit the proposed schedule for the event before Friday. I want to consult you regarding my ideas for the program. I would appreciate your help.

STEP 2 지문에서 질문의 핵심 어구와 관련된 내용을 찾는다

STEP 1 질문을 읽고 의문사와 핵심 어구를 확인한다

Q. What should Mr. Jones give the client by Friday?
　(A) A cost estimate
　(B) Plans for the launch
　(C) Product samples

STEP 3 정답의 단서를 그대로 언급하거나 paraphrasing한 보기를 선택한다

해설　**육하원칙 문제** Mr. Jones가 무엇(What)을 금요일까지 의뢰인에게 주어야 하는지를 묻는 육하원칙 문제이다. 질문의 핵심 어구인 Mr. Jones give ~ by Friday와 관련하여, 'I have to submit the proposed schedule for the event before Friday.'에서 Mr. Jones가 금요일 전에 행사를 위한 일정안을 제출해야 한다고 했으므로, 정답의 단서 the proposed schedule for the event를 paraphrasing한 (B) Plans for the launch가 정답이다.

정답　(B)

지문 해석 p.117

Paraphrasing 연습　지문의 내용과 일치하는 문장을 고르세요.

01

> Staff evaluations are an important training tool that can help your staff stay on course and make adjustments for improvement. Regular one-on-one discussions should be conducted between the immediate supervisor and the staff being evaluated.

(A) Regular feedback improves the relationship between supervisor and subordinate.
(B) Assessment of employees' work encourages improvement in performance.

02

> To reduce the incidence of mold in your home, you need to keep moisture to the minimum. You can do this by keeping all rooms well-ventilated. Turn on your electric fan when you are cooking or when you notice the windows becoming misty.

(A) To prevent mold, keep the air flowing in your home.
(B) To reduce moisture, keep an electric fan on at all times.

03

> The Watley Department Store is holding a sweepstakes for all brides-to-be. To be eligible for the events, you must have made plans to get married between January 1 and May 31, next year. Register at the wedding gown section of the women's clothing department.

(A) Entrants must have a definite wedding date to qualify for the sweepstakes.
(B) The Watley Department Store is having a sale on wedding gowns.

04

> Tree planting is considered as an inexpensive means of reducing carbon dioxide in the atmosphere. Trees absorb carbon dioxide, to the degree that it actually offsets carbon emissions by fossil fuels. However, the extent to which trees will be planted depends on local policies and technology.

(A) Tree planting will reduce the amount of fossil fuels used.
(B) Cultivation of trees is a cost-effective way to offset carbon dioxide emissions.

05

Recommendation: Please supply a replacement unit for the customer mentioned at the top of this form, as the heater she purchased is clearly defective.

(A) The defective heater will be repaired at no cost.
(B) The customer should be sent a new product.

06

To reduce the cost of delivery services, the Piedmont Corporation is changing its policy regarding outsourcing. The company has discovered that by accepting outsourcing proposals and hiring fewer staff, it can save on support services costs.

(A) Costs can be decreased by hiring an outside firm.
(B) Costs can be reduced by limiting outside contracts.

07

Tenants must report any problems with rodents and bugs. We have a contract with a pest control company who will examine your apartment unit and provide possible solutions. Tenants may book an appointment with this vendor at no charge.

(A) Tenants should hire the services of a pest control vendor.
(B) Tenants can schedule a time and date for inspection.

08

Mark your calendars for Saturday, March 23, when a large benefit dinner will be held at the city's convention center. The event is sponsored by Branding Consultancy, a marketing company in Hollywood.

(A) A company based in Hollywood has supported Branding Consultancy.
(B) Branding Consultancy has funded and organized a gathering.

09 기사

World Trek Travel magazine published the results of its latest hotel survey in this month's issue and the Grand Ching Hotel in Beijing received the highest ranking from guests. Respondents gave high marks to the hotel for its innovative design and exemplary customer care. Rounding out the top three hotels were the Stanley Hotel in Vancouver and the Orchid Terrace in Bangkok. The publication surveyed more than 4,000 guests and travelers to compile the results.

Q. What did *World Trek Travel* recently do?

(A) Published an article on luxury hotels
(B) Conducted a study
(C) Launched a new section

10 이메일

I am sorry to inform you that the vehicle you reserved on our agency's Web site yesterday will not be available on the dates indicated. Unfortunately, it is peak season and those types of minivans have all been booked. However, I can offer you one of our larger vans. It seats eight passengers and only costs $20 more than the one you wanted. I hope you will find this offer suitable. Please let me know.

Q. Why is the requested vehicle unavailable?

(A) It is no longer offered as an option.
(B) It has already been scheduled for use.
(C) It costs more than the customer has budgeted.

11 안내문

Drivers applying for a new license should fill out a form and proceed to window 3. For vehicle registration, please take a number and wait by window 5. To have your picture taken, wait for your name to be called at window 4. To retrieve a confiscated license, please pay the fine at window 8 and wait for further instructions. Thank you.

Q. Where can visitors make a payment?

(A) At window 3
(B) At window 4
(C) At window 8

정답·해설·해석 p.117

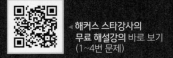
🕐 제한 시간 6분

Questions 01-04 refer to the following flyer.

Oberlin Community Youth Center Summer Ceramics Class!

Looking for something fun and educational to do this summer? Enroll in Oberlin Community Youth Center's (OCYC) series of ceramics classes! Learn basic techniques for sculpting simple household objects from our expert instructors. Local potter Arnold Robson and art teacher Marilyn Davis will guide you through the processes step by step. Learn about a vast variety of sculpting methods from Mr. Robson, and how to apply glaze and use a kiln from Ms. Davis.

DETAILS:

The classes will be held at the youth center located at 436 Westpoint Avenue. Classes are scheduled for Mondays and Thursdays from 3 P.M. to 5 P.M., from July 9 to August 22. Upon completion of the series, a show exhibiting students' work will be held on August 24 at 7:30 P.M. in the OCYC's own event hall.

REGISTRATION:

To reserve a spot for the classes, come by the OCYC administrative office. The fee for the class is $220, inclusive of materials. Participants need to be residents of Oberlin between the ages of 13 and 19. Deadline for enrollment is June 30. Payment can be made in cash or by credit card. Fees are nonrefundable. For further details, call Eve Wilson at 555-9907.

---

01 What is the purpose of the flyer?

(A) To announce the opening of a facility
(B) To request volunteers for a community center
(C) To advertise a workshop for local teachers
(D) To publicize an art course

02 When will the courses begin?

(A) On June 30
(B) On July 9
(C) On August 22
(D) On August 24

03 Who will participate in the program?

(A) Amateur artists
(B) Local teenagers
(C) High school teachers
(D) Gallery owners

04 What type of class will be taught by Mr. Robson?

(A) Sculpting techniques
(B) Advanced pottery
(C) Painting methods
(D) Applying a glaze

Questions 05-06 refer to the following letter and article.

November 18

Kelly Simon
Perlman International
30 Bent Street
Perth, WA 6015

Dear Ms. Simon,

It was nice to meet you at the Property Expo. I want to thank you for providing a pamphlet about the properties that Perlman International represents. Our firm is interested in submitting an offer for Francis Tower in Sydney.

Star Pacifica is a unit of Singapore's CK Wong Group, which has a long history of owning and developing land across Asia. It was established for the purpose of developing property in Australia. Our first acquisition was at 20 Carlisle Street in Melbourne. This was followed by 811 Harbor Way in Sydney. Francis Tower will be our third project.

We would like to schedule a site visit, as well as a meeting to discuss terms. I will follow up in a few days, but if you need to contact me sooner, I can be reached at 555-9034.

Sincerely,

Ronald Lee
Managing director
Star Pacifica

Francis Tower Sells for $19 million in Year's First Major Sale

January 14—The Robinson family has sold the Francis Tower in Sydney for $19 million to Star Pacifica. The new owner, a subsidiary of Singapore's CK Wong Group, aims to replace the former apartment building with commercial and office spaces. It currently owns the Maritime Plaza in Sydney and the Union Building in Melbourne. It is also in negotiations to purchase Astor Terrace in Brisbane.

Perlman International's Kelly Simon, who brokered the deal, says the building attracted numerous buyers. "Star Pacifica won because of their superior offer," she says. Star Pacifica's managing director, Ronald Lee, says he was delighted with the acquisition. "Although the area is not as upscale as other parts of the city," he says, "it is only a matter of time before that changes."

---

05 How did Mr. Lee learn about Francis Tower?

(A) He read an advertisement on a Web site.
(B) He received a brochure during an event.
(C) He was asked to participate in an auction.
(D) He saw the building during a site visit.

06 Which property did Star Pacifica acquire first?

(A) Francis Tower
(B) Maritime Plaza
(C) Union Building
(D) Astor Terrace

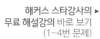

해커스 스타강사의 ▶
무료 해설강의 바로 보기
(1~4번 문제)

정답·해설·해석 p.119 / [별책] 토익 RC 필수 어휘 p.38

READING Part 7
Ch 02 육하원칙 문제 Hackers TOEIC Reading

Not/True 문제

토익 이렇게 나온다!

Not/True 문제는 지문 내용을 바탕으로 보기 4개 중 옳은 것 또는 틀린 것을 골라냄으로써 세부 내용을 정확히 이해하고 있는지를 확인하는 문제이다. 이 유형의 문제는 각 보기와 지문 내용을 하나하나 대조해 보면서 확인해야 하므로 시간이 많이 소요된다. 육하원칙 문제 다음으로 토익 리딩 Part 7에서 많이 출제되는 빈출 유형 중 하나이며, 평균 11~12문제가 출제된다.

토익 질문 유형 및 전략

빈출 질문 유형

Not 문제	[언급되지 않은 것]	What is **NOT indicated/stated** about Ms. Brown? Ms. Brown에 대해 언급되지 않은 것은?
		What is **NOT mentioned** in the article? 기사에서 언급되지 않은 것은?
	[사실이 아닌 것]	What is **NOT true** about the renovation project? 수리 작업에 대해 사실이 아닌 것은?
	[~이 아닌 것]	What is **NOT** provided in the brochure? 브로슈어에서 제공되지 않은 것은?
True 문제	[언급된 것]	What is **indicated** about online orders? 온라인 주문에 대해 언급된 것은?
		What is **mentioned/stated** in the advertisement? 광고에서 언급된 것은?
		What does the e-mail **indicate/mention** about the upcoming construction? 곧 있을 공사에 대해 이메일이 언급하는 것은?
	[사실인 것]	What is **true** about the company policy? 회사 규정에 대해 사실인 것은?

문제 풀이 전략

STEP 1 질문 또는 보기를 읽고 핵심 어구를 확인한다.

STEP 2 지문에서 질문 또는 보기의 핵심 어구와 관련된 내용을 찾는다.

질문이나 보기의 핵심 어구를 그대로 언급하거나 paraphrasing한 부분의 주변에서 정답의 단서를 찾는다. Double/Triple passages의 경우, 각 보기와 관련된 내용이 다른 지문 곳곳에서 제시될 수도 있다.

STEP 3 각 보기와 지문 내용을 하나씩 대조하여 정답을 선택한다.

Not 문제는 지문의 내용과 일치하지 않거나 지문에 언급되지 않은 보기를, True 문제는 지문의 내용과 일치하는 보기를 선택한다.

예제 공고

> **Reminders regarding Medford Incorporated's Audio-Visual Room**
> * ^AMake sure to reserve the audio-visual room at least three days in advance. •——
> * ^CLet us know ahead of time whether you need to borrow equipment.
> * Reservations may only be made for a maximum of four hours.
> * Food and drinks are strictly prohibited.

STEP 2 지문에서 질문 또는 보기의 핵심 어구와 관련된 내용을 찾는다

STEP 1 질문 또는 보기를 읽고 핵심 어구를 확인한다

Q. What is indicated about reservations? •——
   (A) They can be made on the day they are needed.
   (B) They must be booked separately for meals and parties.
   (C) They may include equipment with advance notice. •——

STEP 3 각 보기와 지문 내용을 하나씩 대조하여 정답을 선택한다

해설 **Not/True 문제** 질문의 핵심 어구인 reservations와 관련된 내용을 지문에서 찾아 보기와 대조하는 Not/True 문제이다. (A)는 'Make sure to reserve ~ at least three days in advance.'에서 적어도 3일 전에 예약해야 한다고 했으므로 지문의 내용과 일치하지 않고, (B)는 지문에 언급되지 않은 내용이다. (C)는 'Let us know ahead of time whether you need to borrow equipment.'에서 장비를 대여해야 하는지 미리 알려달라고 했으므로 지문의 Let ~ know ahead of time이 with advance notice로 바뀌어 표현된 (C) They may include equipment with advance notice가 정답이다.

정답 (C)

지문 해석 p.120

Paraphrasing 연습   지문의 내용과 일치하는 문장을 고르세요.

01

> We are holding a job opportunities information session for university seniors and recent graduates. This is a one-day session scheduled for May 25. Registration is not required, as admission will be on a first-come-first-served basis only.

(A) Only university students may attend the session.
(B) Participants will be admitted in the order they arrive.

02

> The Bergerson Industries Corporation will be relocating its factory to the east side of the city. Roger Bergerson, sole proprietor, said the transfer will facilitate delivery of materials to the warehouse.

(A) Roger Bergerson is the owner of the company.
(B) Roger Bergerson is the company's shipping manager.

03

> Do you find dust balls under your dressers and beds even if you've already swept the floor? Our new Whoosh vacuum cleaners are so powerful that floors, carpets, and even curtains can become spotless in just a few minutes.

(A) The Whoosh vacuum cleaner can make draperies clean.
(B) There's no need to dust the furniture after you've used Whoosh.

04

> The governor's travel schedule tomorrow includes a stopover at Lincoln, Nebraska, where he intends to deliver a speech on his plans to run for a second term. The talk will be delivered at the Lincoln Chamber of Commerce.

(A) The governor will talk about issues on commerce.
(B) The governor will discuss his plans for re-election.

05

From 8:00 A.M. to 11:00 P.M., the prices of children's bicycles at the Mega Bike Shop will be marked down by as much as 20 to 25 percent!

(A) The store is selling all bicycles at marked-down prices.
(B) The store will hold a sale on select items.

06

The Carmichael Group Incorporated said that plans for the construction of a 450 million dollar office building had been approved but that work on the building would not proceed until investors provide the initial outlay needed.

(A) Construction will begin when financial backing is given.
(B) The Carmichael Group will invest in the building when the plans are finalized.

07

The owner of the building was informed that renovations are needed to meet the accessibility requirements of workers with disabilities. One important change mentioned is the installation of suitable door handles on all building entrances.

(A) Properly installed doors are needed at all building entrances.
(B) Renovations will enable disabled workers to use door handles.

08

Write to Home Remodeling Contractors for a home remodeling guide. Aside from home reconstruction ideas and plans, the guide includes a picture catalog for every room in your house. You can also get a free quote on any room you want to remodel.

(A) The company does not charge for estimates.
(B) The guide is free for contractors.

09 공고

The Bank of Labrador is pleased to offer clients a free series of workshops on financial planning for retirement. The first session will take place on Thursday, April 6 at 7:30 P.M. at our branch on 322 Callahan Avenue. Three other sessions will follow every Thursday at the same time and location. Through our workshops, we want to help you prepare for retirement. We will cover such topics as retirement savings plans, short- and long-term investments, high-interest savings accounts, and setting up accounts to receive pension payments. If you are interested in attending, please call 555-9835.

Q. What is mentioned in the notice?

  (A) Participants will learn about several subjects.
  (B) The bank will host three different workshops.
  (C) A financial institution will conduct employee training.

10 광고

Introducing the Palazzo Dining Room Set!

Palazzo Designs unveils its newest line of elegant dining room furnishings. The Palazzo Dining Room Set includes a carved oak table which seats six, along with matching chairs. Rounding out the set are a wooden china cabinet with a glass display case and three storage cupboards. All pieces are handcrafted in Lombardia, Italy by traditional craftspeople. The set is adorned with carved roses and vines and is truly a magnificent addition to any home. Look for the Palazzo Dining Room Set and other Palazzo furnishings at home decor stores near you!

Q. What is NOT true about the Palazzo Dining Room Set?

  (A) It is manufactured in Italy.
  (B) It can accommodate six diners.
  (C) It is available for sale online.

11 기사

Award-winning pop sensation, Lucille DeForest, can add "fashion designer" to her already impressive résumé. In partnership with clothing retailer Y&C, DeForest launched a line of clothing and accessories last year. Sales for the new collection have been high, and the items have become some of the store's bestsellers. A spokesperson for Y&C said the company plans to collaborate with the singer again for a fall and winter collection. DeForest's designs are described as "edgy" and "very current," which has helped Y&C attract more young, female shoppers.

Q. What is NOT indicated about Y&C?

  (A) It recently collaborated with a musician.
  (B) It offers seasonal collections.
  (C) It designs all its own products.

정답·해설·해석 p.120

🕐 제한 시간 6분

Questions 01-04 refer to the following brochure.

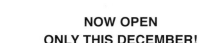

NOW OPEN
ONLY THIS DECEMBER!

Come to Miami's Dream Land
for a unique holiday attraction

Winter World

Enter a magical world covered in ice and snow and take part in some of the delightful outdoor traditions of winter, such as building ice castles and snowmen. Or simply walk along snow-covered paths as you view sculptures created by professional ice carvers from around the world.

Don't forget to check out our improved ice slide, which is now wider and longer!

Until December 31 only, you may visit Winter World from Mondays to Fridays, between 4 P.M. and 11 P.M., and Saturdays and Sundays, from 3 P.M. to midnight.

Please note that temperatures at Winter World can reach −15 degrees Celsius. Visitors are advised to dress warmly before entering the facility. Although taking photographs is allowed on the premises, extremely cold temperatures can damage electronic devices. Bring cameras at your own risk.

Admission is $8.50 on top of regular park entrance fees. All passes are available for purchase on www.dreamland.com/winter. Also, find out more about our yearly passes for all attractions by visiting www.dreamland.com.

01 What can visitors do in Winter World?

(A) Watch some sporting events
(B) Participate in traditional activities
(C) Go on a guided tour
(D) Purchase clothing for cold weather

02 What does the brochure indicate about Winter World?

(A) It is open to the public for a limited time.
(B) It is included in the admission fee to Dream Land.
(C) It is open until 11 P.M. everyday.
(D) It offers ice sculpting classes for beginners.

03 What is NOT stated about Dream Land?

(A) It is located in Miami.
(B) It permits photography in some areas.
(C) It offers annual admission rates.
(D) It closes some facilities during the winter.

04 According to the brochure, how can people book tickets?

(A) By contacting a travel agency
(B) By dialing a number
(C) By visiting an online site
(D) By going to the administrative office

Questions 05-06 refer to the following e-mail and information on a Web page.

TO:	\<Undisclosed recipients>
FROM:	Jaime Buenaventura \<Jaime.buenaventura@apollohealthclub.com>
DATE:	December 6
SUBJECT:	New Online Services

Dear members,

Apollo Health Club is pleased to announce new features on our Web site. You may now take advantage of different payment modes, including credit card and online transfers, to renew or upgrade a membership.

A Goldstar membership is only $940 and will give you access to various club areas, admittance to all classes, and consultations with training staff. Regular memberships are still $780.

In addition, the Web site now provides online enrollment. All you need is a computer to register for any class being offered. Just click on the registration link. The health club also offers new member forums on its Web site. Chat with other members or get advice from our health and wellness experts.

We hope that you will find these new features a convenient and welcome addition to our services.

Jaime Buenaventura
Operations Manager, Apollo Health Club

---

www.apollohealthclub.com/membership/renewal

Where wellness is a way of life · APOLLO HEALTH CLUB

HOME	CLASS SCHEDULES	MEMBERSHIP	FORUM

Thank you for your business!

Customer Information:

Name: Carolyn Wentz	Date: December 15
Contact number: 555-6633	Member number: CW-99876
Home address: 3426 Pinewood Drive, Libertyville, IL 60048	Membership validity: 12 months
E-mail: carolyn.wentz@recordmail.com	Payment received: $940.00

This is an automatic message to notify you about your membership renewal. You will be forwarded a copy of this message to the e-mail address you provided.

To learn more about your membership, click on the "HOME" tab or call our 24-hour hotline at 555-9696. Our representatives will be happy to assist you.

Regards,

Gerry Yuson
Customer Service Manager, Apollo Health Club

---

05 What is NOT offered by Apollo Health Club?

(A) A telephone service for customers
(B) Personal advice from health experts
(C) A variety of payment methods
(D) Spa and massage treatments

06 What is true about Carolyn Wentz?

(A) She is a Goldstar member.
(B) She has not yet paid her gym fee.
(C) She is uninterested in taking any classes.
(D) She recently called a hotline.

해커스 스타강사의 ▶
무료 해설강의 바로 보기
(5~6번 문제)

정답·해설·해석 p.122 / [별책] 토익 RC 필수 어휘 p.39

CHAPTER 04

추론 문제

토익 이렇게 나온다!

추론 문제는 지문의 내용을 근거로 새로운 사실을 추론할 수 있는지를 확인하는 문제이다. 추론 문제는 글의 대상이나 출처를 묻는 문제처럼 지문 전체가 단서인 전체 정보 추론 문제와, 지문 일부를 단서로 하여 특정 세부 사항을 추론하는 세부 정보 추론 문제로 나눌 수 있다. 반드시 지문에 근거해서 답을 찾아야 하는 문제이며, 평균 10문제가 출제된다.

토익 질문 유형 및 전략

빈출 질문 유형

전체 정보 추론	[글의 대상]	**For whom** is the announcement **(most likely) intended**? 공고는 누구를 대상으로 하는가?
	[글의 출처]	**Where** would this notice **most likely** be found? 이 공고는 어디서 볼 수 있을 것 같은가?
세부 정보 추론	[~에 대해 암시/추론되는 것]	**What** is **suggested/implied** about Ms. Collins? Ms. Collins에 대해 암시/추론되는 것은?
		What is **indicated** about Denton Manufacturing? Denton 제조 회사에 대해 암시되는 것은?
		* What is indicated ~? 형태는 Not/True 문제뿐만 아니라 추론 문제로도 출제된다.
		What does Mr. Lim **suggest** about his trip? Mr. Lim이 그의 여행에 대해 암시하는 것은?
	[~의 신분/ ~할 것 같은 사람]	**Who most likely** is Jennifer Carter? Jennifer Carter는 누구일 것 같은가?
		Who will **probably** lead the discussion? 누가 토론을 이끌 것 같은가?
	[~할 것 같은 것]	**What** will **most likely** happen on October 9? 10월 9일에 무엇이 일어날 것 같은가?

문제 풀이 전략

STEP 1 질문을 읽고 핵심 어구를 확인한다.
질문에 핵심 어구가 없는 전체 추론 문제의 경우, 각 보기들을 먼저 확인해 둔다.

STEP 2 지문에서 질문의 핵심 어구와 관련된 내용을 찾는다.
질문의 핵심 어구를 그대로 언급하거나 paraphrasing한 부분의 주변에서 정답의 단서를 찾는다. 질문에 핵심 어구가 없는 경우, 지문 전체를 읽으며 대상이나 출처를 암시하는 단서를 찾는다. Double/Triple passages의 경우, 다른 지문에서 정답의 단서를 찾아야 할 수도 있다.

STEP 3 지문을 바탕으로 추론할 수 있는 내용의 보기를 선택한다.

예제 송장

> Carrington Shipping Agency
> Branch: 342 Richmond Avenue, Castledale AZ 99867   Invoice Date: April 27 ● ─── **STEP 2** 지문에서 질문의 핵심 어구와 관련된 내용을 찾는다
>   Name: Joanna Peterson   Client Code: JP-98667
>   Payment Due: $238.96   Date Due: May 2
> You may pay the fee by credit card at www.carringtonshipping.com or mail a personal check to the branch office indicated above.

Q. What is suggested about Carrington Shipping Agency? ● ─── **STEP 1** 질문을 읽고 핵심 어구를 확인한다
     (A) It has more than one location. ● ─── **STEP 3** 지문을 바탕으로 추론할 수 있는 내용의 보기를 선택한다
     (B) It only accepts online service requests.
     (C) It offers discounts for domestic shipments.

해설 **추론 문제** 질문의 핵심 어구인 Carrington Shipping Agency에 대해 추론하는 문제이다. 'Carrington Shipping Agency, Branch: 342 Richmond Avenue, Castledale AZ 99867'에서 Carrington 운송사의 지점 주소가 명시되었으므로 Carrington 운송사는 여러 개의 지점이 있다는 사실을 추론할 수 있다. 따라서 (A) It has more than one location이 정답이다.

정답 (A)

지문 해석 p.124

HACKERS PRACTICE 토익 고득점을 위한 필수 연습

Paraphrasing 연습 지문의 내용과 일치하는 문장을 고르세요.

01

> For those interested in becoming a Large Goods Vehicle (LGV) driver, we recommend Veritas Training, the only training company that provides free retest training should the driver fail the first test.

(A) The training may be repeated once without charge.
(B) Veritas recommends that an LGV driver sign up for training.

02

> Henson Speakers provides the finest quality speakers available in the market. With zero tolerance for defects, Henson has made an enormous investment in high-tech factory equipment.

(A) Henson invested a great deal of money in production machinery.
(B) Henson has purchased a new factory to increase production rates.

03

> Our cellular service plans are individually tailored to fit the financial situation of each of our customers. Aside from the basic plan, Cell-Com provides extra services to make your entire cellular package fit your wireless communication needs.

(A) The basic plan is suitable for all communication needs.
(B) Pricing options are available for all budgets.

04

> Management has noted some opposition to the proposal for the company's reorganization. To address your concerns, we will be issuing a memorandum that will provide answers to your questions. We hope that this memo will lay your worries to rest.

(A) A conference is being scheduled for management and employees.
(B) There is an existing plan to restructure the company.

Doctors have been looking into alternative medicine as one way of speeding up a patient's recovery from an operation. In particular, herbs look very promising.

(A) Herbs may promote faster healing from surgery.
(B) Doctors use herbs during surgical operations.

We specialize in the installation of security systems, closed-circuit cameras, and flood lights. Our products are tested and approved by security professionals. For those making a purchase or service request for the first time, mention this advertisement and we will give you 10 percent off.

(A) Installations are free of charge when purchasing any security equipment.
(B) The customer can take advantage of a discount if he or she refers to the advertisement.

The Kennedy Business Center is giving a free one-time seminar on business financing options on August 24. Pre-registration is required as seating is limited.

(A) You need to sign up in advance to attend the seminar.
(B) The seminar is limited to employees only.

This Sunday at the beachfront by the pavilion the City Council will be hosting a community breakfast. The goal is to gather residents of the neighborhood for a morning outdoors, in support of reconstructing the pavilion's floor. Coffee and pastries, courtesy of Henry's Bakery, will be available from 8 A.M. to noon.

(A) A bakery is hosting a fundraiser to build a pavilion.
(B) A bakery will give out free food before noon.

09 광고

Enjoy all the sights, sounds, and sensations of Los Angeles by purchasing a public transportation day pass! Simply ask for a 24-hour tourist pass at any ticket counter or purchase one at a vending machine, and take advantage of unlimited use of subways and buses. Touch the card at subway turnstiles or bus fareboxes and get on board! Passes are $18 for adults and $14 for children and senior citizens.

Q. Where would the advertisement most likely be found?

(A) In a journal on transportation
(B) In a local tourist brochure
(C) In a senior citizen's magazine

10 편지

Dear Ms. Leary,

I just wanted to inform you about a change to Ms. Clarkson's schedule when she visits the branch here in San Diego next week. She will be visiting the head of research, Dr. Leo Menkin, at the laboratory facilities at 9:30 A.M. on Monday. Unfortunately, branch director Kyle Mason will not be back from his business trip at that time, so we'll change that appointment to Wednesday at 10 A.M. Please reply if you have any questions.

Sincerely,
Andy White

Q. What is indicated about Ms. Clarkson?

(A) She will be speaking to Dr. Leo Menkin about a job on Wednesday morning.
(B) She was previously scheduled to meet with Kyle Mason on Monday.
(C) She has already left for a business trip to a company branch.

11 이메일

TO: Soniajuarez@sunsetagency.com
FROM: LeonLee@sunsetagency.com

I just got your message this morning about the interview scheduled for 12:30 this afternoon. Don't worry about anything. I will contact Mr. Hanks and inform him that you have an emergency dental appointment and that I will be interviewing him for the position instead. I will send you a message after the meeting and let you know how it went. I hope you feel better soon!

Q. Who most likely is Mr. Hanks?

(A) An employee at a dental clinic
(B) An agent at a real estate firm
(C) An applicant for a job position

정답·해설·해석 p.124

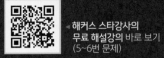

⏱ 제한 시간 6분

Questions 01-04 refer to the following article.

Colton City to Become Regional Medical Provider

The state's Department of Health announced that an expansion of the Colton City Medical Center will begin this summer. The additions will nearly double the size of the current facilities at a cost of $48 million. The new building will take three years to complete and will include a pediatrics ward, additional surgery facilities, a cancer treatment unit, and space for extra 80 beds. In addition, renovation work will be carried out on the current wards and emergency room.

The Department of Health said the enlarged medical center will serve residents of Colton City as well as those in smaller, nearby towns including Rosedale, Lavington, and Freemont. At the moment, all towns have their own hospitals, but plans are to downsize the facilities and make them into walk-in clinics only. However, Rosedale and Freemont will keep their emergency rooms open. Staff currently employed at the hospitals will either work at the clinics or be transferred to Colton City. Ellen Raines, spokesperson for the Department of Health said, "Residents with medical problems that cannot be taken care of at the clinics will be referred to Colton Medical Center." She also stated that the expanded center will become the primary medical care provider in the region.

01 Which city will NOT have an emergency room?

(A) Colton City
(B) Rosedale
(C) Lavington
(D) Freemont

02 What does the article suggest about the upcoming expansion?

(A) It will be completed by the end of the year.
(B) It is being paid for with borrowed funds.
(C) It will allow a hospital to accommodate more patients.
(D) It is being carried out at numerous regional hospitals.

03 What will most likely happen to current hospital employees?

(A) They will not lose their jobs because of changes.
(B) They will be expected to accept cuts in pay.
(C) They will renegotiate the terms of their contracts.
(D) They will go through additional training.

04 Who is Ellen Raines?

(A) A representative for a construction firm
(B) A physician at a local clinic
(C) A representative for a government agency
(D) A patient at a medical center

Questions 05-06 refer to the following advertisement and e-mail.

 Haven Studios: Casting Call

Haven Studios is announcing a casting call for its new film production, *Home Away from Home*. The movie will be a comedy directed by Alex Jones about an American exchange student in China. We are looking for actors and actresses to audition for the following roles:

Character: Sam Evans (American male, aged 20-25)
Character: Ming Na Chin (Asian female, aged 20-25, fluent in English and Chinese)
Character: Mr. Ping (Asian male, aged 50-60, fluent in English and Chinese)
Character: Mrs. Evans (American female, aged 40-50)

If you fit the description we are looking for and are willing to work overseas for two months, send a copy of your résumé and head shot to homeaway@havenstudios.com by April 14. Only those selected for auditions will be contacted. Please do not come to the auditions unless we have requested that you do so. Tryouts will take place on April 16-17 at Haven Studios, 334 Bradbury Boulevard. Specific times for auditions will be sent by our casting director, Maureen O'Donnell, to selected performers by e-mail. If you have any questions, contact one of our production staff at 555-8877.

FROM Gina Poole <ginapoole@coolmail.com>
TO Henry Chan <hchan@instamail.com>
SUBJECT Audition
DATE April 12

Hi Henry,

My friend Dennis Lowe showed me an advertisement the other day about a casting call for an upcoming movie. I'm actually going to audition for a role myself on April 16, and thought you might also want to contact the studio. There is a character that you would be perfect for, as they are looking for a male actor who can also speak Chinese. The movie is being produced by Haven Studios, and you can send your résumé and headshot to their casting director at homeaway@havenstudios.com. Let me know if they contact you!

Good luck!

05 For whom is the advertisement most likely intended?

(A) Student film directors
(B) Audience members for a show
(C) Performers looking for movie roles
(D) Participants in an acting competition

06 What role will Mr. Chan most likely inquire about?

(A) Sam Evans
(B) Mr. Ping
(C) Ming Na Chen
(D) Mrs. Evans

정답·해설·해석 p.126 / [별책] 토익 RC 필수 어휘 p.40

해커스 스타강사의 ▶
무료 해설강의 바로 보기
(5~6번 문제)

의도 파악 문제

토익 이렇게 나온다!

의도 파악 문제는 주로 메시지 대화문에서 인용구가 쓰인 의도를 정확히 파악할 수 있는지를 확인하는 문제이다. 해당 인용구의 의미를 확인하고, 인용구의 주변 문장을 통해 문맥상 의미를 파악하여 일치하는 보기를 선택하면 된다. 인용구 자체만으로는 여러 방향의 해석이 가능하므로, 반드시 지문의 내용에 근거하여 답을 선택해야 한다. 매회 2문제가 출제된다.

토익 질문 유형 및 전략

빈출 질문 유형

의도 파악   At 12:15, what does Mr. Landry mean when he writes, "I believe so"?
12시 15분에, Mr. Landry가 "I believe so"라고 썼을 때, 그가 의도한 것은?

At 10:48 A.M., what does Mr. Bernard most likely mean when he writes, "Go ahead"?
오전 10시 48분에, Mr. Bernard가 "Go ahead"라고 썼을 때, 그가 의도한 것 같은 것은?

문제 풀이 전략

STEP 1 질문을 읽고 인용구와 그 위치를 확인한다.

STEP 2 지문에서 인용구의 주변 문장을 읽고 인용구의 문맥상 의미를 파악한다.

인용구의 주변에서 인용구가 어떤 의미로 쓰였는지 파악한다. 인용구의 주변 문장만 읽고 정답을 찾기 힘들 경우, 지문 전체의 흐름을 이해한 후 인용구의 의미를 파악한다.

STEP 3 인용구가 쓰인 의도를 가장 잘 나타낸 보기를 선택한다.

예제   메시지 대화문

Nancy Hillard	13:44
Are you on your way to the airport?	
Kyle Larson	13:47
Yes. Just picked up the rental car, so I'm about 20 minutes away.	
Nancy Hillard	13:48
Take your time. I just got word that Mr. Gupta's flight has been delayed by up to an hour and a half.	
Kyle Larson	13:53
That long? Should I turn back and wait at the office?	
Nancy Hillard	14:01
<u>Just go ahead</u>. Make sure you meet Mr. Gupta at the arrival area. It's his first time here.	

STEP 2
지문에서 인용구의 주변 문장을 읽고 인용구의 문맥상 의미를 파악한다

STEP 1
질문을 읽고 인용구와 그 위치를 확인한다

STEP 3
지문을 바탕으로 추론할 수 있는 내용의 보기를 선택한다

Q. At 14:01, what does Ms. Hillard mean when she writes, "Just go ahead"?
(A) She thinks Mr. Larson should return to the office.
(B) She will follow Mr. Larson to the airport at a later time.
(C) She wants Mr. Larson to proceed as originally planned.

해설   **의도 파악 문제** Ms. Hillard가 의도한 것을 묻는 문제이므로, 질문의 인용어구(Just go ahead)가 언급된 주변 문맥을 확인한다. 'Should I turn back and wait at the office?'(13:53)에서 Mr. Larson이 되돌아가서 사무실에서 기다려야 할지 묻자 Ms. Hillard가 'Just go ahead'(그냥 가세요)라고 한 후, 'Make sure you meet Mr. Gupta at the arrival area.'(14:01)에서 반드시 Mr. Gupta를 도착 구역에서 만나라고 한 것을 통해, Ms. Hillard는 Mr. Larson이 원래 계획한 대로 공항으로 가기를 원한다는 것을 알 수 있다. 따라서 (C) She wants Mr. Larson to proceed as originally planned가 정답이다.

정답   (C)

지문 해석 p.127

Paraphrasing 연습   지문의 내용과 일치하는 문장을 고르세요.

01

> The International Association of Business Speakers is holding its yearly speech competition beginning July 1. Contestants must give a five-minute talk on a subject of their choosing. The winners from each division will compete in a final event at our annual gathering on September 10.

(A) Contestants were assigned a topic to speak about.
(B) Participants may decide on the subjects of their speeches.

02

> At chef Daniella Esparza's new bistro La Graella, the menu revolves around simple yet hearty dishes made from carefully chosen ingredients. Located along Water Street, it has quickly become a favored lunch spot for executives working in the nearby financial district. Reservations from 12 P.M. through 2 P.M. are highly advised.

(A) Diners should call to book a table for lunch.
(B) La Graella is usually only open for lunch.

03

> In a survey conducted by the Reedville Public Library, it was revealed that 48 percent of respondents visited the facility regularly. Of that number, the majority expressed satisfaction with the programs and services offered by the library.

(A) Reedville residents rarely visit the public library.
(B) The public library's frequent visitors are pleased with its offerings.

04

> On Monday, city transport officials announced a series of subway station closures that will begin in May. In total, 16 stations around Hanford City will be closed for up to 14 months at a time to make way for much needed renovations.

(A) Several subway stations will be closed for over a year.
(B) City officials plan to construct 16 new subway stations in the coming years.

05

At the time of booking, reservations must be guaranteed by a deposit equivalent to one night's stay. Guests may cancel a reservation up to three days prior to arrival. In the event of a late cancellation, the deposit will not be returned.

(A) Guests only need to pay for one night upon making a reservation.
(B) Guests staying more than one night must pay a higher deposit.

06

Louisville sports fans will have to wait another year for the city's new stadium to open. Construction has been pushed back on account of a plan to increase the structure's capacity further. When completed, the facility will hold 55 thousand people.

(A) Sports fans are unhappy about a stadium's delayed construction.
(B) Altered plans for a sports facility have resulted in a delay.

07

The turnout at the recently concluded trade fair has been the largest yet in the event's 15-year history. Many of those in attendance praised the way organizers handled it, and said they would gladly come back next year if invited.

(A) Attendance at next year's event is expected to double.
(B) A number of participants are interested in taking part in an event again.

08

Your satisfaction is our main concern. Visit our Web site to view a list of frequently asked questions about your electric bill. If your concern is not listed, you may send an e-mail to customerservice@volectra.com, or call 555-2302 during our regular business hours.

(A) Billing complaints must be handled by following a set of procedures.
(B) Customers can address billing concerns in a variety of ways.

09 메시지 대화문

Jack Parker	7:35 P.M.
Why don't we take the city bus together tomorrow? It stops near our office every 30 minutes or so.	
Beth Kim	7:36 P.M.
I don't know. I have a meeting downtown in the morning. It'll be easier for me to take a taxi.	
Jack Parker	7:38 P.M.
No problem. Text me when you get there. We can grab something to eat before the conference begins.	
Beth Kim	7:40 P.M.
Good idea. That'll give us a chance to review the materials for the presentation.	

Q. At 7:36 P.M., what does Ms. Kim most likely mean when she writes, "I don't know"?

(A) She thinks Mr. Parker's information is inaccurate.
(B) She is uncertain about a bus's departure time.
(C) She disagrees with Mr. Parker's suggestion.

10 메시지 대화문

Jerry King	16:06
Cindy, I was wondering if the commercial's been recorded. We have to make some changes to the script.	
Cindy Adams	16:08
You're in luck. The recording session's been pushed to Thursday. Why are additional changes needed?	
Jerry King	16:11
Mr. Blum requested them. I'll e-mail the details to you first thing tomorrow morning.	

Q. At 16:08, what does Ms. Adams mean when she writes, "You're in luck"?

(A) She will try to secure a deadline extension.
(B) Mr. King has a chance to revise a script.
(C) Mr. Blum gave his approval to record a commercial.

11 메시지 대화문

Anne Walker	[12:06]	Did you take the contract to Mr. Boyle's office yet?
Bill Hooper	[12:08]	He just signed it. Why? Is there a problem?
Anne Walker	[12:10]	Yeah. I noticed that the lease expiration date is wrong.
Bill Hooper	[12:13]	Can you make the correction right now? Have your assistant Kevin bring it here for Mr. Boyle to sign.
Anne Walker	[12:14]	I'm on it. It'll be ready within an hour. Sorry about this.

Q. At 12:14, what does Ms. Walker indicate she will do when she writes, "I'm on it"?

(A) Personally deliver a document
(B) Apologize to a real estate agent
(C) Give an assistant a task

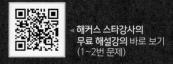
🕐 제한 시간 6분

Questions 01-02 refer to the following text message chain.

Libby Pike	10:05 A.M.

I heard that you've been promoted to manager of the Shelby branch! When are you moving?

Clyde O'Neill	10:05 A.M.

I leave in about two weeks.

Libby Pike	10:07 A.M.

You're going to be busy packing.

Clyde O'Neill	10:08 A.M.

I know. And I need to find a place to rent in Shelby. Since you worked at that branch last year, can you recommend any neighborhoods close to the office?

Libby Pike	10:12 A.M.

My apartment was in Crystal Heights, which might be OK for you. It's only a 15-minute walk to the office and in a really nice part of Shelby. What's your budget?

Clyde O'Neill	10:14 A.M.

I don't want to spend more than $700 a month.

Libby Pike	10:15 A.M.

I'm not sure. It'd be very hard to find an apartment for under $900 in that neighborhood.

Clyde O'Neill	10:16 A.M.

Then I might try looking in another area. Thanks anyway!

01 What is suggested about Ms. Pike?

(A) She will transfer to another branch.
(B) She pays over $700 per month in rent.
(C) She was once Mr. O'Neill's manager.
(D) She has lived in Shelby before.

02 At 10:15 A.M., what does Ms. Pike most likely mean when she writes, "I'm not sure"?

(A) She is not certain that a unit is vacant.
(B) She believes a budget is unrealistic.
(C) She thinks an area is inconveniently located.
(D) She was not informed about a promotion.

Questions 03-06 refer to the following online discussion chain.

Maria Jasso	3:45 P.M.	Hello, managers. I'm sorry for the short notice, but a group of students from the Loewing Institute of Technology will visit us at the automobile plant tomorrow for a tour. I'll be leading it, but I need your cooperation.
Alex Rocha	3:46 P.M.	Sure. What will we have to do?
Maria Jasso	3:47 P.M.	Well, the students are all engineering majors, and they are hoping to see how we implement automated processes. When they visit each area, I'd like you to give the students a brief overview of what your teams do and answer their questions.
Alex Rocha	3:48 P.M.	OK, I think I can manage that.
Maria Jasso	3:48 P.M.	In your case, Alex, it would also be great if you could show them how the robotic arms work.
Hitomi Yasui	3:49 P.M.	I'm happy to help, too. Out of curiosity, that's the same school that visited a couple of years ago, right? I recall doing something like this before.
Henry Lee	3:49 P.M.	I'll need to check whether I'm free.
Maria Jasso	3:49 P.M.	Correct. They sent some students here two years ago.
Henry Lee	3:50 P.M.	I want to know when this group tour starts. If it's after 1 P.M., then it's fine. I need to attend an event at my daughter's school in the morning.
Maria Jasso	3:52 P.M.	Oh, I forgot. It's actually going to be first thing in the morning. Please ask your assistant manager to cover for you.

| Send |

03 Why did Ms. Jasso contact a group of people?

(A) To go over some regulations
(B) To request some assistance
(C) To change a schedule
(D) To announce a transition

04 What has Mr. Rocha NOT been asked to do?

(A) Respond to inquiries
(B) Summarize team duties
(C) Give a demonstration
(D) Discuss job opportunities

05 At 3:49 P.M., what does Ms. Jasso mean when she writes, "Correct"?

(A) The plant has a partnership with several colleges.
(B) A program has been running for years.
(C) Students from Loewing have visited before.
(D) The student tour program has been prepared well.

06 What is suggested about Mr. Lee?

(A) He is in charge of production.
(B) He has participated in a student tour before.
(C) He was recently promoted to his current position.
(D) He has tomorrow morning off.

정답·해설·해석 p.129 / [별책] 토익 RC 필수 어휘 p.41

해커스 스타강사의 ▶
무료 해설강의 바로 보기
(1~2번 문제)

문장 위치 찾기 문제

토익 이렇게 나온다!
문장 위치 찾기 문제는 지문의 흐름을 파악하여 주어진 문장이 들어가기에 가장 알맞은 위치를 고를 수 있는지를 확인하는 문제이다. 주어진 문장 내의 단서를 이용해서 해당 문장이 들어갈 위치를 찾을 수 있다. 따라서 주어진 문장의 내용과 지문의 흐름을 정확하게 파악한 후 주어진 문장이 들어가기에 적절한 위치를 선택하면 된다. 매회 2문제가 출제된다.

토익 질문 유형 및 전략

빈출 질문 유형

문장 위치   In which of the positions marked [1], [2], [3], and [4] does the following sentence best belong?
"This offer is valid only in the downtown hotel, and not in other branch accommodation in Columbia."
[1], [2], [3], [4]로 표시된 위치 중, 다음 문장이 들어갈 곳으로 가장 적절한 것은?
"이 할인은 시내 호텔에서만 유효하며, 콜롬비아 내 다른 지사의 숙박 시설에서는 유효하지 않습니다."

문제 풀이 전략

STEP 1 주어진 문장을 읽고 문장이 들어갈 위치의 앞뒤 내용을 예상한다.

STEP 2 주어진 문장 내의 단서를 이용하여 지문에서 예상한 내용이 나오는 부분을 찾아 주어진 문장을 삽입해본다.
• 주어진 문장 내의 핵심 어구를 파악한 후, 지문에서 핵심 어구와 관련된 내용을 찾아 빈칸이 있는 위치에 주어진 문장을 삽입해본다.
• 주어진 문장 내에 지시대명사(it, that, these 등)가 있다면 지문에서 지시대명사가 가리키는 것을 찾아 뒤에 있는 빈칸에 주어진 문장을 삽입해본다.
• 주어진 문장 내에 연결어(however, yet, also 등)가 있다면 빈칸이 있는 위치의 앞뒤 맥락을 파악하여 주어진 문장을 삽입해본다.

STEP 3 주어진 문장을 삽입했을 때 가장 자연스러운 위치를 정답으로 선택한다.

예제   기사

> **Sales Up but Profits Down for Fashion Retailer Majeste**
> Despite a boom in sales, profits declined by 10 percent at British retailer Majeste. — [1] —. Over the past 10 months, store sales rose 14 percent, thanks to three new franchise stores in Dubai, Singapore, and Shanghai. — [2] —. However, profits were ultimately eroded by the company's decision to move production out of Bangladesh. Executives predict a recovery next year as its factories in Myanmar gain momentum. — [3] —.

STEP 2
주어진 문장 내의 단서를 이용하여 지문에서 예상한 내용이 나오는 부분을 찾아 주어진 문장을 삽입해본다

Q. In which of the positions marked [1], [2], and [3] does the following sentence best belong?
"Online sales have been equally strong and grew by 30 percent."
(A) [1]
(B) [2]
(C) [3]

STEP 1
질문을 읽고 문장이 들어갈 위치의 앞뒤 내용을 예상한다

STEP 3
주어진 문장을 삽입했을 때 가장 자연스러운 위치를 정답으로 선택한다

해설   **문장 위치 찾기 문제** 지문의 흐름상 주어진 문장이 들어가기에 가장 적절한 곳을 고르는 문제이다. Online Sales have been equally strong and grew by 30 percent에서 온라인 매출이 동등하게 강세였으며 30퍼센트만큼 증가했다고 했으므로, 주어진 문장 앞에 매출과 관련된 내용이 있을 것임을 예상할 수 있다. [2]의 앞 문장인 'store sales rose 14 percent, thanks to three new franchise stores'(2번째 줄)에서 세 곳의 신규 가맹점 덕분에 매장 매출이 14퍼센트 증가했다고 했으므로, [2]에 주어진 문장이 들어가면 매장 매출 증가에 이어 온라인 매출 증가에 대해 이야기하는 자연스러운 문맥이 된다는 것을 알 수 있다. 따라서 (B) [2]가 정답이다.

정답   (B)

지문 해석 p.131

HACKERS PRACTICE 토익 고득점을 위한 필수 연습

Paraphrasing 연습   지문의 내용과 일치하는 문장을 고르세요.

01

The Blaze X8 is our thinnest tablet yet. It features a fast processor, a stunning display, and up to 32 gigabytes of storage when you choose the highest model. Prices start at $149.99 and for a limited time, we are offering free shipping.

(A) The most expensive model of the Blaze X8 costs $149.99.
(B) The Blaze X8 is slimmer than all previous models.

02

Frustrated with the amount of garbage littering coastal waters, a group of students invented a unique trash-collecting device made of plastic materials. The invention is currently being tested, and if successful, could attract investment.

(A) A project's success will depend on the amount of investment it receives.
(B) An invention may get financial support if it is found to actually work.

03

While this projector has been designed with the user's safety in mind, incorrect use could result in injury. Before operating the projector, please read the accompanying user manual and observe the guidelines contained therein. After reading, store the manual for future reference.

(A) Safety issues were considered when the projector was made.
(B) Users have recommended the proper way to handle a product.

04

According to a proposal by the Office of Labor and Employment, the salary limit that determines when a worker is eligible for overtime pay could be raised to $50,000 a year from its current level. If passed, the change could affect millions of workers.

(A) Those making $50,000 a year or less will benefit from a proposed change.
(B) Millions of dollars a year are already being spent to pay for overtime.

05

Regulators have approved broadband provider BDI's roughly $15 billion takeover of mobile phone carrier Elemeno. Commenting on the buyout, a spokesperson for BDI has given assurances that customers of either company should not expect service to decline as a result.

(A) A proposed buyout will lead to improvements in service.
(B) A company's actions will not diminish service in any way.

06

Photographer Kate Booth opened her latest exhibit at the Durham Gallery this week. Entitled "Feminine," it showcases a series of portraits of influential women. Accompanying the exhibit is a limited set of coffee-table books offering bonus photographs from the series. The book is also available for sale on www.katebooth.com.

(A) All of the photographs in a series are also featured in a book.
(B) A book being sold will include pictures not seen in an exhibit.

07

The Hammond Foundation wishes to thank all those who responded to its recent appeal for help. The group collected over $12 million in donations. In addition to providing food and medical aid, the funds will be used to build housing for the victims of Hurricane Wendy.

(A) A charitable group collected food and medicine for storm casualties.
(B) Storm victims can expect to receive various forms of assistance.

08

Routine maintenance is the responsibility of the building manager. If you have a maintenance request, please fill out the appropriate form available in the administration office. Requests will be dealt with in the order that they come in and every effort will be made to handle each one in a timely manner. In case of emergency, dial 555-2307.

(A) Requests will be handled based on the order that they are received.
(B) The building management will respond to each request right away.

09 안내문

> **VISITOR PARKING**
> Winslow University requires permits for use of its on-campus parking lots. Visitors may leave their vehicles only in lots designated with a "P" sign. — [1] —. There is a two-hour limit at metered spaces unless the vehicle displays a permit issued from a vending machine. — [2] —. Parking in these spaces costs $1.50 per hour between 8:00 A.M. and 4:00 P.M., Monday through Friday. Parking lots are open on weekends as well as holidays. — [3] —. For detailed information about on-campus parking, including a map, please visit www.winslow.edu/parking or download our mobile application.

Q. In which of the positions marked [1], [2], and [3] does the following sentence best belong?

"They are all available to visitors for parking free of charge on these days."

(A) [1]
(B) [2]
(C) [3]

10 기사

> First-time author Marsha Bachman will be signing copies of her book, *Stride to Success*, at the Orville Bookshop on June 23 at 1 P.M. Ms. Bachman is a retired US army captain with a 20-year career in the military. — [1] —. The book gives an account of Ms. Bachman's experiences and how they helped to shape her into the person she is today. Critics call it a touching yet light-hearted tale of triumph in the face of adversity. — [2] —. "A must-read," says Mandy Coleman of *The Denver Sentinel*. — [3] —.

Q. In which of the positions marked [1], [2], and [3] does the following sentence best belong?

"Now she gives motivational speeches at colleges and offices around the country."

(A) [1]
(B) [2]
(C) [3]

11 기사

> Norwegian oil company Borfinne could be betting on a massive spike in oil prices over the coming years. — [1] —. Analysts reached this conclusion following reports of the firm's worldwide fleet expansion plans. — [2] —. According to an unnamed source, the company placed an order for 15 new vessels to be delivered over the next two years. — [3] —. Borfinne has locations in the North Sea, the Gulf of Mexico, and the coastal waters of Western Africa. A spokesperson for Borfinne could not be reached for comment at the time of writing.

Q. In which of the positions marked [1], [2], and [3] does the following sentence best belong?

"The ships could conceivably be deployed in one of three offshore operations."

(A) [1]
(B) [2]
(C) [3]

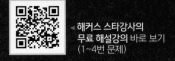
⏱ 제한 시간 8분

Questions 01-04 refer to the following e-mail.

From: Norma Lewis <nlewis@bestfurniture.com>
To: James Vogel <jvogel@smail.com>
Subject: Furniture order
Date: September 10

Dear Mr. Vogel,

We received your order of a rectangular Edgewood-series dining table with four matching chairs in light oak. However, we are sorry to say that the size you ordered is sold out at all our locations and will not be restocked by our supplier until the end of the month. — [1] —. We have given your order the highest priority and can ship it to you as soon as we receive it. — [2] —. If you need a table sooner, we would like to suggest the same model in a slightly larger size. It is also rectangular but measures 1.1 by 1.3 meters. — [3] —. Or you can check out other designs available that are in your preferred size. We hope to receive your reply as soon as possible so that we know how to proceed with your order. — [4] —.

Our deepest apologies for any inconvenience. Do let me know if you have any questions.

Very sincerely yours,
Norma Lewis
Customer Service
Best Furniture

01 What is the main purpose of the e-mail?

(A) To confirm shipment of an order
(B) To respond to a catalog request
(C) To inform a customer of a problem
(D) To provide furniture specifications

02 What is indicated about Best Furniture?

(A) It ships products internationally.
(B) It manufactures its own line of goods.
(C) It operates more than one store.
(D) It is holding a sale at the end of the month.

03 What is NOT an option that Ms. Lewis offers?

(A) Getting a larger size
(B) Paying a rush fee
(C) Viewing other available products
(D) Waiting for an item to be in stock

04 In which of the positions marked [1], [2], [3], and [4] does the following sentence best belong?

"To help you decide, we have attached a catalog so that you can compare each of the two table sizes."

(A) [1]
(B) [2]
(C) [3]
(D) [4]

Questions 05-08 refer to the following announcement.

The Hastings Gallery is delighted to reveal that the Paul and Marina Novak Collection will be returning for public viewing in September. — [1] —. Featuring over 300 works of art produced by Australian artists between 1924 and 1988, the collection exhibit was closed last year for minor refurbishments of the gallery space. A small event has been planned to commemorate the occasion. — [2] —. Please await further announcements.

About the collection:
The collection was donated to the Hastings Gallery by Melbourne residents Paul and Marina Novak. Ms. Novak was a fashion designer in the 1940s when she married the physician Dr. Paul Novak. — [3] —. The couple shared a passion for art, which led Ms. Novak to become an art dealer in 1951. With the goal of promoting Australia's artists around the world, she labored for decades to identify the best emerging Australian artists and to generate interest in the work of Australian artists. — [4] —. Shortly after Ms. Novak's passing in 1991, all of the paintings were donated to the Hastings Gallery. It remains one of the largest gifts of art ever made to a gallery in the country.

05 What is mainly being announced?

(A) The sale of an art gallery
(B) The reopening of an exhibit
(C) The hiring of a curator
(D) The recognition of an artist

06 What is true about Marina Novak?

(A) She worked in fashion before dealing in art.
(B) Her art has appeared in galleries across Australia.
(C) She helped to fund the construction of a gallery.
(D) Her husband collected art from around the world.

07 What is NOT mentioned about the Paul and Marina Novak Collection?

(A) It consists of more than 300 pieces.
(B) It was given to a gallery for free.
(C) It contains pieces made from 1924 to 1988.
(D) It was partially damaged during a renovation.

08 In which of the following positions marked [1], [2], [3] and [4] does the following sentence best belong?

She simultaneously built up an outstanding private collection.

(A) [1]
(B) [2]
(C) [3]
(D) [4]

정답·해설·해석 p.133 / [별책] 토익 RC 필수 어휘 p.42

해커스 스타강사의 ▶
무료 해설강의 바로 보기
(1~4번 문제)

CHAPTER 07

동의어 찾기 문제

토익 이렇게 나온다!

동의어 찾기 문제는 지문에 나온 특정 단어와 뜻이 같은 단어를 보기 중에서 찾을 수 있는지를 확인하는 문제이다. 해당 단어가 들어있는 부분의 문맥을 파악한 후, 문맥 속의 뜻과 일치하는 단어를 보기에서 선택하면 된다. 한 가지 이상의 뜻을 가진 단어를 출제한 후, 그것의 동의어 여러 개가 보기에 출제되는 경우가 있으므로 문맥을 확인한 후 답을 선택해야 한다. 동의어 찾기 문제는 평균 2~4문제 정도 출제된다.

토익 질문 유형 및 전략

빈출 질문 유형

[Single passage]   The word "place" in paragraph 1, line 4 is closest in meaning to
1문단 네 번째 줄의 단어 "place"는 의미상 –와 가장 가깝다.

[Multiple passages]   In the letter, the word "class" in paragraph 3, line 2 is closest in meaning to
편지에서, 3문단 두 번째 줄의 단어 "class"는 의미상 –와 가장 가깝다.

문제 풀이 전략

STEP 1   질문에서 단어와 그 위치를 확인한다.
질문의 The word "~"에서 단어를 확인하고, in paragraph ~, line ~에서 해당 단어가 위치한 문단과 줄 수를 확인한다.

STEP 2   지문에서 해당 단어가 포함된 문장을 찾아 문맥상 의미를 파악한다.
해당 단어를 포함한 문장을 지문에서 찾아 문장 내에서 해당 단어가 어떠한 의미로 쓰였는지 파악한다. 해당 단어의 동의어이지만 문맥에서 쓰인 뜻과 다른 의미를 가진 단어가 오답 보기로 나오는 경우도 있으므로, 반드시 문맥을 통해 의미를 확인한다.

STEP 3   문맥상 가장 비슷한 의미의 보기를 선택한다.

예제   기사

> **The Trend of Online Retailing**
>
> A large number of small businesses no longer rent out store spaces or sign expensive leases. Opening an online shop or service is becoming more popular as rent fees continue to climb. Additionally, business owners are able to manage their accounting much more easily, and they can also avoid hiring too many additional employees.
>
> In addition, many retailers claim they are able to increase sales through online stores. The lower operational costs means they can offer lower prices to customers. Even with shipping fees, many Internet retailers can sell items at a lower cost than regular stores.

STEP 2
지문에서 해당 단어가 포함된 문장을 찾아 문맥상 의미를 파악한다

STEP 1
지문에서 단어와 그 위치를 확인한다

Q. The word "climb" in paragraph 1, line 3 is closest in meaning to
   (A) improve
   (B) rise
   (C) expand

STEP 3
문맥상 가장 비슷한 의미의 보기를 선택한다

해설   **동의어 찾기 문제** 1문단 세 번째 줄의 climb을 포함하고 있는 문장 'Opening an online shop or service is becoming more popular as rent fees continue to climb.'에서 climb이 '오르다'라는 뜻으로 사용되었다. 따라서 '오르다'라는 뜻을 가진 (B) rise가 정답이다. (C) expand도 climb의 동의어이지만, climb이 이 문맥에서 크기나 양, 또는 수적인 면에서 '확대되다'라는 의미로 쓰이지 않았으므로 답이 될 수 없다.

정답   (B)

지문 해석 p.134

핵심 동의어 리스트

동사

01 appreciate
[əprí:ʃièit]

이해하다 = understand

I can appreciate(=understand) your concern regarding this matter and would be happy to meet with you to discuss it further.
저는 이 문제에 대한 당신의 염려를 이해하며 기꺼이 당신과 만나서 이에 대해 더 논의하길 원합니다.

감사하다 = give thanks for

We appreciate(=give thanks for) all the hard work the team has done on this project and would like to invite you all to a celebratory dinner.
우리는 이 프로젝트에 대해 팀이 들인 모든 노고에 감사드리고 축하 만찬에 여러분 모두를 초청하고자 합니다.

02 assume
[əsú:m]

생각하다, 추측하다 = suppose

The clients assume(=suppose) that rumors of the company's financial problems are exaggerated. 고객들은 그 회사의 재정 문제에 관한 소문이 과장되었다고 생각한다.

(책임 등을) 지다, 떠맡다 = take on

Most students assume(=take on) a large amount of debt during their time at university. 대부분의 학생들은 대학에 다니는 기간 동안 많은 빚을 진다.

03 attract
[ətrǽkt]

(관심·흥미를) 끌다, 유인하다 = draw, appeal to

Our new line of skin products aims to attract(=draw, appeal to) mostly middle-aged women. 우리의 새로운 스킨 제품 라인은 주로 중년 여성들의 관심을 끄는 것을 목표로 한다.

04 cover
[kʌ́vər]

포함하다 = include

The cost estimates cover(=include) all shipping, handling fees, and taxes.
비용 견적은 모든 배송, 취급 수수료와 세금을 포함한다.

논의하다 = address, discuss

The topic of greenhouse gas emissions was covered(=addressed, discussed) at the seminar. 온실가스 배출에 관한 주제는 그 세미나에서 논의되었다.

지불하다 = pay for

Sara brought only enough cash to cover(=pay for) her own accommodation expenses. Sara는 그녀의 숙박비를 지불하기에 충분할 만큼의 돈만 가져왔다.

보도하다 = report on

The journalist covered(=reported on) the hotel's grand opening.
그 기자는 그 호텔의 대개장에 대해 보도했다.

(분실·상해 등에 대해 보험으로) 보장하다 = insure

Many complained that the new health insurance does not cover(=insure) preexisting medical conditions. 많은 사람들은 새로운 건강 보험이 기존에 가지고 있는 질병들을 보장하지 않는다고 항의했다.

감추다, 숨기다 = conceal

The management decided not to cover(=conceal) the defects of the products but rather to recall the items immediately. 경영진은 제품의 결함을 감추기보다는 오히려 제품을 즉시 회수하기로 결정했다.

05 decline
[dikláin]

거절하다, 사양하다 = reject

The credit card was declined(=rejected) because the customer had exceeded his monthly limit. 그 고객은 그의 월 한도를 초과했기 때문에 신용카드가 거절되었다.

06 keep [ki:p]	계속 유지하다, 보유하다 = **retain, maintain** Make sure to keep(=retain, maintain) accurate records of your travel expenses. 반드시 계속해서 여행 경비의 정확한 기록을 유지하세요.
07 reflect [riflékt]	반영하다, 나타내다 = **indicate** His work has reflected(=indicated) a high level of competency and professionalism. 그의 작업은 높은 수준의 능력과 전문성을 반영해 왔다.
08 renew [rinʲúː]	연장하다 = **extend, lengthen** The law firm decided to renew(=extend, lengthen) its office lease for another two years. 그 법률 회사는 사무실 임대차 계약을 2년 더 연장하기로 결정했다.
09 submit [səbmít]	제출하다 = **file, send in, place** Applicants for the marketing position must submit(=file, send in, place) their forms and résumés by June 27. 마케팅직 지원자들은 그들의 서류와 이력서를 6월 27일까지 제출해야 한다.
10 serve [səːrv]	제공하다 = **provide** The airline will serve(=provide) hot meals to all passengers on flights to Beijing. 그 항공사는 베이징으로 가는 항공편의 모든 승객들에게 따뜻한 식사를 제공할 것이다. 근무하다 = **act, work** Mr. Brian Davis will serve(=act, work) as the temporary director until a replacement can be found. Mr. Brian Davis는 후임자가 구해질 때까지 임시 국장으로 근무할 것이다.
11 stress [stres]	강조하다 = **emphasize** Skyview's factory managers always stress(=emphasize) the importance of safety in the workplace. Skyview사의 공장장들은 작업장 내 안전의 중요성을 항상 강조한다. 걱정하게 하다 = **trouble** Mr. Arthur is stressed(=troubled) by the planning of the annual investors' meeting. Mr. Arthur는 연례 투자자 회의 준비로 걱정했다.
12 sustain [səstéin]	부양하다, 유지하다 = **maintain** The company produces enough wheat to sustain(=maintain) the entire nation's population. 그 회사는 나라 전체의 인구를 부양하기에 충분한 밀을 생산한다. (큰 손실·충격을) 입다, 경험하다 = **suffer** Many investors sustained(=suffered) heavy losses last week after the stock market crashed. 많은 투자자들이 주식 시장이 폭락한 후인 지난주에 큰 손실을 입었다.
13 treat [triːt]	대우하다, 다루다 = **deal with** The workshop will show employees how to treat(=deal with) customers with complaints. 그 워크숍은 직원들에게 불만이 있는 고객들을 어떻게 대우하는지 보여줄 것이다.

명사

14 atmosphere [ǽtməsfìər]	분위기, 환경 = **environment** The hotel created an exotic atmosphere(=environment) by filling their lobby with plants and flowers. 그 호텔은 로비를 식물과 꽃으로 채움으로써 이국적인 분위기를 만들어 냈다.

15 commission
[kəmíʃən]

수수료 = **fee**

All store clerks receive a 20 percent commission(=fee) for every sale they make.
모든 상점 직원들은 그들이 이뤄낸 모든 판매에 대해 20퍼센트의 수수료를 받는다.

위원회 = **committee**

A meeting on the history preservation was publicly announced by commission
(=committee). 역사 보존에 관한 회의가 위원회에 의해 공식적으로 발표되었다.

16 consideration
[kənsìdəréiʃən]

고려, 숙고, 관심 = **attention**

The director recommended several filming locations for the studio's consideration
(=attention). 감독은 영화사가 고려해 볼 만한 영화 촬영 장소 몇 곳을 추천했다.

17 course
[kɔːrs]

방향 = **direction**

In today's meeting, we will discuss the course(=direction) of our corporate strategy
for next year. 오늘 회의에서, 우리는 내년을 위한 회사 전략의 방향에 대해서 논의할 것이다.

18 effect
[ifékt]

영향, 결과 = **result, outcome**

The CEO's resignation is having a negative effect(=result, outcome) on the
company's public image. 최고 경영자의 사임은 회사의 대외 이미지에 부정적인 영향을 미치고 있다.

소지품, 소유물 = **possession**

During work hours, employees' personal effects(=possessions) should be stored in
their lockers. 작업 시간 동안, 직원들의 개인 소지품은 각자의 물품 보관함에 보관되어야 한다.

19 facility
[fəsíləti]

시설, 기관 = **establishment**

Potential clients from around the world are visiting next week to meet with our
executive staff and tour our facility(=establishment).
전 세계의 잠재적 고객들이 자사의 간부들을 만나고 시설을 견학하기 위해 다음 주에 방문할 것이다.

수월함, 쉬움 = **ease**

Mr. Kent is an accomplished musician who is able to perform some of the most
difficult piano compositions with great facility(=ease).
Mr. Kent는 가장 어려운 몇몇 피아노 악곡을 매우 수월하게 연주할 수 있는 뛰어난 음악가이다.

20 feasibility
[fìːzəbíliti]

(실행) 가능성 = **possibility, viability**

The accountants will assess the feasibility(=possibility, viability) of marketing in
China. 그 회계사들은 중국에서의 마케팅의 가능성을 평가할 것이다.

21 paycheck
[péitʃèk]

급여 = **salary, wage**

Greyson Enterprises offers monthly rather than weekly paychecks(=salaries,
wages) to their employees. Greyson사는 직원들에게 주급이 아닌 월급을 준다.

22 provision
[prəvíʒən]

보급품, 공급품 = **supply**

Mr. White suggested we place the order this week before we run out of provisions
(=supplies). Mr. White는 우리가 보급품이 떨어지기 전인 이번 주에 주문을 해야 한다고 제안했다.

준비 = **arrangements**

CAN-Rail makes special seating provisions(=arrangements) for senior citizens and
passengers traveling with young children.
CAN-Rail사는 노인들 또는 어린이와 함께 여행하는 승객들을 위한 특별 좌석을 준비한다.

23 proprietor
[prəpráiətər]

소유주 = owner

It is the responsibility of the building proprietor(=owner) to maintain and repair the elevators. 승강기를 유지 및 보수하는 것은 건물 소유주의 책임이다.

24 stock
[stɑk]

재고, 재고품 = inventory, supply

The supplier's stock(=inventory, supply) of computer keyboards is nearly depleted. 공급자의 컴퓨터 자판 재고가 거의 바닥났다.

주식 = shares

The textile manufacturer decided to sell 30 percent of their company's stock (=shares). 그 섬유 제조사는 자사 주식의 30퍼센트를 매각하기로 결정했다.

25 term
[tə:rm]

조건 = condition

All staff are permitted two weeks of vacation according to the terms(=conditions) of their contracts. 모든 직원들은 그들의 계약 조건에 따라 2주의 휴가가 허용된다.

기간 = period

After the two-year term(=period) is complete, the tenant has the option of renewing the rental contract. 2년의 기간이 끝난 후에, 세입자는 임대 계약을 갱신할 선택권을 갖는다.

26 variety
[vəráiəti]

다양성 = diversity

Delmonico Restaurant is famous for the variety(=diversity) of flavors in its dishes. Delmonico 식당은 다양한 맛의 요리로 유명하다.

종류, 범위 = kind, range

Our laptops are offered in many varieties(=kinds, ranges) to suit everyone's needs. 우리의 노트북 컴퓨터는 모든 사람의 요구에 부합할 수 있도록 다양한 종류로 제공됩니다.

형용사

27 certain
[sə:rtn]

특정한 = specific

Recycling centers will be made available to residents only at certain(=specific) locations throughout the city. 재활용 센터는 도시 전역의 특정 지역에서만 주민들에게 이용 가능하게 될 것이다.

28 due
[dju:]

~할 예정인 = scheduled

Construction of Fairview Children's Hospital is due(=scheduled) for completion at the end of March. Fairview 아동 병원의 건설은 3월 말에 완공될 예정이다.

29 effective
[iféktiv]

효율적인 = efficient

Ms. Getty conducted a workshop that focused on more effective(=efficient) production methods. Ms. Getty는 더 효율적인 생산 방법에 초점을 둔 워크숍을 실시했다.

유효한 = valid

The discount offered by the bookstore is effective(=valid) until the end of the month. 그 서점에서 제공되는 할인은 이달 말까지 유효하다.

30 notable
[nóutəbl]

중요한 = important

Beatrice Zbornak is a notable(=important) figure in the civil rights movement. Beatrice Zbornak은 시민권 운동에서 중요한 인물이다.

31 immediate
[imíːdiət]

즉각적인, 당장의 = instant

The public is asking for immediate(=instant) action by the government over the high unemployment rate. 대중은 높은 실업률에 대해 정부의 즉각적인 대응을 요구하고 있다.

당면한 = current

The firm is too busy with a particular case of immediate(=current) concern to take on any new clients. 그 회사는 당면한 우려와 관련된 특정 사건으로 너무 바빠서 새로운 고객들을 유치할 수 없다.

32 liable
[láiəbl]

~하기 쉬운 = likely

Computers are more liable(=likely) to crash when four or more applications are running at once. 컴퓨터는 4개 이상의 응용 프로그램이 동시에 실행될 때 더 고장 나기 쉽다.

책임이 있는 = responsible

The court decided that the supplier was liable(=responsible) for the cost of damage to the shipment. 법원은 공급자가 배송 손상 비용에 대한 책임이 있다고 판결을 내렸다.

33 prominent
[prámənənt]

유명한 = well-known

Professor McClanahan is a prominent(=well-known) expert in the field of alternative energy. McClanahan 교수는 대체 에너지 분야에서 유명한 전문가이다.

34 sharp
[ʃɑːrp]

급격한 = rapid

Snowstorms and a sharp(=rapid) drop in temperatures are expected for this weekend. 눈보라와 급격한 기온 하락이 이번 주말 동안 예상된다.

35 sound
[saund]

견고한 = solid

The city authority called in a team of top engineers to ensure that the new bridge is as structurally sound(=solid) as possible.
시 당국은 새로운 다리가 가능한 한 구조적으로 견고하다는 것을 확실히 하기 위해 최고의 엔지니어팀을 초빙했다.

부사

36 consecutively
[kənsékjutivli]

연속적으로 = successively

Employees working for more than seven days consecutively(=successively) are eligible for a bonus. 7일 이상 연속으로 근무하는 직원들은 상여금을 받을 자격이 있다.

37 exceptionally
[iksépʃənəli]

특히 = especially

Lindstrom Jewelers is famous for making exceptionally(=especially) fine jewelry.
Lindstrom Jewelers사는 특히 정교한 보석을 제작하는 것으로 유명하다.

38 primarily
[praimérəli]

주로 = mainly

Movers Plus primarily(=mainly) serves people relocating within North America.
Movers Plus사는 주로 북미 내에서 이사하는 사람들에게 서비스를 제공한다.

39 randomly
[rǽndəmli]

무작위로, 불규칙적으로 = irregularly

Safety inspections at the factory seemed to be conducted quite randomly (=irregularly). 공장에서의 안전 검사는 완전히 무작위로 이루어지는 것처럼 보였다.

의미가 가장 가까운 단어를 고르세요.

01 **Place** your bag in the locker.   ⓐ Put ⓑ Select

02 The brochure **informed** customers about products.   ⓐ mentioned ⓑ told

03 **chance** to meet the guest speaker   ⓐ assembly ⓑ opportunity

04 the company's newest sports car **model**   ⓐ design ⓑ example

05 The sale had the merchandise **moved** quickly.   ⓐ sold ⓑ relocated

06 current **status** of employment   ⓐ state ⓑ fact

07 **regarding** the customer's request   ⓐ concerning ⓑ worrying

08 very **modest** energy consumption   ⓐ slight ⓑ limited

09 Financial experts **supported** the testimony.   ⓐ confirmed ⓑ looked after

10 will cost **a great deal of** money   ⓐ a reduction of ⓑ a large amount of

11 **expedite** the delivery schedule   ⓐ turn down ⓑ speed up

12 **track** the location of the shipment   ⓐ monitor ⓑ guide

13 The vehicle **performs** well in the winter.   ⓐ functions ⓑ acts

14 the company's **rotating** work schedule   ⓐ alternating ⓑ turning

15 **learn** new methods for accounting   ⓐ find out ⓑ look up

16 an **account** of her trip to Africa   ⓐ narrative ⓑ figure

17 **overlook** your special request   ⓐ accomplish ⓑ neglect

18 will forward you the **right** information   ⓐ correct ⓑ requested

19 **observe** the rules   ⓐ follow ⓑ establish

20 **confirm** a corporate agreement   ⓐ approve ⓑ reject

21 The speaker offered **tips** on Web marketing.   ⓐ summits ⓑ suggestions

22 Ms. Baines has an **outgoing** personality.   ⓐ friendly ⓑ leaving

23 a **finish** to protect it from rain and snow   ⓐ completion ⓑ coating

24 **launch** a new perfume   ⓐ develop ⓑ introduce

25 a **vacancy** for a mailroom assistant   ⓐ opening ⓑ career

26 have a previous **engagement**   ⓐ reservation ⓑ appointment

27 **maintain** the company's reputation   ⓐ preserve ⓑ assert

28 **complimentary** copies of the new book   ⓐ free ⓑ praiseworthy

29 assess the financial **damage**   ⓐ risk ⓑ loss

30 Gas prices are **falling**.   ⓐ inflating ⓑ decreasing

31 transfer the **balance** of the funds   ⓐ stability ⓑ remainder

32 Imports have **markedly** increased.	ⓐ distinctly ⓑ primarily
33 **meet** the board's requirements	ⓐ satisfy ⓑ encounter
34 **operate** a business	ⓐ work ⓑ run
35 his **impending** retirement	ⓐ approaching ⓑ voluntary
36 **demonstrate** how to use the fax machine	ⓐ explain ⓑ protest
37 Consumption of luxury goods dropped **abruptly**.	ⓐ significantly ⓑ suddenly
38 The editor **highlighted** the problems in the article.	ⓐ featured ⓑ corrected
39 The final meeting will **occur** next week.	ⓐ conclude ⓑ happen
40 Cooking aromas **draw** diners.	ⓐ attract ⓑ carry
41 Our license **expires** next month.	ⓐ perishes ⓑ finishes
42 **raise** the quality of our products	ⓐ elevate ⓑ gather
43 Ms. Haught was **honored** for her contribution.	ⓐ recognized ⓑ remembered
44 **face** the competition	ⓐ defeat ⓑ confront
45 a **thorough** search for missing luggage	ⓐ complete ⓑ random
46 **suspend** Internet service	ⓐ cancel ⓑ defend
47 **accrue** interest at 12 percent per year	ⓐ pay ⓑ accumulate
48 women's **apparel** production	ⓐ garment ⓑ jewelry
49 **affect** the economic state	ⓐ influence ⓑ pretend
50 be **anxious** to begin the new project	ⓐ hesitant ⓑ eager
51 a drop in industrial **output**	ⓐ profit ⓑ production
52 **relieve** his heavy workload	ⓐ alleviate ⓑ endure
53 a supermarket **patron**	ⓐ supporter ⓑ customer
54 The task **entails** much stress.	ⓐ involves ⓑ causes
55 as a **consequence** of the decision	ⓐ result ⓑ objective
56 **aggravate** the downturn in economic activity	ⓐ intensify ⓑ extend
57 the **provision** in the contract	ⓐ clause ⓑ supply
58 **outstanding** natural beauty	ⓐ exceptional ⓑ excessive
59 a nice **spot** for a picnic	ⓐ property ⓑ place
60 There was a lot of **speculation** about the new design.	ⓐ conjecture ⓑ configuration
61 **surpass** everyone's expectations	ⓐ exceed ⓑ increase
62 **assess** the value of the property	ⓐ depreciate ⓑ evaluate

정답 p.135

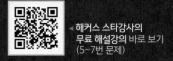
⏰ 제한 시간 7분

Questions 01-04 refer to the following e-mail.

From	Mario Martinez <mmartinez@rosenblattcorp.com>
To	All research coordinators <researchdept@rosenblattcorp.com>
Date	April 7
Subject	Improving Quality of Research

I finished looking over the research projects from last month and noticed a decline in the quality of work submitted by our staff. Our editor, Marcel Russolini, also mentioned that he has been spending twice as much time correcting technical errors. In addition, there has been an increase in cases where writers do not present sufficient details about statistics on the results of studies conducted by others.

Rosenblatt Corporation distributes information to several notable government agencies, foundations, and corporations. They depend on our research and analysis to guide them in policy making, decision making, and creating outreach programs around the globe. Therefore, it is crucial for us to follow strict standards and provide high quality research reports.

After a meeting with our director, Sonia Lieberman, we came up with possible solutions to these problems:
- Conducting workshops to address writing issues
- Providing additional time for the completion of projects
- Asking staff for suggestions on online research resources and which current subscriptions they would like to renew
- Scheduling longer breaks to give writers some downtime
- Holding more group meetings to discuss difficulties with projects

Should you think of other suggestions regarding this matter, let me know.

Mario Martinez

---

01 The word "notable" in paragraph 2, line 1 is closest in meaning to

(A) written
(B) important
(C) obvious
(D) common

02 What is NOT a suggestion offered by Ms. Lieberman and Mr. Martinez?

(A) Arranging staff workshops
(B) Having more frequent meetings
(C) Providing longer breaks
(D) Scheduling shorter deadlines

03 The word "renew" in paragraph 3, line 6 is closest in meaning to

(A) determine
(B) study
(C) extend
(D) renovate

04 What is indicated about Rosenblatt Corporation?

(A) It conducts research for several types of clients.
(B) It is controlled by the government.
(C) It publishes a variety of materials.
(D) It sponsors local outreach programs.

Questions 05-07 refer to the following brochure and review.

 ## Visionary Hotels and Convention Centers!
Making Business Events Enjoyable!

Have your next corporate event at one of our world-renowned hotels and see what everyone is talking about!

Visionary Hotel and Convention Center: Guam
Enjoy incredible scenery, beaches, and activities at our recently renovated facility. We offer three event halls, a business center, wireless Internet access, meeting rooms, and airport shuttles.

Visionary Hotel and Convention Center: Goa
Located on an expansive, private beach, the hotel includes an auditorium, two event halls, a business center, airport shuttles, and wireless Internet.

Visionary Hotel and Convention Center: Cebu
Make use of any of our five event halls, and take a scuba excursion or lounge on our beaches during your free time. A business center, meeting rooms, and wireless Internet are also available.

Visionary Hotel and Convention Center: Trinidad
Guests are raving about our newly renovated business center and swimming area. Two large event halls and an auditorium are also available.

To learn more about Visionary Hotels and Convention Centers or to book your next corporate event with us, log on to www.visionaryfacilities.com today!

Convention Center Review   p.284

(continued from p.283) The remodeled business center is truly the most amazing part of this hotel, offering 20 computers for use as well as a video-conference room. I did, however, find the lack of wireless Internet service an inconvenience for conference attendees. I was impressed with the event halls, as they were exceptionally well-maintained and included audiovisual equipment. Most noteworthy is the hotel's recently constructed swimming area, which has two large pools and a waterfall. As for accommodation, the rooms were clean and spacious. I highly recommend this convention center and hotel.

---

05 In the brochure, the word "facility" in paragraph 2, line 1 is closest in meaning to

(A) terminal　　　　(B) establishment
(C) division　　　　(D) region

06 In the review, the word "exceptionally" in line 4 is closest in meaning to

(A) especially　　　　(B) usually
(C) rarely　　　　(D) frequently

07 Which hotel did the author of the review visit?

(A) Guam　　　　(B) Goa
(C) Cebu　　　　(D) Trinidad

정답·해설·해석 p.138 / [별책] 토익 RC 필수 어휘 p.43

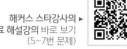 해커스 스타강사의 ▶
무료 해설강의 바로 보기
(5~7번 문제)

SECTION 2

지문 유형별 공략 - Single Passage

CHAPTER 08

이메일(E-mail)/편지(Letter)

토익 이렇게 나온다!

이메일/편지는 비즈니스 또는 개인 생활과 관련하여 정보를 주고 받는 글이다. 비즈니스와 관련된 이메일/편지에는 사내에서 또는 다른 회사 간에 직원들이 업무상 주고 받는 다양한 내용이 나오고, 개인 생활과 관련된 이메일/편지는 상점, 은행, 부동산업체 등의 시설과 고객 간에 오가는 것과 같이 실생활과 관련된 상황을 다룬다. 토익 리딩 Part 7에서 가장 많이 출제되는 지문 유형으로, 평균 2지문 정도 출제된다.

토익 질문 유형 및 전략

빈출 질문 유형

주제/목적 찾기 문제	이메일/편지의 목적을 묻는다.
	What is the purpose of the e-mail/letter? 이메일/편지의 목적은 무엇인가?
	Why was the e-mail sent? / Why was the letter written? 이메일은 왜 보내졌는가?/편지는 왜 쓰였는가?
	Why did Ms. Wellington write the e-mail/letter? Ms. Wellington은 왜 이메일/편지를 썼는가?
육하원칙 문제	요청 사항, 해야 할 일이나 기타 세부 사항을 주로 묻는다.
	What was Mr. Windfield required to do? Mr. Windfield는 무엇을 하도록 요구되었는가?
	What do residents have to do by Friday? 거주자들은 금요일까지 무엇을 해야 하는가?
	Why will the staff meeting be changed to Monday? 직원 회의는 왜 월요일로 변경될 것인가?
Not/True 문제	이메일/편지에 언급된 사람, 회사나 시설 등에 대해 일치하거나 일치하지 않는 것을 주로 묻는다.
	What is indicated about Ms. Rowan? Ms. Rowan에 대해 언급된 것은?
	What is NOT mentioned about Pro-Tech? Pro-Tech사에 대해 언급되지 않은 것은?
추론 문제	이메일/편지에 언급된 사람, 회사 등 특정 대상에 대해 추론할 수 있는 것을 주로 묻는다.
	Who most likely is May Adamson? May Adamson은 누구일 것 같은가?
	What is indicated about Abraham Jewelers? Abraham Jewelers사에 대해 암시되는 것은?

핵심 전략

1. 이메일/편지를 보내고 받는 사람이 누구인지 확인한다.
이메일/편지의 앞부분과 마지막에서 각각 받는 사람(Dear ~)이 누구인지, 보내는 사람이 누구인지 확인한다. 이메일의 경우, 지문 처음의 "From: ~"과 "To: ~"에서도 보내는 사람과 받는 사람을 알 수 있다.

2. 이메일/편지의 흐름을 알아야 한다.
주로 이메일/편지의 앞부분에는 목적이 언급되고, 이후에는 그에 따른 세부 사항 및 첨부된 것, 그리고 요청 사항이 이어진다.

3. 이메일/편지의 목적, 첨부된 것, 요청 사항 및 해야 할 일에 대한 내용은 관련 표현을 익혀 두면 쉽게 찾을 수 있다.

From: Harold Leighton <hleighton@sylvanbank.com>
To: Charlotte Bryant <c_bryant@webmail.net>
Subject: Online Banking Service Now Active   📄 servicecontract.word
Date: April 30

Dear Ms. Bryant,

Thank you for signing up for Sylvan Bank's online banking services. This e-mail serves as confirmation that your request has been approved. You will now be able to keep track of your accounts, pay bills, request overdrafts or extensions, activate a credit card, and wire funds to other accounts.

To activate your account, visit www.sylvanbank.com and log in to the Web site using the user name and password you registered at one of our branches.

Once you have successfully logged in, you will be asked to change your password again. Please use a mixture of numerals and letters no shorter than eight characters in length. We highly recommend that you change your password on a regular basis for the safety of your accounts. In addition, for extra protection you will be prompted to provide us with answers for three security questions. On occasion, you will have to give answers for these questions when logging in.

I have attached a copy of the service registration contract you signed for your reference. Please confirm your registration by replying to this e-mail. It will simply let us know that this is your correct e-mail address, and that you have received notification.

Thank you again, and we hope you will find our online banking services both convenient and efficient.

Sincerely,

Harold Leighton
Online Account Representative, Sylvan Bank

보내는 사람
받는 사람
받는 사람
목적
세부 사항
첨부된 것
요청 사항
보내는 사람

Q1. What is the purpose of the e-mail?

(A) To request answers to security questions
(B) To notify a customer of new Web site features
(C) To give information about using services
(D) To confirm personal details of a current client

Q2. What is mentioned about Ms. Bryant?

(A) She has already activated her account.
(B) She requested a change of password.
(C) She must answer a short survey.
(D) She signed an agreement with a bank.

해설 Q1 **주제/목적 찾기 문제** 이메일의 목적을 묻는 목적 찾기 문제이다. 'To activate your account, visit www.sylvanbank.com and log in to the Web site using your user name and password you registered'에서 계좌를 활성화하려면 www.sylvanbank.com에 방문하여 등록한 사용자 이름과 비밀번호를 사용하여 웹사이트에 로그인하라고 한 후, 이후에 해야 할 것들에 대해 알려주고 있으므로 (C) To give information about using services가 정답이다.

Q2 **Not/True 문제** 질문의 핵심 어구인 Ms. Bryant와 관련된 내용을 지문에서 찾아 보기와 대조하는 Not/True 문제이다. (A)는 'To activate your account, visit www.sylvanbank.com and log in to the Web site using your user name and password'에서 계좌를 활성화하려면 www.sylvanbank.com에 방문하여 사용자 이름과 비밀번호를 사용하여 웹사이트에 로그인하라고 했으므로 지문의 내용과 일치하지 않는다. (B)와 (C)는 지문에 언급되지 않은 내용이다. (D)는 'I have attached a copy of the service registration contract you signed'에서 서명한 서비스 등록 계약서의 사본을 첨부한다고 했으므로 (D) She signed an agreement with a bank가 정답이다.

정답 Q1 (C)   Q2 (D)

지문 해석 p.140

이메일/편지에 자주 나오는 ★핵심 표현

1. 이메일/편지의 목적

I'm pleased to ~ : ~하게 되어 기쁩니다

I'm pleased to inform you that your application for a small business loan has been accepted.
소기업 대출을 위한 귀하의 신청이 승인되었음을 알려 드리게 되어 기쁩니다.

I'm writing to ~ : ~하기 위해 이메일/편지를 씁니다

I'm writing to provide you with details on your most recent employee evaluation.
귀하의 가장 최근 직원 평가에 대한 세부 내용을 제공해 드리기 위해 이메일/편지를 씁니다.

2. 첨부된 것

I have attached/enclosed ~ : 저는 ~을 첨부/동봉했습니다

I have attached a copy of your delivery schedule, which shows when each purchase will arrive.
귀하의 배송 일정표 사본 한 부를 첨부했으며, 이는 각 구매품이 언제 도착할지를 보여주고 있습니다.

3. 요청 사항 및 해야 할 일

Could you ~? : ~해 주실 수 있으십니까?

Could you possibly have the items delivered by June 17 at the latest?
혹시 늦어도 6월 17일까지 물품들이 배달되도록 해 주실 수 있으십니까?

Be sure to ~ : 반드시 ~해 주십시오

Be sure to send the articles to the editor so she has a chance to look them over.
편집자가 기사들을 훑어볼 수 있도록 반드시 그것들을 편집자에게 보내 주십시오.

이메일/편지에 자주 나오는 ★필수 어휘

1. 성과 및 평가

avid adj. 열심인, 욕심 많은 　　　　= enthusiastic	**intelligent** adj. 똑똑한, 총명한
boost v. (사기를) 북돋우다, 신장시키다	**memorable** adj. 기억할 만한, 인상적인
creative adj. 창조적인, 독창적인	**praiseworthy** adj. 칭찬할 만한, 훌륭한
critical adj. 중요한, 비판적인	**proud** adj. 자랑스러운, 거만한
dedication n. 헌신, 전념 　　= devotion, commitment	**recommendation** n. 추천, 권고
efficiency n. 효율(성), 능률	**rewarding** adj. 보람 있는, 수익이 많이 나는
eminent adj. 탁월한, 저명한 　　　　= notable	**robust** adj. (신념이나 정신이) 확고한, 튼튼한
enhance v. 향상시키다, 높이다	**satisfaction** n. 만족, 만족함
expert n. 전문가; adj. 노련한	**self-confidence** 자신
influential adj. 영향력 있는, 유력한	**spectacular** adj. 장관을 이루는, 극적인
inspiring adj. 영감을 주는, 용기를 주는	**unique** adj. 유일한, 독특한

2. 제품 배송

authorization n. 공인, 허가

back order 재고가 없어 미룬 주문, 이월 주문; 이월 주문하다

contractor n. 계약자, 도급업자

crack n. 결함, 틈; v. 깨지다, 금이 가다

customer service department 고객 서비스부

exclusive adj. 독점적인, 한정된

faulty adj. 흠이 있는, 부적절한　　　　　= defective, flawed

figure n. 수치, 계산

flexibility n. 유연성, 융통성

function n. 기능, 작용; v. 기능을 하다, 작용하다　　= work

incident n. 사건, 일

instruction n. 설명, 지시

load n. 화물, 짐

malfunction n. 고장, 기능 부전; v. 제대로 작동하지 않다

missing adj. 없어진, 분실한

on-site 현장의, 현지의

prompt adj. 신속한, 즉석의; v. 부추기다　　= immediate, timely

query n. 질문, 문의

replacement n. 교체, 교환품

resolve v. 해결하다, 결정하다; n. 결심, 결의

shipment n. 수송, 발송

technician n. 기술자, 기사

3. 출판

audible adj. 들을 수 있는, 들리는

author n. 저자, 작가　　　　　　　　　　= writer

authorship n. 원작자, 출처

biography n. 전기, 일대기

biweekly adj. 격주의; adv. 격주로

book signing 책 사인회

censorship n. 검열

conceal v. 숨기다, 감추다

contain v. 담고 있다, 포함하다

coverage n. 보도, 범위

fictional adj. 허구적인, 소설의

handwritten adj. 손으로 쓴

literary adj. 문학의, 문학적인

manuscript n. 원고, 사본

nonfiction n. 논픽션, 소설이나 이야기 외의 산문

novel n. 소설; adj. 새로운

periodical n. 정기 간행물, 잡지

praise n. 찬사, 칭찬; v. 칭찬하다

press n. 신문, 언론계

publication n. 출판물, 발행

renowned adj. 유명한, 명성 있는　　= prominent, well-known, celebrated, noted

report n. 보도, 보고; v. 공표하다

subscription n. 예약 구독, 신청

4. 금융 및 경제

bank statement 은행 계좌 통지서

bankrupt adj. 파산한, 지불 능력이 없는

bounced check 부도 수표

capital adj. 자본의; n. 자본, 자산

cash a check 수표를 현금으로 바꾸다

checking account 당좌 예금 계좌

collection notice 수금 통지서

currency n. 통화, 유통

endorse v. (어음이나 증권에) 배서하다, 보증하다

exchange rate 환율, 외환 시세

fluctuate v. 변동하다, 불안정하다

interest n. 이자, 흥미

monetary adj. 통화의, 화폐의

monopoly n. 독점, 전매

mortgage n. 저당, 융자

outstanding balance 예금 잔고, 미변제 잔고

overdraw v. 초과 인출하다

overdue adj. (지불) 기한이 지난, 미불의

recession n. 불경기, 경기 침체　　　　= stagnation

remit v. 송금하다, (빚 등을) 면제하다

savings account 보통 예금 (계좌)

sluggish adj. 불경기의, 부진한

유형 연습   지문을 읽고 질문에 답하세요.

01 이메일

TO: Timothy Carey <tcarey@fastmail.com>
FROM: Gina Anderson <ganderson@pendletongolfclub.com>

I received your inquiry about registering for membership at the Pendleton Golf Club. Attached, you will find a copy of an application form and a handbook on our facilities and events. Please fill in the required details and submit the form to one of our staff members. Once your membership has been approved, you will be sent a membership card and may start using the facilities.

Q. What does Ms. Anderson request Mr. Carey to do?

(A) Send her a membership card
(B) Submit an application form
(C) Give her a copy of a brochure

02 편지

January 19
Gordon De Leon
85 Westlake Avenue
Windsor, ON N8T 1W2

Dear Mr. De Leon,

Thank you so much for facilitating our company's conflict management workshop last Friday. Several of our managerial staff members told me they found the material you covered very practical and enlightening. We plan to hold similar training sessions for our staff in the future, and would be delighted to have you conduct them as well. If you are interested in my offer, I will let you know of our plans soon.

Q. Why was the letter written?

(A) To request future services
(B) To schedule an upcoming event
(C) To provide information on training

03 편지

Dear Ms. Ogilvy,

This letter confirms your firm's participation in the upcoming Food and Beverage Fair in Paris. I have included three exhibitor's passes and a list of participants at the fair. Along with this letter, I've also sent you a brochure that includes useful information about accommodation, dining, and transportation in Paris.

Q. Who most likely is Ms. Ogilvy?

(A) An event organizer
(B) An applicant for a fair
(C) A travel agent

정답·해설·해석 p.140

🕐 제한 시간 12분

Questions 01-04 refer to the following letter.

Weber Jones
Apartment 34, Baronial Arms Building
1531 Lakewood Drive
Chicago, IL 73456

Dear Mr. Jones,

I'm writing to inform you that your partial manuscript for *No Second Chances* was received with much enthusiasm by the editors at Scout Publications. We feel it has tremendous potential in the non-fiction category and are requesting that you submit a copy of the complete manuscript for review. This is required of all first-time authors. Please note that the manuscript review process could take up to 12 months to finish as extensive fact-checking will be involved.

Once your work has been fully reviewed, we will notify you of our intention to publish by sending you an offer letter containing our proposed contract terms. If an agreement is successfully negotiated, your manuscript will undergo an editorial process in preparation for publication and release. Please note that your work will always be handled by the editors at Scout Publications with the utmost professionalism.

Enclosed with this letter is a document containing the formatting guidelines you must follow when submitting your manuscript. Be sure to read each item carefully. Far from being arbitrary, these guidelines have been carefully designed based on our 30 years of experience in the industry. We have rejected promising manuscripts in the past simply because these instructions were not followed.

In closing, we would like to remind you that your submission of a completed manuscript will indicate to us that you have not submitted your work for review to any other publisher.

James Carrington
Scout Publications

01 Why did Mr. Carrington write the letter?

(A) To recommend a writer for an editorial position
(B) To request a copy of a manuscript
(C) To approve a completed novel for publication
(D) To criticize an aspiring author's work

02 The word "terms" in paragraph 2, line 2 is closest in meaning to

(A) conditions
(B) words
(C) periods
(D) relations

03 What has Mr. Jones been asked to do?

(A) Revise a lengthy document
(B) Follow the editor's recommendations
(C) Read the enclosed instructions
(D) Evaluate a contract proposal

04 What is NOT mentioned about Scout Publications?

(A) It deals in works of non-fiction.
(B) It owns the rights to Mr. Jones's book.
(C) It has been around for three decades.
(D) It maintains strict formatting guidelines.

Questions 05-08 refer to the following e-mail.

To:	Steve Corcoran <scorcoran@lunettes.com>
From:	Mary Henry <mhenry@lunettes.com>
Date:	April 4
Subject:	Urgent Request
Attachment:	Oakland_event.word

Steve,

I was notified by the courier company this morning that a shipment of merchandise is on its way here to Lunette's design studio in L.A. It should arrive sometime between 2 p.m. and 5 p.m. this afternoon. The shipment contains finished samples that we ordered from a factory in Mexico, some of which I'd like to exhibit at next week's Fashion Expo in Oakland. While I would prefer to receive the items myself, I will be departing for Oakland at 1 p.m. I am needed there to oversee preparations for the coming event. Please accept the shipment on my behalf. And don't worry about payment, as I've already taken care of that.

When you receive the merchandise, make sure that the quantities are correct and that there is no visible damage to any of the pieces. Then, I need you to pick out specific articles of clothing and repack them for overnight delivery to Oakland using AirExpress. I've attached to this e-mail a list of the items that I need. It indicates the model numbers and colors I am looking for.

Send the package to me at Room 44B of the Grand Excelsior Hotel, 82 Whitehall Boulevard, Oakland, CA 94603. Call me at 555-7540 if there are any problems.

05 What is the purpose of the e-mail?

(A) To place an order for merchandise
(B) To arrange transport to an event
(C) To report on a firm's activities
(D) To request assistance with an upcoming delivery

06 What is indicated about Lunette's?

(A) It has a branch in Oakland.
(B) It closes after 5 P.M.
(C) It has a supplier in Mexico.
(D) It is hosting an expo.

07 Where will Mr. Corcoran send the items of clothing?

(A) To an office
(B) To an accommodation facility
(C) To an exhibition center
(D) To a department store

08 What is attached to the e-mail?

(A) Directions to a venue
(B) A list of specifications
(C) Packing instructions
(D) A product catalog

Questions 09-12 refer to the following e-mail.

TO:	Wendy Armstrong <warmstrong@polsonpc.com>
FROM:	Derek Ling <dling@polsonpc.com>
SUBJECT:	Keep up the good work!
DATE:	July 19

📄 employee_profile.word

Hi Wendy,

I'm pleased to inform you that, based on a review of the sales results from all of our branches in the region, yours was found to have had the best overall performance this past quarter.

For the period covering April to June, store receipts show that you consistently exceeded the monthly sales targets set at the beginning of the year. More specifically, sales figures in every department but one surpassed those for the same period last year. The only exception was desktop computers, but this is unsurprising given that many of our customers are switching to laptops these days.

As the top sales performing branch manager, you will be receiving a bonus of $1,000 on your next paycheck. You will also be named in our bimonthly newsletter. As you know, the newsletter is distributed nationally to all our branches and is frequently read by the CEO, Mr. Tom Robbins.

Furthermore, if you maintain the same level of performance for the next three consecutive quarters, you will become eligible to be nominated for the Branch Manager of the Year Award, which is presented annually during a ceremony at our headquarters in Dallas. Employees who receive the award are automatically guaranteed a salary increase and become candidates for promotion to regional supervisors later on.

In closing, could you take a look at your employee information file that I have attached to this e-mail and make sure that it is up to date? I'll need to send the information to our head office so that they have a record of your achievement. Please return it to me by the end of the day.

Thank you and congratulations.

Derek Ling
Regional Supervisor
Polson PC

09 What is suggested about Ms. Armstrong?

(A) She is responsible for sales at a computer store.
(B) She was recently rewarded with a salary increase.
(C) She was recommended by the CEO of a company.
(D) She successfully launched a new line of products.

10 Why did sales of desktop computers decline?

(A) Low employee productivity
(B) An accounting mistake
(C) Inefficient management practices
(D) A change in consumer preferences

11 What is indicated about Polson PC?

(A) It regularly collects feedback from customers.
(B) It holds a yearly event at its main office.
(C) It presently has an opening for a regional supervisor.
(D) It publishes a company newsletter every month.

12 What does Mr. Ling require of Ms. Armstrong?

(A) Her contact details
(B) The name of her direct supervisor
(C) An update on her personnel file
(D) A sales report for the month

CHAPTER 09 양식 및 기타(Forms)

토익 이렇게 나온다!

양식 및 기타는 생활 속에 자주 사용되는 양식과 기타 실용문 형식의 글이다. 일정표(schedule), 초대장(invitation), 영수증(receipt)이나 송장(invoice), 광고지(flyer) 등 여러 가지가 양식 및 기타에 속하며, 평균 1지문 정도 출제된다.

토익 질문 유형 및 전략

빈출 질문 유형

주제/목적 찾기 문제
양식에 언급된 행사의 목적이나 양식의 주제를 묻는다.
What is the purpose of the ceremony? 의식의 목적은 무엇인가?
What does the flyer promote? 광고지가 홍보하는 것은 무엇인가?
What is being announced? 공고되고 있는 것은 무엇인가?

육하원칙 문제
어떤 일에 대한 이유, 추후 일정 계획이나 기타 세부 사항을 주로 묻는다.
Why did Ms. Lang pay an additional fee? Ms. Lang은 왜 추가 요금을 냈는가?
What will take place in the main hall? 대강당에서 무엇이 일어날 것인가?
How often will employees be evaluated? 직원들은 얼마나 자주 평가될 것인가?

Not/True 문제
양식에 언급된 행사, 사람 등에 대해 일치하거나 일치하지 않는 것을 주로 묻는다.
What is indicated about the promotional workshops? 홍보 워크숍에 대해 언급된 것은?
What is NOT mentioned about Ms. Lane? Ms. Lane에 대해 언급되지 않은 것은?

추론 문제
양식의 대상이나 양식에 언급된 특정 사항에 대해 추론할 수 있는 것을 주로 묻는다.
For whom is the schedule probably intended? 일정표는 누구를 대상으로 할 것 같은가?
What benefit will Monica Chambers most likely receive? Monica Chambers는 어떤 혜택을 받을 것 같은가?

핵심 전략

1. 각 양식의 패턴을 알아 둬야 한다.
일정표는 관련 회사나 행사 이름을 명시한 후, 세부 일정이 나열된다. 전체 세부 일정이 달력 형태로 나오기도 한다.
초대장은 행사 종류나 제목, 날짜 및 시간, 장소 등 간략한 개요가 제시된 후에 세부 행사 내용이 이어진다.
영수증과 송장은 발행한 상점이나 식당의 이름, 주소가 나오고, 그 아래에 거래 번호, 거래 날짜, 세부 항목별 금액 등이 나온다.
광고지는 광고하는 것의 종류, 세부 내용, 홈페이지 주소와 같은 연락처 순으로 나열된다.
전화 메모의 경우 메모를 전달받을 사람(For/To: ~), 전화를 건 사람(From: ~), 세부 메모 내용 등의 순서로 나온다.

2. 양식의 대상이 누구인지 파악해야 한다.
양식의 대상은 지문에 직접 제시되지 않고 추론 문제로 묻는 경우가 자주 있으므로 글의 전체적인 상황을 보고 유추해내야 한다.

Bearing the Torch of Knowledge

Brightman University 50th Anniversary Celebrations
June 12 to 15 on campus grounds
88 Ludlow Canyon Road, Hamilton, MO 65401

□ 행사 제목
□ 행사 종류
□ 날짜 및 시간
□ 장소

The community of Hamilton is invited to join Brightman University in celebrating 50 years of academic excellence. We have prepared a series of activities for the town's enjoyment. Below are some highlights:

On Thursday, June 12,	On Friday, June 13,	On Saturday, June 14,
A multimedia exhibit covering the university's history opens at the newly refurbished Sarah J. Meier Building.	A formal dinner and dance will be held at Wakefield Memorial Hall. Tickets are $25 each.	The alumni association hosts a free concert at Ryder Field, which will be accompanied by a fundraiser organized by current students.

세부 행사 내용

In addition, chancellor Howard Bain will be leading commencement ceremonies on June 15 at the Main Events Center.

For tickets, directions, and other details, contact Event Services at 555-0196, ext. 48, or go to www.brightmanuniv.edu. All are welcome, and we hope to see you there!

Q1. For whom is the invitation most likely intended?

(A) Members of the press
(B) Participants in a program
(C) Instructors at a college
(D) Residents of a town

Q2. What is being announced?

(A) The opening of a town's historical exhibit
(B) The start of a community building project
(C) The commemoration of an institute's founding
(D) The annual gathering of professionals in a field

Q3. What is indicated about the planned activities?

(A) They were organized by an elected council.
(B) They will take place over a period of four days.
(C) They are being offered free of charge.
(D) They will be held at various places around Hamilton.

해설 　Q1 **추론 문제** 초대장의 대상을 추론하는 문제이다. 'The community of Hamilton is invited'에서 해밀턴 지역 사회가 초청된다고 했으므로 해밀턴 지역에 사는 주민들을 대상으로 하는 초대장임을 추론할 수 있다. 따라서 (D) Residents of a town이 정답이다.

Q2 **주제/목적 찾기 문제** 　공고되는 것을 묻는 주제 찾기 문제이다. 'Brightman University 50th Anniversary Celebrations'에서 Brightman 대학교의 50주년 기념일 축하 행사임을 알린 후, 세부 일정을 나열하고 있으므로 (C) The commemoration of an institute's founding이 정답이다.

Q3 **Not/True 문제** 질문의 핵심 어구인 the planned activities와 관련된 내용을 지문에서 찾아 보기와 대조하는 Not/True 문제이다. (A)는 지문에 언급되지 않은 내용이다. (B)는 'June 12 to 15'에서 행사가 6월 12일부터 15일까지 총 4일간 진행된다고 했으므로 (B) They will take place over a period of four days가 정답이다. (C)는 'A formal dinner and dance will be held ~ Tickets are $25 each.'에서 공식 만찬 및 무도회의 티켓이 25달러라고 했으므로 지문의 내용과 일치하지 않는다. (D)는 'on campus grounds'에서 학교 부지에서 진행된다고 했으므로 지문의 내용과 일치하지 않는다.

정답 　Q1 (D) 　　Q2 (C) 　　Q3 (B)

지문 해석 p.143

양식에 자주 나오는 ★필수 어휘

1. 대금 청구

accept v. 받아들이다, 받다	**payment** n. 지불(금), 납입
apologize v. 사과하다, 변명하다	**purchase** v. 사다, 얻다; n. 구매, 구입
balance due 차감 부족액, 미불액, 잔금	**routine** n. 일과; adj. 정기적인 = regular, usual
billing n. 청구서 발부, 거래 총액	**subtotal** n. 소계
comment n. 언급, 지적; v. 견해를 밝히다	**summary** n. 요약; adj. 요약한, 간략한 = outline
discount v. 할인하다; n. 할인, 할인액	**tax** n. 세금; v. 과세하다
electronic adj. 전자의, 컴퓨터의	**total** adj. 총계의, 전체의; n. 총액, 합계
fail v. 실패하다, ~하지 못하다	**transaction** n. 거래, 매매
income n. 수입, 소득	**vendor** n. 행상인, 매각인 = seller
interrupt v. 중단하다, 차단하다	**voucher** n. 상품권, 할인권 = gift certificate

2. 기념 및 축하 행사

amusement park 유원지	**festival** n. 축제, 축하 행사 = festivity
attendance n. 출석, 참석	**formal** adj. 형식적인, 공식적인
auction n. 경매; v. 경매하다	**instrument** n. 기구, 악기
banquet n. 연회, 축하연	**international** adj. 국제적인
beverage n. 음료	**invitation** n. 초대, 초대장
book signing 책 사인회	**membership** n. 회원, 회원권
celebrate v. 축하하다, 기념하다 = commemorate	**museum** n. 박물관, 미술관
ceremony n. 식, 의식	**offer** v. 제안하다, 제공하다; n. 제안, 제공
classical adj. 고전적인, 전통적인	**performance** n. 상연, 연기, 연주
community n. 지역 사회, 공동체	**proceed** v. 진행하다, 시작하다
cost n. 비용, 대가; v. 비용이 들다, 노력이 들다	**rain date** 우천시 행사 변경일
donate v. 기부하다, 기증하다 = contribute	**reception** n. 환영, 환영회

3. 일정 및 스케줄

agenda n. 의사 일정, 의제

assemble v. 모이다, 집합시키다

break n. 휴식, 중단; v. 휴식하다, 중단되다

brief adj. 잠시의, 간결한

call off 취소하다, 중지하다

cancellation n. 취소, 해제

content n. 내용, 목차, 취지

draft n. 초안; adj. 초안의

guideline n. 지침, 정책

layout n. 배치, 구획

make arrangement 준비하다

meal n. 식사, 식사 시간

overview n. 개관, 개요

permanent adj. 영구적인, 상설의

registration n. 등록

tentative adj. 잠정적인, 불확실한

4. 전화

answer the phone 전화를 받다

call back 나중에 다시 전화하다

caller n. 전화 거는 사람, 발신자

disconnect v. 전화를 끊다

emergency n. 비상 사태; adj. 긴급한

extension n. 내선, 구내 전화

follow-up 후속 조치

give a person a call ~에게 전화하다

hang up 전화를 끊다

leave a message 전할 말을 남기다

pick up the phone 수화기를 들다

return one's call ~의 전화에 답하다

take a message 전할 말을 받아두다

voice mail 음성 메시지

HACKERS PRACTICE 토익 고득점을 위한 필수 연습

유형 연습 지문을 읽고 질문에 답하세요.

01 전화 메모

WHILE YOU WERE OUT

To: Jacqueline Stamos
Date/Time: January 19, 3:18 P.M.
MESSAGE: Gail Anderson from World Electronics would like you to contact her about some changes to the upcoming schedule for the robotics conference next month. Please contact her as soon as possible.
Call Received By: Liam Connelly

Q. What was the purpose of Ms. Anderson's call?

(A) To inform Ms. Stamos of changes to a schedule
(B) To confirm attendance to a conference
(C) To request a copy of an itinerary

02 일정표

Thanks for registering for the Annual Oregon State Student Science Exhibition! Please look through the following week-long schedule:

May 9	9 A.M.-5 P.M.	All entries must be submitted at the Pinewood Exhibition Center.
May 10-14	9 A.M.-6:30 P.M.	The exhibit will open to the public. Participants must be on site to offer explanations of their projects to the judges and attendees.
May 15	10:30 A.M.-12 P.M.	Awards will be handed out at the exhibition center.

Q. How often does the event take place?

(A) Every week
(B) Every month
(C) Every year

03 광고지

LEARN HOW TO SAVE ON ENERGY COSTS!

Want to make your home more energy-efficient? Learn how to cut household costs and become more environmentally-friendly by attending next week's seminar sponsored by the Ministry of the Environment. Entitled "Saving Money by Lowering Energy Consumption", the seminar will be held on March 8 from 7 P.M. to 9:30 P.M. at the Richland Community Center on 1232 Monarch Avenue. Tom Singh, environmental science professor at Western Prairie University, will be on hand to give a special presentation and answer any questions following his talk. For additional information, or to sign up for the seminar, send a query to events@ministryenvironment.org.

Q. What does the flyer promote?

(A) An educational event
(B) An energy saving device
(C) A series of college lectures

정답·해설·해석 p.144

🕐 제한 시간 10분

Questions 01-02 refer to the following receipt.

Deskman Co.
For all your office needs
521 Conference Center Way
Benton, PA 1795
555-6323
VAT TIN# 002-3632-0963

S#645545210   03/01 7:00 P.M.

PRODUCT # 52541
Abacus FX-63II Calculator   4 @ $15.99 $63.96

PRODUCT # 20152
Deskman Multipurpose
Paper Case   1 @ $20.25 $20.25

PRODUCT # 30046
Scribble Ballpoint Pen
Box of 12   3 @ $4.00 $12.00

PRODUCT # 96510
Baklushi Printer Black Ink
Cartridge 130 ml   1 @ $68.22 $68.22

PRODUCT # 75230
Stevens Chair mat   5 @ $29.99 $149.95

Total $314.38
Cash $500.00
Change $185.62

THANKS for your BUSINESS!

This is your official receipt. Merchandise may be returned for replacement within seven days from the date of purchase.

---

01 What type of business is Deskman Company?

(A) A convenience shop
(B) An appliance center
(C) A home decor establishment
(D) An office supplies outlet

02 What information is NOT stated in the receipt?

(A) Exchanges are permissible.
(B) Items are nonrefundable.
(C) Pens are sold by the dozen.
(D) The transaction was made at night.

READING Part 7 Ch 09 양식 및 기타 Hackers TOEIC Reading

Questions 03-06 refer to the following schedule.

**Work Schedule for Upcoming Renovations at Bella Vista Apartment Complex
August 1-August 19**

Repainting of all walls in the lobby, halls, and entrances
August 1-7
Crew manager: Dan Parsons

Carpet and wooden flooring replacement in main lobby
August 8-19
Crew manager: Doris Schmidt

Retiling of shower and changing rooms at sports facility
August 7-11
Crew manager: Harry Seymour

Repaving of underground parking facility (B1)
August 5-18
Crew manager: Larry Smithers

Please contact your crew managers for details on the projects. So that there will be minimal disturbance for residents, work will only take place between 8:30 A.M. to 6:30 P.M. The schedule above is open to change, depending on work progress. Staff will be notified of any changes by their crew managers. Please use only entrance G-3 to move equipment and supplies in and out of the building.

03 What is NOT indicated in the schedule?

(A) Work will be conducted during the month of August.
(B) Several areas of the facility will undergo renovations.
(C) Dan Parsons will lead a crew of painters.
(D) The lobby floors will be retiled.

04 What will most likely happen on August 15?

(A) Renovations at Bella Vista will be completed.
(B) Larry Smithers will supervise workers in the parking area.
(C) Some walls in a reception area will be painted.
(D) Tiles will be installed in a shower area.

05 Why are staff only permitted to work during certain hours?

(A) The company doesn't want to pay overtime wages.
(B) The building closes before that time.
(C) The residents of the facility may be bothered.
(D) The managers are booked for other jobs.

06 What is suggested about the Bella Vista Apartment Complex?

(A) It currently has no vacant units.
(B) It was built many years ago.
(C) It has more than one entrance.
(D) It is under construction.

Questions 07-10 refer to the following form.

Springdale Art Festival

The annual Springdale Art Festival will be held this year from June 1-4. The venue will be the Springdale Community Center at 156 Donovan Avenue. Doors will open at 10 A.M. and close at 7 P.M.

Artists interested in participating are urged to reserve a booth as soon as possible, as space is limited. Reservations must be made by the artists themselves and not by resellers or agents. Booths include lighting, a table, partitions for hanging artwork, and two chairs. Payment must be made before May 15 or reservations will be forfeited. We regret that we are unable to offer refunds for any cancellations. Fill in this form and submit it to Leona Helms at Springdale Art Council, 5998 Larch Crescent. Payments by cash, credit card, or money order are accepted. If you have questions, call 555-0967.

Name	Terry Clark	Address	18 Rose Street, Springdale
Phone	555-4453	E-mail	terryc@speedmail.com
Type of art	Paintings		

Select a booth:
☐10/8 feet ☐10/20 feet ☐12/24 feet ☒14/28 feet

Payment method:
☒cash ☐money order ☐credit card number: _____

Signature: *Terry Clark*

07 What is the purpose of the form?

(A) To enroll in an art course
(B) To register for a festival
(C) To apply for membership
(D) To enter a competition

08 What will happen on May 15?

(A) Selections will be made for an exhibit.
(B) The venue of an art festival will open.
(C) Unpaid reservations will be canceled.
(D) Refunds will no longer be given.

09 What is stated about the event?

(A) It is being organized by Leona Helms.
(B) It is scheduled to last for four days.
(C) It is taking place at a local gallery.
(D) It is free to the general public.

10 What is suggested about Mr. Clark?

(A) He will only attend two days of the event.
(B) He is a member of the art council.
(C) He has previously taken part in the festival.
(D) He will display some of his own artwork.

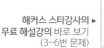

해커스 스타강사의 ▶
무료 해설강의 바로 보기
(3~6번 문제)

기사(Article & Report)

토익 이렇게 나온다!

기사는 신문이나 잡지 등을 통해 새로운 소식을 전달하는 글로서, 보고서나 보도 자료의 형태도 포함한다. 지역사회에서 부터 회사 및 개인의 동향, 문화행사 소식에 이르기까지 다양한 분야의 주제를 다룬다. 어휘 능력이 많이 요구되고 지문이 긴 경우가 많아 다소 어려운 지문 유형으로서, 평균 1~2지문 정도 출제된다.

토익 질문 유형 및 전략

빈출 질문 유형

주제/목적 찾기 문제	기사의 목적, 주제를 묻는다.
	What is the purpose of the article? 기사의 목적은 무엇인가?
	What is the article mainly about? 기사는 주로 무엇에 대한 것인가?
육하원칙 문제	기사에 언급된 사람, 날짜 및 시간이나 기타 세부 사항을 주로 묻는다.
	Who founded the Global Environment Forum? 누가 세계 환경 포럼을 설립했는가?
	When will the companies sign the agreement? 회사들은 언제 계약서에 서명을 할 것인가?
	Why was the production plant shut down? 왜 제조 공장이 폐쇄되었는가?
Not/True 문제	기사에 언급된 행사, 회사나 시설 등에 대해 일치하거나 일치하지 않는 것을 주로 묻는다.
	What is NOT indicated about the music festival? 음악 축제에 대해 언급되지 않은 것은?
	What is mentioned about the National Museum? 국립 박물관에 대해 언급된 것은?
추론 문제	기사가 발행될 만한 곳이나 기사에 언급된 특정 사항에 대해 추론할 수 있는 것을 주로 묻는다.
	Where would the article most likely be published? 기사는 어디에서 발행될 것 같은가?
	What is suggested about Raven Industries? Raven Industries사에 대해 암시되는 것은?

핵심 전략

1. 기사의 제목이나 앞부분에서 주제를 정확히 파악하면 지문의 세부 내용을 파악하기 쉽다.

앞부분에서 글의 주제를 제대로 파악하면 이하 본문은 주제를 뒷받침하는 세부 내용이므로 흐름을 수월하게 따라갈 수 있다. 지문 처음에 제목이 있는 경우, 제목을 통해서도 미리 주제를 예측하고 파악할 수 있다.

2. 기사의 주제는 주제를 나타내는 관련 표현을 익혀두면 쉽게 찾을 수 있다.

3. 다양한 분야의 수준 높은 어휘를 익혀두면 지문 내용 파악에 도움이 된다.

기사에서는 어휘 능력이 많이 요구되므로 책에 수록된 '파트 7 핵심 표현 및 필수 어휘(p.420~421)'를 익혀두면 기사의 내용을 빠르고 정확하게 파악할 수 있다.

Countries around the Globe Report Record-breaking Summer Temperatures

September 30 – Dr. Christian Mulligan, a researcher at the World Weather Organization (WWO), announced that four countries recorded dramatic increases in temperature this year. In a press statement from the WWO yesterday, Dr. Mulligan said some countries endured severe heat waves over the past year, a condition that is at least partially due to climate change, according to statistics collected by the institute.

주제

In January, Colombia recorded a temperature of 42 degrees Celsius, the hottest ever in recent decades. Four months later in May, Pakistan topped records for the entire Asian continent, with a temperature of 53 degrees Celsius. It was followed by Russia, with 44 degrees in July, the country's hottest summer in 130 years. Surpassing its own maximum was Finland, which registered a temperature of 37 degrees this year, up from 35 degrees a century ago.

세부 사항

The WWO says that these changes in temperature are caused by several factors. Global warming has increased the rate at which the arctic icecap is melting, driving temperatures upwards. Pollution is also a factor, as it affects the ozone layer which protects the Earth from the sun. An increase of UV rays entering the atmosphere is raising temperatures around the globe.

Q1. What is the purpose of the article?

(A) To offer a forecast of weather patterns
(B) To report observations regarding climate change
(C) To inform readers of an organization's activities
(D) To recommend that countries take certain measures

Q2. When was the hottest temperature recorded?

(A) In January
(B) In May
(C) In July
(D) In September

Q3. What is suggested about the World Weather Organization?

(A) It recently hired Dr. Mulligan.
(B) It has a branch office in Finland.
(C) It gathers data about global temperatures.
(D) It releases annual reports to the public.

해설 Q1 **주제/목적 찾기 문제** 기사의 목적을 묻는 목적 찾기 문제이다. 'Countries around the Globe Report Record-breaking Summer Temperatures'와 'four countries recorded dramatic increases in temperature this year'에서 세계의 국가들이 유례없는 여름 기온을 기록했으며 올해 4개 국가가 극적인 기온 상승을 기록했다고 언급한 후, 각 나라에서 관측된 기온 상승 및 원인에 대한 세부 정보를 제공하고 있으므로 (B) To report observations regarding climate change가 정답이다.

Q2 **육하원칙 문제** 가장 높은 기온이 언제(When) 기록되었는지를 묻는 육하원칙 문제이다. 질문의 핵심 어구인 hottest temperature와 관련하여, 'in May, Pakistan topped records for the entire Asian continent, with a temperature of 53 degrees Celsius'에서 5월에 파키스탄이 기온 섭씨 53도로 아시아 대륙 전체에서 최고 기록을 세웠다고 했으므로 (B) In May가 정답이다.

Q3 **추론 문제** 질문의 핵심 어구인 World Weather Organization에 대해 추론하는 문제이다. 'In a press statement from the WWO yesterday, Dr. Mulligan said some countries endured severe heat waves over the past year, ~ according to statistics collected by the institute.'에서 WWO의 언론 발표에서, Dr. Mulligan이 지난해 동안 몇몇 국가들이 심한 혹서를 견뎠다고 했고, 이는 해당 기관인 WWO가 수집한 통계에 따른 것이라고 했으므로 WWO는 세계 기온에 대한 자료를 수집한다는 사실을 추론할 수 있다. 따라서 (C) It gathers data about global temperatures가 정답이다.

정답 Q1 (B) Q2 (B) Q3 (C)

지문 해석 p.146

기사에 자주 나오는 ⭐핵심 표현

1. 기사의 주제

사람/기관 announced that ~ : (사람/기관)이 ~라고 발표했다

The department of transport announced that the highway construction has been delayed.
운수부는 고속도로 건설이 지연되어 왔다고 발표했다.

사람/기관 will hold ~ : (사람/기관)은 ~을 열 것이다

The city council will hold a public forum to discuss municipal improvement ideas.
시 의회는 도시 개선 아이디어를 논의하기 위한 공개 포럼을 열 것이다.

사람/기관 recently launched ~ : (사람/기관)은 최근에 ~을 시작했다/출시했다

The Ministry of Environment recently launched a campaign to raise awareness of water resource preservation.
환경부는 최근에 수자원 보존에 대한 인식을 높이기 위한 캠페인을 시작했다.

사람/기관 recently published ~ : (사람/기관)은 최근에 ~을 발표했다/출간했다

Dr. Mendel recently published the results of his study on natural vitamins in a medical journal.
Dr. Mendel은 최근에 천연 비타민에 대한 그의 연구 결과를 의학 잡지에 발표했다.

2. 인용

"~" said 사람 : (사람)이 ~라고 말했다

"The protection of human rights is a major goal of our organization," said Leo Winters.
Leo Winters는 "인권 보호가 저희 조직의 주요 목표입니다."라고 말했다.

사람 explain "~" : (사람)이 ~라고 설명한다

Dr. Will Mason from Davenport Hospital explained, "The additional space will help us provide better care."
Davenport 병원의 Dr. Will Mason은 "추가적인 공간은 우리가 더 나은 서비스를 제공하도록 할 것입니다."라고 설명했다.

사람 pointed out "~" : (사람)이 ~라고 지적했다

Mayor Dickens pointed out, "The subway system is 30 years old and needs renovations."
Dickens 시장은 "전철 시스템은 30년이 되었으며 보수를 필요로 합니다."라고 지적했다.

기사에 자주 나오는 ⭐필수 어휘

1. 사회 및 정치

arbitration n. 중재, 조정	illegal adj. 불법적인, 위법의	
commit v. 저지르다, 위탁하다	indict v. 기소하다, 고발하다	
consulate n. 영사관	infringement n. 위반, 침해	
controversial adj. 논쟁의 여지가 있는	legislation n. 입법, 법률	
custody n. 보호, 구류	litigation n. 소송, 고소	
detention n. 구치, 유치	ordinance n. 법령, 조례	
enactment n. 입법, 법률	plaintiff n. 원고, 고소인	
federal adj. 연방 정부의, 연방제의	prosecutor n. 검사, 검찰관	
forfeit n. 벌금, 박탈; v. 몰수당하다, 상실하다	punishment n. 처벌, 형벌 = penalty	
forgery n. 위조, 허위 = counterfeit	strike n. 파업; v. 파업하다	
fraud n. 사기, 가짜	summit n. 정상 회담	

2. 통신 및 운수 산업

aircraft   n. 항공기

bypass   n. 우회도로   = detour

coach   n. (대형) 버스

commute   v. 통근하다; n. 통근

congestion   n. 혼잡, 정체

destination   n. 목적지, 도착지

exit   n. 출구; v. 나가다, 떠나다

expressway   n. 고속도로   = highway

freight   n. 화물, 화물 운송

fuel   n. 연료

intersection   n. 교차로, 교차 지점

lane   n. 차로, 좁은 길

motorcyclist   n. 오토바이 운전자

passageway   n. 통로, 복도

passenger   n. 승객, 탑승객

pedestrian   n. 보행자; adj. 보행의

public transportation   대중교통

shortcut   n. 지름길

traffic jam   교통 체증, 교통 혼잡

transfer   v. 이동하다, 갈아타다

vehicle   n. 차량, 운송 수단

vessel   n. (대형) 선박   = boat

3. 환경

blizzard   n. 눈보라

climate   n. 기후

conserve   v. 보호하다, 보존하다   = save, preserve

contamination   n. 오염

drought   n. 가뭄

ecology   n. 생태학, 생태

endangered   adj. 멸종 위기에 처한

flood   n. 홍수

generate   v. 발생시키다, 만들어 내다

habitat   n. 서식지, 자생지

hail   n. 우박

hazardous   adj. 위험한   = risky, unsafe

humidity   n. 습도, 습기

inclement   adj. (날씨가) 궂은, 추운

precipitation   n. 강수, 강수량   = rainfall

purify   v. 정화하다, 깨끗이 하다

shower   n. 소나기, 모래 바람

temperature   n. 기온, 온도

timber   n. 목재, 목재용 산림   = lumber, wood

torrential   adj. 억수같이 쏟아지는, 급류의

wildlife   n. 야생 생물; adj. 야생 생물의

wind power   풍력

4. 건강

antibiotic   adj. 항생의, 항생 물질의; n. 항생 물질

diagnosis   n. 진단

discover   v. 발견하다, 알다

exercise   n. 운동, 훈련; v. 운동하다, 훈련하다

fatigue   n. 피로, 피곤

finding   n. 조사 결과

interfere   v. 간섭하다, 해치다

jet lag   시차로 인한 피로

medication   n. 약, 약물 치료

nutrition   n. 영양, 영양물

prescription   n. 처방, 처방전, 처방약

relationship   n. 관계, 관련

relax   v. 쉬게 하다, 긴장을 풀다

researcher   n. 연구원, 조사원

response   n. 반응, 응답

symptom   n. 증상, 징후

vaccination   n. 예방 접종

wellness   n. 건강, 호조

유형 연습 지문을 읽고 질문에 답하세요.

01 기사

Outside Columbus this week, construction began on a $200 million mixed-use development for Kepler Pharmaceuticals. The company, which now ranks second in the world on sales of medicinal products, has a staff of 900 at its headquarters, representing an increase of 12 percent from last year and 47 percent for the decade. The new complex will house additional office space, research laboratories, testing centers, and an auditorium. Rapid corporate growth has created overcrowding in the current facility, which was built 18 years ago.

Q. Where would the article probably be published?

(A) In a real estate brochure
(B) In a business journal
(C) In a health publication

02 기사

Sales reports in leading warehouse clubs show that a lint remover is one of the top-selling products of the year. More than one million Clean-Well Lint Removers, which are manufactured by Cleaners Corporation, have been sold in the United States since April. This is an average of approximately 150,000 units per month. The product's popularity has risen over the past few months because it is effective in removing lint from washing machines, clothing, rugs, and other objects.

Q. What is the article mainly about?

(A) A leading warehouse club
(B) A manufacturing company
(C) A best-selling cleaning product

03 기사

It was revealed on Friday that Nelly Stadlin's *All Gather Round* has been picked up for production by Rosebud Pictures. The best-selling novel, Stadlin's last in a three-part series, depicts a fictional family's struggles living in Depression-era Oklahoma. Shooting is expected to begin in six months with actor Kelly Rader playing the lead role of Beth Abney. Other cast selections are unconfirmed at this time.

Q. Who is Nelly Stadlin?

(A) A fiction author
(B) A film producer
(C) A retired historian

정답·해설·해석 p.147

🕐 제한 시간 12분

Questions 01-04 refer to the following article.

Douglas Museum to Renovate the Randolph Building

The Douglas Museum announced today that it has been awarded a $5 million grant from the Lauderhill Foundation, which raises money to preserve notable architecture. The money will be used to restore the exterior of the Randolph Building, a historically significant structure on the Douglas Museum's sprawling grounds.

The Randolph Building was constructed 110 years ago, and it contains some of the nation's rarest and most valuable books, music manuscripts, artworks, and antiques. Its interior underwent extensive renovations a decade ago, including the installation of new lighting and exhibition cases throughout the building, as well as the restoration of antique furnishings.

On April 15, work will begin on the exterior of the building, with the goal of returning it to its original condition. To achieve this, the services of two specialists have been secured. Martin Walker, an expert in early 20th-century architecture, will take the lead on the project. Working closely with him will be Beth Anders, who specializes in art restoration. She will focus on the sculptures and other decorative elements that adorn the building. The project is expected to take a minimum of three months, and the building will be closed to visitors during this period.

---

01 How did the Douglas Museum get the funds for the renovation work?

(A) It received an award from the government.
(B) It sold several works of art from its collection.
(C) It collected many donations from visitors.
(D) It accepted a grant from an organization.

02 What is NOT mentioned about the Randolph Building?

(A) It houses precious items.
(B) It is over a century old.
(C) It was closed for a decade.
(D) It has a restored interior.

03 The word "secured" in paragraph 3, line 5, is closest in meaning to

(A) obtained
(B) withheld
(C) protected
(D) attached

04 What can be inferred about Ms. Anders?

(A) She is an employee of the Douglas Museum.
(B) She studied architecture as a university student.
(C) She purchased new artwork for the Randolph Building.
(D) She will work under the supervision of Mr. Walker.

Questions 05-08 refer to the following article.

JUNE 6. A crowd of students, faculty, and medical professionals gathered Tuesday at New Jersey's Logan University to attend the release of a study by visiting scholar Dr. Steve Manning. Dr. Manning, director of child healthcare research at California's De Anda University, presented his findings from a study on the influence of diet and exercise on children's performance in school.

Over a period of five years, he observed a cross section of students from different grade levels and determined that children with healthy lifestyles performed better at school than their peers. "For instance," he explained, "those who received proper nutrition at home and in school tended to display higher cognitive ability. When this condition was coupled with regular physical exercise, the same students were also more likely to engage in classroom learning." He also added that it seems the right combination of food and exercise produces children who are more attentive in school and thus are better disposed to absorb knowledge. — [1] —.

The results shed light on why some students might be having academic problems. — [2] —. Dr. Manning found that 16 percent of the study participants were clearly not getting enough to eat at home. Of those that were, 30 percent regularly consumed foods that were high in fat or sugar. — [3] —. Dr. Manning supplemented his report by recommending specific foods and exercise routines. He also encouraged schools to cooperate with parents in ensuring that children receive the right amount of each factor. — [4] —.

The event was part of a regular undertaking by Logan University, which seeks to educate the public on developments concerning health, academics, culture, and society. Transcripts of Dr. Manning's presentation are available for download on www.loganedu.com. Those interested in exploring Dr. Manning's complete body of research are directed to his online database at www.deanda.edu/manning.

05 Where did Dr. Manning release his study results?

(A) At a local community center
(B) At an organization's headquarters
(C) At an educational institution
(D) At a corporate research facility

06 What is NOT mentioned about Dr. Manning?

(A) He normally performs his work in California.
(B) He is an expert on intelligence in children.
(C) He gave fitness and diet suggestions at the event.
(D) He collected several years' worth of research.

07 What is indicated about the study?

(A) It was limited to elementary school students.
(B) It focused solely on conditions for academic success.
(C) It proposed supplementing children's diets with vitamins.
(D) It revealed why some children may have learning difficulties.

08 In which of the positions marked [1], [2], [3], and [4] does the following sentence best belong?

"Making matters worse, half of the tested participants exercised for less than 20 minutes a day."

(A) [1]
(B) [2]
(C) [3]
(D) [4]

Questions 09-12 refer to the following article.

Mayor Unveils Symbol of the City
by Donna Wood

Monday morning at City Hall, Mayor Joel Weeks held a press conference to present the new logo for Riverbend, Illinois. The adoption of a logo comes just two years after Riverbend's population surpassed 2,500 and it was officially declared a city.

The design is based on a winning entry submitted by artist Ralph McCord during a contest held last year. It features a representation of the Candle River flowing between two hills toward a rising sun. On the left bank of the river stands a tree with one branch extending over the water. On the other side, a black bull sits beside the river's edge. Magnolia flowers were later added to the tree.

According to standards and selection committee chair Sylvia Morris, "Mr. McCord's design fulfilled the guidelines we prepared and we feel that his final image best symbolizes the values of our city — nobility, hard work, and our heritage as an agricultural town." The image is enclosed within a disc bordered by gold stars against a blue band. In addition, a slogan created by local author Kyle Holmes reads "From the earth comes life" and appears underneath the new logo.

The logo will be used in all official correspondence beginning later this month. In addition, a version of the image will be carved into stone and placed above the entrance to City Hall. The logo has also been added to the home page of the Riverbend Web site at www.riverbend.il.gov.

09 What is the article mainly about?

(A) The unveiling of a public monument
(B) The adoption of a city logo
(C) The requirements for a competition
(D) The announcement of a mayor's campaign

10 Which is NOT a feature of Mr. McCord's original design?

(A) A seated animal
(B) A type of flower
(C) A decorative border
(D) A river image

11 What is suggested about Sylvia Morris?

(A) She participated in choosing the best design.
(B) She is in charge of official correspondence.
(C) She received training as an artist.
(D) She designed the local city hall.

12 What will Mr. McCord's design be used on?

(A) All government buildings
(B) City hall letters
(C) Street signs
(D) Tourist brochures

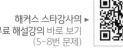

CHAPTER 11

메시지 대화문(Text message chain)

토익 이렇게 나온다!
메시지 대화문은 2인 이상이 메시지를 주고 받는 글로서, 크게 두 사람간의 메시지 대화문이나 여러 사람간의 채팅 대화문으로 나뉠 수 있다. 주로 사내 또는 다른 회사 직원들간의 비즈니스 관련 대화나 일상 생활에서 나누는 지인간의 대화 등의 다양한 상황을 다룬다. 평균 2지문 정도 출제된다.

토익 질문 유형 및 전략

빈출 질문 유형

의도 파악 문제
대화문에서 특정 어구가 어떤 의도로 쓰였는지를 묻는다.
At 12:17, what does Ms. Ludeau mean when she writes, "I see"?
12시 17분에, Ms. Ludeau가 "I see"라고 썼을 때, 그녀가 의도한 것은?

주제/목적 찾기 문제
대화문의 주제나 대화자가 연락한 목적을 묻는다.
What is the main topic being discussed? 논의되고 있는 주요 주제는 무엇인가?
Why did Ms. Kim send the message? Ms. Kim은 왜 메시지를 보냈는가?
Why did Mr. Landry contact Ms. Goff? Mr. Landry는 왜 Ms. Goff에게 연락했는가?

육하원칙 문제
대화자의 요청 사항이나 제안 사항 또는 어떤 일에 대한 장소, 일정 계획이나 기타 세부 사항을 주로 묻는다.
What is Mr. Marcelo asked to do? Mr. Marcelo가 무엇을 하도록 요청되는가?
Where will Mr. Johns meet Mr. Simon? Mr. Johns는 어디서 Mr. Simon을 만날 것인가?

Not/True 문제
대화자 또는 대화문에 언급된 사람, 회사나 행사 등에 대해 일치하거나 일치하지 않는 것을 주로 묻는다.
What is indicated about Mr. Lee? Mr. Lee에 대해 언급된 것은?
What is NOT mentioned about the concert? 콘서트에 대해 언급되지 않은 것은?

추론 문제
대화자 또는 대화문에 언급된 사람이나 특정 사항에 대해 추론할 수 있는 것을 주로 묻는다.
What is suggested about Mr. Hanson? Mr. Hanson에 대해 암시되는 것은?
Where does Mr. Ito most likely work? Mr. Ito는 어디에서 일할 것 같은가?
Who most likely is Ms. Taylor? Ms. Taylor는 누구인 것 같은가?
What will Mr. Wang most likely do next? Mr. Wang은 다음에 무엇을 할 것 같은가?

핵심 전략

1. 메시지 대화문의 흐름을 정확히 파악해야 한다.
메시지 대화문에서는 지문에서 언급된 어구나 문장의 의미를 의도 파악 문제로 묻는 경우가 자주 있으므로 지문의 전체적인 흐름을 파악하여 유추해야 한다. 앞부분에서 대화문의 주제나 목적을 제대로 파악하면 뒷부분의 세부 대화 흐름을 수월하게 따라갈 수 있다. 이때 대화에 참여하는 사람이 여러 명인 경우가 있으므로 메시지를 보낸 사람이 누구인지 확인하면서 대화문의 흐름을 정확하게 파악한다.

2. 대화자의 요청 및 제안 사항에 대한 내용은 관련 표현을 익혀두면 쉽게 파악할 수 있다.
메시지 대화문에서는 의사 표현이 자주 등장하므로, 책에 수록된 '파트 7 핵심 표현 및 필수 어휘(p.428~429)'를 익혀두면 대화문의 내용을 빠르고 정확하게 파악할 수 있다.

예제 메시지 대화문

Jeff Simmons	8:12
Hi Ms. Gotti. Just got to the conference center. I'm at delivery bay 21.	
Miriam Gotti	8:15
OK, Jeff. I'm headed over right now with a few of my team members. Should be there in 20 minutes.	
Jeff Simmons	8:17
Noted. Would you like me to start unloading stuff for the event?	
Miriam Gotti	8:21
Sure. I just got off the phone with Mr. Cooper. He's in the lobby upstairs. I've asked him to go down and meet you.	
Jeff Simmons	8:22
Great! Is it all right if we start setting up then?	
Miriam Gotti	8:23
By all means! Mr. Cooper's got the forms you'll need to get past security.	
Miriam Gotti	8:24
We're in Hall D, by the way.	
Jeff Simmons	8:25
Got it! See you there in a bit, Ms. Gotti.	

연락한 목적

세부 내용

Q1. Why did Mr. Simmons contact Ms. Gotti?

(A) To ask for further instructions
(B) To notify her about a delivery
(C) To confirm her attendance at an event
(D) To inquire about some documents

Q2. Where will Mr. Cooper meet Mr. Simmons?

(A) In Hall D
(B) In the lobby
(C) At delivery bay 21
(D) At a security office

Q3. At 8:23, what does Ms. Gotti mean when she writes, "By all means"?

(A) She will try to get to a venue as soon as possible.
(B) She would like Mr. Simmons to follow through with his idea.
(C) She expects a task to be completed within a time frame.
(D) She wants Mr. Simmons to find people who can assist him.

해설　Q1　**주제/목적 찾기 문제** Mr. Simmons가 Ms. Gotti에게 연락한 목적을 묻는 목적 찾기 문제이므로 지문의 앞부분을 주의 깊게 확인한다. 'Just got to the conference center.'(8:12)에서 Mr. Simmons가 회의장에 도착했다고 한 후, 'Would you like me to start unloading stuff for the event?'(8:17)에서 행사를 위한 비품을 내려야 할지 의견을 구하고 있으므로 (A) To ask for further instructions가 정답이다.

Q2　**육하원칙 문제** Mr. Cooper가 어디에서(Where) Mr. Simmons를 만날 것인지를 묻는 육하원칙 문제이다. 질문의 핵심 어구인 Mr. Cooper meet Mr. Simmons와 관련하여, 'I'm at delivery bay 21.'(8:12)에서 Mr. Simmons가 21번 배달 구역에 있다고 한 후, 'I've asked him to go down and meet you.'(8:21)에서 Ms. Gotti가 Mr. Cooper에게 내려가서 Mr. Simmons를 만나라고 부탁했다고 했으므로 Mr. Cooper는 21번 배달 구역에서 Mr. Simmons를 만날 것임을 알 수 있다. 따라서 (C) At delivery bay 21이 정답이다.

Q3　**의도 파악 문제** Ms. Gotti가 의도한 것을 묻는 문제이므로, 질문의 인용어구(By all means)가 언급된 주변 문맥을 확인한다. 'Is it all right if we start setting up then?'(8:22)에서 Mr. Simmons가 그때 준비를 시작해도 괜찮겠느냐고 문의하는 말에 Ms. Gotti가 'By all means!'(물론이죠)라고 한 것을 통해, Ms. Gotti는 Mr. Simmons가 그의 계획을 이행하기를 바란다는 것을 알 수 있다. 따라서 (B) She would like Mr. Simmons to follow through with his idea가 정답이다.

정답　Q1 (A)　　Q2 (C)　　Q3 (B)

지문 해석 p.150

메시지 대화문에 자주 나오는 ⭐핵심 표현

1. 요청 사항

Do you mind ~? : ~해 주실 수 있으십니까?

Do you mind giving me a lift downtown tonight after work if you're going there anyway?
오늘 혹시 시내로 나가시면, 오늘 밤 퇴근 후에 저 좀 태워다 주실 수 있으십니까?

Can you help me with ~? : ~을 도와주실 수 있나요?

Can you help me with installing an update on my computer when you have a moment?
잠깐 시간 있으실 때 제 컴퓨터에 업데이트를 설치하는 것을 도와주실 수 있나요?

2. 제안 사항

What about ~? : ~은 어때요?

What about trying the new Vietnamese restaurant around the corner for lunch today?
오늘 점심에 근처에 있는 새로운 베트남 식당에 가보는 것은 어때요?

I would like 사람 **to ~ :** 저는 (사람)이 ~하는 것이 좋을 것 같아요

I would like you to pass the information on to my assistant as soon as you get back.
저는 당신이 돌아오는 대로 제 비서에게 그 정보를 전달해주시는 것이 좋을 것 같아요.

메시지 대화문에 자주 나오는 ⭐구어체 표현

1. 의견 및 요청에 대한 동의

Exactly. 맞아요.	= Correct.	Absolutely. 그럼요. 물론이지요.
No problem. 그럼요. (전혀 문제 없어요.)		You have a point. 당신의 말도 일리가 있어요.
That/It works (for me). (제게) 그것이 괜찮네요.		I don't see why not. 되고 말고요.

Absolutely. 그럼요. 물론이지요. = Sure.

2. 업무 처리

I will see to it. 제가 그것을 처리할게요.	= I will take care of it.	I will get to it. 제가 그것을 시작할게요.
I will set it up. 제가 그것을 준비할게요.		Done. (일이) 완료되었어요.

메시지 대화문에 자주 나오는 ⭐필수 어휘

1. 사내 업무

approval n. 승인		overtime n. 초과 근무
attach v. 첨부하다		placement n. 일자리
branch n. 지점		post v. 게시하다
company newsletter 사보		progress n. 진행, 진척
confirm v. 확인하다	= verify	promote v. 승진시키다
deadline n. 마감일자		review n. 검토

in charge 담당하는, ~을 맡고 있는	shift n. 교대 근무 (시간)
in-house 사내의	submit v. 제출하다
instruct v. 지시하다, 알려 주다	supervise v. 감독하다
notify v. 알리다, 통지하다　　=inform, give notice	supply room 비품실
office supply 사무용품	transfer v. 전근 가다, 이동하다　　= relocate

2. 회의 및 행사 참가

affiliate n. 계열사; v. 제휴하다	participant n. 참가자, 참여자　　= attendee
assistance n. 도움, 보조	participate in ~에 참가하다
conduct a seminar 세미나를 개최하다	patron n. 손님, 후원자
convention hall (호텔 등의) 회의장　　= conference hall	pick up (차로 사람을) 마중 나가다
department n. 부, 부서	presentation n. 발표
delay n. 지연; v. 지연되다, 연기하다	registration form 신청서
display n. 진열; v. 전시하다	release v. 발표하다, 공개하다　　= announce, publicize
enroll v. 등록하다　　= register	set up 설치하다
exposition n. 전시회, 박람회　　= exhibition	sign up 등록하다, 가입하다
headquarters n. 본부, 본사	trade fair 무역 박람회

3. 시설 이용

amenity n. 편의 시설	equipment n. 장비, 장치
availability n. 이용성, 가능성	facility n. 시설, 기관
cafeteria n. 구내식당	fee n. 요금, 수수료
check into ~에 투숙하다	parking lot 주차장
comfortable adj. 쾌적한, 편안한	rating n. 평가, 등급　　= assessment
decent adj. 괜찮은, 적당한	reasonable adj. 합리적인, 적정한
estimate n. 견적서; v. 추산하다	utilize v. 이용하다

4. 약속 및 일정

arrangement n. 준비, 계획	one-way adj. 편도의
appointment n. 예약, (특히 업무 관련) 약속	pack v. 짐을 꾸리다
be scheduled for ~로 예정되어 있다	postpone v. 연기하다, 미루다
business day 영업일	prepare v. 준비하다
business trip 출장	provisional adj. 잠정적인, 일시적인　　= tentative
cancel v. 취소하다	reschedule v. 일정을 변경하다
flight ticket 항공권	round-trip adj. 왕복 여행의
head v. 향하다, 가다	unexpectedly adv. 갑자기, 예상외로
modification n. 수정, 변경	timetable n. 일정표

HACKERS PRACTICE 토익 고득점을 위한 필수 연습

유형 연습 지문을 읽고 질문에 답하세요.

01 메시지 대화문

Betsy Lindhof	8:52
Did you get my e-mail last Friday? About Ms. Farrow?	
Daniel Sung	8:55
No, what about her? Is there a problem?	
Betsy Lindhof	8:56
Oh, it's just that she won't be able to start work today. Had a personal emergency. She can come in tomorrow, though.	
Daniel Sung	8:57
OK, no problem. We're mostly just doing orientation today. She can catch up.	
Betsy Lindhof	8:58
That's what I thought. Just wanted to let you know.	
Daniel Sung	8:59
Thanks. The rest of the new employees are waiting in the training room. I'll be there in a few minutes.	

Q. At 8:58, what does Ms. Lindhof mean when she writes, "That's what I thought"?

    (A) She was certain that Mr. Sung could take her place.
    (B) She did not believe Ms. Farrow's absence would be an issue.
    (C) She assumed that an extra session would need to be held.

02 메시지 대화문

Emma Browning	15:39
Hi Sarah. It looks like I won't be making it back to the office this afternoon. My meeting is running long. Could you send me your presentation by e-mail instead?	
Sarah Clapp	15:41
Hi Emma. Sure thing. But do you think you'll have time to look it over before tomorrow?	
Emma Browning	15:46
Absolutely. I can read it on my way home on the train and send you my notes at around 7 P.M.	
Sarah Clapp	15:47
I really appreciate that, but I hope I'm not putting you out. You must have a lot on your plate.	
Emma Browning	15:48
Yes, but it's quite all right. It's your first client meeting, and I promised I'd help... which is not to say I don't think you'll do well. I'm sure you will.	
Sarah Clapp	15:51
Thank you, Emma! I'm sending the documents to you as we speak.	

Q. What is NOT indicated about Ms. Browning?

    (A) Her meeting will probably end late.
    (B) She commutes to work on a train.
    (C) She is uncertain about Ms. Clapp's abilities.

정답·해설·해석 p.150

🕐 제한 시간 10분

Questions 01-02 refer to the following text message chain.

Claire Fontaine   9:38 A.M.
Sorry to bother you. Have you been to the print shop yet?

Joe Greyson   9:39 A.M.
No. Still at the post office. Why?

Claire Fontaine   9:43 A.M.
Can you get an extra 20 copies of the company newsletter?
They're for my new trainees.

Joe Greyson   9:46 A.M.
No problem. Do you have enough company handbooks to give
them?

Claire Fontaine   9:48 A.M.
I believe so. There's a box of them in the supply room. Near
the back. I saw them there last month.

Joe Greyson   9:51 A.M.
Mr. Jennings used all of those last week. I'll ask them to print
some more for us.

Claire Fontaine   9:55 A.M.
Just get 20. We plan to make changes to the handbook soon, so
we won't need more than that.

Joe Greyson   9:57 A.M.
Will do. I can bring them to your office after I pick them up.

---

01 At 9:48 A.M., what does Ms. Fontaine mean
when she writes, "I believe so"?

(A) She agrees that extra newsletters should be
printed.
(B) She supposes she can drop by the print
shop.
(C) She thinks there are a sufficient number of
handbooks.
(D) She understands that newsletters have
been distributed.

02 What does Mr. Greyson offer to do?

(A) Make some modifications to a company
handbook
(B) Drop off some extra copies at
Ms. Fontaine's workplace
(C) Call a store to order more of a product
(D) Pick up some boxes from a supply room

Questions 03-06 refer to the following online chat discussion.

Steve Williams 9:10 A.M.		Laura, there is a problem with the curtains we ordered for the offices of Winston Legal Services. Our supplier has run out of the fabric that we originally chose.
Laura Davis 9:13 A.M.		I see. We are supposed to be done with that project by the end of the month. What should we do?
Michael Smith 9:15 A.M.		I was able to locate some new fabric samples last night, Steve. It took me hours, but I think I found some that we can use. I e-mailed photographs of them to you.
Steve Williams 9:18 A.M.		Thank you, Michael! If we can find something suitable, we may still be able to make the deadline.
Laura Davis 9:20 A.M.		I hope so. I'd like to avoid informing the client that their project's been delayed again.
Steve Williams 9:22 A.M.		Michael, some of these could work. I'll show them to the client now.
Laura Davis 9:24 A.M.		Keep me posted as well, Steve. I need to know if I have to readjust the schedule for this project.

Send

03 In which field do the writers most likely work?

(A) Accounting
(B) Law
(C) Textile manufacturing
(D) Interior design

04 What did Mr. Smith do yesterday?

(A) Discussed a problem with a client
(B) Attended the opening of a new office space
(C) Attempted to find out substitutes for a product
(D) Completed an urgent project report

05 At 9:22 A.M., what does Mr. Williams mean when he writes, "some of these could work"?

(A) Some e-mail addresses are correct.
(B) He will be testing the quality of a material.
(C) A client will probably approve of a selection.
(D) He needs to make a few changes to a business plan.

06 What is true about Ms. Davis?

(A) She is eager to change a deadline.
(B) She is in charge of a project timeline.
(C) She prepares for a client presentation.
(D) She will be away from the office.

Questions 07-10 refer to the following text-message chain.

Hank Warden	(11:26 A.M.)

Good morning. I'm with Bene-Connect Wireless. I've come to your apartment to install a router, but no one is home. Are you nearby?

Michaela Howe	(11:28 A.M.)

Oh. That completely slipped my mind. I'm actually at the airport right now. I'm about to catch a flight.

Hank Warden	(11:29 A.M.)

OK. That's fine. We can reschedule easily enough.

Michaela Howe	(11:35 A.M.)

But I really need the new router set up because the one your company installed last year isn't working anymore. I'll contact the building manager to see if she can give you access to my apartment.

Michaela Howe	(11:40 A.M.)

I just spoke to the manager, Susan Lewis, and she said she will let you in. Just go meet her at the office on the second floor.

Hank Warden	(11:42 A.M.)

All right. Is it OK if she sign the work order form? The company requires authorization before I start any work.

Michaela Howe	(11:43 A.M.)

That shouldn't be a problem.

Hank Warden	(11:44 A.M.)

Great. Your new router should be all set up when you get back from your trip. If it gives you any trouble, just let us know and we will change it for free as long as it's still under warranty.

07 Who most likely is Mr. Warden?

(A) A technician
(B) A salesperson
(C) A landlord
(D) A plumber

08 What is suggested about Ms. Howe?

(A) She will meet Ms. Lewis later in the day.
(B) She is an existing customer of Bene-Connect.
(C) She is employed by an Internet provider.
(D) She just returned from a business trip.

09 At 11:43 A.M., what does Ms. Howe mean when she writes, "That shouldn't be a problem"?

(A) She is willing to repair a device on her own.
(B) She does not mind if someone else signs for her.
(C) She can go down to a lobby to meet a technician.
(D) She is familiar with a software installation process.

10 What is indicated about Bene-Connect Wireless?

(A) It offers services seven days a week.
(B) It is planning to release a new product.
(C) It does not charge to replace items under warranty.
(D) It is conducting a survey among its customers.

정답·해설·해석 p.151 / [별책] 토익 RC 필수 어휘 p.47

해커스 스타강사의 ▶
무료 해설강의 바로 보기
(1~2번 문제)

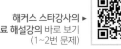

Chapter 11 메시지 대화문(Text message chain) | 433

READING Part 7   Ch 11 메시지 대화문   Hackers TOEIC Reading

CHAPTER 12 광고(Advertisement)

토익 이렇게 나온다!

광고는 홍보하고자 하는 여러 가지 것들을 광고하는 글로서, 크게 일반 광고와 구인 광고로 나뉠 수 있다. 일반 광고는 제품이나 서비스뿐만 아니라 식당 및 상점, 부동산, 각종 프로그램 등 다양한 것을 다루고, 구인 광고는 인턴, 관리자 등 여러 직급을 다룬다. 평균 1~2지문 정도 출제된다.

토익 질문 유형 및 전략

빈출 질문 유형

[일반 광고]

주제/목적 찾기 문제	광고되는 것, 광고의 목적을 묻는다.
	What is being advertised? 광고되고 있는 것은 무엇인가?
	What is the purpose of the advertisement? 광고의 목적은 무엇인가?
육하원칙 문제	제공되는 것, 특정 종류나 기타 세부 사항을 주로 묻는다.
	What does the store provide for free with a purchase? 상점은 구입품과 함께 무엇을 무료로 제공하는가?
	Which item is temporarily unavailable? 어떤 물품이 일시적으로 이용 불가능한가?
Not/True 문제	회사나 시설과 같은 광고주, 광고되는 제품이나 서비스 등에 대해 일치하거나 일치하지 않는 것을 주로 묻는다.
	What is indicated about the Helena Society? Helena 협회에 대해 언급된 것은?
	What is NOT mentioned about items on sale? 판매 중인 품목에 대해 언급되지 않은 것은?
추론 문제	광고의 타깃, 광고가 게재된 곳이나 광고에 언급된 특정 사항에 대해 추론할 수 있는 것을 주로 묻는다.
	For whom is the advertisement intended? 광고는 누구를 대상으로 하는가?
	Where would the advertisement most likely be found? 광고는 어디에서 볼 수 있을 것 같은가?
	What is indicated about the office furniture? 사무용 가구에 대해 암시되는 것은?

[구인 광고]

육하원칙 문제	지원자가 해야 할 일, 지원 자격이나 기타 세부 사항을 주로 묻는다.
	What do applicants need to submit in person? 지원자들은 무엇을 직접 제출해야 하는가?
	What is listed as a requirement for the accounting job? 회계직의 요구 조건으로서 무엇이 열거되어 있는가?
Not/True 문제	구직자나 고용주, 광고된 직책의 책무 등에 대해 일치하거나 일치하지 않는 것을 주로 묻는다.
	What is indicated about job seekers contacted for interviews?
	면접을 위해 연락받은 구직자들에 대해 언급된 것은?
	What is NOT a responsibility of the sales director? 영업 이사의 책무가 아닌 것은?
추론 문제	광고의 타깃을 주로 묻는다.
	For whom is the advertisement intended? 광고는 누구를 대상으로 하는가?

핵심 전략

1. 일반 광고는 제목 및 앞부분에서 광고되는 것을 파악한 후 세부 내용을 확인한다.
제목이나 앞부분에서 광고되는 것을 파악한 후, 그것의 장점 및 혜택 등의 세부 내용을 확인한다.

2. 구인 광고의 흐름을 알면 지문의 세부 내용을 파악하기 쉽다.
채용하려는 직급은 Intern Opportunity와 같은 제목으로 지문 상단 또는 앞부분에 제시된다. 직급이 제시된 이후에는 주로 담당하게 될 업무, 지원 자격 등이 제시되고, 지문 마지막에 지원 방법이 나온다.

3. 일반 광고에서 광고되는 것과 장점 및 혜택, 구인 광고에서 담당 업무 및 지원 자격과 지원 방법에 대한 내용은 관련 표현을 익혀두면 쉽게 찾을 수 있다.

Pinewood Towers
The Perfect Location to Conduct Business!

〕 광고되는 것

Located in the financial district of Portland, Pinewood Towers is the perfect location to house your business. In addition to our spacious units, the building provides:

- 24-hour security services
- Three basement floors for parking
- A coffee shop and cafeteria
- A full maintenance staff

Just minutes from public transportation, Pinewood Towers is very conveniently situated on 776 Poplar Avenue. We now have vacancies for spaces that can comfortably hold 10 to 40 persons. Each unit includes its own lobby, restrooms, and storage areas. All spaces are equipped with Internet and telephone access and can also be furnished for an extra fee.

장점

For a guided tour of the vacant units at Pinewood Towers, please speak to one of our agents by calling 555-8877 between 9 A.M. and 6 P.M. Monday through Friday. And for this month only, all tenants leasing a unit for one year or longer are eligible to receive a 15 percent deduction. Call us today to take advantage of this rare opportunity!

혜택

Q1. What is being advertised?

(A) A corporate moving service
(B) A real estate investment firm
(C) A building containing office spaces
(D) A storage facility

Q2. What is indicated about Pinewood Towers?

(A) Its construction is nearing completion.
(B) It only offers short-term leases.
(C) It can provide furnishing to tenants.
(D) It is hiring 40 extra staff members.

Q3. According to the advertisement, who is eligible to receive a reduced rate?

(A) Current tenants of the facility
(B) Those renting large office spaces
(C) Owners of small businesses
(D) People leasing for 12 months or longer

해설 Q1 **주제/목적 찾기 문제** 광고되는 것을 묻는 주제 찾기 문제이다. 제목 'Pinewood Towers, The Perfect Location to Conduct Business!' 에서 Pinewood Towers가 사업을 운영하기 위한 최적의 장소라고 한 후, 건물의 장점 및 임대 혜택을 설명하고 있으므로 (C) A building containing office spaces가 정답이다.

Q2 **Not/True 문제** 질문의 핵심 어구인 Pinewood Towers와 관련된 내용을 지문에서 찾아 보기와 대조하는 Not/True 문제이다. (A)는 지문에 언급되지 않은 내용이다. (B)는 'all tenants leasing a unit for one year or longer'에서 한 공간을 1년 혹은 그 이상 임대하는 모든 세입자들이라고 했으므로 지문의 내용과 일치하지 않는다. (C)는 'All spaces ~ can also be furnished for an extra fee'에서 모든 공간은 추가 요금을 내면 가구가 비치될 수 있다고 했으므로 (C) It can provide furnishing to tenants가 정답이다. (D)는 지문에 언급되지 않은 내용이다.

Q3 **육하원칙 문제** 광고에 따르면, 할인 요금을 받을 자격이 있는 사람이 누구인지(who)를 묻는 육하원칙 문제이다. 질문의 핵심 어구인 eligible to receive a reduced rate와 관련하여, 'all tenants leasing a unit for one year or longer are eligible to receive a 15 percent deduction'에서 한 공간을 1년 혹은 그 이상 임차하는 모든 세입자들은 15퍼센트 공제를 받을 자격이 있다고 했으므로 (D) People leasing for 12 months or longer가 정답이다.

정답 Q1 (C)   Q2 (C)   Q3 (D)

지문 해석 p.153

광고에 자주 나오는 ⭐핵심 표현

[일반 광고]

1. 광고되는 것 소개

(Are you) looking for ~? : ~을 찾고 계십니까?

Are you looking for a place that serves home-cooked meals? 집에서 요리된 식사를 제공하는 곳을 찾고 계십니까?

2. 장점 및 혜택

We offer ~ : 저희는 ~을 제공합니다

We offer a large variety of shoes for every occasion. 저희는 모든 경우를 위한 매우 다양한 신발을 제공합니다.

[구인 광고]

1. 담당 업무

The responsibilities of 직종 **are ~ :** (직종)의 책무는 ~하는 것입니다

The responsibilities of the bank manager are overseeing branch operations and meeting the company's financial goals. 은행 지점장의 책무는 지점 운영을 감독하고 회사의 재정 목표를 달성하는 것입니다.

2. 지원 자격

~ is required : ~이 요구됩니다

Availability to work weekend shifts is required. 주말 교대 근무 가능함이 요구됩니다.

~ is mandatory : ~은 필수입니다

A degree in business administration is mandatory for the managerial position. 관리직에 경영학 학위는 필수입니다.

3. 지원 방법

e-mail a cover letter and résumé to 사람 **at** 주소 **:** (사람)에게 (주소)로 자기소개서와 이력서를 이메일로 보내십시오

To apply, e-mail a cover letter and résumé to Lily Chambers at lilcham@regentbank.com.
지원하시려면, Lily Chambers에게 lilcham@regentbank.com으로 자기소개서와 이력서를 이메일로 보내십시오.

광고에 자주 나오는 ⭐필수 어휘

1. 식당 및 상점

ambience n. 분위기, 환경	= atmosphere	**franchise** n. 체인점, 가맹점 영업권
appetizer n. 전채 요리, 식욕을 돋우는 것		**grocery store** 식료품점
bargain n. 특가품, 거래; v. 흥정하다	= deal, negotiate	**licensed** adj. 허가된, 면허를 받은
bustling adj. 부산한, 붐비는	= busy	**patron** n. 고객, 단골손님
certified adj. 공인의, 보증된		**pricey** adj. 값비싼, 돈이 드는 = expensive
cuisine n. 요리, 요리법		**serving** n. 1인분, 음식 시중, 접대
diner n. 식사하는 손님		**showroom** n. 전시실, 진열실
dish n. 요리, 접시		**storage** n. 저장, 창고
entrée n. 주요 요리		**unparalleled** adj. 견줄 데 없는, 비할 바 없는
family-owned 가족이 운영하는		**vegetarian** n. 채식주의자; adj. 채식의

2. 채용

administrative adj. 경영상의, 행정상의	**job opening** 공석
application n. 지원, 신청서	**layoff** n. 해고
apply for ~에 지원하다	**payroll** n. 급여 대상자 명단, 급여 지급 총액
candidate n. 후보자, 지원자	**pension** n. 연금, 수당
cover letter 자기소개서	**prerequisite** n. 필요 조건; adj. 필수의
dismiss v. 해고하다, 내쫓다　　= fire	**probationary period** 시험 채용 기간
dispatch v. 파견하다, 보내다	**recruit** v. 모집하다; n. 신입 사원
employment n. 고용, 채용	**reference letter** 추천서
get a promotion 승진하다	**resignation** n. 사직, 사임
human resources(= personnel) **department** 인사부	**résumé** n. 이력서
internship n. 인턴 사원 근무, 인턴직	**retirement** n. 퇴직, 은퇴

3. 부동산

accompany v. 동행하다, 수반하다, 동반하다	**landlord** n. 집주인, 지주
architectural adj. 건축의, 구성적인	**lease** n. 임대차, 임대차 계약; v. 임대(임차)하다　　= rent
ceiling n. 천장	**outskirt** n. 교외, 변두리
couch n. 소파, 긴 의자	**parlor** n. 응접실, 객실
cozy adj. 아늑한, 편안한	**premises** n. 토지, 부동산
evacuate v. (집을) 비우다, 떠나다, 대피하다　　= vacate	**property** n. 부동산, 토지
flat n. 아파트	**real estate** 부동산, 부동산 중개업
furnished adj. 가구가 비치된	**remote** adj. 외진, 먼
garage n. 차고, 주차장, 차량 정비소	**spacious** adj. 넓은, 훤히 트인
housing n. 주거, 주택	**stroll** v. 거닐다, 산책하다; n. 산책
inhabitant n. 주민, 거주자　　= dweller, occupant, resident, tenant	**tenure** n. (부동산의) 보유, 보유 기간
	vacant adj. 비어 있는, 사람이 없는

4. 프로그램(교육/TV/여행)

accommodation n. 숙소, 거처	**inn** n. 여관, 작은 호텔
air n. 전파 통신 매체; v. 방송되다	**lodge** n. 오두막, 여관; v. 숙박하다, 묵다
attraction n. 명소, 인기거리	**make a reservation** 예약하다
boast v. 자랑하다, 큰소리치다	**marketplace** n. 시장, 장터
confirmation n. 확인, 확정	**package** n. 패키지, 일괄 프로그램
deal n. 거래, 처리; v. (주제 등을) 다루다, 처리하다	**premiere** n. 초연, 개봉; v. 초연을 하다, 처음으로 주연을 맡다
distance n. 거리, 먼 거리	**scenery** n. 경치, 배경
episode n. 1회 방송	**souvenir** n. 기념품, 토산품
experience n. 경험, 체험; v. 경험하다, 체험하다	**sponsor** n. 후원 업체, 광고주; v. 후원하다, 광고주가 되다
explore v. 탐험하다, 조사하다	**stay** v. 머무르다, 숙박하다
fabulous adj. 굉장한, 믿어지지 않는　　= fantastic, terrific	**tropical** adj. 열대 지방의, 열대의
guided tour 안내원이 딸린 여행	**tune in** 채널을 맞추다

유형 연습   지문을 읽고 질문에 답하세요.

01 일반 광고

Riverdale Antique Auction!

Come on down to Henderson's Antiques on 354 Dalecourt Avenue in downtown Riverdale for its annual antique auction, this Sunday from 1:30 P.M. This special event is held to raise funds for the local children's hospital. Items on auction are donated by residents and businesses in the region and include furniture, housewares, artwork, and collectibles! Visit www.hendersonantiques.com to take a look at the list of items up for auction.

Q. What is the purpose of the event?

(A) To make room for new stock
(B) To collect money for a charitable cause
(C) To solicit donations from local residents

02 구인 광고

WANTED: Breakfast Shift Head Cook

Duties: Hal's Diner is looking for a head cook to cover our breakfast shift from 5:30 A.M. to 11 A.M. Monday through Friday. The selected applicant will be responsible for the preparation of breakfast grill items including eggs, pancakes, and meats. He or she will also be in charge of overseeing the other two cooks and making daily lists of supplies needed for the next shift.

Qualifications: We are looking for a cook who has worked as a member of kitchen staff for a minimum of six years. Experience in management is also an asset.

Q. What is a required task for the advertised position?

(A) Purchasing of food items
(B) Managing a team
(C) Weekend work

03 일반 광고

Looking for an economical way to get around? Try the Yorktown Cycle, a bike made specifically for city dwellers:
• Comfortable, upright seating position
• Foldable, lightweight frame
• Durable, all-weather tires
Find the basic kit at most major retailers and customize it with accessories. View our catalog at www. yorktowncycle.com.

Q. For whom is the advertisement most likely intended?

(A) Fitness enthusiasts
(B) Business travelers
(C) Urban commuters

정답·해설·해석 **p.154**

🕐 제한 시간 12분

Questions 01-04 refer to the following advertisement.

Management Opportunity

The Dilly Dogs N' Fries Franchise is accepting applications for a full-time district manager position. We would prefer to offer the opportunity to staff within the company. The responsibilities of the position include overseeing all aspects of operations for the restaurant's 12 locations in eastern New Jersey, ensuring that each one meets the company's standards for food and service quality. The duties of the district manager will include hiring and training new personnel, analyzing and reporting sales figures, and guaranteeing compliance with state food and work safety regulations. He or she will communicate often with the executive for the purpose of discussing the business's growth. Local travel is required. The candidate must have a master's degree in business management and some familiarity with basic accounting. Strong leadership and coaching skills are mandatory. Current employees who wish to apply for this job are asked to e-mail a cover letter and résumé to Blake Carlton of administrative services at blacarl@dilly.com.

01 For whom is the advertisement intended?

(A) New trainees
(B) Business specialists
(C) Existing employees
(D) Sales managers

02 According to the advertisement, what is NOT a responsibility of the job?

(A) Meeting with upper management
(B) Keeping track of sales data
(C) Traveling between various locations
(D) Conducting market research

03 What is mentioned about the advertised position?

(A) It is a temporary job.
(B) It offers a full benefits package.
(C) It will require some leading skills.
(D) It requires completion of training.

04 What is indicated about Dilly Dogs N' Fries?

(A) It maintains a training facility for its employees.
(B) It failed to comply with the state's food safety guidelines.
(C) It operates a dozen branches around New Jersey.
(D) It requires letters of reference for all incoming staff members.

READING Part 7   Ch 12 광고   Hackers TOEIC Reading

Questions 05-08 refer to the following advertisement.

Alladin Shopping Mall-A Great New Place to Shop!

Are you looking for the ideal place to do all your shopping? After the recent completion of construction, the Alladin Shopping Mall is now open to all residents and visitors and is sure to meet all your shopping needs. Located in the heart of Dubai, the mall houses the Mercato Department Store, which features six floors of retail space. This famed shopping destination offers men's and women's wear, children's clothing, sporting and household goods, and a cosmetics and perfume department. The women's department boasts a variety of accessories and a vast footwear department.

And if you need a bite to eat, come to our sixth-floor food court which has Arabic, Italian, Chinese, Japanese, and American fast food favorites as well as fine dining fare. Need something for dinner later on? Our supermarket on the basement floor features a wide selection of quality imported and local food items.

Also, take advantage of the many benefits offered to holders of a Priority Shopper Card. Register for the card at any of our service counters, and enjoy year-round discounts and savings at selected stores in the mall. Save up points on your card to qualify for free gifts. Just present your card whenever you pay for a purchase!

For more information on Alladin Mall's stores, products, events and promotions, simply visit www.alladinmall.com. Alladin Mall is open every day from 10 A.M. to 9 P.M.

Alladin Mall... Shop to your heart's desire!

05 What is indicated about the Alladin Shopping Mall?

(A) It is operated by a foreign company.
(B) It has seven floors of shopping area.
(C) It provides a shuttle for visiting tourists.
(D) It is located beside a hotel.

06 What is NOT mentioned about Mercato?

(A) It is a well-known department store.
(B) It offers clothing for men and women.
(C) It contains a large shoe collection.
(D) It closes later on the weekends.

07 What will the mall provide to cardholders?

(A) Access to private lounges
(B) Reduced prices on some products
(C) Invitations to special events
(D) Complimentary product samples

08 How can readers find out about promotions?

(A) By calling a number
(B) By visiting an administrative office
(C) By sending an e-mail
(D) By looking at a Web site

Questions 09-12 refer to the following advertisement.

2Storage is Florida's largest chain of storage providers. It offers four convenient options to temporarily store your items.

JUNIOR	DELUXE
From $30 6.75 square meters Ideal for small appliances, sports equipment, and other personal belongings	From $100 13.5 square meters Ideal for the contents of small homes and offices
PREMIUM	PREFERRED
From $200 18 square meters Ideal for the contents of large homes and offices	Prices and sizes vary Includes document storage containers, covered vehicle parking, and units with temperature controls

* For more information, call 555-5044. Complimentary handcarts, packing materials, and security locks are provided. For an extra charge, customers may arrange for pickup and delivery. Also, if you are a new customer, get discount coupons on our free 2Storage mobile application.

09 What is indicated about 2Storage?

(A) It recently added a service.
(B) Its biggest unit size is 200 square meters.
(C) It has more than one location.
(D) Its facilities are open 24 hours a day.

10 Which option comes in different sizes?

(A) Junior
(B) Deluxe
(C) Premium
(D) Preferred

11 What is NOT offered for free by 2Storage?

(A) Handcarts
(B) Pickup services
(C) Packing materials
(D) Security locks

12 What is true about the mobile application?

(A) It allows customers to submit special requests.
(B) It is available at no cost to users.
(C) It does not require registration.
(D) It offers a one-month trial period.

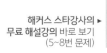

CHAPTER 13

공고(Notice & Announcement)

토익 이렇게 나온다!

공고는 앞으로 있을 행사나 각종 공지 사항 등에 대해 알리는 글로서, 크게 사내 공고와 일반 공고로 나뉠 수 있다. 사내 공고는 회사 내 시스템이나 시설, 회의나 출장 관련 사항 등을 다루고, 일반 공고는 비즈니스나 학술 세미나 및 강연, 상점에서 볼 수 있는 안내 사항 등 실생활 범위의 다양한 내용을 주로 다룬다. 평균 1지문 정도 출제된다.

토익 질문 유형 및 전략

빈출 질문 유형

주제/목적 찾기 문제	공고의 목적, 주제를 묻는다.
	What is the purpose of the notice? 공고의 목적은 무엇인가?
	What is being announced? 공고되고 있는 것은 무엇인가?
육하원칙 문제	요청 사항, 추후 일정 계획이나 기타 세부 사항을 주로 묻는다.
	What are the staff members asked to do? 직원들은 무엇을 하도록 요청되는가?
	What is scheduled for July 18? 7월 18일에 무엇이 예정되어 있는가?
	When will the orientation be held? 오리엔테이션은 언제 열릴 것인가?
Not/True 문제	공고에 언급된 사람이나 회사, 행사 등에 대해 일치하거나 일치하지 않는 것을 주로 묻는다.
	What is indicated about Ms. Singh? Ms. Singh에 대해 언급된 것은?
	What is NOT a planned event? 계획된 행사가 아닌 것은?
추론 문제	공고의 대상, 공고가 게재된 곳이나 공고에 언급된 특정 사항에 대해 추론할 수 있는 것을 주로 묻는다.
	To whom is the notice most likely addressed? 공고는 누구를 대상으로 낸 것 같은가?
	Where would the notice most likely be found? 공고는 어디서 볼 수 있을 것 같은가?
	What is suggested about new employees? 신입 사원들에 대해 암시되는 것은?

핵심 전략

1. 공고의 기본 구성을 알면 글의 핵심을 빠르게 파악할 수 있다.

앞부분에는 공고의 목적이나 주제가 명시된다. 중간에는 요청 사항, 추후 일정 계획, 시간 및 장소, 관련된 사람 등 세부 사항이 언급된다. 마지막에는 문의할 수 있는 연락처가 나온다.

2. 공고의 목적 및 주제, 요청 사항에 대한 내용은 관련 표현을 익혀두면 쉽게 찾을 수 있다.

NOTICE:
All Grosvenor Electronics Customers

We would like to inform our customers that beginning April 1, our revised policy on product exchange will take effect. If a purchased item is defective or does not operate properly, it may be exchanged for the same item only. We will not offer cash refunds on returned merchandise.

To request an exchange, bring the merchandise in its original packaging along with the bill of sale to a service counter at the outlet where it was purchased. You will be asked to fill in a form with a brief description of the problem. After you submit the form, one of our technicians will examine the product to determine whether it can be repaired. If a repair is possible, we will do so free of charge within five business days. If the merchandise is irreparable, we will replace it with a new one unless the item is no longer in stock. In this case, you will have the option of taking store credit in lieu of a replacement.

Thank you for your understanding. If you have questions, please contact a customer service representative. Our Web site at www.grosvenorelectronics.com will be updated shortly to reflect this policy change.

목적

세부 사항

연락처

Q1. What is the purpose of the notice?

    (A) To inform shoppers of new store guidelines
    (B) To request feedback on shop services
    (C) To announce the opening of a repair department
    (D) To provide details on store credit

Q2. What is indicated about Grosvenor Electronics?

    (A) It will be moving to a new area.
    (B) It provides cash rebates in some cases.
    (C) It is open five days per week.
    (D) It has a staff of technicians.

Q3. According to the notice, what will happen soon?

    (A) New products will arrive at the store.
    (B) The store's Web page will be changed.
    (C) Prices of merchandise will be adjusted.
    (D) Staff will undergo additional training.

해설 **Q1** **주제/목적 찾기 문제** 공고의 목적을 묻는 목적 찾기 문제이다. 'We would like to inform our customers that ~ our revised policy on product exchange will take effect.'에서 제품 교환에 대한 수정된 방침이 시행될 예정임을 자사 고객들에게 알리고 싶다고 한 후, 교환 절차에 대해 안내하고 있으므로 (A) To inform shoppers of new store guidelines가 정답이다.

    Q2 **Not/True 문제** 질문의 핵심 어구인 Grosvenor Electronics와 관련된 내용을 지문에서 찾아 보기와 대조하는 Not/True 문제이다. (A)는 지문에 언급되지 않은 내용이다. (B)는 'We will not offer cash refunds'에서 현금 환불을 제공하지 않을 것이라고 했으므로 지문의 내용과 일치하지 않는다. (C)는 지문에 언급되지 않은 내용이다. (D)는 'one of our technicians will examine the product'에서 자사 기술자들 중 한 명이 제품을 검사할 것이라고 했으므로 (D) It has a staff of technicians가 정답이다.

    Q3 **육하원칙 문제** 곧 일어날 일이 무엇인지(what)를 묻는 육하원칙 문제이다. 질문의 핵심 어구인 happen soon과 관련하여 'Our Web site ~ will be updated shortly'에서 웹사이트가 곧 업데이트될 것이라고 했으므로 (B) The store's Web page will be changed가 정답이다.

정답 Q1 (A)   Q2 (D)   Q3 (B)

지문 해석 p.157

공고에 자주 나오는 ⭐핵심 표현

1. 공고의 목적 및 주제

행사 will be held ~ : (행사)는 열릴 것입니다

The seminar will be held at the Moresby Convention Center on January 15 at 5:30 P.M.
세미나는 1월 15일 오후 5시 30분에 Moresby 컨벤션 센터에서 열릴 것입니다.

We would like to ~ : 저희는 ~하고 싶습니다

We would like to ask you to meet with the board next Monday at 10:30 A.M.
저희는 여러분이 다음 월요일 오전 10시 30분에 이사회와 만나기를 요청하고 싶습니다.

2. 요청 사항

You must ~ : 여러분은 ~해야 합니다

You must present your original receipt to request a refund or exchange of any purchase.
구매에 대해서 환불이나 교환을 요청하려면 원본 영수증을 제출해야 합니다.

Please make sure ~ : 반드시 ~해 주십시오

Please make sure to forward us your itinerary for the upcoming business trip to Southeast Asia.
동남아시아로 가는 곧 있을 출장에 대한 귀하의 일정표를 저희에게 반드시 전송해 주십시오.

사람 need to ~ : (사람)은 ~할 필요가 있습니다

Guests need to bring their invitations to the event.
내빈들은 행사 초대장을 가져올 필요가 있습니다.

공고에 자주 나오는 ⭐필수 어휘

1. 세미나 및 강연

associate v. 참가시키다; n. 준회원	**institute** n. 협회, 집회
attendee n. 참가자, 출석자	**keynote speaker** 기조 연설자
auditorium n. 강당, 청중석	**professional** adj. 전문적인, 직업의; n. 전문가
development n. 전개, 확장	**refreshment** n. 다과, 가벼운 음식물
distribute v. 분배하다, 나누어 주다 = hand out	**resource** n. 원천, 자료
host n. 진행자, 주최자; v. 사회를 맡다, 주최하다	**share** v. 공유하다, 분배하다; n. 할당, 몫
improve v. 개선하다, 향상시키다 = enhance	**title** n. 표제, 제목; n. 제목을 붙이다 = entitle

2. 회사 일반 업무

accomplish v. 완수하다, 성취하다	= achieve	
acquaint v. 익히 알게 하다, 숙지하다		
assert v. 주장하다, 단언하다	= insist, maintain	
compromise n. 타협, 양보; v. 타협하다, 절충하다		
consensus n. 합의, 의견 일치		
cooperation n. 협력, 협동	= collaboration, partnership	
correspondence n. 일치, 상응, 통신		
deadlock n. 교착상태		
debate v. 토론하다, 숙고하다; n. 토론, 논쟁		
disapprove v. 거절하다, 찬성하지 않다	= refuse, reject, decline	
mediate v. 중재하다, 조정하다		

negotiate v. 교섭하다, 협상하다	
object to ~에 반대하다	= oppose
opposition n. 반대, 항의	
persuade v. 설득하다, 확신시키다	
procedure n. 절차, 방법	
proponent n. 지지자, 제안자	= supporter
propose v. 제안하다, 제출하다	= suggest
pursue v. 추구하다, 수행하다	
set out 시작하다, 착수하다	
undertake v. (일·책임을) 맡다, 착수하다	= take over
withstand v. 견뎌내다, 이겨내다	

3. 회의 및 출장

airline n. 항공사	
arrangement n. 조정, 준비	
assembly n. 집회, 회의	
book v. 예약하다	= reserve
choose v. 선택하다, 선출하다	= select, name, pick
compact adj. 소형의, 치밀한; n. 계약, 동의	
convention n. 집회, 대회	= conference
division manager 부장, 부서장	
entertainment n. 접대, 여흥	
finalize v. 마무리 짓다, 완결하다	
flight n. 항공편, 비행	
handle v. 다루다, 취급하다; n. 손잡이	
in advance 미리, 사전에	

incur v. 초래하다, 발생시키다	
investor n. 투자자	
itinerary n. 여행 일정	
leave v. 떠나다, 출발하다	= depart from
lift v. 향상시키다; n. 차에 태워줌	
lodging n. 숙박, 숙소	
preliminary adj. 예비의, 준비의	
preside over a meeting 사회를 보다	
publicize v. 광고하다, 알리다	= promote, advertise
reimburse v. 배상하다, 변제하다	= refund
renovate v. 혁신하다, 보수하다	
revise v. 수정하다, 변경하다	= alter, modify
travel v. 여행하다, 이동하다; n. 여행, 이동	

4. 교환 및 환불

check n. 점검, 수표; v. 점검하다, 조사하다	
copy n. 사본, 복사	
credit card 신용카드	
delivery n. 배송, 배달	
exchange v. 교환하다, 교체하다; n. 교환, 교환물	
fault n. 결점, 책임, 잘못	= defect, flaw, mistake
in accordance with ~에 따라서	
inconvenience n. 불편	
investigate v. 살피다, 조사하다	= look into
invoice n. 청구서, 송장	= statement

offer an apology 사과하다	= extend an apology
patronage n. 단골, 후원	
place an order 주문하다	
policy n. 방침, 정책	
postal code 우편번호	
refund v. 환불하다; n. 환불, 상환액	
restore v. 회복시키다, 복원하다	
return department 반송 담당 부서	
shipping n. 선적, 해상 운송	
wrong adj. 잘못된, 틀린	

유형 연습 지문을 읽고 질문에 답하세요.

01 공고

All passengers are informed that photography in the immigration area is not permitted. Also, make sure that you have your passport and completed customs form ready for the officer. Proceed to the immigration desk only when instructed to come forward. Only one person at a time will be served, apart from families traveling with children under age of 10.

Q. Why was the notice written?

(A) To give instructions on filling out a form
(B) To announce changes in departure policies
(C) To provide guidelines for an immigration check

02 공고

Submit an entry registration form, five photographs of your sculpture, and a brief description of your work to the National Art Association (NAA) office. Those applicants selected to compete in the competition will be called by one of our representatives. A participation fee of $38 must be paid prior to January 26.

Q. How will selected participants be notified?

(A) They will be sent a letter.
(B) They will be contacted by phone.
(C) They will be visited by a representative.

03 공고

Commuters are informed that Bus #33 will not be passing on Rainforest Avenue from April 9 to April 22 due to road construction. Instead, the route will be changed, and the bus will travel down Ogden Street. Those going to destinations on Rainforest Avenue are urged to take Subway line 2 and exit at Waterford Station.

Q. Where would the notice most likely be found?

(A) At a bus stop
(B) On an online map
(C) At a construction site

정답·해설·해석 p.157

🕐 제한 시간 12분

Questions 01-04 refer to the following notice.

NOTICE

The Rushmore Building's management has heard your complaints and agreed to replace the building's current elevators with new ones. The new elevators will require less maintenance and also provide faster service. To cover the cost of improvements, we will be raising the monthly dues collected from each tenant by $10.00 effective May 1. Please expect delays in elevator service as the work is underway. To minimize any inconvenience, the work will proceed in stages as follows:

- West lobby: April 1 to 4
- East lobby: April 8 to 10
- South lobby: April 18 to 22
- North lobby: May 1 to 4

During this time, the elevators in the east lobby and north lobby will be reserved for residents of floors 1 through 15, while the other two will be for residents of floors 16 through 32. All elevators will provide access to the underground parking garage.

For questions or concerns, contact the building administrator at 555-0418.

01 What is the notice mainly about?

(A) A change in security procedures
(B) A recent set of complaints from tenants
(C) An improvement to a building
(D) An opportunity to rent some apartments

02 What will happen in May?

(A) A special ceremony will be held.
(B) Some charges will be increased.
(C) A management office will be closed.
(D) Some parking spaces will be made available.

03 What is stated about the north lobby?

(A) It will require additional maintenance.
(B) It is reserved for building management.
(C) It has the largest number of elevators.
(D) It will be the last to receive an upgrade.

04 What can be inferred about Rushmore Building?

(A) It is 32 floors above the ground.
(B) It leases spaces to commercial tenants.
(C) It has four floors of parking for residents.
(D) It is managed by an outside company.

Questions 05-08 refer to the following notice.

22nd Annual Conference on Finance and the Economy

The International Council on Economic Relations (ICER), in cooperation with *Capital Magazine*, invites you to attend its conference, "A Forecast of the Economic Climate of the Future", September 18 and 19 at the Grand Ballroom of the Palace Hotel in Manhattan, New York. Join us as we examine the changing role of the financial industry in today's global economy and plot the way forward for professionals in the field.

At the conference, you will learn about the impact recent events have had on the financial industry and the policy trends that will shape it in the years to come. Topics for discussion include factors affecting the role that the global banking industry plays, the regulation of international finance in an increasingly connected world, and how corporate investment decisions affect the development of emerging economies. Invited keynote speakers are the chair of the Liberty America Bank, Mr. Arthur Lowenstein, and current president of Germany's Wachstum Investment Bank, Ms. Bettina Kaufmann.

Registration for this event is required and will not be available at the venue. Please visit our Web site at www.icer.com/eventreg to sign up. Fees are $60 for those who are part of ICER member organizations and $120 for those who are not. Subscribers to *Capital Magazine* may also take advantage of a special offer on hotel lodgings. To book a room at a hotel near the conference venue, contact Susan Garnier at s.garnier@icer.org.

05 To whom is the notice most likely addressed?

(A) Event organizers
(B) Publishing executives
(C) Government employees
(D) Banking professionals

06 Where is the conference being held?

(A) At the offices of a publishing company
(B) At the headquarters of a hosting organization
(C) At an accommodation facility
(D) At an investment bank

07 What are interested participants asked to do?

(A) Mail in a payment
(B) Bring a membership card
(C) Sign up on a Web site
(D) Register at the event

08 How can attendees obtain a discount on accommodations?

(A) By subscribing to a publication
(B) By booking before a specified date
(C) By sending an e-mail to Ms. Garnier
(D) By downloading a coupon

Questions 09-12 refer to the following announcement.

Announcement to All Personnel

In response to client complaints about the usability of our products, King Industries has established a quality assurance department that will be responsible for testing and evaluating all products developed by the company. — [1] —. In connection with this, we are looking for volunteers to participate in testing our latest networking product, the QX2B router, which is scheduled for release in six months.

Participants will need to perform a series of tasks to determine how difficult it is to set up the product using the accompanying software. — [2] —. Feedback from the exercise will be used to correct any mistakes with functionality and to develop a complete user manual. Because the product is intended for consumers with limited technical knowledge, advanced computing skills are not required. — [3] —. Detailed testing guidelines will be provided in a document prepared by Tim Jenkins from the engineering department.

Testing has been tentatively scheduled for the afternoon of Thursday, May 14, in the meeting room on the fourth floor. If you are interested in joining, please make sure that you have your supervisor's permission and that you will not be interrupted during the three-hour span of the test. — [4] —. To sign up, look for the post titled "QX2B testing" on the company's online bulletin board. A further announcement will be made next Wednesday with the list of chosen participants.

09 What is the notice about?

(A) Taking part in a company event
(B) Addressing customer feedback
(C) Participating in a training seminar
(D) Joining a departmental meeting

10 What is indicated about King Industries?

(A) It is recruiting new personnel.
(B) It manufactures faulty products.
(C) It is hosting a networking event.
(D) It sells consumer devices.

11 What is NOT stated about testing?

(A) It will facilitate the use of products.
(B) It will take up a portion of one afternoon.
(C) It will require approval for applicants.
(D) It will be conducted online.

12 In which of the positions marked [1], [2], [3], and [4] does the following sentence best belong?

"The volunteers might encounter outstanding problems that our product engineers missed regarding this process."

(A) [1]
(B) [2]
(C) [3]
(D) [4]

회람(Memo)

토익 이렇게 나온다!

회람은 회사 내에서 공지 사항 및 새로운 소식을 전달하는 글로서, 양식은 이메일과 비슷하지만 앞뒤에 인사말 없이 내용 중심으로 쓰여 있다. 내용은 회사 내 공고와 유사하게 회사 시설 및 업무 관련 안내 사항이나 기타 사내 소식 등을 주제로 다룬다. 평균 1지문 정도 출제되며, 연계지문으로 종종 출제하기 때문에 지문 유형을 알아놓도록 한다.

토익 질문 유형 및 전략

빈출 질문 유형

주제/목적 찾기 문제	회람의 목적, 주제를 묻는다.
	What is the purpose of the memo? 회람의 목적은 무엇인가?
	What is mainly discussed in the memo? 회람에서 주로 논의되는 것은 무엇인가?
육하원칙 문제	추후 일정 계획, 요청되거나 해야 할 일, 기타 세부 사항을 주로 묻는다.
	What will take place on April 12? 4월 12일에 일어날 일은 무엇인가?
	What must accounting staff do on October 16? 회계 직원들은 10월 16일에 무엇을 해야 하는가?
	When will the departmental meeting be held? 부서 회의는 언제 열릴 것인가?
Not/True 문제	회람에 언급된 회사 및 부서, 사람 등에 대해 일치하거나 일치하지 않는 것을 주로 묻는다.
	What is indicated about Redheart Financial? Redheart 금융 회사에 대해 언급된 것은?
	What is NOT mentioned about participants at the workshop? 워크숍 참가자들에 대해 언급되지 않은 것은?
추론 문제	회람을 받는 대상이나 회람에 언급된 특정 사항에 대해 추론할 수 있는 것을 주로 묻는다.
	To whom was the memo most likely sent? 회람은 누구에게 보내졌을 것 같은가?
	What is suggested about Sunnydale Airport? Sunnydale 공항에 대해 암시되는 것은?

핵심 전략

1. 회람의 양식을 알아두면 본문 내용을 예측할 수 있다.

주로 처음에 수신자(To: ~)와 발신자(From: ~)가 나온다. 그리고 'Subject: ~' 또는 'Re: ~' 다음에 주제가 명시되고 그 아래에 본문이 이어진다. 따라서 본문을 읽기 전 누가 누구에게 무엇에 대한 회람을 보내는 것인지를 확인하여 본문의 내용을 미리 예측한다.

2. 회람 본문의 기본 구성을 알면 글의 흐름을 예상하면서 세부 내용을 정확히 파악할 수 있다.

먼저 회람의 목적이 명시된 후, 추후 일정 계획, 요청 사항이나 해야 할 일 등 세부 사항이 언급된다.

3. 회람의 목적 및 주제, 추후 일정 계획, 요청되거나 해야 할 일에 대한 내용은 관련 표현을 익혀 두면 쉽게 찾을 수 있다.

Sauriol Railway Corporation (SRC)

To: Station managers
From: Antoine Bellefeuille, Operations Head
Date: April 19
Subject: Construction Work

수신자
발신자
작성일자
주제

On April 25, construction will begin on new express ticketing areas at Sauriol Railway's locations throughout Europe. Station managers are informed that these zones will include new ticketing machines which passengers can use at their convenience. Managers are also asked to check up on the construction periodically to ensure that the ongoing work does not pose a safety risk to any member of the riding public.

목적

The Sauriol Railway Corporation is dedicated to providing fast and efficient transportation. As you know, thousands of people rely on our trains for their travels to any of our destinations. As passenger numbers have gone up with each passing year, it has become more important than ever to address the growing volume without inconveniencing our customers. Hence, we are going to add the express ticketing counters for our recently purchased machines in an effort to address this issue.

세부 사항

Each construction job will take no more than a week, though this will depend of course on the size of the station and the number of machines to be installed. Regardless, all work should be completed by mid-July.

Q1. What is the purpose of the memo?

(A) To notify employees of train schedule changes
(B) To inform staff of the installation of machines
(C) To request feedback on work performance
(D) To give instructions on the usage of equipment

Q2. What is NOT mentioned about Sauriol Railway Corporation?

(A) Its customer base has been increasing.
(B) It provides transport services in Europe.
(C) It recently got some new equipment.
(D) It is planning to purchase additional trains.

Q3. What will happen in the middle of July?

(A) Work on ticketing areas will begin.
(B) Managers will conduct safety inspections.
(C) Express ticketing counters will be relocated.
(D) Construction at stations will be finished.

해설 Q1 **주제/목적 찾기 문제** 회람의 목적을 묻는 목적 찾기 문제이다. 'construction will begin on new express ticketing areas', 'these zones will include new ticketing machines'에서 매표 구역에 새로운 기계를 설치하는 공사가 시작될 것이라고 했으므로 (B) To inform staff of the installation of machines가 정답이다.

Q2 **Not/True 문제** 질문의 핵심 어구인 Sauriol Railway Corporation과 관련된 내용을 지문에서 찾아 보기와 대조하는 Not/True 문제이다. (A)는 'passenger numbers have gone up with each passing year'에서 매년 승객 수가 늘고 있다고 했고, (B)는 'Sauriol Railway's locations throughout Europe'에서 유럽 전역에 Sauriol 철도 회사의 역이 있다고 했으며, (C)는 'our recently purchased machines'에서 최근에 기계를 구입했다고 했으므로 모두 지문의 내용과 일치한다. (D)는 지문에 언급되지 않은 내용이므로 (D) It is planning to purchase additional trains가 정답이다.

Q3 **육하원칙 문제** 7월 중순에 일어날 일이 무엇인지(What)를 묻는 육하원칙 문제이다. 질문의 핵심 어구인 the middle of July와 관련하여, 'all work should be completed by mid-July'에서 모든 작업이 7월 중순쯤에 완료될 것이라고 했으므로 (D) Construction at stations will be finished가 정답이다.

정답 Q1 (B)   Q2 (D)   Q3 (D)

지문 해석 p.160

회람에 자주 나오는 ⭐핵심 표현

1. 회람의 목적 및 주제

I'd like to inform ~ : 저는 ~을 알리고 싶습니다

I'd like to inform all staff that company policy requires business attire in the office.
저는 모든 직원들에게 회사 규정이 사무실 내에서 비즈니스 복장을 요구한다는 것을 알리고 싶습니다.

2. 추후 일정 계획

~ is expected to resume on 날짜/시간 : ~이 (날짜/시간)에 재개될 것으로 예상됩니다

Construction of the event hall is expected to resume on July 9.
행사장의 건설이 7월 9일에 재개될 것으로 예상됩니다.

On 날짜/시간, ~ will begin : (날짜/시간)에 ~이 시작될 것입니다

On May 18, office equipment inspections will begin in all departments.
5월 18일에, 모든 부서에서 사무실 비품 점검이 시작될 것입니다.

3. 의무 및 권장 사항

You should ~ : 여러분은 ~해야 합니다

You should remember to turn off all electronic devices before the performance begins.
여러분은 공연이 시작하기 전에 모든 전자 기기의 전원을 끄는 것을 기억하셔야 합니다.

We encourage our employees to ~ : 우리는 직원들이 ~하기를 권장합니다

We encourage our employees to use the new staff lounge on the second floor.
우리는 직원들이 2층의 새로운 직원 휴게실을 이용하기를 권장합니다.

회람에 자주 나오는 ⭐필수 어휘

1. 건설

architect n. 건축가, 설계자	**furniture** n. 가구, 부속품
contract n. 계약, 약정	**hallway** n. 복도, 현관
corridor n. 복도, 통로	**inaccessible** adj. 접근하기 어려운, 접근할 수 없는
cost-efficient 비용 효율이 높은	**installation** n. 설치, 장치
deadline n. 최종 기한, 마감일자	**labor** n. 노동, 업무
disruption n. 붕괴, 중단	**official** adj. 공식적인; n. 공무원
ensure v. 안전하게 하다, 보증하다 = assure, guarantee	**personnel** n. 직원; adj. 직원의
equipment n. 장비, 용품	**rate** n. 비율, 요금, 임금; v. 평가하다 = evaluate, assess, appraise
essential adj. 필수적인, 매우 중요한 = necessary, vital	**rear** n. 뒤쪽; adj. 뒤쪽의
expect v. 예상하다, 기대하다 = anticipate	**reliability** n. 신뢰도, 확실성
floor n. 층, 바닥	**safety** n. 안전, 안전성

2. 회사 방침 및 경영

accounting n. 회계	**inspection** n. 점검, 검사
audit n. 회계 감사, 결산	**maintenance** n. 유지, 보수 관리
competitor n. 경쟁자, 경쟁 상대 = competition, rival	**market share** 시장 점유율
consignment n. 위탁 (판매), 배송	**merger** n. 합병, 합동 = consolidation
deficit n. 부족, 부족액	**observe** v. 지키다, 관찰하다 = adhere to, comply with, conform to, follow, abide by
dividend n. 이익 배당, 배당금	**outsourcing** n. 아웃소싱, 외부조달
downsize v. 줄이다, 축소하다	**ownership** n. 소유, 소유권
earnings n. 소득, 수입	**partnership** n. 공동, 협력, 제휴 = alliance
entrepreneur n. 기업가, 사업가	**profitable** adj. 수익성이 있는, 유익한
executive board 이사회	**shareholder** n. 주주
expenditure n. 지출, 소비	**streamline** v. 간소화하다, 능률적으로 하다
gross income 총소득, 총수입	**yield** v. 산출하다, 초래하다 = produce
headquarters n. 본사, 본부	

3. 공연 및 전시

acclaim v. 환호하다, 갈채하다	**multiple** adj. 다양한, 다수의
association n. 협회, 연합, 제휴	**nominate** v. 지명하다, 임명하다
audience n. 청중, 관중	**occasion** n. 일, 행사
charity n. 자선, 자선단체	**open house** 개방 파티, 공개일
choir n. 합창단, 성가대	**organizer** n. 조직자, 주최자
concertgoer n. 음악회에 자주 가는 사람	**participant** n. 참가자, 관계자
curator n. 큐레이터, 전시 책임자	**performer** n. 공연자, 연주자
enjoyment n. 누림, 즐거움	**portrait** n. 초상화, 인물 사진
exhibit v. 전시하다, 출품하다; n. 전시, 전시회 = show, display	**preview** n. 시사회, 시연
fascinating adj. 매력적인, 황홀한	**session** n. 회의, 시간
fund-raising 모금 활동의; 모금 활동	**trade show** 시사회, 무역 박람회
keynote address 기조 연설 = keynote speech	**voluntary** adj. 자발적인, 지원의

4. 시설 이용

abide v. 머물다, 체류하다	**complimentary** adj. 무료의, 칭찬하는
adjust v. 조절하다, 정비하다	**detail** n. 세부, 항목
agent n. 대리인, 중개자	**entrance** n. 입장, 입구 = entry, admission
allow v. 허가하다, 허락하다 = permit	**inquiry** n. 질문, 문의, 조회
antique adj. 골동의, 옛날의; n. 골동품	**install** v. 설치하다, 설비하다
arena n. 경기장, 공연장 = stadium	**laboratory** n. 실험실, 실습실
athletic adj. (운동) 경기의, 체육의	**locate** v. (어떤 장소에) 정하다, 설치하다
cater v. 음식을 조달하다	**pleasant** adj. 즐거운, 쾌적한
check out 퇴실하다	**scenic** adj. 경치가 좋은, 풍경의
closure n. 폐쇄, 폐점	**suspend** v. 중지하다, 보류하다

유형 연습   지문을 읽고 질문에 답하세요.

01 회람

On Friday, September 20, the entire sales and marketing team will be needed at an event in Sacramento. As a result, the company picnic scheduled for that day has been moved to the following week. Furthermore, the venue has been changed from the Wright Museum to Chimney Park. To arrange transportation to Chimney Park, please contact Ethel Grey at extension 44.

Q. What event will take place at Chimney Park?

(A) A sales convention
(B) A product launch
(C) A company outing

02 회람

We would like to inform all staff that a team of safety inspectors will be visiting the factory on Thursday from 9:30 A.M. to 5:30 P.M. Please make certain that all your work areas are tidy and that safety equipment has been checked. Please answer all questions the inspectors ask. If you have any questions, you should speak to your supervisors.

Q. To whom was the memo most likely sent?

(A) Members of an inspection team
(B) Supervisors at an equipment supplier
(C) Workers at a manufacturing plant

03 회람

Our company will be participating in the upcoming Organic Agriculture Trade Fair in Seattle from May 3-5. We encourage our employees to volunteer at the booth for different shifts. You will be paid an additional incentive of $50 per four-hour shift on top of your regular hourly rates. Those interested should speak to Martine Kotter at the public relations office.

Q. What is indicated about the company?

(A) It is looking for participants for an upcoming event.
(B) It is currently restructuring its pay scales.
(C) It recently revised its work shift policies.

정답·해설·해석 p.160

🕐 제한 시간 12분

Questions 01-04 refer to the following memo.

TO: XT Radio Staff
FROM: Samantha Garrison
SUBJECT: Update
DATE: July 28

Because we've been drawing more listeners lately, we've decided to expand the range of programs that we offer on our station. After conducting a survey, we learned that lots of our listeners would enjoy a sports-themed show of some sort. Therefore, we're going to launch a one-hour sports talk show that will focus on local teams in the Milwaukee area.

The show is going to cover news and stories related to football, basketball, hockey, baseball, and more. We would like it to have at least three different presenters. Next month, we're going to post job advertisements for radio hosts on our Web site. If you know any talented broadcasters with an extensive knowledge of local sports, by all means recommend them to us. They can contact us by sending an e-mail to jobs@xtradio.com. We would prefer to hire people who have some previous experience in radio or another broadcast media. Someone like Mitch Bergman would be our ideal candidate. However, he's still under contract elsewhere.

---

01 What is one purpose of the memo?

(A) To discuss a new initiative
(B) To announce a new sports league
(C) To report on a program's success
(D) To request ideas for a product name

02 What is NOT stated about the sports radio show?

(A) It will feature multiple hosts.
(B) It will focus on local teams.
(C) It will last for 60 minutes.
(D) It will interview athletes.

03 What will the station do in August?

(A) Introduce a new talk host
(B) Invite people to apply for a job
(C) Hold a special contest for listeners
(D) Broadcast a game live

04 What is suggested about Mitch Bergman?

(A) He used to be a professional athlete.
(B) He gave some ideas for a show.
(C) He has experience in broadcasting.
(D) He asked for a high salary.

Questions 05-08 refer to the following memo.

Date:	May 11
To:	All Departments
From:	Meredith Glover, Human Resources Director
Subject:	Notice about parking

With the addition of new employees to the staff at Penumbra, it has become necessary to review the rules regarding the usage of the company parking lot. As you know, fewer spaces are now available for employees, so we will all need to make some adjustments.

Beginning next month, our current policy of permitting parking on a first-come-first-served basis will be scrapped. Instead, numbered spaces will be assigned to specific groups or departments. The five spaces closest to the entrance will stay designated solely for the disabled. — [1] —. The next 10 will be reserved for upper management. Every 20 spaces after that will be assigned, in this order, to finance and accounting, human resources, and sales and marketing. Anyone unable to find a space may park their vehicles at the garage on Anderson Avenue. — [2] —.

Please be reminded that when parking on the company lot, a permit is required. Make sure it is visible through your windshield by placing it on the dashboard of your vehicle or hanging it from the rear-view mirror. — [3] —. If you must leave your car parked in the lot for more than 48 hours, permission must be obtained from the human resources department. Vehicles found in violation of this rule will be towed. — [4] —. Thank you for your cooperation. Please address questions or concerns to your respective department supervisors.

05 What is mainly discussed?

(A) A schedule for upcoming work assignments
(B) Instructions for the use of a facility
(C) New staff hired by the company
(D) Information on a parking lot construction

06 What will happen next month?

(A) Parking permits will be issued.
(B) A construction job will begin.
(C) A revised regulation will take effect.
(D) Travel allowances will be given.

07 How can employees obtain permission for long-term parking?

(A) By speaking to an immediate superior
(B) By replacing their existing permits
(C) By paying for a special license
(D) By contacting a particular department

08 In which of the positions marked [1], [2], [3], and [4] does the following sentence best belong?

"Clients visiting the office for meetings must also be directed to that location."

(A) [1]
(B) [2]
(C) [3]
(D) [4]

Questions 09-12 refer to the following memo.

To: All Personnel
From: George Andrews, Chief Operating Officer
Date: February 1
Subject: Upcoming Plans for Operations

Longwave Instruments will be implementing changes to our current operational system, including timetabling, production, and recruitment procedures. We have contracted the services of Maxwell Consulting to carry out studies in these particular areas. Based on their research and suggestions, changes will be made to our current policies and processes.

The team from Maxwell Consulting will start analyzing our existing procedures to identify areas of concern. It is vital that everyone be as cooperative as possible and answer any questions they might have. After a two-month assessment phase, we will be presented with a list of recommendations. This list will be refined over a one-month period through discussions between management and department heads. At the same time, a chosen group of employees will undergo training for the next phase of this process–implementation of operational changes.

Implementation will be led by our operations manager Wendy Fansler. She and her team will be responsible for adopting the recommendations and ensuring that our policies and procedures are documented in a comprehensive manual of operations. When this 9-month process begins, Maxwell Consulting will no longer be looking into our day-to-day activities. However, they will continue to check in every three months.

At the end of the 12-month period, we will conduct an evaluation to determine whether or not the changes have been beneficial. Staff will provide feedback, and any necessary modifications to the systems will be made at that time.

09 What will the team from Maxwell Consulting do?

(A) Identify potential clients
(B) Evaluate employee concerns
(C) Make suggestions for changes
(D) Conduct seminars for staff

10 When will the implementation phase begin?

(A) After one month
(B) After three months
(C) After nine months
(D) After twelve months

11 What is mentioned about Wendy Fansler?

(A) She is a top executive at Maxwell Consulting.
(B) She will be conducting a survey.
(C) She will be documenting a set of activities.
(D) She must train a group of new employees.

12 What is suggested about Longwave Instruments?

(A) It is planning to relocate its manufacturing plant.
(B) It passed a test administered by Maxwell Consulting.
(C) It is preparing to merge with another corporation.
(D) It may make further system changes after a year.

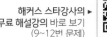

CHAPTER 15 · 안내문(Information)

토익 이렇게 나온다!

안내문은 실생활에서 접할 수 있는 다양한 소재에 대해 정보를 제공하는 글이다. 제품 설명서나 행사 소개문, 시설이나 서비스 관련 각종 설명문 등이 안내문에 속하며, 평균 1지문 정도 출제되며, 연계지문으로 종종 출제되기 때문에 지문 유형을 알아놓도록 한다.

토익 질문 유형 및 전략

빈출 질문 유형

주제/목적 찾기 문제	안내문의 목적, 주제를 묻는다.
	What is the purpose of the information? 안내문의 목적은 무엇인가?
	What is the information about? 안내문은 무엇에 대한 것인가?
육하원칙 문제	얻을 수 있는 정보, 어떤 것을 하기 위한 방법이나 기타 세부 사항을 주로 묻는다.
	What can be found in the catalog? 카탈로그에서 얻을 수 있는 것은 무엇인가?
	How can users access the Web site? 사용자들은 어떻게 웹사이트에 접속할 수 있는가?
	When must interested participants register? 관심 있는 참가자들은 언제 등록을 해야 하는가?
Not/True 문제	안내문에 언급된 사람, 제품 등에 대해 일치하거나 일치하지 않는 것을 주로 묻는다.
	What is indicated about members of the tour group? 관광객들에 대해 언급된 것은?
	What is NOT mentioned about the Kitchen-Helper oven? Kitchen-Helper 오븐에 대해 언급되지 않은 것은?
추론 문제	안내문이 게재된 곳이나 안내문에 언급된 특정 사항에 대해 추론할 수 있는 것을 주로 묻는다.
	Where would the information most likely appear? 안내문은 어디에서 볼 수 있을 것 같은가?
	What will probably be discussed at the meeting on Wednesday? 수요일 회의에서 무엇이 논의될 것 같은가?

핵심 전략

1. 무엇을 안내하는지 구체적인 상황을 파악해야 한다.

지문 처음이나 각 단락 앞에 있는 제목을 통해 먼저 주제를 파악하고, 제목 아래의 세부 내용을 읽어가면서 무엇에 관한 안내이며 어떤 상황인지를 파악한다. 제목이 없는 경우에는 지문 앞부분에서 주제를 파악하고 세부 내용을 읽어 나간다.

2. 안내문을 어디에서 볼 수 있을지 파악해야 한다.

안내문을 볼 수 있는 곳은 지문에 직접 제시되지 않고 추론 문제로 묻는 경우가 자주 있으므로 글의 전체적인 상황을 보고 유추해 내야 한다.

AirConnect Transport Service

When you need to get to or from the airport, don't leave things to chance – rely on AirConnect for rapid, convenient, and affordable airport transfer services. We are a nationally recognized provider serving a number of international airports around the country.

Shuttle Vans
Traveling alone? Save money by sharing a ride with other passengers. Each shuttle van can comfortably seat up to eight passengers and their luggage. Our vans operate around the clock from most major airports with departures every hour. Please note that travel times may vary depending on the number of passengers and their destinations.

Executive Limousine
When time is of the essence, book our executive limo service for quick and efficient round-trip transfers from your home or office. You may also arrange airport pick-ups for distinguished visitors. Choose a vehicle from our fleet of luxury sedans and SUVs, each one driven by courteous and professional staff member.

New! VIP Service
Take advantage of our VIP transport service throughout your visit. Enjoy the convenience of having a car and driver ready and waiting to take you wherever you may wish to go. Private tours may also be arranged.

AirConnect is open 24/7. Call 555-9989 to make a reservation. Book through our Web site www.airconnect.com to get special discounts.

주제

세부 내용

Q1. Where would the information most likely be found?

(A) On an airline's Web site
(B) At a railway station
(C) On a company brochure
(D) In the automotive section of a newspaper

Q2. What is indicated about the shuttle vans?

(A) They operate continuously.
(B) They may be rented out for tours.
(C) They are ideal for people in a hurry.
(D) They can accommodate 10 people.

해설 Q1 **추론 문제** 안내문을 찾을 수 있는 곳을 추론하는 문제이다. 첫 문장인 'When you need to get to or from the airport, ~ rely on AirConnect'에서 공항으로, 또는 공항으로부터 이동해야 할 때, AirConnect사에 의지하라고 한 후, 'Shuttle Vans', 'Executive Limousine', 'New! VIP Service'에서 각 서비스에 대해 알려 주고 있으므로, 공항 수송 업체에서 제공하는 서비스를 설명하는 안내문임을 추론할 수 있다. 따라서 (C) On a company brochure가 정답이다.

Q2 **Not/True 문제** 질문의 핵심 어구인 the shuttle vans와 관련된 내용을 지문에서 찾아 보기와 대조하는 Not/True 문제이다. (A)는 'Our vans operate around the clock'에서 승합차는 24시간 내내 운행한다고 했으므로 around the clock을 continuously로 Paraphrasing한 (A) They operate continuously가 정답이다. (B)는 'Private tours may also be arranged.'에서 개인적인 관광 역시 준비될 수 있다고 했지만 VIP 서비스에 대한 내용이므로 지문의 내용과 일치하지 않는다. (C)는 'When time is of the essence, book our executive limo service'에서 시간이 아주 중요할 때는 고급 리무진 서비스를 예약하라고 했으므로 지문의 내용과 일치하지 않는다. (D)는 'Each shuttle van can comfortably seat up to eight passengers'에서 승합차는 최대 8명의 승객을 수용할 수 있다고 했으므로 지문의 내용과 일치하지 않는다. 참고로, 지문의 time is of the essence가 (C)의 in a hurry로, comfortably seat ~ passengers가 (D)의 accommodate ~ people로 Paraphrasing되었다.

정답 Q1 (C)   Q2 (A)

지문 해석 p.164

안내문에 자주 나오는 ⭐필수 어휘

1. 시설 소개

amenity n. 편의 시설

artwork n. 예술품, 수공예품

authentic adj. 진정한, 확실한   = real, genuine

box office 매표소

clubhouse n. (스포츠클럽 등을 위한) 클럽 회관

complex n. 복합 건물, 단지

comprehensive adj. 포괄적인, 이해가 빠른

district n. 지구, 구역

downtown adv. 도심지에서; adj. 도심지의; n. 도심지

energy-efficient adj. 연료 효율이 좋은

grand opening 개장, 개점

inaugural adj. 개시의, 취임의

landscape n. 풍경, 경치

medieval adj. 중세의, 구식의

municipal adj. 자치 도시의, 시립의

navigate v. 길을 찾다, 돌아다니다

noise n. 소음, 소리

outdoor adj. 야외의, 옥외의

premium adj. 고급의, 값비싼

private adj. 사유의, 개인의

remodel v. 개조하다, 고치다

sculpture n. 조각, 조각물

state-of-the-art adj. 최신식의   = cutting-edge

technique n. 기법, 기술

tranquil adj. 조용한, 평화로운

undergo v. 겪다, 받다

2. 제품 구매

ample adj. 충분한, 풍부한

appliance n. 기구, 장치

artisan n. 장인, 기능공   = craftsman

bid v. 값을 매기다, 입찰하다

booklet n. 소책자, 팸플릿   = brochure, leaflet, flyer

brand-new 새로운, 신품의

browse v. 훑어보다, 검색하다

built-in adj. 붙박이의, 내장된

business day 영업일

come in (상품 등이) 들어오다

commodity n. 상품, 필수품

convenient adj. 편리한, 간편한

cost-effective adj. 비용 효율이 높은

dealer n. 상인, 판매업자   = seller

distribution n. 유통, 분배

enduring adj. 영구적인, 오래가는   = lasting, durable

flavor n. 특징, 특색

fragile adj. 부서지기 쉬운, 연약한

fuel-efficient adj. 연료 효율이 좋은

leather n. 가죽, 가죽 제품

lifelong adj. 평생의, 일생의

measurement n. 측정, 치수

net price 정가

outlet n. 소매점, 직판점

payable adj. 지불해야 할, 지불할 수 있는

portable adj. 휴대용의, 휴대가 쉬운

prolong v. 연장하다, 늘이다   = lengthen

purchase order 구입 주문, 구입 주문서

quantity n. 양, 수량

raffle n. 추첨식 판매; v. 추첨식 판매에 가입하다

retailer n. 소매업자, 소매업

standard n. 표준, 기준; adj. 표준의

supplier n. 공급자, 부품 제조업자

toll-free 무료 장거리 전화의, 무료의

transport v. 수송하다, 운송하다; n. 수송, 운송

trend n. 동향, 추세

up-to-date adj. 최신의, 첨단의

user-friendly adj. 사용하기 쉬운

valid adj. 유효한, 타당한

versatile adj. 다재다능한, 다용도의

waterproof adj. 방수의, 방수가 되는

wholesale adj. 도매의; adv. 도매로; n. 도매

3. 서비스 이용

administer v. 관리하다, 실시하다   = manage, implement

affiliate v. 제휴하다, 가입하다

appropriate v. 전유하다, 충당하다; adj. 적당한   = suitable

archive n. 공문서, 기록 보관소; v. (문서를) 보관하다

automatic adj. 자동의, 기계적인

claim v. 요구하다, 주장하다

compensation n. 보상, 보상금

connection n. 관계, 연결

conservation n. 보존, 보호

consultant n. 상의자, 고문

customize v. 주문에 응하여 만들다

domestic adj. 가정의, 국내의

door-to-door adj. 집집마다의, 집집마다

exist v. 존재하다, 있다

expiration date 유효기간, 계약 만료일

frequent adj. 빈번한, 잦은

household n. 가족, 세대; adj. 가정용의

identify v. 확인하다, 식별하다

insurance n. 보험, 보험금

intermediate adj. 중간의; n. 매개

label n. 상표, 표시

manual adj. 수동의; n. 설명서

newsletter n. 회보, 소식지

questionnaire n. 설문지, 질문서

recall v. 철회하다, 상기하다

revolutionary adj. 획기적인, 혁명의

scale n. 등급, 단계

setup n. 기구, 장치

supplemental adj. 보충의, 추가의

task n. 일, 과업   = duty, assignment

timesaving adj. 시간을 절약해 주는

vary v. 바꾸다, 변경하다, 달라지다

4. 사내 행사

anniversary n. 기념일

assignment n. 임무, 배치

celebration n. 축하, 의식

competitive adj. 경쟁적인, 경쟁할 수 있는

conflict n. 논쟁, 충돌

courteous adj. 예의 바른, 정중한

disregard v. 무시하다, 소홀히 하다   = ignore

disrupt v. 중단시키다, 방해하다

field n. 분야, 범위

forecast v. 예상하다, 예측하다; n. 예상, 예측

heavy adj. 대량의, 힘겨운, 무거운

interdepartmental adj. 각 부서 간의

list n. 목록, 명부; v. 명단에 올리다

normal adj. 정규의, 평균의

operation n. 실시, 사업

oral adj. 구두의

qualification n. 자격, 제한

receptionist n. 접수원, 접수 담당자

turn out 참석하다, 모이다

willingly adv. 자진해서, 기꺼이

HACKERS PRACTICE 토익 고득점을 위한 필수 연습

유형 연습   지문을 읽고 질문에 답하세요.

01 안내문

Ray Block should be applied on the skin prior to being in direct sunlight. Spread the product evenly using your fingertips. Do not put Ray Block on sensitive areas around the eyes or mouth. Avoid using it near any cuts, scratches, or open wounds. Should the product cause any skin irritation, wash it off with soap and water right away. Do not use Ray Block with any other skin product or with your makeup. The product protects the skin from harmful UV rays for up to six hours.

Q. What is the information about?

(A) A body soap
(B) A medication
(C) A skin product

02 안내문

Thank you for purchasing an Electro-Lite product. All our items are sold with a one-year warranty that is valid from the date of purchase. To activate your warranty, the enclosed card must be filled out and sent to us within seven days of purchase along with a copy of your receipt. If you experience any problems with your product, contact our 24-hour hotline at 1-800-555-7436 and one of our agents will gladly assist you.

Q. When must customers submit the warranty card?

(A) Within a day of purchase
(B) Within a week of purchase
(C) Within a month of purchase

03 안내문

Simply complete the registration card and hand it to a flight attendant to register for our Club Cumulus frequent flyer program today! To claim mileage for your current trip, visit one of our service counters and have your boarding pass, a photo ID, and your membership number ready. Statements on accumulated mileage are sent monthly to your specified e-mail address.

Q. What is NOT needed to claim mileage for the current flight?

(A) A boarding pass
(B) A registration form
(C) A piece of identification

정답·해설·해석 p.164

🕐 제한 시간 12분

Questions 01-04 refer to the following information.

Nomadica H2OXP®

Thanks for choosing the Nomadica H2OXP®. This product is a specially designed portable hydration device made of durable high-grade plastic that is both tasteless and odorless. Carry the bottle in your bag or around your waist for quick and easy access. It features a leak-proof cap with an easy-grip handle and a flexible drinking tube, both of which you can easily take apart for cleaning and replacement. Furthermore, the product comes with a patented water filtration system to ensure the purity of your drinking water.

This item must be cleaned after each use. Wash by hand using clean water and mild detergent only. Allow to air-dry before storing. Do not place the product in the dishwasher.

Limited time offer!

Get a free ThermaCool insulated carrying case when you register to receive details about our products, promotions, and future releases. The carrying case keeps liquids cool all day long and includes a belt-loop attachment and bag fasteners. E-mail custreg@nomadica.com or call our toll-free hotline at 1-888-555-0770.

For over 30 years, Nomadica has been known for making high-quality travel accessories that are built to last a lifetime. Our products are used and recommended by experienced travelers and outdoor enthusiasts everywhere. For replacement parts and a list of repair centers, please go to www.nomadica.com.

01 What is the purpose of the information?

(A) To encourage people to shop on a Web site
(B) To remind customers to renew their warranties
(C) To instruct recent buyers on the use of a product
(D) To inform employees at a store about a new service

02 What is indicated about the H2OXP®?

(A) It is available in different colors.
(B) It should not be filled with hot liquid.
(C) It is safe to use in a dishwasher.
(D) It may be disassembled for cleaning.

03 Why should readers call Nomadica?

(A) To register to receive information
(B) To request a product manual
(C) To complete a brief survey
(D) To take advantage of a discount offer

04 What information is available on the Web site?

(A) A directory of Nomadica's branches
(B) Details about repairs and replacements
(C) Travel suggestions for outdoor enthusiasts
(D) A coupon for obtaining a free bag

READING Part 7

Ch 15 안내문

Hackers TOEIC Reading

Questions 05-08 refer to the following information.

Welcome to the main branch of the Blount Memorial Library, which, along with three other branches in Victoria, Kimball, and New Hope, serves all of Marion County.

This three-story structure was completed in 1985 with a grant from the Alfred Blount Foundation. Mr. Blount, a Marion County native, is also a former governor of the state of Tennessee. Daily operations of the facility are funded by the City of Jasper and County of Marion. Additional support comes from the State of Tennessee.

The first floor of the building houses administrative offices, meeting rooms, a copy center, and a community daycare center. The second floor contains our main collection of reading materials, including children's books, bestselling titles in a variety of genres, and current magazine and newspaper subscriptions. The top floor includes our newspaper archives and a research library with a special focus on history, genealogy, and earth sciences. Scattered throughout the library are study desks, computer workstations, and reading lounges. The premises are completely wheelchair accessible.

The main library is open Monday to Friday from 8 a.m. to 8 p.m., Saturdays from 9 a.m. to 6 p.m., and Sundays from 1 p.m. to 5 p.m. We are closed on all major public holidays. The hours may differ at our other branches, so please inquire at the reception desk. To reserve one of the meeting rooms, visitors are asked to contact the library's administration office at 555-2120, extension 14.

05 Where would the information most likely appear?

(A) In a local newspaper
(B) In a librarian's manual
(C) In a brochure of a library
(D) In a literary magazine

06 What is NOT mentioned about Alfred Blount?

(A) He was born in Marion County.
(B) He owned a large collection of books.
(C) He was once a public official.
(D) His foundation provided financial support.

07 What can visitors most likely do on the building's third floor?

(A) Browse through magazines
(B) Find popular novels
(C) Study old publications
(D) Participate in meetings

08 How can a meeting facility be booked?

(A) By visiting an administration office
(B) By filling out a form
(C) By going to a branch
(D) By dialing a number

Questions 09-12 refer to the following information.

On behalf of Baron Studios' director Michelle Devries and producer Dario Mantovani, we would like to thank all the cast and crew for their hard work during this film production. Next week is our final week of shooting, after which we plan to have a party, screen the final film version, and hold a movie premiere. Please find details on all of the upcoming events below.

Wrap-Up Party:
On the final day of filming on August 5, Baron Studios will be hosting a wrap-up party at the Orange Grove Hotel at 6654 Melrose Avenue at 7 P.M. A buffet dinner will be served along with drinks. There will be a live band later for dancing. All cast and crew will be sent invitations this week. The invitation allows you to bring one guest. However, please confirm whether you are coming or not by July 30 with Preethi Samraj at extension #443 so that she can make reservations as soon as possible.

Film Screening:
The final day of film editing is scheduled for September 2. We will be hosting a screening of the film for the entire cast and crew on September 5 at the studio. Snacks and refreshments will be served during the show, and you are free to bring up to four family members or friends. However, please notify Colin Huntington in public relations if you plan on coming and how many passes you will need. Those without passes will not be permitted on studio grounds.

Premiere:
Trade Winds will have its public premiere the following night at the Oakland Movie Theater on 334 Hollywood Boulevard at 8 P.M. The event will be by invitation only, as seats are limited and we will be exclusively inviting studio executives and members of the press. The premiere is a black-tie event, so those invited should dress appropriately. Please bring your invitation with you, as you will not be allowed to enter without it.

09 According to the information, what will take place in August?

(A) Cast and crew will assemble to begin a new project.
(B) A movie will premiere at a theater.
(C) Filming of a production will be completed.
(D) Reservations for an event at a hotel will be made.

10 Who should be contacted to request passes to a movie screening?

(A) Colin Huntington
(B) Dario Mantovani
(C) Preethi Samraj
(D) Michelle Devries

11 What is NOT mentioned about *Trade Winds*?

(A) It will be screened for Baron Studios' executives.
(B) It has not yet been released to the public.
(C) It was directed by Michelle Devries.
(D) It received positive reviews from members of the press.

12 What is suggested about the premiere?

(A) It will include a question period with the press.
(B) It is not for all members of the cast and crew.
(C) It will be held on the studio grounds.
(D) It does not have a dress code requirement.

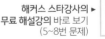

무료 토익·토스·오픽·지텔프 자료 제공
Hackers.co.kr

SECTION 3

지문 유형별 공략 – Multiple Passages

이메일(편지) 연계 지문

토익 이렇게 나온다!

이메일(편지) 연계 지문은 첫 번째 지문으로 이메일(편지)이 나오고, 두 번째나 세 번째 지문으로 또 다른 이메일(편지), 양식, 공고, 광고, 안내문 등이 연계된 지문이다. 주로 이메일이나 양식과 가장 많이 연계된다.

토익 지문 유형 및 연계 문제 핵심 전략

빈출 지문 유형

[Double Passages]

이메일(편지) & 이메일	행사나 일정에 대해 안내하는 이메일(편지) & 행사 등록이나 일정 변경을 요청하는 이메일
이메일(편지) & 양식	특정 사안에 대해 설명하거나 요청하는 이메일(편지) & 그와 관련된 표나 기타 양식

[Triple Passages]

이메일(편지) & 이메일 & 양식	각종 신청을 하거나 업무를 요청하는 이메일(편지) & 신청 결과나 요청한 업무와 관련된 사항을 알려주는 이메일 & 그와 관련된 일정이나 양식
이메일(편지) & 양식 & 공고	행사와 관련된 제안을 하는 이메일(편지) & 행사 일정을 알리는 양식 & 행사 개최나 변경 사항을 안내하는 공고

연계 문제 핵심 전략

STEP 1 질문의 핵심 어구를 통해 먼저 확인할 지문을 결정한다.

STEP 2 해당 지문에서 첫 번째 단서를 찾고, 추가로 필요한 두 번째 단서를 다른 지문에서 찾는다.

   * Triple passages의 경우, 첫 번째 단서를 찾은 후 남은 두 지문 중 추가로 필요한 내용과 관련된 지문을 선택하여 두 번째 단서를 찾는다.

STEP 3 두 개의 단서를 종합하여 정답을 선택한다.

예제   이메일 & 이메일

To: Emmanuel Turner <emmanuel.turner@rocketmail.com>
From: Pauline Buenaventura <pauline.buenaventura@atlantahikers.com>

Thank you for joining the Atlanta Hikers Club. As requested, here is a list of events scheduled for March:
   • March 4, hike at Stone Mountain   • March 21, charity gala ●──
   • March 12, fun run at Pele Park   • March 28, awards ceremony

STEP 2-2
추가로 필요한 두 번째 단서를 다른 지문에서 찾는다

To: Pauline Buenaventura <pauline.buenaventura@atlantahikers.com>
From: Emmanuel Turner <emmanuel.turner@rocketmail.com>

Allow me to thank you for the wonderful event you held on March 4. I registered to ●── participate in the fun run, but unfortunately I will not be able to make it. However, I'll see you at the fundraising activity on the 21st!

STEP 2-1
해당 지문에서 첫 번째 단서를 찾는다

Q. Which event did Mr. Turner recently attend? ●──
   (A) A mountain hike
   (B) A fun run
   (C) A fundraising gala
   (D) An awards ceremony

STEP 1
질문의 핵심 어구를 통해 먼저 확인할 지문을 결정한다

STEP 3
두 개의 단서를 종합하여 정답을 선택한다

정답 (A)

지문 해석 p.167

유형 연습   지문을 읽고 질문에 답하세요.

01~02 편지 & 편지

Dear Ms. Kimmel,

The college is holding a fundraising campaign as we are planning to purchase some property adjacent to the campus in order to construct a new science building. Therefore, we are appealing to alumni members to make a contribution. A donation in any amount would be highly appreciated. In gratitude for your generous support, your name will be engraved on a sponsors' plaque which will be placed on a wall in the lobby.

Alan Blanche, Alumni Association, Buckeye College

Dear Mr. Blanche,

I would be happy to lend my support. Being a chemistry graduate from the college, I'm delighted to hear that a new science building is being planned. I'm sure it will benefit generations of students to come. Enclosed you will find a check in the amount of $1,000. I hope that this helps in some small way.

Diane Kimmel

01 What is mentioned about the campaign?

(A) It will raise money to build a student center.
(B) It will fund a scholarship program.
(C) It is targeting former students of the college.

02 What will Ms. Kimmel be eligible for?

(A) An honorary degree
(B) Her name on a plaque
(C) A tax benefit

03~04 이메일 & 공고

TO   <service@mayberrylibrary.com>
FROM   Dan Hastings <hasty@zoomail.com>

Dear Madam or Sir,

I'm a regular user of the Mayberry Library and have a suggestion. You don't have many publications for younger people in your periodicals section. People my age would like to see more magazines about movies, entertainment, or pop culture. I hope you will consider adding more of these publications in the future.

Dan Hastings

MAYBERRY PUBLIC LIBRARY
Your suggestions help us improve our facility and better serve the public. We are pleased to now offer the following titles of magazines for your reading pleasure in our periodicals section:
• *Sensational Seniors*: A monthly magazine for the active senior citizen
• *Silver Screen Journal*: A weekly publication for young movie lovers
• *Pets and Play*: A quarterly magazine for pet-owners
If you have recommendations for titles you would like to see in the library, send us a message at service@ mayberrylibrary.com.

03 Which publication would Mr. Hastings most likely enjoy reading?

(A) *Sensational Seniors*
(B) *Silver Screen Journal*
(C) *Pets and Play*

04 How often is *Pets and Play* published?

(A) Four times a year
(B) Every three weeks
(C) Twice a month

정답·해설·해석 p.168

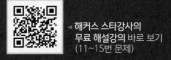
🕐 제한 시간 20분

Questions 01-05 refer to the following e-mails.

To	John Walton <jwalton@mountainpromotions.com>
From	Mary Allen <mallen@mountainpromotions.com>
Subject	Equipment Installation 📄 workschedule.word
Date	May 5

Dear Mr. Walton,

Our technicians were scheduled to do a computer equipment installation in your department on Wednesday, May 7. Unfortunately, I will have to delay the work, as we've been asked to do a computer system upgrade in the accounting department on that date. The work is urgent, so we have no other option. Would it be possible for our technicians to do the installation on Thursday morning instead? If this is inconvenient for you, please refer to the attached work schedule which shows when we are available. As you can see, there wouldn't be any other time to do the work until Monday, May 12. The installation shouldn't take more than a few hours.

Also, some of your staff members will be getting new desktop computers. Please instruct them to save all needed files from their computers. They may upload the files to the company Web board, or save them onto a USB flash drive.

Thanks for your patience and cooperation.

Mary Allen
Technical Support Director
Mountain Promotions

To: Mary Allen <mallen@mountainpromotions.com>
From: John Walton <jwalton@mountainpromotions.com>
Subject: Re: Equipment Installation
Date: May 5

Hi Mary,

Thanks for the message. Actually, we have an important deadline on Thursday, so that's probably not the best time for us. Part of the work your technicians will be doing is the installation of Web cameras, which we need for an online conference with the marketing departments of our other branches on Friday. So, the installation is rather urgent for my department also, as we will need the equipment to be operational in time for the conference. I spoke to the supervisor, Tina Ryder, and she said her department could probably wait until Thursday morning to have their system upgraded. So, if you could schedule the installation work for Wednesday once again, I would be very grateful.

Sorry for the confusion, but I think it will all work out. You can confirm the schedule with Tina. I will inform my staff about your instructions as well. Thanks for your assistance, and I will see you on Wednesday.

John Walton
Associate Director of Marketing
Mountain Promotions

01 Why did Ms. Allen write to Mr. Walton?

(A) To arrange a conference call
(B) To change a work schedule
(C) To order some computers
(D) To ask for a system upgrade

02 What did Ms. Allen forward to Mr. Walton?

(A) Notes on an upcoming presentation
(B) The schedule for a future conference
(C) Instructions for setting up a program
(D) A copy of a work timetable

03 What is mentioned about the conference?

(A) It requires that some devices be installed.
(B) It has been moved to a later date.
(C) It will be taking place outside the office.
(D) It was organized by Mary Allen.

04 Who most likely is Tina Ryder?

(A) A computer technician
(B) A marketing staff member
(C) A manager of the accounting department
(D) A personal assistant for Mr. Walton

05 What does Mr. Walton say he will do?

(A) Delay a conference call to another date
(B) Remind his staff to save some files
(C) Speak with Ms. Ryder about the schedule
(D) Contact the director of another branch

Questions 06-10 refer to the following letter and e-mail.

October 15

Lourdes Finch
Purchasing Director
Serendipity Resorts

Dear Ms. Finch,

I recently came across an advertisement in *Hospitality Asia* which indicated that your company is looking for food suppliers for two resorts that will be opening in Thailand in December. Singha Foods Incorporated is a company located in Singapore that sells a vast variety of fresh produce, meat, and dairy products throughout the Southeast Asian region. We would be very interested in entering a partnership with you.

Singha Foods has an excellent reputation, and we already have numerous clients similar to your company that we work with. We can provide your resorts with the freshest local items, as well as a large selection of imported foods and beverages. I have enclosed our catalog, which includes all the products we currently offer. And if you need items not included in the list, we would be more than happy to find them for you.

I will be visiting Bangkok in three days and would be pleased to meet with you to discuss a possible partnership. Please let me know if you are free at any time between October 18-21. You may contact me at alchan@singhafoods.com.

I hope to hear from you soon.

Sincerely,

Alexis Chan

Alexis Chan
Sales Associate
Singha Foods Incorporated

To	Alexis Chan <alchan@singhafoods.com>
From	Lourdes Finch <lourdesf@serendipityresorts.com>
Subject	Your Inquiry
Date	October 17

Dear Ms. Chan,

Thank you for responding to our advertisement for a supplier. My staff and I had a look through your catalog and were very impressed of the variety and quality of food products you supply. We have already found suppliers for local items including fresh fruits, vegetables, fish and meats, and dairy products. However, we would be interested in meeting with you to discuss your company supplying us with imported foods and beverages.

I am completely booked on the first day of your visit, but would be happy to meet with you on the second day. I will schedule you for a tentative appointment for 12:30 at our corporate headquarters at 446-D Gautama Road. Please let me know if this is convenient for you.

I am looking forward to speaking with you and hope this is the beginning of a long and beneficial business partnership.

Sincerely,

Lourdes Finch
Purchasing Director
Serendipity Resorts

06 Why was the letter written?

(A) To apply for a job with a hotel chain
(B) To respond to an advertisement in a publication
(C) To inquire about the status of a supply delivery
(D) To request information about available products

07 What is indicated about Singha Foods Incorporated?

(A) It works with several accommodation facilities.
(B) It caters special events at hospitality establishments.
(C) Its headquarters are located in Bangkok.
(D) It is expanding its operations to regions outside of Asia.

08 In the letter, the word "entering" in paragraph 1, line 5 is closest in meaning to

(A) ending
(B) going
(C) returning
(D) starting

09 On what date will Ms. Finch and Ms. Chan most likely meet?

(A) October 16
(B) October 18
(C) October 19
(D) October 21

10 What is indicated about Serendipity Resorts in the e-mail?

(A) It is looking for a supplier of dairy products.
(B) It is hiring additional staff for its head office.
(C) It is looking for ways to cut operation costs.
(D) It is planning to purchase imported items.

Questions 11-15 refer to the following e-mails and schedule.

To	Julia Richmond <julr@templetontour.co.nz>
From	June Perry <jupe@templetontour.co.nz>
Subject	New guide
Date	November 1

Hi Julia,

I just got a message from Vincent Peale, and he gave his two months notice today. Apparently, he got a job offer from a tour agency in Auckland. He has been very pleased with the time he has spent working for us, but as Auckland is where his family lives, he accepted the offer.

We will all be sad to see Vincent go, but we need to find a replacement for peak tourist season in January and February. What do you think about Robert Phong for the job? If I remember correctly, he speaks several languages, which was very helpful for some of our foreign clients. Also, please let me know if you have other suggestions for candidates to fill the role.

Thanks!

June Perry

To	June Perry <jupe@templetontour.co.nz>
From	Julia Richmond <julr@templetontour.co.nz>
Subject	Re: New guide
Date	November 2

Hi June,

It's a shame that Vincent will be leaving us. He is one of the best tour guides our agency has ever had, and I have enjoyed working with him very much.

Regarding a replacement, Robert would be great in the position. He exhibited a lot of great communication and interpersonal skills while he was an intern here at the agency. However, during his internship he told me that he was thinking about attending graduate school, so he may be unavailable. If that is the case, I would recommend Veronica Santini. She performed equally well as an intern, is knowledgeable about sites, and has a friendly personality. And I think she's capable of doing more than her current position requires.

Julia

Templeton Tour Agency: *Tour Guide Work Schedule, January 2-8*

	Monday	Tuesday	Wednesday	Thursday	Friday	Saturday	Sunday
1/2 day city tour	Veronica Santini, 2 p.m.	Veronica Santini, 9 a.m.	Harry Dennis, 9 a.m.	Veronica Santini, 2 p.m.	Veronica Santini, 9 a.m.	Harry Dennis, 9 a.m.	Veronica Santini, 2 p.m.
Full day city tour	Harry Dennis, 10 a.m.	Kenneth Albright, 10 a.m.	Kenneth Albright, 10 a.m.	Harry Dennis, 10 a.m.	Kenneth Albright, 10 a.m.	Veronica Santini, Kenneth Albright, 10 a.m.	Harry Dennis, 10 a.m.

If you have any questions regarding your schedule, speak with director of tours Julia Richmond. Also, notify our booking associate Brenda Lane regarding any dates that you will be unavailable. Staff must arrive at points of departure 30 minutes before tours begin.

11 What does Ms. Perry say she received?

(A) A message from a foreign client
(B) An inquiry regarding an apprentice program
(C) A résumé from a job applicant
(D) An employee's notice of resignation

12 What is indicated about Robert Phong?

(A) He works for Templeton Tour Agency as a booking agent.
(B) He handled foreign clients during his internship at Templeton Tour Agency.
(C) He underwent training to become an officially certified tour guide.
(D) He has accepted a job position with another tour company located in Auckland.

13 Why was the second e-mail written?

(A) To provide opinions on a staffing decision
(B) To ask for suggestions about internship applicants
(C) To answer questions about education qualifications
(D) To respond to an offer for a promotion

14 What can be inferred about Veronica Santini?

(A) She was promoted to a tour guide position.
(B) She recently applied for a job at the agency.
(C) She is unavailable as she is attending graduate school.
(D) She was hired as Julia Richmond's personal assistant.

15 What is NOT true about Templeton Tour Agency?

(A) It operates tour programs every day of the week.
(B) It has assigned only full-day tours to Harry Dennis.
(C) It offers daily excursions for tourists at 10 A.M.
(D) It will run the most city visits on Saturday.

Questions 16-20 refer to the following e-mails and receipt.

To: Customer Service <help@glitterngloss.com>
From: Macy Plummer <m.plummer@flexmail.com>
Subject: My purchase
Date: January 4

To Whom It May Concern,

I have a couple of questions about making a return. I bought a sweater at your Trenton branch during your year-end sale last Saturday, and I'd like to return it to the local Glitter N' Gloss store here in Cherry Hill.

I was also wondering whether I could get a refund or if I would have to exchange the item for something else. I paid for it with a credit card and have the original receipt. Please let me know what my options are. Thank you.

Sincerely,

Macy Plummer

To: Macy Plummer <m.plummer@flexmail.com>
From: Customer Service <help@glitterngloss.com>
Subject: Re: My purchase
Date: January 5

Dear Ms. Plummer,

Thank you for your e-mail. To answer your question, we do allow customers to return items to any store regardless of where they were originally purchased, even online. You only need to present the original receipt within 30 days of a purchase. For your convenience, I've posted some other important guidelines below.

• Swimwear, cosmetics, and gift cards may not be returned;
• All refunds will be in the original form of payment;
• For online purchases, refunds will not include the cost of shipping, except when items are found to be faulty.

I hope I've answered all your questions. We may e-mail you some questions about your customer service experience. If you receive this questionnaire, please fill it out and return it to us. Thank you.

Sincerely,

Keith Nance
Glitter N' Gloss Customer Service Associate

Glitter N' Gloss

Thank you for your purchase!

Trenton, NJ

Date: December 30   Time: 4:16 P.M.

Member no.: (not applicable)

- -

Item	Quantity	Price
Beach Sandals	1	$6.40
Sweater	1	$14.99
Hair bands	3	$2.49
Lipstick	1	$4.90
Towel set	1	$12.00

Charge: xxxxxxxxxxxx5437

Subtotal	$40.78
Taxes	$2.38
Total	$43.16

We offer special discounts and exclusive benefits to all Glitter N' Gloss members! If you are interested, visit www.glitterngloss.com.

16 What does Ms. Plummer need assistance with?

(A) Locating a particular store
(B) Understanding a return policy
(C) Learning the date of a store sale
(D) Finding an item in a different size

17 What is suggested about Ms. Plummer?

(A) She usually shops on weekends.
(B) She is a frequent customer at Glitter N' Gloss.
(C) She recently moved from a different city.
(D) She is entitled to a refund on her credit card.

18 What is NOT true about Glitter N' Gloss?

(A) It has more than one store.
(B) It refunds shipping costs on occasion.
(C) It recently launched an online store.
(D) It operates a membership program.

19 According to Mr. Nance, what can Ms. Plummer expect to receive?

(A) A gift card
(B) A product catalog
(C) A survey request
(D) A free gift

20 Which item on the receipt cannot be returned to Glitter N' Gloss?

(A) The sweater
(B) The hair bands
(C) The lipstick
(D) The towel set

해커스 스타강사의 ▶
무료 해설강의 바로 보기
(11~15번 문제)

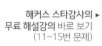

READING Part 7

Ch 16 이메일(편지) 연계 지문   Hackers TOEIC Reading

양식 연계 지문

토익 이렇게 나온다!

양식 연계 지문은 첫 번째 지문으로 양식이 나오고, 두 번째나 세 번째 지문으로 이메일(편지), 공고, 또 다른 양식, 기사 등이 연계된 지문이다. 주로 이메일이나 또 다른 양식과 가장 많이 연계된다.

토익 지문 유형 및 연계 문제 핵심 전략

빈출 지문 유형

[Double Passages]

양식 & 이메일(편지)	주문한 물품에 대한 청구서나 송장 & 주문 및 배송에 문제가 있음을 알리는 이메일(편지)
양식 & 양식	상품이나 시설의 안내 양식 & 상품이나 시설 이용 후기

[Triple Passages]

양식 & 공고 & 이메일(편지)	특정 사안에 대해 설명하는 매뉴얼 & 매뉴얼의 추가 사항이나 변경 사항을 알리는 공고 & 매뉴얼에 관해 문의하는 이메일(편지)
양식 & 이메일(편지) & 기사	상품이나 시설 관련 신청 양식 & 신청에 대한 변동 사항을 알리는 이메일(편지) & 시설 이용 후기 또는 상품 관련 내용을 소개하는 기사

연계 문제 핵심 전략

STEP 1 질문의 핵심 어구를 통해 먼저 확인해야 할 지문을 결정한다.

STEP 2 해당 지문에서 첫 번째 단서를 찾고, 추가로 필요한 두 번째 단서를 다른 지문에서 찾는다.

    * Triple passages의 경우, 첫 번째 단서를 찾은 후 남은 두 지문 중 추가로 필요한 내용과 관련된 지문을 선택하여 두 번째 단서를 찾는다.

STEP 3 두 개의 단서를 종합하여 정답을 선택한다.

예제   메뉴 & 리뷰 & 이메일

> CHEVEUX SOYEUX'S NEWEST HAIR TREATMENTS!
> * Shine enhancing ($15)   * Deep conditioning ($20)
> * Scalp treatment ($60)   * Corrective conditioning ($40)

STEP 2-2 추가로 필요한 두 번째 단서를 다른 지문에서 찾는다

> Review   by Cheryl Aiden(chai@everymail.com)
> On a recent visit to Cheveux, I spent only $20 on my hair treatment and found the results to be quite remarkable. I've also found the salon's other hair treatments to be beneficial and of good value. I highly recommend them.

STEP 2-1 해당 지문에서 첫 번째 단서를 찾는다

> TO: Cheryl Aiden <chai@everymail.com>
> FROM: <clientservices@cheveuxsoyeux.com>
> Thank you for writing a review about Cheveux Soyeux on our Web site. In doing so, you were automatically entered to into a draw to receive a $150 gift card, and you won. Please let us know your address so that we can mail it to you.

STEP 1 질문의 핵심 어구를 통해 먼저 확인해야 할 지문을 결정한다

Q. What type of service did the writer pay for?
    (A) Shine enhancing
    (B) Deep conditioning
    (C) Scalp treatment
    (D) Corrective conditioning

STEP 3 두 개의 단서를 종합하여 정답을 선택한다

정답 (B)

지문 해석 p.174

유형 연습   지문을 읽고 질문에 답하세요.

01~02 전단지 & 이메일

Code Sources Internet Services, 1776 Olsen Ave. (ph.) 555-9978
Fast, Efficient, and Dependable!
Tired of having a poor Internet connection that always seems to be down? Then look no further than Code Sources Internet Services! We offer high-speed connection for both work and home. Downloading is fast and easy, and our security system helps protect your computer. Visit www.codesourcesinternet.com for full details on our regular, business, and premium packages. Present this flyer when you sign up for our premium service during the month of June, and receive 50 percent off your first bill!

TO	<customerservice@codesourcesinternet.com>
FROM	Ellen Delain <edelain@shopsmart.com>

Dear Madam or Sir,

I signed up for Internet service for my store last month and have been very happy with the speed and dependability of the connection. However, I received my first bill yesterday and was charged the full amount. Your flyer indicated that I would only pay half the fee for the first month. So, I should not be paying the regular rate until August, as my package qualifies me for a discount. Please let me know if an error has been made.

Ellen Delain

01 What can be found on the Web site?

(A) A subscription application
(B) A list of outlets
(C) A description of packages

02 What is suggested about Ms. Delain?

(A) She wants to cancel her subscription.
(B) She subscribed for the premium service.
(C) She has not received a billing statement.

03~04 일정표 & 기사

Fountainview Film Festival
September 12-15 at the Powerhouse Theater
SCREENINGS:
A Time of Passion, Sept. 12, 8 P.M.*
The Summer Queen, Sept. 13, 7 P.M.*
Danger Dolls, Sept. 14, 8 P.M.
Over the Hill, Sept. 15, 9 P.M.*
*Screening will be followed by a question and answer period with the director.

Up-and-coming film director Melanie Hayes has been slated to direct San Pedro Studio's newest production, *Bridge to Heaven*. The director spoke about her new project during a discussion period at the Fountainview Film Festival. "I'm really excited about this movie. We are scheduled to begin working on it within two weeks," she said. Hayes was at the festival showing her film, *The Summer Queen*, which has been both a critical and financial success.

03 What is indicated about Ms. Hayes?

(A) She has shown her films at the festival before.
(B) She is scheduled to direct a new film.
(C) She was the recipient of a film award.

04 At what time was Ms. Hayes' film screened during the festival?

(A) At 7 o'clock
(B) At 8 o'clock
(C) At 9 o'clock

정답·해설·해석 p.174

🕐 제한 시간 20분

Questions 01-05 refer to the following invoice and e-mail.

Big Wheels
928 Grandview Avenue
Pittsburgh, PA 15122

Transaction Number: 78954
Date: June 5
Name: Vince Morgan

ITEM	ITEM CODE	AMOUNT	COST
Biking shirts	ST3110	3	$49.98
Water bottle	QK1932	2	$11.98
Sunglasses	OJ3821	1	$69.99
Helmet	SJ0503	1	$89.99
Biking shorts	HW1027	1	$20.10
Bike lock	YB1991	1	$15.25
			TOTAL: $257.29

Thank you for buying from Big Wheels, your one-stop bicycle accessories and apparel store. Please check all the merchandise against the invoice in the package. Also, if anything was damaged during shipment, call one of our representatives right away at 555-7273 or send us a message at service@bigwheels.net. Make sure you have your transaction number when calling or include it in your e-mail.

Big Wheels guarantees all of its merchandise. If for any reason you are not pleased with your purchase, you may return it within 30 days. A store credit or exchange will be provided. Be certain to send back all purchases in their original packaging.

To:	Customer Service, Big Wheels <cservice@bigwheels.com>
From:	Vince Morgan <v.morgan@znet.com>
Subject:	Recent Delivery ▤orderform.word
Date:	June 5

Thank you for your speedy service. I received my order (#78954) this morning, but I have a few issues with my purchase. First, I noticed that I was charged for the sunglasses. Actually, this item was a replacement for a previous purchase which was damaged during shipment, so I don't believe I should be billed for it. In addition, I requested a yellow helmet, but it didn't arrive. Also, the biking shorts came in the wrong size. I ordered a small, but I got a large. I would be grateful if you could send me the correct items as soon as possible. I am attaching a copy of my order form for your convenience. I've never had problems like this with your company before, and would appreciate it if you could fix these errors right away. I hope to hear from you soon.

Sincerely,
Vince Morgan

01 What is NOT mentioned in the invoice?

(A) Any item can be returned within a month of purchase.
(B) Customers unsatisfied with a purchase can get a cash refund.
(C) Representatives can be contacted to report product damage.
(D) Returned purchases must be sent in their original packages.

02 What is indicated about Mr. Morgan?

(A) He was billed for under $200 of purchases.
(B) He requested a store credit for a damaged item.
(C) He forgot to provide his order number.
(D) He recently ordered some athletic clothing.

03 How much was Mr. Morgan incorrectly charged?

(A) $49.98
(B) $11.98
(C) $69.99
(D) $89.99

04 What is offered as an option for item HW1027?

(A) Color
(B) Size
(C) Material
(D) Brand

05 What is suggested about Big Wheels?

(A) It has done business with Mr. Morgan before.
(B) It only sells items on its Web site.
(C) It charges a fee for deliveries.
(D) It has recently launched a new product line.

Questions 06-10 refer to the following invitation and article.

You are formally invited to the 15th Annual Special Events Expo

This is the city's largest occasion for
showcasing the products and services of caterers, suppliers,
event planners, and other party-related industry experts.

The Special Events Expo is by invitation only for guests who have a special interest in the industry.
The event will be held at the Daisyland Convention Center
beginning Thursday, August 11 through Sunday, August 14, from 11 A.M. to 6 P.M. daily.

The attached brochure gives details on all planned events,
including demonstrations on cake decoration techniques in Hall A, cookie baking tools in Hall B,
party planning on a budget in Hall C, and unique event theme creation in Hall D.

To attend the event, simply present this invitation at the entrance.

We look forward to seeing everyone at the expo.

Local Baker Shines at Expo
August 20

Beth Spellman, of Berlin Bakery in downtown Stafford, was recognized for her outstanding food displays at the Special Events Expo last Friday at the Daisyland Convention Center. Industry experts from around the country commended Ms. Spellman's fun and unique cake presentations and romantic, flower-themed wedding cake designs.

Ms. Spellman's shop, Berlin Bakery, has long been a co-sponsor of the expo and was proud to have such a wonderful turnout this year. A Stafford local and daughter of professional baker Elinor Spellman, Beth Spellman went overseas to Germany and France to study baking and food decorating in her twenties. Once she returned from Europe, she put her education to use and continued her mother's baking legacy. Since then, she has become a caterer for a wide variety of parties and celebrations in the city.

Ms. Spellman said that she plans to give her special demonstration again at an international cake decorating seminar next month for culinary students in New York City. Until then, be sure to pick up some of Ms. Spellman's delicious creations at Berlin Bakery in downtown Stafford Square (www.berlinbakes.com).

06 What will happen on August 14?

(A) The special event will begin.
(B) The expo will come to an end.
(C) The guest list will be finalized.
(D) The center will close temporarily.

07 What is NOT included on the invitation?

(A) The dates for the expo
(B) The names of presenters
(C) The location of the event
(D) The types of attendees

08 What happened at the Special Events Expo?

(A) Berlin Bakery was honored as a long-term sponsor.
(B) International students hosted a seminar.
(C) The mayor of Stafford gave a welcome speech.
(D) Ms. Spellman received some special recognition.

09 Where did Ms. Spellman's demonstration most likely take place?

(A) Hall A
(B) Hall B
(C) Hall C
(D) Hall D

10 What is mentioned about Ms. Spellman?

(A) She is originally from Germany.
(B) Her cakes are for birthday parties.
(C) Her mother was a baker as well.
(D) She learned food decoration in Stafford.

Questions 11-15 refer to the following order form, e-mail, and online review.

www.meadowcrestfurniture.com

MEADOWCREST FURNITURE

HOME I PRODUCTS I **ORDERS** I CUSTOMER TESTIMONIALS I CONTACT US

Order number: PQ413957L
Order date: April 25

Ship to: Clair Walker
Walk Tall Marketing
11126 Hayslip Lane
Houston, TX 77041

Item description	Quantity	Price	Total price
Item no. LV29116B - Blaine Taylor "Oasis" two-seater sofa - Dimensions: 180 x 86 x 61 cm	1	$440.00	$440.00
Custom fabric upholstery - Pattern Z810 (blue cotton and polyester blend) - $1.20 per yard	10 yards	$1.20	$12.00

Note: Shipping is $15 within the state of Texas and $25 for elsewhere in the country. All deliveries are made within 10 days of payment confirmation. To request changes, returns, and refunds, or for other concerns, send an e-mail to cs@meadowcrestfurniture.com. We also now offer a furniture removal service at a cost of $60 per item. For orders totaling $500 or more, the service is free.		
Subtotal	$452.00
Discounts	($0.00)
Taxes	$27.12
Shipping	$15.00
TOTAL	$494.12

PRINT

To: Meadowcrest Furniture <cs@meadowcrestfurniture.com>
From: Clair Walker <c.walker@mailranch.com>
Subject: Order PQ413957L
Date: April 26

To whom it may concern,

I placed an order for a sofa yesterday. Unfortunately, I incorrectly measured the space it is intended for and would like to replace it with a larger one. I've looked through your online catalog and have settled on item number LV68423A. It's made by the same manufacturer, but has three seats instead of two. I'd also like to add three tan-colored throw pillows by Lerner Home (item number PW14692K).

With the changes I've requested, I see that I qualify for the free furniture removal service, so I'd like to have my old sofa disposed of responsibly. Thank you for attending to my concern.

Sincerely,

Clair Walker

MEADOWCREST FURNITURE

HOME | PRODUCTS | ORDERS | **CUSTOMER TESTIMONIALS** | CONTACT US

Only customers who have made a verified purchase on www.meadowcrestfurniture.com may submit reviews.

PRODUCT NAME: Blaine Taylor "Oasis" three-seater sofa

See <u>all</u> reviews about this product

Love this product! ★ ★ ★ ★ ★

Posted by Clair Walker, May 12

I decided it was time to do a little redecorating around my office, and after getting a new coffee table and some chairs, I replaced an old sofa in my reception area with the item above. Almost immediately, I received several compliments on it from clients. The sofa is well made, fills the space nicely, and is extremely comfortable. And although the item was not inexpensive, knowing that my clients feel welcome because of it makes it well worth the expense.

---

11 What is NOT true about Meadowcrest Furniture?

(A) It can take over a week to deliver an order.
(B) It sells textiles by the yard.
(C) It charges a single rate for shipping.
(D) It will accept returns on its merchandise.

12 Why did Ms. Walker send the e-mail?

(A) To request a different fabric
(B) To change an item size
(C) To report a payment delay
(D) To correct a delivery address

13 What is suggested about Ms. Walker?

(A) She received a catalog in the mail.
(B) Her pillow was made by Blaine Taylor.
(C) She paid for expedited shipping.
(D) Her updated order cost at least $500.

14 In the e-mail, the phrase "attending to" in paragraph 2, line 2, is closest in meaning to

(A) going to
(B) dealing with
(C) helping out
(D) serving up

15 What is indicated about Walk Tall Marketing?

(A) Its new location is much larger.
(B) Its reception area has been refurnished.
(C) It experienced a growth in sales.
(D) It hired a new assistant.

READING Part 7

Ch 17 양식 연계 지문

Hackers TOEIC Reading

Questions 16-20 refer to the following personnel file, memo and pay statement.

Pittsburgh Express
Serving passengers throughout Pittsburgh for over 50 years

EMPLOYEE PERSONNEL FILE No. 6-425
The information in this file is confidential. Please exercise discretion when handling or disclosing to other parties.

Name: Harold White
Complete address: 1730 Fallowfield Avenue, Pittsburgh PA 15216

Telephone: 555-6364   E-mail: h.white@writeme.com
Emergency contact: Rebecca Simpson   Relationship: Sister
Emergency telephone: 555-9027

Department: Operations   Position: City bus driver
Contract valid until: June 15   Years with company: 10
Hourly rate: $15
Benefits: Medical insurance, pension fund, sick leave, holiday leave

Grievances: None
Disciplinary actions: None
Accident reports: 1

Pittsburgh Express
MEMO

To: All employees
From: Michael O'Rourke, Head of Human Resources
Subject: Employment terms
Date: March 16

As you know, Pittsburgh Express has been acquired by Felton Capital, which will assume ownership on June 1 of this year. The new owner has agreed to retain all existing staff who choose to remain. For those who decide to stay, Felton Capital will honor your current contracts until their dates of expiration. However, benefits will now include medical insurance, pensions, sick leave, holiday leave, and a night-shift allowance. After your respective contracts end, you will be asked to negotiate new contracts that may include additional terms.

Alternatively, you may choose to terminate your employment before the new owners take over. In that case, you will receive a severance package based on your years of service. Your decisions are needed by May 15 and will be shared with Felton Capital along with other employment information. Thank you.

EMPLOYEE PAY STATEMENT

Company subsidiary: Pittsburgh Express

Employee name: Harold White   Pay period: July 1 to July 31

Payment by: _X_ Company check

_____ Bank transfer

INCOME SUMMARY	DEDUCTIONS
Hours worked: 80	National tax: $111.60
Hourly rate: $20.00	State tax: $13.39
Base pay: $900.00	Medical insurance: $15.00
Overtime: $216.00	Pension fund: $12.50
Night shift allowances: $135.00	Other deductions: $0.00
Bonuses: $0.00	

Net pay: $1,098.51   Payable: August 10

Sick leave: 0   Holiday leave: 0

Days taken: 0   Days taken: 0

Days remaining: 5   Days remaining: 10

---

16 What most likely is Pittsburgh Express?

(A) A shipping firm
(B) A city newspaper
(C) A bus company
(D) A medical services provider

17 What is the purpose of the memo?

(A) To announce a new disciplinary policy
(B) To notify staff about a change of ownership
(C) To report a plan to hire new staff
(D) To remind employees about their evaluations

18 What is true about Felton Capital?

(A) It will give bonuses to employees who choose to stay.
(B) It has plans to change the name of the company.
(C) It added a night-shift allowance as a new benefit.
(D) It gave employees one week to make a decision.

19 What is suggested about Mr. White?

(A) He was offered a job at a different firm.
(B) He was asked to move to another department.
(C) He normally works 50 hours a week.
(D) He received an increase in his hourly rate.

20 What is NOT included in the pay statement?

(A) The number of hours worked
(B) The kinds of taxes that are paid
(C) The start date of employment
(D) The preferred payment method

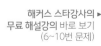
해커스 스타강사의 ▶
무료 해설강의 바로 보기
(6~10번 문제)

CHAPTER 18

기사 연계 지문

토익 이렇게 나온다!

기사 연계 지문은 첫 번째 지문으로 기사가 나오고, 두 번째나 세 번째 지문으로 이메일(편지), 양식, 또 다른 기사, 공고 등이 연계된 지문이다. 주로 이메일이나 양식과 가장 많이 연계된다.

토익 지문 유형 및 연계 문제 핵심 전략

빈출 지문 유형

[Double Passages]

기사 & 이메일(편지)	비즈니스 업계의 새로운 소식을 알리는 기사 & 해당 소식과 관련하여 논의하는 이메일
기사 & 양식	제품/서비스를 소개하는 기사 & 제품/서비스 주문 및 예약 확인서

[Triple Passages]

기사 & 양식 & 이메일(편지)	행사나 상점, 시설을 소개하는 기사 & 행사나 시설 관련 신청 양식 & 행사 참가자들이나 관련자에게 협조를 요청하는 이메일(편지)
기사 & 양식 & 공고	행사 개최를 알리는 기사 & 행사 후기나 관련 서류 & 행사 관련 공고

연계 문제 핵심 전략

STEP 1 질문의 핵심 어구를 통해 먼저 확인할 지문을 결정한다.

STEP 2 해당 지문에서 첫 번째 단서를 찾고, 추가로 필요한 두 번째 단서를 다른 지문에서 찾는다.

　　　　* Triple passages의 경우, 첫 번째 단서를 찾은 후 남은 두 지문 중 추가로 필요한 내용과 관련된 지문을 선택하여 두 번째 단서를 찾는다.

STEP 3 두 개의 단서를 종합하여 정답을 선택한다.

예제　기사 & 이메일

Dallas-based television channel KVBS has announced that it will soon be merging with the Peak Media Conglomeration (PMC). Starting on September 6, KVBS will begin airing programming from PMC. In addition, PMC said it has plans to add a morning news program to the viewing schedule of the channel, which will start broadcasting in January of next year.

STEP 2-2
추가로 필요한 두 번째 단서를 다른 지문에서 찾는다

To: Erik Wade <erikwade@PMC.com>
From: Iris Svenson <irissvenson@KVBS.com>
I would like to meet with you sometime this week to discuss hiring a host for our new program. I've contacted several potential candidates and they have all expressed interest in the position. I'd like to go over the options with you so that we can decide who to contact for interviews. Let me know when you are free.

STEP 2-1
해당 지문에서 첫 번째 단서를 찾는다

STEP 1
질문의 핵심 어구를 통해 먼저 확인할 지문을 결정한다

Q. What is suggested about Iris Svenson?
(A) She wants to apply for a television presenter job.
(B) She is trying to recruit a host for a news program.
(C) She recently conducted some interviews.
(D) She is compiling terms for a merger.

STEP 3
두 개의 단서를 종합하여 정답을 선택한다

정답　(B)

지문 해석 p.181

유형 연습 지문을 읽고 질문에 답하세요.

01~02 기사 & 기사

New Scholarship Program for Young Artists

According to a press release from the Ministry of the Arts, a new scholarship program will soon be launched. The ministry has created the Young Artists Scholarship Program for which 10 applicants from across the province will be selected. Winners will receive full funding for any school located within the province of Saskatchewan. Gary Brown, spokesperson for the ministry, said, "The program is part of our ongoing efforts to promote the growth of fine art within the region."

Local Artist Granted Scholarship

Local painter Brenda Kahn was awarded a full scholarship from the Ministry of the Arts last week, and said she plans to study at the Royal Victoria Art Academy. The scholarship is one of just ten given out to artists in the province every year. Kahn applied for the scholarship in the fall and stated that she is thrilled that the ministry is putting forth such effort to support young artists.

---

01 Who is Brenda Kahn?

(A) An instructor at a school
(B) A spokesperson for the Ministry of the Arts
(C) The recipient of a scholarship

02 What is suggested about Royal Victoria Art Academy?

(A) It is located in Saskatchewan.
(B) It is operated by the Ministry of the Arts.
(C) It offers scholarships to local students.

03~04 기사 & 도표

Online Marketing Seen to Grow

As the trend toward online marketing grows, companies are eager to learn how it measures up against other forms of advertising. In order to address this concern, it is necessary to use comparable data, such as the cost of one ad versus the number of people it reaches. For instance, a company must spend an average of $7 online to reach 1,000 of its target consumers. This figure is more than four times lower than the next most affordable option, and nearly 60 times cheaper than the most expensive one. The main reason for such stark differences is that online ads are mostly paid per click, whereas for other forms, companies must cover large expenses up front.

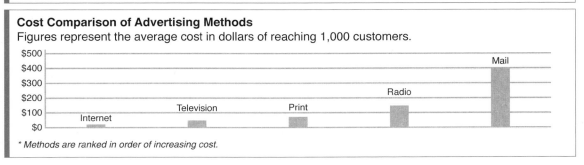

Cost Comparison of Advertising Methods

Figures represent the average cost in dollars of reaching 1,000 customers.

Methods are ranked in order of increasing cost.

---

03 How much is spent on average to reach 1,000 customers online?

(A) $1
(B) $7
(C) $60

04 What is indicated about advertising by mail?

(A) It reaches twice as many viewers as radio.
(B) It is half as effective as all other forms.
(C) It is almost 60 times more costly than online advertising.

정답·해설·해석 p.181

🕐 제한 시간 20분

Questions 01-05 refer to the following article and letter.

Author Wendy Armstrong To Visit Helena

Award-winning author Wendy Armstrong will make a stop in Helena next week on Thursday, September 22, during the North American leg of her book tour to publicize her newest work.

Armstrong is well-known for her Pioneer series of novels, which tell the tale of the Warren family and their struggle to create a life for themselves in the West during the gold rush of the mid-1800s. She is now attempting to bring the same success to a new series based on a family of immigrants to New York in the 1920s. Entitled *Arrivals*, her newest novel will introduce readers to the Pucci family from Naples and their story of coming to America. Released just two weeks ago, *Arrivals* is already on the literary best-seller list, and critics are raving about the work, saying it is Armstrong's best writing in years.

Armstrong has written 14 novels during her writing career, and won numerous awards as an author. She lives with her husband Nathan in Boise, Idaho where they run a small ranch. In her free time, Armstrong often visits universities to give talks to aspiring writers, offering them valuable advice and suggestions.

Armstrong will give a short reading and presentation at Spencer & Chang Bookstore at 11:30 A.M. Following that, she will sign copies of her new book, which will be on sale. The public is invited to attend the event and urged to arrive early as seating is limited. For further information, contact Spencer & Chang Bookstore at 555-3876.

September 17

Wendy Armstrong
87 Upland Heights Road
Boise, ID 86701

Dear Ms. Armstrong,

I came across an article in a local newspaper about an upcoming visit you are having in Helena to publicize your newest novel. I am a professor of modern literature at Northwestern University of the Arts, also located in Helena. The article mentioned that you occasionally speak at universities, and I am writing to inquire whether you might have some free time during your visit to give a similar presentation to our departments. I understand it is short notice, but I decided to contact you anyway as I am sure the avid readers among our students would appreciate the opportunity to listen to a successful writer. I completely understand if you are unable to come, but hope you will consider our invitation. We would happily provide you with a speaker's fee if necessary.

Thank you, and please contact me at leodaniels@nua.edu or by phone at (406) 555-9907.

Sincerely,

Leo Daniels
Professor of Modern Literature
Northwestern University of the Arts

01 What is the main purpose of the article?

(A) To notify readers of a bookstore expansion
(B) To promote a famous guest's upcoming visit
(C) To inform the public of a newly released publication
(D) To provide background information on an author

02 What is suggested about Spencer & Chang?

(A) It is located on a university campus.
(B) It has a special section for Armstrong's novels.
(C) It will be hosting a literary event on September 22.
(D) It accepts advance reservations for special events.

03 What is mentioned about Wendy Armstrong?

(A) She majored in modern literature at Northwestern University.
(B) She will write a series of novels based on her family's story.
(C) She received critical acclaim for her latest novel.
(D) She charges a fee to speak at educational institutions.

04 The word "consider" in paragraph 1, line 7 of the letter is closest in meaning to

(A) believe in
(B) schedule
(C) think about
(D) accept

05 Who would most likely attend a talk given by Ms. Armstrong at the Northwestern University?

(A) Professors of literature
(B) Young people who want to be authors
(C) Participants in a writing contest
(D) Members of writers' association

Questions 06-10 refer to the following report and article.

Summary of Canalvia Transit Authority Annual Report

Usage of public transportation in Canalvia fell by 6.4 percent compared to the previous year. The decline is a continuing trend over the past three years. Buses and trains have been running at only 72 percent passenger capacity.

The actual cost of running the bus and train systems was $52 million for the year. However, passengers only purchased $43 million of tickets. This is the third year in a row that the systems have ended up losing money for the city.

Many of the bus stops and train stations are very outdated and urgently need renovation. Also, security on public transport has become an issue with many local residents. More than 400 complaints were filed last year about security problems. Many passengers also complained about the increase in fares this year, and sales of annual passes were down by 7 percent.

The upcoming opening of two new train stations this March will help increase ticket sales, but other changes are necessary to stop the loss of money.

Canalvia Transit Authority Opens Stations and Announces Changes

By Sheldon Drake

Mayor Ellen Carrington officially opened two new train stations in the Lakeland and Harbor districts of Canalvia yesterday. The stations become operational today and will link the mostly residential areas with downtown and the financial district. The new stations include parking facilities, ticketing offices, retail outlets, and dining establishments.

Following the ceremony at Lakeland, Canalvia Transit Authority Director, Melvin Banks gave a short speech in which he announced several changes for this year. Starting in April, security personnel on the bus and train systems will be increased by 14 percent. In addition, the city council has approved a plan to start renovating old stations and bus stops. The project will begin in June and will last for two years at a cost of $82 million. Funds will come from local taxes and corporate sponsorships.

Mr. Banks said the changes are in response to the demands of residents, and the findings of the transit authority's annual report. The transit systems lost $9 million last year. Mr. Banks hopes the improvements will help attract more passengers and decrease losses.

06 What is the report mainly about?

(A) The annual budget of Canalvia
(B) A city's public transportation systems
(C) The expansion plans for a bus line
(D) An increase in passenger fees

07 What is suggested about the city of Canalvia?

(A) Its bus line isn't running at full capacity.
(B) It is experiencing a drop in population.
(C) It is planning to raise passenger fares.
(D) Its neighborhoods need additional security.

08 When did the Harbor Train Station become operational?

(A) In March
(B) In April
(C) In May
(D) In June

09 What will take place in April?

(A) Stations will temporarily close.
(B) A new budget will be implemented.
(C) Security staff will be increased.
(D) Bus stops will be constructed.

10 Why is the transit authority making the changes?

(A) To cut down on operation costs
(B) To increase ticket sales
(C) To respond to a growing population
(D) To attract more businesses

Questions 11-15 refer to the following article, Web page, and e-mail.

Oz-Air Now Operating Daily Flights to Singapore

Oz-Air has announced daily trips between Sydney and the hub of Southeast Asia-Singapore. Nonstop eight-hour flights will depart daily from Sydney at 9:40 A.M. In addition, return flights will head back to Sydney every day at 6:20 P.M.

"Whether traveling for business or pleasure, passengers can expect the same exceptional service from staff," says Oz-Air marketing director Jennifer Hogan. "We will take care of you on your trip with gourmet meals and attentive service." Singapore has increasingly become a popular destination, offering sights, shopping, cuisine, and unique experiences in a multicultural setting.

To celebrate the new route, Oz-Air is offering return tickets to Singapore for only $569. Further details can be found on the airline's Web site at www.oz-air.co.au/singaporepromotion.

---

www.oz-air.co.au/flights/ticketing/confirmation

PASSENGER NAME: Edmund Chang	
ADDRESS: 3098 42nd Street, Sydney NSW, Australia	
E-MAIL: chang@nswenterprises.com	PHONE: (902)555-9388

FLIGHT NUMBER: ZA 909	DEPARTURE: March 15, 9:40 A.M., Sydney
RETURN FLIGHT NUMBER: ZA 908	DEPARTURE: March 18, 6:20 P.M., Singapore
CLASS: Economy Plus	FREQUENT FLYER NUMBER: None

Note: Cancellations are not possible on any promotional fare offered by the airline. However, other changes are possible provided notice is given at least 10 days before the scheduled date of departure. A $100 fee is applicable in such cases.

SEND

To	\<bookings@ozair.co.au\>
From	Edmund Chang \<chang@nswenterprises.com\>
Subject	Flight
Date	January 14

Dear Madam or Sir,

I recently purchased a ticket for a flight to Singapore on March 15. I am attending the Biological Studies Conference there. I was discussing the conference with an associate at NSW Enterprises, Fred Banks, and told him about your promotional offer. As our work is directly related to the subject of the conference, he would like to accompany me. However, there are no seats available for him on the day I was planning to return. But there are many seats available the next day. Would it be possible to change my ticket so that my colleague and I can travel together? Please let me know as soon as possible as we would like to book quickly while seats are still vacant for the return flight.

Regards,
Edmund Chang

11 Why is Oz-Air offering the special?

(A) To promote its new route
(B) To commemorate the date of its establishment
(C) To publicize its frequent traveler program
(D) To outsell a competing airline

12 What is suggested about Mr. Chang?

(A) He requested an upgrade to business class.
(B) He is not a member of Oz-Air's frequent flyer program.
(C) He frequently travels out of Sydney for his job.
(D) He did not provide all the necessary contact information.

13 What is indicated about Mr. Chang's upcoming flight?

(A) It cannot be combined with other special offers.
(B) It will last for approximately eight hours.
(C) It is scheduled to depart in the evening.
(D) It will only be a one-way journey.

14 Based on the e-mail, in which field does Mr. Chang most likely work?

(A) Travel and tourism
(B) Scientific research
(C) Economic studies
(D) Advertising and promotions

15 What does Mr. Chang want to do?

(A) Book two seats for a flight on March 19
(B) Change his colleague's date of arrival
(C) Get a cancellation charge refunded
(D) Sign up a coworker for a conference

Questions 16-20 refer to the following article, letter, and e-mail.

SCOPE BROADCASTING CORPORATION MAKES MASSIVE DONATION TO AWPS

The Australia Wildlife Protection Society (AWPS) announced at a special ceremony on Monday that Scope Broadcasting Corporation (SBC) had donated $1.2 million to its efforts. President of the AWPS, Cindy Stubbs, was on hand to accept a check from SBC's regional president, Audrey McKay. McKay explained that half the funds were from the channel's viewers and were gathered during a month-long fundraising campaign. Short ads were broadcast on SBC urging viewers to make online donations. The remaining funds were a corporate match from SBC. Stubbs graciously thanked McKay for the donation in a short speech and said that the money would be used for the operation of several wildlife reserves around the country.

Although SBC will not be matching additional contributions until next year's fundraising promotion, donations are still being accepted at www.sbc.co.au/donate. Furthermore, SBC will add an extra $100 to the contributions of those signing up as premium supporters.

February 2

Miriam Smythe
987 Eucalyptus Avenue
Melbourne, VIC 3001

Dear Ms. Smythe,

Thank you so much for signing up as a premium sponsor of Scope Broadcasting Corporation's fundraising program! Your funds will go towards the protection of wildlife across the nation through a range of programs and organizations. Your credit card has been charged the donation amount of $400, and a receipt for your personal records has been e-mailed to you.

Enclosed you will find an informational brochure about SBC's support network, including a list of all the organizations we make donations to worldwide. And as you selected, a medium T-shirt with the AWPS logo has been included as a free gift!

We appreciate your continued viewership, and thank you for your patronage of such important groups. Our efforts can make a difference in protecting life on our planet. Should you have any questions or concerns, feel free to contact me at any time at charbell@sbc.co.au.

Sincerely yours,
Charmaine Bell
Fundraising Department
Scope Broadcasting Corporation

TO	Charmaine Bell <charbell@sbc.co.au>
FROM	Miriam Smythe <smire@victoriamail.com>
SUBJECT	Sponsor package
DATE	February 7

Dear Ms. Bell,

I received the package yesterday from SBC and appreciate the brochure and letter. Unfortunately, the gift contained in the package was not medium as requested. Someone must have enclosed a large one by accident. Would it be possible to get my correct size? I can send the one I have back to you if necessary.

Also, I have not yet received an e-mail containing a receipt. Could you please send it to me? As the donation is tax deductible, my accountant will need a copy of it.

I appreciate your assistance with these matters.

Regards,
Miriam Smythe

---

16 What is the article mainly about?

(A) The appointment of a company executive
(B) The operations of a charitable group
(C) The launch of an online promotion
(D) The success of a fund-raising campaign

17 What can be inferred about Ms. Smythe?

(A) She recently attended a special ceremony.
(B) She rarely watches television programs on SBC.
(C) She holds membership in a support network.
(D) She regularly supports AWPS initiatives.

18 What is suggested about Scope Broadcasting Corporation?

(A) It matched Ms. Smythe's financial donation.
(B) It gives all funds raised to the AWPS.
(C) It will donate an extra $100 in the name of Ms. Smythe.
(D) It will send free gifts to all sponsors.

19 What is indicated about the package sent to Ms. Smythe?

(A) It included a promotional T-shirt that does not fit.
(B) It was missing an informational pamphlet on the AWPS.
(C) It arrived at her residence on February 7.
(D) It contained an item that was accidentally damaged.

20 What will Charmaine Bell most likely do?

(A) Update Ms. Smythe's donor status
(B) Forward a copy of a financial document
(C) Contact Ms. Smythe's personal accountant
(D) Send a product in a larger size

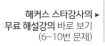

광고 연계 지문

토익 이렇게 나온다!

광고 연계 지문은 첫 번째 지문으로 일반 광고나 구인 광고가 나오고, 두 번째나 세 번째 지문으로 양식, 이메일(편지), 공고, 또 다른 광고 등이 연계된 지문이다. 주로 이메일이나 양식과 가장 많이 연계된다.

토익 지문 유형 및 연계 문제 핵심 전략

빈출 지문 유형

[Double Passages]

광고 & 이메일(편지)   회사나 행사 등을 홍보하는 광고나 구인 광고 & 고객의 문의나 구직 관련 문의에 답변하는 이메일

광고 & 양식   제품/서비스를 홍보하는 광고 & 고객에게 보내는 견적서나 제품/서비스 주문 양식

[Triple Passages]

광고 & 양식 & 이메일   새로운 매장이나 신제품을 홍보하는 광고 & 신제품 관련 안내 양식이나 행사 일정표 & 제품 구매나 행사 관련 내용을 전달하는 이메일

광고 & 이메일 & 공고   회사나 시설/서비스를 홍보하는 광고 & 시설/서비스 이용을 신청하는 이메일 & 특별 행사나 서비스에 대해 안내하는 공고

연계 문제 핵심 전략

STEP 1   질문의 핵심 어구를 통해 먼저 확인할 지문을 결정한다.

STEP 2   해당 지문에서 첫 번째 단서를 찾고, 추가로 필요한 두 번째 단서를 다른 지문에서 찾는다.

       * Triple passages의 경우, 첫 번째 단서를 찾은 후 남은 두 지문 중 추가로 필요한 내용과 관련된 지문을 선택하여 두 번째 단서를 찾는다.

STEP 3   두 개의 단서를 종합하여 정답을 선택한다.

예제   광고 & 광고 & 이메일

> Clockwork's newest timepiece, the Chrono-Watch 3000, was designed with the athletic man in mind. Priced at $2,200, Clockwork's Chrono-Watch 3000 is available at Bullion Fine Jewelry outlets across the country.

STEP 2-1 해당 지문에서 첫 번째 단서를 찾는다

> If you're looking for the perfect gift for the active man in your life, then look no further. Genevex's Metrowatch makes an ideal gift for any occasion. Metrowatch is operated by solar energy and has a watch face set with two carats of diamonds.

STEP 2-2 추가로 필요한 두 번째 단서를 다른 지문에서 찾는다

> To: Charlotte Becker <c.becker@mailroom.com>
> From: Brent Oldwood <b.oldwood@monomail.com>
> If you haven't picked out a gift yet for Allan's birthday, I might be able to help you. I found a store that sells all sorts of watches while I was browsing online last week. Check out the link: www.watchfinder.com.

STEP 1 질문의 핵심 어구를 통해 먼저 확인할 지문을 결정한다

Q. What is indicated about the Chrono-Watch 3000?
    (A) It is more expensive than the Metrowatch.
    (B) It is decorated with precious stones and metals.
    (C) It is for the same type of user as the Metrowatch.
    (D) It is available for purchase from a Web site.

STEP 3 두 개의 단서를 종합하여 정답을 선택한다

정답 (C)

지문 해석 p.187

유형 연습 지문을 읽고 질문에 답하세요.

01~02 광고 & 안내문

Interlingua Toys and Games

Interlingua is a trusted maker of toys and games for children. Choose online from hundreds of products that are fun and educational. Click on the links below to view complete information about specific items for sale.

- Preschool toys (ages 3 and up)
- Building toys (ages 4 and up)
- Puzzle games (ages 5 and up)
- Board games (ages 6 and up)

Please note that the prices listed on our Web site do not include shipping and taxes.

A Day at the Zoo

Teaches children how to identify animals and the sounds they make. Suitable for children 3 years of age and older.

- Price without shipping: $44.95
- Product dimensions: 5.1 x 4.2 x 10.8 inches
- Shipping weight: 2.4 pounds
- Item ships within three days.

---

01 What information can be viewed on the Web site?

(A) Store hours
(B) Delivery charges
(C) Item descriptions

02 What most likely is A Day at the Zoo?

(A) A children's book
(B) A preschool toy
(C) A puzzle game

03~04 광고 & 이메일

COPYWRITER WANTED: Harlequin Advertising

Harlequin Advertising is seeking a copywriter to join its team in Los Angeles. Applicants must have a background in professional writing and be familiar with the advertising industry. Furthermore, preference will be given to those who can demonstrate fluency in a second language. In addition, applicants must be current residents of Los Angeles or be willing to relocate before August 15. To apply, please send a complete work history and copies of your written work to Arlene Sorkin at a.sorkin@harlequinads.com.

To: Pamela Lopez <pamlo@mmail.com>
From: Jane Duvall <j.duvall@starmail.com>
Subject: Job prospect

Hi Pam,
I heard you just moved to Los Angeles and are searching for a job. Actually, an advertising agency I know of is looking for a copywriter. It's a different field than you're used to, but your experience with the bilingual magazine *Linguesa* will count to your advantage. Read the attachment for more details.

---

03 What does Harlequin Advertising ask applicants to provide?

(A) Letters of reference
(B) Copies of a diploma
(C) Writing samples

04 Which necessary qualifications for the position does Ms. Lopez not have?

(A) Residency in a city
(B) Knowledge of advertising
(C) Expertise in a second language

정답·해설·해석 p.188

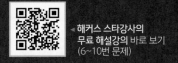

해커스 스타강사의
무료 해설강의 바로 보기
(6~10번 문제)

🕐 제한 시간 15분

Questions 01-05 refer to the following advertisement and e-mail.

TRIPOD PHOTO AND VIDEO SERVICES

Tripod Photo and Video Services takes pride in providing quality photography and video coverage of any occasion. The company covers different kinds of events, including birthday parties, anniversaries, weddings, and more. By using high-resolution and high-definition cameras as well as professional editing software, we ensure that our output is of the best quality. Additionally, the company is made up of a team of professional photographers, videographers, and graphic artists who work before, during, and after an event to fulfill all client requests.

Tripod Photo and Video Services provides a variety of packages, depending on the event to be covered and the required output, which can consist of photo albums or CDs, framed pictures, DVDs of raw and edited videos, or combinations of these items.

And for this month only, get a $50 gift certificate when ordering a video package deal of $800 or more!* Simply e-mail us at customersupport@tripodvideo.com to make a reservation before the month is over, and we will send you a certificate to use on any of our services in the future.

To learn more regarding Tripod Photo and Video Services, our special promotions, and our package deals, check out our Web site at www.tripodvideo.com.

*Reservations must be made by May 31 to be eligible for the special gift certificate offer.

To	Adrian Winston <a.winston@giantredmail.com>
From	Deanna Lloyd <customersupport@tripodvideo.com>
Date	May 28
Subject	Inquiries

Dear Mr. Winston,

Thank you for your message yesterday about booking our services to film your company's 20th anniversary celebration on June 22. I understand that you want the entire celebration to be documented on video within a budget of $600. We would be very happy to do that for you, but we do require some additional information first.

First, you mentioned that the party starts at 7 p.m. at the Breckinridge Hotel, but could you let me know how long it will last? Also, how would you prefer the video files delivered? We can copy them onto discs or send them via e-mail. If you want discs, let us know how many copies are necessary. Finally, we need to find out how large the celebration will be. It will give us an idea of how many camera operators we will have to send.

Once I have these details, I can send you a cost estimate. If you need to speak to me, my number is 555-9004.

Sincerely,

Deanna Lloyd

01 What is the advertisement mainly about?

(A) Editing software for professional photographers
(B) Equipment available for rent from a photography studio
(C) An upcoming promotion for complimentary items
(D) Media-related services offered by a company

02 In the advertisement, the phrase "consist of" in paragraph 2, line 2 is closest in meaning to

(A) be made of
(B) include
(C) be created for
(D) develop

03 What is NOT mentioned as a service provided by Tripod Photo and Video Services?

(A) Raw output to DVD
(B) Social event coverage
(C) Photograph enlargement
(D) Online delivery of videos

04 Why is Mr. Winston ineligible for the special promotion?

(A) His budget is under the minimum purchase requirement.
(B) He did not place a request before a specific date.
(C) He is requesting photography rather than video.
(D) He did not ask for a package deal.

05 What is suggested about Ms. Lloyd?

(A) She is a member of the video production team.
(B) She doesn't know where the venue for the celebration is located.
(C) She is unable to provide services for the anniversary event.
(D) She compiles price estimates for Tripod Photo and Video Services.

Questions 06-10 refer to the following advertisement and letter.

VOLUNTEERS NEEDED

Walton Senior Citizens Center, 3324 29th Street Williamsburg, VA

The Walton Senior Citizens Center is in urgent need of volunteers to plan and facilitate events and activities. With over 700 members, the center aims to provide educational and entertaining activities for the local senior citizen population.

DUTIES:

Volunteers will work together with Evelyn Parsons, our activities coordinator, to plan and carry out a variety of activities. These will include arts and crafts, and simple classes in music, cooking, and languages. The selected applicants will also help with organizing outings to local sites, entertainment venues, and parks. In addition, the volunteers will help prepare music and theatrical performances put on by members twice per year.

REQUIREMENTS:

Applicants must be at least 19 years of age and in possession of a valid driver's license. Previous experience working with senior citizens is also preferred. All applicants must also have passed a first aid course within the past two years.

To apply to be a volunteer, please drop by the center's administration office between 9 A.M. and 6 P.M. from Monday through Saturday. Simply fill out a form and submit it to one of our personnel. We will contact all applicants by letter to inform them whether they have been selected or not. If you have additional questions, call the center at 555-7982.

June 16

Gianni Forno
18-B Westchester Avenue
Williamsburg, VA

Dear Mr. Forno,

Thank you so much for your interest in becoming a volunteer at the Walton Senior Citizens Center. We appreciate your willingness to help us arrange special activities and functions for our members.

We are very impressed with your application and that you have previously done volunteer work for a similar organization in Charleston. Unfortunately, we will not be able to accept you as a volunteer at this time. Should you take a first aid course again in the near future, we would be happy to welcome you as one of our volunteer staff.

Regretfully, this requirement is state law, so we are unable to make an exception in this particular case.

Once again, thank you for applying to be a volunteer. Please feel free to call me at 555-7982 if you have any questions or I can be of any assistance.

Sincerely yours,

Evelyn Parsons

Evelyn Parsons
Activities Coordinator
Walton Senior Citizens Center

06 Why was the advertisement written?

(A) To promote a senior citizens facility
(B) To announce job openings for caretakers
(C) To request people to assist with activities
(D) To ask for volunteers in a study

07 What is a required qualification for applicants?

(A) A degree in nursing
(B) Previous experience with senior citizens
(C) A current license to drive
(D) The ability to speak other languages

08 What is suggested about the members of the center?

(A) They reside at the facility.
(B) They must pay an annual fee.
(C) They need constant medical attention.
(D) They are encouraged to pursue hobbies.

09 What must Mr. Forno do in order to become a volunteer at the center?

(A) Pass a medical training course
(B) Get a current driver's license
(C) Provide a character reference
(D) Wait a year to meet the age requirement

10 What is indicated about Mr. Forno?

(A) He has not worked with senior citizens before.
(B) He plans to take a medical course.
(C) He was previously employed by Ms. Parsons.
(D) He lives in the city the Walton Senior Citizens Center is located in.

Questions 11-15 refer to the following advertisement, invoice, and e-mail.

MOORELAND PUBLISHING

Promote your products and services in our magazines. Established a decade ago, our company's publications attract a diverse audience of readers across the US, and we have won the Media Publisher Award for the past four years. Below is just a small sample of the titles that we carry:

- *Tech Today* features the latest high-tech devices from the world of computing.
- *Fan World* allows you to keep up with your favorite sports teams and athletes.
- *Modern Living* highlights trends in fashion, travel, home design, and more.
- *Political Summit* provides in-depth analyses of contemporary global issues.

Choose from quarter-, half-, and full-page ads. Prices vary for each magazine. To get information about our other available titles, visit www.moorelandpub.com. Register to advertise in a single magazine for three months and receive a 15 percent discount. Members of the Mooreland Business Association are eligible to receive an additional 10 percent discount.

Mooreland Publishing   Invoice number: 4547

Customer name: Cassandra Harding
Organization: Active Life
E-mail: c.harding@activelife.com
Telephone: 555-0913

Magazine	Month advertisement will appear	Cost
Political Summit	March	$350.00
Fan World	April	$150.00
Modern Living	May	$200.00
Tech Today	June-July	$270.00
	Subtotal	$970.00
	10% discount	($97.00)
	Total	$873.00
	Payment due	February 10

* The advertisements may be sent as high-resolution image files to advertising@moorelandpub.com. To request changes or to revise any information in the files, please contact us two weeks before a publication is due to be released.

To: Oscar Lawrence <advertising@moorelandpub.com>
From: Cassandra Harding <c.harding@activelife.com>
Subject: Error
Date: March 3

Dear Mr. Lawrence,

I was very satisfied with the advertising your company provided for our last tennis tournament, so I contacted you to promote one of our biggest events this year. But I am disappointed to report an error in the advertisement published for my organization in one of your magazines this month. The advertisement states that registration for our summer marathon in Dayton must be completed before July 10. As was indicated in the revised version of the advertisement I sent on February 7, registration actually closes on July 20. I assume you must have mistakenly referred to the original version, which included the wrong date. Please put a correction notice on your Web site and send notification e-mails to the subscribers.

Sincerely,

Cassandra Harding

---

11 What is NOT indicated about Mooreland Publishing?

(A) It prints advertisements in three sizes.
(B) It distributes its magazines nationwide.
(C) It publishes more than four types of magazines.
(D) It was founded four years ago.

12 What can be inferred about Active Life?

(A) It organized an event for a politician.
(B) It is raising funds for a special project.
(C) It is a member of a business association.
(D) It provides discounts to select customers.

13 What is suggested about Ms. Harding?

(A) She is the owner of an advertising company.
(B) She has used Mooreland Publishing's services before.
(C) She will receive free copies of some publications.
(D) She will be signing up for a marathon.

14 Which magazine includes an advertisement with an error?

(A) *Political Summit*
(B) *Fan World*
(C) *Modern Living*
(D) *Tech Today*

15 What does Ms. Harding ask Mr. Lawrence to do?

(A) Post a revision
(B) Mail a second invoice
(C) Confirm a payment
(D) Attend an event

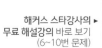

CHAPTER 20 공고 연계 지문

토익 이렇게 나온다!

공고 연계 지문은 첫 번째 지문으로 공고가 나오고, 두 번째나 세 번째 지문으로 이메일(편지), 양식, 기사 등이 연계된 지문이다. 주로 양식이나 이메일과 가장 많이 연계된다.

토익 지문 유형 및 연계 문제 핵심 전략

빈출 지문 유형

[Double Passages]

공고 & 이메일	행사나 사내 규칙에 대해 안내하는 공고 & 행사 등록이나 사내 규칙 변경과 관련된 이메일
공고 & 양식	행사에 대해 안내하는 공고 & 행사 등록이나 기타 신청서

[Triple Passages]

공고 & 양식 & 이메일	회사에서 새롭게 진행하는 사항을 알리는 공고 & 관련된 서류나 양식 & 관련 업무 진행을 요청하는 이메일
공고 & 기사 & 이메일	행사에 대해 안내하는 공고 & 행사 후기를 소개하는 기사 & 행사 제안 사항이나 차후 계획과 관련된 내용의 이메일

연계 문제 핵심 전략

STEP 1 질문의 핵심 어구를 통해 먼저 확인할 지문을 결정한다.

STEP 2 해당 지문에서 첫 번째 단서를 찾고, 추가로 필요한 두 번째 단서를 다른 지문에서 찾는다.

    * Triple passages의 경우, 첫 번째 단서를 찾은 후 남은 두 지문 중 추가로 필요한 내용과 관련된 지문을 선택하여 두 번째 단서를 찾는다.

STEP 3 두 개의 단서를 종합하여 정답을 선택한다.

예제 공고 & 이메일

The Wallingford Community Center Hosts Parenting Seminars in May

The Wallingford Community Center will host two seminars for parents of young children. The first is on May 12 and entitled *Early Childhood Education*, and the second is *Home Safety for Toddlers* and takes place on May 14. Interested participants may contact Glenda Ingram at (709) 555-8249 for registration from May 9 to 11.

— **STEP 2-2** 추가로 필요한 두 번째 단서를 다른 지문에서 찾는다

To: Anna Grimes <annagrimes@filter.com>
From: Donna Wilson <donnawilson@tonomail.com>
I saw a notice from the Wallingford Community Center about a couple of seminars they are holding and felt that one in particular might interest you. We were talking the other day about methods for teaching our kids, so I thought we could attend the seminar together. Let me know, and I can sign us up.

— **STEP 2-1** 해당 지문에서 첫 번째 단서를 찾는다

Q. On what date will Ms. Wilson most likely attend a seminar session?
(A) May 9
(B) May 11
(C) May 12
(D) May 14

— **STEP 1** 질문의 핵심 어구를 통해 먼저 확인할 지문을 결정한다

— **STEP 3** 두 개의 단서를 종합하여 정답을 선택한다

정답 (C)

지문 해석 p.193

HACKERS PRACTICE 토익 고득점을 위한 필수 연습

유형 연습   지문을 읽고 질문에 답하세요.

01~02 공고 & 양식

MAKE A COMMITMENT TO A CHILD IN NEED

The Caroline Becker Foundation provides assistance to needy children around the world with food, clean water, health care, and education. By sponsoring a child, you can help us in our mission. In addition to our annual newsletter, sponsors receive quarterly updates about their child.

We are currently in need of sponsors in the following areas:

Lima, Peru   Donate $100 to provide school age children with textbooks.
Kampala, Uganda   Donate $50 to provide one child with a month of school lunches.

To make a contribution, please clip the attached form and mail it to us.

The Caroline Becker Foundation
SPONSORSHIP FORM
Name: *Mary Martin*   Tel. *555-9382*   Mob. *003-555-7898*
Address: *1485 Oakwood Avenue, Raleigh, NC*
Send my donation to: ☐ Lima, Peru   ■ Kampala, Uganda
In the amount of: *$50*
Method of payment: ☐ Credit card   ■ Cash   ☐ Personal check

---

01 What is mentioned about the foundation?

(A) It publishes a newsletter once a year.
(B) It provides homes for needy children.
(C) It needs volunteers in two countries.

02 What is Ms. Martin providing assistance with?

(A) Health care
(B) Education
(C) Food

03~04 공고 & 이메일

Evergreen Publishing Firm Workshop Schedule

The personnel department will be arranging three workshops on editorial techniques. Staff may sign up for any class they are interested in. The planned sessions are as follows:

WORKSHOP	Facilitator	DATE
Making Language Flow	Rosalind Beatty	May 2
Linguistic Changes in Modern English	Elizabeth Lim	June 3
Using Editing Software	George Thomas	July 1

For more information or to register, send an e-mail to personnel@evergreen.com.

To: Personnel Department <personnel@evergreen.com>
From: Colm Meaney <colmmeaney@evergreen.com>
Subject: Workshop
Date: May 1

Last week, I registered for one of the workshops your department arranged. However, I would like to make a change to my selection. I will be on vacation on the day the editorial software workshop will be held. Could I sign up for Ms. Lim's class instead? Please let me know.

---

03 Why was the announcement written?

(A) To invite employees to attend some events
(B) To inform staff of a change in schedule
(C) To provide information about facilitators

04 Which workshop will Mr. Meaney most likely participate in?

(A) Making Language Flow
(B) Linguistic Changes in Modern English
(C) Using Editing Software

정답·해설·해석 p.193

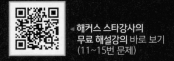
🕐 제한 시간 15분

Questions 01-05 refer to the following announcement and membership form.

METROPOLITAN MUSEUM OF HISTORY (MMH)
Treasures from the Middle Kingdom Exhibition

Date and Time: February 28, 10:00 A.M.
Location: MMH Exhibit Hall D

The Metropolitan Museum of History is pleased to present its newest exhibit of treasures from the Middle Kingdom of ancient Egypt. Over 300 items will be on display, including weapons, jewelry, sculpture, paintings, and other articles from this period of history.

The items are partly from the MMH's collection, with other items on loan from museums in Cairo, Turin, Berlin, and London. The display will continue until May 31.

In addition, Associate Minister of Antiquities for the nation of Egypt, Mustafa Khalil, will visit the exhibit on February 27 at 7 P.M. He will speak about the importance of archaeology in the modern age, and a short film about the history of the Middle Kingdom will be shown. Following these events, refreshments and appetizers will be served. Reservations for this event are necessary. Cost of attendance is $75 per person; however, gold sponsors of the MMH may attend for free. Call our public relations manager to make a booking.

If you are not yet a sponsor of the MMH, please feel free to fill out the enclosed form. Your support is appreciated.

Metropolitan Museum of History (MMH)
SPONSORSHIP APPLICATION:

BENEFITS	MEMBERSHIPS
Free entry to the museum for one year	gold and silver
Quarterly copies of *Contemporary Archaeologist Journal*	
Tickets for the annual Grand Ball	
Admission to all special events, talks, and lectures series	gold only
Reserved private viewings	

Fees are $120 for a silver sponsor and $200 for a gold sponsor. Please fill in the following information and return the form along with your payment to our public relations office.

Name: Rachel Conrad

Address: 6522 Lark Crescent

Family Members: David Conrad (husband)

Phone Number: _____(309) 555-9905_____

E-mail: _____racon@tmail.com_____

Type of sponsorship requested: ◙ gold ☐ silver

Method of payment: ◙ check ☐ credit card ☐ money order

All sponsors who wish to make reservations for the events can call our public relations manager, Mark Lee, at 555-4323. For additional details, visit our Web site at www.mmh.org.

01 What is the announcement mainly about?

(A) An excursion the museum is sponsoring
(B) A tour of an educational institution
(C) An event hosted by the museum
(D) A fundraiser for historic preservation

02 What is suggested about Mustafa Khalil?

(A) He is the director of the MMH.
(B) He loaned items to the museum for the exhibit.
(C) He is an expert on archaeology.
(D) He will be showing one of his documentaries.

03 In the announcement, the phrase "fill out" in paragraph 4, line 1 is closest in meaning to

(A) return
(B) complete
(C) attend
(D) inspect

04 What must sponsors do to hear Mr. Khalil's talk?

(A) Purchase a ticket
(B) Visit an office
(C) Contact Mark Lee
(D) Fill in a form

05 What is indicated about Ms. Conrad?

(A) She has been a previous supporter of the organization.
(B) She will be charged a $200 sponsorship fee.
(C) She has attended events at the museum before.
(D) She is planning to attend a film screening.

Questions 06-10 refer to the following notice and article.

Webdeals Auction and Retail Web Site

NOTICE:

Webdeals, world-famous auction and retail Web site, is pleased to announce that 30 percent of its shares are now publicly traded. Investors may buy shares in the company, which has recorded a stock value increase of 6.4 percent over the past year. The shares were made public yesterday, May 19 at a starting cost of $43.82 per share.

Webdeals will soon be expanding its market to include five new online sites targeted towards customers in China, India, Indonesia, Russia, and Japan. These sites will be made available in the local languages and take into consideration the trends and tastes of consumers in those countries. These expansions are expected to increase net profits for Webdeals by a minimum of 12 percent. The new sites should be operational by October 1. Now is a great chance to take advantage of an incredible investment opportunity.

Investors may buy general shares in Webdeals as a whole, or individual stocks for sites of particular nations. Stock prices for the countries mentioned above are lower at this time with purchase prices starting at $28 per share, while stable markets such as the United States are higher at $49 per share. Additional information on investment opportunities can be accessed at www.webdeals.com/investmentrelations. Or, you can simply get details from your financial advisor or banking institution.

Investors Already Earning Profits from Webdeals Shares

After announcing that 30 percent of its stocks would be publicly traded just one week ago, investors are already seeing their shares in Webdeals rise in value. Opening value for shares was $43.82, and within five business days the stock exchange reports current value at $44.12. The increase surprised financial experts, who didn't predict such interest from investors because the company had not shown any increase in profitability in recent years.

Webdeals opened the shares to the public in an effort to raise capital for expansions into new markets. The company offered the option of purchasing a general stock or investing in individual shares of any of the Web sites being planned for particular countries. Although not as significant as the increase for general shares, all stocks did gain value:

Region	Opening value May 22	Closing value May 26
China	$30.32	$30.78
India	$29.74	$29.97
Indonesia	$32.87	$33.02
Russia	$28.34	$28.44

In spite of the sites not yet being operational, rises were reported across the board as most investors had confidence in the potential of the sites. Initially, Webdeals had planned to open sites in five new markets, using the local language of each country. However, the retailer found that there was not enough interest in one of the previously planned locations, and now plans to launch only four sites.

06 When were Webdeals' stock shares first offered to the public?

(A) May 19
(B) May 20
(C) May 22
(D) May 26

07 What is NOT mentioned about Webdeals' new online sites?

(A) They are going to be available in October.
(B) They will increase in value by 12 percent.
(C) They are going to be in local languages.
(D) They have earned investors' confidence.

08 According to the article, why were some experts surprised by the rise in share value?

(A) Many of the sites are not yet operational.
(B) Webdeals' earnings had stopped growing.
(C) Shares had been made public for only a short time.
(D) The company had to shut down several sites.

09 For which country has Webdeals decided not to launch a Web site?

(A) The United States
(B) China
(C) Indonesia
(D) Japan

10 Why did Webdeals make some of their company shares public?

(A) To enter into several new markets
(B) To get money to pay off loans
(C) To respond to public pressure
(D) To improve their corporate image

Questions 11-15 refer to the following notice, schedule, and e-mail.

NOTICE: All Tech-Train Fitness Center Instructors

As you may know, the additions to our instructional facilities are nearly complete. This will affect the location of some scheduled courses. From October 1, we will begin using the new large exercise room for our aerobics and self-defense classes. Also, all yoga courses will be held in a specialized room located next to the indoor swimming pool. The yoga room now has its own private changing area and shower for the use of instructors and their assistants. These will also be available for use starting in October. Finally, two medium-sized workout rooms have been added on the second floor. They will be used for all of our small-group dance fitness workouts. Please check future work schedules to find out where your classes will be taught. Thank you for your patience over the past two months of construction, and we hope our staff will find the changes and additions beneficial.

Tech-Train Fitness Center: Fall Class Schedule (October-December)

Class	Day/Time	Instructor/Location
Introduction to Yoga	Mon./Thurs. 9-10 A.M.	Bev Peabody, Yoga Room
Intermediate Yoga	Tues./Fri. 9-10:30 A.M.	Raine Lewis, Yoga Room
Advanced Yoga	Wed./Sat. 10-11:30 A.M.	Bev Peabody, Yoga Room
Introduction to Dance Fitness	Tues./Fri. 8:30-10 A.M.	Jay Ang, Workout room A (2nd floor)
Intermediate Dance Fitness	Wed./Sat. 9-10:30 A.M.	Jay Ang, Workout room A (2nd floor)
Advanced Dance Fitness	Thurs./Fri. 6:30-8 P.M.	Jay Ang, Workout room B (2nd floor)
Beginner Self-Defense	Mon./Thurs. 8-9:30 A.M.	Helen Boyd, Exercise Room
Intermediate Self-Defense	Tues./Fri. 8-9:30 A.M.	Jay Ang, Exercise Room
Advanced Self-Defense	Wed./Sat. 2-3:30 P.M.	Helen Boyd, Exercise Room
Aerobics	Tues./Wed. 8-9:30 A.M.	Raine Lewis, Exercise Room

Contact the center's assistant director by e-mail if you have any questions or concerns regarding the schedule.

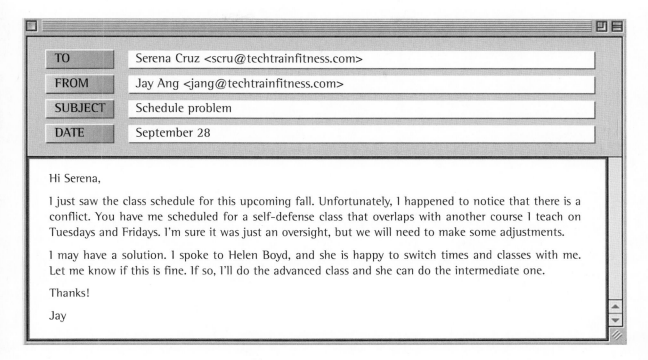

TO	Serena Cruz <scru@techtrainfitness.com>
FROM	Jay Ang <jang@techtrainfitness.com>
SUBJECT	Schedule problem
DATE	September 28

Hi Serena,

I just saw the class schedule for this upcoming fall. Unfortunately, I happened to notice that there is a conflict. You have me scheduled for a self-defense class that overlaps with another course I teach on Tuesdays and Fridays. I'm sure it was just an oversight, but we will need to make some adjustments.

I may have a solution. I spoke to Helen Boyd, and she is happy to switch times and classes with me. Let me know if this is fine. If so, I'll do the advanced class and she can do the intermediate one.

Thanks!

Jay

11 What is the notice mainly about?

(A) Changes to a work scheduling system
(B) Added facilities at a fitness center
(C) New classes being offered by an instructor
(D) Temporary closures of some workout rooms

12 What is indicated about Bev Peabody?

(A) She will teach in a room located on the second floor.
(B) She will have access to a reserved dressing room and shower.
(C) She will train an assistant instructor during her sessions.
(D) She will only lead courses on weekdays this fall.

13 What is true about Tech-Train Fitness Center?

(A) It will have fewer classes than usual for a short period.
(B) It offers aerobics classes for different levels.
(C) Its courses take place once every week.
(D) It will not conduct classes on Sundays.

14 Who most likely is Serena Cruz?

(A) A self-defense instructor at a fitness center
(B) A participant in a dance-oriented course
(C) An assistant director at a fitness club
(D) An applicant for a private trainer position

15 What has Helen Boyd agreed to do?

(A) Trade a scheduled class with a colleague
(B) Notify students about a schedule change
(C) Switch rooms with a coworker
(D) Enroll in a less advanced course

Hackers TOEIC Reading

실전모의고사

1, 2

잠깐! 테스트 전 확인 사항

1. 휴대 전화의 전원을 끄셨나요?
2. Answer Sheet, 연필, 지우개가 준비되셨나요?
3. 시계가 준비되셨나요?
(제한시간: 75분)

* Answer Sheet는 교재 마지막 페이지(p.574)에 수록되어 있습니다.

READING TEST

In this section, you must demonstrate your ability to read and comprehend English. You will be given a variety of texts and asked to answer questions about these texts. This section is divided into three parts and will take 75 minutes to complete.

Do not mark the answers in your test book. Use the answer sheet that is separately provided.

PART 5

Directions: In each question, you will be asked to review a statement that is missing a word or phrase. Four answer choices will be provided for each statement. Select the best answer and mark the corresponding letter (A), (B), (C), or (D) on the answer sheet.

101 In order to ------- the Opreme Gym, people must pay a one-time fee of $200.

(A) train   (B) fit
(C) add   (D) join

102 Employees at Inslee Solutions are asked to alert a supervisor whenever they detect ------- unusual online activity.

(A) several   (B) any
(C) these   (D) none

103 The bonus will be paid ------- the team meets its sales goals for the third quarter.

(A) despite   (B) according to
(C) even so   (D) only if

104 During popular holidays when flowers are in great demand, bouquets ------- higher than usual.

(A) pricing   (B) are priced
(C) can price   (D) have priced

105 The Tenglide razor can operate for more than an hour if its batteries are ------- charged.

(A) locally   (B) formally
(C) accurately   (D) sufficiently

106 You can return or exchange items you buy from the store within 30 days ------- purchase.

(A) about   (B) of
(C) for   (D) until

107 The newly released electric car has a number of ------- features, including a more efficient battery.

(A) obsolete
(B) permissible
(C) improved
(D) probable

108 Job candidates must present a portfolio and pass an aptitude test ------- they can be invited for an interview.

(A) since
(B) while
(C) by
(D) before

109 ------- for the first semester of the new school year will take place from July 6 to 8.

(A) Content
(B) Requirement
(C) Registration
(D) Procedure

110 The band Tiers couldn't rehearse for its performance at the Harrison Theater ------- a technical error.

(A) due to
(B) apart from
(C) such as
(D) but for

111 The promise of higher pay in urban areas ------- a labor shortage in rural parts of the country.

(A) were creating
(B) has created
(C) to create
(D) creating

112 A number of flights at Atlanta International Airport were ------- delayed following the sudden announcement of an approaching storm.

(A) alertly
(B) expertly
(C) carefully
(D) unexpectedly

113 Management would like the employees to work fewer hours yet ------- the same amount that they do now.

(A) produce
(B) produces
(C) produced
(D) will produce

114 To ensure maximum freshness, Gebita Catering's chef buys ingredients at a local market every morning instead of ------- in advance.

(A) order
(B) to order
(C) ordering
(D) orders

115 Verra Department Store is ------- known for selling discounted designer wear from previous seasons.

(A) widely
(B) wide
(C) wider
(D) widen

116 The CEO of Hayes Hotels is said to have an ------- net worth of $500 million.

(A) approximate
(B) approximately
(C) approximation
(D) approximating

117 ------- a driver's license in the state of Massachusetts, one must undergo an eye test once every 10 years.

(A) Maintains
(B) Has maintained
(C) To maintain
(D) Maintenance

118 ------- packing up all of the equipment, Mr. Kramer does not have much to do on the last day of the trade fair.

(A) As though
(B) Regarding
(C) Along with
(D) Except for

GO ON TO THE NEXT PAGE

119 Hartford University scholarship candidates are asked to submit ------- documents so that the committee responsible can properly evaluate their applications.

(A) agreeable
(B) cooperative
(C) supplemental
(D) respectable

120 Each week, Brushla's Web site summarizes for consumers the latest beauty trends ------- in today's major fashion magazines.

(A) highlighting
(B) highlight
(C) highlighted
(D) highlighter

121 While Ms. Brunson is away on leave, the position of ------- supervisor will be given to Mr. Hart.

(A) acting
(B) complete
(C) timely
(D) highest

122 If the virus had been found earlier, it ------- across the country.

(A) has not spread
(B) will not spread
(C) would not have spread
(D) did not spread

123 Ms. Martin's shop became profitable ------- to justify opening a second location.

(A) necessarily
(B) somehow
(C) most
(D) enough

124 According to the convention center's Web site, conference ------- will have an opportunity to ask questions at the end of each presentation.

(A) respondents
(B) commuters
(C) recipients
(D) participants

125 To resolve its financial issues, Gerber & Partners decided to decrease everyone's salaries ------- reducing the number of staff.

(A) as much as
(B) rather than
(C) by all means
(D) assuming that

126 Francis Woods praised the recycling program, ------- saved the company a large amount of money.

(A) which
(B) what
(C) who
(D) where

127 ------- for the Sacramento Film Prize will be invited to screen their movies on the last day of the festival.

(A) Finally
(B) Finale
(C) Finalists
(D) Finalize

128 At the shareholders' meeting next month, Jackson Solutions CEO Doug Stevenson will ------- the details of his expansion plan.

(A) conduct
(B) reveal
(C) prompt
(D) apply

129 Sarah Vasquez instructs staff members to periodically adopt ------- sales techniques so that they always have a new approach with customers.

(A) different
(B) differently
(C) differentiate
(D) differentiation

130 At last night's Leadership in Philanthropy gala, Connor Michaels ------- accepted an award for his contribution to environmental causes.

(A) frequently
(B) routinely
(C) closely
(D) gratefully

PART 6

Directions: In this part, you will be asked to read four English texts. Each text is missing a word, phrase, or sentence. Select the answer choice that correctly completes the text and mark the corresponding letter (A), (B), (C), or (D) on the answer sheet.

Questions 131-134 refer to the following Web page.

www.mandyashtonfashions.com/new

The summer collection from Mandy Ashton is still available online. However, quantities are limited. -------, customers should hurry if they want to pick up any remaining items.
131

For this collection, Mandy Ashton was inspired by the serene color combinations ------- found in the
132
waters of the South Pacific. -------. Mandy Ashton has always felt a connection with the waters and
133
islands of the South Pacific but is concerned about the threat of pollution. She believes that
protecting sensitive ------- is important. That's why Mandy Ashton Fashions will continue to donate
134
10 percent of all proceeds to cleanup efforts. You can support these efforts by shopping at Mandy
Ashton Fashions.

131 (A) Likewise
(B) Accordingly
(C) Besides
(D) Occasionally

132 (A) could be
(B) are being
(C) that are
(D) that will have been

133 (A) Items made from recycled materials are marked down.
(B) Some products are selling faster than we anticipated.
(C) Mandy Ashton Fashions partners with charitable groups.
(D) Each piece features calming green and blue tones.

134 (A) investments
(B) details
(C) environments
(D) textiles

GO ON TO THE NEXT PAGE

Questions 135-138 refer to the following information.

The following are instructions for the Ormevivi Cosmetics home peeling procedure. For the best results, do this procedure twice a week for oily skin and once a week for dry skin. Start by applying Agepro Massage Cream ------- to your face. Without rinsing off, add the ReViVi mask and let it sit for
135
three minutes. A slight stinging sensation is normal. -------. Next, wash your face with a cotton pad,
136
and then carefully ------- it. When this is done, you may want to apply moisturizer. We ------- a
137   138
water-based product. Ideally, you should try ReViVi Day Cream, which is sold separately.

135 (A) generous
(B) generously
(C) generosity
(D) generousness

136 (A) Therefore, you should inform us as soon
as possible.
(B) Sunlight can damage the top layer of skin
permanently.
(C) However, remove it immediately if you feel
any significant pain.
(D) Mixing them together will limit the mask's
effectiveness.

137 (A) drying
(B) dried
(C) will dry
(D) dry

138 (A) recommend
(B) include
(C) demonstrate
(D) direct

Questions 139-142 refer to the following e-mail.

From: Taylor Lim, Vice President <t.lim@corefinance.com>
To: All staff <staff@corefinance.com>
Date: November 2
Subject: Cybersecurity Issues
Attachment: Official Statement

Dear Staff,

Our system detected multiple ------- transactions. Upon further review, we learned that customers
were not even aware of these wire transfers. -------, our security team discovered potential security
issues with several accounts. For now, I've drafted an official public statement. ------- will explain the
situation and the measures the company is taking. Eventually, we will also have to notify all of our
clients via text message and e-mail. -------. Lastly, do not hesitate to contact security if you see
anything unusual yourself. Thank you for your cooperation.

Sincerely,
Taylor Lim

139 (A) personal
    (B) suspicious
    (C) international
    (D) identical

140 (A) Moreover
    (B) Instead
    (C) Except
    (D) Otherwise

141 (A) It
    (B) Both
    (C) They
    (D) Some

142 (A) This has been pointed out by some of our
        clients.
    (B) Some amounts were even above $1
        million.
    (C) Information will be posted on our Web site
        as well.
    (D) The team fully resolved this matter in a
        timely fashion.

GO ON TO THE NEXT PAGE

Questions 143-146 refer to the following article.

Own a Piece of Architectural History

One of ------- architect Chan-mi Gwon's early works has just been put up for sale. A perfect example
143
of her celebrated cubic style, this wooden, five-bedroom structure sits on a two-acre property on the
outskirts of Silverton. -------. Most of Ms. Gwon's residential buildings have become official landmarks
144
and are no longer under private ownership on account of their historical status and architectural
excellence. An auction will be held on August 27. Those interested in ------- are encouraged to
145
register before that date. The starting price is $12 million, but experts ------- the final price will rise
146
much higher.

143 (A) new
     (B) unknown
     (C) amateur
     (D) admired

144 (A) News of the sale has attracted great
         interest.
     (B) These were recently converted into
         museums.
     (C) It is located in the heart of the downtown
         area.
     (D) The figure will probably not discourage
         offers.

145 (A) bid
     (B) bids
     (C) to bid
     (D) bidding

146 (A) will expect
     (B) expect
     (C) had expected
     (D) expected

PART 7

Directions: In this part, you will be asked to read several texts, such as advertisements, articles, instant messages, or examples of business correspondence. Each text is followed by several questions. Select the best answer and mark the corresponding letter (A), (B), (C), or (D) on your answer sheet.

Questions 147-148 refer to the following advertisement.

Bothered by dry, dusty air? Troubled by allergies or asthma?
Keep your home or office comfortable with the EasyBreathe Cool Mist Humidifier!

Features:
- No noisy motors or fans
- No expensive filters to replace
- No heat or steam
- Easy to care for and clean
- Lightweight and compact—bring it everywhere you go
- Power-saving mode to keep your electricity bill low
- Sleek and stylish design that suits any room in the house

Buy the EasyBreathe Cool Mist Humidifier and enjoy the sensation of breathing in fresh, clean air all the time. You can order it online at www.easybreathe.com.

147 What is NOT listed as a feature of the product?

(A) Silent operation
(B) Portability
(C) Steam emission
(D) Energy efficiency

148 How can customers buy the product?

(A) By visiting a Web site
(B) By going to a store
(C) By calling a number
(D) By attending an event

GO ON TO THE NEXT PAGE

Questions 149-150 refer to the following notice.

Notice to All Doveport Apartment Complex Residents

In response to concerns from older residents, overnight alarm systems will now be activated in all common facilities aside from the lobby between 11 P.M. and 6 A.M. This includes the laundry room, the gym, and the pool.

During these times, your personal key code will not open the doors in these locations. Forcing them open will automatically trigger the security alarm. You will still have access to everywhere else, including your personal storage space. If you need special access to any of the restricted areas, please contact our security staff who will remain available around the clock. As a reminder, the main parking lot will remain closed until further notice while repairs are ongoing.

149 According to the notice, which facility will remain accessible between 11 P.M. and 6 A.M.?

(A) The fitness center
(B) The main parking lot
(C) The swimming pool
(D) The storage area

150 What is indicated about Doveport Apartment Complex?

(A) It recently opened.
(B) Its residents are mostly seniors.
(C) It does not allow pets.
(D) It offers 24-hour security.

Questions 151-152 refer to the following text message chain.

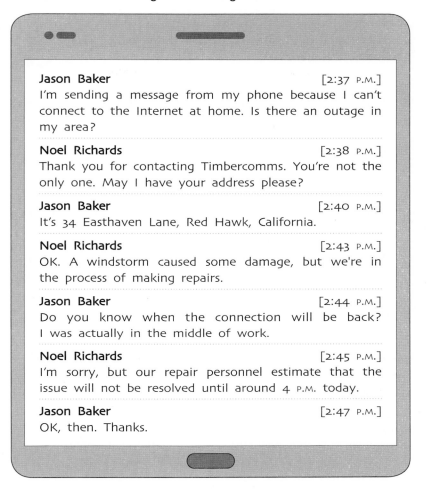

Jason Baker [2:37 P.M.]
I'm sending a message from my phone because I can't connect to the Internet at home. Is there an outage in my area?

Noel Richards [2:38 P.M.]
Thank you for contacting Timbercomms. You're not the only one. May I have your address please?

Jason Baker [2:40 P.M.]
It's 34 Easthaven Lane, Red Hawk, California.

Noel Richards [2:43 P.M.]
OK. A windstorm caused some damage, but we're in the process of making repairs.

Jason Baker [2:44 P.M.]
Do you know when the connection will be back? I was actually in the middle of work.

Noel Richards [2:45 P.M.]
I'm sorry, but our repair personnel estimate that the issue will not be resolved until around 4 P.M. today.

Jason Baker [2:47 P.M.]
OK, then. Thanks.

151 At 2:38 P.M., what does Mr. Richards mean when he writes, "You're not the only one"?

(A) Similar issues have been reported.
(B) It takes some time to register.
(C) Many people want to take part in a promotion.
(D) A number of homes were damaged.

152 What is true about Mr. Baker?

(A) He was working from home.
(B) He often has connection issues.
(C) He has decided to upgrade an Internet plan.
(D) He recently moved to a new location.

GO ON TO THE NEXT PAGE

Questions 153-154 refer to the following flyer.

**Oak Grove Farms Invites You to Join Us for Apple Picking
Sunday, October 21**

Admission $3. Children under 12 get in free. Pick your own apples—we provide baskets. Apples are $1 per pound—pick as many as you like! Free parking is available for all visitors.

After you've finished picking your apples, join us for lunch at our restaurant, the Red Kettle Café. The café is open from 11 A.M. to 3 P.M. and serves a wide variety of soups, sandwiches, and pies made from fresh-picked apples. A pie-making contest will take place at the café from 2 to 3 P.M.

Oak Grove Farms is also fun after dark! Our annual bonfire begins at 6:30 P.M. Hot apple cider will be served around the bonfire.

To get to Oak Grove Farms, take Interstate Highway 76 west and exit at Kenmar Avenue.

---

153 What is implied about Oak Grove Farms?

(A) It sells some of its items on a Web site.
(B) It uses its own products in its restaurant.
(C) It grows a variety of fruits throughout the year.
(D) It charges reduced entry fees for children.

154 What will happen on the evening of October 21?

(A) A buffet dinner
(B) An outdoor fire
(C) Apple picking
(D) Pie making

Unity Nail Salon
Frequent Customer Program

We know that many of our customers enjoy coming to Unity Nail Salon regularly for their salon services. That's why we're proud to offer a discount program for our most frequent customers.

The program includes the following benefits:
- Purchase 10 manicures or pedicures and get the 11th one free. Keep track of your purchases using our discount card.
- Get 10 percent off your total bill when you use any salon service as a group. This offer is available to groups of four or more.
- Get coupons for $5 off when you use more than three services in a month. These coupons can be used for any salon service or product.

* Remember to have your discount card stamped whenever you pay for a service. Coupons and discounts cannot be combined, and customers may use only one discount offer per service.

155 The word "benefits" in paragraph 2, line 1, is closest in meaning to

(A) payments
(B) accounts
(C) advantages
(D) events

156 What is true about Unity Nail Salon's customer program?

(A) It is offered at more than one location.
(B) It is limited to a specific set of services.
(C) It is expiring at the end of the month.
(D) It is packaged for both individuals and groups.

157 What are customers reminded to do?

(A) Book appointments in advance
(B) Schedule weekly services
(C) Combine several discounts
(D) Get a discount card stamped

Wickford Public Library

Changing Hours of Operation

The Wickford Public Library is changing its daily hours of operation to accommodate changes in the public's visiting habits. These changes will allow the library to reduce its operating costs and to devote more resources to the maintenance of its collection of publications.

Beginning on November 3, the following schedule will take effect:
Monday to Wednesday, 9 A.M. to 7 P.M.
Thursday and Friday, 9 A.M. to 6 P.M.
Saturdays and Sundays, 9 A.M. to 4 P.M.

Please note that on weekends, the main desk closes at 2 P.M., and so librarian services will not be available from that time until closing. Patrons may continue to use other building facilities, but they will not be able to check out any books. Furthermore, all library patrons must exit the building by 4 P.M. Some library employees will remain on-site to remind patrons about closing times and to offer other forms of assistance.

For patrons who need additional library services, Bridgestead Library is open from 8 A.M. to 8 P.M. daily.

---

158 What is true about the Wickford Public Library?

(A) It will close earlier on the weekends.
(B) It is renovating a section of the building.
(C) It changed hours on the suggestion of patrons.
(D) It will be replacing its computer system.

159 What will happen at 2 P.M. on the weekends?

(A) Librarian services resume for the afternoon.
(B) Patrons are required to exit the building.
(C) Returned books are considered late.
(D) Checkout services are halted for the day.

160 What should patrons do if they need additional services?

(A) Contact the head librarian
(B) Visit a different library
(C) Make a special appointment
(D) Go to a library's Web site

Sky-High Hot-air Balloons Offer the Ride of Your Life

Ever dreamed of floating through the clouds on an exciting hot-air balloon ride? — [1] —. Make your dream a reality with Sky-High Hot-air Balloons!

- Create memories with your family or friends
- Enjoy a romantic ride with your spouse or partner
- Provide a unique thank-you to your most valued clients

No matter what you're celebrating, Sky-High Hot-air Balloons provides an exciting and unforgettable ride. We offer special dining-and-photography packages for anniversaries, marriage proposals, and more. — [2] —. Want to share a special picnic in the clouds or have professional photos taken of your ride? We'll take care of everything!

You can be sure Sky-High is an established business with a trusted name. *East Metro Weekly* recently listed Sky-High Hot-air Balloons as one of the top five providers of recreational activities in the Somerville area for the 10th year in a row. We've been in business for more than 15 years and follow all safety protocols. — [3] —.

To learn more about prices or to book a ride, call our booking coordinator at 555-3928. — [4] —. Special rates are available for groups.

---

161 What is offered by Sky-High Hot-air Balloons?

(A) Packages for special events
(B) Discounts at partner restaurants
(C) Free commemorative videos
(D) Group pricing for companies

162 What is NOT true about Sky-High Hot-air Balloons?

(A) It has been open for over 15 years.
(B) It is well-regarded in the community.
(C) It takes reservations over the phone.
(D) It publishes a newsletter for its customers.

163 In which of the positions marked [1], [2], [3], and [4] does the following sentence best belong?

"As a result, Sky-High has never had an accident in its entire history."

(A) [1]
(B) [2]
(C) [3]
(D) [4]

Questions 164-167 refer to the following article.

May 15—In recent years, people have become increasingly aware of what they consume. In Chicago alone, dozens of restaurants have opened that specifically serve organic and healthy foods, while thousands of others have expanded their menus to satisfy health-conscious diners.

As a result of this trend, many healthy food products have become more difficult to buy. The average prices of certain fruits and vegetables have more than doubled in the last decade. In addition, access to healthy produce has become a luxury available mostly in upscale urban areas or in rural areas where people maintain gardens. In between these places are food deserts, where there is no grocery store or farmers' market within walking distance of most houses. In areas like these, people are forced to buy packaged food from convenience stores.

Thankfully, things are changing in the Chicago area. The city council passed a bill last month that requires convenience stores to carry fresh fruits and vegetables. These ingredients have to make up at least 20 percent of the store's inventory. Moreover, Mayor Ellison has pledged to organize 30 more farmers' markets around the city to improve accessibility. Even supermarket chain Lovell Stores is doing its part. It has reduced costs by obtaining more produce locally and now offers promotions in its stores. All together, these measures should make healthy food cheaper and more accessible to the buying public.

164 What is the article mostly about?

(A) The availability of healthy food choices
(B) Tax incentives for area businesses
(C) The food intake of local students
(D) Newly established neighborhood zoning laws

165 What is mentioned about upscale urban neighborhoods?

(A) They are a major environmental concern.
(B) They experience rising crime rates.
(C) They provide access to produce.
(D) They attract the best restaurants.

166 The word "chain" in paragraph 3, line 4, is closest in meaning to

(A) cable
(B) group
(C) structure
(D) sequence

167 What can be inferred about Lovell Stores?

(A) It was acquired by a larger company.
(B) It will open new stores in Chicago.
(C) It made its products more affordable.
(D) It plans to sponsor a weekly farmers market.

Questions 168-171 refer to the following e-mail.

To: Cordelia Bryant <cordeliabryant@bernstein.com>
From: Madison Stanley <maddiestanley@mymail.com>
Subject: Items
Date: April 3
Attachments: 2 images

Hi, Ms. Bryant. I'm reaching out because of a problem with my recent order from Bernstein Furniture. — [1] —.

I ordered a sofa and two chairs on March 17. The items arrived as scheduled on April 2. Unfortunately, I was not at home, so I wasn't able to inspect them. — [2] —. My husband accepted the delivery and had the items placed inside the house.

When I got home, I immediately noticed a large stain on the left side of the sofa. One of the chairs also showed signs of water damage. I think perhaps the items were exposed to some sort of moisture during transit. — [3] —.

I'd like to arrange to have these items replaced as soon as possible. I have attached photos of the items to this e-mail for your review. — [4] —. We'll be traveling between May 1 and June 15, so it's essential that the damaged items are removed and the new ones delivered before our departure.

Please let me know when I can expect the new delivery.

Regards,

Madison Stanley

---

168 What kind of business does Ms. Bryant most likely work for?

(A) A furniture retailer
(B) A storage facility
(C) A moving company
(D) A cleaning agency

169 What is indicated about Ms. Stanley's items?

(A) They were delivered late.
(B) They arrived damaged.
(C) They are the wrong color.
(D) They showed signs of use.

170 What does Ms. Stanley request that Ms. Bryant do?

(A) Acknowledge receipt of some photos
(B) Pick up some items before May 1
(C) Pay for a refund with a company check
(D) Schedule a repair as soon as possible

171 In which of the positions marked [1], [2], [3], and [4] does the following sentence best belong?

"As you may know, there was heavy rain on April 1."

(A) [1]
(B) [2]
(C) [3]
(D) [4]

GO ON TO THE NEXT PAGE

Questions 172-175 refer to the following online chat discussion.

Gilbert Cassidy [8:47 A.M.]	Good morning, Catherine and Marc! I wanted to check on the progress we've made with the Landmax project in Greenville so far.
Catherine Sherrill [8:49 A.M.]	Hi, Gilbert! We're moving forward as planned. The town council has reviewed our blueprints and approved our proposal to build townhouses on the property we're buying.
Gilbert Cassidy [8:50 A.M.]	That's great news! What about you, Marc? Are you ready to supervise your first project?
Marc Hernandez [8:51 A.M.]	Yes, absolutely. I've been going over the schedule of construction with our contractor. He's ready to begin the work whenever we are.
Gilbert Cassidy [8:53 A.M.]	Excellent. And when exactly do you think construction can begin?
Catherine Sherrill [8:55 A.M.]	I know that is Marc's area, but, if I may say something first, we can't begin until after the sale of the property has been finalized. I spoke to the owner on Monday, and she expects it to be done by February 28.
Gilbert Cassidy [8:58 A.M.]	OK. Can you remind me what the estimated construction time will be?
Marc Hernandez [9:00 A.M.]	The contractor and I have agreed that the project will take 9 to 10 months to finish, which means all of the townhouses should be ready for occupancy by January of next year.
Gilbert Cassidy [9:03 A.M.]	Good. Please keep me updated. Once construction starts, the sales team can begin selling individual townhouses to buyers.

	Send

172 In which industry do the writers most likely work?

(A) Construction
(B) Advertising
(C) Retail
(D) Accounting

173 At 8:55 A.M., what does Ms. Sherrill mean when she writes, "I know that is Marc's area"?

(A) She gave an assignment to Marc.
(B) She is not in charge of a schedule.
(C) She would like Marc to answer a question.
(D) She needs Marc's permission to complete a task.

174 Who did Ms. Sherrill speak to about a project?

(A) A client
(B) A council head
(C) A property owner
(D) A lead contractor

175 What is expected to happen in the following year?

(A) Plans for new projects will be proposed.
(B) Sales teams will begin selling properties.
(C) Residences will be available to move into.
(D) Monthly payments to a bank will end.

GO ON TO THE NEXT PAGE

Get in Tune at Harmony World

Starting a band? Need an instrument for school? Or have you always just wanted to learn how to play music? Come to Harmony World today, and get in tune with your musical side.

Harmony World is Washington County's largest music store. We carry a wide variety of musical instruments. Buy new instruments from the world's leading brands or trade in your old gear for credit toward your new purchase. We also offer affordable equipment rentals and repair services. Go to www.harmonyworld.com today to browse our complete line of products and services.

On weekdays, we hold one-on-one lessons in guitar, piano, and drums at one of three private, on-site studios. Our instructors are trained musicians who have all played professionally. They cater to every skill level from beginner to advanced. To sign up for lessons, visit the "Lessons" page on our Web site.

If you buy over $50 in merchandise from our store, you will receive a free copy of *Music Master*. This book contains a variety of lessons that are sure to help you become a proficient musician.

Harmony World
102 Conner Street
Fayetteville, AK 72701
Tel. 555-1091

	Product	Price
1	Harding Electric Guitar	$239.99
2	Guitar pick	$2.99
3	Metronome	$17.99
4	Harding miniature amplifier	$32.99
	SUBTOTAL	$293.96
	Store credit	$44.10
	Sales tax (6.5%)	$16.24
	TOTAL	$266.10

PAYMENT: SHARP CREDIT CARD
CUSTOMER NAME: Kelsey Usher
XXXX-XXXX-XXXX-1241

All sales are considered final. Requests for refunds will not be accepted. However, customers may exchange items for something of equal or lesser value. For further assistance, please call us at 555-2109 during normal work hours, Monday to Friday.

176 What can people do on Harmony World's Web site?

(A) Sign up for a newsletter
(B) Find rental equipment
(C) Download music collections
(D) Chat with customer service

177 What is mentioned about the lessons?

(A) They are only for people with advanced skills.
(B) They take place on the weekends.
(C) They are designed for groups.
(D) They are given by experienced professionals.

178 What is probably true about Harmony World?

(A) It could not repair a guitar.
(B) It accepted Ms. Usher's trade-in offer.
(C) It refunded a rental fee.
(D) It provided Ms. Usher with a discount.

179 What will Ms. Usher receive?

(A) A complimentary accessory
(B) A gift card for future purchases
(C) An instructional publication
(D) An extended warranty

180 What information is NOT included in the receipt?

(A) The business hours during holidays
(B) The store's contact information
(C) The user's payment method
(D) The official return policy

GO ON TO THE NEXT PAGE

Questions 181-185 refer to the following letter and e-mail.

THE RADCLIFFE HOTEL

Sam Cohen
120 Millville Road
London, N1 3LJ

August 4

Dear Mr. Cohen,

Thank you for booking a room at the Radcliffe Hotel in Oxford. This confirms your three-night stay from September 9 to 11. We are delighted to have you with us.

Your room comes equipped with a minibar, a television, and free Wi-Fi. The television has over 500 channels offering a variety of news and entertainment options, as well as information about the hotel.

For your convenience, the hotel has a restaurant on the first floor serving contemporary international cuisine as well as a café where you may enjoy your daily complimentary breakfast. Breakfast is served each day from 6 to 10 A.M. You can also order room service 24 hours a day. A pool is located on the second floor and a gym on the third. You can access both with your room keycard. They are open from 6 A.M. to 8 P.M.

Sincerely,

The Guest Services Team
The Radcliffe Hotel
Oxford, England

TO: Staff <staff@radcliffehotel.com>
FROM: Sam Cohen <s.cohen@unimail.com>
SUBJECT: Problem
DATE: September 12

To Whom It May Concern:

My name is Sam Cohen, and I was a recent guest at your hotel. I attended an urban planning conference that took place on the fourth floor. I can't recall my exact room number, but I was right next to the pool.

I'm writing because I left my athletic shoes at the gym. I planned to retrieve them before checking out, but I found myself running late for the airport shuttle. I tried informing your employee on the bus, but he advised me to contact you by e-mail.

If you find the shoes, please mail them back to my registered home address. I am happy to pay for expedited shipping to get them back as soon as possible. Thank you, and I look forward to staying at your hotel again in the future!

Best regards,

Sam Cohen

181　Why was the letter written?

(A) To extend an offer
(B) To solicit some business
(C) To answer a request
(D) To confirm a booking

182　Why was Mr. Cohen staying at the hotel?

(A) He was taking part in a convention.
(B) He was invited to a social event.
(C) He was visiting a branch office.
(D) He was taking time off from work.

183　On which floor was Mr. Cohen's room located?

(A) The first floor
(B) The second floor
(C) The third floor
(D) The fourth floor

184　What did Mr. Cohen leave behind?

(A) A swimsuit
(B) Footwear
(C) Writing material
(D) A file

185　What can be inferred about the Radcliffe Hotel?

(A) It offers a special price for three-night stays.
(B) It has security cameras in public areas.
(C) It has a lost-and-found department.
(D) It provides guests with airport transportation.

GO ON TO THE NEXT PAGE

Questions 186-190 refer to the following Web page, customer review, and e-mail.

Brownwood Vineyards

www.brownwoodvineyardsnapa.com/groups

Group packages
Available Tuesday through Sunday

Brownwood Vineyards is the prime location for wine tastings in Napa. Enjoy exquisite wines such as our Malbec, Merlot, and Cabernet Sauvignon. We also have an award-winning white wine, our Chardonnay, that is the only white wine in our tastings. Tour our winemaking operation, and enjoy the beautiful scenery with one of the following group packages.

- Standard
  Three wines paired with snacks, $60 per person
- Extra
  Five wines paired with three-course meal, $120 per person
- Premium
  Five wines paired with five-course meal, $170 per person
- Platinum
  Unlimited tastings paired with seven-course meal and a grape-pressing experience, $300 per person

Contact groups@brownwoodvineyardsnapa.com for availability and booking.

Napa Winery Reviews

www.napawineryreviews.com/brownwoodvineyards

Name: Kenichi Yamamoto

Date of Visit: June 2

Rating: ★★★★★

Review: I booked a group package for a team outing. Winery employees picked us up from our hotel and took us to their beautiful property, where we enjoyed their selection of wines alongside delicious meals prepared by the chef. One of the highlights was definitely the grape-pressing activity. Everyone had a lot of fun doing that. If I had one complaint, it would be that the van we took was uncomfortable. Still, I would give the whole experience 5 out of 5 stars.

To: Kenichi Yamamoto <k.yamamoto@stansonlink.com>
From: Brenda Meyers <b.meyers@stansonlink.com>
Date: June 3
Subject: Thank you

Kenichi,

Thank you again for arranging our trip. It's a shame that I have to return to the head office in Chicago so soon. I have some urgent business to attend to. Anyway, it was delightful to meet you and share the experience with the rest of the team at Stanson Link's San Francisco office. I was highly impressed with your organization skills and will make a note of that in the report that I submit to management about my trip.

Could I ask you for a small favor? I'd like to order a few cases of the white wine we tasted. I think it would make an excellent gift for our clients.

Thank you,

Brenda Meyers
Stanson Link

---

186 What is NOT true about Brownwood Vineyards?

(A) It is open every day for tours.
(B) It charges for packages by the person.
(C) It provides food with every tasting.
(D) It won an award for one of its wines.

187 Which package did Mr. Yamamoto most likely book?

(A) Standard
(B) Extra
(C) Premium
(D) Platinum

188 What did Mr. Yamamoto like least about his visit to Brownwood Vineyards?

(A) The friendliness of the guide
(B) The taste of some meals
(C) The transportation service
(D) The value of the package tour

189 What does Ms. Meyers suggest about Stanson Link?

(A) It is promoting an executive.
(B) It is being reorganized soon.
(C) It has offices in two cities.
(D) It has scheduled a video meeting.

190 What can be inferred about Ms. Meyers?

(A) She wants to give the Chardonnay as a gift.
(B) She brought more guests than originally planned.
(C) She will be returning to the winery soon.
(D) She has expert knowledge of wines.

GO ON TO THE NEXT PAGE

Questions 191-195 refer to the following e-mails and order confirmation.

To: Jeffrey Bolton <jeffrey@cholawservices.com>
From: Office Market <info@officemarketstore.net>
Date: May 3
Subject: Promotion

Dear Mr. Bolton,

Because you are a member of our loyalty program, we would like to offer you a special promotion. You can get your office supplies at a 30 percent discount. This is a limited time deal, so take advantage while supplies last. All items are currently on sale because we need to make room for new merchandise.

You may go to www.officemarketstore.net to shop for items in stock now. The Web site is continuously updated, so if an item is not listed, that means it has sold out. Customers who purchase items on May 7 will also be provided with a complimentary box of memo pads.

As always, standard shipping is free, and you can expect delivery within five to seven business days. Expedited, two-day shipping is available for an extra fee based on distance.

Thank you for your business,

Your Office Market Team

To: Jeffrey Bolton <jeffrey@cholawservices.com>
From: Angela Mercer <angela@cholawservices.com>
Date: May 7
Subject: Order

Jeffrey,

Thanks for telling me about the Office Market sale. Here's the list of items we need for our department. I restocked everything else earlier this year from Office Barn. Note that only the paper is urgent. The rest isn't critical but would be great to buy at a discount with the sale. I tried to look for printer ink too, but I couldn't find it on the Web site, so we may have to buy it elsewhere. Please order the items below from Office Market tomorrow. Thanks again!

- 20 boxes of standard paper
- 10 boxes of premium paper
- 1,000 large envelopes
- 10 Pens

Angela Mercer
Cho Law Services

Thank you for your order
www.officemarketstore.net

Customer Name: Jeffrey Bolton
Member Account Number: 3774-2201
Order Number: F838-32
Order Date: May 8
Payment Method: Credit Card

Item	Item Number	Price	Quantity	Total
Standard paper	88291	$30 per box	20	$600
Premium paper	88242	$50 per box	10	$500
Envelopes large	83210	$0.03 per piece	1,000	$30
Pens	72919	$1 per pack	10	$10
* Prices above include 30% discount			Subtotal	$1,140
			Shipping	$50
			Total	$1,190

If items are missing from your order, please contact us immediately at orders@officemarketstore.net or through our 24-hour customer service hotline at 555-3083.

191 What is the purpose of the first e-mail?

(A) To introduce an online store
(B) To explain an offer to a customer
(C) To announce new opening times
(D) To inform about changes with a supplier

192 What is Office Market in the process of doing?

(A) Renovating a store location
(B) Replacing a payment system
(C) Merging with a competitor
(D) Disposing of old stock

193 What is stated about Ms. Mercer?

(A) She purchased some items earlier.
(B) She is in charge of the sales department.
(C) She urgently needs some envelopes.
(D) She prefers to shop at Office Barn.

194 Why most likely was Ms. Mercer unable to find printer ink?

(A) It is handled by a different department.
(B) It was sold out on a Web site.
(C) It was not included in an offer.
(D) It is no longer manufactured.

195 What is indicated about Mr. Bolton's order?

(A) It will be shipped from overseas.
(B) It includes items no longer in inventory.
(C) It met the store's deadline for a free gift.
(D) It will be delivered in two days.

GO ON TO THE NEXT PAGE

Bibliography

Below is a list of books by author Martha Nelson. All are available to download in audio format on www.victarpublishing.com.

Telling Stories

In the author's autobiography, she writes a love letter to her hometown of Boston.

Boston Guards

Boston Detective Dolores Sanchez is on a quest to solve a crime in this suspenseful thriller.

Sanchez Strong

In the sequel to *Boston Guards*, Detective Sanchez is on an international assignment in Spain.

Before the Sun Sets

This romance novel centers on Maria, a dying woman with a final wish.

Upcoming novels from Victar Publishing

Dolores Rising

The third and final book of the series that started with *Boston Guards*. Back home, Dolores confronts an old enemy.

Short Stories

Previously unpublished stories are gathered in one collection.

To: Jackie Dennett <j.dennet@bookscafe.com>
From: Ming Oh <ming@ohliteraryagency.com>
Date: August 14
Subject: Book release

Hi Jackie,

I just want to double-check on preparations for the event at Books Café. Ms. Nelson has agreed to participate in a book-signing session provided you can keep the event well organized. Due to her popularity, she tends to attract large crowds and we have had some unfortunate incidents at past events held in small venues. You will need to make sure that you can accommodate at least a thousand visitors. If that isn't possible, we will have to rent a different location.

Let me know, as I am currently wrapping up all of her promotional activities.

Sincerely,

Ming Oh

Boston Central Newspaper

Martha Nelson's Homecoming

September 9—Internationally acclaimed author Martha Nelson came home yesterday to celebrate the release of the third book in her famous detective series, which critics have given rave reviews. First-week sales projections are already on track to surpass its predecessor. Ms. Nelson's popularity was evident at her book signing event, held yesterday at the Boston Star Theater. The signing of her newest book attracted almost 5,000 people. A few visitors were also lucky enough to witness a spontaneous reading by the author that ended in loud applause.

196 What is NOT indicated about Ms. Nelson's works?

(A) They have been recognized with awards.
(B) One of them is about Ms. Nelson's life.
(C) They have been released as audio versions.
(D) Some of them have not been printed yet.

197 What most likely is Mr. Oh responsible for?

(A) Proofreading literary work
(B) Providing legal advice
(C) Organizing promotional events
(D) Handling an author's finances

198 What can be inferred about Ms. Nelson?

(A) She signed copies of *Dolores Rising*.
(B) She is moving back to Boston.
(C) She has a 10-book deal with Victar Publishing.
(D) She has not released any work internationally.

199 Why most likely did Ms. Nelson hold an event at the Boston Star Theater?

(A) It was the closest venue to her hotel.
(B) Her book is being made into a movie.
(C) It was featured in one of her stories.
(D) Books Café would have been too small.

200 According to the article, what is predicted about Ms. Nelson's latest book in her detective series?

(A) It will be turned into a feature film.
(B) It will sell 5,000 copies in the first week.
(C) It will be at least as popular as her previous book.
(D) It will probably lead to a fourth book.

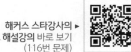

해커스 스타강사의 ▶
무료 해설강의 바로 보기
(116번 문제)

READING TEST

In this section, you must demonstrate your ability to read and comprehend English. You will be given a variety of texts and asked to answer questions about these texts. This section is divided into three parts and will take 75 minutes to complete.

Do not mark the answers in your test book. Use the answer sheet that is separately provided.

PART 5

Directions: In each question, you will be asked to review a statement that is missing a word or phrase. Four answer choices will be provided for each statement. Select the best answer and mark the corresponding letter (A), (B), (C), or (D) on the answer sheet.

101 Many of the team's members were in disagreement about the design concept which the entire project was based -------.

(A) to   (B) in
(C) at   (D) on

102 Despite being a new business, the company has been closely ------- with all client projects, earning it an excellent reputation.

(A) involves   (B) involving
(C) involved   (D) involve

103 During the meeting, one of the board members questioned the firm's intentions ------- overseas investment initiatives.

(A) with respect to   (B) across from
(C) by means of   (D) next to

104 A few speakers experienced traffic delays on the way to the conference, ------- all made it there in time for the opening presentation.

(A) for   (B) but
(C) or   (D) so

105 The car's engine will have to be ------- before mechanics can properly diagnose the source of the problem.

(A) inaugurated   (B) lessened
(C) taken apart   (D) turned up

106 Even though other firms started outsourcing manufacturing overseas, Herdigen remained -------, making all of its products domestically.

(A) locality   (B) local
(C) locals   (D) location

107 Organizers of the trade exhibition were happy to learn that several successful deals ------- by the event participants.

(A) have concluded
(B) conclude
(C) were concluded
(D) are concluded

108 Should anything out of the ordinary ------- in the office facilities, employees must immediately dial building security.

(A) happen
(B) happens
(C) happened
(D) happening

109 The new model will be launched ------- the end of year.

(A) into
(B) on
(C) through
(D) around

110 The furniture items are specially ------- to make them easier to ship in compact boxes.

(A) diminished
(B) committed
(C) redeemed
(D) crafted

111 Mr. Jenkins was compelled ------- a meeting of all of his employees after noticing they made a number of careless accounting mistakes.

(A) to call
(B) calling
(C) call
(D) calls

112 The ------- position will be filled next week by an intern joining the information technology department for the summer.

(A) vacant
(B) enhanced
(C) agreeable
(D) selective

113 The fire department ordered tenants of Pillar Towers to evacuate the structure shortly after a potentially harmful gas ------- was reported.

(A) damage
(B) repair
(C) barrier
(D) leak

114 If initial tests conducted by two separate laboratories return ------- results, the researchers will have to seek out a third provider.

(A) contradictory
(B) contradict
(C) contradicts
(D) contradiction

115 Government officials were unsure of ------- the scope and risks associated with such a large residential development project.

(A) either
(B) each
(C) both
(D) whether

116 The recently constructed terminal for ------- passengers at Carson International Airport is expected to open to the public on May 31.

(A) arrive
(B) arrived
(C) arriving
(D) arrival

117 The local news has issued a severe weather warning ------- the entire county and recommended staying off the roads.

(A) upon
(B) inside
(C) throughout
(D) above

118 The head of the machine maintenance department noticed that the engine needed replacement of vital ------- to function properly.

(A) part
(B) parts
(C) partial
(D) parted

GO ON TO THE NEXT PAGE

119 The professor said many bosses find it difficult to deal with employees ------- and to not let personal opinions interfere with decisions.

(A) conditionally   (B) objectively
(C) compassionately   (D) approvingly

120 The firm will be able to increase ------- by 50 percent as soon as its new factories are completed.

(A) product   (B) produce
(C) productive   (D) production

121 Derry Milk hopes that its newly redesigned packaging will make its products more easily ------- on store shelves.

(A) fashionable   (B) compatible
(C) recognizable   (D) preferable

122 The budget committee approved the project proposal, allowing for enough time to ------- allocate appropriate human resources.

(A) reason   (B) reasoning
(C) reasonably   (D) reasonable

123 Many customers have been unwilling to switch to Beat Cellular ------- some attractive promotional offers.

(A) despite   (B) therefore
(C) conversely   (D) accordingly

124 Signal Inn employs a team of inspectors who check on the ------- of every one of the hotel chain's rooms and facilities.

(A) relevance   (B) elimination
(C) condition   (D) concentration

125 Mr. Anderson left KPI for Thornwoode because he wanted to work for a company that was ------- aligned with his values and aspirations.

(A) closer   (B) less close
(C) more closely   (D) close

126 Mr. Bloom's hectic schedule ------- allows him time to have in-depth one-on-one conversations with his team members.

(A) frequently   (B) rarely
(C) consistently   (D) typically

127 GMT's top executives are expected to ------- further updates on its merger with Hawkland Electric in the coming weeks.

(A) inform   (B) release
(C) exhibit   (D) propose

128 The city council quickly approved legislation that would improve ------- to public buildings for those in wheelchairs.

(A) operation   (B) capability
(C) evaluation   (D) accessibility

129 Moda-Lita has several openings for ------- wishing to work with a team of dedicated and passionate designers hoping to bring new perspectives to the industry.

(A) who   (B) its
(C) that   (D) those

130 The banquet tomorrow evening is ------- for members of the Ravenport Country Club, so invitations must be presented before entry is permitted.

(A) supremely   (B) debatably
(C) strictly   (D) widely

정답·해설·해석 p.217 / [별책] 토익 RC 필수 어휘 p.60

PART 6

Directions: In this part, you will be asked to read four English texts. Each text is missing a word, phrase, or sentence. Select the answer choice that correctly completes the text and mark the corresponding letter (A), (B), (C), or (D) on the answer sheet.

Questions 131-134 refer to the following advertisement.

Are you an avid reader? Then try the new ShockRead mobile e-reader! Perfect for readers on the go, it can be taken almost anywhere and runs for 20 hours on a single charge. It ------- offers incredible
131
convenience.

In addition, ShockRead has a substantial 20 gigabytes of storage. So you need not worry if your digital library is -------. And if you don't feel like reading, ShockRead can turn any book into an audio
132
book at the touch of a button. -------.
133

Buy ShockRead online from July 10. Enjoy a 10 percent discount if you visit www.shockread.com and order it a week -------.
134

131 (A) truly
(B) lastly
(C) originally
(D) rarely

132 (A) affordable
(B) adjustable
(C) simplistic
(D) extensive

133 (A) The space will allow you to download thousands of books.
(B) Some readers do not know what books are in their collection.
(C) The shopping service is available only in select locations.
(D) You can select from several natural voices and speeds.

134 (A) anytime
(B) beforehand
(C) lately
(D) instantly

GO ON TO THE NEXT PAGE

Questions 135-138 refer to the following letter.

Brad Warren
6809 Harvest Rd.
Boulder, CO 80301

Dear Mr. Warren,

When we spoke on the phone, you said that you are planning to open a restaurant in downtown Boulder. I ------- the ideal location for your new business. Not only ------- your size requirements, but it's also within your price range.
    135   136

You should be aware of one condition, however. -------. I know that there is risk involved with these kinds of long-term leases, but he is willing to rent the place out rather cheaply. He's asking for about
                                              137
15 percent less than I expected.

Let me know if you are interested in ------- this property this week. If not, I've come up with a few
                                     138
other alternatives that I can share with you instead. Please call me at (303) 555-9276.

Sincerely,

Hillary Evans
City Realtors

135 (A) have found
    (B) will find
    (C) had found
    (D) finding

136 (A) to be met
    (B) does it meet
    (C) be meeting
    (D) does meet

137 (A) The owner is looking for a tenant who can stay at least five years.
    (B) Construction has already gotten underway on certain sections.
    (C) The building did not pass its most recent safety inspection.
    (D) I'm afraid it is somewhat smaller than what you hoped for.

138 (A) viewing
    (B) designing
    (C) showing
    (D) selling

Questions 139-142 refer to the following notice.

Notice to All Cheswick Towers Residents

A number of you have contacted the management office ------- unusually high gas bills. After
conducting a thorough inspection, we have found that many of the meters are -------. They are not
accurately measuring the amount of gas used each month because they are getting old. Therefore,
we have arranged for the meter in each apartment to be replaced. -------. This should solve the
problem and ensure that you are billed correctly in the future.

In addition, those of you who have overpaid will be reimbursed. The exact amount that will be
returned to you will appear on your billing statement next month.

We apologize for ------- this has caused you.

139 (A) between
(B) concerning
(C) except
(D) during

140 (A) absent
(B) defective
(C) hazardous
(D) complex

141 (A) There are things you can do to use less
energy.
(B) The cost of electricity has been
decreasing lately.
(C) You will no longer receive paper billing
statements.
(D) The work will be carried out sometime
next week.

142 (A) any inconveniences
(B) more inconvenient
(C) very inconveniently
(D) too inconvenient

GO ON TO THE NEXT PAGE

Questions 143-146 refer to the following article.

A New Leader in Beverages

Fizz Devil has taken the lead in the beverage manufacturing sector, ------- a Regalia Research report
released on Thursday.
143

Researchers at Regalia remark that Fizz Devil has successfully distinguished itself from competitors.
Responding to a ------- in the beverage industry, Fizz Devil modified its products. Marketing chief
144
Andrea Thompson stated, "We identified a new pattern in people's drink preferences. -------. We then
145
used this to develop a line of healthy bottled drinks."

The products can be found in stores across the country. The line ------- drinks with names like
146
Homerun Thirst and Yoga Refresh.

143 (A) counting on
     (B) according to
     (C) apart from
     (D) along with

144 (A) source
     (B) trend
     (C) decline
     (D) control

145 (A) They hoped to buy bottled water that is
         purer than tap water.
     (B) They preferred carbonated drinks over
         fruit juices.
     (C) They were seeking better alternatives to
         sugary soft drinks.
     (D) They wanted manufacturers to produce
         drinks in smaller bottles.

146 (A) features
     (B) featured
     (C) featuring
     (D) will feature

PART 7

Directions: In this part, you will be asked to read several texts, such as advertisements, articles, instant messages, or examples of business correspondence. Each text is followed by several questions. Select the best answer and mark the corresponding letter (A), (B), (C), or (D) on your answer sheet.

Questions 147-148 refer to the following flyer.

Carbury Plumbing
Plumbing & Drain Services

With more than 20 years of experience in the business, our plumbing specialists are truly the best!

We offer a number of specialized services to address any of your plumbing needs, including:

✓ Clog and leak repairs
✓ Sink renovations
✓ Water filter installations
✓ Boiler replacements
✓ Water pump repairs
✓ ... And so much more!

Bring in this flyer to receive a free consultation and 10 percent off your first visit from one of our specialists.
Note that this promotion cannot be combined with other offers.

Carbury Plumbing
22 Pewter Drive
Albuquerque, NM 87111
555-8829

147 What is the purpose of the flyer?

(A) To promote a limited-time offer
(B) To announce office plumbing work
(C) To recruit for new plumbers
(D) To advertise various services

148 What is mentioned about Carbury Plumbing's specialists?

(A) They have three decades of experience.
(B) They can fix broken water heaters.
(C) They specialize in bathroom remodeling.
(D) They have a promotion on their Web site.

GO ON TO THE NEXT PAGE

Questions 149-150 refer to the following invoice.

Arbinton Landscaping

INVOICE

37 Cauliflower Way
Dallas, TX 75201
Phone: 555-9273
Fax: 555-9274
www.arbintonland.com

Today's Date	July 6
Invoice Number	347528
Customer ID	893A
Due Date	July 31

Bill To

Mr. Cameron Reynolds
Poindexter Pharmaceuticals
500 Emory Avenue
Dallas, TX 75221
555-6723

Description	Amount
Service fee: garden design	$ 230.00
Labor charge: 18 hours at $20 per hour	$ 360.00
Subtotal	$ 590.00

Comments

1. Please include the invoice number on your check.
2. *Charge was added to correct a pricing error for an item on the June 6 invoice.

Tax at 4.5%	$ 26.55
*Other	$ 75.50
Total	**$ 692.05**

Make all checks payable to:
Arbinton Landscaping

If you have any questions, please contact:
Mark Devers, 555-2268, m_devers@arbintonland.com
We appreciate your business!

149 What should Mr. Reynolds do by July 31?

(A) Confirm his customer identification number
(B) Contact Arbinton for a new invoice
(C) Inquire about additional charges
(D) Pay the total invoice amount

150 What is NOT indicated on the invoice?

(A) Design fees were charged by the hour.
(B) Tax was added to the total amount.
(C) Mr. Devers can be called with inquiries.
(D) There was a mistake on last month's invoice.

Questions 151-152 refer to the following text-message chain.

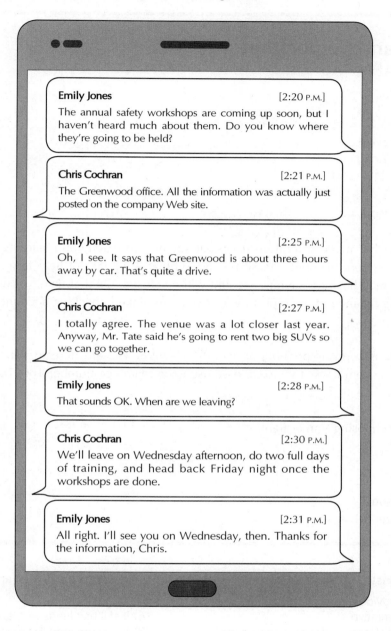

Emily Jones [2:20 P.M.]

The annual safety workshops are coming up soon, but I haven't heard much about them. Do you know where they're going to be held?

Chris Cochran [2:21 P.M.]

The Greenwood office. All the information was actually just posted on the company Web site.

Emily Jones [2:25 P.M.]

Oh, I see. It says that Greenwood is about three hours away by car. That's quite a drive.

Chris Cochran [2:27 P.M.]

I totally agree. The venue was a lot closer last year. Anyway, Mr. Tate said he's going to rent two big SUVs so we can go together.

Emily Jones [2:28 P.M.]

That sounds OK. When are we leaving?

Chris Cochran [2:30 P.M.]

We'll leave on Wednesday afternoon, do two full days of training, and head back Friday night once the workshops are done.

Emily Jones [2:31 P.M.]

All right. I'll see you on Wednesday, then. Thanks for the information, Chris.

---

151 What is NOT mentioned about the safety workshops?

(A) They are held every year.
(B) Details about them can be found online.
(C) They include two days of training.
(D) It is not mandatory to attend them.

152 At 2:27 P.M., what does Mr. Cochran mean when he writes, "I totally agree"?

(A) He is concerned about the distance to a venue.
(B) He is concerned about the size of a vehicle.
(C) He thinks additional sessions need to be provided.
(D) He thinks that they should get back on Thursday.

GO ON TO THE NEXT PAGE

Vanter Bank Corporation

790 West 32nd Street, New York, NY 10105

June 10

Mr. Oscar Morrison
63 Packerston Road
Poughkeepsie, NY 12601

Dear Mr. Morrison,

Our call center has made several unsuccessful attempts to reach you regarding a question we have concerning your account. Please be advised that if we do not hear from you by Friday, July 11, your small business savings account will be closed. On that date, we will also transfer your remaining balance of $350.00 to your externally linked checking account at the Bank of Fulton.

Please call us as soon as possible at 1-800-555-2996. We are here to help you Mondays through Fridays, from 8 A.M. to 9 P.M. Please use issue reference number 100076965 when you contact us.

Thank you for choosing Vanter Bank.

Sincerely,

Louise Robertson
Vanter Bank Deposit Associate

---

153 What is suggested about Mr. Morrison?

(A) He will provide a reference code to a representative.
(B) He asked Vanter to close his business account.
(C) He would like to be contacted by telephone.
(D) He forgot to provide Ms. Robertson his e-mail address.

154 What is NOT mentioned about the savings account?

(A) It still has funds available for withdrawal.
(B) It has reached the monthly transfer limit.
(C) It may be closed if no action is taken.
(D) It is connected to an account at another institution.

Questions 155-157 refer to the following information.

Non-Disclosure Agreement

For all intentions and purposes of this agreement, "confidential information" will refer to any corporate data revealed to employees of Viridian International throughout their employment with the company. Such information will be considered solely the property of the company and not for individual and personal use. The non-disclosure agreement applies to all forms, reports, proposals, designs, techniques, models, and research data, along with any other related details of the company and its business. All verbal and written communication should also be considered confidential information.

In signing this agreement, the employee agrees that:

1. Confidential information will not be transferred in any way to others without prior permission from the company.

2. No confidential information will be duplicated for any reason.

3. Any creation of company-related material throughout the employee's placement at the company will also be considered confidential information.

4. Upon termination of an employment contract, employees will lose all privileges, including access to confidential information.

---

155 What is the purpose of the information?

(A) To educate staff on company policy
(B) To highlight policy changes
(C) To protect employee rights
(D) To make a job offer

156 What is NOT mentioned about confidential information?

(A) It can be spoken between two people.
(B) It involves a variety of different documents.
(C) It includes material that employees create for the company.
(D) It can be copied with managerial consent.

157 What must employees do at the end of their contracts?

(A) Give up access to company data
(B) Sign a separate agreement
(C) Participate in an exit interview
(D) Find work in an unrelated industry

Questions 158-160 refer to the following notice.

Mount Victory Chairlift Hours Changing

One of the top tourist attractions in the region, the Mount Victory chairlift, is extending its hours for the summer season. — [1] —. In the winter, the chairlift carries skiers to the top of the mountain so they can enjoy coming down one of the peak's many trails. During the summer, visitors can ride up to the top and enjoy the view at Mountaineer Restaurant. — [2] —.

In order to take advantage of the longer summer days, the Mount Victory chairlift is now running from 8 A.M. to 10 P.M. — [3] —. Mountaineer Restaurant is also extending its service hours from 8 A.M. through 9 P.M. for the convenience of guests. — [4] —.

For those who wish to hike on the paths, park rangers would like to remind everyone that while the tracks are open at any time of day, it is best to avoid them at night. In addition to the danger posed by wild animals, it can be difficult to see, and hikers can get lost or injured. Also, all routes that are marked "Off Limits" must be avoided at all times.

158 What is indicated about the chairlift?

(A) It is reserved for the use of hikers.
(B) It only operates during the winter months.
(C) It ends at the top of the mountain.
(D) It has the same hours as the dining establishment.

159 What is suggested about the mountain paths?

(A) They are often blocked by trees.
(B) They are inaccessible in the summer.
(C) They are safer during the day.
(D) They are intended for viewing wildlife.

160 In which of the positions marked [1], [2], [3], and [4] does the following sentence best belong?

"They can then either take the lift or hike back down the mountain."

(A) [1]
(B) [2]
(C) [3]
(D) [4]

Town of Redfield
Official Web site for Redfield Town Hall

Home I Online Services I Notifications I **FAQs**

Frequently Asked Questions

1. What are Redfield Town Hall office hours?

All departments for Redfield Town Hall are open from 8 A.M. to 5 P.M., Mondays through Fridays. The office is also open on weekends from 8 A.M. to 2 P.M. Please note that Redfield Town Hall is closed on all national holidays.

2. Where can I find a list of departments?

Departments and respective division heads can be found by clicking on Online Services on the main navigation bar above. Contact information for each department will be listed under Town Hall Divisions on that page. E-mail addresses for division committee members will also be listed under each department head.

3. How can I sign up for Redfield Town Hall weekly e-mail notifications?

To register your e-mail address with us, navigate to Notifications on the main toolbar. Then click the link on the left labeled E-mail Notifications and follow the steps to subscribe. Note that certain e-mail providers may not recognize e-mail notifications from Redfield Town Hall. Be sure to uncheck e-mail notifications labeled as spam to allow for proper transmission.

---

161 Why was the Web page created?

(A) To encourage citizens to register to vote
(B) To inform residents of town hall directions
(C) To provide answers to common questions
(D) To explain the town's history to visitors

162 How can visitors find contact information for department heads?

(A) By e-mailing a committee member
(B) By calling the main office directly
(C) By creating an account on the Web site
(D) By clicking on a link at the top

163 What is indicated about e-mail notifications?

(A) They can be requested by filling out a form.
(B) They are recognized by all e-mail providers.
(C) They are sent out twice each week.
(D) They may be mistaken for spam messages.

GO ON TO THE NEXT PAGE

Questions 164-167 refer to the following online chat discussion.

Wendy Tran	3:32 P.M.	Hi. Can we talk about the glasses for Hogan's Fish and Chips?
Vincent Chou	3:33 P.M.	That's order number 27248, right?
Wendy Tran	3:35 P.M.	Yes, that's the one. Ms. Lin, the owner, wants to change her logo design, but I'm still waiting for her to send me the revised image.
Vincent Chou	3:36 P.M.	Oh. We were about to finish up her sample product.
Wendy Tran	3:37 P.M.	I understand it's a bother, but we need to satisfy her request. If it's any help, she said she could e-mail us the new design by July 8.
Vincent Chou	3:38 P.M.	But we have another project coming up. We need to start working on the Kerala Curry House designs on Thursday. I'm afraid Ms. Lin will need to extend the deadline.
Wendy Tran	3:40 P.M.	I don't think that's possible. Hogan's is supposed to open on August 1, and everything has to be ready within two weeks. Let me talk to Ms. Lin.
Wendy Tran	3:46 P.M.	All right, I got her to agree to send the new design by 8 A.M. on July 6. That should be enough time, right?
Vincent Chou	3:47 P.M.	Sounds good. We can ship out the sample product the same afternoon so she receives it the following morning. Please remind her that she can expect to wait two weeks for the full order after confirmation. That is our policy for all clients unless they pay for our one-week expedited work plan.
Wendy Tran	3:48 P.M.	That reminds me—the manager of Abelardo's called about his coffee cups. He needs them as soon as possible and purchased that option.

Send

164 What is mainly being discussed?

(A) Creating a sample image
(B) Visiting a production facility
(C) Accommodating a client's request
(D) Attending a product launch

165 When will Ms. Lin receive the sample product?

(A) July 6
(B) July 7
(C) July 8
(D) August 1

166 At 3:40 P.M., what does Ms. Tran mean when she writes, "I don't think that's possible"?

(A) A design cannot be approved.
(B) A deadline cannot be extended.
(C) A customer cannot be contacted.
(D) An order cannot be delivered.

167 What is suggested about Abelardo's?

(A) It will be opening on August 1.
(B) It has launched a new beverage line.
(C) Its order will be ready in a week.
(D) Its management has recently changed.

Questions 168-171 refer to the following e-mail.

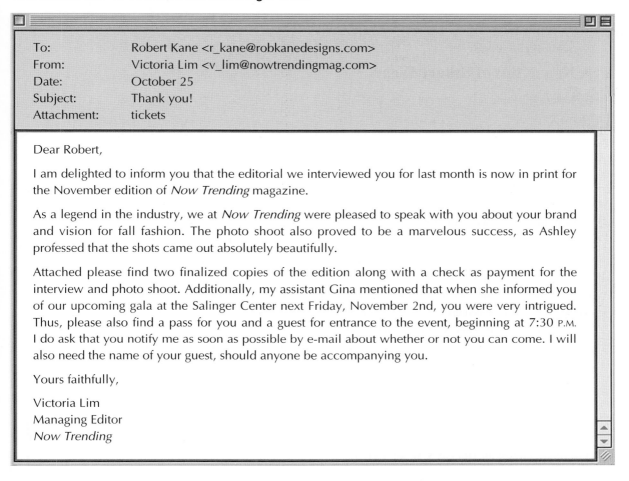

To: Robert Kane <r_kane@robkanedesigns.com>
From: Victoria Lim <v_lim@nowtrendingmag.com>
Date: October 25
Subject: Thank you!
Attachment: tickets

Dear Robert,

I am delighted to inform you that the editorial we interviewed you for last month is now in print for the November edition of *Now Trending* magazine.

As a legend in the industry, we at *Now Trending* were pleased to speak with you about your brand and vision for fall fashion. The photo shoot also proved to be a marvelous success, as Ashley professed that the shots came out absolutely beautifully.

Attached please find two finalized copies of the edition along with a check as payment for the interview and photo shoot. Additionally, my assistant Gina mentioned that when she informed you of our upcoming gala at the Salinger Center next Friday, November 2nd, you were very intrigued. Thus, please also find a pass for you and a guest for entrance to the event, beginning at 7:30 P.M. I do ask that you notify me as soon as possible by e-mail about whether or not you can come. I will also need the name of your guest, should anyone be accompanying you.

Yours faithfully,

Victoria Lim
Managing Editor
Now Trending

---

168 Why was the e-mail written?

(A) To arrange for a business consultation
(B) To ask for approval of photo shoot images
(C) To invite a client to an annual celebration
(D) To provide payment for services rendered

169 When did the interview take place?

(A) September
(B) October
(C) November
(D) December

170 Who told Robert about the gala?

(A) Victoria
(B) Ashley
(C) Gina
(D) Leo

171 What is suggested about Mr. Kane?

(A) He will be attending next Friday's event by himself.
(B) He has never done paid work for *Now Trending* before.
(C) He will have to contact Ms. Lim if he brings a guest.
(D) He will be interviewed by the magazine again next spring.

GO ON TO THE NEXT PAGE

Questions 172-175 refer to the following article.

Tech Speculation Weekly

A New Kind of Smart Wear

By Joshua Hutchins
March 20

There has been a great deal of talk lately about the new line of smart watches soon to be released by technology giant, BurTex Co. The company hopes to make its new smart watch designs the forerunner for future trends in health and fitness.

A recently published report found that approximately 75 percent of consumers cited the field of health care as the most promising industry for wearable technologies like BurTex's smart watch line. — [1] —. People place the most trust in their primary care physicians when it comes to their health. Thus, if more of these doctors approve the usefulness of smart watches, consumers may be encouraged to incorporate the devices into their daily exercise routines.

The report also stated, however, that overall consumer interest in BurTex's smart watches has apparently declined since the product launch announcement. — [2] —. Such devices are largely viewed as specialty items, most likely because of their current scarcity in the marketplace. One quarter of consumers who purchased a smart watch within the last two years noted how they used the technology very infrequently in their daily lives. These consumers cited incorrect or inaccurate data as the number one reason for their doubts about wearable technology. — [3] —.

Additionally, a massive 85 percent of those intrigued by BurTex's new line of watches expressed concern over privacy. Smart watches include functions to share health data with friends and family. — [4] —. However, many feel that such information is highly sensitive and, when shared, could lead to a number of social issues.

172 What is indicated about BurTex Corporation?

(A) They are not big relative to their competitors.
(B) They do not see opportunities in the fitness market.
(C) They are about to launch some new merchandise.
(D) They have recently announced policy changes.

173 According to Mr. Hutchins, what is most likely true about primary care physicians?

(A) Some have found wearable technology to be dangerous.
(B) Some see practicality in smart watches.
(C) Many currently use a wearable device while exercising.
(D) Many are demanding a more accurate way to track patient health data.

174 What percentage of consumers said they rarely use their smart watches?

(A) 25 percent
(B) 50 percent
(C) 75 percent
(D) 85 percent

175 In which of the positions marked [1], [2], [3], and [4] does the following sentence best belong?

"This is due to the fact that some consumers are still unsure of wearable health technology."

(A) [1]
(B) [2]
(C) [3]
(D) [4]

GO ON TO THE NEXT PAGE

To: David Marsh <davemarsh@careconstruction.com>
From: Gary Brent <gbrent@placidpaints.com>
Date: September 2
Subject: Paint order
Attachment: catalog

Dear Mr. Marsh,

Thank you for your recent paint order. We are currently mixing the requested colors but have several questions about some items that require further clarification.

There were two separate entries for the color B227 sky blue paint, each requesting a single four-liter pail. Could you please confirm that this was not an error and that you would actually like to place both orders?

Also, I am afraid that two of the colors you requested correspond to old color codes from last year's catalog. We do have the same items, but they are now Y866 for canary yellow and P306 for violet. I have attached a copy of this year's catalog and have highlighted the colors you selected. If these are incorrect, please contact us as soon as possible to fix the error.

We appreciate your continued patronage and assure you that the other paints are already being prepared. Please send confirmation for these details within the next 24 hours to ensure that the order will be delivered on time.

Sincerely,

Gary Brent
Customer Representative, Placid Paints

To: Gary Brent <gbrent@placidpaints.com>
From: David Marsh <davemarsh@careconstruction.com>
Date: September 10
Subject: Completed paint order

Dear Gary,

We received the paints today. I apologize again for being late in getting the information to you, but our interior designer was away, so we couldn't get the details immediately. In any event, the paints have arrived, which still gives us enough time to stay within our schedule.

Also, I wanted to apologize again for all of the problems on the form. I'm afraid a few different people were adding items to the order, and some of them didn't realize that there had been some changes. Unfortunately, they also didn't notice that one order had been made twice for the same paint shade. It's a good thing you wrote to us so we could resolve the issues here in our office. Rest assured all our staff has now been updated on the changes, so this shouldn't happen again.

Best wishes,

David Marsh
Manager, Care Construction

---

176 According to the first e-mail, why did Mr. Brent send a catalog?

(A) To check order accuracy
(B) To advertise new paint shades
(C) To recommend different colors
(D) To explain a calculation error

177 In the second e-mail, the word "shade" in paragraph 2, line 3, is closest in meaning to

(A) reflection
(B) tone
(C) expression
(D) shelter

178 What is indicated about Care Construction?

(A) Its schedule had to be altered.
(B) It recently completed a project for Mr. Marsh.
(C) It has just hired several new design staff.
(D) Its order referred to outdated information.

179 According to Mr. Marsh, why was there a delay sending information?

(A) The interior designer was not present.
(B) The manager could not find any problems.
(C) The numbers for the paint colors changed.
(D) The designer had trouble making a decision.

180 What is suggested about Mr. Marsh's order?

(A) It was sent to the incorrect address.
(B) It contained a quantity error for color B227.
(C) It was shipped from a foreign supplier.
(D) It cost him more than expected.

GO ON TO THE NEXT PAGE

Dover Community Outreach

Dover Community Outreach (DCO) has provided assistance to low-income families in the town of Dover for over 50 years. DCO works in partnership with local government-funded social service agencies. Families in need are offered small grants through these groups for the following:

Housing and Medical Care
· Rent support
· Security deposit assistance
· Medical care assistance

Education and Job Training
· Field-specific training programs for job-seekers
· Technology development classes to improve technical skills

How You Can Help
Your charitable contribution to DCO can help us do more. To make a donation to Dover Community Outreach, visit our Contributions Page at www.doveroutreach.org/donation. For any questions regarding DCO, please contact the administrative head, Ms. Laura Kingsley at 555-2338 or by sending her an e-mail at l_kingsley@doveroutreach.org.

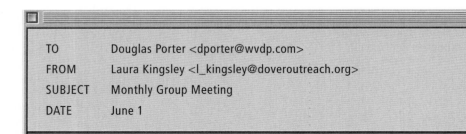

TO	Douglas Porter <dporter@wvdp.com>
FROM	Laura Kingsley <l_kingsley@doveroutreach.org>
SUBJECT	Monthly Group Meeting
DATE	June 1

Dear Dr. Porter,

As usual, the monthly group meeting for Dover Community Outreach members will take place on the second Monday of the month (June 10). As your dental practice, West Victoria Dental, has been a dedicated member and supporter of Dover Community Outreach for the past 10 years, we are delighted that you will be giving a presentation at this month's meeting. I understand that you will need a projector and a microphone system, so we will be sure to have those items ready for you.

Please take a look at this month's meeting agenda:

· Concerns regarding lack of incoming donations; suggestions for methods other than Contributions Page
· Recruiting instructors for new programs
· Housing price increases; discussion on economic data
· Special presentation by Dr. Douglas Porter on senior citizen dental care

As always, your comments and questions on any DCO-related topics are also welcome.

Yours faithfully,

Laura Kingsley
Head of Administration, Dover Community Outreach

---

181 Who does Dover Community Outreach work with?

(A) Pharmaceutical companies
(B) Internet service providers
(C) Internationally run businesses
(D) State welfare groups

182 How does Dover Community Outreach provide support to families?

(A) They pay for all costs related to home ownership.
(B) They completely cover health expenses for people over 70.
(C) They offer classes for people looking for employment.
(D) They install computers for people who work from home.

183 What is indicated about Dr. Porter?

(A) He is gathering research data for a publication.
(B) He is invited to a DCO meeting every second Monday of the month.
(C) He has been a supporter of DCO since its establishment.
(D) He owns a number of dental offices in the town of Dover.

184 What is suggested about Dover Community Outreach?

(A) They are not raising enough funds through their Web site.
(B) They are considering cutting back on certain services offered.
(C) They are recruiting new employees for administrative positions.
(D) They are unaware of recent housing price increases.

185 According to the e-mail, what will be discussed in the monthly meeting?

(A) Where the organization should give donated fund
(B) New technology programs at DCO
(C) How to increase the value of personal residences
(D) Providing dental care for the elderly

GO ON TO THE NEXT PAGE

May 1

Dear Mr. Borden,

This is to inform you that my company will not be renewing its lease once it expires on May 9. There is nothing wrong with the facilities, services, or you as the building owner. My business has simply grown too large, and we need more room. I have appreciated all your assistance over the past five years. We will be relocating to our new offices in Facade Towers on May 10 and 11.

We have hired a cleaning company to return the office to the same condition as it was when we first moved in. As agreed in our contract, I will pay for those services. You may contact me at any time at emoses@emstranslation.com if you need more clarification.

Regards,

Elizabeth Moses
Owner, EMS Translation Services

OFFICINA SERVICES INC.   **INVOICE: #DTS-3987**
4204 Grandville Boulevard, Nashville, TN 37207
Tel. 555-2350

NAME: Elizabeth Moses	DATE: May 11
ADDRESS: EMS Translation Services Unit 56, 4th floor, Stembridge Commercial Building Nashville, TN 37207	**E-MAIL:** emoses@emstranslation.com

SERVICES PROVIDED	COST
Steam clean carpets	$230
Polish floors	$170
Clean restrooms and staff room	$120
Wash all windows	$200
Clean two private offices	$150
Clean conference room	$75
Subtotal	$945
Tax	$90
Amount Owed	$1,035

Payment for this invoice is due within five days of the final date of service. Late payments may incur a penalty.

TO	Elizabeth Moses <emoses@emstranslation.com>
FROM	Harris Lloyd <h.lloyd@officinaservices.com>
SUBJECT	Urgent
DATE	May 17

Ms. Moses,

I am writing about the services my business performed for you. The final date of service was May 11, and an invoice was left with the building manager as you asked. I am not sure if you got the bill, but I have yet to receive payment. It has been six days since services were rendered.

I kindly ask that you send payment by tomorrow. Thereafter, Officina Services will charge you a $50 late fee as indicated in our service contract, which you signed. Should you have any concerns, please respond to this e-mail or contact me at 555-2350.

Regards,
Harris Lloyd

---

186 Why is EMS moving out of its office?

(A) It needs more space.
(B) It has too many complaints.
(C) It is looking for better services.
(D) It was acquired by another firm.

187 What has Ms. Moses agreed to do?

(A) Lease a different unit in the same building
(B) Cover the cost of cleaning a fourth-floor office
(C) Hire Mr. Borden to help her move a business
(D) Have flooring replaced in her previous office space

188 What is true about Officina Services?

(A) It is a provider of relocation services.
(B) It demands full payment by May 12.
(C) It offers a carpet cleaning service.
(D) It is in the Stembridge Commercial Building.

189 What is the main purpose of the e-mail?

(A) To confirm a date for cleaning services
(B) To notify a client of an outstanding bill
(C) To report an error on a financial statement
(D) To inform a manager of a problem with a unit

190 What is suggested about Harris Lloyd?

(A) He mailed a document to an incorrect location.
(B) He owns a business located in Nashville.
(C) He made some calculation errors on an invoice.
(D) He mistakenly left a bill with Mr. Borden's assistant.

GO ON TO THE NEXT PAGE

Questions 191-195 refer to the following article, memo, and e-mail.

Brayden Realty to Open Branch in Reno

Following the success of its first Nevada branch, which launched early last year in Las Vegas, Brayden Realty has announced it will be opening a second office in Reno. "The market in both cities is similar," says Marjorie Olsen, CEO of Brayden Realty. "That's why we're certain this new venture will be profitable." Olsen also explained that the firm would be hiring locally for all of the positions in Reno. The branch will be recruiting a total of 18 managers and staff.

Brayden Realty primarily deals in commercial properties, including hotels and shopping centers. Headquartered in Denver, Colorado, the firm operates in 12 states in the Western US. Reno will become the firm's 28th location when it opens on February 14. After the Reno location is opened, Brayden has its sights set on Arizona and envisions offices in Phoenix and Tucson to start.

MEMO

DATE: February 3

TO: Agent Trainees
FROM: Michelle Larsen

There are some changes to next week's training schedule. First, I've been requested to fly to our headquarters to help with some recruitment issues. So, I will be unavailable to conduct your morning training sessions next week. Substituting for me will be Adrian Gist, who led your office system training session on Tuesday this week. He will be leading all remaining sessions in Reno.

Also, next Friday, we will be celebrating the completion of training with dinner at Paolo's Grill. Please let Adrian know whether you are coming by sending an e-mail to agist@braydenrealestate.com. Each person is allowed one guest.

To:	Adrian Gist <agist@braydenrealestate.com>
From:	Sofia Suarez <ssuar@braydenrealestate.com>
Subject:	Celebration dinner
Date:	February 4

Hello Adrian,

I'd like to attend the meal next week on February 11. I will not be bringing a guest because my husband will be away on a business trip.

Also, I have a question about the business cards you distributed to all the new agents at the end of the office training session. My e-mail address was misprinted. I wasn't sure who to contact about this. Please let me know, as I will need to hand out business cards when the office opens to the public on the 14th.

Thanks for your help, and I look forward to our training sessions next week.

Regards,
Sofia Suarez

191 What is NOT indicated about Brayden Realty?

(A) It plans to launch operations in Phoenix.
(B) It is currently under the leadership of Marjorie Olsen.
(C) It will move its offices from Las Vegas to Reno.
(D) It specializes in commercial facilities and structures.

192 What is stated about the real estate market in Reno?

(A) It is comparable to the market in Las Vegas.
(B) Its demands are not being met by current providers.
(C) It is the fastest-growing market in the Western US.
(D) It provides substantial employment for Reno residents.

193 What does Michelle Larsen mention about Adrian Gist?

(A) He was introduced to trainees at the head office.
(B) He facilitated a session on office systems this week.
(C) He was recently hired as a recruitment manager.
(D) He has met agent trainees on numerous occasions.

194 What is suggested about Sofia Suarez?

(A) She will be training as a manager.
(B) She will be going on a business trip.
(C) She is unable to attend an annual meeting.
(D) She is a resident of Reno.

195 What will Ms. Suarez do next week?

(A) Arrive at the Reno office for a managerial training program
(B) Attend a celebratory event with other trainees at Paolo's Grill
(C) Pick up some new business cards at the end of a session
(D) Lead members of the public on a tour of properties for sale

GO ON TO THE NEXT PAGE

Questions 196-200 refer to the following e-mail, form, and article.

TO   Harvey Lee <h.lee@deltadawn.com>
FROM   Sarah Holland <s.holland@deltadawn.com>
SUBJECT Registration
DATE   October 20

Dear Harvey,

I'm sorry that I wasn't able to attend the weekly meeting yesterday, but how are preparations coming along for the annual travel exposition? I just wanted to let you know that before we can register for it, there is something that I need to confirm. If I remember correctly, Ms. Tucker said that the size of our promotional banners should be appropriate for the type of booth we get. But I haven't received the measurements for them, so I have no way of knowing what sort of booth to choose. Please let me know what they are. I can proceed with registration as soon as I have this information.

Also note that all registration costs will be paid for with the company credit card. Thanks!

Best regards,

Sarah Holland

REGISTRATION FORM: Fifth Annual Travel Exposition, Penner Exhibit Hall, Nov. 11-13

NAME	Sarah Holland	DEPARTMENT	Marketing
COMPANY	Delta Dawn Travel Agency	PHONE	555-8376
ADDRESS	345 Union Building, Unit 23, New Orleans, LA		

Please select one of the following options. Prices listed are for the full three-day event from 10 A.M. through 8 P.M. Participants are required to set up their booths 24 hours prior to the start of the fair.

Large Booth, 6 by 4 meters .... $967 ■
Medium Booth, 5 by 3 meters .... $838 ☐
Small Booth, 4 by 2 meters .... $767 ☐

Penner Exhibit Hall accepts all major credit cards and online payments. All credit card payments are subject to a $5 processing fee. Once payment has been confirmed, you'll be sent a packet containing four passes, a schedule of events, and a list of all participating businesses.

Fifth Annual Travel Exposition Enjoys Another Resounding Success!

Penner Exhibit Hall's fifth yearly travel exposition was the largest in its history, attracting 182 businesses and over 30,000 attendees during the event last weekend. Karen Moore, a representative from travel agency Broad Horizons, said, "The response to the event was tremendous." She claimed that despite her agency's comparatively small presence at the event, her business is still being inundated with calls and e-mails from expo attendees.

Event organizer Barbara Romano attributes the success of the event to online promotion and the use of social media. "We urged all participating companies and businesses to advertise online and to publicize the expo on social media." When asked about plans for next year's travel exposition, Romano reported that an additional 25 booths would be made available.

196 According to the e-mail, what does Ms. Holland ask Mr. Lee to provide?

(A) The rental cost per day
(B) The size of advertising materials
(C) The location of a venue
(D) The dimensions of booths

197 What is the purpose of the form?

(A) To register for a travel industry conference
(B) To specify the terms of an advertising contract
(C) To pay for the rental of a storage unit
(D) To purchase three-day passes to a trade fair

198 What will Delta Dawn Travel Agency probably have to do?

(A) Pay a surcharge for processing
(B) Reserve an additional exhibit booth
(C) Reduce the size of promotional banners
(D) Report the number of people on its staff

199 What is NOT true about Ms. Moore?

(A) She was asked to do promotions on social media.
(B) Her company has received many inquiries from event attendees.
(C) She runs a business similar to that of Delta Dawn Travel Agency.
(D) Her booth was being assembled at a venue on November 11.

200 What does Barbara Romano plan to do?

(A) Participate as a vendor at a future event
(B) Offer additional spaces at next year's exposition
(C) Enlarge Penner Exhibit Hall's facilities
(D) Launch an online advertising campaign

점수 환산표

아래는 교재에 수록된 실전모의고사를 위한 점수 환산표입니다. 문제 풀이 후, 정답 개수를 세어 자신의 토익 리딩 점수를 예상해봅니다.

정답 수	리딩 점수	정답 수	리딩 점수	정답 수	리딩 점수
100	495	66	305	32	125
99	495	65	300	31	120
98	495	64	295	30	115
97	485	63	290	29	110
96	480	62	280	28	105
95	475	61	275	27	100
94	470	60	270	26	95
93	465	59	265	25	90
92	460	58	260	24	85
91	450	57	255	23	80
90	445	56	250	22	75
89	440	55	245	21	70
88	435	54	240	20	70
87	430	53	235	19	65
86	420	52	230	18	60
85	415	51	220	17	60
84	410	50	215	16	55
83	405	49	210	15	50
82	400	48	205	14	45
81	390	47	200	13	40
80	385	46	195	12	35
79	380	45	190	11	30
78	375	44	185	10	30
77	370	43	180	9	25
76	360	42	175	8	20
75	355	41	170	7	20
74	350	40	165	6	15
73	345	39	160	5	15
72	340	38	155	4	10
71	335	37	150	3	5
70	330	36	145	2	5
69	320	35	140	1	5
68	315	34	135	0	5
67	310	33	130		

※ 점수 환산표는 해커스토익 사이트 유저 데이터를 근거로 제작되었으며, 주기적으로 업데이트되고 있습니다. 해커스토익 사이트(Hackers.co.kr)에서 최신 경향을 반영하여 업데이트된 점수환산기를 이용하실 수 있습니다. (토익 > 토익게시판 > 토익점수환산기)

Answer Sheet

진단고사

READING (Part V~VII)

	A	B	C	D		A	B	C	D		A	B	C	D
1	Ⓐ	Ⓑ	Ⓒ	Ⓓ	21	Ⓐ	Ⓑ	Ⓒ	Ⓓ	41	Ⓐ	Ⓑ	Ⓒ	Ⓓ
2	Ⓐ	Ⓑ	Ⓒ	Ⓓ	22	Ⓐ	Ⓑ	Ⓒ	Ⓓ	42	Ⓐ	Ⓑ	Ⓒ	Ⓓ
3	Ⓐ	Ⓑ	Ⓒ	Ⓓ	23	Ⓐ	Ⓑ	Ⓒ	Ⓓ	43	Ⓐ	Ⓑ	Ⓒ	Ⓓ
4	Ⓐ	Ⓑ	Ⓒ	Ⓓ	24	Ⓐ	Ⓑ	Ⓒ	Ⓓ	44	Ⓐ	Ⓑ	Ⓒ	Ⓓ
5	Ⓐ	Ⓑ	Ⓒ	Ⓓ	25	Ⓐ	Ⓑ	Ⓒ	Ⓓ	45	Ⓐ	Ⓑ	Ⓒ	Ⓓ
6	Ⓐ	Ⓑ	Ⓒ	Ⓓ	26	Ⓐ	Ⓑ	Ⓒ	Ⓓ	46	Ⓐ	Ⓑ	Ⓒ	Ⓓ
7	Ⓐ	Ⓑ	Ⓒ	Ⓓ	27	Ⓐ	Ⓑ	Ⓒ	Ⓓ	47	Ⓐ	Ⓑ	Ⓒ	Ⓓ
8	Ⓐ	Ⓑ	Ⓒ	Ⓓ	28	Ⓐ	Ⓑ	Ⓒ	Ⓓ	48	Ⓐ	Ⓑ	Ⓒ	Ⓓ
9	Ⓐ	Ⓑ	Ⓒ	Ⓓ	29	Ⓐ	Ⓑ	Ⓒ	Ⓓ	49	Ⓐ	Ⓑ	Ⓒ	Ⓓ
10	Ⓐ	Ⓑ	Ⓒ	Ⓓ	30	Ⓐ	Ⓑ	Ⓒ	Ⓓ	50	Ⓐ	Ⓑ	Ⓒ	Ⓓ
11	Ⓐ	Ⓑ	Ⓒ	Ⓓ	31	Ⓐ	Ⓑ	Ⓒ	Ⓓ					
12	Ⓐ	Ⓑ	Ⓒ	Ⓓ	32	Ⓐ	Ⓑ	Ⓒ	Ⓓ					
13	Ⓐ	Ⓑ	Ⓒ	Ⓓ	33	Ⓐ	Ⓑ	Ⓒ	Ⓓ					
14	Ⓐ	Ⓑ	Ⓒ	Ⓓ	34	Ⓐ	Ⓑ	Ⓒ	Ⓓ					
15	Ⓐ	Ⓑ	Ⓒ	Ⓓ	35	Ⓐ	Ⓑ	Ⓒ	Ⓓ					
16	Ⓐ	Ⓑ	Ⓒ	Ⓓ	36	Ⓐ	Ⓑ	Ⓒ	Ⓓ					
17	Ⓐ	Ⓑ	Ⓒ	Ⓓ	37	Ⓐ	Ⓑ	Ⓒ	Ⓓ					
18	Ⓐ	Ⓑ	Ⓒ	Ⓓ	38	Ⓐ	Ⓑ	Ⓒ	Ⓓ					
19	Ⓐ	Ⓑ	Ⓒ	Ⓓ	39	Ⓐ	Ⓑ	Ⓒ	Ⓓ					
20	Ⓐ	Ⓑ	Ⓒ	Ⓓ	40	Ⓐ	Ⓑ	Ⓒ	Ⓓ					

맞은 문제 개수: ___ /50

자르는 선 ✂

자르는 선 ✂

Answer Sheet 200% 활용법

교재에 수록된 진단고사와 실전모의고사 1, 2
문제풀이에 활용할 수 있는 Answer Sheet입니다.

시험을 시작하기 전에 Answer Sheet를 잘라내어 사용하고,
정해진 시간 내에 답안지 마킹까지 완료하세요.

실제 시험처럼 연습해봄으로써,
시간 관리 방법을 익히고
실전 감각을 더욱 극대화할 수 있습니다.

Answer Sheet

실전모의고사 2

READING (Part V~VII)

맞은 문제 개수: ____ /100

(Answer bubbles 101–200, columns A B C D)

Answer Sheet

실전모의고사 1

READING (Part V~VII)

맞은 문제 개수: ____ /100

(Answer bubbles 101–200, columns A B C D)

토익 리딩의 기본서 · **최신개정판**

최신기출경향
완벽 반영

해커스 토익
READING RC

개정 9판 5쇄 발행 2024년 8월 19일

개정 9판 1쇄 발행 2023년 1월 2일

지은이	David Cho
펴낸곳	㈜해커스 어학연구소
펴낸이	해커스 어학연구소 출판팀

주소	서울특별시 서초구 강남대로61길 23 ㈜해커스 어학연구소
고객센터	02-537-5000
교재 관련 문의	publishing@hackers.com
동영상강의	HackersIngang.com

ISBN	978-89-6542-476-5 (13740)
Serial Number	09-05-01

영어 전문 포털, 해커스토익
Hackers.co.kr
해커스토익

· **무료 문법&어휘 동영상강의**
· 최신 출제경향이 반영된 **무료 온라인 실전모의고사**
· **매월 무료 적중예상특강 및 실시간 토익시험 정답확인&해설강의**
· 본 교재 **연습문제 무료 해설 PDF**
· 매일 실전 RC/LC 및 토익 보카 TEST 등 **다양한 무료 학습 콘텐츠**

외국어인강 1위, 해커스인강
HackersIngang.com
해커스인강

· 들으면서 외우는 **무료 단어암기 MP3**
· 교재 내 수록된 **진단고사 및 실전문제 무료 해설강의**
· 토익 스타강사의 고득점 전략이 담긴 **본 교재 인강**

토익 리딩의 기본서 · 최신개정판

해커스 토익

최신기출경향
완벽 반영

READING RC

David Cho

정답·해설·해석

해설집

해커스 어학연구소

토익 리딩의 기본서 · 최신개정판

해커스 토익

최신기출경향
완벽 반영

READING RC

정답·해설·해석

해설집

해커스 어학연구소

부사를 뒤에서 꾸며주는 부사임을 알아둔다.

해석 Sunrise 부동산 회사의 50층짜리 오피스 타워의 건축 설계도는 프로젝트 담당자인 Mr. Collins에 의해 이미 검토되었다.

어휘 structural adj. 건축의, 구조의 story n. (건물의) 층 review v. 검토하다

Part 5				p.28
01 (B)	02 (B)	03 (B)	04 (A)	05 (A)
06 (B)	07 (A)	08 (C)	09 (C)	10 (B)
11 (D)	12 (D)	13 (B)	14 (C)	15 (B)
Part 6				**p.30**
16 (C)	17 (D)	18 (C)	19 (C)	20 (D)
21 (B)	22 (B)	23 (D)		
Part 7				**p.32**
24 (D)	25 (C)	26 (C)	27 (B)	28 (A)
29 (C)	30 (B)	31 (D)	32 (D)	33 (B)
34 (C)	35 (D)	36 (C)	37 (D)	38 (B)
39 (D)	40 (C)	41 (D)	42 (D)	43 (B)
44 (D)	45 (D)	46 (B)	47 (B)	48 (B)
49 (C)	50 (D)			

01 격에 맞는 인칭대명사 채우기 ▶ Grammar Ch. 11 대명사

해설 명사(sense) 앞에서 형용사처럼 쓰일 수 있는 인칭대명사는 소유격이므로 (B) his(그의)가 정답이다. 전치사(With) 다음의 목적어 자리로 생각하여 목적격인 (A) him(그에게)을 선택하지 않도록 주의한다.

해석 세부 사항에 대한 그의 예리한 감각으로, Mr. Watson은 연구 프로젝트에 포괄적인 자료 분석을 제공할 수 있었다.

어휘 keen adj. 예리한 comprehensive adj. 포괄적인, 종합적인 analysis n. 분석

02 형용사 자리 채우기 ▶ Grammar Ch. 12 형용사

해설 빈칸은 be동사(was) 다음에 나온 주격 보어 자리이므로 명사 (A)나 (D) 또는 형용사 (B)가 정답의 후보이다. '세미나 참석이 직원들에게 도움이 되다'라는 의미가 되어야 하므로 주어(Attending ~ service)를 설명해 주는 형용사 (B) helpful(도움이 되는)이 정답이다. 명사 (A) help(도움, 종업원)나 (D) helpfulness(유익함)는 주어(Attending ~ service)와 동격을 이루었을 때 어색한 의미가 되므로 답이 될 수 없다.

해석 고객 서비스에 관한 분기별 세미나에 참석하는 것은 Moon River 호텔 직원들에게 도움이 되었다.

어휘 quarterly adj. 분기별의 helpfully adv. 도움이 되도록, 유용하게

03 동사 어휘 고르기 ▶ Vocabulary Ch. 01 동사

해설 '프린터를 수리받는 비용'이라는 의미이므로 '수리하다'라는 뜻을 가진 동사 repair의 p.p.형인 (B) repaired가 정답이다. (A)의 affirm은 '단언하다', (C)의 identify는 '확인하다', (D)의 recognize는 '인정하다, 알아보다'라는 의미이다. 참고로, getting the printer repaired에서 get은 '~하게 하다, 당하다'라는 사역의 의미를 갖는 동사로 to 부정사를 목적격 보어로 취하지만, 이 경우에는 '프린터를 수리받다'라는 수동의 의미로 해석되므로 to 부정사가 아닌 p.p.형인 repaired를 목적격 보어로 취했음을 알아둔다.

해석 프린터를 수리받는 비용이 원래 제품 가격과 거의 같기 때문에, 경영진은 새로운 모델을 구입하기로 결정했다.

어휘 nearly adv. 거의 management n. 경영진

04 부사 어휘 고르기 ▶ Vocabulary Ch. 04 부사

해설 문장의 시제가 현재완료(has _____ been)이고 '프로젝트 담당자에 의해 이미 검토되었다'는 문맥이므로 (A) already(이미)가 정답이다. (B) by chance는 '우연히, 뜻밖에', (C) enough는 '충분히', (D) yet은 부정문에서는 '아직', 의문문에서는 '벌써'라는 의미이다. 참고로, enough는 형용사나

05 명사와 수/인칭 일치된 대명사 채우기 ▶ Grammar Ch. 11 대명사

해설 'Carmoan Industries사의 회계부에서 일할 담당자가 필요하다'는 의미이므로 빈칸에 들어갈 대명사가 가리키게 되는 것은 Carmoan Industries이다. 따라서 단수 사물명사(Carmoan Industries)를 가리키면서 형용사처럼 명사(accounting department) 앞에 쓰이는 소유격 (A) its(그것의)가 정답이다. 회사는 3인칭 복수형 대명사로 받을 수 있지만 목적격인 (B) them(그들에게)과 소유대명사인 (D) theirs(그들의 것)는 명사(accounting department) 앞에 올 수 없으므로 답이 될 수 없다.

해석 Carmoan Industries사는 회사의 회계부에서 일할 경력이 있는 회계 장부 담당자 두 명을 현재 필요로 한다.

어휘 experienced adj. 경력 있는, 경험이 풍부한 bookkeeper n. 회계 장부 담당자 accounting department 회계부

06 동사 어휘 고르기 ▶ Vocabulary Ch. 01 동사

해설 '매장을 방문하거나 매표소에서 찾음으로써 티켓을 얻다'라는 문맥이므로 (B) claim(얻다)이 정답이다. (A) charge는 '청구하다', (C) gives는 '주다', (D) refund는 '환불하다'라는 의미이다.

해석 참석자들은 어떤 World Pass 매장을 방문하거나 매표소에서 티켓을 찾음으로써 Cornerstone 영화 시사회의 무료 티켓을 얻을 수 있다.

어휘 complimentary adj. 무료의 movie premiere 영화 시사회

07 동사 자리 채우기 ▶ Grammar Ch. 01 주어 · 동사

해설 문장에 동사가 없으므로 동사로 사용될 수 있는 (A)와 (B)가 정답의 후보이다. 빈칸 다음에 목적어로 사용되는 명사(difficulties)가 왔으므로 능동형인 (A) have caused가 정답이다. (B)는 수동태이므로 뒤에 목적어로 사용되는 명사(difficulties)가 나올 수 없다. 형용사인 (C)와 동명사 또는 현재분사인 (D)는 동사 자리에 올 수 없다.

해석 현장에서 있었던 시청각 시스템과 관련된 기술적인 문제들이 진로 세미나의 주최자들에게 곤란을 야기했다.

어휘 audio-visual adj. 시청각의 venue n. 현장, 장소 difficulties n. 곤란, 말썽 organizer n. 주최자, 조직자 cause v. ~을 야기하다, 초래하다 causative adj. 야기시키는, 원인이 되는

08 동사 관련 어구 완성하기 ▶ Vocabulary Ch. 06 동사 관련 어구 1

해설 '사용되던 컴퓨터가 새로운 컴퓨터로 교체되다'라는 문맥이므로 빈칸 앞의 have been과 빈칸 뒤의 전치사 with와 함께 '~로 교체되다'라는 의미의 어구를 이루는 동사 replace의 p.p.형 (C) replaced가 정답이다. (replace A with B: A를 B로 교체하다) (A)의 inspect는 '점검하다', (B)의 reject는 '거절하다', (D)의 purchase는 '구입하다'라는 의미이다.

해석 그래픽 팀에 의해 사용되는 컴퓨터들은 최신 사진 편집 소프트웨어를 실행할 수 있는 새로운 것들로 교체되었다.

어휘 capable of ~할 수 있는 run v. (소프트웨어 등을) 실행하다, 운영하다

09 분사 채우기 ▶ Grammar Ch. 09 분사

해설 명사(areas)를 앞에서 꾸밀 수 있는 것은 형용사 역할을 하는 분사이므로 (C) affected가 정답이다. 동사 (A)와 부사 (B)는 명사를 꾸밀 수 없고, 명사 (D)도 areas와 함께 복합 명사로 사용될 수 없으므로 답이 될 수 없다.

해석 정전인 동안, 영향을 받은 지역의 주민들은 전력이 복구되었을 때 전류 급증 현

상의 위험을 줄이기 위해 모든 전기 제품의 플러그를 뽑아야 한다.

어휘 **blackout** n. 정전 **unplug** v. (전기) 플러그를 뽑다
appliance n. 전기 제품, (가정용) 기기 **risk** n. 위험
power surge 전류 급증 현상 **affect** v. 영향을 미치다
affectively adv. 감정적으로 **affected** adj. 영향을 받은, (병 등에) 걸린
affection n. 감정, 감동

10 부사 어휘 고르기 ▶ Vocabulary Ch. 04 부사

해설 '시 의회가 제안서를 공식적으로 수락하다'라는 문맥이므로 (B) formally
(공식적으로)가 정답이다. (A) intermittently는 '때때로, 간헐적으로', (C)
customarily는 '관습적으로', (D) externally는 '외부적으로'라는 의미이다.

해석 지난 금요일에, 시 의회는 Maple Ridge 지역에 새로운 주민 체육 회관을 건
설하기 위한 제안서를 공식적으로 수락했다.

어휘 **city council** 시의회 **athletics** n. 체육

11 도치 구문 채우기 ▶ Grammar Ch. 20 병치·도치 구문

해설 부정어(Never)가 문장 맨 앞에 와서 주어와 동사가 도치된 문장이다. 현
재완료 시제의 도치 문장은 'have + 주어 + p.p.'이므로 Never has the
customer service department 다음에는 p.p.형이 와야 한다. 따라서 (D)
received가 정답이다.

해석 고객 서비스 부서는 할인 중에 구매된 상품은 반품될 수 없음이 발표되었던 지
난달만큼 많은 항의를 받아 본 적이 없다.

어휘 **complaint** n. 항의, 불만 **announce** v. 발표하다, 공표하다
purchase v. 구매하다 **on sale** 할인 중인 **receipt** n. 영수증

12 부사 자리 채우기 ▶ Grammar Ch. 13 부사

해설 빈칸 뒤의 부사(more)를 꾸며 줄 수 있는 것은 부사이므로 (D) marginally
(아주 조금)가 정답이다. 형용사 (A)와 동사 (B), 명사 (C)는 부사를 꾸며 줄
수 없다.

해석 *Public Pulse*지에 실린 시장에서 현재 구매 가능한 제품들에 대한 소비자 평
가는 비슷한 출판물에서 제공된 것들보다 아주 조금 더 믿을 만하다.

어휘 **review** n. 평가 **reliable** adj. 믿을 만한, 믿을 수 있는
publication n. 출판물 **marginal** adj. (자격·능력 등이) 최저의, 한계의
marginalize v. 사회의 주류에서 몰아내다
marginalization n. 사회에서 소외함

13 부사절 접속사 자리 채우기 ▶ Grammar Ch. 17 부사절

해설 문장은 주어(The final payment)와 동사(cannot be released)를 갖춘 완
전한 절이므로, ____ the missing ~ warehouse는 수식어 거품으로 보아
야 한다. 이 수식어 거품은 동사(are delivered)가 있는 거품절이므로, 거품
절을 이끌 수 있는 부사절 접속사 (B) until(~할 때까지)이 정답이다. 전치사
나 부사로 사용되는 (A) through와 (D) beyond, 전치사 (C) toward는 거
품절을 이끌 수 없다.

해석 빠진 주문품들이 창고에 도착하기 전까지 원단과 재봉 물품들에 대한 최종 대
금은 양도될 수 없다.

어휘 **payment** n. 대금, 납입 **release** v. 양도하다, 놓아주다

14 명사 어휘 채우기 ▶ Vocabulary Ch. 02 명사

해설 '시장들은 유명한 역사적 건물들 및 유적지들과의 가까움 때문에 인기 있다'
라는 문맥이므로 명사 (C) proximity가 정답이다. (proximity to: ~에 가
까움) (A) immediacy는 '직접성', (B) availability는 '효용, (입수) 가능성',
(D) vacancy는 '결원, 공석'이라는 의미이다.

해석 로마의 Trastevere 지역에 있는 시장들은 몇몇 유명한 역사적인 건물들 및 유
적지들에 가깝기 때문에 인기 있다.

어휘 **due to** ~ 때문에 **landmark** n. (문화적으로 지정된) 역사적인 건물
historic site 유적지

15 제안·요청·의무의 주절을 뒤따르는 that절에 '동사원형' 채우기
▶ Grammar Ch. 03 동사의 형태와 종류

해설 주절에 요청을 나타내는 동사(demanded)가 왔으므로 종속절의 동사로는
원형이 와야 한다. 따라서 (B) be conducted가 정답이다. 참고로, that절

주어(further studies)와 동사(conduct)가 '추가 연구가 실시되다'라는 의
미의 수동 관계이므로 수동태 동사(be conducted)가 쓰였다.

해석 세법에 대해 제안된 변경의 효과가 입증되지 않았기 때문에, 정부는 추가 연구
가 실시될 것을 요구했다.

어휘 **effect** n. 효과, 영향 **confirm** v. 입증하다, 확인하다 **demand** v. 요구하다
conduct v. 실시하다 **conduction** n. (전기나 열의) 전도

16-19는 다음 회람에 관한 문제입니다.

수신: 전 직원
발신: 건물 관리실
날짜: 11월 27일
제목: 엘리베이터 보수 작업

[16]건물 관리실은 건물의 짝수 층을 운행하는 승객용 엘리베이터에 대한 정기
점검을 가까운 시일 내에 실시하도록 예정되어 있습니다. 12월 3일부터 이용할 수 없을 것입니다. [17]그러므로, 보통 이 엘리베이터를 이
용하는 건물 입주자들은 모든 층을 운행하는 엘리베이터를 사용하도록 요구됩니
다. [18]기술자들은 리프트 장치의 주요 부품들뿐만 아니라 전기 배선도 점검할 것
이므로, 엘리베이터에 적어도 3일간 접근하실 수 없을 것입니다. 부품이 교체될
필요가 있거나 수리가 요구되는 경우에 엘리베이터가 더 오랜 시간 동안 정지될
필요가 있을 수도 있다는 점을 유의해 주시기 바랍니다. [19]저희가 시간을 더 필요
로 한다면 별도의 공지를 드리겠습니다. 이것이 불편할 것임을 이해하지만, 저
희 주민들의 안전이 저희의 최우선 사항입니다.

그렇지만, 가능한 한 빨리 정상적인 작동을 복구하기 위해 저희가 할 수 있는 모
든 것을 할 것임을 보장해 드립니다. 이 문제에 대한 여러분의 인내와 이해에 매
우 감사드립니다.

감사합니다.

conduct v. 실시하다, 실행하다 **even-numbered** adj. 짝수의
in a few days 가까운 시일 내에 **occupant** n. (주택·방·건물 등의) 입주자
check v. 점검하다 **electrical wiring** 전기 배선
as well as ~뿐만 아니라 **part** n. (기계·컴퓨터 등의) 부품
at least 적어도, 최소한 **inconvenience** n. 불편 **tenant** n. 주민, 세입자
utmost adj. 최고의 **priority** n. 우선 사항 **assure** v. 보장하다, 확신하다
restore v. 복구하다 **operation** n. 작동 **regarding** prep. ~에 대하여

16 명사 어휘 고르기 전체 문맥 파악 ▶ Vocabulary Ch. 02 명사

해설 '정기적인 ____을 실시할 것이다'라는 문맥이므로 (C) inspection(점
검), (D) demonstration(시범 설명)이 정답의 후보이다. 빈칸이 있는 문장
만으로 정답을 고를 수 없으므로 주변 문맥이나 전체 문맥을 파악한다. 뒤
문장에서 그 엘리베이터는 이용할 수 없을 것이다(That elevator will
be unavailable)'라고 한 후, '기술자들이 리프트 장치를 점검할 것이다
(our technicians will be checking ~ the lifting device)'라고 했으므
로, 엘리베이터에 대한 점검을 실시할 것임을 알 수 있다. 따라서 명사 (C)
inspection이 정답이다.

어휘 **consideration** n. 고려, 숙고 **experiment** n. 실험

17 부사 자리 채우기 ▶ Grammar Ch. 13 부사

해설 빈칸이 관계대명사 who로 시작되는 관계절의 동사(take)를 꾸미는 자리이
므로 부사 (D) normally(보통)가 정답이다. 형용사 (A)와 동사 (B), 명사 (C)
는 동사를 꾸밀 수 없다.

어휘 **normal** adj. 보통의, 정상적인 **normalize** v. 정상화하다
normality n. 정상 상태

18 형용사 어휘 고르기 ▶ Vocabulary Ch. 03 형용사

해설 '기술자들이 리프트 장치를 점검할 것이기 때문에 엘리베이터에 접근할 수 없
다'는 문맥이므로 형용사 (C) inaccessible(접근할 수 없는)이 정답이다.

어휘 **impossible** adj. 불가능한 **undisclosed** adj. 나타나지 않은, 발표되지 않은
undetermined adj. 미확인의, 결단을 못 내리는

19 알맞은 문장 고르기

해석 (A) 수리가 완료되면 보수 작업 팀원들에게 알려주시기 바랍니다.
(B) 세입자들이 이 기간에 그들의 방을 비워야 하는 것은 필수입니다.

(C) 저희가 시간을 더 필요로 한다면 별도의 공지를 드리겠습니다.
(D) 건물의 모든 엘리베이터는 동시에 점검될 것입니다.

해설 빈칸에 들어갈 알맞은 문장을 고르는 문제이므로 빈칸의 주변 문맥이나 전체 문맥을 파악한다. 앞 문장 'it may be necessary to keep the elevator closed for longer'에서 엘리베이터가 더 오랜 시간 동안 정지될 필요가 있을 수도 있다고 했으므로 빈칸에는 시간을 더 필요로 하게 될 경우 별도의 공지를 하겠다는 내용이 들어가야 함을 알 수 있다. 따라서 (C) We will send another notice if we need more time이 정답이다.

어휘 mandatory adj. 필수의, 명령의 vacate v. 비우다
simultaneously adv. 동시에

20-23은 다음 이메일에 관한 문제입니다.

수신: Jeanne Parton <careers@writemoves.com>
발신: Carson Diaz <cdiaz@mailpal.com>
날짜: 9월 2일
제목: 취업 기회

Ms. Parton께,

²⁰WriteMoves 웹사이트에 현재 게시되어 있는 스페인어 번역가 직위에 대해 관심을 표하고 싶습니다. ²¹저는 몬터레이 대학의 통번역학과에서 석사 학위를 취득했는데, 이곳은 혁신적인 프로그램으로 명성이 높습니다.

저는 댈러스에 위치한 NoroSoft라는 소프트웨어 회사에서 기술 관련 문서작성자로 4년을 보냈습니다. 이 직위에 있는 기간 동안, 저는 설명서들을 영어에서 스페인어로 번역했습니다. ²²제 제작물을 보실 수 있도록 그것들 중 하나를 첨부했습니다. 이에 앞서, 저는 외무부에서 스페인어를 사용하는 고위 인사들을 돕는 인턴으로 일했습니다. ²³특히, 저는 특별 행사에서 그들에게 전달되는 모든 것을 통역하였습니다. 이러한 지난 두 경력으로, 저는 서면 번역과 구두 통역에 동일하게 능숙합니다.

질문이 있으시다면, 주저하지 마시고 제게 연락 주십시오.

Carson Diaz 드림

---

position n. 직위, 자리 post v. 게시하다, 발송하다; n. 우편
master's degree 석사 학위 be renowned for ~으로 명성이 높다
innovative adj. 혁신적인, 획기적인 translate v. 번역하다
manual n. 설명서; adj. 수동의 prior to ~에 앞서 assist v. 돕다, 조력하다
dignitary n. 고위 인사, 고관 interpret v. 통역하다, (의미를) 해석하다
be skilled at ~에 능숙하다, 숙련되다 equally adv. 동일하게, 똑같이

20 부사 어휘 고르기　　　► Vocabulary Ch. 04 부사

해설 '웹사이트에 현재 게시되어 있는 직위에 대해 관심을 표하고 싶다'라는 문맥이므로 부사 (D) currently(현재, 지금)가 정답이다.

어휘 immediately adv. 즉시 previously adv. 이전에
abruptly adv. 갑작스럽게

21 관계대명사와 관계부사 구별하여 채우기　► Grammar Ch. 16 관계절

해설 빈칸 뒤에 주어가 없는 불완전한 절(is renowned for ~ program)이 와서 빈칸 앞의 명사(Monterey University's Department of Translation and Interpretation)를 꾸며 주고 있으므로, 불완전한 절을 이끌 수 있는 관계대명사 (B)와 (D)가 정답의 후보이다. 이 관계절에는 주어가 없으므로 주격 관계대명사 (B) which가 정답이다. 목적격 관계대명사 (D) whom은 관계절 내에서 목적어 역할을 한다. 완전한 절을 이끄는 관계부사 (A) where와 (C) when은 답이 될 수 없다.

22 알맞은 문장 고르기

해석 (A) 면접에 초대해주신 것에 대해 대단히 감사합니다.
(B) 제 제작물을 보실 수 있도록 그것들 중 하나를 첨부했습니다.
(C) 당신이 기재한 추천인들 중 한 명에게 연락할 수 없었습니다.
(D) 그 직위가 단지 임시직이라는 것을 알고 있습니다.

해설 빈칸에 들어갈 알맞은 문장을 고르는 문제이므로 빈칸의 주변 문맥이나 전체 문맥을 파악한다. 앞 문장 'During my time in this position, I translated manuals from English into Spanish.'에서 이 직위, 즉 기술 관련 문서작성자 직위에 있는 기간 동안 설명서들을 영어에서 스페인어로 번역했다고 했

으므로 빈칸에는 번역한 설명서와 관련된 내용이 들어가야 함을 알 수 있다. 따라서 (B) I have attached one of them so you can view my work가 정답이다.

어휘 appreciative adj. 감사하는, 감상을 즐기는 reference n. 추천인, 참고

23 접속부사 채우기　주변 문맥 파악　　► Grammar Ch. 13 부사

해설 빈칸이 콤마와 함께 문장의 맨 앞에 온 접속부사 자리이므로, 앞 문장과 빈칸이 있는 문장의 의미 관계를 파악하여 접속부사인 (A), (C), (D) 중 하나를 정답으로 골라야 한다. 앞 문장에서 자신이 외무부에서 스페인어를 사용하는 고위 인사들을 돕는 인턴으로 일했다고 했고, 빈칸이 있는 문장에서는 자신이 특별 행사에서 그들에게 전달되는 모든 것을 통역했다고 했으므로 앞 문장과 관련하여 구체적인 사항을 추가할 때 사용되는 (D) In particular(특히, 특별히)가 정답이다.

어휘 even so 그렇기는 하지만 instead of ~ 대신에
regardless adv. 그럼에도 불구하고

24-25는 다음 온라인 채팅 대화문에 관한 문제입니다.

Jared Reed [오후 12:05]
²⁴저희 팀이 내년 예산안을 검토할 수 있도록 오늘 오후에 회의실이 필요할 거예요. 오후 2시부터 4시까지 회의실 B를 예약할 수 있나요?

Jessica Chavez [오후 12:10]
죄송하지만, 다른 그룹이 이미 그 시간을 예약했어요. 오후 4시부터 6시까지는 괜찮으세요?

Jared Reed [오후 12:12]
유감스럽지만 안 돼요. ²⁴저희 팀원 3명이 오후 5시에 부사장님께 재무제표를 발표해야 해요. 다른 방이 있나요?

Jessica Chavez [오후 12:14]
음, ²⁵6층에 이용 가능한 장소가 있어요. 모든 동일한 장비를 갖추고 있지만, 상당히 더 좁아요.

Jared Reed [오후 12:16]
다른 선택권이 없는 것 같네요. ²⁵예약해 주세요. 감사합니다.

---

budget proposal 예산안 conference room 회의실
financial statement 재무제표 vice president 부사장
equipment n. 장비, 용품

24 추론 문제

문제 Mr. Reed에 대해 암시되는 것은?
(A) 오늘 아침에 회의를 했다.
(B) 최근에 새로운 팀원을 고용했다.
(C) 오늘 Ms. Chavez를 찾아갈 것이다.
(D) 재무 부서에서 일한다.

해설 질문의 핵심 어구인 Mr. Reed에 대해 추론하는 문제이다. 'my team ~ review next year's budget proposal'(12:05 P.M.)에서 Mr. Reed가 자신의 팀이 내년 예산안을 검토한다고 한 후, 'Three members of my team have to present our financial statements to the vice president at 5 P.M.'(12:12 P.M.)에서 오후 5시에 자신의 팀원 3명이 부사장에게 재무제표를 발표해야 한다고 했으므로 Mr. Reed가 예산안과 재무제표 관련 업무를 처리하는 재무 부서에서 일한다는 사실을 추론할 수 있다. 따라서 (D) He works in the finance department가 정답이다.

어휘 finance department 재무 부서

25 의도 파악 문제

문제 오후 12시 16분에, Mr. Reed가 "I guess I have no other choice"라고 썼을 때, 그가 의도한 것은?
(A) 예약 없이 장소를 방문할 계획이다.
(B) 발표 장비를 이용할 권한이 없을 것이다.
(C) 덜 넓은 방을 사용하기로 결정했다.
(D) 회의 시간을 변경해야 할 것이다.

해설 Mr. Reed가 의도한 것을 묻는 문제이므로, 질문의 인용어구(I guess I have no other choice)가 언급된 주변 문맥을 확인한다. 'there is an available space on the sixth floor. It's got all the same equipment, but it's quite a bit smaller.'(12:14 P.M.)에서 Ms. Chavez가 6층에 이용 가능한 장소가 있는데, 모든 동일한 장비를 갖추고 있지만 상당히 더 좁은 장소라고 하자, Mr. Reed가 'I guess I have no other choice'(다른 선택권이 없는 것 같네요)라고 한 후, 'Please book it for me.'(12:16 P.M.)에서 그 방을 예약해 달라고 한 것을 통해, Mr. Reed가 6층에 있는 더 좁은 장소, 즉 덜 넓은 회의실을 사용하기로 결정했음을 알 수 있다. 따라서 (C) He has decided to use a less spacious room이 정답이다.

Paraphrasing
smaller 더 좁은 → less spacious 덜 넓은

어휘 **reservation** n. 예약 **spacious** adj. 넓은, 널찍한

26-28은 다음 광고에 관한 문제입니다.

[28-C]Vibrastep으로 과체중 감량!

[26]Vibrastep은 체육관에서 한 시간 동안 운동하는 것으로부터 얻는 것과 동일한 효과를 제공합니다. 유명한 운동기기 제조업체인 Athletrex사에서 제조한 이 최첨단 기기는 사용자가 진동 금속판 위에 서 있는 동안 긴장을 푸는 데 도움이 되는 진동을 몸 전체에 전달합니다. 시장에 출시되기 앞서, 이 기기는 진료소와 병원에서 사용되었고, 그 효과는 의사들에 의해 검증되었습니다.

진동 운동은 근육의 수축을 일으켜서 효과를 냅니다. 이는 지방과 피하지방을 연소하는 것 뿐만 아니라 혈액 순환과 신진대사를 향상시키는 것에도 도움을 줍니다. 다른 이점들로는 다음이 포함됩니다:
· [28-D]탄력 있고 팽팽한 피부
· 기분과 전반적인 행복감 향상을 위한 높은 세로토닌 수치
· 한 달 이내에 50퍼센트까지의 [28-B]근력 증가
· 골다공증을 예방하는 향상된 골밀도
· 콜라겐 생성의 증가

하루에 15분씩만으로, 매일, 체중을 효과적으로 감량할 수 있습니다! [27]주문을 하기 위해서는 1-800-555-4880으로 연락해 주십시오. [27]우리 제품은 2년짜리 품질 보증서가 딸려 있고 매장에서는 구입하실 수 없습니다. 오늘 한 대 주문하십시오!

lose weight 체중을 감량하다 work out 운동하다
state-of-the-art adj. 최첨단의 well-known adj. 유명한, 잘 알려진
deliver v. 전달하다 therapeutic adj. 긴장을 푸는 데 도움이 되는, 치료상의
vibration n. 진동, 떨림 prior to ~에 앞서, 먼저
release n. 출시, 발표; v. 출시하다, 공개하다 clinic n. 진료소
verify v. 검증하다, 확인하다 contraction n. 수축, 축소 cellulite n. 피하지방
blood circulation 혈액 순환 metabolism n. 신진대사
tone v. (근육·피부를) 탄력 있게 만들다 elevate v. 높이다
enhance v. 향상시키다 bone density 골밀도
osteoporosis n. 골다공증 boost n. 증가; v. 신장시키다
come with ~이 딸려 있다

---

26 추론 문제

문제 광고는 누구를 대상으로 할 것 같은가?
(A) 운동 시설의 소유주들
(B) 의료업계에 종사하는 전문가들
(C) 건강을 증진하기를 원하는 사람들
(D) 운동기기 소매업자들

해설 광고의 대상을 추론하는 문제이다. 'Vibrastep provides the same benefits that you can get from working out at the gym for an hour.'(1문단 1번째 줄)에서 Vibrastep은 체육관에서 한 시간 운동하는 것과 동일한 효과를 제공한다고 한 후, 건강에 도움이 되는 Vibrastep의 이점들을 설명하고 있으므로 건강을 증진하기를 원하는 사람들을 대상으로 하는 광고임을 추론할 수 있다. 따라서 (C) People wanting to improve their health가 정답이다.

어휘 **proprietor** n. 소유주 **expert** n. 전문가 **retailer** n. 소매업자

---

27 추론 문제

문제 Vibrastep에 대해 암시되는 것은?
(A) 가격은 체육관 회원권과 같다.
(B) 오직 전화로만 구매할 수 있다.

(C) 사용은 의사의 감독을 필요로 한다.
(D) 많은 운동 시설에서 찾아볼 수 있다.

해설 질문의 핵심 어구인 Vibrastep에 대해 추론하는 문제이다. 'Contact us at 1-800-555-4880 to make your order. Our product ~ is not available in stores.'(3문단 1번째 줄)에서 주문을 하기 위해서는 전화를 해야 하며 매장에서는 구입이 불가능하다고 했으므로 전화상으로만 구매가 가능하다는 사실을 추론할 수 있다. 따라서 (B) It can be purchased over the phone only가 정답이다.

어휘 **equivalent to** ~와 같은 **supervision** n. 감독, 관리, 지휘

---

28 Not/True 문제

문제 Vibrastep을 사용하는 것에 대한 이점이 아닌 것은?
(A) 스포츠 활동을 위한 더 강한 체력
(B) 근육의 강화
(C) 과체중 감량
(D) 개선된 피부 상태

해설 질문의 핵심 어구인 a benefit of using the Vibrastep과 관련된 내용을 지문에서 찾아 보기와 대조하는 Not/True 문제이다. (A)는 지문에 언급되지 않은 내용이다. 따라서 (A) Greater stamina for sports activities가 정답이다. (B)는 'An increase in muscle strength'(2문단 6번째 줄)에서 근력 증가라고 했으므로 지문의 내용과 일치한다. (C)는 'Lose that extra weight with Vibrastep!'(제목)에서 Vibrastep으로 과체중을 감량하라고 했으므로 지문의 내용과 일치한다. (D)는 'Skin toning and tightening'(2문단 4번째 줄)에서 탄력 있고 팽팽한 피부라고 했으므로 지문의 내용과 일치한다.

Paraphrasing
An increase in muscle strength 근력 증가 → Strengthening of muscles 근육의 강화
extra weight 과체중 → excess weight 과체중
Skin toning and tightening 탄력 있고 팽팽한 피부 → Improved skin condition 개선된 피부 상태

어휘 **stamina** n. 체력 **excess** adj. 과잉의 **improved** adj. 개선된

29-31은 다음 보도 자료에 관한 문제입니다.

Pacific Film사
707번지 Sycamore가
새너제이, 캘리포니아주 95131
전화: (408) 555-2552~2560
팩스: (408) 555-2565
www.pacificfilm.com

연락: Janina Compton
전화번호: (408) 555-2556
이메일: jcompton@pacificfilm.com

Pacific Film사 1월에 개선할 예정

새너제이, 캘리포니아주, 12월 4일 – 이번 주에, [29]Pacific Film사의 대변인은 내년 초에 회사가 조직 내 일련의 변화에 착수할 것이라고 밝혔다.

1월에, [30]Pacific Film사는 경쟁사들에 뒤지지 않기 위해 새로운 전략들을 시행할 것이다. [30]이 중 하나는 카메라, 메모리 카드 및 디지털 사진에 사용되는 다른 기기들과 같은 제품의 연구 개발에 대한 투자를 늘리는 것을 포함한다. 또 다른 전략은 운용비용과 생산비용을 줄이기 위해 지사와 생산 공장을 중국과 베트남에 설립하는 것이다.

"수년 동안, 디지털 사진업계에서 많은 회사들이 부상하여 Pacific Film사에 도전해 왔습니다. 따라서, 우리는 Pacific Film사의 제품들의 경쟁력 유지를 확실히 하기 위한 조치를 취해야 합니다."라고 최고 경영자인 Anthony Villman이 말했다.

미국에 기반을 둔 다국적 기업인 [31]Pacific Film사는 10년 전에 디지털 사진 제품들을 시장에 처음 소개한 기업 중 하나이다.

representative n. 대변인 reveal v. 밝히다, 드러내 보이다
undertake v. 착수하다 a series of 일련의 implement v. 시행하다
strategy n. 전략 keep pace with ~에 뒤지지 않다, ~에 따라가다

---

investment n. 투자 **research** n. 연구 **development** n. 개발
establishment n. 설립 **regional office** 지사 **cut down on** ~을 줄이다
emerge v. 부상하다, 드러나다 **take steps** 조치를 취하다
competitive adj. 경쟁력이 있는 **multinational** adj. 다국적의
based in ~에 기반을 둔 **introduce** v. 소개하다, 도입하다

29 주제/목적 찾기 문제

문제   보도 자료는 왜 쓰였는가?
(A) 영화 촬영소의 설립을 알리기 위해
(B) 새로운 제품군에 대한 정보를 제공하기 위해
(C) 회사의 계획된 활동들에 대한 정보를 제공하기 위해
(D) 곧 있을 영화 제작을 설명하기 위해

해설   보도 자료가 쓰인 목적을 묻는 목적 찾기 문제이다. 'a representative from Pacific Film revealed that the company would be undertaking a series of changes'(1문단 1번째 줄)에서 Pacific Film사의 대변인이 회사가 일련의 변화에 착수할 것임을 밝혔다고 한 후, 구체적인 전략들을 언급하고 있으므로 (C) To give details on a company's planned activities가 정답이다.

Paraphrasing
revealed 밝히다 → give details 정보를 제공하다

어휘   **planned** adj. 계획된, 예정대로의 **upcoming** adj. 곧 있을, 다가오는

30 추론 문제

문제   Pacific Film사에 대해 암시되는 것은?
(A) 다른 도시로 본사를 이전할 것이다.
(B) 제품군을 개선하기 위해 노력하고 있다.
(C) 아시아에 생산 공장을 열었다.
(D) 새로운 최고 경영자가 있다.

해설   질문의 핵심 어구인 Pacific Film에 대해 추론하는 문제이다. 'Pacific Film will be implementing new strategies'(2문단 1번째 줄)와 'One of these includes increasing investments in research and development of products'(2문단 1번째 줄)에서 Pacific Film사가 시행할 새로운 전략들에 제품 연구 개발에 대한 투자를 늘리는 것이 포함된다고 했으므로 제품군을 개선하기 위해 노력하고 있다는 사실을 추론할 수 있다. 따라서 (B) It is aiming to improve a line of goods가 정답이다.

어휘   **relocate** v. 이전하다, 이동하다 **main office** 본사
aim to do ~하려고 노력하다 **production plant** 생산 공장

31 추론 문제

문제   회사의 디지털 사진 제품들에 대해 암시되는 것은?
(A) Pacific Film사의 가장 잘 팔리는 품목이다.
(B) 다른 상표들과 비교해서 더 비싸다.
(C) 최근에 판매 증가를 경험했다.
(D) 10년 전에 시장에 처음 출시되었다.

해설   질문의 핵심 어구인 digital photography products에 대해 추론하는 문제이다. 'Pacific Film was among the first to introduce digital photography products to the market 10 years ago'(4문단 1번째 줄)에서 Pacific Film사가 10년 전에 디지털 사진 제품들을 시장에 처음 소개한 기업 중 하나라고 했으므로 디지털 사진 제품들은 10년 전에 시장에 처음 출시되었다는 사실을 추론할 수 있다. 따라서 (D) They were first launched on the market a decade ago가 정답이다.

Paraphrasing
10 years 10년 → a decade 10년

어휘   **rise** n. 증가 **launch** v. 출시하다, 진출하다; n. 출시

32-35는 다음 편지에 관한 문제입니다.

Cater Source사
1602번지 Hampstead가
라스베이거스, 네바다주 89101
전화번호: (702) 555-7596 / 팩스: (702) 555-7600
www.catersource.com

8월 27일

Giada Durand

Le Cuisine Francois
952번지 Oakway로
로스앤젤레스, 캘리포니아주 90017

Ms. Durand께,

³²Cater Source사는 귀하의 관심에 감사드립니다. 전화로 말씀드린 것을 되풀이하자면, ³³ᴮ자사는 자기, 유리 및 광택 혹은 무광택 마감칠 처리된 플라스틱 소재로 만든 다양한 종류의 현대 및 전통 식기를 제공합니다. 또한, 자사 제품들은 대부분의 식당 영업 수요를 충족하도록 고안된 접대용 부속품과 함께 다양한 무늬로 나옵니다.

참고하실 수 있도록, ³⁵전체 제품 카탈로그를 보내드렸습니다. 주문하실 준비가 되면, ³³ᴬ간단히 주문서를 작성하셔서 우편을 통해 자사로 돌려 보내 주십시오. 더 신속한 처리를 위해, ³³ᴬ/³⁴자사 웹사이트를 방문해서 주문하실 수도 있습니다. 대량으로 주문하시는 고객께는 할인이 가능합니다. ³³ᴰ자사의 모든 제품은 제조업체 보증서와 더불어 6개월짜리 품질 보증서를 포함합니다.

더 질문이 있으시면, awilson@catersource.com으로 제게 이메일을 보내 주십시오.

Anthony Wilson 드림
마케팅 책임자
Cater Source사

appreciate v. 감사하다, 고마워하다 **reiterate** v. 되풀이하다, 반복하다
contemporary adj. 현대적인, 동시대의 **traditional** adj. 전통의
dinnerware n. 식기 **porcelain** n. 자기
glazed adj. 광택 있는, 유약을 칠한 **matte** adj. 무광택의 **finish** n. 마감칠
be designed to ~하도록 고안되다, 제작되다 **reference** n. 참고
product catalog 제품 카탈로그, 상품 안내 책자 **in bulk** 대량으로

32 주제/목적 찾기 문제

문제   편지의 주 목적은 무엇인가?
(A) 비품의 주문을 확인하기 위해
(B) 식당 행사에 대해 자세한 정보를 제공하기 위해
(C) 제품에 대한 정보를 요청하기 위해
(D) 잠재 고객의 질문에 답하기 위해

해설   편지의 목적을 묻는 목적 찾기 문제이다. 'We at Cater Source appreciate your interest.'(1문단 1번째 줄)에서 Cater Source사에 대한 관심에 감사하다고 한 후, 회사 제품과 주문에 대한 세부 사항을 설명하고 있으므로 (D) To address a potential customer's questions가 정답이다.

어휘   **confirm** v. 확인하다 **address** v. 답하다, 말을 하다
potential adj. 잠재적인, 가능성이 있는

33 Not/True 문제

문제   Cater Source사의 제품들에 대해 언급된 것은?
(A) 여러 소매 판매점에서 구입할 수 있다.
(B) 다양한 소재로 만들어졌다.
(C) 식당들에만 판매된다.
(D) 1년 동안 보증된다.

해설   질문의 핵심 어구인 Cater Source's products와 관련된 내용을 지문에서 찾아 보기와 대조하는 Not/True 문제이다. (A)는 'just fill out the order form and mail it back to us'(2문단 1번째 줄)와 'you may also go to our Web site and place your order there'(2문단 2번째 줄)에서 우편 및 웹사이트를 통한 주문 방법을 언급했으므로 지문의 내용과 일치하지 않는다. (B)는 'we offer a wide selection of ~ dinnerware made of porcelain, glass, and plastic'(1문단 1번째 줄)에서 자기, 유리 및 플라스틱 소재로 만든 다양한 종류의 식기를 제공한다고 했으므로 지문의 내용과 일치한다. 따라서 (B) They are made of a variety of different materials가 정답이다. (C)는 지문에 언급되지 않은 내용이다. (D)는 'All our products include a six-month warranty'(2문단 3번째 줄)에서 모든 제품은 6개월짜리 품질 보증서를 포함한다고 했으므로 지문의 내용과 일치하지 않는다.

Paraphrasing
a wide selection of 다양한 종류의 ~ → a variety of 다양한 ~

어휘 retail outlet 소매 판매점

34 동의어 찾기 문제

문제 2문단 세 번째 줄의 단어 "place"는 의미상 -와 가장 가깝다.
(A) 배치하다
(B) 위치하다
(C) 제출하다
(D) 평가하다

해설 place를 포함하고 있는 구절 'you may also go to our Web site and place your order there'(2문단 2번째 줄)에서 place는 order와 함께 사용되어 '주문을 하다'라는 뜻으로 사용되었다. 따라서 '(주문서를) 제출하다'라는 뜻을 가진 (C) submit이 정답이다.

어휘 rate v. 평가하다

35 육하원칙 문제

문제 Mr. Wilson은 Ms. Durand에게 무엇을 보냈는가?
(A) 보증서 카드
(B) 상품의 샘플
(C) 청구 내역서
(D) 제품들의 목록

해설 Mr. Wilson이 Ms. Durand에게 무엇(What)을 보냈는지를 묻는 육하원칙 문제이다. 질문의 핵심 어구인 Mr. Wilson send to Ms. Durand와 관련하여, 'I have sent you a complete product catalog'(2문단 1번째 줄)에서 전체 제품 카탈로그를 보냈다고 했으므로 (D) A listing of products가 정답이다.

Paraphrasing
product catalog 제품 카탈로그 → A listing of products 제품들의 목록

어휘 merchandise n. 상품, 물품 billing statement 청구 내역서

36-40은 다음 두 편지에 관한 문제입니다.

4월 12일

Lorraine Amici
고객 관리팀
Pacific Waterworks사

Ms. Amici,

저는 귀사의 매장에서 양수기를 구매해서 지난 금요일에 저의 집에 설치했습니다. 월요일에, 저는 양수기가 짧은 간격으로 켜졌다 꺼졌다 하는 것을 발견했고, 이는 도움을 얻기 위해 제가 귀사의 직통 전화로 전화하도록 했습니다. ³⁸저는 24시간 안에 도움을 받아서 기뻤습니다. 그러나, 화요일에 제 집을 방문한 수리팀의 서비스에는 만족하지 못했습니다.

양수기에 결함이 있는 것을 발견한 후, 저는 수리팀이 그것을 새것으로 교체해 줄 것이라 생각했습니다. 대신, 그들은 기기의 몇몇 부품만 교체했습니다. 제가 예상했던 대로, 문제는 그 다음 날 다시 발생했습니다.

³⁶귀사의 수준 이하의 제품은 제 가족을 충분히 오랫동안 불편하게 했고, 그러므로 ³⁶/³⁹저는 귀사가 즉시 제품 전체를 교체해 줄 것을 요구합니다. ³⁷/³⁹만약 귀사에서 이 문제를 3일 안에 처리해주지 않는다면, ³⁹저는 손해에 따른 전액 환불을 요구할 것입니다.

참고하실 수 있도록 공식 영수증과 보증서 카드의 사본을 동봉합니다.

Benito Garcia 드림

water pump 양수기 observe v. 발견하다, 목격하다 interval n. 간격 prompt v. (~에게 결정을 내리도록) 하다 crew n. 팀, 수리반 defective adj. 결함이 있는, 불량인 component n. 부품 occur v. 발생하다, 일어나다 substandard adj. 수준 이하의, 조약한 address v. (어려운 문제 등) 처리하다, 다루다 enclose v. 동봉하다

Pacific Waterworks사
1016번지 West Jackson대로, 시카고, 일리노이주 60607 〇

---

www.pacificwater.com
555-6392

4월 14일

Benito Garcia
6035번지 St. Lawrence가
시카고, 일리노이주 60637

Mr. Garcia께,

Pacific Waterworks사의 경영진을 대신해, 발생했던 문제에 대해 진심으로 사과드리고자 합니다. ³⁹우리 직원 몇 명을 새 양수기와 함께 이 편지를 직접 전달하도록 보냈고, 그들이 새 양수기를 오늘 설치해 드릴 것입니다.

또한, 이 문제를 알려주신 것에 대해 감사드리고 싶습니다. 그러한 사고가 다시 발생하는 것을 방지하기 위해 적절한 조치가 현재 취해지고 있습니다. ⁴⁰이 편지에 동봉된 100달러의 상품권으로 귀하께 보상해 드릴 수 있도록 허락해 주십시오. Pacific Waterworks사의 어떤 제품이든 다음 번에 구매하실 때 이 상품권을 사용하실 수 있습니다.

귀하의 이해에 감사드립니다.

Lorraine Amici 드림
고객 관리 담당자
Pacific Waterworks사

on behalf of ~을 대표하여 express regret for ~을 사과하다 sincere adj. 진심의, 진실된 prevent v. 방지하다, 막다 incident n. 사고, 사건 make it up to ~에게 보상하다 gift certificate 상품권

---

36 주제/목적 찾기 문제

문제 고객은 왜 편지를 보냈는가?
(A) 특별 배송 지침을 제공하기 위해
(B) 주문을 완료하는 데 도움을 구하기 위해
(C) 장비의 교환을 요청하기 위해
(D) 지연된 수송품의 상태를 확인하기 위해

해설 고객이 편지를 쓴 목적을 묻는 목적 찾기 문제이므로 제품 구매자인 Benito Garcia가 작성한 편지를 확인한다. 첫 번째 편지의 'Your substandard product has inconvenienced my family long enough, so I demand that you replace the entire unit immediately.'(3문단 1번째 줄)에서 수준 이하의 제품이 가족을 오랫동안 불편하게 했으므로 즉시 제품을 교체해 줄 것을 요구한다고 했으므로 (C) To ask for an exchange of equipment가 정답이다.

Paraphrasing
replace the entire unit 제품 전체를 교체하다 → an exchange of equipment 장비의 교환

어휘 seek v. 구하다, 추구하다 shipment n. 수송품

37 동의어 찾기 문제

문제 첫 번째 편지에서, 3문단 두 번째 줄의 단어 "address"는 의미상 -와 가장 가깝다.
(A) 지시하다
(B) 보내다
(C) 표시하다
(D) 해결하다

해설 첫 번째 편지의 address를 포함한 구절 'If you do not address this matter'(3문단 2번째 줄)에서 address는 '(어려운 문제 등을) 처리하다, 다루다'라는 뜻으로 사용되었다. 따라서 '(문제 등을) 해결하다'라는 뜻을 가진 (D) resolve가 정답이다.

어휘 direct v. 지시하다 send v. 보내다 mark v. 표시하다

38 추론 문제

문제 Pacific Waterworks사에 대해 암시되는 것은?
(A) 가정 방문에 대한 요금을 소비자들에게 청구한다.
(B) 서비스 요청에 빠른 대응을 제공한다.
(C) 예비 부품을 다른 나라에서 수입한다.

(D) 건설 회사와 제휴하고 있다.

해설 질문의 핵심 어구인 Pacific Waterworks에 대해 추론하는 문제이므로 Pacific Waterworks사로 보내진 편지에서 관련 내용을 확인한다. 첫 번째 편지의 'I was pleased to receive help within 24 hours.'(1문단 3번째 줄)에서 24시간 안에 도움을 받아서 기뻤다고 했으므로 Pacific Waterworks사가 서비스 요청에 빠르게 대응한다는 사실을 추론할 수 있다. 따라서 (B) It provides quick responses to service requests가 정답이다.

어휘 **charge** v. 요금을 청구하다　**house call** (왕진 등의) 가정 방문
response n. 대응, 반응　**spare** adj. 예비의　**part** n. 부품

39 육하원칙 문제 │ 연계

문제 Pacific Waterworks사는 어떻게 Mr. Garcia의 우려에 대응했는가?
(A) 회장의 공식적인 사과문을 전달함으로써
(B) 기계의 품질 보증 기간을 늘려줌으로써
(C) 그의 항의 중 처음 요구 사항을 들어줌으로써
(D) 그의 은행 계좌로 환불 금액을 입금함으로써

해설 두 지문의 내용을 종합해서 풀어야 하는 연계 문제이다. 질문의 핵심 어구인 respond to Mr. Garcia's concerns에서 Pacific Waterworks사가 어떻게 (How) Mr. Garcia의 우려에 대응했는지를 묻고 있으므로 Mr. Garcia가 작성한 편지를 먼저 확인한다.
첫 번째 편지의 'I demand that you replace the entire unit immediately'(3문단 1번째 줄)와 'If you do not address this matter within three days, I will ask for a full refund'(3문단 2번째 줄)에서 Mr. Garcia는 즉시 제품 전체를 교체해 달라고 요구했고, 3일 안에 처리해 주지 않으면 전액 환불을 요청할 것이라는 첫 번째 단서를 확인할 수 있다. 그런데 이에 대해 Pacific Waterworks사가 어떻게 대응했는지 제시되지 않았으므로 Pacific Waterworks사가 보낸 편지에서 관련 내용을 확인한다. 두 번째 편지의 'I have sent some of our staff ~ along with a new water pump, which they will install today.'(1문단 2번째 줄)에서 직원 몇 명을 새 양수기와 함께 보냈으며 그들이 새로운 양수기를 오늘 설치해줄 것이라는 두 번째 단서를 확인할 수 있다.
Mr. Garcia가 즉시 제품 전체를 교체해 달라고 요구했고 그것을 처리해 주지 않으면 전액 환불을 요청할 것이라는 첫 번째 단서와 Pacific Waterworks사가 직원들을 보내 새로운 양수기를 설치하도록 했다는 두 번째 단서를 종합할 때, Pacific Waterworks사가 Mr. Garcia의 처음 요구 사항을 들어주었음을 알 수 있다. 따라서 (C) By granting the initial request in his complaint가 정답이다.

어휘 **grant** v. 들어주다, 승인하다　**initial** adj. 처음의, 초기의　**deposit** v. 입금하다

40 추론 문제

문제 Mr. Garcia에 대해 암시되는 것은?
(A) Pacific Waterworks사의 단골 고객이다.
(B) 품질 보증 기간을 연장받고 싶어 한다.
(C) 추후의 구입품에 돈을 절약할 수 있다.
(D) 이전에도 비슷한 문제를 겪었다.

해설 질문의 핵심 어구인 Mr. Garcia에 대해 추론하는 문제이므로 Mr. Garcia에게 보내진 편지를 확인한다. 두 번째 편지의 'Please allow us to make it up to you with a $100 gift certificate ~. You may use the certificate the next time you buy any product from Pacific Waterworks.'(2문단 2번째 줄)에서 Pacific Waterworks사가 Mr. Garcia에게 100달러의 상품권으로 보상하고 싶다고 했고 이 상품권은 다음 번 제품 구매 시 사용할 수 있다고 했으므로 Mr. Garcia가 추후 구입품에 돈을 절약할 수 있음을 추론할 수 있다. 따라서 (C) He can save money on a purchase in the future가 정답이다.

어휘 **regular customer** 단골 고객　**extend** v. 연장하다

41-45는 다음 편지, 행사 일정표, 이메일에 관한 문제입니다.

시카고 출판 협회
355-345번지 Lawson가
시카고, 일리노이주 60615
cgott@cpubassoc.org

10월 17일

Claude Hutchins
3301 Bellevue 사무소
시애틀, 워싱턴주 98101

Mr. Hutchins께,

⁴¹/⁴³시카고 출판 협회는 올해의 아동 도서상 수상자로 귀하를 선정했다는 사실을 알려드리게 되어 기쁩니다. 귀하의 저서 *Digging for Treasure*는 현재까지 1년간 국내 베스트셀러 1위를 해왔으며 평론가들과 독자들 양쪽 모두에게 찬사를 받고 있습니다.

시상식은 시카고에 있는 Alexandria 호텔에서 개최될 것입니다. ⁴²동봉된 것은 귀하가 검토해야 할 잠정적인 일정표입니다. 본 협회는 수상을 위해 귀하께서 참석하시기를 진심으로 희망하며, 참석 여부를 늦어도 10월 20일까지 저희에게 알려주시기를 정중히 요청드립니다.

Cecilia Gott 드림
관리자

recipient n. (어떤 것을) 받는 사람, 수취인　**top** v. 1위를 하다, 더 높다
critic n. 평론가, 비평가　**alike** adv. 양쪽 모두, 둘 다　**enclose** v. 동봉하다
tentative adj. 잠정적인　**present** v. 참석하다　**at the latest** 늦어도

시카고 출판 협회　　　　　　　　　　　　　　　　　　　*11월 15일*
올해의 도서 시상식
Alexandria 호텔 연회장

프로그램

오후 7시 - 오후 7시 15분	환영사
오후 7시 15분 - 오후 8시 30분	⁴³/⁴⁵시상식
오후 7시 15분 - 오후 7시 30분	올해의 문학 소설
오후 7시 30분 - 오후 7시 45분	올해의 시집
⁴³오후 7시 45분 - 오후 8시	올해의 아동 도서
오후 8시 - 오후 8시 15분	올해의 단편선집
오후 8시 15분 - 오후 8시 30분	⁴⁵올해의 비소설
오후 8시 30분 - 오후 8시 45분	폐회사

⁴³참고: 수상자들은 시상식 중에 수상작에서 발췌한 부분을 낭독할 것입니다.

시상식이 시작될 때 저녁 식사와 음료가 제공될 것입니다. 폐회사 후에는 라이브 음악이 연주될 것입니다.

ballroom n. 연회장, 무도회장　**remark** n. 발언, 말　**literary** adj. 문학의
poetry n. 시, 시가　**anthology** n. 선집, 문집
excerpt n. 발췌한 부분, 인용

발신: Robert Magee <rmagee@smail.com>
수신: Cecilia Gott <cgott@cpubassoc.org>
제목: 유감입니다
날짜: 10월 19일

Ms. Gott께,

저는 현재 런던에 있는 Julia Conde를 대신하여, 이 이메일을 씁니다. 세계 경제 공황에 관한 ⁴⁵그녀의 사실에 기반한 저서가 이곳 영국에서도 베스트셀러가 되었기 때문에, 그녀를 찾는 곳이 매우 많아서 그녀는 전국을 돌아다니며 북투어를 하고 있습니다. ⁴⁵Ms. Conde는 이와 같은 명망 높은 상을 받게 된 것에 대해 진심 어린 감사를 표하고자 하지만, 시상식에 참여할 수는 없을 것입니다. 영국 이후로는, 그녀는 남은 10월 동안 유럽에서의 다른 용무들을 위해 이동하게 될 것입니다. 그리고 나서, 그녀는 11월에 아시아에서 몇몇 행사에 참석할 것입니다. 짐작하실 수 있듯이 지금은 바쁜 시기이며 ⁴⁴Ms. Conde는 1월에 그녀의 새 저서를 위한 연구를 시작하기 전에 남은 한 해 동안 휴식을 취하고자 합니다.

Ms. Conde는 제게 시카고 출판 협회에 그녀의 진심 어린 바람을 전하는 것과 다시 한번 이와 같은 영예에 대해 감사를 표해줄 것을 부탁하였습니다.

Robert Magee 드림

factual adj. 사실에 기반한, 사실의　**account** n. 저서, 설명, 이야기
accord v. 주다, 수여하다　**engagement** n. (약속 시간을 정해서 하는) 용무, 약속
make an appearance 참석하다, 모습을 나타내다
remainder n. 남은 것, 나머지　**honor** n. 영예

41 주제/목적 찾기 문제

문제 편지의 주 목적은 무엇인가?
(A) 작가의 새 작품을 축하하기 위해
(B) 수취인을 공연 관람에 초대하기 위해
(C) 작가에게 그가 상에 선정되었다는 것을 알리기 위해
(D) 베스트셀러 도서의 사본을 요청하기 위해

해설 편지의 목적을 묻는 목적 찾기 문제이므로 편지의 내용을 확인한다. 첫 번째 지문인 편지의 'the Chicago Publishers Association has chosen you as the recipient of the Children's Book of The Year award'(1문단 1번째 줄)에서 시카고 출판 협회가 올해의 아동 도서상 수상자로 편지의 수신인인 Mr. Hutchins를 선정했다고 한 후, 수상을 위한 시상식에 대해 안내하고 있으므로 (C) To notify an author that he was selected for an award 가 정답이다.

Paraphrasing
chosen 선정하다 → selected 선정되다

어휘 congratulate v. 축하하다, 기념하다 notify v. 알리다

42 추론 문제

문제 Ms. Gott가 일정표에 대해 암시하는 것은?
(A) 행사 장소에 게시될 것이다.
(B) 기밀로 유지되어야 한다.
(C) Alexandria 호텔에 의해 승인을 받을 필요가 있다.
(D) 추가 수정을 필요로 한다.

해설 Ms. Gott가 일정표에 대해 암시하는 것을 추론하는 문제이므로 Ms. Gott가 보낸 편지에서 관련 내용을 확인한다. 첫 번째 지문인 편지의 'Enclosed is a tentative schedule for you to review.'(2문단 1번째 줄)에서 동봉된 것은 편지의 수신자가 검토해야 할 잠정적인 일정표라고 했으므로 일정표가 추가로 수정될 수 있다는 사실을 추론할 수 있다. 따라서 (D) It is subject to further revision이 정답이다.

어휘 venue n. 장소 confidential adj. 기밀의, 비밀의 approval n. 승인
subject adj. 필요로 하는, 영향을 받는 revision n. 수정, 변경

43 육하원칙 문제 연계

문제 Mr. Hutchins는 시상식에서 몇 시에 연설을 하도록 요청받을 것인가?
(A) 오후 7시 30분에
(B) 오후 7시 45분에
(C) 오후 8시에
(D) 오후 8시 15분에

해설 두 지문의 내용을 종합해서 풀어야 하는 연계 문제이다. 질문의 핵심 어구인 Mr. Hutchins be asked to speak에서 Mr. Hutchins가 몇 시에(what time) 연설을 하도록 요청받을 것인지를 묻고 있으므로 Mr. Hutchins가 언급된 편지를 먼저 확인한다.

첫 번째 지문인 편지의 'the Chicago Publishers Association has chosen you as the recipient of the Children's Book of The Year award'(1문단 1번째 줄)에서 시카고 출판 협회가 올해의 아동 도서상 수상자로 Mr. Hutchins를 선정했다는 첫 번째 단서를 확인할 수 있다. 그런데 올해의 아동 도서상 수상자가 언제 연설을 하는지가 제시되지 않았으므로 일정표에서 관련 내용을 확인한다. 두 번째 지문인 일정표의 'NOTE: Award recipients will read excerpts from their winning books during the ceremony.'(일정표 하단)에서 수상자들은 시상식 중에 수상작에서 발췌한 부분을 낭독할 것이라고 했고, 'Awards Ceremony, 7:45 P.M. – 8:00 P.M., Children's Book of the Year'(일정표 프로그램 5번째 줄)에서 올해의 아동 도서 시상은 오후 7시 45분이라고 했으므로 아동 도서상 수상자는 오후 7시 45분에 수상작에서 발췌한 부분을 낭독할 것이라는 두 번째 단서를 확인할 수 있다.

Mr. Hutchins가 올해의 아동 도서상 수상자로 선정되었다는 첫 번째 단서와 올해의 아동 도서상 수상자가 오후 7시 45분에 수상작에서 발췌한 부분을 낭독할 것이라는 두 번째 단서를 종합할 때, Mr. Hutchins는 오후 7시 45분에 연설을 하도록 요청받을 것임을 알 수 있다. 따라서 (B) At 7:45 P.M. 이 정답이다.

44 육하원칙 문제

문제 Mr. Magee에 따르면, Ms. Conde의 남은 한 해 계획에는 무엇이 포함되는

가?
(A) 텔레비전으로 방송되는 인터뷰에 참여하는 것
(B) 향후 저서를 위해 초기 연구를 실시하는 것
(C) 바쁜 일정으로부터 휴식을 가지는 것
(D) 휴가 동안에 아시아 일부 지역으로 여행하는 것

해설 Ms. Conde의 남은 한 해 계획에 무엇이(What) 포함되는지를 묻는 육하원칙 문제이므로 질문의 핵심 어구인 Ms. Conde's plans for the rest of the year가 언급된 이메일을 확인한다. 세 번째 지문인 이메일의 'Ms. Conde would like to get some rest for the remainder of the year'(1문단 7번째 줄)에서 Ms. Conde는 남은 한 해 동안 휴식을 취하고자 한다고 했으므로 (C) Taking some time off from a hectic schedule이 정답이다.

Paraphrasing
get rest 휴식을 취하다 → take time off 휴식을 가지다

어휘 televise v. 텔레비전으로 방송하다 conduct v. (업무 따위를) 실시하다
initial adj. 초기의, 처음의 hectic adj. 정신 없이 바쁜

45 추론 문제 연계

문제 Ms. Conde는 어떤 상에 선정된 것 같은가?
(A) 올해의 문학 소설
(B) 올해의 시집
(C) 올해의 단편선집
(D) 올해의 비소설

해설 두 지문의 내용을 종합적으로 확인한 후 추론해서 풀어야 하는 연계 문제이다. 질문의 핵심 어구인 Ms. Conde ~ chosen에서 Ms. Conde가 어떤(which) 상에 선정된 것 같은지를 묻고 있으므로 Ms. Conde에게 보내진 이메일을 먼저 확인한다.

세 번째 지문인 이메일의 'Her factual account ~ became a best-seller ~ in the United Kingdom'(1문단 1번째 줄)에서 Ms. Conde의 사실에 기반한 저서가 영국에서 베스트셀러가 되었다고 했고, 'Ms. Conde would like to express her sincere gratitude ~ for being accorded such a prestigious award'(1문단 3번째 줄)에서 Ms. Conde는 이와 같은 명망 높은 상을 받게 된 것에 대해 진심 어린 감사를 표하고자 한다고 했으므로 Ms. Conde의 사실에 기반한 저서가 수상작에 선정되었다는 첫 번째 단서를 확인할 수 있다. 그런데 Ms. Conde가 어떤 상에 선정된 것인지가 제시되지 않았으므로 일정표에서 관련 내용을 확인한다. 두 번째 지문인 일정표의 'Awards Ceremony, Nonfiction Book of the Year'(일정표 프로그램 7번째 줄)에서 시상식에 올해의 비소설이 포함되어 있다는 두 번째 단서를 확인할 수 있다.

Ms. Conde의 사실에 기반한 저서가 수상작에 선정되었다는 첫 번째 단서와 시상식에 올해의 비소설이 포함되어 있다는 두 번째 단서를 종합할 때, Ms. Conde가 선정된 상이 올해의 비소설이라는 사실을 추론할 수 있다. 따라서 (D) Nonfiction Book of the Year가 정답이다.

46-50은 다음 광고, 주문 양식, 편지에 관한 문제입니다.

Baldwin's Uniform Services사:
귀사의 모든 맞춤 제작 의복 요구에 적합합니다

귀사의 유니폼과 맞춤 제작 의복 요구를 위해 Baldwin's사를 넘어 더 찾아보실 필요는 없습니다!⁴⁶Baldwin's사는 회사명과 로고가 들어간 티셔츠, 폴로 셔츠, 그리고 재킷을 만들 수 있습니다. 저희는 또한 바지, 치마, 그리고 원피스를 귀사의 요구에 맞춰 재단해드립니다. 귀사가 식당, 호텔, 혹은 다른 서비스업을 운영하든 상관없이, 저희의 친절한 직원이 이상적인 스타일, 색상, 천을 선택하는 것에 있어서 귀사와 함께 작업할 것입니다. 디자인 카탈로그를 훑어보시거나, 아니면 저희가 귀사를 위해 유니폼을 맞춤 제작하도록 해주세요! 회사 로고를 인쇄한 기본 티셔츠의 가격이 10달러부터 시작되며 천의 선택과 디자인의 복잡성에 따라 인상됩니다. 대량 구매 시 할인이 적용됩니다. ⁴⁸Carlton 시내의 Gambit로 112번지에 있는 저희 가게에 방문하셔서 저희가 제공하는 모든 것을 확인해보세요!

customize v. 맞춤 제작하다 tailor v. 재단하다
establishment n. 회사, 설립 ideal adj. 이상적인 fabric n. 천, 직물, 섬유
browse through 훑어보다, 읽다 complexity n. 복잡성

BALDWIN'S UNIFORM SERVICES사

맞춤 제작 주문 양식: 4903948	날짜: 4월 9일
성함: Jerod Walton	48회사: Dade Security 은행
48주소: 498번지 Gambit로, Carlton시 와이오밍주, 74898	47-A연락처: 555-4938
	47-A이메일: J-Walt@dadesecuritybank.com

다음의 세부사항을 제공해주시기 바랍니다:

의복 종류	티셔츠
47-C각 사이즈 요청 수량	엑스트라 라지 30장, 라지 120장, 미디움 150장, 스몰 80장
색상	연한 파란색
47-D지시 사항	정면 가운데에 빨간색으로 은행 로고가 인쇄된 기본 프린트 티셔츠를 원합니다.

일단 주문이 제출되면, Baldwin's Uniform Services사는 4영업일 이내에 최초 샘플들을 제공할 것입니다. 49추가 샘플 및 원래의 요청에 대한 변경 사항들은 25달러의 추가 요금을 발생시킬 것입니다. 만약 고객께서 의복에 만족하신다면, 전체 주문 금액의 50퍼센트의 보증금이 요구되며, 남은 금액은 배송 날짜의 이틀 이내에 지불가능합니다.

following adj. 다음의, 뒤따르는   garment n. 의복, 옷   submit v. 제출하다
initial adj. 최초의, 초기의   incur v. 발생시키다, 초래하다
surcharge n. 추가 요금   due adj. 기한인, ~할 예정인

수신 Susanna Baldwin <susanna@baldwinuniforms.com>
발신 Jerod Walton <J-Walt@dadesecuritybank.com>
제목 맞춤 제작 샘플
날짜 4월 13일

Ms. Baldwin께,

저희를 위해 제작하고 있는 50맞춤 제작 티셔츠의 샘플을 보내주셔서 감사합니다. 저는 프린팅의 품질과 색상에 대단히 만족했습니다. 그러나, 제가 생각했던 것만큼 49셔츠의 색상이 로고의 색상과 잘 어울리지는 않는 것 같습니다. 49/50이 로고의 색상이 검정색이나 회색 티셔츠에서는 어떻게 보일지 제가 확인해볼 수 있을까요? 이것이 상당히 대량의 주문이기 때문에, 저는 정말 모든 것이 완벽하도록 확인하고 싶습니다. 50만약 귀하께서 제 요청을 들어주실 수 있다면 제게 이 이메일로 답장을 보내서 알려주시기 바랍니다. 적합한 색상을 찾으면, 귀하께 신용카드로 보증금을 드릴 것이고, 그러면 귀하께서는 작업을 진행하실 수 있습니다.

감사합니다!

Jerod Walton

be pleased with ~에 만족하다   large order 대량 주문   ensure v. 확인하다
suitable adj. 적합한, 적절한   proceed v. 진행하다

---

46 주제/목적 찾기 문제

문제   광고되고 있는 것은 무엇인가?
(A) 유니폼 세탁 서비스
(B) 사업체들을 위한 의복 공급 회사
(C) 패션 부티크 체인점
(D) 그래픽 디자인 회사

해설   광고되고 있는 것을 묻는 주제 찾기 문제이므로 광고의 내용을 확인한다. 첫 번째 지문인 광고의 'Baldwin's can create T-shirts, polo shirts, and jackets with company names or logos. We also tailor trousers, skirts, and dresses to fit the needs of your establishment.'(2번째 줄)에서 회사명과 로고가 들어간 티셔츠, 폴로 셔츠, 그리고 재킷을 만든다고 했고, 또한 바지, 치마, 그리고 원피스를 회사의 요구에 맞춰 재단한다고 했으므로 (B) A clothing supplier for businesses가 정답이다.

어휘   supplier n. 공급 회사, 공급자   chain n. 체인점

---

47 Not/True 문제

문제   주문 양식에 포함되지 않은 것은?
(A) 고객의 연락처

(B) 구매된 각 상품의 가격
(C) 요청된 상품의 수
(D) 주문에 대한 상세한 지시 사항

해설   양식에 언급된 내용을 지문에서 찾아 보기와 대조하는 Not/True 문제이다. 이 문제는 질문에 핵심 어구가 없으므로 각 보기의 핵심 어구와 관련된 내용을 두 번째 지문인 주문 양식에서 확인한다. (A)는 'PHONE: 555-4938, E-MAIL: J-Walt@dadesecuritybank.com'(첫 번째 표 3행 2열)에서 전화 번호와 이메일 주소가 포함되어 있으므로 지문의 내용과 일치한다. (B)는 지문에 언급되지 않은 내용이다. 따라서 (B) The cost of each item purchased가 정답이다. (C)는 'NUMBER OF EACH SIZE WANTED, 30 extra-large, 120 large, 150 medium, 80 small'(두 번째 표 2행)에서 엑스트라 라지 120장, 라지 120장, 미디움 150장, 스몰 80장을 요청한다고 했으므로 지문의 내용과 일치한다. (D)는 'INSTRUCTIONS, I would like basic printed T-shirts with the bank's logo printed in the center of the front side, in red.'(두 번째 표 4행)에서 정면 가운데에 빨간색으로 은행 로고가 인쇄된 기본 프린트 티셔츠를 원한다고 했으므로 지문의 내용과 일치한다.

---

48 Not/True 문제   연계

문제   Dade Security 은행에 대해 언급된 것은?
(A) 행사에서 티셔츠를 나눠주고 있다.
(B) Baldwin's사와 같은 거리에 위치해 있다.
(C) 직원들에게 비즈니스 정장을 입도록 요구하지 않는다.
(D) 로고를 다시 디자인할 것을 계획하고 있다.

해설   두 지문의 내용을 종합해서 풀어야 하는 연계 문제이다. 질문의 핵심 어구인 Dade Security Bank가 언급된 주문 양식을 먼저 확인한다. 두 번째 지문인 주문 양식의 'COMPANY: Dade Security Bank, ADDRESS: 498 Gambit Lane, Carlton City WY, 74898'(첫 번째 표 2행 2열, 3행 1열)에서 Dade Security 은행이 Carlton시의 Gambit로에 있다는 첫 번째 단서를 확인할 수 있다. 그런데 Baldwin's사가 어디에 있는지는 제시되지 않았으므로 Baldwin's사가 작성한 광고에서 관련 내용을 확인한다. 첫 번째 지문인 광고의 'Drop by our shop at 112 Gambit Lane in downtown Carlton City'(9번째 줄)에서 Baldwin's사가 Carlton 시내의 Gambit로에 있다는 두 번째 단서를 확인할 수 있다.
Dade Security 은행이 Carlton시의 Gambit로에 있다는 첫 번째 단서와 Baldwin's사가 Carlton 시내의 Gambit로에 있다는 두 번째 단서를 종합할 때, Dade Security 은행은 Baldwin's사와 같은 거리에 위치해 있다는 것을 알 수 있다. 따라서 (B) It is located on the same street as Baldwin's가 정답이다. (A), (C), (D)는 지문에 언급되지 않은 내용이다.

어휘   give away 나눠주다   locate v. 위치시키다   attire n. 의복, 옷

---

49 추론 문제   연계

문제   Mr. Walton의 주문에 대해 암시되는 것은?
(A) 5개의 다른 사이즈로 나올 것이다.
(B) 4일의 기일 내에 배송되어야만 한다.
(C) 추가 요금의 대상이다.
(D) 4월 13일까지 부분적으로 지불되어야만 한다.

해설   두 지문의 내용을 종합적으로 확인한 후 추론해서 풀어야 하는 연계 문제이다. 질문의 핵심 어구인 Mr. Walton's order와 관련된 내용이 언급된 이메일에서 관련 내용을 먼저 확인한다.
세 번째 지문인 이메일의 'the color of the shirt doesn't match the color of the logo ~. Could I see how it would look on a black or gray shirt?'(2번째 줄)를 통해 발신자인 Mr. Walton이 셔츠의 색상이 로고의 색상과 잘 어울리지 않는 것 같고, 이 로고의 색상이 검정색이나 회색 티셔츠에서는 어떻게 보일지 확인하고 싶다고 요청한다는 첫 번째 단서를 확인할 수 있다. 그런데 추가 요청에 대한 정보가 제시되어 있지 않으므로 Mr. Walton이 작성한 주문 양식에서 샘플 요청과 관련된 내용을 확인한다. 두 번째 지문인 주문 양식의 'Additional samples ~ will incur a $25 surcharge.'(양식 하단 2번째 줄)에서 추가 샘플은 25달러의 추가 요금을 발생시킬 것이라는 두 번째 단서를 확인할 수 있다.
Mr. Walton이 로고의 색상이 검정색이나 회색 티셔츠에서 어떻게 보일지 확인하고 싶다고 요청한다는 첫 번째 단서와 추가 샘플은 25달러의 추가 요금을 발생시킬 것이라는 두 번째 단서를 종합할 때, Mr. Walton의 주문이 추가 요금의 대상이라는 사실을 추론할 수 있다. 따라서 (C) It will be subject to

an added cost가 정답이다.

어휘   **be subject to** ~의 대상이다   **partially** adv. 부분적으로

50 추론 문제

문제   Ms. Baldwin은 왜 이메일에 답장을 할 것 같은가?
(A) 송금을 위한 은행 계좌 정보를 제공하기 위해
(B) 현재 가능한 사이즈에 대해 고객에게 알려주기 위해
(C) 로고 디자인에 대한 고객의 만족도를 확인하기 위해
(D) 샘플 상품에 대한 요청에 응답하기 위해

해설   질문의 핵심 어구인 Ms. Baldwin reply to the e-mail에 대해 추론하는 문제이므로 Ms. Baldwin에게 보내진 이메일에서 관련 내용을 확인한다. 세번째 지문인 이메일의 'Thanks for sending over the sample of the customized T-shirts'(1번째 줄)와 'Could I see how it would look on a black or gray shirt?'(4번째 줄)에서 이메일의 발신자인 Mr. Walton이 맞춤 제작 티셔츠의 샘플을 보내줘서 고맙다고 하며 로고의 색상이 검정색이나 회색의 티셔츠에서 어떻게 보일지 확인해보고 싶다고 한 후, 'Please reply to this e-mail to let me know if you could do that for me.'(5번째 줄)에서 Ms. Baldwin에게 요청을 들어줄 수 있다면 이 이메일로 답장해달라고 했으므로 Ms. Baldwin이 샘플 상품에 대한 요청에 응답하기 위해 이메일에 답장할 것임을 추론할 수 있다. 따라서 (D) To respond to a request for sample merchandise가 정답이다.

어휘   **wire transfer** 송금   **currently** adv. 현재, 지금
confirm v. 확인하다, 확정 짓다   **merchandise** n. 상품

Section 1 문장패턴

Chapter 01 주어 · 동사

1 주어 자리에 올 수 있는 것 : 명사 역할을 하는 것   p.49
    1. (A)   2. (C)   3. (D)

1. 주어 자리 채우기

해설   that절의 주어 자리가 비어 있다. 주어가 될 수 있는 것은 명사이므로 명사인 (A)와 (D)가 정답의 후보이다. '로비의 수리가 연기되다'라는 의미가 자연스러우므로 (A) renovation(수리)이 정답이다. (D) renovator(수리자)는 '수리자가 연기되다'라는 어색한 의미를 만들기 때문에 답이 될 수 없다. 동사 (B)와 (C)는 주어 자리에 올 수 없다.

해석   건물 관리자는 세입자들에게 로비의 수리가 일주일 동안 연기될 수 있다고 통지했다.

어휘   **notify** v. 통지하다, 통보하다   **tenant** n. 세입자, 주민
    postpone v. 연기하다, 뒤로 미루다   **renovate** v. 수리하다

2. 주어 자리 채우기

해설   문장의 주어 자리가 비어 있다. 주어가 될 수 있는 것은 명사이므로 명사인 (A)와 (C)가 정답의 후보이다. 복수 동사(are generating)가 왔으므로 복수 주어 (C) findings(조사 결과)가 정답이다. in a study published in the *Journal of Science*는 주어(Archeological findings)를 꾸미는 수식어이다. 형용사 (B)와 동사 (D)는 주어 자리에 올 수 없다.

해석   *Journal of Science*지에 게재된 연구에 있는 고고학 조사 결과들은 그리스 유물에 대해 연구하는 과학자들 사이에서 흥미를 자아내고 있다.

어휘   **archeological** adj. 고고학의   **publish** v. 게재하다, 싣다
    generate v. 자아내다, 발생시키다   **relic** n. 유물, 유적
    finding n. (조사·연구) 결과, 결론

3. 주어 자리 채우기

해설   문장의 주어 자리가 비어 있다. 주어가 될 수 있는 것은 명사이므로 명사인 (D) structure(건물)가 정답이다. 형용사 (A), 부사 (B), 동사 (C)는 주어 자리에 올 수 없다.

해석   Williams가에 들어설 새로운 건물은 수백 개의 영리 기업들을 수용할 것이다.

어휘   **accommodate** v. 수용하다   **commercial** adj. 영리적인, 상업상의
    enterprise n. 기업, 회사   **structural** adj. 구조상의, 조직상의
    structure v. 구성하다, 조직화하다: n. 건물, 구조

2 가짜 주어 it / there   p.50
    1. (C)   2. (A)   3. (B)

1. 진짜 주어 자리 채우기

해설   there are 다음의 빈칸에는 진짜 주어가 와야 하므로 동명사 (A), 명사 (B)와 (C)가 정답의 후보이다. 빈칸 앞에 복수 동사(are)가 나왔으므로 진짜 주어 자리에도 복수 명사가 와야 한다. 따라서 (C) mistakes(오류)가 정답이다.

해석   이전 발행물에 오류가 있을 때 그 출판사는 정정한 것들을 잡지의 두 번째 페이지에 게재한다.

어휘   **print** v. 게재하다, 인쇄하다   **correction** n. 정정한 것   **issue** n. 발행물, 쟁점

2. 진짜 주어 자리 채우기

해설   가짜 주어 it에 대한 진짜 주어로 올 수 있는 것은 to 부정사나 that절이다. 따라서 빈칸 앞의 to와 함께 to 부정사를 만드는 동사원형 (A) obtain이 정답이다.

해석   공공 도로에서 차량을 운전하기 전에 운전면허증을 취득하는 것은 필수이다.

어휘   **mandatory** adj. 필수의, 의무의   **operate** v. 운전하다, 조종하다
    obtain v. 취득하다, 획득하다   **obtainment** n. 입수, 획득

3. 가짜 주어 자리 채우기

해설   빈칸 뒤에 동사(remain)와 진짜 주어(significant challenges)가 왔으므로, 빈칸에는 가짜 주어가 와야 한다. 따라서 동사 remain의 가짜 주어로 올 수 있는 (B) There가 정답이다.

해석   경쟁이 매우 치열한 시장에서 기반을 구축하기 위해 노력하는 동안 그 신생 기업에게 아주 큰 어려움이 남아 있다.

어휘   **significant** adj. 아주 큰, 현저한, 상당한   **challenge** n. 어려움, 난제
    fledgling adj. 신생의, 미숙한   **gain a foothold in** ~에 기반을 구축하다
    highly ad. 매우   **competitive** adj. 경쟁을 하는, 경쟁적인

3 동사 자리에 올 수 있는 것 : '(조동사 +) 동사'   p.51
    1. (D)   2. (D)   3. (C)

1. 동사 자리 채우기

해설   문장에 동사가 없으므로 동사 (D) soared가 정답이다. 준동사 (A)와 (B), 명사 (C)는 동사 자리에 올 수 없다.

해석   미국산 수입품이 증가했음이 발표된 것에 뒤이어 일본 엔화 대비 달러화의 가치가 어제 폭등했다.

어휘   **soar** v. 폭등하다, 날아오르다   **soarer** n. 나는 것

2. 동사 자리 채우기

해설   문장에 동사가 없으므로 빈칸에는 동사 (A), (B), 또는 (D)가 와야 한다. 단수 주어(An announcement)가 왔으므로 (D) will be posted가 정답이다. 복수 동사 (A) were posted나 (B) have posted는 단수 주어와 함께 쓸 수 없다.

해석   새로운 위생 관리 규정에 대한 공고가 식당의 주방에 게시될 것이다.

어휘   **sanitation** n. 위생 관리, 공중위생   **post** v. 게시하다

3. 동사 자리 채우기

해설   문장에 동사가 없으므로 동사 (C) acquired가 정답이다. 명사 (A)와 준동사 (B), (D)는 동사 자리에 올 수 없다.

해석   봉급을 받는 직원들은 생산 수준을 높이기 위한 장려금으로 작년에 급여의 10퍼센트 인상을 얻었다.

어휘   **salaried** adj. 봉급을 받는   **wage** n. 급여, 임금   **incentive** n. 장려금, 격려
    acquirement n. 취득, 획득   **acquire** v. 얻다, 취득하다

4 명령문은 주어 없이 동사원형으로 시작된다.   p.52
    1. (D)   2. (B)   3. (C)

1. 명령문의 동사 자리 채우기

해설   When절(When ~ presentation) 뒤에 나온 명령문의 동사 자리이므로 동사원형 (D) avoid가 정답이다.

해석   발표를 할 때는, 청중에게 이미 알려진 문제에 대해 논하는 것을 피하십시오.

어휘 **when -ing** ~할 때 **avoid -ing** ~하는 것을 피하다

2. 명령문의 동사 자리 채우기

해설 전치사구(For ~ security) 뒤에 나온 명령문의 동사 자리이므로 동사원형 (B) rely가 정답이다.

해석 여러분 가정의 재정상 안전을 위해, 의료 비상 사태의 경우에 보상을 제공하는 North Star 보험 회사에 의지하세요.

어휘 **compensation** n. 보상, 배상 **rely on** ~에 의지하다

3. 명령문의 동사 자리 채우기

해설 If절(If ~ objectives) 뒤에 나온 명령문의 동사 자리이므로 동사원형 (C) evaluate가 정답이다.

해석 만약 그 전략이 팀의 목표를 충족시키지 못한다면, 불충분한 점이 무엇인지 알아내기 위해 계획을 검토하십시오.

어휘 **objective** n. 목표, 목적 **shortcoming** n. 불충분한 점, 결점 **evaluate** v. 검토하다, 평가하다 **evaluation** n. 평가, 감정

Hackers Practice
p.53

01 ⓑ [토익 공식 3]		02 ⓑ [토익 공식 2]	
03 ⓑ [토익 공식 3]		04 ⓑ [토익 공식 1]	
05 ⓐ [토익 공식 3]		06 ⓐ [토익 공식 2]	
07 ⓑ [토익 공식 3]			

08 Efficient → Efficiency [토익 공식 1]
09 finishes → finished [토익 공식 3]
10 requests → request [토익 공식 4]
11 맞는 문장 [토익 공식 3]   12 There → It [토익 공식 2]
13 evaluation → evaluated [토익 공식 3]
14 omit → omission [토익 공식 1]

해석 01 회계팀은 연례 보고서를 완성하기 위해 주말 동안 일했다.
02 직원들이 새 프로그램 사용을 시작할 수 있기 전에 실시되어야 할 교육이 하나 더 남아 있다.
03 그 식당의 메인 코스 메뉴는 계절에 따라 다르다.
04 회의에서 보내는 시간을 줄이는 것은 사무실에서의 생산성을 증대시킬 것이다.
05 정기 총회의 청중은 의사들과 그 밖의 다른 의료인들로 구성된다.
06 신입 사원들에게 회사의 행동 수칙에 대해 교육하는 것은 중요하다.
07 다음 분기의 예산안은 이번 금요일까지 이사의 사무실로 보내져야 한다.
08 효율성은 Hoovers사에서 업무 과제를 수행할 때 대단히 중요하다.
09 Mr. Miller는 어제 회람 작성을 끝냈을 때, 오류가 있는지 주의 깊게 검토했다.
10 만약 마감 시간을 맞추는 것이 불확실하다면, 관리자에게 연장을 요청하십시오.
11 Mr. Clark가 디자인한 안내 책자는 한 부서장에 의해 수정되고 있다.
12 미국 가정의 40퍼센트는 광대역 인터넷에 접속하지 않는 것으로 알려져 있다.
13 지난밤 회의에서, 제작 진행 책임자는 그 프로젝트를 평가했다.
14 연구 논문에서 그 자료의 누락은 그것이 중요하지 않았다는 것을 보여 준다.

Hackers Test
p.54

Part 5

01 (C)	02 (C)	03 (B)	04 (A)	05 (C)
06 (D)	07 (B)	08 (B)	09 (C)	10 (B)
11 (B)	12 (A)	13 (C)	14 (B)	15 (B)
16 (A)	17 (D)	18 (D)		

Part 6

19 (B)	20 (C)	21 (C)	22 (B)

01 주어 자리 채우기

해설 문장의 주어 자리가 비어 있다. 주어가 될 수 있는 것은 명사이므로 명사 (C) selections(선발)가 정답이다. 동사 (A)와 (B), 형용사 (D)는 주어 자리에 올 수 없다.

해석 고용 위원회에 의해 제안된 지역 영업부장직의 최종 선발은 회사 내에서 이미 일하고 있는 세 명의 후보들을 포함한다.

02 동사 자리 채우기

해설 문장에 동사가 없으므로 동사 (A)와 (C)가 정답의 후보이다. 단수 주어(The unemployment rate)가 왔으므로 단수 동사 (C) excludes가 정답이다. (A) exclude는 복수 동사이므로 답이 될 수 없으며, 준동사 (B)와 명사 (D)는 동사 자리에 올 수 없다.

해석 실업률은 9개월 이상 실업 중인 사람들을 제외한다.

어휘 **exclude** v. 제외하다 **exclusion** n. 제외, 차단

03 주어 자리 채우기

해설 that절의 주어 자리가 비어 있다. 주어가 될 수 있는 것은 명사이므로 명사인 (B)와 (D)가 정답의 후보이다. '서류가 도착하지 않았다'는 의미가 자연스러우므로 (B) document(문서)가 정답이다. (D) documentation(문서화)은 '문서화가 도착하지 않았다'는 어색한 의미를 만들기 때문에 답이 될 수 없다. 참고로, (D) documentation은 '서류'라는 뜻으로도 쓰이는데, 불가산 명사이므로 빈칸 앞의 부정관사 an과 함께 쓸 수 없다. 동사 (A)는 주어 자리에 올 수 없다.

해석 Mr. Jenson은 중요한 서류가 예정대로 도착하지 않았음을 항의하기 위해 택배 회사에 전화했다.

어휘 **courier** n. 택배 회사 **documented** adj. 문서로 기록된
document n. 서류, 문서; v. (상세한 내용을) 기록하다
documentation n. 문서화, 서류, 기록

04 동사 자리 채우기

해설 문장에 동사가 없으므로 동사 (A), (B), (C)가 정답의 후보이다. '립스틱 샘플이 보내졌다'는 수동의 의미이므로 수동태 동사 (A) were sent가 정답이다. (B), (C)는 능동태 동사이므로 답이 될 수 없다. '동사원형 + -ing'(being)로 시작되는 (D)는 준동사이므로 동사 자리에 올 수 없다.

해석 많은 제품 케이스가 손상되었음이 밝혀졌을 때 그 립스틱 샘플들은 제조 회사로 돌려보내졌다.

어휘 **manufacturer** n. 제조 회사 **discover** v. 밝히다, 발견하다
damage v. 손상을 주다, 훼손하다

05 동사 자리 채우기

해설 문장에 동사가 없으므로 빈칸에는 동사 (A), (B), 또는 (C)가 와야 한다. 단수 주어(Consumer spending)가 왔으므로 단수 또는 복수 동사 (B)와 단수 동사 (C)가 정답의 후보이다. '지난 석 달 동안 소비자 지출이 증가해 왔다'는 문맥이므로, 과거에서 현재까지 계속된 일을 표현하는 현재완료 시제 (C) has risen이 정답이다. 복수 동사 (A) rise와 '증가할 것이다'를 표현하는 미래 시제 (B) will rise는 답이 될 수 없다.

해석 소비자 지출이 지난 석 달 동안 상당히 증가해 왔고, 그 결과 전국적인 경제 회복을 가져왔다.

어휘 **consumer spending** 소비자 지출 **significantly** adv. 상당히, 두드러지게
recovery n. 회복

06 동사 자리 채우기

해설 that으로 시작되는 명사절에 동사가 없으므로 동사 (D) adhere가 정답이다. 형용사 (A), 준동사 (B), 명사 (C)는 동사 자리에 올 수 없다. 참고로, they make는 앞의 주어(the changes)를 꾸미는 수식어 거품이며, 목적격 관계대명사 that이 생략된 관계절이다. 이처럼 목적격 관계대명사가 생략된 경우, 관계절의 동사(make)를 문장의 동사로 혼동하지 않도록 주의해야 한다.

해석 아파트를 수리할 예정인 세입자들이 그들이 진행하는 변경 사항들이 임대차 계약의 관련 조항들을 충실히 지키는지 확인해야 한다.

어휘 **renovate** v. 수리하다 **relevant** adj. 관련된, 상응하는 **clause** n. 조항
lease n. 임대차 계약 **adherable** adj. 들러붙을 수 있는

adherence n. 충실, 고수 adhere to 충실히 지키다, 고수하다

07 주어 자리 채우기

해설 as절의 주어 자리가 비어 있다. 주어가 될 수 있는 것은 명사이므로 명사 (B) construction(건설)이 정답이다. 동사 (A), 형용사 (D)는 답이 될 수 없으며 (C) to construct(to 부정사)는 명사(highways)를 전치사 없이 바로 취해야 하므로, to construct가 답이 되려면 additional state highways 앞의 of가 삭제되어야 한다.

해석 주지사는 교통부에 추가적인 자금을 제공할 것인데, 이는 추가적인 주 고속도로의 건설이 우선 사항이기 때문이다.

어휘 funding n. 자금, 재정 지원 highway n. 고속도로
priority n. 우선 사항, 우선권 constructible adj. 건설할 수 있는

08 동사 자리 채우기

해설 문장에 동사가 없으므로 빈칸에는 동사 (B) 또는 (C)가 와야 한다. '운영비가 회사의 추정치를 초과하다'라는 능동의 의미이므로 능동태 동사 (B) had surpassed가 정답이다. (C) was surpassed는 수동태 동사이므로 답이 될 수 없다.

해석 일사분기 말까지, 운영비는 회사의 추정치를 10퍼센트 이상 초과했다.

어휘 operating expense 운영비 estimate n. 추정(치), 견적서; v. 추정하다
surpass v. 초과하다, 넘다

09 주어 자리 채우기

해설 문장의 주어 자리가 비어 있다. 주어가 될 수 있는 것은 명사이므로 명사 (A)와 (C)가 정답의 후보이다. 위원 한 사람을 의미하는 commissioner와 여러 명으로 구성된 위원회를 의미하는 commission 중에서, '특별 위원회가 구성되다'라는 의미를 만드는 (C) commission(위원회)이 정답이다. 준동사 (B)와 (D)는 주어 자리에 올 수 없다.

해석 개발 회사가 모든 조세 정책을 지키고 있는지 밝히기 위해 재정 활동을 조사하도록 특별 위원회가 정부에 의해 구성되었다.

어휘 form v. (단체·위원회 등을) 구성하다, 결성하다 look into ~을 조사하다
determine v. 밝히다, 결정하다 obey v. (명령·법 등을) 지키다
tax policy 조세 정책 commissioner n. (위원회의) 위원
commission v. (미술·음악 작품 등을) 의뢰하다, 주문하다; n. 위원회

10 명령문의 동사 자리 채우기

해설 When절(When ~ buyers) 뒤에 나온 명령문의 동사 자리가 비어 있으므로 동사원형 (B) inform(알리다, 통지하다)이 정답이다.

해석 요청된 샘플을 바이어에게 보낼 때, 그들에게 소포가 가는 중이라는 것을 알려 주십시오.

어휘 requested adj. 요청된 inform v. 알리다, 통지하다

11 주어 자리 채우기

해설 문장의 주어 자리가 비어 있다. 주어가 될 수 있는 것은 명사이므로 명사 (B) acquisition(인수)이 정답이다. 동사 (A)와 (D), 형용사 (C)는 주어 자리에 올 수 없다.

해석 Sartek사의 최근 Telstar사 인수는 이동 통신 시장에서 우위를 차지하게 해줄 것이다.

어휘 dominate v. 우위를 차지하다, 지배력을 발휘하다 acquire v. 취득하다, 얻다
acquisition n. (기업) 인수, 획득, 매입 acquired adj. 획득한, 후천적인

12 동사 자리 채우기

해설 문장에 동사가 없으므로 빈칸에는 동사 (A), (C), 또는 (D)가 와야 한다. 단수 주어(The committee)가 왔으므로 단·복수 모두 쓰일 수 있는 과거 시제 동사 (A)와 단수 동사 (D)가 정답의 후보이다. '위원회가 권고 사항을 검토하다'라는 능동의 의미이므로 능동태 동사 (A) studied가 정답이다. (C) study는 복수 동사이고, (D) was studied는 수동태 동사이므로 답이 될 수 없다.

해석 위원회는 직원 안내서의 휴가 규정을 변경하기 전에 자문 위원의 권고 사항을 신중하게 검토했다.

13 동사 자리 채우기

해설 문장에 동사가 없으므로 동사 (B), (C), (D)가 정답의 후보이다. 과거 시간 표현(40 years ago)이 있으므로 과거 시제 동사 (C) entered가 정답이다.

해석 Katherine Bryant는 Purcell사에 40년 전에 입사하였는데, 이는 그녀가 회사가 처음 설립된 이래 가장 오래 근무한 직원 중 한 사람이 되게 했다.

어휘 serve v. 근무하다, 임기 동안 일하다 establish v. 설립하다, 수립하다

14 주어 자리 채우기

해설 문장의 주어 자리가 비어 있다. 주어가 될 수 있는 것은 명사이므로 명사 (B) termination(종료)이 정답이다. 동사 (A)와 (D)는 주어 자리에 올 수 없으며, 타동사 terminate의 동명사인 (C) terminating은 뒤에 목적어 없이 혼자 쓰일 수 없으므로 답이 될 수 없다.

해석 계약의 종료는 Ms. Zhang이 원료 공급 회사의 소유주와 새로운 계약을 협상하도록 만들었다.

어휘 agreement n. 계약, 협정 negotiate v. 협상하다, 교섭하다
raw material 원료 supplier n. 공급 회사, 공급자
terminate v. 종료하다, 끝내다

15 동사 자리 채우기

해설 문장에 동사가 없으므로 동사 (A)와 (B)가 정답의 후보이다. 단수 주어(The manager)가 왔으므로 단수 동사 (B) affirms가 정답이다. (A) have affirmed는 복수 동사이므로 답이 될 수 없다.

해석 그 부장은 영업팀에 의해 청구된 비용이 근거가 없으며 상환되지 않을 것이라고 단언한다.

어휘 claim v. 청구하다, 요구하다 invalid adj. 근거 없는, 무효한
reimburse v. 상환하다, 배상하다 affirm v. 단언하다, 확언하다

16 동사 자리 채우기

해설 문장에 동사가 없으므로 동사 (A), (B), (C), (D) 모두 정답의 후보이다. half of와 같이 부분을 나타내는 표현이 주어로 오면, half of 뒤에 나온 명사의 수에 동사의 수를 일치시켜야 한다. half of 뒤에 복수 명사(the survey respondents)가 왔으므로 복수 동사 (A) consider가 정답이다. 단수 동사 (B), (C), (D)는 답이 될 수 없다.

해석 설문 조사 응답자들의 절반 이상은 시의 쓰레기 수거 요금이 너무 비싸다고 생각한다.

어휘 respondent n. 응답자 fee n. 요금, 수수료 consider v. ~이라고 생각하다

17 가짜 주어 자리 채우기

해설 동사 is 앞에 문장의 주어 자리가 비어 있다. 빈칸 뒤에 진짜 주어(that employees ~ accounts)가 왔으므로 가짜 주어가 될 수 있는 (D) It이 정답이다.

해석 그들의 계정으로의 승인되지 않은 접근을 방지하기 위해 직원들이 이메일 비밀번호를 주기적으로 변경하는 것은 필수적이다.

어휘 vital adj. 필수적인 periodically adv. 주기적으로
unauthorized adj. 승인되지 않은 access n. 접근 account n. 계정, 계좌

18 주어 자리 채우기

해설 등위접속사 but 다음에 오는 절의 주어가 비어 있다. 주어가 될 수 있는 것은 명사와 to 부정사이므로 (B)와 (D)가 정답의 후보이다. his academic 다음의 빈칸에 와서 주어 역할을 할 수 있는 것은 명사이므로 명사 (D) qualifications(자격)가 정답이다. to 부정사 (B)가 주어 역할을 하려면 주어 자리 맨 앞에 와야 한다.

해석 그 지원자가 관련 업무 경력이 있기는 하지만, 그의 학문적 자격은 직책에 명시된 필요조건을 충족시키지 못한다.

어휘 requirement n. 필요조건 specify v. (구체적으로) 명시하다

19-22는 다음 이메일에 관한 문제입니다.

날짜: 4월 10일
수신: Steve Vickers

발신: Susan White
제목: 실행할 수 있는 워크숍

안녕하세요 Steve,

저는 덴버에 있었던 마케팅 회의에서 이제 막 돌아왔으며 제가 이 행사에서 얻은 정보를 바탕으로 제 팀을 위한 워크숍을 준비하는 것에 대해 생각하고 있었습니다. [19]워크숍의 목적은 직원들에게 현재의 방송 광고 동향에 대한 최신 정보를 제공하기 위함이 될 것입니다.

저는 팀이 새로운 텔레비전 광고 방송들을 개발하고 있으므로 이 정보가 그들에게 매우 유용할 것이라고 생각합니다. [20]저는 우리가 두 번의 회합을 가지되, 5월 9일 월요일에 한 번, 5월 12일 목요일에 또 다른 한 번의 회합을 가지는 것을 제안하는데, 이는 다루어야 할 자료가 많을 것이기 때문입니다. [21]당신에게 간단히 계획을 말씀드리자면, 인터넷이 연결된 텔레비전에 광고하는 것은 우리가 반드시 탐구해야 하는 것입니다. 더 많은 대중에게 도달하기 위해 우리는 전통적인 텔레비전을 많이 보지 않을 수도 있는 시청자들에게 호소하는 방법에 대한 더 깊은 이해가 필요합니다. [22]우리의 고객들이 혁신적인 방법으로 광고하는 것을 희망하고 있기 때문에 이는 매우 중요합니다.

당신이 어떻게 생각하시는지, 그리고 제가 워크숍을 진행시켜서 일정을 잡기를 바라시는지 알려 주십시오.

possible adj. 실행할 수 있는, 가능한 organize v. 준비하다, 계획하다, 구성하다
update v. 최신 정보를 제공하다 broadcast n. 방송; v. 방송하다
trend n. 동향, 경향 commercial n. 광고 방송; adj. 상업상의
session n. 회합, 회의, 수업 material n. 자료 appeal v. 호소하다
go ahead 진행시키다, 진행하다, 앞으로 나아가다

19 의미 구별하여 명사 채우기

해설 '목적은 최신 정보를 제공하기 위함이다'라는 의미이므로 명사 (B) objective(목적)가 정답이다. (C) objection(반대)을 쓰면 '반대는 최신 정보를 제공하기 위함이다'라는 어색한 의미가 된다.

어휘 object v. 반대하다. n. 대상, 목표 objective n. 목적, 목표
objection n. 반대 objectionable adj. 불쾌한, 무례한

20 동사 자리 채우기

해설 문장에 동사가 없으므로 동사 (C) suggest(제안하다)가 정답이다. 명사 (A), 준동사 (B)와 형용사 (D)는 동사 자리에 올 수 없다.

어휘 suggestive adj. ~을 연상시키는

21 동사 어휘 고르기 전체 문맥 파악

해설 '인터넷이 연결된 텔레비전에 광고하는 것을 반드시 _____해야 하다'라는 문맥이므로 모든 보기가 정답의 후보이다. 빈칸이 있는 문장만으로 정답을 고를 수 없으므로 주변 문맥이나 전체 문맥을 파악한다. 지문 앞부분에서 글쓴이가 현재의 방송 광고 동향에 대한 최신 정보를 제공하기 위해 워크숍을 준비하는 것을 생각하고 있었다고 한 후, '전통적인 텔레비전을 많이 보지 않을 수도 있는 시청자들에게 호소하는 방법에 대한 더 깊은 이해가 필요하다'(we require a better understanding of how to appeal to viewers who may not watch much traditional television)고 했으므로 새로운 분야인 인터넷이 연결된 텔레비전에 광고하는 방법에 대해 탐구할 것임을 알 수 있다. 따라서 동사 (C) explore(탐구하다)가 정답이다.

어휘 dispute v. 반박하다 limit v. 제한하다 terminate v. 종료되다, 끝내다

22 알맞은 문장 고르기

해석 (A) 우리가 작업하고 있는 광고들은 일주일 안에 공개되어야 합니다.
(B) 우리의 고객들이 혁신적인 방법으로 광고하는 것을 희망하고 있기 때문에 이는 매우 중요합니다.
(C) 당신이 제안한 것처럼 두 번의 회합을 가지는 것은 불필요해 보입니다.
(D) 팀은 그들이 참석할 수 있는지 이번 주에 우리에게 말해주어야 합니다.

해설 빈칸에 들어갈 알맞은 문장을 고르는 문제이므로 빈칸의 주변 문맥이나 전체 문맥을 파악한다. 앞 문장 'we require a better understanding of how to appeal to viewers who may not watch much traditional television'에서 전통적인 텔레비전을 많이 보지 않을 수도 있는 시청자들에게 호소하는 방법에 대한 더 깊은 이해가 필요하다고 했으므로 빈칸에는 고객들이 혁신적인 방법으로 광고하는 것을 희망하고 있기 때문에 이것이 중요

하다는 내용이 들어가야 함을 알 수 있다. 따라서 (B) This is crucial as our clients hope to advertise in innovative ways가 정답이다.

어휘 crucial adj. 중요한 innovative adj. 혁신적인

Chapter 02 목적어 · 보어 · 수식어

1 목적어 자리에 올 수 있는 것 : 명사 역할을 하는 것 p.57
1. (B) 2. (C) 3. (D)

1. 목적어 자리 채우기

해설 타동사(paid) 뒤에 목적어 자리를 채우는 문제이므로 목적어가 될 수 있는 명사 (B) attention(주의)이 정답이다. 동사 (A), (D)와 형용사 (C)는 목적어 자리에 올 수 없다.

해석 Reliance 여행사는 고객들이 예약한 비행편들이 항공사에 의해 마지막 순간에 취소된 것에 대한 불평에 많은 주의를 기울였다.

어휘 complaint n. 불평, 불만 book v. 예약하다 attentive adj. 주의 깊은, 친절한

2. 목적어 자리 채우기

해설 타동사(implement) 뒤에 목적어 자리를 채우는 문제이므로 목적어가 될 수 있는 명사 (C) regulation(규정)이 정답이다. 형용사 (A), 부사 (B), 동사 (D)는 목적어 자리에 올 수 없다.

해석 회사의 재정난에 대응하여, 재무부장은 운영 경비를 제한하는 규정을 시행하도록 요청받았다.

어휘 in response to ~에 대응하여 implement v. 시행하다
operating adj. 운영상의 cost n. 경비, 비용
regulatory adj. 규제력을 지닌 regulatively adv. 규제하여, 조절하여

3. 목적어 자리 채우기

해설 타동사(analyze) 뒤에 목적어 자리를 채우는 문제이므로 목적어가 될 수 있는 명사 (D) developments(개발, 발전)가 정답이다. 동사 (A), (B)와 형용사 (C)는 목적어 자리에 올 수 없다.

해석 그 연구원은 노트북 컴퓨터의 새로운 디자인에 대해 제안을 하기 전에 무선 기술의 최근 개발을 분석할 것이다.

어휘 analyze v. 분석하다 wireless adj. 무선의 suggestion n. 제안, 암시

2 가목적어 it 구문 p.58
1. (C) 2. (C) 3. (B)

1. 진목적어 자리 채우기

해설 가목적어 it이 있으므로 빈칸에는 진목적어가 와야 한다. 진목적어로 올 수 있는 것은 to 부정사 또는 that절이므로, 보기 중 to 부정사 (C) to give가 정답이다.

해석 제안된 예산 증액은 회사의 각 부서에 추가 지원을 제공하는 것을 가능하게 할 것이다.

어휘 proposed adj. 제안된 budget n. 예산 increase n. 증액, 증가
support n. 지원, 후원; v. 떠받치다, 지원하다 sector n. 부서

2. 진목적어 자리 채우기

해설 가목적어 it이 있으므로 빈칸에는 진목적어가 와야 한다. 진목적어로 올 수 있는 것은 to 부정사 또는 that절이므로, 뒤의 절(the local government ~ area)을 이끄는 (C) that이 정답이다.

해석 지역 시민 단체들은 지방 정부가 주택지 옆에 쓰레기 매립지 건설을 건의하는 것이 불합리하다고 생각한다.

어휘 unreasonable adj. 불합리한 make a proposition 건의하다
landfill n. 쓰레기 매립지

3. 진목적어 자리 채우기

해설 가목적어 it이 있으므로 빈칸에는 진목적어가 와야 한다. 진목적어로 올 수 있는 것은 to 부정사 또는 that절이므로, 보기 중 to 부정사 (B) to comply가 정답이다. 참고로, 문장에 it이 없다면 make a point of -ing를 만드는 (C) of complying이 빈칸에 와야 한다.

해석 창고 근로자들은 사고의 가능성을 줄이기 위해 모든 안전 수칙들을 반드시 준수해야 한다.

어휘 make it a point to do 반드시 ~하다, ~을 중시하다(=make a point of doing) potential n. 가능성 comply with 준수하다, 따르다

---

3 보어 자리에 올 수 있는 것 : 명사 또는 형용사   p.59

1. (B)   2. (D)   3. (A)

1. 보어 자리 채우기

해설 be동사(was)의 보어가 될 수 있는 것은 명사나 형용사이므로 형용사 (B) influential(영향력이 큰)이 정답이다. 동사 (A)는 보어 자리에 올 수 없다. be동사 다음에 (C) influencing이 오면 진행형 동사를 만드는데, 이때 목적어를 필요로 하는 타동사(influence) 뒤에 목적어가 없으므로, (C)는 답이 될 수 없다. be동사 다음에 (D) influenced가 오면 수동태 동사를 만드는데, 이때 '~에 의해 영향을 받다'라는 자연스러운 의미가 되려면 influenced 다음에 전치사 by가 나와야 하므로 (D)는 답이 될 수 없다.

해석 Frank McKenzie는 홍콩 금융 시장으로 확장하려는 회사의 최근 결정에 있어 특히 영향력이 컸다.

어휘 particularly adv. 특히, 특별히 expand v. (사업을) 확장시키다 influence v. 영향을 주다 influential adj. 영향력이 큰, 영향력 있는

2. 보어 자리 채우기

해설 be동사(was)의 보어가 될 수 있는 것은 명사나 형용사이고 보어 자리에 부정관사(a)가 왔으므로 명사 (D) oversight(착오)가 정답이다. 형용사나 분사가 명사를 수식하지 않고 단독으로 쓰였을 경우, 앞에 관사 a/an이 올 수 없다는 것을 알아두자.

해석 Brian Mann은 상을 받을 만했기 때문에 모든 사람들은 그가 올해의 직원상을 수상하지 못했던 것이 큰 착오라고 느꼈다.

어휘 deserve v. ~을 받을 만하다 oversee v. 감독하다 oversight n. 착오, 실수

3. 보어 자리 채우기

해설 be동사(was)의 보어가 될 수 있는 것은 명사나 형용사이므로 형용사 (A) instructive(유익한)가 정답이다. be동사 다음에 (B) instructed가 오면 수동태 동사(was instructed)가 만들어지는데, 이 경우 'Mr. Simm의 강연이 특히 교육을 받았다'라는 어색한 의미가 되므로 (B)는 답이 될 수 없다. 동사 (C)는 보어 자리에 올 수 없다. be동사 다음에 (D) instructing이 오면 진행형 동사(was instructing)가 만들어지는데, 이 경우 목적어를 필요로 하는 타동사(instruct) 뒤에 목적어가 없으므로 (D)는 답이 될 수 없다.

해석 참석자들은 세미나 동안 모든 발표들을 즐겁게 들었고, 모든 사람들이 Mr. Simm의 강연이 특히 유익했다는 것에 동의했다.

어휘 attendee n. 참석자 presentation n. 발표 talk n. 강연, 강의 especially adv. 특히 instructive adj. 유익한, 교육적인

---

4 명사 보어 vs. 형용사 보어   p.60

1. (A)   2. (B)   3. (B)

1. 보어 자리 채우기

해설 be동사(was) 다음에 보어로 올 수 있는 것은 형용사 (A)와 명사 (B), (C)이다. 형용사 (A)를 사용하여 주어를 설명하면 '경영진은 ~하는 데 성공하다'라는 자연스러운 문맥이 되므로 (A) successful(성공한)이 정답이다. 명사 (B)나 (C)가 주어와 동격 관계를 이루면 '경영진은 ~하는 데 성공이다/후임자이다'라는 어색한 의미가 된다.

해석 경영진은 지난달에 노조와 노동 협약의 조건을 재교섭하는 데 성공했다.

어휘 renegotiate v. 재교섭하다, 재조정하다 terms n. 조건 union n. 노조 successful adj. 성공한, 성공적인 successor n. 후임자, 계승자

2. 보어 자리 채우기

해설 be동사(was) 다음에 보어로 올 수 있는 것은 명사 (A)와 형용사 (B)이다. 형용사 (B)를 사용하여 주어를 설명하면 '가격이 적정하다'라는 자연스러운 문맥이 되므로 (B) reasonable(가격이 적정한)이 정답이다. 명사 (A)를 사용하여 주어와 동격 관계를 이루면 '가격이 이유다'라는 어색한 의미가 된다. 부사 (C)는 보어 자리에 올 수 없다. (D) reasoned가 오면 수동태 동사를 만드는데, 이때 '가격이 추론되다'라는 어색한 의미를 만들기 때문에 답이 될 수 없다.

해석 공급자에 의해 제안된 가격이 적정했기 때문에, 회사는 구매 주문을 늘리는 것에 동의했다.

어휘 purchase order 구매 주문(서) reasonable adj. (가격 등이) 적정한, 비싸지 않은

3. 보어 자리 채우기

해설 가짜 주어(it)−진짜 주어(to check ~)의 보어 자리에 올 수 있는 것은 명사 (A), (D)와 형용사 (B)이다. 형용사 (B)를 사용하여 진짜 주어를 설명하면 '~을 확인하는 것이 현명하다'라는 자연스러운 문맥이 되므로 (B) sensible (현명한, 합리적인)이 정답이다. 명사 (A)나 (D)는 소유격이나 관사 없이 혼자 오면 틀린 문장이 된다.

해석 투자자들은 어떤 주식이든 매입하기 전에 회사의 실적을 확인하는 것이 현명하다.

어휘 investor n. 투자자 performance n. 실적, 성과, 성취 share n. 주식, 지분 sense n. 감각, 관념; v. 감지하다, 느끼다 sensible adj. 현명한, 합리적인 sensor n. 센서, 감지기

---

5 수식어 거품   p.61

1. (D)   2. (B)   3. (A)

1. 수식어 거품 채우기

해설 이 문장은 주어(he), 동사(is), 보어(strict)를 갖춘 완전한 절이므로 ____ the new ~ soft-spoken은 수식어 거품이어야 한다. 따라서 수식어 거품을 이끌 수 있는 부사절 접속사 (C)와 (D)가 정답의 후보이다. '~한 반면에 ~하다'라는 의미가 되어야 하므로, (D) While(~한 반면에)이 정답이다.

해석 새로 들어온 관리자는 온화하고 말씨가 부드러운 반면에, 직원의 시간 엄수에 대해서는 매우 엄격하다.

어휘 supervisor n. 관리자, 감독자 mild-mannered adj. 온화한, 온순한 soft-spoken adj. (말씨가) 부드러운, 상냥한 strict adj. 엄격한, 꼼꼼한 punctuality n. 시간 엄수, 기한을 어기지 않음

2. 수식어 거품 채우기

해설 이 문장은 주어(The membership rates)와 동사(will be raised)를 갖춘 완전한 절이므로 주어와 동사 사이에 있는 ____ are charged는 수식어 거품으로 보아야 한다. 따라서 보기 중 수식어 거품이 될 수 있는 관계사 (B) that이 정답이다. 대명사 (A), (C), (D)는 수식어 거품이 될 수 없다.

해석 Southtown 독서 클럽에 의해 청구되는 회원 요금은 주요 경쟁사들의 요금에 맞추도록 인상될 것이다.

어휘 membership n. 회원 (자격·신분) rate n. 요금, 비율 charge v. 청구하다, 고소하다 book club 독서 클럽, 독서회 match v. 맞추다, 필적하다 competitor n. 경쟁 상대, 경쟁자

3. 수식어 거품 채우기

해설 이 문장은 주어(The suspect)와 동사(didn't respond)를 갖춘 완전한 절이므로 ____ that he ~ himself는 수식어 거품으로 보아야 한다. 따라서 보기 중 수식어 거품이 될 수 있는 분사 (A) insisting이 정답이다. 수동태 동사 (B), 동사 (C)와 (D)는 수식어 거품이 될 수 없다. 참고로, only when ~ lawyer는 수식어 거품(____ that he ~ himself)에 의미를 더해 주는 또 다른 수식어 거품이다.

해석 그 용의자는 경찰 소환에 응하지 않았는데, 이는 그가 변호사와 동행했을 때에

만 출두하겠다고 고집했기 때문이다.

어휘 **suspect** n. 용의자 **respond** v. 응하다 **summons** n. 소환, 호출 **present** v. 출두하다, 출석하다 **accompany** v. 동행하다, 동반하다 **insist** v. 고집하다, 강요하다

6 수식어 거품 '구'와 수식어 거품 '절'을 이끄는 것은 다르다. p.62
1. (A)　　2. (B)　　3. (D)

1. 수식어 거품을 이끄는 것 채우기

해설 이 문장은 주어(she), 동사(has ~ become), 보어(a standout)를 갖춘 완전한 절이므로 ____ this ~ company는 수식어 거품으로 보아야 한다. 이 수식어 거품은 동사(is)가 있는 거품절이므로, 보기 중 거품절을 이끌 수 있는 부사절 접속사 (A)나 (D)가 와야 한다. '겨우 3주째이긴 하지만'이라는 의미가 되어야 하므로 (A) Although(비록 ~이긴 하지만)가 정답이다.

해석 비록 그 회사에 근무한 지 겨우 3주째이긴 하지만, Ms. Planter는 금세 마케팅부에서 뛰어난 사람이 되었다.

어휘 **with** prep. ~에 근무하고, ~와 함께 **standout** n. 뛰어난 사람 **in spite of** ~에도 불구하고 **nevertheless** adv. 그럼에도 불구하고 **however** conj. 어떤 방법으로라도; adv. 그러나

2. 수식어 거품을 이끄는 것 채우기

해설 이 문장은 주어(The breakdown), 동사(forced), 목적어(the owner)를 갖춘 완전한 절이므로 ____ production은 수식어 거품으로 보아야 한다. 이 수식어 거품은 동사가 없는 거품구이므로, 거품구를 이끌 수 있는 전치사 (A), (B), (D)가 정답의 후보이다. '생산 중에'라는 의미가 되어야 하므로 (B) during(~하는 중에)이 정답이다.

해석 생산 중에 기계 주요 부품의 고장은 사장이 일시적인 공장 휴업을 발표하도록 만들었다.

어휘 **breakdown** n. 고장, 파손 **piece** n. 부품, 부분 **force A to do** A에게 ~하게 만들다, ~할 것을 강요하다 **temporary** adj. 일시적인 **plant** n. 공장 **shutdown** n. 휴업, 폐업

3. 수식어 거품을 이끄는 것 채우기

해설 이 문장은 주어(the manager), 동사(decided), 목적어(that 이하)를 갖춘 완전한 절이므로 ____ the problems는 수식어 거품으로 보아야 한다. 이 수식어 거품은 동사가 없는 거품구이므로, 거품구를 이끌 수 있는 전치사 (B)와 (D)가 정답의 후보이다. '문제들 때문에'라는 의미가 되어야 하므로 (D) Because of(~ 때문에)가 정답이다. 참고로, Team B is experiencing은 the problems를 꾸미는 수식어 거품으로, 목적격 관계대명사 that이 생략되어 있는 관계절이다.

해석 B팀이 겪고 있는 문제들 때문에, 부장은 팀원들에게 프로젝트 평가 보고서를 작성할 시간을 좀 더 주는 것이 최선이라고 결정했다.

어휘 **assessment** n. 평가 **in case** (~할) 경우에 대비해서

Hackers Practice
p.63

01 who purchased the printer [토익 공식 5]
02 of several staff from the main office [토익 공식 5]
03 While Erica set the table for dinner [토익 공식 5]
04 ⓐ [토익 공식 3]　　　　05 ⓐ [토익 공식 6]
06 ⓑ [토익 공식 1]　　　　07 ⓑ [토익 공식 5]
08 ⓑ [토익 공식 4]　　　　09 ⓐ [토익 공식 6]
10 ⓐ [토익 공식 1]
11 raise → to raise [토익 공식 2]
12 admiration → admirable [토익 공식 4]
13 맞는 문장 [토익 공식 3]
14 submit → to submit [토익 공식 1]

해석 01 프린터를 구매했던 소비자는 환불을 원한다.
　　 02 회사는 몇몇 직원에 대한 본사로부터의 전근을 발표했다.
　　 03 Erica가 저녁을 차리는 동안, Donald는 샐러드를 만들었다.

---

04 그 항공사는 다리를 뻗을 수 있는 공간이 있는 넓은 좌석을 제공함으로써 승객들을 편안하게 해주었다.
05 James는 실행 가능성에 대한 확신이 없었음에도 불구하고 제안서를 제출했다.
06 관중들은 지역 농구팀의 예기치 않은 승리에 놀란 모습을 보였다.
07 Jose는 그의 사무실 근처에 위치한 아파트를 구하고 있다.
08 Wendy는 여행 일정 변경 사항에 대한 최신 정보를 계속 알려 줄 것을 그녀의 비서에게 요청했다.
09 직원 평가는 10월 중에 실시될 것이다.
10 서면 허가증을 받은 방문객들만 공장을 견학할 수 있다.
11 높은 생산 비용은 상품 가격을 인상하는 것이 필요하게 했다.
12 많은 사람들은 최고경영자의 업적이 존경할만하다고 생각한다.
13 그 조립 라인은 장비가 설치되는 대로 가동될 것이다.
14 기업 대출을 신청할 때, 은행 계좌 정보를 제출해야 한다.

Hackers Test
p.64

Part 5				
01 (B)	02 (A)	03 (D)	04 (D)	05 (C)
06 (C)	07 (D)	08 (B)	09 (D)	10 (A)
11 (D)	12 (A)	13 (A)	14 (D)	15 (A)
16 (B)	17 (B)	18 (C)		

Part 6			
19 (C)	20 (D)	21 (B)	22 (A)

01 목적어 자리 채우기

해설 타동사(grant)의 목적어 자리를 채우는 문제이므로 목적어가 될 수 있는 명사 (B) approval(허가)이 정답이다. 동사 (A), 동사 또는 분사 (C), 형용사 (D)는 목적어 자리에 올 수 없다.

해석 시 의회는 환경 훼손이 두드러지게 심각할 경우에는 건설에 대한 허가를 주지 않을 것이다.

어휘 **city council** 시 의회 **grant** v. 주다, 수여하다

02 보어 자리 채우기

해설 가짜 주어(it)의 보어 자리를 채우는 문제이다. 보어가 될 수 있는 것은 명사나 형용사이므로 명사 (A)와 형용사 (C)가 정답의 후보이다. 이 중 빈칸 앞에 부정관사 a와 함께 쓰일 수 있는 것은 명사이므로 (A) benefit(이득)이 정답이다.

해석 대부분의 인사 담당자들은 지원자가 적어도 하나의 외국어에 탄탄한 배경 지식을 가지고 있는 것이 이득이라는 점을 인정한다.

어휘 **recruiter** n. 인사 담당자 **admit** v. 인정하다 **candidate** n. 지원자, 후보자 **at least** 적어도 **benefit** n. 이득; v. 유용하다 **beneficial** adj. 유익한, 이로운

03 보어 자리 채우기

해설 동사(keeps)의 목적격 보어 자리를 채우는 문제이다. 보어가 될 수 있는 것은 명사나 형용사이므로 (A)와 (D)가 정답의 후보이다. 이 중 목적어의 상태를 설명해 주는 형용사 (D) productive(생산적인)가 정답이다. 명사 (A) production(생산)은 목적어(its employees)와 의미적으로 동격 관계를 이루지 못하므로 답이 될 수 없다. 동사 (B)와 부사 (C)는 보어 자리에 올 수 없다. 참고로, (B) produce는 명사로 '생산물, 농작물'이라는 뜻을 갖는데, 명사로 쓰였을 때 문맥에 어울리지 않으므로 정답이 될 수 없다.

해석 Cerda 전자 회사는 정기적인 실적 평가를 실시하고 연간 보너스를 제공함으로써 직원들이 계속 생산적이게 한다.

어휘 **administer** v. 실시하다, 운영하다 **evaluation** n. 평가 **annual** adj. 연간의

04 수식어 거품 채우기

해설 이 문장은 주어(All products), 동사(are), 보어(available)를 갖춘 완전한 절이므로 ____ clients는 수식어 거품으로 보아야 한다. 보기 중 수식어 거품이 될 수 있는 분사 (D) enabling이 정답이다.

해석 상품 목록에 있는 모든 제품들은 자사의 온라인 상점에서 구하실 수 있으며,

이는 고객님들께서 댁에서 편리한 때에 쇼핑하실 수 있도록 해줍니다.

어휘 **available** adj. 구할 수 있는, 이용할 수 있는 **shop** v. 쇼핑하다, 사다
convenience n. 편리한 때

05 주어 자리 채우기

해설 문장의 주어 자리가 비어 있으므로 주어가 될 수 있는 명사 (C) determination (투지, 결심, 결정)이 정답이다. 동사 또는 분사 (A), 부사 (B), 동사 (D)는 주어 자리에 올 수 없다.

해석 제품 소개를 성공으로 만들기 위한 John Carlyle의 투지는 그의 동료들에게 환영받았다.

어휘 **sales presentation** 제품 소개 **appreciate** v. 환영하다, 고마워하다

06 보어 자리 채우기

해설 be동사(are)의 보어가 될 수 있는 것은 형용사 (C) 또는 명사 (D)이다. '항공사 마일리지는 교환할 수 있다'라는 의미가 되어야 하므로 주어(Frequent flyer miles)를 설명해 주는 형용사 (C) redeemable(교환할 수 있는)이 정답이다. 명사 (D) redemption(구함, 상환)은 주어(Frequent flyer miles)와 동격을 이루었을 때 어색한 의미가 되므로 답이 될 수 없다. 참고로, earned ~ passengers는 주어를 꾸며주는 분사이므로 이를 제외하고 문제를 푼다.

해석 Consolidated 항공사 승객에 의해 적립된 항공 마일리지는 Sky-High 연합체의 어떠한 회원 항공사와도 교환할 수 있습니다.

어휘 **frequent flyer miles** 항공 마일리지 **redeem** v. 교환하다, 상환하다
redemption n. 구함, 상환, 현금화

07 수식어 거품을 이끄는 것 채우기

해설 이 문장은 주어(The expertise)와 동사(was gained)를 갖춘 완전한 절이므로 _____ three decades는 수식어 거품으로 보아야 한다. 이 수식어 거품은 동사가 없는 거품구이므로, 거품구를 이끌 수 있는 전치사 (A), (D)가 정답의 후보이다. '30년간의 근무를 통해'라는 의미가 되어야 하므로 (D) through(~을 통해)가 정답이다.

해석 Steve Holden이 성공적인 투자 회사를 개업할 수 있도록 했던 전문 지식은 다국적 은행에서 30년간의 근무를 통해 얻어졌다.

어휘 **expertise** n. 전문 지식 **investment firm** 투자 회사

08 목적어 자리 채우기

해설 타동사(request)의 목적어 자리를 채우는 문제이므로 목적어가 될 수 있는 명사 (B) exemption(면제, 공제)이 정답이다. 형용사 (A), 동사 (C)와 분사 (D)는 목적어 자리에 올 수 없다.

해석 배심원 임무가 미국 시민의 의무이기는 하지만, 건강상의 이유에 대해서는 면제를 요청할 수 있다.

어휘 **jury** n. 배심원 **duty** n. 임무, 의무 **mandatory** adj. 의무의, 필수의
exemptible adj. 면제할 수 있는 **exempt** v. 면제하다

09 목적어 자리 채우기

해설 타동사(has given) 뒤에 목적어를 채우는 문제이다. 목적어가 될 수 있는 명사 (D) motivation(동기)이 정답이다. 동사 (A), 분사 또는 동사 (C)는 목적어 자리에 올 수 없다. 동명사 (B) motivating의 동사원형 motivate(동기를 부여하다)는 뒤에 목적어가 있어야 하는 타동사인데, 이 경우 뒤에 목적어 없이 혼자 쓰일 수 없으므로 빈칸에 올 수 없다.

해석 현재 Parkinson 미술관에 그림이 전시되고 있는 Lyle Stevens는 분투하는 젊은 예술가들에게 동기를 부여해 왔다.

어휘 **currently** adv. 현재 **on exhibit** 전시되어, 진열되어
struggling adj. 분투하는, 기를 쓰는

10 수식어 거품을 이끄는 것 채우기

해설 이 문장은 주어(Several experts)와 동사(met)를 갖춘 완전한 절이므로 _____ practical options는 수식어 거품으로 보아야 한다. 따라서 수식어 거품이 될 수 있는 to 부정사 (A) to discuss가 정답이다.

해석 몇몇 기후변화 전문가들이 새롭고 가격이 알맞은 에너지원을 만들어내기 위한 실제적인 방안을 논의하기 위해 모였다.

어휘 **climate** n. 기후 **practical** adj. 실제적인, 실용적인 **option** n. 방안, 선택
affordable adj. 가격이 알맞은 **discuss** v. 논의하다
discusser n. 의논하는 사람 **discussion** n. 논의

11 보어 자리 채우기

해설 가짜 주어(It)의 보어 자리를 채우는 문제이다. 보어가 될 수 있는 것은 명사나 형용사이므로 형용사 (D) clear(분명한, 명확한)가 정답이다. 동사 (A)와 부사 (B)는 보어 자리에 올 수 없고, 형용사의 최상급 (C) clearest(가장 명백한)를 쓰려면, 적어도 세 개의 비교 대상이 있어야 하는데, 문장에는 비교 대상이 없으므로 (C)는 답이 될 수 없다.

해석 시장에 들어오는 디지털 제품의 공급 과잉으로 전자 산업은 힘든 단계에 진입하고 있는 것이 분명하다.

어휘 **glut** n. (상품의) 공급 과잉, 과도한 양 **challenging** adj. 힘든, 도전적인
phase n. 단계 **clearly** adv. 분명히, 명확하게

12 수식어 거품을 이끄는 것 채우기

해설 이 문장은 필수성분으로 명령문(Please check with Mr. Davidson)이 와 있으므로 _____ he ~ documents는 수식어 거품으로 보아야 한다. 이 수식어 거품은 동사(requires)가 있는 거품절이므로, 거품절을 이끌 수 있는 부사절 접속사 (A)와 (B)가 정답의 후보이다. '추가적인 자료를 요구할 경우에 대비하여'라는 의미가 되어야 하므로 (A) in case(~한 경우에 대비하여)가 정답이다.

해석 Mr. Davidson이 추가 자료를 요구할 경우에 대비하여 오늘 오후 마케팅 발표가 시작하기 전에 그와 의논하세요.

어휘 **check with** ~와 의논하다 **additional** adj. 추가의, 추가적인
furthermore adv. 더욱이, 게다가

13 동사 자리 채우기

해설 문장에 동사가 없으므로 동사 (A)와 (C)가 정답의 후보이다. 주어가 단수이므로 단수 동사 (A) reviews가 정답이다. 복수 동사 (C) are reviewed는 답이 될 수 없다. 또한 'Mr. Kelly가 검토한다'라는 능동의 의미이므로 수동태 동사 (C)는 답이 될 수 없다.

해석 매 금요일마다, Mr. Kelly는 모든 경비 상환 청구들이 타당한지를 확실하게 하기 위해 영업팀의 출장 비용을 검토한다.

어휘 **reimbursement** n. 상환 **legitimate** adj. 타당한, 적당한
review v. 검토하다, 확인하다; n. 검토, 평가

14 수식어 거품을 이끄는 것 채우기

해설 이 문장은 주어(가짜 주어 it, 진짜 주어 that 이하)와 동사(is expected)를 갖춘 완전한 절이므로 _____ worries는 수식어 거품으로 보아야 한다. 이 수식어 거품은 동사가 없는 거품구이므로, 거품구를 이끌 수 있는 전치사 (B)나 (C)가 와야 한다. '우려에도 불구하고'라는 의미가 되어야 하므로 (B) Despite(~에도 불구하고)가 정답이다. 참고로, (C) After는 거품절을 이끄는 부사절 접속사로도 쓰일 수 있다.

해석 정부가 재정 적자를 억제하지 못할 것이라는 우려에도 불구하고, 국가 지출이 최고 기록에 이를 것으로 예상된다.

어휘 **budget deficit** 재정 적자 **an all-time high** 최고 기록

15 보어 자리 채우기

해설 동사(made)의 목적격 보어 자리를 채우는 문제이다. 보어 자리에 올 수 있는 것은 명사나 형용사이므로 형용사 (A), (B)와 명사 (D)가 정답의 후보이다. '오페라를 감동적으로 만들다'라는 의미가 되어야 하므로 형용사 (A) moving(감동적인)이 정답이다. 형용사 (B) movable은 '이동시킬 수 있는'이라는 뜻이므로 의미상 알맞지 않고, 부사 (C)는 보어 자리에 올 수 없다. 명사 (D) movement(움직임)는 목적어(last night's opera)와 의미적으로 동격 관계를 이루지 못한다. 참고로, at the Metropolitan Concert Hall은 목적어(last night's opera)를 꾸미는 전치사구이다.

해석 훌륭한 테너 가수와 매력적인 줄거리가 어젯밤 Metropolitan 콘서트홀에서 열린 오페라를 매우 감동적으로 만들었다.

어휘 **outstanding** adj. 훌륭한 **captivating** adj. 매력적인
plot n. (연극, 소설의) 줄거리, 구상 **movingly** adv. 감동적으로

16 수식어 거품을 이끄는 것 채우기

해설 이 문장은 주어(Companies), 동사(are decreasing), 목적어(the amount of fuel)를 갖춘 완전한 절이므로 ____ increased prices ~ profits는 수식어 거품으로 봐야 한다. 이 수식어 거품은 동사(have begun)가 있는 거품절이므로, 거품절을 이끌 수 있는 부사절 접속사 (B)나 (C)가 와야 한다. '증가한 가격이 ~하기 시작함에 따라'라는 의미가 되어야 하므로 (B) as(~함에 따라)가 정답이다. 참고로, they use는 fuel을 꾸미는 수식어 거품으로, 목적격 관계대명사 that이 생략되어 있는 관계절이다.

해석 에너지 자원의 증가한 가격이 수익을 줄이기 시작함에 따라, 기업들은 그들이 사용하는 연료의 양을 감축하고 있다.

어휘 **cut into** ~을 줄이다 **as** conj. ~함에 따라, ~ 때, ~ 때문에; prep. ~처럼, ~로서
until conj. ~ 때까지

17 진목적어 자리 채우기

해설 동사 consider 뒤에 가목적어 it이 있으므로 빈칸에는 진목적어가 와야 한다. 보기 중 진목적어가 될 수 있는 to 부정사 (B) to conduct가 정답이다.

해설 투자자들이 그 벤처 사업을 위험하다고 여기기 때문에, 경영진은 타당성 조사를 실시하는 것이 최선이라고 생각한다.

어휘 **executives** n. 경영진, 실무자
feasibility study (개발 계획 등의) 타당성 조사, 예비 조사
regard v. ~을 ~으로 여기다, 보다 **risky** adj. 위험한
conduct v. 실시하다, 수행하다

18 수식어 거품을 이끄는 것 채우기

해설 이 문장은 주어(The studio), 동사(is expected)를 갖춘 완전한 절이므로 ____ it can ~ leading actor는 수식어 거품으로 봐야 한다. 이 수식어 거품은 동사(can negotiate)가 있는 거품절이므로, 거품절을 이끌 수 있는 부사절 접속사 (C)나 (D)가 와야 한다. '협상할 수 있다면'이라는 의미가 되어야 하므로 (C) if가 정답이다. 참고로, 등위접속사 (B) for도 절과 절 사이에 올 수 있지만, for(왜냐하면)가 접속사로 사용되려면 앞에 콤마가 필요하므로 답이 될 수 없다.

해석 그 영화사는 감독 및 주연 배우와 협상할 수 있다면 여름 블록버스터에 이은 속편을 제작할 것으로 예상된다.

어휘 **studio** n. 영화사 **sequel** n. 속편 **negotiate** v. 협상하다, 교섭하다

19~22는 다음 기사에 관한 문제입니다.

Renwood 대학교 경영학 교수인 Hae-Eun Kang이 이끄는 연구팀은 최근에 국내 소기업들에 관한 보고서를 발표하였다. 그 보고서에 따르면, 소기업들은 놀라운 속도로 성장하고 있다. ¹⁹지난 두 분기 동안 신생 기업들의 성장으로 10만 개 이상의 새로운 일자리가 창출되었다. 게다가, 새로운 기업들은 5년 전에 그랬던 것에 비해 운영 첫 해에 20퍼센트 넘게 살아남는 것으로 보인다. ²⁰이는 더 많은 사람들이 사업을 시작하는 것을 고려하게 했다.

하지만, Kang 교수는 소기업을 시작하는 것과 관련하여 내재된 위험 요소가 있으며, 계속해서 주의가 기울여져야 한다고 경고한다. ²¹"지역 시장들은 경쟁적이어서, 기업가들은 새롭고 독창적인 제품들을 소비자들에게 제공함으로써 자신들을 돋보이게 만들어야 합니다. ²²이러한 방식으로 획기적이 되는 것은 소기업 소유주들에게 더 큰 장기적인 성공 가능성을 제공합니다."라고 그녀는 말했다.

release v. 발표하다, 풀어주다 **small business** 소기업
remarkable adj. 놀라운, 주목할 만한 **pace** n. 속도
start-up n. 신생 기업 **inherent** adj. 내재하는, 타고난, 고유의
risk n. 위험 요소 **exercise caution** 주의를 기울이다
entrepreneur n. 기업가, 사업가 **set ~ apart** ~을 돋보이게 만들다
original adj. 독창적인, 원래의

19 동사 자리 채우기

해설 문장에 동사가 없으므로 동사 (C) have been created가 정답이다. 명사 (A), 준동사 (B)와 (D)는 동사 자리에 올 수 없다.

어휘 **creation** n. 창출, 창조 **create** v. 창출하다, 창조하다

20 알맞은 문장 고르기

해석 (A) 그러한 기업들이 이런 종류의 대출을 받을 수 있는 것은 놀랍지 않다.
(B) 실업률은 지역마다 상당히 다르다.
(C) 새로운 정책들이 이번 침체를 야기한다고 여겨지는 데에 이유가 있다.
(D) 이는 더 많은 사람들이 사업을 시작하는 것을 고려하게 했다.

해설 빈칸에 들어갈 알맞은 문장을 고르는 문제이므로 빈칸의 주변 문맥이나 전체 문맥을 파악한다. 앞부분에서 소기업들이 놀라운 속도로 성장하고 있으며 새로운 기업들의 생존 가능성도 높아졌다고 했고, 뒤 문장 'However, ~ there are inherent risks involved with starting a small business and that caution should continue to be exercised.'에서 하지만 소기업을 시작하는 것과 관련하여 내재된 위험 요소가 있으므로 계속해서 주의가 기울여져야 한다고 경고했으므로 빈칸에는 소기업들의 성장과 가능성으로 인해 많은 사람들이 새로운 기업을 시작하는 것에 대해 긍정적으로 생각한다는 내용이 들어가야 함을 알 수 있다. 따라서 (D) This has led many people to consider going into business가 정답이다.

어휘 **unemployment rate** 실업률 **vary** v. 다르다, 변경하다
significantly adv. 상당히 **policy** n. 정책, 방책 **downturn** n. 침체
lead v. (사람으로 하여금 어떤 행동·생각을) 하게 하다, 이끌다

21 보어 자리 채우기

해설 be동사(are)의 보어가 될 수 있는 것은 명사 (A), (C) 또는 형용사 (B)이다. '지역 시장들이 경쟁적이다'라는 의미가 되어야 하므로 주어(Local markets)를 설명해 주는 형용사 (B) competitive(경쟁적인)가 정답이다. 명사 (A) competitor(경쟁자)와 (C) competition(경쟁)은 주어(Local markets)와 동격을 이루었을 때 어색한 의미가 되므로 답이 될 수 없다.

어휘 **competitor** n. 경쟁자 **competition** n. 경쟁, 대회
competitively adv. 경쟁적으로

22 형용사 어휘 고르기 주변 문맥 파악

해설 '이러한 방식으로 ____ 되는 것은 장기적인 성공 가능성을 제공한다'라는 문맥이므로 모든 보기가 정답의 후보이다. 빈칸이 있는 문장만으로 정답을 고를 수 없으므로 주변 문맥이나 전체 문맥을 파악한다. 앞 문장에서 '기업가들은 새롭고 독창적인 제품들을 소비자들에게 제공함으로써 자신들을 돋보이게 만들어야 한다(entrepreneurs need to set themselves apart by offering new and original products to consumers)'고 했으므로 (A) innovative(획기적인, 혁신적인)가 정답이다.

어휘 **elaborate** adj. 정교한, 공을 들인 **arbitrary** adj. 임의적인
generous adj. 너그러운, 넉넉한

Section 2 동사구

Chapter 03 동사의 형태와 종류

1 조동사 + 동사원형 p.69
  1. (B) 2. (C) 3. (B)

1. 조동사 다음에 동사원형 채우기

해설 조동사(will) 다음에는 동사원형이 와야 하므로 (B) proceed가 정답이다.

해석 직원 혜택 프로그램을 점검하려는 회사의 계획은 경영진의 전폭적인 지지를 얻고 있으므로 계속 진행될 것이다.

어휘 **plan to do** ~할 계획 **overhaul** v. 점검하다 **benefit** n. 혜택
proceed v. (계속) 진행되다, 나아가다

2. 조동사 다음에 동사원형 채우기

해설 조동사(should) 다음에는 동사원형이 와야 하므로 (C) create가 정답이다.

해석 오늘날의 경쟁적인 환경에서 좋은 성과를 이루기 위해, 기업들은 내용이 충실한 사업 계획을 만들어야 한다.

어휘 achieve v. (일, 목적 등을) 이루다, 성취하다 favorable adj. 좋은, 호의적인
outcome n. 성과, 결과 environment n. 환경
solid adj. 내용이 충실한, 견고한, 단단한

3. 조동사 다음에 동사원형 채우기

해설 조동사(could) 다음에는 동사원형이 와야 하므로 (B) retrieve가 정답이다. 조동사 다음에 과거형 동사 (D)는 나올 수 없다. 참고로, 조동사와 동사원형 자리 사이에 있는 not은 정답 선택에 영향을 주지 않는다.

해석 컴퓨터 기술자는 파일들이 바이러스에 의해 손상되었기 때문에 하드디스크로부터 그것들을 복구하지 못했다.

어휘 technician n. 기술자 retrieve v. 복구하다

---

2 진행형(be + -ing)/수동형(be + p.p.)/완료형(have + p.p.) p.70
1. (D)   2. (B)   3. (D)

1. 'be동사 + p.p.' 채우기

해설 '전략적인 계획이 실시되다'라는 의미가 되기 위해서는 수동형 문장이 되어야 한다. 따라서 be동사(is)와 함께 수동형 동사를 만드는 p.p.형 (D) implemented가 정답이다. 동사원형 (A)는 be동사 다음에 올 수 없다.

해석 프로젝트 분석가는 전략적인 계획에 있는 어떠한 잠재적인 문제점이라도 계획이 실시되기 전에 발견할 수 있어야 한다.

어휘 analyst n. 분석가 spot v. 발견하다, 찾아내다
potential adj. 잠재적인, 가능성 있는; n. 잠재력, 가능성
strategic adj. 전략적인 implement v. 실시하다

2. 'have동사 + p.p.' 채우기

해설 빈칸 뒤에 목적어(the president's decision)가 온 것으로 보아, have동사(has)와 함께 완료형 동사를 만드는 p.p.형 (B) commended가 정답이다. 동사원형 (D)는 have동사 다음에 올 수 없다.

해석 Owens 상원 의원은 전자 산업에 추가적인 보조금을 제공하겠다는 대통령의 결정을 공개적으로 칭찬했다.

어휘 senator n. 상원 의원 publicly adv. 공개적으로
subsidies n. 보조금 commend v. 칭찬하다, 추천하다

3. 'be동사 + -ing' 채우기

해설 '떠나다, 이사하다'라는 의미로 쓰이는 동사 move는 자동사이므로, 수동태 문장을 만들 수 없다. 따라서 be동사(have been) 다음에 와서 능동 진행형을 만드는 (D) moving이 정답이다. 동사원형 (A)는 be동사 다음에 올 수 없으며, 명사 (B)는 소유격이나 관사 없이 혼자 오면 틀린 문장이 된다. (C) moved는 과거형으로 쓰인 경우 be동사 다음에 올 수 없고 p.p.형으로 쓰이더라도 be동사 다음에 와서 수동태를 만들 수 없는 자동사이므로 답이 될 수 없다.

해석 최근의 인구 밀도 그래프는 지방의 젊은 거주자들이 대학 교육을 받고 직장을 구하기 위해 주요 도시들로 이사하고 있다는 것을 보여준다.

어휘 density n. 밀도 rural adj. 지방의, 시골의 resident n. 거주자

---

3 혼동하기 쉬운 자동사와 타동사, 3형식과 4형식 동사 p.71
1. (D)   2. (A)   3. (B)

1. 쓰임에 맞는 동사 채우기

해설 빈칸 뒤에 목적어(that절)가 하나만 온 것으로 보아, 빈칸에는 목적어를 하나만 갖는 3형식 동사가 와야 한다. 따라서 보기 중 3형식 동사인 (D) mentioned가 정답이다. to all staffs는 전치사구이므로, 목적어로 간주될 수 없다.

해석 보안실장은 어떠한 정보도 언론에 새어 나가지 않게 하기 위해 예방 조치가 취해져야 함을 전 직원에게 말했다.

어휘 precaution n. 예방 조치 leak to ~로 새어 나가다

---

press n. 언론, 신문, 잡지사 convince v. 확신시키다, 설득하다
mention v. 말하다, 언급하다

2. 쓰임에 맞는 동사 채우기

해설 빈칸 뒤에 목적어가 2개(the director와 that절) 온 것으로 보아, 빈칸에는 목적어를 2개 갖는 4형식 동사가 와야 한다. 따라서 보기 중 4형식 동사인 (A) advised가 정답이다.

해석 위원회는 Baker 프로젝트에 대한 계속되는 지원이 재정 손실로 이어질 수도 있다고 이사에게 조언했다.

어휘 council n. 위원회, 의회 result in ~으로 이어지다, ~한 결과를 초래하다
financial loss 재정 손실

3. 쓰임에 맞는 동사 채우기

해설 '~에게'라고 해석되는 간접 목적어(the investors)를 전치사 없이 바로 가질 수 있는 4형식 동사 (B) told가 정답이다. (C)와 (D)는 전치사(to) 없이 간접 목적어를 바로 가질 수 없다. tell은 tell me A와 tell me about A의 형태로 모두 쓰일 수 있는 반면에, (A)의 give는 give me A로만 쓰일 수 있고, give me about A의 형태로는 쓰이지 못하므로 답이 될 수 없다.

해석 증권 중개인은 금융 선물 거래를 안전하게 지켜 주는 안전 투자 계획에 대해 투자자들에게 말했다.

어휘 stockbroker n. 증권 중개인 investment n. 투자
secure v. 안전하게 지키다, 보장하다 financial future 금융 선물 (거래)

---

4 제안·요청·의무의 주절을 뒤따르는 that절엔 동사원형이 와야 한다. p.72
1. (D)   2. (B)   3. (C)

1. 제안·요청·의무의 주절을 뒤따르는 that절에 '동사원형' 채우기

해설 주절에 제안을 나타내는 동사(suggests)가 왔으므로 동사원형 (D) order가 정답이다.

해석 그 대학은 학생들이 적어도 개강 2주 전에는 교재를 주문하기를 제안한다.

어휘 at least 적어도, 최소한 prior to ~ 전에, ~에 앞서

2. 제안·요청·의무의 주절을 뒤따르는 that절에 '동사원형' 채우기

해설 주절에 요청을 나타내는 동사(requested)가 왔으므로 종속절의 동사로는 원형 (B) 또는 (C)가 와야 한다. that절의 주어(the operating system)와 동사(restore)가 '운영 체제가 복구되다'라는 의미의 수동 관계이므로 restored 앞에 와서 수동형 동사를 만드는 (B) be가 정답이다.

해석 그 고객은 그 운영 체제가 다른 프로그램들과 호환성이 없기 때문에 이전 버전으로 복구되도록 요청했다.

어휘 restore v. 복구하다, 복원하다 previous adj. 이전의
incompatibility n. (컴퓨터) 호환성 없음, 부조화

3. 제안·요청·의무의 주절을 뒤따르는 that절에 '동사원형' 채우기

해설 주절에 의무를 나타내는 형용사(important)가 왔으므로 동사원형 (C) visit가 정답이다.

해석 이 문제의 긴급함 때문에, Mr. Lambert가 추가 자금의 필요성을 논의하기 위해 이번 주에 본사를 방문하는 것이 중요하다.

어휘 urgency n. 긴급함, 절박함 headquarters n. 본사, 본사 직원들

Hackers Practice p.73

01 ⓐ [토익 공식 1]	02 ⓐ [토익 공식 4]
03 ⓑ [토익 공식 3]	04 ⓐ [토익 공식 1]
05 ⓐ [토익 공식 1]	06 ⓑ [토익 공식 3]
07 ⓑ [토익 공식 3]	08 called → call [토익 공식 1]
09 agree → agreed [토익 공식 2]	
10 will write → write [토익 공식 4]	

11 be sponsor → be sponsored [토익 공식 2]
12 provides → provide [토익 공식 1]
13 is study → is studying, studies [토익 공식 2]
14 to remain → remain [토익 공식 4]

해석 01 Dr. Jensen은 그의 최근 연구 조사를 명확하게 설명할 것이다.
02 모든 손님이 항상 방문자 배지를 착용하는 것은 중요하다.
03 그 상원 의원은 새로운 세금 법률 제정에 대해 국회 의원들과 이야기하기 위해 초대되었다.
04 전문 운동선수가 되기 위해 그는 결코 그의 꿈을 포기하지 않았다.
05 주유소 점원은 우리가 엔진이 정기적으로 점검되게 하고 싶은지 물어보았다.
06 현지 주민들은 새로운 고속도로에 대한 계획을 반대하는데, 이는 고속도로가 자연 서식지를 파괴할 것이기 때문이다.
07 그 여행사 직원은 도쿄에서 단기 체류가 있음을 나에게 말하는 것을 잊었다.
08 내가 너의 상사에게 전화를 해서 네가 아프다는 것을 그녀에게 알리는 게 좋겠다.
09 Eric은 제품 조사를 돕는 것에 동의했다.
10 그 회사는 직원들이 매달 말에 진행 상황 보고서를 작성하기를 요구한다.
11 그 마라톤은 몇몇 지역 회사들에 의해 후원될 것이다.
12 Fairfield 슈퍼마켓은 구매한 것에 대한 환불을 좀처럼 제공하지 않는다.
13 Helen은 지구 온난화와 환경 오염 간의 관계를 공부하고 있다.
14 우리가 경쟁사들의 활동을 계속 인지하는 것은 필수적이다.

Hackers Test
p.74

Part 5

01 (B)	02 (C)	03 (C)	04 (B)	05 (A)
06 (D)	07 (C)	08 (C)	09 (C)	10 (B)
11 (C)	12 (C)	13 (A)	14 (C)	15 (D)
16 (C)	17 (B)	18 (C)		

Part 6

19 (A)	20 (D)	21 (B)	22 (C)

01 조동사 다음에 동사원형 채우기

해설 조동사(should) 다음에는 동사원형 (A), (B) 또는 (D)가 올 수 있다. '등록 서류가 제출되다'라는 수동의 의미가 되어야 하므로 수동태 (B) be submitted가 정답이다. 능동태를 만드는 (A)와 (D)는 답이 될 수 없다.

해석 신청자들이 그들의 예약이 취소되는 것을 원하지 않는다면 모든 등록 서류가 이틀 내로 제출되어야 한다.

어휘 paperwork n. 서류, 서류 작업 forfeit v. 취소당하다, 박탈당하다, 상실하다
reservation n. 예약, 예약석(실)

02 조동사 다음에 동사원형 채우기

해설 조동사처럼 쓰이는 표현(used to) 다음에도 동사원형이 와야 하므로 (C) work가 정답이다. 참고로, 'used to + 동사원형'은 '~했었다'라는 의미이고, 'be used to + -ing'는 '~하는 데 익숙하다'라는 의미인 것도 알아두자.

해석 Steve Pearson은 민간 회사에서 통계 분석가로 일했었지만, 그는 현재 정부의 재정 고문이다.

어휘 statistical adj. 통계의 financial adj. 재정의 consultant n. 고문, 상담가

03 제안·요청·의무의 주절을 뒤따르는 that절에 '동사원형' 채우기

해설 주절에 의무를 나타내는 형용사(imperative)가 왔으므로 종속절 동사로는 원형 (B) 또는 (C)가 와야 한다. 주어(employees)와 동사(instruct)가 '직원들이 교육을 받다'라는 의미의 수동 관계이므로 수동태 (C) be instructed가 정답이다.

해석 인사부장은 점점 경쟁이 치열해지는 시장에서 직원들이 그들의 가치를 높이기 위해서는 반드시 정기적으로 교육을 받아야 한다고 생각한다.

어휘 human resources 인사부, 인적 자원 imperative adj. 반드시 ~해야 하는

04 'be동사 + -ing' 채우기

해설 문장에 동사가 없으므로, 빈칸에는 -ing(generating) 앞에 와서 동사 형태를 만드는 be동사 (A)와 (B)가 정답의 후보이다. 과거 시간 표현(Until recently)이 있으므로 과거 시제인 (B) was가 정답이다.

해석 최근까지, 쇼핑몰에 위치한 Family Entertainment 게임 센터는 소유주가 기대했던 만큼의 수익을 창출하지 못하고 있었다.

어휘 arcade n. 게임(오락) 센터 generate v. 창출하다, 발생시키다
revenue n. 수익, 수입, 세입

05 동사 자리 채우기

해설 주절에 온 동사 suggest가 제안을 나타낼 때는 종속절의 동사로 원형을 쓴다. 그러나 이 문장에서처럼 suggest가 제안을 의미하지 않고 '완곡하게 말하다(imply), 암시하다'를 의미할 때는 that절에 원형이 아니라 일반 동사를 쓴다. 종속절에 단수 취급되는 동명사 주어(setting aside cash)가 왔으므로 단수 동사 (A) makes가 정답이다.

해석 재정 고문들은 비상사태에 대비해 현금을 확보해 두는 것이 초보 투자가들이 손실에서 회복하는 것을 더 용이하게 한다고 말한다.

어휘 adviser n. 고문, 충고자 set aside 확보하다, 챙겨 놓다
emergency n. 비상사태 recover v. 회복하다, 벌충하다 loss n. 손실

06 조동사 다음에 동사원형 채우기

해설 조동사(must) 다음에는 동사원형 (A) 또는 (D)가 와야 한다. '지원서에 소인이 찍히다'라는 수동의 의미가 되어야 하므로 수동태 (D) be postmarked가 정답이다.

해석 그 직책들은 즉시 충원되야 할 필요가 있으므로, 지원서는 늦어도 3월 21일까지는 소인이 찍혀야 한다.

어휘 immediately adv. 즉시 no later than 늦어도 ~까지는
postmark v. 소인을 찍다

07 제안·요청·의무의 주절을 뒤따르는 that절에 '동사원형' 채우기

해설 주절에 의무를 나타내는 동사(insists)가 왔으므로 동사원형 (C) be provided가 정답이다.

해석 그 관리자는 프로젝트 마감 일자가 지켜지지 못한다면 최소한 한 달 전에는 통지받아야 한다고 강조한다.

어휘 insist v. 강조하다, 주장하다 notification n. 통지 in advance 사전에, 미리

08 목적어 자리 채우기

해설 타동사(has caused) 뒤에 목적어 자리를 채우는 문제이다. 목적어가 될 수 있는 명사 (C) damage(피해)가 정답이다. to 부정사 (D) to damage의 동사원형 damage(피해를 입히다)는 뒤에 목적어가 있어야 하는 타동사인데, 이 경우 뒤에 목적어 없이 혼자 쓰일 수 없으므로 답이 될 수 없다.

해석 일련의 지진은 동남아시아 몇몇 주요 도시의 주거 지역과 상업 지역에 피해를 야기했다.

어휘 a series of 일련의 residential adj. 주거의 commercial adj. 상업의

09 쓰임에 맞는 동사 채우기

해설 목적어(the need) 앞에 전치사(about)가 있는 것으로 보아 빈칸에는 자동사 (A) 또는 (C)가 와야 한다. 전치사 about과 함께 쓰여 '~에 대해 이야기하다'라는 의미를 만드는 자동사 (C) talk가 정답이다. (B)와 (D)는 전치사 없이 목적어를 바로 가져야 하는 타동사이므로 답이 될 수 없다. (A) object는 전치사 to와 함께 쓰이며 about과는 같이 쓰이지 않는다.

해석 발표하는 동안에, 마케팅팀장은 신제품으로 주요 인구층의 소비자들을 겨냥해야 할 필요성에 대해 이야기할 것이다.

어휘 target v. 겨냥하다, 목표로 삼다 demographic adj. 인구의, 인구(통계)학의

10 조동사 다음에 동사원형 채우기

해설 조동사(will) 다음에는 동사원형이 와야 하므로 (B) celebrate가 정답이다.

해석 올해는 기업의 50주년을 기념하는 해이기 때문에, Maguire사는 대규모 파티와 함께 그 행사를 축하할 것이다.

11 조동사 다음에 동사원형 채우기

해설   조동사(did) 다음에는 동사원형이 와야 하므로 (C) concur가 정답이다.

해석   관리자는 화장품 부문으로 진출해야 한다는 생각에 동의하지 않았는데, 이는 경쟁이 너무 치열하다고 느꼈기 때문이다.

어휘   expand v. 진출하다, 확장하다   cosmetics n. 화장품   sector n. 부문
competition n. 경쟁   intense adj. 치열한   concur v. 동의하다

12 제안·요청·의무의 주절을 뒤따르는 that절에 '동사원형' 채우기

해설   주절에 제안을 나타내는 동사(recommends)가 왔으므로 종속절의 동사로는 원형 (A) 또는 (C)가 와야 한다. that절의 주어(the factory's waste disposal equipment)와 동사(upgrade)가 '공장의 폐기물 처리 설비가 개선되다'라는 의미의 수동 관계이므로 수동태 (C) be upgraded가 정답이다.

해석   그 조사관은 환경 훼손의 위험을 줄이기 위해 공장의 폐기물 처리 설비가 개선되어야 한다고 권고한다.

어휘   inspector n. 조사관, 감독관   waste disposal 폐기물 처리
lessen v. 줄이다   environmental damage 환경 훼손

13 조동사 다음에 동사원형 채우기

해설   조동사(do) 다음에는 동사원형 (A) 또는 (C)가 와야 한다. '사람들이 요건을 충족시키다'라는 능동의 의미가 되어야 하므로 능동태 동사 (A) satisfy가 정답이다.

해석   그 직업에 대한 기본 지식 요건을 충족시키지 못하는 사람들을 탈락시키기 위해 지원자들에게 테스트가 주어졌다.

어휘   eliminate v. 탈락시키다, 제거하다   requirement n. 요건, 필요조건
satisfy v. 충족시키다

14 조동사 다음에 동사원형 채우기

해설   조동사(should) 다음에는 동사원형 (A) 또는 (C)가 와야 한다. '~에 바탕을 두다'는 be based on으로 표현하므로 (C) be based가 정답이다.

해석   최종 보고서는 몇 달 전에 수집된 자료보다는 더 최근 자료에 바탕을 두어야 한다.

어휘   finding n. 자료, 재료, 발견(물)   rather than ~보다는
be based on ~에 바탕을 두다, ~에 입각하다

15 수식어 거품을 이끄는 것 채우기

해설   이 문장은 주어(hundreds of people), 동사(found), 목적어(themselves)를 갖춘 완전한 절이므로 ＿＿ the sudden collapse of the firm은 수식어 거품으로 보아야 한다. 이 수식어 거품은 동사가 없는 거품구이므로, 거품구를 이끌 수 있는 전치사 (A) 또는 (D)가 와야 한다. '갑작스러운 실패 때문에'라는 의미가 되어야 하므로 (D) Because of(~ 때문에)가 정답이다. (A) As는 전치사로 쓰일 때 '~로서'를 의미하므로 이 문맥에 어울리지 않는다. 참고로, as는 뒤에 절을 이끌면 부사절 접속사이다.

해석   회사의 갑작스러운 실패 때문에, 수백 명의 사람들이 일자리를 잃었다.

어휘   sudden adj. 갑작스러운   collapse n. 실패, 와해, 붕괴; v. 무너지다
hundreds of 수백의

16 동사 자리 채우기

해설   문장에 동사가 없으므로 빈칸에는 동사 (A), (C) 또는 (D)가 와야 한다. 주어(the finance team)가 단수 주어이며, '재무팀이 비용을 삭감하다'라는 능동의 의미가 되어야 하므로 능동태 동사 (C) trimmed가 정답이다. (A) trim은 복수 동사이므로 답이 될 수 없다.

해석   재정 적자를 초래하는 것을 피하기 위해, 재무팀은 꼭 필요한 것이 아니라고 생각되는 비용들을 삭감했다.

어휘   incur v. 초래하다   deficit n. 적자   expense n. 비용, 경비
inessential adj. 꼭 필요한 것이 아닌   trim v. (예산 등을) 삭감하다, 다듬다

17 쓰임에 맞는 동사 채우기

해설   빈칸 뒤에 목적어 2개(assembly participants와 that절)가 온 것으로 보아,

빈칸에는 목적어를 2개 갖는 4형식 동사가 와야 한다. 보기 중 4형식 동사 (B) informed가 정답이다.

해석   관리직 비서는 회의 참가자들에게 장소가 버스 정류장과 좀 더 가까운 곳으로 변경되었다고 알렸다.

어휘   assembly n. 회의, 집회   venue n. (경기, 회담 등의) 장소
depot n. (작은) 정류장, 역

18 'have동사 + p.p.' 채우기

해설   빈칸이 has와 that절(that ~ October) 사이에 있으므로, that절을 목적어로 취하면서 has와 함께 완료형 동사를 만드는 p.p.형 (C) requested가 정답이다. 참고로, requested가 요청을 나타내는 동사이기 때문에 that절에 동사원형(be)이 쓰인 것이다.

해석   많은 직원들이 8월에 휴가 일정을 잡기 때문에, 편집장은 사진집에 대한 마감일을 10월로 연장해 줄 것을 요청했다.

어휘   editor n. 편집장   extend v. 연장하다

19-22는 다음 기사에 관한 문제입니다.

> ### 새로운 농업용 유기농 비료
>
> 20세기 초반 이래로, 많은 국내 농가들은 토양에 쉽게 용해되고 식물에 빠르게 흡수되기 때문에 무기질 비료를 사용해왔다. 하지만, 빠른 흡수 속도는 식물의 성장과 토질에 부정적으로 영향을 준다는 것이 마침내 밝혀졌다. [19]이제, Green Agri-Company는 GreenGrowth라고 불리는 새로운 유기농 퇴비를 소개하려고 하는데, 이 퇴비는 식물이 영양분을 너무 빠르게 흡수하는 것을 방지해 줄 수 있다.
>
> [20]GreenGrowth의 효율성을 시험하기 위해, 웨스트버지니아주의 한 농장주는 몇 달 동안 농장의 조그마한 채소 농사 대지에 제품을 이용했다. 회사가 발행한 보고서에서, 그 농장주는 농작물 수확량이 증가했다고 진술했다. [21]그것은 비료가 토양에 적합했으며 식물들이 영양분을 천천히 흡수하도록 했기 때문인데, 이는 식물들이 영양소와 수분을 둘 다 유지할 수 있게 했다. 더욱이, 토양의 비옥함은 현저하게 개선되었는데, 이는 농작물의 성장을 위한 이상적인 환경을 조성했다. [22]더 자세한 결과는 회사의 웹사이트에서 이용할 수 있다.
>
> GreenGrowth는 현재 농업용 제품 소매상에서 구할 수 있다.
>
> organic adj. 유기농의   fertilizer n. 비료   inorganic adj. 무기질의, 인위적인
> readily adv. 쉽게   dissolve v. 용해하다, 녹다   soil n. 토양
> absorb v. 흡수하다   negatively adv. 부정적으로   introduce v. 소개하다
> compost n. 퇴비, 혼합물   nutrient n. 영양분   crop n. 농작물
> take in ~을 흡수하다   enable v. 할 수 있게 하다, 가능하게 하다
> retain v. 유지하다, 보유하다   retailer n. 소매상, 소매업자

19 조동사 다음에 동사원형 채우기

해설   조동사(can) 뒤에는 동사원형이 와야 하므로 (A) prevent(방지하다, 예방하다)가 정답이다.

20 'have동사 + p.p.' 채우기

해설   빈칸이 has와 명사(the product) 사이에 있으므로, the product를 목적어로 취하면서 has와 함께 완료형 동사를 만드는 p.p.형 (D) utilized가 정답이다. 동사원형 (A) utilize는 조동사 has 다음에 올 수 없다.

어휘   utilize v. 이용하다   utility n. 유용(성), 공공시설, 공공요금

21 형용사 어구 완성하기 전체 문맥 파악

해설   '비료가 토양에 ＿＿＿이다'라는 문맥이므로 (B) suitable(적합한), (C) essential(필수적인)이 정답의 후보이다. 빈칸이 있는 문장만으로 정답을 고를 수 없으므로 주변 문맥이나 전체 문맥을 파악해야 한다. 지문 앞부분에서 무기질 비료가 식물의 성장을 방해한다고 한 후, 새로운 유기농 퇴비를 이용했을 때 '농작물 수확량이 증가했다(crop yields increased)'고 했으므로 농작물 수확량이 증가했다는 것은 새로운 비료가 토양에 적합했기 때문임을 알 수 있다. 따라서 빈칸 앞의 was와 빈칸 뒤의 for와 함께 쓰여 '~에 적합하다'라는 의미의 어구를 이루는 형용사 (B) suitable이 정답이다.

어휘   notable adj. 주목할 만한   relevant adj. 관련 있는, 유의미한

22 알맞은 문장 고르기

해석 (A) GreenGrowth는 유통을 위한 허가를 받기 전에 추가적인 검사를 필요로 한다.
(B) 연구원들은 GreenGrowth가 왜 그렇게 잘 작용하는지 아직 알지 못한다.
(C) 더 자세한 결과는 회사의 웹사이트에서 이용할 수 있다.
(D) GreenGrowth에 의해 야기되는 토질 악화는 심각하지 않은 일이다.

해설 빈칸에 들어갈 알맞은 문장을 고르는 문제이므로 빈칸의 주변 문맥이나 전체 문맥을 파악한다. 앞부분에서 회사는 GreenGrowth의 효율성을 시험했고, 'In a report published by the company, the farmer stated that crop yields increased.'에서 회사가 발행한 보고서에서 효율성을 시험한 농장주가 농작물 수확량이 증가했다고 한 후, 제품의 시험 결과들에 대해 설명하고 있으므로 빈칸에는 보고서의 더 자세한 결과는 회사의 웹사이트에서 이용할 수 있다는 내용이 들어가야 함을 알 수 있다. 따라서 (C) More detailed results can be accessed through the company's Web site가 정답이다.

어휘 require v. 필요로 하다, 요구하다　distribution n. 유통, 분배
access v. 이용하다, 접근하다　deterioration n. 악화

Chapter 04 주어와의 수일치

1 단수 주어 뒤에는 단수 동사, 복수 주어 뒤에는 복수 동사를 쓴다.
p.77
1. (B)　　2. (A)　　3. (B)

1. 주어와 수일치하는 동사 채우기

해설 주어(The recent meeting)가 단수이므로 단수 동사인 (B)와 (C)가 정답의 후보이다. that절을 목적어로 취하면서 '회의가 ~을 암시하다'라는 능동의 의미를 만들어내는 능동형의 동사가 와야 하며, that절에 현재 동사(is)가 있으므로 주절의 동사인 빈칸에도 현재 시제가 와야 한다. 따라서 능동의 현재 단수 동사인 (B) suggests가 정답이다. 주어와 동사 사이에 있는 수식어 거품(between the two companies)은 동사의 수 결정에 아무런 영향을 주지 않으므로, 동사 자리 앞에 온 companies를 보고 복수 동사인 (A)를 선택하는 일이 없도록 주의해야 한다.

해석 두 회사 사이의 최근 회의는 거래가 임박함을 암시한다.

어휘 deal n. 거래, 협정　suggest v. 암시하다, 시사하다

2. 동사와 수일치하는 주어 채우기

해설 빈칸은 that절의 주어 자리인데, 주어가 될 수 있는 것은 명사이므로 명사 (A)와 (C)가 정답의 후보이다. 동사(needs)가 단수이므로 단수 주어 (A) decision이 정답이다. 주어와 동사 사이에 있는 수식어 거품(to implement ~ month)은 동사의 수 결정에 영향을 주지 않는다.

해석 경영진은 새로운 회계 제도를 다음 달에 실행하려는 그들의 결정이 재고되어야 한다는 것을 깨닫게 되었다.

어휘 management n. 경영진　realize v. 깨닫다, 이해하다
implement v. 실행하다

3. 주어와 수일치하는 동사 채우기

해설 주어(The government's program)가 단수이므로 단수 동사 (B)와 (D)가 정답의 후보이다. '정부의 프로그램이 학생들을 돕는다'는 능동의 의미가 맞으므로 (B) aids가 정답이다. 주어와 동사 사이에 있는 수식어 거품(to reduce ~ fees)은 동사의 수 결정에 영향을 주지 않으므로 동사 자리 앞에 온 fees를 보고 복수 동사를 선택하는 일이 없도록 주의해야 한다.

해석 수업료를 줄이기 위한 정부의 프로그램은 교육 비용을 지불하려고 애쓰고 있는 학생들을 돕는다.

어휘 reduce v. 줄이다, 감소시키다　tuition fee 수업료
struggle v. 애쓰다, 발버둥치다　aid v. 도와주다

---

2 주어로 쓰인 수량 표현·부분/전체 표현과의 수일치
p.78
1. (A)　　2. (B)　　3. (D)

1. 수량 표현 주어와 수일치하는 동사 채우기

해설 주어로 복수 취급되는 수량 표현 'a number of + 복수 명사'(A ~ number of refund requests)가 와 있으므로, 복수 동사 (A)와 (D)가 정답의 후보이다. occur는 자동사로 수동태가 될 수 없으므로 능동태 동사 (A) occur가 정답이다.

해석 안정상의 문제와 결함 때문에 구매 물품들이 회수되면 굉장히 많은 환불 요청이 발생한다.

어휘 refund n. 환불　recall n. 회수, 상기; v. 상기하다　defect n. 결함
occur v. 발생하다

2. 수량 표현 주어와 수일치하는 동사 채우기

해설 주어로 단수 취급되는 수량 표현 'every + 명사'(Every employee)가 와 있으므로, 단수 동사 (B) needs가 정답이다.

해석 모든 직원은 승진과 개인의 성장을 위한 자신의 전망이 무엇인지 고려할 필요가 있다.

어휘 prospect n. 전망, 가능성　advancement n. 승진, 출세

3. 부분/전체 표현 주어와 수일치하는 동사 채우기

해설 주어로 전체를 나타내는 표현(All)이 와 있으므로 of 뒤의 복수 명사(the consultants' suggestions)에 알맞은 복수 동사 (D) have been taken이 정답이다. '제안이 고려되다'라는 수동의 의미가 되어야 하므로 능동태인 (C) will take는 답이 될 수 없다.

해석 이번 합병에 관한 회사의 입장에 대한 고문의 모든 제안들이 최고 경영자에 의해 고려되었다.

어휘 consultant n. 고문, 상담가　suggestion n. 제안, 암시
position n. 입장, 상태, 위치　regarding prep. ~에 관하여
upcoming adj. 이번의, 다가오는　merger n. 합병
take A into consideration A를 고려하다

---

3 접속사로 연결된 주어와의 수일치
p.79
1. (B)　　2. (C)　　3. (A)

1. 접속사로 연결된 주어와 수일치하는 동사 채우기

해설 주어로 단수 명사 Mr. Burns와 the secretary가 접속사 and로 연결되어 있으므로, 복수 동사 (B) are coming이 정답이다.

해석 회사 알링턴 지사의 Mr. Burns와 그의 비서는 주말 모임에 올 것이다.

어휘 secretary n. 비서, 서기관　branch n. 지사, 분과, 가지
gathering n. 모임

2. 접속사로 연결된 주어와 수일치하는 동사 채우기

해설 주어로 단수 명사 The chef's assistant와 I가 접속사 and로 연결되어 있으므로, 복수 동사 (C) are preparing이 정답이다. I에 맞춰 (A) am preparing을 쓰지 않도록 주의해야 한다.

해석 요리사의 조수와 나는 오늘 밤 와인 시음 행사를 위한 특별 메뉴를 준비하고 있는데, 여기에 몇몇 수석 음식 평론가들이 참석할 것이다.

어휘 chef n. 요리사　assistant n. 조수, 보조자　taste v. 시음하다, 맛을 보다

3. 주어와 수일치하는 동사 채우기

해설 문장의 주어(The federal government)가 단수이므로 단수 동사 (A) is pushing이 정답이다. along with(~와 함께)는 접속사처럼 보이지만 동사의 수 결정에 영향을 주지 않는 수식어 거품을 이끈다.

해석 주요 산업체들과 함께, 연방 정부는 숙련된 근로자들을 위한 더 많은 일자리를 창출하기 위해 노력하고 있다.

어휘 leading adj. 주요한, 선도하는, 뛰어난

push v. (목적을 달성하기 위하여) 노력하다, 떠밀다

4 주격 관계절의 선행사와 동사의 수일치 p.80

1. (A) 2. (B) 3. (A)

1. 선행사와 수일치하는 주격 관계절의 동사 채우기

해설 주격 관계사(that)의 선행사(Files)가 복수이므로 관계절에는 복수 동사 (A) 또는 (B)가 와야 한다. '서류가 보관되다'라는 수동의 의미가 되어야 하므로 수동태 동사 (A) were stored가 정답이다.

해석 본사에 보관되었던 서류들이 모든 기록을 통합해 보려는 노력으로 새로운 기록 보관소에 재배치되어 왔다.

어휘 relocate v. 재배치하다, 이동시키다 archive n. 기록 보관소
in an effort to ~하기 위한 노력으로 consolidate v. 통합하다
store v. 보관하다, 저장하다

2. 선행사와 수일치하는 주격 관계절의 동사 채우기

해설 주격 관계사(that)의 선행사(the technology conferences)가 복수이므로 관계절에는 복수 동사 (B), (C) 또는 단, 복수에 모두 쓸 수 있는 과거동사 (A)가 와야 한다. host로 '주최되다'를 표현하기 위해서는 수동태 동사를 써야 하므로 수동태 동사 (B) are hosted가 정답이다.

해석 매년, 그 제조업체는 전국 각지의 대학들에 의해 주최되는 기술 학회에 직원들을 파견한다.

어휘 representative n. 직원, 대표자 conference n. 학회
throughout the country 전국 각지의 host v. 주최하다, 진행하다

3. 선행사와 수일치하는 주격 관계절의 동사 채우기

해설 이 문장에서 주격 관계절 who ____ support가 수식하는 것은 단수 명사 The number가 아니라 복수 명사 users이므로, 복수 동사 (A)와 (D)가 정답의 후보이다. '지원을 요구하다'라는 능동의 의미가 되어야 하므로 능동태 동사 (A) require가 정답이다.

해석 그 회사에서 자사 소프트웨어의 최신 버전을 출시한 이래로 지원을 요구하는 사용자들의 수가 증가해 왔다.

어휘 the number of ~의 수 support n. (컴퓨터·컴퓨터 시스템과 관련된) 지원
release v. 출시하다, 풀어놓다, 공개하다 latest adj. 최신의, 최근의
version n. 버전, 판

Hackers Practice p.81

01 ⓑ [토익 공식 1]
02 ⓑ [토익 공식 4]
03 ⓐ [토익 공식 2]
04 ⓑ [토익 공식 2]
05 ⓑ [토익 공식 1]
06 ⓑ [토익 공식 1]
07 ⓐ [토익 공식 3]
08 is → are [토익 공식 3]
09 opens → open [토익 공식 2]
10 맞는 문장 [토익 공식 1]
11 report → reports [토익 공식 1]
12 is → are / The passengers → The passenger [토익 공식 1]
13 맞는 문장 [토익 공식 1]
14 are → is [토익 공식 1]

해석 01 다가오는 회사 야유회에 대한 세부 사항들은 전 직원들에게 이메일로 발송되었다.
02 발표를 할 학회 참석자들은 그들의 연락처를 주최자들에게 제공하도록 요구된다.
03 많은 사람들은 그 회사의 예산안이 터무니없다고 생각한다.
04 기록 보관소에 있는 모든 문서들은 전자 형식으로 변환되었다.
05 학술 토론회가 시작될 때 소개된 연사들은 온라인 광고 전문가들이다.
06 그 도시 내 인터넷 카페들은 더 비싼 요금을 청구하기 시작했다.
07 그 영화감독은 제작진들과 함께 한 장면을 다시 촬영할 것이다.
08 희귀한 다이아몬드와 큰 사파이어가 이번 주말까지 전시된다.
09 그 지역 커피숍의 절반이 자정까지 영업한다.
10 일부 기고가들은 한 달에 한 번만 잡지에 기고한다.
11 뉴스는 추후 통지가 있을 때까지 그 고속도로가 폐쇄될 것이라고 보도한다.

12 일등석 티켓을 지닌 승객(들)은 탑승 수속을 할 때 신속 탑승 줄을 이용하는 것이 허용된다.
13 현재의 자료는 재무 분석을 수행할 때 필수적이다.
14 판촉 할인을 통해 매출을 늘리는 것은 기업가들에 의해 흔히 사용되는 전략이다.

Hackers Test p.82

Part 5

01 (D)	02 (C)	03 (C)	04 (A)	05 (C)
06 (A)	07 (D)	08 (A)	09 (C)	10 (C)
11 (B)	12 (D)	13 (A)	14 (B)	15 (C)
16 (A)	17 (C)	18 (A)		

Part 6

19 (A)	20 (C)	21 (D)	22 (B)

01 동사와 수일치하는 주어 채우기

해설 빈칸은 주어 자리이다. 동사(are handled)가 복수이므로 복수 주어 (D) requests가 정답이다. 주어와 동사 사이에 있는 for information ~ products는 수식어 거품이다.

해석 곧 공개될 제품 정보에 대한 모든 요청 사항들은 홍보부에 의해 처리된다.

어휘 upcoming adj. 곧 공개될, 이번의 handle v. 처리하다, 다루다
public relations department 홍보부

02 동사와 수일치하는 수량 표현 주어 채우기

해설 접속사(because) 뒤에 온 절의 동사(offer)가 복수이므로 복수 취급되는 수량 표현 (C) both가 정답이다. 단수 취급되는 수량 표현 (A)와 (D)는 답이 될 수 없다. 목적어 자리에 오는 목적격 대명사 (B)는 주어 자리에 올 수 없다.

해석 Price-Rite와 Herald 체인점은 두 곳 모두 적정한 가격에 우수한 제품을 제공하기 때문에 사람들에게 인기가 있다.

어휘 quality goods 우수한 제품, 우량품
affordable adj. (가격이) 적정한, 알맞은, (비용을) 감당할 수 있는

03 주어와 수일치하는 동사 채우기

해설 문장에 동사가 없으므로 동사 (A), (C), (D)가 정답의 후보이다. 주어 (American Social Trends)가 -s로 끝났지만 고유명사로 단수 취급되므로 (C) will be broadcast가 정답이다. (A)와 (D)는 복수 동사이므로 답이 될 수 없다.

해석 개인주의와 자본주의 사이의 관계를 탐구하는 다큐멘터리인 American Social Trends가 8월에 방영될 것이다.

어휘 explore v. 탐구하다, 분석하다 individualism n. 개인주의
capitalism n. 자본주의 broadcast v. 방영하다

04 수식어 거품 채우기

해설 이 문장은 주어(Questions)와 동사(should be addressed)를 갖춘 완전한 절이므로 ____ the recent changes ~ eligibility는 수식어 거품으로 보아야 한다. 따라서 수식어 거품을 이끌 수 있는 전치사 (A) concerning이 정답이다. 과거분사 (C) concerned는 뒤에 목적어(the recent changes)를 이끌지 못하므로 답이 될 수 없다.

해석 직원 혜택과 직원 적격성의 최근 변경에 관한 질문들은 인사부의 Mr. Henderson에게 제기되어야 합니다.

어휘 eligibility n. 적격성 address v. 제기하다 concerning prep. ~에 관한

05 주어와 수일치하는 동사 채우기

해설 문장에 동사가 없고, 주어(The proposed layout)가 단수이므로 단수 동사 (C)와 (D)가 정답의 후보이다. 빈칸 뒤에 과거를 나타내는 표현(two months ago)이 있으므로 과거 동사 (C) was approved가 정답이다.

해석 사무실을 위해 제안된 배치도는 두 달 전에 승인되었지만, 추가적인 작업 장소를 설비하자는 결정이 변경을 야기할 것이다.

어휘 **proposed** adj. 제안된 **layout** n. 배치도, 설계 **install** v. 설비하다, 설치하다 **workstation** n. 작업 장소 **result in** ~을 야기하다

06 선행사와 수일치하는 주격 관계절의 동사 채우기

해설 주격 관계절(who ~ basis)의 동사가 없으므로 동사 (A), (B), (C)가 정답의 후보이다. 주격 관계사(who)의 선행사(Salespeople)가 복수이므로 관계절에는 복수 동사 (A) 또는 (C)가 올 수 있다. '판매원들이 고객과의 상호 작용을 다루다'라는 능동의 의미가 맞으므로 능동태 동사 (A) handle이 정답이다.

해석 고객과의 상호 작용을 사례별로 다루는 판매원들은 모두에게 같은 접근법을 고수하는 사람들보다 더 능률적이다.

어휘 **interaction** n. 상호 작용 **on a case-by-case basis** 사례별로 **effective** adj. 능률적인, 효과적인 **stick to** 고수하다, ~에 집착하다 **approach** n. 접근법, 접근; v. 다가오다 **handle** v. 다루다, 처리하다

07 조동사 다음에 동사원형 채우기

해설 조동사(will) 다음에는 동사원형이 와야 하므로 (D) generate가 정답이다.

해석 유행성 독감은 아마도 처방전 없이 살 수 있는 약에 대한 수요 증가를 발생시킬 것이다.

어휘 **epidemic** n. 유행, 전염병, 보급 **demand** n. 수요, 요구; v. 요구하다 **over-the-counter** adj. 처방전 없이 살 수 있는 **medication** n. 약 **generate** v. 발생시키다, 만들어 내다

08 주어와 수일치하는 동사 채우기

해설 문장에 동사가 없고, 주어(The growing middle class)가 단수이므로 단수 동사 (A)와 (B)가 정답의 후보이다. '증가하는 중산층은 ~로 판단되다'라는 수동의 의미가 맞으므로 수동태 동사 (A) is viewed가 정답이다.

해석 인도에서 증가하는 중산층은 많은 다국적 기업들에게 장래성 있는 시장으로 판단된다.

어휘 **middle class** 중산층 **promising** adj. 장래성 있는, 전도유망한 **multinational** adj. 다국적의 **view** v. 판단하다, 간주하다

09 주어와 수일치하는 동사 채우기

해설 문장에 동사가 없고, 주어(The purchase button)가 단수이므로 단수 동사 (A)와 (C)가 정답의 후보이다. (A)는 수동태 동사이고 (C)는 능동태 동사인데, 동사 disappear는 자동사로 수동태가 될 수 없으므로 능동태 동사인 (C) has disappeared가 정답이다.

해석 쇼핑 웹사이트에 있는 몇몇 제품들에 대한 구매 버튼이 일시적으로 사라졌으며, 이 물품들을 장바구니에 추가할 수 없게 하였다.

어휘 **purchase** n. 구매, 구입; v. 구입하다 **temporarily** adv. 일시적으로 **disappear** v. 사라지다

10 주어와 수일치하는 동사 채우기

해설 문장에 동사가 없으므로 동사 (C)와 (D)가 정답의 후보이다. 주어(The government's proposed plan)가 단수이므로 단수 동사 (C) has taken이 정답이다. 주어와 동사 사이에 있는 to expand ~ reservoir는 수식어 거품으로 동사의 수 결정에 영향을 주지 않는다.

해석 새로운 발전소와 저수지를 건설함으로써 그 지역의 사회 기반 시설을 확장시키려는 정부의 제안된 계획이 지난 두 달 동안 구체화되어 왔다.

어휘 **expand** v. 확장시키다 **infrastructure** n. 사회 기반 시설 **construct** v. 건설하다 **power plant** 발전소 **reservoir** n. 저수지 **take shape** 구체화하다, 형태를 갖추다

11 주어와 수일치하는 동사 채우기

해설 문장에 동사가 없으므로 동사 (B)와 (D)가 정답의 후보이다. 동명사 주어(Applying an incentive system)는 단수 주어로 취급되므로 단수 동사 (B) motivates가 정답이다.

해석 직장에서 성과급 제도를 적용하는 것은 직원들이 성과를 향상시키도록 동기를 부여한다.

어휘 **incentive** n. 성과급, 장려금 **performance** n. 성과 **motivate** v. 동기를 부여하다

12 선행사와 수일치하는 주격 관계절의 동사 채우기

해설 주격 관계절(who ~ study)에 동사가 없으므로 빈칸에는 동사 (B) 또는 (D)가 올 수 있다. 주격 관계사(who)의 선행사(anyone)가 단수 취급되는 수량 표현이므로 단수 동사 (D) maintains가 정답이다.

해석 장학금은 학업의 첫 2년 동안 4.0의 평균 평점을 유지하는 모든 학생에게 제공된다.

어휘 **grade point average** 평균 평점(GPA) **maintain** v. 유지하다

13 주어와 수일치하는 동사 채우기

해설 that절의 동사가 없으므로 동사 (A), (C), (D)가 정답의 후보이다. that절의 주어(the fees)가 복수이므로 복수 동사 (A) include가 정답이다. 주어와 동사 사이에 있는 수식어 거품(for the two-day educational event)은 동사의 수 결정에 영향을 주지 않는다.

해석 참가자들은 이틀간의 교육 행사를 위한 비용이 참고 자료, 숙박, 그리고 식사 비용을 포함한다는 것을 통지받았다.

어휘 **participant** n. 참가자, 관계자 **inform** v. 통지하다 **fee** n. 비용, 요금 **reference** adj. 참고(용)의; n. 참조 **material** n. 자료, 재료 **lodging** n. 숙박, 하숙 **include** v. ~을 포함하다

14 선행사와 수일치하는 주격 관계절의 동사 채우기

해설 주격 관계절(that ~ development)의 동사가 없고, 빈칸 앞의 주격 관계사(that)의 선행사(an investment trust company)가 단수이므로 단수 동사 (B)와 (C)가 정답의 후보이다. '투자 신탁 회사가 ~을 제공하다'라는 능동의 의미가 맞으므로 능동태 동사 (B) provides가 정답이다.

해석 마이애미에 있는 부동산을 매입하기 전에, Jeff Damon은 부동산 개발에 대한 조언을 제공하는 투자 신탁 회사와 만날 약속을 잡았다.

어휘 **property** n. 부동산, 재산 **investment** n. 투자 **trust** n. 신탁, 위탁; v. 신뢰하다

15 주격 관계절의 동사와 수일치하는 선행사 채우기

해설 빈칸은 주격 관계대명사(who)의 선행사 자리이다. 주격 관계절의 동사(accept)가 복수 동사이므로 선행사 역시 복수 명사 (C) recruits가 정답이다.

해석 한 달 급여에 상응하는 계약 보너스는 2년간의 고용 계약을 수락하는 신입 사원들에게 지급되고 있다.

어휘 **signing bonus** (계약 체결 시 선지급하는) 계약 보너스 **recruit** n. 신입 사원

16 주어와 수일치하는 동사 채우기

해설 문장에 동사가 없으므로 동사 (A)와 (C)가 정답의 후보이다. 주어(The regulations)가 복수이므로 동사도 복수 동사 (A) describe가 정답이다. 주어와 동사 사이에 있는 수식어 거품(listed ~ handbook)은 동사의 수 결정에 영향을 주지 않는다.

해석 직원 안내서의 첫 장에 기입된 규정들은 근로자들이 충실히 지키도록 요구되는 행동 수칙을 설명한다.

어휘 **regulations** n. 규정, 규칙 **list** v. 기입하다, 열거하다; n. 목록, 명단 **handbook** n. 안내서 **code of conduct** 행동 수칙 **adhere to** ~을 충실히 지키다, 고수하다

17 수량 표현 주어와 수일치하는 동사 채우기

해설 문장에 동사가 없으므로 동사 (C)와 (D)가 정답의 후보이다. 주어로 복수 취급되는 수량 표현 many가 와 있으므로, 복수 동사 (C) estimate가 정답이다.

해석 만약 중국의 경제가 현재 속도로 계속 확장한다면, 많은 사람들은 6년 이내에 중국의 국내 총생산이 미국의 국내 총생산을 능가할 것이라고 추정한다.

어휘 **expand** v. 확장하다 **current** adj. 현재의 **GDP** 국내 총생산(gross domestic product) **surpass** v. 능가하다, 뛰어나다 **estimate** v. 추정하다, 평가하다

18 주어와 수일치하는 동사 채우기

해설 문장에 동사가 없고, 주어(The number)가 단수이므로 단수 동사 (A)와 (C)가 정답의 후보이다. '~의 수가 50을 초과할 것으로 예상된다'는 수동의 의미가 되어야 하므로 수동태 동사 (A) is expected가 정답이다. 참고로 'a number of + 복수 명사'가 주어로 오면 복수 동사를 써야 한다. 주어와 동사

사이에 온 수식어 거품(being ~ jobs)은 동사의 수 결정에 영향을 주지 않는다.

해석 이번 여름에 임시직으로 그 회사에 고용되는 사람의 수는 50명을 초과할 것으로 예상된다.

어휘 **hire** v. 고용하다 **temporary** adj. 임시의, 일시적인 **exceed** v. 초과하다

19-22는 다음 편지에 관한 문제입니다.

Noel Velasquez
1015번지 Meriwether로
버밍햄, 미시간주 48009

Mr. Velasquez께,

Harrison's 온라인 몰은 자사 웹사이트에 대한 귀하의 의견을 받게 되어 감사하게 생각하는데, 이는 자사에 주문 과정을 능률화할 기회를 주기 때문입니다. [19]우리는 귀하께서 많은 수의 제품 종류로 인해 사이트를 돌아다니시는 데 어려움을 겪으셨다는 것을 이해합니다. 우리는 제품들을 유사한 특성에 따라 분류하려고 계획하고 있습니다. 이는 고객들이 필요로 하는 것을 찾기 쉽게 만들어줄 것입니다.

[20]또한, 귀하의 서신은 귀하께서 관심 없었던 여러 물품들이 나타난 장황한 검색들에 대해 설명하고 있습니다. 이 문제를 처리하기 위해, 자사 웹사이트 개발자들이 검색 결과를 개선할 간소화된 시스템을 현재 설계하고 있습니다. [21]웹사이트는 월말이 되기 전에 업데이트될 것입니다. 아마, 귀하께서 제기하신 사안들은 더 이상 문제가 되지 않을 것입니다.

[22]다시 한번 귀하의 의견에 감사드리며, 귀하의 지속적인 지지를 기대하겠습니다.

Pierre Leon 드림

streamline v. 능률화하다, 간소화하다 **navigate** v. 돌아다니다
group v. 분류하다 **attribute** n. 특성, 속성 **an array of** 여럿의, 다수의
address v. 처리하다, 다루다 **refine** v. 개선하다, 정제하다

---

19 동사 자리 채우기

해설 빈칸이 문장의 동사 자리이므로 동사 (A) understand(이해하다)가 정답이다. 명사 (B)와 to 부정사 (C), 형용사 (D)는 모두 동사 자리에 올 수 없다.

20 주어와 수일치하는 동사 채우기

해설 that절의 동사 자리가 비어 있으므로 빈칸에는 동사가 와야 한다. 주격 관계사(that)의 선행사(searches)가 복수이므로 관계절에는 복수 동사 (C), (D)가 와야 한다. '웹사이트에서 관심 없었던 물품들이 함께 검색되는 결과가 발생한다'라는 현재의 상황을 나타내므로 현재 동사 (C) result가 정답이다.

어휘 **result** v. 결과로서 생기다, 기인하다

21 알맞은 문장 고르기

해석 (A) 쇼핑객들은 다가오는 판매 행사에 대해 통지를 받을 것입니다.
(B) 좀 더 다양성을 더하기 위해 제품 종류의 수가 늘어날 것입니다.
(C) 귀하께서 주문하신 물품의 재고가 있으면 통지를 받게 되실 것입니다.
(D) 웹사이트는 월말이 되기 전에 업데이트될 것입니다.

해설 빈칸에 들어갈 알맞은 문장을 고르는 문제이므로 빈칸의 주변 문장이나 전체 문맥을 파악한다. 앞 문장 'To address this problem, our Web site developers are currently designing a simplified system'에서 문제를 처리하기 위해 개발자들이 새로운 웹사이트 시스템을 설계하고 있다고 한 후, 뒤 문장 'Hopefully, the issues you raised will no longer be a concern.'에서 편지의 수신자가 제기한 사안이 더 이상 문제가 되지 않을 것이라고 했으므로 빈칸에는 웹사이트가 월말이 되기 전에 업데이트될 것이라는 내용이 들어가야 함을 알 수 있다. 따라서 (D) The Web site will be updated before the end of the month가 정답이다.

어휘 **inform** v. 통지하다, 알리다 **notify** v. 통지하다 **in stock** 재고의

22 명사 어휘 고르기 전체 문맥 파악

해설 '다시 한번 귀하의 _____에 감사한다'는 문맥이므로 모든 보기가 정답의 후보이다. 빈칸이 있는 문장만으로 정답을 고를 수 없으므로 주변 문장이나 전체 문맥을 파악한다. 지문 앞부분에서 '의견을 주어서 고맙다(appreciates

---

receiving your feedback)'고 했으므로 빈칸을 포함한 구절은 '다시 한번 의견을 주어 감사한다'는 의미가 되어야 한다. 따라서 명사 (B) comments (의견)가 정답이다.

어휘 **work** n. 일, 수고 **order** n. 주문 **request** n. 요청

Chapter 05 능동태·수동태

1 능동태와 수동태의 구별   p.85
1. (C)   2. (A)   3. (D)

1. 태에 맞는 동사 채우기

해설 '이름과 전화번호가 기입되다'라는 수동의 의미이고 동사 뒤에 목적어가 없으므로 should be 다음에 와서 수동태 동사를 만드는 p.p.형 (C) written이 정답이다. be동사 다음에는 동사가 올 수 없으므로 (A)와 (B)는 답이 될 수 없다. -ing형 (D) writing은 should be 다음에 와서 능동태를 만들기 때문에 답이 될 수 없다.

해석 귀하의 이름과 전화번호는 아래 제시된 공간에 명확하게 기입되어야 합니다.

어휘 **clearly** adv. 명확하게, 분명하게

2. 태에 맞는 동사 채우기

해설 동사가 없는 수식어 거품구(the delivery of the package) 앞에 빈칸이 있으므로 수식어 거품구를 이끌 수 있는 to 부정사 (A)와 (C)가 정답의 후보이다. '배송을 서두르다'라는 능동의 의미이고 뒤에 목적어(the delivery)가 있으므로 to 부정사의 능동태 (A) To hasten이 정답이다. 수식어 거품이 될 수 없는 동사 (B)와 (D)는 답이 될 수 없다.

해석 소포의 배송을 서두르기 위해서, 택배 요금에 5달러를 추가해야 할 것입니다.

어휘 **package** n. 소포, 포장 **add A to B** A를 B에 추가하다, 더하다
courier n. 택배 회사 **fee** n. 요금, 수수료 **hasten** v. 서두르다

3. 태에 맞는 동사 채우기

해설 관계절 내에 동사가 없으므로 동사 (A), (C), (D)가 정답의 후보이다. 타동사(attach) 뒤에 목적어가 없고, 관계절의 주어(a copy)와 동사(attach)가 '사본이 첨부되다'라는 수동의 의미를 가지므로 수동태 동사 (D) is attached가 정답이다.

해석 새로 고용된 모든 직원들은 개인 정보 양식을 작성하도록 요구되는데, 양식의 사본 한 부가 계약서에 첨부되어 있습니다.

어휘 **newly** adv. 새로이 **require** v. 요구하다 **fill out** 작성하다
contract n. 계약서

2 4형식/5형식 동사의 수동태   p.86
1. (C)   2. (D)   3. (B)

1. 태에 맞는 동사 채우기

해설 명사절(that ~ package)에서 4형식 동사(offer)의 태를 구별하는 문제이다. '그 유망한 지원자는 제공받다'라는 수동의 의미가 되어야 하므로 수동태 동사 (C) be offered가 정답이다. 이 문장은 능동태 문장이 수동태가 되면서 간접 목적어가 주어(the promising candidate)로 오고 직접 목적어(a better salary and benefits package)가 동사 뒤에 남은 형태이다.

해석 관리자는 유망한 지원자가 더 나은 급여와 복지 혜택을 제공받아야 한다는 것을 제안했다.

어휘 **promising** adj. 유망한 **candidate** n. 지원자
benefits package 복지 혜택

2. 태에 맞는 동사 채우기

해설 5형식 동사(consider)의 태를 구별하는 문제이다. 'Paul이 ~로 여겨지다'라는 수동의 의미이므로 수동태 동사 (D) is considered가 정답이다. 이 문장은

능동태 문장이 수동태가 되면서 목적어(Paul)가 주어 자리로 가고 동사 뒤에 목적격 보어(the best public speaker)가 남은 형태이다.

해석 발표를 하는 것이 다소 생소하기는 하지만, Paul은 부서에서 최고의 연설가로 여겨진다.

어휘 somewhat adv. 다소, 약간
consider A (as) B A를 B라고 여기다, 생각하다

3. 태에 맞는 동사 채우기

해설 5형식 동사(remind)의 태를 구별하는 문제이다. '사람들이 ~하라는 말을 상기하다'라는 수동의 의미이므로 수동태 동사 (B) was reminded가 정답이다. 이 문장은 능동태 문장이 수동태가 되면서 목적어(The research team)가 주어 자리로 가고 뒤에 목적격 보어(to make ~)가 남은 형태이다.

해석 연구팀은 귀중한 자료의 손실을 방지하기 위해 모든 업무의 백업 파일을 만들라는 말을 상기했다.

어휘 backup file 백업 파일, 여벌 파일   prevent v. 방지하다, 예방하다
valuable adj. 귀중한, 소중한

---

3 감정 동사의 능동태/수동태 구별   p.87
1. (B)   2. (D)   3. (D)

1. 태에 맞는 동사 채우기

해설 주어(Young entrepreneurs)가 실망감을 느끼므로 수동태를 써야 한다. be와 함께 수동태 동사를 만드는 p.p.형 (B) disappointed가 정답이다. be 다음에는 보어로 명사 (D)도 올 수 있지만 '사업가가 실망이다'라는 어색한 의미를 만들기 때문에 (D)는 답이 될 수 없다.

해석 벤처 기업을 설립하는 젊은 사업가들은 초기에 판매가 저조하더라도 실망해서는 안 된다.

어휘 entrepreneur n. 사업가, 기업가   set up 설립하다, 세우다

2. 태에 맞는 동사 채우기

해설 주어(Jerry Porter)가 기쁨을 느끼므로 수동태를 써야 한다. be동사(was)와 함께 수동태를 만드는 p.p.형 (D) fascinated가 정답이다. (C)도 was와 함께 수동태를 만들지만, 감정 동사(fascinate)는 진행형(was being fascinated)으로 쓰일 수 없다.

해석 Jerry Porter가 요리를 시작했을 때, 그는 저렴하고 아주 맛이 좋은 음식을 만드는 것이 얼마나 쉬운지 알아가는 데 매료되었다.

어휘 take up (일 등을) 시작하다   fascinate v. 매료시키다, 반하게 하다

3. 태에 맞는 동사 채우기

해설 주어(The manager)가 직원들을 격려해 주는 주체이므로 능동태 동사 (D) encouraged가 정답이다. 주어가 단수이므로 복수 동사 (A)는 답이 될 수 없다.

해석 분기가 끝나기 전에 회사의 목표를 달성해 보려는 노력으로 관리자는 곧 있을 보너스에 대한 소식으로 그녀의 직원들을 격려했다.

어휘 upcoming adj. 곧 있을, 다가오는   in an effort to do ~해보려는 노력으로
encourage v. 격려하다, ~의 용기를 북돋우다

---

4 수동태 동사 숙어   p.88
1. (B)   2. (B)   3. (C)

1. 태에 맞는 동사 채우기

해설 '~에 전념하다'라는 표현은 be dedicated to이므로 (B) is dedicated가 정답이다.

해석 회계팀은 정확한 요금 청구서를 제공하고 모든 고객 문의를 24시간 이내에 해결하는 일에 전념한다.

어휘 accounting n. 회계, 경리   accurate adj. 정확한
billing statement 요금 청구서   resolve v. 해결하다

---

inquiry n. 문의, 조사   be dedicated to -ing ~하는 것에 전념하다, 헌신하다

2. 5형식 수동태 동사 뒤에 to 부정사 채우기

해설 to 부정사를 목적격 보어로 갖는 5형식 동사(ask)가 수동태(are asked)가 되면 그 뒤에는 to 부정사가 남게 되므로 (B) to participate가 정답이다.

해석 Coretek사의 영업 사원들은 고객 관련 사항 워크숍에 참석할 것을 요청받았고, 이는 6월 14일 오후 2시에 개최될 것이다.

어휘 sales associate 영업 사원   customer relations 고객 관련 사항
be asked to ~할 것을 요청받다

3. 태에 맞는 동사 채우기

해설 '~에 기뻐하다'라는 표현은 be delighted with이므로 (C) delighted가 정답이다.

해석 이사회 구성원들은 회사의 새로운 광고 캠페인에 대한 소비자의 긍정적인 반응을 진심으로 기뻐했다.

어휘 the board 이사회   truly adv. 진심으로   be delighted with ~을 기뻐하다

Hackers Practice   p.89

01 ⓐ [토익 공식 1]
02 ⓑ [토익 공식 2, 4]
03 ⓐ [토익 공식 1]
04 ⓑ [토익 공식 3]
05 ⓐ [토익 공식 1]
06 ⓐ [토익 공식 1]
07 ⓑ [토익 공식 3]
08 relating → related [토익 공식 4]
09 맞는 문장 [토익 공식 1]
10 has suggested → has been suggested / was suggested [토익 공식 1]
11 designed → was designed [토익 공식 1]
12 wearing → to wear [토익 공식 2, 4]
13 awarded → was awarded [토익 공식 2]
14 맞는 문장 [토익 공식 4]

해석 01 Bill은 그 프로젝트를 11월 이전에 끝내기 위해 또 다른 조수가 필요하다고 말했다.
02 궂은 날씨에도 불구하고 항공기들은 예정대로 도착할 것으로 기대된다.
03 상점 주인은 고객의 전액 환불 요구를 수락했다.
04 Dr. Menkin은 진료소의 불충분한 시설 때문에 실망했다.
05 한 지역 영화사는 음악 산업에 대한 다큐멘터리를 제작해 왔다.
06 이삿짐 운송업자들은 가구를 그 회사의 새 본사로 운송할 것이다.
07 Joshua는 그가 파리 지사로 전근간다는 것을 알게 되어 흥분했다.
08 아파트 가격은 위치와 밀접하게 관련되어 있다.
09 강한 바람 때문에, 승객들은 비행 중에 난기류를 경험할 것이다.
10 신입 사원을 위한 추가적인 교육이 자문 위원에 의해 제안되었다.
11 그 차량은 장거리를 통근해야 하는 교외 지역의 사람들을 위해 고안되었다.
12 연구실 직원들은 항상 보호안경과 장갑을 착용하도록 권고받는다.
13 훌륭한 관리 능력 때문에 Ms. King에게 승진이 주어졌다.
14 그 단체는 가난한 아이들에게 교육 기회를 제공하는 데 헌신한다.

Hackers Test   p.90

Part 5

01 (C)	02 (C)	03 (B)	04 (D)	05 (C)
06 (B)	07 (D)	08 (C)	09 (D)	10 (B)
11 (A)	12 (B)	13 (D)	14 (B)	15 (C)
16 (D)	17 (C)	18 (C)		

Part 6

19 (D)	20 (C)	21 (B)	22 (A)

01 태에 맞는 동사 채우기

해설 '돈이 인출되다'라는 수동의 의미이고 동사 뒤에 목적어가 없으므로, has just

been 다음에 와서 수동태 동사를 만드는 p.p.형 (C) withdrawn이 정답이다. be동사(has been) 다음에는 보어로 명사 (B)도 올 수 있지만, 주어(A substantial sum of money)와 명사(withdrawal)가 의미적으로 동격 관계를 이루지 않기 때문에 (B)는 답이 될 수 없다.

해석 　새 연구 시설 건축 공사를 위한 대금을 지불하기 위해 상당한 액수의 돈이 그 기업의 은행 계좌에서 방금 인출되었다.

어휘 　**substantial** adj. 상당한　**sum** n. 액수, 합계　**pay for** 대금을 지불하다
withdraw v. (계좌에서 돈을) 인출하다, 취소하다

02 태에 맞는 동사 채우기

해설 　'~하도록 요구되다'라는 표현은 be required to이므로 (C) are required가 정답이다.

해석 　연방법은 모든 회사가 직원들에게 최소 10일의 유급 휴가를 매년 제공하도록 요구된다고 규정한다.

어휘 　**federal** adj. 연방의　**stipulate** v. 규정하다, 명기하다
paid adj. 유급의, 보수가 주어지는

03 태에 맞는 동사 채우기

해설 　관계절(that ~ division)에서 동사(assign)의 태를 구별하는 문제이다. 관계절 앞에 있는 명사(The campaigns)와 동사(assign)가 '캠페인이 배정되다'라는 수동의 의미이고, 동사 뒤에 목적어가 없으므로 수동태 동사 (B) were assigned가 정답이다. (A), (C), (D)는 모두 능동태 동사이므로 답이 될 수 없다.

해석 　방송부에 배정되었던 캠페인은 효과적이지 않았기 때문에 취소되었다.

어휘 　**broadcasting** n. 방송, 방영　**scrap** v. 취소하다, 폐기하다
effective adj. 효과적인　**assign** v. 배정하다, 맡기다, 할당하다

04 5형식 수동태 동사 뒤에 to 부정사 채우기

해설 　to 부정사를 목적격 보어로 갖는 5형식 동사(mean)가 수동태(is meant)가 되면 그 뒤에는 to 부정사가 남게 된다. 따라서 to 뒤에 와서 to 부정사를 만드는 동사원형 (B)와 (D)가 정답의 후보이다. to 부정사 자리 뒤에 목적어(the reimbursement process)가 있으므로, 목적어를 취할 수 있는 능동태 to 부정사를 만드는 (D) simplify가 정답이다.

해석 　Mr. Stuart에 의해 지난 금요일에 발표된 정책 변경은 직원 출장비에 대한 상환 절차를 간소화할 예정이다.

어휘 　**be meant to do** ~할 예정이다, ~하기로 되어 있다
reimbursement n. 상환, 배상　**travel expense** 출장비
simplify v. 간소화하다

05 태에 맞는 동사 채우기

해설 　'~을 갖추고 있다'라는 표현은 be equipped with이므로 (C) are equipped가 정답이다.

해석 　일등석은 Ray 항공사 승객들의 편의를 위해 인터넷 접속, 국제 전화, 그리고 팩스기를 갖추고 있다.

어휘 　**first class seat** 일등석　**connection** n. 접속, 연결
convenience n. 편의, 편리　**be equipped with** ~을 갖추고 있다

06 태에 맞는 동사 채우기

해설 　감정 동사(please)의 태를 구별하는 문제이다. 주어(Morgan Corporation)가 기쁨을 느끼므로 수동태를 써야 한다. be동사(is)와 함께 수동태 동사를 만드는 p.p.형 (B) pleased가 정답이다.

해석 　Morgan사는 회사가 주식 매입 선택권을 전 직원에게 제공할 것이라는 사실을 알리게 되어 기쁩니다.

어휘 　**stock option** 주식 매입 선택권　**please** v. 기쁘게 하다
be pleased to do ~하게 되어 기뻐하다　**pleasurable** adj. 즐거운, 유쾌한

07 태에 맞는 동사 채우기

해설 　'그 기관이 시행하다'는 능동의 의미이고 동사 뒤에 목적어(current regulations)가 있으므로, will be 다음에 와서 능동태를 만드는 -ing형 (D) enforcing이 정답이다. be동사(will be) 다음에는 보어로 명사 (A)도 올 수 있지만, 주어(the agency)와 명사(enforcement)가 의미적으로 동격

관계를 이루지 못하므로 (A)는 답이 될 수 없다.

해석 　무역 재정 위원회가 투자에 대한 변경된 정책을 승인할 때까지, 그 기관은 현재 규정을 모든 신생 기업들에게 시행할 것이다.

어휘 　**commission** n. 위원회　**approve** v. 승인하다, 찬성하다
agency n. 기관, 대리점　**regulation** n. 규정, 규칙
enforce v. (법률 등을) 시행하다

08 수동태 동사 뒤에 전치사 채우기

해설 　to 부정사의 수동태(to be escorted) 뒤에서 행위의 주체(the floor manager)를 나타내는 전치사 (C) by가 정답이다.

해석 　제조 시설의 방문객들은 현장 관리자의 수행을 받게 될 것인데, 그는 공장을 시찰시켜 줄 것이다.

어휘 　**manufacturing** adj. 제조의　**facility** n. 시설　**escort** v. 수행하다, 동행하다

09 'be동사 + -ing' 채우기

해설 　will be 다음에 와서 올바른 동사 형태를 이루는 것은 진행형을 만드는 -ing이므로 (D) releasing이 정답이다. be동사 다음에는 동사원형 (A)나 단수 현재 동사 (B)는 올 수 없다.

해석 　캘리포니아주의 Jordan 상원 의원은 오늘 오후에 세법과 관련하여 제안된 변경 사항에 대해 언론에 성명을 발표할 것이다.

어휘 　**senator** n. 상원 의원　**tax code** 세법　**release** v. 발표하다, 공개하다

10 태에 맞는 동사 채우기

해설 　4형식 동사(send)의 태를 구별하는 문제이다. '참석자들에게 보고서가 발송된다'는 수동의 의미가 되어야 하므로, will 뒤에 와서 수동태를 만드는 (B) be sent가 정답이다. 이 문장은 능동태 문장이 수동태가 되면서 직접 목적어(several pertinent reports)가 주어 자리에 오고 뒤에 '전치사 + 간접 목적어'(to all those)가 남은 형태이다. 참고로, in attendance at the workshop은 those를 꾸며 주는 수식어 거품구이다.

해석 　회계 연도를 위한 계획을 수월하게 하기 위해, 몇몇 관련 보고서가 워크숍에 참석한 모든 이들에게 발송될 것이다.

어휘 　**facilitate** v. 수월하게 하다, 촉진하다　**planning** n. 계획, 입안
fiscal year 회계 연도　**pertinent** adj. 관련 있는, 적절한　**in attendance** 참석한

11 주어와 수일치하는 동사 채우기

해설 　문장의 동사 자리가 비어 있으므로, 동사 (A)와 (C)가 정답의 후보이다. 주어(The receipt)가 단수이므로 단수 동사 (A) lists가 정답이다. 주어와 동사 사이에 있는 수식어 거품(for the shipment from the supplier)은 동사의 수 결정에 영향을 주지 않는다.

해석 　공급자로부터 받은 수송 영수증은 모든 관련 세금, 관세, 그리고 국제 배송비를 열거한다.

어휘 　**list** v. 열거하다, 목록에 포함시키다

12 태에 맞는 동사 채우기

해설 　'~할 것으로 기대되다'라는 표현은 be expected to이므로 (B) is expected가 정답이다.

해석 　특별히 훈련된 분쟁 해결 고문의 채용이 회사 내 경영진과 직원들 사이의 긴장을 완화할 것으로 기대된다.

어휘 　**introduction** n. 채용, 도입　**conflict resolution** 분쟁 해결　**advisor** n. 고문
management n. 경영진　**be expected to do** ~하도록 기대된다, 예상된다

13 태에 맞는 동사 채우기

해설 　4형식 동사(inform)의 태를 구별하는 문제이다. '관리자가 ~을 통지받다'라는 수동의 의미이므로 수동태 동사 (D) had been informed가 정답이다. 이 문장은 능동태 문장이 수동태가 되면서 간접 목적어(the director)가 주어로 오고 직접 목적어(that ~ Incorporated)가 동사 뒤에 남은 형태이다.

해석 　만약 그 관리자가 가장 유력한 후보자가 아직도 Master Lines사의 고문이라는 사실을 통지받았다면, 그는 다른 후보자들에게 더 큰 우선권을 주었을 것이다.

어휘 　**director** n. 관리자, 이사　**consultant** n. 고문　**priority** n. 우선권

14 태에 맞는 동사 채우기

해설 동사가 없는 수식어 거품구(the plant's production output) 앞에 빈칸이 있으므로 to 부정사 (A)와 (B)가 정답의 후보이다. '극대화하다'라는 능동의 의미이고, 뒤에 목적어(the plant's production output)가 있으므로 to 부정사의 능동태 (B) To maximize가 정답이다. 수식어 거품이 될 수 없는 동사 (C)와 (D)는 답이 될 수 없다.

해석 공장 생산량을 극대화하기 위해서, 작업 과정에서의 비능률적인 점을 찾기 위한 검사가 수행될 것이다.

어휘 inspection n. 검사 identify v. 찾다, 확인하다
inefficiency n. 비능률적인 것, 비능률 maximize v. 극대화하다

15 태에 맞는 동사 채우기

해설 '우승자들이 참석할 계획이다'라는 능동의 의미가 되어야 하므로 be동사 (are) 뒤에 와서 능동 진행형을 만드는 (C) planning이 정답이다. be동사 (are) 다음에는 동사원형 (A) plan도 단수 동사 (B) plans도 올 수 없다. (A)와 (B)를 명사로 간주하여 주어(The winners)와 주격 보어 자리에 온 명사(plan, plans)가 의미적으로 동격 관계를 이루지 않기 때문에 답이 될 수 없다. (D) planned는 수동태를 만드므로 답이 될 수 없다.

해석 표어 경연 우승자들이 오늘 저녁 만찬에 참석할 계획이며, 만찬은 Lawrence 컨벤션 센터의 가장 큰 식당에서 저녁 8시에 시작될 것이다.

16 태에 맞는 동사 채우기

해설 '참석자들이 권고받다'라는 수동의 의미이므로, be동사 (are) 다음에 와서 수동태 동사를 만드는 p.p.형 (D) advised가 정답이다.

해석 행사 장소 근처에 머물고 싶은 세미나 참석자들은 일찍 호텔을 예약하도록 권고받는다.

어휘 participant n. 참석자 venue n. (경기, 회담 등의) 장소 book v. 예약하다
advisory adj. 조언의, 충고의; n. 경보, 주의보
be advised to do ~하도록 권고받다

17 태에 맞는 동사 채우기

해설 조동사(cannot) 다음에는 동사원형 (C) 또는 (D)가 올 수 있다. 주어(tenants)와 동사(enter)가 '세입자들이 로비에 출입하다'라는 능동의 의미이고 동사 뒤에 목적어(the lobby)가 있으므로 능동태 동사 (C) enter가 정답이다.

해석 구조상의 수리가 시작되고 나면, 세입자들은 건물 관리진에게 공지를 받을 때까지 로비에 출입할 수 없다.

어휘 structural adj. 구조상의 renovation n. 수리, 혁신 tenant n. 세입자
entrant n. 신입생, 참가자 entrance n. 입구, 현관

18 태에 맞는 동사 채우기

해설 주어(The use)와 동사(prohibit)가 '사용이 금지되다'라는 수동의 의미이고 동사 자리인 빈칸 뒤에 목적어가 없으므로 수동태 동사 (C) is prohibited가 정답이다.

해석 개인적인 지출을 위한 법인 카드 사용은 금지되어 있으며 즉각적인 징계 조치가 취해질 수 있다.

어휘 personal adj. 개인적인 expense n. 지출, 경비 immediate adj. 즉각적인
disciplinary action 징계 조치 prohibit v. 금지하다

19-22는 다음 회람에 관한 문제입니다.

수신: 모든 Carver Media사 직원들
발신: Jean Dubois, 인사부
제목: 재활용
날짜: 12월 12일

우리가 만들어내는 쓰레기의 양을 줄이기 위해 재활용 프로그램을 시작할 것입니다. [19]별개의 컨테이너 네 개가 휴게실에 추가되었습니다. 재활용 가능한 물품들이 반드시 알맞은 통에 놓이도록 해주십시오. [20]그것들은 모두 알기 쉽게 분류되어 있으므로, 유리, 고철 용기, 플라스틱, 종이가 함께 놓이지 않아야 합니다. [21]음식물이 담긴 용기들을 헹구는 것은 매우 중요합니다. 이는 재활용이 일주일에 한 번씩만 수거될 것이기 때문이며, 우리는 사무실을 가능한 한 청결하게 ⟳

유지하고자 합니다. [22]가끔 유해한 화학물질이 새어 나오는 건전지는 복사기 옆에 있는 종이 상자 안에 놓여야 합니다. 이 사안에 관한 여러분의 협조에 감사드립니다.

reduce v. 줄이다, 감소시키다 trash n. 쓰레기 recyclable adj. 재활용 가능한
appropriate adj. 알맞은, 적절한 bin n. 통 clearly adv. 알기 쉽게, 분명히
label v. (라벨을 붙여) 분류하다; n. 라벨 rinse out 헹구다
harmful adj. 유해한 cardboard n. 종이, 판지 cooperation n. 협조

19 알맞은 문장 고르기 문제

해석 (A) 공간 부족에 대한 몇몇 불만 사항들이 있어 왔습니다.
(B) 주민들은 더 이상 쓰레기 수거를 위해 비용을 지불하지 않아도 됩니다.
(C) 자원봉사자들은 해결책을 제시하는 것을 도와야 할 수도 있습니다.
(D) 별개의 컨테이너 네 개가 휴게실에 추가되었습니다.

해설 빈칸에 들어갈 알맞은 문장을 고르는 문제이므로 빈칸의 주변 문맥이나 전체 문맥을 파악한다. 앞 문장 'We are starting a recycling program'에서 자신들이 재활용 프로그램을 시작할 것이라고 했고, 뒤 문장 'Please make sure to put any recyclable items in the appropriate bin.'에서 재활용 가능한 물품이 반드시 알맞은 통에 놓이도록 해달라고 했으므로 빈칸에는 재활용 프로그램에 활용될 통이 새로 놓였다는 내용이 들어가야 함을 알 수 있다. 따라서 (D) Four separate containers have been added to the break room이 정답이다.

어휘 complaint n. 불만 사항 pay v. (비용 등을) 지불하다
come up with ~을 제시하다 solution n. 해결책
separate adj. 별개의, 개별적인

20 태에 맞는 동사 채우기

해설 조동사(should) 다음에는 동사원형 (A), (C), (D)가 올 수 있다. 주어(glass, tin, plastic, and paper)와 동사(place)가 '유리, 고철 용기, 플라스틱, 종이가 놓이다'라는 수동의 의미이고 동사 자리인 빈칸 뒤에 목적어가 없으므로 수동태 동사 (C) be placed가 정답이다.

21 형용사 어휘 고르기 주변 문맥 파악

해설 '음식물이 담긴 용기들을 헹구는 것이 _____하다'라는 문맥이므로 (A) difficult (어려운), (B) essential(매우 중요한), (C) unnecessary(불필요한)가 정답의 후보이다. 빈칸이 있는 문장만으로 정답을 고를 수 없으므로 주변 문맥이나 전체 문맥을 파악한다. 뒤 문장에서 '이는 재활용이 일주일에 한 번씩만 수거될 것이기 때문이고, 사무실을 가능한 한 청결하게 유지하고자 한다(This is because the recycling will only be collected once each week, and we'd like to keep the office as clean as possible.)'고 했으므로 음식물이 담긴 용기를 헹구는 것이 매우 중요하다고 강조하고 있음을 알 수 있다. 따라서 형용사 (B) essential(매우 중요한)이 정답이다.

어휘 unnecessary adj. 불필요한 various adj. 다양한

22 선행사와 수일치하는 주격 관계절의 동사 채우기

해설 주격 관계절(which ~ chemicals)에 동사가 없으므로 동사 (A)와 (B)가 정답의 후보이다. 주격 관계사(which)의 선행사(Batteries)가 복수이므로 복수 동사 (A) leak가 정답이다.

어휘 leak v. 새어 나오다, 새다

Chapter 06 시제와 가정법

1 현재 / 과거 / 미래   p.93
   1. (D)   2. (B)   3. (B)

1. 올바른 시제의 동사 채우기

해설 who절(who ~ retiring)에 동사가 없으므로 동사 (C)와 (D)가 정답의 후보이다. 과거에 단체를 설립했다는 문맥이므로 과거 시제 (D) established가 정답이다. 준동사 (A)와 명사 (B)는 동사 자리에 올 수 없다. 단체를 설립하는 일은 반복되는 동작이나 일반적인 특징이 될 수 없기 때문에 현재 시제 (C)는

해석 은퇴 후에 자선 사업 단체를 설립한 Steve Malkin은 청년들을 어떻게 도울 수 있을지 결정하기 위해서 사하라 사막 이남의 아프리카를 방문 중이다.

어휘 **philanthropic** adj. 자선 사업의, 박애주의의 **Sub-Saharan** 사하라 사막 이남의 **determine** v. 결정하다

2. 올바른 시제의 동사 채우기

해설 이번 주말까지 출장 중일 것이라는 미래의 상황을 추측하는 문맥이므로 미래 시제 (B) will be가 정답이다. 미래완료 (C) will have been은 until과 함께 쓰이지 못하므로 답이 될 수 없다. 참고로 until the end of this week도 미래 시제를 나타내는 단서이다.

해석 Mr. Sanders는 이번 주말까지 도쿄 출장 중일 것이므로, 예정대로 매출 보고서를 완성하지 못할 것이다.

3. 올바른 시제의 동사 채우기

해설 If절은 Ms. Lee가 사무실 수리를 빨리 마치는 것을 요구할 것이라는 미래의 사건을 나타낸다. if로 시작되는 조건절에서는 미래를 나타내기 위해 현재 시제를 쓰므로 (B) requires가 정답이다.

해석 Ms. Lee가 사무실 수리를 예정보다 빨리 마치는 것을 요구한다면, 추가적인 인부들의 고용을 허가해야 할 것이다.

어휘 **ahead of time** 예정보다 빨리 **authorize** v. 허가하다, 인가하다 **require** v. 요구하다, 필요로 하다

---

2 현재진행 / 과거진행 / 미래진행   p.94
   1. (C)   2. (B)   3. (C)

1. 올바른 시제의 동사 채우기

해설 미래 표현(next Wednesday)이 있으므로 미래진행 시제 (C) will be meeting이 정답이다.

해석 Kamata 중공업의 직원들은 다음 주 수요일 오후 4시에 KLX사와의 합병 제의에 관한 우려를 제기하기 위해 주주들과 만나고 있을 것이다.

어휘 **representative** n. 직원, 대표(자), 대리인 **heavy industries** 중공업 **shareholder** n. 주주 **address** v. 제기하다, (문제, 상황 등을) 다루다 **concern** n. 우려, 걱정 **regarding** prep. ~에 관하여

2. 올바른 시제의 동사 채우기

해설 복수 주어(facilities)가 왔으므로 복수 동사 (A)와 (B)가 정답의 후보이다. 시설의 특징을 설명하고 있으므로 현재 시제 (B) consist가 정답이다. 상태 동사(consist)는 진행 시제로 쓸 수 없기 때문에 (A) are consisting은 답이 될 수 없다.

해석 Gentech사의 최근 건설된 연구 시설들은 건강 검진 센터뿐만 아니라 최첨단의 생물학 및 화학 실험실로 이루어져 있다.

어휘 **state-of-the-art** adj. 최첨단의, 최신식의 **laboratory** n. 실험실 **as well as** ~뿐만 아니라, ~에 더하여 **consist of** 이루어져 있다, ~로 구성되다

3. 올바른 시제의 동사 채우기

해설 '사람이 놀라다'라는 수동의 의미가 맞으므로, be동사와 함께 수동태 동사를 만드는 (C) surprised가 정답이다. 감정 동사(surprise)는 진행 시제로 쓸 수 없으므로, 빈칸 앞의 be동사(was)와 함께 진행 시제를 만드는 (A), (D)는 답이 될 수 없다. 동사원형 (B) surprise는 be동사 뒤에 올 수 없다.

해석 가장 신뢰받는 직원들 중 몇 명이 사임한 다음에 경쟁사에 입사한 사실을 발견하고 회사 사장보다 더 크게 놀란 사람은 없었다.

어휘 **company president** 회사 사장 **resign** v. 사임하다 **competitor** n. 경쟁 상대

---

3 현재완료 / 과거완료 / 미래완료   p.95
   1. (B)   2. (D)   3. (D)

1. 올바른 시제의 동사 채우기

해설 문장에 동사가 없으며, 단수 주어(the car industry)가 왔으므로 현재완료 동사의 단수 형태인 (B)와 과거완료 동사인 (D)가 정답의 후보이다. 수개월 간(For several months), 즉 몇 달 전부터 현재까지 발생해 온 일을 나타내야 하므로 현재완료 시제 (B) has interested가 정답이다. 과거완료 시제 (D) had interested는 과거의 특정 시점 이전에 발생한 일을 나타낸다.

해석 자동차 제품이 이제 국가 수출의 15퍼센트를 차지하기 때문에 수개월 동안 자동차 산업은 많은 투자자들의 관심을 끌어왔다.

어휘 **automotive** adj. 자동차의 **make up** 차지하다, 구성하다 **export** n. 수출; v. 수출하다 **interest** v. 관심을 끌다

2. 올바른 시제의 동사 채우기

해설 과거의 특정 시점(스트레스를 푼 시점) 이전에 발생한 일(스트레스가 쌓인 일)을 표현하기 위해서 과거완료 시제를 쓴다. 빈칸 뒤의 p.p.형 caused와 함께 과거완료 시제를 만드는 (D) had been이 정답이다.

해석 점심시간 동안 체육관에서 운동을 함으로써, Linda는 바쁜 오전 시간으로 인해 생긴 업무 관련 스트레스를 완화할 수 있었다.

어휘 **relieve** v. 완화하다, 덜어 주다

3. 올바른 시제의 동사 채우기

해설 이전부터 사용된 비용이 특정 미래 시점(By next month)에 3천 8백만 달러가 되는 것을 표현하기 위해서 미래완료 시제를 쓴다. 따라서 빈칸 뒤의 spent와 함께 미래완료 시제를 만드는 (D) will have been이 정답이다.

해석 다음 달까지, 3천 8백만 달러가 화석 연료 사용과 기후 변화의 관계에 대한 연구에 소비될 것이다.

어휘 **fossil fuel** 화석 연료 **climate change** 기후 변화

---

4 시제 일치   p.96
   1. (C)   2. (C)   3. (B)

1. 시간 표현과 일치하는 시제의 동사 채우기

해설 과거 특정 시점 이래를 의미하는 표현인 'since + 과거 사건(the advent ~ computer)'이 왔으므로 현재완료 시제 (C) has dropped가 정답이다.

해석 정보화 시대의 도래와 개인용 컴퓨터의 발명 이래로 텔레비전 시청률은 조금씩 감소해 왔다.

어휘 **viewership** n. 시청률, 시청자 **slightly** adv. 조금, 약간 **advent** n. 도래

2. 시간 표현과 일치하는 시제의 동사 채우기

해설 과거 시간 표현(Last week)이 있으므로 과거 시제 (C) wrote가 정답이다.

해석 지난주에, 한 신문 논설위원은 대학의 입학 관행에 대한 조사를 유발하는 사설을 썼다.

어휘 **trigger** v. 유발하다, 불러일으키다 **investigation** n. 조사 **admission** n. 입학 **practice** n. 관행, 관례

3. 올바른 시제의 동사 채우기

해설 주절 동사(was notified)가 과거이므로 종속절에도 과거 동사 (B) would be delayed가 정답이다.

해석 경영진은 통관 수속 문제 때문에 파리 사무소로 발송된 선적의 도착이 지연될 것이라고 통지받았다.

어휘 **management** n. 경영진 **shipment** n. 선적, 수송, 수송품 **customs** n. 통관 수속, 관세, 세관 **delay** v. 지연시키다, 연기하다

---

5 가정법 미래 / 과거 / 과거완료   p.97
   1. (B)   2. (C)   3. (A)

1. 가정법 동사 채우기

해설 If절에 had p.p.(had not been taken)가 왔으므로 주절에는 이와 짝을 이루는 would have p.p.가 와야 한다. 빈칸 앞에 would가 있으므로 (B) have been assumed가 정답이다. 조동사(would) 다음에는 동사원형이 와야 하므로 had로 시작하는 (C)는 답이 될 수 없다.

해석 운송비를 절감하기 위한 조치가 취해지지 않았었다면, 추가된 비용은 소비자들이 떠맡았을 것이다.

어휘 take measure 조치를 취하다, 대책을 강구하다 curtail v. (비용을) 절감하다
expense n. 비용, 지출 assume v. (권력, 책임을) 떠맡다, 가정하다

2. 가정법 동사 채우기

해설 If절에 had p.p.(had been reduced)가 왔으므로 주절에는 이와 짝을 이루는 would have p.p.가 와야 한다. 따라서 (C) would have improved가 정답이다. 주절에는 would와 같은 조동사가 꼭 와야 하므로 would가 없는 나머지 보기들은 답이 될 수 없다.

해석 개인 소득세가 감면됐었다면, 국가 경제는 훨씬 더 빨리 개선되었을 것이다.

어휘 income tax 소득세 improve v. 개선되다, 나아지다

3. 가정법 동사 채우기

해설 If절에 had p.p.(had come)가 왔으므로 주절에는 이와 짝을 이루는 would have p.p.가 와야 한다. 그러나 주절에 현재 시제를 나타내는 단서(now)가 와 있으므로, 주절에는 가정법 과거 'would + 동사원형'을 써서 혼합가정법을 만들어야 한다. 따라서 (A) would be가 정답이다.

해석 기술자가 오늘 아침에 왔다면, 에어컨이 지금 작동하고 있을 것이다.

어휘 technician n. 기술자

---

6 if 없는 가정법 : 가정법 도치와 without구문 p.98
1. (C) 2. (D) 3. (D)

1. 가정법 동사 채우기

해설 주절에 might have p.p.(might have fulfilled)가 왔으므로 if절에는 이와 짝을 이루는 had p.p.가 와야 한다. 이 경우 주어와 조동사의 자리가 바뀌면서 had가 이미 문장 앞으로 나와 있으므로 빈칸에는 p.p.형이 와야 한다. p.p.형으로 시작된 (B)와 (C) 중, 주어(the materials)와 동사(order)가 '재료들이 주문되다'라는 의미의 수동 관계이므로 수동태 동사 (C) been ordered가 정답이다.

해석 재료들이 시간에 맞추어 주문됐었다면, 회사는 고객의 급한 주문 요청을 완수했을 것이다.

어휘 on time 시간에 맞추어 fulfill v. 완수하다, 이행하다

2. 가정법 동사 채우기

해설 if가 생략되어 주어(the team)와 조동사(Had)가 도치된 절에 had submitted가 왔으므로 주절에는 이와 짝을 이루는 would have p.p.형이 와야 한다. 따라서 (D) would not have had가 정답이다.

해석 그 팀이 예정대로 보고서를 제출했었다면, 부장이 이사회 회의를 연기할 필요는 없었을 것이다.

어휘 submit v. 제출하다 on schedule 예정대로 postpone v. 연기하다

3. 가정법 동사 채우기

해설 의문문이 아닌 평서문의 맨 처음에 들어가야 할 조동사를 선택하는 문제이므로, 가정법에서 if가 생략되어 주어와 동사가 도치된 문장임을 알 수 있다. 주절의 시제가 미래(will refund)이므로 가정법 미래 문장임을 알 수 있다. 따라서 가정법 미래에 사용되는 조동사 (D) Should가 정답이다.

해석 귀하의 대출 신청이 거절된다면, 금융 기관은 신청 처리 비용을 환불해줄 것이다.

어휘 loan n. 대출 deny v. 거절하다 financial institution 금융 기관
refund v. 환불하다

Hackers Practice p.99

01 ⓑ [토익 공식 1, 4] 02 ⓐ [토익 공식 3, 4]
03 ⓑ [토익 공식 5] 04 ⓑ [토익 공식 1]
05 ⓑ [토익 공식 6] 06 ⓐ [토익 공식 1]
07 ⓐ [토익 공식 5] 08 ⓐ [토익 공식 1]
09 ⓑ [토익 공식 6] 10 ⓐ [토익 공식 2]
11 by the time [토익 공식 4]
12 be [토익 공식 5]
13 at the moment [토익 공식 2]
14 usually [토익 공식 1]

해석
01 Mr. Ryes가 임대용 거처를 점검했을 때, 그는 세입자가 부엌을 개조했다는 것을 알아차렸다.
02 그 기술자는 바이러스가 몇몇 컴퓨터를 감염시켰다는 것을 발견했다.
03 통역사가 없었다면, 우리는 그 고객의 말을 알아듣지 못했을 것이다.
04 그 시장 조사는 우리가 신제품 라인을 출시할 장소들을 선정할 때 유용할 것이다.
05 환경 보호 활동가들의 노력이 없었다면, 그 공원은 주거 지역으로 바뀌었을 것이다.
06 경제학자들이 대출 금리가 상승할 것이라고 생각한다면, 우리는 다른 자금원을 찾아야 한다.
07 그 상점이 가격을 더 적게 청구한다면, 고객들은 그곳에서 더 쇼핑하고 싶어할 것이다.
08 상품이 포장되자마자, 운송부 직원이 그것을 트럭에 실을 것이다.
09 내 집이 더 컸다면, 나는 그 소파를 샀을 것이다.
10 인사부는 직원의 능률을 증대시킬 교육 과정을 고안하고 싶어 한다.
11 새 프린터가 생산 준비가 될 때쯤이면 Sabre-Tech사는 자사 공장을 개선했을 것이다.
12 내가 좀 더 일찍 집을 나섰었다면, 지금쯤 공항에 있을 것이다.
13 일류 레스토랑에서 한때 일했던 Maria는 현재 대사관의 식사를 준비한다.
14 사설 개업 치과 의사들은 발치 하나에 보통 60달러를 청구한다.

Hackers Test p.100

Part 5

01 (C)	02 (D)	03 (D)	04 (C)	05 (D)
06 (C)	07 (C)	08 (D)	09 (B)	10 (C)
11 (B)	12 (D)	13 (C)	14 (C)	15 (D)
16 (C)	17 (A)	18 (C)		

Part 6

19 (B)	20 (D)	21 (C)	22 (B)

01 올바른 시제의 동사 채우기

해설 주절 동사(were delighted)가 과거이므로, that절(종속절)에는 과거완료 동사 (A)나 (C), 과거 동사 (D)가 올 수 있다. 'Sam Warner가 승진되었다'는 수동의 의미가 맞으므로 수동태 동사 (C) had been promoted가 정답이다.

해석 회계부 직원들은 그들의 동료 Sam Warner가 부팀장으로 승진되었다는 사실을 알고 매우 기뻐했다.

어휘 accounting n. 회계 delight v. 매우 기뻐하다, 즐기다 co-worker n. 동료
promote v. 승진시키다, 촉진하다

02 시간 표현과 일치하는 시제의 동사 채우기

해설 과거 시간 표현(last week)이 있으므로 과거 동사 (D) designated가 정답이다.

해석 Keating 시장은 새로 구성된 교통 대책 위원회의 책임자 직무를 맡도록 Veronica Moore를 지난주에 지명했다.

어휘 serve as ~의 직무를 맡다, ~의 역할을 하다 director n. 책임자, 감독
transportation n. 교통, 운송업
task force (특정한 문제를 해결하기 위한) 대책 위원회, 프로젝트 팀
designate v. (특정한 자리나 직책에) 지명하다

03 가정법 동사 채우기

해설 if절에 'had + 주어(it) + p.p.(been)'가 도치되어 온 것으로 보아 주절에는 이와 짝을 이루는 would have p.p.가 와야 한다. 따라서 (D) would not have won이 정답이다.

해석 광고부의 매우 유능한 카피라이터들의 지원이 없었다면, 그 회사는 거래를 성사시키지 못했을 것이다.

어휘 **account** n. 거래, 거래 관계 **talented** adj. 유능한, 재능 있는 **advertising** n. 광고 **division** n. (회사) 부, 국, 과

04 올바른 시제의 동사 채우기

해설 Once절은 연구 보고서를 수정하는 미래의 일을 나타낸다. Once로 시작되는 시간절에서는 미래를 나타내기 위해 현재 시제를 쓰므로 (C) revise가 정답이다.

해석 팀원들이 연구 보고서를 수정하고 나면, 그들은 그것의 사본들을 모든 이사회 임원들에게 전송할 것이다.

어휘 **revise** v. 수정하다, 개정하다

05 가정법 표현 채우기

해설 주절에 would have p.p.(would not have been completed)가 온 것으로 보아 가정법 과거완료 문장임을 알 수 있다. 따라서 가정법 문장에 쓰이는 (D) without이 정답이다. 이때, without 대신에 if it had not been for가 쓰일 수도 있다.

해석 Bio-Data사의 헌신적이고 철두철미한 연구팀의 지속적인 수고가 없었다면 보고서는 완성될 수 없었을 것이다.

어휘 **dedicated** adj. 헌신적인, 전념하는 **thorough** adj. 철두철미한, 꼼꼼한

06 주어와 수일치하는 동사 채우기

해설 문장에 동사가 없고, 주어(The two accounting firms)가 복수이므로 복수동사 (C)와 (D)가 정답의 후보이다. '회계 법인들이 협상 중이다'라는 능동의 의미가 맞으므로 능동태 동사 (C) are negotiating이 정답이다.

해석 두 회계 법인들은 합병의 조건을 협상 중이며 계약의 세부 사항들을 다음 주 월요일에 언론에 공개할 것으로 예상된다.

어휘 **accounting** n. 회계 **term** n. (합의, 계약 등의) 조건, 가격, 비용 **merger** n. 합병 **likely** adj. ~할 것으로 예상되는 **agreement** n. 계약 **negotiate** v. 협상하다, 성사시키다

07 수식어 거품을 이끄는 것 채우기

해설 이 문장은 주어(the company's market share)와 동사(has not increased)를 갖춘 완전한 절이므로 _____ a new promotion was launched ~는 수식어 거품으로 보아야 한다. 이 수식어 거품은 동사(was launched)가 있는 거품절이므로, 거품절을 이끌 수 있는 부사절 접속사 (C) Although가 정답이다. 전치사 (A)와 부사 (B), (D)는 거품절을 이끌 수 없다.

해석 새로운 판촉 상품이 마케팅부에 의해 한 달 전에 출시되었지만, 회사의 시장 점유율은 증가하지 않았다.

어휘 **launch** v. 출시하다, 개시하다 **market share** 시장 점유율

08 가정법 동사 채우기

해설 that절에 속해 있는 또 다른 종속절에 가정법 과거완료의 도치 문장(had the company hired an editor)이 왔으므로 that절의 동사로는 이와 짝을 이루는 would have p.p.가 와야 한다. 빈칸 앞에 would 대신 쓸 수 있는 could가 있으므로 have p.p.형인 (C)와 (D)가 정답의 후보이다. 주어와 동사가 '설명서가 준비되다'라는 의미의 수동 관계이므로 수동태 (D) have been arranged가 정답이다.

해석 관리자는 그 자료가 인쇄되기 전에 그것을 검토할 편집자를 회사에서 고용했었다면 설명서가 더 잘 준비되었을 것이라고 지적했다.

어휘 **manual** n. 설명서, (안내)책자 **editor** n. 편집자 **go over** ~을 검토하다, 점검하다 **arrange** v. 준비하다, 배열하다

09 올바른 시제의 동사 채우기

해설 If절은 문제 발생이라는 미래에 일어날 가능성이 있는 사건을 나타낸다. if로 시작되는 조건절에서는 미래를 나타내기 위해 현재 시제를 쓰므로 (B) encounter가 정답이다.

해석 세관 신고서를 작성할 때 어려움에 직면하면, 승무원에게 말씀하셔서 도움을 받으시기 바랍니다.

어휘 **complete** v. 작성하다, 끝마치다 **customs declaration form** 세관 신고서 **assistance** n. 도움, 지원 **encounter** v. 직면하다, 접하다

10 시간 표현과 일치하는 시제의 동사 채우기

해설 '최근에 사람들이 등록해 오고 있다'라는 문맥에서 부사 Recently와 함께 쓰일 수 있는 (C) have been registering이 정답이다. (B) are to be registering의 'be동사 + to 부정사'는 이 경우 계획이나 예정을 의미하여 '최근에 사람들이 등록할 예정이다'라는 어색한 문맥을 만들기 때문에 (B)는 정답이 될 수 없다.

해석 최근, 관리직에 있는 사람들은 긍정적인 리더십과 직원들의 동기 부여에 관한 더 많은 강의에 등록해 오고 있다.

어휘 **supervisory** adj. 관리의, 감독의 **motivation** n. 동기 부여 **register in** ~에 등록하다

11 시간 표현과 일치하는 시제의 동사 채우기

해설 과거 시간 표현(last Friday)이 있으므로 과거 시제 (B) submitted가 정답이다.

해석 Ms. Ross는 지난 금요일에 해외 시장의 고객층을 확대할 내년 마케팅 방안을 제출했다.

어휘 **expand** v. 확대하다 **customer base** 고객층 **overseas market** 해외 시장 **submit** v. 제출하다

12 시간 표현과 일치하는 시제의 동사 채우기

해설 미래완료 시제와 함께 쓰이는 표현 'By the time + 현재동사(are installed)'가 왔으므로 미래완료 시제 (D) will have increased가 정답이다.

해석 두 대의 새 대형 프린터가 설치될 즈음이면, 그 인기 간행물에 대한 수요는 두 배로 증가해 있을 것이다.

어휘 **by the time** ~할 즈음 **install** v. 설치하다 **demand for** ~에 대한 수요, 요구 **publication** n. 간행(물), 출판 **twofold** adv. 두 배로; adj. 두 배의

13 가정법 동사 채우기

해설 '계획들이 확정됐었다면'에서 볼 수 있듯이 과거의 반대 상황을 가정하고 있으므로 가정법 과거완료 (C) had been이 정답이다. 참고로, 이 문장은 혼합 가정법 문장으로 If절에는 과거 사실의 반대를 나타내는 과거완료(had been)를 썼고, 주절에는 현재 사실의 반대를 나타내는 가정법 과거(would be)를 썼다.

해석 계획들이 예정대로 확정됐다면, Gilbert & Sons사는 이미 Safeway Water 프로젝트의 예비 조사를 수행하고 있을 것이다.

어휘 **confirm** v. 확정하다, 확인하다 **feasibility study** (개발 계획 등의 실현 가능성을 조사하는) 예비 조사, 타당성 조사

14 올바른 시제의 동사 채우기

해설 조건을 나타내는 Unless절에 현재 시제(ends)가 쓰였으므로 회의가 늦게 끝나지 않는다는 미래의 일을 나타내고 있음을 알 수 있다. 따라서 주절에도 미래 시제를 써야 하므로 (C) will return이 정답이다.

해석 고객과의 회의가 늦게 끝나지 않는다면, 우리는 오후 5시가 되기 직전에 사무실로 돌아올 것이다.

어휘 **client** n. 고객

15 시간 표현과 일치하는 시제의 동사 채우기

해설 현재완료 시간 표현(over the past week)이 있으므로 현재완료 시제 (D) has stabilized가 정답이다.

해석 지난주 동안에 금의 가격이 1온스당 1,300달러로 안정되었지만, 대부분의 금

융 전문가들은 주식 시장에서의 투자자 신뢰 부족 때문에 가격이 오를 것 같다는 데 동의한다.

어휘 **confidence** n. 신뢰, 자신감 **stabilize** v. 안정되다, 안정시키다

16 제안·요청·의무의 주절을 뒤따르는 that절에 '동사원형' 채우기

해설 주절에 제안을 나타내는 동사(suggests)가 왔으므로 동사원형 (C) sign이 정답이다.

해석 행정 자문 위원은 사업 계약 개정이 경영진에 의해 승인을 받은 이후에 고객들이 그것에 서명하는 것을 제안한다.

어휘 **administrative** adj. 행정상의 **revision** n. 개정, 수정

17 가정법 동사 채우기

해설 If절에 were가 왔으므로 주절에는 이와 짝을 이루는 'would + 동사원형'이 와야 한다. 따라서 (A) would gain이 정답이다.

해석 Cargill Sportswear사의 광고 캠페인이 좀 더 효과적이라면, 회사는 더 큰 시장 점유율을 얻게 될 것이다.

어휘 **advertisement** n. 광고 **effective** adj. 효과적인 **gain** v. 얻게 되다

18 시간 표현과 일치하는 시제의 동사 채우기

해설 현재완료 시간 표현(over the last 25 years)이 있으므로 현재완료 시제 (C) has established가 정답이다. 과거완료 시제 (B) had established는 과거의 특정 시점 이전에 발생한 일을 나타낸다.

해석 국제적인 고급 호텔 체인 Mirage Hotels & Resorts사는 지난 25년간 600개가 넘는 호텔과 리조트를 설립하였다.

어휘 **luxury** adj. 고급의, 호화로운 **establish** v. 설립하다

19-22는 다음 이메일에 관한 문제입니다.

수신: Morgan Clark <mclark@mproj.com>
발신: Lisa Ross <lisross@envirofirst.org>
제목: 직원 채용에 대한 정보

Mr. Clark께,

¹⁹우리는 오하이오주 Hampton에서의 수질 관리 프로젝트에 관한 귀하의 제안서를 2주 전에 받았습니다. 그것을 읽고 난 후, 자사 재정 지원 기구는 이 사업이 실행 가능하며 수혜 대상자들에게 이롭다는 것을 알아냈습니다. 그러나, 그 제안서는 인력 요구 사항에 대한 상세한 설명을 포함하고 있지 않습니다. ²⁰이 점에 대해 귀하에게 추가 정보를 제공해 주시길 요청해도 되겠습니까?

그 외에는, 제안서에 대해 만족스럽게 생각하며 제안서의 목표들이 저희의 목표와 일치한다고 생각합니다. ²¹이전에 이 사업에 관해 대화를 나누셨던 저희 직원 James Gray가 다음 2주 안에 인력 세부 사항에 관하여 귀하에게 연락할 것입니다. 위원회는 가능한 한 빨리 귀하의 수정된 제안서를 보기 원합니다. ²²위원회가 최종 승인을 허가하면, 즉시 귀하에게 알리도록 하겠습니다. 저희의 전적인 지원에 대해 안심하셔도 됩니다. 감사합니다.

Lisa Ross

staffing n. 직원 채용 **proposal** n. 제안서, 제의
undertaking n. 사업, (중요한·힘든) 일 **feasible** adj. 실행 가능한
advantageous adj. 이로운, 유익한 **intended** adj. 대상으로 삼은, 의도하는
beneficiary n. 수혜자 **requirement** n. 요구, 필요 조건
pleased adj. 만족스러운, 기쁜 **objective** n. 목표, 목적
be in line with ~과 일치하다 **aim** n. 목표, 목적
representative n. 직원, 대표 **revise** v. 수정하다

19 올바른 시제의 동사 채우기

해설 '2주 전에 당신의 제안서를 받았다'라는 문맥에서 과거를 나타내는 표현 'two weeks ago'와 함께 쓰일 수 있는 과거 시제 동사 (B) received가 정답이다.

20 형용사 어휘 고르기 주변 문맥 파악

해설 '_____한 정보를 요청하다'라는 문맥이므로 모든 보기가 정답의 후보이다. 빈칸이 있는 문장만으로 정답을 고를 수 없으므로 주변 문맥이나 전체 문맥을 파악한다. 앞 문장에서 '제안서에 상세한 설명이 포함되어 있지 않다(the

proposal does not include a full description)'고 했으므로 빈칸이 있는 문장에서 추가적인 정보를 요청하고 있음을 알 수 있다. 따라서 형용사 (D) additional(추가의)이 정답이다.

어휘 **early** adj. 이른 **recent** adj. 최근의 **preceding** adj. 이전의, 선행하는

21 올바른 시제의 동사 채우기

해설 '직원이 다음 2주 안에 연락할 것이다'라는 문맥에서 미래를 나타내는 전치사구 'within the next two weeks'와 함께 쓰일 수 있는 미래 시제 (C) will contact가 정답이다.

22 알맞은 문장 고르기

해석 (A) Hampton 댐의 복구 공사는 현재 진행 중입니다.
(B) 위원회가 최종 승인을 허가하면, 즉시 귀하에게 알리도록 하겠습니다.
(C) 기술적인 문제 때문에 귀하의 제안서를 검토하지 못했습니다.
(D) 관리직의 자격 요건은 아래에 나와 있습니다.

해설 빈칸에 들어갈 알맞은 문장을 고르는 문제이므로 빈칸의 주변 문맥이나 전체 문맥을 파악한다. 앞 문장 'The committee would like to see your revised proposal as soon as possible.'에서 위원회는 가능한 한 빨리 수정된 제안서를 보기 원한다고 했으므로 빈칸에는 위원회가 수정된 제안서에 대해 최종 승인을 허가하면 즉시 알리겠다는 내용이 들어가야 함을 알 수 있다. 따라서 (B) Should the board grant final approval, we will notify you immediately가 정답이다.

어휘 **restoration** n. 복구 **grant** v. 허가하다, 승인하다
qualification n. 자격 요건

Section 3 준동사구

Chapter 07 to 부정사

1 to 부정사의 역할 p.105
1. (D) 2. (D) 3. (A)

1. to 부정사 채우기

해설 이 문장은 주어(The firm), 동사(closed), 목적어(one of its smallest offices)를 갖춘 완전한 절이므로 _____ operating costs는 부사 역할을 하는 수식어 거품으로 보아야 한다. 따라서 수식어 거품이 될 수 있는 to 부정사 (D) to decrease가 정답이다. 이 경우 to decrease는 목적(삭감하기 위해)을 나타내는 to 부정사이다. 동사 (A), (B), (C)는 수식어 거품이 될 수 없다.

해석 그 회사는 운영 비용을 삭감하기 위해 회사의 가장 작은 사무실들 중 한 곳을 일시적으로 폐쇄했다.

어휘 **temporarily** adv. 일시적으로, 임시로 **operating** adj. 운영상의, 경영상의

2. to 부정사 채우기

해설 '카탈로그의 목적은 ~을 제공하는 것이다'라는 의미가 되어야 하므로 _____ detailed ~ gallery는 주격 보어 자리이다. 따라서 명사 역할을 하는 to 부정사 (D) to supply가 정답이다. be동사(is) 다음에는 동사원형이 올 수 없으므로 (A) supply는 답이 될 수 없다. (B) supplied를 빈칸에 넣으면 수동태 동사(is supplied)가 되는데, 이때 '박물관 카탈로그의 목적이 제공받다'라는 어색한 문맥이 만들어진다. 명사 (C) supplies(공급품)를 be동사(is) 다음에 나온 명사 보어로 볼 수 있지만, 주어(The purpose)와 동격을 이루지 못하므로 정답이 될 수 없다.

해석 박물관 카탈로그의 목적은 미술품 진열실에서 현재 전시 중인 미술품에 대한 상세한 정보를 제공하는 것이다.

어휘 **purpose** n. 목적, 취지 **detailed** adj. 상세한 **artwork** n. 미술품, 예술품
display v. 전시하다, 진열하다 **gallery** n. 미술품, 진열실, 화랑

3. to 부정사 채우기

해설 이 문장은 주어(The Dogwood Company)와 동사(is pleased)를 갖춘 완전한 절이므로 ____ that ~ Web site는 부사 역할을 하는 수식어 거품으로 보아야 한다. 따라서 수식어 거품이 될 수 있는 to 부정사 (A) to report가 정답이다. 이 경우 to report는 이유(전해드리게 되어서)를 나타내는 to 부정사이며, be pleased(is pleased)는 뒤에 to 부정사를 자주 취하는 구문이다. 명사 또는 동사 (B)와 동사 (C), (D)는 수식어 거품이 될 수 없다.

해석 Dogwood사는 고객들이 이제 자사 웹사이트에서 원예 장비를 직접 구매할 수 있음을 전해드리게 되어서 기쁩니다.

어휘 be pleased to do ~하게 되어서 기쁘다 gardening n. 원예
equipment n. 장비, 비품 directly adv. 직접, 곧바로

---

2 to 부정사의 형태와 의미상 주어 p.106
1. (B) 2. (A) 3. (C)

1. to 부정사의 to 채우기

해설 '아이디어를 내기 위해'라는 의미가 되어야 하므로, 목적을 나타내는 to 부정사를 만들 수 있는 (B) to가 정답이다.

해석 새 프로젝트를 이끌고 있는 Mr. Cummings는 마케팅 전략에 대한 아이디어를 내기 위해 모든 팀 구성원들이 모이기를 원한다.

어휘 lead v. 이끌다, 지휘(인솔)하다 convene v. 모이다, 회합하다
brainstorm v. 브레인스토밍으로 아이디어를 내다 strategy n. 전략

2. to 부정사의 동사원형 채우기

해설 '확보하기를 기대하다'라는 의미가 되어야 하므로, 명사 역할을 하는 to 부정사를 만들어야 한다. to 다음에는 동사원형이 와야 하므로 (A) secure가 정답이다. 이 경우 to 부정사에 확보를 완료했다는 의미는 없으므로 완료형 to 부정사를 만드는 (D) have secured는 답이 될 수 없다.

해석 아르헨티나에 새로운 분점을 설립함에 따라, 그 회사는 라틴 아메리카 내에서 더 넓은 고객층을 확보하기를 기대한다.

어휘 establishment n. 설립, 확립 branch n. 분점, 지사
customer base 고객층 secure v. 확보하다

3. to 부정사의 in order to 채우기

해설 '알아내기 위해'라는 의미가 되어야 하므로, 목적을 나타내는 to 부정사를 만들기 위해 동사원형(determine) 앞에 to가 와야 한다. 그러나 보기 중 to가 없으므로 to 대신 쓰일 수 있는 (C) in order to가 정답이다. 참고로, to 부정사가 목적을 나타낼 때는 to 대신 in order to나 so as to를 쓸 수 있다.

해석 임대주는 몇 개 층이 제대로 따뜻해지지 않는 이유를 알아내기 위해 건물 전체의 난방 장치를 끌 것이다.

어휘 landlord n. 임대주, 토지 소유자 shut off 끄다, 잠그다
determine v. 알아내다, 결정하다 heat v. 따뜻하게 만들다, 가열하다; n. 열, 더위
in order to do ~하기 위해 in case of ~의 경우에는

---

3 to 부정사를 취하는 동사, 명사, 형용사 p.107
1. (D) 2. (C) 3. (D)

1. to 부정사 채우기

해설 동사 fail(Having failed) 다음에는 to 부정사가 와야 하므로 (D) to reach가 정답이다.

해석 합의에 도달하지 못했기 때문에, 관리자는 결정이 연기되는 것을 요청했다.

어휘 consensus n. 합의, 일치 fail to do ~하지 못하다 reach v. ~에 도달하다

2. to 부정사 채우기

해설 명사 right 다음에는 명사를 꾸며 주어 형용사 역할을 하는 to 부정사가 와야 하므로 (C) to examine이 정답이다.

해석 재무 담당 이사에 의해 고용된 외부 회계 감사관에게 조사 기간 동안 그 회사

의 회계 자료를 검토할 수 있는 권한이 주어졌다.

어휘 external adj. 외부의 auditor n. 회계 감사관
finance director 재무 담당 이사 examine v. 검토하다, 조사하다

3. to 부정사 채우기

해설 형용사 able 다음에는 to 부정사가 와야 하므로 (D) to complete가 정답이다.

해석 그 최고 경영자는 새로운 직원들이 고용된다면 그 팀이 마감 일자 전에 연구 프로젝트를 끝마칠 수 있을 것이라고 생각한다.

---

4 to 부정사가 아닌 원형 부정사를 목적격 보어로 갖는 동사 p.108
1. (B) 2. (A) 3. (A)

1. 원형 부정사 채우기

해설 준 사역동사 help(can help) 다음에 동사가 올 때는 원형 부정사나 to 부정사가 와야 하므로, 보기 중 원형 부정사 (B) widen이 정답이다.

해석 그들의 분야와 관련된 학회에 참석하는 것은 사람들의 직업상 연락망을 넓히는 데 도움이 될 수 있다.

어휘 network n. 연락망, 통신망 widen v. 넓히다

2. 원형 부정사 채우기

해설 사역동사 have(will have)의 목적격 보어로는 원형 부정사가 와야 하므로 (A)와 (D)가 정답의 후보이다. '지원자에게 통지하는 중이다'라는 진행 중인 동작을 나타낼 필요가 없기 때문에 진행형 원형 부정사 (D) be notifying이 아닌 (A) notify가 정답이다. 목적어(her secretary)와 목적격 보어(notify)가 '그녀의 비서가 통지받다'라고 수동으로 해석되면 문맥에 맞지 않으므로, 목적격 보어 자리에 p.p.형 (C) notified는 올 수 없다.

해석 인사부장은 면접 일정 변경에 대해 자신의 비서가 지원자에게 통지하도록 할 것이라고 말했다.

어휘 applicant n. 지원자 notify v. 통지하다, 알리다

3. 원형 부정사 채우기

해설 사역동사 let(to let)의 목적격 보어로는 원형 부정사가 와야 하므로 (A) leave가 정답이다. 이 경우 목적어(their employees)와 목적격 보어(leave)가 '직원들이 보내지다'라는 수동 관계를 이루고 있지 않으므로, 목적격 보어 자리에 p.p.형인 (C) left는 올 수 없다.

해석 관리자들은 직원들이 회사의 자원봉사 프로그램에 참여하기 위해 매주 수요일에 일찍 퇴근하는 것을 허락해 달라고 요청받는다.

어휘 volunteer n. 자원봉사자; adj. 자원의, 자발적인

Hackers Practice p.109

01 ⓑ [토익 공식 3]	02 ⓐ [토익 공식 2]
03 ⓑ [토익 공식 1]	04 ⓑ [토익 공식 4]
05 ⓐ [토익 공식 2]	06 ⓑ [토익 공식 4]
07 ⓑ [토익 공식 3]	
08 requesting → to request [토익 공식 3]	
09 맞는 문장 [토익 공식 3]	
10 finish → to finish [토익 공식 2]	
11 reschedule → rescheduled [토익 공식 4]	
12 approve → to approve [토익 공식 3]	
13 맞는 문장 [토익 공식 4]	
14 improve → to improve [토익 공식 1]	

해석 01 그 관리자는 그녀의 놀라운 성과 덕분에 임금 인상을 받게 되어 기쁠 것이다.
02 모든 소프트웨어 프로그램에 대해 정기적인 개정판을 배포하는 것은 필수적이다.
03 특정 지원자들에게는 추천서 제출 요건이 면제될 수 있다.

04 Ms. MacGregor는 직원에 대한 그녀의 배려가 마감일에 대한 그녀의 결정에 영향을 미치도록 했다.

05 생물학과의 연구를 지속하려면 대학으로부터 추가적인 재정 지원이 필요하다.

06 Mr. Wilkins는 그의 자동차를 공인 정비공에게 점검받기로 결정했다.

07 Davis 교수는 학생들이 시험 중에 휴대폰을 사용하는 것을 금지한다.

08 소비자는 제품에 결함이 있거나 손상되면 환불을 요구할 권리가 있다.

09 Patricia는 그 책의 삽화를 11월 8일까지 끝마치기를 희망한다.

10 그 최고 경영자는 회계팀이 거래를 완료할 수 있도록 승인해 주어야 한다.

11 Mr. Williams는 그의 비서를 통해 항공편의 일정이 변경되도록 할 것이다.

12 그 장비가 비싸지 않아서, 경영진은 그것의 구매를 기꺼이 승인해 줄 것이다.

13 에어컨이 고장 났기 때문에, Ms. Jones는 직원에게 기술자를 부르게 했다.

14 그 제조사는 시애틀 공장의 능률을 향상시키기 위한 방법들을 개발해야 한다.

Hackers Test   p.110

Part 5

01 (A)	02 (B)	03 (C)	04 (C)	05 (B)
06 (B)	07 (B)	08 (A)	09 (C)	10 (B)
11 (A)	12 (C)	13 (C)	14 (C)	15 (B)
16 (A)	17 (D)	18 (A)		

Part 6

19 (C)	20 (B)	21 (C)	22 (D)

01 to 부정사 채우기

해설 'in order to + 동사원형'은 목적을 나타내는 to 부정사 대신 쓰일 수 있다. 따라서 빈칸에는 in order와 연결되어 목적(예방하기 위해서)을 나타내는 'to + 동사원형' 형태인 (A)와 (B)가 정답의 후보이다. 주어(Mr. Coulter)와 to 부정사가 'Mr. Coulter는 ~을 예방하다'라는 의미의 능동 관계이므로 능동형 to 부정사 (A) to prevent가 정답이다. to 부정사 뒤에 목적어(the loss or damage)가 있는 것도 능동형을 선택하는 단서가 될 수 있다.

해석 Mr. Coulter는 중요 문서들의 분실이나 손상을 예방하기 위해 기록 보관을 위한 장소를 지정했다.

어휘 **designate** v. 지정하다, 지명하다   **storage** n. 보관(실), 저장(소)   **document** n. 문서, 서류   **prevent** v. 예방하다

02 to 부정사 채우기

해설 동사 need 다음에는 능동형 to 부정사 (B), 또는 need 다음에 와서 수동형 to 부정사(to be obtained)와 같은 의미를 가지는 -ing형 (C)가 올 수 있다. '신고서의 사본을 입수하다'라는 능동의 의미이므로 능동형 to 부정사 (B) to obtain이 정답이다.

해석 이전에 제출된 납세 신고서의 사본을 입수해야 하는 기업들은 요청서를 세무서에 제출해야 한다.

어휘 **previously** adv. 이전에   **file** v. 제출하다   **tax return** 납세 신고서   **submit** v. 제출하다   **taxation office** 세무서   **obtain** v. 입수하다, 얻다

03 to 부정사 채우기

해설 빈칸은 가주어 it의 진주어 자리이다. 진주어가 될 수 있는 것은 to 부정사나 명사절이므로 보기 중 to 부정사 (C) to develop이 정답이다. 동사 (A)와 (D), 명사 (B)는 진주어 자리에 올 수 없다. 참고로, for the company는 to 부정사의 의미상 주어이다.

해석 Ms. Collins는 시장 내 증가한 경쟁 때문에 회사가 획기적인 상품을 개발하는 것이 필요하다고 생각한다.

어휘 **innovative** adj. 획기적인, 혁신적인   **competition** n. 경쟁

04 to 부정사의 to 채우기

해설 빈칸 뒤의 동사원형(approve) 앞에서 to 부정사를 만드는 (C) to가 정답이다. 이 경우 to approve는 authority를 꾸며 주어 형용사 역할을 하는 to 부정사이다. (A), (B), (D)와 같은 전치사 다음에는 동사원형이 올 수 없고 동명사나 명사가 와야 한다. 참고로, authority는 to 부정사를 취하는 명사임을 기억하자.

해석 임원과 재정 관리자만이 월간 예산에 대한 중대한 변경을 승인할 권한을 가지고 있다.

어휘 **executive officer** 임원   **finance** n. 재정, 자금   **authority** n. 권한, 권위   **approve** v. 승인하다   **monthly** adj. 월간의, 한 달의   **budget** n. 예산

05 원형 부정사 채우기

해설 준 사역동사 help(will help)의 목적격 보어로는 원형 부정사나 to 부정사가 와야 하므로 원형 부정사 (B) prepare가 정답이다.

해석 수학과에서 마련한 내일 밤의 개인 교습은 학생들이 곧 있을 시험을 준비하도록 도울 것이다.

어휘 **tutoring session** 개인 교습   **arrange** v. 마련하다, 준비하다, 배열하다   **upcoming** adj. 곧 있을, 다가오는   **examination** n. 시험

06 to 부정사 채우기

해설 명사 information을 뒤에서 꾸밀 수 있는 to 부정사 (B)와 과거분사 (C)가 정답의 후보이다. '적합한 노트북 모델을 고르기 위한 정보'라는 문맥으로 보아 목적어(a ~ notebook model)를 취하면서 명사(information)를 뒤에서 꾸밀 수 있는 to 부정사 (B) to select가 정답이다. 과거분사 (C) selected는 뒤에 목적어를 취할 수 없으므로 답이 될 수 없다.

해석 적합한 노트북 모델을 고르기 위한 추가 정보가 필요하신 고객들은 회사 홈페이지의 제품 설명서 부분을 참고하셔야 합니다.

어휘 **require** v. 필요로 하다, 요구하다   **additional** adj. 추가의   **suitable** adj. 적합한   **consult** v. 참고하다   **description** n. 설명서, 서술적 묘사

07 to 부정사 채우기

해설 명사 need(a need) 다음에는 to 부정사가 와야 하므로 (B) to improve가 정답이다. 참고로, 'for + 명사'(for Net Manage)는 to 부정사의 의미상 주어이다.

해석 고객의 불만 사항들은 Net Manage사가 현재의 품질 보증과 모니터링 체계를 개선할 필요가 있을지도 모른다는 것을 보여준다.

어휘 **present** adj. 현재의, 존재하는   **assurance** n. 보증   **monitoring** n. 모니터링, 감시   **improve** v. 개선하다, 향상시키다

08 to 부정사 채우기

해설 동사 aim(aims) 다음에는 to 부정사가 와야 하므로, to 다음에 올 수 있는 동사원형 (A) express가 정답이다. '분위기를 표현해 왔다'는 완료의 의미가 필요하지 않으므로 완료형 to 부정사 (D) have expressed는 답이 될 수 없다.

해석 정물 사진작가로서, Mr. Bryant는 사진 모음집을 만들 때 특별한 분위기를 표현하려고 애쓴다.

어휘 **still-life** adj. 정물(화)의   **particular** adj. 특별한, 특유의   **create** v. 새로 만들다, 창조하다   **collection** n. 모음집, 컬렉션   **aim to do** ~하려고 애쓰다, ~할 작정이다   **express** v. 표현하다

09 보어 자리 채우기

해설 be동사(was)의 보어가 될 수 있는 것은 명사나 형용사이다. 보어 자리에 부정관사(a)가 왔으므로 명사 (C) consideration이 정답이다.

해석 아시아에서 Pitman Works사 제품의 올라가는 인기는 회사의 최근 확장과 관련하여 중요한 고려 사항이다.

어휘 **popularity** n. 인기   **significant** adj. 중요한   **with regard to** ~과 관련하여   **recent** adj. 최근의   **expansion** n. 확장, 확대   **consideration** n. 고려 사항

10 to 부정사의 동사원형 채우기

해설   동사 promise(promised) 다음에는 to 부정사가 와야 하므로, to 다음의 빈칸에 올 수 있는 동사원형 (B) update가 정답이다.

해석   Ms. Evans는 지사장에게 공급업체와의 합의 과정에 대해 매주 최신 정보를 전달할 것을 약속했다.

어휘   regional director 지사장   weekly adv. 주마다, 주 1회씩
progress n. 과정   negotiation n. 합의
update v. 최신 정보를 주다

11 to 부정사의 의미상 주어 for 채우기

해설   to 부정사(to sign)의 의미상의 주어로는 'for + 명사'가 쓰이므로, 명사 factory employees와 함께 쓰여 to 부정사의 의미상 주어를 이루는 (A) for가 정답이다.

해석   공장 직원들이 서명하고 사용할 공구를 대여해서 근무가 끝날 때 반납하는 것은 의무이다.

어휘   mandatory adj. 의무의, 필수의   sign out 서명하고 (물건을) 대여하다
tool n. 공구, 연장

12 to 부정사 채우기

해설   명사 way(ways) 다음에는 to 부정사가 와야 하므로 (C) to promote가 정답이다. 참고로, ways는 'way of + -ing' 형태로도 쓰일 수 있으므로 to promote 대신 of promoting을 쓸 수도 있음을 알아 둔다.

해석   노동조합은 경영진과 직원 간의 협력 증대를 활성화시킬 수 있는 방법들을 개발하기 위한 목적으로 회사 임원들과 함께 일하는 데 동의했다.

어휘   official n. 임원, 간부   cooperation n. 협력, 협동
management n. 경영진, 관리   promote v. 활성화시키다, 장려하다

13 수동태 동사 뒤에 전치사 채우기

해설   수동태 동사 are satisfied 다음에 오는 전치사 (C) with가 정답이다.

해석   쇼핑객들이 가게의 서비스에 만족하는 것을 확실히 하기 위해, 고객 담당 직원들은 정기적으로 교육받는다.

어휘   ensure v. 확실하게 하다, 보증하다
customer representative 고객 담당 직원   train v. 교육하다, 훈련하다
regularly adv. 정기적으로   be satisfied with ~에 만족하다

14 to 부정사 채우기

해설   동사 ask(are ~ asking)의 목적격 보어로는 to 부정사가 와야 하므로 (C) to reduce가 정답이다.

해석   천연가스와 다른 석유 제품들의 가격이 상승함에 따라, 공익 기업들은 현재 사람들에게 연료 소비를 줄여 달라고 요청하고 있다.

어휘   natural gas 천연가스   petroleum n. 석유
utility company 공익 기업   fuel n. 연료   consumption n. 소비
reduce v. 줄이다, 감소시키다

15 태에 맞는 동사 채우기

해설   Until절의 주어(a complete inspection)와 보기의 동사(perform)가 '완벽한 점검이 실행되다'라는 의미의 수동 관계에 있고 빈칸 뒤에 목적어가 없으므로 수동태 (B) is performed가 정답이다. until로 시작되는 시간절에서는 미래를 나타내기 위해 현재 시제를 쓰므로, 미래 시제 (D) will be performed는 빈칸에 올 수 없다.

해석   그 장비에 대한 완벽한 점검이 실행될 때까지, 공장의 안전 규정에는 변동 사항이 없을 것이다.

어휘   inspection n. 점검, 정밀 검사   safety n. 안전(성)
regulation n. 규정, 규칙   perform v. 실행하다, 수행하다

16 to 부정사 채우기

해설   동사 remain(remains) 다음에는 명사, 형용사, 또는 to 부정사가 올 수 있다. 따라서 to 부정사 (A) to be가 정답이다.

해석   청량음료의 새로운 제조법에 대중들이 좋게 반응할지 아닐지는 두고 봐야 한다.

어휘   public n. 대중, 일반 사람들; adj. 일반 대중의, 공공의
react v. 반응하다, 대응하다   formula n. 제조법, 방식
remain to be seen 두고 보아야 한다

17 to 부정사 채우기

해설   동사 remind(reminded)의 목적격 보어 자리에는 to 부정사가 와야 하므로 (D) to call이 정답이다.

해석   보조원은 그 국회의원에게 곧 있을 그녀의 발표와 관련하여 무역 공개 토론회의 회장에게 전화하라고 상기시켜 주었다.

어휘   remind v. 상기시키다, 알려 주다   congressperson n. 국회의원
trade n. 무역, 상업; v. 무역하다, 거래하다   forum n. 공개 토론회, 포럼

18 to 부정사 채우기

해설   '고객들에 대응하기 위해서'라는 의미가 되어야 하므로 목적을 나타내는 to 부정사 (A) to cope가 정답이다. '대응하고 있기 위해서'라는 진행의 의미가 필요하지 않으므로 진행형 to 부정사 (C) to be coping은 답이 될 수 없다. '대응되기 위해서'라는 수동의 의미 역시 틀리므로 수동태 to 부정사 (D) to be coped도 답이 될 수 없다.

해석   긴 연휴 동안 고객들의 쇄도에 대응하기 위해 몇 명의 새로운 계산원과 판매원이 고용되었다.

어휘   cashier n. 계산원, 출납원   influx n. 쇄도, 유입
cope with ~에 대응하다, 대처하다

19-22는 다음 편지에 관한 문제입니다.

Edward Mitchell
1505번지 Main가
페어팩스, 버지니아주 20151

Mr. Mitchell께,

[19]종합적인 검토를 한 후, 저희는 귀하의 단체를 후원하는 것을 계속하기로 결정했습니다. [20]저희는 귀하께서 제공해주신 연간 개요를 꼼꼼히 읽어 보았으며, 지구 온난화에 관한 정확한 정보를 제공하려는 귀하의 노력이 성공을 거두고 있다고 확신합니다. 따라서, Sanford 협회는 귀하에 대한 재정 지원을 추가로 1년 더 연장하기로 결정했습니다. [21]저희는 또한 그것이 15퍼센트까지 늘어날 것임을 알리게 되어 기쁩니다. 추가적인 지원이 귀하께서 더욱 긍정적인 결과를 거두실 수 있게 하기를 진심으로 바랍니다.

[22]저는 귀하께서 동봉된 보조금 동의서에 서명하시고 이번 주 금요일 전에 택배 회사를 통해 돌려보내 주시기를 권합니다. 감사드리며, 계속해서 좋은 일을 해 주시기를 바랍니다.

Scott Hernandez 드림

conduct v. 하다, 지휘하다   comprehensive adj. 종합적인, 이해하는
review n. 검토   sponsor v. 후원하다; n. 후원자   organization n. 단체
read through ~을 꼼꼼히 읽어보다   global warming 지구 온난화
meet with success 성공을 거두다   extend v. 연장하다
funding n. 재정 지원, 자금   additional adj. 추가의, 추가적인
enable v. ~할 수 있게 하다   enclose v. 동봉하다   grant n. 보조금
courier service 택배 회사   keep up ~을 계속하다, 유지하다

19 동사 어휘 고르기   전체 문맥 파악

해설   '후원하는 것을 _____ 하기로 결정하다'라는 문맥이므로 모든 보기가 정답의 후보이다. 빈칸이 있는 문장만으로 정답을 고를 수 없으므로 주변 문맥이나 전체 문맥을 파악한다. 뒷부분에서 Sanford 협회가 Mr. Mitchell의 단체에 대한 재정 지원을 추가로 1년 더 연장하기로 결정했다고 했으므로 후원하는 것을 계속하기로 결정했음을 알 수 있다. 따라서 동사 (C) continue가 정답이다.

어휘   question v. 이의를 제기하다   prohibit v. 금지하다   begin v. 시작하다

20 보어 자리 채우기

해설   be동사(are) 다음에는 주어 We의 상태를 설명할 수 있는 주격 보어가 필요하므로 보어가 될 수 있는 형용사 (B)와 (C)가 정답의 후보이다. '우리는 ~라고 확신한다'는 문맥이므로 (B) convinced(확신을 가진)가 정답이다.

(C) convincing(설득력 있는)을 쓰면 '우리는 ~라는 설득력 있다'는 어색한 의미가 된다. 동사 (A)와 부사 (D)는 보어 자리에 올 수 없다.

어휘   convince v. 확신시키다, 신념을 가지다   convinced adj. 확신을 가진, 신념 있는
convincing adj. 설득력 있는, 남을 납득시키는

21 알맞은 문장 고르기

해석   (A) 저희 협회에 대한 귀하의 관대한 후원에 매우 감사드립니다.
(B) 문제를 해결하기 위해 귀하의 프로그램에 관한 더 많은 세부 사항이 필요합니다.
(C) 저희는 또한 그것이 15퍼센트까지 늘어날 것임을 알리게 되어 기쁩니다.
(D) 저희가 귀하의 단체를 위해 할 수 있는 것은 그 정도밖에 없습니다.

해설   빈칸에 들어갈 알맞은 문장을 고르는 문제이므로 빈칸의 주변 문맥이나 전체 문맥을 파악한다. 앞 문장 'the Sanford Institute has chosen to extend your funding for an additional year'에서 Sanford 협회가 상대방, 즉 Mr. Mitchell의 단체에 대한 재정 지원을 추가로 1년 더 연장하기로 결정했다고 한 후, 뒤 문장 'We sincerely hope that the extra support will enable you to achieve even more positive results.'에서 추가적인 지원이 더욱 긍정적인 결과를 거둘 수 있게 하기를 바란다고 했으므로 빈칸에는 단체에 대한 추가적인 재정 지원 결정과 관련된 내용이 들어가야 함을 알 수 있다. 따라서 (C) We are also pleased to say that it will be increased by 15 percent가 정답이다.

어휘   generous adj. 관대한   sponsorship n. 후원
association n. 협회, 단체   detail n. 세부 사항   resolve v. 해결하다

22 to 부정사 채우기

해설   동사 encourage의 목적격 보어 자리에는 to 부정사가 와야 하므로 (D) to sign이 정답이다.

어휘   sign v. 서명하다

Chapter 08 동명사

1 동명사의 역할, 형태, 의미상 주어   p.113
1. (C)   2. (B)   3. (B)

1. 동명사 채우기

해설   문장에서 동사(helps) 앞에 위치한 _____ regular donations는 주어 자리이다. 주어 자리에 와서 명사 역할을 할 수 있는 것은 동명사이므로 (C) Making이 정답이다. 동사 (A), (B)와 동사 또는 분사 (D)는 명사 자리에 올 수 없다.

해석   지역 자선 단체에 정기적인 기부를 하는 것은 다른 사람들을 도울 뿐만 아니라, 상당한 절세도 제공한다.

어휘   donation n. 기부   charity n. 자선 단체   significant adj. 상당한
tax advantage 절세

2. 동명사 채우기

해설   전치사(from)의 목적어 자리에는 동명사 (B) 또는 명사 (C), (D)가 올 수 있다. 명사(friends)를 목적어로 취하면서 전치사의 목적어 자리에 올 수 있는 동명사 (B) contacting이 정답이다. 명사 앞에 다른 명사가 연결이나 전치사 없이 바로 올 수 없으므로 명사 (C)와 (D)는 답이 될 수 없다.

해석   부서장들은 근무 시간 중에 친구들과 온라인으로 연락하는 것을 삼가도록 직원들을 상기시키는 회람을 배부했다.

어휘   distribute v. 배부하다, 나누어 주다   refrain from ~을 삼가다

3. 동명사 채우기

해설   전치사(by)의 목적어 자리에는 명사나 동명사가 와야 하므로 동명사 (B) adjusting이 정답이다. 동사 (A)와 (D), 동사 또는 분사 (C)는 목적어 자리에 올 수 없다.

해석   조명 조건에 상관없이, 사진사들은 그들의 카메라의 설정을 조절함으로써 선명한 이미지를 정확히 담아낸다.

어휘   capture v. 정확히 담아내다, 붙잡다   adjust v. 조절하다

2 동명사를 목적어로 갖는 동사   p.114
1. (C)   2. (D)   3. (C)

1. 동명사와 to 부정사 구별하여 채우기

해설   동사 begin(began)은 동명사와 to 부정사 모두를 목적어로 가질 수 있으므로 동명사 (C) offering이 정답이다.

해석   작년에, 오하이오 대학교의 언어학과는 아랍어 상급 과정들을 제공하기 시작했다.

2. 동명사와 to 부정사 구별하여 채우기

해설   동명사를 목적어로 취하는 동사 consider(to consider)의 목적어 자리가 비어 있으므로 동명사 (D) consulting이 정답이다.

해석   중역들이 신입 사원들을 채용하기 전에 인사부와 상의하는 것을 고려하는 것은 현명하다.

어휘   consult v. 상의하다, 상담하다

3. 동명사와 to 부정사 구별하여 채우기

해설   동사 forget은 동명사와 to 부정사를 모두 목적어로 가질 수 있으므로 동명사 (A)와 to 부정사 (C)가 정답의 후보이다. 미래에 명시해야 한다는 문맥이므로 to 부정사 (C) to specify가 정답이다. 참고로, 동명사는 '과거'를, to 부정사는 '미래 또는 목적'을 나타낸다.

해석   사용자들은 기술적 도움을 요청할 때 어떤 버전의 소프트웨어가 설치되어 있는지 명시하는 것을 잊어서는 안 된다.

어휘   specify v. 명시하다

3 동명사 vs. 명사   p.115
1. (C)   2. (A)   3. (C)

1. 동명사와 명사 구별하여 채우기

해설   전치사(By)의 목적어 자리에는 동명사 (C) 또는 명사 (A), (D)가 올 수 있다. 이 중, 뒤에 목적어(the amount)를 가질 수 있는 것은 동명사이므로 (C) limiting이 정답이다.

해석   서류 작업의 양을 제한함으로써, Stamford사는 더 효율적으로 일상적인 업무들을 완수할 수 있다.

어휘   paperwork n. 서류 작업   accomplish v. 완수하다, 성취하다
routine adj. 일상적인; n. 일과, 관례

2. 동명사와 명사 구별하여 채우기

해설   타동사(used)의 목적어 자리에는 명사 (A) 또는 동명사 (C)가 올 수 있다. 빈칸 뒤에 목적어가 없으므로 명사 (A) study가 정답이다. 동명사 (C) studying은 뒤에 목적어가 와야 한다.

해석   소매 체인점 주인은 가게의 배치를 결정하기 위해 소비자 행동에 대해 최근 출판된 연구를 활용했다.

어휘   determine v. 결정하다   layout n. 배치(도)   study n. 연구; v. 연구하다

3. 동명사와 명사 구별하여 채우기

해설   전치사(for)의 목적어 자리에는 명사 (A) 또는 동명사 (C)가 올 수 있다. 이 중, 뒤에 목적어(the distribution needs)를 가질 수 있는 것은 동명사이므로 (C) satisfying이 정답이다.

해석   그 팀은 중소기업들의 유통 수요를 충족하기 위한 전략들을 논의하기 위해 세 시간 동안 만났다.

어휘   distribution n. 유통, 분배

4 동명사 관련 표현
p.116

1. (B) 2. (D) 3. (D)

1. 동명사 채우기

해설 look forward to(looks forward to)의 to는 전치사이므로 to 다음에는 동명사가 와야 한다. 따라서 (B) learning이 정답이다.

해석 Mr. Gray는 Gen-Ex사와 관련된 투자 기회에 대해 많이 알게 되기를 기대하는데, 이 회사는 현저한 성장을 보여 왔다.

어휘 significant adj. 현저한, 상당한 look forward to ~을 기대하다

2. 동명사 채우기

해설 have difficulty in(have had ~ difficulty in)의 전치사 in 다음에는 동명사가 와야 한다. 따라서 (D) modifying이 정답이다.

해석 해외 지사들은 새로운 회계 시스템을 따르기 위해 그들의 경영 방식을 변경하는 데 많은 어려움을 겪어 왔다.

어휘 conform v. 따르다, 순응하다 modify v. 변경하다, 수정하다

3. 동명사 채우기

해설 object to의 to는 전치사이므로 to 다음에는 동명사가 와야 한다. 따라서 동명사 (D) traveling이 정답이다.

해석 직원들은 워크숍 프로그램에 만족하지만, 교육 센터를 오고 가는 데 한 시간씩 이동하는 것에는 반대한다.

어휘 object to ~에 반대하다 travel v. 이동하다, 가다

Hackers Practice
p.117

01 ⓑ [토익 공식 4]   02 ⓐ [토익 공식 2]
03 ⓑ [토익 공식 3]   04 ⓐ [토익 공식 4]
05 ⓐ [토익 공식 3]   06 ⓑ [토익 공식 4]
07 ⓑ [토익 공식 4]
08 examine → examining/to examine [토익 공식 1]
09 맞는 문장 [토익 공식 1]
10 drive → driving [토익 공식 1]
11 to eat → eating [토익 공식 2]
12 choose → choosing [토익 공식 1]
13 맞는 문장 [토익 공식 2]
14 help → helping [토익 공식 4]

해석 01 Daniel은 많은 사람으로 이루어진 팀과 함께 일하는 것에 익숙하다.
02 Melanie는 기차역에 도착했을 때 내게 전화하는 것을 잊었고, 그래서 나는 그녀를 데리러 가지 않았다.
03 계약서를 쓸 때는 적절한 용어를 사용하도록 주의하십시오.
04 버스 터미널에 도착하려면 이 도로를 따라 계속 걸어야 한다.
05 교육적인 프로그램을 시청하는 것이 아이의 지식을 확장한다고 입증되었다.
06 그 프로젝트는 환경에 대한 인식을 높이는 데 기여했다.
07 직원들은 회사가 올해 상여금을 지급할 것인지 아닌지 궁금해하지 않을 수 없다.
08 Dr. Prasad의 책무들 중 하나는 환자들을 진찰하는 것이다.
09 Mr. Roberts는 우리가 이 벽을 제거해서 그의 사무실을 넓혀 주기를 원한다.
10 휘발유 값이 오르면 차를 운전하는 비용은 증가할 것이다.
11 Tina는 다이어트 중이기 때문에 설탕 먹는 것을 피한다.
12 그녀는 옷을 디자인하는 데는 능숙한 반면, 무슨 천을 사용할지 고르는 데는 서투르다.
13 그 손님은 든든한 식사보다 샐러드를 먹는 것을 선호했다.
14 Jessica의 인상적인 봉사 활동 기록은 그녀가 어려운 사람들을 돕는 데 헌신적이라는 사실을 입증한다.

Hackers Test
p.118

Part 5

01 (D)	02 (A)	03 (B)	04 (B)	05 (D)
06 (D)	07 (B)	08 (B)	09 (C)	10 (D)
11 (A)	12 (D)	13 (B)	14 (A)	15 (C)
16 (B)	17 (C)	18 (B)		

Part 6

19 (D)	20 (D)	21 (B)	22 (B)

01 동명사 채우기

해설 have a problem(having problems) 다음에는 동명사가 와야 하므로 (D) concentrating이 정답이다.

해석 너무 많은 스트레스와 휴식의 부족은 개인이 직장에서 집중하는 데 어려움을 겪는 원인이 될 수 있다.

어휘 contribute v. (~의) 한 원인이 되다

02 동명사 채우기

해설 전치사(Despite)의 목적어 자리에는 명사나 동명사가 와야 하므로 동명사의 완료형인 (A) having hired가 정답이다.

해석 공장에 더 많은 직원들을 채용했음에도 불구하고, 생산부장은 여전히 시설에 인원이 부족하다고 생각한다.

어휘 understaffed adj. 인원 부족의

03 동명사 채우기

해설 동사 discontinue의 목적어 자리에는 동명사가 와야 하므로 (B) producing이 정답이다.

해석 이동 통신 시장에 집중하기 위해, ASD Technologies사는 개인용 컴퓨터 라인의 생산을 중단할 것이다.

어휘 mobile communications 이동 통신 discontinue v. 중단하다

04 동명사 채우기

해설 be committed to(is committed to)의 to는 전치사이므로 to 다음에는 동명사가 와야 한다. 따라서 (B) publishing이 정답이다.

해석 Northfield Books사는 다양한 교과 영역에서 가격이 알맞고 고품질인 교재를 출판하는 데 전념한다.

어휘 committed to ~에 전념하는 a wide range of 다양한, 광범위한

05 동명사와 명사 구별하여 채우기

해설 전치사(of)의 목적어 자리에 올 수 있는 것은 명사 (B) 또는 동명사 (D)이다. 이 중 뒤에 목적어(a competing business)를 가질 수 있는 것은 동명사이므로 (D) obtaining이 정답이다.

해석 ANX사는 주주들에게 경쟁사를 사들이려는 의사를 발표하는 서신을 보냈다.

어휘 shareholder n. 주주 disclose v. 발표하다, 공개하다
intention n. 의사, 의도 compete v. 경쟁하다 obtain v. 사들이다, 얻다

06 주어와 수일치하는 동사 채우기

해설 빈칸은 동사 자리이고, 주어(The factory supervisor)가 단수이므로 단수 동사 (D) acquires가 정답이다. 준동사 (A)와 (C)는 동사 자리에 올 수 없다.

해석 그 공장 관리자는 약간 사용된 물건들을 할인 가격에 판매하는 중고품 중개인으로부터 장비와 기계를 얻는다.

어휘 second-hand adj. 중고의 bargain price 할인 가격 acquire v. 얻다

07 동명사 채우기

해설 동사 consider(is considering)의 목적어 자리에는 동명사가 와야 하므로 (B) implementing이 정답이다.

해석 Express Parcel사는 국제 배송 요금을 7퍼센트 인상하는 변경 사항을 회사의 요금 체계에 시행하는 것을 고려하고 있다.

어휘 **implement** v. 시행하다

08 to 부정사의 동사원형 채우기

해설 동사 continue는 동명사와 to 부정사를 모두 목적어로 가질 수 있지만, continue 뒤에 to가 왔으므로 to 부정사를 만드는 동사원형 (B) impress가 정답이다.

해석 온라인 쇼핑 사이트들은 양질의 제품, 저렴한 가격 및 신속한 배송을 제공함으로써 구매자들에게 계속해서 깊은 인상을 주고 있다.

어휘 **quality** adj. 양질의, 고급의 **impress** v. ~에게 (깊은) 인상을 주다

09 동명사와 명사 구별하여 채우기

해설 전치사(at)의 목적어 자리에 올 수 있는 것은 동명사 (C) 또는 명사 (D)이다. 이 중, 뒤에 목적어(the organization's year-end deficit)를 가질 수 있는 것은 동명사이므로 (C) resolving이 정답이다. 명사 (D) resolution은 뒤에 목적어를 가질 수 없다.

해석 예산 책정액의 최근 감축은 그 단체의 연말 적자를 해결하는 것을 목표로 했다.

어휘 **cut** n. 감축, 인하 **appropriation** n. (돈의) 책정(액) **aimed at** ~을 목표로 한 **year-end** 연말의 **deficit** n. 적자 **resolve** v. 해결하다, 결심하다 **resolution** n. 결의, 해답

10 동명사와 명사 구별하여 채우기

해설 타동사 reach(to reach)의 목적어 자리에 올 수 있는 것은 동명사 (C) 또는 명사 (D)이다. 이 중, 목적어 자리 앞에 부정관사(a)가 와 있으므로 명사 (D) agreement가 정답이다. 부정관사 뒤에 동명사 (C) agreeing은 올 수 없다.

해석 두 회사의 경영자들은 계약 조건과 관련해 남아 있는 의견 차이를 해결함으로써 상호 간에 이로운 협정에 이르기 위해 노력하고 있다.

어휘 **mutually** adv. 상호 간에, 공통으로 **beneficial** adj. 이로운, 유익한 **settle** v. (문제 등을) 해결하다 **remaining** adj. 남아 있는 **differences** n. 의견 차이 **contract term** 계약 조건

11 동명사 채우기

해설 '~하러 가다'는 go -ing로 표현하므로 동명사 (A) traveling이 정답이다.

해석 Mr. Warren은 많은 사람들과 함께 단체로 여행하기보다는 혼자서 여행을 가고 싶어 하는데, 그가 자신만의 여행 일정을 세우는 것을 좋아하기 때문이다.

어휘 **would rather** (~하기보다는 차라리) ~하고 싶다 **set** v. 세우다, 마련하다

12 동명사 채우기

해설 문장에서 동사(enables) 앞에 위치한 ___ business expenditures는 주어 자리이다. 주어 자리 맨 앞에 오면서 뒤에 목적어(business expenditures)를 가질 수 있는 것은 동명사이므로 (D) Reviewing이 정답이다.

해석 사업 비용을 매달 꼼꼼하게 검토하는 것은 회사들이 불필요한 비용을 찾아서 없앨 수 있도록 해 준다.

어휘 **expenditure** n. 비용, 지출 **identify** v. 찾다, 발견하다 **eliminate** v. 없애다, 삭제하다 **expense** n. 비용

13 동명사와 명사 구별하여 채우기

해설 전치사(on)의 목적어 자리에 올 수 있는 것은 동명사 (B) 또는 명사 (D)이다. 이 중, 뒤에 목적어(a discounted rate)를 가질 수 있는 것은 동명사이므로 (B) receiving이 정답이다. 명사 (D) receipt는 뒤에 목적어를 가질 수 없다.

해석 회원들은 체육관 회원권 연장에 할인 요금을 받는 것에 대한 추가 정보를 얻기 위해 접수처를 방문할 수 있다.

어휘 **reception desk** 접수처 **detail** n. 정보, 세부 사항 **rate** n. 요금, ~료 **renewal** n. (기한) 연장, 갱신

14 태에 맞는 동사 채우기

해설 빈칸 다음에 목적어가 없고, 빈칸에 들어가야 할 동사(coincide)가 자동사이므로 능동태 동사 (A) will coincide가 정답이다. 목적어를 가질 수 없는 자동사는 수동태로 쓸 수 없으므로 수동태 동사 (B)와 (C)는 답이 될 수 없다.

해석 그 회사의 최신 카메라 라인의 출시는 다음 주에 시작하는 대규모 마케팅 캠페인과 동시에 일어날 것이다.

어휘 **release** n. 출시, 발표 **coincide with** ~과 동시에 일어나다 **massive** adj. 대규모의, 거대한

15 동명사와 명사 구별하여 채우기

해설 동사 permit의 목적어 자리에 올 수 있는 명사 (A)와 동명사 (C)가 정답의 후보이다. 이 중, 목적어(a vehicle)를 가질 수 있는 것은 동명사이므로 (C) leaving이 정답이다. 참고로, (A) leave가 명사로 쓰일 때에는 '휴가, 허가'라는 의미로 사용된다. 추가로, permit은 'permit + 목적어 + to 부정사'로도 사용될 수 있음을 알아두자.

해석 마을은 거리 청소가 실시되는 일요일 새벽 1시와 새벽 4시 사이에는 이 구역에 차를 세워 두는 것을 허용하지 않는다.

어휘 **permit** v. 허용하다, 허가하다 **conduct** v. 실시하다 **leave** n. 휴가; v. (남겨) 두다

16 to 부정사 채우기

해설 '높은 점수를 받기 위해서'라는 의미가 되어야 하므로 빈칸에는 '~하기 위해서'를 의미하는 (A) 또는 (B)가 올 수 있다. 사람의 행동 목적을 나타내기 위해서는 to 부정사가 와야 하므로 to 부정사 (B) To earn이 정답이다. for -ing인 (A) For earning은 사물의 용도를 나타낸다.

해석 사법 고시에서 높은 점수를 받기 위해, Tom Byers는 깨어 있는 순간의 대부분을 도서관에서 참고 자료들을 읽으며 보냈다.

어휘 **bar exam** 사법 고시 **reference** n. 참고, 참조 **earn** v. 받다, 벌다

17 동명사 채우기

해설 동사 enjoy(enjoys)의 목적어 자리에는 동명사가 와야 하므로 (C) meeting이 정답이다.

해석 생물학과장은 유전학 분야의 최근 발전을 논의하기 위해 다른 교수진들과 만나는 것을 즐거워한다.

어휘 **head** n. (조직의) 장, 우두머리 **department** n. 학과, 부서 **faculty member** 교수진 **genetics** n. 유전학

18 동명사와 명사 구별하여 채우기

해설 전치사(in)의 목적어 자리에 올 수 있는 것은 동명사 (B) 또는 명사 (D)이다. 이 중, 뒤에 목적어(the various aquatic species)를 가질 수 있는 것은 동명사이므로 (B) protecting이 정답이다. 명사 (D) protection은 뒤에 목적어를 가질 수 없다.

해석 연안 석유 채굴의 금지는 해안 생태계에 서식하는 다양한 해양 생물들을 보호하는 데 매우 중요했다.

어휘 **ban** n. 금지 **offshore** adj. 연안의, 앞바다의 **oil drilling** 석유 채굴 **crucial** adj. 매우 중요한, 필수적인 **inhabit** v. 서식하다 **coastal** adj. 해안의, 연안의 **ecosystem** n. 생태계

19-22는 다음 이메일에 관한 문제입니다.

발신: tharris@comdev.com
수신: ebryant@comdev.com
제목: 태국 지사 관련 소식

저는 새로운 방콕 사무실을 방문하고 어제 본사로 돌아왔습니다. [19]이 지사는 태국어와 영어 수업들을 운영해오고 있습니다. 명백히, 그것들의 목적은 현지 직원들과 파견된 관리자들 사이의 의사소통을 돕기 위함입니다. [20]그럼에도 불구하고, 이 지사는 여전히 의사소통 문제에 직면하고 있습니다. 저는 이 문제가 언어뿐만 아니라 업무 방식에 있어서의 문화적 차이도 포함한다고 생각합니다.

[21]저는 자사의 교육 프로그램이 태국과 서양의 기업 문화에 대한 관련 있는 차이점들을 아우르는 수업을 포함하도록 조정하는 것을 제안하고 싶습니다. 이런 수업들은 현지 직원들과 외국 직원들 사이의 개선되는 관계에 기여할 것입니다.

[22]저는 프로그램에 대한 정보를 담고 있는 보고서를 첨부하였으며 또한 귀하에게 보여드리고 싶은 추가적인 몇 개의 방안들도 첨부하였습니다. 저는 귀하의 생각을 알고 싶으므로, 저의 의견을 살펴보고 답변을 주시기 바랍니다. 귀하 ⊙

께서 저의 제안이 적절하다고 여기신다면 제가 교육 담당 직원에게 연락을 취하겠습니다. 저는 개정된 교육 과정이 필요한 변화들을 가져올 것이라고 확신합니다.

headquarters n. 본사 **facilitate** v. (남)의 일 따위를 돕다, ~을 용이하게 하다
dispatch v. 파견하다 **encounter** v. 직면하다, 접하다
involve v. 포함하다, 관련시키다 **session** n. 수업 (시간)
relevant adj. (당면 문제에) 관련 있는, 적절한 **additional** adj. 추가적인
run by ~에게 보여주다

19 알맞은 문장 고르기

해석 (A) 이 지사에 곧 긴축 재정이 시행될 것입니다.
(B) 직원들은 그곳의 고객들과 좋은 관계를 구축해왔습니다.
(C) 그곳의 위치는 이전보다 접근하는 것이 더 용이해졌습니다.
(D) 이 지사는 태국어와 영어 수업들을 운영해오고 있습니다.

해설 빈칸에 들어갈 알맞은 문장을 고르는 문제이므로 빈칸의 주변 문맥이나 전체 문맥을 파악한다. 앞 문장 'I arrived back at headquarters yesterday after visiting the new Bangkok office.'에서 새로운 방콕 사무실을 방문하고 어제 본사로 돌아왔다고 한 후, 뒤 문장 'Apparently, their objective is to facilitate communication between local staff and our dispatched managers.'에서 명백히 그것들의 목적은 현지 직원들과 파견된 관리자들 사이의 의사소통을 돕기 위함이라고 했으므로 빈칸에는 새로운 방콕 사무실에서 태국어와 영어 수업을 운영해오고 있다는 내용이 들어가야 함을 알 수 있다. 따라서 (D) The branch has been running Thai and English courses가 정답이다.

어휘 **fiscal austerity** 긴축 재정 **impose** v. 시행하다, 도입하다
access v. 접근하다 **run** v. 운영하다, 달리다

20 접속부사 채우기 주변 문맥 파악

해설 빈칸이 콤마와 함께 문장의 맨 앞에 온 접속부사 자리이므로, 앞 문장과 빈칸이 있는 문장의 의미 관계를 파악하여 접속부사인 네 개의 보기 중 하나를 정답으로 골라야 한다. 앞 문장에서 의사소통을 위한 언어 수업을 운영하고 있음을 언급했고, 빈칸이 있는 문장에서는 여전히 의사소통 문제에 직면하고 있다고 했으므로, 앞 문장과 대조되는 내용의 문장에서 사용되는 (D) Nevertheless(그럼에도 불구하고)가 정답이다.

어휘 **otherwise** adv. 그렇지 않으면 **consequently** adv. 결과적으로
furthermore adv. 게다가

21 동명사 채우기

해설 동사 suggest(to suggest)는 동명사를 목적어로 취하므로 (B) adapting이 정답이다.

어휘 **adapt** v. 조정하다, 맞추다

22 'have동사 + p.p.' 채우기

해설 빈칸 뒤에 목적어(a report)가 온 것으로 보아, 빈칸에는 have동사와 함께 완료형 동사를 만드는 p.p.형 (B) 또는 (D)가 와야 한다. '보고서를 첨부했다'는 능동의 의미가 맞으므로 (B) attached가 정답이다.

어휘 **attachment** n. 첨부 파일, 부착 **attach** v. 첨부하다, 붙이다

Chapter 09 분사

1 분사의 역할 p.121
1. (D) 2. (B) 3. (C)

1. 분사 채우기

해설 명사(unemployment problem)를 앞에서 꾸밀 수 있는 것은 형용사 역할을 하는 분사이므로 (D) existing이 정답이다. 동사 (A)와 (B)는 명사를 꾸밀 수 없고, 명사 (C) 역시 복합 명사가 아닌 이상 명사를 꾸밀 수 없다.

해석 현존하는 실업 문제를 해결하기 위해, 정부는 그 지역 내 신생 기업들에게 소

액 대출을 제공할 것이다.

어휘 **small loan** 소액 대출 **start-up company** 신생 기업
exist v. 현존하다, 존재하다 **existing** adj. 현존하는, 현재의

2. 분사 채우기

해설 명사(An e-mail newsletter) 뒤에서 명사를 꾸미는 것은 분사이므로 (B) transmitted가 정답이다. 동사 (A), (C), (D)는 명사를 꾸밀 수 없다. 명사 뒤에서 명사를 꾸미는 분사는 수식어 거품이므로, 수식어 거품 채우기 문제를 푸는 방법을 쓸 수도 있다. 이 문장은 주어(An e-mail newsletter), 동사(helps), 목적어(subscribers), 목적격 보어(stay ~ depression)를 갖춘 완전한 절이므로, _____ by the Psychology Network는 수식어 거품으로 보아야 한다. 보기 중 수식어 거품이 될 수 있는 분사 (B) transmitted가 정답이다. 동사 (A), (C), (D)는 수식어 거품이 될 수 없다.

해석 Psychology Network에 의해 발신되는 이메일 소식지는 구독자들이 우울증에 관한 새로운 연구에 대해 계속해서 정보를 제공받을 수 있도록 도와준다.

어휘 **newsletter** n. 소식지 **subscriber** n. 구독자
depression n. 우울증, 불황, 불경기 **transmit** v. 발신하다, 전달하다

3. 분사 채우기

해설 5형식 동사(keep)의 목적격 보어로 올 수 있는 것은 형용사 역할을 하는 분사이므로 (C) protected가 정답이다.

해석 호텔 투숙객들은 모든 객실에 포함되어 있는 전자 금고를 이용함으로써 그들의 귀중품을 계속 보호한다.

어휘 **valuables** n. 귀중품 **utilize** v. 이용하다 **protect** v. 보호하다

2 분사구문 p.122
1. (B) 2. (A) 3. (C)

1. 분사구문 채우기

해설 빈칸에는 '~한 후에'라는 의미의 시간을 나타내는 분사구문이 와야 하므로 (B) Having이 정답이다. 참고로, 분사구문은 수식어 거품이므로, 수식어 거품 채우기 문제를 푸는 방법을 쓸 수도 있다. 빈칸은 수식어 거품(_____ terminated ~ Gardens)을 이끄는 자리이므로 분사 (B) Having이 정답이다. 동사 (A), (C), (D)는 수식어 거품이 될 수 없다.

해석 Lee Gardens에서의 임대 계약이 끝난 후에, Ms. Pascual은 좀 더 편리한 장소로 이사할 수 있었다.

어휘 **terminate** v. 끝나다, 종료되다 **convenient** adj. 편리한

2. 부사절 접속사 + 분사구문 채우기

해설 부사절 접속사(Although) 다음에는 동사 (B), (C), (D)가 바로 올 수 없으므로 분사 (A) completed가 정답이다.

해석 완료가 되었더라도, 원고는 편집자가 최종안에 오류가 없음을 확신할 때까지 출간되지 않을 것이다.

어휘 **manuscript** n. 원고 **publish** v. 출간하다 **final draft** 최종안

3. 부사절 접속사 + 분사구문 채우기

해설 부사절 접속사(After) 다음에는 동사 (A), (B), (D)가 바로 올 수 없으므로 분사 (C) verifying이 정답이다. 참고로, 부사(hastily)는 분사(verifying)를 꾸미는 역할을 하고 있다.

해석 주방 도구에 결함이 있다는 항의를 서둘러 확인한 후에, Kitchen Works사는 즉각적인 결함 제품 회수를 공표했다.

어휘 **hastily** adv. 서둘러서, 급히 **defective** adj. 결함이 있는
issue v. 공표하다 **immediate** adj. 즉각적인 **recall** n. (결함 제품) 회수
verify v. 확인하다

3 현재분사 vs. 과거분사 p.123
1. (C) 2. (C) 3. (B)

1. 현재분사와 과거분사 구별하여 채우기

해설　이 문장은 주어(The attachment), 동사(contains), 목적어(the information)를 갖춘 완전한 절이므로, ＿＿＿ to the sales report 이하는 수식어 거품으로 보아야 한다. 보기 중 수식어 거품이 될 수 있는 것은 분사 (C)와 (D)이다. 분사의 수식을 받는 명사(the information)와 분사가 '정보가 추가되다'라는 의미의 수동 관계이므로 과거분사 (C) added가 정답이다. 수식어 거품이 될 수 없는 명사 (A)와 동사 (B)는 답이 될 수 없다. 참고로, sent to the regional manager는 주어(The attachment)를 꾸며 주는 수식어 거품이다.

해석　지역 관리자에게 발송된 첨부 파일은 회계팀이 판매 보고서에 추가한 정보를 포함한다.

어휘　**regional** adj. 지역의, 지방의   **sales report** 판매 보고서

2. 현재분사와 과거분사 구별하여 채우기

해설　when절의 주어(the voiceover)와 보어가 '해설 소리가 매력적이다'라는 의미의 능동 관계이므로 현재분사 (C) appealing이 정답이다. 참고로, appeal과 같은 감정동사의 현재분사와 과거분사를 구별할 때, 주어가 감정을 느끼면 과거분사 p.p., 주어가 감정의 원인이면 현재분사 -ing를 쓴다. 이 경우 주어(the voiceover)가 매력을 느끼게 하는 원인이므로 현재분사 (appealing)를 써야 한다.

해석　고객들은 광고에서 해설 소리가 매력적으로 들릴 때 제품을 구매하는 것에 관심을 보일 가능성이 더 많다.

어휘　**interest** n. 관심, 흥미; v. 관심을 갖게 하다   **voiceover** n. 해설 소리
　　　appeal v. 매력적이다, 호소하다   **appealing** adj. 매력적인, 흥미로운

3. 현재분사와 과거분사 구별하여 채우기

해설　이 문장은 주어(the tourism center), 동사(provides), 목적어(information)를 갖춘 완전한 절이므로, ＿＿＿ in the downtown area는 수식어 거품으로 보아야 한다. 보기 중 수식어 거품이 될 수 있는 것은 분사 (A)와 (B)이다. 주절의 주어(the tourism center)와 분사구문이 '관광 센터가 위치해 있다'는 의미의 수동 관계이므로 과거분사 (B) Situated가 정답이다. 수식어 거품이 될 수 없는 동사 (C)와 명사 (D)는 답이 될 수 없다.

해석　도심지에 위치해 있기 때문에, 그 관광 센터는 여행과 숙박 시설 준비에 관한 도움뿐만 아니라 지역의 역사적 건물에 대한 정보도 제공한다.

어휘　**downtown** adj. 도심의, 중심가의; n. 도심지, 중심가
　　　landmark n. 역사적 건물, 주요 지형지물   **as well as** ~뿐만 아니라 ~도
　　　assistance n. 도움, 지원   **accommodation** n. 숙박 시설

---

4 현재분사와 과거분사를 혼동하기 쉬운 표현   p.124
　1. (A)　2. (C)　3. (C)

1. 현재분사와 과거분사 구별하여 채우기

해설　수식받는 명사(means)와 분사가 '선호되는 수단'이라는 의미의 수동 관계이므로 과거분사 (A) preferred가 정답이다.

해석　코르크 마개가 와인병에 뚜껑을 씌우기 위해 선호되는 수단이기는 하지만, 금속 나사 마개가 제조업체들 사이에서 점점 인기가 더해져 왔다.

어휘　**means** n. 수단, 방법   **cap** v. 뚜껑을 씌우다; n. 뚜껑, 캡
　　　screw cap 나사 마개, 틀어서 여는 뚜껑   **increasingly** adv. 점점, 더욱더
　　　prefer v. 선호하다   **preference** n. 더 좋아함, 선택

2. 현재분사와 과거분사 구별하여 채우기

해설　수식받는 명사(applicants)와 분사가 '경력이 있는 지원자들'이라는 의미의 수동 관계이므로 과거분사 (C) experienced가 정답이다. 참고로, 형용사 (D) experiential(경험에 의한)을 빈칸에 넣으면 '경험에 의한 지원자들'이라는 어색한 의미가 만들어지므로 답이 될 수 없다.

해석　정부 정책은 모든 경력 지원자들이 공석인 공무원직에 대해 동등한 고려를 받아야 한다고 명시한다.

어휘　**specify** v. 명시하다, 상술하다   **open** adj. 공석인   **civil service** 공무원
　　　experienced adj. 경력이 있는, 경험이 있는
　　　experiential adj. 경험에 의한, 경험상의

3. 현재분사와 과거분사 구별하여 채우기

해설　수식받는 명사(dressers)와 분사가 '손으로 만들어진 화장대'라는 의미의 수동 관계이므로 과거분사 (C) handcrafted가 정답이다.

해석　아일랜드의 Blue Deer Furniture사는 수공예 화장대에 대한 독창성과 전반적인 우수성으로 세계적으로 유명하다.

어휘　**world-renowned** 세계적으로 유명한   **originality** n. 독창성
　　　overall adj. 전반적인, 종합적인   **quality** n. 우수성, 고급
　　　dresser n. 화장대, 경대   **handcraft** n. 수공예; v. 손으로 만들다

Hackers Practice   p.125

01 ⓑ [토익 공식 3]	02 ⓐ [토익 공식 4]
03 ⓑ [토익 공식 3]	04 ⓐ [토익 공식 1]
05 ⓑ [토익 공식 2]	06 ⓑ [토익 공식 3]
07 ⓐ [토익 공식 3]	
08 handled → handling [토익 공식 3]	
09 맞는 문장 [토익 공식 4]	
10 Knew → Knowing [토익 공식 3]	
11 revise → revised [토익 공식 1]	
12 맞는 문장 [토익 공식 2]	
13 issuing → issued [토익 공식 3]	
14 promised → promising [토익 공식 4]	

해석　01 쇼핑객들은 온라인에서 제품을 구입할 때 신용카드를 사용하도록 장려된다.
　　　02 고객들과 장기적인 관계를 유지하기 위해서는 그들에게 오래도록 기억에 남는 인상을 심어 주어야 한다.
　　　03 역무원은 승객들에게 승차권에 명시된 시간까지 기차에 탑승해야 한다고 말했다.
　　　04 Jane은 건물 관리자로부터 집세를 내라고 상기시키는 공고문을 받았다.
　　　05 그 은행원에게 몇 통의 전화가 와서, 그가 하고 있는 업무를 끝내지 못하게 했다.
　　　06 서비스가 불만족스러운 고객들은 서비스 안내 직원에게 연락하도록 요구된다.
　　　07 회사 네트워크 시스템이 감염되는 것을 방지하기 위해 바이러스 퇴치 프로그램이 최신 버전으로 유지되게 하십시오.
　　　08 경비 상환을 처리하는 직원에게 영수증을 제출하시기 바랍니다.
　　　09 제출된 기획안은 위원회 전원의 마음에 들었다.
　　　10 그 계획에 대해 아무것도 몰라서, Maureen은 동료에게 최신 정보를 제공해 달라고 요청했다.
　　　11 은행은 그 고객에게 수정된 거래 내역서를 보낼 것이다.
　　　12 매일 밤 퇴근하기 전에, 관리인은 모든 조명이 꺼졌는지 확인한다.
　　　13 그녀는 관리자가 교부한 회람을 읽으며 몇 분을 보냈다.
　　　14 많은 유망한 지원자들이 우리 회사의 면접에 지원했다.

Hackers Test   p.126

Part 5

01 (D)	02 (B)	03 (B)	04 (C)	05 (C)
06 (D)	07 (C)	08 (B)	09 (C)	10 (D)
11 (B)	12 (B)	13 (D)	14 (D)	15 (D)
16 (A)	17 (A)	18 (C)		

Part 6

19 (D)	20 (B)	21 (B)	22 (C)

01 분사구문 채우기

해설　이 문장은 주어(The hotel), 동사(provides), 목적어(personal service)를 갖춘 완전한 절이므로, ＿＿＿ that 이하는 수식어 거품으로 보아야 한다. 따라서 보기 중 수식어 거품이 될 수 있는 분사 (D) guaranteeing이 정답이다. 참고로, guaranteeing ~은 '그리고 ~을 장담하다, 보증하다'라는 의미의 연속동작을 나타내는 분사구문이며 and it guarantees ~로 대신 쓸 수도 있다.

해석 그 호텔은 사소한 일에도 세심한 정성을 기울이는 개인 전용 서비스를 제공하고, 투숙객들이 편하고 기분 좋게 머무르는 것을 장담한다.

어휘 **attention** n. 정성, 배려 **stay** n. 머무름, 체류
guarantee v. 장담하다, 보증하다, 약속하다

02 현재분사와 과거분사 구별하여 채우기

해설 빈칸은 명사(package)를 꾸미는 형용사 역할을 하는 분사 자리이므로 과거분사 (B)와 현재분사 (C)가 정답의 후보이다. 수식받는 명사(package)와 분사가 '소포가 배달되다'라는 의미의 수동 관계이므로 과거분사 (B) delivered가 정답이다. 현재분사 (C) delivering은 능동 관계를 나타내기 때문에 답이 될 수 없다.

해석 사용 설명서는 귀하의 사무실로 배달되는 소포에 있을 것입니다.

어휘 **manual** n. 설명서, 소책자

03 동명사 채우기

해설 '전치사 to + 동명사'의 동명사를 채우는 문제이다. 등위접속사(and)가 is looking forward to ~의 전치사 to를 연결하고 있으므로 동명사 (B) resolving이 정답이다.

해석 그 최고 경영자는 지점 대표들을 만나 지난 분기에 발생했던 모든 문제를 해결하기를 기대하고 있다.

어휘 **look forward to -ing** ~할 것을 기대하다 **representative** n. 대표
arise v. 발생하다, 생기다 **resolve** v. 해결하다

04 현재분사와 과거분사 구별하여 채우기

해설 5형식 동사(get)의 목적격 보어 자리에 분사를 채우는 문제이므로 분사 (C)와 (D)가 정답의 후보이다. 목적어와 목적격 보어가 '직원들에게 ~하는 동기가 부여되다'라는 의미의 수동 관계이므로 과거분사 (C) motivated가 정답이다. 현재분사 (D) motivating은 능동 관계를 나타내기 때문에 답이 될 수 없다.

해석 부서장들은 직원들에게 적시에 업무를 끝마치고자 하는 동기가 부여될 수 있는 방법을 논의하기 위해 모였다.

어휘 **head** n. 장, 우두머리; v. 지휘하다, 인솔하다 **convene** v. 모이다, 회합하다
in a timely manner 적시에, 시기적절하게 **motivate** v. 동기를 부여하다

05 현재분사와 과거분사 구별하여 채우기

해설 빈칸은 복합 명사(networking solutions)를 꾸미는 형용사 역할을 하는 분사 자리이므로 과거분사 (C)와 현재분사 (D)가 정답의 후보이다. 수식받는 명사(solutions)와 분사가 '솔루션이 전문화되다'라는 의미의 수동 관계이므로 과거분사 (C) specialized가 정답이다.

해석 Net Connect사는 고객들에게 파일 및 프린터 공유부터 일정 및 달력 동기화에 이르는 전문화된 네트워킹 솔루션을 제공한다.

어휘 **furnish A with B** A에게 B를 제공하다
range from A to B (범위가) A에서 B까지 이르다
synchronization n. 동기화

06 현재분사와 과거분사 구별하여 채우기

해설 '부사절 접속사(when) + 분사구문' 표현에서 분사구문을 채우는 문제이므로 현재분사 (B)와 과거분사 (D)가 정답의 후보이다. '~에 직면하다'라는 의미의 'be confronted with'를 분사구문으로 만들려면 being을 생략해야 하므로 과거분사 (D) confronted가 정답이다.

해석 Rebecca Lewis는 회사에서 겨우 세 달 동안 근무했지만, 스트레스가 많은 상황에 직면했을 때 대처할 수 있다는 것을 이미 증명했다.

어휘 **cope** v. 대처하다, 대응하다 **stressful** adj. 스트레스가 많은
be confronted with ~에 직면하다, 마주치다

07 현재분사와 과거분사 구별하여 채우기

해설 5형식 동사(found)의 목적격 보어 자리에 분사를 채우는 문제이므로 현재분사 (C)와 과거분사 (D)가 정답의 후보이다. 목적어(the director's latest movie)와 목적격 보어가 '영화가 (사람들에게) 영감을 주다'라는 의미의 능동 관계이므로 현재분사 (C) inspiring이 정답이다. 목적어와 목적격 보어가 동격 관계를 이루지 못하므로 명사 (B)는 답이 될 수 없다. find의 목적격 보어 자리에 동사 (A) inspire는 올 수 없다.

해석 일부 평론가들은 줄거리에 상상력이 부족하다고 주장했지만 많은 관람객들은 그 감독의 최신 영화가 영감을 준다고 생각했다.

어휘 **maintain** v. 주장하다, 유지하다 **plot** n. 줄거리, 구성
unimaginative adj. 상상력이 부족한 **inspiring** adj. 영감을 주는

08 현재분사와 과거분사 구별하여 채우기

해설 이 문장은 주어(Many of the tax breaks), 동사(will be canceled)를 갖춘 완전한 절이므로, 주어와 동사 사이에 온 ____ to strengthen ~ industry는 수식어 거품으로 보아야 한다. 보기 중 수식어 거품이 될 수 있는 것은 과거분사 (B)와 현재분사 (C)이다. 분사는 이 문장에서 앞에 있는 명사(the tax breaks)를 꾸며 주는 역할을 하게 된다. 수식받는 명사(the tax breaks)와 분사가 '감세 조치가 제공되다'라는 의미의 수동 관계이므로 과거분사 (B) provided가 정답이다.

해석 국내 철강 산업을 강화하기 위해 제공된 많은 감세 조치들은 새로운 정부가 취임하자마자 취소될 것이다.

어휘 **tax break** 감세 조치 **strengthen** v. 강화하다 **once** conj. ~하자마자
administration n. 정부, 내각 **take office** 취임하다

09 현재분사와 과거분사 구별하여 채우기

해설 be동사(were) 다음에 보어로 올 수 있는 것은 형용사 역할을 하는 분사 (B), (C), 그리고 명사 (D)이다. 주어(the product's patent negotiations)와 보어가 '협상이 (사람을) 피로하게 하다'라는 의미의 능동 관계이므로 현재분사 (C) exhausting이 정답이다. 명사 (D)를 보어 자리에 넣으면 주어(the product's patent negotiations)와 동격을 이루어야 하는데, 이 경우 '협상은 소모이다'라는 어색한 의미가 되므로 명사 (D)는 답이 될 수 없다.

해석 비록 제품 특허 협상은 소모적이었지만, 두 회사 모두 최종 계약 조건에 만족한다.

어휘 **negotiation** n. 협상 **term** n. 조건, 조항, 기간
exhausting adj. 소모적인, 진을 빼는 **exhaustion** n. 소모, 고갈

10 부사절 접속사 + 분사구문 채우기

해설 부사절 접속사(after) 다음에 올 수 있는 분사 (D) consulting이 정답이다. 동사 (A), (B) 또는 명사 (C)는 부사절 접속사 다음에 올 수 없다.

해석 이미지 편집 소프트웨어를 설치할 수 없는 고객분들은 설명서를 참고하신 후에 기술 지원 상담 전화로 연락하셔야 합니다.

어휘 **hotline** n. 상담 전화 **consult** v. 참고하다, 상의하다

11 현재분사와 과거분사 구별하여 채우기

해설 이 문장은 주어(The bank), 동사(will conduct), 목적어(an information seminar)를 갖춘 완전한 절이므로, ____ to open ~ accounts는 수식어 거품으로 보아야 한다. 보기 중 수식어 거품이 될 수 있는 것은 분사 (A)와 (B)이다. 수식받는 명사(clients)와 분사가 '고객들이 계획하다'라는 의미의 능동 관계이므로 현재분사 (B) planning이 정답이다. 과거분사 (A) planned는 수동 관계를 나타낸다.

해석 그 은행은 공인된 연금 저축 계좌를 개설하려고 계획하는 고객들을 위해 다음 주에 안내 세미나를 진행할 예정이다.

어휘 **conduct** v. (특정 활동을) 하다, 수행하다 **open** v. (계좌 따위를) 개설하다
registered adj. 공인된, 등록된 **retirement** n. 연금, 퇴직

12 현재분사와 과거분사 구별하여 채우기

해설 빈칸은 명사(event)를 꾸미는 형용사 역할을 하는 분사 자리이므로 현재분사 (C)와 과거분사 (D)가 정답의 후보이다. '학술 토론회의 최종 행사'라는 문맥이므로 '최종의'를 뜻하는 현재분사 (C) concluding이 정답이다.

해석 학술 토론회의 최종 행사는 Peace 무도회로, 여기서 대표단은 지역 사회 구성원들을 만날 수 있다.

어휘 **symposium** n. 학술 토론회 **delegate** n. 대표단 **conclude** v. 끝내다
conclusion n. 결론 **concluding** adj. 최종의

13 분사 채우기

해설 이 문장은 주어(Employees), 동사(must meet), 목적어(the requirements)를 갖춘 완전한 절이므로 ____ transfer 이하는 수식어 거품으로 보아야 한

다. 보기 중 수식어 거품이 될 수 있는 분사 (D) requesting이 정답이다. 동사 또는 명사 (A)와 동사 (B)는 수식어 거품 자리에 올 수 없다. 참고로, 현재분사는 -ing로, 과거분사는 (being) p.p.로 표현되지만, been p.p.는 올바른 분사 형태가 아니므로 (C) been requested는 답이 될 수 없다.

해석 해외 지점으로의 이동을 요청하는 직원들은 전근을 위한 조건을 충족시켜야 한다.

어휘 transfer n. 이동; v. 이동하다 overseas branch 해외 지점
meet the requirements 조건을 충족시키다 relocation n. 전근, 이전

14 분사 채우기

해설 빈칸이 명사(sales)를 앞에서 꾸미는 형용사 자리이므로 보기 중 명사를 앞에서 꾸밀 수 있는 분사 (D) reduced가 정답이다.

해석 출판사들이 더 많은 디지털 형식의 교과서를 제작함에 따라, 대학 서점들은 매출 감소를 겪을 것으로 예상된다.

어휘 publisher n. 출판사

15 주어와 수일치하는 동사 채우기

해설 주어로 단수 명사 Mr. Morris와 대명사 I가 접속사 and로 연결되어 있으면 복수 취급하므로, 복수 동사 (D) are deleting이 정답이다. I에 동사를 맞춰 (B) am deleting을 쓰지 않도록 주의해야 한다.

해석 Ms. Wood의 결론이 시대에 뒤처진 정보에 근거했기 때문에 Mr. Morris와 나는 보고서에서 그녀가 쓴 부분을 삭제하고 있다.

어휘 be based on ~에 근거하다 outdated adj. 시대에 뒤진, 구식의
delete v. 삭제하다

16 현재분사와 과거분사 구별하여 채우기

해설 빈칸은 복합 명사(reference materials)를 꾸미는 형용사 자리이므로 과거분사 (A)와 현재분사 (B)가 정답의 후보이다. 수식받는 명사(reference materials)와 분사가 '참고 자료가 주문되다'라는 의미의 수동 관계이므로 과거분사 (A) ordered가 정답이다.

해석 직원들은 통신 소프트웨어에 대한 이해력을 넓히기 위해 최근에 주문된 참고 자료를 이용해야 한다.

어휘 recently adv. 최근에 reference material 참고 자료

17 원형 부정사 채우기

해설 지각동사 see(to see)의 목적격 보어로는 원형 부정사나 현재분사가 와야 하므로 원형 부정사 (A) perform이 정답이다. 목적어(the famous rock band)와 목적격 보어(perform)가 '록 밴드가 공연되다'라는 수동 의미로 해석되면 문맥에 맞지 않으므로 목적격 보어 자리에 p.p.형인 (B) performed는 올 수 없다.

해석 그 경기장은 유명한 록 밴드가 공연하는 것을 보기 위해 기다리는 수많은 사람들로 가득했다.

어휘 be packed with ~로 가득하다 perform v. 공연하다, 수행하다

18 분사 채우기

해설 이 문장은 주어(The institute), 동사(has initiated), 목적어(a policy)를 갖춘 완전한 절이므로 ＿＿＿ to increase 이하는 수식어 거품으로 보아야 한다. 보기 중 수식어 거품이 될 수 있는 것은 분사이므로 (C) trying이 정답이다. 참고로, offering cash incentives는 명사 a policy를 꾸며 주는 수식어 거품이다.

해석 그 연구소는 직원 생산성을 높이기 위해 노력하는 감독관들에게 현금 장려금을 제공하는 정책을 시작했다.

어휘 initiate v. 시작하다, 개시하다 cash incentive 현금 장려금, 상금 제도

19-22는 다음 편지에 관한 문제입니다.

Mr. Colby께,

[19]주택 보호를 제공하는 일체형 패키지인, HomeShield 시스템에 대한 귀하의 관심에 감사드립니다. ↻

HomeShield 시스템은 동작 및 연기 감지기, 화재 스프링클러, 그리고 BYT 보안 요원에 의해 감시되는 경보 시스템을 포함합니다. [20]이 보안 시스템은 모바일 기기를 위한 HomeShield 애플리케이션을 사용해서 원격으로 작동될 수 있습니다. 이 앱은 귀하가 시스템 구성 요소를 관리할 수 있도록 해주며 그것들이 제대로 작동하고 있음을 보장합니다. 이것은 귀하의 가족이 집을 떠나 시간을 보내게 되어 귀하의 주택을 점검해야 할 때 큰 장점입니다.

[21]저희 측 직원이 귀하의 가정을 방문하는 것에 관심이 있으시다면 555-6835로 전화하셔서 귀하의 안전 요구 사항을 저희에게 말씀해주십시오. 혹은, inquiries@bytsolutions.com으로 이메일을 보내주십시오. [22]저희가 귀하께 설치 견적서를 다음 날까지 제공해 드릴 것입니다. 예약은 그 후 아무 때나 정해질 수 있습니다.

기억해주십시오, BYT Solutions와 함께라면 귀하의 안전에 대해서는 안심하셔도 됩니다. 귀하로부터 소식을 들을 수 있기를 기대합니다.

Marilou Eaglin, BYT Solutions사 드림

---

all-in-one adj. 일체형의 detector n. 감지기 monitor v. 감시하다
security personnel 보안 요원 component n. 구성 요소
function v. 작동하다, 기능하다 check on ~을 점검하다, 확인하다
residence n. 주택, 거주지 in good hands 안심할 수 있는

19 현재분사와 과거분사 구별하여 채우기

해설 이 문장은 주어(We), 동사(appreciate), 목적어(your interest)를 갖춘 완전한 절이므로, an all-in-one package ＿＿＿ home protection은 수식어 거품이다. 따라서 과거분사 (B)와 현재분사 (D)가 정답의 후보이다. 수식 받는 명사(an all-in-one package)와 분사가 '일체형 패키지가 ~을 제공하다'라는 의미의 능동 관계이므로 현재분사 (D) providing이 정답이다.

어휘 provide v. 제공하다

20 동사 어휘 고르기 주변 문맥 파악

해설 '보안 시스템은 원격으로 ＿＿＿될 수 있다'는 문맥이므로 네 개의 보기 모두 정답의 후보이다. 빈칸이 있는 문장만으로 정답을 고를 수 없으므로 주변 문맥이나 전체 문맥을 파악한다. 뒤 문장에서 '이 앱, 즉 모바일 기기 애플리케이션을 통해 시스템 구성 요소를 관리할 수 있도록 해주며 제대로 작동하고 있음을 보장한다(The app allows you to manage system components and ensure that they are functioning properly.)'고 했으므로 보안 시스템은 원격으로 작동될 수 있음을 알 수 있다. 따라서 동사 (B) operated(작동하다)가 정답이다. (A) turned on(켜다)은 시스템의 전원이 켜지는 것만을 의미하므로 답이 될 수 없다.

어휘 turn on 켜다 update v. 최신식으로 하다 close down 종료하다, 폐쇄하다

21 원형 부정사 채우기

해설 사역동사 have(having)의 목적격 보어로는 원형 부정사가 와야 하므로 (B) visit이 정답이다. 목적어(a representative)와 목적격 보어(visit)가 '직원이 방문되다'라는 수동의 의미로 해석되면 문맥에 맞지 않으므로 보어 자리에 p.p.형인 (A) visited는 올 수 없다.

22 알맞은 문장 고르기

해석 (A) 주택 소유주들은 두 번 다시 난방 시스템에 대해 걱정할 필요가 없을 것입니다.
(B) 귀하의 가정을 위한 보안 시스템은 귀하의 요구 사항에 따라 설정되었습니다.
(C) 저희가 귀하께 설치 견적서를 다음 날까지 제공해 드릴 것입니다.
(D) 패키지는 동작 감지기를 포함하도록 최근에 업데이트되었습니다.

해설 빈칸에 들어갈 알맞은 문장을 고르는 문제이므로 빈칸의 주변 문맥이나 전체 문맥을 파악한다. 앞부분에서 직원이 가정에 방문하기를 원한다면 전화나 이메일로 안전 요구 사항을 말해달라고 했고, 뒤 문장 'Appointments can be arranged any time after that.'에서 예약은 그 후 아무 때나 정해질 수 있다고 했으므로 빈칸에는 편지의 수신자에게 다음 날까지 설치 견적서를 제공할 것이라는 내용이 들어가야 함을 알 수 있다. 따라서 (C) We will provide you with an installation estimate by the next day가 정답이다.

어휘 configure v. 설정하다

Chapter 10 명사

1 명사 자리   p.131

1. (D)   2. (B)   3. (D)

1. 명사 자리 채우기

해설 타동사(followed)의 목적어 자리에 올 수 있는 것은 명사이므로 명사 (D) advice가 정답이다. 빈칸 앞에 정관사(the)가 있는 것도 명사 자리를 알려 주는 단서가 된다. 동사 또는 분사 (A), 동사 (B)와 형용사 (C)는 명사 자리에 올 수 없다.

해석 그 소유주는 마케팅 컨설턴트의 조언을 따라서 그녀의 사업에 대한 광고 캠페인을 전개했다.

어휘 owner n. 소유주, 주인 follow v. 따르다 consultant n. 컨설턴트, 고문 develop v. 전개하다, 개발하다

2. 명사 자리 채우기

해설 전치사(for)의 목적어 자리인 동시에 소유격(the project committee's) 다음에 올 수 있는 것은 명사이므로 명사 (B) assessment가 정답이다. 동사 또는 분사 (A), 형용사 (C)와 동사 (D)는 명사 자리에 올 수 없다.

해석 몇 개월 전에 미뤄졌던 예비 조사는 프로젝트 위원회의 평가에 맞춰 재개할 것으로 예상된다.

어휘 feasibility study (개발 계획 등의 실현 가능성을 조사하는) 예비 조사, 타당성 조사 postpone v. 미루다, 연기하다 resume v. 재개하다, 다시 시작하다 in time 때 맞추어 assessment n. 평가

3. 명사 자리 채우기

해설 전치사(at)의 목적어 자리에 올 수 있는 것은 명사이므로 명사 (D) expense가 정답이다. 빈칸 앞에 형용사(great)가 있는 것도 명사 자리를 알려 주는 단서가 된다. 동사 또는 분사 (A), 형용사 (B)와 부사 (C)는 명사 자리에 올 수 없다.

해석 노인들을 위한 건강 관리 서비스와 처방약은 정부의 막대한 비용으로 제공된다.

어휘 healthcare n. 건강 관리, 의료 prescription n. 처방(전) the elderly 노인들 at great expense 막대한 비용으로

2 가산 명사와 불가산 명사   p.132

1. (A)   2. (B)   3. (D)

1. 단수와 복수 명사 구별하여 채우기

해설 타동사(expect)의 목적어 자리에는 동명사나 명사가 와야 하므로, 명사 (A), (C)와 동명사 (B)가 정답의 후보이다. 목적어 자리 앞에 부정관사(a)가 와 있으므로 단수 명사 (A) standard가 정답이다. 동명사 (B)는 부정관사와 함께 쓰일 수 없다. 동사 또는 과거분사 (D)는 명사 자리에 올 수 없다.

해석 설문 조사 결과에 따르면, 응답자들은 기술이 발달하고 임금이 상승함에 따라 더 나은 생활 수준을 기대한다.

어휘 survey n. 설문 조사; v. 조사하다 respondent n. 응답자

2. 단수와 복수 명사 구별하여 채우기

해설 타동사(recommends)의 목적어 자리에는 동명사나 명사가 와야 하므로, 명사 (A), (B)와 동명사 (C)가 정답의 후보이다. 빈칸 뒤에 목적어가 없으므로 동명사 (C) changing이 아닌 명사 (A) 또는 (B)를 써야 한다. change는 가산 명사이므로 앞에 관사가 오거나 복수형이어야 하는데, 앞에 관사가 없으므로 복수형 (B) changes가 정답이다. 동사 또는 과거분사 (D)는 명사 자리에 올 수 없다.

해석 주요 시민 단체의 보고서는 정부의 이민 정책에 중대한 변화를 권한다.

어휘 civic adj. 시민의 significant adj. 중대한 immigration n. 이민, 이주

3. 가산 명사와 불가산 명사 구별하여 채우기

해설 전치사(through)의 목적어 자리에 올 수 있는 것은 명사이므로 명사 (C)와 (D)가 정답의 후보이다. 빈칸 앞에 부정관사(an)가 있으므로 가산 단수 명사 (D) advertisement가 정답이다. (C) advertising은 불가산 명사이므로 부정관사와 함께 쓰일 수 없다. 동사 (A)와 형용사 (B)는 명사 자리에 올 수 없다.

해석 Mr. Williams는 손꼽히는 비즈니스 잡지에 게재된 광고를 통해 J-Stone Industries사의 홍보 담당자 공석에 대해 알게 되었다.

어휘 open adj. 공석인, 비어 있는 publicist n. 홍보 담당자

3 한정사와 명사   p.133

1. (C)   2. (D)   3. (C)

1. 명사에 맞는 한정사 채우기

해설 이 문장은 주어(merchandise)와 동사(must be checked)가 갖추어진 완전한 절이므로, 주어(merchandise)를 앞에서 한정해 주는 한정사 (A)와 (C)가 정답의 후보이다. merchandise는 불가산 명사이므로 불가산 명사 앞에 올 수 있는 (C) Any가 정답이다. 부정관사 (A) An은 불가산 명사와 함께 쓰일 수 없다.

해석 가게로 반품되는 어떤 상품이라도 선반에 다시 놓여지기 전에 손상 및 기능성이 반드시 점검되어야 한다.

어휘 merchandise n. 상품 damage n. 손상, 피해; v. 손상을 주다 functionality n. 기능성 put back 다시 놓다

2. 한정사에 맞는 명사 채우기

해설 복수 명사 앞에 오는 수량 형용사 several이 있으므로, 복수 명사 (D) closures가 정답이다.

해석 회사는 직원들에게 전국에 있는 몇몇 공장의 폐쇄를 알리기 위한 공식 성명을 발표했다.

어휘 issue a statement 성명을 발표하다 closure n. 폐쇄

3. 한정사에 맞는 명사 채우기

해설 단수 명사 앞에 오는 수량 형용사 Each가 있으므로 단수 명사 (C) trainee가 정답이다.

해석 각 수습사원은 전임 회계사 직책으로 승진하기 전에 6개월간의 교육을 받아야 한다.

어휘 probationary adj. 수습(견습) 중의 undergo v. 받다, 겪다 instruction n. 교육, 훈련 advance v. 승진하다, 나아가다 full-time adj. 전임의 accountant n. 회계사 trainee n. 수습사원, 훈련생

4 사람명사 vs. 사물/추상명사   p.134

1. (D)   2. (C)   3. (B)

1. 사람명사 추상명사 구별하여 채우기

해설 목적어 자리에 올 수 있는 것은 명사이므로 명사 (B)와 (D)가 정답의 후보이다. '근로자들이 정규 고용직을 얻으려고 한다'는 의미이므로 추상명사 (D) employment(고용)가 정답이다. 사람명사 (B) employee(피고용인)를 쓰면 '근로자들이 정규 피고용인을 얻으려고 한다'는 어색한 의미가 된다.

해석 대부분의 근로자들은 정규직 자리의 경제적 안정성을 선호하기 때문에 정규 고용직을 얻으려고 한다.

어휘 seek v. 얻으려고 하다, 추구하다 permanent adj. 정규직의, 영원한

2. 사람명사 추상명사 구별하여 채우기

해설 전치사(of)의 목적어 자리에 올 수 있는 것은 명사이므로 명사 (B), (C), (D)가 정답의 후보이다. '언론 분야'라는 의미이므로 추상명사 (C) journalism

(언론, 언론학)이 정답이다. 사람명사 (B) journalist(기자)나 사물명사 (D) journal(잡지, 학술지)는 어색한 의미를 만들기 때문에 답이 될 수 없다.

해석 뛰어난 조사 능력과 세부 사항에 대한 주의는 언론 분야에서 일하는 데 필요한 자질이다.

어휘 attention n. 주의 necessary adj. 필요한 quality n. (사람의) 자질, 품질
field n. 분야 journalistic adj. 신문 잡지 특유의

3. 사람명사 추상명사 구별하여 채우기

해설 전치사(as)의 목적어 자리에 올 수 있는 것은 명사이므로 명사 (B), (C), (D)가 정답의 후보이다. '심리학자를 컨설턴트로 고용하다'라는 의미이므로 사람명사 (B) consultants(컨설턴트, 고문)가 정답이다. 추상명사 (C) consultancy(컨설팅사)나 (D) consultations(상담)를 쓰면 '심리학자를 컨설팅사/상담으로 고용하다'라는 어색한 의미가 된다.

해석 제조업자들은 종종 심리학자들을 자문 위원으로 고용하여 다양한 연령대의 아동을 위한 장난감을 디자인하는 데 그들의 통찰력을 구한다.

어휘 manufacturer n. 제조업자 frequently adv. 종종, 자주
psychologist n. 심리학자 obtain v. 구하다, 얻다 insight n. 통찰력

5 복합 명사   p.135

1. (C)   2. (A)   3. (C)

1. 다른 명사를 수식하는 명사 채우기

해설 '연구 프로그램'이라는 복합 명사의 의미이므로 복합 명사를 만드는 명사 (C) research가 정답이다. 분사 (A) 또는 (B)를 빈칸에 넣으면 '연구하는/연구된 프로그램'이라는 어색한 의미가 되어 버린다. 참고로, 복합 명사에서 앞의 명사에는 -(e)s를 붙일 수 없으므로 (D) researches는 빈칸에 올 수 없다.

해석 그 연구 프로그램은 정부 기관에서 자금을 받아 그 대학 공학 기술 시설의 유능한 과학자들에 의해 실시되었다.

어휘 fund v. 자금을 대다; n. 자금 carry out (실험, 시험) 실시하다, 실행하다
capable adj. 유능한, 능력 있는 engineering n. 공학 (기술)

2. 다른 명사를 수식하는 명사 채우기

해설 '운동 기구'라는 복합 명사의 의미이므로 복합 명사를 만드는 명사 (A) exercise가 정답이다. 복합 명사는 특별한 경우가 아니면 앞의 명사에 -(e)s를 붙이지 않으므로 (B) exercises는 답이 될 수 없다. 분사 (C) 또는 (D)를 넣으면 '운동하는/운동된 기구'라는 어색한 의미가 되어 버린다.

해석 광고에 나온 운동 기구는 사람들이 단 몇 주 만에 보다 탄력 있는 근육을 얻는 데 도움을 준다는 것이 보장된다.

어휘 equipment n. 기구, 장비 guarantee v. 보장하다, 장담하다
help + 목적어 + 동사원형 목적어가 ~하는 데 도움이 되다
achieve v. 얻다, 달성하다 muscle n. 근육 tone n. (근육의) 탄력

3. 다른 명사를 수식하는 명사 채우기

해설 '유효 기간'이라는 복합 명사의 의미이므로 복합 명사를 만드는 명사 (C) expiration이 정답이다. 분사 (A)를 넣으면 '만료된 날짜'라는 어색한 의미가 되어 버린다. 동사 (B), (D)는 명사를 꾸밀 수 없으므로 답이 될 수 없다.

해석 그 소매업자는 주문한 화장용 크림의 유효 기간이 이미 지났다고 주장하며 공급 회사에 항의를 제기했다.

어휘 file a complaint 항의를 제기하다 claim v. 주장하다

6 혼동하기 쉬운 명사   p.136

1. (B)   2. (A)   3. (D)

1. 의미 구별하여 명사 채우기

해설 '출품작들을 검토하다'라는 의미이므로 명사 (B) entries(출품작, 참가 등록)가 정답이다. (D) entrance(입장)를 쓰면 '입장을 검토하다'라는 어색한 의미가 되어 버린다.

해석 출간 작가 심사위원단은 올해의 청년 작가상 수상작을 결정하기 위해 마감일인 5월 12일까지 제출된 모든 출품작들을 검토할 것이다.

어휘 panel n. 심사위원단 determine v. 결정하다, 결심하다
entry n. 출품작, 참가 등록 entrance n. 입장

2. 의미 구별하여 명사 채우기

해설 '안내원으로부터 주차 허가증을 받다'라는 의미이므로 (A) permit(허가증)이 정답이다. (B) permission(허가)을 쓰면 '안내원으로부터 허가를 받다'라는 어색한 의미가 된다.

해석 방문객들이 안내원으로부터 주차 허가증을 먼저 받지 않고 건물 뒤쪽 부지에 차를 두고 가는 것은 허용되지 않는다.

어휘 leave v. 두고 가다, 남기다 lot n. 부지, 지역 attendant n. 안내원, 참석자
permit n. 허가증, 면허장; v. 허락하다 permission n. 허가, 승인

3. 의미 구별하여 명사 채우기

해설 '경제 관념을 갖는 것'이라는 의미이므로 (D) sense(관념, 감각)가 정답이다. (B) sensor(감지기)나 (C) sensation(감동, 흥분)을 쓰면 '경제 감지기/경제 감동을 갖는 것'이라는 어색한 의미가 되어 버린다.

해석 올바른 경제 관념을 갖는 것은 장기간의 안락한 생활 방식에 대해 준비하기 위한 개인 퇴직금 적립 계획을 수립하는 데 도움이 될 수 있다.

어휘 retirement plan 개인 퇴직금 적립 계획 provide for ~에 대해 준비하다
sense n. 관념, 감각 sensor n. 감지기 sensation n. 감동, 흥분

Hackers Practice   p.137

01 ⓑ [토익 공식 1]		02 ⓐ [토익 공식 6]	
03 ⓑ [토익 공식 6]		04 ⓑ [토익 공식 6]	
05 ⓐ [토익 공식 1]		06 ⓑ [토익 공식 5]	
07 ⓐ [토익 공식 5]			

08 arrive → arrival [토익 공식 1]
09 applicants → applicant [토익 공식 3]
10 developer → development [토익 공식 4]
11 supervisor → supervision [토익 공식 4]
12 traveling → traveler [토익 공식 2]
13 occupancy → occupation [토익 공식 4]
14 beneficiaries → benefits [토익 공식 4]

해석 01 Portside 병원 직원들은 힘닿는 데까지 환자들에게 봉사하는 데 헌신적인 것으로 알려져 있다.
02 귀중품이 안전한 장소에 보관되도록 하는 것은 호텔 투숙객들의 책임이다.
03 영화 제작 일정표는 주연 여배우의 다른 약속된 일에 맞추어 변경되었다.
04 허리케인이 홍수를 일으킬 가능성 때문에, 연안 지역 주민들은 대피하도록 권고된다.
05 여성이 바지를 입는 유행은 1900년대 초반에 생겨났다.
06 그 은행의 컨설턴트들은 뮤추얼 펀드를 구매하는 데 관심이 있는 고객들에게 투자 조언을 해준다.
07 Marshall은 마케팅 부서의 출근 기록 확인 및 정리를 맡고 있다.
08 영업부장은 중요한 고객의 도착을 기다리러 공항 기차역으로 갔다.
09 모든 지원자는 지불된 비용에 대해 공식 영수증을 받았다.
10 EU와 일본 간의 경제 관계 발전에 관한 워크숍이 도쿄에서 열렸다.
11 총지배인은 전 직원의 감독을 맡는다.
12 Mr. Lee는 출장이 잦은 비즈니스 여행객이기 때문에, 전용 공항 라운지 입장이 허용되었다.
13 비록 그의 직업은 가르치는 것이었지만, 그는 취미 삼아 주식 거래도 조금 했다.
14 Power 헬스클럽은 체계적인 운동의 이점을 발견할 것을 사람들에게 권고한다.

Hackers Test   p.138

Part 5

01 (D)   02 (D)   03 (C)   04 (B)   05 (B)

06 (A)	07 (D)	08 (B)	09 (D)	10 (A)
11 (B)	12 (D)	13 (D)	14 (C)	15 (A)
16 (A)	17 (C)	18 (C)		

Part 6			
19 (C)	20 (A)	21 (B)	22 (B)

01 사람명사 추상명사 구별하여 채우기

해설 　타동사(reviewed)의 목적어 자리에 올 수 있는 것은 명사나 동명사이므로 동명사 (A)와 명사 (C), (D)가 정답의 후보이다. '작성한 지원서를 검토한다'는 문맥이므로 (D) application(지원서, 지원)이 정답이다. (C) applicant(지원자)를 쓰면 '작성한 지원자를 검토한다'는 어색한 의미가 된다. 참고로, 빈칸 앞에 명사를 꾸미는 분사(completed)가 있는 것도 명사 자리를 알려 주는 단서가 된다. 빈칸 뒤에 목적어가 없으므로 동명사 (A)는 답이 될 수 없다.

해석 　Denise Samson은 인사 담당자에게 건네주기 전에 오류가 없는지 확실하게 하기 위해 작성한 지원서를 검토했다.

어휘 　completed adj. 작성한　hand v. 건네주다　application n. 지원(서)

02 명사 자리 채우기

해설 　타동사(will consider)의 목적어 자리에 올 수 있는 것은 명사나 동명사이므로 동명사 (B)와 명사 (D)가 정답의 후보이다. 빈칸 뒤에 목적어가 없으므로 명사 (D) termination이 정답이다. 동명사 (B) terminating은 뒤에 목적어가 와야 한다. 빈칸 앞에 정관사(the)가 있는 것도 명사 자리를 알려 주는 단서가 된다.

해석 　행정 관리자는 그의 비서가 다른 직원들과 잘 지내지 못하는 점을 감안하여 계약 종료를 고려할 것이다.

어휘 　administrative adj. 행정상의, 경영상의　in light of ~을 감안하여, ~에 비추어　get along with ~와 잘 지내다　termination n. 종료

03 다른 명사의 수식을 받는 명사 채우기

해설 　주어 자리에 올 수 있는 것은 명사이므로 명사 (C) growth가 정답이다. 동사 (A), (D) 또는 분사 (B)는 주어 자리에 올 수 없다. 참고로, earnings growth (수익 성장)는 [명사s + 명사]의 형태를 가지는 복합 명사이다.

해석 　그 보고서는 회사의 연평균 수익 성장이 분석가들이 추정했던 것보다 훨씬 더 높다는 것을 보여주었다.

어휘 　indicate v. 보이다, 가리키다, 나타내다　annual adj. 연간의, 1년의　analyst n. 분석가　estimate v. 추정하다, 평가하다

04 사람명사 추상명사 구별하여 채우기

해설 　주어 자리에 올 수 있는 것은 명사이므로 명사 (B)와 (C)가 정답의 후보이다. '새 책장의 조립이 어려웠다'라는 의미가 되어야 하므로 추상명사 (B) assembly(조립)가 정답이다. 사람명사 (C) assembler(조립공)를 쓰면 '새 책장의 조립공이 어려웠다'라는 어색한 의미가 된다. 동사 (A)와 동사 또는 분사 (D)는 주어 자리에 올 수 없다.

해석 　새 책장의 조립은 예상했던 것보다 더 어려웠다.

어휘 　bookcase n. 책장　assemble v. 조립하다

05 의미 구별하여 명사 채우기

해설 　전치사(in)의 목적어 자리에 올 수 있는 것은 명사나 동명사이므로 명사 (A), (B), (D)가 정답의 후보이다. '공장 근로자들에 의해 달성된 생산성 증가'라는 의미가 되어야 하므로 (B) productivity(생산성, 생산율)가 정답이다. (A) product(생산품)나 (D) produce(농산물)를 쓰면 생산품이나 농산물을 달성했다는 의미가 되므로 답이 될 수 없다.

해석 　경영진은 회사의 산호세 공장 근로자들에 의해 달성된 생산성 증가에 감명받았다.

어휘 　be impressed with 감명받다　achieve v. 달성하다, 성취하다

06 현재분사와 과거분사 구별하여 채우기

해설 　명사(text) 앞의 빈칸에는 명사를 꾸며 주는 형용사 역할을 하는 과거분사 (A)나 현재분사 (C), 또는 복합 명사(명사 + 명사)를 만드는 명사 (B)가 올 수 있다. '수정된 문서'라는 의미가 되어야 하므로 '수정된'을 의미하는 과거

분사 (A) revised가 정답이다. 능동 의미를 갖는 현재분사 (C) revising(수정하는)은 답이 될 수 없다. 참고로, (B) revision(수정)은 text와 결합할 때, revision text가 아니라, '편집'이라는 의미의 text revision으로 쓰인다.

해석 　수정된 문서 한 부는 책 출간에 앞서 오류가 있는지 편집장에 의해 검토되어야 한다.

어휘 　managing editor 편집장　inaccuracy n. 오류, 틀림, 부정확

07 한정사에 맞는 명사 채우기

해설 　타동사(has attracted)의 목적어 자리에 올 수 있는 것은 명사이므로 명사 (C)와 (D)가 정답의 후보이다. 복수 명사와 함께 쓰이는 수량 형용사 fewer가 와 있으므로, 복수 명사 (D) registrants(등록자)가 정답이다. 동사 (A)와 동사 또는 분사 (B)는 목적어 자리에 올 수 없다.

해석 　최근 정부에 의해 설립된 연금 제도는 본래 예상했던 것보다 더 적은 등록자들을 끌어모았다.

어휘 　pension scheme 연금 제도　attract v. 끌어모으다　registration n. 등록　registrant n. 등록자

08 명사 자리 채우기

해설 　가짜 주어(there)에 대하여 진짜 주어 자리에 올 수 있는 것은 명사이므로 명사 (B)와 (C)가 정답의 후보이다. '계획 중지 외의 대안'이라는 의미가 되어야 하므로 (B) alternative(대안)가 정답이다. (C) alternation(교대, 교체)을 쓰면 '계획 중지 외의 교대'라는 어색한 의미가 된다.

해석 　그 최고 경영자는 회사가 충분한 자본금을 모을 때까지는 확장 계획을 그만두는 것 외에 대안이 없다고 말했다.

어휘 　drop v. 그만두다　raise v. 모으다, 마련하다　capital n. 자본금, 자산

09 의미 구별하여 명사 채우기

해설 　타동사(require)의 목적어 자리에 올 수 있는 것은 명사이므로 (A)와 (D)가 정답의 후보이다. '몇몇 도로 및 다리의 폐쇄를 필요로 하다'라는 의미가 되어야 하므로 (D) closing(폐쇄)이 정답이다. (A) close(종말, 끝)를 쓰면 '몇몇 도로 및 다리의 종말을 필요로 하다'라는 어색한 의미가 된다.

해석 　시 공무원들에 따르면, 오클라호마시의 개량 공사 프로젝트는 최대 6개월 동안 몇몇 도로 및 다리의 폐쇄를 필요로 할 것이다.

어휘 　city official 시 공무원　improvement n. 개량 공사　require v. 필요로 하다

10 다른 명사를 수식하는 명사 채우기

해설 　명사(numbers) 앞 빈칸에는 명사를 꾸며 주는 형용사 (D) 또는 복합 명사(명사 + 명사)를 만드는 명사 (A), (B), (C)가 올 수 있다. '계좌 번호'라는 의미가 되어야 하므로 명사 (A) Account가 정답이다. 형용사 (D) Accountable(책임이 있는)을 쓰면 '책임이 있는 번호'라는 어색한 의미가 된다. 복합 명사에서 앞의 명사에는 -s가 붙을 수 없으므로 (B) Accounts는 numbers 앞에 올 수 없다. (C) Accounting(회계학)을 쓰면 '회계학 번호'라는 어색한 의미가 된다.

해석 　이전 고객들의 계좌 번호는 회사의 새로운 정책의 일환으로 6개월 동안 데이터베이스에 보존될 것이다.

어휘 　maintain v. 보존하다, 유지하다　account number 계좌 번호

11 단수와 복수 명사 구별하여 채우기

해설 　동사(collect)의 목적어 자리에는 동명사나 명사가 와야 하므로, 명사 (A)와 (B)가 정답의 후보이다. '설문 조사로부터 나온 결과들을 모으다'라는 의미로, 가산 명사 result의 복수형 (B) results가 정답이다. to 부정사 (C)와 동사 또는 과거분사 (D)는 명사 자리에 올 수 없다.

해석 　Mr. Barrett은 지난달의 고객 설문 조사로부터 나온 결과들을 모아서 상세한 보고서를 준비할 것이다.

어휘 　collect v. 모으다, 수집하다　detailed adj. 상세한, 세부에 걸친

12 동명사와 명사 구별하여 채우기

해설 　전치사(in)의 목적어 자리에는 동명사 (A) 또는 명사 (D)가 올 수 있다. 빈칸 뒤에 목적어가 없으므로 명사 (D) motion이 정답이다. 동명사 (A) moving은 목적어와 함께 써야 한다. (C) move도 명사로 쓰일 수 있지만, '작동 중인, 움직

이고 있는'을 의미하는 표현은 in motion이므로 (C) move는 답이 될 수 없다.

해석 그 운영자는 필요한 모든 원자재들이 준비가 될 때까지 기계에 시동을 걸지 않을 것이다.

어휘 operator n. 운영자, 경영자 raw material 원자재, 원료
in place ~할 준비가 되어 있는 set A in motion A에 시동을 걸다

13 명사 자리 채우기

해설 '안전을 보장하기 위한 노력'이라는 의미가 되어야 하므로 빈칸에는 타동사 (to ensure)의 목적어가 와야 한다. 목적어 자리에 올 수 있는 것은 명사이므로 명사 (D) safety(안전)가 정답이다.

해석 작업장 내의 안전을 보장하기 위한 노력으로, 정부는 장비 관리와 위험 물질 사용 및 보관에 관한 법을 수립했다.

어휘 in an effort to do ~하기 위한 노력으로 maintenance n. 관리, 정비
hazardous adj. 위험한 substance n. 물질

14 주어와 수일치하는 동사 채우기

해설 문장에 동사가 없으며, 주어(Demands)가 복수이므로 단수, 복수에 모두 쓰일 수 있는 과거 동사 (C) rose가 정답이다. 단수 동사 (A)와 (B)는 복수 주어와 함께 쓸 수 없다.

해석 새로운 의료 보상 프로그램 수정에 대한 요구가 급격히 증가했으며, 이는 몇몇 주요 병원들이 파업하는 결과를 낳았다.

어휘 modification n. 수정, 변경 coverage n. 보상 (범위) strike n. 파업

15 명사 자리 채우기

해설 전치사(Out of)의 목적어 자리에는 명사가 와야 하므로 (A) respect가 정답이다. (B) respecting은 '~에 관하여'를 의미하는 전치사로 명사 자리에 올 수 없다. respecting을 동명사로 본다 하더라도 뒤에 목적어가 없기 때문에 정답이 될 수 없다. 참고로, out of respect는 '경의를 표하여'라는 뜻의 표현이다.

해석 대학 설립자의 바람에 경의를 표하여, 학문적으로 재능이 있는 빈곤 가정의 학생들은 전액 장학금을 제공받는다.

어휘 out of respect 경의를 표하여 wish n. 바람, 소망; v. 바라다

16 사람명사 추상명사 구별하여 채우기

해설 If절의 주어 자리가 비어 있다. 주어가 될 수 있는 것은 명사이므로 (A), (B), (C)가 정답의 후보이다. '부착된 사진'이라는 의미가 되어야 하므로 (A) photographs(사진들)가 정답이다. (B) photography(사진술)나 (C) photographers(사진가들)를 쓰면 '부착된 사진술/사진가'라는 어색한 의미가 된다.

해석 양식에 부착된 사진이 크기 요건을 충족하지 않을 경우, 외무부는 여권을 발행해 줄 수 없을 것이다.

어휘 attach v. 부착하다 requirement n. (필요) 요건 issue v. 발행하다

17 단수와 복수 명사 구별하여 채우기

해설 전치사(with)의 목적어 자리에는 동명사나 명사가 와야 하므로, 명사 (B)와 (C)가 정답의 후보이다. retiree는 가산 명사이므로 앞에 관사가 오거나 복수형이어야 하는데, 빈칸 앞에 관사가 없으므로 복수형 (C) retirees가 정답이다. 동사 (A)와 동사 또는 과거분사 (D)는 명사 자리에 올 수 없다.

해석 플로리다주는 1년의 대부분 동안 따뜻한 기후가 계속되기 때문에 은퇴자들에게 인기가 있다.

어휘 retiree n. 은퇴자, 퇴직자

18 사람명사 추상명사 구별하여 채우기

해설 전치사(to)의 목적어 자리에 올 수 있는 것은 명사이므로 명사 (C)와 (D)가 정답의 후보이다. '판매자에게 전달되다'라는 의미가 되어야 하므로 사람명사 (C) seller(판매자)가 정답이다. 추상명사 (D) selling(판매)을 쓰면 '판매에게 전달되다'라는 어색한 의미가 된다.

해석 신용카드나 온라인 은행 이체를 통한 납입은 상품이 요청된 날짜에 운송되는 것을 보장하기 위해 판매자에게 이틀 이내로 전달되어야 합니다.

어휘 payment n. 납입, 지불(금) ship v. 운송하다

19-22는 다음 회람에 관한 문제입니다.

수신: 전 지점장
발신: Jane Dawson, 지역 관리자 – 동남아시아
날짜: 6월 7일

지난달 싱가포르에서의 회의 중에 논의했던 바와 같이, GLE사는 영업 사원들을 위한 새로운 장려금 프로그램을 시행할 것입니다. [19]모든 지점들은 7월 1일에 이를 적용할 것입니다.

[20]이것은 대규모 거래들에 대한 수수료 지급을 포함합니다. 직원들은 총 500달러 이상의 그들이 내는 모든 매출에 대해 5퍼센트의 상여금을 받을 것입니다. [21]이에 더하여, 직원들이 계속 의욕을 가지도록 돕기 위해, 연간 최고 기록을 가진 판매 사원은 매년 12월에 한 달 급여에 상당하는 금액을 받게 될 것입니다.

[22]이 프로그램이 직원 만족도를 향상시키고 회사에 증가된 이윤을 가져올 것이라고 확신합니다. 장려금 제도가 실시되기 전에 직원들과 이에 대해 논의하시고, 질문이 있으시다면 제게 알려주시기 바랍니다. 항상 그렇듯이, 여러분의 노고에 감사드립니다.

discuss v. 논의하다 incentive n. 장려금 sales personnel 영업 사원들
branch n. 지점 total v. 합계가 ~이 되다
furthermore adv. 이에 더하여, 게다가 motivated adj. 의욕을 가진
reward v. (상을) 주다; n. 보상 salary n. 급여 improve v. 향상시키다
profit n. 이윤 go into effect 실시하다, 효력이 발생되다

19 올바른 시제의 동사 채우기 전체 문맥 파악

해설 '모든 지점들이 7월 1일에 이를 적용하다'라는 문맥인데, 이 경우 빈칸이 있는 문장만으로는 올바른 시제의 동사를 고를 수 없으므로 주변 문맥이나 전체 문맥을 파악하여 정답을 고른다. '7월 1일(July 1)'은 회람의 발신 날짜인 '6월 7일(Date: June 7)' 이후이고, 앞 문장에서 'GLE사가 새로운 장려금 프로그램을 시행할 것이다(GLE Inc. is implementing a new incentive program)'라고 했으므로 모든 지점들에 새로운 프로그램이 적용되는 시점은 회람을 작성한 시점보다 미래임을 알 수 있다. 따라서 미래 시제 (C) will adopt가 정답이다.

어휘 adopt v. 적용하다, 채택하다

20 알맞은 문장 고르기

해석 (A) 이것은 대규모 거래들에 대한 수수료 지급을 포함합니다.
(B) 유사한 프로그램들은 회사가 너무 많은 돈을 잃게 했습니다.
(C) 저희 영업 사원들은 정기적인 교육을 받습니다.
(D) 저희는 아직 최소 매출액을 결정하지 못했습니다.

해설 빈칸에 들어갈 알맞은 문장을 고르는 문제이므로 빈칸의 주변 문맥이나 전체 문맥을 파악한다. 앞부분에서 회사가 새로운 장려금 프로그램을 시행한다고 한 후, 뒤 문장 'Staff members will be given a 5 percent bonus for any sale they make totaling $500 or more.'에서 직원들은 총 500달러 이상이 되는 모든 매출에 대해 5퍼센트의 상여금을 받을 것이라고 했으므로 빈칸에는 새로운 장려금 프로그램의 상여금과 관련된 내용이 들어가야 함을 알 수 있다. 따라서 (A) It will involve providing commissions on big transactions가 정답이다.

어휘 commission n. 수수료 big adj. 대규모의, 큰 transaction n. 거래
cost v. 잃게 하다; n. 비용 sales representative 영업 사원

21 형용사 어휘 고르기

해설 '한 달 급여에 상당하는 금액'이라는 문맥이 되어야 하므로 형용사 (B) equivalent(상당하는)가 정답이다.

어휘 remaining adj. 나머지의 accessible adj. 접근 가능한
refundable adj. 환불 가능한, 반환할 수 있는

22 다른 명사의 수식을 받는 명사 채우기

해설 타동사(will improve)의 목적어 자리에는 명사나 동명사가 와야 하므로, 명사 (B)와 동명사 (C)가 정답의 후보이다. 빈칸 뒤에 목적어가 없으므로 명사 (B) satisfaction이 정답이다. 참고로, employee satisfaction은 '직원 만족도'라는 의미의 복합 명사이다.

어휘　satisfactorily adv. 만족하게　satisfaction n. 만족
　　　satisfactory adj. 만족스러운, 충분한

1 인칭대명사의 격　　　　　　　　　　　　　p.141
1. (D)　2. (B)　3. (B)

1. 격에 맞는 인칭대명사 채우기

해설　주어 자리에는 소유대명사 (B)나 주격 (D)가 올 수 있다. '그들이 마중받다'라는 의미이므로 주격 (D) they(그들이)가 정답이다. '그들의 것이 마중받다'가 아니므로 소유대명사 (B) theirs(그들의 것)는 답이 될 수 없다.

해석　무역 협상자들이 공항에 도착했을 때, 그들은 마중을 받아 현지 호텔로 안내되었다.

어휘　trade n. 무역, 교역　negotiator n. 협상자　pick up (차로 사람을) 마중 나가다

2. 격에 맞는 인칭대명사 채우기

해설　명사(report) 앞에서 형용사처럼 쓰일 수 있는 인칭대명사는 소유격이므로 (B) her(그녀의)가 정답이다.

해석　Ms. Seaward는 그녀의 보고서를 수정한 후, 변경 사항을 검토하기 위해 지역 담당자와 만났다.

어휘　revise v. 수정하다, 개정하다　go over ~을 검토하다, 점검하다

3. 격에 맞는 인칭대명사 채우기

해설　타동사(may reach)의 목적어 자리에 올 수 있는 인칭대명사는 목적격 (B) 또는 소유대명사 (D)이다. '우리의 것에게 연락하다'가 아니라 '우리에게 연락하다'라는 의미이므로 소유대명사 (D) ours(우리의 것)가 아닌 목적격 (B) us(우리에게)가 정답이다.

해석　웹사이트를 이용하는 데 어려움을 겪는 고객들은 이메일을 보내시거나 서비스 안내 직원에게 전화하셔서 우리에게 연락하실 수 있습니다.

어휘　reach v. 연락하다, 이르다; n. 범위, 세력

2 재귀대명사　　　　　　　　　　　　　　p.142
1. (B)　2. (A)　3. (C)

1. 재귀대명사 채우기

해설　'내가 직접 발표하다'라는 의미이므로 주어(I)를 강조하는 재귀대명사 (B) myself가 정답이다. 3형식 동사(give) 뒤에는 목적어가 하나만 올 수 있으므로, 목적어(the presentation) 외에 또 다른 목적어 (A) me나 (C) mine은 올 수 없다. 소유격 (D) my는 꾸밈을 받는 명사와 함께 와야 한다.

해석　내가 직접 고객에게 발표할 수 없었기 때문에, 그녀와 제품 정보를 훑어봐 줄 것을 Mr. Perez에게 요청했다.

어휘　go over ~을 훑어보다, 검토하다

2. 격에 맞는 인칭대명사 채우기

해설　타동사(offered)의 목적어 자리이므로 목적격 (A), 소유대명사 (C), 재귀대명사 (D)가 정답의 후보이다. 관리자가 스스로에게 상여금을 준 것이 아니라 다른 사람(Chad Reyes)에게 상여금을 준 것이므로 재귀대명사 (D) himself가 아닌 (A) him이 정답이다. '그의 것에 상여금을 주다'가 아니라 '그에게 상여금을 주다'라는 의미이므로 소유대명사 (C) his는 답이 될 수 없다. 참고로, (C) his를 뒤의 명사구(a substantial bonus)를 꾸며 주는 소유격으로 본다 해도, 소유격(his)과 부정관사(a)는 나란히 올 수 없으므로 his는 답이 될 수 없다.

해석　Chad Reyes의 올해 총 매출액이 영업부의 다른 모든 이들의 총 매출액보다 높아서, 관리자는 그에게 상당한 액수의 상여금을 주었다.

어휘　substantial adj. 상당한

3. 재귀대명사 채우기

해설　전치사(by)의 목적어 자리에 올 수 있는 것은 목적격 (A), 재귀대명사 (C), 또는 소유대명사 (D)이다. '홀로 건설 현장을 방문하다'라는 의미이므로, by oneself(홀로, 혼자 힘으로)를 만드는 재귀대명사 (C) herself가 정답이다.

해석　Ms. Cole은 건설되고 있는 창고의 진행 상황을 확인하기 위해 홀로 건설 현장을 방문했다.

어휘　construction site 건설 현장　check up on (~가 옳은지) 확인하다　progress n. 진행, 진척　warehouse n. 창고

3 지시대명사 / 지시형용사　　　　　　　　　p.143
1. (D)　2. (A)　3. (B)

1. those 채우기

해설　'다른 주요 대학들의 연구소 시설들'(the laboratory facilities of other major universities)이라는 의미이다. 복수 명사(facilities)를 대신해서 사용할 수 있는 지시대명사가 필요하므로 (D) those가 정답이다.

해석　뉴욕대학의 연구소 시설들은 지역 내 다른 주요 대학들의 연구소 시설들에 비길 만하다.

어휘　laboratory n. 연구소, 실험실　comparable adj. 비길 만한, 비교할 만한

2. those 채우기

해설　뒤에 분사(hoping)를 수식어로 받아 '희망하는 사람들'을 의미하므로 (A) those가 정답이다. 관계대명사 (B)는 앞에 선행사가 있어야 하므로 답이 될 수 없다. (C) ones는 앞에 나온 명사를 대신해서 쓰이는 대명사인데 앞에 제시된 명사가 없으므로 답이 될 수 없다.

해석　올해 마라톤에 참가하기를 희망하는 사람들을 위해, 빠르고 쉬운 등록이 가능하도록 신청서가 온라인상에서 이용 가능하게 되었다.

어휘　application form 신청서　available adj. 이용할 수 있는　facilitate v. 가능하게 하다　registration n. 등록

3. that 채우기

해설　'채소 가격'(the cost of vegetables)이라는 의미이다. 앞의 단수 명사(the cost)를 대신해서 사용할 수 있는 지시대명사가 필요하므로 (B) that이 정답이다.

해석　식품 가격은 작년에 전반적으로 상승했는데, 육류 가격이 거의 두 배 증가하고 채소 가격이 거의 15퍼센트 올랐다.

어휘　in general 전반적으로, 대체로　nearly adv. 거의　double v. 두 배가 되다

4 부정대명사 / 부정형용사 1 : one/another/other　p.144
1. (D)　2. (B)　3. (B)

1. 부정대명사/형용사 채우기

해설　'또 다른 한 종류의 의류를 4월에 출시하다'라는 의미이므로 (D) another(또 다른 하나)가 정답이다. (A) each one은 '하나하나', (B) one another는 '서로서로'를 의미한다. (C) other는 앞에 the가 없을 때 형용사로만 쓰이므로 명사가 와야 하는 목적어 자리에 올 수 없다.

해석　XTD Design사의 상품에 대한 수요가 매우 높아서 그 회사는 한 종류의 의류를 1월에 출시하고 또 다른 한 종류의 의류를 4월에 출시할 것이다.

어휘　demand n. 수요　launch v. 출시하다, 개시하다　clothing n. 의류

2. 부정대명사/형용사 채우기

해설　'다른 업체들은 제품 가격을 낮추고 싶어 하지 않는다'는 의미이므로 (B) others(다른 것들)가 정답이다. (A) other는 앞에 the가 없을 때 형용사로만 쓰이므로 명사가 와야 하는 주어 자리에는 올 수 없다.

해석　몇몇 공급업체들은 그 회사의 할인 요청에 응했지만, 다른 업체들은 그들의 제

품 가격을 낮추고 싶어 하지 않았다.

어휘 be unwilling to do ~하고 싶어 하지 않다

3. 부정대명사/형용사 채우기

해설 '서로를 알다'라는 의미이므로 each 다음에 other가 와야 한다. 따라서 (B) other가 정답이다.

해석 신입 사원을 위한 오리엔테이션 중에, 직원들 중 두 명이 이미 서로 아는 사이였음이 밝혀졌다.

---

5 부정대명사 / 부정형용사 2 : some/any, no/none, most/almost   p.145

1. (C)   2. (A)   3. (A)

1. 부정대명사/형용사 채우기

해설 '직원들 중 몇몇이 마감일 연장을 다행이라고 여기다'라는 의미이므로 '몇몇'을 의미하는 (C) Some이 정답이다. (A) No는 형용사이므로 명사가 와야 하는 주어 자리에는 올 수 없다. (B) One은 뒤의 are와 수일치되지 않으므로 답이 될 수 없으며, (D) Any는 긍정문에서 '어떤 ~라도'를 의미하므로 이 문맥에는 맞지 않는다.

해석 출판부 직원들 중 몇몇은 지면 배치 프로젝트의 마감일이 연장된 것이 다행이라고 여긴다.

어휘 relieved adj. 다행이라고 여기는, 안도하는   layout n. 지면 배치, 레이아웃

2. 부정대명사/형용사 채우기

해설 '요리에 대해 다소 전문가라고 생각하다'라는 의미이므로 긍정문에서 전치사 of와 함께 쓰여 '다소, 약간의'라는 의미를 만드는 (A) something이 정답이다. 참고로 'something of + 추상명사'는 '다소 ~', '약간의 ~'라는 의미의 관용 표현이다.

해석 Mr. Spencer는 로마에서 10년 가까이 살았기 때문에, 그 자신이 이탈리아 요리에 대해 다소 전문가라고 생각한다.

어휘 expert n. 전문가   cuisine n. 요리

3. 부정대명사/형용사 채우기

해설 빈칸은 관계절의 주어 자리로 명사가 와야 한다. '대부분이 관련되어 있다'는 의미가 되어야 하므로 '대부분'을 의미하는 (A) most가 정답이다. (B) the most는 '가장 많은'이나 '가장 ~을'을 의미하는 최상급 표현에 쓰이며, (D) almost는 부사로 주로 'almost all (of) the + 명사'의 형태로 쓰인다.

해석 프로젝트 승인 위원회는 40건의 제안서를 받았는데, 이들 중 대부분은 시골 지역으로의 전력 송전과 관련되어 있었다.

어휘 approval n. 승인   proposal n. 제안(서)   be related to ~과 관련되어 있다   transmission n. 송전, 전송

---

6 명사-대명사 일치   p.146

1. (C)   2. (A)   3. (A)

1. 명사와 수/인칭 일치된 대명사 채우기

해설 '그 작가의 최신 소설이 찬사를 받다'라는 의미가 되어야 하므로 빈칸에 들어갈 대명사가 가리키게 되는 것은 The author's latest novel이다. 따라서 단수 사물명사(The ~ novel)를 가리키는 대명사 (C) it이 정답이다.

해석 그 작가의 최신 소설은 일반 대중에게 인기 있었고, 여러 저명한 평론가들로부터 찬사 또한 받았다.

어휘 latest adj. 최신의, 최근의   praise n. 찬사, 칭찬   critic n. 평론가

2. 명사와 수/인칭 일치된 대명사 채우기

해설 '그녀가 예약한 객실'이라는 의미이므로 빈칸에 들어갈 대명사가 가리키게 되는 것은 Ms. Davidson이다. 따라서 여성인 단수 사람명사(Ms. Davidson)를 가리키는 대명사 (A) she가 정답이다.

해석 Ms. Davidson은 그녀가 예약한 객실이 네 명을 수용할 수 있는지 재확인하기 위해 호텔에 전화했다.

어휘 double-check 재확인하다   accommodate v. 수용하다

3. 명사와 수/인칭 일치된 대명사 채우기

해설 '재정 위원회가 예산 집행 계획안을 제출하다'라는 의미이므로 빈칸에 들어갈 대명사가 가리키게 되는 것은 the finance committee이다. 따라서 단수 사물명사(the finance committee)를 가리키면서 형용사처럼 복합 명사(budget recommendations) 앞에 쓰이는 소유격 (A) its가 정답이다.

해석 Ms. Lee는 재정 위원회에 예산 집행 계획안을 검토하기 위해 회계부장에게 제출하도록 지시했다.

어휘 instruct v. 지시하다   budget n. 예산 집행 계획, 예산(안)   review n. 검토

Hackers Practice   p.147

01 ⓑ [토익 공식 1]		02 ⓑ [토익 공식 3]	
03 ⓐ [토익 공식 1]		04 ⓐ [토익 공식 4]	
05 ⓑ [토익 공식 2]		06 ⓐ [토익 공식 1]	
07 ⓑ [토익 공식 3]			

08 someone → anyone [토익 공식 5]
09 its → their [토익 공식 6]   10 our → its [토익 공식 6]
11 them → it [토익 공식 6]   12 its → their [토익 공식 6]
13 its → our [토익 공식 6]
14 themselves → them [토익 공식 2]

해석 01 모든 직원들은 매주 그들의 직속 상사에게 경과 보고서를 제출하도록 요구된다.
02 자메이카는 해변들이 근처 국가들의 해변들보다 더 멋지기 때문에 인기 있는 관광지이다.
03 임금의 선불을 받으려면 월말까지 신청서를 제출해야 한다.
04 팀장들은 또 다른 직원을 프로젝트에 배정하기 위해 부장으로부터 허가를 받아야 한다.
05 Jack은 모든 친구들이 주말에 바빴기 때문에 혼자 영화를 보러 가기로 결정했다.
06 Mr. Edwards는 그녀가 운영 관리자 자리에 가장 적합한 후보라고 생각한다.
07 오늘 아침 배달원을 통해 발송된 그 문서들은 댈러스 사무실에 내일 도착할 것이다.
08 관광객들이 안내 데스크로 갔지만, 그들을 도와줄 사람이 아무도 없었다.
09 문제는 시 근로자들이 6퍼센트의 임금 인상에 대한 요구를 재고하기를 거부한다는 것이다.
10 Sunrise 리조트는 맛있는 식사를 제공하며 그것만의 수영장을 가지고 있다.
11 비록 Forrest Hills가 극장가에서 성공적이지는 않았지만, 대부분의 영화 평론가들은 그것을 걸작으로 여긴다.
12 학생들은 늦어도 8월 3일까지 가을 학기 강좌에 등록해야 한다.
13 우리는 우리의 고객들에게 양질의 상품과 훌륭한 서비스를 제공하는 데 전념한다.
14 Ms. Jenson은 여행 일정이 변경되었다고 알리기 위해 여행 단체 일원들에게 연락했다.

Hackers Test   p.148

Part 5				
01 (A)	02 (D)	03 (D)	04 (B)	05 (A)
06 (B)	07 (D)	08 (B)	09 (C)	10 (D)
11 (B)	12 (B)	13 (B)	14 (A)	15 (D)
16 (D)	17 (C)	18 (B)		

Part 6			
19 (A)	20 (A)	21 (B)	22 (D)

01 명사의 수/인칭 일치된 대명사 채우기

해설 'Drake Industries사의 생산 능력'이라는 의미가 되어야 하므로 빈칸에 들어갈 대명사가 가리키게 되는 것은 Drake Industries이다. 따라서 단수 사물 명사(Drake Industries)를 가리키면서 형용사처럼 복합 명사(production capacity) 앞에 쓰이는 소유격 (A) its가 정답이다.

해석 Mr. Harrington은 Drake Industries사가 자사의 생산 능력을 확대하기 위해 유럽에 몇몇 제조 공장을 개설하는 것을 결정했을 수도 있음을 시사했다.

02 부정대명사/형용사 채우기

해설 '또 다른 한 직원은 자율 근무 시간제를 높이 평가한다'는 의미가 되어야 하므로 (D) another(또 다른 하나/한 사람)가 정답이다. (A) no는 형용사이므로 뒤에 명사 없이 혼자 주어 자리에 올 수 없으며, (B) other는 앞에 the가 없을 때 형용사로만 쓰이므로 명사가 와야 하는 주어 자리에 올 수 없다. (C) neither는 앞에 언급된 2개의 대상 모두를 가리키는데, 앞에 언급된 대상이 1개이므로 답이 될 수 없다.

해석 그 회사의 한 직원은 정해진 시간 동안 일하는 것을 선호하는 반면, 또 다른 한 직원은 관리자에 의해 최근 마련된 자율 근무 시간제를 높이 평가한다.

어휘 **fixed** adj. 정해진, 결정된
appreciate v. 높이 평가하다, (좋은 점을) 인정하다, 감상하다
flexible working hours system 자율 근무 시간제

03 격에 맞는 인칭대명사 채우기

해설 타동사(haven't completed)의 목적어 자리에 올 수 있는 것은 목적격 (A), 재귀대명사 (C), 또는 소유대명사 (D)이다. '우리의 것(예산안)을 완성하지 못하다'라는 의미가 되어야 하므로 소유대명사 (D) ours(우리의 것)가 정답이다.

해석 마케팅부는 그들의 내년 예산안을 끝냈지만, 홍보부에 있는 우리는 아직 우리의 것을 완성하지 못했다.

어휘 **public relations** 홍보 (활동)

04 부정대명사/형용사 채우기

해설 빈칸 이하는 '어느 직책도 정확히 그가 찾고 있던 것은 아니다'라는 의미가 되어야 하므로 (B) none(아무것도 ~ 아니다)이 정답이다.

해석 Mr. Eisenhower는 그 회사에서 많은 직책을 제의받았지만, 그 중 어느 것도 정확히 그가 찾고 있던 것이 아니었다.

어휘 **a number of** 많은 **position** n. 직(=job), 위치, 직장

05 원형 부정사 채우기

해설 사역동사 let(could not let)의 목적격 보어로는 원형 부정사가 필요하므로 (A) damage가 정답이다. 참고로, let의 목적어는 its current patent dispute이고 with a competitor는 목적어를 꾸며 주는 전치사구이다.

해석 최고 경영자는 GED 자동차 회사가 경쟁사와의 현 특허 분쟁이 대중에게 보여지는 회사의 명성을 손상시키게 놔둘 수 없음을 강조했다.

어휘 **emphasize** v. (중요성을) 강조하다, 역설하다
let + 목적어 + 동사원형 목적어를 ~하게 하다 **current** adj. 현재의
patent n. 특허 **dispute** n. 분쟁 **reputation** n. 명성

06 격에 맞는 인칭대명사 채우기

해설 명사(celebrity status) 앞에서 형용사처럼 쓰일 수 있는 인칭대명사가 필요하므로 소유격 (B) their가 정답이다.

해석 유명인들은 제품 라인을 시장에 출시함으로써 그들의 유명한 지위를 가끔 활용한다.

어휘 **make good use of** ~을 활용하다 **celebrity** n. 유명인, 명성
product line 제품 라인, 제품군

07 부정대명사/형용사 채우기

해설 '어떠한 권한도 주어지지 않는다'는 의미가 되어야 하므로 (D) any(어떠한)가 정답이다. 앞에 부정의 의미를 만드는 has not이 왔으므로 no를 중복하여 쓸 필요는 없다.

해석 부 경리부장에게는 고객이 요청하는 문서를 공개할 수 있는 어떠한 권한도 주어지지 않았다.

어휘 **authority** n. 권한, 권위 **release** v. 공개하다, 풀어 주다

08 재귀대명사 채우기

해설 명사(the director) 뒤에서 명사를 강조할 수 있는 것은 재귀대명사이므로 (B) herself가 정답이다. 주어(the director)가 이미 있으므로 또 다른 주어가 되는 주격 (C)나 소유대명사 (A)는 올 수 없다. 뒤에 명사가 없으므로 소유격 (D) 역시 올 수 없다.

해석 관리자 자신은 그녀의 공무를 수행하는 동안 어떠한 정치적인 참여도 삼가야 한다는 것이 그 회사의 정책이다.

어휘 **abstain from** 삼가다, 그만두다 **involvement** n. 참여, 연루, 말려들게 함
carry out 수행하다

09 those 채우기

해설 빈칸 이하는 '고정 수당이나 월급을 받는 직원들'(employees who receive a fixed wage or salary)이라는 의미가 되어야 한다. 이때 앞의 복수 명사 (employees)를 대신해서 사용할 수 있는 지시대명사가 필요하므로 (C) those가 정답이다. (A) such는 형용사이므로 뒤에 명사가 와야 하며, 지시대명사 (B) that은 단수 명사를 대신해서 사용된다. 부정대명사 (D) anyone은 정해지지 않은 막연한 사람을 나타낸다.

해석 성과급제로 일하는 직원들은 고정 수당이나 급여를 받는 직원들보다 더 능률적이다.

어휘 **incentive** n. 성과급, 장려금 **efficient** adj. 능률적인, 유능한
fixed adj. 고정된, 변치 않는 **wage** n. 수당, 임금 **salary** n. 급여, 월급

10 no/none/not 구별하여 채우기

해설 부정관사(a)를 앞에서 강조할 수 있어야 하므로 (D) Not이 정답이다. no는 not a(n) 또는 not any와 같은 뜻으로, 이 표현들을 빈칸에 넣으면 not a single이나 not any a single이라는 잘못된 표현이 되므로 (A) No는 답이 될 수 없다. (B) Any가 오면 역시 any a single이라는 잘못된 표현이 되며, (C) None은 명사이므로 또 다른 명사(a single file) 앞에 올 수 없다.

해석 사무실의 컴퓨터 서버가 작동을 멈춘 이래로 단 한 개의 파일도 복구되지 못했지만, 다행히도 대부분의 직원들은 그들의 작업에 대한 백업 파일을 만들어 두었다.

어휘 **recover** v. 복구하다 **crash** v. (컴퓨터 시스템이) 작동을 멈추다
fortunately adv. 다행히도

11 부정대명사/형용사 채우기

해설 '나머지 한 명이 서둘러 나갔다'는 의미가 되어야 하고 주어 자리이므로 주어가 될 수 있는 (B) the other(나머지 한 명)가 정답이다. (A) other는 형용사로만 쓰여 명사가 있어야 하는 주어 자리에 혼자 올 수 없으며, (C)와 (D)는 '서로'를 의미하므로 문맥에 맞지 않아 답이 될 수 없다.

해석 나머지 한 명이 인쇄된 보고서와 서류를 가지러 서둘러 나간 사이, 한 동료는 방문한 중역들과 함께 사무실에 남아 있었다.

어휘 **associate** n. 동료, 친구

12 부정대명사/형용사 채우기

해설 '웹사이트 디자이너들 중 대부분은 경력이 있다'는 의미가 되어야 하므로 (B) Most of(~ 중 대부분)가 정답이다. (A) Most(대부분, 대부분의)와 (D) Some (약간의, 몇몇의)은 형용사로 쓰였을 때 명사를 꾸밀 수 있지만 정관사(the) 앞에 나올 수 없다. (C) Almost는 부사이므로 명사나 대명사를 꾸밀 수 없고 주로 형용사 all을 꾸며 'almost all (of) the + 명사'의 형태로 쓰인다.

해석 웹사이트 디자이너들 중 대부분은 Windermere 스튜디오에서 일하기 전 그래픽 디자인 분야에서 2, 3년의 경력을 가지고 있었다.

13 격에 맞는 인칭대명사 채우기

해설 '회사들의 수입'이라는 의미가 되어야 하므로 빈칸에 들어갈 대명사가 가리키게 되는 것은 Companies이다. 따라서 명사(earnings) 앞에 와서 복수 사물 명사(Companies)를 가리키는 인칭대명사가 필요하므로 소유격 (B) their가 정답이다.

해석 자사 수입의 일정 부분을 자선 단체에 기부하는 회사들은 종종 긍정적인 대외 이미지를 발전시킨다.

어휘	donate v. 기부하다, 기증하다　certain adj. 일정한, 약간의

어휘 donate v. 기부하다, 기증하다　certain adj. 일정한, 약간의
portion n. 부분, 일부　earnings n. 수입, 소득　charitable adj. 자선의
organization n. 단체, 조직　public image 대외 이미지

14 that 채우기

해설 빈칸에는 명사(suggestion)를 꾸미는 역할을 하는 지시형용사 (A) 또는 (B), 소유격 (D)가 올 수 있다. suggestion이 단수이므로 단수 명사와 어울리는 (A) that이 정답이다. (B) those는 복수 명사 앞에서 사용되므로 답이 될 수 없다. (D) its는 사람명사(The financial consultant)를 대신하여 사용될 수 없다.

해석 재정 자문 위원은 비용을 줄이기 위해 임금 동결을 권고했으나, 그 제안은 이사회에 의해 거부되었다.

어휘 freeze n. (임금, 가격 등의) 동결　reject v. 거부하다

15 태에 맞는 동사 채우기

해설 '상사가 통지받다'라는 수동태 의미가 되어야 하므로 be 다음에 와서 수동태 동사를 만드는 p.p.형 (D) informed가 정답이다. (B) information은 주어(a superior)와 동격을 이루지 못하므로 빈칸에 와서 주격 보어가 될 수 없다.

해석 어떤 직원이라도 하루 이상 휴가를 내려면, 적어도 일주일 전에 상사가 통지받아야만 할 것이다.

어휘 take off 휴가를 내다, 떠나다　superior n. 상사, 상관; adj. 우수한
in advance 사전에, 미리　inform v. 통지하다, 알리다

16 부정대명사/형용사 채우기

해설 '오직 서로에게만 밝히다'라는 의미가 되어야 하므로 '서로'를 의미하는 (D) each other가 정답이다.

해석 두 기업은 연구 조사 결과를 오직 서로에게만 밝히고, 결과를 공개적으로 발표하거나 제3자를 관여시키지 않기로 합의했다.

어휘 reveal v. 밝히다, 드러내다　finding n. 조사 결과
publicly adv. 공개적으로, 공적으로　third party (당사자 이외의) 제3자

17 those 채우기

해설 빈칸 뒤의 분사(determined)를 수식어로 받아 '~하기로 결심한 사람들'을 나타내는 (C) Those가 정답이다.

해석 회사에서 경영직을 위한 자격을 얻기로 결심한 사람들은 통솔력을 발전시키기 위해 노력해야 한다.

어휘 determined to ~하기로 결심한　qualify v. 자격을 얻다, 자격을 주다
managerial adj. 경영의, 관리의　make an effort 노력하다, 애쓰다

18 명사와 수/인칭 일치된 대명사 채우기

해설 '기획안들을 꼼꼼히 읽다'라는 의미가 되어야 하므로 빈칸에 들어갈 대명사가 가리키게 되는 것은 the proposals이다. 따라서 복수 명사(the proposals)를 가리키는 대명사 (B) them이 정답이다. 소유대명사 (C)와 (D)는 '~의 것'을 의미하여 문맥과 어울리지 않는다.

해석 재정 전문가는 기획안들을 받았고 어느 것이 회사의 이익을 위해 가장 적합한지를 결정하기 전에 그것들을 이제 꼼꼼히 읽어 볼 것이다.

어휘 read through ~을 꼼꼼히 읽다　suit v. 적합하다, ~에 알맞다

19-22는 다음 편지에 관한 문제입니다.

11월 4일
Eileen Rivera
213번지 West 35번가, 1301호
뉴욕, 뉴욕주 10001

Ms. Rivera께,

귀하의 초고를 받아 보았으며 저희 출판사에서 그것을 출판하는 것에 대한 귀하의 관심에 감사드립니다. [19]저희는 귀하의 창조성과 재능을 높이 평가하며 귀하와 함께 일하는 것을 매우 기대하고 있습니다.

[20]그러나, 실제 출판 작업에 앞서, 귀하의 원 자료에 대한 전반적인 검토가 진행될 것입니다. 이와 관련하여, 귀하의 집필에 사용된 참고 문헌의 목록을 저희에게 제공해 주시길 요청드려도 되겠습니까? 이 절차는 모든 표절 문제를 방지 ⟳

하기 위해 필수적입니다. [21]저희는 귀하께서 양해해 주시고 저희의 요청에 응해 주시기를 희망합니다. 저희가 귀하께 이것을 부탁 드리는 이유가 귀하의 작품과는 특별히 연관이 없다는 것을 알아두시기 바랍니다. 이는 저희가 출판하는 모든 작품의 저자들에게 요청하는 것입니다. [22]귀하로부터 소식을 들을 수 있기를 기대합니다.

Bill Patterson, 출판국장 드림

prior to ~에 앞서　review n. 검토, 논평

prior to ~에 앞서　review n. 검토, 논평
source material (연구·조사 등의) 원 자료
in this regard 이와 관련하여, 이 점에 있어서　reference n. 참고 문헌, 참조
procedure n. 절차, 순서, 차례　mandatory adj. 필수의, 의무의
plagiarism n. 표절　to do with ~과 연관이 있는

19 동사 어휘 고르기

해설 '창조성과 재능을 높이 평가하다'라는 문맥이므로 '높이 평가하다'라는 뜻의 (A) appreciate가 정답이다.

어휘 assure v. 보증하다　address v. 말하다, 연설하다　anticipate v. 예상하다

20 올바른 시제의 동사 채우기　주변 문맥 파악

해설 '출판 작업에 앞서, 전반적인 검토가 진행되다'라는 문맥인데, 이 경우 빈칸이 있는 문장만으로는 정답을 고를 수 없으므로 주변 문맥이나 전체 문맥을 파악한다. 뒤 문장에서 '이와 관련하여, 사용된 참고 문헌의 목록을 제공해 달라(may we ask you to provide ~ a list of the references used in your writing)'고 했으므로 편지에서 요청하고 있는 참고 문헌의 목록을 받은 후에 검토가 이루어질 것임을 알 수 있다. 따라서 미래 시제 (A) will be held가 정답이다.

21 알맞은 문장 고르기

해석 (A) 귀하의 작품을 받아들일 수 없어 유감입니다.
(B) 저희는 귀하께서 양해해 주시고 저희의 요청에 응해 주시기를 희망합니다.
(C) 귀하의 서류는 요청하신 대로 전달되었습니다.
(D) 회사는 미출판 작가를 구하고 있습니다.

해설 빈칸에 들어갈 알맞은 문장을 고르는 문제이므로 빈칸의 주변 문맥이나 전체 문맥을 파악한다. 앞 문장 'This procedure is mandatory in order to prevent any plagiarism issues.'에서 이 절차는 표절 문제를 방지하기 위해 필수적이라고 했으므로 빈칸에는 이를 양해하고 요청에 응해주기를 바란다는 내용이 들어가야 함을 알 수 있다. 따라서 (B) We hope you understand and will comply with our request가 정답이다.

어휘 unfortunate adj. 유감인, 불행한　comply v. 응하다, 준수하다
unpublished writer 미출판 작가

22 인칭대명사 채우기　전체 문맥 파악

해설 '____로부터 소식을 들을 수 있기를 기대한다'는 문맥에서 빈칸이 전치사의 목적어 자리이므로, 목적격 대명사인 모든 보기가 정답의 후보가 된다. 빈칸이 있는 문장만으로 정답을 고를 수 없으므로 주변 문맥이나 전체 문맥을 파악한다. 편지의 수신자가 Ms. Rivera(Dear Ms. Rivera)라고 했고, 그녀의 원고를 출간하는 데 필요한 요청 사항(may we ask you)에 대한 소식을 듣기 기대한다고 했으므로 빈칸에 들어갈 대명사는 Ms. Rivera, 즉 '편지의 수신자'를 가리킨다. 따라서 편지의 수신자를 가리키는 2인칭 대명사 (D) you가 정답이다.

Chapter 12 형용사

1 형용사 자리　p.151
1. (D)　2. (A)　3. (A)

1. 형용사 자리 채우기

해설 명사(action)를 꾸며 줄 수 있는 형용사 (D) direct(직접적인)가 정답이다.

해석 시중 은행들은 심각한 통화 부족에 대처하기 위해 직접적인 행동을 취하도록 권고받는다.

어휘　commercial bank 시중 은행　be advised to ~하도록 권고받다
　　　deal with 대처하다, ~를 다루다　currency n. 통화　shortfall n. 부족, 부족액
　　　directness n. 단순 명쾌함　direction n. 방향　directly adv. 곧장, 똑바로

2. 형용사 자리 채우기

해설　복합 명사(installation instructions)를 꾸미기 위해서는 형용사 (A) 또는
　　　분사 (B), (D)가 올 수 있다. '쉬운 설치 설명'이라는 의미를 만드는 형용사가
　　　필요하므로 (A) easy가 정답이다. 분사 (B) 또는 (D)를 쓰면 '수월해진 설치
　　　설명 '또는 '수월하게 하는 설치 설명'이라는 어색한 의미가 된다.

해설　안내 책자에 나온 쉬운 설치 설명은 기계를 사용하기 위해 준비하는 것을 간단
　　　하게 했다.

어휘　installation n. 설치　instruction n. 설명, 지시
　　　manual n. 안내 책자, 설명서　ease v. 수월하게 하다, 완화하다

3. 형용사 자리 채우기

해설　빈칸은 주격 보어 자리이므로 형용사 (A) 또는 명사 (B), (D)가 올 수 있다. '근
　　　로자들이 덜 생산적이다'라는 문맥에서 주어(Workers)를 설명해 주는 형용사
　　　가 필요하므로 (A) productive(생산적인)가 정답이다. 명사 (B) production
　　　(생산)이나 (D) productiveness(다작, 생산적임)는 주어(Workers)와 의미적
　　　으로 동격 관계에 있지 않으므로 답이 될 수 없다.

해설　근로자들은 충분한 수면을 취하지 못하면 일반적으로 낮 동안 훨씬 덜 생산적
　　　이다.

어휘　in general 일반적으로, 대개　day n. 낮　sufficient adj. 충분한

---

2 수량 표현　　　　　　　　　　　　　　　p.152
　　1. (C)　2. (A)　3. (C)

1. 명사에 맞는 수량 표현 채우기

해설　단수 가산 명사(order) 앞에 빈칸이 있으므로 단수 명사 앞에 쓰는 (C)
　　　Every가 정답이다. (A) Many는 복수 가산 명사 앞에, (B) Some과 (D)
　　　More는 복수 가산 명사나 불가산 명사 앞에 올 수 있다.

해설　배송부로 들어오는 모든 주문은 최고의 정성과 관심을 가지고 처리된다.

어휘　process v. 처리하다　utmost adj. 최고의, 최대한의

2. 명사에 맞는 수량 표현 채우기

해설　anxiety는 가산, 불가산으로 모두 쓰이는 명사인데, 이 문장에서는 앞에 부정
　　　관사 a가 없고 뒤에 복수형을 만드는 -s도 갖지 않았으므로, 불가산 명사이다.
　　　따라서 불가산 명사 앞에 오는 (A) much가 정답이다. (B) many는 복수 가
　　　산 명사 앞에 오는 수량 표현이므로 답이 될 수 없다. 명사(anxiety)를 앞에서
　　　꾸며 줄 수 있는 것은 형용사이므로 부사 (C)와 (D)는 답이 될 수 없다.

해설　새 정부 규제가 금융 시장에 불안정을 일으킬 것이라는 소문은 투자자들 사이
　　　에 많은 불안을 야기했다.

어휘　rumor n. 소문　instability n. 불안정　anxiety n. 불안, 걱정

3. 명사에 맞는 수량 표현 채우기

해설　복수 명사(benefits) 앞에 빈칸이 있으므로 복수 명사 앞에 쓰는 (C) many
　　　가 정답이다. (B) a lot은 a lot of가 되어야 명사 앞에 올 수 있다. (D) some
　　　of 다음에는 the나 소유격이 있어야 명사 앞에 올 수 있다.

해설　Ceylon 화장품 회사의 새로운 핸드 크림을 사용해 온 고객들은 그 제품의 많
　　　은 효과들로 인해 호평을 한다.

어휘　rave review 호평　benefit n. 효과, 혜택

---

3 혼동하기 쉬운 형용사　　　　　　　　　　p.153
　　1. (C)　2. (C)　3. (D)

1. 문맥에 어울리는 형용사 채우기

해설　명사(effort)를 꾸미기 위해서는 형용사 (B) 또는 (C)가 와야 한다. '상당한

노력'이라는 의미가 되어야 하므로 (B) considerate(사려 깊은)가 아닌 (C)
considerable(상당한)이 정답이다.

해설　프로젝트의 시작에 앞서, Mr. Hanks는 건설 계획의 실행 가능성을 밝히는 데
　　　상당한 노력을 가했다.

어휘　prior to ~에 앞서, 먼저　exert v. 가하다, 행사하다
　　　determine v. 밝히다, 결정하다　feasibility n. 실행 가능성

2. 문맥에 어울리는 형용사 채우기

해설　빈칸은 주격 보어 자리이므로 형용사 (A)와 (C)가 정답의 후보이다. '가격이
　　　~에 좌우되다'라는 의미가 되어야 하므로 (C) dependent(~에 좌우되는, 의
　　　존적인)가 정답이다. (A) dependable(신뢰할 만한, 믿을 수 있는)을 쓰면 '가
　　　격이 ~에 신뢰할 만하다'라는 어색한 의미가 된다.

해설　제품의 가격은 제조 과정 중에 사용된 원자재의 가격에 여전히 좌우된다.

어휘　remain v. 여전히 ~이다　raw material 원자재
　　　depend v. 신뢰하다, 의지하다　dependent upon ~에 좌우되는

3. 문맥에 어울리는 형용사 채우기

해설　명사(performance)를 꾸미기 위해서는 형용사 (B) 또는 (D)가 와야 한다.
　　　'인상적인 연주'라는 의미가 되어야 하므로 (B) impressed(감명받은)가 아닌
　　　(D) impressive(인상적인)가 정답이다.

해설　바이올리니스트의 인상적인 연주에 큰 감동을 받은 후에, 음악 평론가는 그 연
　　　주회에 대한 평을 쓰려고 앉았을 때 무슨 말을 해야 할지 몰랐다.

어휘　stun v. 큰 감동을 주다, 망연자실하게 하다　critic n. 평론가
　　　be at a loss for words 무슨 말을 해야 할지 모르다

---

4 'be + 형용사' 숙어　　　　　　　　　　p.154
　　1. (C)　2. (A)　3. (C)

1. 형용사 관용 표현 채우기

해설　'하락할 것 같다'는 의미가 되어야 하므로 be likely to do(~할 것 같다)를 만
　　　드는 (C) likely가 정답이다.

해설　최근 유가 증권의 동향을 고려해 볼 때, 시가는 다음 분기 동안 2퍼센트 하락할
　　　것 같다.

어휘　given prep. ~을 고려해 볼 때　stocks and bonds 유가 증권
　　　market n. 시가, 시세, 시장　alike adj. 서로 같은, 비슷한
　　　likely adj. ~할 것 같은, 그럴듯한　likelihood n. 있음직함, 가능성, 가망

2. 형용사 관용 표현 채우기

해설　'거부되기 쉽다'는 의미가 되어야 하므로 be subject to(~되기 쉽다)를 만드
　　　는 (A) subject가 정답이다.

해설　연령 요건에 대한 증명이 충족되지 않으면, 온라인 쇼핑 클럽 회원 신청은 거부
　　　되기 쉽다.

어휘　proof n. 증명, 증거　rejection n. 거부, 거절, 폐기
　　　subject adj. ~될 수 있는, ~을 받아야 하는　subjective adj. 주관적인, 개인의

3. 형용사 관용 표현 채우기

해설　'수령할 자격이 없다'는 의미가 되어야 하므로 be eligible to do(~할 자격이
　　　있다)를 만드는 (C) eligible이 정답이다.

해설　시민들은 정년퇴직 연령이 될 때까지는 정부 연금을 수령할 자격이 없다.

어휘　pension n. 연금, 생활 보조금　mandatory retirement 정년퇴직
　　　eligibleness n. 바람직함, 적격임　eligible adj. 자격이 있는, 적격의

Hackers Practice　　　　　　　　　　　　p.155

01 ⓐ [토익 공식 3]	02 ⓑ [토익 공식 3]
03 ⓐ [토익 공식 2]	04 ⓑ [토익 공식 3]
05 ⓐ [토익 공식 1]	06 ⓑ [토익 공식 2]
07 ⓑ [토익 공식 3]	

08 economical → economic [토익 공식 3]
09 newly → new [토익 공식 1]
10 awareness → aware [토익 공식 4]
11 like → likely [토익 공식 4]
12 Difference → Different [토익 공식 1]
13 understandable → understanding [토익 공식 3]
14 regionally → regional [토익 공식 1]

해석 01 조종사가 안전벨트 착용 표시등을 켜서 탑승객들이 각자의 자리로 돌아갔다.
02 David Williams는 Brookstone 대학에서 다섯 학기 연속으로 좋은 성적을 받지 못했다.
03 Mr. Walton은 매일 아침을 먹는 동안 신문을 읽는다.
04 대체로, 올해 총 생산량은 지난 3년간의 총 생산량에 필적한다.
05 그 여행사 직원은 Mr. Kang의 곧 있을 출장의 수정된 일정표를 요청했다.
06 통근 시간대의 교통량이 너무 많아서, 통근자들은 흔히 도로 위에서 몇 시간을 보낸다.
07 그 이사가 이번 연휴에 근로자들에게 휴가를 더 준 것은 매우 사려 깊었다.
08 경기 침체는 공공 지출에 악영향을 미쳐 왔다.
09 정부는 도급업자들에게 올림픽을 위한 새 경기장 건립에 입찰할 것을 요청했다.
10 저희 호텔이 직불카드를 받지 않는다는 규정을 알아 두십시오.
11 기자에 따르면, Ogden 은행은 다음 분기에 사업을 확장할 것 같다.
12 다양한 쟁점들이 지난 이사회 중에 논의되었다.
13 Dr. Menkin은 관심과 배려로 환자들을 치료하는 이해심 있는 의사이다.
14 상공 회의소의 목표는 지역 기업에 도움을 주는 것이다.

Hackers Test
p.156

Part 5

01 (C)	02 (B)	03 (B)	04 (D)	05 (D)
06 (B)	07 (C)	08 (B)	09 (D)	10 (A)
11 (B)	12 (C)	13 (A)	14 (B)	15 (C)
16 (D)	17 (A)	18 (D)		

Part 6

19 (D)	20 (C)	21 (B)	22 (C)

01 형용사 자리 채우기

해설 명사(solutions)를 꾸미기 위해서는 형용사가 와야 하므로 (C) innovative (혁신적인, 독창적인)가 정답이다.

해석 Mr. Jefferson은 훌륭한 협상자로 여겨지는데 그가 사람들이 흥미롭다고 생각하는 방식으로 혁신적인 해결책을 제시하기 때문이다.

어휘 consider v. ~을 ~라고 여기다, 숙고하다 negotiator n. 협상자, 교섭자
appealing adj. 흥미로운, 매력적인 innovate v. 혁신하다, 도입하다
innovator n. 혁신자, 도입자 innovation n. 혁신

02 형용사 자리 채우기

해설 명사(consultants)를 꾸미기 위해서는 형용사 (B) 또는 분사 (C)가 올 수 있다. '법률 고문'이라는 의미를 만드는 형용사 (B) legal(법률의)이 정답이다. 빈칸에 분사 (C) legalized를 쓰면 '적법화된 고문'이라는 어색한 의미가 된다.

해석 Coleridge사는 제안된 합병에 대한 의견을 묻기 위해 다수의 유능한 법률 고문들을 불렀다.

어휘 call in 부르다, ~에 전화하다 competent adj. 유능한 merger n. 합병
legalize v. 적법화하다 legally adv. 법률(합법)적으로, 법률상

03 문맥에 어울리는 형용사 채우기

해설 빈칸은 관계사 that절의 보어 자리이다. '정보가 신뢰할 만하다'라는 의미가 되어야 하므로 (C) reliant(의지하는)가 아닌 (B) reliable(신뢰할 만한, 믿을 수 있는)이 정답이다. 선행사(information)와 명사(reliability)가 의미적으로 동격 관계에 있지 않으므로 명사 (A)는 답이 될 수 없다. 분사 (D)를 쓰면 수동태 동사(is relied)가 되는데 rely는 자동사이므로 수동태를 만들 수 없어 역

시 답이 될 수 없다.

해석 중개인들은 고객들이 현명한 투자 결정을 내릴 수 있도록 완전히 신뢰할 만한 정보를 고객들에게 제공해야 한다.

어휘 broker n. 중개인 reliability n. 신뢰도, 확실성 rely v. 의지하다, 의존하다

04 형용사 자리 채우기

해설 명사(details)를 꾸미기 위해서는 부사 (A), (B), (C)가 아니라 형용사가 와야 하므로 (D) more가 정답이다. 참고로, (C) quite는 부사임에도 명사 앞에 올 수 있지만, 'a/an + 명사' 앞에만 올 수 있다.

해석 마케팅부장은 제품에 대해 더 많은 세부 사항을 받을 때까지 광고 전략에 대해서 어떠한 충고도 하기를 꺼린다.

어휘 unwilling adj. 꺼리는, 싫어하는, 마지못해 strategy n. 전략
mostly adv. 주로, 일반적으로 quite adv. 꽤, 상당히

05 사람명사 추상명사 구별하여 채우기

해설 주어 자리에 올 수 있는 것은 명사이므로 (A), (C), (D)가 정답의 후보이다. 직원들에게 일정을 알리는 주체는 사람이어야 하므로 사람명사 (D) supervisor(감독자)가 정답이다. 추상명사 (A) supervision(감독)이나 (C) supervising(감독, 감리)을 쓰면 '감독이 직원들에게 일정을 알리다'라는 어색한 의미가 된다.

해석 기술자가 모든 사무실 컴퓨터의 소프트웨어를 업데이트하기 전에, 사무실 감독자가 이메일을 통해서 직원들에게 일정을 알릴 것이다.

어휘 via prep. (특정한 사람, 시스템 등을) 통해서 supervise v. 감독하다

06 문맥에 어울리는 형용사 채우기

해설 빈칸은 보어 자리이므로 형용사 (B), (D)와 명사 (C)가 정답의 후보이다. 보어가 주어를 설명해서 '참석자들이 ~할 책임이 있다'라는 의미가 되어야 하므로 형용사 (B) responsible(책임이 있는)이 정답이다. be responsible for는 '~에 책임이 있다'라는 표현임을 기억해 두자. 참고로, (D) responsive(민감하게 반응하는)는 be responsive to(~에 민감하게 반응하다)의 형태로 쓰인다. 주어(attendees)와 명사(responsibility)가 동격 관계에 있지 않으므로 명사 (C)는 답이 될 수 없다.

해석 회의 기획자들은 참석자들이 본인의 숙소를 스스로 마련할 책임이 있다는 것을 명시한 편지를 보냈다.

어휘 state v. 명시하다 arrange v. 마련하다 accommodation n. 숙소
responsibly adv. 책임감 있게, 틀림없이 responsibility n. 책임

07 문맥에 어울리는 형용사 채우기

해설 명사(effort)를 꾸미기 위해서는 형용사 (C)나 (D)가 와야 한다. '공동의 노력'이라는 의미가 되어야 하므로 (C) collective(공동의, 집단의)가 정답이다. 형용사 (D) collecting은 '모금용의 노력'이라는 어색한 의미가 되므로 답이 될 수 없다.

해석 상을 받은 로고 디자인의 창작은 그래픽팀의 여러 멤버들에 의한 공동의 노력의 결과였다.

어휘 award-winning adj. 상을 받은 collecting adj. 모금용의; n. 수집, 모금

08 형용사 자리 채우기

해설 빈칸은 주격 보어 자리이므로 형용사 (B)와 명사 (D)가 정답의 후보이다. '지시를 따른다'라는 의미가 되어야 하므로 형용사 (B) compliant(따르는, 부응하는)가 정답이다. 주어(The employees)와 명사(compliancy)가 동격 관계에 있지 않으므로 명사 (D)는 답이 될 수 없다.

해석 직원들은 공장 시설 점검 중에 보건부 직원에 의해 전달된 지시들을 따랐다.

어휘 representative n. 직원, 대리인, 대표자 inspection n. 점검, 검사
comply v. 따르다, 준수하다 compliancy n. 준수, 따름

09 명사에 맞는 수량 표현 채우기

해설 복수 명사(small business owners) 앞에는 복수 명사 앞에 쓰는 수량 표현이 와야 하므로 (D) most가 정답이다. 최상급 표현 (A) the most가 오면 '가장 소규모 자영업자'라는 어색한 의미가 된다. 부사 (B) almost가 오면 '거의 소규모 자영업자'라는 어색한 의미가 되며 (C) most of가 빈칸에 오려면 빈

칸 뒤에 the가 있어야 한다.

해석 그 조사는 대부분의 소규모 자영업자들이 세법을 개선하려는 정부의 노력에 불만족스러워한다는 것을 보여준다.

어휘 demonstrate v. 보여주다, 입증하다 reform v. 개선하다 tax code 세법

10 형용사 자리 채우기

해설 명사(process)를 꾸미기 위해서는 형용사가 필요하므로 (A) creative(창조적인)가 정답이다. 분사 (B)도 형용사 역할을 할 수 있지만, '창조된 과정'이라는 어색한 의미를 만든다.

해석 James Davis는 비평적으로 호평을 받은 그의 소설을 쓰는 것은 3년 동안 지속된 힘든 창조적인 과정이었다고 인터뷰에서 말했다.

어휘 state v. 말하다 critically adv. 비평적으로 acclaimed adj. 호평을 받은
last v. 지속하다; adj. 마지막의 create v. 창조하다

11 형용사 자리 채우기

해설 빈칸은 주격 보어 자리이므로 분사 (A), 형용사 (B), 명사 (C)가 정답의 후보이다. '출장을 자주 다니는 사람들에게 매력적이다'라는 의미가 되어야 하므로 be attractive to(~에게 매력적이다)를 만드는 (B) attractive가 정답이다. 분사 (A)는 be동사(is)와 함께 수동태 문장을 만들어 '여행 가방 라인이 매혹됐다'라는 어색한 의미가 되므로 답이 될 수 없다. 명사 (C)는 주어(line of luggage)와 명사(attraction)가 동격 관계에 있지 않으므로 답이 될 수 없다.

해석 그 제조사의 가장 최신의 여행 가방 라인은 출장을 자주 다니는 사람들에게 매력적인데, 그 가방이 그들의 필요를 염두에 두고 만들어졌기 때문이다.

어휘 with ~ in mind ~을 염두에 두고 need n. 필요(한 것), 요구
attract v. 매혹하다, 끌다 attractive adj. 매력적인, 마음을 끄는
attraction n. 매력, 명소 attractively adv. 보기 좋게

12 형용사 자리 채우기

해설 명사(Web site)를 꾸미는 것은 형용사 역할을 할 수 있는 분사이므로 (C) personalized(개인화된)가 정답이다. 동사 (A), 부사 (B), 명사 (D)는 형용사 자리에 올 수 없다.

해석 새로운 소셜 네트워킹 서비스는 등록된 사용자들이 친구들과 가족들이 볼 수 있는 개인화된 웹사이트에 콘텐츠를 게시하도록 해준다.

어휘 registered adj. 등록된 post v. 게시하다 content n. 콘텐츠, 내용물
personalize v. (개인의 필요에) 맞추다, 개인화하다
personally adv. 직접, 개인적으로 personalization n. 개인화, 인격화

13 형용사 자리 채우기

해설 명사(reason)를 꾸미기 위해서는 형용사 (A)나 분사 (C)가 와야 한다. '특정한 원인'이라는 의미가 되어야 하므로 (C) specified(명시된, 지정된)가 아닌 (A) specific(특정한)이 정답이다.

해석 그 회사의 감소하는 시장 점유율의 특정한 원인이 아직 밝혀지지 않았지만, 고조된 경쟁이 한 요인인 것 같다.

어휘 decline v. 감소하다 determine v. 밝히다, 알아내다 factor n. 요인
specifics n. 세목, 상세한 특성 specifically adv. 특히, 구체적으로

14 형용사 자리 채우기

해설 명사(method)를 꾸미기 위해서는 형용사가 필요하므로 (B) available(이용 가능한)이 정답이다. 이처럼 available은 명사를 뒤에서 수식할 수 있다.

해석 여성 의류 시장에서의 자사 시장 점유율을 높이려는 회사의 시도에서 모든 이용 가능한 방법들이 고려될 것이다.

어휘 attempt n. 시도, 도전 share n. 시장 점유율 apparel n. 의류
availability n. 유용성, (입수) 가능성 availably adv. 쓸모 있게, 유효하게

15 현재분사와 과거분사 구별하여 채우기

해설 명사(design)를 꾸미기 위해서는 분사 (B) 또는 (C)가 와야 한다. 수식 받는 명사(design)와 분사가 '디자인이 개선되다'라는 의미의 수동 관계이므로 과거분사 (C) improved(개선된)가 정답이다. 복합 명사(명사 + 명사)가 아닌 경우, 명사(improvement)는 명사(design)를 꾸밀 수 없으므로 명사 (D) improvement는 답이 될 수 없다.

해석 새 휴대용 컴퓨터의 개선된 디자인은 더 커진 화면과 더욱 강력해진 처리 장치를 포함하기 때문에 많은 소비자들의 마음을 끈다.

어휘 appeal v. 마음을 끌다, 간청하다 improve v. 개선하다, 향상시키다

16 명사에 맞는 수량 표현 채우기

해설 불가산 명사(trouble) 앞에는 불가산 명사 앞에 쓰는 수량 표현인 (B) 또는 (D)가 와야 한다. '작년보다 더 적은 문제'라는 의미가 되어야 하므로 (B) least(가장 적은)가 아닌 (D) less(더 적은)가 정답이다.

해석 연간 재고 조사는 경영진이 세부 계획을 제시했기 때문에 작년보다 문제가 적을 것이다.

어휘 come up with (해답 등을) 제시하다, 찾아내다

17 명사와 수 일치된 지시형용사 채우기

해설 명사(report)를 앞에서 꾸밀 수 있는 것은 지시형용사 (A) 또는 (C)이다. 명사(report)가 단수이므로 (A) This가 정답이다. (C) These는 복수 명사 앞에 오는 지시형용사이다.

해석 Ms. Sanders가 쓴 이 보고서는 회사의 해외 지점 각각의 재무 실적에 대한 철저한 비교를 포함한다.

어휘 thorough adj. 철저한 comparison n. 비교
financial performance 재무 실적

18 문맥에 어울리는 형용사 채우기

해설 명사(story)를 꾸미기 위해서는 형용사 (B), (D), 또는 분사 (C)가 와야 한다. '성공적인 기사로 상을 타다'라는 의미가 되어야 하므로 (D) successful (성공적인)이 정답이다. (B) successive(연속의)를 쓰면 '연속적인 기사로 상을 타다'라는 어색한 의미가 된다. 타동사 succeed(~을 잇따르다)로 과거분사(succeeded)로 만들면 '매우 잇따르는 기사'라는 어색한 의미를 만들기 때문에 (C) succeeded는 답이 될 수 없다.

해석 파티에서, Jack의 많은 신문사 동료들은 Jack이 지구 온난화의 영향에 대한 매우 성공적인 기사로 상을 탄 것에 대해 그를 축하해 주었다.

어휘 colleague n. 동료 win an award 상을 타다
global warming 지구 온난화 succeed v. 잇따르다, 성공하다

19-22는 다음 이메일에 관한 문제입니다.

수신: Janet Burke
발신: Pat Summers, 인사부 관리자

Ms. Burke께,

[19]우리는 독일 베를린에 있는 자사 해외 지점으로의 귀하의 전근 요청이 승인되었음을 알려 드리고자 합니다. [20]우리는 귀하의 취업 비자를 신청하기 위해 6월 4일까지 독일 대사관에 방문하려고 계획하고 있으므로, 첨부된 파일에 명시된 서류를 최대한 빨리 제출하셔야 합니다.

전근에 앞서, 귀하는 서로 다른 문화 사이의 대처 기술에 관한 프로그램뿐만 아니라 독일어 집중 강좌 코스도 끝마쳐야 할 것입니다. 그 후에, 귀하는 베를린 지점에서의 오리엔테이션에 참석하게 될 것입니다. [21]이 프로그램들은 귀하가 새로운 환경에 익숙해지게 할 것입니다. 우리는 이러한 수업들이 매우 유용한 것으로 판명될 것이라고 믿습니다.

[22]교육을 받는 동안, 귀하는 우리가 후임자를 찾게 될 때까지 홍보부 조수로서의 현 직책에서 계속 활동할 것인데, 이는 3, 4주 이내가 될 것입니다.

귀하의 새로운 발령에 대한 문의 사항이 있으시면, 저에게 연락하여 주십시오.

Pat Summers 드림

---

transfer v. 전근 가다, 이동하다 embassy n. 대사관 work visa 취업 비자
relocation n. 전근, 재배치 intensive course 집중 (강좌) 코스
coping skills 대처 기술 undergo v. 받다(겪다) replacement n. 후임자
appointment n. 발령, 임명, 약속 get in touch with ~와 연락(접촉)하다

---

19 동사 어휘 고르기 전체 문맥 파악

해설 '해외 지점으로의 전근 요청이 ____되다'라는 문맥이므로 빈칸 앞의 has been과 함께 수동태를 만드는 p.p.형 (A) received(접수하다), (C) declined (거절하다), (D) approved(승인하다)가 정답의 후보이다. 빈칸이 있는 문장만으로 정답을 고를 수 없으므로 주변 문맥이나 전체 문맥을 파악한다. 뒤 문장에서 '취업비자를 신청할 계획이므로 서류를 제출하라(We plan ~ to apply for your work visa, so you must submit the documents)'고 한 후, 전근 이전에 받아야 할 교육에 대해 설명하고 있으므로 전근을 가기 위한 준비를 하는 이유는 요청이 승인되었기 때문임을 알 수 있다. 따라서 (D) approved가 정답이다.

어휘　add v. 더하다

20 현재분사와 과거분사 구별하여 채우기

해설　빈칸이 명사(documents) 뒤에 있으므로 명사를 꾸밀 수 있는 분사 (B)와 (C)가 정답의 후보이다. 명사와 분사가 '서류가 명시되다'라는 의미의 수동 관계이므로 과거분사 (C) specified가 정답이다.

21 알맞은 문장 고르기

해석　(A) 강의가 시작하기 전에 귀하가 만드신 커리큘럼을 제출하십시오.
　　　(B) 이 프로그램들은 귀하가 새로운 환경에 익숙해지게 할 것입니다.
　　　(C) 귀하는 후임자가 될 사람을 교육하셔야 합니다.
　　　(D) 우리는 귀하가 그 지점에 완전히 적응하였음을 확신합니다.

해설　빈칸에 들어갈 알맞은 문장을 고르는 문제이므로 빈칸의 주변 문맥이나 전체 문맥을 파악한다. 앞부분에서 전근에 앞서 독일어 강좌 코스와 서로 다른 문화 사이의 대처 기술에 관한 프로그램 및 새로운 지점에서의 오리엔테이션에 참석해야 할 것이라고 했고, 뒤 문장 'We have every confidence that these sessions will prove very helpful.'에서 이러한 수업이 유용한 것으로 판명될 것이라고 믿는다고 했으므로 빈칸에는 이 프로그램들이 이메일의 수신자가 새로운 환경에 익숙해지게 할 것이라는 내용이 들어가야 함을 알 수 있다. 따라서 (B) These programs should familiarize you with your new surroundings가 정답이다.

어휘　submit v. 제출하다　familiarize v. 익숙해지게 하다
　　　surrounding n. (주변)환경　replace v. ~의 후임자가 되다, 대체하다
　　　adapt v. 적응하다

22 보어 자리 채우기

해설　stay는 주격 보어를 갖는 동사이므로 보어로 사용될 수 있는 명사 (A), (D) 또는 형용사 (C)가 와야 한다. '현 직책에서 계속 활동하게 될 것이다'라는 의미가 되어야 하므로 빈칸에는 주어(you)를 설명해 주는 형용사 (C) active(활동적인)가 정답이다. 분사 (B) acted는 '행동된'을 의미하므로 문맥에 어울리지 않는다.

어휘　act v. 행동하다, 연기하다　activity n. 활동

Chapter 13 부사

1 부사 자리　　p.159
　1. (A)　2. (D)　3. (C)

1. 부사 자리 채우기

해설　형용사(unsound)를 꾸미기 위해서는 부사가 와야 하므로 부사 (A) structurally(구조적으로)가 정답이다. 명사 (B), 동사 또는 분사 (C), 형용사 (D)는 형용사를 꾸밀 수 없다.

해석　한 측량 기사의 정밀 조사는 그 건물이 공사 동안에 표준 이하의 재료를 사용했기 때문에 구조적으로 견고하지 않을 수 있음을 보여준다.

어휘　surveyor n. 측량 기사, 감독자　inspection n. 정밀 조사
　　　unsound adj. 견고하지 못한, 불안정한　substandard adj. 표준 이하의, 열악한

2. 부사 자리 채우기

해설　동사(access)를 꾸미기 위해서는 부사가 와야 하므로 부사 (D) freely(자유롭게)가 정답이다. 형용사 (A), (B), (C)는 동사를 꾸밀 수 없다.

해석　최근 전기 통신의 발전은 휴대 전화 소유자들이 다양한 디지털 매체 콘텐츠에

자유롭게 접근하는 것을 가능하게 했다.

어휘　advance in ~에서의 발전, 진보
　　　telecommunications n. (원거리) 전기 통신　a wide range of 다양한

3. 부사 자리 채우기

해설　전치사구(after ~ Inglewood Financial)를 꾸미기 위해서는 부사가 와야 하므로 부사 (C) shortly(바로, 곧)가 정답이다. 형용사 (A), (B)와 동사 (D)는 전치사를 꾸밀 수 없다.

해석　Mr. Ling은 Inglewood 금융 회사의 보스턴 지점에 있는 관리직 면접을 본 후에 바로 고용되었다.

어휘　managerial adj. 관리의, 경영의　branch n. 지점

2 비슷한 형태를 갖고 있지만 의미가 다른 부사　p.160
　1. (D)　2. (A)　3. (C)

1. 의미에 맞는 부사 채우기

해설　동사(submitted)를 꾸미기 위해서는 부사가 와야 하므로 (A), (D)가 정답의 후보이다. '늦게 제출한 직원들을 책망하다'라는 의미가 되어야 하므로 (D) late(늦게)가 정답이다. (A) lately(최근에는)는 어색한 문맥을 만든다.

해석　그 관리자는 마감 일자를 맞춘 직원들을 칭찬하고 보고서를 하루나 이틀 늦게 제출한 직원들을 책망하는 내용의 회람을 보냈다.

어휘　commend v. 칭찬하다　meet the deadline 마감 일자를 맞추다
　　　admonish v. 책망하다, (강력히) 충고하다　submit v. 제출하다

2. 의미에 맞는 부사 채우기

해설　'거의 13퍼센트 증가하다'라는 의미가 되어야 하므로 (A) nearly(거의)가 정답이다. (B) near(가까이)는 어색한 문맥을 만든다.

해석　쌀과 옥수수 같은 기초 농산물의 가격이 1월 이래로 거의 13퍼센트 증가했다.

어휘　commodity n. 농산물

3. 의미에 맞는 부사 채우기

해설　동사(practice)를 꾸미기 위해서는 부사가 와야 하므로 (A)와 (C)가 정답의 후보이다. '열심히 연습하다'라는 의미가 되어야 하므로 (C) hard(열심히)가 정답이다. (A) hardly(거의 ~않다)를 쓰면 '거의 연습하지 않다'라는 의미가 되므로 답이 될 수 없다. 동사 (B)와 동명사 (D)는 동사를 꾸밀 수 없다.

해석　연주자들은 공연 전에 반드시 그들이 연주하는 음악 작품에 완전히 익숙해지도록 열심히 연습한다.

어휘　make it a point to 반드시 ~하다　piece n. 작품, 조각

3 부사 선택 1 : 시간 부사 already/still/yet, ever/ago/once　p.161
　1. (B)　2. (A)　3. (C)

1. 시간 부사 채우기

해설　'벌써 시작했다'는 의미가 되어야 하므로 '벌써'를 의미하는 (B) already가 정답이다. (A) yet은 'have yet to + 동사원형'의 형태가 아닌 이상 긍정문에 올 수 없다. (C) never(결코 ~않다)와 (D) then(그러고 나서)은 어색한 문맥을 만든다.

해석　교통이 너무 복잡해서 우리가 극장에 도착했을 때쯤에는, 벌써 수상작 연극이 시작했다.

어휘　by the time ~할 때쯤　award-winning 상을 받은

2. 시간 부사 채우기

해설　'아직 고안하지 못했다'는 의미가 되어야 하므로 '아직'을 의미하는 (A) yet 또는 (B) still이 정답의 후보이다. 이 중 not 뒤에 올 수 있는 (A) yet이 정답이다. 참고로, still은 'I still don't understand it.(나는 아직도 이해하지 못한다.)'처럼 not 앞에 온다.

해석 기반 시설 계약이 공개 입찰을 통해 주어져야 함에도 불구하고, 행정당국은 그
것을 감안하는 정책을 아직 고안하지 못했다.

어휘 infrastructure n. 기반 시설, 하부 구조 award v. 주다, 수여하다; n. 상
open bid 공개 입찰 administration n. 행정당국, 정부
devise v. 고안하다 allow for ~을 감안하다, 고려하다, 참작하다

3. 시간 부사 채우기

해설 '이틀 전에'라는 의미가 되어야 하므로 '이전에'를 의미하는 (B) once 또는
(C) ago가 정답의 후보이다. 이 중 시간 표현(two days) 바로 다음에 와서
그 시간 이전에 일어난 일을 나타내는 (C) ago가 정답이다.

해석 노동조합 지도자들은 약 이틀 전쯤 대부분의 회사 사원들이 파업에 들어간 이
래로 줄곧 경영진 대표들과 협상을 해오고 있다.

어휘 negotiate with ~와 협상하다 management n. 경영진
representative n. 대표(자) go on strike 파업하다

---

4 부사 선택 2 : 빈도 부사 always, usually, often, hardly p.162
1. (D) 2. (B) 3. (C)

1. 빈도 부사 채우기

해설 '평가는 보통 매 분기 말에 이루어진다'는 의미가 되어야 하므로 (D) usually
(보통)가 정답이다.

해석 Calvin's 할인점에서, 팀장들에 대한 평가는 보통 매 분기 말에 이루어진다.

어휘 evaluation n. 평가, 사정 quarter n. 분기, 4분의 1
constantly adv. 끊임없이

2. 빈도 부사 채우기

해설 '최신 정보를 제공하기 위해 보고서를 자주 작성하다'라는 의미가 되어야
하므로 (B) often(자주)이 정답이다. 잠시 후에 어떤 일이 일어날 것이라는
문맥, 또는 잠시 후에 어떤 일이 일어났다는 상황에 쓰이는 시간 부사 (A)
soon(곧) 또는 (C) shortly(곧)를 정답으로 선택하지 않도록 주의해야 한다.

해석 연구원들은 부장들과 중역들에게 최신 정보를 제공하기 위해 프로젝트 현황
보고서를 자주 작성한다.

어휘 status n. 현황, 상황 update n. 최신 정보

3. 빈도 부사 채우기

해설 '그렇게 열심히 하는 사원은 거의 본 적이 없다'는 의미가 되어야 하므로 부정
의 의미(거의 ~않다)를 담고 있는 부사 (C) Rarely가 정답이다. 참고로, 이 문
장은 부정 부사 rarely가 문장 맨 앞으로 나와 주어와 동사가 도치된 형태이다.

해석 Mr. Conrad는 소프트웨어 설계 분야에 많은 경력을 가지고 있으면서 그렇게
열성적이고 열중하는 신입 사원은 거의 본 적이 없다.

어휘 eager adj. 열성적인 enthusiastic adj. 열중하는 recruit n. 신입 사원

---

5 부사 선택 3 : 접속부사 besides, therefore, however,
otherwise p.163
1. (D) 2. (B) 3. (B)

1. 접속부사 채우기

해설 '제안이 받아들여지지만 나중에 실행된다'는 의미가 되어야 하므로 (D)
however(그러나)가 정답이다.

해석 직원들이 내는 제안은 언제나 경영진에 의해 받아들여지지만, 대부분의 제안
들은 보통 이사회가 열리고 난 후에야 실행된다.

어휘 not A until B B하고 나서야 A하다 act upon(= on) 실행하다

2. 부사 otherwise 채우기

해설 '달리 명시되어 있지 않은 한'이라는 의미가 되어야 하므로 (B) otherwise(달
리)가 정답이다.

해석 달리 명시되어 있지 않은 한, 이 데이터베이스에 있는 연락처 정보는 6월 30일
현재 최신입니다.

어휘 unless conj. ~하지 않는 한 state v. 명시하다
up-to-date adj. 최신의, 최근의 as of ~ 현재로

3. 접속부사 채우기

해설 접속사 and가 명령문(Please check ~ statement)과 명령문(make ~
transfer)을 연결하고 있으며, '이름을 확인하고 나서 지불하라'는 의미가 되
어야 하므로 (B) then(그러고 나서)이 정답이다.

해석 대금 청구서에 인쇄된 수령인의 이름을 확인하고 나서 신용카드나 온라인 이
체를 통해 결제해 주시기 바랍니다.

어휘 recipient n. 수령인, 받는 사람 billing statement 대금 청구서
make a payment 결제하다 transfer n. 이체, 환승; v. 이동하다

---

6 부사 선택 4 : 강조 부사 just, right, only, well, even, quite
p.164
1. (B) 2. (C) 3. (C)

1. 강조 부사 채우기

해설 전치사구(for the period indicated)를 강조하면서 '오직 명시된 기간에만'
이라는 의미가 되어야 하므로 (B) only(오직)가 정답이다.

해석 이 사업 비자는 여권 소지자가 오직 명시된 기간에만 그 나라 내에서 여행할
수 있도록 한다.

어휘 allow A to do A가 ~할 것을 허락하다 indicate v. 명시하다, 표시하다

2. 강조 부사 채우기

해설 전치사구(below the market value)를 강조하면서 '~보다 훨씬 아래'라는
의미를 만드는 (C) well(훨씬)이 정답이다. 형용사나 다른 부사를 꾸미는 (A)
very와 (B) so는 전치사구를 강조하지 못한다. 명사를 꾸미는 (D) such 역
시 전치사구를 강조하지 못한다.

해석 Parmalac사는 ImClone사 주식을 판매 당시의 시장 가치보다 훨씬 낮은 가
격에 매각했다.

어휘 stock n. 주식 market value 시장 가치

3. 강조 부사 채우기

해설 비교급(more aggressive) 앞의 빈칸에는 비교급을 강조하는 부사가 와야
하므로 (C) much가 정답이다. (A) just는 원급을 강조하는 부사이고 (D)
quite는 최상급을 강조하는 부사이므로 비교급을 강조하지 못한다. (B) very
는 형용사나 부사를 꾸미는 역할을 하며 비교급을 강조하지 못한다.

해석 그 회사는 경쟁에서 앞서려면 광고에 대해 훨씬 더 적극적인 접근이 필요하다
는 결정을 내렸다.

어휘 aggressive adj. 적극적인, 공격적인 pull ahead of ~을 앞서다, 앞지르다

---

7 부사 선택 5 : so, such, very, too p.165
1. (C) 2. (D) 3. (A)

1. so/such/very/too 구별하여 채우기

해설 부정관사 a 앞에 와서 명사(event)를 꾸밀 수 있어야 하므로 (C) such(매우)
가 정답이다. (B) far(훨씬)는 비교급을 강조하는 부사이며 부정관사 a 앞에
올 수 없으므로 답이 될 수 없다. 참고로, such는 뒤에 온 that절과 연결되어
'매우 ~여서 ~하다'는 의미를 가진다.

해석 그 도시의 문화 전시회는 매우 큰 행사여서 여러 위원회들이 축제 행사들을 계
획하는 데 필요해요.

어휘 cultural adj. 문화의 exposition n. 전시회, 박람회
sizable adj. 꽤 큰, 상당한 크기의 festivity n. 축제 행사

2. so/such/very/too 구별하여 채우기

해설   분사(satisfied)를 꾸밀 수 있어야 하므로 (D) very가 정답이다. 부정적인 문장이 아니므로 (A) too는 쓸 수 없다. (B) enough는 분사를 뒤에서 수식하고, (C) even은 비교급을 강조하는 역할을 하므로 답이 될 수 없다.

해석   그 일이 급히 이루어졌다는 것을 고려하면 그 이사가 결과에 매우 만족했다는 것은 놀라웠다.

어휘   **considering that**절 ~을 고려하면   **in a rush** 급히, 서둘러서

3. so/such/very/too 구별하여 채우기

해설   '세금은 감당하기에 너무 부담스럽다'는 부정적인 의미가 되어야 하므로 부정의 의미를 갖는 too를 포함한 (A) much too가 정답이다.

해석   만일 제안된 세율 인상이 승인된다면, 그 지역의 세금은 중소기업들이 감당하기에는 너무나 부담스러울 것이다.

어휘   **burdensome** adj. 부담스러운, 힘든   **handle** v. 감당하다, 다루다

---

8 부사 선택 6 : also/too/as well/either, later/thereafter, forward/ahead   p.166

    1. (C)   2. (B)   3. (B)

1. 부사 채우기

해설   '또한 확인할 필요가 있다'는 의미가 되어야 하므로 '또한'을 의미하는 부사 (B), (C) 또는 (D)가 정답의 후보이다. 빈칸이 문장 중간에 있으므로 문장 앞이나 중간에 쓸 수 있는 (C) also가 정답이다. 부정문에 또 다른 부정문을 덧붙일 때 쓰는 (B) either와 문장 끝에 와야 하는 (D) as well은 답이 될 수 없다.

해석   Ms. Peters는 그 디자인이 훌륭하다고 생각하지만, 그녀는 그것들이 진열창에서 어떻게 보이는지 또한 확인할 필요가 있다.

어휘   **marvelous** adj. 훌륭한, 놀라운   **display** n. 진열; v. 전시하다

2. 부사 채우기

해설   '그 이후에 제공되다'라는 의미가 되어야 하므로 (B) thereafter(그 이후에)가 정답이다. (A) later는 시간 표현 없이 쓰일 때 '지금 이후에'를 의미하므로 문맥에 어울리지 않는다.

해석   비행기는 오후 3시 15분에 이륙할 것이고, 그 이후에 곧 가벼운 간식이 승객들에게 제공될 것이다.

어휘   **take off** 이륙하다   **shortly** adv. 곧   **suddenly** adv. 갑자기, 돌연히

3. 부사 채우기

해설   '앞을 향해서 진보하다'라는 의미가 되어야 하므로 상태를 가리키는 (A) ahead(앞에)가 아닌 방향을 가리키는 (B) forward(앞을 향해서)가 정답이다. (C) toward는 전치사이므로 뒤에 명사 없이 쓰일 수 없다.

해석   경영진은 Ms. Bernal의 전문 지식 때문에 그녀를 회사의 최고 경영자로 임명한 것이 커다란 진보라고 여겼다.

어휘   **executive** n. 경영진   **appointment** n. 임명   **expertise** n. 전문 지식

Hackers Practice   p.167

01 ⓑ [토익 공식 3]   02 ⓐ [토익 공식 7]
03 ⓑ [토익 공식 7]   04 ⓐ [토익 공식 5]
05 ⓑ [토익 공식 7]   06 ⓐ [토익 공식 8]
07 ⓑ [토익 공식 6]
08 Always → Usually [토익 공식 4]
09 great → greatly [토익 공식 2]
10 맞는 문장 [토익 공식 1]
11 significance → significantly [토익 공식 1]
12 never → ever [토익 공식 4]
13 맞는 문장 [토익 공식 1]
14 slight → slightly [토익 공식 1]

해석   01   이사회는 회사가 건설하려고 계획하는 컨벤션 센터의 위치를 아직 고르지 못했다.

       02   실험실에서 필요로 하는 장비가 매우 값비싸서 경영진은 구매를 미뤘다.

       03   많은 사람들이 참석할 것이라는 생각에, 그들은 너무 많은 음식을 준비했다.

       04   오늘 안으로 호텔 예약을 취소하지 않으면, 우리는 25퍼센트의 취소 수수료를 내야 한다.

       05   직원들은 관리자에 의해 제안된 수수료 제도에 매우 만족했다.

       06   Online Solutions사는 고객들에게 통신망 관리, 웹사이트 디자인, 그리고 또한 검색 엔진 최적화 서비스도 제공한다.

       07   그의 예정된 연설 바로 직전에, Mr. Richards는 사무실로부터 급한 전화가 왔다는 이야기를 들었다.

       08   보통, 나는 업무 일정이 바쁠 때 점심으로 샌드위치를 먹는다.

       09   Ciko 화장품사는 새로운 마케팅 전략을 적용함으로써 매출을 대단히 증가시킬 수 있었다.

       10   그 최고 경영자는 모든 지점에서 복장 규정 방침이 엄격히 시행될 것을 요구한다.

       11   추가 직원을 고용하는 것은 공장의 생산 능력이 크게 확대되는 결과를 가져왔다.

       12   그 회계사는 출장 경비에 대한 상환을 거의 승인하지 않는다.

       13   연구원들은 정확히 무엇이 견본에 문제를 일으켰는지 밝혀내야 한다.

       14   최근의 보고서는 지난 분기 동안 개인 소비 지출이 약간 증가했음을 보여준다.

Hackers Test   p.168

Part 5

01 (C)	02 (C)	03 (D)	04 (C)	05 (B)
06 (D)	07 (B)	08 (D)	09 (A)	10 (D)
11 (A)	12 (A)	13 (B)	14 (A)	15 (B)
16 (D)	17 (D)	18 (B)		

Part 6

19 (B)	20 (C)	21 (A)	22 (A)

01 부사 자리 채우기

해설   동명사(investigating)를 꾸미기 위해서는 부사가 와야 하므로 부사 (C) extensively(대대적으로, 광범위하게)가 정답이다. 명사 (A), 형용사 (B), 분사 (D)는 답이 될 수 없다.

해석   당국은 비행기 충돌의 원인을 대대적으로 조사하는 데에 꼬박 1년을 보냈다.

어휘   **official** n. 당국(자), 공무원   **investigate** v. 조사하다, 수사하다

02 의미에 맞는 부사 채우기

해설   최상급을 만드는 the most가 있으며 '가장 높게 추천되는 사무용 소프트웨어'라는 의미가 되어야 하므로 '(위상·평가·금액 등이) 높게, 매우'를 의미하는 (C) highly가 정답이다. (A) high는 '(높이·목표 등이) 높이'를 의미한다. 명사 (B)는 분사(recommended)를 수식하는 부사 자리에 올 수 없으며, 최상급 (D) highest는 most와 함께 쓰일 수 없다. 참고로, 빈칸 뒤의 recommended와 어구를 이루는 highly를 정답으로 선택하는 식으로 문제를 풀 수도 있다. (highly recommended: 적극적으로 추천되는)

해석   새로운 Perfect Presenter는 오늘날 시장에서 가장 높게 추천되는 사무용 소프트웨어이다.

03 강조 부사 채우기

해설   부정적인 의미를 갖는 too(너무)는 much나 far로 강조되므로 (D) far가 정답이다. 참고로, much와 far는 비교급을 강조하기도 한다.

해석   우리 회사에서 이용 가능한 제도 프로그램은 너무나 고급용이라 수습직원들은 사용할 수 없다.

어휘   **drafting** n. 제도   **trainee** n. 수습직원, 실습생   **pretty** adv. 꽤, 상당히

04 강조 부사 채우기

해설   원급(as comfortable)을 강조해야 하므로 (C) just(꼭)가 정답이다.

해석 게스트 하우스에서 머무르는 것은 일류 호텔에 투숙하는 것보다 더 저렴하고, 그곳의 편의 시설 또한 꼭 (일류 호텔의 편의 시설 만큼이나) 쾌적하다.

어휘 guest house 게스트 하우스, 소규모 호텔 check into ~에 투숙하다
first-class adj. 일류의 amenity n. 편의 시설
comfortable adj. 쾌적한, 편안한

05 부사 자리 채우기

해설 비교급 표현(as ~ as)을 걷어 내면 빈칸에 동사(will be restored)를 꾸미기 위해서 부사가 와야 한다는 것을 알 수 있다. 따라서 부사 (B) promptly(신속하게)가 정답이다.

해석 일단 2층의 정전 문제가 해결되면, 건물 전체의 전기 공급은 가능한 한 신속하게 복구될 것이다.

어휘 power outage 정전 prompt adj. 즉각적인, 지체 없는; v. 촉발하다, 유발하다
promptness n. 재빠름, 신속

06 의미에 맞는 부사 채우기

해설 '좀처럼 근무일을 거르지 않는다'라는 의미를 만들기 위해서는 hardly ever (좀처럼 ~않다)가 와야 하므로 (D) hardly(거의 ~않다)가 정답이다. (C) nearly를 쓰려면 문장에 not이 있어야 '거의 ~않다'는 의미가 된다.

해석 Mr. Richards는 절대로 지각하지 않고 좀처럼 근무일을 거르지 않는 매우 헌신적인 직원으로 알려져 있다.

어휘 dedicated adj. 헌신적인, 열심인

07 부정형용사 채우기

해설 all of와 명사(restaurant rating services) 사이에는 정관사 the가 와야 하므로, the를 포함하고 있는 (B) the other가 정답이다. 참고로, the 대신 소유격이 올 수도 있다.

해석 그 식당은 새로 생겼음에도 불구하고, 이미 Food Review지와 다른 모든 식당 평가 기관에서 호평을 받아 왔다.

어휘 rating n. 평가, 등급 service n. 기관, 공공사업

08 부사 자리 채우기

해설 형용사(important)를 꾸미기 위해서는 부사가 와야 하므로 부사 (D) progressively(계속해서)가 정답이다. 동사 또는 명사 (A), 분사 (B), 형용사 (C)는 형용사를 꾸밀 수 없다.

해석 소비자의 의견은 제품이 보여지고 포장되는 방식을 결정하는 데 있어 계속해서 더욱 중요한 요소가 되고 있다.

어휘 factor n. 요소 present v. 보여주다, 내놓다; n. 선물
progress v. 진전을 보이다, 진행하다 progressive adj. 진보적인, 점진적인

09 부사 자리 채우기

해설 '미리 전화를 하라'는 의미가 되어야 하므로 '미리'라는 뜻의 부사 (A) ahead가 정답이다. (B) once(한 때)는 막연한 과거의 시점을 나타내는 ever와 비슷하게 쓰이는 부사이므로, 미래의 행동을 나타내는 표현에는 올 수 없다. (C) whether는 절과 절을 연결하는 역할을 하므로 답이 될 수 없다. 명사 (D) advance는 전치사 in과 함께 쓰여 in advance(미리)가 되어야 ahead와 같은 의미의 부사로 쓰일 수 있다.

해석 Pendleton사는 카탈로그에 있는 모든 상품의 재고가 공인 대리점에 있다고 항시 보장할 수 없으니, 확인하기 위해 미리 전화 주십시오.

어휘 in stock 재고로, 비축되어 authorized adj. 공인된
outlet n. 대리점, 판매점, 출구 make sure 확인하다

10 의미에 맞는 부사 채우기

해설 동사(have sprung)를 꾸미기 위해서는 부사가 와야 하므로 (B), (C), (D)가 정답의 후보이다. '최근에 생겨났다'는 의미가 되어야 하므로 (B) late(늦게) 또는 (C) later(나중에)가 아닌 (D) lately(최근에)가 정답이다.

해석 농업이 주요 산업인 시골 지역에 많은 대형 투자 프로젝트들이 최근 생겨났다.

어휘 spring up 생기다, (갑자기) 발생하다 rural adj. 시골의 agriculture n. 농업

11 부사 자리 채우기

해설 빈칸 앞의 명령문(proceed to the Web site) 전체를 꾸미기 위해서는 부사가 와야 하므로 부사 (A) immediately(즉시)가 정답이다. 형용사 (B)와 명사 (C), (D)는 문장 전체를 꾸밀 수 없다.

해석 온라인 계좌를 신청하려면, 즉시 웹사이트로 이동하여 가입 버튼을 클릭하세요.

어휘 register v. 신청하다, 등록하다 online account 온라인 계좌
proceed v. 이동하다, 진행하다 immediate adj. 즉각적인
immediateness n. 곧 일어남 immediacy n. 신속성, 속도

12 접속부사 채우기

해설 현재완료 시제(has agreed)의 has와 agreed 사이에는 부사가 와야 하며 '생산성을 증대시켜야 하므로 급여 인상에 동의했다'는 의미가 되어야 하므로 접속부사인 (A) therefore(그러므로)가 정답이다. 부사절 접속사 (C)는 절의 맨 처음에 와야 하므로 답이 될 수 없다.

해석 Synco-Vac사는 생산성을 증대시켜야 하므로, 회사는 급여 인상을 연간 수익에 기반을 두는 것에 동의했다.

어휘 boost v. ~을 증대시키다 productivity n. 생산성
base on ~에 기반을 두다, 근거를 두다 in contrast 반대로

13 빈도 부사 채우기

해설 '필요한 만큼 자주 수분 공급 크림이 사용된다'라는 의미가 되어야 하므로 (B) often(자주)이 정답이다.

해석 추운 날에 피부가 건조해지는 것을 예방하기 위해, 수분 공급 크림은 필요한 만큼 자주 사용될 수 있습니다.

어휘 dry out 건조하게 하다 moisturizer n. 수분 공급 크림

14 부사 채우기

해설 '완전히 끝내지 못했다'는 의미를 만들기 위해서는 not quite(완전히 ~하지 않다)가 와야 하므로 (A) quite가 정답이다. 참고로, 'I'm not quite ready.'는 '완전히 준비되지 않았다.'는 의미이다.

해석 Ms. Jones는 직원들에게 비록 분석을 완전히 끝내지 못했더라도 연구 결과를 제출하라고 요청했다.

15 부사 자리 채우기

해설 동사(Had been divided)를 꾸미기 위해서는 부사가 필요하므로 (B) equally(똑같이)가 정답이다. 참고로, Had ~ researchers는 가정법의 if절(If the information collection work had been divided ~ researchers)의 if가 생략된 후 주어와 조동사 had의 위치가 바뀐 도치 구문이다.

해석 정보 수집 작업이 연구원들 사이에 똑같이 나눠졌다면, 응답자 설문 조사는 지금쯤 끝났을 것이다.

어휘 equality n. 평등 equalize v. 균등하게 하다

16 부사 자리 채우기

해설 문장 전체를 수식하기 위해서는 부사가 와야 하므로 부사 (D) Interestingly (흥미롭게도, 재미있게)가 정답이다. 명사 또는 동사 (A), 동사 또는 분사 (B), 분사 (C)는 답이 될 수 없다.

해석 흥미롭게도, 그 제품에 대해 부정적인 의견을 남긴 사람들 중 누구도 실제로 그 제품을 구매하지 않았다.

어휘 negative adj. 부정적인 comment n. 의견, 논평

17 수식어 거품 채우기

해설 이 문장은 주어(Mr. Bennett)와 동사(works)를 갖춘 완전한 절이므로 ____ serving ~ Giltmore Corporation은 수식어 거품으로 보아야 한다. 이 수식어 거품은 동사가 없는 거품구이므로, 보기 중 거품구를 이끌 수 있는 전치사 (D) Besides(~ 외에도)가 정답이다.

해석 Giltmore사의 이사회 구성원으로 근무하는 것 외에, Mr. Bennett은 몇몇 중소기업의 자문 위원으로도 일한다.

어휘 serve v. 근무하다, 일하다 board n. 이사회
smaller enterprise 중소기업 as good as ~나 다름없는

18 부사 자리 채우기

해설 동사(should be summarized)를 꾸미기 위해서는 부사가 필요하므로 (B) simply(간단히, 단순히)가 정답이다. 참고로, 부사 more가 부사 simply를 강조하고 부사 much가 more를 강조하여 '훨씬 더 간단히'라는 의미를 나타낸다.

해석 슈퍼마켓에서 판매되는 식료품의 영양소 함유량은 사람들이 라벨에 있는 것이 무엇인지 이해하는 데 도움이 되도록 훨씬 더 간단히 요약되어야 한다.

어휘 nutrient n. 영양소 content n. 함유량, 내용물, 항목
summarize v. 요약하다 simplicity n. 간단함, 평이함

19-22는 다음 편지에 관한 문제입니다.

Marsha Berger
Tyrrell 제조 회사

Ms. Berger께,

¹⁹제가 회의에 참석할 수 없음을 귀하께 알려드리기 위해 편지를 씁니다. 자사가 현재 구조 조정을 겪고 있기 때문에, 제가 뉴욕을 떠날 수 없습니다. ²⁰저희가 귀사의 제품을 자사의 제품 라인에 포함시키자는 귀하의 제안을 발전시키기를 간절히 바라고 있다는 것에 대해 안심하셔도 됩니다.

저의 불참을 대신하여, 귀하를 7월 7일에 Tilton 호텔에서 있을 조찬 회의에 초대하고자 합니다. ²¹그러나, 그날 저와 만날 수 없다면, 저는 7월 8일 저녁에도 시간이 있습니다. 어떤 날이 더 편할지 제게 알려주시기 바랍니다. ²²7월 10일에 자사 이사회에 귀하의 아이디어를 제출할 수 있도록 귀하와 함께 그 아이디어에 대해 곧 논의하고 싶습니다. 저희는 이전부터 다른 제조사들과의 협력 시도를 추구해왔습니다. 그러므로, 귀하의 제안은 경영진에게 큰 관심사가 될 것입니다.

저는 양사가 같은 방향으로 나아가고 있고, 합작 사업이 상호 간에 이익이 될 것이라고 믿습니다. 이번 주에 귀하와 만날 기회가 있기를 기대하겠습니다.

Justin White
Garnet Distribution사

undergo v. ~을 겪다, 받다 restructuring n. 구조 조정
assure v. 안심시키다, 확신하다 incorporate v. 포함하다, 합병하다
free adj. 시간이 있는, 선약이 없는 board of directors 이사회
cooperative adj. 협력의 endeavor n. 시도
head v. (특정 방향으로) 가다, 향하다 joint venture 합작 사업
mutually adv. 상호 간에 beneficial adj. 이익이 되는
look forward to ~을 기대하다 opportunity n. 기회

19 알맞은 문장 고르기

해석 (A) 이는 제안서가 결국 거절되었음을 알리기 위함입니다.
(B) 제가 회의에 참석할 수 없음을 귀하께 알려드리기 위해 편지를 씁니다.
(C) 이는 저희가 합의했던 것이 예정대로 진행될 것임을 보장하기 위함입니다.
(D) 귀하께서 어떤 장소에서 만나기를 원하시는지를 묻기 위해 편지를 씁니다.

해설 빈칸에 들어갈 알맞은 문장을 고르는 문제이므로 빈칸의 주변 문맥이나 전체 문맥을 파악한다. 뒤 문장 'As our company is currently undergoing restructuring, it is impossible for me to leave New York.'에서 회사가 현재 구조 조정을 겪고 있기 때문에 편지의 발신자(I)가 뉴욕을 떠날 수 없다고 한 후, 뒷부분에서 불참을 대신하여 다른 날짜에 있을 조찬 회의에 초대하고자 한다고 했으므로 빈칸에는 회의에 참석할 수 없다는 것을 알리기 위해 편지를 쓴다는 내용이 들어가야 함을 알 수 있다. 따라서 (B) I am writing to inform you that I will be unable to attend the conference가 정답이다.

어휘 turn down 거절하다 proceed v. 진행하다 as scheduled 예정대로

20 to 부정사 채우기

해설 eager는 'be eager to 부정사'의 형식으로 사용되는 형용사이므로 (C) to develop이 정답이다.

어휘 be eager to do 간절히 ~하고 싶다 develop v. 발전시키다, 개발하다

21 접속부사 채우기 주변 문맥 파악

해설 빈칸이 콤마와 함께 문장 맨 앞에 온 접속부사 자리이므로, 앞 문장과 빈칸이 있는 문장의 의미 관계를 파악하여 접속부사인 (A), (B), (C) 중 하나를 정답으로 골라야 한다. 앞 문장에서 7월 7일에 열릴 조찬 회의에 초대하고 싶다고 했고, 빈칸이 있는 문장에서 '만일 그날 만날 수 없다면(if you are unable to meet ~ on that day)'이라고 했으므로 앞 문장과 대조되는 내용의 문장에서 사용되는 (A) However(그러나)가 정답이다. 부사절 접속사 (D) While(~인 데 반하여)는 콤마 없이 바로 문장이 와야 하므로 답이 될 수 없다.

어휘 furthermore adv. 더욱이, 게다가 besides adv. 게다가, 그밖에는

22 시간 부사 채우기

해설 '곧 논의하고 싶다'는 의미가 되어야 하므로 '곧'을 의미하는 (A) soon이 정답이다.

어휘 since adv. ~한 때로부터 still adv. 아직 often adv. 자주

Chapter 14 전치사

1 전치사 선택 1 : 시간과 장소 in/at/on   p.171
1. (B) 2. (B) 3. (C)

1. in/at/on 구별하여 채우기

해설 시각(4 o'clock) 앞에는 전치사 at을 쓰므로 (B) at이 정답이다.

해석 부동산 중개인과의 인터뷰는 내일 오후 4시로 예정되어 있다.

어휘 real estate agent 부동산 중개인 be scheduled for ~로 예정되어 있다

2. in/at/on 구별하여 채우기

해설 큰 공간 내의 장소(urban centers) 앞에는 전치사 in을 쓰므로 (B) in이 정답이다.

해석 신제품 저지방 감자칩이 스프링필드에서 인기 상품이 된다면, 그것은 미국 전역의 몇몇 다른 도심지에서 시험 판매될 것이다.

어휘 low-fat 저지방의 hot seller 인기 상품 test-market 시험 판매하다
urban center 도심지, 도시 중심가

3. in/at/on 구별하여 채우기

해설 '기계들이 제자리에 있다'라는 의미를 만들기 위해서는 in place(제자리에)가 와야 하므로 (C) in이 정답이다.

해석 모든 시추기들은 제자리에 있으며 최고 책임자의 지시에 맞춰 석유 추출을 시작할 준비가 되어 있다.

어휘 drilling machine 시추기, 천공기 (땅속 깊이 구멍을 뚫는 장치)
extraction n. 추출

2 전치사 선택 2 : 시점과 기간   p.172
1. (C) 2. (C) 3. (B)

1. 시점/기간 전치사 구별하여 채우기

해설 '오늘로부터 2주 후로 연기되었다'라는 의미가 되어야 하므로 (C) from(~로부터)이 정답이다.

해석 최고 경영자가 모스크바 지사의 경영 문제를 처리하기 위해 갑자기 유럽으로 떠나야 했었기 때문에, 회식은 오늘로부터 2주 후로 연기되었다.

어휘 unexpectedly adv. 갑자기, 예상외로 postpone v. 연기하다, 미루다

2. 시점/기간 전치사 구별하여 채우기

해설 '전입일 15일 이전에'라는 의미가 되어야 하므로 (C) prior to(~ 전에)가 정답

이다. 이처럼 prior to 앞에는 시간 표현(15 days)이 와서 '얼마간의 시간 이전'을 의미할 수 있다.

해석   임대 보증금은 전입일 최소 15일 이전에 집주인의 은행 계좌로 이체되어야 한다.

어휘   rental adj. 임대의; n. 집세   deposit n. 보증금   transfer v. 이체하다
landlord n. 집주인, 주인, 지주   moving-in 전입(move in: 이사 오다)

3. 시점/기간 전치사 구별하여 채우기

해설   기간을 나타내는 표현(one month)이 있으므로 기간을 나타내는 전치사 (B) within(~ 이내에)이 정답이다. 전치사 (A), (C), (D)는 시점을 나타내므로 답이 될 수 없다.

해석   부품 및 서비스 보증이 유효하려면 품질 보증서는 상품 수령 한 달 이내에 회사로 반송되어야 한다.

어휘   warranty n. 품질 보증서   valid adj. 유효한, 타당한

---

3   전치사 선택 3 : 위치   p.173
    1. (A)   2. (D)   3. (B)

1. 전치사 채우기

해설   '사람들 사이에서'라는 의미가 되어야 하므로 '~ 사이에'를 나타내는 전치사 (A) 또는 (C)가 정답의 후보이다. 이 중 '셋 이상의 사람'(people aged 45 years and above) 앞에 쓰이는 전치사 (A) among이 정답이다. (C) between은 두 개의 사물이나 두 사람 사이를 나타낼 때 쓰인다.

해석   최근의 한 연구는 지난 20년간 45세 이상의 사람들 사이에서 처방약 복용이 꾸준히 증가해 왔음을 말해 준다.

어휘   prescription drug 처방약   steadily adv. 꾸준히   decade n. 10년

2. 전치사 채우기

해설   '공사 중이다'라는 의미를 만들기 위해서 under construction(공사 중인)이 와야 하므로 (D) under가 정답이다.

해석   Lester가 있는 사무실 건물의 별관은 4월까지 공사 중일 것이다.

어휘   annex n. 별관, 부가물

3. 전치사 채우기

해설   '평균보다 20퍼센트 이하로 떨어졌다'라는 의미가 되어야 하므로 (B) below(~ 이하)가 정답이다.

해석   지난 여름의 많은 강수량은 비치웨어 판매량이 평균보다 20퍼센트 이하로 하락하는 것을 야기했다.

어휘   precipitation n. 강수량

---

4   전치사 선택 4 : 방향   p.174
    1. (B)   2. (A)   3. (B)

1. 전치사 채우기

해설   '명단에서 삭제되다'라는 의미가 되어야 하므로 (B) from(~에서)이 정답이다.

해석   온라인 소식지 구독자들은 정기 구독 갱신을 요청하는 이메일에 답하지 않는다면 그들의 이름이 우편 수취인 명단에서 삭제될 것이라는 공지를 받았다.

어휘   newsletter n. (클럽, 조직의) 소식지, 회보   mailing list 우편 수취인 명단
request v. 요청하다, 신청하다   renewal n. 갱신, 부활

2. 전치사 채우기

해설   '도로가 산을 통과하여 나 있다'는 의미가 되어야 하므로 (A) through(~을 통과하여)가 정답이다.

해석   산을 관통하게 될 새 고속도로는 야생 생물과 생태계에 돌이킬 수 없는 피해를 입힐 것으로 예상된다.

어휘   be expected to do ~할 거라 예상되다   cause damage 피해를 입히다
irreversible adj. 돌이킬 수 없는   wildlife n. 야생 생물
ecosystem n. 생태계   run through ~을 관통하다

3. 전치사 채우기

해설   '설치물이 손이 닿지 않는 곳에 매달려 있었기 때문에'라는 의미를 만들기 위해서 out of reach(손이 닿지 않는)가 와야 하므로 (B) out of가 정답이다.

해석   고장 난 조명 설치물이 손이 닿지 않는 곳에 매달려 있었기 때문에, 기술자는 발판 사다리를 요청했다.

어휘   broken adj. 고장 난   fixture n. 설치물, 고정물   stepladder n. 발판 사다리

---

5   전치사 선택 5 : 이유, 양보, 목적, 제외, 부가   p.175
    1. (B)   2. (B)   3. (A)

1. 전치사 채우기

해설   '그를 위해서 특별 행사를 개최하다'라는 의미가 되어야 하므로 (B) for(~를 위해서)가 정답이다.

해석   회사는 Kyle Wood의 뛰어난 판매 기록을 인정하여 그를 위한 특별 행사를 개최할 것이라고 발표했다.

어휘   in recognition of ~을 인정하여, ~의 답례로   outstanding adj. 뛰어난

2. 전치사 채우기

해설   that절은 주어(the proposal)와 동사(would be presented)를 갖춘 완전한 절이므로 ____ any changes는 수식어 거품으로 보아야 한다. 이 수식어 거품은 동사가 없는 거품구이므로, 보기 중 거품구를 이끌 수 있는 전치사 (A)와 (B)가 정답의 후보이다. '어떠한 변동 사항도 없다면'이라는 의미가 되어야 하므로 (B) barring(~이 없다면)이 정답이다.

해석   관리자는 어떠한 변동 사항도 없다면, 지속 가능한 개발 단체들의 특별 회의에서 그 제안이 제출될 것이라고 말했다.

어휘   sustainable development 지속 가능한 개발, 환경친화적 개발

3. 전치사 채우기

해설   이 문장은 주어(Western Steel's stock price)와 동사(rose)를 갖춘 완전한 절이므로 ____ the overall decline은 수식어 거품으로 보아야 한다. 이 수식어 거품은 동사가 없는 거품구이므로, 보기 중 거품구를 이끌 수 있는 전치사 (A), (B), (D)가 정답의 후보이다. '철강 산업의 수익성의 전반적인 감소에도 불구하고 Western Steel의 주가가 올랐다'는 의미가 되어야 하므로 (A) in spite of가 정답이다.

해석   철강 산업의 수익성의 전반적인 감소에도 불구하고 Western Steel의 주가가 크게 올랐다.

어휘   steel n. 철강, 강철   stock price 주가   decline n. 감소, 쇠퇴
profitability n. 수익성   except(= excepting) prep. ~을 제외하고
apart from ~ 이외에는, ~뿐만 아니라

---

6   전치사 선택 6 : of, ~에 관하여   p.176
    1. (C)   2. (C)   3. (A)

1. 전치사 채우기

해설   the end가 this month의 부분이므로, 부분을 나타내는 전치사 (C) of가 정답이다.

해석   그 회사의 독립 회계 감사는 이달 말까지 완료될 것으로 예상된다.

어휘   audit n. 회계 감사, 심사, 회계 보고서

2. 전치사 채우기

해설   공개 토론회(a panel discussion)의 토론 주제가 새 의학 기술과 관련된 윤리적 문제들(ethical issues related to new medical technology)이므로, 특정한 주제 앞에 쓰이는 (C) on(~에 관하여)이 정답이다.

해석 Dr. Wilson은 새 의학 기술과 관련된 윤리적 문제들에 관한 공개 토론회의 사회를 보기 위해 워크숍에 참석할 것이다.

어휘 **moderate** v. ~의 사회를 보다 **panel discussion** 공개 토론회
ethical adj. 윤리적인

3. 전치사 채우기

해설 '노동자 급여에 관한 분쟁'이라는 의미가 되어야 하므로 (A) over(~에 관하여)가 정답이다.

해석 노동자 급여에 관한 분쟁은 공장에 고용된 조합원들이 파업에 들어가는 결과를 초래했다.

어휘 **dispute** n. 분쟁, 논쟁 **union member** 조합원
go on strike 파업에 들어가다

---

7 전치사 선택 7 : 기타 전치사   p.177
　　1. (A)　　2. (B)　　3. (D)

1. 전치사 채우기

해설 '조세 규정 준수의 증거로서 사본을 보관하다'라는 의미가 되어야 하므로 (A) as(~로서)가 정답이다.

해석 정부는 모든 기업들이 그들의 재무제표 사본을 조세 규정 준수의 증거로서 보관해야 한다고 제안한다.

어휘 **financial statements** 재무제표 **compliance** n. 준수, 순종

2. 전치사 채우기

해설 '화상 회의를 통해 많은 항공료를 절약한다'라는 의미가 되어야 하므로 (B) through(~을 통해서)가 정답이다.

해석 기업들은 화상 회의를 통해 항공 요금을 절약할 수 있는데, 화상 회의는 사무실을 떠나지 않고도 국제 회의가 가능하도록 한다.

어휘 **airfare** n. 항공 요금 **video conference** 화상 회의
international meeting 국제 회의

3. 전치사 채우기

해설 '발송부 직원들을 제외하고'라는 의미를 만들기 위해서 exception과 함께 쓰일 수 있는 전치사는 with이므로 정답은 (D) with이다. 참고로, with the exception of는 '~을 제외하고'라는 뜻으로 사용되는 표현이라는 것을 알아두자.

해석 임금 인상을 요구했던 발송부 직원들을 제외하고, 모든 근로자들은 봉급과 근무 시간에 대해 만족을 표시했다.

어휘 **contentment** n. 만족, 흡족감 **shipping** n. 발송, 선적
with the exception of ~을 제외하고

---

8 동사, 형용사, 명사와 함께 쓰인 전치사 표현   p.178
　　1. (C)　　2. (C)　　3. (B)

1. 전치사 채우기

해설 동사 transfer와 함께 쓰이는 전치사 (C) to가 정답이다.

해석 경영진은 이전에 관리부가 맡았던 특정 책무들을 회계부로 이양하기로 결정했다.

어휘 **administrative** adj. 관리상의, 행정의, 경영상의 **accounting** n. 회계(학), 경리

2. 전치사 채우기

해설 명사 advocate와 함께 쓰이는 전치사 (C) of가 정답이다.

해석 Mr. Han은 가정과 학교 기반의 프로그램을 통한 효과적인 조기 교육의 옹호자이다.

어휘 **advocate** n. 옹호자, 변호사; v. 변호하다, 옹호하다
early education 조기 교육

---

3. 전치사 채우기

해설 '고객들의 불만에 응하여'라는 의미가 되어야 하므로 (B) In response to (~에 응하여)가 정답이다.

해석 장시간 기다림에 대한 투숙객들의 불만에 응하여, 호텔은 2개의 엘리베이터를 더 추가할 예정이다.

Hackers Practice   p.179

01 ⓐ [토익 공식 2]	**02** ⓐ [토익 공식 5]
03 ⓑ [토익 공식 6]	**04** ⓑ [토익 공식 2]
05 ⓐ [토익 공식 5]	**06** ⓑ [토익 공식 7]
07 ⓐ [토익 공식 5]	**08** on → at/by [토익 공식 1, 2]
09 on → in [토익 공식 1]	**10** 맞는 문장 [토익 공식 1]
11 At → In [토익 공식 4]	**12** for → of [토익 공식 8]
13 to → for [토익 공식 5]	
14 below → under [토익 공식 3]	

해석 **01** 그 나라는 정치적 불안정의 결과로 지난 10년 동안 투자가 거의 없어 어려움을 겪어 왔다.
02 상승하는 원자재 가격으로 인해, 수입 물가는 8월에 16퍼센트만큼 상승했다.
03 최근 몇 년간, 개인 투자자들은 도시의 이 지역에 점점 매력을 느꼈다.
04 이메일이나 실시간 인터넷 지원을 통한 도움 요청은 업무 시간 동안에만 처리된다.
05 다가오는 재정 위기에도 불구하고, 국가 경제는 불황에서 회복되었다.
06 이력서 작성을 포함한 다양한 구직 기술에 관한 워크숍이 연중 내내 제공된다.
07 매입 비용을 제외하고, 그 관리자는 운영과 구조 조정에 대한 추가적인 지출을 예상했다.
08 최근 보고서는 다음 분기 초에 물가 상승률이 4퍼센트에 달할 수 있다고 했다.
09 Green Garden은 그 도시에서 가장 인기 있는 채식 식당이다.
10 손님들은 보관을 위해 호텔의 안내 데스크에 개인 물품을 맡길 수 있다.
11 품행의 관점에서, 직원들은 서로를 존중하여 대하는 것이 기대된다.
12 노동절을 기념하여, 미국의 모든 거래소는 9월 6일에 영업을 하지 않을 것이다.
13 승객들은 연결 항공편을 위해 탑승권을 반드시 소지해야 함을 다시 한번 알려 드립니다.
14 그 금융 회사는 탈세에 관해 조사 중이지만, 대부분의 기업 변호사들은 위반된 법이 없었다는 데 동의한다.

Hackers Test   p.180

Part 5

01 (C)	02 (B)	03 (C)	04 (B)	05 (B)
06 (A)	07 (C)	08 (D)	09 (C)	10 (D)
11 (C)	12 (A)	13 (C)	14 (A)	15 (D)
16 (C)	17 (C)	18 (A)		

Part 6

19 (A)	20 (C)	21 (B)	22 (C)

01 in/at/on 구별하여 채우기

해설 날짜(August 26)에 사용되는 전치사 (C) on이 정답이다.

해석 그 회사의 기념 행사가 8월 26일에 열릴 것이므로, 참석자들은 이 날짜를 메모해 두어야 한다.

어휘 **anniversary** n. 기념일 **make a note of** ~을 메모해 두다

02 전치사 채우기

해설 '~에서 여행하기 가까운 거리에 위치하다'라는 의미를 만들기 위해서 within easy traveling distance of(~에서 여행하기 가까운 거리에)가 와야 하므로 (B) within이 정답이다.

해석 그 혁신적인 웹사이트는 여행객들이 그들의 호텔에서 여행하기 가까운 거리에 있는 흥미로운 장소들을 찾을 수 있게 해준다.

어휘 innovative adj. 혁신적인 search for ~을 찾다
within easy distance 가까운 거리에

03 시점/기간 전치사 구별하여 채우기

해설 '11월 5일까지 신청서를 제출하다'라는 의미가 되어야 하므로 '~까지'를 의미하는 전치사 (C)와 (D)가 정답의 후보이다. 그 중 '행동이 발생할 때까지'를 의미하는 전치사 (C) by가 정답이다. (D) until은 '상태가 계속될 때까지'를 의미하기 때문에 답이 될 수 없다.

해석 보스턴 기술 박람회에 참가하기를 희망하는 기업들은 11월 5일까지 신청서를 제출해야 한다.

어휘 participate in ~에 참가하다 exhibition n. 박람회, 전시회

04 전치사 채우기

해설 '팀에 의해 제출된 디자인 대신 원래 디자인을 사용한다'라는 의미가 되어야 하므로 (B) instead of(~ 대신에)가 정답이다.

해석 Ms. Turner는 우리에게 마케팅팀이 제출했던 디자인 대신 원래의 디자인을 제품 전시에 사용해 달라고 부탁했다.

어휘 original adj. 원래의, 최초의, 독창적인 display n. 전시, 진열

05 전치사 채우기

해설 이 문장은 주어(The workshop), 동사(teaches), 간접 목적어(managers and employees), 직접 목적어(how to dispute someone else's ideas)를 갖춘 완전한 절이므로 _____ causing offense는 수식어 거품으로 보아야 한다. 이 수식어 거품은 동사가 없는 거품구이므로, 거품구를 이끌 수 있는 전치사 (A)와 (B)가 정답의 후보이다. '무례하지 않게, 무례한 일 없이'라는 의미가 되어야 하므로 (B) without(~ 없이)이 정답이다.

해석 그 워크숍은 관리자와 직원들에게 상대방의 의견에 무례하지 않게 이의를 제기하는 방법을 가르친다.

어휘 dispute v. 이의를 제기하다 offense n. 무례, 불쾌한 것
whereas conj. ~인 반면 otherwise adv. 그렇지 않으면

06 전치사 채우기

해설 '비용에 관계없이'라는 의미가 되어야 하므로 of와 함께 사용되어 '~에 관계없이, 상관없이'를 의미하는 전치사 역할을 하는 (A) regardless가 정답이다. 참고로, (C) regarding(~에 관하여)은 of 없이 혼자 와야 전치사 역할을 할 수 있다.

해석 그 관리자는 비용에 관계없이 모든 상품들이 주말까지 운송되기를 원한다.

어휘 item n. 상품, 항목, 조항 by the end of ~의 말까지
regardless of ~에 관계없이, 상관없이 regardful adj. 주의 깊은, 유의하는
regarding prep. ~에 관해서는 regard v. ~로 여기다, 간주하다

07 부사 자리 채우기

해설 전치사구(in New Zealand)를 꾸미기 위해서는 부사가 와야 하므로 부사 (C) primarily(주로)가 정답이다. 형용사 또는 명사 (A), 동사 또는 분사 (B), 형용사 (D)는 전치사구를 꾸밀 수 없다.

해석 그 영화감독의 최신 작품은 주로 뉴질랜드에서 촬영되었지만, 몇몇 장면은 로스앤젤레스와 뉴욕에서 촬영되었다.

어휘 shoot v. 촬영하다, 쏘다 prime adj. 가장 중요한; n. 전성기; v. 준비하다
primarily adv. 주로 primary adj. 주요한, 기본적인

08 전치사 채우기

해설 '공간 부족 때문에'라는 의미가 되어야 하므로 (D) because of(~ 때문에)가 정답이다.

해석 몇몇 직원들은 본사 내의 공간 부족 때문에 회의실에 있는 작업 장소를 사용할 것을 요청받았다.

어휘 workstation n. 작업 장소 conference room 회의실 lack n. 부족
main office 본사 except for ~을 제외하고는
thanks to ~ 덕분에 aside from ~을 제외하고는

09 시점/기간 전치사 구별하여 채우기

해설 시점을 나타내는 표현(early next year)이 있으며 내년 초까지 신청 받지 않는 '상태가 계속된다'는 의미이므로 (A) by가 아닌 (C) until이 정답이다. 부사절 접속사 (B) when은 거품절을 이끄는 역할을 하며, 거품구(early next year)를 이끄는 자리에는 올 수 없다. 기간을 나타내는 전치사 (D) through는 답이 될 수 없다.

해석 자금 압박 때문에, BCN사는 내년 초까지 해외 지점으로의 전근 신청을 받지 않을 것이다.

어휘 funding n. 자금, 재정 지원 constraint n. 압박, 제약, 통제
transfer n. 전근, 이동; v. 이동하다 overseas adj. 해외의

10 전치사 채우기

해설 '둘 사이의 차이점'이라는 의미를 만들기 위해서 difference between A and B(A와 B의 차이)가 와야 하므로 (D) between이 정답이다.

해석 가구 감정사들은 진짜 골동품과 복제품의 차이점을 구별할 수 있다.

어휘 appraiser n. 감정사, 감정관 tell v. 구별하다, 말하다
genuine adj. 진짜의 antique n. 골동품
reproduction n. 복제품, 복제

11 전치사 채우기

해설 동사 congratulate와 함께 쓰여 '축하하다'라는 의미를 만드는 (C) on이 정답이다.

해석 Field 미술관은 David Young이 국내 미술 작품상 후보에 오른 것을 축하하기 위하여 7월 3일에 행사를 개최할 것이다.

어휘 congratulate A on B A에게 B를 축하하다
nomination n. 후보에 오름, 추천, 지명

12 in/at/on 구별하여 채우기

해설 기간(the last ten years) 앞에는 전치사 in(~ 동안)을 사용하므로 (A) In이 정답이다.

해석 지난 10년 동안, 전문 비즈니스 서비스는 Washington 지역 내 전체 일자리 증가의 38퍼센트를 차지해왔다.

어휘 comprise v. (비율이) 차지하다, 구성되다 region n. 지역, 영역

13 전치사 채우기

해설 '돕기를 고대하다'라는 의미가 되어야 하므로 동사 look과 함께 쓰여 '~을 고대하다'라는 의미를 만드는 (C) forward가 정답이다. look out(~을 찾아보다), look on(방관하다, 구경하다)은 뒤에 전치사 to를 갖지 않는다. look down은 to가 아니라 on과 함께 쓰여 '~을 얕보다, 무시하다'라는 의미를 갖는다.

해석 언제나처럼, Gray Consulting사는 법률상의 도움이 필요하실 때 귀하를 돕기를 고대합니다.

어휘 as always 언제나처럼, 평소와 같이 assist A with B B에 관해 A를 돕다
legal adj. 법률상의, 법률에 관한, 합법의

14 in/at/on 구별하여 채우기

해설 모퉁이(the corner)는 두 길이 교차하는 '지점'을 가리키므로 (A) at이 정답이다.

해석 그 대리점의 급여 지급 사무소는 무역 위원회 센터 맞은편인 Faribault가와 23번가 사이 모퉁이에 위치해 있다.

어휘 payroll n. 급여 지급, 급여 대장 across from ~의 맞은편에

15 시점/기간 전치사 구별하여 채우기

해설 빈칸 뒤에 기간을 나타내는 표현(the next couple of days)이 있으므로 기간을 나타내는 전치사 (D) over가 정답이다. 전치사 (B) by와 (C) from은 시점을 나타내므로 답이 될 수 없다. 특정일 앞에 쓰이는 (A) on도 올 수 없다.

해석 Wageworks사는 앞으로 며칠 동안 거의 절반가량의 컴퓨터 장비를 최신 장치로 교체할 계획이다.

어휘　**replace A with B** A를 B로 교체하다　**nearly** adv. 거의, 대략, 간신히
　　　equipment n. 장비, 장치　**updated** adj. 최신의　**device** n. 장치

16 전치사 채우기

해설　동사 associate(associated)와 함께 '~과 관련되다'라는 뜻으로 쓰이는 (C) with가 정답이다.

해석　많은 사람들은 관리비, 재산세와 같이 자택 소유와 관련된 높은 비용에 대해 걱정한다.

어휘　**be concerned about** ~에 대해 걱정하다　**homeownership** n. 자택 소유
　　　maintenance fee 관리비　**property tax** 재산세
　　　associated with ~과 관련된

17 사람명사 추상명사 구별하여 채우기

해설　동사(entitles)의 목적어 자리에는 동명사 (B) 또는 명사 (C), (D)가 올 수 있다. '구독자들에게 상품권을 준다'는 의미가 되어야 하므로 (C) subscribers (구독자들)가 정답이다.

해석　*Teen*지는 특별 판촉 행사를 하고 있는데, 그것은 정기 구독자에게 일류 의상실 상품권을 주는 것이다.

어휘　**promotion** n. 판촉 행사, 승진, 촉진, 장려　**gift certificate** 상품권
　　　boutique n. 의상실, 부티크　**subscribe** v. 구독하다, 가입하다, 청약하다
　　　entitle A to B A에게 B의 권리를 주다

18 전치사 채우기

해설　'상여금을 도입함으로써 생산량을 증가시키다'라는 의미가 되어야 하므로 (A) by(~함으로써)가 정답이다.

해석　그 부장은 생산 할당량을 채운 모든 직원들을 위한 상여금을 도입함으로써 생산량을 증가시키고자 한다.

어휘　**production** n. 생산량　**introduce** v. 도입하다　**bonus** n. 상여금, 특별 수당
　　　quota n. 할당량

19-22는 다음 기사에 관한 문제입니다.

Orashi 항공이 새로운 노선을 시작하다

9월 9일—나이지리아의 Orashi 항공은 서아프리카에서 가장 빠르게 성장하는 항공사 중 하나이다. ¹⁹지난 10년 동안, 그 항공사는 가나, 차드, 그리고 카메룬으로의 빈번한 항공편에서 세계 최상급의 서비스를 제공함으로써 독자적으로 유명해져 왔다. ²⁰이제, 이 기업은 첫 번째 유럽 노선을 시작함으로써 확장할 것을 기대하고 있다.

Orashi 항공은 아부자에서 파리까지의 직항편을 개설함으로써 시작할 것이다. 이는 유럽 여행의 증가 추세에 대응하는 것이다. ²¹이 노선에 더하여, 빠른 시일 내에 런던으로의 항공편 서비스를 개시할 계획이다.

²²확장을 용이하게 하기 위해, Orashi 항공은 새로운 AeroJet 540-XW 비행기 두 대를 구입할 예정인데, 이것들은 연비가 더 높고 350명의 승객을 탑승시킬 수 있는 수용력을 가지고 있다.

---

route n. 노선, 경로　**airline** n. 항공사　**decade** n. 10년
make a name 유명해지다　**offer** v. 제공하다, 권하다
world-class adj. 세계 최상급의　**frequent** adj. 빈번한, 자주 있는
establish v. 개설하다, 설립하다　**direct flight** 직항편
initiate v. 개시하다, 시작하다　**facilitate** v. 용이하게 하다, 가능하게 하다
expansion n. 확장　**be set to** ~할 예정이다
purchase v. 구입하다; n. 구입(품)　**fuel efficient** 연비가 높은, 연료 효율이 좋은
seat v. 앉히다, 앉다; n. 좌석　**passenger** n. 승객

19 전치사 채우기

해설　'지난 10년 동안 유명해져 왔다'라는 의미가 되어야 하므로 기간을 나타내는 전치사 (A) Throughout(~ 동안, ~ 내내)이 정답이다. (B) Before는 '~ 전에'라는 의미로 시점을, (C) Along은 '~을 따라'라는 의미로 방향을, (D) Between은 '~ 사이에'라는 의미로 시간이나 위치를 나타내는데, 시간을 나타낼 때에는 두 가지 대상 사이를 가리킨다.

20 알맞은 문장 고르기

해석　(A) 이것은 비자 신청 과정에 막대하게 영향을 끼쳤다.

(B) 그 결과, 공항들은 더 엄격한 보안 조치를 필요로 한다.

(C) 이제, 이 기업은 첫 번째 유럽 노선을 시작함으로써 확장할 것을 기대하고 있다.

(D) 연료비가 항공업계의 티켓 가격에 직접적인 영향을 준다.

해설　빈칸에 들어갈 알맞은 문장을 고르는 문제이므로 빈칸의 주변 문맥이나 전체 문맥을 파악한다. 뒤 문장 'Orashi will begin by establishing a direct flight from Abuja to Paris.'에서 Orashi 항공이 아부자에서 파리까지의 직항편을 개설함으로써 시작할 것이라고 한 후, 뒷부분에서 빠른 시일 내에 런던으로의 항공편 서비스도 개시할 계획이라고 했으므로 빈칸에는 파리와 런던으로의 새로운 노선들을 추가하는 것과 관련된 내용이 들어가야 함을 알 수 있다. 따라서 (C) Now, the company hopes to expand by starting its first European route가 정답이다.

어휘　**drastically** adv. 심하게, 철저하게　**visa** n. 비자, 허가증
　　　tight adj. 엄격한, 단단한　**security measure** 보안 조치

21 전치사 채우기　전체 문맥 파악

해설　이 문장은 주어(가짜 주어 there, 진짜 주어 plans)와 동사(are)를 갖춘 완전한 절이므로 ____ this route는 수식어 거품으로 보아야 한다. 이 수식어 거품은 동사가 없는 거품구이므로 거품구를 이끌 수 있는 전치사 (A), (B), (D)가 정답의 후보이다. 이 경우, 빈칸이 빈칸 뒤의 명사구(this route)와 함께 전치사구를 이루어 콤마와 함께 문장 맨 앞에 왔으므로 앞 문장과 빈칸이 있는 문장을 의미적으로 연결하는 접속부사의 역할을 한다. 앞부분에서 Orashi 항공이 파리까지의 직항편을 개설할 것이라고 했고, 빈칸이 있는 문장에서는 빠른 시일 내에 런던으로의 항공편 서비스도 개시할 계획이라고 했으므로 추가적인 내용을 덧붙이는 문장에서 사용되는 (B) In addition to(~에 더하여)가 정답이다. (C) As long as는 부사절 접속사이므로 거품절을 이끈다.

어휘　**instead of** ~ 대신에　**as long as** 오직 ~하는 경우에만
　　　in preparation for ~에 대비하여

22 명사 어휘 고르기

해설　'비행기가 350명의 승객들을 탑승시킬 수 있는 수용력을 가지고 있다'라는 문맥이 되어야 하므로 명사 (C) capacity(수용력, 용량)가 정답이다.

어휘　**quantity** n. 양, 수량　**reservation** n. 예약　**principle** n. 원칙, 주의

Section 5　접속사와 절

Chapter 15　등위접속사와 상관접속사

1　등위접속사　　　　　　　　　　　　　　　p.185
　1. (B)　　2. (B)　　3. (D)

1. 등위접속사 채우기

해설　'미국 13개 주와 25개국'이라는 의미가 되어야 하므로 (B) and(그리고)가 정답이다.

해석　그 기업의 고객 명부는 미국 13개 주와 25개국의 고객들로 구성되었다.

어휘　**portfolio** n. 고객 명부　**consist of** ~로 구성되다

2. 등위접속사 채우기

해설　'흥미로운 기획안이지만 효과적일지는 모르겠다'는 의미가 되어야 하므로 (B) but(그러나)이 정답이다.

해석　Ms. Lee는 그 마케팅 회사의 광고 기획안이 아주 흥미롭다고 생각했지만, 그것이 그녀의 회사에 효과적일 것이라는 확신은 없었다.

어휘　**find** v. 생각하다, 깨닫다, 찾다　**proposal** n. 안, 제안
　　　intriguing adj. 아주 흥미로운, 매력적인
　　　uncertain adj. 확신이 없는, 잘 모르는

3. 등위접속사 채우기

해설 단수 동사(is)가 온 것으로 보아, 단수 주어(Sky Tower)와 또 다른 단수 주어 (the Erickson Building)를 연결하여 단수 주어를 만드는 (D) or가 정답이다. (B) and를 쓰면 단수 동사가 아닌 복수 동사가 와야 한다.

해석 Sky 타워나 Erickson 빌딩이 Jacob and Associates사의 새 지사를 수용할 것이다.

어휘 house v. 수용하다, 장소를 제공하다 regional office 지사

2 상관접속사   p.186

1. (A)   2. (D)   3. (C)

1. 상관접속사 채우기

해설 상관접속사 either와 맞는 짝인 (A) or가 정답이다. 참고로, either A or B가 전치사구(by visiting a bookstore)와 전치사구(by ordering it online)를 연결하고 있다.

해석 고객들은 서점을 방문하거나 온라인으로 주문함으로써 Ben Rand의 최신 소설책을 구매할 수 있다.

2. 상관접속사 채우기

해설 but 다음에 (D) not이 와야 전치사구(for transportation and hotel expenses)와 전치사구(for entertainment or personal needs)를 연결하는 B but not A(A가 아닌 B)가 된다. 따라서 (D) not이 정답이다.

해석 현장에 있는 영업 담당자들을 위한 수당은 유흥비나 개인적인 필요를 위해서가 아닌, 교통 경비와 숙박 비용을 위해 주어진다.

어휘 allowance n. 수당, 용돈   sales representative 영업 담당자 in the field 현장에서   expense n. 경비, 비용

3. 상관접속사 채우기

해설 상관접속사 but also와 맞는 짝인 (C) not only가 정답이다. 이 경우 (B) not이나 (A) only를 단독으로 쓰지 않도록 주의해야 한다.

해석 그 이사는 관리자가 제출한 보고서가 미완성일 뿐만 아니라 솜씨 없게 작성되었다고 불평했다.

어휘 incomplete adj. 미완성의, 불충분한

Hackers Practice   p.187

01 ⓑ [토익 공식 1]	02 ⓐ [토익 공식 1]
03 ⓐ [토익 공식 1]	04 ⓐ [토익 공식 1]
05 ⓑ [토익 공식 1]	06 ⓑ [토익 공식 1]
07 ⓐ [토익 공식 1]	

08 not only → both [토익 공식 2]
09 neither → not [토익 공식 2]
10 and → but [토익 공식 2]
11 Both → Either [토익 공식 2]
12 or → nor [토익 공식 2]
13 yet → and [토익 공식 2]
14 also → or [토익 공식 2]

해석 01 Janet은 그녀의 아이의 생일 파티를 위한 몇몇 선물을 구매하고 포장했다.
02 그는 건물에 들어가려고 시도했으나, 보안 요원이 이미 정문을 잠갔다.
03 소매상들은 소비자들을 끌어모으기 위해 할인을 해주거나 추가 서비스를 제공해야 한다.
04 나는 그 영화를 여러 번 봤는데도 여전히 그것을 보는 것을 즐긴다.
05 Greg은 1월에 휴가를 신청했는데, 왜냐하면 친구들과 스키를 타러 가고 싶었기 때문이다.
06 항구 옆에 있는 전망대와 시내에 있는 전통 시장은 그 도시의 주요 관광 명소들이다.
07 오늘 아침 내 차의 시동이 걸리지 않았고, 그래서 나는 견인차를 불러야 했다.
08 최근의 의료법은 의사와 환자 모두에게 유익하다.

09 온라인이 아닌 공인 중개인으로부터 중고차를 구매하는 것이 권장된다.
10 판촉 스파 패키지는 1시간 동안의 마사지뿐만 아니라 손톱 손질도 포함한다.
11 Mr. Porter 또는 Ms. Hale 중 한 명이 이사회에 연구 결과를 제출할 것이다.
12 Sandy는 내일 오전에 수술이 있기 때문에 오늘 밤에 먹지도 마시지도 않을 것이다.
13 Jays 식당에 의해 제공되는 저녁 식사 세트는 전채 요리와 후식을 모두 포함한다.
14 고장 난 모니터는 환불 받거나 다른 제품으로 교환될 수 있다.

Hackers Test   p.188

Part 5

01 (C)	02 (D)	03 (D)	04 (A)	05 (A)
06 (D)	07 (C)	08 (B)	09 (C)	10 (A)
11 (C)	12 (B)	13 (C)	14 (D)	15 (D)
16 (B)	17 (A)	18 (B)		

Part 6

19 (C)	20 (D)	21 (C)	22 (D)

01 등위접속사 채우기

해설 '현대적이고 효율적인 경영 기반'이라는 의미가 되어야 하므로 (C) and(그리고)가 정답이다.

해석 Maxwell Byrd사는 해당 산업에서 타의 추종을 불허하는 현대적이고 효율적인 경영 기반을 설립했다는 것에 자부심을 갖고 있다.

어휘 pride on ~에 자부심을 갖다   infrastructure n. 기반, 기본적 시설 unmatched adj. 타의 추종을 불허하는

02 상관접속사 채우기

해설 상관접속사 or와 맞는 짝인 (D) either가 정답이다. 참고로, either A or B가 명사구(the event's headquarters)와 명사구(Web site)를 연결하고 있다.

해석 뉴욕 마라톤에 참가하기를 희망하는 선수들은 신청서를 제출하기 위해 행사 본부나 웹사이트를 방문해야 한다.

어휘 headquarters n. 본부, 본사   registration form 신청서

03 등위접속사 채우기

해설 '아침 일찍 또는 저녁 늦게'라는 의미가 되어야 하므로 (D) or(또는)가 정답이다.

해석 전력 공급이 안정적이지 않은 지역에서 정전을 예방하기 위해, 주요 가전제품들을 아침 일찍 또는 저녁 늦게 사용하십시오.

어휘 power supply 전력 공급   stable adj. 안정적인 appliances n. 가전제품

04 등위접속사 채우기

해설 If절에서 두 개의 동사(place, do not receive)를 연결하는 등위접속사를 채우는 문제이다. '주문했지만 물건을 받지 못하다'라는 의미가 되어야 하므로 (A) but(그러나)이 정답이다. 부사 (B), (C), (D)는 2개의 동사를 연결하는 역할을 하지 못한다.

해석 주문하고 영업일 기준으로 7일 이내에 물건을 받지 못했다면, 고객들은 문의를 하기 위해 운송부에 연락할 수 있다.

어휘 place an order 주문하다   business day 영업일   inquiry n. 문의

05 등위접속사 채우기

해설 '금요일까지 제출하라고 전달받았지만 마감 일자를 놓쳤다'는 의미가 되어야 하므로 (A) yet(그러나)이 정답이다.

해석 모든 근로자들은 그들의 세금 서류를 회계사에게 금요일까지 제출하라고 전달받았지만, 대부분의 사람들이 마감 일자를 놓쳤다.

어휘 tell v. 전달하다, 말하다   accountant n. 회계사

06 상관접속사 채우기

해설 상관접속사 both와 맞는 짝인 (D) and가 정답이다. 참고로, both A and B가 조동사 has에 이어지는 동사구(improved ~)와 동사구(increased ~)를 연결하고 있다.

해석 사무실의 새로운 실내 장식은 직원들의 사기를 높이고 전반적인 업무 효율을 증대시켰다.

어휘 interior n. 실내 장식, 인테리어; adj. 내부의, 안쪽의 morale n. 사기, 의욕 overall adj. 전반적인 efficiency n. 효율

07 등위접속사 채우기

해설 '개인 또는 팀 전체'라는 의미가 되어야 하므로 (C) or(또는)가 정답이다.

해석 최고 책임자는 지난주의 행사를 평가하는 일을 개인에게 맡길지 또는 팀 전체에게 맡길지 결정하려 하고 있다.

어휘 chief executive 최고 책임자 assign v. 맡기다, 할당하다

08 상관접속사 채우기

해설 빈칸 뒤의 also와 함께 쓰여 상관접속사 not only와 맞는 짝인 (B) but also를 만드는 (B) but이 정답이다. 참고로, not only A but also B가 동사구(grabs ~)와 동사구(stimulates ~)를 연결하고 있다.

해석 소비자의 관심을 끌 뿐만 아니라 상품에 대한 흥미도 불러일으키는 더욱 효과적인 광고가 필요하다.

어휘 grab attention 관심을 끌다 stimulate v. 흥미를 불러일으키다, 자극하다

09 상관접속사 채우기

해설 전치사 on 다음의 명사구 2개(the basis ~, their level ~)를 연결하는 자리이므로 'A뿐만 아니라 B도'라는 뜻의 (C) as well as가 정답이다.

해석 승진은 후보자들의 헌신과 성실함의 정도뿐만 아니라 그들의 이전 경력에 근거하여 고려될 것이다.

어휘 on the basis of ~에 근거하여 prior adj. 이전의, 사전의 dedication n. 헌신, 전념 loyalty n. 성실, 충실

10 등위접속사 채우기

해설 '명사 + 전치사'(Participation in)와 '명사 + 전치사'(support of)를 연결하기 위해서는 접속사가 와야 한다. '참여와 후원'이라는 의미를 만들면서 2개의 '명사 + 전치사'를 연결할 수 있는 등위접속사 (A) and(그리고)가 정답이다. 수식어 거품절을 이끄는 부사절 접속사 (C)와 접속사의 역할을 할 수 없는 부사 (D), 그리고 절과 절만을 연결할 수 있는 (B) so는 답이 될 수 없다.

해석 그 단체의 자선 행사에 대한 참여와 지원은 가난한 사회 구성원들을 위한 주거지 건설 대금을 지급하도록 도와줄 것이다.

어휘 charity n. 자선 benefit n. (모금을 위한) 자선 행사 pay for 대금을 지급하다 shelter n. 주거지 underprivileged adj. 가난한, 불우한

11 상관접속사 채우기

해설 not 앞에 (C) but이 와야 전치사구(by the head office)와 전치사구(by the accounting department)를 연결하는 B but not A(A가 아닌 B)가 된다. 따라서 (C) but이 정답이다.

해석 Mr. Carrington의 퇴직 수당은 회계부가 아닌 본사에 의해 처리되었다.

어휘 severance package 퇴직 수당 process v. 처리하다, 가공하다

12 상관접속사 채우기

해설 and와 맞는 상관접속사 짝이 필요하므로 (B) both가 정답이다. 참고로, both A and B는 명사구(her daily accomplishments)와 명사구(her total output)를 연결하고 있다. (C) plus는 and와 같은 의미를 가지고 등위접속사처럼 쓰이지만 상관접속사 자리에는 올 수 없다. so는 오직 절과 절을 연결하는 역할을 한다.

해석 Sarah의 근무 첫째 달 말에, 회사는 그녀의 일일 성과와 총 생산량을 평가했다.

어휘 employment n. 근무, 고용 accomplishment n. 성과, 업적 output n. 생산량

13 태에 맞는 동사 채우기

해설 주어(Copies ~ report)와 동사(send)가 '보고서의 사본들이 보내지다'라는 수동의 의미를 가지므로 수동태 동사 (C) have been sent가 정답이다.

해석 연간 재무 보고서 사본들이 인사부와 전략 기획부의 부장들에게 보내졌다.

어휘 financial report 재무 보고서 strategic adj. 전략의, 전략적인

14 현재분사와 과거분사 구별하여 채우기

해설 빈칸이 명사(effect) 앞에 있으므로 명사를 꾸밀 수 있는 형용사 (A), 분사인 (B) 또는 (D)가 정답의 후보이다. '효과가 지속적이다'라는 의미를 나타내야 하므로 현재분사인 (D) lasting이 정답이다. 'lasting effect'(지속적인 영향)를 관용 표현처럼 알아두자. last가 형용사로 쓰일 때에는 '맨 마지막의, 지난'이라는 뜻이므로 문맥에 맞지 않아 오답이다.

해석 무료 사용자 제작 온라인 미디어의 풍부함은 예능 산업의 비즈니스 모델에 지속적인 영향을 미쳐 왔다.

어휘 abundance n. 풍부함 lasting adj. 지속적인

15 상관접속사 채우기

해설 상관접속사 nor와 맞는 짝인 (D) neither가 정답이다. 참고로, neither A nor B가 명사(layoffs)와 명사구(pay reductions)를 연결하고 있다.

해석 그 기업은 회사의 재정 상태가 안정적이며 강제 해고나 급여 삭감을 고려하고 있지 않다고 전 직원들을 안심시키기를 바란다.

어휘 reassure v. 안심시키다 layoff n. 강제 해고

16 상관접속사 채우기

해설 and와 맞는 상관접속사 짝이 필요하므로 (B) both가 정답이다. 참고로, both A and B가 to 부정사구(to save on long-term interest rates)와 to 부정사구(to ensure a solid credit rating)를 연결하고 있다.

해석 Albom사는 장기 금리를 절약하는 것과 탄탄한 신용등급을 보장하는 것 모두를 위해 재정이 재건될 것이다.

어휘 refinance v. 재정을 재건하다, 자금을 보충하다 save on ~를 절약하다

17 상관접속사 채우기

해설 상관접속사 either와 맞는 짝인 (A) or가 정답이다. 참고로, either A or B는 동사구(mail ~ address)와 동사구(send them by e-mail)를 연결하고 있다.

해석 변호사 보조직 지원자들은 서류를 그 기업의 사무실 주소로 우편 발송하거나 이메일을 통해 보낼 수 있다.

어휘 paralegal n. 변호사 보조원, 준법률가 business address 사무 주소

18 형용사 자리 채우기

해설 '포괄적이고 적절한 정보'라는 의미로 보아 빈칸에는 information을 꾸미는 품사가 와야 한다. 명사(information)를 꾸미는 것은 형용사이므로 (B) comprehensive가 정답이다.

해석 사업 투자 기회에 관심이 있는 사람들은 그들이 알맞은 결정을 내릴 수 있도록 돕는 포괄적이고 적절한 정보를 제공받을 것이다.

어휘 relevant adj. 적절한, 관련 있는 appropriate adj. 알맞은 comprehensive adj. 포괄적인, 종합적인

19-22는 다음 기사에 관한 문제입니다.

> **샌디에이고 이동통신 시장으로 진출할 New Horizon사**
>
> [19]국내의 가장 빠르게 성장하는 인터넷 및 이동 전화 서비스 제공업체인 New Horizon 통신사가 샌디에이고로 확장한다는 것을 알리게 되어 기뻐하고 있다.
>
> [20]회사는 올해 초 컨설팅 회사인 DataVision사에 설문 조사를 실시해 줄 것을 요청했고, 결과는 New Horizon 통신사의 빠른 인터넷과 고품질 통화 서비스에 대한 커다란 수요를 보여주었다. 더욱이, 경쟁 통신사인 NationTel사와 Dash Wireless사에 의해 제공되는 신통치 않은 서비스는 수천 명의 고객들이 New Horizon사로 바꿀 것이라는 가능성을 암시한다. 최고 경영자인 Desmond Chang은 그런 움직임이 회사를 위한 경제적 이치에 잘 맞는 것이라고 말한다. [21]구체적으로, Chang은 New Horizon사가 약 5천만 달러의 ○

추가적인 연간 수익을 볼 것으로 기대한다.

서비스는 연말 전에 샌디에이고에서 정상적으로 가동될 것이다. ²²그러나, 정확한 일정은 아직 결정되지 않았다. 최신 정보는 더 많은 정보가 공개됨에 따라 회사의 웹사이트에 게재될 것이다.

> cellular service 이동 전화 서비스 lackluster adj. 신통치 않은
> potential n. 가능성, 잠재력 switch over 바꾸다, 돌리다
> make sense 이치에 맞다 be up and running 정상적으로 가동하고 있다
> post on 게재하다

19 동사 어휘 고르기

해설 '회사가 샌디에이고로 확장한다는 것을 알리게 되어 기쁘다'는 문맥이 되어야 하므로 (C) announce(알리다)가 정답이다.

어휘 request v. 요구하다 support v. 지원하다 certify v. 보증하다

20 상관접속사 채우기

해설 and와 맞는 상관접속사 짝이 필요하므로 (D) both가 정답이다.

21 접속부사 채우기 주변 문맥 파악

해설 빈칸이 콤마와 함께 문장의 맨 앞에 온 접속부사 자리이므로, 앞 문장과 빈칸이 있는 문장의 의미 관계를 파악하여 접속부사인 (A), (C)와 접속부사처럼 쓰일 수 있는 부사구 (B) 중 하나를 정답으로 골라야 한다. 앞 문장에서 고객들이 New Horizon사로 움직이고 있는 것은 경제적 이치에 잘 맞음을 언급했고, 빈칸이 있는 문장에서는 회사가 5천만 달러의 추가 수익을 볼 것이라고 했으므로, 구체적인 예를 들 때 사용되는 (C) Specifically(구체적으로)가 정답이다.

어휘 on the other hand 반면에 in contrast 대조적으로, 반면에
regardless adv. 상관없이

22 알맞은 문장 고르기

해석 (A) NationTel사와 Dash Wireless사는 비슷한 협정을 체결했다.
(B) 추가 수입은 회사가 결정을 내리는 데 도움이 될 것이다.
(C) 지역 사무소의 직원들이 본사의 직원들보다 업무를 더 잘 수행한다.
(D) 그러나, 정확한 일정은 아직 결정되지 않았다.

해설 빈칸에 들어갈 알맞은 문장을 고르는 문제이므로 빈칸의 주변 문맥이나 전체 문맥을 파악한다. 앞 문장 'The service should be up and running ~ before the end of the year.'에서 서비스가 연말 전에 정상적으로 가동될 것이라고 했고, 뒤 문장 'Updates will be posted on the company's Web site as more information is disclosed.'에서 최신 정보는 더 많은 정보가 공개됨에 따라 회사의 웹사이트에 게재될 것이라고 했으므로 빈칸에는 정확한 일정은 아직 결정되지 않았다는 내용이 들어가야 함을 알 수 있다. 따라서 (D) However, a definite timetable has yet to be finalized가 정답이다.

어휘 finalize v. 결정하다, 마무리 짓다

Chapter 16 관계절

1 관계절의 자리와 쓰임 p.191
1. (C) 2. (C) 3. (D)

1. 관계사 자리 채우기

해설 이 문장은 주어(The discounts)와 동사(are)를 갖춘 완전한 절이므로, 주어와 동사 사이에 온 ____ are available on the company's Web site는 수식어 거품으로 보아야 한다. 따라서 보기 중 수식어 거품이 될 수 있는 관계사 (C) that이 정답이다. 이 수식어 거품은 앞의 명사(The discounts)를 꾸미는 형용사 역할을 하는 관계절이다. 참고로, 대명사 (A), (B), (D)는 수식어 거품이 될 수 없다.

해석 회사의 웹사이트에서 이용할 수 있는 할인은 제한된 기간 동안에만 유효하다.

어휘 available adj. 이용할 수 있는 valid adj. 유효한, 타당한

2. 관계절 내 동사 채우기

해설 관계절(who ~ project)의 선행사(engineers)와 동사(select)가 '기술자들이 선발되다'라는 의미의 수동 관계이므로, 수동태 동사 (C) have been selected가 정답이다. 능동태 동사 (A), (B), (D)는 답이 될 수 없다.

해석 최근에, 그 이사는 교량 건설 프로젝트를 지휘하도록 선발된 기술자들의 명단을 발표했다.

어휘 release v. 발표하다, 공개하다 lead v. ~을 지휘하다

3. 관계사 자리 채우기

해설 이 문장은 주어(Dietary supplements)와 동사(are)를 갖춘 완전한 절이므로, ____ are produced from synthetic materials는 수식어 거품으로 보아야 한다. 이 수식어 거품은 주어를 뒤에서 꾸미는 역할을 하는 관계절이므로 관계사 (D) which가 정답이다. 명사절 또는 부사절 접속사 (A) whatever와 (C) whichever, 명사절 접속사 (B) what은 관계사 자리에 올 수 없다.

해석 합성 물질로부터 제조된 건강 보조 식품은 일반적으로 안전하지만, 소비자들은 이를 사용하기 전에 의사와 상의해야 한다.

어휘 dietary supplement 건강 보조 식품 synthetic adj. 합성의, 인조의
consult v. 상의하다, 상담하다 physician n. 의사

2 관계대명사의 선택과 격 p.192
1. (B) 2. (D) 3. (A)

1. 관계대명사 채우기

해설 선행사(A contract)가 사물이며, 빈칸에 들어갈 관계대명사가 관계절(has not yet been confirmed by the management) 안에서 주어 역할을 해야 한다. 따라서 주격 사물 관계대명사 (B) which가 정답이다.

해석 경영진에 의해 아직 확인되지 않은 계약은 그 조항들이 직원들에 의해 합의가 되었다 하더라도 법적 지위를 갖지 못할 것이다.

어휘 standing n. 지위, 평판 agree v. 합의가 되다, 의견이 일치하다

2. 관계대명사 채우기

해설 관계절(president ~ markets)에는 명사(president)를 꾸며 주어 '회사의 회장'이라는 의미를 만드는 소유격 관계대명사가 필요하므로 (D) whose가 정답이다.

해석 Genex-Co사는 회사의 회장이 수익성이 좋은 유럽 시장과 아시아 시장으로 진출하는 데 전념하는 기업이다.

어휘 be committed to -ing ~에 전념하다, 헌신하다 lucrative adj. 수익성이 좋은

3. 관계대명사 채우기

해설 선행사(Job candidates)가 사람이며, 빈칸에 들어갈 관계대명사가 관계절(are currently employed) 안에서 주어 역할을 해야 한다. 따라서 주격 사람 관계대명사 (A) who가 정답이다.

해석 현재 취직 상태인 입사 지원자들은 지원서에 근무 시작 가능일을 포함시켜야 한다.

어휘 candidate n. 지원자 currently adv. 현재 employed adj. 취직하고 있는
include v. 포함시키다, 넣다 availability n. 가능성, 유용성

3 전치사 + 관계대명사/수량 표현 + 관계대명사/관계대명사의 생략 p.193
1. (C) 2. (B) 3. (B)

1. '전치사 + 관계대명사' 채우기

해설 이 문장은 주어(The inclusion)와 동사(is)를 갖춘 완전한 절이므로 by ____ textbook publishers ~ their products는 수식어 거품으로 보아야

한다. 이 수식어 거품은 주어(textbook publishers), 동사(increase), 목적어(the educational value)가 있는 완전한 절이므로, 빈칸 앞의 전치사 by와 함께 '전치사 + 관계대명사' 형태로 완전한 절을 이끌 수 있는 관계대명사 (C) which가 정답이다.

해석 CD와 다른 보충 자료의 포함은 교과서 출판사들이 자사 상품의 교육적 가치를 증대시키는 방법이다.

어휘 inclusion n. 포함, 함유 supplemental adj. 보충의
publisher n. 출판사

2. '수량 표현 + 관계대명사' 채우기

해설 이 문장은 주어(A lot of automotive manufacturers)와 동사(participated)를 갖춘 완전한 절이므로 some of _____ took advantage of ~ models는 수식어 거품으로 보아야 한다. 이 수식어 거품은 수량 표현 (some of)으로 시작하고 있으므로 이 뒤의 빈칸에는 관계대명사가 와야 한다. 수량 표현(some of) 다음에는 주격 관계대명사 (A) who가 아닌 목적격 관계대명사가 와야 하므로 (B) whom이 정답이다. (D) that은 전치사(of) 바로 뒤에 올 수 없으므로 답이 될 수 없다.

해석 많은 자동차 제조 회사들이 박람회에 참가했으며, 그 중 일부는 내년도 모델을 소개할 수 있는 기회로 활용했다.

어휘 automotive adj. 자동차의 exhibition n. 박람회, 전시회
take advantage of ~을 기회로 활용하다, 이용하다

3. '관계대명사 + be동사' 생략 뒤에 오는 형태 채우기

해설 _____ for ~ position은 앞의 명사(the three applicants)를 꾸미는 관계절로, 명사와 관계절 사이에는 '관계대명사 + be동사(who are)'가 생략되어 있다. 이때, 이 뒤에 명사가 오면 선행사와 동격을 이루고 형용사가 오면 선행사를 설명해 주는 역할을 한다. '임명하기에 적합한 지원자'라는 의미가 되어야 하므로 형용사 (B) suitable이 정답이다. 명사 (A) suitability와 (D) suitableness는 선행사(the three applicants)와 의미적으로 동격을 이루지 못하므로 답이 될 수 없다. 참고로, 보통 '관계대명사 + be동사' 생략 뒤에는 명사보다 형용사가 자주 온다는 것도 알아 두자.

해석 관리자 자리에 임명하기에 적합한 세 명의 지원자들 중에, 두 명은 해외 지사에서 근무했던 경험이 있다.

어휘 applicant n. 지원자 appointment n. 임명
managerial adj. 관리의, 지배의 suitable adj. 적합한, 알맞은

---

4 관계부사 p.194

1. (A) 2. (B) 3. (D)

1. 관계대명사와 관계부사 구별하여 채우기

해설 빈칸은 명사(Staff members)를 뒤에서 꾸미는 관계절을 이끄는 자리이다. 빈칸 뒤의 절(would like to visit the food and beverages trade fair)에 주어가 빠진 불완전한 절이 왔으므로, 주격 관계대명사 (A)와 (C)가 정답의 후보이다. 선행사(Staff members)가 사물이 아닌 사람이므로, 사람 관계대명사인 (A) who가 정답이다. 완전한 절을 이끄는 관계부사 (B) when은 답이 될 수 없다.

해석 이번 주에 식료품 무역 박람회를 방문하고자 하는 직원들은 그들의 관리자로부터 허가를 얻어야 한다.

어휘 trade fair 무역 박람회 obtain v. 얻다, 획득하다
permission n. 허가, 승인, 동의 supervisor n. 관리자, 감독관

2. 관계대명사와 관계부사 구별하여 채우기

해설 빈칸은 명사(The new shuttle service)를 뒤에서 꾸미는 관계절을 이끄는 자리이다. 빈칸 뒤의 절(has been operating since last year)에 주어가 없으므로, 주격 관계대명사 (A)와 (B)가 정답의 후보이다. 선행사(The new shuttle service)가 사람이 아닌 사물이므로, 사물 관계대명사인 (B) which가 정답이다. 명사절을 이끄는 접속사인 (C) what과 완전한 절을 이끄는 관계부사 (D) where는 답이 될 수 없다.

해석 지난해부터 운행되고 있는 새로운 셔틀버스는 그 도시의 모든 주요 쇼핑 지역에 서비스를 제공한다.

어휘 operate v. 운행하다, 운영하다 district n. 지역, 지구

3. 관계대명사와 관계부사 구별하여 채우기

해설 빈칸 뒤에 완전한 절(she did volunteer work)이 와 있으므로, 완전한 절을 이끌 수 있는 관계부사 (B) 또는 (D)가 와야 한다. 선행사(the hospital)가 장소를 가리키므로, 장소 선행사와 함께 쓰이는 관계부사 (D) where가 정답이다. 불완전한 절을 이끄는 관계대명사 (A) which와 (C) who는 답이 될 수 없다.

해석 Ms. Torres는 대학에 다니는 동안 자원봉사를 했던 병원의 일자리에 지원했다.

어휘 apply v. 지원하다
volunteer adj. 자원하는, 자발적인; v. 자원하다; n. 자원봉사자

Hackers Practice p.195

01 ⓐ [토익 공식 1]		02 ⓑ [토익 공식 2]	
03 ⓐ [토익 공식 2]		04 ⓑ [토익 공식 1]	
05 ⓐ [토익 공식 1]		06 ⓐ [토익 공식 2]	
07 ⓒ [토익 공식 2]			

08 where → which/that [토익 공식 2]
09 is targeted → are targeted [토익 공식 1]
10 having → has [토익 공식 1]
11 when → which/that [토익 공식 4]
12 that → which [토익 공식 2]
13 them → which [토익 공식 3]
14 맞는 문장 [토익 공식 4]

해석 01 Susan은 몇몇 언어를 구사할 수 있는데, 이는 그녀가 외국 고객들과 일할 때 이점이다.
02 줄 서 있는 탑승객들은 그들의 여행 서류들을 준비해 두어야 한다.
03 기획안이 선정된 모든 필자들은 보상으로 특별 휴가가 주어질 것이다.
04 Mr. Ing은 누군가 방에 들어오면 자동으로 불이 켜지는 보안등을 설치했다.
05 상점 회원권을 신청하고 싶은 고객들은 안내 데스크에 들르시면 됩니다.
06 그 프린터 모델은 6개의 무료 잉크 카트리지와 함께 제공되며, 이 제공은 제한된 시간 동안만 이용 가능하다.
07 식별 번호가 대기자 명단에 있는 사람들은 내일 다시 전화해야 한다.
08 당신 책상 위에 있는 것은 내일 회의에서 논의될 프로젝트 일정표이다.
09 청소년들을 대상으로 하는 오락 프로그램의 수는 꾸준히 증가해 왔다.
10 다가오는 워크숍은 그 부서가 준비해 온 시리즈의 첫 번째이다.
11 변화하는 기후는 환경 운동가들 사이에서 많은 우려를 야기해 온 문제이다.
12 2층으로 이어지는 계단은 재건되고 있다.
13 나는 백화점에서 새 정장과 넥타이를 구매했는데, 둘 다 할인 중이었다.
14 Jake가 일하는 빵집은 케이크로 인기가 있다.

Hackers Test p.196

Part 5

01 (A)	02 (A)	03 (B)	04 (C)	05 (C)
06 (A)	07 (B)	08 (B)	09 (C)	10 (D)
11 (B)	12 (C)	13 (B)	14 (C)	15 (D)
16 (A)	17 (C)	18 (C)		

Part 6

19 (C)	20 (A)	21 (C)	22 (B)

01 관계대명사 채우기

해설 명사(a dress code policy)를 뒤에서 꾸미는 절(she ~ environment)은 형용사 역할을 하는 관계절이므로, 명사절을 이끄는 접속사 (C) what은 답에서 제외된다. 또한 콤마(,) 바로 뒤에 올 수 없는 관계대명사 (B) that 역시 답이 될 수 없다. 관계절 안에 삽입절(she believes)이 있을 때는 삽입절을 빼고 관계대명사의 격을 선택해야 한다. 사물 선행사(a dress code policy)

가 왔고 절(will result in ~ environment) 안에 주어가 없으므로, 사물 선행사에 쓰는 주격 관계대명사 (A) which가 정답이다.

해석　관리자는 복장 규정 방침을 시행했는데, 그녀는 이것이 좀 더 전문적인 근무 환경을 낳을 것이라고 생각한다.

어휘　**dress code** 복장 규정　**result in** (결과를) 낳다　**professional** adj. 전문적인

02 관계대명사 채우기

해설　____ had important ~ latest product는 명사(all)를 뒤에서 꾸며 주는 관계절이다. 이 관계절 안에 주어가 없으므로, 주격 관계대명사 (A) who가 정답이다. 소유격 관계대명사 (B) whose는 바로 뒤에 관계대명사의 꾸밈을 받는 명사가 와서 'whose + 명사'의 형태가 되어야 빈칸에 올 수 있다. 절을 이끌 수 없는 지시대명사 (C) these와 (D) those는 답이 될 수 없다. 참고로, 대명사 all은 '모든 것, 모든 일'이라는 의미와 '모든 사람'이라는 의미를 모두 가지며 문맥에 맞게 해석한다.

해석　회사의 최신 제품 출시에 중요한 역할을 한 모든 사람들의 공로를 인정하여 기념식이 열릴 것이다.

어휘　**ceremony** n. 기념식　**in recognition of** (~의 공로를) 인정하여, ~의 답례로　**launch** n. 출시; v. 출시하다

03 '수량 표현 + 관계대명사' 채우기

해설　이 문장은 주어(Boundless Air), 동사(hired), 목적어(eight certified pilots)를 갖춘 완전한 절이므로, all of ____ were trained는 수식어 거품으로 보아야 한다. 이 수식어 거품이 수량 표현(all of)으로 시작하고 있으므로 목적격 관계대명사 (B) whom이 정답이다.

해석　Boundless 항공사는 면허증을 가진 조종사 8명을 고용했는데, 그들 모두는 맨해튼에 있는 같은 기관에서 교육받았다.

어휘　**certified** adj. 면허증을 가진, 공인의, 보증된　**institute** n. 기관, 연구소, 학원

04 관계대명사와 관계부사 구별하여 채우기

해설　빈칸은 명사(the most recently proposed financial plan)를 뒤에서 꾸미는 관계절을 이끄는 자리이다. 관계절 안에 삽입절(the CEO believes)이 있을 때는 삽입절을 빼고 관계대명사의 격을 선택해야 한다. 빈칸 뒤의 절(will help ~ debt) 안에 주어가 없으므로, 주격 관계대명사 (C) which가 정답이다. 부사절 접속사 (A) while과 완전한 절을 이끄는 관계부사 (B) when, 콤마(,) 바로 뒤에 올 수 없는 관계대명사 (D) that은 답이 될 수 없다.

해석　어제 회의에서, 직원들은 가장 최근에 제안된 재무 계획을 검토했는데, 최고 경영자는 이것이 회사가 부채에서 빠져나오는 데 도움이 될 것이라고 생각한다.

어휘　**financial** adj. 재무의, 금융의　**corporation** n. 회사　**debt** n. 부채, 빚

05 관계사 자리 채우기

해설　이 문장은 주어(The government's latest expansion), 동사(has provided), 목적어(students)를 모두 갖춘 완전한 절이므로 ____ were formerly unavailable은 수식어 거품으로 보아야 한다. 따라서 수식어 거품을 이끌 수 있는 관계대명사 (C) that이 정답이다. 이 수식어 거품은 명사(assistance)를 뒤에서 꾸미는 역할을 하는 관계절이다. (A) what은 명사절을 이끄는 접속사이므로 답이 될 수 없다.

해석　정부의 교육 지원 프로그램의 최근 확대는 이전에는 이용할 수 없었던 등록금 지원 전형을 학생들에게 제공해 왔다.

어휘　**latest** adj. 최근의, 최신의　**type** n. 전형, 유형　**tuition** n. 등록금, 수업료　**assistance** n. 지원, 도움　**formerly** adv. 이전에는

06 관계대명사 채우기

해설　in ____ they will reside는 명사(the country)를 뒤에서 꾸며 주는 관계절이다. 이 관계절은 전치사(in)로 시작하고 있으므로 이 뒤의 빈칸에는 목적격 관계대명사 (A) 또는 (C)가 와야 한다. 선행사(the country)가 사람이 아니라 사물이므로, 사물 관계대명사 (A) which가 정답이다. (B) that이 빈칸에 들어가면 in that(~이므로, ~라는 점에서)이 되는데, 빈칸 앞뒤의 절이 인과 관계를 이룬다고 할 수 없으므로 (B)는 답이 될 수 없다.

해석　의사소통 문제를 예방하기 위해, 해외에서 근무하도록 배정된 직원들은 그들이 거주할 나라의 언어를 공부할 것이 요구된다.

어휘　**avoid** v. 예방하다, 막다, 피하다　**reside** v. 거주하다

07 부정대명사 채우기

해설　'모든 사람과 직접 이야기하다'라는 의미가 자연스러우므로 (B) everyone이 정답이다. (A) anyone은 긍정문에 쓰이면 '누구든지, 아무라도'를 의미하는데, 이 문맥에는 맞지 않으므로 답이 될 수 없다. (C) neither one(어떤 사람도 ~ 아니다)과 (D) no one(아무도 ~ 않다)도 문맥에 맞지 않아 답이 될 수 없다.

해석　부하 직원들과의 관계를 개선하고 그들의 능력을 더 잘 이해하기 위한 시도로 사장은 모든 직원과 직접 이야기할 것이다.

어휘　**in an attempt to do** ~하려는 시도　**improve relations** 관계를 개선하다　**subordinate** n. 부하, 하급자

08 '전치사 + 관계대명사' 채우기

해설　'전치사 + 관계대명사' 뒤에는 완전한 절 대신 to 부정사가 올 수 있다. 따라서 to 부정사(to place ~ club) 앞에 올 수 있는 것은 '전치사 + 관계대명사' 형태인 (A)와 (B)이다. 선행사(envelope)가 사물이므로 (B) in which가 정답이다. 빈칸에 (C) what을 넣으면 빈칸 이하는 '의문사 + to 부정사'라는 명사절 형태가 되어 버린다. 그러나 빈칸 이하는 명사(a pre-addressed, stamped envelope)를 꾸며 주는 형용사절(관계절)이므로, 명사절을 만드는 (C)는 답이 될 수 없다. (D) wherever는 부사절을 이끄는 복합관계부사이므로 답이 될 수 없다.

해석　이 편지에 첨부된 것은 우리 클럽의 회원 신청서를 안에 넣을 수 있는 주소가 적혀 있고 우표가 붙여진 봉투이다.

어휘　**attached** adj. 첨부된, 덧붙여진　**pre-addressed** 주소가 적힌　**stamp** v. (봉투에) 우표를 붙이다　**envelope** n. 봉투

09 등위접속사 채우기

해설　완전한 두 개의 절 사이에 빈칸이 있으므로, 두 절을 연결해 주는 접속사 (A)와 (C)가 정답의 후보이다. '프린터에 문제가 있었고, 그래서 시간이 오래 걸린다'는 문맥이 되어야 하므로 '그래서'를 의미하는 등위접속사 (C) so가 정답이다. (A) that은 앞에 so/such와 함께 쓰일 때만 '결과적으로 ~하다'라는 의미를 갖게 되므로 답이 될 수 없으며 (B) moreover(게다가, 더욱이)와 (D) therefore(그러므로)는 부사이므로 접속사 역할을 하지 못한다.

해석　프린터에 몇 가지 문제가 있었고, 그래서 마케팅부가 광고 포스터를 만드는 것이 예상했던 것보다 더 오래 걸리고 있다.

10 관계절 내 동사 채우기

해설　선행사(The information packet)와 관계절의 동사(mail)가 '자료 묶음이 보내지다'라는 의미의 수동 관계이므로, 수동태 동사 (B)와 (D)가 정답의 후보이다. 이 중, 단수 명사인 선행사(The information packet)에 수일치하는 단수 동사 (D) was mailed가 정답이다.

해석　참가자들에게 보내진 자료 묶음은 워크숍에서 논의될 주제들의 개요를 서술한다.

어휘　**information packet** 자료 묶음　**outline** v. 개요를 서술하다, 약술하다

11 '수량 표현 + 관계대명사' 채우기

해설　이 문장은 주어(A budget overrun), 동사(has been reported)를 갖춘 완전한 절이므로 most of ____ is accounted for는 수식어 거품으로 보아야 한다. 이 수식어 거품이 수량 표현(most of)으로 시작하고 있으므로 관계대명사 (B)와 (D)가 정답의 후보이다. 수량 표현(most of) 다음에는 목적격 관계대명사가 와야 하므로 (B) which가 정답이다. 소유격 관계대명사 (D) whose는 'whose + 명사'의 형태로 쓰여야 하므로 답이 될 수 없다.

해석　32억엔의 예산 초과가 이번 분기에 Tekeda 건설 회사에 의해 보고되었는데, 초과액의 대부분은 정유 공장 프로젝트가 차지한다.

어휘　**overrun** n. 초과　**account for** 차지하다, ~의 이유가 되다　**oil refinery** 정유 공장

12 부사절 접속사 + 분사구문 채우기

해설　부사절 접속사(After) 다음에는 주어 없이 동사 (A)나 (D)가 올 수 없고 분사구문이 올 수 있으므로, 올바른 분사구문의 형태인 (C) being informed가 정답이다. (B) been informed는 올바른 분사구문의 형태가 아니므로 답이

될 수 없다.

해석 연방 최저 임금의 계획된 인상을 통지 받은 후에, Howser 전자 회사는 있을 수 있는 미래의 손실을 상쇄하기 위해 자사 소프트웨어의 가격을 인상했다.

어휘 **federal** adj. 연방 (정부)의 **minimum wage** 최저 임금
raise v. 인상하다, 올리다 **offset** v. 상쇄하다

13 관계대명사와 관계부사 구별하여 채우기

해설 빈칸 뒤에 주어가 없는 불완전한 절(annually ~ horticulture)이 와서 빈칸 앞의 명사(The Mother Nature Garden Show)를 꾸며 주고 있으므로, 불완전한 절을 이끌 수 있는 관계대명사 (B)와 (D)가 정답의 후보이다. 이 관계절에는 주어가 없으므로 주격 관계대명사 (B) which가 정답이다. 소유격 관계대명사 (D) whose는 바로 뒤에 관계대명사의 꾸밈을 받는 명사가 와서 'whose + 명사'의 형태가 되어야 빈칸에 올 수 있다. 완전한 절을 이끄는 관계부사 (A) when과 (C) where는 답이 될 수 없다.

해석 원예 분야의 최신 기술을 매년 보여주는 Mother Nature 원예 전시회는 한 주간 열리는 행사 동안 5,000명 이상의 참석자들을 끌어모은다.

어휘 **annually** adv. 매년 **demonstrate** v. 보여주다 **horticulture** n. 원예
run n. 행사, 공연

14 관계사 자리 채우기

해설 명사(a qualified operations manager)를 뒤에서 꾸미는 절(____ has ~ skills)은 형용사 역할을 하는 관계절이므로 관계사 (C) who가 정답이다. 대명사 (A) she나 부사절 접속사 (B) if, (D) because는 답이 될 수 없다.

해석 Terra사는 뛰어난 문제 해결 능력을 가진 자격 있는 업무팀장을 채용하려는 계획을 발표했다.

어휘 **intention** n. 계획, 의도 **qualified** adj. 자격 있는, 적임의
operations manager 업무팀장

15 '관계대명사 + be동사' 생략 뒤에 오는 형태 채우기

해설 ____ with the governor's reelection campaign은 앞의 명사(the advisors)를 꾸미는 관계절로, 명사와 관계절 사이에는 '관계대명사 + be동사(who are)'가 생략되어 있다. 이 경우 선행사(the advisors)와 관계절의 동사(associate)가 '고문들이 ~과 관련되다'라는 의미의 수동 관계가 되어야 하므로 be associated with(~와 관련되다)를 써서 the advisors who are associated with the governor's reelection campaign이라고 쓸 수 있다. 이때, who are를 생략할 수 있으므로 (D) associated가 정답이다. 참고로, 이 문제를 명사 뒤에서 명사를 꾸며 주는 분사 채우기 문제로 볼 수도 있다. 수식받는 명사(the advisors)와 분사가 '고문들이 관련되다'라는 의미의 수동 관계이므로 과거분사 (D) associated가 정답이다.

해석 그 주지사의 재선 운동과 관련된 모든 고문들 중에, Mr. McKenzie가 경제 문제에 가장 정통하다.

어휘 **advisor** n. 고문, 조언자 **reelection** n. 재선
knowledgeable adj. 정통한, 박식한, 아는 것이 많은
be associated with ~와 관련되다

16 관계대명사 채우기

해설 사람 선행사(Richard Perkins)가 왔고 관계절(____ has been ~ years) 안에 주어가 없으므로 사람 선행사에 쓰는 주격 관계대명사 (A) who가 정답이다.

해석 30년 이상 이 은행의 소중한 직원이었던 Richard Perkins를 예우하는 만찬이 다음 주 금요일에 열릴 것이다.

어휘 **honor** v. 예우하다; n. 명예 **valued** adj. 소중한, 존중되는

17 관계절 내 동사 채우기

해설 whose ~ plans는 앞의 명사(a personnel director)를 꾸미는 관계절이다. 이 관계절에는 동사가 없으므로 동사가 포함된 (C)와 (D)가 정답의 후보이다. 관계절의 주어(whose professional goals)가 복수이므로 복수 동사가 포함된 (C) are compatible이 정답이다.

해석 Neo International사는 회사의 장기 계획과 양립할 수 있는 직무 목표를 갖는 인사부장 자리를 광고해 왔다.

어휘 **compatible with** ~와 양립할 수 있는

18 관계대명사 채우기

해설 이 문장은 주어(An employee), 동사(may receive), 목적어(a raise)를 갖춘 완전한 절이므로, ____ performance ~ satisfactory는 수식어 거품으로 보아야 한다. 이 수식어 거품은 주어(An employee)를 꾸며 주는 관계절이다. 보기의 관계대명사 중, 빈칸 뒤의 명사(performance)와 함께 관계절 내의 주어가 될 수 있는 소유격 관계대명사 (C) whose가 정답이다.

해석 명시된 기간 동안 실적이 만족스러운 직원은 현재 임금 기준에 근거하여 임금 인상을 받을 수 있다.

어휘 **performance** n. 실적, 성과 **specified** adj. 명시된, 지정된
satisfactory adj. 만족스러운 **raise** n. 임금 인상 **based on** ~에 근거하여

19-22는 다음 이메일에 관한 문제입니다.

발신: murphy@harebuilders.com
수신: williams@houston.com
날짜: 5월 22일
제목: 경기장 청사진

Mr. Williams께,

[19]저희 기술자들이 자사가 건설하게 될 새 경기장의 도면들을 검토했습니다. [20]건축 준비로, 그들이 부지의 크기를 저희 청사진과 비교했고 몇몇 불일치가 있음을 발견했습니다. 어떻게 이런 일이 일어났는지에 상관없이, 저희는 시정 조치를 취해야 합니다.

[21]그러므로, 귀하는 정확한 크기를 보여주는 새로운 도면을 작성해야 할 것입니다. 청사진이 확정되지 않으면, 저희는 이 프로젝트 작업을 시작할 수 없습니다. [22]이는 관련된 모두에게 막대한 비용이 드는 지연을 야기할 수 있습니다. 추가적인 비용에 있어서 단 하루가 수천 달러로 이어질 수 있다는 것을 고려할 때, 저희의 고객은 어떤 지연에도 반대할 것입니다. 그러므로 귀하가 즉시 청사진을 업데이트해주신다면 감사하겠습니다.

Terry Murphy, Hare 건축 회사

arena n. 경기장, 공연장 **blueprint** n. 청사진, 계획 **plan** n. 도면, 설계도
construction n. 건축 **measurement** n. 크기, 측정
draw up 작성하다, 만들다 **object to** ~에 반대하다
postponement n. 지연, 연기

---

19 올바른 시제의 동사 채우기 전체 문맥 파악

해설 '자사가 경기장을 건설하다'라는 문맥인데, 이 경우 빈칸이 있는 문장만으로는 올바른 시제의 동사를 고를 수 없으므로 주변 문맥이나 전체 문맥을 파악하여 정답을 고른다. 뒷부분에서 '청사진이 확정되지 않으면 프로젝트 작업을 시작할 수 없다(Unless the blueprints are fixed, we cannot begin work on the project.)'고 했으므로 회사가 경기장을 건설할 시점은 미래임을 알 수 있다. 따라서 미래에 예정된 일을 나타내는 be + -ing 형태의 (C) is building이 정답이다.

20 명사 어휘 고르기 주변 문맥 파악

해설 '몇몇 ____가 있음을 발견했다'라는 문맥이므로 모든 보기가 정답의 후보이다. 빈칸이 있는 문장만으로 정답을 고를 수 없으므로 주변 문맥이나 전체 문맥을 파악한다. 빈칸이 있는 문장에서 '부지의 크기를 청사진과 비교했다(compared measurements of the site with our blueprints)'고 했고, 뒤 문장에서 '시정 조치를 취해야 한다(have to take corrective action)'고 했으므로 부지의 크기와 청사진 간의 불일치를 발견했음을 알 수 있다. 따라서 명사 (A) discrepancies(불일치)가 정답이다.

어휘 **statistics** n. 통계 **diagram** n. 도형, 도표 **pattern** n. 양식, 패턴

21 관계사 자리 채우기

해설 이 문장은 주어(you), 동사(will need), 목적어(to draw up)를 갖춘 완전한 절이므로 ____ the right measurements는 수식어 거품으로 보아야 한다. 따라서 수식어 거품이 될 수 있는 관계절을 만드는 (B)와 (C)가 정답의 후보이다. 새로운 도면이 정확한 크기를 보여주는 것은 현재의 상태가 되어야 하므로 현재 시제를 포함한 (C) that display가 정답이다. 접속사 + 동사인 (D) and are displaying이 빈칸에 와서 and가 절(you will need to draw up new plans)과 절((you) are displaying the right measurements)을 연

결하는 구조로 본다 하더라도, '새로운 도면을 작성해야 할 것이고 정확한 크기를 보여주고 있다'라는 어색한 문맥이 되어 답이 될 수 없다.

22 알맞은 문장 고르기

해석 (A) 저희 기술자들이 언급한 것을 제가 정확히 명시하겠습니다.
(B) 이는 관련된 모두에게 막대한 비용이 드는 지연을 야기할 수 있습니다.
(C) 시간이 더 필요하시다면 귀하는 연기를 요청하실 수 있습니다.
(D) 우리는 어떻게 그 오류들이 발생했는지에 대해 확신하지 못합니다.

해설 빈칸에 들어갈 알맞은 문장을 고르는 문제이므로 빈칸의 주변 문맥이나 전체 문맥을 파악한다. 앞 문장 'Unless the blueprints are fixed, we cannot begin work on the project.'에서 청사진이 확정되지 않으면 프로젝트 작업을 시작할 수 없다고 했고, 뒤 문장 'Our client will object to any postponement considering that a single day can lead to thousands of dollars in additional expenses.'에서 추가적인 비용에 있어서 단 하루가 수천 달러로 이어질 수 있다는 것을 고려할 때 고객이 어떤 지연에도 반대할 것이라고 했으므로 빈칸에는 프로젝트의 지연과 손실에 대한 내용이 들어가야 함을 알 수 있다. 따라서 (B) It could result in costly delays for everyone involved가 정답이다.

어휘 specify v. 명시하다 costly adj. 막대한 비용이 드는

Chapter 17 부사절

1 부사절의 자리와 쓰임 p.199
1. (C) 2. (C) 3. (D)

1. 부사절 접속사 자리 채우기

해설 이 문장은 주어(가짜 주어 there와 진짜 주어 an open position)와 동사(will be)를 갖춘 완전한 절이므로, ____ the marketing ~ Singapore는 수식어 거품으로 보아야 한다. 이 수식어 거품은 필수성분 앞에 와 있으므로, 보기 중 필수성분 앞에 온 수식어 거품을 이끌 수 있는 부사절 접속사 (B)와 (C)가 정답의 후보이다. '만약 이전하게 된다면'이라는 의미가 되어야 하므로 (C) If(~라면)가 정답이다. 관계대명사 (D) That은 필수성분 앞에 온 수식어 거품을 이끌지 못하므로 답이 될 수 없다. 절과 절을 연결하는 접속부사 (A) Therefore는 절을 이끌 수 없으므로 답이 될 수 없다.

해석 마케팅 대표가 싱가포르로 전근하면, 본사에 공석이 생길 것이다.

어휘 relocate v. 전근하다, 이동하다 open adj. 공석인, 비어 있는, 개방된

2. 부사절 접속사 자리 채우기

해설 이 문장은 필수성분(it is ~ nations)을 갖춘 완전한 절이므로, ____ the minimum ~ years는 수식어 거품으로 보아야 한다. 이 수식어 거품은 필수성분 앞에 와 있으므로, 보기 중 필수성분 앞에 온 수식어 거품을 이끌 수 있는 부사절 접속사 (C) Whereas(~이지만, ~한 반면에)가 정답이다. (A) However도 부사절 접속사로 쓰일 수 있지만 '어떻게 ~하든 상관없이'를 의미하므로 이 문맥에 어울리지 않는다.

해석 지난 몇 년 사이 몇몇 국가에서 최저 임금이 상승했다고는 하지만, 많은 나라들은 아직 빈곤선 이하에 있다.

어휘 minimum wage 최저 임금 poverty level 빈곤선

3. 부사절 접속사 자리 채우기

해설 who절(who ~ hold)은 주어(주격 관계대명사 who), 동사(hear), 목적어(music)를 갖춘 완전한 절이므로 ____ placed on hold는 수식어 거품으로 보아야 한다. 수식어 거품 자리에 온 분사구문(placed on hold) 앞에 올 수 있는 것은 부사절 접속사 (B) 또는 (D)이다. '기다리는 동안'이라는 의미가 되어야 하므로 (D) while(~ 동안)이 정답이다. 전치사 (A)는 과거분사 구문을 이끌 수 없으며 부사 (C)는 분사구문을 꾸밀 수 있지만 이 경우 '앞서 통화를 기다리다'라는 어색한 의미가 되므로 답이 될 수 없다.

해석 통화 연결을 기다리는 동안 연결된 전화선으로 음악을 듣는 고객들은 전화를 끊을 가능성이 더 적다.

어휘 place v. 놓다, 두다; n. 장소 on hold (사람이) 통화를 기다리는 hang up 전화를 끊다 ahead adv. (시간적으로) 앞에, 앞으로

2 부사절 접속사 1 : 시간 p.200
1. (B) 2. (D) 3. (A)

1. 부사절 접속사 채우기

해설 '서류가 제출되는 대로'라는 의미가 되어야 하므로 (B) Once(~하는 대로)가 정답이다. 등위접속사 (D) Yet은 두 개의 절 사이에 와야 하며, 두 개의 절 맨 앞에는 오지 못한다.

해석 모든 적절한 서류가 제출되는 대로, 당신은 Royers 금융 회사의 회계사로서 정식 등록될 것입니다.

어휘 paperwork n. 서류, 서류 작업, 문서 업무 file v. 제출하다

2. 부사절 접속사 채우기

해설 이 문장은 필수성분(The author ~ requests)을 갖춘 완전한 절이므로 ____ a positive book review ~ Wednesday는 수식어 거품으로 보아야 한다. 이 수식어 거품은 동사(was published)가 있는 거품절이므로, 거품절을 이끌 수 있는 부사절 접속사 (B)와 (D)가 정답의 후보이다. '서평이 신문에 발행된 이래로 인터뷰 요청을 받아 왔다'는 의미가 되어야 하므로 (D) since(~한 이래로)가 정답이다.

해석 지난주 수요일에 긍정적인 서평이 한 주요 신문에서 발행된 이래로 그 작가는 몇 건의 인터뷰 요청을 받아 왔다.

어휘 request n. 요청 book review (특히 신간 서적의) 서평

3. 부사절 접속사 채우기

해설 '오페라가 시작되기 20분 전보다 더 이전에 도착하다'라는 의미가 되어야 하므로 (A) before(~ 전에)가 정답이다.

해석 오페라가 시작되기 20분 전보다 더 이전에 도착하신 손님들은 대강당 문이 열릴 때까지 로비에서 기다려야 합니다.

어휘 patron n. 손님, 후원자

3 부사절 접속사 2 : 조건, 양보 p.201
1. (A) 2. (C) 3. (D)

1. 부사절 접속사 채우기

해설 이 문장은 필수성분(The value ~ drop)을 갖춘 완전한 절이므로 ____ the government ~ downswing은 수식어 거품으로 보아야 한다. 이 수식어 거품은 동사(intervenes)가 있는 거품절이므로, 거품절을 이끌 수 있는 부사절 접속사 (A)와 (B)가 정답의 후보이다. '만약 정부가 개입하지 않는다면 달러 가치가 계속 떨어진다'는 의미가 되어야 하므로 (A) unless(만약 ~이 아니라면)가 정답이다. 절과 절 사이에 오는 등위접속사 (D) or(또는)도 빈칸에 올 수 있지만, 이 문장에서는 '달러 가치가 계속 떨어지거나 또는 정부가 개입한다'는 어색한 의미를 만든다.

해석 하락을 멈추기 위해 정부가 개입하지 않는다면 달러 가치는 계속해서 떨어질 것이다.

어휘 continue to do 계속해서 ~하다 intervene v. (상황 개선을 돕기 위해) 개입하다 halt v. 멈추다, 중지시키다 downswing n. (경기·출생률 등의) 하락, 위축 except conj. ~을 제외하고는; prep. ~을 제외하고는

2. 부사절 접속사 채우기

해설 '비록 다음 달까지 근무를 시작하지는 않지만 일자리를 얻었다'는 의미가 되어야 하므로 (C) although(비록 ~이지만)가 정답이다. 등위접속사 (B) so(그래서)는 절과 절 사이에 올 수 있지만 이 문장에서는 '원하는 일자리를 얻었으므로 다음 달까지 근무를 시작하지 않는다'라는 어색한 의미를 만든다.

해석 아주 우수한 면접을 본 후에, Perry James는 비록 다음 달까지 근무를 시작하지는 않을지라도 그가 지원한 일자리를 얻었다.

어휘 exceptional adj. 아주 우수한 apply v. 지원하다, 신청하다

3. 부사절 접속사 채우기

해설 '만약 컴퓨터가 인터넷에 접속하지 못한다면'이라는 의미가 되어야 하므로 (D) if(만약 ~라면)가 정답이다. (C) whether는 부사절에 쓰일 때 '~이든 아니든'을 의미하므로 이 문맥에 어울리지 않는다.

해석 고객들은 그들의 컴퓨터가 라우터를 이용해서 인터넷에 접속하지 못한다면 서비스 상담 전화로 연락하면 된다.

어휘 hotline n. 상담 전화 access v. 접속하다
router n. 라우터(네트워크에서 데이터의 전달을 촉진하는 중계 장치)

---

4 부사절 접속사 3 : 이유, 목적, 결과 p.202
1. (B) 2. (B) 3. (A)

1. 부사절 접속사 채우기

해설 이 문장은 필수성분(A conference call ~ organized)을 갖춘 완전한 절이므로 ____ they ~ dissatisfaction은 수식어 거품으로 보아야 한다. 이 수식어 거품은 동사(can discuss)가 있는 거품절이므로, 거품절에 올 수 있는 부사절 접속사 (B)와 (C)가 정답의 후보이다. 빈칸 뒤에 can이 있으므로 함께 쓰여 '문제들을 논의할 수 있도록'이라는 의미를 만드는 (B) so that(~할 수 있도록)이 정답이다. 참고로, (A)에 that이 붙어 in order that이 되면 so that과 같은 의미의 부사절 접속사가 된다.

해석 고객 불만을 포함한 문제들을 논의할 수 있도록 회사의 수석 관리자 전원을 참가시키는 전화 회의가 준비되어 왔다.

어휘 senior adj. 수석의, 상위의 dissatisfaction n. 불만, 불평

2. 부사절 접속사 채우기

해설 '기차가 선로에서 꼼짝 못하게 되었기 때문에 직원들이 늦었다'는 의미가 되어야 하므로 (B) because(~이기 때문에)가 정답이다. 참고로, (C) that은 앞에 so/such와 함께 쓰일 때만 부사절 접속사 역할을 하여 '결과적으로 ~하다'라는 의미를 갖는다. 여기서는 앞에 so나 such가 없고, so나 such가 있다 하더라도 문맥에 어울리지 않으므로 (C) that은 답이 될 수 없다.

해석 동부행 A선 기차가 선로에서 꼼짝 못하게 되었기 때문에 많은 직원들이 사무실에 늦게 도착했다.

어휘 bound adj. ~행의 get stuck 꼼짝 못하게 되다 track n. 선로

3. 부사절 접속사 채우기

해설 이 문장은 필수성분(farmers are likely to appeal)이 있는 완전한 절이므로 ____ that wheat exports ~ year는 수식어 거품으로 보아야 한다. 이 수식어 거품은 동사(have declined)가 있는 거품절이므로, that 앞에 와서 거품절을 이끌 수 있는 부사절 접속사 (A), (B) (C)가 정답의 후보이다. '감소한 것을 고려했을 때'라는 의미가 되어야 하므로 (A) Considering(~을 고려했을 때, ~을 고려하여)이 정답이다. (D) Unless(만약 ~이 아니라면) 다음에는 that 없이 바로 절이 와야 한다.

해석 밀 수출이 작년 한 해 동안 크게 감소한 것을 고려했을 때, 농부들이 정부에 지원을 호소할 가능성이 크다.

어휘 export n. 수출 decline v. 감소하다 significantly adv. 크게, 상당히
appeal v. 호소하다 assistance n. 지원, 도움

---

5 부사절 접속사 4 : 복합관계부사 whenever, wherever, however p.203
1. (C) 2. (B) 3. (C)

1. 복합관계부사 채우기

해설 '차량을 정비받을 때는 언제든'이라는 의미가 되어야 하고, 뒤에 완전한 문장이 왔기 때문에 복합관계부사 (C) whenever(언제 ~하든)가 정답이다. 복합관계대명사 (A), (B), (D)는 뒤에 불완전한 문장이 오므로 답이 될 수 없다.

해석 Grayson Automotive사는 고객들이 차량을 정비받을 때는 언제든 서비스 평가 양식을 작성해 달라고 요청한다.

어휘 fill out 작성하다, 기입하다 service v. (차량, 기계를) 정비하다, 점검하다

2. 복합관계부사 채우기

해설 much와 같은 부사와 함께 올 수 있는 복합관계부사 (B) However가 정답이다. 'however much + 주어 + 동사'는 '얼마나 많이 ~하든'을 의미한다.

해석 Mr. Taylor의 고용주가 그에게 얼마나 많이 지급하든 상관없이, Carson Agency는 그가 자신들의 일자리 제안을 수락하는 경우에 월급을 두 배로 올려 주겠다고 제안했다.

어휘 double v. 두 배로 하다 accept v. 수락하다, 받아들이다

3. 복합관계부사 채우기

해설 '고객들이 어디에 있든 상관없다'는 의미가 되어야 하므로 (C) wherever(어디에서 ~하든 상관없이)가 정답이다.

해석 고도로 발전된 신기술은 고객이 어디에 있든 상관없이 인터넷을 통한 안전하고 빠른 거래를 가능하게 한다.

어휘 highly-advanced 고도로 발전된 transaction n. 거래, 처리

---

6 부사절 접속사 vs. 전치사 p.204
1. (A) 2. (C) 3. (D)

1. 부사절 접속사 자리 채우기

해설 이 문장은 필수성분(The documents will be delivered by courier)을 갖춘 완전한 절이므로 ____ a completed ~ machine은 수식어 거품으로 보아야 한다. 이 수식어 거품은 동사(is submitted)가 있는 거품절이므로, 거품절을 이끌 수 있는 부사절 접속사 (A) once가 정답이다. 전치사 (C) upon은 거품절을 이끌지 못한다.

해석 완성된 요청서가 온라인 또는 팩스를 통해 제출되는 대로 배달원에 의해 문서가 배달될 것이다.

어휘 courier n. (택배) 배달원 via prep. ~을 통하여

2. 부사절 접속사 자리 채우기

해설 이 문장은 필수성분(Gold prices have stabilized)을 갖춘 완전한 절이므로 ____ oil prices ~ the Middle East는 수식어 거품으로 보아야 한다. 이 수식어 거품은 동사(have risen)가 있는 거품절이므로, 거품절을 이끌 수 있는 부사절 접속사 (C) while이 정답이다. 전치사 (A) during은 거품절을 이끌지 못한다.

해석 중동에서의 생산 부족으로 인해 석유 가격이 급격히 상승한 반면에 금값은 안정되었다.

어휘 stabilize v. 안정되다, 고정되다 sharply adv. 급격하게, 심하게
shortage n. 부족

3. 부사절 접속사 자리 채우기

해설 이 문장은 필수성분(it is still popular)을 갖춘 완전한 절이므로 ____ the company's ~ years는 수식어 거품으로 보아야 한다. 이 수식어 거품은 동사(has remained)가 있는 거품절이므로, 거품절을 이끌 수 있는 부사절 접속사 (D) Although가 정답이다. 전치사 (A)와 접속부사 (B), (C)는 절을 이끌 수 없으므로 답이 될 수 없다.

해석 비록 그 회사의 제품 종류는 지난 몇 년간 계속 바뀌지 않았지만, 전국에 있는 소비자들에게 여전히 인기가 있다.

어휘 remain v. 계속(여전히) ~이다, 남아 있다

Hackers Practice p.205

01 ⓐ [토익 공식 4]		02 ⓑ [토익 공식 3]
03 ⓐ [토익 공식 2]		04 ⓐ [토익 공식 5]
05 ⓑ [토익 공식 3]		06 ⓑ [토익 공식 3]
07 ⓐ [토익 공식 4]		

08 even → even though [토익 공식 3]
09 Despite → Although [토익 공식 6]
10 during → while [토익 공식 6]
11 from → before [토익 공식 1]
12 as soon → as soon as [토익 공식 2]
13 while → because [토익 공식 4]
14 unless when → unless [토익 공식 3]

해석 01 나는 지갑을 잃어버려서, 어떤 신분증도 가지고 있지 않았다.
02 그 구두는 내가 예산 세운 것보다 비용이 더 들었지만, 나는 어쨌든 그것들을 구매했다.
03 나는 마케팅 조사가 끝날 때까지 그 프로젝트를 시작할 수 없다.
04 그 식당이 붐빌 때는 언제라도 사람들은 자리를 잡으려고 몇 시간을 기다린다.
05 대용량 파일을 보낼 경우에 대비하여 용량 제한이 없는 이메일 계정 주소를 알려주세요.
06 만약 공사가 완료되면, 새 버스 터미널이 5월에 운영을 시작할 것이다.
07 내 팸플릿을 직접 인쇄할 수 있도록 컬러 프린터를 샀다.
08 얼마나 많은 사람들이 올 것인지 확실하지 않았지만 나는 예약을 했다.
09 그 방송은 시청률이 좋지 않았지만, 방송국은 그것을 연장했다.
10 Mr. Jameson이 그 회사의 회장이었던 동안에 총 수익은 200퍼센트 증가했다.
11 수석 회계사는 새 예산안을 작성하기 전에 그 회사의 연간 지출 보고서를 참조해야 한다.
12 인쇄소에서 초대장들이 도착하자마자 여주인은 우편으로 그것들을 보낼 것이다.
13 미디어 캠페인이 준비되지 않았기 때문에 나는 출시 일정을 변경했다.
14 아프지 않다면 관리자조차 통지 없이 일찍 퇴근할 수 없다.

Hackers Test
p.206

Part 5

01 (D)	02 (A)	03 (D)	04 (D)	05 (A)
06 (D)	07 (C)	08 (A)	09 (C)	10 (D)
11 (C)	12 (B)	13 (C)	14 (D)	15 (B)
16 (A)	17 (B)	18 (C)		

Part 6

19 (D)	20 (C)	21 (C)	22 (D)

01 부사절 접속사 채우기

해설 이 문장은 필수성분(Everyone ~ personnel)을 갖춘 완전한 절이므로 ____ they are ~ time은 수식어 거품으로 보아야 한다. 이 수식어 거품은 동사(are entering)가 있는 거품절이므로, 거품절을 이끌 수 있는 부사절 접속사 (B)와 (D)가 정답의 후보이다. '잠시 동안만 들어올지라도 신분을 증명해야 한다'라는 의미가 되어야 하므로 (D) even if(비록 ~일지라도, 비록 ~이지만)가 정답이다. 전치사 (A) regarding과 (C) in spite of는 절을 이끌 수 없으므로 답이 될 수 없다.

해석 비록 잠시 동안만 들어올지라도 모든 사람은 반드시 안내 데스크 직원에게 자기 신분을 증명해야 한다.

어휘 identify oneself (자기) 신분을 증명하다 personnel n. 직원

02 부사절 접속사 채우기

해설 '연료비도 절약해 주면서 모든 편의 시설을 제공한다'는 의미가 되어야 하므로 (A) while(~하면서, ~하는 동안)이 정답이다. 참고로, 여기서 while은 분사구문 (saving ~ consumption)을 이끌고 있다.

해석 Ventress사가 생산한 새로운 세단형 자동차는 연료 소비 비용을 절약해 주면서 운전자들에게 최신식 차량의 모든 편의 시설을 제공한다.

어휘 comfort n. 편의 시설; v. 위로하다 fuel n. 연료 consumption n. 소비

03 부사절 접속사 채우기

해설 이 문장은 필수성분(quarterly bonuses are awarded)을 갖춘 완전한 절이므로, ____ the sales goals are met은 수식어 거품으로 보아야 한다. 이 수식어 거품은 동사(are met)가 있는 거품절이므로, 거품절을 이끌 수 있는 부사절 접속사 (B), (C), (D)가 정답의 후보이다. '상여금은 오직 목표가 달성되는 경우에만 주어진다'는 의미가 되어야 하므로 (D) provided that(오직 ~하는 경우에만)이 정답이다. 이때 that은 생략될 수도 있다. (B) in case는 '목표가 달성될 경우에 대비하여 상여금이 주어진다', (C) rather than은 '목표가 달성되기 보다는 상여금이 주어진다'는 어색한 의미를 만들기 때문에 답이 될 수 없다. 참고로, A rather than B(B보다는 A)는 등위접속사처럼 같은 품사나 같은 구조를 연결하는 역할을 한다.

해석 Pemberton 섬유 회사에서, 분기별 상여금은 오직 매출 목표가 달성되는 경우에만 주어진다.

어휘 quarterly adj. 분기별의, 한 해 네 번의 award v. 주다, 수여하다 sales goal 매출 목표 meet v. 달성하다, 충족시키다

04 부사절 접속사 채우기

해설 이 문장은 필수성분(The manager ~ firms)을 갖춘 완전한 절이므로 ____ approval ~ given은 수식어 거품으로 보아야 한다. 이 수식어 거품은 동사(was given)가 있는 거품절이므로, 거품절을 이끌 수 있는 부사절 접속사 (A)와 (D)가 정답의 후보이다. '승인을 받은 이래로 보안 회사에 연락했다'는 의미가 되어야 하므로 (D) since(~한 이래로)가 정답이다.

해석 회의장 관리자는 경보 장치를 개선하기 위한 승인을 받은 이래로 몇몇 보안 회사에 연락했다.

어휘 convention hall (호텔 등의) 회의장 contact v. 연락하다, 접촉하다

05 부사절 접속사 채우기

해설 이 문장은 필수성분(Please tell ~ researcher)을 갖춘 완전한 절이므로 ____ the survey ~ forms는 수식어 거품으로 보아야 한다. 이 수식어 거품은 동사(have completed)가 있는 거품절이므로, 거품절을 이끌 수 있는 부사절 접속사 (A) when(~하면, ~할 때)이 정답이다. 수식어 거품이 완전한 절이므로 불완전한 절 앞에 오는 관계대명사 (B) which, (C) who와 복합관계대명사 (D) whatever는 답이 될 수 없다.

해석 설문 조사 참가자들이 평가 양식을 작성하면 연구원에게 알리라고 담당자에게 말해 주세요.

어휘 in charge 담당하는, ~을 맡고 있는 notify v. 알리다, 통지하다 participant n. 참가자, 참여자 assessment n. 평가

06 부사절 접속사 자리 채우기

해설 that절은 필수성분(applicants ~ membership)을 갖춘 완전한 절이므로 ____ recommended by a current member는 수식어 거품으로 보아야 한다. 이 수식어 거품 자리에 온 분사구문 앞에 올 수 있는 부사절 접속사 (D) unless(~이 아닌 한)가 정답이다. 전치사 (A) except for와 접속부사 (B) or else는 과거분사가 이끄는 구문 앞에 올 수 없으며, 등위접속사 (C) but(그러나)은 두 개의 과거분사(granted ~와 recommended ~) 사이에 올 수 있지만 이 문장에서 어색한 의미를 만들기 때문에 답이 될 수 없다.

해석 그 클럽은 매우 폐쇄적이어서 현 회원에 의해 추천되지 않는 한 신청자들에게 회원권이 주어지지 않을 것이다.

어휘 exclusive adj. 폐쇄적인, 독점적인, 배타적인 grant v. 주다, 승인하다, 허가하다

07 부사절 접속사 채우기

해설 이 문장은 필수성분(The policy ~ management)을 갖춘 완전한 절이므로 ____ the current package ~ expansive는 수식어 거품으로 보아야 한다. 이 수식어 거품은 동사(was considered)가 있는 거품절이므로, 거품절에 올 수 있는 부사절 접속사 (A)와 (C)가 정답의 후보이다. '현행 정책이 너무 광범위하다고 여겨졌기 때문에 방침이 수정되었다'라는 의미가 되어야 하므로 (C) because(~이기 때문에)가 정답이다.

해석 현행 정책이 너무 광범위하다고 여겨졌기 때문에 직원 혜택에 관한 방침은 경영진에 의해 수정되었다.

어휘 benefit n. 혜택 package n. (종합) 정책 expansive adj. 광범위한

08 부사절 접속사 채우기

해설 빈칸 뒤에 that이 있고 '전문가들은 국가 경제가 빠르게 성장하고 있다는 점에서 정확하다'는 의미가 되어야 하므로 부사절 접속사 in that(~라는 점에서)을 만드는 (A) in이 정답이다. (D) so도 that과 함께 부사절 접속사 so that(~할 수 있도록)을 만들지만 '국가 경제가 성장할 수 있도록 정확하다'라는 어색한 의미가 되어 답이 될 수 없다.

해석 전문가들은 국가 경제가 다른 나라의 경제보다 더 빠르게 성장하고 있다는 점에서 정확하다.

어휘 correct adj. 정확한, 옳은 nation n. 나라, 국가

09 부사절 접속사 채우기

해설 이 문장은 필수성분(The executive ~ job)을 갖춘 완전한 절이므로 ____ all ~ met은 수식어 거품으로 보아야 한다. 이 수식어 거품은 동사(are met)가 있는 거품절이므로, 거품절을 이끌 수 있는 부사절 접속사 (C)와 (D)가 정답의 후보이다. '모든 조건들이 충족되는 경우에만 그 일을 수락할 것이다'라는 의미가 되어야 하므로 (C) only if(오직 ~하는 경우에만)가 정답이다. (A) up to는 전치사이므로 절을 이끌 수 없다.

해석 그 임원은 그의 모든 조건들이 충족되는 경우에만 그 일을 수락할 것이다.

어휘 executive n. 임원, 이사 meet v. 충족하다, 응하다

10 복합관계부사 채우기

해설 '구매 여부를 결정할 때는 언제라도'라는 의미가 되어야 하므로 (D) Whenever(언제 ~하더라도)가 정답이다. 참고로, 'whenever + -ing'는 'when + -ing'에서 나온 형태로 볼 수 있다.

해석 아파트 구매 여부를 결정할 때는 언제라도 재산세와 유지 비용을 계산해 보는 것이 필요하다.

어휘 property tax 재산세
maintenance n. (건물·기계 등을 정기적으로 보수·점검하는) 유지

11 부사절 접속사 자리 채우기

해설 이 문장은 필수성분(The National Review ~ country)을 갖춘 완전한 절이므로 ____ hiring ~ publications는 수식어 거품으로 보아야 한다. -ing(hiring)를 보아, 이 수식어 거품은 분사구문일 수도 있고 동명사구일 수도 있다. 따라서 빈칸에는 분사구문을 이끄는 부사절 접속사도, 동명사구를 이끄는 전치사도 올 수 있다. '몇몇 유명한 기자들을 고용한 후에 가장 잘 팔리는 신문이 되었다'라는 의미가 되어야 하므로 (C) after(~한 후에)가 정답이다. 참고로, after는 부사절 접속사와 전치사 역할을 모두 할 수 있다.

해석 다른 신문사로부터 몇몇 유명한 기자들을 고용한 후에 The National Review지는 전국에서 가장 잘 팔리는 신문이 되었다.

어휘 notable adj. 유명한, 중요한 journalist n. 기자

12 부사절 접속사 채우기

해설 이 문장은 필수성분(Members ~ hours)을 갖춘 완전한 절이므로 ____ the contract negotiations are complete은 수식어 거품으로 보아야 한다. 이 수식어 거품은 동사(are)가 있는 거품절이므로, 거품절에 올 수 있는 부사절 접속사 (A)와 (B)가 정답의 후보이다. '계약 협상이 완료될 때까지 초과 근무를 요구받다'라는 의미가 되어야 하므로 (B) until(~할 때까지)이 정답이다.

해석 법무팀 직원들은 계약 협상이 완료될 때까지 초과 근무를 하도록 요구되고 있다.

어휘 be asked to do ~하도록 요구되다 negotiation n. 협상
complete adj. 완료된, 완성된; v. 끝마치다, 완료하다

13 상관접속사 채우기

해설 but 다음에 와서 to 부정사구(to pay ~ business trips)를 to 부정사구(to purchase personal items)를 연결하여 B but not A(A가 아닌 B)라는 형태를 이루는 (C) not이 정답이다. 참고로, 여기서는 B 자리에 온 to 부정사구 앞에 only가 와서 'A가 아닌 오직 B'라는 의미가 되었다.

해석 관리자들은 개인 물품을 구매하기 위해서가 아니라, 오직 출장 동안의 식사와 숙박 비용을 결제하기 위해서만 법인 카드를 사용할 수 있다.

14 부사절 접속사 채우기

해설 '부품이 정기적으로 점검 및 관리되는 경우에만 선명하게 복사할 것이다'라는 의미가 되어야 하므로 (D) as long as(오직 ~하는 경우에만)가 정답이다. (B) in case는 앞으로 일어날 상황에 대처할 일을 계획하고 있다는 문맥에 쓰이므로 답이 될 수 없다.

해석 오직 기계 부품들이 정기적으로 점검되고 관리되는 경우에만, 이 컬러 복사기는 놀라울 만큼 선명하게 그림과 글을 복사할 것이다.

어휘 reproduce v. 복사하다 remarkable adj. 놀라운, 주목할 만한
clarity n. 선명도

15 부사절 접속사 채우기

해설 이 문장은 주어(An account)와 동사(cannot be accessed or reactivated)를 갖춘 완전한 절이므로 ____ deleted by ~ user는 수식어 거품으로 보아야 한다. 이 수식어 거품 자리에 온 분사구문(deleted by the registered user) 앞에 올 수 있는 것은 부사절 접속사 (B) 또는 (C)이다. p.p.(deleted)를 포함한 분사구문의 바로 앞에 올 수 있는 것이 와야 하므로 (B) once(일단 ~하면)가 정답이다. (C) after(~한 후에)는 뒤에 과거분사가 포함된 분사구문이 올 경우, p.p.가 뒤에 올 수 없고 'being + p.p.' 형태가 와야 한다.

해석 등록된 사용자에 의해 일단 삭제되면 TikTak의 음악 스트리밍 서비스의 계정은 접속되거나 재활성화될 수 없다.

어휘 account n. 계정 access v. 접속하다; n. 접근, 입장
reactivate v. 재활성화하다

16 부사절 접속사 채우기

해설 이 문장은 필수성분(Gary ~ shop)을 갖춘 완전한 절이므로 ____ the bank ~ loan은 수식어 거품으로 보아야 한다. 이 수식어 거품은 동사(approves)가 있는 거품절이므로, 거품절을 이끌 수 있는 부사절 접속사 (A)와 (D)가 정답의 후보이다. '은행이 대출 신청을 승인하는 경우에만 가게를 열 계획이다'라는 의미가 되어야 하므로 (A) Providing(오직 ~하는 경우에만)이 정답이다.

해석 오직 은행이 그의 소기업 대출 신청을 승인하는 경우에만, Gary는 연말까지 가게를 열 계획이다.

어휘 approve v. 승인하다, 인정하다 application n. 신청(서), 지원 loan n. 대출

17 부사절 접속사 채우기

해설 이 문장은 필수성분(Included ~ coupon)을 갖춘 완전한 절이므로 ____ readers ~ friends는 수식어 거품으로 보아야 한다. 이 수식어 거품은 동사(can introduce)가 있는 거품절이므로, 거품절을 이끌 수 있는 부사절 접속사 (A)와 (B)가 정답의 후보이다. '잡지를 소개할 수 있도록 쿠폰이 포함되다'라는 의미가 되어야 하므로 (B) so that(~할 수 있도록)이 정답이다. 참고로, 이 문장의 필수성분은 보어로 사용된 형용사 분사 Included가 문장 앞으로 나와 주어(a coupon)와 동사(is)의 자리가 바뀐 형태이다.

해석 독자들이 친구들에게 잡지를 소개할 수 있도록 할인된 1년 구독 쿠폰이 이번 달 호에 포함되어 있다.

어휘 include v. 포함하다, 넣다 in addition to ~에 더해서

18 수식어 거품 채우기

해설 이 문장은 필수성분(Addison Manufacturing ~ means)을 갖춘 완전한 절이므로 ____ the amount of raw materials needed는 수식어 거품으로 보아야 한다. 보기 중 수식어 거품을 이끌 수 있는 전치사 (C) Considering(~을 고려했을 때)이 정답이다.

해석 필요한 원자재의 양을 고려했을 때, Addison 제조 회사는 필요로 하는 공급량을 얻을 다른 방법을 알아볼 것이다.

어휘 explore v. 알아보다, 조사하다, 탐구하다 means n. 방법, 수단
supply n. 공급량 consideration n. 고려

날짜: 8월 9일
발신: jdemers@starwaysfurniture.com
수신: bkent@filconsulting.com
제목: 직업 소개 지원

Mr. Kent께,

¹⁹캘리포니아 주에 있는 제조 공장의 최근 확장은 Starways 가구 회사가 이 시설에서의 생산 능력과 인력을 증가시키는 것을 가능하게 했습니다. ²⁰저희는 위스콘신 주와 캔자스 주에 있는 공장을 닫으려고 계획하고 있으며, 모든 가구 생산이 9월 1일에 로스앤젤레스 공장으로 이전될 것입니다.

저희는 이 두 공장의 근로자들에게 전근할 것을 요청하였으나, 몇몇은 제안을 거절했습니다. ²¹그러므로, 저희는 그들이 사직 합의서에 서명한다면 그들에게 직업 소개 지원을 제공하기로 결정했습니다.

직업 소개를 신속히 처리하기 위해 저희는 귀사가 이 직원들을 위한 고용 교육 워크숍을 제공해 주셨으면 합니다. ²²교육은 가능한 한 빨리 이루어져야 합니다. 위스콘신 주와 캔자스 주의 공장들은 다음 2주에 걸쳐 문을 닫을 것입니다. 이 문제를 논의하기 위해 다음 주 월요일에 만날 수 있겠습니까?

Josie Demers

job placement 직업 소개, 취업 알선   **expansion** n. 확장, 확대
relocate v. 전근하다   **assistance** n. 지원, 보조, 도움
resignation n. 사직   **expedite** v. 신속히 처리하다

19 유사의미 형용사 중에서 고르기

해설   (A), (C), (D)는 모두 가까움을 의미하는 형용사이다. '최근 확장이 캘리포니아 주에 있는 시설에서의 생산 능력과 인력을 증가시키는 것을 가능하게 했다'라는 문맥이 되어야 하므로 최근의 사건, 시간을 나타내는 형용사 (D) recent가 정답이다. (recent news: 최근 소식) (A) adjacent는 '(거리상) 가까운, 인접한' (adjacent to the station: 역에서 가까운), (C) nearest는 '(거리상, 공간상) 가장 가까운'(the nearest coffee shop: 가장 가까운 커피숍)이라는 뜻이다.

20 올바른 시제의 동사 채우기   주변 문맥 파악

해설   '9월 1일에 모든 가구 생산이 로스앤젤레스 공장으로 이전된다'라는 문맥인데, 이 경우 빈칸이 있는 문장만으로는 올바른 시제의 동사를 고를 수 없으므로 주변 문맥이나 전체 문맥을 파악하여 정답을 고른다. '9월 1일(September 1)'은 이메일의 발신 날짜인 '8월 9일(Date: August 9)'이후이므로 생산이 이전되는 시점은 이메일을 작성한 시점보다 미래임을 알 수 있다. 따라서 미래 시제 (C) will be shifted가 정답이다.

어휘   **shift** v. (장소를) 옮기다, 이동하다

21 부사절 접속사 채우기

해설   '그들이 사직 합의서에 서명한다면 직업 소개 지원을 제공할 것이다'라는 의미가 되어야 하므로 '(만약) ~라면'의 뜻으로 조건을 나타내는 부사절 접속사 (C) provided가 정답이다.

어휘   **provided** conj. (만약) ~라면, 오직 ~하는 경우에만

22 알맞은 문장 고르기

해석   (A) 새로 고용되었기 때문에, 그들에게 종합적인 오리엔테이션이 필요할 수도 있습니다.
(B) 그들은 수업이 그들의 경력에 도움이 된다고 생각했습니다.
(C) 캘리포니아 공장은 우리의 필요를 처리할 장비가 잘 갖추어져 있습니다.
(D) 교육은 가능한 한 빨리 이루어져야 합니다.

해설   빈칸에 들어갈 알맞은 문장을 고르는 문제이므로 빈칸의 주변 문맥이나 전체 문맥을 파악한다. 앞 문장 'To expedite job placement, we would like your company to provide ~ training workshops.'에서 직업 소개를 신속히 처리하기 위해 수신자의 회사가 교육 워크숍을 제공해주길 바란다고 했고, 뒤 문장 'The Wisconsin and Kansas plants will close over the next two weeks.'에서 위스콘신 주와 캔자스 주의 공장이 다음 2주에 걸쳐 문을 닫을 것이라고 했으므로 빈칸에는 교육이 가능한 한 빨리 이루어져야 한다는 내용이 들어가야 함을 알 수 있다. 따라서 (D) The trainings should take

---

place as soon as possible이 정답이다.

어휘   **comprehensive** adj. 종합적인

Chapter 18 명사절

1 명사절의 자리와 쓰임   p.209
   1. (C)   2. (D)   3. (C)

1. 명사절 접속사 채우기

해설   타동사(confirmed)의 목적어 자리에 온 절(Selectric Incorporated ~ pagers) 앞에는 명사절 접속사가 와야 하므로 (C) that이 정답이다. 전치사 (A)와 (B), 대명사 (D)는 절을 이끌 수 없으므로 답이 될 수 없다.

해석   그 회사의 언론 담당 직원은 Selectric사가 더 이상 무선 호출기를 제조하지 않을 것임을 확인했다.

어휘   **no longer** 더 이상 ~않다   **manufacture** v. 제조하다; n. 제조(업)
   pager n. (휴대용 소형) 무선 호출기

2. 명사절 접속사 채우기

해설   동사(indicated)의 목적어 자리에 온 절(the past year ~ sales) 앞에는 명사절 접속사가 와야 하므로 (D) that이 정답이다. 전치사 (A)와 (C), 대명사 (B)는 절을 이끌 수 없으므로 답이 될 수 없다.

해석   United Plastics사는 지난해 해외 매출이 10퍼센트 감소했다고 말했다.

어휘   **indicate** v. ~을 (간단히) 말하다, 시사하다, 나타내다   **past** adj. 지난, 이전의

3. 명사절 접속사 채우기

해설   동명사(determining)의 목적어 자리에 온 절(____ will be given the award) 앞에는 명사절 접속사가 와야 하므로 (C) who가 정답이다. 대명사 (A)와 (B)는 절을 이끌 수 없고, (D)는 부사절 접속사로 명사절 앞에 올 수 없으므로 답이 될 수 없다.

해석   누가 상을 받을지 결정하는 데에 경영진을 도울 수 있도록 직원들은 이달의 직원상을 받을 사람을 선택하여 제출할 것을 요청받는다.

어휘   **pick** n. 선택된(뽑힌) 사람(것); v. 선택하다   **give award** 상을 주다

2 명사절 접속사 1: that   p.210
   1. (A)   2. (B)   3. (B)

1. that 채우기

해설   주어 자리에 온 절(the holiday ~ days)은 명사절이므로 명사절 접속사 (A) That이 정답이다. 부사절 접속사 (B), (C)와 등위접속사 (D)는 명사절 접속사 자리에 올 수 없으므로 답이 될 수 없다. 참고로, 주어로 쓰인 that절의 that은 생략될 수 없음을 알아두자.

해석   휴일이 오직 3일만 지속된다는 것은 전 직원에게 실망스러운 일이다.

어휘   **last** v. 지속되다, 계속하다   **disappointment** n. 실망   **entire** adj. 전체의

2. that 채우기

해설   형용사 convinced와 절(his decision ~ correct) 사이에는 명사절 접속사가 와야 하므로 (B) that이 정답이다. 관계대명사 (A) whom 뒤에는 불완전한 절이 와야 하며 전치사 (C)와 등위접속사 (D)는 명사절 접속사 자리에 올 수 없으므로 답이 될 수 없다.

해석   다음 날 그 회사가 기록적인 손실을 발표하자 Mr. Forster는 주식을 매각하기로 했던 그의 결정이 옳았음을 확인했다.

어휘   **stock** n. 주식   **record** adj. 기록적인; v. 기록하다; n. 기록
   be convinced that ~을 확신하다

3. that 채우기

해설 명사 rumor와 동격을 이루는 절(the company was in financial trouble) 사이에는 명사절 접속사가 와야 한다. 따라서 (B) that이 정답이다.

해석 투자자들과의 회의 중에, 상무 이사는 회사가 재정적인 어려움에 빠졌다는 소문을 부인했다.

어휘 refute v. 부인하다   rumor that ~라는 소문
be in financial trouble 재정적인 어려움에 빠지다

---

3 명사절 접속사 2 : if, whether   p.211
   1. (A)   2. (B)   3. (C)

1. if 채우기

해설 동사(know)의 목적어 자리에 온 명사절(the in-house trainers ~ evenings)의 접속사를 채우는 문제이다. '추가 리더십 세미나를 개최하고자 하는지 알고 싶어 한다'는 문맥에서 '~인지 아닌지'라는 의미를 갖는 명사절 접속사 (A) if가 정답이다. 부사절 접속사 (B)와 (D)는 명사절 접속사 자리에 올 수 없고, 접속부사 (C)는 두 개의 절을 연결할 수 없으므로 답이 될 수 없다.

해석 인사부장은 사내 교육 담당자들이 저녁에 추가 리더십 세미나를 기꺼이 개최하고자 하는지 알고 싶어 한다.

어휘 in-house 사내의   trainer n. 교육 시키는 사람
be willing to do 기꺼이 ~하다
conduct(=hold) a seminar 세미나를 개최하다
supplementary adj. 추가의, 보충의

2. whether (or not) 채우기

해설 whether 다음에 단 하나의 to 부정사(to install ~ system)가 와 있으므로 'whether or not + to 부정사' 형태를 이룰 수 있는 (B) or not이 정답이다.

해석 Chambers Tech사는 최신 버전의 운영 체제를 사무실 컴퓨터에 설치할지 말지에 대해 아직 고려하고 있는 중이다.

어휘 latest adj. 최신의   whether or not ~인지 아닌지

3. if와 whether 구별하여 채우기

해설 '자금을 할당할지 말지에 대해 논의를 가질 것이다'라는 의미에 어울리는 접속사는 (A) if 또는 (C) whether이다. 이 중 (A) if는 전치사(about) 다음에 올 수 없으므로 (C) whether가 정답이다.

해석 위원회는 온라인 마케팅 캠페인에 자금을 할당할지 말지에 대해 논의를 가질 것이다.

어휘 committee n. 위원회   allocate v. 할당하다, 배분하다

---

4 명사절 접속사 3 : 의문사 who, what, which, when, where, how, why   p.212
   1. (D)   2. (C)   3. (A)

1. 의문사 채우기

해설 동사(know)의 목적어 역할을 하는 명사절의 접속사를 채우는 문제이다. 명사절 자리에 주어가 없는 불완전한 절(prepared ~ Web site)이 와 있으므로 의문대명사 (C)와 (D)가 정답의 후보이다. '누가 준비했는지 알고 싶다'는 의미가 되어야 하므로 (D) who(누가)가 정답이다. 의문부사 (A) why와 명사절 접속사 (B) that 다음에는 완전한 절이 나와야 하므로 답이 될 수 없다.

해석 그 관리자는 회사 웹사이트에 있는 직원 프로필이 상세하고 잘 작성되었다는 것을 발견하고 누가 그것들을 준비했는지 알고 싶어 한다.

어휘 prepare v. 준비하다   detailed adj. 상세한

2. 의문사 채우기

해설 타동사(asked)의 목적어 역할을 하는 명사절을 이끄는 접속사가 빈칸에 와야 하므로 (C)와 (D)가 정답의 후보이다. '얼마나 많은 사람들'이라는 의미가 되어야 하므로 (D) what(무엇이)가 아닌 (C) how(얼마나)가 정답이다. 전치사

(A)와 (B)는 절을 이끌 수 없으므로 답이 될 수 없다.

해석 행사를 준비하기 위해, 음식 공급자는 얼마나 많은 사람들이 만찬에 참석할 것인지 물었다.

어휘 make preparation 준비하다   caterer n. 음식 공급자

3. 의문사 채우기

해설 to 부정사(to do ~) 앞에 의문사를 채우는 문제이므로 (A), (C), (D)가 정답의 후보이다. '무엇을 해야 할지 알다'라는 의미가 되어야 하므로 (A) what (무엇이)이 정답이다. 의문사가 아닌 (B) that은 답에서 제외된다.

해석 Mr. Albertson은 회사 변호사와 상의할 것인데, 이는 그녀가 그 법률상의 문제에 대해 무엇을 해야 할지 알 것이기 때문이다.

어휘 consult v. 상의하다

---

5 명사절 접속사 4 : 복합관계대명사 who(m)ever, whatever, whichever   p.213
   1. (B)   2. (C)   3. (C)

1. 복합관계대명사 채우기

해설 '논의된 것은 무엇이든 기밀이다'라는 의미가 되어야 하므로 (B) Whatever (무엇이든 간에)가 정답이다. (A) Whichever는 '셀 수 있는 몇 가지 중에서 어느 것이든 간에'를 의미하므로 문맥에 맞지 않아 답이 될 수 없다.

해석 이사진 회의에서 논의된 것은 무엇이든 기밀이며 어떤 이유로든 다른 직원들에게 알려지면 안 된다.

어휘 confidential adj. 기밀의   divulge v. (비밀을) 알려주다, 누설하다

2. 복합관계대명사/복합관계형용사와 의문사 구별하여 채우기

해설 that절의 주어 자리에 온 명사절(needs a certificate ~ reasons) 안에는 주어가 와야 하므로 목적격 (D) whomever를 제외한 (A), (B), (C)가 정답의 후보이다. '필요로 하는 누구든'이라는 의미가 되어야 하므로, 의문사 (A) who가 아닌 복합관계대명사 (C) whoever가 정답이다. (B) whenever는 when처럼 빠진 요소가 없는 완벽한 절 앞에 오며, 주어가 없는 불완전한 절 앞에 올 수 없다.

해석 그 관리자는 개인적인 이유로 재직 증명서가 필요한 사람은 누구든지 Ms. Simon에게 도움을 요청하라고 직원들에게 다시 한번 말해 주었다.

어휘 remind v. 다시 한번 말해 주다, 상기시키다
certificate of employment 재직 증명서   ask for ~을 요청하다
assistance n. 도움, 보조

3. 복합관계대명사/복합관계형용사와 의문사 구별하여 채우기

해설 빈칸에는 문장 안에서 주어로 쓰인 명사절(team of sales ~ units)을 이끄는 접속사가 와야 하며, '어느 팀이든지'라는 의미가 되어야 하므로 의문형용사 (A) Which가 아닌 복합관계형용사 (C) Whichever가 정답이다. 형용사 또는 대명사 (B)와 대명사 (D)는 절을 이끌 수 없으므로 답이 될 수 없다.

해석 가장 많은 수량의 물품을 판매한 영업 사원의 팀은 어느 팀이든지 이달의 팀 상을 받을 것이다.

어휘 sales representative 영업 사원   unit n. (상품의) 한 개

---

6 what과 that의 구별   p.214
   1. (C)   2. (D)   3. (A)

1. what과 that 구별하여 채우기

해설 동사(determine)의 목적어 자리에 온 명사절의 접속사를 채우는 문제이다. '고객들이 필요로 하는 것'이라는 의미가 되어야 하며, 빈칸 뒤에 동사(need)의 목적어가 빠진 불완전한 절이 왔으므로 불완전한 절을 이끄는 (C) what이 정답이다. (A) how(어떻게)와 (D) if(~인지 아닌지)는 문맥에 맞지 않아 답이 될 수 없다.

해석 호텔 업계에서, 잘 훈련되고 경험이 풍부한 직원들은 고객들이 무엇을 필요로

하는지 신속히 알아낼 수 있다.

어휘 experienced adj. 경험이 풍부한 determine v. 알아내다, 밝히다

2. what과 that 구별하여 채우기

해설 동사(understand)의 목적어 자리에 온 명사절(the company ~ director)의 접속사를 채우는 문제이다. 빈칸 뒤에 완전한 절이 왔으므로 완전한 절을 이끄는 (D) that이 정답이다.

해석 그 직원은 기업 활동을 위한 회사 자금이 임원의 사전 승인 없이는 지출될 수 없다는 것을 알고 있다.

어휘 understand v. 알다, 이해하다 corporate adj. 기업의
disburse v. 지출하다, 분배하다 prior adj. 사전의 approval n. 승인

3. what과 that 구별하여 채우기

해설 '매우 쉬워서 그 결과 ~하다'라는 의미이므로 so 뒤에 온 절(even a beginner ~ data) 앞에는 부사절을 이끄는 that이 와야 한다. 따라서 (A) that이 정답이다. (C) what은 명사절만 이끌 수 있으므로 답이 될 수 없다.

해석 새 컴퓨터 프로그램들이 정보를 정리하는 것을 매우 쉽게 해주어서 초보자조차 어떠한 자료로도 인상적인 도표를 만들어낼 수 있다.

어휘 organize v. 정리하다, 체계화하다

Hackers Practice
p.215

01 ⓐ [토익 공식 2]
02 ⓑ [토익 공식 4]
03 ⓐ [토익 공식 3, 6]
04 ⓑ [토익 공식 3]
05 ⓑ [토익 공식 5]
06 ⓑ [토익 공식 4]
07 ⓐ [토익 공식 2]
08 when the moment is right to make a change
 → 동사의 목적어 [토익 공식 1, 4]
09 How the offices will be assigned → 주어 [토익 공식 1, 4]
10 what questions would appear on the test
 → 전치사의 목적어 [토익 공식 1, 4]
11 what customers have been complaining about
 → 보어 [토익 공식 1, 4]
12 that good education should be available to all youths
 → 명사 idea의 동격절 [토익 공식 1, 2]
13 why the staff were being trained again
 → 동사의 목적어 [토익 공식 1, 4]
14 that many people dislike telemarketing
 → 보어 [토익 공식 1, 2]

해석 01 나는 Hank가 휴스턴 지점의 운영을 인계받을 것이라고 확신한다.
02 그 소유주가 두 가지 제안 중 어떤 것을 선택할지는 불분명하다.
03 주민들은 교외의 성장이 소중한 토지의 부주의한 사용을 낳을 것이라고 걱정한다.
04 그 기자는 Ms. Lee에게 현행 프로젝트들이 있는지 여부 대신 그녀의 배경에 대해 질문했다.
05 현장 관리직에 지원하고 싶은 사람은 누구든지 본사에 이력서를 제출해야 한다.
06 Sarah는 다음 주 남미 여행을 위해 무엇을 싸야 할지 고르는 데 어려움을 겪고 있다.
07 최고 경영자는 회사가 반도체 시장으로 확장하고 있었다는 보도가 사실임을 확인했다.
08 공급 회사들은 변화를 주기에 적당한 시점이 언제인지를 결정해야 할 것이다.
09 사무실이 어떻게 배정될지는 관리자의 책임이다.
10 학생들은 시험에서 어떤 문제들이 나올지 걱정했다.
11 계산대의 긴 줄은 고객들이 불평해 왔던 것이다.
12 그 재단은 좋은 교육이 모든 젊은이들에게 이용 가능해야 한다는 생각으로 설립되었다.
13 관리자는 직원들이 왜 다시 교육 받고 있었는지 설명하지 않았다.
14 문제는 많은 사람들이 전화 판매를 싫어한다는 것이다.

Hackers Test
p.216

Part 5

01 (D)	02 (D)	03 (A)	04 (D)	05 (D)
06 (C)	07 (B)	08 (C)	09 (A)	10 (B)
11 (C)	12 (B)	13 (C)	14 (A)	15 (D)
16 (B)	17 (A)	18 (C)		

Part 6

19 (D)	20 (B)	21 (D)	22 (C)

01 의문사 채우기

해설 동사(reveals)의 목적어 자리에 온 명사절(brands ~ most)을 이끌 수 있는 것은 명사절 접속사이므로 (B), (C), (D)가 정답의 후보이다. 빈칸 뒤에 명사(brands)가 있고, '어떤 브랜드를 가장 좋아하는지를 보여주다'라는 의미가 되어야 하므로 brands와 함께 명사절의 주어 역할을 하는 의문형용사 (D) which가 정답이다. 부사절 접속사 (A) as는 수식어 거품절을 이끈다.

해석 그 설문 조사는 소비자들이 어떤 브랜드를 가장 좋아하는지를 보여준다.

어휘 reveal v. 보여주다, 드러내다 admire v. 좋아하다, 감탄하다

02 의문사 채우기

해설 타동사(know)의 목적어 자리에 온 절(the final ~ contract) 앞에 명사절 접속사를 채우는 문제이다. 빈칸 다음에 주어(the final revisions), 동사(will be made)를 갖춘 완벽한 절이 왔으며, '최종 수정이 언제 이루어질 것인지'라는 의미가 되어야 하므로 의문사 (D) when(언제)이 정답이다. 전치사인 (A)와 (B)는 절을 이끌 수 없고, 관계대명사 (C)는 불완전한 절을 취하므로 답이 될 수 없다.

해석 마케팅 이사는 계약서에 최종 수정이 언제 이루어질지 알고 싶어 한다.

03 수량 표현 자리 채우기

해설 문장의 주어인 명사(club members)를 꾸미는 자리이므로 형용사 (A) all이 정답이다. 부사 (B)는 명사를 꾸밀 수 없으므로 답이 될 수 없다. 빈칸은 필수성분 앞이므로, 수식어 거품 앞에 오는 부사절 접속사 (C)도 답이 될 수 없다. (D)가 복합관계형용사로 쓰여 whichever club members(=any club members that)가 되려면 그 뒤에 -ing(joining)가 아닌 동사가 와야 한다.

해석 6시에, 해안가에서의 특별 만찬에 참가하는 모든 클럽 회원들은 Lakeside 센터 입구에 모여야 한다.

04 복합관계대명사/복합관계형용사와 의문사 구별하여 채우기

해설 that절 안에서 주어 역할을 하는 절(reports they needed) 앞에는 명사절 접속사가 와야 하므로 접속사 (C)와 (D)가 정답의 후보이다. '어떤 보고서든지'라는 의미가 되어야 하므로, 의문형용사 (C) whose가 아닌 복합관계형용사 (D) whichever가 정답이다. 참고로 whichever가 명사(reports)를 꾸미면서 that절 내에서 주어 역할을 하는 명사절을 이끌고 있다. 지시대명사 (A)와 형용사 (B)는 절을 이끌 수 없다.

해석 언어학 학술회 참가자들은 미리 요청된다면 그들이 필요로 하는 어떤 보고서든지 제공받을 수 있음을 보장받았다.

어휘 linguistics n. 언어학 in advance 미리

05 what과 that 구별하여 채우기

해설 명사(the documents)를 뒤에서 꾸미는 절(he ~ desk)은 형용사절(관계절)이므로, 형용사절을 이끌 수 있는 관계대명사 (D) that이 정답이다. 명사절 접속사 (A)와 (B)는 형용사절을 이끌 수 없으며, 지시대명사 (C) those는 접속사 역할을 할 수 없다.

해석 Mr. Turner는 부주의로 그의 책상에 두고 나온 문서들을 가져오기 위해 사무실로 돌아가야 했다.

어휘 inadvertently adv. 부주의로, 무심코

06 등위접속사 채우기

해설 '주문은 결제가 이루어진 날에 발송되고 배송은 도착지에 따라 3주에서 6주가 필요하다'라는 의미가 되어야 하므로 등위접속사 (C) and(그리고)가 정답

이다. 전치사 (B), (D)는 동사(require)를 목적어로 가질 수 없으므로 답이 될 수 없다.

해석 해외 주문은 일반적으로 결제가 이루어진 날에 발송되고 배송은 도착지에 따라 3주에서 6주가 필요하다.

어휘 depending on ~에 따라   destination n. 도착지, 목적지

07 whether A or B 채우기

해설 문장에 Whether가 있고 '세미나가 이번 달에 열리는지 4월에 열리는지'라는 의미가 되어야 하므로 whether A or B를 이룰 수 있는 (B) or가 정답이다.

해석 세미나가 이번 달에 열리는지 4월에 열리는지는 오늘 오후 회의에서 결정될 것이다.

어휘 hold v. 열다, 개최하다

08 that 채우기

해설 형용사 mindful과 절(steel beams ~ structure) 사이에는 명사절 접속사가 와야 하므로 (C) that이 정답이다. 전치사 (A)와 (B)는 절을 이끌 수 없다. 참고로, 의문사 (D) who 다음에는 주어나 목적어 등이 빠진 불완전한 절이 오는데, 이 문장에는 완전한 절이 와 있으므로 (D)는 답이 될 수 없다.

해석 그 현장 주임은 철제 기둥이 구조물의 가장 꼭대기로 끌어올려질 것임을 염두에 두라고 팀원들을 상기시켰다.

어휘 foreman n. 현장 주임   be mindful that ~을 염두에 두다, 주의하다
steel n. 철강   beam n. 기둥
hoist v. (흔히 밧줄이나 장비를 이용하여) 끌어올리다

09 명사 자리 채우기

해설 전치사(for)의 목적어 자리에 올 수 있는 것은 명사이므로 명사 (A) admittance가 정답이다. 동사 또는 과거분사 (B), 형용사 (C)와 동사 (D)는 전치사의 목적어 자리에 올 수 없다.

해석 간호사는 건강 검진 일정을 잡고 입원에 필요한 양식에 기입하는 데 있어 개개인을 돕는 것을 담당한다.

어휘 be in charge of ~을 담당하다, 책임지다   admittance n. 입원, 입장
admit v. 입원시키다, 인정하다   admittable adj. 용인할 수 있는, 허용할 수 있는

10 의문사 채우기

해설 전치사(on)의 목적어 역할을 하면서 to 부정사(to be ~)를 이끌 수 있는 의문사를 채우는 문제이다. '어떻게 유능하고 신뢰할 만한 지도자가 되는가'라는 의미가 되어야 하므로 (B) how(어떻게)가 정답이다.

해석 다음 주의 워크숍은 어떻게 기업계에서 유능하고 신뢰할 만한 지도자가 될 수 있는가에 초점을 맞출 것이다.

어휘 focus on ~에 초점을 맞추다   effective adj. 유능한, 효과적인
trustworthy adj. 신뢰할 수 있는   corporate n. 기업; adj. 조직의

11 의문사 채우기

해설 빈칸 뒤에 단수 명사(account)가 있고 '누구의 계좌로 사업 비용이 청구되어야 하는지를 알기 원한다'라는 의미가 되어야 하므로 의문형용사 (C) whose가 정답이다. 이 문장에서 whose는 '의문형용사 + 명사'의 형태로 뒤에 나온 명사를 꾸미면서 동사(know)의 목적어 자리에 온 명사절(to ___ ~ charged)을 이끄는 명사절 접속사로 쓰였다. 소유격 대명사 (A) its와 (B) their가 account 앞에 와서 account ば 관계대명사가 생략된 관계절 the business expenses should be charged의 수식을 받는 것으로 볼 수도 있지만 '사업 비용이 청구되어야 하는 그것의/그들의 계좌를 알기 원한다'라는 어색한 의미가 되고, its와 their가 지칭하는 대상이 문장에 없으므로 답이 될 수 없다. 지시형용사 (D) those는 복수 명사 앞에 오므로 답이 될 수 없다.

해석 Ms. Corning은 누구의 계좌로 사업 비용이 청구되어야 하는지를 알기 원한다.

어휘 account n. 계좌, 계정   charge v. 청구하다, 부과하다

12 명사절 접속사 채우기

해설 'advise + 목적어 + 명사절'이 수동태가 되면서 목적어가 주어(All personnel) 자리로 가고 수동태 동사(are advised) 뒤에 명사절이 온 형태이다. 따라서 명사절(they ~ supplies) 앞에서 명사절을 이끌 수 있는 접속

사 (B) that이 정답이다. (A) if는 '~인지 아닌지 권고받다'라는 어색한 의미를 만들기 때문에 답이 될 수 없다.

해석 모든 직원들은 사무용품 신청을 제한하도록 권고받는데, 비용 삭감이 즉시 시행될 것이기 때문이다.

어휘 personnel n. 직원; adj. 직원의   expenditure n. 비용, 지출   cut n. 삭감
take effect (법 등이) 시행되다, 효력이 발생하다

13 복합관계대명사/복합관계형용사와 의문사 구별하여 채우기

해설 전치사(by) 뒤에는 목적어만 올 수 있으므로 (C)와 (D)가 정답의 후보이다. '누구에 의해서 수행될지'라는 의미가 되어야 하므로, 복합관계대명사 (D) whomever(누구든 간에)가 아닌 의문사 (C) whom(누구)이 정답이다.

해석 비록 직원들이 일상활동에 관해서는 어느 정도 통제권을 갖지만, 어떤 업무가 누구에 의해 수행될지는 감독관이 결정한다.

어휘 when it comes to ~에 관해서는, ~의 문제라면

14 what과 that 구별하여 채우기

해설 '너무 힘들어서 그 결과 ~하다'라는 의미로 보아 so 뒤에 온 절(he takes an occasional personal day) 앞에서 부사절을 이끄는 (A) that이 정답이다. what절은 문장 내에서 명사 역할만 할 수 있으므로 (C) what은 답이 될 수 없다.

해석 Martin의 일은 너무나 힘들어서 그는 직장의 압박감에서 벗어나기 위해 가끔씩 휴가를 갖는다.

어휘 demanding adj. (일이) 힘든, 큰 노력을 요하는
occasional adj. 가끔의, 임시의   pressure n. 압박감
so ~ that - 너무 ~해서 -하다

15 복합관계대명사 채우기

해설 주어 자리에 온 절(exits the building last) 앞에는 명사절 접속사가 와야 하므로 (B)와 (D)가 정답의 후보이다. 빈칸은 명사절 내의 주어 자리이므로 주격 복합관계대명사 (D) Whoever가 정답이다. 목적격 복합관계대명사 (B) Whomever는 답이 될 수 없다. 참고로, (A) Anyone과 (C) Someone도 '누구든지'라는 의미이지만 대명사는 절을 이끌 수 없으므로 답이 될 수 없다.

해석 건물을 마지막으로 나가는 사람은 누구든지 사무실 경보장치를 설정하고 중앙 출입문을 잠가야 한다.

16 that 채우기

해설 opinion은 동격절을 취하는 명사이므로, opinion과 동격을 이루는 절(the company ~ staff) 사이에는 명사절 접속사가 와야 한다. 따라서 명사절 앞에 쓰여 동격절을 만드는 (B) that이 정답이다.

해석 대부분의 경영진들은 회사가 더 많은 직원을 고용해야 한다는 의견을 공통적으로 갖고 있다.

어휘 share v. 공통적으로 갖다, 공유하다   opinion n. 의견, 견해

17 명사절 접속사 채우기

해설 타동사(decide)의 목적어 자리에서 명사절(needs ~ signed)을 이끌 수 있는 것은 명사절 접속사이므로 (A)와 (C)가 정답의 후보이다. 이 명사절은 '무엇이 수정되어야 하는지'라는 의미가 되어야 하므로 (A) what(무엇)이 정답이다. (C) whether(~인지 아닌지)는 문맥에 맞지 않는다.

해석 법무부는 계약서에 서명하기 전에 무엇이 수정되어야 하는지 결정하기 위해 계약서에 대한 회의를 오늘 오후에 열 것이다.

어휘 hold a meeting 회의를 열다   contract n. 계약(서)   revise v. 수정하다

18 what과 that 구별하여 채우기

해설 주어 자리에 온 명사절(happens during the first year)을 이끌 수 있는 것은 명사절 접속사이므로 (A), (C), (D)가 정답의 후보이다. 이 명사절은 주어가 없는 불완전한 절이므로, 불완전한 명사절 앞에 오는 (C) what이 정답이다. 완전한 명사절 앞에 오는 (A) that이나 (D) how는 답이 될 수 없다.

해석 새로운 사업체를 연 사람들에게, 첫해 동안 일어나는 일은 성공의 중요한 예측 지표이다.

어휘 predictor n. 예측 지표, 예보자

19-22는 다음 이메일에 관한 문제입니다.

수신: Joe Jackson <jjack@kpwritersassociation.com>
발신: Eileen Davis <eileen_d@kremshainc.com>
제목: 연례 작가 회의
날짜: 11월 1일

Mr. Jackson께,

저는 이전에 연례 작가 회의에 가본 적이 있고 제가 참석했던 모든 강의들을 대단히 즐겼었기 때문에 한 달 전쯤에 올해의 것에 등록했습니다. ¹⁹그러나, 계획에 변동이 생겼습니다. 결국 저는 가지 못할 것입니다. ²⁰중요한 비즈니스 회의가 소집되었고, 제가 참석해야만 합니다.

그러므로 저는 등록을 철회하고 싶습니다. ²¹저는 또한 제가 환불을 받을 수 있는지 없는지 알고 싶습니다. 그것의 자격을 얻기 위해 충분히 미리 취소를 알려드리고 있다고 생각하지만, 만약 그렇지 않다면 알려주십시오. ²²불편에 대해 진심으로 사과드립니다. 성공적인 행사가 되기를 바랍니다.

Eileen Davis 드림

register v. 등록하다 thoroughly adv. 대단히, 철저히
after all (예상과 달리) 결국에는, 어쨌든 withdraw v. 철회하다, 중단하다, 빼내다
refund n. 환불 notify v. 알리다, 통지하다 in advance 미리, 사전에
qualify v. ~의 자격을 얻다 apologize v. 사과하다 sincerely adv. 진심으로

19 접속부사 채우기 주변 문맥 파악

해설 빈칸이 콤마와 함께 문장의 맨 앞에 온 접속부사 자리이므로, 앞 문장과 빈칸이 있는 문장의 의미 관계를 파악하여 접속부사인 (A), (C), (D) 중 하나를 정답으로 골라야 한다. 앞 문장에서 행사에 등록했음을 언급했고, 빈칸이 있는 문장에서는 계획에 변동이 생겼다고 한 후, 올해의 행사에 가지 못할 것이라고 했으므로, 앞 문장과 대조되는 내용의 문장에서 사용되는 (D) However (그러나)가 정답이다. 전치사 (B) Despite(~에도 불구하고)는 뒤에 명사가 와야 하므로 답이 될 수 없다.

어휘 besides adv. 게다가 likewise adv. 마찬가지로, 게다가

20 알맞은 문장 고르기

해석 (A) 저는 그녀를 대신할 적합한 발표자를 찾을 수 없었습니다.
(B) 중요한 비즈니스 회의가 소집되었고, 제가 참석해야만 합니다.
(C) 저는 강의들 대부분에 그다지 감명받지 않았습니다.
(D) 평생 회원으로서, 저는 반값 티켓을 받을 자격이 있습니다.

해설 빈칸에 들어갈 알맞은 문장을 고르는 문제이므로 빈칸의 주변 문맥이나 전체 문맥을 파악한다. 앞 문장 'I will not be able to go after all.'에서 결국 자신이 가지 못할 것이라고 했고, 뒷부분에서 등록을 철회하고 환불받고 싶다고 했으므로 빈칸에는 참석할 수 없는 이유와 관련된 내용이 들어가야 함을 알 수 있다. 따라서 (B) A vital business meeting was called, and I must attend가 정답이다.

어휘 suitable adj. 적합한, 적당한 replace v. 대신하다, 대체하다
vital adj. 중요한, 필수적인 majority n. 대부분, 대다수
lifetime adj. 평생의, 일생의 entitle v. 자격을 주다

21 명사절 접속사 채우기

해설 동사(know)의 목적어 자리에 온 명사절(it is possible for me to get a refund)의 접속사를 채우는 문제이므로 명사절 접속사 (A)와 (D)가 정답의 후보이다. '환불을 받을 수 있는지 없는지'라는 의미가 되어야 하므로 (D) whether(~인지 아닌지)가 정답이다. 빈칸 뒤에 완전한 절이 왔으므로 불완전한 절을 이끄는 (A) what은 답이 될 수 없다.

어휘 though conj. 비록 ~이지만 whereas conj. ~한 반면에

22 명사 어휘 고르기 전체 문맥 파악

해설 '___에 대해 사과하다'라는 문맥이므로 모든 보기가 정답의 후보이다. 빈칸이 있는 문장만으로 정답을 고를 수 없으므로 주변 문맥이나 전체 문맥을 파악한다. 앞부분에서 이미 행사에 등록했지만 이것을 철회하고 환불을 받고 싶다고 했으므로 자신이 초래한 불편에 대해 사과를 하고 있음을 알 수 있다. 따라서 명사 (C) inconvenience가 정답이다.

어휘 interruption n. 방해, 중단

Section 6 특수구문

Chapter 19 비교 구문

1 원급 p.221
1. (B)   2. (C)   3. (C)

1. 원급 표현 채우기

해설 as ~ as 사이에는 동명사 working을 꾸미는 부사가 필요하므로 부사 (B) effectively가 정답이다.

해석 가채용 평가에서, Kevin Edwards는 그 부서의 경력 있는 직원들만큼 효과적으로 일한 것에 대해 칭찬을 받았다.

어휘 probationary adj. 가채용의, 견습중인 praise v. 칭찬하다
experienced adj. 경력 있는, 숙련된 effectively adv. 효과적으로

2. 원급 표현 채우기

해설 빈칸 뒤에 as가 왔으므로 함께 원급 표현(as ~ as)을 만드는 (C) as many가 정답이다.

해석 연구는 육체 노동자들이 어떤 분야에 있는 숙련된 전문직 종사자들보다도 평균적으로 두 배의 시간만큼 더 많이 일한다는 것을 보여준다.

어휘 laborer n. 육체 노동자, 인부 on average 평균적으로, 대체로
skilled adj. 숙련된, 노련한 professional n. 전문직 종사자, 전문가
field n. 분야, 현장

3. 원급 표현 채우기

해설 빈칸 뒤에 as가 왔으므로 이와 함께 원급 표현(as ~ as)을 만드는 (A)와 (C)가 정답의 후보이다. as ~ as 사이에 명사(detail)가 들어가는 원급 표현은 'as + 명사 + as'가 아니라 'as + many/much + 명사'이므로, (A) as가 아닌 (C) as much가 정답이다.

해석 훈련 목적으로, 신입 사원들은 가능한 한 매우 상세하게 업무 진행 보고서를 작성하도록 요구된다.

어휘 write up 작성하다 progress report (업무) 진행 보고서

2 비교급 p.222
1. (D)   2. (D)   3. (C)

1. 비교급 표현 채우기

해설 비교급(more media interest)이 왔으므로 함께 비교급 표현을 만드는 (D) than이 정답이다.

해석 생물학 연구 센터는 멸종 위기종에 대한 두 번째 학회를 주최할 것이라고 발표했는데, 이는 첫 번째 학회가 예상보다 많은 언론의 관심을 받았기 때문이다.

어휘 host v. 주최하다 endangered adj. 멸종될 위기에 이른
species n. 종(생물 분류의 기초 단위)

2. 비교급 표현 채우기

해설 뒤에 'the 비교급'(the earlier)이 온 것으로 보아 'the 비교급 ~, the 비교급 -'(~할수록 점점 더 -하다)를 만드는 문제이다. 따라서 'the 비교급'인 (D) The sooner가 정답이다.

해석 재무 보고서가 이사에게 빨리 제출될수록, 그가 다음 해 예산에 대한 결정을 내리는 것이 점점 더 빨라질 것이다.

어휘 make a decision 결정을 내리다

3. 비교급 표현 채우기

해설 뒤에 than이 왔으므로 함께 비교급 표현을 만드는 비교급 (C) fairer가 정답이다.

해석   Spokane 내 토지에 대해 최근 제의한 액수는 지난주에 한 개발업자가 제안했던 것보다 훨씬 더 많다.

어휘   **offer** n. 제의한 액수, 제안   **property** n. 토지, 재산   **fair** adj. 많은, 상당한

3 최상급   p.223
1. (B)   2. (D)   3. (D)

1. 최상급 표현 채우기

해설   '~ 중에서 (가장 –한)'를 의미하는 of the workers가 왔으므로 함께 최상급을 만드는 (B) most가 정답이다. 참고로, capable 다음에 명사 worker가 생략되어 있는데, 이는 worker가 올 것이 명확하므로 생략된 경우이다.

해석   이 공장의 근로자들 중 가장 유능한 사람은 새로 개설된 시설로 이동될 것이다.

어휘   **capable** adj. 유능한, 능력 있는   **newly** adv. 새로이, 최근에

2. 최상급 표현 채우기

해설   '~ 중에서 (가장 –한)'를 의미하는 of the hand-held devices가 왔으므로 최상급 (C)와 (D)가 정답의 후보이다. '~ 중에서 가장 큰 수익이다'보다는 '~ 중에서 가장 수익성이 있다'는 의미가 자연스러우므로, (C) most profits가 아닌 (D) most profitable이 정답이다. 참고로, profitable 다음에 명사 device가 생략되어 있는데, 이는 device가 올 것이 명확하므로 생략된 경우이다.

해석   대부분의 휴대 전화들보다 적은 기능을 가졌지만, Belmar사의 새로운 모델은 올해 출시된 휴대용 단말기들 중 가장 수익성이 있다.

어휘   **hand-held device** 휴대용 단말기   **release** v. 출시하다, 풀어놓다
       profitable adj. 수익성이 있는

3. 최상급 표현 채우기

해설   '~ 중에서 (가장 –한)'를 의미하는 that절이 왔으므로 함께 최상급을 만드는 (C)와 (D)가 정답의 후보이다. 명사(building)를 꾸며야 하므로 부사의 최상급(most largely)이 아닌 형용사의 최상급 (D) largest가 정답이다.

해석   Harborview 리조트는 Rising Star사가 건설한 것들 중에서 가장 큰 건물이다.

어휘   **construct** v. 건설하다

4 기타 원급, 비교급, 최상급 표현   p.224
1. (B)   2. (A)   3. (B)

1. 원급/비교급/최상급 표현 채우기

해설   '3년 이상을 보냈다'는 의미가 되어야 하므로 (B) more than(~ 이상)이 정답이다.

해석   Knight 교수는 아마존 계곡의 식물을 연구하는 데 3년 이상을 보냈는데, 그 기간은 그가 계획했던 것보다 훨씬 더 길었다.

어휘   **vegetation** n. 식물

2. 원급/비교급/최상급 표현 채우기

해설   빈칸 앞에 would rather가 있으므로 'would rather ~ than –'(-하느니 차라리 ~하다)을 만들 수 있는 (A) than이 정답이다.

해석   Mr. Clemens는 그의 사업을 확장하는 데 더 좋은 때를 기다리느니 차라리 지금 투자하고 싶어 한다.

어휘   **wait for** ~를 기다리다   **expand** v. 확장하다

3. 원급/비교급/최상급 표현 채우기

해설   빈칸 뒤에 than any other ~가 있으므로, '비교급 + than any other ~'를 만들 수 있는 비교급 (B) stronger가 정답이다.

해석   Garson's Steel 제조 회사는 자사 웹사이트에 A-1 철골이 그 회사가 생산하

는 다른 어떤 종류보다 더 튼튼하다는 것을 명시한다.

어휘   **steel rod** 철골

Hackers Practice   p.225

01 ⓑ [토익 공식 4]		02 ⓑ [토익 공식 2]	
03 ⓐ [토익 공식 1]		04 ⓑ [토익 공식 4]	
05 ⓐ [토익 공식 3]		06 ⓐ [토익 공식 1]	
07 ⓑ [토익 공식 1]			

08 more → the more [토익 공식 2]
09 to → as [토익 공식 1]
10 more → most [토익 공식 3]
11 conveniently → convenient [토익 공식 2]
12 when → than [토익 공식 2]
13 much → many [토익 공식 1]
14 low → lower [토익 공식 2]

해석   01   궂은 기상 상태 때문에, 그 회의는 오늘보다는 내일 개최될 것이다.
       02   새 기계는 우리가 사용했던 이전 장비보다 더 효율적으로 작동했다.
       03   바쁜 시간제 근무 일정에도 불구하고, 나는 내가 할 수 있는 한 규칙적으로 그 수업에 참석했다.
       04   비행기가 이륙하자마자 조종사는 난기류를 경험할 것 같다고 방송했다.
       05   이 건물의 디자인은 단연코 그 도시에 있는 모든 건물 중 가장 혁신적이다.
       06   오래된 박물관을 개조하는 것은 새로운 시설을 건설하는 것보다 더 비쌀 것이다.
       07   나는 Cheryl이 꼭 우리의 이전 관리자만큼이나 체계적일 것이라고 생각한다.
       08   도시에 더 가까워질수록, 교통은 더 혼잡할 것이다.
       09   새 일자리를 얻었지만, 내 책무는 이전 것과 같다.
       10   Henry는 내가 함께 일해 봤던 사람들 중에서 가장 창의적인 사람이다.
       11   온라인으로 쇼핑하는 것은 여러 상점들을 돌아다니는 것보다 더 편리하다.
       12   우리의 지난 분기 이익은 우리가 예상했던 것보다 훨씬 크다.
       13   학생들이 모든 것을 분명하게 이해할 수 있도록 가능한 한 많은 예시들을 제공하기 바랍니다.
       14   우리 강의 오염량은 10년 전보다 훨씬 더 적다.

Hackers Test   p.226

Part 5

01 (B)	02 (B)	03 (A)	04 (C)	05 (D)
06 (D)	07 (A)	08 (B)	09 (C)	10 (C)
11 (C)	12 (C)	13 (B)	14 (D)	15 (A)
16 (D)	17 (D)	18 (A)		

Part 6

19 (B)	20 (A)	21 (C)	22 (B)

01 비교급 표현 채우기

해설   빈칸 뒤에 than이 왔으므로 함께 비교급 표현을 만드는 비교급(-er 또는 more + 형용사/부사)이 와야 한다. 빈칸 뒤에 형용사(imperative)가 와 있으므로 (B) more가 정답이다. (A) better를 넣으면 '더 잘 긴급하다'라는 어색한 의미가 된다. (D) larger는 형용사의 비교급이므로, 또 다른 형용사(imperative) 앞에 올 수 없다.

해석   그 회사는 고객 지원 활동 프로그램을 개발하는 것이 영업 사원들을 교육하는 것보다 더 긴급하다고 결론 내렸다.

어휘   **decide** v. (~라고) 결론 내리다, 결정하다   **develop** v. 개발하다, 전개하다
       outreach n. 지원 활동   **imperative** adj. 긴급한, 필수적인

02 원급/비교급/최상급 표현 채우기

해설   빈칸 앞에 No sooner가 왔으므로 함께 비교급 표현 no sooner ~ than –(~하자마자 –하다)를 만드는 (B) than이 정답이다.

해석 그 기업이 음악 재생기를 출시하자마자 다른 제조업체가 유사한 기기를 발표했다.

어휘 **launch** v. 출시하다, 시작하다 **introduce** v. (신제품 등을) 발표하다, 도입하다
similar adj. 유사한, 닮은

03 비교급 표현 채우기

해설 빈칸 뒤에 than이 왔으므로 함께 비교급 표현을 만드는 비교급 (A) better가 정답이다. (D) any good은 부정어(not, no)와 함께 쓰여 '소용이 없다'라는 의미를 만든다.

해석 프로젝트 마감 일자 이후에 회의를 개최하는 것이 이번 주에 회의를 하려고 시도하는 것보다 대부분의 직원들에게 더 도움이 될 것이다.

어휘 **hold** v. 개최하다, 열다 **deadline** n. 마감 일자
work v. 도움이 되다, 영향을 미치다

04 원급 표현 채우기

해설 빈칸 뒤에 as가 왔으므로 함께 원급 표현(as ~ as)을 만드는 (C) as much가 정답이다.

해석 영업 부서에서, 열의와 의욕을 가진 신입 점원들은 고객들에게 전문적인 외판원들만큼 많은 만족감을 제공한다.

어휘 **enthusiasm** n. 의욕, 열광 **satisfaction** n. 만족감, 만족

05 비교급 표현 채우기

해설 '더 적은 정부의 규제가 있는 시장에서 더 큰 수익을 낳는다'는 의미가 되어야 하므로 (D) less가 정답이다. (A) fewer는 가산 명사 앞에 오는 비교급 표현이므로 답이 될 수 없다.

해석 정부의 규제가 더 적은 시장에 진입하는 게 더 큰 수익을 낳는다는 것이 회사의 입장이다.

어휘 **position** n. 입장, 태도 **result in** ~을 낳다 **gain** n. 수익, 이익

06 전치사 채우기

해설 a timely manner와 함께 쓰여 '제때에, 적절한 시기에'라는 뜻을 이루는 전치사 (D) in이 정답이다.

해석 미국 대사관의 규정과 절차의 최근 변경 사항들은 제때에 비자를 발급받는 것을 더 어렵게 만들었다.

어휘 **regulation** n. 규정, 단속, 규제 **procedure** n. 절차, 순서
embassy n. 대사관

07 부사절 접속사 자리 채우기

해설 that절은 주어(his film), 동사(had been released)를 갖춘 완전한 절이므로 _____ public interest ~ greatest는 수식어 거품으로 보아야 한다. 따라서 수식어 거품을 이끌 수 있는 부사절 접속사 (A)와 (C)가 정답의 후보이다. '주연 배우에 대한 대중의 관심이 최고조에 달했을 때 영화가 개봉된다'라는 의미가 되어야 하므로 (A) when(~할 때)이 정답이다.

해석 그 영화감독은 주연 배우에 대한 대중의 관심이 최고조에 달했을 때 그의 영화가 개봉된 것에 기뻐했다.

어휘 **release** v. (영화 등을) 개봉하다 **lead actor** 주연 배우

08 명사에 맞는 수량 표현 채우기

해설 복수 가산 명사(positions) 앞에는 가산 명사에 올 수 있는 수량 표현 few가 와야 하므로 few의 비교급 표현인 (B) fewer가 정답이다. (A) lesser는 little의 이중 비교급 형태로 '(가치나 중요성이) 덜한'을 의미하므로, '(수가) 적은'을 의미하는 문맥에는 올 수 없다. (D) much는 불가산 명사 앞에 오는 수량 표현이므로 답이 될 수 없다.

해석 최근 보고서에 따르면, 아주 적은 일자리가 산업 미술과 응용 과학 분야의 말단직 지원자들에게 열려 있다.

어휘 **position** n. 일자리, 직위 **entry-level** 말단의, 초보의
candidate n. 지원자, 후보자

09 원급 표현 채우기

해설 as ~ as 사이에는 동사(will proceed)를 꾸미는 부사가 와야 하므로 (C) smoothly(순조롭게, 원활하게)가 정답이다.

해석 비록 그 사업에 임명된 직원들의 수가 감소했지만, 경영진은 그 일이 이전처럼 순조롭게 진행되기를 바란다.

어휘 **appointed** adj. 임명된, 정해진 **proceed** v. 진행되다
smooth adj. 매끄러운

10 최상급 표현 채우기

해설 빈칸 뒤에 ever(여태껏)가 왔고, 'Ms. Okada는 여태껏 전국 골프대회에서 우승한 모든 선수 중에 가장 어린 선수다'라는 의미가 되어야 하므로 최상급인 (C) youngest가 정답이다.

해석 Ms. Okada는 새크라멘토에서 매년 열리는 전국 골프대회에서 우승한 여태껏 가장 어린 선수다.

11 원급/비교급/최상급 표현 채우기

해설 '충분함 이상이다'라는 의미가 되어야 하므로 (C) more than(~ 이상)이 정답이다. (A) enough가 답이 되려면 형용사(sufficient) 뒤에 와서 sufficient enough가 되어야 한다. (B) too much(너무 많이, 너무 많은)는 형용사(sufficient)를 꾸미지 못하며, (D) such 역시 명사를 꾸밀 수는 있지만 형용사를 꾸미지는 못한다.

해석 그 회사의 기술자들은 사무실 컴퓨터들을 점검했고 직원들의 필요에 부응하는 데 그것들이 충분함 이상이라는 것을 확인했다.

어휘 **inspect** v. 점검하다, 검사하다 **verify** v. 확인하다, 입증하다
sufficient adj. 충분한

12 비교급 표현 채우기

해설 Of the two가 온 것으로 보아 'of the two ~ + the 비교급'(둘 중에 더 ~한 사람/것)이 되어야 하므로 비교급 (C) higher가 정답이다.

해석 정치 연설회에 참석한 두 명의 국가 공무원들 중, 더 높은 직위의 사람이 가장 많은 언론의 주목을 받았다.

어휘 **government official** 국가 공무원 **present** adj. 참석한, 있는
campaign meeting 정치 연설회 **attention** n. 주목, 주의

13 비교급 표현 채우기

해설 빈칸 앞부분에 'the 비교급'(The more)이 온 것으로 보아 'the 비교급 ~, the 비교급 -'(~할수록 점점 더 -하다)을 만드는 문제이다. '부품이 전문화되다'라는 의미가 되어야 하므로 형용사 보어 (B) specialized(전문화된, 전문적인)가 정답이다. 명사 보어 (D) specialization(전문화)은 주어(a piece of factory equipment)와 의미적으로 동격 관계를 이루지 못한다. 참고로, 비교급 표현의 품사 문제는 비교급 표현을 걷어내고 원래 형태(a piece of factory equipment is _____)로 만들어 풀어야 한다. 주어(a piece of factory equipment)와 명사(specialization)가 의미적으로 동격 관계에 있지 않으므로 주어를 설명해 주는 형용사(specialized)가 와야 한다.

해석 공장 설비의 부품이 더 전문화될수록, 조작자는 그것을 제대로 작동시키기 위해 점점 더 숙련되어야 한다.

어휘 **piece** n. 부품, 부분 **operator** n. 조작자, 기사 **run** v. 작동시키다, 작동하다
specialize v. 전공하다, 전문적으로 다루다
specialized adj. 전문화된, 전문적인 **specialization** n. 전문화, 특수화

14 원급/비교급/최상급 표현 채우기

해설 '11월 10일 이후에는 더 이상 받아들여지지 않다'라는 의미가 되어야 하므로 no longer(더 이상 ~ 않다)를 써야 한다. 빈칸 앞에 no가 와 있으므로 (D) longer가 정답이다. (C) later가 빈칸에 오려면 빈칸 뒤에 than과 시간 표현이 바로 있어야 하고, '늦어도 11월 10일까지 받아들여지다'라는 문맥이어야 한다.

해석 이것은 10월 지출에 대한 상환 요청이 11월 10일 이후에는 더 이상 받아들여지지 않을 것임을 모든 직원들에게 상기시키기 위함입니다.

어휘 **reimbursement** n. 상환, 변제 **expense** n. 지출, 비용

15 최상급 표현 채우기

해설 빈칸 앞에 최상급(best)이 있으므로 '~ 중에 가장 -한'이라는 의미의 최상급 표현 '최상급 + of ~/in ~/that절'을 만드는 (A) of가 정답이다.

해석 모든 사람들은 1등 상을 받은 영화가 후보에 오른 모든 영화들 중에서 진정으로 최고였다고 생각한다.

어휘 nominate v. 후보에 오르다, 임명하다

16 원급/비교급/최상급 표현 채우기

해설 '팀장들에 의해 허가되기보다 부서장에 의해 승인된다'라는 의미가 되어야 하므로 (D) rather than(~보다)이 정답이다.

해석 계약된 횟수 이상의 휴가에 대한 신청은 팀장들에 의해 허가되기보다 부서장에 의해 승인돼야 한다.

어휘 in excess of ~ 이상의, ~을 초과하여 permit v. 허가하다, 허락하다

17 원급/비교급/최상급 표현 채우기

해설 'have _____ been + 비교급'(has _____ been greater)이 와 있고 '더 ~해 본 적이 없다'는 의미가 되어야 한다. 따라서 'have never been + 비교급' 표현을 만들 수 있는 (D) never가 정답이다.

해석 증가하는 도시 내 근로자들의 수로 인해 지하철을 타는 통근자들의 수가 오늘날보다 더 많았던 적은 없다.

어휘 commuter n. 통근자 subway n. 지하철

18 원급 표현 채우기

해설 '토론토행 비행편과 샌프란시스코행 비행편의 출발 시각이 같다'는 의미가 되어야 하므로 (A) the same as(~와 똑같은)가 정답이다.

해석 가장 늦은 토론토행 비행편 출발 시각은 샌프란시스코를 향해 출발할 예정인 비행편의 출발 시각과 같습니다.

어휘 departure n. 출발

19-22는 다음 이메일에 관한 문제입니다.

> 날짜: 8월 12일
> 발신: curtisneil@mricksupply.com
> 수신: jtanner@mricksupply.com
> 제목: 회신: 신규 사무용품 목록
>
> [19]우리의 고객들에게 신규 사무용품 목록을 보내는 일이 지연된 것에 대해 사과의 말씀을 드립니다. 저는 그 일을 즉시 하려고 했으나, 완성해야 할 긴급한 보고서가 있어 귀하가 요청하신 대로 할 시간이 없었습니다.
>
> [20]게다가, 저는 과거에 우리에게서 용품을 구매했던 여러 회사들의 현재 주소를 확인할 수가 없었습니다. 제 비서가 이메일 주소를 확인하기 위해 지금 이 회사들에 연락을 취하려고 시도하고 있습니다.
>
> 일단 이것이 완료되면, 저는 이메일로 귀하께 업데이트된 연락처 파일을 보내겠습니다. [21]저는 업데이트를 늦어도 오늘 오후 5시까지 완료할 수 있을 것입니다. 귀하께서 근무 시간이 끝나기 전에 그 파일을 확인해주신다면 감사하겠습니다. [22]귀하의 확인 후 즉시 고객들에게 목록을 발송할 것입니다. 이제부터 고객 정보를 반드시 최신 상태로 유지하는 것을 확실히 하도록 하겠습니다.
>
> Curtis Neil 드림

buyer n. 고객, 구매자 **confirm** v. 확인하다 **assistant** n. 비서
verify v. 확인하다 **workday** n. 근무 시간(= working day)
make sure 확실하게 하다 **up to date** 최신(식)의, 지금 유행하는

19 명사 어휘 고르기 전체 문맥 파악

해설 '사무용품 목록을 보내는 일이 _____에 대해 사과하고자 한다'는 문맥이므로 모든 보기가 정답의 후보이다. 빈칸이 있는 문장만으로 정답을 고를 수 없으므로 주변 문맥이나 전체 문맥을 파악한다. '그 일을 즉시 하려고 했으나 당신이 요청한 대로 할 시간이 없었다(I had intended to do that right away, but I ~ didn't have time to do as you requested.)'고 했으므로 보내기로 한 목록의 발송이 지연되어 아직 처리되지 않았음을 알 수 있다. 따라서 명사 (B) delay(지연)가 정답이다. (D) error(틀림, 잘못)는 '요청한 정보가 아닌

다른 정보를 보내다'라는 의미이므로 문맥에 맞지 않아 답이 될 수 없다.

어휘 refusal n. 거절 negligence n. 무관심, 등한 error n. 틀림, 잘못

20 명사에 맞는 수량 표현 채우기

해설 복수 가산 명사(companies) 앞에 빈칸이 있으므로 복수 명사 앞에 쓰는 수량 표현 (B) many가 정답이다.

21 비교급 표현 채우기

해설 빈칸이 than 앞에 있으므로 비교급인 (C) later가 정답이다. no later than은 '늦어도 ~까지'라는 뜻의 표현임을 알아 둔다. (D) more lately는 '더 최근에'라는 뜻으로 no와 함께 쓰이면 의미가 어색해지므로 답이 될 수 없다.

22 알맞은 문장 고르기

해석 (A) 그 문제를 정정할 충분한 시간이 없을 것입니다.
(B) 귀하의 확인 후 즉시 고객들에게 목록을 발송할 것입니다.
(C) 네트워크를 업데이트하는 것은 앞으로 한 시간이 더 걸릴 것입니다.
(D) 모든 사람들이 신규 사무용품에 대해 기대하고 있습니다.

해설 빈칸에 들어갈 알맞은 문장을 고르는 문제이므로 빈칸의 주변 문맥이나 전체 문맥을 파악한다. 앞부분에서 연락처 파일을 업데이트하여 이메일의 수신자에게 보내겠다고 했고, 앞 문장 'I would appreciate if you could confirm the file'에서 그것을 확인해주기를 바란다고 했으므로 빈칸에는 수신자가 연락처 파일을 확인하는 즉시 사무용품 목록을 고객들에게 발송하겠다는 내용이 들어가야 함을 알 수 있다. 따라서 (B) I will send the list out to the buyers right after your verification이 정답이다.

Chapter 20 병치·도치 구문

1 병치 구문   p.229
1. (D)   2. (B)   3. (B)

1. 병치 구문 채우기

해설 등위접속사(and) 앞에 형용사(effective)가 연결되어 있으므로 and 뒤에도 형용사가 와야 한다. 따라서 (D) affordable(가격이 알맞은)이 정답이다. 분사 (C) affording은 진행형을 만드는 분사로 쓰이고, 형용사로는 잘 쓰이지 않는다. 참고로, and로 연결된 두 형용사는 2형식 동사 has proven의 보어이다.

해석 많은 회사들에게, 중개인을 이용하는 것은 외국 시장으로의 진입을 시도할 때 효과적이며 가격도 알맞다는 것이 판명되어 왔다.

어휘 intermediary n. 중개인, 중재자 afford v. ~을 할 여유가 되다

2. 병치 구문 채우기

해설 'Ms. Saunders는 항공편을 예약하고 숙소를 예약한다'는 문맥으로 보아, 등위접속사(and)에 연결되는 것은 동사 books와 또 다른 동사이다. 앞의 동사가 단수(books)이므로 단수 동사 (B) makes가 정답이다. 참고로, and로 연결된 두 동사의 주어는 Ms. Saunders이다.

해석 Ms. Saunders는 모든 직원들이 출장을 갈 때 그들을 위해 항공편과 숙소를 예약한다.

어휘 book v. 예약하다 accommodation n. 숙소, 숙박 시설
business trip 출장 make reservations 예약하다

3. 병치 구문 채우기

해설 등위접속사(and) 뒤에 동명사(managing)가 연결되어 있으므로 (B) providing이 정답이다. 참고로, and로 연결된 두 개의 -ing는 동사구 consist of의 목적어 자리에 온 동명사이다.

해석 직원의 책무는 회사 제품에 대한 정보를 제공하는 것과 고객들의 특별 요청을 처리하는 것으로 이루어져 있다.

어휘 consist of ~으로 이루어져 있다 manage v. 처리하다, 다루다

2 도치 구문
p.230

1. (B) 2. (D) 3. (A)

1. 도치 구문 채우기

해설 주절에 would have p.p.(would have canceled)가 온 것으로 보아 가정법 과거완료 문장이다. 가정법 과거완료의 도치 문장은 'Had + 주어 + p.p.'이므로 Had the department store 다음에는 p.p.형인 (B) 또는 (C)가 와야 한다. 주어(the department store)와 동사(realize)가 '그 백화점이 ~을 알아차리다'라는 의미의 능동 관계이므로 have 조동사(Had) 뒤에 와서 능동태 동사를 만드는 (B) realized가 정답이다.

해석 판촉 판매가 고객들에게 인기가 없을 것임을 백화점이 알아차렸다면, 그 행사를 취소했을 것이다.

어휘 **promotional** adj. 판촉의, 홍보의 **popular with** ~에게 인기 있는
realize v. 알아차리다, 인식하다

2. 도치 구문 채우기

해설 부정어(Seldom)가 앞에 와서 주어와 동사가 도치된 문장이다. do 조동사(does)가 문장의 앞에 나가 있으면 주어 다음에는 동사원형이 와야 하므로 (D) affect가 정답이다.

해석 Ms. Lerner의 세부 사항에 대한 주의는 경영상의 결정을 내릴 때 전체 그림을 보는 그녀의 능력에 거의 영향을 미치지 않는다.

어휘 **seldom** adv. 거의(좀처럼) ~ 않는 **detail** n. 세부 사항, 정보

3. 도치 구문 채우기

해설 'Only + 부사절'(Only after a consensus was reached)이 앞에 와서 주어와 동사가 도치된 문장이다. do 조동사(did)가 문장의 앞에 나가 있으므로, 동사원형 (A) decide가 정답이다.

해석 합의에 이르고 나서야 총괄 책임자는 직원들에게 의무적인 초과 근무를 하게 하는 것을 포기하기로 결정했다.

어휘 **consensus** n. 합의 **forgo** v. 포기하다 **mandatory** adj. 의무적인, 필수의

Hackers Practice
p.231

01 ⓐ [토익 공식 1]		02 ⓑ [토익 공식 2]	
03 ⓐ [토익 공식 1]		04 ⓑ [토익 공식 1]	
05 ⓐ [토익 공식 2]		06 ⓐ [토익 공식 2]	
07 ⓑ [토익 공식 1]			
08 energize → energy [토익 공식 1]			
09 맞는 문장 [토익 공식 1]		10 Have → Had [토익 공식 2]	
11 employ → employees [토익 공식 1]			
12 meet → meets [토익 공식 1]			
13 reputable → reputation [토익 공식 1]			
14 맞는 문장 [토익 공식 2]			

해석 01 신상 여행 가방 제품군은 튼튼하며 쉽게 가지고 다닐 수 있도록 개발되었다.
02 이 상점은 좀처럼 제품을 할인하지 않는데, 왜냐하면 가격이 이미 낮기 때문이다.
03 운동하는 것과 지방이 많은 음식을 적게 먹는 것은 과체중을 뺄 수 있는 최선의 방법 중 두 가지이다.
04 그 프랑스 식당 종업원들은 손님들에게 주문을 받고 주문한 음식을 서빙할 것이다.
05 약속을 취소하시려면, 저희 접수원에게 연락주시기 바랍니다.
06 최근에서야 Ms. Soper는 건물 디자인에 결함이 있다는 것을 알아챘다.
07 그 여행 가이드는 재미있고 재치 있었는데, 이는 여행을 매우 즐겁게 해주었다.
08 그 음료수는 격렬한 신체 활동을 하는 사람들에게 체력과 기력을 제공한다.
09 매표소는 1층 정문 옆에 있다.
10 당신이 좀 더 일찍 알려 줬다면, 나는 그 회의에 참석할 수 있었을 것이다.

11 정규직 직원들과 시간제 직원들 모두 정책 변경에 영향을 받을 것이다.
12 Julia는 정기적으로 해외로 여행을 가서 외국 고객들과 만난다.
13 그 회사는 전례 없는 판매 기록과 서비스 부문 수상의 명성을 갖고 있다.
14 올해의 무역 박람회는 작년 박람회보다 더 순조롭게 진행되었다.

Hackers Test
p.232

Part 5

01 (B)	02 (A)	03 (C)	04 (C)	05 (D)
06 (D)	07 (C)	08 (D)	09 (A)	10 (D)
11 (D)	12 (A)	13 (B)	14 (C)	15 (C)
16 (D)	17 (A)	18 (D)		

Part 6

19 (B)	20 (D)	21 (D)	22 (C)

01 병치 구문 채우기

해설 등위접속사(and) 뒤에 형용사(competitive)가 연결되어 있으므로 and 앞에도 형용사가 와야 한다. 따라서 '안정된, 확립된'을 의미하는 형용사로 쓰이는 (B) established가 정답이다. (D) establishing은 형용사로는 잘 쓰이지 않고 진행형 동사를 만들 때 쓰인다. 참고로, and로 연결된 두 형용사는 명사 markets를 꾸미고 있다.

해석 안정되고 경쟁적인 시장으로 사업을 확장시키려는 소매업자들은 그들의 상품을 다른 회사의 상품들과 구분 짓기 위해 효과적인 광고 방법을 개발해야 한다.

어휘 **expand** v. (사업을) 확장시키다 **differentiate** v. 구분 짓다, 구별하다
establish v. 설립하다 **established** adj. 안정된, 확립된

02 도치 구문 채우기

해설 주어와 동사가 도치된 절(did many of the other tenants) 앞에서 도치 구문을 이끌 수 있는 접속사 (A) as가 정답이다. 부사 (B), (C), (D)는 두 절을 연결하는 접속사 역할을 할 수 없다.

해석 Cullman and Sons사는 건물 관리인에게 오작동하는 에어컨에 대해 항의했는데, 이는 다른 많은 세입자들도 마찬가지였다.

어휘 **malfunctioning** adj. 오작동하는 **tenant** n. 세입자, 임차인

03 부사절 접속사 자리 채우기

해설 이 문장은 필수성분(Mr. Royce ~ airport)을 갖춘 완전한 절이므로 ____ boarding his flight to Dallas는 수식어 거품으로 보아야 한다. 수식어 거품 자리에 온 분사구문(boarding ~ Dallas) 앞에는 부사와 부사절 접속사가 모두 올 수 있으므로, 부사절 접속사 (A), (B)와 부사 (B), (D) 모두 정답의 후보이다. '댈러스행 비행기에 탑승하기 전에'라는 의미가 되어야 자연스러우므로 부사절 접속사 (C) Before(~하기 전에)가 정답이다. (A), (B), (D)를 사용하면 어색한 의미가 되므로 답이 될 수 없다.

해석 댈러스행 비행기에 탑승하기 전에, Mr. Royce는 공항으로부터의 교통편을 마련하기 위해 그의 호텔에 연락했다.

어휘 **board** v. 탑승하다 **arrange** v. 마련하다, 처리하다

04 도치 구문 채우기

해설 주어와 동사가 도치된 절(will those) 앞에서 도치 구문을 이끌 수 있는 부정어 (C) neither가 정답이다. (D) only는 부사(구, 절)와 함께 절 앞으로 나갔을 때에만 주어와 동사를 도치시킬 수 있다. 참고로, that lack ~ estimate는 those를 꾸며 주는 수식어 거품이다. 그리고 문장 마지막에 be reviewed가 생략되었다.

해석 목적에 대해 명확한 설명을 제공하지 않는 기획안은 검토되지 않을 것이며, 이는 예산액이 없는 기획안도 마찬가지일 것이다.

어휘 **proposal** n. 안, 제의 **budget estimate** 예산액

05 병치 구문 채우기

해설 상관접속사(both A and B)의 both 뒤에 형용사(detailed)가 연결되어 있으므로 and 뒤에도 형용사가 와야 한다. 따라서 (D) substantial이 정답이

다. 참고로, 두 형용사는 be동사(is)의 보어이다.

해석 그 박물관은 미술사에 대한 지식이 상세하고 상당한 큐레이터를 구하고 있다.

어휘 seek v. 구하다, 찾다 understanding n. 지식, 이해
substance n. 물질 substantial adj. 상당한, 튼튼한

06 관계사 자리 채우기

해설 명사(a task)를 뒤에서 꾸미는 형용사절(occupies ~ time)에 주어가 없으므로 주격 관계대명사 (D) that이 정답이다. 명사절 접속사 (A) what은 관계사 자리에 올 수 없으며, 관계부사 (B) when은 뒤에 완전한 절을 이끌므로 답이 될 수 없다.

해석 인사 기록의 관리는 행정 비서의 많은 시간을 차지하는 업무이다.

어휘 occupy v. 차지하다, 사용하다 a great deal of 많은, 다량의

07 병치 구문 채우기

해설 '직원들의 헌신과 성과를 보상하다'라는 의미로 보아, 등위접속사 and가 연결해야 하는 것은 reward의 목적어 두 개이다. reward의 목적어로 and 뒤에 명사 achievements가 왔으므로 명사 (C) dedication이 정답이다.

해석 Michelle Sanders의 책인 *Successful Leadership*은 관리자들을 위해 직원들의 헌신과 성과를 어떻게 보상하는지에 대한 조언을 포함한다.

어휘 reward v. 보상하다, 사례하다 dedicate v. 바치다, 전념하다
dedication n. 헌신, 전념 dedicational adj. 바치는, 헌신적으로

08 도치 구문 채우기

해설 주절에 might have p.p.(might have considered)가 온 것으로 보아 가정법 과거완료 문장이다. 가정법 과거완료의 도치 문장은 'Had + 주어 + p.p.'이므로 Had the marketing report 다음에는 p.p.형인 (B)와 (D)가 정답의 후보이다. 주어(the marketing report)와 동사(present)가 '마케팅 보고서가 제시되다'라는 의미의 수동 관계이므로 Had와 함께 수동태 동사를 만드는 (D) been presented가 정답이다.

해석 마케팅 보고서가 좀 더 설득력 있게 제시됐다면, 투자자들은 전기차 신규 개발 사업에 돈을 투자하는 것을 고려했을 것이다.

어휘 convincingly adv. 설득력 있게, 납득이 가도록 electric adj. 전기의
venture n. 신규 개발 사업 present v. 제시하다, 제출하다

09 병치 구문 채우기

해설 '남성용 정장 그리고 평상복'이라는 의미로 보아, 등위접속사 and가 연결해야 하는 것은 clothing을 꾸며 주는 형용사 두 개이다. clothing을 꾸며 주는 형용사로 and 뒤에 casual이 왔으므로 and 앞 빈칸에도 형용사가 와야 한다. 따라서 (A) formal(정식용의, 격식 차린, 공식적인)이 정답이다. (C) formalizing은 형용사로는 잘 쓰이지 않고 진행형 동사를 만들 때 쓰인다.

해석 그 백화점은 남성 정장과 평상복에 대해 일주일 동안 세일을 개최할 것이라고 발표하는 간판을 내걸었다.

어휘 put up a sign 간판을 내걸다 casual adj. 평상시의, 격식을 차리지 않는
formally adv. 정식으로 formalize v. 공식화하다
formality n. 형식상의 절차

10 부사절 접속사 채우기

해설 이 문장은 필수성분(Companies ~ tax records)을 갖춘 완전한 절이므로 _____ the government ~ an audit은 수식어 거품으로 보아야 한다. 이 수식어 거품은 동사(decides)가 있는 거품절이므로, 거품절을 이끌 수 있는 부사절 접속사 (B)와 (D)가 정답의 후보이다. '만약 ~한 경우를 대비하여 보관하다'라는 의미가 되어야 하므로 (D) in case(~에 대비하여)가 정답이다.

해석 기업들은 정부가 회계 감사를 수행하기로 결정할 경우를 대비하여 최소 5년 동안 세무 기록을 보관해야 한다.

어휘 audit n. 회계 감사 in case (~할) 경우에 대비하여

11 도치 구문 채우기

해설 주어와 동사가 도치된 절(have motorcycle ~ in sales) 앞에서 도치 구문을 이끌 수 있는 부정어 (D) Seldom(거의 ~ 않는)이 정답이다.

해석 오토바이와 스쿠터 제조업자들은 올해 이사분기 동안 겪었던 것과 같은 매출

의 증가를 경험해 본 적이 거의 없다.

어휘 experience v. 경험하다, 겪다

12 도치 구문 채우기

해설 필수성분(Mr. Desmond ~ department) 뒤에 온 절은 should로 시작하는 가정법 미래 도치 구문이다. should 다음은 주어 자리이므로 주격 (A) he가 정답이다.

해석 고용 계약서 조항에 관한 문의 사항이 있을 경우, Mr. Desmond는 인사부에 연락할 수 있다.

어휘 concerning prep. ~에 관한, 관하여 terms n. 조항, 조건
contract n. 계약서

13 도치 구문 채우기

해설 주어와 동사가 도치된 절(will it provide ~ items) 앞에서 도치 구문을 이끌 수 있는 접속사 (B) nor가 정답이다. 나머지 접속사들은 도치 구문을 이끌지 못한다.

해석 Online Auction Services사는 제3의 판매 회사에 의해 판매된 상품들에 대한 문의나 항의에 응답하지 않을 것이며, 이 물품들에 대한 환불 역시 제공하지 않을 것이다.

어휘 third-party adj. 제3자의 vendor n. 판매 회사, 노점상 refund n. 환불(금)

14 병치 구문 채우기

해설 '충분한 수면을 취하고 균형 잡힌 식생활을 유지하는 것'이라는 의미로 보아 등위접속사 and가 연결해야 하는 것은 문장의 주어 두 개이다. and 앞에 동명사구 getting sufficient sleep이 왔으므로 and 뒤의 빈칸에도 동명사가 와야 한다. 따라서 (C) maintaining이 정답이다.

해석 규칙적인 운동뿐만 아니라, 충분한 수면을 취하고 균형 잡힌 식생활을 유지하는 것이 건강한 생활 방식의 중요한 요소들이다.

어휘 sufficient adj. 충분한 balanced adj. 균형 잡힌, 안정된
diet n. 식생활, 식단 element n. 요소, 성분 maintain v. 유지하다

15 도치 구문 채우기

해설 주어와 동사가 도치된 절(are we) 앞에 도치 구문을 이끌 수 있는 (A)와 (C)가 정답의 후보이다. '우리 역시 그렇게 하고 있다'라는 의미이므로 (C) so(~도 역시 그러하다)가 정답이다. (D) as가 빈칸에 오려면 빈칸 앞에 and가 삭제되어야 한다.

해석 다른 건축 회사들은 곧 있을 도시 건물 법규 변경에 대비하고 있으며, 이는 우리 회사 역시 그러하다.

어휘 architectural adj. 건축(학)의 upcoming adj. 곧 있을, 다가오는
code n. 법규, 규정

16 최상급 표현 채우기

해설 '~ 중에서 (가장 -한)'를 의미하는 of information available이 왔으므로 최상급 (D) largest가 정답이다.

해석 *The Entrepreneur's Guidebook*은 직접 사업을 시작할 때 준비해야 하는 것에 대한 이용 가능한 정보 중에서 가장 광범위한 모음집이다.

어휘 compilation n. 모음집, 편집본 large adj. 광범위한, 큰

17 병치 구문 채우기

해설 '금융 정보를 얻고 주식을 매입하기 위해'라는 의미로 보아 등위접속사 and가 연결해야 하는 것은 to 부정사 두 개이다. and 앞에 to 부정사(to acquire)가 왔으므로 and 뒤의 빈칸에도 to 부정사가 와야 한다. 이때, and 뒤에 온 to 부정사의 to는 생략이 가능하므로 to purchase를 대신하는 (A) purchase가 정답이다. (C)도 to 부정사의 완료형(to have p.p.)을 만들 수 있지만 정보를 얻는 것보다 주식을 매입하는 것이 먼저 일어난 일임을 나타내는 문맥은 아니므로 답이 될 수 없다.

해석 개인 투자자들은 금융 정보를 얻고 주식을 매입하기 위해 온라인 서비스를 점점 더 많이 사용하고 있다.

어휘 increasingly adv. 점점 더, 갈수록 더 acquire v. 얻다, 획득하다
stock n. 주식, 재고품

18 병치 구문 채우기

해설 '좋은 교육을 받고 경험이 많은 후임자'라는 의미로 보아 등위접속사 and가 연결해야 하는 것은 명사(replacement)를 꾸며 주는 '부사 + 분사' 두 개이다. and 뒤에 '부사 + 분사(highly experienced)'가 왔으므로 앞의 부사(well) 다음에는 분사 (C) 또는 (D)가 와야 한다. 이때, 수식받는 명사 (replacement)와 분사가 '후임자가 좋은 교육을 받다'라는 의미로 수동 관계에 있으므로 과거분사 (D) educated가 정답이다.

해석 수석 연구원의 임박한 사임에 따라, 좋은 교육을 받고 경험이 많은 후임자를 위한 공석이 지금 광고되고 있다.

어휘 impending adj. 임박한, 곧 닥칠 resignation n. 사임, 사직
replacement n. 후임자, 대체

19-22는 다음 이메일에 관한 문제입니다.

수신: Janice King <jking@smail.com>
발신: Geoff Greer <ggreer@altenergy.com>
제목: 회의 발표
날짜: 12월 16일

[19]저는 우리가 대체 에너지 회의에서 제공하기로 계획하고 있는 발표에 대해 경영진으로부터 의견을 받았습니다. 그들은 발표가 우리 제품들의 특징에 초점을 맞추지 않고 대부분 연구 결과에 관한 것임에 대해 우려를 표명했습니다. [20]태양열 동력 난방기들의 우리의 최신 제품군을 홍보하고 고객층을 넓히기 위해, 그들은 우리가 발표 중에 품목들에 대한 더 많은 세부 사항을 제공하기를 원합니다.

따라서, 저는 발표를 수정하기 위해 귀하와 만나고 싶습니다. [21]첨부된 것은 해당되는 제품들의 가격, 기능, 그리고 사양에 대한 요약본입니다.

포함된 자료를 꼼꼼히 읽어 주십시오. [22]특히, 마지막 페이지는 상세히 검토되어야 합니다. 그것에 경영진이 발표의 주안점이 되기를 바라는 정보가 있습니다. 다 읽으신 뒤에는 약속을 정할 수 있도록 제게 통보해 주십시오. 저는 우리가 오늘 오후에 만날 수 있기를 바라는데 이는 이 작업이 최대한 빨리 끝나야 하기 때문입니다.

---

feedback n. 의견, 피드백 alternative energy 대체 에너지
express concern 우려를 표명하다 findings n. (조사·연구 등의) 결과
solar-powered adj. 태양열 동력의 client base 고객층
specification n. 사양, 설명서 applicable adj. 해당되는, 적용할 수 있는

---

19 인칭대명사 채우기 _전체 문맥 파악_

해설 '____가 제공하기로 계획하고 있는 발표'라는 문맥에서 빈칸이 관계절 (____ are planning ~)의 주어 자리이므로, 모든 보기가 정답의 후보이다. 빈칸이 있는 문장만으로 정답을 고를 수 없으므로 주변 문맥이나 전체 문맥을 파악한다. 발표 내용에 대해 경영진으로부터 받은 의견을 설명한 후, 이메일 발신자(I)가 수신자(you)에게 만나서 발표 자료를 수정하자고 했으므로 발표를 준비하는 사람은 이메일 발신자(I)와 수신자(you) 둘 다임을 알 수 있다. 따라서 1인칭 복수 대명사 (B) we가 정답이다.

20 병치 구문 채우기

해설 '태양열 동력 난방기들의 우리의 최신 제품군을 홍보하고 고객층을 넓히기 위해'라는 의미로 보아 등위접속사 and가 연결해야 하는 것은 to 부정사 두 개이다. and 앞에 to 부정사(to promote)가 왔으므로 and 뒤의 빈칸에도 to 부정사가 와야 한다. 이때, and 뒤에 온 to 부정사의 to는 생략이 가능하므로 to expand를 대신하는 (D) expand가 정답이다.

21 형용사 어휘 고르기 _주변 문맥 파악_

해설 '____은 해당되는 제품들의 가격, 기능, 그리고 사양에 대한 요약본이다'라는 문맥이므로 모든 보기가 정답의 후보이다. 빈칸이 있는 문장만으로 정답을 고를 수 없으므로 주변 문맥이나 전체 문맥을 파악한다. 뒤 문장에서 '꼼꼼히 읽어 달라'고 했으므로 제품에 대한 세부 사항이 본 이메일에 첨부되어 보내졌음을 알 수 있다. 따라서 형용사 (D) Attached(첨부된)가 정답이다. 참고로, 이 문장은 분사 형태의 형용사 보어(Attached)가 문장의 맨 앞으로 나와 주어와 동사의 도치가 일어났다.

어휘 mentioned adj. 언급한 requested adj. 요청된
considered adj. 깊이 생각한, 숙고한 끝의

22 알맞은 문장 고르기

해석 (A) 저는 귀하의 모든 요청에 답변할 수는 없었습니다.
(B) 우리의 조사 결과는 수정 중에 더 면밀히 이해되어야 합니다.
(C) 특히, 마지막 페이지는 상세히 검토되어야 합니다.
(D) 그것을 명시된 기한까지 반드시 제출하십시오.

해설 빈칸에 들어갈 알맞은 문장을 고르는 문제이므로 빈칸의 주변 문장이나 전체 문맥을 파악한다. 앞 문장 'Please read through the included materials carefully.'에서 포함된 자료를 꼼꼼히 읽어 달라고 했고, 뒤 문장 'It has the information that management wants to be the focus of the presentation.'에서 그것에 경영진이 발표의 주안점이 되기를 바라는 정보가 있다고 했으므로 빈칸에는 포함된 자료의 마지막 페이지는 특히 상세히 검토되어야 한다는 내용이 들어가야 함을 알 수 있다. 따라서 (C) In particular, the last page should be reviewed in depth가 정답이다.

어휘 follow v. 이해하다, (내용을) 따라잡다 revision n. 수정 hand in 제출하다
indicated adj. 명시된

Section 1 어휘

Chapter 01 동사

Hackers Practice
p.244

01 ⓑ support 지원하다	02 ⓐ acknowledge 알리다
03 ⓑ appear ~한 것 같이 보이다	04 ⓑ witness 보이다, 목격하다
05 ⓑ arrange 정하다	06 ⓐ assist 돕다
07 ⓑ cancel 취소하다	08 ⓑ secure 마련하다
09 ⓐ assemble 조립하다	10 ⓑ intend 목적을 가지다
11 ⓑ operate 수술하다	12 ⓐ utilize 이용하다
13 ⓑ brief 간단히 설명하다	14 ⓐ supply 공급하다
15 ⓑ prevent 예방하다	16 ⓐ match 일치하다
17 ⓑ encounter 직면하다	18 ⓐ certify 보증하다
19 ⓐ cooperate 협력하다	20 ⓐ strive 노력하다
21 ⓑ reveal 공개하다	22 ⓑ gauge 평가하다
23 ⓐ schedule 예정하다	24 ⓑ prohibit 금지하다
25 ⓐ proceed 진행되다	26 ⓐ attract 유인하다
27 ⓐ benefit ~에 도움이 되다	28 ⓑ expedite 신속히 처리하다
29 ⓐ reject 거절하다	30 ⓑ preside 주재하다
31 ⓑ obtain 취득하다	32 ⓐ release 풀다, 방출하다
33 ⓐ handle 다루다	34 ⓑ remain 남다, 남아있다
35 ⓑ order 주문하다	36 ⓑ finalize 마무리짓다
37 ⓐ speculate 추측하다	38 ⓐ enforce 시행하다
39 ⓑ divert 우회하다	40 ⓑ perceive 인지하다
41 ⓐ ship 수송하다	42 ⓐ apply 적용하다
43 ⓑ oversee 감독하다	44 ⓐ authorize 허가하다
45 ⓐ confirm 확인하다	46 ⓑ present 제시하다
47 ⓑ submit 제출하다	48 ⓐ duplicate 재현하다
49 ⓑ follow 따르다	50 ⓐ assert 단언하다
51 ⓑ mark 표시하다	52 ⓐ ensure 확실히 하다
53 ⓐ occupy 사용하다	54 ⓐ require 요청하다
55 feature 특별히 포함하다	56 decline 거절하다
57 cause 야기하다	58 visit 방문하다
59 expect 예상하다	60 compile 수집하다
61 use 이용하다	62 include 포함하다
63 predict 예측하다	64 organize 정리하다
65 complete 완성하다	66 administer 시행하다
67 examine 검토하다	68 expand 확대하다
69 receive 받다	70 exhibit 전시하다
71 remind 상기시키다	72 tolerate 견디다
73 offer 제공하다	74 insert 삽입하다

Hackers Test
p.247

Part 5

01 (C)	02 (B)	03 (C)	04 (D)	05 (C)
06 (C)	07 (C)	08 (C)	09 (D)	10 (A)
11 (A)	12 (A)	13 (D)	14 (D)	15 (C)
16 (B)	17 (C)	18 (B)	19 (C)	20 (B)

Part 6

21 (B)	22 (B)	23 (D)	24 (C)

01 동사 어휘 고르기

해설 '다른 시험이 있으므로 과제물 마감일을 연장하다'라는 문맥이므로 동사 extend의 진행형 (C) extending(연장하다)이 정답이다. (A)의 place는 '놓다, 두다', (B)의 supply는 '공급하다', (D)의 provide는 '제공하다'라는 의미이다.

해석 Wilson 교수는 많은 학생들이 다음 주에 다른 수업들의 시험이 있으므로 과제물 마감일을 연장할 것이다.

어휘 essay n. 과제물, 에세이 deadline n. 마감일

02 동사 어휘 고르기

해설 '광고는 제품이 ~라는 것을 명시하다'라는 문맥이므로 동사 (B) specifies(명시하다)가 정답이다. (A)의 retail은 '(특정 가격에) 팔리다', (C)의 distribute는 '나누어 주다, 유통시키다', (D)의 solicit은 '요청하다'라는 의미이다.

해석 광고는 그 기업의 제품에 최대 2년짜리 품질 보증서가 딸려 있다는 것을 명시한다.

어휘 warranty n. 품질 보증서

03 동사 어휘 고르기

해설 '고객들은 어떤 제품이 그들에게 최선인지 알아볼 수 있다'라는 문맥이므로 동사 (C) determine(알아내다, 밝히다)이 정답이다. (A) accept는 '받아들이다, 수락하다', (B) convince는 '납득시키다, 설득하다', (D) commit은 '저지르다, 약속하다'라는 의미이다.

해석 고객들은 그 업체의 웹사이트에 방문함으로써 어떤 제품이 그들에게 최선인지 알아볼 수 있다.

어휘 product n. 제품, 생산품

04 동사 어휘 고르기

해설 '환경 운동가 단체가 ~에 대한 문제를 제기하다'라는 문맥이므로 동사 address의 과거형 (D) addressed(제기하다)가 정답이다. (A)의 request는 '요구하다', (B)의 leave는 '떠나다, 남기다', (C)의 conform은 '따르다, 일치하다'라는 의미이다.

해석 한 환경 운동가 단체가 캐나다 북부와 러시아의 기온 상승을 언급하면서 기후 변화에 대한 문제를 제기했다.

어휘 make reference to ~을 언급하다

05 동사 어휘 고르기

해설 '감소하는 승객 수로 인해 항공편을 중단하다'라는 문맥이므로 동사 suspend의 진행형 (C) suspending(중단하다)이 정답이다. (A)의 reflect는 '비추다, 반영하다', (B)의 enclose는 '둘러싸다, 동봉하다', (D)의 depart는 '떠나다'라는 의미이다.

해석 Turwind 항공은 감소하는 승객 수로 인해 올랜도에서 밴쿠버로 가는 항공편을 중단할 것이라고 발표했다.

어휘 decline v. 감소하다 passenger n. 승객

06 동사 어휘 고르기

해설 '운송을 더 신속히 처리하는 것이 가능한지 문의하다'라는 문맥이므로 동사 (C) expedite(더 신속히 처리하다)가 정답이다. (A) emphasize는 '강조하다', (B) demonstrate는 '보여주다, 설명하다', (D) recognize는 '알아보다, 인정하다'라는 의미이다.

해석 월요일 회의 전에 소포를 받아야 했기 때문에, Mr. Kim은 운송을 더 신속히 처리하는 것이 가능한지 문의했다.

어휘 parcel n. 소포 inquire v. 문의하다

어휘 increase n. 상승; v. 상승하다 offer v. 제공하다 package n. 패키지 여행(상품)

07 동사 어휘 고르기

해설 '많은 보고서들이 ~라는 것을 보여 주다'라는 문맥이므로 동사 (C) indicate (보여 주다)가 정답이다. (A) inspect는 '점검하다', (B) interfere는 '간섭하다', (D) invoke는 '(느낌·상상을) 불러일으키다'라는 의미이다.

해석 많은 보고서들이 직원들에게 더 많은 결정의 자유를 제공하는 것은 그들이 직장에서 더 큰 책임감을 가지게 한다는 것을 보여 준다.

어휘 workplace n. 직장, 업무 현장

08 동사 어휘 고르기

해설 '영사기와 관련한 문제에 부닥치다'라는 문맥이므로 동사 encounter의 과거형 (C) encountered(곤란·반대 등에 부닥치다, 직면하다)가 정답이다. (A) 의 duplicate는 '복제하다', (B)의 issue는 '발급하다', (D)의 return은 '반납하다'라는 의미이다.

해석 Ms. Choi가 영사기와 관련한 문제에 부닥쳤을 때, 그녀는 발표를 중단하고 도움을 요청해야 했다.

어휘 assistance n. 도움, 지원

09 동사 어휘 고르기

해설 문맥상 목적어인 a building permit(건축 허가증)과 어울려 사용될 수 있는 동사 (D) obtain(취득하다, 얻다)이 정답이다. (A) tear는 '찢다, 뜯다'라는 의미이다. (B) contain은 '포함하다, 함유하다'의 의미를 갖지만 주로 '물질이 어떤 성분을 포함하다'와 같은 문맥에서 사용되므로 답이 될 수 없다. (C) restore는 '회복시키다'라는 의미이다.

해석 주민들은 웹사이트에서 신청서를 다운로드하고 작성한 양식을 시청에 제출함으로써 건축 허가증을 취득할 수 있다.

어휘 city hall 시청, 시 당국

10 동사 어휘 고르기

해설 'Jack Phillips를 새로운 회계부장으로 임명하다'라는 문맥이므로 동사 name의 과거형 (A) named(임명하다, 지명하다)가 정답이다. (B)의 point는 '(손가락으로) 가리키다', (C)의 found는 '설립하다', (D)의 practice는 '실행하다, 실천하다'라는 의미이다.

해석 Mason Electronics사의 최고경영자는 Jack Phillips를 새로운 회계부장으로 임명했다.

어휘 head n. 장, 책임자 accounting department 회계부

11 동사 어휘 고르기

해설 'Ms. Hawkins가 일자리 제안을 거절하다'라는 문맥이므로 동사 (A) reject (거절하다)가 정답이다. (B) adapt는 '맞추다, 조정하다', (C) convene은 '소집하다', (D) benefit은 '이익을 주다, 유익하다'라는 의미이다.

해석 Ms. Hawkins는 Milestone Media사가 보충 건강 보험을 제공하려고 하지 않기 때문에 그 회사의 일자리 제안을 거절할 것이다.

어휘 supplementary adj. 보충의, 추가의 insurance n. 보험, 보험금

12 동사 어휘 고르기

해설 '올해의 총회 참석자 수는 작년의 수를 앞섰다'라는 문맥이므로 동사 surpass 의 과거형 (A) surpassed(앞서다, 뛰어넘다)가 정답이다. (B)의 repeat는 '반복하다, 되풀이하다', (C)의 accomplish는 '성취하다, 달성하다', (D)의 impress는 '깊은 인상을 주다, 감명시키다'라는 의미이다.

해석 올해의 총회 참석자 수는 작년의 수를 3천 명을 넘게 앞섰다.

어휘 attendance n. 참석자 수, 참석 conference n. 총회, 회의

13 동사 어휘 고르기

해설 '매출에서 14퍼센트의 상승을 보이다'라는 문맥이므로 동사 witness의 과거형 (D) witnessed(보이다, 목격하다)가 정답이다. (A)의 combine은 '결합하다', (B)의 commend는 '칭찬하다, 추천하다', (C)의 adjust는 '조정하다, 적응하다'라는 의미이다.

해석 Westwood 여행사는 남미로 가는 단체 패키지 여행을 제공하기 시작하자마자 매출에서 14퍼센트의 상승을 보였다.

14 동사 어휘 고르기

해설 '출장비는 회람에 명시된 금액을 초과할 수 없다'는 문맥이므로 동사 (D) exceed(초과하다)가 정답이다. (A) exist는 '존재하다', (B) prevent는 '막다, 예방하다', (C) delay는 '미루다, 연기하다'라는 의미이다.

해석 직원들에 의해 청구되는 출장비는 회계부에서 온 회람에 명시된 금액을 초과할 수 없다.

어휘 travel expense 출장비 claim v. 청구하다, 요청하다 specified adj. 명시된

15 동사 어휘 고르기

해설 '주문을 확인하기 위해 전화하다'라는 문맥이므로 동사 (C) confirm(확인하다)이 정답이다. (A) contact는 '연락하다', (B) confront는 '~에 직면하다, 맞서다', (D) contend는 '주장하다, 겨루다'라는 의미이다.

해석 Mr. Ewing은 맨체스터에 있는 그의 새로운 가게를 위한 상품 주문을 확인하기 위해 그의 공급자에게 전화했다.

어휘 merchandise n. 상품, 물품

16 동사 어휘 고르기

해설 '정보를 얻으려면 화면 표시 장치를 참고해야 한다'는 문맥이므로 동사 (B) consult(참고하다)가 정답이다. (A) browse는 '둘러보다, 훑어보다', (C) pursue는 '추구하다', (D) inform은 '알리다'라는 의미이다.

해석 비행 일정에 대한 정보를 얻으려면, 승객들은 터미널의 탑승 구역 도처에 위치한 화면 표시 장치를 참고해야 한다.

어휘 display n. 화면 표시 장치

17 동사 어휘 고르기

해설 '경기 침체가 값을 오르게 할 것이라고 추측하다'라는 문맥이므로 동사 speculate의 과거형 (C) speculated(추측하다, 짐작하다)가 정답이다. (A)의 survey는 '설문 조사하다', (B)의 perform은 '수행하다', (D)의 characterize는 '~의 특징을 나타내다'라는 의미이다.

해석 그 재정 자문가는 경기 침체가 금값을 급격히 오르게 할 것이라고 추측했다.

어휘 financial advisor 재정 자문가 economic downturn 경기 침체 cause v. ~하게 하다 rise v. 오르다 sharply adv. 급격히, 날카롭게

18 동사 어휘 고르기

해설 '어느 것을 구매할지 결정하기 전에 여러 종류의 회계 소프트웨어를 알아보았다'라는 문맥이므로 동사 explore의 과거형 (B) explored(알아보다, 답사하다)가 정답이다. (A)의 publish는 '출판하다, 게재하다', (C)의 invite는 '초대하다, 청하다', (D)의 remark는 '언급하다, 논평하다'라는 의미이다.

해석 경영진은 어느 것을 구매할지 결정하기 전에 여러 종류의 회계 소프트웨어를 알아보았다.

어휘 management n. 경영진, 관리 accounting n. 회계, 경리

19 동사 어휘 고르기

해설 '항공편 티켓을 예약하다'라는 문맥이므로 동사 (C) reserve(예약하다)가 정답이다. (A) appoint는 '임명하다', (B) require는 '필요로 하다', (D) attach는 '붙이다'라는 의미이다.

해석 Mr. Jenkins는 여행사 직원에게 다음 주 화요일에 토론토로 가는 이른 아침 항공편 티켓을 예약해 달라고 요청했다.

20 동사 어휘 고르기

해설 '3층에 있는 사무실을 5년 간 사용하다'라는 문맥이므로 동사 occupy의 p.p.형 (B) occupied(사용하다)가 정답이다. (A)의 subscribe는 '구독하다', (C)의 divide는 '나누다', (D)의 associate는 '연상하다, 관련시키다'라는 의미이다.

해석 Ms. Anderson은 지금까지 5년 간 3층에 있는 사무실을 사용했는데, 그녀의 승진 이후에 한 층 위에 있는 곳으로 옮길 것이다.

Downtown 금융 센터 개조

²¹Downtown 금융 센터는 건물 전면 및 로비 재설계를 포함한, 대규모의 수리를 곧 겪을 것입니다. 이 작업의 목적은 고급 기업 세입자를 센터의 사무 공간으로 끌어들이는 데 있어 금융 센터가 경쟁 우위를 갖도록 하는 것입니다.

²²작업 완료 후에는, 하루의 시간에 따라 색이 변하는 거울로 된 유리 외관의 추가로 인해 건물이 상당히 달라 보일 것입니다. ²³또한, 로비의 개선된 좌석 공간은 편안함과 널찍함에 특히 신경 써서, 전보다 더 많은 사람들을 수용할 것입니다.

주목할 만한 것은 Downtown 금융 센터가 수리와 관련해 아주 색다른 조치를 취했다는 것입니다. 센터는 Vernon Design 협회의 젊은 건축가상을 수상한 후 건축계에 최근 진출한 프리랜서 건축가 Janice Pana를 채용했습니다. ²⁴회사가 아닌 개인 토건업자를 고용하는 것은 흔치 않은 결정입니다. 그러나, 센터는 그녀의 능력이 그녀를 이 도전에 잘 대처하게 할 것이라고 믿습니다.

수리는 9월 1일부터 시작할 것이며 연말이 되기 전에 완료될 것으로 예상됩니다.

---

renovation n. 수리, 개조 extensive adj. 대규모의, 광범위한
redesign n. 재설계 facade n. (건물의) 전면, 앞쪽 면
competitive adj. 경쟁적인 edge n. 우위, 우세 high-end adj. 고급의
tenant n. 세입자, 임차인 exterior n. 외관, 외면
remarkable adj. 주목할 만한 unconventional adj. 색다른, 독특한
move n. 조치, 행동 appoint v. 채용하다, 임명하다
make one's debut 진출하다 meet the challenge 도전(시련)에 잘 대처하다

21 동사 어휘 고르기 전체 문맥 파악

해설 'Downtown 금융 센터가 대규모의 수리를 곧 _____할 것이다'라는 문맥이므로 (A) deliberate(심사숙고하다)와 (B) undergo(겪다)가 정답의 후보이다. 빈칸이 있는 문장만으로 정답을 고를 수 없으므로 주변 문맥이나 전체 문맥을 파악한다. 지문 뒷부분에서 수리는 9월 1일부터 시작할 것이라고 했으므로 Downtown 금융 센터는 이미 수리를 하기로 결정했다는 것을 알 수 있다. 따라서 동사 (B) undergo가 정답이다.

어휘 alleviate v. 완화하다 retrieve v. 회수하다

22 부사 어휘 고르기

해설 '색이 변하는 유리 외관 때문에 작업 완료 후에는 건물이 상당히 달라 보일 것이다'라는 문맥이므로 부사 (B) substantially(상당히, 크게)가 정답이다.

어휘 commonly adv. 흔히, 보통 supposedly adv. 추정상, 아마
temporarily adv. 일시적으로

23 동사 어휘 고르기

해설 '로비의 개선된 좌석 공간은 더 많은 사람들을 수용할 것이다'라는 문맥이므로 동사 (D) accommodate(수용하다)가 정답이다.

어휘 escalate v. 확대시키다, 증가시키다 empathize v. 공감하다
isolate v. 격리시키다

24 알맞은 문장 고르기

해석 (A) 많은 사람들이 건물의 색이 변하는 조명을 칭찬했습니다.
(B) 세입자들은 로비가 재설계되었으므로 이제 그곳에 앉아 있는 것을 좋아합니다.
(C) 회사가 아닌 개인 토건업자를 고용하는 것은 흔치 않은 결정입니다.
(D) 그 구역의 작업은 계속되고 있으나 곧 완료될 것입니다.

해설 빈칸에 들어갈 알맞은 문장을 고르는 문제이므로 빈칸의 주변 문맥이나 전체 문맥을 파악한다. 앞부분에서 Downtown 금융 센터가 수리와 관련해 아주 색다른 조치를 취했다고 한 후, 앞 문장 'The center appointed freelance architect'에서 센터가 프리랜서 건축가를 채용했다고 했으므로 빈칸에는 회사가 아닌 개인 토건업자를 고용하는 것은 흔치 않은 결정이라는 내용이 들어가야 함을 알 수 있다. 따라서 (C) Employing an individual contractor rather than a firm is a rare decision이 정답이다.

어휘 compliment v. 칭찬하다 contractor n. 토건업자, 계약자
firm n. 회사, 기업 ongoing adj. 계속되는, 진행 중인

Chapter 02 명사

Hackers Practice p.254

01 ⓐ disposal 처리	02 ⓐ scarcity 부족
03 ⓑ facility 시설	04 ⓑ qualification 자격
05 ⓑ requirement 요건	06 ⓐ contestant 참가자
07 ⓐ coordination 합동	08 ⓐ feedback 의견
09 ⓐ forum 토론의 장	10 ⓐ performance 성과
11 ⓑ inquiry 문의	12 ⓑ proposal 제안서
13 ⓐ approach 접근법	14 ⓐ concern 우려
15 ⓑ breakdown 고장	16 ⓑ shortcoming 결점
17 ⓐ outlook 관점	18 ⓑ reference 추천서, 참고
19 ⓐ warranty 보증 기간	20 ⓑ nomination 추천
21 ⓐ perspective 시각	22 ⓐ replica 복제품
23 ⓑ premise 전제	24 ⓑ stage 단계
25 ⓑ capacity 수용력	26 ⓐ renovation 수리
27 ⓐ publicity 평판	28 ⓐ complaint 불만
29 ⓑ advancement 승진	30 ⓑ foundation 토대
31 ⓑ agreement 합의	32 ⓐ study 연구
33 ⓐ demand 수요	34 ⓑ progress 진척
35 ⓐ request 요청	36 ⓑ transmission 전송
37 ⓐ entry 출품작	38 ⓑ volunteer 지원자, 자원봉사자
39 ⓑ jeopardy 위험	40 ⓑ specification 사양
41 ⓑ amenity 편의시설	42 ⓑ variety 다양함
43 ⓐ violation 위반	44 ⓑ position 직위
45 ⓐ expansion 확장	46 ⓑ selection 선발
47 ⓐ purpose 목적	48 ⓐ notice 통지
49 candidate 후보자	50 approval 허가, 승인
51 completion 완료, 수료	52 reminder 상기시켜 주는 메모
53 transaction 거래	54 durability 내구성
55 evaluation 평가	56 exception 예외
57 lecture 강의	58 testimonial 추천의 글
59 responsibility 책임, 부담	60 promotion 홍보 활동
61 improvement 개선	62 inconvenience 불편
63 development 개발, 발달	64 collection 소장품
65 diversity 다양성	66 occurrence 발생
67 appreciation 감사	68 review 평가

Hackers Test p.257

Part 5

01 (B)	02 (D)	03 (B)	04 (D)	05 (C)
06 (C)	07 (B)	08 (D)	09 (B)	10 (A)
11 (D)	12 (C)	13 (D)	14 (A)	15 (B)
16 (D)	17 (C)	18 (D)	19 (C)	20 (C)

Part 6

21 (B)	22 (C)	23 (B)	24 (D)

01 명사 어휘 고르기

해설 '뉴스 보도 분야에서 경력을 쌓으려는 Mr. Archer의 끈기는 보상받았다'는 문맥이므로 명사 (B) persistence(끈기, 고집)가 정답이다. (A) adequacy는 '타당성', (C) regularity는 '규칙적임', (D) acceptance는 '수락'이라는 의미이다.

해석 뉴스 보도 분야에서 경력을 쌓으려는 Mr. Archer의 끈기는 그가 지역 TV 방송국의 뉴스 기자직을 제안받았을 때 마침내 보상받았다.

02 명사 어휘 고르기

해설 '추가적인 교대 근무를 하다'라는 문맥이므로 명사 (D) shift(교대 근무, 전환)가 정답이다. (A) division은 '부서', (B) system은 '제도, 체계', (C) operation은 '(기계·컴퓨터 등의) 작동, 작업'이라는 의미이다.

해석 회사에 직원이 부족하기 때문에 Ms. Lee는 이번 주에 추가적인 교대 근무를 하도록 요청받았다.

어휘 extra adj. 추가의 be short of ~이 부족하다

03 명사 어휘 고르기

해설 '갈등을 해소하려고 시도하다'라는 문맥이므로 명사 (B) conflicts(갈등, 충돌)가 정답이다. (A)의 estimate는 '견적, 추정', (C)의 announcement는 '발표', (D)의 confirmation은 '확인'이라는 의미이다.

해석 노조 대표는 제조 공장의 직원들과 경영진 사이의 갈등을 해소하려고 시도한다.

어휘 union n. 노조 representative n. 대표 attempt v. 시도하다, 애써 해보다 management n. 경영진 manufacturing plant 제조 공장

04 명사 어휘 고르기

해설 '새로운 임원은 전문 지식을 갖추고 있다'는 문맥이므로 명사 (D) expertise (전문 지식)가 정답이다. (A) inspection은 '점검, 검사', (B) purpose는 '목적', (C) commission은 '위원회, 수수료'라는 의미이다.

해석 그 새로운 임원은 정책 입안, 전략 공식화, 그리고 사업 인수 분야에 대한 전문 지식을 갖추고 있다.

어휘 executive officer 임원 possess v. 갖추고 있다 area n. 분야, 지역 formulation n. 공식화, 형성 acquisition n. 인수, 획득

05 명사 어휘 고르기

해설 '쓰레기를 줍는 것을 도울 자원 봉사자들을 구하다'라는 문맥이므로 명사 (C) volunteers(자원봉사자, 지원자)가 정답이다. (A)의 application은 '지원서', (B)의 investor는 '투자자', (D)의 champion은 '우승자'라는 의미이다.

해석 환경단체 Green Planet은 이번 주말에 시립 공원에서 쓰레기를 줍는 것을 도울 자원 봉사자들을 구한다.

어휘 environmental adj. 환경의 organization n. 단체, 조직 seek v. 구하다, 찾다 pick up ~을 줍다

06 명사 어휘 고르기

해설 '상승하는 인건비가 이윤 감소를 초래하다'라는 문맥이므로 명사 (C) reduction(감소)이 정답이다. (A) deliberation은 '심사)숙고', (B) specification은 '설명서, 열거, 상술', (D) precaution은 '예방 조치'라는 의미이다.

해석 경제학자들은 상승하는 인건비가 서비스 분야에 있는 많은 회사들의 이윤 감소를 초래할 것이라고 예상한다.

어휘 economist n. 경제학자 expect v. 예상하다, 기대하다 labor cost 인건비 lead to ~을 초래하다 profit n. 이윤, 수익 sector n. 분야

07 명사 어휘 고르기

해설 '신문사들이 배포 전략을 변경하고 있다'라는 문맥이므로 명사 (B) distribution (배포)이 정답이다. (A) identification은 '신분증', (C) procedure는 '절차, 방법', (D) transfer는 '이동, 전근'이라는 의미이다.

해석 점점 더 많은 구독자들이 온라인 콘텐츠 이용을 선호하기 때문에 신문사들은 그들의 배포 전략을 변경하고 있다.

어휘 strategy n. 전략, 계획 now that ~이기 때문에, ~이니까 subscriber n. 구독자 prefer v. 선호하다

08 명사 어휘 고르기

해설 '컴퓨터 모니터 설정에 간단한 조정을 하다'라는 문맥이므로 명사 (D) adjustments(조정)가 정답이다. (A)의 disruption은 '분열, 혼란', (B)의 reminder는 '상기시키는 것', (C)의 statement는 '성명, 성명서'라는 의미이다.

해석 당신의 컴퓨터 모니터 설정에 약간의 간단한 조정을 하는 것은 눈을 보호하는 데 도움을 줄 수 있다.

어휘 protect v. 보호하다 vision n. 눈, 시력

09 명사 어휘 고르기

해설 '10월호는 보도를 포함할 것이다'라는 문맥이므로 명사 (B) issue(호, 발행물)

가 정답이다. (A) cost는 '가격, 비용', (C) guarantee는 '보증', (D) state는 '상태'라는 의미이다.

해석 *Starburst*지의 10월호는 인도네시아에 있는 Carlton 전자 회사의 제조 공장에 대한 보도를 포함할 것이다.

어휘 contain v. 포함하다, 담고 있다 manufacturing n. 제조(업)

10 명사 어휘 고르기

해설 '허가를 받은 누구에게든지 웹사이트에서 다운로드 될 수 있다'라는 문맥이므로 명사 (A) permission(허가, 허락)이 정답이다. 명사 (B) significance는 '중요성', (C) maintenance는 '유지', (D) experience는 '경험'이라는 의미이다.

해석 Carlos Modano의 사진은 그의 허가를 받은 누구에게든지 그의 웹사이트에서 다운로드 될 수 있다.

어휘 photography n. 사진

11 명사 어휘 고르기

해설 '해변과 대형 쇼핑센터 둘 다와의 근접함'이라는 문맥이므로 명사 (D) proximity(근접함)가 정답이다. (A) region은 '지역, 지방', (B) direction은 '방향', (C) benefit은 '혜택, 이익'이라는 의미이다.

해석 Fenwood 호텔의 해변과 대형 쇼핑센터 둘 다와의 근접함은 많은 여행객들에게 그곳이 매력적인 선택이 되도록 한다.

어휘 attractive adj. 매력적인

12 명사 어휘 고르기

해설 '기술 특허권 모음은 회사의 최고 자산이다'라는 문맥이므로 명사 (C) asset (자산)이 정답이다. (A) loss는 '손실, 손해' (B) sign은 '기호, 신호', (D) notice는 '통지, 예고'라는 의미이다.

해석 SPS사 매입을 통해 획득한 기술 특허권 모음은 Telcore사의 최고 자산이다.

어휘 patent n. 특허권, 특허증 acquire v. 획득하다, 얻다

13 명사 어휘 고르기

해설 '재활용하지 않는 주민에 대한 벌금을 인상하는 발안'이라는 문맥이므로 (B) initiative(발안, 계획)가 정답이다. (A) outreach는 '봉사 활동', (C) union은 '연합', (D) election은 '선거'라는 의미이다.

해석 그 시장은 재활용하지 않는 주민에 대한 벌금을 인상하는 발안을 지지한다.

어휘 in support of ~을 지지하여 penalty n. 벌금, 형벌

14 명사 어휘 고르기

해설 '지불 금액을 수령하는 즉시 주문을 처리하여 발송하다'라는 문맥이므로 명사 (A) receipt(수령, 받음)가 정답이다. (B) admittance는 '입장 허가', (C) allowance는 '허용, 허가', (D) occupation은 '직업'이라는 의미이다.

해석 Wagner's Online Store사는 지불 금액을 수령하는 즉시 하루 또는 이틀 내로 고객의 주문을 처리하여 발송할 것입니다.

어휘 process v. 처리하다; n. 과정 ship v. 발송하다

15 명사 어휘 고르기

해설 '유전학 분야에서의 최근 발전'이라는 문맥이므로 명사 (B) developments (발전)가 정답이다. (A)의 figure는 '수치, 숫자', (C)의 repetition은 '반복, 되풀이', (D)의 decision은 '결정, 판단'이라는 의미이다.

해석 유전학 분야에서의 최근 발전은 의사들에게 여러 가지 유전적 건강 상태를 검사할 수 있는 능력을 제공해 왔다.

어휘 genetics n. 유전학 a variety of 여러 가지의 hereditary adj. 유전적인

16 명사 어휘 고르기

해설 '생산성을 20퍼센트 정도 높이는 목표를 달성하다'라는 문맥이므로 (D) objective(목표, 목적)가 정답이다. (A) contraction은 '수축, 축소', (B) approval은 '찬성, 승인', (C) compensation은 '보상'이라는 의미이다.

해석 새 장비를 구입하는 것은 공장이 생산성을 20퍼센트 정도 높이는 목표를 달성하는 데에 도움이 될 것이다.

어휘 equipment n. 장비, 설비 achieve v. 달성하다, 성취하다
productivity n. 생산성

17 명사 어휘 고르기

해설 '자금을 확보하는 문제에도 불구하고 대학교는 기숙사를 건설할 것이다'라는
문맥이므로 명사 (C) challenge(문제)가 정답이다. (A) prelude는 '전주곡,
서막', (B) orientation은 '지향, 예비 교육', (D) contest는 '대회, 시합'이라
는 의미이다.

해석 자금을 확보하는 데 있어 직면한 문제에도 불구하고, 밴쿠버 대학교는 더 많은
학생들을 수용하기 위해 새로운 기숙사 건설을 계속할 것이다.

어휘 proceed with ~을 계속하다 dormitory n. 기숙사
accommodate v. 수용하다 secure v. 확보하다 funding n. 자금

18 명사 어휘 고르기

해설 '도시로 오는 방문객들의 유입'이라는 문맥이므로 명사 (D) influx(유입, 쇄도)
가 정답이다. (A) incorporation은 '결합, 법인 조직', (B) assumption은
'추측, 가정', (C) allowance는 '용돈, 수당'이라는 의미이다.

해석 축구 토너먼트 동안 도시로 오는 방문객들의 유입은 호텔 방을 예약하는 것을
불가능하게 만들었다.

어휘 tournament n. 토너먼트, 대회 impossible adj. 불가능한
book v. 예약하다

19 명사 어휘 고르기

해설 '더 많은 고객의 유치를 기대하며 수리를 받다'라는 문맥이므로 명사 (C)
renovation(수리)이 정답이다. (A) formation은 '형성'이라는 의미이다.
(B) magnification은 '확대'의 의미를 갖지만 '물체를 확대해서 보다'와 같
은 문맥에서 사용되므로 답이 될 수 없다. (D) premonition은 '(특히 불길
한) 예감, 징후'라는 의미이다.

해석 그 식당은 더 많은 비즈니스 클래스 고객의 유치를 기대하며 수리를 받는 중이다.

어휘 undergo v. ~을 받다, 겪다 attract v. 유치하다, 끌어모으다

20 명사 어휘 고르기

해설 '팀의 주된 우선 사항'이라는 문맥이므로 명사 (C) priority(우선 사항)가 정
답이다. (A) suitability는 '적합, 어울림', (B) productivity는 '생산성', (D)
satisfaction은 '만족'이라는 의미이다.

해석 Ms. Cooper의 팀의 주된 우선 사항은 완성된 웹사이트의 오류를 점검하는
것이 될 것이다.

어휘 complete v. 완성하다, 완료하다 error n. 오류

21-24는 다음 회람에 관한 문제입니다.

발신: Warran Reynolds, 홍보부
수신: 전 직원

²¹Burrows Design Limited사의 모든 직원들에게 품질 보증에 대한 새로운
시스템이 다음 달부터 시행될 것임을 알려 드립니다. 엄격한 품질 규정 절차가
우수성에 대한 자사의 명성이 유지되는 것을 보장하기 위해 도입될 것입니다.

모든 직원들은, 설계부터 생산까지, 자사의 기준이 충족되고 있는지 확인하고
이러한 점검들을 기록으로 보관하도록 요청받을 것입니다. ²²그 기록은 그 후에
평가를 위해 부서 관리자들에게 제출될 것입니다. 결과물에 대해 논의하기 위해
회의가 곧 마련될 것이고 간부진이 기록에 기반하여 피드백과 권고 사항을 제
시할 것입니다. ²³간부들로부터의 제안 사항은 모든 직원들에게 바로 전달될
것입니다. 그러면 그들은 그들의 업무에 상응하는 변화를 주어야 할 것입니다.

하루 동안의 특별 입문 세미나가 2월 19일 토요일에 101호 회의실에서 예정되
었으며, 새로운 시스템이 자세히 설명될 것입니다. ²⁴모든 직원들이 참석해야 합
니다. 초과 근무에 대해서는 그에 알맞게 수당이 지급될 것입니다.

---

implement v. 시행하다 strict adj. 엄격한 reputation n. 명성, 평판
excellence n. 우수성, 훌륭함, 탁월함 departmental adj. 부서의
come up with ~을 제시하다 corresponding adj. 상응하는, 해당하는
introductory adj. 입문의, 예비의 accordingly adv. 그에 알맞게

21 명사 어휘 고르기 전체 문맥 파악

해설 '새로운 품질 _____에 대한 시스템이 다음 달부터 시행될 것이다'라는 문맥
이므로 (A) coverage(보상)와 (B) assurance(보증)가 정답의 후보이다. 빈
칸이 있는 문장만으로 정답을 고를 수 없으므로 주변 문맥이나 전체 문맥을
파악한다. 뒤 문장에서 '엄격한 품질 규정 절차(Strict quality regulation
procedures)'를 시행한다고 한 후, '모든 직원들이 자사의 기준이 충족되고
있는지 확인하도록 요청받는다(All employees ~ will be asked to check
whether our standards are being met)'고 했으므로 새로 시행되는 시스
템이 품질 보증과 관련된 것임을 알 수 있다. 따라서 빈칸 앞의 명사 quality
와 함께 복합명사를 이루어 '품질 보증'이라는 의미를 나타내는 명사 (B)
assurance가 정답이다.

어휘 revenue n. 수입 affiliation n. 합병, 제휴

22 명사 어휘 고르기 주변 문맥 파악

해설 '기록이 _____을 위해 제출되다'라는 문맥이므로 모든 보기가 정답의 후보
이다. 빈칸이 있는 문장만으로 정답을 고를 수 없으므로 주변 문맥이나 전
체 문맥을 파악한다. 뒤 문장에서 '결과물을 논의하기 위해 회의가 마련된
다(Meetings will be arranged to discuss the findings)'고 했고, '피드
백(feedback)'과 '권고 사항(recommendations)'이 제시될 것이라고 했
으므로 기록에 대한 평가가 이루어질 것임을 알 수 있다. 따라서 명사 (C)
evaluation(평가)이 정답이다.

어휘 conversion n. 전환 revision n. 수정 accumulation n. 누적

23 알맞은 문장 고르기

해석 (A) 그 결과물은 수정을 해야 할 필요성을 보여 줍니다.
(B) 간부들로부터의 제안 사항들은 모든 직원들에게 바로 전달될 것입니다.
(C) 직원들 중 누구도 회의에 참석할 수 없을 것입니다.
(D) 품질 평가 제도는 수 년간 효과적이었음이 판명되었습니다.

해설 빈칸에 들어갈 알맞은 문장을 고르는 문제이므로 빈칸의 주변 문맥이나 전
체 문맥을 파악한다. 앞 문장 'the managing staff will come up with
feedback and recommendations based on the reports'에서 간부
진이 기록에 기반하여 피드백과 권고 사항을 제시할 것이라고 한 후, 뒤 문
장 'They are then expected to make corresponding changes to
their work.'에서 그러면 직원들은 그들의 업무에 상응하는 변화를 주어야
할 것이라고 했으므로 빈칸에는 간부들로부터 받은 제안 사항들이 모든 직
원들에게 바로 전달될 것이라는 내용이 들어가야 함을 알 수 있다. 따라서 (B)
The suggestions from executives are to be sent to all employees
immediately가 정답이다.

어휘 make adjustments 수정하다, 조절하다 assessment n. 평가

24 형용사 어휘 고르기

해설 '모든 직원들이 참석하는 것은 필수적이다'라는 문맥이 되어야 하므로 형용사
(D) imperative(필수적인)가 정답이다. 'It is imperative to + 동사원형 / It
is imperative that절'은 '~해야 한다, ~할 필요가 있다'라는 뜻으로 사용됨
을 알아 두자.

어휘 decisive adj. 결정적인, 결단력 있는 applicable adj. 적용할 수 있는
resourceful adj. 지략 있는, 자원이 풍부한

Chapter 03 형용사

Hackers Practice   p.264

01 ⓐ conclusive 결정적인		02 ⓑ effective 효과적인	
03 ⓐ inactive 비활성 상태의		04 ⓑ urgent 시급한	
05 ⓑ proficient 능숙한		06 ⓐ cautious 조심하는	
07 ⓐ initial 최초의		08 ⓐ diverse 다양한	
09 ⓑ routine 정기적인		10 ⓐ active 적극적인	
11 ⓑ accurate 정확한		12 ⓐ vast 방대한	
13 ⓑ perpetual 끊임없는		14 ⓑ concentrated 집중적인	

15 ⓐ chief 주된
16 ⓑ efficient 효율적인
17 ⓐ unavailable 이용할 수 없는
18 ⓐ challenging 어려운
19 ⓑ delicate 민감한
20 ⓑ preliminary 예비의
21 ⓑ comprehensive 종합적인
22 ⓑ potential 잠재적인
23 ⓐ desired 원하는
24 ⓐ harsh 혹독한
25 ⓑ imperative 꼭 필요한, 필수의
26 ⓑ principal 주요한
27 ⓑ distinguished 뛰어난
28 ⓑ beneficial 유익한
29 ⓐ accessible 이용할 수 있는
30 ⓐ pending 미결인
31 ⓑ hazardous 유해한
32 ⓑ advisable 바람직한
33 ⓐ customary 관례적인
34 ⓐ updated 최신의
35 ⓐ artificial 인공적인
36 ⓑ ambitious 야심찬
37 popular 인기 있는
38 worth ~할 가치가 있는
39 reasonable 적당한, 합리적인
40 confident 자신감 있는
41 equivalent 동등한
42 coming 다음의
43 exhausting 지치게 하는
44 existing 현재의, 현존하는
45 apologetic 미안해 하는
46 complimentary 무료로 제공되는
47 official 공식적인
48 crucial 중요한
49 authentic 정통의

Hackers Test

p.267

Part 5

01 (D)	02 (B)	03 (C)	04 (C)	05 (D)
06 (D)	07 (D)	08 (A)	09 (B)	10 (A)
11 (D)	12 (C)	13 (B)	14 (A)	15 (C)
16 (A)	17 (B)	18 (D)	19 (A)	20 (B)

Part 6

21 (A)	22 (B)	23 (C)	24 (A)

01 형용사 어휘 고르기

해설 '충분한 자금 없이는 재개발이 지연될 것이다'라는 문맥이므로 형용사 (D) adequate(충분한)이 정답이다. (A) multiple은 '다수의'의 의미를 갖지만 가산 명사와 함께 사용되므로 답이 될 수 없다. (B) frustrating은 '좌절감을 일으키는', (C) receptive는 '잘 받아들이는, 수용하는'이라는 의미이다.

해석 충분한 자금 없이는, 도심 지역의 재개발이 한 해 더 지연될 것이다.

어휘 funding n. 자금 redevelopment n. 재개발

02 형용사 어휘 고르기

해설 '과도한 차량 배기가스'라는 문맥이므로 형용사 (B) Excessive(과도한)가 정답이다. (A) Impressed는 '감명받은', (C) Official은 '공식적인', (D) Experienced는 '숙련된'이라는 의미이다.

해석 과도한 차량 배기가스는 대체로 나쁜 대기 질의 원인이다.

어휘 emission n. 배기가스, 배출물 largely adv. 대체로, 크게, 주로
responsible for ~에 원인이 있는

03 형용사 어휘 고르기

해설 빈칸 뒤의 명사 analysis(분석)를 수식하여 '상세한 분석'이라는 뜻을 나타내는 형용사 (C) thorough(상세한)가 정답이다. (A) comfortable은 '편안한', (B) punctual은 '시간을 지키는', (D) remaining은 '남아있는'이라는 의미이다.

해석 그녀의 다큐멘터리에서 Tracy Hasan은 바이킹 문화의 기원과 전통을 다루는 상세한 분석을 제공한다.

어휘 documentary n. 다큐멘터리 analysis n. 분석, 조사 origin n. 기원, 근원

04 형용사 어휘 고르기

해설 '100명의 작업량에 맞먹는다'라는 문맥이므로 형용사 (C) equivalent(맞먹는, 동등한)가 정답이다. 특히 'be equivalent to + 명사'의 어구로 자주 쓰인다는 것을 기억해두자. (A) seasonal은 '계절적인', (B) contrary는 '반대되는', (D) established는 '확립된'이라는 의미이다.

해석 그 기계에 의해 하루 동안 생산되는 제품 수는 100명의 작업량에 맞먹는다.

어휘 goods n. 제품, 상품 produce v. 생산하다

05 형용사 어휘 고르기

해설 '흥미진진한 줄거리가 영화 팬들을 매료시키다'라는 문맥이므로 형용사 (D) compelling(흥미진진한)이 정답이다. (A) visible은 '보이는, 가시적인', (B) durable은 '내구성이 있는, 오래가는', (C) predictable는 '예측할 수 있는, 너무 뻔한'이라는 의미이다.

해석 David Wilkin의 최신 영화의 흥미진진한 줄거리는 영화 팬들을 매료시켰고 전문 비평가들로부터 찬사를 받았다.

어휘 plot n. 줄거리 latest adj. 최신의, 최근의
fascinate v. 매료시키다, 반하게 하다 moviegoer n. 영화 팬
earn v. 받다, 얻다 praise n. 찬사, 칭찬; v. 칭찬하다
professional adj. 전문가의, 전문적인 critic n. 비평가

06 형용사 어휘 고르기

해설 '초기의 차량들은 인기가 없었지만 그 후의 것들은 관심을 끌었다'는 문맥이므로 형용사 (D) subsequent(그 후의)가 정답이다. (A) previous는 '이전의', (B) subordinate는 '하급의', (C) overdue는 '기한이 지난'이라는 의미이다.

해석 그 회사가 생산한 초기의 차량들은 인기가 없었지만, 그 후의 것들은 소비자들의 많은 관심을 끌어들였다.

어휘 attract v. 끌어들이다, 마음을 끌다 a great deal 많이, 상당량

07 형용사 어휘 고르기

해설 Although 이하의 부사절과 뒤 문장의 연결이 자연스러워야 한다. '비회원도 웹사이트에서 주문할 수 있지만, 환불은 회원인 사람들만이 이용할 수 있다'는 문맥이므로 형용사 (D) available(이용할 수 있는)이 정답이다. (A) respectable은 '존경할 만한, 훌륭한', (B) noticeable은 '뚜렷한, 분명한', (C) sociable은 '사교적인'이라는 의미이다.

해석 비회원도 웹사이트에서 상품을 주문할 수 있지만, 환불은 클럽 회원인 사람들만이 이용할 수 있다.

어휘 rebate n. (지급한 대금의 일부를) 환불, 리베이트

08 형용사 어휘 고르기

해설 '안전 워크숍이 모든 직원들에게 의무적이다'라는 문맥이므로 형용사 (A) mandatory(의무적인)가 정답이다. (B) marginal은 '미미한, 중요하지 않은', (C) distinct는 '뚜렷한, 분명한', (D) plausible은 '그럴듯한'이라는 의미이다.

해석 Mr. Bradshaw는 토요일에 열리는 안전 워크숍이 모든 직원들에게 예외 없이 의무적이라고 알렸다.

어휘 announce v. 알리다, 발표하다 workshop n. 워크숍 exception n. 예외

09 형용사 어휘 고르기

해설 빈칸 뒤의 명사 offer와 함께 쓰여 '최근 제의한 액수'라는 뜻을 나타내는 형용사 (B) latest(최근의)가 정답이다. (A) correct는 '정확한', (C) instant는 '즉시의', (D) longest는 '가장 긴'이라는 의미이다.

해석 Ms. Gomez는 그녀의 집을 팔고 싶어 했지만, 구매자가 최근 제의한 액수는 불충분하다고 생각했다.

어휘 be eager to ~을 하고 싶어 하다 offer n. 제의한 액수, (금전적) 제의
insufficient adj. 불충분한

10 형용사 어휘 고르기

해설 '거대한 수영장을 포함하다'라는 문맥이므로 형용사 (A) immense(거대한)가 정답이다. (B) mobile은 '이동하는, 움직임이 자유로운', (C) imaginative는 '상상력이 풍부한, 창의적인', (D) dense는 '빽빽한, 밀집한'이라는 의미이다.

해석 Tropical Island 리조트는 어린이들을 위한 물 미끄럼틀을 특징으로 하는 거대한 수영장을 포함하고 있다.

어휘 include v. 포함하다 feature v. 특징으로 하다, 특별히 포함하다

11 형용사 어휘 고르기

해설 '휠체어를 탄 사람들에게 모든 층이 이용 가능하도록 엘리베이터를 설치하다'라는 문맥이므로 형용사 (D) accessible(이용할 수 있는)이 정답이다. (A) extendable은 '연장할 수 있는', (B) accomplished는 '완성된, 재주가 많은', (C) comprehensive는 '포괄적인'이라는 의미이다.

해석 휠체어를 탄 사람들에게 모든 층이 이용 가능하도록 엘리베이터가 건물에 설치되었다.

어휘 install v. 설치하다

12 형용사 어휘 고르기

해설 '시간제 근로자들에게 제한된 의료 혜택을 제공하다'라는 문맥이므로 형용사 (C) limited(제한된, 한정된)가 정답이다. limited는 범위나 자원의 양이 제한되어 있다는 의미이지만 (B) restrained는 '(표현·문체 등이) 자제된'이라는 의미이므로 오답이다. (A) intended는 '목표로 삼은, 의도된', (D) confined는 '갇힌'이라는 의미이다.

해석 Chang and Nobel 법률 회사는 시간제 근로자들에게 제한된 의료 혜택을 제공한다.

어휘 medical coverage 의료 혜택

13 형용사 어휘 고르기

해설 '계획은 아직 잠정적이지만 준비가 되면 대표자가 전화할 것이다'라는 문맥이므로 형용사 (B) tentative(잠정적인)가 정답이다. (A) vigilant는 '조금도 방심하지 않는', (C) contemporary는 '동시대의, 현대의', (D) infinite는 '무한한, 한계가 없는'이라는 의미이다.

해석 컨설턴트의 회사 방문 계획은 아직 잠정적이지만, 일단 준비가 되면 Mr. Lim에게 전화할 것이다.

어휘 consultant n. 컨설턴트, 고문 representative n. 대표자, 대리인 once conj. 일단 ~하면, ~하자마자 arrangement n. 준비, 예정

14 형용사 어휘 고르기

해설 빈칸 뒤의 명사 attribute(자질)를 수식하여 '유용한 자질'이라는 뜻을 나타내는 형용사 (A) beneficial(유용한)이 정답이다. (B) repetitive는 '반복적인', (C) superficial은 '피상적인', (D) expensive는 '비싼'이라는 의미이다.

해석 사업 분석가로 일하고자 하는 사람들에게, 시장 조사 경력은 매우 유용한 자질이다.

어휘 analyst n. 분석가 attribute n. 자질, 속성

15 형용사 어휘 고르기

해설 '최소한 6개월 동안 유효한 여권'이라는 문맥이므로 형용사 (C) valid(유효한)가 정답이다. (A) ordinary는 '보통의, 일상적인', (B) local은 '지역의, 현지의', (D) returning은 '돌아가는'이라는 의미이다.

해석 그 국가를 방문하기 위해서, 여행객들은 최소 6개월 동안 유효한 여권을 가지고 있어야 한다.

어휘 passport n. 여권 at least 최소한

16 형용사 어휘 고르기

해설 '기밀 의료 정보는 제3자에게 제공되지 않을 것이다'라는 문맥이므로 형용사 (A) confidential(기밀의)이 정답이다. (B) accidental은 '우연한', (C) deliberate는 '신중한', (D) precise는 '정확한'이라는 의미이다.

해석 Clover 진료소의 환자들은 기밀 의료 정보가 제3자에게 절대 제공되지 않을 것임에 안심할 수 있다.

어휘 patient n. 환자 rest assured ~에 안심하다 third party 제3자

17 형용사 어휘 고르기

해설 Although 이하의 부사절과 뒤 문장의 연결이 자연스러워야 한다. '이전에는 경영진에게만 주식 매입 선택권이 제공되었으나, 지금은 평사원도 지분을 매입할 자격이 있다'는 문맥이므로 형용사 (B) eligible(~할 자격이 있는)이 정답이다. 특히 'be eligible to + 동사원형'의 어구로 자주 쓰인다는 것을 기억해두자. (A) appropriate는 '적절한', (C) dependable은 '믿을 수 있는, 신뢰

할 수 있는', (D) proper는 '적절한, 제대로 된'이라는 의미이다.

해석 이전에는 경영진에게만 주식 매입 선택권이 제공되었지만, 지금은 평사원들도 지분을 매입할 자격이 있다.

어휘 stock option 주식 매입 선택권 previously adv. 이전에 management n. 경영진 share n. 지분, 주식

18 형용사 어휘 고르기

해설 '하나의 계정이 손상될 경우를 대비하여 추가적인 이메일 주소를 제공하도록 요구되다'라는 문맥이므로 형용사 (D) additional(추가의)이 정답이다. (A) improvisational은 '즉흥의', (B) occasional은 '가끔의', (C) intentional은 '고의적인, 계획된'이라는 의미이다.

해석 온라인 서점의 고객들은 하나의 계정이 손상될 경우를 대비하여 추가 이메일 주소를 제공하도록 요구된다.

어휘 compromise v. 손상하다; n. 타협

19 형용사 어휘 고르기

해설 '물품 배송이 여전히 계류 중이다'라는 문맥이므로 형용사 (A) pending(계류 중인, 남아있는)이 정답이다. (B) initial은 '처음의', (C) dependent는 '의존하는', (D) representative는 '대표하는'이라는 의미이다.

해석 아직 지불금이 수령되지 않았기 때문에 물품 배송이 여전히 계류 중이다.

어휘 delivery n. 배송 payment n. 지불금, 지급

20 형용사 어휘 고르기

해설 '세법의 변화에 주의를 기울이는 회계 전문가들을 고용하다'라는 문맥이므로 형용사 (B) attentive(주의를 기울이는)가 정답이다. 특히 'be attentive to + 명사'의 어구로 자주 쓰인다는 것을 기억해두자. (A) firm은 '확고한, 단단한', (C) unresponsive는 '둔감한, 반응이 없는', (D) anxious는 '염려하는, 불안해하는'이라는 의미이다.

해석 Brixton Accounting Services사는 세법의 변화에 주의를 기울이는 많은 회계 전문가들을 고용하고 있다.

어휘 employ v. 고용하다 accounting n. 회계 specialist n. 전문가 tax law 세법

21-24는 다음 편지에 관한 문제입니다.

Carmen Anders
657번지 Wentworth Heights
시애틀, 워싱턴주 99362

Ms. Anders께,

자사의 웹사이트를 개설한 귀하의 노고에 매우 감사드립니다. ²¹매출이 지난 분기에 28퍼센트라는 전례 없는 비율로 상승했고, 그 매출의 대부분은 사이트를 통해서 이루어졌습니다.

²²쇠퇴하고 있는 경제는 올해 초 몇 개월 간 자사의 미용 제품 매출에 부정적으로 영향을 주었지만, 웹사이트가 그러한 흐름을 역전시켰고 회사에 대단히 도움이 되었습니다.

²³우리는 귀하의 노고와 사이트의 혁신적인 외관 및 디자인을 높이 평가하고 있습니다. 실제로, 우리의 고객들은 우리에게 사이트의 독특한 특징과 독창적인 지면 배치에 대해 긍정적인 의견들을 보내 왔습니다.

우리는 귀하의 작업의 우수함과 결과에 아주 만족하고 있으며, 우리의 다음 프로젝트에 대해 알려드리고자 합니다. 우리는 이전부터 채용 페이지를 개설하려고 계획해왔습니다. ²⁴우리는 귀하께서 이 프로젝트 또한 맡아주실 수 있기를 바랍니다. 관심이 있으시다면 제게 연락해 주시기 바랍니다.

귀하에게서 소식을 듣기를 기대하며, 노고에 다시 한번 매우 감사드립니다.

Mathew Lucas 드림
최고 경영자, Maxton Cosmetics사

set up 개설하다, 설립하다 quarter n. 분기, 4분의 1 declining adj. 쇠퇴하는 impact v. 영향을 주다 reverse v. 역전시키다, 뒤집다 appreciate v. 높이 평가하다, 고마워하다 look n. 외관

21 형용사 어휘 고르기

해설 '매출이 전례 없는 비율로 상승했다'는 문맥이므로 형용사 (A) unprecedented (전례 없는)가 정답이다.

어휘 unacceptable adj. 용납할 수 없는 underestimated adj. 과소평가된
uncontrolled adj. 제어되지 않는

22 부사 어휘 고르기

해설 '쇠퇴하고 있는 경제가 제품 매출에 부정적으로 영향을 주었다'는 문맥이므로 부사 (B) adversely(부정적으로)가 정답이다.

어휘 resentfully adv. 분개하여 skeptically adv. 회의적으로
contrarily adv. (문장을 수식하여) 이에 반하여

23 형용사 어휘 고르기   주변 문맥 파악

해설 '웹사이트의 ____한 외관과 디자인'이라는 문맥이므로 (A) detailed(정교한), (C) innovative(혁신적인), (D) diverse(다양한)가 정답의 후보이다. 빈칸이 있는 문장만으로 정답을 고를 수 없으므로 주변 문맥이나 전체 문맥을 파악한다. 뒤 문장에서 고객들이 사이트의 '독특한 특징(unique features)'과 '독창적인 지면 배치(ingenious layout)'에 대해 긍정적인 의견들을 보냈다고 했으므로 외관과 디자인이 혁신적이었음을 알 수 있다. 따라서 형용사 (C) innovative가 정답이다.

어휘 informative adj. 유익한

24 알맞은 문장 고르기

해석 (A) 우리는 귀하께서 이 프로젝트 또한 맡아주실 수 있기를 바랍니다.
(B) 온라인 매출은 사이트의 기술적인 문제들 때문에 상당히 손해를 입었습니다.
(C) 경제 호전은 화장품 가게들에게 불균형적으로 영향을 미쳤습니다.
(D) 사용자들은 귀하의 수정 사항들이 사이트를 돌아다니는 것을 더 어렵게 만들었다고 생각합니다.

해설 빈칸에 들어갈 알맞은 문장을 고르는 문제이므로 빈칸의 주변 문맥이나 전체 문맥을 파악한다. 앞부분에서 이전의 작업에 만족하고 있다고 했고, 앞 문장 'We have been planning to create our recruitment page for some time now.'에서 이전부터 채용 페이지를 개설하려고 계획해왔다고 한 후, 뒤 문장 'Please contact me if you are interested.'에서 관심이 있다면 연락하라고 했으므로 빈칸에는 이 프로젝트 또한 맡아주기를 바란다는 내용이 들어가야 함을 알 수 있다. 따라서 (A) We hope that you will be able to work on this project as well이 정답이다.

어휘 as well - 또한 suffer v. 손해를 입다, 악화되다 significantly adv. 상당히
upswing n. 호전 disproportionately adv. 불균형적으로
modification n. 수정 사항 navigate v. 돌아다니다, 길을 찾다

Chapter 04 부사

Hackers Practice   p.273

01 ⓑ hardly 거의 없다
02 ⓑ specifically 특별히
03 ⓑ formerly 전에
04 ⓐ unfortunately 안타깝게도
05 ⓐ permanently 영구히
06 ⓑ randomly 무작위로
07 ⓐ briefly 간단히, 잠시
08 ⓑ unexpectedly 예상치 못하게
09 ⓑ markedly 현저하게
10 ⓐ nearly 거의
11 ⓐ routinely 정기적으로
12 ⓐ unusually 유별나게, 현저하게
13 ⓐ entirely 전부
14 ⓐ thoroughly 철저하게
15 ⓐ reassuringly 안심이 되게
16 ⓑ intentionally 의도적으로
17 ⓐ barely 간신히
18 ⓐ properly 제대로
19 ⓑ regretfully 유감스럽게도
20 ⓐ gradually 서서히
21 ⓑ simultaneously 동시에
22 ⓐ accurately 정확하게
23 ⓑ patiently 참을성 있게
24 ⓑ collectively 집단으로
25 ⓐ comprehensively 포괄적으로
26 ⓑ periodically 주기적으로

27 ⓐ purposely 일부러
28 ⓐ implicitly 절대적으로
29 ⓑ openly 숨김없이
30 ⓐ temporarily 일시적으로
31 ⓐ conveniently 편리하게
32 ⓑ eventually 결국
33 exceptionally 매우
34 rarely 드물게
35 slightly 조금, 약간
36 presently 현재
37 initially 처음에
38 frequently 자주
39 unanimously 만장일치로
40 especially 특히
41 gently 조용하게
42 finally 마침내
43 regularly 규칙적으로
44 elsewhere 다른 곳에서
45 accordingly 그에 알맞게
46 tastefully 고상하게, 멋있게
47 widely 널리
48 possibly 아마도

Hackers Test   p.276

Part 5

01 (B)	02 (C)	03 (D)	04 (B)	05 (A)
06 (C)	07 (D)	08 (A)	09 (C)	10 (A)

Part 6

11 (A)	12 (D)	13 (D)	14 (D)

01 부사 어휘 고르기

해설 빈칸 뒤의 동사구 monitor the humidity level을 수식하여 '습도를 정확하게 측정하다'라는 문맥을 이루는 부사 (B) precisely(정확하게)가 정답이다. (A) newly는 '최근에, 새로이', (C) regretfully는 '유감스럽게' (D) highly는 '매우'라는 의미이다.

해석 그 에어컨은 방안의 습도를 정확하게 측정할 수 있다.

어휘 humidity level 습도

02 부사 어휘 고르기

해설 'Bill Mathewson은 최고의 금융 컨설턴트 중 한 명이라고 널리 여겨진다'라는 문맥이므로 부사 (C) generally(널리, 일반적으로)가 정답이다. (A) closely는 '긴밀하게', (B) evenly는 '균등하게', (D) adversely는 '역으로, 반대로'라는 의미이다.

해석 Bill Mathewson은 중소기업 소유주들에게 최고의 금융 컨설턴트 중 한 명이라고 널리 여겨진다.

어휘 regard v. 여기다 financial consultant 금융 컨설턴트

03 부사 어휘 고르기

해설 직원 행사를 보통 휴게실에서 연다는 내용 다음에 but이 나왔으므로 but 다음은 앞 문장과 상반되는 내용을 전달해야 한다. 빈칸을 포함한 절이 '가끔은 식당이나 호텔에서도 개최되다'라는 문맥이므로, 부사 (D) occasionally(가끔)가 정답이다. (A) early는 '일찍', (B) considerably는 '상당히, 많이', (C) remotely는 '멀리서'라는 의미이다.

해석 시의회 부서 직원들을 위한 직원 행사는 보통 사무실의 휴게실에서 열리지만, 특별 행사는 가끔 식당이나 호텔에서 개최되기도 한다.

어휘 function n. 행사, 의식 lounge n. 휴게실, 라운지 host v. 개최하다

04 부사 어휘 고르기

해설 '고객 서비스 직원들이 일반적으로 3일 이내에 응답한다'라는 문맥이므로 부사 (B) typically(일반적으로, 보통)가 정답이다. (A) overly는 '지나치게, 너무', (C) greatly는 '대단히', (D) tightly는 '단단히, 꽉'이라는 의미이다.

해석 NQ사의 고객 서비스 직원들은 일반적으로 3일 이내에 고객 문의에 응답한다.

어휘 representative n. 직원, 대리인 respond v. 응답하다, 대답하다
inquiry n. 문의, 질문

05 부사 어휘 고르기

해설 '사무실로 불려가기를 참을성 있게 기다리다'라는 문맥이므로 부사 (A) patiently(참을성 있게, 끈기 있게)가 정답이다. (B) expertly는 '훌륭하게, 전

문적으로', (C) cautiously는 '신중하게, 조심스럽게', (D) jointly는 '공동으로'라는 의미이다.

해석 로비에 있는 지원자들은 면접을 보기 위해 사무실로 불려가기를 참을성 있게 기다렸다.

어휘 **applicant** n. 지원자 **call into** ~로 불러들이다, 소환하다

06 부사 어휘 고르기

해설 because 이하의 부사절에서 Baker 가에 있는 선물 가게가 인기 있는 이유를 설명하고 있으므로 inexpensive를 수식하여 '비교적 비싸지 않은 상품들'이라는 문맥을 이루는 부사 (C) relatively(비교적, 상대적으로)가 정답이다. (A) exactly는 '정확히', (B) narrowly는 '가까스로, 좁게', (D) rarely는 '드물게'라는 의미이다.

해석 Baker 가에 있는 선물 가게는 편리한 위치에 있고, 상품들도 비교적 비싸지 않기 때문에 소비자들에게 인기 있다.

어휘 **be popular with** ~에게 인기 있다 **locate** v. ~에 위치하다, ~에 두다

07 부사 어휘 고르기

해설 '오후에 다른 일에 집중할 수 있도록 일부러 아침에 회의를 잡다'라는 문맥이므로 부사 (D) purposely(일부러, 고의로)가 정답이다. (A) scarcely는 '거의 ~ 않다', (B) potentially는 '어쩌면, 잠재적으로', (C) explicitly는 '명백하게, 명확하게'라는 의미이다.

해석 Mr. Waters는 그가 오후에 다른 일에 집중할 수 있도록 일부러 아침에 회의를 잡는다.

어휘 **schedule** v. 일정을 잡다 **focus on** ~에 집중하다

08 부사 어휘 고르기

해설 '작문 워크숍이 이전에 책을 출간해본 적이 없는 경험 없는 작가들을 위해 준비되다'라는 문맥이므로 부사 (A) previously(이전에)가 정답이다. (B) eagerly는 '간절히, 열심히', (C) shortly는 '곧, 금방', (D) urgently는 '급히'라는 의미이다.

해석 그 작문 워크숍은 이전에 책을 출간해본 적이 없는 경험 없는 작가들을 위해 준비되었다.

어휘 **organize** v. 준비하다 **inexperienced** adj. 경험이 없는, 미숙한 **publish** v. 출간하다

09 부사 어휘 고르기

해설 as 이하의 부사절과 앞 문장의 연결이 자연스러워야 한다. '관리자가 도착하자마자 즉시 회의가 재개될 것이다'라는 문맥이므로 부사 (C) promptly(즉시, 정시에)가 정답이다. (A) assertively는 '단정적으로', (B) cordially는 '다정하게', (D) particularly는 '특히'라는 의미이다.

해석 직원들은 오전 10시까지 회의실로 돌아와야 하는데, 이는 관리자가 도착하자마자 즉시 회의가 재개될 것이기 때문이다.

어휘 **resume** v. 재개되다, 다시 시작되다 **once** conj. ~하자마자, ~할 때

10 부사 어휘 고르기

해설 '몇 명의 새로운 직원을 최근에 채용했다'라는 문맥이므로 부사 (A) recently (최근에)가 정답이다. (B) usually는 '주로, 보통', (C) certainly는 '확실히'라는 의미이다. (D) freshly는 주로 물건의 상태를 묘사하는 과거분사를 수식하여 '새롭게'라는 의미로 쓰이므로 hire라는 동사를 수식하기에는 부적절하다. (freshly baked bread: 갓 구운 빵)

해석 회사에서 최근에 새로운 직원 몇 명을 채용했으므로, 그들을 소개하기 위한 모임이 구내 식당에서 열릴 것이다.

어휘 **gathering** n. 모임 **hold** v. 열다, 개최하다 **cafeteria** n. 구내 식당

11-14는 다음 공고에 관한 문제입니다.

시카고 클래식 음악 홀
입장권 발매에 대한 추가 정보

올해, 우리는 클래식 콘서트 시리즈에 10개의 추가 공연을 포함시켰습니다. 〇

---

[11]입장권에 대한 엄청난 수요와 각 공연당 이용 가능한 한정된 좌석 때문에, 콘서트 참석에 관심 있으신 분들은 미리 온라인 예약을 하시는 것이 권고됩니다.

입장권은 예약을 하신 후 언제든지 매표소에서 찾아가실 수 있습니다. 인터넷으로 예약하실 때, 여러분은 청구 번호를 받으실 것입니다. [12]입장권을 수령하기 위해서는 여러분의 신분증과 청구 번호가 동시에 제시되어야 합니다. 우리의 방침에 따라, 운전면허증과 같이, 사진이 부착된 정부 발행 신분증만이 인정됩니다. [13]이 규정은 다른 사람들이 여러분의 입장권을 수령하는 것을 방지하기 위해 시행됩니다. 여러분은 유효한 신분증 없이는 입장권을 수령할 수 없을 것입니다.

[14]여러분께 감사를 표하기 위해, 이번 시즌에 특별 판촉 상품을 제공하고 있으니, 입장권을 반드시 보관하세요. 공연이 끝난 뒤에 무료 콘서트 티셔츠를 얻는 데 사용하실 수 있습니다.

어떠한 문의라도, 1-500-555-1588로 전화하셔서 우리 고객 상담원들 중 한 명에게 말씀해 주시기 바랍니다.

---

additional adj. 추가의 **overwhelming** adj. 엄청난, 압도적인
demand n. 수요 **performance** n. 공연 **urge** v. 권고하다, 재촉하다
pick up 찾아가다 **box office** 매표소 **claim** n. 청구; v. 얻다, 요구하다
present v. 제시하다 **obtain** v. 수령하다, 얻다 **driver's license** 운전면허증
acceptable adj. 인정되는, 허용되는 **valid** adj. 유효한, 타당한
appreciation n. 감사 **inquiry** n. 문의

11 형용사 어휘 고르기

해설 '한정된 좌석 때문에, 미리 예약하는 것이 권고된다'라는 문맥이므로 '한정된, 부족한'이라는 뜻을 가진 형용사 (A) limited(한정된)가 정답이다.

어휘 **spacious** adj. 넓은 **discreet** adj. 신중한 **previous** adj. 이전의

12 부사 어휘 고르기

해설 '입장권을 수령하기 위해서는 신분증과 청구 번호가 동시에 제시되어야 한다'는 문맥이므로 부사 (D) simultaneously(동시에)가 정답이다.

어휘 **primarily** adv. 주로 **mutually** adv. 상호적으로 **frequently** adv. 자주

13 알맞은 문장 고르기

해석 (A) 클래식 음악 공연은 인기가 계속 하락하고 있습니다.
(B) 콘서트가 취소될 경우 여러분은 연락을 받을 것입니다.
(C) 예약은 오직 매표소에서만 가능합니다.
(D) 이 규정은 다른 사람들이 여러분의 입장권을 수령하는 것을 방지하기 위해 시행됩니다.

해설 빈칸에 들어갈 알맞은 문장을 고르는 문제이므로 빈칸의 주변 문맥이나 전체 문맥을 파악한다. 뒤 문장 'You will not be able to receive your tickets without a valid ID.'에서 유효한 신분증 없이는 입장권을 수령할 수 없을 것이라고 했으므로 빈칸에는 이 규정이 다른 사람들이 입장권을 수령하는 것을 방지하기 위해 시행된다는 내용이 들어가야 함을 알 수 있다. 따라서 (D) The rule is in effect to prevent others from collecting your tickets가 정답이다.

어휘 **decline in popularity** 인기가 하락하다 **be in effect** 시행되다

14 동사 어휘 고르기 주변 문맥 파악

해설 '특별 판촉 상품을 제공하고 있으니, 입장권을 반드시 _____하라'는 문맥이므로 (B) examine(검토하다), (C) select(선택하다), (D) retain(보관하다)이 정답의 후보이다. 빈칸이 있는 문장만으로 정답을 고를 수 없으므로 주변 문맥이나 전체 문맥을 파악한다. 뒤 문장에서 '공연이 끝난 뒤에 무료 콘서트 티셔츠를 얻는 데 사용할 수 있다(You can use it to claim a free concert T-shirt after the show.)'고 했으므로 공연 후에 특별 판촉 상품을 얻기 위해 입장권을 보관해야 함을 알 수 있다. 따라서 동사 (D) retain이 정답이다.

어휘 **commit** v. (범죄를) 저지르다, 약속하다

Section 2 어구

Chapter 05 형용사 관련 어구

Hackers Practice

p.283

01 to (be enough to ~에 충분하다)
02 for (be favorable for ~에 적합하다)
03 required (be required to ~하도록 요구되다)
04 irrelevant (be irrelevant to ~와 무관하다)
05 integral (be integral to ~에 필수적이다)
06 notable (be notable for ~로 유명하다)
07 with (be consistent with ~와 일치하다)
08 for (be scheduled for ~로 예정되다)
09 from (be absent from ~에 불참하다)
10 of (be aware of ~을 인식하다)
11 dedicated (be dedicated to ~에 전념하다)
12 to (be opposite to ~와 반대이다)
13 of (be cognizant of ~에 대해 알고 있다)
14 willing (be willing to 기꺼이 ~하다)

Hackers Test

p.284

Part 5

01 (C)	02 (D)	03 (B)	04 (A)	05 (D)
06 (C)	07 (B)	08 (D)	09 (C)	10 (D)

Part 6

11 (B)	12 (C)	13 (A)	14 (C)

01 형용사 관련 어구 완성하기

해설 '영화 팬들은 그 영화의 개봉에 대해 열광하고 있다'라는 문맥에서 빈칸 앞의 are와 빈칸 뒤의 전치사 about과 함께 '~에 대해 열광하다'라는 의미의 어구를 이루는 형용사 (C) enthusiastic이 정답이다. (be enthusiastic about: ~에 대해 열광하다, 열중하다) (A) potent는 '강력한, 강한', (B) creative는 '창의적인, 창조적인', (D) articulate는 '명료한, 조리 있는'이라는 의미이다.

해석 영화 팬들은 그 영화의 개봉에 대해 열광하고 있고 이미 극장 밖에서 줄을 서 있다.

어휘 opening n. 개봉, 개막 line up 줄 서다, 줄 세우다

02 형용사 관련 어구 완성하기

해설 빈칸 앞의 was와 빈칸 뒤의 전치사 for와 함께 쓰여 '~에 자격이 있다'라는 어구를 이루는 형용사 (D) eligible이 정답이다. (be eligible for: ~에 자격이 있다) (A) economic은 '경제의', (B) effective는 '효과적인'이라는 의미이며, (C) eager는 '열망하는, 간절한'이라는 의미로 전치사 to와 함께 쓰인다.

해석 그 사업가는 웹사이트에 나열된 필요 요건을 확인했을 때, 그가 대출에 자격이 있음을 알게 되었다.

어휘 entrepreneur n. 사업가, 기업가 loan n. 대출

03 형용사 관련 어구 완성하기

해설 빈칸 앞의 is와 빈칸 뒤의 전치사 for와 함께 쓰여 '~에 이상적이다'라는 의미의 어구를 이루는 형용사 (B) ideal이 정답이다. (be ideal for: ~에 이상적이다) (A) known은 '알려진', (C) simple은 '간단한, 단순한', (D) alert는 '민첩한, 방심하지 않는'이라는 의미이다.

해석 Star Tower에 있는 침실 2개짜리 아파트는 도심지역에서 일하는 누구에게나 이상적이다.

어휘 downtown area 도심지역

04 형용사 관련 어구 완성하기

해설 '티켓이 한 달 쯤 전에 판매될 것 같다'라는 문맥에서 빈칸 앞의 are와 빈칸 뒤의 전치사 to와 함께 쓰여 '~할 것 같다'라는 의미의 어구를 이루는 형용사 (A) likely가 정답이다. (be likely to: ~할 것 같다) (B) inserted는 '삽입된'이라는 의미이며, (C) comparable은 '필적하는, 비길 만한'이라는 의미로 전치사 to와 함께 쓰인다. (D) increased는 '증가한'이라는 의미이다.

해석 아직 공식적인 발표가 되지 않았지만, 음악 공연 한 달 쯤 전에 티켓이 판매될 것 같다.

어휘 official adj. 공식적인 announcement n. 발표, 공고 go on sale 판매하다

05 형용사 관련 어구 완성하기

해설 빈칸 앞의 are와 빈칸 뒤의 전치사 from과 함께 쓰여 '~가 면제되다'라는 의미의 어구를 이루는 형용사 (D) exempt가 정답이다. (be exempt from: ~가 면제되다) (A) complimentary는 '무료의, 칭찬하는', (B) provided는 '제공되는', (C) insolent는 '오만한, 무례한'이라는 의미이다.

해석 Cubicle Supply사의 웹사이트에 따르면, 500달러 또는 이상을 구매한 쇼핑객들은 모든 운송비 및 취급 수수료가 면제된다.

어휘 or more 또는 그 이상, ~ 정도 shipping n. 운송 handling charge 취급 수수료

06 형용사 관련 어구 완성하기

해설 빈칸 앞의 is와 빈칸 뒤의 전치사 to와 함께 쓰여 '기꺼이 ~하다'라는 의미의 어구를 이루는 형용사 (C) willing이 정답이다. (be willing to: 기꺼이 ~하다) (A) relevant는 '적절한', (B) relaxing은 '편한', (D) necessary는 '필수적인'이라는 의미이다.

해석 Ms. Stein은 회사가 기꺼이 그녀에게 필요 시 집에서 일하도록 해주었기 때문에 일자리 제의를 받아들였다.

어휘 accept v. 받아들이다, 수락하다 job offer 일자리 제의

07 형용사 관련 어구 완성하기

해설 빈칸 앞의 is와 빈칸 뒤의 전치사 to와 함께 쓰여 '~을 받아야 한다'라는 의미의 어구를 이루는 형용사 (B) subject가 정답이다. (be subject to: 승인 등을 받아야 한다) (A) compulsory는 '강제적인, 필수의', (C) uncovered는 '아무것도 덮여 있지 않은, 노출된, 폭로된', (D) interior는 '내부의'라는 의미이다.

해석 공장에서 나오는 탄소 배출에 대한 제안된 규정 변경은 환경부의 검토 대상이다.

어휘 propose v. 제안하다, 건의하다 regulation n. 규정, 규제 regarding prep. ~에 대하여 carbon n. 탄소 emission n. 배출

08 형용사 관련 어구 완성하기

해설 빈칸 앞의 is와 빈칸 뒤의 전치사 for와 함께 쓰여 '~에 대해 책임이 있다'라는 의미의 어구를 이루는 형용사 (D) responsible이 정답이다. (be responsible for: ~에 대해 책임이 있다) (A) dependable은 '믿을 수 있는', (B) debatable은 '논쟁의 여지가 있는', (C) inevitable은 '피할 수 없는'이라는 의미이다.

해석 도서관은 귀하의 개인 소지품에 대해 책임이 없으므로, 소지품을 내버려 두지 마십시오.

어휘 possession n. 소지품, 소유 belongings n. 소지품, 재산 unattended adj. 내버려 둔, 주인이 옆에 없는

09 형용사 관련 어구 완성하기

해설 '임원들은 고객들을 상실한 것에 대해 걱정한다'는 문맥에서 빈칸 앞의 are와 빈칸 뒤의 전치사 about과 함께 쓰여 '~에 대해 걱정하다'라는 의미의 어구를 이루는 형용사 (C) concerned가 정답이다. (be concerned about: ~에 대해 걱정하다) (A) connected는 '연결된', (B) considered는 '깊이 생각한', (D) convinced는 '확신하는'이라는 의미이다.

해석 Coleman 법률 사무소의 임원들은 최근 경쟁 법률 사무소에 몇몇 중요 고객들을 상실한 것에 대해 걱정한다.

어휘 recent adj. 최근의 loss n. 상실, 손실 prominent adj. 중요한, 유명한

10 형용사 관련 어구 완성하기

해설 '서비스 제공에 헌신적이다'라는 문맥에서 빈칸 앞의 is와 빈칸 뒤의 전치사 to와 함께 쓰여 '~에 헌신적이다'라는 의미의 어구를 이루는 형용사 (D) dedicated가 정답이다. (be dedicated to: ~에 헌신적이다) (A) assured는 '자신감 있는, 확신하는'이라는 의미로 전치사 of와 함께 쓰인다. (B) concentrated는 '집중된, 응집된', (C) offered는 '제공된, 개설된'이라는 의미이다.

해석 Blue Ribbon사는 고객들에게 일관성 있고 시기적절한 양질의 서비스를 제공하는 데 헌신적이다.

어휘 consistent adj. 일관성 있는 timely adj. 시기적절한, 적시의

11-14는 다음 회람에 관한 문제입니다.

발신: Richard Garfield, 부사장
수신: 마케팅부 전 직원
제목: 발표
날짜: 10월 13일

계속 진행 중인 세계 불황의 결과로 올해에 자사의 매출액이 하락했다는 것을 여러분 모두 알고 있을 것입니다. ¹¹경기 침체의 특성에 대해 잘 알고 있는 분들은 소비자들이 실업이나 침체된 소득에 대처하기 위해 소비를 억제한다는 것을 아실 겁니다. ¹²예상대로, 최근의 매출액 하락은 이러한 소비자 성향을 반영합니다.

¹³숙고 후에, 고위 경영진은 몇 가지 대책을 고안했습니다. 이는 자사 상품에 대해 감소한 수요를 상쇄하기 위해 시행될 것입니다. ¹⁴우리는 여러분에게 자사 계획의 상세한 개요를 제공할 발표 일정을 잡을 예정인데, 이는 주로 광고의 주안점을 바꾸는 것과 관련이 있습니다. 발표의 날짜, 시간, 장소는 내일 오후까지는 결정될 것입니다.

drop v. 하락하다, 떨어지다 as a result of ~의 결과로
ongoing adj. 계속 진행 중인 slump n. 불황, 급감
economic downturn 경기 침체 curb v. 억제하다, 제한하다
cope with ~에 대처하다, 대응하다 stagnant adj. 침체된, 불경기의
senior management 고위 경영진 devise v. 고안하다, 창안하다
several adj. 몇 가지의 offset v. 상쇄하다, 보완하다
overview n. 개요 renew v. 바꾸다, 새롭게 하다, 재개하다
focus n. 주안점, 초점 determine v. 결정하다

11 형용사 관련 어구 완성하기

해설 '경기 침체의 특성에 대해 잘 알고 있는 사람들'이라는 문맥에서 빈칸 앞의 are와 빈칸 뒤의 전치사 with와 함께 쓰여 '~에 대해 잘 알다'라는 의미의 어구를 이루는 형용사 (B) familiar(~을 잘 아는)가 정답이다. (be familiar with: ~에 대해 잘 알다) (A) reliant는 '의존하는, 신뢰하는'이라는 의미로 주로 전치사 on/upon과 함께 사용되므로 답이 될 수 없다.

어휘 consistent adj. 일관된, 일치하는 friendly adj. 친절한

12 알맞은 문장 고르기

해석 (A) 이를 염두에 두고, 지금은 이 성과를 축하할 시기입니다.
(B) 금융 전문가들은 불경기가 끝났다고 분명히 말했습니다.
(C) 예상대로, 최근의 매출액 하락은 이러한 소비자 성향을 반영합니다.
(D) 저희의 웹사이트를 방문해서 최신 구인 공고를 보시기를 권해드립니다.

해설 빈칸에 들어갈 알맞은 문장을 고르는 문제이므로 빈칸의 주변 문맥이나 전체 문맥을 파악한다. 앞부분에서 올해에 회사의 매출액이 하락했다고 한 후, 앞 문장 'consumers curb their spending to cope with job losses or stagnant incomes'에서 소비자들이 실업이나 침체된 소득에 대처하기 위해 소비를 억제한다고 했으므로 빈칸에는 최근의 매출액 하락이 소비자들의 소비 억제와 관련이 있다는 내용이 들어가야 함을 알 수 있다. 따라서 (C) Unsurprisingly, the recent decline in sales reflects this consumer tendency가 정답이다.

어휘 with in mind 염두에 두고 financial analyst 금융 전문가
declare v. 분명히 말하다, 선언하다 recession n. 불경기, 불황
unsurprisingly adv. 예상대로, 놀랄 것도 없이
decline n. 하락, 감소; v. 감소하다 reflect v. 반영하다
tendency n. 성향, 경향 advise v. 권하다, 조언하다

13 명사 어휘 고르기 전체 문맥 파악

해설 '숙고 후에 고위 경영진은 몇 가지 ____을 고안했다'라는 문맥이므로 모든 보기가 정답의 후보이다. 빈칸이 있는 문장만으로는 정답을 고를 수 없으므로 주변 문맥이나 전체 문맥을 파악한다. 뒤 문장에서 '이는 자사 상품에 대해 감소한 수요를 상쇄하기 위해 시행될 것(These will be implemented to offset decreased demand for our products.)'이라고 한 후, 뒷부분에서 광고의 주안점을 바꾸는 것과 관련된 계획들을 발표할 것이라고 했으므로 고위 경영진이 숙고 후에 상품에 대해 감소한 수요를 상쇄하기 위해 몇 가지 대책을 고안했음을 알 수 있다. 따라서 명사 (A) measures(대책)가 정답이다.

어휘 alliance n. 연합, 동맹 regulation n. 규제 standard n. 기준

14 형용사 어휘 고르기

해설 '계획의 상세한 개요'라는 문맥이므로 형용사 (C) detailed(상세한)가 정답이다.

어휘 extreme adj. 극도의, 극심한 vulnerable adj. 취약한, 연약한
continuous adj. 계속되는, 지속적인

Chapter 06 동사 관련 어구 1

Hackers Practice   p.289

01 to (credit A to B A를 B의 공으로 믿다)
02 on (be based on ~에 기반을 두다)
03 on (advertise on ~에 광고를 하다)
04 in (result in ~을 야기하다)
05 on (depend on ~에 달려 있다)
06 of (consist of ~로 구성되다)
07 in (engage in ~에 참여하다)
08 to (lead to ~로 이어지다)
09 for (compete for ~을 위해 경쟁하다)
10 assigned (assign A to B A를 B에 배당하다)
11 entitled (be entitled to ~을 받을 자격이 있다)
12 as (regard A as B A를 B로 여기다)
13 to (be related to ~와 관련되다)
14 by (be accompanied by ~이 동봉되다)
15 from (prohibit A from -ing A가 ~하는 것을 금지하다)
16 in (be involved in ~에 종사하다)
17 to (subject A to B A를 B에 노출시키다)

Hackers Test   p.290

Part 5

| 01 (B) | 02 (A) | 03 (C) | 04 (C) | 05 (C) |
| 06 (B) | 07 (B) | 08 (C) | 09 (B) | 10 (D) |

Part 6

| 11 (D) | 12 (D) | 13 (D) | 14 (A) |

01 동사 관련 어구 채우기

해설 '냉장고에 정수기와 자동 얼음 제조기가 갖춰져 있다'라는 문맥이므로 빈칸 앞의 is와 빈칸 뒤의 전치사 with와 함께 쓰여 'A에 B가 갖춰져 있다'라는 의미의 어구를 이루는 동사 equip의 p.p.형 (B) equipped(갖추다, 장착하다)가 정답이다. (equip A with B: A에 B를 갖추다, 장착하다) (A)의 assign은 '배정하다, 배치하다', (C)의 insert는 '끼우다, 삽입하다', (D)의 attract는 '끌어당기다, 유인하다'라는 의미이다.

해석 그 냉장고에는 정수기와 자동 얼음 제조기가 갖춰져 있다.

어휘 water dispenser 정수기 automatic adj. 자동의

02 동사 관련 어구 완성하기

해설 '재활용품을 버리다'라는 문맥이므로 빈칸 뒤의 전치사 of와 함께 쓰여 '~을 버리다'라는 의미의 어구를 이루는 동사 (A) dispose가 정답이다. (dispose of: ~을 버리다, 처분하다) (B) compose는 '구성하다'라는 의미이며, (C) exclude는 '제외하다, 배제하다'라는 의미로 'exclude A from B(B에서 A를 제외하다)'의 형태로 주로 쓰인다. (D) abandon은 '버리다'라는 의미로 dispose와 다르게 뒤에 전치사 없이 바로 목적어를 쓴다는 점을 알아 두자.

해석 입주자들은 건물 뒤쪽에서 찾을 수 있는 표시된 쓰레기통에만 재활용품을 버리는 것이 허용된다.

어휘 occupant n. 입주자, 사용자 be allowed to ~하는 것이 허용되다
recyclable n. 재활용품; adj. 재활용할 수 있는 bin n. 쓰레기통
rear n. (어떤 것의) 뒤쪽

03 동사 관련 어구 완성하기

해설 '오래된 건물의 수리를 전문적으로 하다'라는 문맥이므로 빈칸 뒤의 전치사 in과 함께 쓰여 '~을 전문적으로 하다'라는 의미의 어구를 이루는 동사 (C) specializes가 정답이다. (specialize in: ~을 전문적으로 하다) (A)의 create는 '창조하다', (B)의 research는 '연구하다, 조사하다', (D)의 delegate는 '위임하다'라는 의미이다.

해석 Oakley Properties사는 오래된 건물의 수리를 전문적으로 하며, 건물들 특유의 외관을 유지하면서 그 건물들을 현대적이고 편리하게 만든다.

어휘 renovation n. 수리 modern adj. 현대적인, 최신의
convenient adj. 편리한 retain v. 유지하다, 보유하다
unique adj. 특유의, 고유한 appearance n. 외관, (겉)모습

04 동사 관련 어구 완성하기

해설 '수정한 로고를 원래의 형태와 구별하는 것이 어렵다'라는 문맥이므로 전치사 from과 함께 쓰여 '~과 구별하다'라는 의미의 어구를 이루는 동사 (C) differentiate이 정답이다. (differentiate from: ~과 구별하다) (A) reproduce는 '복제하다', (B) market은 '거래하다, 내놓다', (D) expand는 '확대하다'라는 의미이다.

해석 그 그래픽 디자인 회사가 Radix Sportwear사의 로고에 약간의 수정만 했기 때문에, 그것을 원래의 형태와 구별하는 것은 어렵다.

어휘 slight adj. 약간의, 조금의 modification n. 수정, 변경

05 동사 관련 어구 완성하기

해설 빈칸을 포함한 구는 주절의 내용인 택배 회사의 새로운 트럭 구매의 이유를 부연 설명해 줄 분사구문이므로, '증가하는 서비스 수요에 대응하여'라는 문맥이 되어야 한다. 따라서 빈칸 뒤의 전치사 to와 함께 쓰여 '~에 대응하다'라는 의미의 어구를 이루는 동사 respond의 현재분사형 (C) responding이 정답이다. (respond to: ~에 대응하다) (A)의 communicate은 '의사소통하다', (B)의 discuss는 '상의하다', (D)의 interview는 '면접을 보다'라는 의미이다.

해석 그 택배 회사는, 증가하는 서비스 수요에 대응하여, 새로운 한 무리의 트럭을 구입했다.

어휘 courier company 택배 회사 purchase v. 구입하다; n. 구매
fleet n. (한 기관이 소유한 비행기·버스·택시 등의) 무리

06 동사 관련 어구 완성하기

해설 '입장은 교수들과 대학원생들로 한정되다'라는 문맥이므로 빈칸 뒤의 전치사 to와 함께 쓰여 '~로 한정하다'라는 의미의 어구를 이루는 동사 restrict의 p.p.형 (B) restricted가 정답이다. (restrict A to B: A를 B로 한정하다) (A)의 enlist는 '입대하다, 협력하다', (C)의 contradict는 '반박하다, 부정하다'라는 의미이다. (D)의 prevent는 '방해하다'라는 의미로 'prevent A from B'의 형태로 주로 쓰인다.

해석 기록 보관소 입장은 교수들과 대학원생들로 한정된다는 것이 도서관 방침이다.

어휘 admission n. 입장, 입학 archive n. 기록 보관소

07 동사 관련 어구 완성하기

해설 빈칸 뒤의 전치사 for와 함께 쓰여 '신용카드에 대한 자격을 갖추다'라는 문맥에서 '~에 대한 자격을 갖추다'라는 의미의 어구를 이루는 동사 (B) qualify가 정답이다. (qualify for: ~에 대한 자격을 갖추다) (A) propose는 '제안하다', (C) demand는 '요구하다', (D) preserve는 '보호하다'라는 의미이다.

해석 신용카드에 대한 자격을 갖추기 위해, 고객들은 그들이 시기적절한 때에 납부할 능력이 있다는 증거를 제공해야 한다.

어휘 be capable of ~할 능력이 있다 make payment 납부하다, 결제하다
timely adj. 시기적절한, 때맞춘

08 동사 관련 어구 완성하기

해설 '퇴직기념 파티가 회사 50주년 기념일과 동시에 일어나다'라는 문맥이므로 빈칸 뒤의 전치사 with와 함께 쓰여 '~과 동시에 일어나다'라는 의미의 어구를 이루는 동사 (C) coincides가 정답이다. (coincide with: ~과 동시에 일어나다, ~과 일치하다) (A)의 associate는 '연관 짓다', (B)의 deal은 '다루다', (D)의 agree는 '동의하다'라는 의미이다.

해석 다음 달에 열리는 Ms. Jensen의 퇴직기념 파티는 회사 50주년 기념일과 동시에 일어난다.

어휘 retirement n. 퇴직, 은퇴 anniversary n. (주년) 기념일

09 동사 관련 어구 완성하기

해설 '휴대 전화의 갑작스런 판매 증가는 인기 드라마에 휴대 전화가 등장한 덕분이다'라는 문맥이므로 빈칸 뒤의 전치사 to와 함께 쓰여 '~의 덕분으로 돌리다'라는 의미의 어구를 이루는 동사 attribute의 p.p.형 (B) attributed가 정답이다. (attribute A to B: A를 B의 덕분으로 돌리다) (A)의 permit은 '허가하다', (C)의 attest는 '증명하다', (D)의 allocate는 '할당하다, 배분하다'라는 의미이다.

해석 Superslim사 휴대 전화의 갑작스런 판매 증가는 현재 NATV에서 방영 중인 인기 텔레비전 드라마에 그 휴대 전화가 등장한 덕분이다.

어휘 sudden adj. 갑작스런, 급작스런 appearance n. 등장, 출연

10 동사 관련 어구 완성하기

해설 '그들의 실적과 평가에 바탕을 두다'라는 문맥에서 빈칸 앞의 are와 빈칸 뒤의 전치사 on과 함께 쓰여, '~에 바탕을 두다'라는 의미의 어구를 이루는 동사 base의 p.p.형 (D) based가 정답이다. (be based on: ~에 바탕을 두다) (A)의 lift는 '들어 올리다', (B)의 collect는 '모으다, 수집하다', (C)의 relate는 '관련시키다'라는 의미로 'relate A with B(A를 B에 관련시키다)' 또는 'relate with A(A와 부합하다)'의 형태로 주로 쓰인다.

해석 직원들의 연간 보너스는 그들의 관리자들에 의해 제출된 그들의 실적과 평가에 바탕을 두고 있다.

어휘 performance n. 실적 evaluation n. 평가 submit v. 제출하다
supervisor n. 관리자

11-14는 다음 편지에 관한 문제입니다.

Hi-Net 케이블 인터넷 고객 서비스
867번지 East Valley Trail NW
그레이트 폴스, 몬타나주 68750

담당자분께,

저는 어제 귀사로부터 대금 청구서를 받았고 오류가 있다는 점을 알아차렸습니다. 저는 몇 주 전에 인터넷 서비스를 신청했고, 매달 35달러의 비용이 들 것이라고 들었습니다. ¹¹그러나, 첫 번째 청구서를 받았을 때, 저는 그 대신에 제 계좌로 50달러가 청구되었음을 알게 되었습니다. 제 신청서에서 확인하실 수 있듯이, 저는 일반 서비스를 신청했습니다. ¹²하지만 고객 담당 직원이 실수로 저를 초고속 연결망에 등록한 것 같습니다. 자동 납부를 취소하기 위해 은행에 전화했지만, 돈은 이미 보내졌습니다. 즉시 제 요금제를 낮춰주시고, 차액을 환불해주십시오. ¹³아니면 제 다음 청구서에서 그 금액을 공제해주셔도 됩니다. ¹⁴귀하로부터 가능한 한 빨리 답변을 받기를 희망하며, 이 문제가 곧 해결되기를 기대합니다.

Eleanor Briggs 드림

billing statement 대금 청구서 sign up for ~을 신청하다 account n. 계좌
request v. 신청하다, 요구하다 standard adj. 일반적인, 보통의; n. 기준
representative n. 직원 register v. 등록하다 automatic adj. 자동의
payment n. 납부 downgrade v. (등급을) 낮추다 plan n. 요금제, 계획
immediately adv. 즉시 refund v. 환불하다 difference n. 차액, 차이
matter n. 문제; v. 중요하다 shortly adv. 곧, 얼마 안 되어

11 동사 관련 어구 완성하기

해설 '50달러가 발신인(I)의 계좌로 청구되었다'라는 문맥이므로 빈칸 앞의 had been과 빈칸 뒤의 전치사 to가 함께 쓰여 '(대금이) ~로 청구되다'라는 의미의 어구를 이루는 동사 charge의 p.p.형 (D) charged가 정답이다. (charge to: ~로 청구하다)

어휘 calculate v. 계산하다, 산출하다 contribute v. 기여하다, 기부하다
compensate v. 보상하다, 배상하다

12 부사 어휘 고르기 | 주변 문맥 파악

해설 '직원이 초고속 연결망에 ___ 등록했다'라는 문맥이므로 모든 보기가 정답의 후보이다. 빈칸이 있는 문장만으로는 정답을 고를 수 없으므로 주변 문맥이나 전체 문맥을 파악한다. 앞 문장에서 자신이 '일반 서비스를 신청했다 (I requested the standard service)'고 했으므로 직원이 실수로 발신자가 등록하지 않은 서비스에 잘못 등록했음을 알 수 있다. 따라서 부사 (D) mistakenly(실수로, 잘못하여)가 정답이다.

어휘 continually adv. 계속적으로, 줄곧 cautiously adv. 신중히, 조심하여
simultaneously adv. 동시에

13 알맞은 문장 고르기

해석 (A) 현재, 제가 받고 있는 서비스는 예상했던 것만큼 빠르지 않습니다.
(B) 귀하는 다음 달에 높은 등급의 요금제에 자격이 될 수도 있습니다.
(C) 이 요금 지불의 지연에 대해 사과 드립니다.
(D) 아니면 제 다음 청구서에서 그 금액을 공제해주셔도 됩니다.

해설 빈칸에 들어갈 알맞은 문장을 고르는 문제이므로 빈칸의 주변 문맥이나 전체 문맥을 파악한다. 앞부분에서 자신에게 잘못 청구된 요금이 이미 납부되었다고 한 후, 앞 문장 'Please ~ refund the difference.'에서 차액을 환불해달라고 했으므로, 빈칸에는 잘못 청구된 요금에 대한 발신자의 요구 사항과 관련된 내용이 들어가야 함을 알 수 있다. 따라서 (D) Or you can subtract that amount from my next bill이 정답이다.

어휘 expect v. 예상하다 eligible adj. 자격이 있는 delay n. 지연; v. 미루다
subtract v. 공제하다, 빼다

14 동사 어휘 고르기 | 전체 문맥 파악

해설 '이 문제가 곧 ___ 되기를 기대하다'라는 문맥이므로 (A) resolved(해결하다)와 (C) reported(보고하다)가 정답의 후보이다. 빈칸이 있는 문장만으로는 정답을 고를 수 없으므로 주변 문맥이나 전체 문맥을 파악한다. 앞부분에서 자신에게 요금이 잘못 청구되었다고 한 후, 자신의 요금제를 낮추고 차액을 환불해달라고 요청했으므로 발신자는 문제가 곧 해결되기를 기대하고 있음을 알 수 있다. 따라서 동사 (A) resolved가 정답이다.

어휘 remove v. 제거하다, 치우다 reduce v. 줄이다, 감소시키다

Chapter 07 동사 관련 어구 2

Hackers Practice
p.295

01 **from** (refrain from ~을 삼가다)
02 **on** (be passed on 전달되다)
03 **charge** (take charge of ~을 책임지다)
04 **short** (run short of ~이 다 떨어지다, 부족하다)
05 **care** (take care of ~을 처리하다)
06 **shut** (shut down 문을 닫다)
07 **to** (come to an end 종료되다)
08 **set** (set up 준비하다)
09 **bring** (bring up 제기하다)
10 **up** (make up for ~을 만회하다)
11 **advantage** (take advantage of ~을 이용하다)
12 **up on** (follow up on ~에 대해 후속 조치하다)
13 **effect** (come into effect 시행되다)
14 **forth** (set forth 제시하다)

Hackers Test
p.296

Part 5

01 (D)	02 (D)	03 (C)	04 (A)	05 (D)
06 (B)	07 (B)	08 (D)	09 (A)	10 (C)

Part 6

11 (C)	12 (D)	13 (B)	14 (C)

01 동사 관련 어구 완성하기

해설 '방문객들은 신청서를 작성하다'라는 문맥에서 빈칸 뒤의 전치사 out과 함께 쓰여 '~을 작성하다'라는 의미의 어구를 이루는 동사 (D) fill이 정답이다. (fill out: ~을 작성하다) (A) work는 'work out: 운동하다, 산출하다', (B) leave는 'leave out: ~을 빼다, 배제하다', (C) bow는 'bow out: (공손히) 물러나다, 사직하다'라는 의미이다.

해석 무역 박람회에 도착한 방문객들은 신청서를 작성하고 명함을 제시하라는 말을 들었다.

어휘 visitor n. 방문객 trade fair 무역 박람회 present v. 제시하다
business card 명함

02 동사 관련 어구 완성하기

해설 '신상품을 개발하는 데 성공하다'라는 문맥에서 빈칸 뒤의 전치사 in과 함께 쓰여 '~에 성공하다'라는 의미의 어구를 이루는 동사 succeed의 p.p.형 (D) succeeded가 정답이다. (succeed in -ing: ~에 성공하다) (A)의 delegate는 '(대표로서) 파견하다', (B)의 motivate는 '~에 동기 부여를 하다', (C)의 reveal은 '드러내다'라는 의미이다.

해석 대부분의 비평가들은 패션 디자이너 Viola Arancia가 가격이 적당하면서도 최신 유행인 신상품들을 개발하는 데 성공했다는 것에 동의했다.

어휘 critic n. 비평가, 평론가 develop v. 개발하다, 발전시키다
collection n. 신상품들, 컬렉션 affordable adj. 가격이 적당한
trendy adj. 최신 유행의

03 동사 관련 어구 채우기

해설 '박물관을 떠난 후에 지역 시장에 잠깐 들를 것이다'라는 문맥이므로 '잠시 들르다'라는 의미를 갖는 동사 어구 (C) stop by가 정답이다. (A) take up은 '차지하다, 시작하다', (B) sit down은 '앉다', (D) bring in은 '가져오다, 받아들이다'라는 의미이다.

해석 박물관을 떠난 후에, 단체 관광객들은 점심을 위해 지역 시장에 잠시 들를 것이다.

어휘 marketplace n. 시장, 장터

04 동사 관련 어구 채우기

해설 '새로운 기술 동향에 뒤떨어지지 않기 위해 세미나에 참석하고 온라인 강의들을 수강하다'라는 문맥이므로 '~에 뒤떨어지지 않다'라는 의미를 갖는 동사 어구 (A) keep up with가 정답이다. (B) break away from은 '~에서 도망치다', (C) cut down on은 '~을 줄이다', (D) get through with는 '~을 끝내다, 완료하다'라는 의미이다.

해석 Mr. Lee는 새로운 기술 동향에 뒤떨어지지 않기 위해 Newport 기술 학회의 세미나에 참석하고 온라인 강의들을 수강한다.

어휘 trend n. 동향, 유행

05 동사 관련 어구 완성하기

해설 '재료들이 부족할 것을 우려하여, 필요한 것을 사오게 하다'라는 문맥에서 빈칸 앞의 run, 빈칸 뒤의 of와 함께 쓰여 '~이 부족하다'라는 의미의 어구를 이루는 부사 (D) short가 정답이다. (run short of: ~이 부족하다) (A) vast는 '어마어마한, 방대한', (B) lengthy는 '너무 긴, 장황한'이라는 의미를 가진다. (C) fast(빠르게)는 run이 '달리다'라는 의미로 쓰일 때 이를 수식할 수 있는 부사이다.

해석 사진 현상소에 재료들이 부족할 것을 우려하여, Mr. Lark는 필요한 것을 사오도록 그의 조수를 보냈다.

어휘 developing adj. (사진) 현상의 send out ~을 보내다 assistant n. 조수

06 동사 관련 어구 채우기

해설 '고객의 의견이 Ms. Burnham에게 전달되다'라는 문맥이므로 '전달하다'라는 의미의 동사 어구 pass on의 p.p.형 (B) passed on이 정답이다. (A)의 figure out은 '알아내다, 이해하다', (C)의 call off는 '취소하다', (D)의 depend on은 '~에 의존하다'라는 의미이다.

해석 새로 나온 스마트폰 모델에 대한 고객의 의견은 검토를 위해 Ms. Burnham에게 전달되었다.

어휘 **feedback** n. 의견, 피드백 **review** n. 검토; v. 검토하다

07 동사 관련 어구 채우기

해설 '오리엔테이션이 다음 주 본사 회의실에서 열릴 것이다'라는 문맥이므로 '~이 열리다'라는 의미를 갖는 동사 어구 (B) take place가 정답이다. (A) let in은 '들여보내다', (C) move around는 '돌아다니다', (D) keep out은 '~이 들어오지 못하게 막다'라는 의미이다.

해석 신입 회계사들을 위한 오리엔테이션이 다음 주 본사 회의실에서 열릴 것이다.

어휘 **orientation** n. 오리엔테이션, 예비 교육 **accountant** n. 회계사
main office 본사

08 동사 관련 어구 완성하기

해설 '전문분야에 포함되지 않았기 때문에 적절하게 답변할 수 없었다'라는 문맥이므로 빈칸 뒤의 전치사 within과 함께 쓰여 '~에 포함되다'라는 의미의 어구를 이루는 동사 (D) fall이 정답이다. (fall within: ~에 포함되다) (A) find는 '찾다', (B) ask는 '묻다', (C) join은 '연결하다, 결합하다'라는 의미이다.

해석 그 질문은 발표자의 전문분야에 포함되지 않았기 때문에 그는 적절하게 답변할 수 없었다.

어휘 **adequately** adv. 적절하게, 충분히 **area of expertise** 전문분야

09 동사 관련 어구 완성하기

해설 '농산물의 낮은 수확량이 최근 경기 불안정의 원인이 되다'라는 문맥에서 빈칸 뒤의 전치사 for와 함께 쓰여 '~의 원인이 되다'라는 의미의 어구를 이루는 동사 (A) account가 정답이다. (account for: ~의 원인이 되다) (B) change는 'change for: ~로 교환하다, ~행으로 갈아타다', (C) resolve는 '해결하다, 결심하다', (D) require는 '요구하다, 필요로 하다'라는 의미이다.

해석 남아메리카 주요 농산물의 낮은 수확량은 일부 남아메리카 최빈국들의 최근 경기 불안정의 원인이 된다.

어휘 **yield** n. 수확량 **agricultural** adj. 농업의 **instability** n. 불안정

10 동사 관련 어구 채우기

해설 '공연 책임자의 업무를 인계 받을 것이다'라는 문맥이므로 '~을 인계 받다'라는 의미를 갖는 동사 어구 (C) take over가 정답이다. (A) work out은 '해결하다, 운동하다', (B) bring down은 '내리다, 떨어뜨리다', (D) pass through는 '~을 거쳐가다'라는 의미이다.

해석 Ms. Wren은 현재의 공연 책임자가 이번 달 말에 퇴직하면, 그의 업무를 인계 받을 것이다.

어휘 **retire** v. 퇴직하다, 은퇴하다

11-14는 다음 기사에 관한 문제입니다.

자가 투자의 새로운 동향

은행 저축 예금의 금리가 계속 하락함에 따라, 이제 퇴직 기금을 조성하는 것은 30년 전보다 더 어렵다. 다행히도, 이것에 대처할 방법이 있다. ¹¹금융 정보에 대한 지식을 얻는 것은 여러 개의 이용 가능한 선택권들에 의해 갈피를 못 잡는 사람들에게는 자산이다.

일부 사람들은 투자 정보를 복잡하다고 여기며 경력 있는 중개인 서비스에 협력을 요청하는 것을 택한다. 그러나, 몇몇 투자자들은 그들의 자금을 다룰 때 다양한 접근에 의지하는 방법을 배워 왔다. ¹²그들은 그들 스스로 정보를 모으기 위해 온라인 토론, 비즈니스 잡지 및 정기 간행물을 조사한다. ¹³그들은 그들을 위해 그것을 해주는 중개인에 의존하는 것 대신 한 회사가 얼마나 재정상 안정적인지와 언제 투자하기에 가장 좋은 때인지를 배운다. 직접 조사를 한 후에, 투자자들은 그들의 자본을 어디에 투자할 것인지 결정할지 시장에 대해 새로◐

---

¹⁴습득한 지식을 활용할 수 있다. ¹⁴초보자라도 충분한 정보를 가지고 분명히 더 나은 투자 결정을 할 수 있다. 이는 위험하게 들릴 수도 있지만, 많은 성공한 투자자들이 스스로 조사를 함으로써 시작했다.

---

interest rate 금리, 이자율 **savings account** 저축 예금(계좌)
decline v. 하락하다, 감소하다 **build up** 조성하다, (재산·인격 등)을 쌓다
retirement n. 퇴직 **deal with** (문제 따위)에 대처하다
understanding n. 지식, 이해 **bewildered** adj. 갈피를 못 잡는, 당황한
complicated adj. 복잡한 **enlist** v. 협력을 요청하다 **rely on** ~에 의지하다
resource n. 정보, 자원 **handle** v. 다루다, 처리하다
periodical n. 정기 간행물 **gather** v. 모으다 **stable** adj. 안정적인
middle man 중개인 **capital** n. 자본, 자금

11 명사 어휘 고르기 전체 문맥 파악

해설 '금융 정보에 대한 지식을 얻는 것은 ____이다'라는 문맥이므로 (B) obligation(의무)과 (C) asset(자산)이 정답의 후보이다. 빈칸이 있는 문장만으로 정답을 고를 수 없으므로 주변 문맥이나 전체 문맥을 파악한다. 지문 뒷부분에서 투자자들이 '그들 스스로 정보를 얻어(gather information for themselves)'서 '그들의 자본을 어디에 투자할 것인지 결정하는 데 새로 습득한 지식을 활용한다(use their newly acquired knowledge ~ to decide where to put their capital)'고 했으므로 금융 정보에 대한 지식을 얻는 것은 자산이 될 수 있음을 알 수 있다. 따라서 명사 (C) asset이 정답이다.

어휘 **assignment** n. 과제, 임무, 배정 **obligation** n. 의무 **indicator** n. 지표

12 동사 관련 어구 채우기

해설 '스스로 정보를 모으기 위해 다양한 자료를 조사하다'라는 문맥이므로 '조사하다'라는 의미를 갖는 동사 어구 (D) look into가 정답이다.

어휘 **turn in** 제출하다, 안쪽으로 향하다, 휘다 **take over** 인계받다, 양도받다
check in 탑승(숙박) 수속을 밟다

13 동사 관련 어구 완성하기

해설 빈칸 뒤의 전치사 on과 함께 쓰여 '중개인에 의존하기보다는 스스로 배운다'는 문맥에서 '~에 의존하다'라는 의미의 어구를 이루는 depend의 -ing형 (B) depending이 정답이다. (depend on: ~에 의존하다)

어휘 **collect** v. 수집하다 **partner** v. 제휴하다 **merge** v. 합병하다

14 알맞은 문장 고르기

해석 (A) 웹사이트에 제공되어 있는 많은 정보는 상반된다.
(B) 실수를 피하기 위해 중개인에게 조언을 요청하는 것이 더 현명하다.
(C) 초보자라도 충분한 정보를 가지고 분명히 더 나은 투자 결정을 할 수 있다.
(D) 중개인을 고용하는 것이 유일하게 이용 가능한 선택권이다.

해설 빈칸에 들어갈 알맞은 문장을 고르는 문제이므로 빈칸의 주변 문맥이나 전체 문맥을 파악한다. 앞부분에서 투자자들은 스스로 정보를 모으기 위해 온라인 토론, 비즈니스 잡지 및 정기 간행물을 조사한다고 한 후, 뒤 문장 'many successful investors started out by doing research themselves'에서 많은 성공한 투자자들이 스스로 조사를 함으로써 시작했다고 했으므로 빈칸에는 초보자라도 충분한 정보를 가지고 분명히 더 나은 투자 결정을 할 수 있다는 내용이 들어가야 함을 알 수 있다. 따라서 (C) Even beginners can surely make better investment decisions with adequate information 이 정답이다.

어휘 **conflicting** adj. 상반되는, 충돌하는 **advice** n. 정보, 조언
adequate adj. 충분한, 적절한 **broker** n. 중개인

Chapter 08 명사 관련 어구

Hackers Practice
p.301

01 **list** (a list of ~의 목록)
02 **lack** (lack of ~의 부족)
03 **guarantee** (guarantee of ~에 대한 보장)
04 **on** (tax on ~에 대한 세금)

05 **of** (consent of ~의 동의)
06 **on** (an emphasis on ~에 대한 강조)
07 **series** (a series of 일련의)
08 **participants** (conference participants 회의 참가자들)
09 **in** (in a tie 동점으로)
10 **for** (regard for ~에 대한 배려)
11 **of** (advocate of ~의 옹호자)
12 **over** (dispute over ~에 대한 분쟁)
13 **concerning** (questions concerning ~와 관련된 질문)
14 **array** (an array of 다수의 ~)

Hackers Test

Part 5

01 (D)	02 (A)	03 (C)	04 (C)	05 (D)
06 (C)	07 (D)	08 (B)	09 (A)	10 (C)

Part 6

11 (C)	12 (B)	13 (B)	14 (D)

01 명사 관련 어구 완성하기

해설 빈칸 앞의 work와 함께 쓰여 '근무 교대'라는 의미의 어구를 이루는 명사 (D) shift가 정답이다. (work shift: 근무 교대) (A) opportunity는 '기회', (B) authorization은 '허가, 인가', (C) statistic은 '통계(자료)'라는 의미이다.

해석 실험실 책임자는 그 다음 주 근무 교대에 변경 사항이 있을 경우 매 금요일에 게시판에 공지를 올릴 것이다.

어휘 **laboratory** n. 실험실 **notice** n. 공지 **bulletin board** 게시판

02 명사 관련 어구 완성하기

해설 빈칸 앞의 time과 함께 쓰여 '시간 제약'이라는 의미의 어구를 이루는 명사 (A) constraints가 정답이다. (time constraint: 시간 제약) (B)의 operation은 '작동, 작용', (C)의 measurement는 '측량, 치수', (D)의 unit은 '단위'라는 의미이다.

해석 워크숍 마지막에는 시간 제약으로 인해 몇 개의 질문만 답변되었다.

03 명사 관련 어구 완성하기

해설 빈칸 앞의 명사 employee와 함께 쓰여 '직원 생산성'이라는 의미의 어구를 이루는 명사 (C) productivity가 정답이다. (employee productivity: 직원 생산성) (A) applicability는 '적용 가능성, 응용할 수 있음', (B) quantity는 '양, 수량', (D) utility는 '유용성, 공공시설'이라는 의미이다.

해석 그 자문 위원은 Argento 인테리어 회사 관리자들에게 최신 기술을 사용함으로써 직원 생산성이 향상될 수 있다고 조언했다.

어휘 **advise** v. 조언하다, 권고하다 **newest** adj. 최신의

04 명사 관련 어구 완성하기

해설 빈칸 앞의 job과 함께 쓰여 '채용 공고'라는 의미의 어구를 이루는 명사 (C) openings가 정답이다. (job opening: 채용 공고) (A)의 achievement는 '업적', (B)의 publication은 '출간', (D)의 investment는 '투자'라는 의미이다.

해석 고용주들은 채용 공고를 게시하고 잠재적인 후보자들의 이력서를 훑어보기 위해 웹사이트를 활용한다.

어휘 **post** v. 게시하다 **browse** v. 훑어보다, 검색하다 **résumé** n. 이력서
potential adj. 잠재적인, 가능성이 있는 **candidate** n. 후보자, 지원자

05 명사 관련 어구 완성하기

해설 빈칸 앞의 sales와 함께 쓰여 '매출 예측'이라는 의미의 어구를 이루는 명사 (D) projection이 정답이다. (sales projection: 매출 예측, 판매 전망) (A) engagement는 '약속, 계약', (B) recruitment는 '채용, 보충', (C) commission은 '수수료, 위탁'이라는 의미이다.

해석 만약 매출 예측이 정확하다면, 그 회사는 올해에 수익을 30퍼센트 정도 증가

시킬 것이다.

어휘 **accurate** adj. 정확한, 정밀한 **revenue** n. 수익, 세입

06 명사 관련 어구 완성하기

해설 빈칸 뒤의 전치사 to와 함께 쓰여 '~에 대한 의무'라는 의미의 어구를 이루는 명사 (C) obligation이 정답이다. (obligation to: ~에 대한 의무) (A) designation은 '지정, 임명', (B) delegation은 '대표단, 대표 파견', (D) reservation은 '예약'이라는 의미이다. 참고로, under obligation to가 '~할 의무가 있는'이라는 뜻으로 쓰였다.

해석 Thomas 엔지니어링 건설 회사는 새로운 건축 프로젝트를 다음 달까지 완성할 의무가 있다.

어휘 **complete** v. 완성하다

07 명사 관련 어구 완성하기

해설 '연간 판매 보고서 전부가 인쇄되었다'라는 문맥이므로 빈칸 앞의 in its와 함께 쓰여 '전부, 통째로'라는 의미의 어구를 이루는 명사 (D) entirety가 정답이다. (in its entirety: 전부, 통째로) (A) summary는 '요약', (B) order는 '순서, 주문', (C) facility는 '시설'이라는 의미이다.

해석 연간 판매 보고서 전부가 인쇄되었고 부서장들 사이에 배부되었다.

어휘 **annual** adj. 연간의 **sales report** 판매 보고서
distribute v. 배부하다, 배포하다

08 명사 관련 어구 완성하기

해설 빈칸 앞의 baggage와 함께 쓰여 '수하물 허용량'이라는 의미의 어구를 이루는 명사 (B) allowance가 정답이다. (baggage allowance: 수하물 허용량) (A) consent는 '동의', (C) assessment는 '평가', (D) mass는 '질량, 다량'이라는 의미이다. (D) mass의 경우 빈칸 뒤의 문맥과 연결이 어색하므로 답이 될 수 없음에 유의한다.

해석 대부분의 항공사들은 탑승한 모든 승객의 편안함을 보장하기 위해 수하물 허용량을 승객 1인당 한 개로 축소하였다.

어휘 **reduce** v. 축소하다, 줄이다 **hand baggage** (여행자의) 수하물
ensure v. 보장하다, 확실하게 하다 **comfort** n. 편안함, 안락

09 명사 관련 어구 완성하기

해설 빈칸 뒤의 전치사 to와 함께 쓰여 '~에 기부'라는 의미의 어구를 이루는 명사 (A) contribution이 정답이다. (contribution to: ~에 기부, 공헌) (B) addition은 '추가', (C) concession은 '양보', (D) subsidy는 '(국가의) 보조금, 장려금'이라는 의미이다.

해석 Dr. Rosen이 어린이 병원에 많은 기부를 했는데, 이는 오래된 소아과 병동을 개조하는 것을 가능하게 했다.

어휘 **renovate** v. 개조(보수)하다 **pediatric** adj. 소아과의 **wing** n. 동(부속 건물)

10 명사 관련 어구 완성하기

해설 빈칸 뒤의 전치사 to와 함께 쓰여 '~에 대한 전념, 헌신'이라는 의미의 어구를 이루는 명사 (C) commitment가 정답이다. (commitment to: ~에 대한 전념, 헌신) (A) coordination은 '조정', (B) cooperation은 '협동, 협력', (D) compromise는 '타협, 절충안'이라는 의미이다.

해석 그 상점의 계속되는 성공은 주로 합리적인 가격에 최고 품질의 상품만 판매하는 것에 대한 그 상점의 전념 때문이다.

어휘 **continued** adj. 계속되는 **primarily** adv. 주로 **reasonable** adj. 합리적인

11-14는 다음 기사에 관한 문제입니다.

온라인으로 안전하게 쇼핑하다

[11]최근 몇 년간, 온라인 쇼핑은 모든 연령층 사이에서 점점 더 인기 있어져 왔다. 하지만 더욱더 많은 사람들이 버튼 클릭만으로 구매를 하게 되면서, 사이버 범죄 발생률이 증가하고 있다. [12]어제 공공 안전부에서 발표한 보도 자료는 온라인 쇼핑객들에게 주의를 기울이도록 촉구했다. 그 중에서도, 제품을 찾기 위해서는 검색 엔진보다 신뢰할 수 있는 온라인 소매업체를 항상 이용하라고 말했다. 비밀번호를 자주 변경하는 것도 매우 권장되었다. [13]이렇게 하는 것은 공인되지 ◑

않은 사람들이 사용자 계정에 접근하는 것을 더욱 어렵게 만든다. [14]뿐만 아니라, 신용카드 명세서를 면밀히 확인하고 의심스러운 청구 금액을 즉시 신고하는 것이 빠르게 문제를 발견하고 해결하는 가장 좋은 방법으로 확인되었다. 보도 전문을 읽으려면, www.dps.com/tips를 방문하면 된다.

safely adv. 안전하게 **increasingly** adv. 점점 더, 점차 **age group** 연령대
incidence n. 발생률 **cybercrime** n. 사이버 범죄 **rise** v. 증가하다
urge v. 촉구하다, 강력히 권고하다 **caution** n. 주의, 경고 **retailer** n. 소매업체
frequently adv. 자주 **highly** adv. 매우 **recommend** v. 권장하다
statement n. 명세서 **suspicious** adj. 의심스러운
identify v. 확인하다, 증명하다 **spot** v. 발견하다, 알아채다; n. 얼룩, 장소
resolve v. 해결하다

11 형용사 어휘 고르기 주변 문맥 파악

해설 '온라인 쇼핑은 모든 연령층 사이에서 점점 더 ____해왔다'라는 문맥이므로 (A) rare(드문), (B) unnecessary(불필요한), (C) popular(인기 있는)가 정답의 후보이다. 빈칸이 있는 문장만으로 정답을 고를 수 없으므로 주변 문맥이나 전체 문맥을 파악한다. 뒤 문장에서 '더욱더 많은 사람들이 버튼 클릭만으로 구매를 한다(more and more people making purchases with the click of a button)'고 했으므로 온라인 쇼핑이 점점 더 인기 있어져 왔음을 알 수 있다. 따라서 (C) popular가 정답이다.

어휘 **inconvenient** adj. 불편한

12 명사 관련 어구 완성하기

해설 빈칸 뒤의 명사 release와 함께 쓰여 '보도 자료'라는 의미의 어구를 이루는 명사 (B) press가 정답이다. (press release: 보도 자료) (A) product는 '상품', (C) program은 '프로그램, 계획', (D) preview는 '사전 검토, 시사회'라는 의미이다.

13 알맞은 문장 고르기

해석 (A) 이러한 신용카드에 대한 의존은 재정에 장기적인 영향을 미칠 수 있다.
(B) 이렇게 하는 것은 공인되지 않은 사람들이 사용자 계정에 접근하는 것을 더욱 어렵게 만든다.
(C) 그 기술이 사용될 수 있는지 확실하게 하기 위해서는 추가적인 연구가 필요하다.
(D) 상품의 가격과 서비스를 온라인으로 비교하는 것은 이보다 더 쉬웠던 적이 없다.

해설 빈칸에 들어갈 알맞은 문장을 고르는 문제이므로 빈칸의 주변 문맥이나 전체 문맥을 파악한다. 앞부분에서 안전한 온라인 쇼핑을 위해 쇼핑객들이 주의를 기울여야 한다고 한 후, 앞 문장 'Changing passwords frequently was also highly recommended.'에서 비밀번호를 자주 변경하는 것도 매우 권장되었다고 했으므로 빈칸에는 비밀번호를 자주 변경하는 것이 온라인 쇼핑을 안전하게 하는 데에 도움이 된다는 내용이 들어가야 함을 알 수 있다. 따라서 (B) Doing so makes it more difficult for unauthorized people to access user accounts가 정답이다.

어휘 **dependence** n. 의존, 의존도 **effect** n. 영향; v. 영향을 미치다
finance n. 재정, 재원 **unauthorized** adj. 공인되지 않은
access v. ~에 접근하다 **additional** adj. 추가의, 부가적인
ensure v. 확실하게 하다, 보장하다 **compare** v. 비교하다 **goods** n. 상품

14 부사 어휘 고르기

해설 '신용카드 명세서를 면밀히 확인하는 것'이라는 문맥이므로 부사 (D) closely (면밀히, 엄밀히)가 정답이다.

어휘 **hastily** adv. 급히, 서둘러서 **flexibly** adv. 유연하게, 융통성 있게
randomly adv. 무작위로

Chapter 09 짝을 이루는 표현

Hackers Practice   p.307

01 **make** (make a presentation 발표하다)
02 **reputation** (have a reputation 명성이 있다)
03 **wage** (earn a wage 임금을 받다)
04 **instantly** (instantly recognizable 즉시 알아볼 수 있는)
05 **offers** (promotional offers 판촉용 특별 서비스)
06 **description** (technical description 기술 설명서)
07 **informed** (informed decision 정보에 근거한 결정)
08 **attract** (attract one's attention ~의 이목을 사로잡다)
09 **extreme** (with extreme care 매우 주의 깊게)
10 **cautiously** (cautiously optimistic 조심스럽게 낙관적인)
11 **work** (work from home 재택근무하다)
12 **Prospective** (prospective employee 채용 후보자)
13 **award** (win an award 상을 받다)
14 **visual** (visual aids 시각 보조 교재)
15 **inherently** (inherently risky 본래부터 위험한)
16 **needs** (meet one's needs ~의 필요를 충족시키다)
17 **superb** (superb attention to detail 세부적인 것에 대한 큰 주의)
18 **full** (reach one's full potential ~의 잠재력을 최대로 발휘하다)
19 **accept** (accept an application 원서를 접수하다)
20 **raise** (raise awareness 인식을 높이다)

Hackers Test   p.308

Part 5

01 (B)	02 (B)	03 (D)	04 (A)	05 (C)
06 (B)	07 (B)	08 (A)	09 (C)	10 (C)

Part 6

11 (B)	12 (D)	13 (C)	14 (A)

01 짝을 이루는 표현 완성하기

해설 빈칸 앞의 동사 investigate와 짝표현을 이루어 '(실행) 가능성을 조사하다'라는 의미를 나타내는 명사 (B) feasibility가 정답이다. (investigate the feasibility: (실행) 가능성을 조사하다) (A) sponsorship은 '후원, 지원', (C) authorization은 '권한 부여, 위임', (D) prediction은 '예측'이라는 의미이다.

해석 토지 개발부의 연구원들은 산업용 건물을 주거 단지로 전환하는 것의 가능성을 조사할 것이다.

어휘 **property development** 토지 개발 **transform** v. 전환하다, 바꾸다
industrial adj. 산업용의, 산업의 **residential** adj. 주거의, 주거용의

02 짝을 이루는 표현 완성하기

해설 빈칸 뒤의 명사 subscription과 짝표현을 이루어 '가입을 갱신하다'라는 의미를 나타내는 동사 (B) renew가 정답이다. (renew a subscription: 가입을 갱신하다) (A) permit은 '허락하다', (C) collect는 '모으다, 수집하다', (D) validate는 '입증하다, 인증하다'라는 의미이다.

해석 Cable-Link사와의 케이블 텔레비전 가입을 갱신하기 위해서, 간단히 회사 웹 사이트에 있는 알맞은 양식을 기입하여 귀하의 현재 서비스가 만료되기 전에 제출하십시오.

어휘 **expire** v. 만료되다, 만기가 되다, 끝나다

03 짝을 이루는 표현 완성하기

해설 빈칸 뒤의 명사 employment와 짝표현을 이루어 '직업을 구하다'라는 의미를 나타내는 동사 seek의 현재분사형 (D) seeking이 정답이다. (seek employment: 직업을 구하다) (A)의 hire는 '(단기간) 빌리다, (사람을) 고용하다', (B)의 question은 '질문하다', (C)의 warrant는 '정당화하다, 보증

하다'라는 의미이다.

해석 Ladlaw 부동산에서 직업을 구하려는 사람들은 대학교 성적 증명서와 최소 2부의 추천서를 이력서 사본과 함께 제출해야 합니다.

어휘 **transcript** n. 성적 증명서 **reference letter** 추천서
along with ~와 함께, ~에 따라 **résumé** n. 이력서

04 짝을 이루는 표현 완성하기

해설 빈칸 뒤의 명사 presentation과 짝표현을 이루어 '발표하다'라는 의미를 나타내는 동사 (A) deliver가 정답이다. (deliver a presentation: 발표하다) deliver는 뒤에 a speech, a presentation, an address 등의 명사와 함께 쓰여 '발표하다, 연설하다'의 의미로 사용된다. (B) proceed는 '나아가다', (C) obtain은 '획득하다', (D) agree는 '동의하다'라는 의미이다.

해석 공장의 생산부장인 Virginia Hey는 장비 업그레이드의 실현 가능성에 대해 발표하기로 결정했다.

어휘 **practicality** n. 실현 가능성 **equipment** n. 장비

05 짝을 이루는 표현 완성하기

해설 빈칸 뒤의 명사 employees와 함께 짝표현을 이루어 '채용 후보자들'이라는 의미를 나타내는 형용사 (C) prospective가 정답이다. (prospective employee: 채용 후보자) (A) probable은 '유망한'이라는 의미로 주로 candidate, winner 등의 명사와 짝표현을 이룬다. (a probable presidential candidate: 유망한 대통령 후보) (B) disgruntled는 '불만을 품은, 시무룩한', (D) eventual은 '결과로 일어나는, 궁극적인'이라는 의미이다.

해석 관리부는 채용 후보자들에게 정규직으로 배정되기 전에 3개월간 지속되는 가채용 기간을 거칠 것을 요구한다.

어휘 **administrative** adj. 관리상의, 행정상의
probationary adj. 가채용의, 견습 중의 **last** v. 지속되다, 계속되다
assign v. (일·책임 등을) 배정하다, 맡기다 **permanent position** 정규직

06 짝을 이루는 표현 완성하기

해설 빈칸 뒤의 형용사 unattended와 짝표현을 이루어 '(사람/사물)을 내버려 두다'라는 의미를 나타내는 동사 (B) leave가 정답이다. (leave 사람/사물 unattended: 사람/사물을 내버려 두다) (A) store는 '저장하다', (C) reside는 '존재하다, 거주하다', (D) put은 '놓다'라는 의미이다.

해석 동물 보호 협회는 사람들에게 차량 내에 그들의 반려동물을 내버려 두지 않을 것을 권한다.

어휘 **encourage** v. 권하다, 조장하다

07 짝을 이루는 표현 완성하기

해설 빈칸 뒤의 명사 orders와 짝표현을 이루어 '주문 처리를 완료하다'라는 의미를 나타내는 동사 (B) fulfill이 정답이다. (fulfill orders: 주문 처리를 완료하다) (A) refine는 '정제하다, 개선하다', (C) restrain은 '억제하다', (D) notify는 '통지하다'라는 의미이다.

해석 Farscape 제조 회사는 고객들의 주문 처리를 완료하기 위해 생산직 직원을 2퍼센트 늘려야 할 것이다.

08 짝을 이루는 표현 완성하기

해설 빈칸 뒤의 명사 survey와 짝표현을 이루어 '조사를 실시하다'라는 의미를 나타내는 동사 (A) conduct가 정답이다. (conduct a survey: 조사를 실시하다) survey는 보통 make, do, carry out, conduct 등의 동사와 함께 쓰여 '조사하다'의 의미로 사용된다. (B) pursue는 '추구하다', (C) predict는 '예언하다', (D) mention은 '언급하다'라는 의미이다.

해석 어떤 특징이 다음 제품 라인에 포함되어야 할지 결정하기 위해, Browder 전자 회사의 연구부는 회사의 고객들에게 조사를 실시할 것이다.

어휘 **feature** n. 특징, 특성 **division** n. (관청·회사 등의) 부, 국, 과

09 짝을 이루는 표현 완성하기

해설 빈칸 앞의 동사 gain과 짝표현을 이루어 '인정받다'라는 의미를 나타내는 명사 (C) recognition이 정답이다. (gain recognition: 인정받다)

(A) implication은 '함축, 암시', (B) assimilation은 '동화, 흡수', (D) perception은 '인식, 지각'이라는 의미이다.

해석 Mr. Lavington은 국제 특허법 전문가로서 업계에서 주목할 만한 인정을 받았다.

어휘 **gain** v. 얻다 **significant** adj. 주목할 만한 **patent** n. 특허

10 짝을 이루는 표현 완성하기

해설 빈칸 앞의 동사 work와 빈칸 뒤의 명사 hours와 짝표현을 이루어 '연장 근무하다'라는 의미를 나타내는 형용사 (C) extended가 정답이다. (work extended hours: 연장 근무하다, 초과 근무를 하다) (A) partial은 '일부분의', (B) refreshed는 '(기분이) 상쾌한', (D) former는 '이전의'라는 의미이다.

해석 경영진은 바쁜 명절 시즌 동안에 고객들을 더 잘 응대하기 위해 전 매장 직원들이 연장 근무할 것을 요청했다.

어휘 **request** v. 요청하다 **serve** v. 응대하다

11-14는 다음 광고에 관한 문제입니다.

특가 도서 바자회!

Novel Ideas 서점은 이번 주 토요일 오전 9시부터 오후 4시까지 연례 재고 정리 세일을 열어, 모든 소설, 정기 간행물, 그리고 여행 가이드 서적에 대해 엄청난 할인을 제공할 것입니다. Novel Ideas 서점은 베스트 셀러들과 가장 인기 있는 소설 선집들을 가지고 있지만, 재미만을 위한 독서에 그치지 마십시오. **11여러분은 지식도 넓힐 수 있습니다.** 우리는 비즈니스 예절, 고급 요리, 세계 문화, 그리고 세계사와 같은 광범위한 주제의 비소설 도서들을 보유하고 있습니다.

12이 모든 도서와 훨씬 더 많은 것들을 정가의 50에서 80퍼센트까지 할인된 가격에 고객분들께서 쉽게 구하실 수 있습니다!

우리 서점은 재고 정리 세일을 1년에 한 번만 실시하므로, 할인은 한 분당 여덟 권으로 엄격히 제한될 것입니다. **13한도가 초과된 이후에는 모든 품목에 대해 정상 가격이 적용될 것입니다.** 모든 분들이 특가품을 공정한 몫으로 나누어 가질 수 있도록 손님들께 이 제약을 존중해 주시기를 호소 드립니다.

14이 행사는 7시간 동안 진행되오니, 여러분의 필요를 충족시켜 줄 완벽한 도서를 보유하고 있음을 보장하는 Novel Ideas 서점으로 오십시오!

bargain n. 특가품, 특매품 **bazaar** n. 바자회
clearance sale 재고 정리 세일, 창고 정리 판매 **offer** v. 제공하다, 내놓다
enormous adj. 엄청난, 막대한 **gourmet cooking** 고급 요리
available adj. 구할 수 있는 **fair** adj. 공정한, 타당한 **share** n. 몫, 지분

---

11 동사 어휘 고르기 | 주변 문맥 파악

해설 '지식을 _____ 할 수 있다'는 문맥이므로 (B) broaden(넓히다)과 (D) share(공유하다)가 정답의 후보이다. 빈칸이 있는 문장만으로 정답을 고를 수 없으므로 주변 문맥이나 전체 문맥을 파악한다. 앞 문장에서 '재미만을 위한 독서에 그치지 말라(don't stop at reading just for pleasure)'고 했고, 뒤 문장에서 '광범위한 주제의 도서들을 보유(We have ~ books on a wide array of topics)'하고 있다고 했으므로, 책을 통해 지식을 넓힐 수 있음을 알 수 있다. 따라서 동사 (B) broaden이 정답이다.

어휘 **publish** v. 출판하다 **emphasize** v. 강조하다 **share** v. 나누다, 공유하다

12 짝을 이루는 표현 완성하기

해설 빈칸 뒤의 형용사 available과 짝표현을 이루어 '고객들이 쉽게 구할 수 있다'라는 문맥에서 '쉽게 구할 수 있는'이라는 의미를 나타내는 부사 (D) readily(쉽게)가 정답이다. (readily available: 쉽게 구할 수 있는)

어휘 **improbably** adv. 있음직하지 않게 **eagerly** adv. 열심히
willingly adv. 기꺼이

13 알맞은 문장 고르기

해석 (A) 우리의 상품은 중고이지만, 고품질입니다.
(B) 우리와 제휴하고 있는 다른 서점들이 많이 있습니다.
(C) 한도가 초과된 이후에는 모든 품목에 대해 정상 가격이 적용될 것입니다.
(D) 재고 정리 품목들은 우리의 웹사이트에서 여러분을 위해 특별 주문될 수 있습니다.

빈칸에 들어갈 알맞은 문장을 고르는 문제이므로 빈칸의 주변 문맥이나 전체 문맥을 파악한다. 앞 문장 'discounts will be strictly limited to eight books per person'에서 할인은 한 명당 여덟 권으로 엄격히 제한될 것이라고 한 후, 뒤 문장 'We appeal to shoppers to honor this restriction so that everyone can get a fair share of the bargains.'에서 모든 사람이 특가품을 공정한 몫으로 나누어 가질 수 있도록 손님에게 이 제약을 존중해 주기를 호소한다고 했으므로 빈칸에는 한도가 초과된 이후에는 모든 품목에 대해 정상 가격이 적용될 것이라는 추가적인 내용이 들어가야 함을 알 수 있다. 따라서 (C) Regular prices will apply to all items after the limit is passed가 정답이다.

어휘 secondhanded adj. 중고의 affiliated adj. 제휴하고 있는
in stock 재고, 재고의

14 짝을 이루는 표현 완성하기

해설 빈칸 뒤의 your needs와 짝표현을 이루어 '필요를 충족시키다'라는 의미를 나타내는 동사 (A) meet(충족하다)이 정답이다. (meet one's needs: ~의 필요를 충족시키다)

어휘 solve v. 풀다, 해결하다 inform v. 알리다 announce v. 발표하다

Section 3 유사의미어

Chapter 10 유사의미 동사

Hackers Test
p.316

Part 5

01 (C)	02 (C)	03 (B)	04 (C)	05 (B)
06 (A)	07 (B)	08 (A)	09 (B)	10 (D)

Part 6

11 (B)	12 (B)	13 (A)	14 (D)

01 유사의미 동사 중에서 고르기

해설 '보다 건강에 좋은 식품의 선택을 장려하는 것을 목표로 하다'라는 문맥이므로 동사 (C) promote(장려하다, 홍보하다)가 정답이다. (A) support는 '(사람·정책 등을) 지지하다', (B) guide는 '안내하다', (D) replace는 '대체하다'라는 의미이다.

해석 정부의 후원을 받는 일련의 텔레비전 광고는 비만율을 억제하는 방법의 일환으로 보다 건강에 좋은 식품의 선택을 장려하는 것을 목표로 한다.

어휘 a series of 일련의 aim v. ~을 목표로 하다 healthy adj. 건강에 좋은
means n. 방법, 수단 curb v. 억제하다 obesity n. 비만

02 유사의미 동사 중에서 고르기

해설 빈칸 뒤의 명사 briefing(브리핑, 설명회)을 목적어로 취하면서 '신입 직원들은 안전 브리핑에 참석해야 한다'는 문맥에 적합한 동사 (C) attend(~에 참석하다)가 정답이다. (A) participate도 '참석하다'라는 의미이지만 뒤에 전치사 in이 있어야 목적어가 올 수 있다. (participate in: ~에 참석하다) (B) register는 '등록하다'라는 의미이며 'register for: ~에 등록하다'의 형태로 자주 사용됨을 알아 둔다. (D) depart는 '~을 떠나다'라는 의미이다.

해석 회사 정책에 따라, 모든 신입 직원들은 공장 기계를 작동시키는 것을 시도하기 전에 우선 안전 브리핑에 참석해야 한다.

어휘 in line with ~에 따라 policy n. 정책 attempt to do ~을 시도하다
operate v. 작동시키다 machinery n. 기계, 기계류

03 유사의미 동사 중에서 고르기

해설 (A)와 (B) 모두 '(계약 등이) 끝나다'라는 의미와 관련이 있지만, 주어인 agreement(협정)와 함께 쓰여 '~이 만기가 되다'라는 의미를 나타내는 자동사 (B) expire(만기가 되다)가 정답이다. (A) invalidate(~을 무효화하다)

는 타동사이므로 '무효화되다'라는 의미로 쓰일 때 수동태로 사용된다. (C) violate는 '(법률·규칙 등을) 위반하다'라는 의미의 타동사이고, (D) submit은 '제출하다'라는 의미의 타동사이다. (submit an application: 신청서를 제출하다)

해석 갱신을 위한 재교섭에 성과를 거두지 않는 한, 계약상의 협정은 7월 말에 만기가 될 것이다.

어휘 renegotiation n. 재교섭, 재검토 renewal n. 갱신
succeed v. 성과를 거두다, 성공하다, 잘 되다 contractual adj. 계약상의
agreement n. 협정, 계약, 협약

04 유사의미 동사 중에서 고르기

해설 '누군가에게 특정 사실을 통지하다'라는 의미를 나타내면서, 사람 목적어를 취하는 동사가 와야 하므로 (C) notify(~에게 통지하다)가 정답이다. (B) announce도 '알리다'라는 의미이지만 공지 내용을 직접 목적어로 받는다. (announce the director's retirement: 이사의 퇴임을 알리다) (A) advance는 '진전시키다, 제출하다'라는 의미이며 (D) devise는 '(방법 등을) 고안하다'라는 의미로 쓰인다. (devise a new plan: 새로운 계획을 고안하다)

해석 그 계약서는 세입자들이 아파트에 가하고자 하는 모든 주요 구조 변화를 소유주에게 통지해야 한다는 점을 규정한다.

어휘 stipulate v. 규정하다, 명기하다 tenant n. 세입자

05 유사의미 동사 중에서 고르기

해설 '관리자에게 말하다'라는 의미를 나타내면서 전치사 없이 사람을 목적어로 취하는 동사가 와야 하므로 동사 tell의 과거형 (B) told(말하다)가 정답이다. (C)의 express는 '(감정, 생각 등을) 표현하다'라는 의미이며 표현 대상을 직접 목적어로 받는다. (A)의 agree는 '동의하다', (D)의 direct는 '안내하다'라는 의미이다.

해석 Mr. Kang은 관리자에게 공장의 기계 중 하나가 점검되어야 한다고 말했다.

어휘 service v. (차량·기계를) 점검하다; n. 서비스, 봉사

06 유사의미 동사 중에서 고르기

해설 (A), (B), (D) 모두 '빌려주다'라는 의미와 관련이 있지만 '은행이 자금을 대출해 주다'라는 문맥이므로 동사 (A) lend(대출하다, 물건·돈을 빌려주다)가 정답이다. (B) lease는 '(차량·집 등을) 임대하다', (C) borrow는 '빌리다', (D) rent는 '(차량·집 등을 요금을 내고) 빌리다, 빌려주다'라는 의미이다.

해석 로드아일랜드 주 은행은 현지 사업 계획을 개발하는 사람들에게 낮은 이율로 자금을 대출해 주는 특별 프로그램을 수립했다.

어휘 establish v. 수립하다, 확립하다 interest n. 이율
initiative n. 계획, 자주성

07 유사의미 동사 중에서 고르기

해설 '수익성이 있는지 판단하기 위해 평가하다'라는 문맥이므로 동사 (B) evaluate(평가하다)가 정답이다. (A) coordinate는 '조직화하다', (C) estimate는 '예측하다', (D) address는 '(문제·상황을) 고심하다'라는 의미이므로 문맥에 어울리지 않는다.

해석 잠재적 투자자는 수익성이 있는 벤처 사업인지 아닌지 판단하기 위해 제안서를 평가할 것이다.

어휘 potential adj. 잠재적인, 가능성이 있는 profitable adj. 수익성이 있는, 유익한
venture n. 벤처 (사업), (사업 상의) 모험

08 유사의미 동사 중에서 고르기

해설 '백화점의 보상 프로그램에 등록하기를 원하는 고객들'이라는 문맥에서, 빈칸 뒤의 전치사 in과 함께 쓰여 '~에 등록하다'라는 의미를 나타내는 동사 (A) enroll(등록하다)이 정답이다. (B) apply가 '신청하다'라는 의미가 되기 위해서는 전치사 for가 필요하고, (C) instruct는 '지시하다, 가르치다', (D) interview는 '인터뷰하다'라는 의미이므로 문맥에 어울리지 않는다.

해석 Central 백화점의 보상 프로그램에 등록하기를 원하는 고객님께서는 안내 데스크에 신청서를 제출하셔야 합니다.

어휘 reward n. 보상 application n. 신청(서) information desk 안내 데스크

09 유사의미 동사 중에서 고르기

해설 '결혼을 늦은 나이까지 뒤로 미루다'라는 문맥이므로 동사 (B) postpone(뒤로 미루다)이 정답이다. (A) appoint는 '지목하다', (C) reschedule은 '일정을 변경하다', (D) preview는 '미리 보다'라는 의미이므로 문맥에 어울리지 않는다.

해석 결혼을 늦은 나이까지 뒤로 미루는 것은 요즘 젊은 사람들에게 꽤 흔한 일이 되었다.

10 유사의미 동사 중에서 고르기

해설 '경보 장치를 작동시키는 방법을 실제로 해 보이다'라는 문맥이므로 동사 (D) demonstrate(실제로 해 보이다)가 정답이다. (A)와 (C) 역시 '보이다'라는 의미와 관련이 있지만 (A) expose는 '드러내다, 노출시키다', (C) display는 '(물건 등을) 전시하다'라는 의미이므로 문맥에 어울리지 않는다. (B) persuade는 '설득하다'라는 의미이다.

해석 토요일에, 경비 회사에서 온 기술자가 경보 장치를 설치하고 그것을 작동시키는 방법을 실제로 해 보이기 위해 사무실을 방문할 것이다.

어휘 technician n. 기술자 install v. 설치하다 activate v. 작동시키다

11-14는 다음 안내문에 관한 문제입니다.

태양열 발전에 대해 강연할 수석 연구원

[11]다음 달에 애틀랜타에서 열리는 재생 가능 에너지에 관한 전국 학회에서, Sunbeam Resources사의 수석 연구원인 Dr. Robert Flack은 태양열 발전 분야에서 그의 연구소가 이룩한 기술적 발전들에 대해 강연을 할 것입니다.

대부분의 연구소들은 합성 원료를 사용하여 태양 전지판을 개발합니다. [12]그러나, Dr. Flack의 팀은 가격이 알맞고 입수하기 쉬운 천연 원료를 이용합니다. 그는 두 시간짜리 발표로 그의 팀의 방법을 요약할 것입니다. 기본적으로, Dr. Flack은 원료들의 이용 가능성이 왜 정부의 각료들이 태양 에너지에 전폭적인 지원을 해 주어야 하는 이유인지를 설명할 것입니다. [13]그는 또한 어떻게 태양 에너지가 석탄과 그 밖의 다른 재생 불가능한 에너지원들에 대한 실용적인 대안으로써 점진적으로 발달해 왔는지 설명할 것입니다.

학회는 Southern 기술 기관에서 11월 26일부터 12월 3일까지 개최될 것입니다. 발표는 참석자들이 편한 날짜에 학회에 참석할 수 있도록 하기 위해 매일 반복됩니다. 온라인 등록은 11월 15일까지 가능합니다. [14]등록 기간에, 여러분은 어떤 날짜든 등록하실 수 있습니다. 그러나, 11월 15일 이후에는, 등록자들은 오직 12월 3일 모임에만 등록할 수 있습니다.

solar power 태양열 발전 renewable adj. 재생 가능한
advance n. 발전, 진전 synthetic adj. (인위적으로) 합성한, 인조의
affordable adj. (가격이) 알맞은, 입수 가능한 summarize v. 요약하다
essentially adv. 기본적으로, 본질적으로
availability n. 이용 가능성, (입수) 가능성
evolve v. 점진적으로 발달하다, 진화하다 viable adj. 실용적인, 실행 가능한
coal n. 석탄 so as to ~하기 위해서 enrollee n. 등록자

---

11 유사의미 동사 중에서 고르기

해설 네 개의 보기 모두 '말하다'라는 의미와 관련이 있지만, 빈칸 뒤의 전치사 about과 함께 쓰여 '~에 대해 강연을 하다'라는 의미를 나타내는 동사 (B) speak(강연을 하다)가 정답이다.

어휘 note v. (중요하거나 흥미로운 것을) 언급하다, 유념하다

12 동사 어휘 고르기 _주변 문맥 파악_

해설 'Dr. Flack의 팀은 천연 원료를 ____하다'라는 문맥이므로 모든 보기가 정답의 후보이다. 빈칸이 있는 문장만으로 정답을 고를 수 없으므로 주변 문맥이나 전체 문맥을 파악한다. 이 경우, 빈칸이 있는 문장의 맨 앞에 접속부사(However)가 있으므로 앞 문장과 의미상 대조적인 관계임을 알 수 있다. 앞 문장에서 '대부분의 연구소들은 합성 원료를 사용한다(Most facilities ~ using synthetic materials)'고 했으므로 Dr. Flack의 팀은 합성 원료가 아닌 천연 원료를 사용함을 알 수 있다. 따라서 동사 (B) utilizes(이용하다)가 정답이다.

어휘 study v. 연구하다; n. 연구 secure v. 확보하다 apply v. 적용하다

13 명사 관련 어구 완성하기

해설 '석탄과 그 밖의 다른 재생 불가능한 에너지원들에 대한 실용적인 대안'이라는 문맥에서 빈칸 뒤의 전치사 to와 함께 쓰여 '~에 대한 대안'이라는 의미의 어구를 이루는 명사 (A) alternative(대안)가 정답이다. (an alternative to: ~에 대한 대안)

어휘 divergence n. (의견 등의) 차이 attribute n. 속성, 특성
motivation n. 자극, 동기 부여

14 알맞은 문장 고르기

해설 (A) Dr. Flack은 그의 연구로 인해 12월 이후 연락이 되지 않을 수 있습니다.
(B) 그것은 참석해야 하는 사람들을 허가하기 위해 연기되었습니다.
(C) 그 결과물은 기밀이며 일반 대중들에게는 공개될 수 없습니다.
(D) 등록 기간에, 여러분은 어떤 날짜든 등록하실 수 있습니다.

해설 빈칸에 들어갈 알맞은 문장을 고르는 문제이므로 빈칸의 주변 문맥이나 전체 문맥을 파악한다. 앞부분에서 발표는 학회가 개최되는 동안 매일 반복된다고 했고, 앞 문장 'registration is available until November 15'에서 등록은 11월 15일까지 가능하다고 한 후, 뒤 문장 'After November 15, however, enrollees can only register for the December 3 session.'에서 11월 15일 이후에 등록자들은 오직 12월 3일 모임에만 등록할 수 있다고 했으므로 빈칸에는 등록 기간인 11월 15일 이전에는 등록자들이 어떤 날짜든 등록할 수 있다는 내용이 들어가야 함을 알 수 있다. 따라서 (D) During the enrollment period, you may sign up for any day가 정답이다.

어휘 postpone v. 연기하다 confidential adj. 기밀의
disclose v. 공개하다

Chapter 11 유사의미 명사

Hackers Test
p.322

Part 5

01 (C)	02 (B)	03 (B)	04 (D)	05 (C)
06 (C)	07 (B)	08 (D)	09 (D)	10 (C)

Part 6

11 (B)	12 (C)	13 (D)	14 (B)

01 유사의미 명사 중에서 고르기

해설 네 개의 보기 모두 '요금'이라는 의미와 관련이 있는 어휘들이나, '여분의 수하물을 추가 요금으로 보내다'라는 문맥이므로, 서비스에 대한 '요금, 비용'이라는 뜻을 가진 명사 (C) charge가 정답이다. (A) fare는 '(교통) 요금' (taxi fare: 택시 요금)을 의미하며, (B) toll은 '통행료', (D) estimate은 '견적, 추정액'이라는 의미이다.

해석 여분의 수하물은 가방 당 50달러의 추가 요금으로 보내질 수 있다.

어휘 luggage n. 수하물 check v. (비행기 등을 탈 때 수화물을) 부치다

02 유사의미 명사 중에서 고르기

해설 (A)와 (B) 모두 '선호'라는 의미와 관련이 있는 어휘들이나, 빈칸에는 빈칸 뒤의 전치사 for와 함께 쓰여 '~에 대한 선호'라는 어구를 이루는 명사가 들어가야 하므로 (B) preference가 정답이다. (A) choice는 '선택한 것'을 의미하며 (C) reaction은 '반응', (D) promotion은 '승진'이라는 의미이다.

해석 비즈니스 학술지의 최근호에 실린 보고서는 소비자들 사이에서 온라인 결제 서비스에 대한 선호가 증가했음을 명시했다.

어휘 issue n. (잡지·신문 같은 정기 간행물의) 호 state v. 명시하다, 서술하다

03 유사의미 명사 중에서 고르기

해설 네 개의 보기 모두 비슷한 의미를 지니고 있으나, '회사 자료에 대한 접근 권한'이라는 문맥이므로 '접근 권한'이라는 뜻을 가진 명사 (B) access가 정답이다. 이때 access가 불가산 명사임에 주의한다. (A) pass는 '정기권, 통로, 통행' (a rail pass: 철도 정기권), (C) entrance는 '입구' (the building entrance: 건물 입구), (D) approach는 '출입로, 접근법'이라는 의미이며 가산 명사이다. (a rarely used approach: 잘 사용되지 않는 출입로)

해석 새로운 자문 위원인 Mr. Powell은 실행 가능성 조사에 필요한 정보를 검색하기 위해 회사의 기록 보관소에 대한 접근 권한을 요청했다.

어휘 consultant n. 자문 위원 archive n. 기록 보관소, (보관된) 자료
retrieve v. (정보를) 검색하다, 되찾다 feasibility n. 실행 가능성

04 유사의미 명사 중에서 고르기

해설 빈칸에는 findings와 함께 쓰여 '조사 결과'라는 어구를 만들 수 있는 어휘가 필요하다. (A)와 (D) 모두 '조사'라는 의미와 관련이 있는데, laboratory와 함께 쓰여 실험실에서의 '연구, 학술 조사'를 나타내는 명사가 필요하므로 (D) research가 정답이다. (A) survey는 설문을 통해 정보를 알아내는 '표본 조사'를 의미하며 (B) response는 '응답', (C) question은 '질문'이라는 의미이다.

해석 그 실험실의 연구 결과는 Dawson Beauty Products사의 새로운 화장품 라인이 환경친화적이라는 것을 보여준다.

어휘 laboratory n. 실험실
environmentally friendly 환경친화적인, 환경을 해치지 않는

05 유사의미 명사 중에서 고르기

해설 (A)와 (C) 모두 '크기'라는 의미와 관련이 있는 어휘들이나, 공간의 일부분을 나타낼 수 있는 명사가 빈칸에 들어가야 하므로 (C) proportion(부분, 비율)이 정답이다. (A) size는 물건의 크고 작음, 즉 '크기'를 나타낼 때 쓰이며 (B) content는 '용량, 내용(물)', (D) number는 '숫자'라는 의미이다.

해석 그 병원 신축 병동의 상당 부분은 새로운 산모와 유아를 위한 치료 시설로 사용될 것이다.

어휘 significant adj. 상당한, 중요한 wing n. 동, 부속 건물 infant n. 유아

06 유사의미 명사 중에서 고르기

해설 (A)와 (C)는 유사한 의미이나, '배울 것에 대한 명확한 설명'이라는 문맥이므로 '설명'이라는 뜻을 가진 명사 (C) explanation이 정답이다. (A) direction은 특정 행동을 하도록 안내하는 '지침'을 나타낼 때 쓰이며, (B) suggestion은 '의견', (D) recommendation은 '추천, 권장'이라는 의미이다.

해석 오리엔테이션이 시작될 때, 강사는 신입 직원들에게 그 주 내내 그들이 배울 것에 대한 명확한 설명을 제공했다.

어휘 instructor n. 강사

07 유사의미 명사 중에서 고르기

해설 (A)와 (B)는 유사한 의미이나, 그 중 부정관사 a와 함께 쓰여 '서면상으로 제공되는 상세한 설명'이라는 뜻으로 쓰일 수 있는 명사 (B) description(설명, 해설)이 정답이다. (A) information(정보)은 불가산 명사로 부정관사와 함께 쓰일 수 없다. (C) inquiry는 '문의, 질문', (D) confirmation은 '확인, 확정'이라는 의미이다. (confirmation of reservation: 예약 확인)

해석 Chemtech 제조 회사의 카탈로그는 화학 공장에서 사용되는 장비, 공구 및 기구들에 대한 상세한 설명을 제공한다.

어휘 instrument n. 기구 plant n. 공장

08 유사의미 명사 중에서 고르기

해설 빈칸에는 명성의 '향상'이라는 뜻의 어휘가 들어가야 한다. (A)와 (D) 모두 '증대'라는 의미와 관련이 있는데, 이 중 가치와 품질이 높아짐을 나타내는 명사가 빈칸에 들어가야 하므로 (D) enhancement(향상, 상승)가 정답이다. (A) increment는 수나 양의 '증가'를 의미하며, (B) comparison은 '비교', (C) disruption은 '중단, 분열'이라는 의미이다.

해석 새로운 홍보 캠페인의 목표는 회사 명성의 향상이다.

어휘 public relation 홍보, 섭외 reputation n. 명성, 평판

09 유사의미 명사 중에서 고르기

해설 (B)와 (D) 모두 '값어치'라는 의미와 관련이 있는 어휘들이나, 구체적인 금액 뒤에 쓰여 '(얼마)어치'라는 뜻으로 쓰일 수 있는 명사 (D) worth가 정답이다. (A) class는 '등급'이라는 의미이며, (B) value는 '가치, 값어치'라는 의미

이지만 구체적인 금액과 함께 쓰이지는 않는다. (C) credit은 '신용 거래, 공제액'이라는 의미이다.

해석 호텔의 모든 투숙객들은 지역 식당과 명소들에 대한 200달러어치의 할인권과 상품권이 포함된 환영 패키지를 제공받는다.

어휘 welcome packet 환영 패키지 voucher n. 상품권 attraction n. 명소

10 유사의미 명사 중에서 고르기

해설 빈칸에는 경기 상황을 반영하는 '징후'라는 뜻의 어휘가 들어가야 한다. (B)와 (C) 모두 '표시'라는 의미와 관련이 있는데, 이 중 무언가를 암시하는 '징후'라는 뜻을 가진 명사 (C) indication이 정답이다. (B) show는 의도적으로 감정을 표시하는 것을 의미한다. (in a show of loyalty: 충성심의 표시로써) (A) account는 '설명, 계좌', (D) condition은 '상태'라는 의미이다.

해석 현재의 시장 동향은 어떤 특정 분야가 좋은 투자 기회인지를 보여주는 훌륭한 징후이다.

어휘 trend n. 동향, 추세 particular adj. 특정한 sector n. 분야, 부문
opportunity n. 기회

11-14는 다음 편지에 관한 문제입니다.

Mark Walter
52번지 Southern가
그레이트 폴스, 몬타나 주 86503

Mr. Walter께,

[11]우리 사무실에 있는 냉방 장치와 관련해 문제가 있었음을 알리고자 편지를 씁니다. 저는 2주 전에 Coolair Corporation사에 연락했고, 회사 측에서 필요한 수리를 하기 위해 기술자를 보내주었습니다.

[12]작업은 상당한 비용으로 이루어졌는데, 각 기계의 몇몇 부품들이 손상되어서 교체되어야만 했기 때문입니다. 기술자에 따르면, 기계들은 관리팀에 의해 제대로 설치되지 않았습니다. 냉방기가 설치 중에 파손되었기 때문에, Coolair사는 오작동에 대해 책임을 지는 것을 거부했고, 이것은 우리 측이 직접 수리 비용을 부담해야 함을 의미합니다.

[13]저는 재료비 365달러, 인건비 420달러를 포함하여 총 수리 비용이 785달러라는 것을 나타내는 항목별로 구분된 청구서를 동봉했습니다. 우리의 임대 계약서는 이러한 비용은 건물주가 부담한다고 명시합니다. [14]우리가 배상을 요구하는 것은 타당합니다. 그러므로, 우리는, 비용 전액을 가능한 한 빨리 변상받을 수 있으면 좋겠습니다.

Molly Davison 드림

---

air-conditioning adj. 냉방 장치의 considerable adj. 상당한
component n. 부품 maintenance n. 관리, 정비, 유지
take responsibility for ~에 대해 책임을 지다 malfunction n. 오작동
itemize v. 항목별로 구분하다 invoice n. 청구서, 송장
lease n. 임대 계약서 reimburse v. 변상하다, 상환하다

11 명사 어휘 고르기 전체 문맥 파악

해설 '냉방 장치와 관련해 _____이 있었음을 알리기 위해'라는 문맥이므로 모든 보기가 정답의 후보이다. 빈칸이 있는 문장만으로 정답을 고를 수 없으므로 주변 문맥이나 전체 문맥을 파악한다. 뒤 문장에서 '필요한 수리를 하기 위해 기술자를 보내 주었다(they sent a technician to make the necessary repairs)'고 한 후, 뒷부분에서 냉방기를 수리하는 이유 및 비용에 대해 설명하고 있으므로 냉방 장치에 문제가 있었음을 알 수 있다. 따라서 명사 (B) issues(문제)가 정답이다.

어휘 success n. 성공 satisfaction n. 만족 request n. 요구, 부탁

12 유사의미 명사 중에서 고르기

해설 네 개의 보기 모두 금액을 의미하는 어휘들인데, '작업은 상당한 비용으로 이루어졌다'는 문맥이므로 명사 (C) expense(비용)가 정답이다.

어휘 tariff n. 관세 penalty n. 벌금 fine n. 벌금

13 유사의미 명사 중에서 고르기

해설 (A)와 (D) 모두 '재료'라는 의미와 관련이 있는 어휘들이나, 이 중 물건 수

리에 필요한 '재료'라는 뜻을 가진 명사 (D) materials가 정답이다. (A) ingredients는 음식의 재료나 혼합물의 성분을 말할 때 쓰인다.

어휘 **stationery** n. 문구류, 문방구 **supplement** n. 보충물, 추가물

14 알맞은 문장 고르기

해석 (A) 자사는 수리 비용이 과다 청구되었다고 생각합니다.
(B) 우리가 배상을 요구하는 것은 타당합니다.
(C) 우리는 아직 수리 비용을 지불하지 않았습니다.
(D) 그 기술자는 고장의 원인을 알아내지 못했습니다.

해설 빈칸에 들어갈 알맞은 문장을 고르는 문제이므로 빈칸의 주변 문맥이나 전체 문맥을 파악한다. 앞 문장 'Our lease states that such costs are covered by the owner of the building.'에서 발신자와 수신자 간의 임대 계약서는 수리 비용은 건물주가 부담한다고 명시한다고 했으므로 빈칸에는 발신자가 배상을 요구하는 것이 타당하다는 내용이 들어가야 함을 알 수 있다. 따라서 (B) It is appropriate for us to ask for compensation이 정답이다.

어휘 **overcharge** v. 과다 청구하다 **appropriate** adj. 타당한, 적절한
compensation n. 배상 **breakdown** n. 고장
determine v. 알아내다, 결정하다

Chapter 12 유사의미 형용사·부사

Hackers Test
p.328

Part 5

01 (A)	02 (A)	03 (B)	04 (C)	05 (B)
06 (A)	07 (C)	08 (B)	09 (C)	10 (B)

Part 6

11 (B)	12 (C)	13 (B)	14 (C)

01 유사의미 형용사 중에서 고르기

해설 (A)와 (B) 모두 '명백한'이라는 의미와 관련이 있는 어휘들이나, '기술적인 지식이 부족한 것이 분명하다'라는 문맥이므로, 어떤 사실이 명확하고 확실함을 나타내는 형용사 (A) apparent(분명한)가 정답이다. (B) visible은 '(사람 또는 사물이) 눈에 보이는'이라는 의미이므로 문맥과 어울리지 않는다. (C) substantial은 '상당한', (D) notable은 '주목할 만한'이라는 의미이다.

해석 그 지원자는 가장 기초적인 질문에조차 힘겹게 대답했기 때문에, 그녀가 기술적인 지식이 부족한 것은 분명했다.

어휘 **struggle** v. 힘겹게 하다, 고심하다 **lack** v. ~이 부족하다

02 유사의미 형용사 중에서 고르기

해설 (A)와 (D)는 유사한 의미이나 'Mr. Lewis가 은퇴한 이래로 계속해서 자리가 비어 있다'는 문맥이므로 장소 또는 자리가 '비어 있는, 사용되지 않고 있는'이라는 뜻을 가진 형용사 (A) unoccupied가 정답이다. (D) discarded는 사물이 '더 이상 사용되지 않는, 버려진'이라는 의미이므로 문맥과 어울리지 않는다. (discarded equipment: 더 이상 사용되지 않는 장비) (B) disguised는 '변장한, 속임수의', (C) interrupted는 '중단된'이라는 의미이다.

해석 사내 자문 위원 자리는 Mr. Lewis가 은퇴했을 때 공석이 되었으며 계속해서 비어 있다.

어휘 **in-house** (회사·조직) 내부의 **vacate** v. 공석으로 하다, 비우다

03 유사의미 형용사 중에서 고르기

해설 (A)와 (B)는 유사한 의미이나, '요즘은 작은 기기들이 더 유행한다'는 문맥이므로 '유행하는, 널리 퍼진'이라는 뜻을 가진 형용사 (B) prevalent가 정답이다. (A) leading은 '일류의, 뛰어난'이라는 의미이므로 문맥과 어울리지 않는다. (leading brand: 일류 브랜드) (C) natural은 '자연의, 타고난', (D) precedent는 '이전의, 앞선'이라는 의미이다.

해석 사람들은 CD 플레이어를 가방과 배낭에 넣어서 다니곤 했지만, 요즘은 디지털 파일을 재생하는 아주 작은 기기들이 더 유행한다.

어휘 **compact disk player** CD 플레이어 **device** n. 기기, 장치

04 유사의미 부사 중에서 고르기

해설 'continually(계속해서)'와 'lastingly(지속적으로)'의 차이를 구분해야 하는 문제이다. '계속해서 감시하다'라는 문맥이므로 어떤 일이 계속해서 일어남을 나타내는 부사 (C) continually(계속해서)가 정답이다. (B) lastingly는 '(효과 등이) 지속적으로' 유지되는 것을 나타낼 때 쓰인다. (lastingly effective treatment: 지속적으로 효과적인 치료) (A) everlastingly는 '영원히, 변함없이', (D) stirringly는 '자극해서, 감동시켜서'라는 의미이다.

해석 새로운 감시 시스템은 사실상 그 시설의 모든 부분이 보안 직원들에 의해 계속 감시되도록 한다.

어휘 **surveillance** n. 감시, 감독 **virtually** adv. 사실상, 가상으로
facility n. 시설 **monitor** v. 감시하다, 관리하다

05 유사의미 형용사 중에서 고르기

해설 (B)와 (C)는 유사한 의미이나 '많은 객실들이 비어 있다'라는 문맥이므로 자리나 집 등이 '비어 있는'이라는 뜻을 가진 형용사 (B) vacant가 정답이다. (C) blank는 종이나 벽 등이 '비어 있는'이라는 의미이므로 문맥과 어울리지 않는다. (A) resistant는 '저항력 있는', (D) ongoing은 '계속 진행 중인'이라는 의미이다.

해석 Emperor 호텔의 겨울 판촉 행사에도 불구하고, 이번 주에 많은 객실들이 비어 있는 채로 남아 있다.

어휘 **promotion** n. 판촉 행사 **remain** v. 남아 있다

06 유사의미 부사 중에서 고르기

해설 (A)와 (C)는 유사한 의미이나, '규정을 엄격하게 따르다'라는 문맥이므로 부사 (A) stringently(엄격하게)가 정답이다. (C) strongly는 '강하게'라는 의미이므로 문맥에 어울리지 않는다. (B) objectively는 '객관적으로', (D) evenly는 '균등하게'라는 의미이다.

해석 그 보안 요원은 권한이 없는 사람들의 건물 출입을 금지하는 것에 관한 규정을 엄격하게 따른다.

어휘 **security personnel** 보안 요원 **regulation** n. 규정
bar v. (~하는 것을) 금지하다 **unauthorized** adj. 권한이 없는, 허가받지 않은

07 유사의미 형용사 중에서 고르기

해설 '최근의 회사 주가 하락'이라는 문맥이므로 '최근의'라는 뜻을 가진 형용사 (C) recent가 정답이다. (A) stable은 '안정된'이라는 의미이며, (B) modern은 '근대의, 현대의'라는 의미이므로 문맥과 어울리지 않는다. (D) casual은 '무심한, 임시의'라는 의미이다.

해석 최근의 회사 주가 하락은 투자자들에게 추가 주식을 더 싼 가격에 매입할 기회를 제공했다.

어휘 **investor** n. 투자자 **purchase** v. 매입하다, 구매하다 **share** n. 주식

08 유사의미 형용사 중에서 고르기

해설 (A)와 (B) 모두 '다음'이라는 의미와 관련이 있지만, 빈칸 앞에 정관사 the가 없으므로 형용사 (B) next가 정답이다. next는 현재를 기준으로 하여 '다음의'라는 뜻을 나타낼 때 정관사를 필요로 하지 않지만, (A) following은 앞에 정관사 the가 와야 한다. (C) before는 '이전에'라는 의미로 문맥에 어울리지 않는다. (D) later는 주로 부사로 쓰여 '뒤에, 나중에'라는 뜻을 가지며 형용사로 쓰일 때에는 관사와 함께 'a later date: 후일에'의 형태로 쓰이므로 오답이다.

해석 Cleaver 금융 그룹의 인사부장인 Jerry Mathers는 다음 주에 회계직 면접을 실시할 것이다.

어휘 **conduct** v. 실시하다, 시행하다 **accounting** n. 회계

09 유사의미 부사 중에서 고르기

해설 Mr. Patrick이 그동안 주로 써온 글에 관한 내용이므로 부사 (C) primarily (주로)가 정답이다. (A) firstly는 '우선, 첫째로', (B) completely는 '완전히,

전적으로', (D) categorically는 '절대적으로, 명확히'라는 의미이다.

해석   프리랜서 작가인 Mr. Patrick은 주로 세계 경제 동향에 관해 몇몇 금융 잡지에 글을 써 왔다.

어휘   **trend** n. 동향, 추세   **financial** adj. 금융의

10 유사의미 형용사 중에서 고르기

해석   '조기 퇴직을 알리는 서한을 제출하다'라는 문맥이므로 '조기의, (시기적으로 보통보다) 이른'이라는 뜻을 가진 형용사 (B) early가 정답이다. (A) overdue는 '(결제·반납 등의) 기한이 지난', (C) active는 '적극적인, 활동적인', (D) previous는 '(시간·순서적으로) 이전의, 앞의'라는 의미이다. (previous government: 이전 정부)

해석   예기치 않은 병 때문에, Tom Walton은 그의 조기 퇴직을 알리는 서한을 제출해야만 했다.

어휘   **due to** ~ 때문에   **unexpected** adj. 예기치 않은, 뜻밖의   **illness** n. 병   **be forced to do** ~해야만 한다, ~하도록 강요받다   **resignation** n. 퇴직, 사직, 사임

11-14는 다음 회람에 관한 문제입니다.

발신: 인사부
수신: 전 직원
제목: 새로운 의료 서비스 체계
날짜: 7월 6일

[11]직원들에게 의료 지원을 제공하기 위한 회사측 노력의 일환으로, 인사부는 8월 1일부터 시행될 새로운 의료 서비스 체계를 알리게 되어 기쁩니다.

[12]직원들과의 폭넓은 협의 후에, 이전 보험 제도의 구성 요소가 아니었던 안과 및 치과 종합치료 같은 혜택들을 포함하는 포괄적인 의료 종합 정책을 준비했습니다. 더 많은 세부 사항들을 위해서는, 오늘 아침에 배부된 새로운 직원 안내서를 참고해 주십시오. [13]개선된 종합 정책에 관한 정보가 마지막 장에 있습니다. 만약 여러분이 아직 사본을 받지 못했다면, 알아야 할 모든 것은 웹사이트에서 보실 수 있습니다.

보상 비용은 직원들에 의해 분담될 것이기 때문에, 월급 공제가 자동으로 발생할 것입니다. [14]이에 대한 모든 문의는 인사부의 Zoe Kazan에게 보내시기를 권장합니다. 그녀는 가능한 한 그것들을 충분히 답변하고자 최선을 다할 것입니다.

---

health care 의료 서비스   **scheme** n. 체계, 안   **effort** n. 노력
support n. 지원   **please** v. (~하여) 기쁘다   **implement** v. 시행하다
consultation n. 협의, 상의   **put together** 준비하다, 만들다
comprehensive adj. 포괄적인, 광범위한   **package** n. 종합 정책, 꾸러미
coverage n. 보상, 보험   **deduction** n. 공제
automatically adv. 자동으로

11 유사의미 동사 중에서 고르기

해설   '새로운 의료 서비스 체계를 알리게 되어 기쁘다'라는 문맥이므로 (B) announce(알리다, 발표하다)가 정답이다. (D) notify도 '알리다'라는 의미이지만 notify 뒤의 목적어 자리에는 사람이 와서 'notify + 사람 + of + 내용'의 형태로 쓰여야 하므로 답이 될 수 없다.

어휘   **review** v. 재검토하다, 회상하다   **appreciate** v. 고맙게 여기다

12 유사의미 형용사 중에서 고르기

해설   (A)와 (C) 모두 '넓은'이라는 의미와 관련이 있지만, '폭넓은 협의 후에 의료 종합 정책을 준비했다'라는 문맥이므로 지식이나 품목을 나타내는 어휘들과 함께 쓰여 '폭넓은, 광범위한'이라는 뜻을 가지는 형용사 (C) extensive가 정답이다. (A) spacious(넓은)는 추상적인 범위를 나타내지 못하고 물질적인 장소가 넓다는 의미로 쓰이므로 오답이다.

어휘   **preoccupied** adj. (어떤 생각·걱정에) 사로잡힌, 정신이 팔린   **hesitant** adj. 주저하는, 망설이는

13 알맞은 문장 고르기

해석   (A) 우리 기업의 웹사이트는 직원 평가에 관해 충분히 설명하고 있습니다.
(B) 개선된 종합 정책에 관한 정보가 마지막 장에 있습니다.
(C) 건강 보험이 예전만큼 포괄적이지 않다는 점을 알아 두십시오.

(D) 처방전 갱신 마감 기한이 7월 17일까지로 연장되었습니다.

해설   빈칸에 들어갈 알맞은 문장을 고르는 문제이므로 빈칸의 주변 문맥이나 전체 문맥을 파악한다. 앞 문장 'For more details, please refer to the new employee manual'에서 더 많은 세부 사항들을 위해서는 새로운 직원 안내서를 참고하라고 했으므로 빈칸에는 새로운 안내서에 관련된 정보가 있음을 안내하는 내용이 들어가야 함을 알 수 있다. 따라서 (B) There is information about the improved package on the last page가 정답이다.

어휘   **corporate** adj. 기업의   **fully** adv. 충분히, 완전히   **evaluation** n. 평가
improved adj. 개선된, 향상된   **inclusive** adj. 포괄적인
deadline n. 마감 기한   **prescription** n. 처방전   **renewal** n. 갱신, 기한 연장

14 명사 어휘 고르기   주변 문맥 파악

해설   'Zoe Kazan에게 ____을 보내도록 권장한다'라는 문맥이므로 모든 보기가 정답의 후보이다. 빈칸이 있는 문장만으로 정답을 고를 수 없으므로 주변 문맥이나 전체 문맥을 파악한다. 뒤 문장에서 '그녀는 가능한 한 그것들을 충분히 답변하고자 최선을 다할 것(She will do her best to answer them as thoroughly as possible.)'이라고 했으므로, Zoe Kazan에게 문의를 보내도록 권장하고 있음을 알 수 있다. 따라서 명사 (C) inquiries가 정답이다.

어휘   **image** n. 이미지, 영상   **reminder** n. 상기시키는 것, 조언
document n. 문서, 서류

Chapter 01 문맥 파악 문제 1: 단어 고르기 문제

예제 해석   p.334

문법 접속부사 문제

즉각 배포를 위함

3월 27일

최신 Solaris LT-4 노트북이 4월 10일에 출시될 예정입니다. Solaris 팀은 경쟁 상품보다 더 빠른 처리 속도와 더 긴 배터리 수명을 특징으로 하는 제품을 제공하기 위해 최첨단의 공학 기술 해결책을 사용했습니다. 우선, 이 기기는 해당 종류에서 가장 강력한 중앙 처리 장치와 큰 메모리를 특징으로 합니다. 게다가, 올해 모델의 배터리는 한 번 충전 시 최대 16시간까지 지속될 수 있습니다.

release v. 출시하다 **cutting-edge** adj. 최첨단의
deliver v. 제공하다, 배달하다 **competition** n. 경쟁 상대, 경쟁
feature v. ~을 특징으로 하다, 특별히 포함하다 **class** n. 종류, 등급

Hackers Practice   p.335

유형 연습

01 (A)   02 (B)   03 (C)   04 (B)

01 **문법** 시제 문제

발신: Hugo Woods, 영업 이사
수신: 영업 직원

여러분 중 많은 분들이 아시다시피, 저는 현재 유럽의 최대 화장품 제조업체인 Hartco사와 거래를 논의해왔습니다. 그들의 제품은 미국을 제외한 모든 곳에서 팔리고 있습니다. 제 계획은 미국 내 주요 도시들에 있는 우리 고객들에게 그것들을 유통시키는 것입니다. 그렇게 되게 하기 위해서는, 전체 재무 보고서가 필요합니다. 2주 뒤의 다음 회의 전까지 제가 출력할 수 있도록 그것을 제 이메일로 보내주시기 바랍니다.

deal n. 거래, 합의 **distribute** v. 유통하다, 배포하다
financial report 재무 보고서

해설 **올바른 시제의 동사 채우기** '제품이 미국을 제외한 모든 곳에서 팔리다'라는 문맥인데, 이 경우 빈칸이 있는 문장만으로는 올바른 시제의 동사를 고를 수 없으므로 주변 문맥이나 전체 문맥을 파악하여 정답을 고른다. 뒤 문장에서 '자신의 계획은 미국 내 주요 도시들에 있는 고객들에게 그것들을 유통시키는 것(My plan is to distribute them to our clients in major US cities.)'이라고 했으므로 제품이 미국을 제외한 모든 곳에서 팔리는 것은 현재의 상황임을 알 수 있다. 따라서 현재 시제 (A) are sold가 정답이다.

02 **문법** 대명사 문제

Mr. Browning께,

곧 있을 공관 지구 개발 프로젝트에서 당신과 함께 일하게 되어 기쁩니다. 당신의 프로젝트 관리자로서, 당신이 어떠한 잠재적인 문제들이라도 극복할 수 있도록 제가 도와드리겠습니다. 프로젝트의 규모를 감안할 때, 우리는 몇 가지 우려 사항들을 예상할 수 있습니다. 예를 들어, 지역 시민들이 소음이나 매연과 같은 것들에 대해 항의할 수 있고, 규제 기관들이 추가 서류를 요구할 수 있습니다. 반드시 그들이 프로젝트 상황에 만족하게 하기 위해 조치들이 취해져야 합니다. 논의를 하기 위해 당신이 언제 시간이 되는지 알려주시기 바랍니다. ◎

upcoming adj. 곧 있을, 다가오는 **civic center** 공관 지구, 시민 회관
overcome v. 극복하다, 이겨내다 **potential** adj. 잠재적인, 가능성 있는
object to ~에 항의하다, 반대하다 **fume** n. 매연, 연기
regulator n. 규제 기관, 규제 담당자 **paperwork** n. 서류, 서류 작업
condition n. 상황, 조건

해설 **인칭대명사 채우기** '반드시 _____이 프로젝트 상황에 만족하게 하다'라는 문맥에서 빈칸이 명사절의 주어 자리이므로, 모든 보기가 정답의 후보이다. 빈칸이 있는 문장만으로 정답을 고를 수 없으므로 주변 문맥이나 전체 문맥을 파악한다. 앞 문장에서 지역 시민들(local citizens)이 소음이나 매연과 같은 것들에 대해 항의할 수 있고 규제 기관들(regulators)이 추가 서류를 요구할 수 있다고 했으므로 빈칸에 들어갈 대명사는 지역 시민들과 규제 기관들을 가리킨다. 따라서 3인칭 대명사 (B) they가 정답이다.

03 **문법** 접속부사 문제

이 공고는 사이버 보안의 중요성에 대한 주의입니다. 여러 계정들에 동일한 비밀번호를 사용하지 마십시오. 그렇게 하면, 한 번에 여러 계정을 이용할 수 없게 되는 것에 대해서 걱정하지 않아도 됩니다. 예를 들어, 저희 직원들 중 한 명은 그의 은행 계좌와 이메일 계정에 동일한 비밀번호를 사용했습니다. 그것이 도용되었을 때, 그는 두 가지 모두를 이용할 수 없었습니다. 사이버 보안에 대한 더 많은 정보를 얻고 싶으시다면, IT팀에 연락하시기 바랍니다. 그들은 항상 도울 준비가 되어 있습니다.

reminder n. 주의, 상기시키는 것 **cybersecurity** n. 사이버 보안
account n. 계정, 계좌 **steal** v. 도용하다, 훔치다

해설 **접속부사 채우기** 빈칸이 콤마와 함께 문장의 맨 앞에 온 접속부사 자리이므로, 앞 문장과 빈칸이 있는 문장의 의미 관계를 파악하여 접속부사인 세 개의 보기 중 하나를 정답으로 골라야 한다. 앞 문장에서 그렇게 하면, 즉 여러 계정들에 동일한 비밀번호를 사용하지 않으면 한 번에 여러 계정을 이용할 수 없게 되는 것에 대해서 걱정하지 않아도 된다고 했고, 빈칸이 있는 문장에서는 직원들 중 한 명이 그의 은행 계좌와 이메일 계정에 동일한 비밀번호를 사용했다고 하면서 여러 계정에 동일한 비밀번호를 사용해서 한꺼번에 계정을 이용할 수 없게 된 경우를 예로 들고 있다. 따라서 빈칸 앞 문장에서 언급한 여러 계정에 동일한 비밀번호를 사용하지 않아야 한다는 것에 대한 근거로, 여러 계정에 동일한 비밀번호를 사용해 불편을 겪은 직원의 예시를 언급했으므로 (C) For example(예를 들어)이 정답이다.

어휘 **after all** 결국에는, 어쨌든 **in effect** 사실상, 실제로는

04 **어휘** 명사 어휘 문제

6월 25일—이번 여름의 더운 날씨 때문에, 도시 주민들이 사용 가능한 물이 더 적을 것입니다. 따라서 시 수도국은 모든 주민들이 물을 현명하게 사용할 것을 권장하고 누수는 없는지 그들의 집을 점검할 것을 권고한다. "이 조치는 낭비를 줄이는 데에 도움이 될 것입니다"라고 수도국장 Kyle Brenner는 말한다. 물 절약에 대한 더 많은 제안들을 얻기 위해, Mr. Brenner는 독자들에게 수도국 웹사이트를 방문할 것을 권장하고 있다.

available adj. 사용 가능한 **encourage** v. 권장하다, 장려하다
wisely adv. 현명하게 **water leak** 누수 **conservation** n. 절약, 보호

해설 **명사 어휘 고르기** '이 조치는 _____을 줄이는 데에 도움이 될 것이다'라는 문맥이므로 모든 보기가 정답의 후보이다. 빈칸이 있는 문장만으로 정답을 고를 수 없으므로 주변 문맥이나 전체 문맥을 파악한다. 앞 문장에서 '모든 주민들이 물을 현명하게 사용할 것을 권장하고 누수는 없는지 그들의 집을 점검할 것을 권고한다(encourages all residents to use water wisely and recommends that they check their homes for any water leaks)'고 했고 뒤 문장에서 '물 절약에 대한 더 많은 제안들을 얻기 위해 수도국의 웹사이트를 방문할 것을 권장하고 있다(For more suggestions on water

conservation, ~ encourages ~ to visit the department's Web site.)'
고 했으므로 권고 조치가 물 낭비를 줄이는 데에 도움이 될 것임을 알 수 있다.
따라서 명사 (B) waste(낭비)가 정답이다.

어휘 　heat n. 열기, 열 　noise n. 잡음, 소리

Hackers Test
p.336

01 (D)	02 (C)	03 (A)	04 (C)	05 (B)
06 (D)	07 (A)	08 (D)	09 (D)	10 (B)
11 (D)	12 (B)	13 (D)	14 (C)	15 (D)
16 (A)				

01-04는 다음 보도 자료에 관한 문제입니다.

> **EI Industries사 전기 자동차 출시**
>
> EI Industries사는 대담하고, 새로운 방향으로 나아가고 있다. ⁰¹내년부터, 그 회사가 내놓는 새로운 모델들은 오로지 전기 자동차뿐일 것이다. EI Industries사의 최고 경영자인 Ryan Yang은 그것이 회사의 미래를 보장하는 최선의 방법이라고 생각한다.
>
> EI사의 새로운 라인업 중 첫 번째 차량은 Delta SUV일 예정이다. ⁰²전기로만 움직이는 이 자동차는 큰 인상을 남길 것으로 예상된다. 폭넓은 매력과 동급 최고의 기능들과 함께, Delta는 급격히 성장하는 매출을 보일 것으로 예상된다. ⁰³매출은 심지어 몇 년 안에 EI사의 휘발유로 움직이는 Gamma SUV의 매출을 능가할지도 모른다.
>
> ⁰⁴회사는 휘발유로 움직이는 모델들의 부품과 유지보수를 계속 제공할 것이다. 그러나, 현재의 버전들은 업데이트되지 않을 것이고, EI사는 가까운 미래에 그것들을 판매하는 것을 중단할 계획이다.
>
> **bold** adj. 대담한 **introduce** v. 내놓다, 소개하다
> **secure** v. 보장하다, 안전하게 하다 **appeal** n. 매력; v. 관심을 끌다
> **maintenance** n. 유지보수, 관리

01 부사 자리 채우기

해설 동사구(will be electric vehicles)를 꾸밀 수 있는 것은 부사이므로 부사 (D) exclusively(오로지, 독점적으로)가 정답이다. 동사 (A), 분사 (B), 형용사 (C)는 동사구를 꾸밀 수 없다.

02 알맞은 문장 고르기

해석 (A) 그 회사는 오랜 성공의 기록으로 기억될 것이다.
(B) Delta의 판매량은 예상했던 것보다 더 많았다.
(C) 전기로만 움직이는 이 자동차는 큰 인상을 남길 것으로 예상된다.
(D) 더 새로운 모델들은 휘발유 한 통으로도 더 멀리 간다.

해설 빈칸에 들어갈 알맞은 문장을 고르는 문제이므로 빈칸의 주변 문맥이나 전체 문맥을 파악한다. 앞 문장 'The first vehicle in EI's new lineup will be the Delta SUV.'에서 EI사의 새로운 라인업 중 첫 번째 차량은 Delta SUV일 예정이라고 했고 뒤 문장 'the Delta is expected to have rapidly growing sales'에서 Delta가 급격히 성장하는 매출을 보일 것으로 예상된다고 했으므로 빈칸에는 Delta SUV의 출시에 대한 기대와 관련된 내용이 들어가야 함을 알 수 있다. 따라서 (C) The all-electric vehicle is anticipated to make a big impression이 정답이다.

03 동사 어휘 고르기 　주변 문맥 파악

해설 '매출은 Gamma SUV의 매출을 _____할지도 모른다'라는 문맥이므로 모든 보기가 정답의 후보이다. 빈칸이 있는 문장만으로 정답을 고를 수 없으므로 주변 문맥이나 전체 문맥을 파악한다. 앞 문장에서 'Delta는 급격히 성장하는 매출을 보일 것으로 예상된다(the Delta is expected to have rapidly growing sales)'고 했으므로 Delta의 매출이 Gamma SUV의 매출을 능가할 수도 있다는 것임을 알 수 있다. 따라서 동사 (A) outperform(능가하다)이 정답이다.

어휘 **develop** v. 성장시키다, 개발하다 **assemble** v. 모으다, 조립하다
replace v. 대체하다, 바꾸다

04 올바른 시제의 동사 채우기 　주변 문맥 파악

해설 '휘발유로 움직이는 모델들의 부품과 유지보수를 계속 제공하다'라는 문맥인데, 이 경우 빈칸이 있는 문장만으로는 올바른 시제의 동사를 고를 수 없으므로 주변 문맥이나 전체 문맥을 파악하여 정답을 고른다. 뒤 문장에서 '현재의 버전들은 업데이트되지 않을 것이고, EI사는 가까운 미래에 그것들을 판매하는 것을 중단할 계획이다(the current versions will not be updated, and EI plans to stop selling them in the near future)'이라고 했으므로 당분간은 휘발유로 움직이는 모델들의 부품과 유지보수를 계속 제공할 것임을 알 수 있다. 따라서 미래 시제 (C) will continue가 정답이다.

05-08은 다음 광고에 관한 문제입니다.

> **Sawyer and Associates**
>
> Sawyer and Associates는 상업용 및 주거용 건축에 있어서 중서부 지역의 최고의 선택입니다. ⁰⁵10년 이상 동안, 저희 팀은 그 지역 전역에 있는 건물들을 설계해왔습니다.
>
> 이제, 도면과 청사진을 제작하는 것뿐만 아니라, 저희는 건설 서비스까지 포함하기 위해 사업을 확장하고 있습니다. ⁰⁶이러한 이유로, 저희는 중요한 역할들을 맡을 자질이 있는 사람들을 찾고 있습니다. ⁰⁷여기에는 숙련된 도급업자들과 소매상들이 포함됩니다. 관심이 있으신 분들은 이력서를 jobs@sawyerassociates.com으로 보내서 지원하실 수 있습니다. ⁰⁸추천서 및 과거 프로젝트와 관련된 모든 서류를 포함해주시기 바랍니다. 최소 5년의 관련 경력이 있고 선택한 직무의 요건을 충족시키는 능력을 보여줄 수 있는 지원자들에게 우선권이 주어질 것입니다.
>
> **commercial** adj. 상업의, 상업적인 **residential** adj. 주거의, 주택지의
> **drawing** n. 도면, 그림 **blueprint** n. 청사진 **qualified** adj. 자질이 있는
> **crucial** adj. 중요한, 결정적인 **reference** n. 추천서, 참고 자료
> **applicant** n. 지원자 **demonstrate** v. 보여주다, 입증하다

05 동사 어휘 고르기 　주변 문맥 파악

해설 '우리 팀은 그 지역 전역에 있는 건물들을 _____해왔다'라는 문맥이므로 모든 보기가 정답의 후보이다. 빈칸이 있는 문장만으로 정답을 고를 수 없으므로 주변 문맥이나 전체 문맥을 파악한다. 뒤 문장에서 '도면과 청사진을 제작하는 것뿐만 아니라, 건설 서비스까지 포함하기 위해 사업을 확장하고 있다(in addition to creating drawings and blueprints, we are expanding our business to include construction services)'고 했으므로 그 지역 전역에 있는 건물들을 설계해왔다는 것임을 알 수 있다. 따라서 동사 (B) designed(설계하다)가 정답이다.

어휘 **purchase** v. 구입하다 **maintain** v. 관리하다, 유지하다
inspect v. 점검하다, 검사하다

06 접속부사 채우기 　주변 문맥 파악

해설 빈칸이 콤마와 함께 문장의 맨 앞에 온 접속부사 자리이므로, 앞 문장과 빈칸이 있는 문장의 의미 관계를 파악하여 접속부사인 네 개의 보기 중 하나를 정답으로 골라야 한다. 앞 문장에서 건설 서비스까지 포함하기 위해 사업을 확장하고 있다고 했고, 빈칸이 있는 문장에서는 중요한 역할들을 맡을 자질이 있는 사람들을 찾고 있다고 했으므로, 원인과 결과를 나타내는 문장에서 사용되는 (D) For this reason(이러한 이유로)이 정답이다.

어휘 **on the contrary** 그와는 반대로

07 알맞은 문장 고르기

해석 (A) 여기에는 숙련된 도급업자들과 소매상들이 포함됩니다.
(B) 저희는 고객들에게 여러 비용 효율이 높은 해결책들의 선택 기회를 제공합니다.
(C) 그 행사는 갓 졸업한 대학 졸업자들에게 좋은 기회입니다.
(D) *Davenport Daily News*는 그것을 그 지역 내 최고라고 평가했습니다.

해설 빈칸에 들어갈 알맞은 문장을 고르는 문제이므로 빈칸의 주변 문맥이나 전체 문맥을 파악한다. 앞 문장 'we are seeking qualified individuals to fill crucial roles'에서 중요한 역할들을 맡을 자질이 있는 사람들을 찾고 있다고 했으므로 빈칸에는 모집 중인 일자리와 관련된 내용이 들어가야 함을 알 수 있다. 따라서 (A) These include skilled contractors and tradespeople이 정답이다.

어휘　**contractor** n. 도급업자, 계약자　**tradespeople** n. 소매상, 상인
　　　cost-effective adj. 비용 효율이 높은

08 수식어 거품 채우기

해설　이 문장은 주어(you)가 생략된 명령문으로 동사(include)와 목적어
(references and any documents)를 갖춘 완전한 절이므로 ____ to
past projects는 수식어 거품으로 보아야 한다. 따라서 보기 중 수식어 거
품이 될 수 있는 관계절을 만드는 (C)와 (D)가 정답의 후보이다. 선행사가
any documents이고 '과거 프로젝트와 관련된 모든 서류'라는 의미가 되어
야 하므로 관계절 안에서 주어 역할을 하는 주격 관계대명사 that을 포함한
(D) that relate가 정답이다. (C)는 목적격 관계대명사 that/which가 생략
된 형태의 관계절로, 격이 맞지 않고 '그것이 모든 서류를 과거 프로젝트와 관
련시키다'라는 어색한 문맥이 되어 답이 될 수 없다.

어휘　**relatively** adv. 비교적

09-12는 다음 공고에 관한 문제입니다.

> 저희의 단골 고객님들이 아시다시피, CT Solutions사는 모든 주문을 가능한 한
> 신속하고 안전하게 배송하려고 노력합니다. [09]저희가 20년 전에 시작한 이래로
> 저희의 익일 보장 서비스는 업계의 표준이 되어왔습니다.
>
> 그럼에도 불구하고, 일들은 때때로 저희의 통제를 벗어납니다. [10]이러한 경우,
> 저희가 기대에 부응하지 못할 수도 있습니다. 지난 몇 시간 동안, 북동쪽의 심한
> 눈보라 상황이 도로를 미끄럽게 하고 시야를 좋지 않게 만들었습니다. [11]이것은
> 저희 운전기사들에게 심각한 문제를 야기합니다. 따라서, 기상 상황이 나아지
> 고 저희 트럭들이 안전하게 운행될 수 있을 때까지, 저희는 피해 지역 전역에서
> 배송을 중단할 것입니다. [12]영향을 받는 지역을 확인하시려면, 저희 웹사이트를
> 방문하세요. 고객님들은 또한 저희 모바일 앱에서도 확인하실 수 있습니다. 이
> 것이 발생시킬 수 있는 모든 불편에 대해 진심으로 사과드립니다.
>
> **loyal customer** 단골 고객　　**seek** v. 노력하다, 추구하다
> **swiftly** adv. 신속하게, 즉시　　**securely** adv. 안전하게, 튼튼하게
> **standard** n. 표준, 기준　　**blizzard** n. 눈보라　　**visibility** n. 시야, 가시성
> **suspend** v. 중단하다, 연기하다　　**inconvenience** n. 불편

09 부사절 접속사 채우기

해설　이 문장은 필수성분(Our guaranteed next-day service ~ industry
standard)을 갖춘 완전한 절이므로 ____ we ~ ago는 수식어 거품으
로 보아야 한다. 이 수식어 거품은 동사(started)가 있는 거품절이므로, 거품
절을 이끌 수 있는 부사절 접속사 (A), (C), (D)가 정답의 후보이다. '20년
전에 시작한 이래로 업계의 표준이 되어 왔다'라는 의미가 되어야 하므로
(D) since(~ 이래로)가 정답이다. 전치사 (B) from(~로부터)은 절을 이끌 수
없으므로 답이 될 수 없다.

어휘　**once** conj. 일단 ~하면, ~하는 대로

10 동사 어휘 고르기　주변 문맥 파악

해설　'기대에 부응하는 것을 ____할 수도 있다'라는 문맥이므로 모든 보기가 정
답의 후보이다. 빈칸이 있는 문장만으로 정답을 고를 수 없으므로 주변 문맥
이나 전체 문맥을 파악한다. 앞 문장에서 '일들은 때때로 통제를 벗어난다
(events are sometimes outside of our control)'고 했으므로 기대에 부
응하는 것을 못할 수도 있다는 것을 알 수 있다. 따라서 동사 (B) fail(~하지
않다, 실패하다)이 정답이다.

어휘　**forget** v. 잊다, 잊어버리다　　**happen** v. 우연히 ~하다, 일어나다
　　　decide v. 결정하다, 판단을 내리다

11 명사 어휘 고르기　주변 문맥 파악

해설　'____에게 심각한 문제를 야기한다'라는 문맥이므로 모든 보기가 정답의 후
보이다. 빈칸이 있는 문장만으로 정답을 고를 수 없으므로 주변 문맥이나 전
체 문맥을 파악한다. 뒤 문장에서 '따라서 트럭들이 안전하게 운행될 수 있
을 때까지 피해 지역 전역에서 배송을 중단할 것(Therefore, until ~ our
trucks can be operated safely, we will be suspending deliveries
throughout affected areas.)'이라고 했으므로 트럭을 운행하는 운전기사
들에게 문제를 야기하는 것임을 알 수 있다. 따라서 명사 (D) drivers(운전기
사)가 정답이다.

어휘　**competitor** n. 경쟁자, 참가자　　**technician** n. 기술자　　**parcel** n. 소포, 꾸러미

12 알맞은 문장 고르기

해석　(A) 운송 중에 발생한 손상에 대해 사과드립니다.
　　　(B) 영향을 받는 지역을 확인하시려면, 저희 웹사이트를 방문하세요.
　　　(C) 귀하의 요청은 해당 부서로 전달되었습니다.
　　　(D) 첫 번째 결제 방법이 거절된 경우 다른 결제 방법을 선택하십시오.

해설　빈칸에 들어갈 알맞은 문장을 고르는 문제이므로 빈칸의 주변 문맥이나 전
체 문맥을 파악한다. 앞 문장 'until the weather improves and our
trucks can be operated safely, we will be suspending deliveries
throughout affected areas'에서 기상 상황이 나아지고 트럭들이 안전하
게 운행될 수 있을 때까지 피해 지역 전역에서 배송을 중단할 것이라고 했으
므로 빈칸에는 배송 중단과 관련된 내용이 들어가야 함을 알 수 있다. 따라서
(B) To learn which areas are affected, visit our Web site가 정답이다.

어휘　**transit** n. 운송, 수송　　**appropriate** adj. 알맞은, 적절한

13-16은 다음 이메일에 관한 문제입니다.

> 수신: Gabriela Novak <G_Novak@ecorp.com>
> 발신: Eris사 고객 서비스 <customerservice@eris.com>
> 날짜: 4월 25일
> 제목: E-Max 에스프레소 기계
>
> Gabriela께,
>
> E-Max EM-70에 대한 귀하의 후기에 감사드립니다. [13]귀하께서는 수령하신 제
> 품이 불량인 것 같다고 말씀하셨습니다. 귀하께서는 고운 찌꺼기를 만들어내는
> 것을 방해하는 제품의 분쇄기와 관련된 문제를 언급해주셨습니다.
>
> [14]안타깝게도, 일부 제품들이 불량인 부품과 함께 배송되었습니다. 귀하의 제품
> 이 그것들 중 하나인지 확인하려면, 귀하의 EM-70의 제조일자를 찾아보십시
> 오. [15]이것은 기계의 뒷면에 전원 코드 옆에 인쇄되어 있습니다. 만약 기계가 작
> 년 11월 8일과 11월 15일 사이에 제조되었다면, 그 부품을 포함할 가능성이 높
> 습니다. 이런 경우, 저희는 추가 비용 없이 기꺼이 기계를 새 제품으로 교환해드
> 리겠습니다. [16]귀하께서 선택하신 어떤 주소로든 그것을 배송해드릴 수 있습니
> 다. 만약 그 경우가 아니라면, 저희는 귀하께서 가까운 공인된 수리 센터에 기기
> 를 가져가시기를 추천드립니다.
>
> Ken Sebald 드림
> 고객 서비스 담당자
>
> **review** n. 후기, 검토　　**grinder** n. 분쇄기　　**fine** adj. 고운, 질 높은
> **ground** n. 찌꺼기, 땅　　**defective** adj. 불량의, 결함 있는　　**look up** 찾아보다

13 형용사 어휘 고르기　주변 문맥 파악

해설　'수령한 제품이 ____였다'라는 문맥이므로 모든 보기가 정답의 후보이다.
빈칸이 있는 문장만으로 정답을 고를 수 없으므로 주변 문맥이나 전체 문맥
을 파악한다. 뒤 문장에서 '고운 찌꺼기를 만들어내는 것을 방해하는 제품
의 분쇄기와 관련된 문제를 언급했다(You cited an issue with the unit's
grinder that prevents you from making fine grounds.)'고 했으므로
제품에 문제가 있다는 것을 알 수 있다. 따라서 형용사 (D) faulty(불량인,
잘못된)가 정답이다.

어휘　**satisfactory** adj. 만족스러운, 충분한　　**complete** adj. 완전한, 완성된
　　　genuine adj. 진짜의, 진실한

14 접속부사 채우기　주변 문맥 파악

해설　빈칸이 콤마와 함께 문장의 맨 앞에 온 접속부사 자리이므로, 앞 문장과 빈칸
이 있는 문장의 의미 관계를 파악하여 접속부사인 네 개의 보기 중 하나를 정
답으로 골라야 한다. 앞 문장에서 이메일 수신자가 제품의 분쇄기와 관련된
문제를 언급했다고 했고, 빈칸이 있는 문장에서는 일부 제품들이 불량인 부품
과 함께 배송되었다고 했으므로, 앞에서 언급한 부정적인 상황에 대한 유감을
나타내는 문장에서 사용되는 (C) Unfortunately(안타깝게도, 불행하게도)가
정답이다.

어휘　**later** adv. 나중에, 후에　　**hence** adv. 그러므로
　　　conversely adv. 정반대로, 역으로

15 알맞은 문장 고르기

해석　(A) 저희는 자랑스럽게도 여기 미국에서 저희의 모든 제품들을 생산합니다.

(B) 실제로, 손잡이를 더 높은 곳으로 조정하여 이것을 바로잡을 수 있습니다.
(C) 저희는 귀하의 예약을 더 적절한 시간으로 쉽게 변경할 수 있습니다.
(D) 이것은 기계의 뒷면에 전원 코드 옆에 인쇄되어 있습니다.

해설 빈칸에 들어갈 알맞은 문장을 고르는 문제이므로 빈칸의 주변 문맥이나 전체 문맥을 파악한다. 앞 문장 'please look up the manufacturing date of your EM-70'에서 EM-70의 제조일자를 찾아보라고 했으므로 빈칸에는 제조일자를 확인하는 방법과 관련된 내용이 들어가야 함을 알 수 있다. 따라서 (D) This is printed on the back of the machine next to the power cord가 정답이다.

어휘 correct v. 바로잡다, 수정하다 knob n. 손잡이, 혹

16 인칭대명사 채우기 주변 문맥 파악

해설 '어떤 주소로든 _____을 배송해줄 수 있다'라는 문맥에서 빈칸이 동사의 목적어 자리이므로, 모든 보기가 정답의 후보이다. 빈칸이 있는 문장만으로 정답을 고를 수 없으므로 주변 문맥이나 전체 문맥을 파악한다. 앞 문장에서 기계를 새 제품(a new product)으로 교환해주겠다고 했으므로 빈칸에 들어갈 대명사는 새 제품을 가리킨다. 따라서 3인칭 단수 대명사 (A) it이 정답이다.

Chapter 02 문맥 파악 문제 2: 문장 고르기 문제

예제 해석   p.340

이메일

> 수신: Susan Caldwell <scaldwell@coxfirm.com>
> 발신: Dennis Andrews <dandrews@coxfirm.com>
> 제목: 교육
>
> Ms. Caldwell께,
>
> 관리부는 몇 달 전에 출시된 새로운 회계 소프트웨어를 사용하기로 결정했습니다. 이 프로그램은 사용하기 매우 쉽고 회계사들이 관리부와 재무부에서 하고 있는 업무를 단순화할 것입니다. 이와 관련해서, 저는 전체 회계팀을 위해 당신이 교육을 진행해주시기를 바랍니다. **이것을 당신의 최우선 사항으로 해주시길 바랍니다.** 저희는 다음 달에 이 소프트웨어를 사용할 것으로 예상하기 때문에, 이 강좌는 가능한 한 빨리 열려야 합니다.
>
> Dennis Andrews
> 관리부장
>
> training session 교육 (과정) administrative adj. 관리의
> exceptionally adv. 매우, 유달리 simplify v. 단순화하다
> in this regard 이와 관련해서

해석 (A) 회계 업무는 완료되지 않았습니다.
(B) 저희는 당신이 팀원들에 대해 어떻게 생각하는지 알고 싶습니다.
(C) 이것을 당신의 최우선 사항으로 해주시길 바랍니다.

어휘 priority n. 우선 사항, 우선 순위

Hackers Practice   p.341

유형 연습
01 (A)   02 (B)   03 (C)   04 (B)

01 기사

> 3월 25일 – 미국에 본사를 둔 음료 회사인 BoosTin사는 지난 분기의 성장률이 작년의 같은 기간과 비교하여 두 배가 되었다고 발표했다. 최고 경영자 Robert Cherish은 이 성공을 회사의 시장 조사 덕분으로 돌렸다. 작년에, 회사는 사람들이 그들의 음료에 정말로 원하는 것이 무엇인지를 보여준 소비자 조사를 실시했다. 설문 조사에 근거하여, BoosTin사는 신제품을 발표했는데, 이는 향상된 소비자 만족으로 이어졌다. **그 결과 회사는 이제 훨씬 더 높은 매출을 자랑한다.** Cherish는 "저희의 경험은 소비자의 의견을 얻는 것에 대한 중요성을 보여 ◯

줍니다."라고 덧붙였다.

> beverage n. 음료 base v. ~에 본사를 두다 growth rate 성장률
> quarter n. 분기 attribute A to B A를 B의 덕분으로 돌리다
> consumer n. 소비자 satisfaction n. 만족 demonstrate v. 보여주다

해석 (A) 그 결과 회사는 이제 훨씬 더 높은 매출을 자랑한다.
(B) 소비자들은 회사가 만든 변화를 좋아하지 않았다.
(C) 권장된 변경 사항은 현재 심의 중이다.

해설 **알맞은 문장 고르기** 빈칸에 들어갈 알맞은 문장을 고르는 문제이므로 빈칸의 주변 문맥이나 전체 문맥을 파악한다. 앞 문장 'Based on the survey, BoosTin introduced new products, which led to improved customer satisfaction.'에서 설문 조사에 근거하여 BoosTin사가 신제품을 발표했는데 이는 향상된 소비자 만족으로 이어졌다고 했으므로 빈칸에는 그 결과 회사가 이제 훨씬 더 높은 매출을 자랑한다는 내용이 들어가야 함을 알 수 있다. 따라서 (A) The company now boasts much higher sales as a result가 정답이다.

어휘 boast v. 자랑하다 recommend v. 권장하다, 추천하다
under discussion 심의 중인

02 이메일

> 수신: Gavin Dawson <gdawson@riverviewapartments.com>
> 발신: Vern Casper <vcasper@riverviewapartments.com>
>
> 몇몇 건물 입주자들이 방화문을 열어둔 상태로 방치하는 것을 알게 되었습니다. 방화문은 다른 층으로 불길이 퍼지는 것을 막는 보호벽으로 쓰이기 때문에, 언제나 닫혀 있어야 합니다. 이 규율을 무시하는 것은 위험할 수 있습니다. 그러므로, 귀하께서 복도에 이에 대해 상기시켜 주는 메모를 게시해 주신다면 고맙겠습니다. 그리고 만약 수리가 필요한 방화문을 발견하신다면, 즉시 제게 알려주십시오.
>
> come to one's attention ~을 알게 되다 occupant n. 입주자
> fire door 방화문 leave v. 방치하다, 떠나다 barrier n. 벽 flame n. 불길
> reminder n. 상기시켜 주는 메모, 편지 hallway n. 복도

해석 (A) 저희는 그것들을 없애는 것을 고려하고 있습니다.
(B) 이 규율을 무시하는 것은 위험할 수 있습니다.
(C) 이 문들은 자동으로 닫힐 것입니다.

해설 **알맞은 문장 고르기** 빈칸에 들어갈 알맞은 문장을 고르는 문제이므로 빈칸의 주변 문맥이나 전체 문맥을 파악한다. 앞 문장 'As fire doors serve as a protective barrier, preventing flames from spreading to other floors, they must remain closed at all times.'에서 방화문은 다른 층으로 불길이 퍼지는 것을 막는 보호벽으로 쓰이기 때문에 언제나 닫혀 있어야 한다고 했으므로 빈칸에는 이 규율을 무시하는 것은 위험할 수 있다는 내용이 들어가야 함을 알 수 있다. 따라서 (B) Disregarding this rule can be hazardous가 정답이다.

어휘 disregard v. 무시하다 hazardous adj. 위험한

03 편지

> Mr. Baker께,
>
> 이것은 5월 1일까지 지불하셔야 했던 귀하의 분기 보험료에 대해 상기시켜드리기 위한 것입니다. 납입이 30일 연체되었기 때문에, 저희는 원래 금액에 10퍼센트의 위약금을 적용하여, 총 435.00달러를 지불하실 의무가 있게 되었습니다. 이 문제를 가능한 한 빨리 처리하기 위해 서비스 안내 직원에게 555-0954로 연락하시거나 저희의 지점 중 한 곳을 방문해주십시오. 납입은 늦어도 6월 15일까지 이루어져야 합니다. 그렇지 않으면, 저희는 귀하의 의료 보험을 중단할 수밖에 없습니다.
>
> quarterly adj. 분기의 insurance premium 보험료
> due adj. 지불해야 하는 late adj. 연체된, 지체된 apply v. 적용하다
> penalty n. 위약금, 벌금 owe v. 지불할 의무가 있다
> have no choice but to ~할 수밖에 없다 discontinue v. 중단하다
> coverage n. 보험, 보상

해석 (A) 필요할 경우 회사는 연장을 승인해줄 것입니다.

(B) 보험료는 매월 달라집니다.

(C) 납입은 늦어도 6월 15일까지 이루어져야 합니다.

해설 **알맞은 문장 고르기** 빈칸에 들어갈 알맞은 문장을 고르는 문제이므로 빈칸의 주변 문맥이나 전체 문맥을 파악한다. 앞부분에서 분기 보험료 납입이 연체되었다고 했고, 뒤 문장 'Otherwise, we will have no choice but to discontinue your medical coverage.'에서 그렇지 않으면 의료 보험을 중단할 수밖에 없다고 했으므로 빈칸에는 보험료 납입이 늦어도 6월 15일까지 이루어져야 한다는 내용이 들어가야 함을 알 수 있다. 따라서 (C) Payment must be made by June 15 at the latest가 정답이다.

어휘 **grant** v. 승인하다 **from month to month** 매월 **at the latest** 늦어도

04 광고

> Newtown 문화 센터에서는, 모든 사람들이 멋진 이야기를 말할 수 있는 잠재력을 가지고 있다고 생각합니다. 작문 실력을 발전시키고 싶으시다면, 2주간의 워크숍 또는 일대일 수업에 등록하기 위해 저희를 방문하세요. 저희 프로그램들은 다양한 경험도에 적합합니다. 문법 기본 공부를 다시 하고 싶은 초보자이든 여러 사람들로부터 의견을 구하고 있는 노련한 작가이든, 저희가 드리는 도움은 매우 유용할 것입니다. www.newtownwriting.com에 방문하셔서 저희의 일정을 확인하시고 다가오는 강의에 등록하세요.
>
> **potential** n. 잠재력; adj. 가능성이 있는 **enroll** v. 등록하다
> **one-on-one** adj. 일대일의 **brush up on** ~의 공부를 다시 하다
> **seasoned** adj. 노련한 **invaluable** adj. 매우 유용한

해석 (A) 저희는 현재 초보자를 위한 소설 강좌만 제공하고 있습니다.

(B) 저희 프로그램들은 다양한 경험도에 적합합니다.

(C) 등록은 2주 더 연기되었습니다.

해설 **알맞은 문장 고르기** 빈칸에 들어갈 알맞은 문장을 고르는 문제이므로 빈칸의 주변 문맥이나 전체 문맥을 파악한다. 뒤 문장 'Whether you're a beginner wishing to brush up on grammar essentials or a seasoned author looking for feedback from a group of peers, the help we provide will be invaluable.'에서 문법 기본 공부를 다시 하고 싶은 초보자이든 여러 사람들로부터 의견을 구하고 있는 노련한 작가이든, Newtown 문화 센터에서 주는 도움이 매우 유용할 것이라고 했으므로 빈칸에는 문화 센터의 프로그램이 다양한 경험도에 적합하다는 내용이 들어가야 함을 알 수 있다. 따라서 (B) Our programs are appropriate for various levels of experience가 정답이다.

어휘 **fiction** n. 소설 **appropriate** adj. 적합한 **put off** 연기하다

Hackers Test

p.342

01 (C)	02 (C)	03 (A)	04 (B)	05 (C)
06 (A)	07 (B)	08 (D)	09 (B)	10 (D)
11 (C)	12 (D)	13 (B)	14 (C)	15 (C)
16 (C)				

01-04는 다음 이메일에 관한 문제입니다.

> 발신: Hattie-Mae Slocum <hattie@slocumrealty.com>
> 수신: Peter McAllen <peter@slocumrealty.com>
> 날짜: 8월 4일
> 제목: 영업 기회
>
> Peter께,
>
> 저는 신문에서 Teva 제약 회사가 여기 샬럿에 지사를 열 것이라고 읽었습니다. ⁰¹기사는 6개월 이내에 그 회사가 임원 몇 명을 이곳으로 전근시킬 것임을 언급했습니다. 그들이 새로운 지사로 이동하게 되면, 그들 중 대부분이 집이나, 적어도 임시 숙소 구입에 관심이 있을 것이라고 생각합니다. ⁰²만약 그렇다면, 이것은 우리에게 판매 실적을 낼 수 있는 좋은 기회가 될 것입니다.
>
> ⁰³우리가 회사 숙소를 전문적으로 한다는 것을 알리기 위해 그들의 본사에 연락해볼 수 있을 겁니다. ⁰⁴당신이 그들에게 우리 회사를 소개하는 이메일을 보내주실 수 있나요? 가구가 완전히 갖춰진 우리의 아파트를 특징으로 다루는 소책자를 첨부해주시고, 이곳들이 바로 입주될 수 있다는 점을 반드시 강조해주세요.

> Hattie-Mae 드림
>
> **paper** n. 신문 **regional office** 지사 **article** n. 기사
> **executive** n. 임원, 경영진 **assume** v. ~할 것으로 생각하다
> **in the market for** ~ 구입에 관심이 있는 **at least** 적어도
> **temporary** adj. 임시의, 일시적인 **accommodation** n. 숙소, 적응
> **contact** v. 연락하다 **headquarters** n. 본사 **housing** n. 숙소, 주택
> **firm** n. 회사 **brochure** n. 소책자 **feature** v. 특징으로 삼다, 특별히 포함하다
> **furnished** adj. 가구가 갖춰진 **right away** 바로, 즉시

01 동사 어휘 고르기 주변 문맥 파악

해설 '회사가 임원 몇 명을 이곳으로 ____ 것이다'라는 문맥이므로 (C) transferring (전근시키다)과 (D) hiring(고용하다)이 정답의 후보이다. 빈칸이 있는 문장만으로 정답을 고를 수 없으므로 주변 문맥이나 전체 문맥을 파악한다. 앞 문장에서 'Teva 제약 회사가 이곳에 지사를 열 것(Teva Pharmaceuticals will be opening a regional office here)'이라고 했고, 뒤 문장에서 '그들, 즉 임원들이 새로운 지사로 이동하게 되면(Once they have relocated to the new branch)'이라고 했으므로 임원들이 새로운 지사로 전근할 것임을 알 수 있다. 따라서 동사 (C) transferring이 정답이다.

어휘 **audit** v. (회계 장부 등을) 감사하다; n. 회계 감사 **supply** v. 공급하다, 제공하다

02 알맞은 문장 고르기

해석 (A) 지역 내에 몇몇 다른 새로운 회사들이 있습니다.

(B) 변화는 신입 사원들에게 힘들 수 있습니다.

(C) 만약 그렇다면, 이것은 우리에게 판매 실적을 낼 수 있는 좋은 기회가 될 것입니다.

(D) 이러한 이유로, 저는 귀하의 가장 최근의 매출에 대해 논의하고 싶습니다.

해설 빈칸에 들어갈 알맞은 문장을 고르는 문제이므로 빈칸의 주변 문맥이나 전체 문맥을 파악한다. 앞 문장 'I assume that most of them will be in the market for homes or ~ temporary accommodation'에서 그들, 즉 임원들 대부분이 집이나 임시 숙소 구입에 관심이 있을 것이라고 한 후, 뒷부분에서 아파트에 대한 정보가 포함된 소책자와 함께 자신들의 회사를 소개하는 이메일을 그 회사의 본사로 보내자고 제안했으므로 빈칸에는 임원들의 전근이 자신들의 회사에 미칠 수 있는 영향과 관련된 내용이 들어가야 함을 알 수 있다. 따라서 (C) If so, it would be a great chance for us to make some sales가 정답이다.

어휘 **transition** n. 변화 **make sales** 판매 실적을 내다

03 동사 관련 어구 완성하기

해설 '회사 숙소를 전문적으로 하다'라는 의미가 되어야 하므로 빈칸 뒤의 전치사 in과 함께 쓰여 '~을 전문적으로 하다'라는 의미의 어구를 이루는 동사 (A) specialize가 정답이다. (specialize in: ~을 전문적으로 하다)

어휘 **depend** v. 의존하다, 의지하다 **remain** v. 남다, 머무르다
speculate v. 추측하다

04 현재분사와 과거분사 구별하여 채우기

해설 이 문장은 주어(you), 동사(Could ~ send), 간접 목적어(them), 직접 목적어(an e-mail)를 갖춘 완전한 절이므로 ____ our firm은 수식어 거품으로 보아야 한다. 따라서 명사(e-mail)를 뒤에서 수식할 수 있는 현재분사 (B)와 과거분사 (D)가 정답의 후보이다. 수식 받는 명사(e-mail)와 분사가 '우리 회사를 소개하는 이메일'이라는 의미의 능동 관계이므로 현재분사 (B) introducing이 정답이다. 수식어 거품이 될 수 없는 명사 (A)와 동사 (C)는 답이 될 수 없다.

05-08은 다음 편지에 관한 문제입니다.

> 8월 22일
>
> Mary Slater
> 구매 관리자
> Deli Merchandising사
>
> Ms. Slater께,
>
> 저는 Katz & Picket 냉동 식품 제조사의 직원입니다. ⁰⁵현재까지 몇 달 동안, 저희는 아시아 시장에 진입하는 것을 계획해왔으며 판매업자를 찾고 있습

니다. ⁰⁶귀사가 식료품을 유통하므로, 저희가 제공하는 것을 판매해줄 소매업자를 귀사가 추천해주셨으면 합니다. 저희는 주로 냉동 식품 산업에서 큰 호평을 받은 냉동 채소, 간식, 그리고 유제품을 생산합니다. 저희의 위생적으로 포장된 식품은 모양과 맛뿐만 아니라 영양에 있어서도 우수합니다. 저희의 모든 식품은 식당 직원들과 최고의 요식업자에 의해 맛이 평가됩니다. ⁰⁷귀하께서는 이들의 의견을 저희 웹사이트에서 보실 수 있습니다.

귀하께서 다음 주에 저와 일정을 잡으실 수 있다면, 저는 몇몇 견본품을 가지고 비행편을 마련할 수 있습니다. 귀하께서 이 수익성 있는 기회를 고려하여 저희와 거래를 하셨으면 합니다. ⁰⁸당장은, 저희의 상품 목록 전부를 보실 수 있도록 제가 이 편지에 동봉한 책자를 보시기 바랍니다.

Ross Lange 드림
마케팅 관리자
Katz & Picket 냉동 식품 제조사

representative n. 직원, 대표 frozen food 냉동 식품 look for v. 찾다
dairy product 유제품 acclaim n. 호평, 환호 hygienically adv. 위생적으로
edible n. 식품 superior adj. 우수한 appearance n. 모양, 외관
nutrition n. 영양 personnel n. 직원 profitable adj. 수익성이 있는
for the time being 당장은, 당분간 enclose v. 동봉하다

05 올바른 시제의 동사 채우기

해설 현재까지 몇 달 동안(For some months now) 아시아 시장에 진입하는 것을 계획해왔다는 문맥이므로 몇 달 전부터 현재까지 계속 진행되고 있는 일을 나타내는 현재완료진행 시제 (C) have been planning이 정답이다. 과거완료 시제 (D) had planned는 과거의 특정 시점 이전에 발생한 일을 나타낸다.

06 명사 어휘 고르기 주변 문맥 파악

해설 '자사가 제공하는 것을 판매해줄 _____을 귀사가 추천해주었으면 한다'라는 문맥이므로 (A) retailers(소매업자)와 (D) advertisers(광고주)가 정답의 후보이다. 빈칸이 있는 문장만으로 정답을 고를 수 없으므로 주변 문맥이나 전체 문맥을 파악한다. 앞 문장에서 '우리는 판매업자를 찾고 있다(we ~ are looking for a merchandiser)'고 했으므로 Katz & Picket사가 제공하는 것을 판매해줄 소매업자를 추천해주기를 바라고 있음을 알 수 있다. 따라서 명사 (A) retailers가 정답이다.

어휘 replacement n. 대체, 대체물 commodity n. 상품, 물품

07 알맞은 문장 고르기

해석 (A) 저희는 최고급 식당에서만 식사합니다.
(B) 귀하께서는 이들의 의견을 저희 웹사이트에서 보실 수 있습니다.
(C) 저희는 아시아 시장에 진입했을 때 긍정적인 반응을 얻었습니다.
(D) 저희의 회의는 계획대로 다음 주에 진행될 것입니다.

해설 빈칸에 들어갈 알맞은 문장을 고르는 문제이므로 빈칸의 주변 문맥이나 전체 문맥을 파악한다. 앞 문장 'All of our food items are taste-tested by restaurant personnel and top caterers.'에서 모든 식품이 식당 직원들과 최고의 요식업자에 의해 맛이 평가된다고 하며 평가에 대해 설명하고 있으므로 빈칸에는 이들의 의견과 관련된 내용이 들어가야 함을 알 수 있다. 따라서 (B) You may view their comments on our Web site가 정답이다.

어휘 dine v. 식사하다

08 형용사 자리 채우기

해설 명사(product list)를 꾸미기 위해서는 분사 (B)나 형용사 (D)가 와야 한다. '상품 목록의 전부'라는 의미가 되어야 하므로 (B) completing(완료시키는)이 아닌 형용사 (D) complete(전부의, 완전한)가 정답이다.

09-12는 다음 공고에 관한 문제입니다.

공고: 고등학교 체육관 건설의 입찰

1975년 이후로, Roosevelt 고등학교의 학생들은 체육 수업과 스포츠 활동에 같은 체육관을 사용해왔습니다. ⁰⁹하지만, 이 건물은 이제 낡고 허름하며, 많은 장비들이 교체될 필요가 있습니다. 학교 관계자들은 새로운 체육관을 건설하기 위한 예산안을 최근에 승인했으며 토건업자들에게 이를 짓기 위해 입찰할 것을 요청하고 있습니다. ¹⁰신청하기 위해, 토건업자는 자격증을 소지하고 있어야 ◑

하며 학교 체육관 건설 경력이 있어야 합니다. ¹¹4월 15일 전에 제출되어야 할 신청서와 함께, 입찰자들은 지난 5년간 완공했던 건설 프로젝트의 포트폴리오를 제공해야 합니다. 또한 그들은 프로젝트를 완료하는 데 사용할 자재와 장비의 설명뿐만 아니라, 직원의 목록과 그들의 이력서를 포함해야 합니다. ¹²이 요건을 충족하는 사람들만 연락을 받을 것입니다. 더 자세한 정보를 원하시면, 저희 웹사이트에 방문해주십시오.

bid n. 입찰 gymnasium n. 체육관, 경기장 physical education n. 체육
shabby adj. 허름한 budget n. 예산(안) application n. 신청서
personnel n. 직원, 인원 résumé n. 이력서 description n. 설명, 종류

09 주어와 수일치하는 동사 채우기

해설 접속사(and) 뒤에 온 절에 동사가 없으므로 동사 (A), (B), (D)가 정답의 후보이다. 주어(much of the equipment)가 단수로 취급되는 수량 표현이므로 단수 동사 (B) needs가 정답이다. 참고로, 부분이나 전체를 나타내는 표현이 주어로 쓰이면 of 뒤의 명사에 동사를 수일치시켜야 한다.

10 형용사 어휘 고르기

해설 '신청하기 위해, 토건업자는 자격증을 소지하고 있어야 한다'라는 문맥이 되어야 하므로 형용사 (D) licensed(자격증을 소지한)가 정답이다. (A) realistic은 '현실적인', (B) instructional은 '교육용의', (C) moderate는 '보통의'라는 의미이다.

11 전치사 채우기

해설 '4월 15일 전에 제출되어야 할 신청서와 함께, 포트폴리오를 제공해야 한다'라는 의미가 되어야 하므로 (C) Along with(~와 함께, ~에 덧붙여)가 정답이다.

어휘 except for ~을 제외하고는 in accordance with ~에 따라
as regards ~과 관련하여

12 알맞은 문장 고르기

해설 (A) 체육 수업은 현재 중단되었습니다.
(B) 이 프로젝트는 이제 건설의 두 번째 단계에 있습니다.
(C) 관계자들은 조만간 예산안을 승인할 계획입니다.
(D) 이 요건을 충족하는 사람들만 연락을 받을 것입니다.

해설 빈칸에 들어갈 알맞은 문장을 고르는 문제이므로 빈칸의 주변 문맥이나 전체 문맥을 파악한다. 앞부분에서 입찰자들은 신청서와 함께 지난 5년간 완공했던 건설 프로젝트의 포트폴리오를 제공해야 한다고 했고, 앞 문장 'They must ~ include a list of their personnel and their résumés, as well as a description of the materials and equipment they will use to complete the project.'에서 프로젝트를 완료하는 데 사용할 자재와 장비의 설명뿐만 아니라 직원의 목록과 그들의 이력서를 포함해야 한다고 하며 신청을 위해 필요한 요건을 나열하고 있으므로, 빈칸에는 이 요건을 충족하는 사람들만 연락을 받을 것이라는 내용이 들어가야 함을 알 수 있다. 따라서 (D) Only those who meet the requirements will be contacted가 정답이다.

어휘 suspend v. 중단하다 phase n. 단계, 국면

13-16은 다음 기사에 관한 문제입니다.

¹³지속적인 건강 질환으로 약을 복용하는 환자들에게 좋은 소식이 있다. 보건부는 5월 1일부로 여러 가지 만성 질환으로 고통을 겪는 사람들은 그들의 의사로부터 최초의 처방전을 받기만 하면 된다고 말했다. 그 이후, 환자들은 그들의 처방전대로 조제해줄 약국을 온라인으로 간단히 고를 수 있을 것이다. ¹⁴일단 요청서가 제출되면, 이 요청서에 대한 접근 권한이 선택된 약국에 주어질 것이다. ¹⁵환자들은 유효한 신분증만 가져가면 되고, 약사는 그들의 약을 조제해줄 것이다.

지금까지, 천식이나 알레르기 같은 만성 질환을 가진 많은 사람들은 그저 그들의 처방전을 받기 위해 어쩔 수 없이 여러 차례 의사를 방문해야 했다. ¹⁶보건부 장관 Diedre Meyer는 "이들에게 필요한 약은 항상 일정하기 때문에, 현재의 절차는 사실 매우 비효율적입니다."라고 말했다. Ms. Meyer는 새로운 전자 처방전 서비스가 이 문제를 해결하기를 희망한다.

chronic ailment 만성 질환 initial adj. 최초의, 초기의
prescription n. 처방전 pharmacy n. 약국 fill v. 처방전대로 조제하다
grant v. 주다, 승인하다 medication n. 약 asthma n. 천식 ◑

force v. (어쩔 수 없이) ~하게 하다 repeatedly adv. 여러 차례, 되풀이하여
needs n. 필요한 것 procedure n. 절차, 수순 electronic adj. 전자의

13 알맞은 문장 고르기

해석 (A) 전문가에 따르면, 약제비와 의료 보험 비용이 상승하고 있다.
(B) 지속적인 건강 질환으로 약을 복용하는 환자들에게 좋은 소식이 있다.
(C) 약국들이 엄격한 법률의 적용을 받게 될 것이라고 최근에 발표되었다.
(D) 제의된 보험 제도는 처방 약제의 가격을 현저히 감소시킬 수 있다.

해설 빈칸에 들어갈 알맞은 문장을 고르는 문제이므로 빈칸의 주변 문맥이나 전체
문맥을 파악한다. 뒤 문장 'those suffering from ~ chronic ailments will
only have to get an initial prescription from their doctors starting
May 1'에서 5월 1일부로 만성 질환으로 고통을 겪는 사람들은 의사로부터
최초의 처방전을 받기만 하면 될 것이라고 한 후, 뒷부분에서 만성 질환을 가
진 사람들에게 비효율적이었던 현재의 절차를 대신할 새로운 절차에 대해 설
명하고 있으므로 빈칸에는 만성 질환을 겪는 사람들을 위한 새로운 소식이 있
다는 내용이 들어가야 함을 알 수 있다. 따라서 (B) There is good news
for patients taking medication for persistent health conditions가 정
답이다.

Paraphrasing
chronic ailment 만성 질환 → persistent health conditions 지속적인 건
강 질환

어휘 medicine n. 약제, 약 healthcare n. 의료 보험, 건강 관리
on the rise 상승하는 legislation adj. 법률, 법규
insurance program 보험 제도 prescription medication 처방 약제

14 부사절 접속사 채우기

해설 이 문장은 주어(access to them), 동사(will be granted)를 갖춘 완전한 절
이므로 _____ the requests are submitted는 수식어 거품으로 보아야 한
다. 이 수식어 거품은 동사(are submitted)가 있는 거품절이므로, 거품절을
이끌 수 있는 부사절 접속사 (A), (B), (C), (D)가 모두 정답의 후보이다. '일
단 요청서가 제출되면 접근 권한이 선택된 약국에 주어질 것이다'라는 의미가
되어야 하므로 (C) Once(일단 ~하면)가 정답이다.

어휘 while conj. ~인 반면에 unless conj. ~가 아닌 이상
before conj. ~하기 전에

15 동사 어휘 고르기

해설 '환자들은 유효한 신분증만 가져가면 되고, 약사는 그들의 약을 조제해줄 것
이다'라는 문맥이므로 동사 (C) dispense(조제하다, 내어주다)가 정답이다.
(A) relieve는 '완화하다', (B) separate는 '분리하다', (D) consider는 '고
려하다'라는 의미이다.

16 형용사 어휘 고르기 전체 문맥 파악

해설 '절차가 매우 _____하다'라는 문맥이므로 (B) complicated(복잡한)와 (C)
inefficient(비효율적인)가 정답의 후보이다. 빈칸이 있는 문장만으로 정답을
고를 수 없으므로 주변 문맥이나 전체 문맥을 파악한다. 앞부분에서 만성 질
환으로 고통을 겪는 사람들은 의사로부터 최초의 처방전을 받기만 하면 될
것이라고 한 후, 앞 문장에 '만성 질환을 가진 많은 사람들은 그저 그들의
처방전을 받기 위해 어쩔 수 없이 여러 차례 의사를 방문해야 했다'(many
people with chronic conditions ~ have been forced to visit doctors
repeatedly just to get their prescriptions)고 했으므로 만성 질환 환자들
에게 처방전을 받기 위해 여러 차례 의사를 방문해야 하는 절차는 비효율적임
을 알 수 있다. 따라서 형용사 (C) inefficient가 정답이다.

어휘 unaffected adj. 영향을 받지 않는 incompetent adj. 무능한

Section 1 질문 유형별 공략

Chapter 01 주제/목적 찾기 문제

예제 해석 p.354

광고

> Wiggles 반려동물 용품점 ... 여러분의 반려동물이 필요로 하는 모든 것! 시애틀에 있는 반려동물 주인들은 필요한 모든 반려동물 용품들을 한 곳에서 다 살 수 있는 상점을 원하는데, Renton가 235번지에 새로 개점한 Wiggles 반려동물 용품점이 바로 그들을 위한 상점입니다! 우리는 고양이와 개를 위해 개집, 액세서리, 샴푸 및 빗을 포함한 다양한 제품들을 제공합니다. 오직 이번 주에만, 모든 반려동물용 식품이 정가에서 30퍼센트 할인됩니다. 주중 어느 날이든 오전 9시부터 오후 8시까지 방문해 주십시오.
>
> need v. 필요로 하다; n. 필요한 것 one-stop adj. 한 곳에서 다 살 수 있는
> wide adj. 다양한, 넓은 kennel n. 개집 regular adj. 정규의, 정식의

문제 광고의 목적은 무엇인가?
(A) 최근에 설립된 상점을 홍보하기 위해
(B) 새로운 반려동물 액세서리 라인을 소개하기 위해
(C) 가축병 치료와 관련된 서비스 이용을 장려하기 위해

어휘 established adj. 설립된, 확립된
veterinary adj. 가축병 치료와 관련된, 수의의

Hackers Practice p.355

Paraphrasing 연습
01 (B) 02 (B) 03 (A) 04 (A) 05 (B)
06 (A) 07 (B) 08 (A)

유형 연습
09 (A) 10 (B) 11 (C) 12 (A)

01

> Melrose 은행은 특별 은행 서비스에 가입한 일부 고객들이 추가 현금 자동 입출금기 수수료를 내고 있었음을 최근에 발견했습니다. 이 현금 자동 입출금기 수수료는 다음 주에 고객들의 계좌로 상환될 것입니다.
>
> (A) 은행의 고객들은 더 이상 현금 자동 입출금기 수수료를 내지 않을 것이다.
> (B) 은행은 은행 계좌를 통해 고객들에게 돈을 상환할 것이다.

해설 답의 근거 문장은 'This ATM fee will be reimbursed to our clients' accounts next week.'으로 (B)가 정답이다. reimburse가 repay로 바뀌어 표현되었다.

어휘 sign up for ~에 가입하다, 등록하다 reimburse v. 상환하다

02

> Protect-It 플라스틱 용기는 비바람으로부터 무엇이든 보호하는 데 효과적입니다. 일반 저장 용기는 물이 들어가지 않게 할 수 없지만, Protect-It 제품은 습기가 용기에 스미는 것을 막아주는 특허 받은 뚜껑과 폐쇄 장치를 갖추고 있습니다. ○

(A) Protect-It 용기는 많은 양의 물을 담을 수 있다.
(B) Protect-It 용기는 방수 소재로 만들어진다.

해설 답의 근거가 되는 부분은 'Protect-It products have patented lids and closure mechanisms that prevent moisture from entering the container'로 (B)가 정답이다. prevent moisture from entering이 water-resistant로 바뀌어 표현되었다.

어휘 elements n. 비바람, 자연력 keep out ~이 들어가지 않게 하다
patented adj. 특허 받은 closure n. 폐쇄 moisture n. 습기
water-resistant adj. 방수의

03

> Capital Alliance사는 회계학 학위를 소지한 공인회계사를 찾고 있습니다. 이상적인 후보자는 3년에서 5년의 회계 감사 및 회계 분야 경력이 있어야 합니다.
>
> (A) 대학 학위가 이 직위의 요건이다.
> (B) 최신 회계 원리에 대한 지식이 요구된다.

해설 답의 근거 문장은 'Capital Alliance Incorporated is looking for a CPA with a degree in accounting.'으로 (A)가 정답이다. degree가 diploma로 바뀌어 표현되었다.

어휘 CPA(= certified public accountant) 공인회계사 degree n. 학위
auditing n. 회계 감사 diploma n. 학위 requirement n. 요건, 필요 조건

04

> 상승하는 휘발유 가격이 트럭과 승용차 판매에 장기적인 부진을 초래했기 때문에 최고의 두 자동차 회사는 생산량을 줄이려고 계획 중이다. 재고 산적에 직면한 Ace 자동차 회사와 Townsend 자동차 회사는 다음 두 분기 동안 생산을 15퍼센트 줄일 것이다.
>
> (A) 저조한 판매는 최고의 자동차 제조업체들이 생산을 줄이도록 하고 있다.
> (B) 감소된 생산량은 상승하는 연료비를 상쇄할 수 있다.

해설 답의 근거 문장은 'The top two car companies are planning to trim production as the increasing cost of gasoline has caused a prolonged slump in sales of trucks and cars.'로 (A)가 정답이다. trim이 cut으로, slump in sales가 Poor sales로 바뀌어 표현되었다.

어휘 trim v. 줄이다, 삭감하다 prolonged adj. 장기적인, 오래 끄는
slump n. 부진, 불경기 inventory n. 재고 pileup n. 산적, 쌓임, 밀림
quarter n. 분기 offset v. 상쇄하다

05

> Paradise 해변 리조트에서 여러분의 체류가 즐거울 수 있도록, 청결에 관한 우리 규칙에 엄격한 주의를 기울여 주시기 바랍니다. 쓰레기나 엎질러진 액체는 제거가 어렵고 비용이 많이 들기 때문에, 오두막을 더러운 상태로 방치하는 손님은 오두막 사용을 위한 100달러의 열쇠 보증금을 잃게 될 것입니다.
>
> (A) 방 열쇠를 잃어버린 손님들은 보증금을 받지 못할 것이다.
> (B) 오두막을 깨끗하게 해놓지 않으면 보증금이 환불되지 않을 것이다.

해설 답의 근거가 되는 부분은 'guests who leave their huts dirty will forfeit the $100 key deposit for use of a hut'으로 (B)가 정답이다. leave ~ dirty가 not left clean으로, forfeit이 not be refunded로 바뀌어 표현되었다.

어휘 pay attention to ~에 주의를 기울이다 costly adj. 비용이 많이 드는, 비싼
spill v. 엎지르다 hut n. 오두막 forfeit v. 잃다, 상실하다, 박탈당하다
deposit n. 보증금; v. 예금하다 refund v. 환불하다

06

> Wells 시민 문화 회관은 지역 사회 내 저소득층 가정의 아이들을 위한 컴퓨터 구매 비용을 충당하기 위해 금전 기부를 얻으려 하고 있습니다.
>
> (A) 개인이 낸 돈은 컴퓨터 구매에 자금을 공급하는 데 쓰일 것이다.
> (B) 중고 컴퓨터의 기부가 요청되고 있다.

해설 답의 근거가 되는 부분은 'monetary donations to cover the cost of buying computers'로 (A)가 정답이다. monetary donations가 Private money로, cover the cost가 finance로, buying이 purchase로 바뀌어 표현되었다.

어휘 seek v. 얻으려 하다, 찾다 monetary adj. 금전의, 재정의 donation n. 기부 low-income adj. 저소득의 finance v. ~에 자금을 공급하다

07

> 홍콩의 Cabot Systems사는 미국에 본사를 둔 휴대폰 멀티미디어 기술 회사인 Flexpoint사를 매입하는 과정에 있다. Cabot Systems사는 Flexpoint사의 기술을 이용해 휴대폰 업계에서 우위를 차지하는 공급자가 되고자 한다.
>
> (A) 두 회사가 휴대폰 생산 협정문에 서명했다.
> (B) Cabot Systems사는 시장의 지배권을 잡기 위해 Flexpoint사를 사들이고 있다.

해설 답의 근거가 되는 부분은 'Cabot Systems in Hong Kong is in the process of acquiring US-based Flexpoint'와 'Cabot Systems wants to be the dominant supplier for the mobile industry by using Flexpoint's technologies.'로 (B)가 정답이다. acquiring이 buying out으로 바뀌어 표현되었다. dominant supplier 역시 정답의 to gain control of the market에 대한 단서가 된다.

어휘 be in the process of ~하는 과정이다 acquire v. 매입하다, 취득하다 dominant adj. 우위를 차지하는, 지배적인 buy out 사들이다, 매수하다

08

> 곧 은퇴할 예정인 *JOC*지 편집장 Bill Conley는 객원 편집장이 *The Journal of Commerce (JOC)*지 11월호를 감독하게 한 후, 이제는 편집장 자리에 대한 지원서를 받고 있다. Mr. Conley는 자신의 후임자를 고르는 데 적극적으로 관여하고 있다고 말했다.
>
> (A) *JOC*지의 편집장은 자신의 후임자를 찾고 있다.
> (B) 객원 편집장이 영구적으로 인계받을 것이다.

해설 답의 근거 문장은 'Mr. Conley said that he is having an active hand in selecting his own replacement.'로 (A)가 정답이다. replacement가 successor로 바뀌어 표현되었다.

어휘 supervise v. 감독하다, 관리하다 soon-to-retire adj. 곧 은퇴할 예정인 have a hand in ~에 관여하다 replacement n. 후임자, 대체물 successor n. 후임자 take over 인계받다, 넘겨받다

09 이메일

> 귀하의 일본 출장을 위한 여행 일정표 한 부를 발송하였습니다. 세부 사항을 검토하시고 필요한 어떤 변경이든 제게 알려 주십시오. 일정이 괜찮으시다면, 이 이메일에 답장을 보내 확정해 주십시오.
>
> forward v. 발송하다 itinerary n. 일정표, 여행 계획 confirm v. 확정하다

문제 이메일은 왜 쓰였는가?
(A) 여행 정보의 확인을 요청하기 위해
(B) 숙소 변경에 대한 공지를 제공하기 위해
(C) 출장 일정을 요청하기 위해

해설 **주제/목적 찾기 문제** 이메일이 쓰인 목적을 묻는 목적 찾기 문제이다. 특별히 이 문제는 지문 마지막 부분에 목적 관련 내용이 언급되었음에 유의한다. 'If the schedule is fine, please confirm by replying to this e-mail.'에서 일정이 괜찮다면 이메일에 답장을 보내 확정해 달라고 했으므로 (A) To request confirmation of trip information이 정답이다.

Paraphrasing
schedule 일정 → trip information 여행 정보

어휘 accommodation n. 숙소, 숙박

10 기사

> The National Aviation Authority (NAA)는 국내선 항공권 비용이 지난해에 비해 10퍼센트 가까이 증가했음을 보여주는 보고서를 어제 공개했다. 이 보고서는 오르는 연료비는 단지 부분적으로만 책임이 있다는 것을 보여주었다. 수하물, 유류 할증 및 좌석 선택 요금과 같이 "숨겨진 요금"에 관한 승객들의 부정적인 의견에 대한 반응으로, 많은 국내 항공사들은 이전 가격 체계로 되돌아갔고 이러한 요금들을 항공 운임에 포함시키고 있다. 따라서 항공권 가격이 올라간 것처럼 보일지라도, 이 인상은 사실 승객들에게는 큰 영향을 미치지 않을 수도 있다.
>
> domestic adj. 국내의 be to blame ~에 대한 책임이 있다 partially adv. 부분적으로 hidden adj. 숨겨진 surcharge n. 할증료 carrier n. 항공사

문제 기사에서 주로 논의되는 것은 무엇인가?
(A) 연료비가 항공 산업에 미치는 영향
(B) 오르는 서비스 가격의 원인
(C) 국내에서 여행하는 승객의 증가

해설 **주제/목적 찾기 문제** 기사에서 주로 논의되는 것을 묻는 주제 찾기 문제이다. 특별히 이 문제는 전체 지문을 요약하여 주제를 찾아야 한다. 'the cost of domestic flights has increased by nearly 10 percent compared to last year'에서 국내선 항공권 비용이 지난해에 비해 10퍼센트 가까이 증가했다고 한 후, 'rising gas prices'와 'charges for baggage, fuel surcharges, and seat selection'에서 오르는 연료비와 수하물, 유류 할증 및 좌석 선택 요금을 항공권 비용이 증가한 이유로 나열하고 있으므로 (B) The reasons for rising prices of a service가 정답이다.

Paraphrasing
the cost of domestic flights 국내선 항공권 비용 → prices of a service 서비스의 가격

11 편지

> 저는 귀하의 단체가 다가오는 자선 경매를 위한 미술품 기증을 기다리고 있다는 것을 한 동료로부터 들었습니다. 저는 도자기 조각품들을 만드는 지역 미술가이며 행사를 위해 한 점의 품목을 기꺼이 제공하고자 합니다. 어디로 조각품을 가져가야 하는지와 언제까지 그것이 필요하신지 제게 알려 주시기 바랍니다. 또한, 미술품이 팔리지 않으면 어떤 일이 생길지도 말씀해 주시겠습니까?
>
> charity n. 자선 ceramic n. 도자기 sculpture n. 조각품

문제 편지의 한 가지 목적은 무엇인가?
(A) 미술관의 일자리에 대해 물어보기 위해
(B) 전시회에 입장을 요청하기 위해
(C) 행사를 위한 기증을 제안하기 위해

해설 **주제/목적 찾기 문제** 편지의 목적을 묻는 목적 찾기 문제이다. 특별히 이 문제는 지문의 중반에 목적 관련 내용이 언급되었음에 유의한다. 'I ~ would be happy to provide an item for the event.'에서 행사를 위해 한 점의 품목을 기꺼이 제공하겠다고 했으므로 (C) To offer a donation for an event가 정답이다.

12 공고

> 관리진은 Rockport Towers의 모든 세입자들께 건물이 새로운 재활용 체계를 실시할 것임을 알려 드립니다. 재활용품을 위한 새로운 컨테이너들은 건물 1층의 2번 출구 뒤 쓰레기장에서 이제 이용할 수 있습니다. 컨테이너들은 유리, 종이 및 금속 물질에 대해 이용 가능합니다. 사용된 건전지와 잉크 카트리지와 같은 물품들을 위해 마련된 더 작은 컨테이너 또한 있습니다. 귀하의 물품들을 알맞게 처분해주시기를 정중히 요청드립니다. 또한, 모든 유리 및 금속 용기는 내부에 남은 액체가 없음을 확실히 해주시기 바랍니다. 귀하의 협조에 감사드립니다.
>
> tenant n. 세입자, 임차인 implement v. 실시하다 dispose v. 처분하다 appropriately adv. 알맞게 liquid n. 액체 cooperation n. 협조

문제 공고되고 있는 것은 무엇인가?

(A) 폐기를 위한 지침
(B) 이사를 위한 절차
(C) 건물 직원들을 위한 정책

해설 **주제/목적 찾기 문제** 공고되는 것을 묻는 주제 찾기 문제이므로 지문의 앞부분을 주의 깊게 확인한다. 'the building will be implementing a new recycling system'에서 건물이 새로운 재활용 체계를 실시할 것이라고 한 후, 재활용품을 위한 컨테이너 위치 및 폐기 방법을 안내하고 있으므로 (A) Guidelines for disposal이 정답이다.

Hackers Test

p.358

01 (D)	02 (B)	03 (A)	04 (B)	05 (B)
06 (C)				

01-04는 다음 이메일에 관한 문제입니다.

발신: Patricia Sutherland <psuth@adelaideleather.com>
수신: Timothy Cunning <timcun@zoomail.com>
날짜: 3월 7일
제목: 귀하의 주문

Mr. Cunning께,

2월 2일 자사 웹사이트에서의 ⁰¹여행 가방 주문에 관한 귀하의 메시지를 어제 받았습니다. 귀하께서는 물건이 아직 도착하지 않았다고 말씀하셨습니다. 이것이 제가 가지고 있는 정보입니다:

주문 번호: 887598
품목: Lennox 검은색 에나멜가죽 기내 반입용 여행 가방 모델 344번
가격: 122.76달러 (세금 포함)
⁰²발송일: 2월 5일
수신인: Timothy Cunning, 6522번지 Swan Lake로, Raymont 아이다호주 99877

이 정보가 맞는지 확인해 주시기 바랍니다. 저는 배달 서비스 제공업체에 연락했고, ⁰³그들은 물건의 소재를 파악할 수 없었습니다. 불편에 대해 깊이 사과드립니다. ⁰³저는 귀하께 전액 환불을 제공해 드리거나 또 다른 여행 가방을 보내드릴 수 있습니다. 귀하께서 무엇을 선호하시는지 알려 주시기 바랍니다. 또한, 이 실수를 보상하기 위해, ⁰⁴추후 어떤 구매에도 사용하실 수 있는 30달러 상당의 상품권을 첨부해 드립니다.

다시 한번, 실수에 대한 유감을 표시하고자 합니다. 귀하의 인내와 이해에 진심으로 감사드립니다.

Patricia Sutherland 드림
고객 서비스 상담원
Adelaide Leather Goods사

indicate v. 말하다, 알리다 **patent leather** 에나멜가죽 **locate** v. 소재를 파악하다, 놓다 **make up for** ~을 보상하다, 만회하다 **voucher** n. 상품권, 쿠폰 **express one's regret** 유감을 표시하다

01 주제/목적 찾기 문제

문제 Ms. Sutherland는 왜 Mr. Cunning에게 글을 썼는가?

(A) 기업에 대한 정보를 제공하기 위해
(B) 구매품의 배달을 확인하기 위해
(C) 서비스의 이용 가능성에 대해 문의하기 위해
(D) 그의 이전 문의에 대해 응답하기 위해

해설 Ms. Sutherland가 Mr. Cunning에게 글을 쓴 목적을 묻는 목적 찾기 문제이므로 지문의 앞부분을 주의 깊게 확인한다. 'I received your message yesterday regarding the order of a suitcase'(1문단 1번째 줄)에서 여행 가방 주문에 관한 메시지를 받았다고 한 후, 주문 정보 확인을 요청하고 주문이 어떻게 처리될지를 안내하고 있으므로 받은 메시지에 대해 답변하는 이메일임을 알 수 있다. 따라서 (D) To respond to his previous inquiry가 정답이다.

어휘 **availability** n. 이용 가능성 **inquiry** n. 문의

02 육하원칙 문제

문제 언제 Mr. Cunning의 구매품이 보내졌는가?

(A) 2월 2일에
(B) 2월 5일에
(C) 3월 6일에
(D) 3월 7일에

해설 Mr. Cunning의 구매품이 언제(When) 보내졌는지를 묻는 육하원칙 문제이다. 질문의 핵심 어구인 purchase sent와 관련하여, 'Shipped on: February 5'(2문단 4번째 줄)에서 발송일이 2월 5일이라고 했으므로 (B) On February 5가 정답이다.

Paraphrasing
Shipped 발송된 → sent 보내진

03 육하원칙 문제

문제 Ms. Sutherland는 무엇을 하겠다고 제안하는가?

(A) 분실된 물건에 대한 대체품을 보낸다
(B) 구매품을 더 새로운 모델로 교환한다
(C) 부분 환불을 제공한다
(D) 고객의 정보를 갱신한다

해설 Ms. Sutherland가 무엇(What)을 하겠다고 제안하는지를 묻는 육하원칙 문제이다. 질문의 핵심 어구인 offer to do와 관련하여 'they have been unable to locate the item'(3문단 2번째 줄)에서 배달 서비스 제공업체에서 물건의 소재를 파악할 수 없었다고 한 후, 'I can ~ send out another suitcase.'(3문단 2번째 줄)에서 또 다른 여행 가방을 보내줄 수 있다고 했으므로 (A) Send a replacement for a lost item이 정답이다.

Paraphrasing
unable to locate 소재를 파악할 수 없는 → lost 분실된

어휘 **replacement** n. 대체품, 교환품

04 육하원칙 문제

문제 Ms. Sutherland는 무엇을 Mr. Cunning에게 보냈는가?

(A) 갱신된 송장
(B) 신용 상품권
(C) 주문 양식
(D) 제품 카탈로그

해설 Ms. Sutherland가 무엇(What)을 Mr. Cunning에게 보냈는지를 묻는 육하원칙 문제이다. 질문의 핵심 어구인 send to Mr. Cunning과 관련하여 'I am attaching a voucher for $30 that you may use for any future purchase'(3문단 4번째 줄)에서 추후 어떤 구매에도 사용할 수 있는 30달러 상당의 상품권을 첨부한다고 했으므로 (B) A credit voucher가 정답이다.

05-06은 다음 공고와 이메일에 관한 문제입니다.

*Global Geography*지
⁰⁵지금 자유 기고가들로부터 투고를 받고 있습니다!

*Global Geography*지는 과학, 역사 및 문화계에 관심 있는 자유 기고가들을 지금 찾고 있다는 것을 알려 드리게 되어 기쁩니다. ⁰⁵기사에 대한 아이디어가 있으시면, 다음을 포함한 제안서를 간단하게 제출하십시오:

• 이름, 주소, 전화번호 및 이메일 주소
• 작문 견본 (200단어 이하)
• 집필하고 싶은 기사의 개요
• 집필했던 출판물의 목록 (해당되는 경우)

우리 편집팀이 여러분의 제안서를 검토할 것이고, 여러분의 기사가 출판을 위해 선정되면, 다음의 급여 체계를 제공합니다:

200-500단어 짧은 기사	300달러와 *Global Geography*지 1년 구독
501-800단어 정규 기사	500달러와 *Global Geography*지 1년 구독
801 단어 이상 특집 기사	900달러와 *Global Geography*지 2년 구독
표지 기사	1,200달러와 *Global Geography*지 2년 구독

* 구독은 매년 *12*부에 해당합니다.

*Global Geography*지는 의뢰되지 않은 기사는 받지 않으므로, 먼저 저희에 ↻

게 연락해 주십시오. 문의는 submissions@globalgeography.com으로 보내주십시오.

submission n. 투고, 제출, 제안   **freelance writer** 자유 기고가
editorial adj. 편집의   **unsolicited** adj. 의뢰되지 않은, 자발적인

수신: Christopher Gluck <chrisgluck@dmail.com>
발신: Cassandra Hitchens <submissions@globalgeography.com>
제목: 회신: 투고 제안   writercontract.word
날짜: 9월 21일

Mr. Gluck께,

[06]귀하의 집필 제안서가 편집부 직원들에 의해 승인되었음을 알려 드리게 되어 기쁩니다. 저희는 귀하의 아이디어에 매우 깊은 인상을 받았으며, 귀하의 수중 고고학에 대한 기사를 기대합니다. 기사의 마감일은 12월 1일입니다. 편집과 수정 후에, 2월호에 발행될 것을 기대하실 수 있습니다.

이 이메일에 기고가 계약서를 첨부했습니다. 꼼꼼히 읽어보시고, 서명해서, (509) 555-9988로 팩스를 보내주시거나 스캔한 사본을 이메일로 보내주십시오.

보수는 12월 31일까지 송금될 것입니다. 900달러의 보수가 귀하의 계좌로 송금될 수 있도록 필요한 은행 정보도 보내주셔야 합니다.

귀하의 관심에 감사드리며, 귀하의 기사를 읽게 되기를 간절히 바랍니다.

Cassandra Hitchens, 투고부 부국장 드림

approve v. 승인하다   **underwater archaeology** 수중 고고학
revision n. 수정, 개정   **remit** v. 송금하다   **wire** v. 송금하다; n. 선

05 주제/목적 찾기 문제

문제   공고는 주로 무엇에 대한 것인가?

(A) 구독료 변경
(B) 투고 방법
(C) 다가오는 작문 대회
(D) 새로운 잡지 발매

해설   공고가 주로 무엇에 대한 것인지를 묻는 주제 찾기 문제이므로 공고의 내용을 확인한다. 첫 번째 지문인 공고의 'Now accepting submissions from freelance writers!'(제목 2번째 줄)에서 지금 자유 기고가들로부터 투고를 받고 있다고 했고, 'If you have an idea for an article, simply submit a proposal including the following:'(1문단 2번째 줄)에서 기사에 대한 아이디어가 있으면 제안서를 제출하라고 한 후, 제안서에 포함시켜야 할 내용을 나열하고 제안서가 어떻게 처리되는지 설명하고 있으므로 (B) A system for submissions가 정답이다.

06 주제/목적 찾기 문제

문제   Ms. Hitchens는 왜 이메일을 썼는가?

(A) 요청된 은행 정보를 제공하기 위해
(B) 구독료 납입을 요청하기 위해
(C) 기고가에게 투고에 대해 알리기 위해
(D) 기고가에게 편집상의 변화를 알리기 위해

해설   Ms. Hitchens가 이메일을 쓴 목적을 묻는 목적 찾기 문제이므로 Ms. Hitchens가 작성한 이메일의 내용을 확인한다. 두 번째 지문인 이메일의 'I am pleased to inform you that your writing proposal has been approved by our editorial staff.'(1문단 1번째 줄)에서 집필 제안서가 편집부 직원들에 의해 승인되었음을 알리게 되어 기쁘다고 했으므로 (C) To notify a writer about a submission이 정답이다.

Paraphrasing
inform 알리다 → notify 알리다
writing proposal 집필 제안서 → a submission 투고

Chapter 02 육하원칙 문제

예제 해석   p.360

이메일

수신 Agatha Williams <a_williams@ffm.com>
발신 Richard Jones <r_jones@ffm.com>

Perk-to-Go 병 커피의 출시를 위한 목표 마감일을 확인했습니다. 의뢰인에 따르면, 출시는 8월 27일에 이루어질 것입니다. 저는 금요일 전에 행사를 위한 일정안을 제출해야 합니다. 프로그램에 대한 제 아이디어에 관해 귀하와 상의하고 싶습니다. 도와주시면 감사하겠습니다.

target date 목표 마감일   **launch** n. 출시   **bottled** adj. 병에 담긴
client n. 의뢰인, 고객   **consult** v. 상의하다, 상담하다

문제   Mr. Jones는 무엇을 금요일까지 의뢰인에게 주어야 하는가?

(A) 비용 견적
(B) 출시를 위한 계획
(C) 제품 견본

어휘   **estimate** n. 견적

Hackers Practice   p.361

Paraphrasing 연습
01 (B)   02 (A)   03 (A)   04 (B)   05 (B)
06 (A)   07 (B)   08 (B)

유형 연습
09 (B)   10 (B)   11 (C)

01

직원 평가는 직원들이 예정 방향으로 나아가고 개선을 위해 조정하도록 돕는 중요한 훈련 수단이다. 직속상사와 평가받는 직원 간에 정기적인 일대일 면담이 실시되어야 한다.

(A) 정기적인 피드백은 관리자와 부하직원 간의 관계를 개선해 준다.
(B) 직원 업무 평가는 실적 향상을 장려한다.

해설   답의 근거 문장은 'Staff evaluations are an important training tool that can help your staff stay on course and make adjustments for improvement.'로 (B)가 정답이다. evaluations가 Assessment로 바뀌어 표현되었다.

어휘   **on course** 예정 방향으로 나아가   **make an adjustment** 조정하다
one-on-one 일대일의   **immediate supervisor** 직속상사
subordinate n. 부하직원   **assessment** n. 평가

02

여러분 집에 곰팡이 발생을 줄이려면, 습기를 최소한으로 유지해야 합니다. 여러분은 모든 방을 환기가 잘 되게 함으로써 이렇게 할 수 있습니다. 요리를 할 때나 창문에 습기가 차는 것을 보았을 때 선풍기를 켜십시오.

(A) 곰팡이를 막으려면, 집안에 공기가 흐르게 하십시오.
(B) 습기를 줄이려면, 선풍기를 항상 틀어 두십시오.

해설   답의 근거 문장은 'To reduce the incidence of mold in your home, you need to keep moisture to the minimum. You can do this by keeping all rooms well-ventilated.'로 (A)가 정답이다. well-ventilated가 keep the air flowing으로 바뀌어 표현되었다.

어휘   **incidence** n. 발생(률)   **mold** n. 곰팡이
well-ventilated adj. 환기가 잘 되는   **misty** adj. 습기가 찬, 안개 자욱한

03

Watley 백화점은 모든 예비 신부들을 위해 경품 행사를 개최하고 있습니다. 행사에 참가할 자격이 있으려면, 내년 1월 1일과 5월 31일 사이에 결혼을 할 계획을 세웠어야 합니다. 여성복 매장의 웨딩드레스 코너에서 등록하십시오.

(A) 참가자들은 경품 행사의 자격을 얻기 위해 확실한 결혼 날짜가 잡혀 있어야 한다.
(B) Watley 백화점은 웨딩드레스 할인 판매를 하고 있다.

해설 답의 근거 문장은 'To be eligible for the events, you must have made plans to get married between January 1 and May 31, next year.'로 (A)가 정답이다. be eligible for the events가 qualify for the sweepstakes로 바뀌어 표현되었다.

어휘 sweepstakes n. 경품 행사, (상품을 건) 경쟁 bride-to-be n. 예비 신부 eligible adj. ~할 자격이 있는, 적격의 make plans 계획을 세우다 entrant n. 참가자 qualify for ~할 자격을 얻다

04

나무 심기는 대기 중의 이산화탄소를 줄이는 저렴한 방법으로 여겨진다. 나무는 화석 연료에 의한 탄소 배출을 실제로 상쇄하는 정도까지 이산화탄소를 흡수한다. 그러나, 나무가 어느 정도 심어지는지는 현지 정책과 기술에 달려있다.

(A) 나무 심기는 화석 연료 사용량을 줄일 것이다.
(B) 수목 재배는 이산화탄소 배출을 상쇄하는 데 비용 효율이 높은 방법이다.

해설 답의 근거 문장은 'Tree planting is considered as an inexpensive means of reducing carbon dioxide in the atmosphere.'로 (B)가 정답이다. Tree planting이 Cultivation of trees로, an inexpensive means가 a cost-effective way로, of reducing이 to offset으로 바뀌어 표현되었다.

어휘 inexpensive adj. 저렴한, 비싸지 않은 means n. 방법, 수단 carbon dioxide 이산화탄소 atmosphere n. 대기 absorb v. 흡수하다 offset v. 상쇄하다 emission n. 배출(물) fossil fuel 화석 연료 degree n. 정도, 등급 depend on ~에 달려 있다 cultivation n. 재배, 경작 cost-effective adj. 비용 효율이 높은

05

권장 사항: 고객이 구매한 가열기에 명백히 결함이 있으므로, 이 서식의 상단에 언급한 고객에게 교환품 하나를 제공해 주십시오.

(A) 결함이 있는 가열기는 무료로 수리될 것이다.
(B) 고객에게 새 제품이 보내질 것이다.

해설 답의 근거가 되는 부분은 'Please supply a replacement unit for the customer'로 (B)가 정답이다. supply a replacement unit이 be sent a new product로 바뀌어 표현되었다.

어휘 defective adj. 결함이 있는 at no cost 무료로

06

배송 서비스 비용을 줄이기 위해서, Piedmont사는 외부 위탁에 관한 정책을 바꾸고 있다. 그 회사는 외부 위탁 제의를 받아들이고 직원을 덜 고용함으로써, 지원 서비스 비용을 절약할 수 있음을 알게 되었다.

(A) 외부 업체를 고용함으로써 비용을 줄일 수 있다.
(B) 외부 계약을 제한함으로써 비용을 줄일 수 있다.

해설 답의 근거 문장은 'The company has discovered that by accepting outsourcing proposals and hiring fewer staff, it can save on support services costs.'로 (A)가 정답이다. outsourcing이 hiring an outside firm으로, can save on이 can be decreased로 바뀌어 표현되었다.

어휘 outsourcing n. 외부 위탁 decrease v. 줄이다 limit v. 제한하다

07

세입자들은 설치류나 벌레에 관한 어떤 문제라도 반드시 알려야 합니다. 우 ➲

리는 세입자의 아파트를 점검하고 가능한 해결책을 제시해 해충 구제 회사와 계약을 맺고 있습니다. 세입자들은 무료로 이 업체에 예약할 수 있습니다.

(A) 세입자들은 해충 규제 업체를 고용해야 한다.
(B) 세입자들은 점검을 위한 시간과 날짜를 정할 수 있다.

해설 답의 근거 문장은 'Tenants may book an appointment with this vendor at no charge.'로 (B)가 정답이다. book an appointment가 schedule a time and date로 바뀌어 표현되었다.

어휘 rodent n. 설치류 (쥐, 다람쥐 등) pest n. 해충 vendor n. 업체, 매각인, 상인

08

시립 컨벤션 센터에서 대규모 자선 만찬회가 열리는 3월 23일 토요일을 달력에 표시해 두십시오. 이 행사는 할리우드에 있는 마케팅 회사인 Branding 자문 회사에 의해 후원됩니다.

(A) 할리우드에 기반을 둔 한 회사가 Branding 자문 회사를 후원했다.
(B) Branding 자문 회사가 모임에 자금을 지원하고 계획했다.

해설 답의 근거가 되는 부분은 'The event is sponsored by Branding Consultancy'로 (B)가 정답이다. The event가 a gathering으로, sponsored가 funded and organized로 바뀌어 표현되었다.

어휘 mark v. 표시하다 benefit n. 자선 consultancy n. 자문 회사 organize v. 계획하다, 조직하다 gathering n. 모임

09 기사

*World Trek Travel*지는 최근 호텔 설문 조사 결과를 이번 달 호에 게재했으며 베이징의 Grand Ching 호텔이 투숙객들로부터 가장 높은 등급을 받았다. 응답자들은 호텔의 혁신적인 디자인과 모범적인 고객 서비스에 높은 점수를 주었다. 상위 3개 호텔을 완성한 것은 밴쿠버의 Stanley 호텔과 방콕의 Orchid Terrace였다. 이 출판물은 4천 명 이상의 투숙객들 및 여행객들을 설문하여 결과를 수집했다.

respondent n. 응답자 mark n. 점수, 흔적 innovative adj. 혁신적인 exemplary adj. 모범적인, 훌륭한 customer care 고객 서비스 round out 완성하다. ~을 상세히 설명하다 publication n. 출판물, 발행, 발행물 compile v. (자료 등을) 수집하다

문제 *World Trek Travel*지는 최근에 무엇을 했는가?
(A) 고급 호텔에 대한 기사를 실었다
(B) 조사를 실시했다
(C) 새로운 난을 시작했다

해설 육하원칙 문제 *World Trek Travel*지가 최근에 무엇(What)을 했는지를 묻는 육하원칙 문제이다. 질문의 핵심 어구인 *World Trek Travel* recently do와 관련하여, '*World Trek Travel* magazine published the results of its latest hotel survey in this month's issue'에서 *World Trek Travel*지가 최근의 호텔 설문 조사 결과를 이번 달 호에 게재했다고 했으므로 (B) Conducted a study가 정답이다.

Paraphrasing
survey 설문 조사 → a study 조사

어휘 luxury adj. 고급(품)의, 사치(품)의 launch v. 시작하다, 착수하다

10 이메일

귀하께서 어제 저희 대리점 웹사이트에서 예약하신 차량을 지정된 날짜에 이용하실 수 없음을 알려드리게 되어 유감스럽습니다. 공교롭게도, 현재는 성수기이며 해당 종류의 미니밴들은 모두 예약되었습니다. 그러나, 귀하께 더 큰 밴들 중 한 대를 제공해 드릴 수 있습니다. 그것은 8명의 승객을 수용할 수 있으며 귀하가 원했던 차량보다 비용이 단지 20달러 더 들 뿐입니다. 귀하께서 이 제안이 적당하다고 여기시길 바랍니다. 제게 알려주시기 바랍니다.

vehicle n. 차량 indicate v. 지정하다, 표시하다 unfortunately adv. 공교롭게도 peak season 성수기 seat v. 수용하다

문제 요청된 차량은 왜 이용할 수 없는가?

(A) 더 이상 선택 사항으로 제공되지 않는다.
(B) 이미 사용이 예정되었다.
(C) 고객이 세운 예산보다 비용이 더 든다.

해설 **육하원칙 문제** 요청된 차량을 왜(Why) 이용할 수 없는지를 묻는 육하원칙 문제이다. 질문의 핵심 어구인 unavailable과 관련하여, 'those types of minivans have all been booked'에서 해당 종류의 미니밴들은 모두 예약되었다고 했으므로 (B) It has already been scheduled for use가 정답이다.

Paraphrasing
booked 예약된 → scheduled for use 사용이 예정된

어휘 **option** n. 선택 사항, 선택권 **budget** v. 예산을 세우다

11 안내문

신규 면허를 신청하시는 운전자들은 양식을 작성한 후 3번 창구로 가십시오. 차량 등록을 하시려면, 번호표를 뽑고 5번 창구 옆에서 기다리십시오. 사진을 촬영하시려면, 4번 창구에서 이름이 호명되기를 기다리십시오. 압수된 면허증을 되찾으시려면, 8번 창구에서 벌금을 지불한 후 추가 지시 사항을 기다리십시오. 감사합니다.

apply v. 신청하다 **license** n. 면허(증) **proceed** v. 가다, 계속하다
window n. 창구, 매표구 **retrieve** v. 되찾다
confiscate v. 압수하다, 몰수하다 **fine** n. 벌금 **instruction** n. 지시 사항, 설명

문제 방문객들은 어디에서 납부할 수 있는가?
(A) 3번 창구에서
(B) 4번 창구에서
(C) 8번 창구에서

해설 **육하원칙 문제** 방문객들이 어디에서(Where) 납부할 수 있는지를 묻는 육하원칙 문제이다. 질문의 핵심 어구인 make a payment와 관련하여, 'please pay the fine at window 8'에서 8번 창구에서 벌금을 지불하라고 했으므로 (C) At window 8이 정답이다.

Paraphrasing
make a payment 납부하다 → pay ~을 지불하다

Hackers Test
p.364

01 (D)	02 (B)	03 (B)	04 (A)	05 (B)
06 (C)				

01-04는 다음 광고지에 관한 문제입니다.

Oberlin 지역 청소년 센터 여름 도예 강좌!

이번 여름에 할 즐겁고 교육적인 것을 찾고 계십니까? ⁰¹Oberlin 지역 청소년 센터 (OCYC)의 도예 강좌 시리즈에 등록하십시오! 전문 강사들로부터 간단한 가정용품들을 조각하는 기본 기술들을 배우십시오. 현지 도예가 Arnold Robson과 미술 교사인 Marilyn Davis가 과정 내내 단계적으로 여러분을 지도할 것입니다. ⁰⁴방대한 종류의 조각 방법에 대해서는 Mr. Robson으로부터, 유약을 바르고 가마를 사용하는 법에 대해서는 Ms. Davis로부터 배우십시오.

세부 사항:
강좌는 Westpoint가 436번지에 위치한 청소년 센터에서 열릴 것입니다. ⁰²강좌는 7월 9일부터 8월 22일까지, 월요일과 목요일 오후 3시부터 5시까지로 예정되어 있습니다. 강좌 수료 후에는, 수강생들의 작품 전시회가 8월 24일 오후 7시 30분에 OCYC 자체 이벤트 홀에서 열릴 것입니다.

등록:
강좌에 자리를 예약하시려면, OCYC 행정실에 들러 주시기 바랍니다. 수업료는 220달러로, 재료비를 포함합니다. ⁰³참가자들은 13세에서 19세 사이의 Oberlin 거주자여야 합니다. 등록 마감일은 6월 30일입니다. 납입은 현금이나 신용카드로 할 수 있습니다. 수업료는 환불되지 않습니다. 더 많은 정보를 얻으시려면, Eve Wilson에게 555-9907로 전화주시기 바랍니다.

ceramics n. 도예 **sculpt** v. 조각하다 **household** adj. 가정용의
potter n. 도예가 **process** n. 과정

step by step 단계적으로, 점차로 **vast** adj. 방대한, 굉장히 많은
apply v. 바르다 **glaze** n. 유약 **kiln** n. 가마, 화로 **completion** n. 수료
exhibit v. 전시하다 **inclusive of** ~을 포함하여

01 주제/목적 찾기 문제

문제 광고지의 목적은 무엇인가?
(A) 시설 개장을 알리기 위해
(B) 지역 주민 센터에 자원 봉사자를 요청하기 위해
(C) 지역 교사들을 위한 워크숍을 광고하기 위해
(D) 예술 강좌를 홍보하기 위해

해설 광고지의 목적을 묻는 목적 찾기 문제이므로 지문의 앞부분을 주의 깊게 확인한다. 'Enroll in Oberlin Community Youth Center's (OCYC) series of ceramics classes!'(1문단 1번째 줄)에서 Oberlin 지역 청소년 센터 (OCYC)의 도예 강좌 시리즈에 등록할 것을 언급한 후, 도예 강좌의 세부 사항 및 등록 방법을 설명하고 있으므로 (D) To publicize an art course가 정답이다.

Paraphrasing
ceramics classes 도예 강좌 → an art course 예술 강좌

어휘 **volunteer** n. 자원 봉사자 **publicize** v. 홍보하다, 알리다

02 육하원칙 문제

문제 강좌는 언제 시작될 것인가?
(A) 6월 30일에
(B) 7월 9일에
(C) 8월 22일에
(D) 8월 24일에

해설 강좌가 언제(When) 시작될 것인지를 묻는 육하원칙 문제이다. 질문의 핵심 어구인 the courses begin과 관련하여, 'Classes are scheduled ~ from July 9 to August 22.'(2문단 1번째 줄)에서 강좌는 7월 9일부터 8월 22일까지로 예정되어 있다고 했으므로 (B) On July 9가 정답이다.

Paraphrasing
the courses 강좌 → classes 강좌

03 육하원칙 문제

문제 누가 프로그램에 참석할 것인가?
(A) 아마추어 예술가
(B) 지역 청소년
(C) 고등학교 교사
(D) 미술관 소유주

해설 프로그램에 참석할 사람이 누구(Who)인지를 묻는 육하원칙 문제이다. 질문의 핵심 어구인 participate in과 관련하여, 'Participants need to be residents of Oberlin between the ages of 13 and 19.'(3문단 2번째 줄)에서 참가자들은 13세에서 19세 사이의 Oberlin 거주자여야 한다고 했으므로 (B) Local teenagers가 정답이다.

Paraphrasing
residents ~ between the ages of 13 and 19 13세에서 19세 사이 ~ 거주자 → Local teenagers 지역 청소년

04 육하원칙 문제

문제 Mr. Robson이 어떤 종류의 강좌를 가르칠 것인가?
(A) 조각 기술
(B) 고급 도예
(C) 그림 그리는 방법
(D) 유약 바르기

해설 Mr. Robson이 어떤(What) 종류의 강좌를 가르칠 것인지를 묻는 육하원칙 문제이다. 질문의 핵심 어구인 taught by Mr. Robson과 관련하여, 'Learn about a vast variety of sculpting methods from Mr. Robson'(1문단 5번째 줄)에서 방대한 종류의 조각 방법에 대해서는 Mr. Robson으로부터 배우라고 했으므로 (A) Sculpting techniques가 정답이다.

Paraphrasing
methods 방법 → techniques 기술

05-06은 다음 편지와 기사에 관한 문제입니다.

11월 18일

Kelly Simon
Perlman International사
30번지 Bent가
퍼스, 웨스턴 오스트레일리아주 6015

Ms. Simon께,

⁰⁵부동산 박람회에서 당신을 만나서 기뻤습니다. Perlman International사가 대리를 맡은 부동산에 대한 책자를 제공해주신 것에 대해 감사드리고 싶습니다. 저희 회사는 시드니에 있는 Francis Tower에 가격을 제시하고 싶습니다.

Star Pacifica사는 싱가포르의 CK Wong 그룹의 계열사이며, 이 그룹은 아시아 전역에 토지를 소유하고 개발한 오랜 역사를 가지고 있습니다. 이 회사는 호주에서 부동산을 개발하려는 목적으로 설립되었습니다. ⁰⁶저희가 첫 번째로 매입한 곳은 멜버른의 Carlisle가 20번지에 있었습니다. 이는 시드니의 Harbor Way 811번지로 이어졌습니다. Francis Tower는 저희의 세 번째 사업이 될 것입니다.

저희는 조건을 논의하기 위한 회의뿐만 아니라 현장 방문 일정을 잡고 싶습니다. 제가 며칠 후에 다시 연락드릴 것입니다만, 제게 더 빨리 연락하셔야 한다면 555-9034로 연락하실 수 있습니다.

Ronald Lee 드림
상무이사
Star Pacifica사

---

represent v. 대리하다, 대표하다   offer n. 가격 제시, 제공 가격
unit n. 계열사, 구성단위   acquisition n. 매입한 물건, 인수   site n. 현장, 위치
terms n. (협의, 계약 등의) 조건

올해 첫 번째 주요 거래에서 Francis Tower가 1,900만 달러에 팔리다

1월 14일–Robinson가는 시드니에 있는 Francis Tower를 Star Pacifica사에 1,900만 달러에 매각했다. 싱가포르의 CK Wong 그룹의 계열사인 새로운 소유주는 이전의 아파트 건물을 상업 및 사무 공간으로 바꾸는 것을 목표로 하고 있다. ⁰⁶이 회사는 현재 시드니의 Maritime Plaza와 멜버른의 Union Building을 소유하고 있다. 또한 브리즈번에 있는 Astor Terrace를 매입하기 위한 협상을 진행 중이다.

그 거래를 중개했던 Perlman International사의 Kelly Simon은 그 건물이 수많은 매수자들의 관심을 끌었다고 말한다. "Star Pacifica사는 그들의 높은 제시 가격으로 인해 쟁취해냈습니다"라고 그녀는 말한다. Star Pacifica사의 상무이사 Ronald Lee는 이번 인수에 만족했다고 말한다. "비록 그 지역이 그 도시의 다른 지역들처럼 고급스럽지는 않지만 그것이 바뀌는 것은 그저 시간문제입니다."라고 그는 말한다.

---

subsidiary n. 계열사, 자회사   commercial adj. 상업의, 상업적인
negotiation n. 협상, 협의   broker v. 중개하다; n. 중개인
superior adj. 우월한, 월등한   upscale adj. 고급스러운, 부자의

---

05 육하원칙 문제

문제   Mr. Lee는 Francis Tower에 대해 어떻게 알게 되었는가?
(A) 웹사이트에서 광고를 읽었다.
(B) 행사 중에 책자를 받았다.
(C) 경매에 참여하도록 요청받았다.
(D) 현장 방문 중에 그 건물을 보았다.

해설   Mr. Lee가 Francis Tower에 대해 어떻게(How) 알게 되었는지를 묻는 육하원칙 문제이므로 질문의 핵심 어구인 Mr. Lee가 작성한 편지에서 관련 내용을 확인한다. 첫 번째 지문인 편지의 'It was nice to meet you at the Property Expo. I want to thank you for providing a pamphlet about the properties ~. Our firm is interested in submitting an offer for Francis Tower in Sydney.'(1문단 1번째 줄)에서 Mr. Lee가 부동산 박람회에서 Ms. Simon을 만나서 기뻤다고 하면서 부동산에 대한 책자를 제공해준 것에 대해 감사하고 싶고 시드니에 있는 Francis Tower에 가격을 제시하고 싶다고 했으므로 (B) He received a brochure during an event가 정답이다.

Paraphrasing
pamphlet 책자 → brochure 책자
Property Expo 부동산 박람회 → event 행사

어휘   brochure n. 책자   auction n. 경매

06 육하원칙 문제   연계

문제   Star Pacifica사는 첫 번째로 어떤 건물을 매입했는가?
(A) Francis Tower
(B) Maritime Plaza
(C) Union Building
(D) Astor Terrace

해설   두 지문의 내용을 종합해서 풀어야 하는 연계 문제이다. 질문의 핵심 어구인 property ~ Star Pacifica acquire first에서 Star Pacifica사가 첫 번째로 어떤(Which) 건물을 매입했는지를 묻고 있으므로 Star Pacifica사에서 작성한 편지를 먼저 확인한다.
첫 번째 지문인 편지의 'Our first acquisition was ~ in Melbourne.'(2문단 2번째 줄)에서 Star Pacifica사가 첫 번째로 매입한 곳은 멜버른에 있었다는 첫 번째 단서를 확인할 수 있다. 그런데 해당 건물의 이름이 무엇인지 제시되지 않았으므로 기사에서 관련 내용을 확인한다. 두 번째 지문인 기사의 'It currently owns ~ the Union Building in Melbourne.'(1문단 3번째 줄)에서 Star Pacifica사가 현재 멜버른의 Union Building을 소유하고 있다는 두 번째 단서를 확인할 수 있다.
Star Pacifica사가 첫 번째로 매입한 곳은 멜버른에 있었다는 첫 번째 단서와 Star Pacifica사가 현재 멜버른의 Union Building을 소유하고 있다는 두 번째 단서를 종합할 때, Star Pacifica사가 첫 번째로 매입한 건물은 멜버른의 Union Building임을 알 수 있다. 따라서 (C) Union Building이 정답이다.

Chapter 03 Not/True 문제

예제 해석   p.366

공고

Medford사 시청각실과 관련된 주의 사항

- ^A반드시 적어도 3일 전에 미리 시청각실을 예약해 주십시오.
- 장비를 대여해야 하는지 미리 알려 주십시오.
- 예약은 최대 4시간까지만 할 수 있습니다.
- 음식물과 음료는 엄격히 금지됩니다.

---

reminder n. 주의 사항, 암시   audio-visual adj. 시청각의
in advance 미리   ahead of time 미리, 시간 전에   strictly adv. 엄격히
prohibit v. 금지하다

문제   예약에 대해 언급된 것은?
(A) 필요로 하는 당일에 예약될 수 있다.
(B) 식사와 행사는 개별적으로 예약되어야 한다.
(C) 사전 통보에 따라 장비를 포함시킬 수 있다.

어휘   separately adv. 개별적으로, 단독으로   notice n. 통보, 공지

Hackers Practice   p.367

Paraphrasing 연습

01 (B)	02 (A)	03 (A)	04 (B)	05 (B)
06 (A)	07 (B)	08 (A)		

유형 연습

09 (A)	10 (C)	11 (C)

01

대학교 최상급생들과 최근 졸업생들을 위한 취업 정보 강연회를 개최합니다. ○

강연회는 5월 25일로 예정된 일일 강연회입니다. 입장은 선착순으로만 이루어지기 때문에, 등록은 필요하지 않습니다.

(A) 오직 대학생들만 강연회에 참석할 수 있다.
(B) 참가자들은 도착하는 순서대로 입장이 허락될 것이다.

해설 답의 근거가 되는 부분은 'admission will be on a first-come-first-served basis only'로 (B)가 정답이다. a first-come-first-served basis가 in the order they arrive으로 바뀌어 표현되었다.

어휘 **session** n. 강연회, 교육 **senior** n. (대학 등의) 최상급생; adj. 상급의
graduate n. 졸업생 **registration** n. 등록 **admission** n. 입장
first-come-first-served adj. 선착순의 **participant** n. 참가자
admit v. 입장을 허락하다

02

Bergerson Industries사는 도시 동쪽으로 공장을 이전할 것입니다. 자영업자인 Roger Bergerson은 공장의 이전이 창고로의 자재 운송을 용이하게 할 것이라고 말했습니다.

(A) Roger Bergerson은 회사의 소유자이다.
(B) Roger Bergerson은 회사의 발송부장이다.

해설 답의 근거가 되는 부분은 'Roger Bergerson, sole proprietor'로 (A)가 정답이다. sole proprietor가 owner로 바뀌어 표현되었다.

어휘 **relocate** v. 이전하다 **sole** adj. 단독의, 유일한 **sole proprietor** 자영업자
transfer n. 이전, 이동 **facilitate** v. 용이하게 하다 **warehouse** n. 창고

03

이미 바닥을 닦았는데도 화장대와 침대 밑에서 먼지 더미가 나오나요? 새로 나온 Whoosh 진공청소기는 매우 강력해서 바닥, 카펫, 심지어 커튼까지도 몇 분 만에 티끌 하나 없이 깨끗해질 수 있습니다.

(A) Whoosh 진공청소기는 커튼을 깨끗하게 할 수 있다.
(B) Whoosh 청소기를 사용한 후에는 가구의 먼지를 털 필요가 없다.

해설 답의 근거가 되는 부분은 'even curtains can become spotless in just a few minutes'로 (A)가 정답이다. curtains가 draperies로, spotless가 clean으로 바뀌어 표현되었다.

어휘 **dust ball** 먼지 더미 **dresser** n. 화장대 **sweep** v. 닦다
spotless adj. 티끌 하나 없이 깨끗한 **drapery** n. 커튼, 휘장

04

주지사의 내일 여행 일정은 네브래스카주, 링컨에서의 단기 방문을 포함하며, 그곳에서 그는 두 번째 임기를 위한 자신의 출마 계획에 대하여 연설을 할 계획입니다. 연설은 링컨 상공회의소에서 이루어질 것입니다.

(A) 주지사는 상업 관련 문제들에 대해 연설할 것이다.
(B) 주지사는 재선을 위한 자신의 계획에 대해 논의할 것이다.

해설 답의 근거가 되는 부분은 'he intends to deliver a speech on his plans to run for a second term'으로 (B)가 정답이다. run for a second term이 re-election으로 바뀌어 표현되었다.

어휘 **governor** n. 주지사 **stopover** n. 단기 방문
intend v. ~할 계획이다, 생각이다 **deliver a speech** 연설하다, 강연하다
run for 출마하다, ~에 후보하다 **term** n. 임기, 조건
Chamber of Commerce 상공회의소 **commerce** n. 상업, 통상

05

오전 8시부터 오후 11시까지, Mega 자전거 가게의 어린이용 자전거 가격이 20퍼센트에서 25퍼센트까지 할인될 것입니다!

(A) 상점은 모든 자전거를 할인된 가격에 팔고 있다.
(B) 상점은 선정된 품목에 대해서 할인 판매를 할 것이다.

해설 답의 근거가 되는 부분은 'the prices of children's bicycles at the Mega

Bike Shop will be marked down'으로 (B)가 정답이다. children's bicycles가 select items로, be marked down이 hold a sale로 바뀌어 표현되었다.

어휘 **mark down** (정가의) 할인을 하다, ~을 적어 두다 **select** adj. 선정된, 엄선된

06

Carmichael 그룹은 4억 5천만 달러 규모의 사무실 건물 공사 계획이 허가되었으나 건물에 대한 작업은 필요한 초기 비용을 투자자들이 제공하기 전까지는 진행되지 않을 것이라고 밝혔다.

(A) 재정 지원이 주어지면 공사가 시작될 것이다.
(B) 계획이 확정되면 Carmichael 그룹은 그 건물에 투자할 것이다.

해설 답의 근거가 되는 부분은 'work on the building would not proceed until investors provide the initial outlay needed'로 (A)가 정답이다. work on the building이 Construction으로, proceed가 begin으로, provide the initial outlay가 financial backing is given으로 바뀌어 표현되었다.

어휘 **outlay** n. 비용 **financial backing** 재정 지원

07

건물의 소유주는 장애가 있는 직원들이 접근하기 쉽게 하기 위한 요건들을 충족시키기 위해 개조 공사가 필요하다고 통지받았습니다. 주요 변경 사항으로 언급된 것은 모든 건물 입구에 알맞은 손잡이를 설치하는 것입니다.

(A) 올바르게 설치된 문들이 모든 건물 입구에 필요하다.
(B) 개조 공사는 장애를 가진 직원들이 손잡이를 사용할 수 있게 할 것이다.

해설 답의 근거가 되는 부분은 'renovations are needed to meet the accessibility requirements of workers with disabilities'와 'the installation of suitable door handles on all building entrances'로 (B)가 정답이다. workers with disabilities가 disabled workers로, installation of suitable door handles가 enable ~ to use door handles로 바뀌어 표현되었다.

어휘 **meet** v. 충족시키다, 맞추다 **accessibility** n. 접근하기 쉬움, 접근성
disability n. 장애 **installation** n. 설치, 설비 **door handle** 손잡이, 문고리
entrance n. 입구, 현관 **properly** adv. 올바르게, 적절히
enable v. ~을 할 수 있게 하다

08

주택 개조 안내서를 받으시려면 Home Remodeling Contractors사에 서면으로 신청하세요. 주택 개조 아이디어와 설계도 외에도, 안내서에는 귀댁의 모든 방을 위한 사진 카탈로그가 들어 있습니다. 개조를 원하시는 어떤 방에 대해서든 무료 견적도 받으실 수 있습니다.

(A) 회사는 견적비를 청구하지 않는다.
(B) 안내서는 토건업자에게 무료로 제공된다.

해설 답의 근거 문장은 'You can also get a free quote on any room you want to remodel.'로 (A)가 정답이다. get a free quote가 does not charge for estimates로 바뀌어 표현되었다.

어휘 **aside from** ~ 외에 **quote** n. 견적, 시세, 거래가격

09 공고

[C]Labrador 은행은 고객들에게 은퇴 대비 재무 계획에 관한 일련의 무료 워크숍을 제공하게 되어 기쁩니다. [B]첫 번째 모임은 4월 6일 목요일 오후 7시 30분에 Callahan가 322번지에 있는 우리 지점에서 열릴 것입니다. [B]세 번의 다른 모임은 같은 시간과 장소에서 매주 목요일에 이어질 것입니다. 워크숍을 통해서, 고객분들이 은퇴를 준비하는 것을 도와드리고 싶습니다. [D]퇴직 저축 계획, 단기 및 장기 투자, 고금리 예금 계좌, 연금 지급금 수령을 위한 계좌 개설과 같은 주제들을 다룰 것입니다. 참석하는 데 관심이 있으시면, 555-9835로 연락하시기 바랍니다.

retirement n. 은퇴 **session** n. 모임, 화합 **cover** v. (연구, 주제) 다루다

READING Part 7

Hackers TOEIC Reading

savings n. 저축, 예금 interest n. 금리, 이자 account n. 계좌
pension n. 연금 payment n. 지급금

문제 공고에서 언급된 것은?

(A) 참가자들은 여러 주제에 대해서 배우게 될 것이다.

(B) 은행은 3개의 다른 워크숍을 개최할 것이다.

(C) 금융 기관은 직원 교육을 실시할 것이다.

해설 Not/True 문제 공고에서 언급된 내용을 찾아 보기와 대조하는 Not/True 문제이다. (A)는 'We will cover such topics as retirement savings plans, short-and long-term investments, high-interest savings accounts, and setting up accounts to receive pension payments.' 에서 퇴직 저축 계획, 단기 및 장기 투자, 고금리 예금 계좌, 연금 지급금 수령을 위한 계좌 개설과 같은 주제들을 다룰 것이라고 했으므로 (A) Participants will learn about several subjects가 정답이다. (B)는 'The first session will take place'와 'Three other sessions will follow'에서 첫 번째 모임이 열리고, 세 번의 다른 모임이 이어질 것이라고 했으므로 지문의 내용과 일치하지 않는다. (C)는 'The Bank of Labrador is pleased to offer clients a free series of workshops'에서 Labrador 은행이 고객들을 대상으로 하는 워크숍을 제공한다고 했으므로 지문의 내용과 일치하지 않는다.

10 광고

Palazzo 식당 세트를 소개합니다!

Palazzo Designs사가 우아한 식당 가구의 최신 라인을 공개합니다. [B]Palazzo 식당 세트는 6명을 앉힐 수 있는 참나무를 깎아 만든 식탁과, 이와 어울리는 의자를 포함합니다. 유리 진열장이 있는 목재로 된 도자기 장식품과 3개의 보관용 찬장이 세트를 완성합니다. [A]모든 제품은 이탈리아의 롬바르디아에서 전통 장인이 손으로 만든 것입니다. 이 세트는 조각된 장미와 포도나무로 장식되어 있고 어떤 가정에든 정말로 훌륭한 가구가 됩니다. [C]Palazzo 식당 세트와 다른 Palazzo 가구를 가까운 가정용 실내 장식용품 상점에서 찾으세요!

---

unveil v. 공개하다 elegant adj. 우아한 furnishing n. 가구, 비품
oak n. 참나무 matching adj. 어울리는 round out 완성하다
china n. 도자기 handcraft v. 손으로 만들다 craftspeople n. 장인
adorn v. 장식하다 vine n. 포도나무 magnificent adj. 훌륭한

문제 Palazzo 식당 세트에 대해 사실이 아닌 것은?

(A) 이탈리아에서 제작된다.

(B) 식사하는 사람 여섯 명을 수용할 수 있다.

(C) 온라인으로 판매 가능하다.

해설 Not/True 문제 질문의 핵심 어구인 Palazzo Dining Room Set과 관련된 내용을 지문에서 찾아 보기와 대조하는 Not/True 문제이다. (A)는 'All pieces are handcrafted in Lombardia, Italy'에서 모든 제품은 이탈리아의 롬바르디아에서 손으로 만든 것이라고 했으므로 지문의 내용과 일치한다. (B)는 'The Palazzo Dining Room Set includes a carved oak table which seats six'에서 Palazzo 식당 세트는 6명을 앉힐 수 있는 참나무를 깎아 만든 식탁을 포함한다고 했으므로 지문의 내용과 일치한다. (C)는 'Look for the Palazzo Dining Room Set ~ at home decor stores near you!'에서 Palazzo 식당 세트를 가까운 가정용 실내 장식용품 상점에서 찾으라고 했으므로 지문의 내용과 일치하지 않는다. 따라서 (C) It is available for sale online이 정답이다.

Paraphrasing
handcrafted 손으로 만들다 → manufactured 제작하다
seat 앉히다 → accommodate 수용하다

어휘 manufacture v. 제작하다

11 기사

상을 받은 [A]팝의 돌풍, Lucille DeForest는 이미 인상적인 그녀의 이력서에 "의상 디자이너"를 추가할 수 있다. [A]의류 소매업체 Y&C사와 제휴하여, DeForest는 작년에 의류와 액세서리 라인을 출시했다. 이 새로운 신상품들의 판매량은 높았고, 그 제품들은 상점의 최고 인기 상품의 일부가 되었다. Y&C사의 대변인은 [B]회사가 가을과 겨울 신상품들에 대해 그 가수와 다시 합작할 계획이라고 말했다. DeForest의 디자인은 "혁신적이고" "매우 최신"이라고 묘사되는데, ⟳

이러한 점은 Y&C사가 더 많은 젊은 여성 쇼핑객들을 유치할 수 있게 도와주었다.

collection n. (의류 등의) 신상품들, 컬렉션 spokesperson n. 대변인
collaborate v. 합작하다, 협력하다 edgy adj. 혁신적인

문제 Y&C사에 대해 언급되지 않은 것은?

(A) 최근에 한 음악가와 합작했다.

(B) 계절별 신상품을 제공한다.

(C) 모든 제품을 직접 디자인 한다.

해설 Not/True 문제 질문의 핵심 어구인 Y&C와 관련된 내용을 지문에서 찾아 보기와 대조하는 Not/True 문제이다. (A)는 'pop sensation, Lucille DeForest'와 'In partnership with clothing retailer Y&C, DeForest launched a line of clothing and accessories last year.'에서 Lucille DeForest가 가수이며, 의류 소매업체 Y&C사와의 제휴를 통해 작년에 의류와 액세서리 라인을 출시했다고 했으므로 지문의 내용과 일치한다. (B)는 'the company plans to collaborate with the singer again for a fall and winter collection'에서 회사는 가을과 겨울 신상품들에 대해 그 가수와 다시 합작할 계획이라고 했으므로 지문의 내용과 일치한다. (C)는 지문에 언급되지 않은 내용이다. 따라서 (C) It designs all its own products가 정답이다.

Paraphrasing
In partnership with ~와 제휴하여 → collaborated 합작하다
fall and winter 가을과 겨울 → seasonal 계절별

Hackers Test

01 (B)	02 (A)	03 (D)	04 (C)	05 (D)
06 (A)				

01-04는 다음 브로슈어에 관한 문제입니다.

[02-A]현재 개장 중
오직 이번 12월만!

[03-A]마이애미 Dream Land로 와서 독특한 휴일 명물을 보세요

Winter World

얼음과 눈으로 뒤덮인 신비한 세계에 들어오셔서 얼음 성과 눈사람 만들기와 같은 [01]몇몇 즐거운 겨울 야외 전통 놀이에 참여하세요. 또는 전세계에서 온 전문 얼음 조각가들이 만든 조각품들을 보면서 눈으로 덮인 길을 따라 그냥 걸어보세요.

더 넓어지고 길어져서 더욱 향상된 얼음 썰매를 확인하시는 것을 잊지 마세요!

[02-A]오직 12월 31일까지만, [02-C]여러분은 월요일부터 금요일까지는 오후 4시에서 오후 11시 사이에, 토요일과 일요일은 오후 3시부터 자정까지 Winter World를 방문하실 수 있습니다.

Winter World의 기온은 섭씨 영하 15도까지 내려갈 수 있다는 것을 유념해 주시기 바랍니다. 방문객들은 시설에 입장하시기 전에 따뜻하게 옷을 입으시기 바랍니다. [03-B]구내에서 사진 촬영은 허용되지만, 극도로 찬 기온이 전자 기기를 손상시킬 수도 있습니다. 본인 책임하에 카메라를 가져오시기 바랍니다.

[02-B]입장료는 공원 일반 입장료 외에 8.50달러입니다. [04]모든 입장권은 www.dreamland.com/winter에서 구매하실 수 있습니다. 또한, [03-C]www.dreamland.com에 접속하여 모든 즐길 거리를 위한 연간 입장권에 대해 좀 더 알아보시기 바랍니다.

---

magical adj. 신비한, 매혹적인 take part in 참여하다
delightful adj. 즐거운 path n. 길 sculpture n. 조각품
premises n. 구내, 점포 at one's own risk 자기 책임하에
on top of ~ 외에, ~에 더하여

01 육하원칙 문제

문제 Winter World에서 방문객들은 무엇을 할 수 있는가?

(A) 스포츠 경기를 본다

(B) 전통 놀이에 참여한다

122 | 무료 온라인 실전모의고사 및 학습자료 Hackers.co.kr

(C) 가이드가 있는 여행을 한다
(D) 추운 날씨에 대비하여 옷을 구매한다

해설 　Winter World에서 방문객들이 무엇(What)을 할 수 있는지를 묻는 육하원칙 문제이다. 질문의 핵심 어구인 visitors do와 관련하여, 'take part in some of the delightful outdoor traditions of winter'(1문단 2번째 줄)에서 즐거운 겨울 야외 전통 놀이에 참여하라고 했으므로 (B) Participate in traditional activities가 정답이다.

Paraphrasing
take part in 참여하다 → Participate in 참가하다
outdoor traditions 야외 전통 놀이 → traditional activities 전통 놀이

02 Not/True 문제

문제 　브로슈어가 Winter World에 대해 언급하는 것은?
(A) 제한된 시간 동안만 대중에게 개방된다.
(B) Dream Land 입장료에 포함되어 있다.
(C) 매일 밤 11시까지 개장한다.
(D) 초보자를 위한 얼음 조각 수업을 제공한다.

해설 　질문의 핵심 어구인 Winter World와 관련된 내용을 브로슈어에서 찾아 보기와 대조하는 Not/True 문제이다. (A)는 'NOW OPEN ONLY THIS DECEMBER!'(제목)와 'Until December 31 only'(3문단 1번째 줄)에서 오직 12월 한 달만 개장한다고 했으므로 지문의 내용과 일치한다. 따라서 (A) It is open to the public for a limited time이 정답이다. (B)는 'Admission is $8.50 on top of regular park entrance fees.'(5문단 1번째 줄)에서 입장료는 공원 일반 입장료 외에 8.50달러라고 했으므로 지문의 내용과 일치하지 않는다. (C)는 'you may visit Winter World from Mondays to Fridays, between 4 P.M. and 11 P.M., and Saturdays and Sundays, from 3 P.M. to midnight'(3문단 1번째 줄)에서 월요일부터 금요일까지는 오후 4시에서 오후 11시 사이에, 토요일과 일요일은 오후 3시부터 자정까지 Winter World를 방문할 수 있다고 했으므로 지문의 내용과 일치하지 않는다. (D)는 지문에 언급되지 않은 내용이다.

Paraphrasing
only this December 오직 이번 12월만 → a limited time 제한된 시간

03 Not/True 문제

문제 　Dream Land에 대해 언급되지 않은 것은?
(A) 마이애미에 위치해 있다.
(B) 몇몇 구역에서는 사진 촬영을 허용한다.
(C) 연간 입장 요금제를 제공한다.
(D) 겨울에 몇몇 시설의 문을 닫는다.

해설 　질문의 핵심 어구인 Dream Land와 관련된 내용을 지문에서 찾아 보기와 대조하는 Not/True 문제이다. (A)는 'Come to Miami's Dream Land'(제목 아래 1번째 줄)에서 마이애미 Dream Land로 오라고 했으므로 지문의 내용과 일치한다. (B)는 'taking photographs is allowed on the premises'(4문단 4번째 줄)에서 구내에서 사진 촬영이 허용된다고 했으므로 지문의 내용과 일치한다. (C)는 'find out more about our yearly passes ~ by visiting www.dreamland.com'(5문단 4번째 줄)에서 웹사이트에 접속해서 연간 입장권에 대해 좀 더 알아보라고 했으므로 지문의 내용과 일치한다. (D)는 지문에 언급되지 않은 내용이다. 따라서 (D) It closes some facilities during the winter가 정답이다.

Paraphrasing
taking photographs is allowed 사진 촬영이 허용되다 → permits photography 사진 촬영을 허용하다
premises 구내 → some areas 몇몇 구역

04 육하원칙 문제

문제 　브로슈어에 따르면, 사람들이 어떻게 표를 예약할 수 있는가?
(A) 여행사에 연락해서
(B) 전화를 해서
(C) 온라인 사이트를 방문해서
(D) 관리사무소에 가서

해설 　사람들이 어떻게(how) 표를 예약할 수 있는지를 묻는 육하원칙 문제이다. 질문의 핵심 어구인 book tickets와 관련하여, 'All passes are available for purchase on www.dreamland.com/winter.'(5문단 2번째 줄)에서 모든

입장권은 www.dreamland.com/winter에서 구매할 수 있다고 했으므로
(C) By visiting an online site가 정답이다.

어휘 　travel agency 여행사

05-06은 다음 이메일과 웹페이지에 있는 정보에 관한 문제입니다.

수신: <공개되지 않은 수신자들>
발신: Jaime Buenaventura <Jaime.buenaventura@apollohealthclub.com>
날짜: 12월 6일
제목: 새로운 온라인 서비스

회원님들께,

Apollo 헬스클럽은 자사 웹사이트의 새로운 기능을 알리게 되어 기쁘게 생각합니다. 05-C여러분은 이제 회원권을 갱신하거나 등급을 올리기 위해 신용카드와 온라인 이체를 포함한 여러 결제 방식을 이용할 수 있습니다.

06-AGoldstar 회원권은 단 940달러이며 여러분에게 다양한 클럽 구역으로의 출입, 모든 강좌 입장, 그리고 지도 강사와의 상담을 제공합니다. 일반 회원권은 여전히 780달러입니다.

또한, 웹사이트는 이제 온라인 등록을 제공합니다. 제공되는 모든 강좌에 등록하기 위해서 컴퓨터만 있으면 됩니다. 단지 등록 링크를 클릭하세요. 헬스클럽은 웹사이트에 새로운 회원폼도 제공합니다. 다른 회원들과 이야기를 나누거나 05-B자사의 건강 전문가에게 조언을 받으세요.

여러분이 이 새로운 기능들을 편리하고 환영받을 만한 서비스라고 여기시길 바랍니다.

Jaime Buenaventura
운영 팀장, Apollo 헬스클럽

feature n. 기능, 특징 take advantage of 이용하다 renew v. 갱신하다
admittance n. 입장 (허가) consultation n. 상담 enrollment n. 등록
wellness n. 건강

www.apollohealthclub.com/membership/renewal
건강함이 하나의 생활 방식인 곳　　　　APOLLO 헬스클럽

홈	수업 일정	회원권	포럼

거래해주셔서 감사합니다!

고객 정보:
이름: Carolyn Wentz　　　　　　　　날짜: 12월 15일
연락처: 555-6633　　　　　　　　　　회원 번호: CW-99876
주소: 3426번지 Pinewood로,　　　　회원권 유효: 12개월
　　　리버티빌, 일리노이주 60048
이메일: carolyn.wentz@recordmail.com　06-A/B받은 금액: 940달러

이것은 귀하의 회원권 갱신에 대해 알려드리기 위한 자동 메시지입니다. 귀하는 이 메시지의 사본을 귀하께서 제공하신 이메일 주소로 전송받으실 것입니다.

05-A귀하의 회원권에 대해 더 알고 싶으시면, "홈"을 클릭하시거나 자사의 24시간 전화 상담 서비스 555-9696으로 전화 주십시오. 자사 직원들이 귀하를 기꺼이 도와드릴 것입니다.

Gerry Yuson 드림
고객 서비스 담당자, Apollo 헬스클럽

validity n. 유효 notify v. 알리다 forward v. 전송하다
hotline n. 전화 상담 서비스 representative n. 직원, 대리인

05 Not/True 문제

문제 　Apollo 헬스클럽에 의해 제공되지 않는 것은?
(A) 고객을 위한 전화 서비스
(B) 건강 전문가의 개별적인 조언
(C) 다양한 결제 방식
(D) 스파와 안마 치료

해설 　Apollo 헬스클럽이 제공하는 서비스와 관련된 내용에 대해 묻는 Not/True

문제이다. 질문의 핵심 어구인 Apollo Health Club이 언급된 이메일과 웹페이지 모두에서 관련 내용을 확인한다.

(A)는 두 번째 지문인 웹페이지의 'To learn more about your membership, ~ call our 24-hour hotline'(2문단 1번째 줄)에서 회원권에 대해 더 알고 싶으면 헬스클럽의 24시간 전화 상담 서비스로 전화하라고 했으므로 지문의 내용과 일치한다. (B)는 첫 번째 지문인 이메일의 'get advice from our health and wellness experts'(3문단 3번째 줄)에서 자사의 건강 전문가에게 조언을 받으라고 했으므로 지문의 내용과 일치한다. (C)는 첫 번째 지문인 이메일의 'You may now take advantage of different payment modes, including credit card and online transfers'(1문단 1번째 줄)에서 신용카드와 온라인 이체를 포함한 여러 결제 방식을 이용할 수 있다고 했으므로 지문의 내용과 일치한다. (D)는 지문에 언급되지 않은 내용이다. 따라서 (D) Spa and massage treatments가 정답이다.

Paraphrasing
hotline 전화 상담 서비스 → A telephone service 전화 서비스
different payment modes 여러 결제 방식 → A variety of payment methods 다양한 결제 방식

06 Not/True 문제 연계

문제 Carolyn Wentz에 대해 사실인 것은?

(A) Goldstar 회원이다.
(B) 체육관 이용료를 아직 결제하지 않았다.
(C) 수업을 수강하는 것에 무관심하다.
(D) 최근에 전화 상담 서비스에 전화했다.

해설 두 지문의 내용을 종합해서 풀어야 하는 연계 문제이다. 질문의 핵심 어구인 Carolyn Wentz가 언급된 웹페이지를 먼저 확인한다.
두 번째 지문인 웹페이지의 'Payment received: $940.00'(Customer Information 오른쪽 4번째 줄)에서 Carolyn Wentz가 940달러를 결제했다는 첫 번째 단서를 확인할 수 있다. 그런데 무엇에 대한 대가로 940달러를 지불했는지 제시되지 않았으므로 이메일에서 940달러와 관련된 내용을 확인한다. 첫 번째 지문인 이메일의 'A Goldstar membership is only $940'(2문단 1번째 줄)에서 Goldstar 회원권이 940달러라는 두 번째 단서를 확인할 수 있다.
Carolyn Wentz가 940달러를 지불했다는 첫 번째 단서와 Goldstar 회원권이 940달러라는 두 번째 단서를 종합할 때, Carolyn Wentz는 Goldstar 회원임을 알 수 있다. 따라서 (A) She is a Goldstar member가 정답이다. (B)는 'Payment received: $940.00'(Customer Information 오른쪽 4번째 줄)에서 받은 금액이 940달러라고 했으므로 지문의 내용과 일치하지 않는다. (C)와 (D)는 지문에 언급되지 않은 내용이다.

어휘 uninterested adj. 무관심한

Chapter 04 추론 문제

예제 해석 p.372

송장

Carrington 운송사
지점: 342번지 Richmond가, Castledale 애리조나주 99867

송장 발부일: 4월 27일

이름: Joanna Peterson   고객 번호: JP-98667
납부 금액: 238.96달러   납부 기한: 5월 2일

신용카드로 www.carringtonshipping.com에서 요금을 지불하시거나 개인 수표를 위에 기재된 지점 사무실로 보내시면 됩니다.

문제 Carrington 운송사에 대해 암시되는 것은?

(A) 한 곳 이상 소재하고 있다.
(B) 온라인 서비스 신청만 받는다.
(C) 국내 수송에 대해 할인을 제공한다.

어휘 branch n. 지점, 지사 domestic adj. 국내의, 가정의 shipment n. 수송

Hackers Practice p.373

Paraphrasing 연습

01 (A)	02 (A)	03 (B)	04 (B)	05 (A)
06 (B)	07 (A)	08 (B)		

유형 연습

09 (B)	10 (B)	11 (C)

01

대형 화물 자동차(LGV)의 운전자가 되는 것에 관심이 있는 분들에게, 운전자가 첫 번째 시험에서 떨어질 경우 무료 재시험 훈련을 제공하는 유일한 훈련 업체인 Veritas Training사를 권해 드립니다.

(A) 훈련은 무료로 한 번 재시행될 수 있다.
(B) Veritas사는 LGV 운전자들에게 훈련 과정에 등록할 것을 권한다.

해설 답의 근거가 되는 부분은 'the only training company that provides free retest training should the driver fail the first test'로 (A)가 정답이다. free retest training이 The training ~ repeated once without charge로 바뀌어 표현되었다.

어휘 retest n. 재시험 sign up for ~에 등록하다

02

Henson Speakers사는 시장에서 구할 수 있는 최고 품질의 스피커를 제공한다. 어떠한 결함도 허용하지 않는 Henson사는 최첨단 공장 설비에 막대한 투자를 했다.

(A) Henson사는 생산 기계에 상당히 많은 돈을 투자했다.
(B) Henson사는 생산율을 높이기 위해 새로운 공장을 구매했다.

해설 답의 근거가 되는 부분은 'Henson has made an enormous investment in a high-tech factory equipment'로 (A)가 정답이다. made an enormous investment가 invested a great deal of money로, factory equipment가 production machinery로 바뀌어 표현되었다.

어휘 tolerance n. 허용 오차 defect n. 결함, 결점 a great deal of 상당히 많은 machinery n. 기계(류) production rate 생산율

03

저희의 이동 전화 서비스 제도는 고객들 각자의 재정적 상황에 맞게 개별적으로 맞춰집니다. 기본 제도 외에, Cell-Com사는 귀하의 전체적인 이동 전화 패키지가 귀하의 무선 통신 수요에 적합하도록 추가적인 서비스들을 제공합니다.

(A) 기본 제도는 모든 통신 수요에 적합하다.
(B) 가격 선택제는 모든 지출 규모에 이용이 가능하다.

해설 답의 근거 문장은 'Our cellular service plans are individually tailored to fit the financial situation of each of our customers.'로 (B)가 정답이다. individually tailored to fit the financial situation of each of our customers가 Pricing options are available for all budgets로 바뀌어 표현되었다.

어휘 tailor v. 맞추어 만들다 fit v. 맞추다 aside from ~ 외에 entire adj. 전체적인 wireless adj. 무선의 option n. 선택제 budget n. 지출 규모, 예산

04

경영진은 회사의 구조 조정 안에 대해 반대 의견이 있는 것을 알게 되었습니다. 여러분의 우려를 해결하기 위하여, 여러분의 질문에 응답하는 회람을 발송할 것입니다. 이 회람이 여러분의 염려를 잠재울 수 있기를 바랍니다.

(A) 경영진과 직원들을 위한 회의가 예정되어 있다.
(B) 회사를 재편성하려는 현행 계획이 있다.

해설 답의 근거 문장은 'the proposal for the company's reorganization'으로

(B)가 정답이다. proposal이 plan으로, the company's reorganization 이 restructure the company로 바뀌어 표현되었다.

어휘 **management** n. 경영진 **reorganization** n. 구조 조정
address v. 해결하다, 다루다 **concern** n. 우려, 걱정
lay A to rest A를 잠재우다
restructure v. (조직·제도 등을) 재편성하다, 개혁하다

05

> 의사들은 수술 후 환자의 회복 속도를 높이는 한 가지 방법으로 대체 약품을 연구해 오고 있다. 특히, 약용 식물은 전망이 매우 밝아 보인다.
>
> (A) 약용 식물은 수술 후 치유를 더 빠르게 촉진할 수 있다.
> (B) 의사들은 외과 수술 중에 약용 식물을 사용한다.

해설 답의 근거가 되는 부분은 'alternative medicine as one way of speeding up a patient's recovery from an operation'으로 (A)가 정답이다. speeding up a patient's recovery가 faster healing으로, from an operation이 from surgery로 바뀌어 표현되었다.

어휘 **look into** 연구하다, 조사하다 **alternative** adj. 대체의 **operation** n. 수술
in particular 특히 **herb** n. 약용 식물 **promising** adj. 전망이 밝은
surgery n. (외과) 수술, 외과 **surgical** adj. 외과의, 수술의

06

> 우리는 보안 시스템, 폐쇄 회로 카메라, 그리고 투광 조명 설치를 전문으로 합니다. 자사 제품은 보안 전문가들로부터 시험을 거쳐 승인되었습니다. 제품 구매나 서비스 요청이 처음이신 분들께는, 이 광고를 언급하시면 10퍼센트를 할인해 드릴 것입니다.
>
> (A) 어떤 보안 장비를 구입하더라도 설치는 무료이다.
> (B) 고객이 이 광고를 언급하면 할인을 받을 수 있다.

해설 답의 근거가 되는 부분은 'mention this advertisement and we will give you 10 percent off'로 (B)가 정답이다. mention이 refers to로, give ~ 10 percent off가 a discount로 바뀌어 표현되었다.

어휘 **installation** n. 설치 **closed-circuit** 폐쇄 회로의 **flood light** 투광 조명(등)
approved adj. 승인된 **free of charge** 무료의 **refer to** 언급하다

07

> Kennedy 상업 지구에서 8월 24일 사업 재정 옵션에 관한 무료 세미나를 한 회 엽니다. 좌석이 한정되어 있으므로 사전 등록하셔야 합니다.
>
> (A) 세미나에 참석하기 위해서는 미리 등록해야 한다.
> (B) 이 세미나는 직원들에게만 한정되어 있다.

해설 답의 근거 문장은 'Pre-registration is required as seating is limited.'로 (A)가 정답이다. Pre-registration이 sign up in advance로 바뀌어 표현되었다.

어휘 **pre-registration** 사전 등록 **sign up** 등록하다 **in advance** 미리

08

> 이번 일요일 누각 옆의 해변에서 시 의회가 지역 주민을 위한 조찬회를 열 것입니다. 이 행사의 목적은 누각 바닥 재건축을 후원하여, 이웃의 주민들을 아침 야외 행사에 모으는 것입니다. 커피와 빵과자가 Henry 제과점의 후원으로 오전 8시부터 정오까지 제공됩니다.
>
> (A) 한 제과점에서 누각을 짓기 위한 기금 모금 행사를 연다.
> (B) 한 제과점에서 오전에 무료 음식을 나눠줄 예정이다.

해설 답의 근거 문장은 'Coffee and pastries, courtesy of Henry's Bakery, will be available from 8 A.M. to noon.'으로 (B)가 정답이다. Coffee and pastries, courtesy of Henry's Bakery가 A bakery will give out free food로 바뀌어 표현되었다.

어휘 **beachfront** n. 해변 **pavilion** n. 누각, 정자 **City Council** 시 의회
resident n. 주민 **in support of** ~을 후원하여 **courtesy of** ~의 후원으로
fundraiser n. 기금 모금 행사 **give out** ~을 나눠 주다

09 광고

> 대중교통 일일 승차권을 구매해서 로스앤젤레스의 모든 풍경, 소리, 그리고 느낌을 즐기세요! 그냥 어느 매표소에서나 24시간 여행자 승차권을 달라고 요청하거나 자동판매기에서 하나 구입하시고, 지하철과 버스를 무한정 이용하세요. 지하철 회전식 개찰구나 버스 요금 상자에 카드를 대고 승차하세요! 승차권은 성인용이 18달러이고 어린이용과 노인용은 14달러입니다.

sight n. 풍경, 경치 **sensation** n. 느낌, 기분 **ask for** ~을 달라고 요청하다
take advantage of ~를 이용하다, 활용하다 **unlimited** adj. 무한정의
turnstile n. 회전식 개찰구 **farebox** n. (지하철·버스 등의) 요금 상자
on board 승차한, 승선한 **senior citizen** 노인, 고령 시민

문제 광고는 어디서 볼 수 있을 것 같은가?
(A) 교통에 대한 정기 간행물에서
(B) 지역 여행자 안내문에서
(C) 노인을 위한 잡지에서

해설 **추론 문제** 지문 곳곳에 퍼져 있는 여러 단서를 종합하여 광고가 실릴 만한 곳을 추론하는 문제이다. 'Enjoy all the sights, sounds, and sensations of Los Angeles'와 'ask for a 24-hour tourist pass at any ticket counter ~ take advantage of unlimited use of subways and buses'에서 로스앤젤레스의 모든 풍경, 소리, 그리고 느낌을 즐겨 보라고 한 후, 매표소에서 24시간 여행자 승차권을 달라고 요청하거나 자동판매기에서 구입하고 지하철과 버스를 무한정 이용해 보라고 했으므로 여행자들에게 상품을 광고하는 곳, 즉 (B) In a local tourist brochure가 정답이다.

10 편지

> Ms. Leary께,
>
> Ms. Clarkson이 다음 주에 샌디에이고에 있는 이곳 지사를 방문할 때의 일정 변경 사항에 대해 귀하께 알려 드리고자 합니다. 그녀는 연구부장 Dr. Leo Menkin의 실험실 시설을 월요일 오전 9시 30분에 방문할 것입니다. 유감스럽게도, 지사장 Kyle Mason은 그때 출장에서 돌아오지 않을 것이므로, 그 약속을 수요일 오전 10시로 변경할 것입니다. 질문이 있으면 답장 주시기 바랍니다.
>
> Andy White 드림

laboratory n. 실험실; adj. 연구의 **appointment** n. 약속, 예약

문제 Ms. Clarkson에 대해 암시되는 것은?
(A) 그녀는 일에 대해 Dr. Leo Menkin과 수요일 아침에 이야기할 것이다.
(B) 그녀는 사전에 Kyle Mason과 월요일에 만나기로 예정되어 있었다.
(C) 그녀는 이미 회사 지사로 출장을 떠났다.

해설 **추론 문제** 질문의 핵심 어구인 Ms. Clarkson에 대해 추론하는 문제이다. 'She will be visiting the head of research ~ at 9:30 A.M. on Monday. Unfortunately, branch director Kyle Mason will not be back from his business trip at that time, so we'll change that appointment to Wednesday at 10 A.M.'에서 Ms. Clarkson이 월요일 오전 9시 30분에 연구부장을 방문할 때까지 Kyle Mason은 출장에서 돌아오지 않을 것이므로 그와의 약속을 수요일 오전 10시로 변경할 것이라고 한 내용을 통해 Ms. Clarkson은 이미 Kyle Mason과 월요일에 만나기로 예정되어 있었다는 사실을 추론할 수 있다. 따라서 (B) She was previously scheduled to meet with Kyle Mason on Monday가 정답이다.

11 이메일

> 수신: Soniajuarez@sunsetagency.com
>
> 발신: LeonLee@sunsetagency.com
>
> 저는 오늘 아침에 오늘 오후 12시 30분에 예정된 면접에 대한 귀하의 메시지를 방금 받았습니다. 아무것도 걱정하지 마세요. 제가 Mr. Hanks에게 연락하여 귀하가 긴급한 치과 예약이 있으며 제가 대신 그 일자리에 대해 그를 면접 볼 것임을 통보하겠습니다. 면접 후에 귀하께 메시지를 보내서 어떻게 되었는지 알려 드리겠습니다. 곧 회복하시기를 바랍니다!

emergency adj. 긴급한, 비상용의; n. 비상(사태) **instead** adv. 그 대신에

문제 　Mr. Hanks는 누구일 것 같은가?

    (A) 치과 직원
    (B) 부동산 회사 직원
    (C) 구직 지원자

해설 　**추론 문제** 질문의 핵심 어구인 Mr. Hanks에 대해 추론하는 문제이다. 'I will contact Mr. Hanks and inform him ~ that I will be interviewing him for the position instead.'에서 이메일 작성자가 대신 그 일자리에 대해 Mr. Hanks를 면접 볼 것임을 통보하겠다고 했으므로 Mr. Hanks는 구직 지원자라는 사실을 추론할 수 있다. 따라서 (C) An applicant for a job position이 정답이다.

Hackers Test

p.376

01 (C)	02 (C)	03 (A)	04 (C)	05 (C)
06 (B)				

01-04는 다음 기사에 관한 문제입니다.

Colton시 지역 의료 공급지가 될 예정

주 보건부는 [01-A]Colton시 의료 센터 확장이 올 여름에 시작될 것이라고 발표했다. 이 증축 공사는 4천 8백만 달러의 비용으로 현재 시설의 크기를 거의 두 배로 만들 것이다. [02]새로운 빌딩은 완공되기까지 3년이 걸릴 것이며 소아과 병동, 추가 수술 시설, 암 치료 병동과 80여 개의 여분의 침대를 위한 공간을 포함 할 것이다. 또한, [01-C]수리 작업은 현재 병동과 응급실에 이행될 것이다.

보건부는 확장된 의료 센터가 Colton시 주민들뿐만 아니라 Rosedale, Lavington과 Freemont를 포함한 더 작은 인근 마을에 사는 주민들에게도 서비스를 제공할 것이라고 말했다. 현재는, [01-C]모든 마을들이 각자의 병원을 보유하고 있지만, 그 시설을 축소하고 예약 없이 진찰을 받을 수 있는 진료소로만 만들 계획이다. 하지만, [01-B/D]Rosedale과 Freemont는 응급실을 열어둘 것이다. [03]현재 병원에 고용된 직원들은 진료소에서 근무하거나 Colton시로 이동하게 될 것이다. [04]보건부 대변인인 Ellen Raines는 "진료소에서 해결할 수 없는 의료 문제가 있는 주민들은 Colton시 의료 센터로 보내질 것입니다."라고 말했다. 그녀는 또한 확장된 센터는 지역 내에서 주요 의료 공급자가 될 것이라고 말했다.

department of health 보건부　at a cost of ~의 비용으로
pediatrics n. 소아과　ward n. 병동　treatment n. 치료
carry out 이행하다, ~을 수행하다　enlarged adj. 확장된
downsize v. 축소하다, 줄이다
walk-in adj. 예약이 필요 없는, 예약 없이 출입하는　spokesperson n. 대변인
refer A to B A를 B에게 보내다　primary adj. 주요, 주된

---

01 Not/True 문제

문제 　응급실을 보유하게 될 도시가 아닌 것은?

    (A) Colton시
    (B) Rosedale
    (C) Lavington
    (D) Freemont

해설 　질문의 핵심 어구인 have an emergency room과 관련된 내용을 지문에서 찾아 보기와 대조하는 Not/True 문제이다. (A)는 'an expansion of the Colton City Medical Center will begin this summer'(1문단 2번째 줄)에서 Colton시 의료 센터 확장이 올 여름에 시작될 것이라고 한 후, 'renovation work will be carried out on the current wards and emergency room'(1문단 9번째 줄)에서 수리 작업은 현재 병동과 응급실에 이행될 것이라고 했으므로 지문의 내용과 일치한다. (B)와 (D)는 'Rosedale and Freemont will keep their emergency rooms open'(2문단 7번째 줄)에서 Rosedale과 Freemont는 응급실을 열어둘 것이라고 했으므로 지문의 내용과 일치한다. (C)는 'all towns have their own hospitals, but plans are to downsize the facilities and make them into walk-in clinics only'(2문단 5번째 줄)에서 모든 마을들이 각자의 병원을 보유하고 있지만 시설을 축소하고 예약 없이 진찰을 받을 수 있는 진료소로만 만들 것이라고 했으므로 지문의 내용과 일치하지 않는다. 따라서 (C) Lavington이 정답이다.

02 추론 문제

문제 　기사가 곧 있을 확장에 대해 암시하는 것은?

    (A) 연말까지 완공될 것이다.
    (B) 빌린 자금으로 대금을 지불할 것이다.
    (C) 더 많은 환자들을 수용할 수 있는 병원이 되도록 할 것이다.
    (D) 수많은 지역 병원에서 이행되고 있다.

해설 　질문의 핵심 어구인 upcoming expansion에 대해 추론하는 문제이다. 'The new building ~ will include a pediatrics ward, additional surgery facilities, a cancer treatment unit, and space for extra 80 beds.'(1문단 5번째 줄)에서 새로운 빌딩은 소아과 병동, 추가 수술 시설, 암 치료 병동과 80여 개의 여분의 침대를 위한 공간을 포함할 것이라고 한 내용을 통해 더 많은 환자들을 위한 병동과 침대 공간이 추가될 것이라는 사실을 추론할 수 있다. 따라서 (C) It will allow a hospital to accommodate more patients가 정답이다.

Paraphrasing
include ~ space for extra 80 beds 80여 개의 여분의 침대를 위한 공간을 포함하다 → accommodate more patients 더 많은 환자들을 수용하다

어휘 　pay for 대금을 지불하다　borrowed adj. 빌린, 차용한
allow v. 가능하게 하다, 허락하다　numerous adj. 수많은

03 추론 문제

문제 　현 병원 직원들에게는 무엇이 일어날 것 같은가?

    (A) 변화 때문에 그들의 일자리를 잃지는 않을 것이다.
    (B) 급여 삭감을 받아들일 것으로 예상된다.
    (C) 그들의 계약 조건을 재협상할 것이다.
    (D) 추가 교육을 마칠 것이다.

해설 　질문의 핵심 어구인 current hospital employees에 대해 추론하는 문제이다. 'Staff currently employed at the hospitals will either work at the clinics or be transferred to Colton City.'(2문단 9번째 줄)에서 현재 병원에 고용된 직원들은 진료소에서 근무하거나 Colton시로 이동하게 될 것이라고 했으므로, 현 병원 직원들은 그들의 일자리를 잃지 않고 계속해서 일할 수 있다는 사실을 추론할 수 있다. 따라서 (A) They will not lose their jobs because of changes가 정답이다.

어휘 　pay n. 급여　renegotiate v. 재협상하다　term n. 조건, 조항
go through (일·예정 등을) 다 마치다, ~을 통과하다

04 육하원칙 문제

문제 　Ellen Raines는 누구인가?

    (A) 건설 회사의 대표자
    (B) 지역 진료소의 의사
    (C) 정부 기관의 대표자
    (D) 의료 센터의 환자

해설 　Ellen Raines가 누구인지(Who)를 묻는 육하원칙 문제이다. 질문의 핵심 어구인 Ellen Raines와 관련하여, 'Ellen Raines, spokesperson for the Department of Health'(2문단 11번째 줄)에서 보건부 대변인이 Ellen Raines라고 했으므로 (C) A representative for a government agency가 정답이다.

Paraphrasing
spokesperson 대변인 → representative 대표자

어휘 　physician n. 의사　government n. 정부　agency n. 기관

05-06은 다음 광고와 이메일에 관한 문제입니다.

---

[05]Haven 영화사: 캐스팅 공고

Haven 영화사는 *Home Away from Home*이라는 새로운 영화 제작을 위한 캐스팅 공고를 공지합니다. 이 영화는 Alex Jones가 연출하는 중국에 있는 미국인 교환 학생에 대한 코미디 영화가 될 것입니다. [05]저희는 다음 배역들에 대해 오디션을 볼 남자 배우들과 여자 배우들을 찾고 있습니다.

배역: Sam Evans (미국인 남성, 20-25세)
배역: Ming Na Chin (아시아인 여성, 20-25세, 영어와 중국어가 유창해야 함)
[06]배역: Mr. Ping (아시아인 남성, 50-60세, 영어와 중국어가 유창해야 함) ➡

배역: Mrs. Evans (미국인 여성, 40-50세)

만약 여러분이 우리가 찾고 있는 설명에 적합하고 두 달 동안 해외에서 일하고자 한다면, 이력서 사본과 얼굴 사진 1장을 homeaway@havenstudios.com으로 4월 14일까지 보내 주십시오. 오디션을 위해 선발된 분들만 연락을 받을 것입니다. 저희가 여러분에게 오디션 참가를 요청하지 않았다면 오지 말아 주십시오. 오디션 시험은 4월 16-17일에 Bradbury 대로 334번지, Haven 영화사에서 이루어질 것입니다. 오디션을 위한 특정 시간은 캐스팅 감독인 Maureen O'Donnell이 선발된 연기자들에게 이메일로 보낼 것입니다. 질문이 있으시면, 저희 제작진 중 한 명에게 555-8877로 연락하시기 바랍니다.

studio n. 영화사 **casting** n. 캐스팅, 배역 선정 **production** n. 제작, 생산 **direct** v. 연출하다, 감독하다 **fluent** adj. 유창한 **description** n. 설명, 묘사 **head shot** n. 얼굴 사진 **tryout** n. (능력·적격) 시험 **performer** n. 연기자

발신 Gina Poole <ginapoole@coolmail.com>
수신 Henry Chan <hchan@instamail.com>
제목 오디션
날짜 4월 12일

안녕하세요 Henry,

제 친구 Dennis Lowe가 지난번에 저에게 곧 있을 영화를 위한 캐스팅 공고에 대한 광고를 보여 주었습니다. 저는 사실 4월 16일에 배역을 위한 오디션을 보러 갈 예정이며, 당신도 영화사에 연락하고 싶어 할 것이라고 생각했습니다. [06]당신에게 안성맞춤인 배역이 있는데, 영화사가 중국어로도 말할 수 있는 남자 배우를 찾고 있기 때문입니다. 영화는 Haven 영화사에 의해 제작될 것이며, 당신의 이력서와 얼굴 사진을 캐스팅 감독에게 homeaway@havenstudios.com으로 보낼 수 있습니다. 그들이 당신에게 연락하면 저에게 알려주세요!

행운을 빌어요!

perfect adj. 안성맞춤의, 완벽한 **produce** v. 제작하다, 생산하다

05 추론 문제

문제 광고는 누구를 대상으로 할 것 같은가?
(A) 학생 영화 감독들
(B) 공연의 청중들
(C) 영화 배역을 찾고 있는 연기자들
(D) 연기 대회 참가자들

해설 광고의 대상을 추론하는 문제이다. 첫 번째 지문인 광고의 'Haven Studios: Casting Call'(제목)에서 Haven 영화사에서 캐스팅 공고를 한다고 한 후, 'We are looking for actors and actresses to audition for the following roles:'(1문단 2번째 줄)에서 다음 배역들에 대해 오디션을 볼 남자 배우들과 여자 배우들을 찾고 있다고 했으므로 영화 배역에 대한 오디션을 보고자 하는 배우들을 대상으로 하는 광고임을 추론할 수 있다. 따라서 (C) Performers looking for movie roles가 정답이다.

Paraphrasing
actors and actresses 남자 배우들과 여자 배우들 → Performers 연기자들

06 추론 문제 연계

문제 Mr. Chan은 어떤 배역에 대해 문의할 것 같은가?
(A) Sam Evans
(B) Mr. Ping
(C) Ming Na Chin
(D) Mrs. Evans

해설 두 지문의 내용을 종합적으로 확인한 후 추론해서 풀어야 하는 연계 문제이다. 질문의 핵심 어구인 Mr. Chan ~ inquire about에서 Mr. Chan이 어떤 배역에 대해 문의할 것 같은지를 묻고 있으므로 Mr. Chan에게 보내는 이메일을 먼저 확인한다.
두 번째 지문인 이메일의 'There is a character that you would be perfect for, as they are looking for a male actor who can also speak Chinese.'(1문단 3번째 줄)에서 이메일의 수신자인 Mr. Chan에게 안성맞춤인 배역이 있는데 그 배역을 하려면 중국어를 할 줄 아는 남자 배우여야 한다는 첫 번째 단서를 확인할 수 있다. 그런데 중국어를 할 줄 아는 남자 배우를 위한 배역이 무엇인지 제시되지 않았으므로 광고에서 배역을 확인한다.
첫 번째 지문인 광고의 'Character: Mr. Ping (Asian male, aged 50-60,

---

fluent in English and Chinese)'(2문단 3번째 줄)에서 중국어와 영어가 유창해야 하는 남자 배역은 Mr. Ping이라는 두 번째 단서를 확인할 수 있다.
영화사에서 중국어를 할 줄 아는 남자 배우를 찾고 있으며 Mr. Chan이 안성맞춤일 것이라는 첫 번째 단서와 중국어가 유창해야 하는 남자 배역은 Mr. Ping이라는 두 번째 단서를 종합할 때, Mr. Chan이 문의할 것 같은 배역은 Mr. Ping이라는 사실을 추론할 수 있다. 따라서 (B) Mr. Ping이 정답이다.

Chapter 05 의도 파악 문제

예제 해석   p.378

메시지 대화문

Nancy Hillard	13:44
공항으로 가는 길인가요?	
Kyle Larson	13:47
네. 이제 막 렌터카를 찾아서, 20분 정도 걸릴 거예요.	
Nancy Hillard	13:48
천천히 해요. Mr. Gupta의 항공편이 한 시간 반 정도 지연되었다는 소식을 방금 들었어요.	
Kyle Larson	13:53
그렇게 오래요? 되돌아가서 사무실에서 기다려야 할까요?	
Nancy Hillard	14:01
그냥 가세요. 반드시 Mr. Gupta를 도착 구역에서 만나도록 하세요. 그는 여기가 처음이거든요.	

문제 14시 01분에, Ms. Hillard가 "Just go ahead"라고 썼을 때, 그녀가 의도한 것은?
(A) Mr. Larson이 사무실로 돌아가야 한다고 생각한다.
(B) 나중에 공항으로 Mr. Larson을 따라갈 것이다.
(C) Mr. Larson이 원래 계획한 대로 진행하기를 원한다.

어휘 **on one's way to** ~로 가는 길에 **pick up** ~을 찾다
arrival area 도착 구역 **proceed** v. 진행하다

Hackers Practice   p.379

Paraphrasing 연습				
01 (B)	02 (A)	03 (B)	04 (A)	05 (A)
06 (B)	07 (B)	08 (B)		

유형 연습		
09 (C)	10 (B)	11 (C)

01

국제 상업 연사 협회가 7월 1일에 시작하는 연례 연설 대회를 개최한다. 참가자들은 그들이 선택한 주제에 관한 5분 연설을 해야 한다. 각 조의 우승자는 9월 10일 연례 집회에서 결승전에 참가할 것이다.

(A) 참가자들에게는 연설할 주제가 주어졌다.
(B) 참가자들은 자신의 연설 주제를 결정할 수 있다.

해설 답의 근거 문장은 'Contestants must give a five-minute talk on a subject of their choosing.'으로 (B)가 정답이다. Contestants가 Participants로 바뀌어 표현되었다.

어휘 **association** n. 협회 **speech** n. 연설 **competition** n. 대회 **contestant** n. 참가자 **of one's choosing** ~가 선택한 **division** n. 조, 분할 **compete** v. (경기에) 참가하다, 경쟁하다

02

요리사 Daniella Esparza의 작은 새 식당인 La Graella에서는, 메뉴에 엄선된 재료로 만들어진 간단하면서도 푸짐한 요리를 위주로 삼는다. Water가를 따라 위치한 이곳은 빠르게 인근 금융가에서 일하는 중역들의 인기 있는 점심 식사 장소가 되었다. 오후 12시부터 오후 2시까지는 예약이 매우 권고된다.

(A) 식사하는 손님들은 점심 테이블을 예약하기 위해 전화해야 한다.
(B) La Graella는 보통 점심 시간에만 문을 연다.

해설 답의 근거 문장은 'Reservations from 12 P.M. through 2 P.M. are highly advised.'로 (A)가 정답이다. Reservations from 12 P.M. through 2 P.M.이 book a table for lunch로 바뀌어 표현되었다.

어휘 **bistro** n. 작은 식당 **revolve around** ~을 위주로 삼다 **hearty** adj. 푸짐한
ingredient n. 재료 **favored** adj. 인기 있는 **executive** n. 중역, 경영진
financial district 금융가 **diner** n. 식사하는 손님

03

Reedville 공립 도서관에 의해 실시된 조사에서, 응답자의 48퍼센트가 정기적으로 시설을 방문했다는 것이 밝혀졌다. 그 인원 중에서, 대다수가 도서관에 의해 제공된 프로그램과 서비스에 만족을 표현했다.

(A) Reedville의 주민들은 좀처럼 공립 도서관을 방문하지 않는다.
(B) 공립 도서관을 자주 방문하는 사람들은 제공된 것들에 만족한다.

해설 답의 근거가 되는 부분은 '48 percent of respondents visited the facility regularly'와 'Of that number, the majority expressed satisfaction with the programs and services offered by the library.'로 (B)가 정답이다. 48 percent of respondents visited the facility regularly가 The public library's frequent visitors로, the programs and services offered by the library가 its offerings로 바뀌어 표현되었다.

어휘 **respondent** n. 응답자 **satisfaction** n. 만족 **pleased** adj. 만족한
offering n. 제공된(내놓은) 것

04

월요일에, 시 교통 공무원들은 5월에 시작될 일련의 지하철역 폐쇄를 발표했다. 통틀어서, Hanford시 주변에 있는 16개의 역이 꼭 필요한 수리를 위해 최대 14개월 동안 따로따로 폐쇄될 것이다.

(A) 몇몇 지하철역은 1년 이상 폐쇄될 것이다.
(B) 시 공무원들은 향후 몇 년간 16개의 새로운 지하철역을 건설할 계획이다.

해설 답의 근거가 되는 부분은 '16 stations around Hanford City will be closed for up to 14 months'로 (A)가 정답이다. 16 stations가 Several subway stations로, up to 14 months가 over a year로 바뀌어 표현되었다.

어휘 **subway station** 지하철역 **closure** n. 폐쇄 **at a time** 따로따로
renovation n. 수리, 수선

05

예약하실 때, 예약은 하루 숙박 요금에 상당하는 계약금으로 보증되어야 합니다. 투숙객은 도착 3일 전까지 예약을 취소하실 수 있습니다. 지체된 취소의 경우, 계약금은 반환되지 않을 것입니다.

(A) 투숙객은 예약의 조건으로 하루 숙박 요금을 지불하기만 하면 된다.
(B) 하루 이상 숙박하는 투숙객은 더 높은 계약금을 지불해야 한다.

해설 답의 근거 문장은 'At the time of booking, reservations must be guaranteed by a deposit equivalent to one night's stay.'로 (A)가 정답이다. At the time of booking이 upon making a reservation으로, by a deposit equivalent to one night's stay가 pay for one night로 바뀌어 표현되었다.

어휘 **guarantee** v. 보증하다, 약속하다 **deposit** n. 계약금, 보증금
equivalent adj. (~에) 상당하는 **prior to** ~ 전에

06

Louisville의 스포츠 팬들은 시의 새 경기장이 개장하는 것을 한 해 더 기다려야 할 것이다. 공사는 이 건축물의 수용 인원을 더 늘리려는 계획으로 인해 미뤄졌다. 완료되면, 시설은 5만 5천 명을 수용할 것이다.

(A) 스포츠 팬들은 경기장의 지연된 공사에 대해 불만스러워 한다.
(B) 스포츠 시설의 변경된 계획은 지연을 초래했다.

해설 답의 근거가 되는 부분은 'wait another year for the city's new stadium to open'과 'Construction has been pushed back on account of a plan to increase the structure's capacity further.'로 (B)가 정답이다. city's new stadium이 a sports facility로, has been pushed back이 have resulted in a delay로 바뀌어 표현되었다.

어휘 **stadium** n. 경기장 **construction** n. 공사, 건축 **push back** 미루다
capacity n. 수용 인원 **hold** v. 수용하다, 함유하다 **alter** v. 변경하다
result in ~을 초래하다, 야기하다

07

최근에 끝난 무역 박람회의 참가자 수가 행사의 15년 역사 중 가장 많았다. 참석한 사람들 중 많은 사람들이 주최자들이 그것을 처리한 방식을 칭찬했고, 만약 초대된다면 내년에 기꺼이 다시 올 것이라고 말했다.

(A) 내년 행사의 참석자 수는 두 배가 될 것으로 예상된다.
(B) 다수의 참가자들이 다시 행사에 참가할 의향이 있다.

해설 답의 근거가 되는 부분은 'Many of those in attendance'와 'said they would gladly come back next year if invited'로 (B)가 정답이다. Many of those in attendance가 A number of participants로, gladly come back next year가 interested in taking part in an event again으로 바뀌어 표현되었다.

어휘 **turnout** n. 참가자 수 **trade fair** n. 무역 박람회 **in attendance** 참석한
handle v. 처리하다 **gladly** adv. 기꺼이 **a number of** 다수의
take part 참가하다

08

귀하의 만족은 저희의 주된 관심사입니다. 전기요금 고지서에 대해 자주 묻는 질문 목록을 둘러보시려면 저희의 웹사이트를 방문하십시오. 귀하의 용무가 목록에 포함되어 있지 않다면, customerservice@volectra.com으로 이메일을 보내시거나, 정규 업무 시간에 555-2302로 전화하실 수 있습니다.

(A) 고지서 관련 항의는 일련의 절차를 따라 처리되어야 한다.
(B) 고객들은 다양한 방법으로 고지서 관련 용무를 해결할 수 있다.

해설 답의 근거 문장은 'Visit our Web site to view a list of frequently asked questions about your electric bill.'과 'you may send an e-mail to customerservice@volectra.com, or call 555-2302'로 (B)가 정답이다. a list of frequently asked ~ call 555-2302가 a variety of ways로 바뀌어 표현되었다.

어휘 **concern** n. 관심사, 용무 **electric** adj. 전기의 **list** v. 목록에 포함하다
address v. 해결하다, 처리하다

09 메시지 대화문

Jack Parker	오후 7:35

내일 시내 버스 같이 타는 것 어때요? 버스가 30분쯤마다 우리 사무실 근처에 서요.

Beth Kim	오후 7:36

잘 모르겠어요. 아침에 시내에서 회의가 있어요. 저는 택시를 타는 것이 더 편할 거예요.

Jack Parker	오후 7:38

괜찮아요. 도착하면 저한테 문자해 주세요. 회의가 시작하기 전에 잠깐 뭔가 먹을 수 있을 거예요.

Beth Kim	오후 7:40

좋은 생각이에요. 그건 우리에게 발표 자료를 검토할 기회를 줄 거예요.

downtown adv. 시내에서 **grab** v. 잠깐 ~을 먹다, 급히 먹다

문제　오후 7시 36분에, Ms. Kim이 "I don't know"라고 썼을 때, 그녀가 의도한 것 같은 것은?
(A) Mr. Parker의 정보가 부정확하다고 생각한다.
(B) 버스의 출발 시각에 대해 확신이 없다.
(C) Mr. Parker의 제안에 동의하지 않는다.

해설　**의도 파악 문제** Ms. Kim이 의도한 것 같은 것을 묻는 문제이므로, 질문의 인용어구(I don't know)가 언급된 주변 문맥을 확인한다. 'Why don't we take the city bus together tomorrow?'(7:35 P.M.)에서 Mr. Parker가 내일 시내 버스를 함께 타는 것을 제안하자, Ms. Kim이 'I don't know'(잘 모르겠어요)라고 한 후, 'It'll be easier for me to take a taxi.'(7:36 P.M.)에서 자신은 택시를 타는 것이 더 편할 것이라고 한 것을 통해, Ms. Kim이 Mr. Parker의 제안에 동의하지 않는다는 것을 알 수 있다. 따라서 (C) She disagrees with Mr. Parker's suggestion이 정답이다.

어휘　**inaccurate** adj. 부정확한 **uncertain** adj. 확신이 없는 **departure** n. 출발

10 메시지 대화문

Jerry King	16:06

Cindy, 광고가 녹음되었는지 궁금해서요. 대본을 조금 수정해야 해요.

Cindy Adams	16:08

운이 좋으시네요. 녹음 시간이 목요일로 늦춰졌어요. 추가 수정들이 왜 필요한가요?

Jerry King	16:11

Mr. Blum이 요청했어요. 제가 내일 아침에 제일 먼저 세부 사항을 이메일로 보내드릴게요.

wonder v. 궁금하다 **commercial** n. 광고 **record** v. 녹음하다 **script** n. 대본 **session** n. 시간, 기간 **push** v. 늦추다, 밀다 **additional** adj. 추가의 **request** v. 요청하다 **detail** n. 세부 사항

문제　16시 08분에, Ms. Adams가 "You're in luck"이라고 썼을 때, 그녀가 의도한 것은?
(A) 마감일 연장을 얻어 내려고 노력할 것이다.
(B) Mr. King이 대본을 수정할 기회가 있다.
(C) Mr. Blum이 광고 녹음을 승인해 주었다.

해설　**의도 파악 문제** Ms. Adams가 의도한 것을 묻는 문제이므로, 질문의 인용어구(You're in luck)가 언급된 주변 문맥을 확인한다. 'I was wondering if the commercial's been recorded. We have to make some changes to the script.'(16:06)에서 Mr. King이 광고가 녹음되었는지 궁금하다고 하며 대본을 조금 수정해야 한다고 하자, Ms. Adams가 'You're in luck'(운이 좋으시네요)이라고 한 후, 'The recording session's been pushed to Thursday.'(16:08)에서 녹음 시간이 목요일로 늦춰졌다고 한 것을 통해, Mr. King이 대본을 수정할 기회가 있다는 것을 알 수 있다. 따라서 (B) Mr. King has a chance to revise a script가 정답이다.

어휘　**secure** v. 얻어 내다, 확보하다 **revise** v. 수정하다 **approval** n. 승인, 인정

11 메시지 대화문

Anne Walker	12:06

Mr. Boyle의 사무실에 벌써 계약서를 가지고 가셨나요?

Bill Hooper	12:08

그가 방금 그것에 서명했어요. 왜요? 문제가 있나요?

Anne Walker	12:10

네. 임대차 계약 만료 날짜가 잘못되었다는 것을 알았어요.

Bill Hooper	12:13

지금 바로 수정해줄 수 있나요? Mr. Boyle이 서명할 수 있도록 당신의 비서 Kevin이 그것을 여기로 가져오게 해주세요.

Anne Walker	12:14

그럴게요. 한 시간 이내에 준비될 거예요. 죄송해요.

lease n. 임대차 계약 **expiration** n. 만료 **within an hour** 한 시간 이내에

문제　12시 14분에, Ms. Walker가 "I'm on it"이라고 썼을 때, 그녀가 할 것이라고 나타낸 것은?
(A) 직접 서류를 전달한다
(B) 부동산 중개인에게 사과한다
(C) 비서에게 업무를 준다

해설　**의도 파악 문제** Ms. Walker가 의도한 것을 묻는 문제이므로, 질문의 인용어구(I'm on it)가 언급된 주변 문맥을 확인한다. 'Can you make the correction right now? Have your assistant Kevin bring it here for Mr. Boyle to sign.'(12:13)에서 Mr. Hooper가 Ms. Walker에게 지금 수정해줄 수 있는지 물으며 비서 Kevin이 수정된 계약서를 가져오도록 해달라고 요청하자, Ms. Walker가 'I'm on it'(그럴게요)이라고 한 후, 'It'll be ready within an hour.'(12:14)에서 한 시간 이내에 준비될 것이라고 한 것을 통해, Ms. Walker가 비서에게 업무를 줄 것임을 알 수 있다. 따라서 (C) Give an assistant a task가 정답이다.

Hackers Test

p.382

01 (D)	02 (B)	03 (B)	04 (D)	05 (C)
06 (D)				

01-02는 다음 메시지 대화문에 관한 문제입니다.

Libby Pike	오전 10:05

당신이 셀비 지사의 관리자로 승진했다는 걸 들었어요! 언제 이사하세요?

Clyde O'Neill	오전 10:05

2주쯤 뒤에 떠나요.

Libby Pike	오전 10:07

짐 싸느라 바빠지겠네요.

Clyde O'Neill	오전 10:08

맞아요. 그리고 저는 셀비에서 임차할 집을 찾아야 해요. 당신이 작년에 그 지사에서 일하셨으니, 제게 사무실에서 가까운 동네를 추천해 주실 수 있나요?

Libby Pike	오전 10:12

01제 아파트는 Crystal Heights에 있었는데, 그곳이 당신에게 괜찮을 거예요. 01사무실에서 걸어서 단 15분 거리이고, 셀비의 아주 좋은 지역 내에 있거든요. 02예산은 어느 정도예요?

Clyde O'Neill	오전 10:14

02한 달에 700달러 넘게 쓰고 싶지 않아요.

Libby Pike	오전 10:15

잘 모르겠네요. 02그 동네에서 900달러 미만의 아파트를 찾는 건 정말 어려울 거예요.

Clyde O'Neill	오전 10:16

그럼 다른 지역을 찾아 봐야겠네요. 어쨌든 감사해요!

promote v. 승진하다, 홍보하다 **branch** n. 지사, 지점 **move** v. 이사하다, 옮기다; n. 이동 **pack** v. (짐을) 싸다 **place** n. 집, 장소; v. 배치하다, 놓다 **rent** v. 임차하다, 세내다; n. 집세 **recommend** v. 추천하다, 권장하다 **neighborhood** n. 동네, 지역 **budget** n. 예산, 비용 **spend** v. (돈을) 쓰다, (시간을) 보내다

01 추론 문제

문제　Ms. Pike에 대해 암시되는 것은?
(A) 다른 지사로 전근할 것이다.
(B) 집세로 매달 700달러 넘게 지불한다.
(C) 한동안 Mr. O'Neill의 부장이었다.
(D) 이전에 셀비에 거주한 적이 있다.

해설　질문의 핵심 어구인 Ms. Pike에 대해 추론하는 문제이다. 'My apartment was in Crystal Heights', 'It's ~ in a really nice part of Shelby.'

(10:12 A.M.)에서 Ms. Pike가 자신의 아파트는 Crystal Heights에 있었는데 그곳은 셸비의 아주 좋은 지역 내에 있다고 했으므로 Ms. Pike가 이전에 셸비에 거주한 적이 있다는 사실을 추론할 수 있다. 따라서 (D) She has lived in Shelby before가 정답이다.

어휘 **transfer** v. 전근하다, 이동하다 **once** adv. 한동안, 한때, 언젠가

02 의도 파악 문제

문제 오전 10시 15분에, Ms. Pike가 "I'm not sure"라고 썼을 때, 그녀가 의도한 것 같은 것은?
(A) 세대가 비어 있는지 확신하지 못한다.
(B) 예산이 현실에 맞지 않다고 생각한다.
(C) 지역이 불편한 위치에 있다고 생각한다.
(D) 승진에 대해 통보받지 못했다.

해설 Ms. Pike가 의도한 것 같은 것을 묻는 문제이므로, 질문의 인용어구(I'm not sure)가 언급된 주변 문맥을 확인한다. 'What's your budget?'(10:12 A.M.)에서 Ms. Pike가 Clyde O'Neill에게 예산이 어느 정도인지 물었고, 'I don't want to spend more than $700 a month.'(10:14 A.M.)에서 Clyde O'Neill이 한 달에 700달러 넘게 쓰고 싶지 않다고 하자, Ms. Pike가 'I'm not sure'(잘 모르겠네요)라고 한 후, 'It'd be very hard to find an apartment for under $900 in that neighborhood.'(10:15 A.M.)에서 그 동네에서 900달러 미만의 아파트를 찾는 것이 정말 어려울 거라고 한 것을 통해, Ms. Pike가 700달러의 예산이 현실에 맞지 않다고 생각함을 알 수 있다. 따라서 (B) She believes a budget is unrealistic이 정답이다.

어휘 **certain** adj. 확신하는, 확실한 **vacant** adj. 비어 있는, 사람이 안 사는 **unrealistic** adj. 비현실적인 **inconveniently** adv. 불편하게 **inform** v. 통지하다, 알리다

03-06은 다음 온라인 대화문에 관한 문제입니다.

Maria Jasso 오후 3:45
안녕하세요, 팀장님들. 촉박하게 통보하여 죄송하지만, ⁰⁵Loewing 공과 대학의 학생 단체가 견학을 위해 내일 자동차 공장으로 우리를 방문할 거예요. 제가 그것을 이끌 것이지만, ⁰³저는 여러분의 협조가 필요해요.

Alex Rocha 오후 3:46
그럼요. 저희가 무엇을 해야 할까요?

Maria Jasso 오후 3:47
음, 학생들은 모두 공학을 전공하는 학생들이고, 그들은 우리가 어떻게 자동화된 공정을 시행하는지를 보길 희망해요. 그들이 각 구역을 방문할 때, ^{04-A/B}저는 여러분이 학생들에게 여러분의 팀들이 무엇을 하는지에 대해 간단한 개요를 제공하고 그들의 질문에 답해주기를 바라요.

Alex Rocha 오후 3:48
네, 할 수 있을 것 같아요.

Maria Jasso 오후 3:48
^{04-C}Alex, 당신의 경우에는, 그들에게 로봇 팔이 어떻게 작동하는지도 보여준다면 정말 좋겠어요.

Hitomi Yasui 오후 3:49
저도 돕게 되어 기뻐요. 그저 호기심에서 묻는데, ⁰⁵그건 2년 전쯤에 방문했던 학교와 같은 학교조, 그렇죠? 이전에 이것과 비슷한 것을 했던 것이 기억나요.

Henry Lee 오후 3:49
저는 시간이 될지 확인해 봐야겠어요.

Maria Jasso 오후 3:49
맞아요. ⁰⁵그들은 2년 전에 몇몇 학생들을 여기로 보냈어요.

Henry Lee 오후 3:50
이 단체 견학이 언제 시작되는지 알고 싶어요. ⁰⁶만약 이것이 오후 1시 이후라면, 괜찮아요. 오전에는 제 딸아이의 학교 행사에 참석해야 해요.

Maria Jasso 오후 3:52
아, 제가 깜빡했네요. 사실 이건 오전에 가장 먼저 시작할 일이에요. 부팀장에게 당신을 대신해달라고 부탁해주세요.

short notice 촉박한 통보 **cooperation** n. 협조 **major** n. 전공(하는 학생) **implement** v. 시행하다 **automated** adj. 자동화된 **brief** adj. 간단한, 짧은 ◑

---

overview n. 개요 **robotic** adj. 로봇(식)의 **out of curiosity** 그저 호기심에서 묻는데 **recall** v. 기억해 내다 **cover** v. 대신하다

03 주제/목적 찾기 문제

문제 왜 Ms. Jasso는 사람들에게 연락했는가?
(A) 규정을 검토하기 위해
(B) 도움을 요청하기 위해
(C) 일정을 변경하기 위해
(D) 변화에 대해 발표하기 위해

해설 Ms. Jasso가 사람들에게 연락한 목적을 묻는 목적 찾기 문제이므로 지문의 앞부분을 주의 깊게 확인한다. 'I need your cooperation'(3:45 P.M.)에서 Ms. Jasso가 협조가 필요하다고 했으므로 (B) To request some assistance가 정답이다.

Paraphrasing
cooperation 협조 → assistance 도움

어휘 **go over** ~을 검토하다 **regulation** n. 규정 **transition** n. 변화

04 Not/True 문제

문제 Mr. Rocha가 하도록 요청받은 것이 아닌 것은?
(A) 질문에 응답한다
(B) 팀의 업무를 간략하게 말한다
(C) 시범 설명을 한다
(D) 취업 기회에 대해 논의한다

해설 질문의 핵심 어구인 Mr. Rocha와 관련된 내용을 지문에서 찾아 보기와 대조하는 Not/True 문제이다. (A)는 'I'd like you to ~ answer their questions.'(3:47 P.M.)에서 Maria Jasso가 여러분, 즉 대화에 참여하고 있는 사람들이 그들, 즉 학생들의 질문에 답해주기를 바란다고 했으므로 지문의 내용과 일치한다. (B)는 'I'd like you to give the students a brief overview of what your teams do ~'(3:47 P.M.)에서 Maria Jasso가 여러분, 즉 대화에 참여하고 있는 사람들의 팀들이 무엇을 하는지에 대해 간단한 개요를 제공해주기를 바란다고 했으므로 지문의 내용과 일치한다. (C)는 'In your case, Alex, it would also be great if you could show them how the robotic arms work.'(3:48 P.M.)에서 Maria Jasso가 Alex Rocha에게 로봇 팔이 어떻게 작동하는지도 학생들에게 보여준다면 정말 좋겠다고 했으므로 지문의 내용과 일치한다. (D)는 지문에 언급되지 않은 내용이다. 따라서 (D) Discuss job opportunities가 정답이다.

Paraphrasing
answer ~ questions 질문에 답하다 → Respond to inquires 질문에 대답하다
give ~ a brief overview 간단한 개요를 제공하다 → Summarize 간략하게 말하다

어휘 **respond** v. 대답하다, 응답하다 **duty** n. 업무, 임무 **demonstration** n. (무엇의 작동 과정이나 사용법에 대한 시범) 설명

05 의도 파악 문제

문제 오후 3시 49분에, Ms. Jasso가 "Correct"라고 썼을 때, 그녀가 의도한 것은?
(A) 그 공장은 몇몇 대학과 제휴를 맺고 있다.
(B) 한 프로그램이 몇 년간 운영되어오고 있다.
(C) Loewing의 학생들이 이전에 방문한 적이 있다.
(D) 학생 견학 프로그램은 잘 준비되었다.

해설 Ms. Jasso가 의도한 것을 묻는 문제이므로, 질문의 인용어구(Correct)가 언급된 주변 문맥을 확인한다. 'a group of students from the Loewing Institute of Technology will visit us'(3:45 P.M.)에서 Ms. Jasso가 Loewing 공과 대학의 학생 단체가 우리를 방문할 것이라고 했고, Hitomi Yasui가 'that's the same school that visited a couple of years ago, right?'(3:49 P.M.)에서 그것, 즉 Loewing 공과 대학이 2년 전쯤에 방문했던 학교와 같은 학교인지 묻자, Ms. Jasso가 'Correct(맞아요)'라고 한 후, 'They sent some students here two years ago.'(3:49 P.M.)에서 그들이 2년 전에 몇몇 학생들을 여기로 보냈었다고 한 것을 통해, Loewing 공과 대학의 학생들이 이전에 방문한 적이 있음을 알 수 있다. 따라서 (C) Students from Loewing have visited before가 정답이다.

어휘 **partnership** n. 제휴, 협력 **run** v. 운영되다

06 추론 문제

문제 Mr. Lee에 대해 암시되는 것은?
(A) 생산을 담당하고 있다.
(B) 이전에 학생 견학에 참여한 적이 있다.
(C) 최근에 그의 현재 직책으로 승진했다.
(D) 내일 오전에 휴무이다.

해설 질문의 핵심 어구인 Mr. Lee에 대해 추론하는 문제이다. 'If it's after 1 P.M., then it's fine. I need to attend an event at my daughter's school in the morning.'(3:50 P.M.)에서 Mr. Lee가 만약 이것, 즉 내일 진행되는 단체 견학이 1시 이후라면 괜찮지만 오전에는 딸의 학교 행사에 참석해야 한다고 했으므로, Mr. Lee가 내일 오전에 휴무라는 사실을 추론할 수 있다. 따라서 (D) He has tomorrow morning off가 정답이다.

어휘 **be in charge of** ~을 담당하다 **promote** v. 승진시키다
have ~ off ~에 휴무이다, 쉬다

Chapter 06 문장 위치 찾기 문제

예제 해석   p.384

기사

의류 소매업체 Majeste의 매출 증가에도 불구한 수익 감소
급격한 매출 증가에도 불구하고, 영국 소매업체 Majeste에서는 수익이 10퍼센트 감소했다. — [1] —. 지난 10개월에 걸쳐, 두바이, 싱가포르, 그리고 상하이에 있는 세 곳의 신규 가맹점 덕분에, 매장 매출이 14퍼센트 증가했다. — [2] —. 그러나, 수익은 방글라데시로부터 생산을 이전한다는 회사의 결정에 의해 결국 하락했다. 경영진은 미얀마에 있는 공장들이 탄력이 붙음에 따라 내년에 회복을 예상한다. — [3] —.

문제 [1], [2], [3]으로 표시된 위치 중, 다음 문장이 들어갈 곳으로 가장 적절한 것은?
"온라인 매출이 동등하게 강세였으며 30퍼센트만큼 증가했다."
(A) [1]
(B) [2]
(C) [3]

어휘 **retailer** n. 소매업체, 소매상 **boom** n. 급격한 증가 **thanks to** ~ 덕분에
ultimately adv. 결국 **erode** v. (가치가) 하락하다 **move** v. 이전하다
executive n. 경영진, 중역 **gain momentum** 탄력이 붙다

Hackers Practice   p.385

Paraphrasing 연습
01 (B)   02 (B)   03 (A)   04 (A)   05 (B)
06 (B)   07 (B)   08 (A)

유형 연습
09 (C)   10 (A)   11 (C)

01

Blaze X8은 지금까지 있었던 것 중 가장 얇은 태블릿입니다. 이것은 당신이 최고급 모델을 골랐다는, 빠른 중앙 연산 처리 장치, 근사한 디스플레이, 32기가바이트까지의 저장 공간을 특징으로 합니다. 가격은 149.99달러부터 시작하며 제한된 시간 동안, 저희는 무료 배송을 제공하고 있습니다.
(A) Blaze X8의 가장 비싼 모델은 149.99달러이다.
(B) Blaze X8은 모든 이전 모델들보다 얇다.

해설 답의 근거 문장은 'The Blaze X8 is our thinnest tablet yet.'으로 (B)가 정답이다. thinnest ~ yet이 slimmer than all로 바뀌어 표현되었다.

어휘 **yet** adv. 지금까지 있었던 것 중 가장 ~한, 아직 **feature** v. ~을 특징으로 하다
processor n. 중앙 연산 처리 장치 **stunning** adj. 근사한, 멋진
display n. 디스플레이, 화면 표시 장치

02

연안 해역을 어지럽히는 쓰레기의 양에 낙심하여, 한 무리의 학생들이 단순한 플라스틱 소재로 만들어진 독특한 쓰레기 수거 장치를 발명했다. 발명품은 현재 시험 중에 있으며, 만약 성공적이라면, 투자를 끌어모을 수 있을 것이다.
(A) 프로젝트의 성공은 그것이 받는 투자금의 양에 달렸다.
(B) 발명품은 그것이 실제로 작동한다는 것이 밝혀진다면 재정적인 지원을 받을 것이다.

해설 답의 근거 문장은 'The invention is currently being tested, and if successful, could attract investment.'로 (B)가 정답이다. if successful 이 if it is found to actually work로, could attract investment가 may get financial support로 바뀌어 표현되었다.

어휘 **litter** v. 어지럽히다, 버리다 **coastal waters** 연안 해역
unique adj. 독특한 **attract** v. 끌어모으다
investment n. 투자, 투자금

03

이 영사기는 사용자의 안전을 고려하여 설계되었지만, 잘못된 사용은 부상을 야기할 수 있습니다. 영사기를 작동하기 전에, 첨부한 사용자 설명서를 읽고, 그 안에 포함된 지침을 준수하십시오. 읽은 후에는, 추후 참고를 위해 설명서를 보관하십시오.
(A) 영사기가 만들어졌을 때 안전 문제가 고려되었다.
(B) 사용자들은 상품을 다루는 올바른 방법을 추천했다.

해설 답의 근거가 되는 부분은 'While this projector has been designed with the user's safety in mind'로 (A)가 정답이다. user's safety가 Safety issues로, with ~ in mind가 were considered로 바뀌어 표현되었다.

어휘 **projector** n. 영사기 **with A in mind** A를 고려하여 **operate** v. 작동하다
accompanying adj. 첨부한 **user manual** 사용자 설명서
observe v. 준수하다 **guideline** n. 지침 **therein** adv. 그 안에서
reference n. 참고, 참조

04

노동고용부의 제의에 따르면, 근로자가 언제 초과 근무 수당을 받을 자격이 있는지를 결정하는 급여 한도가 현재 수준으로부터 연간 5만 달러까지 증가될 수도 있습니다. 통과된다면, 이 변화는 수백만 명의 근로자들에게 영향을 미칠 것입니다.
(A) 일 년에 5만 달러나 그 이하를 버는 이들은 제의된 변화로부터 이득을 얻을 것이다.
(B) 일 년에 수백만 달러가 이미 초과 근무 비용을 지불하기 위해 사용되고 있다.

해설 답의 근거가 되는 부분은 'the salary limit that determines when a worker is eligible for overtime pay could be raised to $50,000 a year from its current level'과 'If passed, the change could affect millions of workers.'로 (A)가 정답이다. could affect가 will benefit으로 바뀌어 표현되었다.

어휘 **proposal** n. 제의 **eligible for** 자격이 있는 **overtime pay** 초과 근무 수당

05

규제 기관들이 광대역 제공 기관 BDI의 대략 150억 달러의 Elemeno 휴대폰 회사 인수를 승인했다. 인수에 대해 언급하며, BDI의 대변인은 이 결과로 둘 중 어느 회사의 고객들도 서비스가 축소되는 것을 예상하지 않아도 된다는 것을 보증했다.
(A) 제안된 인수가 서비스의 향상으로 이어질 것이다.
(B) 회사의 조치는 어떤 방법으로든 서비스를 축소하지 않을 것이다.

해설 답의 근거 문장은 'Commenting on the buyout, a spokesperson for BDI has given assurances that customers of either company should not expect service to decline as a result.'로 (B)가 정답이다. the buyout이 A company's actions로, service to decline이 diminish service로 바뀌어 표현되었다.

어휘 **regulator** n. 규제 기관 **broadband** n. 광대역 **provider** n. 제공 기관 **takeover** n. 인수, 인계 **carrier** n. (전화나 인터넷 서비스를 제공하는) 회사 **buyout** n. 인수 **spokesperson** n. 대변인 **give assurance that** ~임을 보증하다 **decline** v. 축소되다, 감소하다 **diminish** v. 축소하다, 줄이다

06

사진사 Kate Booth가 그녀의 가장 최근 전시회를 이번 주에 Durham 전시관에서 열었습니다. 'Feminine'이라고 제목이 붙여진, 이 전시회는 일련의 영향력 있는 여인들의 초상화를 전시합니다. 이 전시회에 딸린 것은 시리즈의 보너스 사진들을 제공하는 한정판 차 탁자용 책입니다. 이 책은 www. katebooth. com에서도 구매할 수 있습니다.

(A) 시리즈에 있는 모든 사진이 책에 또한 특별히 포함되어 있다.
(B) 판매되고 있는 책은 전시회에서 볼 수 없는 사진들을 포함할 것이다.

해설 답의 근거 문장은 'Accompanying the exhibit is a limited set of ~ books offering bonus photographs from the series.'로 (B)가 정답이다. bonus photographs가 pictures not seen in an exhibit으로 바뀌어 표현되었다.

어휘 **exhibit** n. 전시회 **entitle** v. 제목을 붙이다 **showcase** v. 전시하다 **portrait** n. 초상화 **influential** adj. 영향력 있는 **accompany** v. 딸리다, 동반되다 **coffee-table book** 차 탁자용 책 **feature** v. 특별히 포함하다, 특징으로 삼다

07

Hammond 재단은 도움에 대한 최근의 호소에 응답한 모든 이들에게 감사를 표하고 싶어 합니다. 이 단체는 기부로 1천 2백만 달러 이상을 모았습니다. 음식과 의료 지원을 제공하는 것뿐만 아니라, 이 기금은 허리케인 Wendy의 희생자들을 위한 집을 짓는 데 사용될 것입니다.

(A) 자선 단체는 폭풍 희생자들을 위한 음식과 약을 모았다.
(B) 폭풍 희생자들은 다양한 형태의 도움을 받는 것을 기대할 수 있다.

해설 답의 근거 문장은 'In addition to providing food and medical aid, the funds will be used to build housing for the victims of Hurricane Wendy.'로 (B)가 정답이다. providing food and medical aid, ~ build housing이 various forms of assistance로, victims of hurricane이 Storm victims로 바뀌어 표현되었다.

어휘 **foundation** n. 재단 **donation** n. 기부 **fund** n. 기금 **victim** n. 희생자, 피해자 **casualty** n. 희생자, 사상자

08

정기 점검은 건물 관리자의 책임입니다. 점검 요청 사항이 있으시면, 행정실에서 얻으실 수 있는 알맞은 양식을 작성하십시오. 요청은 오는 순서대로 처리될 것이며 각각을 시기 적절하게 처리하기 위해 모든 노력이 취해질 것입니다. 비상 시에는, 555-2307로 전화하십시오.

(A) 요청은 수령되는 순서대로 처리될 것이다.
(B) 건물 관리진은 각각의 요청에 즉시 응답할 것이다.

해설 답의 근거가 되는 부분은 'Requests will be dealt with in the order that they come in'으로 (A)가 정답이다. will be dealt with가 will be handled로, they come in이 they are received로 바뀌어 표현되었다.

어휘 **routine maintenance** 정기 점검 **request** n. 요청 사항, 요청 **administration office** 행정실 **deal with** 처리하다 **handle** v. 처리하다

09 안내문

방문객 주차

Winslow 대학교는 교내 주차장 사용을 위해 허가증을 요구합니다. 방문객들은 "P" 표시로 표기된 구역에만 그들의 차량을 둘 수 있습니다. — [1] —. 차량이 자동 판매기에서 발행된 허가증을 보여주지 않는 한, 미터제 구역에는 두 시간 제한이 있습니다. — [2] —. 이러한 구역에 주차하는 것은 월요일부터 금요일 오전 8시와 오후 4시 사이에 시간당 1.50달러입니다. 주차장은 휴일뿐 아니라 주말에도 개방합니다. — [3] —. 지도를 포함하여, 교내 주차 구역에 대한 자세한 정보를 위해서는, www.winslow.edu/parking를 방문하시거나 저희의 모바일 앱을 다운로드하십시오.

permit n. 허가증 **designate** v. 표기하다 **issue** v. 발행하다 **vending machine** 자동 판매기

문제 [1], [2], [3]으로 표시된 위치 중, 다음 문장이 들어갈 곳으로 가장 적절한 것은?

"이 날에는 그곳들 전역에 방문객들이 무료로 주차하는 것이 가능합니다."

(A) [1]
(B) [2]
(C) [3]

해설 **문장 위치 찾기 문제** 지문의 흐름상 주어진 문장이 들어가기에 가장 적절한 곳을 고르는 문제이다. They are all available to visitors for parking free of charge on these days에서 이 날에는 그곳들 전역에 방문객들이 무료로 주차하는 것이 가능하다고 했으므로, 주어진 문장 앞에 무료로 주차하는 것이 가능한 날과 장소에 관한 내용이 언급된 부분이 있을 것임을 예상할 수 있다. [3]의 앞 문장인 'Parking lots are open on weekends as well as holidays.'(4번째 줄)에서 주차장은 휴일뿐만 아니라 주말에도 개방한다고 했으므로, [3]에 주어진 문장이 들어가면 휴일과 주말의 주차장 이용에 관한 내용을 설명하는 자연스러운 문맥이 된다는 것을 알 수 있다. 따라서 (C) [3]이 정답이다.

어휘 **free of charge** 무료로

10 기사

처음으로 글을 쓴 작가 Marsha Bachman은 6월 23일 오후 1시에 Orville 서점에서 그녀의 책 *Stride to Success*에 사인할 것이다. Ms. Bachman은 군생활 20년 경력의 은퇴한 미군 대위이다. — [1] —. 이 책은 Ms. Bachman의 경험과 그것이 그녀를 오늘날의 그녀로 만드는 데 어떻게 기여했는지에 대한 이야기를 한다. 평론가들은 이것을 감동적이지만 또한 편한 마음으로 즐길 수 있는 역경에 맞선 승리 이야기라고 부른다. — [2] —. *The Denver Sentinel*지의 Mandy Coleman은 '필독서'라고 말한다. — [3] —.

first-time adj. (무엇을) 처음으로 해 보는 **retired** adj. 은퇴한 **captain** n. 대위 **give an account of** ~의 이야기를 하다 **critic** n. 평론가 **touching** adj. 감동적인 **light-hearted** adj. 편한 마음으로 즐길 수 있는 **adversity** n. 역경

문제 [1], [2], [3]으로 표시된 위치 중, 다음 문장이 들어갈 곳으로 가장 적절한 것은?

"현재 그녀는 전국의 대학과 회사에서 동기부여 연설을 한다."

(A) [1]
(B) [2]
(C) [3]

해설 **문장 위치 찾기 문제** 지문의 흐름상 주어진 문장이 들어가기에 가장 적절한 곳을 고르는 문제이다. Now she gives motivational speeches at colleges and offices around the country에서 현재 그녀는 전국의 대학과 회사에서 동기부여 연설을 한다고 했으므로, 주어진 문장 앞에 그녀의 현재나 과거에 관한 내용이 언급된 부분이 있을 것임을 예상할 수 있다. [1]의 앞 문장이 'Ms. Bachman is a retired US army captain with a 20-year career in the military.'(2번째 줄)에서 Ms. Bachman은 군생활 20년 경력의 은퇴한 미군 대위라고 했으므로, [1]에 주어진 문장이 들어가면 그녀의 과거와 현재의 활동에 대해 이야기하는 자연스러운 문맥이 된다는 것을 알 수 있다. 따라서 (A) [1]이 정답이다.

어휘　**motivational** adj. 동기부여의

11 기사

노르웨이 석유 회사 Borfinne는 향후 몇 년에 걸친 거대한 유가 급등에 기대를 걸 수 있을 것이다. — [1] —. 경제 분석가들은 회사의 전 세계적인 선단 확장 계획 발표에 따라 이 결론에 도달했다. — [2] —. 익명의 소식통에 따르면, 회사는 향후 2년에 걸쳐 배달될 15척의 새로운 선박을 주문했다. — [3] —. Borfinne사는 북해, 멕시코 만, 그리고 서부 아프리카의 연안 해역에 소재하고 있다. Borfinne사의 대변인은 이 글을 쓰는 시점에는 설명을 위한 연락이 닿지 않았다.

spike n. 급등　**analyst** n. 경제 분석가, 분석자　**fleet** n. 선단
unnamed adj. 익명의　**source** n. 소식통, 출처　**place an order** 주문하다
vessel n. 선박　**coastal waters** 연안 해역　**spokesperson** n. 대변인

문제　[1], [2], [3]으로 표시된 위치 중, 다음 문장이 들어갈 곳으로 가장 적절한 것은?

"이 선박들은 아마도 세 곳의 연안 사업체 중 하나에 배치될 것이다."

　　(A) [1]
　　(B) [2]
　　(C) [3]

해설　**문장 위치 찾기 문제** 지문의 흐름상 주어진 문장이 들어가기에 가장 적절한 곳을 고르는 문제이다. The ships could conceivably be deployed in one of three offshore operations에서 선박들이 아마도 세 곳의 연안 사업체 중 하나에 배치될 것이라고 했으므로, 주어진 문장 뒤에 세 곳의 연안 사업체에 관한 내용이 언급된 부분이 있을 것임을 예상할 수 있다. [3]의 뒤 문장인 'Borfinne has locations in the North Sea, the Gulf of Mexico, and the coastal waters of Western Africa.'(4번째 줄)에서 Borfinne사는 북해, 멕시코 만, 그리고 서부 아프리카의 연안 해역에 소재하고 있다고 했으므로, [3]에 주어진 문장이 들어가면 선박들이 배치될 수 있는 연안 사업체 세 곳에 대해 설명하는 자연스러운 문맥이 된다는 것을 알 수 있다. 따라서 (C) [3]이 정답이다.

어휘　**conceivably** adv. 아마도, 생각하건대　**deploy** v. 배치하다
offshore adj. 연안의　**operation** n. 사업체, 기업

Hackers Test

p.388

| 01 (C) | 02 (C) | 03 (B) | 04 (C) | 05 (B) |
| 06 (A) | 07 (D) | 08 (D) | | |

01-04는 다음 이메일에 관한 문제입니다.

발신: Norma Lewis <nlewis@bestfurniture.com>
수신: James Vogel <jvogel@smail.com>
제목: 가구 주문
날짜: 9월 10일

Mr. Vogel께,

저희는 귀하로부터 4개의 어울리는 의자가 딸린 옅은 황갈색 직사각형 Edgewood 시리즈 식탁을 주문받았습니다. 그러나, [01/02]귀하께서 주문한 크기가 지사의 모든 곳에서 품절되었으며 월말까지 저희 제조업체로부터 새로 공급되지 않을 것이라는 사실을 전하게 되어 유감입니다. — [1] —. [03-D]저희는 귀하의 주문을 우선으로 하고 있으며 그것을 수령하는 대로 귀하께 보내드릴 수 있습니다. — [2] —. 식탁이 더 빨리 필요하시다면, [03-A/04]저희는 약간 더 큰 크기의 동일한 제품을 추천드리고 싶습니다. [04]이것 또한 직사각형이지만, 가로 1.1미터 세로 1.3미터의 크기입니다. — [3] —. 혹은 귀하께서 선호하는 크기로 [03-C]구입 가능한 다른 디자인을 확인해 보실 수 있습니다. 저희가 귀하의 주문을 어떻게 처리할지 알 수 있도록 가능한 한 빨리 귀하의 답변을 받기를 바랍니다. — [4] —.

불편을 드린 것에 대해 깊이 사과드립니다. 질문이 있으시다면 알려주십시오.

Norma Lewis 드림
고객 서비스팀
Best Furniture사

rectangular adj. 직사각형의　**oak** n. 황갈색, 오크 (나무)
restock v. 새로 공급하다, 보충하다　**supplier** n. 제조업체
priority n. 우선, 우선권　**slightly** adv. 약간, 조금

01 주제/목적 찾기 문제

문제　이메일의 주 목적은 무엇인가?

　　(A) 주문의 발송을 확정하기 위해
　　(B) 카탈로그 요청에 답변하기 위해
　　(C) 고객에게 문제를 알리기 위해
　　(D) 가구 사양을 제공하기 위해

해설　이메일이 쓰인 목적을 묻는 목적 찾기 문제이다. 'we are sorry to say that the size you ordered is sold out'(1문단 2번째 줄)에서 이메일의 수신자가 주문한 크기가 품절되었다는 것을 전하게 되어 유감이라고 했으므로 (C) To inform a customer of a problem이 정답이다.

어휘　**shipment** n. 발송, 수송　**specification** n. 사양, 설명서

02 추론 문제

문제　Best Furniture사에 대해 암시되는 것은?

　　(A) 제품을 국제 수송한다.
　　(B) 자사 상품 라인을 제조한다.
　　(C) 한 곳 이상의 매장을 운영한다.
　　(D) 월말에 할인 판매 행사를 개최할 것이다.

해설　질문의 핵심 어구인 Best Furniture사에 대해 추론하는 문제이다. 'the size you ordered is sold out at all our locations'(1문단 2번째 줄)에서 주문한 크기가 Best Furniture사의 모든 곳에서 품절되었다고 했으므로 매장이 한 곳 이상이라는 사실을 추론할 수 있다. 따라서 (C) It operates more than one store가 정답이다.

03 Not/True 문제

문제　Ms. Lewis가 제안하는 대안이 아닌 것은?

　　(A) 더 큰 크기를 사는 것
　　(B) 빠른 처리를 위한 비용을 지불하는 것
　　(C) 구입 가능한 다른 제품들을 보는 것
　　(D) 물품의 재고가 있을 때까지 기다리는 것

해설　질문의 핵심 어구인 an option that Ms. Lewis offers와 관련된 내용을 지문에서 찾아 보기와 대조하는 Not/True 문제이다. (A)는 'we would like to suggest the same model in a slightly larger size'(1문단 5번째 줄)에서 약간 더 큰 크기의 동일한 제품을 추천하고 싶다고 했으므로 지문의 내용과 일치한다. (B)는 지문에 언급되지 않은 내용이다. 따라서 (B) Paying a rush fee가 정답이다. (C)는 'you can check out other designs available'(1문단 6번째 줄)에서 구입 가능한 다른 디자인을 확인해 볼 수 있다고 했으므로 지문의 내용과 일치한다. (D)는 'We ~ can ship it to you as soon as we receive it.'(1문단 3번째 줄)에서 기존 주문 제품을 수령하는 대로 보내줄 수 있다고 했으므로 지문의 내용과 일치한다.

04 문장 위치 찾기 문제

문제　[1], [2], [3], [4]로 표시된 위치 중, 다음 문장이 들어갈 곳으로 가장 적절한 것은?

"결정하시는 것을 돕기 위해, 저희는 두 식탁의 크기 각각을 비교하실 수 있도록 카탈로그를 첨부했습니다."

　　(A) [1]
　　(B) [2]
　　(C) [3]
　　(D) [4]

해설　지문의 흐름상 주어진 문장이 들어가기에 가장 적절한 곳을 고르는 문제이다. To help you decide, we have attached a catalog so that you can compare each of the two table sizes에서 결정하는 것을 돕기 위해 두 식탁의 크기 각각을 비교할 수 있도록 카탈로그를 첨부했다고 했으므로, 주어진 문장 앞에 두 식탁의 크기에 관한 내용이 있을 것을 예상할 수 있다. [3]의 앞부분 'we ~ suggest the same model in a slightly larger size'(1문단 5번째 줄)에서 약간 더 큰 크기의 동일한 제품을 추천한다고 하며 [3]의 앞 문장인 'It ~ measures 1.1 by 1.3 meters.'(1문단 5번째 줄)에서 그 식탁

의 크기를 언급하고 있으므로, [3]에 주어진 문장이 들어가면 두 개의 식탁의 크기를 비교해 보는 것에 대해 설명하는 자연스러운 문맥이 된다는 것을 알 수 있다. 따라서 (C) [3]이 정답이다.

05-08은 다음 공고에 관한 문제입니다.

> ⁰⁵Hastings 미술관은 Paul and Marina Novak Collection이 9월에 공개 관람으로 돌아올 것임을 알리게 되어 기쁩니다. — [1] —. ^{07-A/C}1924년과 1988년 사이에 호주 예술가들에 의해 제작된 300점이 넘는 예술품들을 포함하는 이 소장품 전시는 미술관 공간의 간단한 정비로 인해 작년에 문을 닫았습니다. 이 날을 기념하기 위해 작은 행사가 계획되었습니다. — [2] —. 추후 공지를 기다려 주시길 바랍니다.
>
> 소장품에 관해:
> 소장품은 멜버른 주민인 Paul Novak과 Marina Novak에 의해 Hastings 미술관에 기증되었습니다. ^{06-A}Ms. Novak은 의사인 Dr. Paul Novak과 결혼했던 때인 1940년대에 패션 디자이너였습니다. — [3] —. ^{06-A}부부는 예술에 대한 열정을 공유했고, 이것은 Ms. Novak이 1951년에 미술상이 되도록 이끌었습니다. 호주의 예술가들을 전 세계에 홍보하는 것을 목표로, ⁰⁸그녀는 최고의 신흥 호주 예술가들을 찾아내고 호주 예술가들의 작품에 대한 관심을 불러일으키기 위해 수십 년 동안 노력했습니다. — [4] —. ^{06-B}1991년에 Ms. Novak의 사망 직후, ^{06-B/07-B}모든 그림들은 Hastings 미술관에 기증되었습니다. 그것은 국내에서 미술관에 한 최대의 예술 작품 기증 중 하나로 남아 있습니다.

refurbishment n. 정비, 단장 **commemorate** v. 기념하다
occasion n. (특정한) 때, 경우 **physician** n. 의사 **art dealer** 미술상
promote v. 홍보하다, 촉진하다 **labor** v. 노력하다, 일하다
identify v. 찾아내다, 확인하다 **emerging** adj. 신흥의, 신생의

05 주제/목적 찾기 문제

문제 주로 공고되고 있는 것은 무엇인가?
(A) 미술관 매각
(B) 전시의 재개장
(C) 큐레이터 고용
(D) 예술가 표창

해설 주로 공고되고 있는 것을 묻는 주제 찾기 문제이다. 'The Hastings Gallery is delighted to reveal that the Paul and Marina Novak Collection will be returning for public viewing in September.'(1문단 1번째 줄)에서 Hastings 미술관이 Paul and Marina Novak Collection이 9월에 공개 관람으로 돌아올 것임을 알리게 되어 기쁘다고 한 후, 전시에 대해 소개하고 있으므로 (B) The reopening of an exhibit이 정답이다.

Paraphrasing
be returning for public viewing 공개 관람으로 돌아오다 → reopening 재개장

어휘 **recognition** n. 표창, 인정

06 Not/True 문제

문제 Marina Novak에 대해 사실인 것은?
(A) 예술품을 취급하기 전에 패션 분야에서 일했다.
(B) 그녀의 예술품은 호주 전역의 미술관에서 보여졌다.
(C) 미술관 건설에 자금을 대는 것을 도왔다.
(D) 그녀의 남편은 전 세계에서 미술품을 수집했다.

해설 질문의 핵심 어구인 Marina Novak과 관련된 내용을 지문에서 찾아 보기와 대조하는 Not/True 문제이다. (A)는 'Ms. Novak was a fashion designer in the 1940s'(2문단 2번째 줄)와 'The couple shared a passion for art, which led Ms. Novak to become an art dealer in 1951.'(2문단 3번째 줄)에서 Ms. Novak은 1940년대에 패션 디자이너였으며 부부는 예술에 대한 열정을 공유했고 이것이 Ms. Novak이 1951년에 미술상이 되도록 이끌었다고 했으므로 지문의 내용과 일치한다. 따라서 (A) She worked in fashion before dealing in art가 정답이다. (B)는 'Shortly after Ms. Novak's passing ~, all of the paintings were donated to the Hastings Gallery.'(2문단 7번째 줄)에서 Ms. Novak의 사망 직후 모든 그림들은 Hastings 미술관에 기증되었다고 했으므로 지문의 내용과 일치하지 않는다. (C)와 (D)는 지문에 언급되지 않은 내용이다.

Paraphrasing
was a fashion designer 패션 디자이너였다 → worked in fashion 패션 분야에서 일했다
art dealer 미술상 → dealing in art 예술품을 취급하다

어휘 **deal in** 취급하다, 거래하다 **fund** v. 자금을 대다; n. 자금

07 Not/True 문제

문제 Paul and Marina Novak Collection에 대해 언급되지 않은 것은?
(A) 300점이 넘는 작품들로 구성된다.
(B) 미술관에 무료로 제공되었다.
(C) 1924년부터 1988년까지 만들어진 작품을 포함한다.
(D) 보수 공사 동안 일부가 손상되었다.

해설 질문의 핵심 어구인 the Paul and Marina Novak Collection과 관련된 내용을 지문에서 찾아 보기와 대조하는 Not/True 문제이다. (A)와 (C)는 'Featuring over 300 works of art produced ~ between 1924 and 1988'(1문단 3번째 줄)에서 1924년과 1988년 사이에 제작된 300점이 넘는 예술품들을 포함한다고 했으므로 지문의 내용과 일치한다. (B)는 'all of the paintings were donated to the Hastings Gallery'(2문단 8번째 줄)에서 모든 그림들은 Hastings 미술관에 기증되었다고 했으므로 지문의 내용과 일치한다. (D)는 지문에 언급되지 않은 내용이다. 따라서 (D) It was partially damaged during a renovation이 정답이다.

Paraphrasing
Featuring over 300 works of art 300점이 넘는 예술품들을 포함하다 → consists of more than 300 pieces 300점이 넘는 작품들로 구성되다
donated 기부하다 → given ~ for free 무료로 제공되다
Featuring ~ works of art produced ~ between 1924 and 1988 1924년과 1988년 사이에 제작된 예술품들을 포함하다 → contains pieces made from 1924 to 1988 1924년부터 1988년까지 만들어진 작품을 포함하다

어휘 **partially** adv. 일부, 부분적으로 **renovation** n. 보수 공사, 개조

08 문장 위치 찾기 문제

문제 [1], [2], [3], [4]로 표시된 위치 중, 다음 문장이 들어갈 곳으로 가장 적절한 것은?
"그녀는 동시에 뛰어난 개인 소장품을 모았습니다."
(A) [1]
(B) [2]
(C) [3]
(D) [4]

해설 지문의 흐름상 주어진 문장이 들어가기에 가장 적절한 곳을 고르는 문제이다. She simultaneously built up an outstanding private collection에서 그녀는 동시에 뛰어난 개인 소장품을 모았다고 했으므로, 주어진 문장 앞에 개인 소장품을 모은 기간에 한 일과 관련된 내용이 있을 것임을 예상할 수 있다. [4]의 앞 문장인 'she labored for decades to identify the best emerging Australian artists and to generate interest in the work of Australian artists'(2문단 5번째 줄)에서 그녀는 최고의 신흥 호주 예술가들을 찾아내고 호주 예술가들의 작품에 대한 관심을 불러일으키기 위해 수십 년 동안 노력했다고 했으므로, [4]에 주어진 문장이 들어가면 수십 년 동안 최고의 신흥 호주 예술가들을 찾아내고 호주 예술가들의 작품에 대한 관심을 불러일으키기 위해 노력하면서 뛰어난 개인 소장품을 모았다는 자연스러운 문맥이 된다는 것을 알 수 있다. 따라서 (D) [4]가 정답이다.

어휘 **simultaneously** adv. 동시에, 일제히

Chapter 07 동의어 찾기 문제

예제 해석 p.390

기사

> 온라인 소매의 동향
> 많은 수의 소기업들은 더 이상 상점 공간을 임대하거나 비싼 임대 계약을 하 ◑

지 않는다. 임대료가 계속 오르고 있기 때문에, 온라인 상점이나 서비스를 여는 것이 점점 인기가 많아지고 있다. 게다가, 기업 소유주들은 훨씬 쉽게 그들의 회계를 관리할 수 있고, 너무 많은 추가 직원들을 고용하는 것을 피할 수 있다.

또한, 많은 소매 상인들은 그들이 온라인 상점을 통해 매출을 증가시킬 수 있다고 주장한다. 보다 낮은 운영 비용은 그들이 고객들에게 더 낮은 가격을 제공할 수 있음을 의미한다. 운송료가 있더라도, 많은 인터넷 소매 상인들은 보통 상점들보다 낮은 가격에 물건을 팔 수 있다.

rent out 임대하다　lease n. 임대 계약　accounting n. 회계, 정산
retailer n. 소매 상인　operational adj. 운영상의, 사용 가능한

문제　1문단 세 번째 줄의 단어 "climb"은 의미상 ~와 가장 가깝다.
(A) 개선되다
(B) 오르다
(C) 확대하다

어휘　improve v. 개선되다　expand v. 확대하다

Hackers Practice

p.396

01 ⓐ	02 ⓑ	03 ⓑ	04 ⓐ	05 ⓐ
06 ⓐ	07 ⓐ	08 ⓑ	09 ⓐ	10 ⓑ
11 ⓑ	12 ⓐ	13 ⓐ	14 ⓐ	15 ⓐ
16 ⓐ	17 ⓐ	18 ⓐ	19 ⓐ	20 ⓐ
21 ⓐ	22 ⓐ	23 ⓐ	24 ⓐ	25 ⓐ
26 ⓐ	27 ⓐ	28 ⓐ	29 ⓐ	30 ⓑ
31 ⓐ	32 ⓐ	33 ⓐ	34 ⓑ	35 ⓐ
36 ⓐ	37 ⓑ	38 ⓑ	39 ⓐ	40 ⓐ
41 ⓐ	42 ⓐ	43 ⓐ	44 ⓑ	45 ⓐ
46 ⓐ	47 ⓑ	48 ⓐ	49 ⓐ	50 ⓑ
51 ⓑ	52 ⓐ	53 ⓑ	54 ⓐ	55 ⓐ
56 ⓐ	57 ⓐ	58 ⓐ	59 ⓑ	60 ⓐ
61 ⓐ	62 ⓑ			

01
해석　당신의 가방을 사물함에 두세요.
해설　Place가 '두다'라는 의미로 쓰였으므로 ⓐ Put(두다)이 정답이다.

02
해석　그 브로셔는 고객들에게 제품들에 대해 알려 주었다.
해설　inform이 '알려 주다'라는 의미로 쓰였으므로 ⓑ told가 정답이다. (tell: 알려 주다)

03
해석　초청 연사를 만날 기회
해설　chance가 '기회'라는 의미로 쓰였으므로 ⓑ opportunity(기회)가 정답이다.
어휘　guest speaker 초청 연사　assembly n. 집회, 회의

04
해석　회사의 최신 스포츠카 모델
해설　model이 '모델', 즉 '디자인'이라는 의미로 쓰였으므로 ⓐ design(디자인)이 정답이다.

05
해석　그 세일은 상품이 빨리 판매되도록 했다.
해설　move가 '판매되다'라는 의미로 쓰였으므로 ⓐ sold가 정답이다. (sell: 판매되다)
어휘　merchandise n. 상품　relocate v. 이전하다

06
해석　현재 고용 상태

해설　status가 '상태, 상황'이라는 의미로 쓰였으므로 ⓐ state(상태)가 정답이다.
어휘　employment n. 고용　fact n. 사실

07
해석　고객의 요구에 관하여
해설　regarding이 '~에 관하여'라는 의미로 쓰였으므로 ⓐ concerning(~에 관련하여)이 정답이다.

08
해석　그리 많지 않은 에너지 소비량
해설　modest가 '많지 않은'이라는 의미로 쓰였으므로 ⓑ limited(아주 많지는 않은, 제한된)가 정답이다.
어휘　consumption n. 소비(량)　slight adj. 약간의

09
해석　재정 전문가들은 그 진술을 확인했다.
해설　support가 '(진술이나 말 등을) 확인하다'라는 의미로 쓰였으므로 ⓐ confirmed가 정답이다. (confirm: 확인하다)
어휘　look after 돌보다, 부양하다

10
해석　많은 돈이 들 것이다
해설　a great deal of가 '많은'이라는 의미로 쓰였으므로 ⓑ a large amount of (많은)가 정답이다.
어휘　reduction n. 감소

11
해석　배송 일정을 신속히 처리하다
해설　expedite가 '신속히 처리하다'라는 의미로 쓰였으므로 ⓑ speed up(속도를 높이다)이 정답이다.
어휘　turn down 거절하다

12
해석　운송 위치를 추적하다
해설　track이 '추적하다'라는 의미로 쓰였으므로 ⓐ monitor(감시하다, 관리하다)가 정답이다.

13
해석　그 차량은 겨울에 잘 작동한다.
해설　perform이 '작동하다'라는 의미로 쓰였으므로 ⓐ functions가 정답이다. (function: 작동하다) ⓑ의 act(실행하다)도 perform의 동의어지만, 문제에서 perform이 '실행하다'의 의미로 쓰이지 않았으므로 답이 될 수 없다.
어휘　vehicle n. 차량

14
해석　회사의 교대 업무 일정
해설　rotate가 '교대하다'라는 의미로 쓰였으므로 ⓐ alternating이 정답이다. (alternate: 교대하다) ⓑ의 turn(돌다)도 rotate의 동의어지만, 문제에서 rotate가 '돌다'의 의미로 쓰이지 않았으므로 답이 될 수 없다.

15
해석　회계의 새로운 방법을 습득하다
해설　learn이 '습득하다', 즉 '알게 되다'라는 의미로 쓰였으므로 ⓐ find out(~에 대해 알게 되다)이 정답이다.
어휘　accounting n. 회계　look up 찾아보다

16
해석　그녀의 아프리카 여행에 대한 이야기
해설　account가 '이야기'라는 의미로 쓰였으므로 ⓐ narrative(이야기, 묘사)가 정

답이다.

어휘 **figure** n. 숫자, 모습

17
해석 당신의 특별한 요청을 못 보고 지나치다

해설 overlook이 '~을 못 보고 지나치다, 빠뜨리다'라는 의미로 쓰였으므로 ⓑ neglect(간과하다)가 정답이다.

어휘 **accomplish** v. 성취하다

18
해석 당신에게 정확한 정보를 전달하겠다

해설 right가 '정확한, 바른'이라는 의미로 쓰였으므로 ⓐ correct(정확한)가 정답이다.

어휘 **forward** v. 전달하다, 보내다   **request** v. 요청하다

19
해석 규칙을 준수하다

해설 observe가 '준수하다'라는 의미로 쓰였으므로 ⓐ follow(준수하다, 따르다)가 정답이다.

어휘 **establish** v. 제정하다, 만들다

20
해석 법인 계약서를 승인하다

해설 confirm이 '승인하다'라는 의미로 쓰였으므로 ⓐ approve(승인하다)가 정답이다.

어휘 **corporate** adj. 법인의   **reject** v. 거절하다

21
해석 그 연설자는 웹 마케팅에 대한 조언을 제공했다.

해설 tip이 '조언'이라는 의미로 쓰였으므로 ⓑ suggestions가 정답이다. (suggestion: 조언) ⓐ summits(정상)도 tip의 동의어지만, 문제에서 tip이 '정상'의 의미로 쓰이지 않았으므로 답이 될 수 없다.

22
해석 Ms. Baines는 사교적인 성격을 가지고 있다.

해설 outgoing이 '사교적인'이라는 의미로 쓰였으므로 ⓐ friendly(사교적인)가 정답이다. ⓑ leaving(떠나는)도 outgoing의 동의어지만, 문제에서 outgoing이 '떠나는'의 의미로 쓰이지 않았으므로 답이 될 수 없다.

어휘 **personality** n. 성격   **leave** v. 떠나다

23
해석 비와 눈으로부터 보호하기 위한 마감 칠

해설 finish가 '마감 칠'이라는 의미로 쓰였으므로 ⓑ coating(칠)이 정답이다.

어휘 **completion** n. 완료

24
해석 새 향수를 출시하다

해설 launch가 '출시하다'라는 의미로 쓰였으므로 ⓑ introduce(발표하다)가 정답이다.

어휘 **perfume** n. 향수   **develop** v. 개발하다

25
해석 우편실 보조원 공석

해설 vacancy가 '공석'이라는 의미로 쓰였으므로 ⓐ opening(빈자리)이 정답이다.

어휘 **assistant** n. 보조원   **career** n. 직업, 이력

26
해석 선약이 있다

해설 engagement가 '약속'이라는 의미로 쓰였으므로 ⓑ appointment(약속)가 정답이다.

어휘 **previous** adj. 이전의   **reservation** n. 예약

27
해석 회사의 명성을 유지하다

해설 maintain이 '유지하다'라는 의미로 쓰였으므로 ⓐ preserve(유지하다)가 정답이다. ⓑ assert(주장하다)도 maintain의 동의어지만, 문제에서 maintain이 '주장하다'의 의미로 쓰이지 않았으므로 답이 될 수 없다.

어휘 **reputation** n. 명성

28
해석 무료 신규 도서

해설 complimentary가 '무료의'라는 의미로 쓰였으므로 ⓐ free(무료의)가 정답이다.

어휘 **praiseworthy** adj. 칭찬할 만한

29
해석 재정 손실을 평가하다

해설 damage가 '손실'이라는 의미로 쓰였으므로 ⓑ loss(손실)가 정답이다.

어휘 **assess** v. 평가하다   **risk** n. 위험

30
해석 휘발유 가격이 떨어지고 있다.

해설 fall이 '떨어지다'라는 의미로 쓰였으므로 ⓑ decreasing이 정답이다. (decrease: 떨어지다)

어휘 **inflate** v. (가격이) 상승하다

31
해석 자금의 잔액을 이체하다

해설 balance가 '잔액'이라는 의미로 쓰였으므로 ⓑ remainder(잔여, 나머지)가 정답이다.

어휘 **stability** n. 안정

32
해석 수입이 현저하게 증가했다.

해설 markedly가 '현저하게'라는 의미로 쓰였으므로 ⓐ distinctly(뚜렷하게)가 정답이다.

어휘 **import** n. 수입   **primarily** adv. 주로, 첫째로

33
해석 이사회의 요구 조건을 충족시키다

해설 meet가 '충족시키다'라는 의미로 쓰였으므로 ⓐ satisfy(충족시키다)가 정답이다. ⓑ encounter(만나다)도 meet의 동의어이지만 문제에서 meet가 '만나다'의 의미로 쓰이지 않았으므로 답이 될 수 없다.

어휘 **board** n. 이사회   **requirement** n. 요구 조건

34
해석 사업을 경영하다

해설 operate가 '경영하다'라는 의미로 쓰였으므로 ⓑ run(경영하다)이 정답이다. ⓐ work(작동하다)도 operate의 동의어이지만, 문제에서 operate가 '작동하다'의 의미로 쓰이지 않았으므로 답이 될 수 없다.

35
해석 그의 임박한 퇴직

해설 impending이 '임박한'이라는 의미로 쓰였으므로 ⓐ approaching(다가오

는)이 정답이다.

어휘 voluntary adj. 자발적인, 자원한

36
해석 팩스 기계 사용법을 설명하다

해설 demonstrate가 '설명하다'라는 의미로 쓰였으므로 ⓐ explain(설명하다)이 정답이다. ⓑ protest(항의하다)도 demonstrate의 동의어이지만, 문제에서 demonstrate가 '항의하다'의 의미로 쓰이지 않았으므로 답이 될 수 없다.

37
해석 사치품 소비가 갑자기 줄어들었다.

해설 abruptly가 '갑자기'라는 의미로 쓰였으므로 ⓑ suddenly(갑자기)가 정답이다.

어휘 consumption n. 소비 luxury goods 사치품 significantly adv. 크게

38
해석 편집자는 기사에서 그 문제점들을 강조했다.

해설 highlight가 '강조하다'라는 의미로 쓰였으므로 ⓐ featured가 정답이다. (feature: ~을 특집으로 하다)

39
해석 마지막 모임은 다음 주에 있을 것이다.

해설 occur가 '일어나다'라는 의미로 쓰였으므로 ⓑ happen(일어나다)이 정답이다.

어휘 conclude v. 끝나다, 종료되다

40
해석 요리하는 냄새는 손님들을 끈다.

해설 draw가 '(주의·흥미 등을) 끌다'라는 의미로 쓰였으므로 ⓐ attract(끌다)가 정답이다.

어휘 carry v. 쟁취하다, 나르다

41
해석 우리의 면허는 다음 달에 만료된다.

해설 expire가 '만료되다'라는 의미로 쓰였으므로 ⓑ finishes가 정답이다. (finish: 끝나다) ⓐ의 perish(죽다)도 expire의 동의어이지만, 문제에서 expire가 '죽다'의 의미로 쓰이지 않았으므로 답이 될 수 없다.

42
해석 자사 제품의 질을 높이다

해설 raise가 '높이다'라는 의미로 쓰였으므로 ⓐ elevate(높이다)가 정답이다. ⓑ gather(모으다)도 raise의 동의어이지만, 문제에서 raise가 '(돈을) 모으다'의 의미로 쓰이지 않았으므로 답이 될 수 없다.

43
해석 Ms. Haught는 그녀의 공헌으로 영예를 받았다.

해설 honor가 '영예를 주다'라는 의미로 쓰였으므로 ⓐ recognized가 정답이다. (recognize: 인정하다)

어휘 contribution n. 공헌

44
해석 경쟁에 직면하다

해설 face가 '직면하다'라는 의미로 쓰였으므로 ⓑ confront(직면하다)가 정답이다.

어휘 defeat v. (전쟁·선거에서) 이기다

45
해석 분실된 수하물에 대한 철저한 수색

해설 thorough가 '철저한'이라는 의미로 쓰였으므로 ⓐ complete(철저한)가 정

답이다.

어휘 luggage n. 수하물 random adj. 닥치는 대로의, 임의의

46
해석 인터넷 서비스를 정지하다

해설 suspend가 '정지하다'라는 의미로 쓰였으므로 ⓐ cancel(정지하다)이 정답이다.

어휘 defend v. 막다, 방어하다

47
해석 연 12퍼센트의 이자가 붙다

해설 accrue가 '(이자가) 붙다, 생기다'라는 의미로 쓰였으므로 ⓑ accumulate (축적되다)가 정답이다.

어휘 interest n. 이자 pay v. 지불하다

48
해석 여성 의류 생산

해설 apparel이 '의류'라는 의미로 쓰였으므로 ⓐ garment(의류)가 정답이다.

49
해석 경제 상황에 영향을 미치다

해설 affect가 '영향을 미치다'라는 의미로 쓰였으므로 ⓐ influence(영향을 주다)가 정답이다. ⓑ pretend(~인 체하다)도 affect의 동의어이지만, 문제에서 affect가 '~인 체하다'의 의미로 쓰이지 않았으므로 답이 될 수 없다.

어휘 economic adj. 경제의

50
해석 새 프로젝트를 시작하고 싶어 하다

해설 anxious가 '~하고 싶어 하는'이라는 의미로 쓰였으므로 ⓑ eager(~하고 싶어 하는)가 정답이다.

51
해석 산업 생산량의 감소

해설 output이 '생산량'이라는 의미로 쓰였으므로 ⓑ production(생산량)이 정답이다.

어휘 drop n. 감소 profit n. 이익

52
해석 과도한 업무량을 덜어 주다

해설 relieve가 '덜어 주다'라는 의미로 쓰였으므로 ⓐ alleviate(완화시키다)가 정답이다.

어휘 workload n. 업무량 endure v. 감당하다, 견디다

53
해석 슈퍼마켓 손님

해설 patron이 '손님'이라는 의미로 쓰였으므로 ⓑ customer(손님)가 정답이다. ⓐ supporter(후원자)도 patron의 동의어이지만, 문제에서 patron이 '후원자'의 의미로 쓰이지 않았으므로 답이 될 수 없다.

54
해석 그 일은 많은 스트레스를 수반한다.

해설 entail이 '수반하다'라는 의미로 쓰였으므로 ⓐ involves가 정답이다. (involve: 수반하다)

어휘 cause v. 야기시키다

55
해석 그 결정에 대한 결과로

해설 consequence가 '결과'라는 의미로 쓰였으므로 ⓐ result(결과)가 정답이다.

어휘 **objective** n. 목적

56

해석 경제 활동의 침체를 악화시키다

해설 aggravate가 '악화시키다'라는 의미로 쓰였으므로 ⓐ intensify(심하게 하다, 도를 더하다)가 정답이다.

어휘 **downturn** n. 침체, 하향세　**extend** v. 확장하다, 연장하다

57

해석 계약서 조항

해설 provision이 '조항'이라는 의미로 쓰였으므로 ⓐ clause(조항)가 정답이다. ⓑ supply(공급, 필수품)도 provision의 동의어지만, 문제에서 provision이 '공급'의 의미로 사용되지 않았으므로 답이 될 수 없다.

58

해석 뛰어난 자연적 아름다움

해설 outstanding이 '뛰어난'이라는 의미로 쓰였으므로 ⓐ exceptional(뛰어난)이 정답이다.

어휘 **excessive** adj. 지나친

59

해석 소풍에 좋은 장소

해설 spot이 '장소'라는 의미로 쓰였으므로 ⓑ place(장소)가 정답이다.

어휘 **property** n. 토지, 건물

60

해석 새 디자인에 대한 많은 추측이 있었다.

해설 speculation이 '추측'이라는 의미로 쓰였으므로 ⓐ conjecture(추측)가 정답이다.

어휘 **configuration** n. 구성, 배치

61

해석 모든 이의 기대를 능가하다

해설 surpass가 '능가하다'라는 의미로 쓰였으므로 ⓐ exceed(넘어서다)가 정답이다.

어휘 **expectation** n. 기대　**increase** v. 증가시키다

62

해석 부동산의 가치를 평가하다

해설 assess가 '평가하다'라는 의미로 쓰였으므로 ⓑ evaluate(평가하다)가 정답이다.

어휘 **property** n. 부동산　**depreciate** v. 가치를 떨어뜨리다

Hackers Test
p.398

01 (B)	02 (D)	03 (C)	04 (A)	05 (B)
06 (A)	07 (D)			

01-04는 다음 이메일에 관한 문제입니다.

발신: Mario Martinez <mmartinez@rosenblattcorp.com>
수신: 모든 연구 진행자 <researchdept@rosenblattcorp.com>
날짜: 4월 7일
제목: 연구의 질 향상

저는 지난달 조사 프로젝트를 검토하는 것을 끝냈으며 우리 직원들에 의해 제출된 작업 품질의 하락을 알아챘습니다. 자사 편집자인 Marcel Russolini도 그가 기술적인 오류들을 교정하는 데 두 배나 되는 시간을 들이고 있다고 언급했습니다. 게다가, 집필자들이 다른 사람들에 의해 실시된 연구 결과의 통계 자료에 관한 충분한 정보를 제시하지 않는 경우가 증가해 왔습니다. ◐

[01/04]Rosenblatt사는 몇몇 중요한 정부 기관, 재단 및 주식회사에 정보를 공급합니다. [04]그들은 정책 입안, 의사 결정 및 전 세계적으로 원조 활동 프로그램을 창설하는 데 지표가 되는 [04]우리의 조사 및 분석에 의존합니다. 그러므로, 우리가 엄격한 기준을 따르고 양질의 조사 보고서를 제공하는 것은 매우 중요합니다.

자사 이사인 Sonia Lieberman과의 회의 후에, 저희는 이러한 문제들에 대해 가능한 해결책을 찾아보았습니다.
– [02-A]집필 문제를 다루는 워크숍 실시
– [02-D]프로젝트 완료를 위한 추가 시간 제공
– 직원들에게 온라인 조사 자원 및 [03]어떤 구독을 연장하고자 하는지에 대한 제안 요청
– [02-C]집필자들에게 약간의 휴식 시간을 주기 위한 더 긴 휴가 계획
– [02-B]프로젝트와 관련한 어려움을 논의하기 위한 더 많은 그룹 회의의 개최

이 문제와 관련하여 다른 제안이 생각나면, 저에게 알려 주십시오.

Mario Martinez

coordinator n. 진행자　**look over** 검토하다
decline n. 하락, 퇴보; v. 거절하다, 하락하다　**statistics** n. 통계 자료
distribute v. 공급하다, 배포하다　**notable** adj. 중요한, 유명한
foundation n. 재단, 기초　**analysis** n. 분석　**policy making** 정책 입안
decision making 의사 결정　**outreach** n. 원조 활동, 봉사 활동
globe n. 세계; adj. 지구의　**crucial** adj. 매우 중요한, 결정적인
come up with (해답 등을) 찾아내다, 생각나다　**address** v. 다루다, 처리하다
resource n. 자원, 공급원　**subscription** n. 구독
renew v. 연장하다, 갱신하다　**downtime** n. 휴식 시간, 중단 기간

01 동의어 찾기 문제

문제 2문단 첫 번째 줄의 단어 "notable"은 의미상 ~와 가장 가깝다.
　(A) 서면으로 된
　(B) 중요한
　(C) 명백한
　(D) 공통의

해설 notable을 포함하고 있는 문장 'Rosenblatt Corporation distributes information to several notable government agencies, foundations, and corporations.'(2문단 1번째 줄)에서 notable은 '중요한'이라는 뜻으로 사용되었다. 따라서 '중요한'이라는 뜻을 가진 (B) important가 정답이다.

어휘 **written** adj. 서면으로 된, 문자로 쓴　**obvious** adj. 명백한
　common adj. 공통의, 보통의

02 Not/True 문제

문제 Ms. Lieberman과 Mr. Martinez에 의해 제시된 제안이 아닌 것은?
　(A) 직원 워크숍 준비하기
　(B) 더 잦은 회의 갖기
　(C) 더 긴 휴가 제공하기
　(D) 더 짧은 원고 마감 시간 계획하기

해설 질문의 핵심 어구인 a suggestion offered by Ms. Lieberman and Mr. Martinez와 관련된 내용을 지문에서 찾아 보기와 대조하는 Not/True 문제이다. (A)는 'Conducting workshops to address writing issues'(3문단 3번째 줄)에서 집필 문제를 다루는 워크숍 실시라고 했으므로 지문의 내용과 일치한다. (B)는 'Holding more group meetings to discuss difficulties with projects'(3문단 8번째 줄)에서 프로젝트와 관련한 어려움을 논의하기 위한 더 많은 그룹 회의 개최라고 했으므로 지문의 내용과 일치한다. (C)는 'Scheduling longer breaks to give writers some downtime'(3문단 7번째 줄)에서 집필자들에게 약간의 휴식 시간을 주기 위한 더 긴 휴가 계획이라고 했으므로 지문의 내용과 일치한다. (D)는 'Providing additional time for the completion of projects'(3문단 4번째 줄)에서 프로젝트 완료를 위한 추가 시간 제공이라고 했으므로 지문의 내용과 일치하지 않는다. 따라서 (D) Scheduling shorter deadlines가 정답이다.

Paraphrasing
Conducting workshops 워크숍 실시 → **Arranging ~ workshops** 워크숍 준비
Holding ~ meetings 회의 개최 → **Having ~ meetings** 회의 갖기
Scheduling longer breaks 더 긴 휴가 계획 → **Providing longer breaks** 더 긴 휴가 제공

어휘   **arrange** v. 준비하다, 배열하다   **frequent** adj. 잦은, 빈번한

03 동의어 찾기 문제

문제   3문단 여섯 번째 줄의 단어 "renew"는 의미상 –와 가장 가깝다.

(A) 결정하다
(B) 연구하다
(C) 연장하다
(D) 수리하다

해설   renew를 포함하고 있는 구절 'which current subscriptions they would like to renew'(3문단 5번째 줄)에서 renew는 '연장하다'라는 뜻으로 사용되었다. 따라서 '연장하다'라는 뜻을 가진 (C) extend가 정답이다.

어휘   **study** v. 연구하다, 공부하다   **renovate** v. 수리하다, ~을 새롭게 하다

04 추론 문제

문제   Rosenblatt사에 대해 암시되는 것은?

(A) 몇몇 유형의 고객들을 위한 조사를 실시한다.
(B) 정부에 의해 관리된다.
(C) 다양한 자료들을 출판한다.
(D) 지역 원조 활동 프로그램을 후원한다.

해설   질문의 핵심 어구인 Rosenblatt Corporation에 대해 추론하는 문제이다. 'Rosenblatt Corporation distributes information to several notable government agencies, foundations, and corporations. They depend on our research and analysis'(2문단 1번째 줄)에서 Rosenblatt사가 몇몇 정부 기관, 재단 및 주식회사에 정보를 공급하며 그들은 Rosenblatt사의 조사와 분석에 의존한다고 했으므로 Rosenblatt사가 몇몇 기관 및 회사를 위해 조사와 분석을 한다는 사실을 추론할 수 있다. 따라서 (A) It conducts research for several types of clients가 정답이다.

어휘   **publish** v. 출판하다   **a variety of** 다양한   **material** n. 자료, 재료

05-07은 다음 브로슈어와 후기에 관한 문제입니다.

Visionary 호텔 및 컨벤션 센터!
기업 행사를 즐겁게 만들기!

여러분의 다음 기업 행사를 우리의 세계적으로 유명한 호텔들 중 한 곳에서 진행하시고 모두가 무엇에 대해 이야기하는지를 알아보세요!

Visionary 호텔 및 컨벤션 센터: 괌
[05]최근 수리한 우리 호텔의 시설에서 놀라운 경치, 해변 및 활동을 즐기세요. 호텔은 세 개의 행사장, 비즈니스 센터, [07]무선 인터넷 접속, 회의실 및 공항 정기 왕복 버스를 제공합니다.

Visionary 호텔 및 컨벤션 센터: 고아
널찍한 전용 해변에 위치해 있는, [07]이 호텔은 강당, 두 개의 행사장, 비즈니스 센터, 공항 정기 왕복 버스 및 무선 인터넷을 포함하고 있습니다.

Visionary 호텔 및 컨벤션 센터: 세부
우리의 다섯 개 행사장들 중 어느 곳이든 이용하시고, 여러분의 여가 시간 동안 스쿠버 여행을 하시거나 해변을 거닐어 보세요. 비즈니스 센터, 회의실 및 [07]무선 인터넷도 이용하실 수 있습니다.

Visionary 호텔 및 컨벤션 센터: 트리니다드섬
[07]투숙객들은 새로 수리한 우리 호텔의 비즈니스 센터와 수영장에 대해 격찬하고 있습니다. 두 개의 넓은 행사장과 강당 또한 이용하실 수 있습니다.

Visionary 호텔 및 컨벤션 센터에 대해 더 알고 싶으시거나, 여러분의 다음 기업 행사를 우리와 예약하시려면, 오늘 www.visionaryfacilities.com에 로그인 하세요!

world-renowned 세계적으로 유명한   **incredible** adj. 놀라운, 광장한   **scenery** n. 경치, 풍경   **shuttle** n. 정기 왕복 버스   **expansive** adj. 널찍한, 광대한   **auditorium** n. 강당, 대강의실   **excursion** n. 여행, 소풍   **lounge** v. 어슬렁어슬렁 거닐다   **available** adj. 이용 가능한   **rave** v. 격찬하다

컨벤션 센터 후기   284페이지

(283페이지에서 계속) [07]개조된 비즈니스 센터는 정말로 이 호텔의 가장 훌 ⟳

룡한 부분으로, 영상 회의실뿐만 아니라 사용할 수 있는 20여 대의 컴퓨터도 제공합니다. [07]하지만, 저는 무선 인터넷 서비스가 없는 것이 회의 참석자들에게 불편함을 준다는 것을 알아차렸습니다. 저는 행사장에 감명을 받았는데, [06]행사장들이 특히 잘 가꾸어져 있었고 시청각 장비를 포함하고 있었기 때문입니다. [07]가장 주목할 만한 것은 호텔의 최근 건설된 수영장인데, 이것은 두 개의 넓은 풀장과 폭포를 갖추고 있습니다. 숙박 시설에 관해서는, 객실들이 깨끗하고 넓었습니다. 이 컨벤션 센터와 호텔을 적극 추천합니다.

☆☆☆☆

lack n. 결여, 부족; v. 결여되다, 부족하다   **attendee** n. 참석자   **exceptionally** adv. 특히   **well-maintained** adj. 잘 가꾸어진   **audiovisual** adj. 시청각의   **noteworthy** adj. 주목할 만한, 두드러진   **as for** ~에 관해서는   **spacious** adj. 넓은

05 동의어 찾기 문제

문제   브로슈어에서, 2문단 첫 번째 줄의 단어 "facility"는 의미상 –와 가장 가깝다.

(A) 터미널
(B) 시설
(C) 구분
(D) 지역

해설   facility를 포함하고 있는 문장 'Enjoy incredible scenery, beaches, and activities at our recently renovated facility.'(2문단 1번째 줄)에서 facility는 '시설'이라는 뜻으로 사용되었다. 따라서 '시설'이라는 뜻을 가진 (B) establishment가 정답이다.

어휘   **terminal** n. 터미널   **division** n. 구분, 분할   **region** n. 지역

06 동의어 찾기 문제

문제   후기에서, 네 번째 줄의 단어 "exceptionally"는 의미상 –와 가장 가깝다.

(A) 특히
(B) 보통
(C) 드물게
(D) 자주

해설   exceptionally를 포함하고 있는 문장 'they were exceptionally well-maintained and included audiovisual equipment'(3번째 줄)에서 exceptionally는 '특히'라는 뜻으로 사용되었다. 따라서 '특히'라는 뜻을 가진 (A) especially가 정답이다.

어휘   **usually** adv. 보통   **rarely** adv. 드물게   **frequently** adv. 자주, 종종

07 육하원칙 문제   연계

문제   어떤 호텔을 후기의 필자가 방문했는가?

(A) 괌
(B) 고아
(C) 세부
(D) 트리니다드섬

해설   두 지문의 내용을 종합해서 풀어야 하는 연계 문제이다. 질문의 핵심 어구인 author ~ visit에서 후기의 필자가 어떤(Which) 호텔을 방문했는지를 묻고 있으므로 필자가 작성한 후기를 먼저 확인한다.
두 번째 지문인 후기의 'The remodeled business center is truly the most amazing part of this hotel'(1번째 줄), 'I did, however, find the lack of wireless Internet service an inconvenience'(2번째 줄), 'Most noteworthy is the hotel's recently constructed swimming area'(4번째 줄)에서 필자가 방문했던 곳은 개조된 비즈니스 센터를 갖추고 있지만 무선 인터넷 서비스가 없는 것이 불편을 주었고, 최근 건설된 수영장을 갖추고 있다는 첫 번째 단서를 확인할 수 있다. 그런데 이러한 특징을 가진 호텔이 어디에 있는 곳인지 제시되지 않았으므로 브로슈어에서 각 호텔의 특징을 확인한다. 첫 번째 지문인 브로슈어의 'Guests are raving about our newly-renovated business center and swimming area.'(5문단 1번째 줄)에서 트리니다드섬의 호텔 및 컨벤션 센터가 새로 수리한 비즈니스 센터와 수영장을 갖추고 있으며 'We offer ~ wireless Internet access'(2문단 1번째 줄), 'the hotel includes ~ wireless Internet'(3문단 1번째 줄), 'wireless Internet are also available'(4문단 2번째 줄)에서 트리니다드섬의 호텔을 제외한 모든 호텔이 무선 인터넷을 제공한다는 두 번째 단서를 확인할 수 있다.

필자가 방문했던 호텔이 개조된 비즈니스 센터와 최근 건설된 수영장을 갖추고 있으나 무선 인터넷 서비스가 없다는 첫 번째 단서와 트리니다드섬의 호텔을 제외한 모든 호텔이 무선 인터넷을 제공한다는 두 번째 단서를 종합할 때, 필자가 방문했던 호텔은 트리니다드섬에 있는 곳임을 알 수 있다. 따라서 (D) Trinidad가 정답이다.

Section 2 지문 유형별 공략 - Single Passage

Chapter 08 이메일(E-mail)/편지(Letter)

예제 해석   p.403

이메일

> 발신: Harold Leighton <hleighton@sylvanbank.com>
> 수신: Charlotte Bryant <c_bryant@webmail.net>
> 제목: 온라인 뱅킹 서비스가 이제 활성화되었습니다   servicecontract.word
> 날짜: 4월 30일
>
> Ms. Bryant께,
>
> Sylvan 은행의 온라인 뱅킹 서비스에 등록해 주셔서 감사합니다. 이 이메일은 귀하의 요청이 승인되었다는 것을 확인하는 역할을 합니다. 귀하께서는 이제 귀하의 계좌를 계속 파악하고, 청구서를 지불하고, 마이너스 통장 설정 혹은 채무 상환 연기 승인을 요청하거나, 신용카드를 활성화하고, 예금을 다른 계좌로 송금할 수 있습니다.
>
> ¹ᐟ²ᴬ귀하의 계정을 활성화하려면, www.sylvanbank.com에 방문하여 자사 지점들 중 한 곳에서 ²ᴬ등록하신 사용자 이름과 비밀번호를 사용하여 웹사이트에 로그인하십시오.
>
> 귀하께서 성공적으로 로그인을 하고 나면, 비밀번호를 다시 변경하도록 요구될 것입니다. 길이가 8자 이상인 숫자와 문자의 조합을 사용해 주십시오. 귀하 계좌의 보안을 위해 비밀번호를 정기적으로 변경할 것을 적극 권장합니다. 또한, 추가적인 보호를 위해 귀하께서는 세 가지 보안 질문에 답을 제공하도록 유도될 것입니다. 귀하께서는 로그인할 때 때때로 그 질문들에 대답해야 할 것입니다.
>
> ²ᴰ귀하께서 서명한 서비스 등록 계약서의 사본을 참고하실 수 있도록 첨부하였습니다. 이 이메일에 답장을 보냄으로써 귀하의 등록을 확인하여 주십시오. 답장은 이 주소가 귀하의 올바른 이메일 주소이며, 귀하가 통지를 받았음을 알려 줄 것입니다.
>
> 재차 감사드리며, 귀하께서 저희의 온라인 뱅킹 서비스가 편리하고 효율적이라고 생각하시기를 바랍니다.
>
> Harold Leighton 드림
> 온라인 계정 담당자, Sylvan 은행

keep track of ~에 대해 계속 파악하다   **account** n. 계좌, 계정
overdraft n. 마이너스 통장 설정 (액수)   **extension** n. 채무 상환 연기 승인
wire v. 송금하다, 배선 공사를 하다   **numeral** n. 숫자; adj. 숫자의
on a regular basis 정기적으로   **prompt** v. 유도하다; adj. 즉시
notification n. 통지

Q1.
문제   이메일의 목적은 무엇인가?
   (A) 보안 질문에 대한 답을 요청하기 위해
   (B) 고객에게 새로운 웹사이트의 특징을 알려주기 위해
   (C) 서비스를 이용하는 것에 대한 정보를 주기 위해
   (D) 현 고객의 개인 정보를 확인하기 위해

어휘   **notify** v. 알리다   **feature** n. 특징   **current** adj. 현재의

Q2.
문제   Ms. Bryant에 대해 언급된 것은?

(A) 이미 그녀의 계정을 활성화했다.
(B) 비밀번호의 변경을 요청했다.
(C) 짧은 조사에 응해야 한다.
(D) 은행과의 계약에 서명했다.

어휘   **survey** n. 조사   **agreement** n. 계약, 동의

Hackers Practice   p.406

01 이메일

> 수신: Timothy Carey <tcarey@fastmail.com>
> 발신: Gina Anderson <ganderson@pendletongolfclub.com>
>
> 저는 Pendleton 골프 클럽 회원 등록에 관한 귀하의 문의를 받았습니다. 첨부된 것에서, 신청서 사본과 저희 시설 및 행사에 관한 안내서를 찾으실 수 있을 것입니다. 필수 세부 사항을 기입해서 저희 직원들 중 한 명에게 제출해 주십시오. 회원 신청이 승인되면, 귀하께서는 회원 카드를 받게 되고 시설을 이용하실 수 있게 됩니다.

inquiry n. 문의   **application** n. 신청   **handbook** n. 안내서
fill in 기입하다   **approve** v. 승인하다

문제   Ms. Anderson이 Mr. Carey에게 무엇을 하라고 요청하는가?
   (A) 회원 카드를 보내라
   (B) 신청서를 제출하라
   (C) 안내 책자 사본을 전달하라

해설   **육하원칙 문제** Ms. Anderson이 Mr. Carey에게 무엇(What)을 하라고 요청하는지를 묻는 육하원칙 문제이다. 질문의 핵심 어구인 Mr. Carey to do와 관련하여, 'Attached, you will find a copy of an application form'과 'Please ~ submit the form to one of our staff members.'에서 첨부된 신청서 사본을 직원들 중 한 명에게 제출해 달라고 했으므로 (B) Submit an application form이 정답이다.

02 편지

> 1월 19일
> Gordon De Leon
> 85번지 Westlake가
> 윈저, 온타리오주 N8T 1W2
>
> Mr. De Leon께,
>
> 지난 금요일에 자사의 갈등 관리 워크숍을 이끌어 주셔서 정말 감사드립니다. 자사의 몇몇 관리 직원들은 귀하가 다뤘던 소재가 매우 실용적이고 계몽적이었다고 제게 말했습니다. 저희는 추후에 자사 직원들을 위해 비슷한 교육들을 가질 계획이고, 귀하께서 그 교육들도 진행해 주신다면 아주 기쁠 것입니다. 저의 제안에 관심이 있으시다면, 귀하께 저희 계획을 곧 알려 드리겠습니다.

facilitate v. 이끌다, 조장하다   **managerial** adj. 관리의
material n. 소재, 자료   **practical** adj. 실용적인, 실제적인
enlightening adj. 계몽적인, 깨우치는   **conduct** v. 진행하다, 운영하다

문제   이 편지는 왜 쓰였는가?
   (A) 추후의 업무를 요청하기 위해
   (B) 곧 있을 행사의 일정을 잡기 위해
   (C) 교육에 대한 정보를 제공하기 위해

해설   **주제/목적 찾기 문제** 편지가 쓰인 목적을 묻는 목적 찾기 문제이다. 'We plan to hold similar training sessions for our staff in the future, and would be delighted to have you conduct them as well.'에서 추후에 직원들을 위해 비슷한 교육들을 가질 계획이고 그 교육들도 진행해 주기를 바란다고 했으므로 (A) To request future services가 정답이다.

03 편지

문제   Ms. Ogilvy는 누구일 것 같은가?

    (A) 행사 주최자
    (B) 박람회 지원자
    (C) 여행사 직원

해설   **추론 문제** 질문의 핵심 어구인 Ms. Ogilvy에 대해 추론하는 문제이다. 'Dear Ms. Ogilvy, This letter confirms your firm's participation in the upcoming Food and Beverage Fair in Paris.'에서 Ms. Ogilvy에게 이 편지는 파리에서 곧 있을 식음료 박람회에 귀사의 참가를 승인하는 것이라고 했으므로 Ms. Ogilvy는 식음료 박람회 참가를 지원한 회사의 직원이라는 사실을 추론할 수 있다. 따라서 (B) An applicant for a fair가 정답이다.

어휘   organizer n. 주최자, 조직자 travel agent 여행사 직원

Hackers Test
p.407

01 (B)	02 (A)	03 (C)	04 (B)	05 (D)
06 (C)	07 (B)	08 (B)	09 (A)	10 (D)
11 (B)	12 (C)			

01-04는 다음 편지에 관한 문제입니다.

release n. 발간 utmost adj. 최고의, 최대의 professionalism n. 전문성
enclose v. 동봉하다 formatting n. 서식 설정 far from 결코 ~이 아닌
arbitrary adj. 임의적인, 제멋대로의 promising adj. 촉망되는, 장래성 있는

01 주제/목적 찾기 문제

문제   Mr. Carrington은 왜 편지를 썼는가?

    (A) 편집자 직책에 작가를 추천하기 위해
    (B) 원고 사본을 요청하기 위해
    (C) 완성된 소설의 출판을 승인하기 위해
    (D) 작가가 되려는 사람의 작품을 비평하기 위해

해설   Mr. Carrington이 편지를 쓴 목적을 묻는 목적 찾기 문제이다. 'We ~ are requesting that you submit a copy of the complete manuscript for review.'(1문단 2번째 줄)에서 검토를 위해 전체 원고의 사본 한 부를 제출해 주기를 요청한다고 했으므로 (B) To request a copy of a manuscript가 정답이다.

어휘   criticize v. 비평하다 aspiring adj. ~이 되려는

02 동의어 찾기 문제

문제   2문단 두 번째 줄의 단어 "terms"는 의미상 –와 가장 가깝다.

    (A) 조건
    (B) 단어
    (C) 기간
    (D) 관계

해설   terms를 포함하고 있는 구절 'we will notify you of our intention to publish by sending you an offer letter containing our proposed contract terms'(2문단 1번째 줄)에서 terms가 '조건'이라는 뜻으로 사용되었다. 따라서 '조건'이라는 뜻을 가진 (A) conditions가 정답이다.

어휘   word n. 단어 period n. 기간 relation n. 관계

03 육하원칙 문제

문제   Mr. Jones는 무엇을 하라고 요청받았는가?

    (A) 긴 문서를 수정하라
    (B) 편집자의 권고를 따라라
    (C) 동봉된 지침들을 읽어라
    (D) 계약 제안서를 평가하라

해설   Mr. Jones가 무엇(What)을 하라고 요청받았는지를 묻는 육하원칙 문제이다. 질문의 핵심 어구인 Mr. Jones ~ asked to do와 관련하여, 'Enclosed with this letter is a document containing the formatting guidelines'(3문단 1번째 줄)와 'Be sure to read each item carefully.'(3문단 2번째 줄)에서 동봉된 서식 설정 관련 지침들을 포함하고 있는 문서의 각 항목을 주의 깊게 읽으라고 했으므로 (C) Read the enclosed instructions가 정답이다.

    Paraphrasing
    guidelines 지침 → instructions 지침

어휘   lengthy adj. 긴, 장황한 evaluate v. 평가하다

04 Not/True 문제

문제   Scout 출판사에 대해 언급되지 않은 것은?

    (A) 비소설 작품을 취급한다.
    (B) Mr. Jones의 책에 대한 판권을 소유한다.
    (C) 30년 동안 활동해 왔다.
    (D) 엄격한 서식 설정 관련 지침들을 유지한다.

해설   질문의 핵심 어구인 Scout Publications와 관련된 내용을 지문에서 찾아 보기와 대조하는 Not/True 문제이다. (A)는 'We feel it has tremendous potential in the non-fiction category and are requesting ~ the complete manuscript for review.'(1문단 2번째 줄)에서 Mr. Jones의 원고가 비소설 분야에서 엄청난 가능성을 가지고 있다고 생각하며 검토를 위해 전체 원고의 사본을 요청한다고 했으므로 지문의 내용과 일치한다. (B)는 지문에 언급되지 않은 내용이다. 따라서 (B) It owns the rights to Mr. Jones's book이 정답이다. (C)는 'our 30 years of experience in the industry'(3문단 3번째 줄)에서 이 업계에서 30년 동안의 경험이 있다고

했으므로 지문의 내용과 일치한다. (D)는 'We have rejected promising manuscripts in the past simply because these instructions were not followed.'(3문단 4번째 줄)에서 과거에 지침들을 따르지 않았다는 이 유만으로 촉망되는 원고를 거절한 적이 있다고 했으므로 지문의 내용과 일 치한다.

Paraphrasing
30 years 30년 → three decades 30년

어휘 **deal in** 취급하다 **right** n. 판권, 권리 **be around** 활동하고 있다

05-08은 다음 이메일에 관한 문제입니다.

수신: Steve Corcoran <scorcoran@⁰⁶lunettes.com>
발신: Mary Henry <mhenry@⁰⁶lunettes.com>
날짜: 4월 4일
제목: 긴급 요청
첨부 파일: Oakland_event.word

Steve,

⁰⁵제품 수송이 여기 로스앤젤레스에 있는 Lunette's사의 디자인 작업실로 오는 중이라는 것을 오늘 아침에 운송 회사로부터 통지받았습니다. 이것은 오늘 오후 2시에서 5시 사이에 도착할 것입니다. ⁰⁶이 수송은 멕시코에 있는 공장으로부터 우리가 주문한 완성된 샘플들을 포함하고 있는데, 이 중 몇몇은 제가 다음 주에 오클랜드에서 있을 Fashion Expo에 전시하고 싶은 것들입니다. 직접 제품을 받고 싶은데, 저는 오후 1시에 오클랜드로 떠날 예정입니다. 다가오는 행사 준비를 감독하기 위해 저는 그곳에 있어야 합니다. ⁰⁵저를 대신해서 수송품을 수령해 주십시오. 결제에 대해서는 제가 이미 처리했으므로 걱정하지 않아도 됩니다.

제품을 수령하면, 수량이 정확한지 그리고 어떤 제품에도 눈에 보이는 손상이 없는지를 확인해 주세요. 그 다음에, AirExpress를 이용하여 당일 배송으로 오클랜드로 보내기 위해 특정 의류 물품들을 골라서 다시 포장해 주시기 바랍니다. ⁰⁸필요한 제품 목록을 이메일에 첨부했습니다. 이것은 제가 찾고 있는 모델 번호와 색상을 보여 줍니다.

캘리포니아주, 오클랜드, Whitehall대로 82번지 94603에 있는 ⁰⁷Grand Excelsior 호텔 객실 44B호로 소포를 보내주세요. 문제가 있으면 저에게 555-7540으로 전화주시기 바랍니다.

urgent adj. 긴급한 **courier** n. 운송 기관 **on one's way** 오는 중인
finished adj. 완성된 **depart** v. 떠나다 **oversee** v. 감독하다
visible adj. 눈에 보이는 **article** n. 물품 **repack** v. 다시 포장하다

---

05 주제/목적 찾기 문제

문제 이메일의 목적은 무엇인가?
(A) 제품을 주문하기 위해
(B) 행사장으로 가는 교통수단을 마련하기 위해
(C) 회사 활동을 보고하기 위해
(D) 곧 올 배송에 대한 도움을 요청하기 위해

해설 이메일이 쓰인 목적을 묻는 목적 찾기 문제이다. 'I was notified by the courier company this morning that a shipment of merchandise is on its way here to Lunette's design studio in L.A.'(1문단 1번째 줄)와 'Please accept the shipment on my behalf.'(1문단 6번째 줄)에서 제품 수송이 로스앤젤레스에 있는 Lunette's사의 디자인 작업실로 오는 중이라는 것을 오늘 아침에 운송 회사로부터 통지받았으며, 수송품을 대신해서 수령해달라고 했으므로 (D) To request assistance with an upcoming delivery가 정답이다.

Paraphrasing
on its way 오는 중인 → upcoming 곧 올
shipment 수송 → delivery 배송

어휘 **arrange** v. 마련하다

06 추론 문제

문제 Lunette's사에 대해 암시되는 것은?
(A) 오클랜드에 지점이 있다.
(B) 오후 5시 이후에 문을 닫는다.
(C) 멕시코에 공급 회사가 있다.
(D) 박람회를 개최할 예정이다.

해설 질문의 핵심 어구인 Lunette's에 대한 내용을 추론하는 문제이다. 수신, 발신 이메일 주소의 lunettes.com(이메일 상단 부분)을 통해 Steve Corcoran과 Mary Henry 모두 Lunette's사에서 근무한다는 것을 알 수 있고, 'The shipment contains finished samples that we ordered from a factory in Mexico'(1문단 3번째 줄)에서 이 수송은 멕시코에 있는 공장으로부터 Lunette's사가 주문한 완성된 샘플들을 포함하고 있다고 했으므로, Lunette's사에 샘플을 공급하는 회사가 멕시코에 있다는 사실을 추론할 수 있다. 따라서 (C) It has a supplier in Mexico가 정답이다.

어휘 **supplier** n. 공급 회사

07 육하원칙 문제

문제 Mr. Corcoran은 어디로 의류 제품을 보낼 것인가?
(A) 사무실로
(B) 숙박 시설로
(C) 전시회장으로
(D) 백화점으로

해설 Mr. Corcoran이 어디(Where)로 의류 제품을 보낼 것인지를 묻는 육하원칙 문제이다. 질문의 핵심 어구인 send the items와 관련하여, 'Send the package to me at Room 44B of the Grand Excelsior Hotel'(3문단 1번째 줄)에서 Grand Excelsior 호텔 객실 44B호로 소포를 보내달라고 했으므로 (B) To an accommodation facility가 정답이다.

08 육하원칙 문제

문제 이메일에 첨부된 것은 무엇인가?
(A) 행사 장소로 가는 길
(B) 세부 내역 목록
(C) 포장 관련 지침
(D) 제품 카탈로그

해설 이메일에 첨부된 것이 무엇인지(What)를 묻는 육하원칙 문제이다. 질문의 핵심 어구인 attached to the e-mail과 관련하여, 'I've attached to this e-mail a list of the items that I need.'(2문단 3번째 줄)에서 필요한 제품 목록을 이메일에 첨부했다고 했으므로 (B) A list of specifications가 정답이다.

어휘 **venue** n. (행사 등의) 장소 **specification** n. 세부 내역

09-12는 다음 이메일에 관한 문제입니다.

수신: Wendy Armstrong <warmstrong@polsonpc.com>
발신: Derek Ling <dling@polsonpc.com>
제목: 계속해서 잘해 주시기 바랍니다   employee_profile.word
날짜: 7월 19일

안녕하세요 Wendy,

지역 내 모든 지점들의 판매 결과 검토를 바탕으로, 당신의 지점이 지난 분기에 최고의 종합 성과를 거두었다는 사실을 알려 드리게 되어 기쁩니다.

4월부터 6월까지의 기간 동안, 상점 수입금은 당신이 연초에 정한 월 판매 목표를 지속적으로 초과했다는 것을 보여 줍니다. 좀 더 구체적으로 말하자면, ¹⁰모든 부문의 매출액은 한 부문을 제외하고 지난해 같은 기간 동안의 매출액을 뛰어넘었습니다. 유일한 예외는 데스크톱 컴퓨터였지만, 요즘 자사의 많은 고객들이 노트북 컴퓨터로 옮겨 가고 있다는 것을 고려하면 이것은 뜻밖의 일이 아닙니다.

⁰⁹최고의 판매 실적을 낸 지점장으로서, 당신은 다음 달 급료 지급 수표에 1,000달러의 특별 수당을 받게 될 것입니다. 당신은 또한 ¹¹ᴰ자사 격월 회보에 이름이 언급될 것입니다. 아시다시피, 회보는 전국적으로 자사의 모든 지점에 배부되고 최고 경영자인 Mr. Tom Robbins가 자주 읽습니다.

뿐만 아니라, 다음 연속 세 분기 동안 동일한 수준의 성과를 유지한다면, 당신은 ¹¹ᴮ올해의 지점장상에 대한 후보자로 지명될 것이며, 이 상은 매년 댈러스에 있는 본사에서 열리는 식에서 주어집니다. 상을 받은 직원들은 자동적으로 봉급 인상을 보장받게 되고 추후에 지역 관리자로의 승진 후보자가 됩니다.

끝으로, ¹²제가 이메일에 첨부한 당신의 직원 정보 파일을 보시고, 그것이 최신 정보인지 확인해주시겠습니까? 당신의 업적에 대한 기록을 본사 측이 보유할 수 있도록 정보를 보내야 합니다. 오늘까지 저에게 ¹²돌려보내 주시기 바랍니다.

감사하며 축하드립니다.   ○

Derek Ling
⁰⁹지역 관리자
⁰⁹Polson 컴퓨터 회사

overall adj. 종합적인, 전반적인 receipt n. 수입금, 수령액
consistently adv. 지속적으로 exceed v. 초과하다
specifically adv. 구체적으로 말하면, 분명히 figure n. 액수, 값
department n. 부문, 부 surpass v. 뛰어넘다 exception n. 예외
given that ~을 고려하면 consecutive adj. 연속적인, 계속되는
nominate v. 지명하다, 임명하다 headquarters n. 본사
achievement n. 업적, 달성

09 추론 문제

문제 Ms. Armstrong에 대해 암시되는 것은?
(A) 컴퓨터 상점의 매출을 책임진다.
(B) 최근 봉급 인상으로 보상받았다.
(C) 회사의 최고 경영자에게 추천받았다.
(D) 새로운 라인의 제품을 성공적으로 출시했다.

해설 질문의 핵심 어구인 Ms. Armstrong에 대한 내용을 추론하는 문제이다. 'As the top sales performing branch manager'(3문단 1번째 줄)에서 최고 판매 실적의 지점장이라는 내용과, 'Regional Supervisor, Polson PC'(이메일 하단)에서 편지가 Polson 컴퓨터 회사의 지역 관리자로부터 보내진 사내 이메일이라는 내용을 통해, Ms. Armstrong이 컴퓨터 판매 회사의 한 지점에서 매출을 관리하는 지점장이라는 사실을 추론할 수 있다. 따라서 (A) She is responsible for sales at a computer store가 정답이다.

10 육하원칙 문제

문제 데스크톱 컴퓨터의 매출은 왜 감소했는가?
(A) 낮은 직원 생산성
(B) 회계상의 실수
(C) 비효율적인 관리 운영
(D) 소비자의 선호 변화

해설 지점 매출이 왜(Why) 감소했는지를 묻는 육하원칙 문제이다. 질문의 핵심 어구인 sales of desktop computers decline과 관련하여, 'sales figures in every department but one surpassed those for the same period last year. The only exception was desktop computers, ~ many of our customers are switching to laptops'(2문단 2번째 줄)에서 모든 부문의 매출액은 한 부문을 제외하고 지난해 같은 기간 동안의 매출액을 뛰어넘었고, 유일한 예외는 데스크톱 컴퓨터인데 많은 고객들이 노트북 컴퓨터로 옮겨 가고 있다고 했으므로 (D) A change in consumer preferences가 정답이다.

Paraphrasing
customers are switching to 고객들이 ~로 옮겨 가고 있다 → A change in consumer preferences 소비자의 선호 변화

어휘 productivity n. 생산성 inefficient adj. 비효율적인 preference n. 선호

11 Not/True 문제

문제 Polson 컴퓨터 회사에 대해 언급된 것은?
(A) 고객들로부터 피드백을 정기적으로 수집한다.
(B) 본사에서 연례 행사를 개최한다.
(C) 현재 지역 관리자 직책은 공석이다.
(D) 매월 회보를 발간한다.

해설 질문의 핵심 어구인 Polson PC와 관련된 내용을 지문에서 찾아 보기와 대조하는 Not/True 문제이다. (A)는 지문에 언급되지 않은 내용이다. (B)는 'the Branch Manager of the Year Award, which is presented annually during a ceremony at our headquarters in Dallas'(4문단 2번째 줄)에서 올해의 지점장상은 매년 댈러스에 있는 본사에서 열리는 식에서 주어진다고 했으므로 (B) It holds a yearly event at its main office가 정답이다. (C)는 지문에 언급되지 않은 내용이고, (D)는 'our bimonthly newsletter'(3문단 2번째 줄)에서 격월 회보가 있다고 했으므로 지문의 내용과 일치하지 않는다.

Paraphrasing
headquarters 본사 → main office 본사

어휘 presently adv. 현재

12 육하원칙 문제

문제 Mr. Ling이 Ms. Armstrong에게 요구하는 것은 무엇인가?
(A) 연락처 세부 사항
(B) 직속 관리자 이름
(C) 인사 파일의 최신 정보
(D) 당월의 판매 보고서

해설 Mr. Ling이 Ms. Armstrong에게 요구하는 것이 무엇인지(What)를 묻는 육하원칙 문제이다. 질문의 핵심 어구인 Mr. Ling require of Ms. Armstrong과 관련하여, 'could you take a look at your employee information file ~ and make sure that it is up to date'(5문단 1번째 줄)와 'Please return it'(5문단 3번째 줄)에서 직원 정보 파일이 최신 정보인지 확인해보고 돌려보내 달라고 했으므로 (C) An update on her personnel file이 정답이다.

Paraphrasing
employee information 직원 정보 → personnel 인사의

Chapter 09 양식 및 기타(Forms)

예제 해석 p.411

초대장

> 지식의 빛을 퍼뜨리다
> ²Brightman 대학교 50주년 기념일 축하
> ³ ᴮ6월 12일부터 15일까지 ³ ᴰ학교 부지에서
> 88번지 Ludlow Canyon로, 해밀턴, 미주리주 65401
>
> 50년 동안의 학문적 우수성을 기념하는 자리에 Brightman 대학교와 함께하도록 ¹해밀턴 지역 사회가 초청됩니다. 우리는 도시의 즐거움을 위해 일련의 활동을 준비했습니다. 아래는 몇몇 볼거리입니다.
>
> | 6월 12일, 목요일에는, 대학의 역사를 다루는 멀티미디어 전시가 새로이 개장한 Sarah J. Meier 건물에서 열립니다. | 6월 13일, 금요일에는, ³ ᶜ공식 만찬과 무도회가 Wakefield 기념홀에서 개최됩니다. ³ ᶜ티켓은 장당 25달러입니다. | 6월 14일, 토요일에는, 동창회가 Ryder 운동장에서 무료 콘서트를 주최하며, 이는 재학생들이 준비한 모금 행사와 동시에 진행될 것입니다. |
> | --- | --- | --- |
>
> 게다가, Howard Bain 총장이 6월 15일에 주행사장에서 학위 수여식을 이끌 것입니다.
>
> 티켓, 위치 및 다른 세부 정보를 얻으시려면, 555-0196 내선 48번의 행사 서비스부로 연락하시거나, www.brightmanuniv.edu를 방문하시기 바랍니다. 모두 환영하며, 그곳에서 뵙기를 희망합니다!

bear v. 퍼뜨리다, 낳다 torch n. 빛, 광명 anniversary n. 기념일
grounds n. 부지, 구내 highlight n. 볼거리, 가장 중요한 점
refurbish v. 개장하다 alumni association 동창회
accompany v. 동시에 진행되다, 동반하다 fundraiser n. 모금 행사
chancellor n. 총장, 학장 commencement n. 학위 수여식, 졸업식

Q1.
문제 초대장은 누구를 대상으로 할 것 같은가?
(A) 보도진들
(B) 프로그램 참가자들
(C) 대학 강사들
(D) 지역 주민들

Q2.
문제 공고되는 것은 무엇인가?
(A) 도시의 역사적인 전시 개막식
(B) 지역 건축 프로젝트 시작

(C) 대학 설립 기념행사

(D) 한 분야의 전문가들의 연례 모임

어휘 commemoration n. 기념행사, 축하 institute n. 대학 founding n. 설립

Q3.

문제 예정된 행사에 대해 언급된 것은?

(A) 선출된 의회에 의해 준비되었다.

(B) 4일의 기간 동안 개최될 것이다.

(C) 무료로 제공될 것이다.

(D) 해밀턴 근방의 여러 장소에서 개최될 것이다.

어휘 free of charge 무료로

Hackers Practice
p.414

유형 연습

| 01 (A) | 02 (C) | 03 (A) |

01 전화 메모

부재 중인 동안에

수신: Jacqueline Stamos
날짜/시간: 1월 19일, 오후 3시 18분
메시지: World 전자회사의 Gail Anderson은 다음 달 로봇 공학 학회의 다가오는 일정에 대한 몇 가지 변경 사항과 관련해 귀하에서 연락해 주시기를 원합니다. 가능한 한 빨리 그녀에게 연락해 주시길 바랍니다.
전화 받은 사람: Liam Connelly

robotics n. 로봇 공학 conference n. 학회, 회의

문제 Ms. Anderson의 전화 목적은 무엇인가?

(A) Ms. Stamos에게 일정에 대한 변경 사항을 알려주기 위해

(B) 학회 참석을 확인하기 위해

(C) 일정표의 사본을 요청하기 위해

해설 **주제/목적 찾기 문제** 전화 메모의 목적을 묻는 목적 찾기 문제이다. 'To: Jacqueline Stamos'에서 메모 수신인인 Jacqueline Stamos에게 'Gail Anderson ~ would like you to contact her about some changes to the upcoming schedule'에서 Gail Anderson이 다가오는 일정에 대한 변경 사항과 관련해 Jacqueline Stamos가 연락해 주기를 원하고 있다고 했으므로 Ms. Anderson은 Ms. Stamos에게 일정에 대한 변경 사항을 알려주기 위해 전화한 것임을 알 수 있다. 따라서 (A) To inform Ms. Stamos of changes to a schedule이 정답이다.

02 일정표

연례 오리건주 학생 과학 전시회에 등록해주셔서 감사합니다! 다음 일주일간의 일정을 검토해 주시기 바랍니다:

5월 9일	오전 9시 – 오후 5시	모든 출품작은 반드시 Pinewood 전시회장에 제출되어야 합니다.
5월 10–14일	오전 9시 – 오후 6시 30분	전시회는 대중에게 개방될 것입니다. 참가자는 자신의 작품에 대한 설명을 심사위원들과 참석자들에게 제공하기 위해 반드시 현장에 있어야 합니다.
5월 15일	오전 10시 30분 – 오후 12시	상은 전시회장에서 주어질 예정입니다.

look through 검토하다 week-long 일주일간의 entry n. 출품작, 응모작
on site 현장의 judge n. 심사위원 hand out (나누어) 주다

문제 이 행사는 얼마나 자주 열리는가?

(A) 매주

(B) 매달

(C) 매년

해설 **육하원칙 문제** 행사가 얼마나 자주(How often) 열리는지를 묻는 육하원칙 문제이다. 질문의 핵심 어구인 the event take place와 관련하여, 'the Annual Oregon State Student Science Exhibition'에서 연례 오리건주 학생 과학 전시회라고 했으므로 전시회는 매년 열리는 행사임을 알 수 있다. 따라서 (C) Every year가 정답이다.

03 광고지

에너지 비용을 절약하는 방법을 배우세요!

여러분의 집을 좀 더 연료 효율이 좋도록 만들고 싶으신가요? 환경부가 후원하는 다음 주 세미나에 참석함으로써 가사 비용을 줄이고 더욱 환경친화적이 되는 방법을 배워보세요. "에너지 소비를 줄임으로써 돈을 절약하기"라는 제목의 이 세미나는 3월 8일 오후 7시부터 오후 9시 30분까지 Monarch가 1232번지의 Richland 지역 주민 센터에서 열릴 예정입니다. Western Prairie 대학교의 환경 과학 교수인 Tom Singh이 참석하여 특별 발표를 하고 그의 발표에 이어 어떠한 질문에라도 답변하실 것입니다. 추가 정보를 위해, 또는 세미나에 등록하기 위해서는, events@ministryenvironment.org로 문의를 보내주시기 바랍니다.

household adj. 가사의 consumption n. 소비 on hand 참석(출석)하여
query n. 문의, 의문

문제 광고지가 홍보하는 것은 무엇인가?

(A) 교육적인 행사

(B) 에너지 절약 기기

(C) 일련의 대학 강좌

해설 **주제/목적 찾기 문제** 광고지가 홍보하는 것을 묻는 주제 찾기 문제이다. 광고지 제목 'LEARN HOW TO SAVE ON ENERGY COSTS!'에서 에너지 비용을 절약하는 방법을 배우라고 한 후, 'Learn how to cut household costs and become more environmentally-friendly by attending next week's seminar sponsored by the Ministry of the Environment.'에서 환경부가 후원하는 세미나에 참석하여 가사 비용을 줄이고 더욱 환경친화적이 되는 방법을 배워보라고 했으므로 (A) An educational event가 정답이다.

어휘 educational adj. 교육적인 device n. 기기

Hackers Test
p.415

| 01 (D) | 02 (B) | 03 (D) | 04 (B) | 05 (C) |
| 06 (C) | 07 (B) | 08 (C) | 09 (B) | 10 (D) |

01–02는 다음 영수증에 관한 문제입니다.

⁰¹Deskman사
모든 사무실 필요 용품을 위해서
521번지 Conference Center로
벤턴, 펜실베이니아주 1795
555-6323
부가 가치세 납세자 인식 번호 002-3632-0963

S#645545210	⁰²ᴰ3월 1일 오후 7시		
상품 번호 52541 Abacus FX-63II 계산기	4개 단가 15.99달러	63.96달러
상품 번호 20152 Deskman 다용도 종이 케이스	1개 단가 20.25달러	20.25달러
상품 번호 30046 ⁰²ᶜScribble 볼펜 12자루들이 상자	3개 단가 4.00달러	12.00달러
상품 번호 96510 Baklushi 프린터 검정색 잉크 카트리지 130ml	1개 단가 68.22달러	68.22달러
상품 번호 75230 Stevens 의자 매트	5개 단가 29.99달러	149.95달러

합계	314.38달러
현금	500.00달러
거스름돈	185.62달러

거래해 주셔서 감사합니다!

이것은 공식적인 영수증입니다. ^{02-A}교환을 하시려면 상품은 구매일로부터 7일 이내에 반품되어야 합니다.

VAT 부가 가치세(value added tax)
TIN 납세자 인식 번호(taxpayer identification number) **calculator** n. 계산기
@ 단가, ~으로(at) **merchandise** n. 상품

01 육하원칙 문제

문제 Deskman사는 어떤 종류의 상점인가?
(A) 편의점
(B) 가정용 기기 센터
(C) 가정용 실내 장식 점포
(D) 사무용품 소매점

해설 Deskman사가 어떤(What) 종류의 상점인지를 묻는 육하원칙 문제이다. 질문의 핵심 어구인 Deskman Company와 관련하여, 'Deskman Co. For all your office needs'(영수증 상단 1번째 줄)에서 Deskman사는 모든 사무실 필요 용품을 위한 회사라고 한 후, 영수증 전체에 걸쳐 사무용품 구매 내역을 나열하고 있으므로 Deskman사는 사무용품을 판매하는 상점임을 알 수 있다. 따라서 (D) An office supplies outlet이 정답이다.

paraphrasing
office needs 사무실 필요 용품 → office supplies 사무용품

어휘 **appliance** n. (가정용) 기기 **decor** n. (건물의 실내) 장식
establishment n. 점포, 설립 **outlet** n. 소매점

02 Not/True 문제

문제 영수증에서 언급되지 않은 정보는?
(A) 교환이 허용된다.
(B) 상품들은 환불이 안 된다.
(C) 펜들은 12개씩 판매된다.
(D) 거래는 밤에 이루어졌다.

해설 영수증에 언급된 내용을 지문에서 찾아 보기와 대조하는 Not/True 문제이다. 이 문제는 질문에 핵심 어구가 없으므로 각 보기의 핵심 어구와 관련된 내용을 지문에서 찾아 대조한다. (A)는 'Merchandise may be returned for replacement within seven days from the date of purchase.'(영수증 하단)에서 교환을 하려면 상품은 구매일로부터 7일 이내에 반품되어야 한다고 했으므로 지문의 내용과 일치한다. (B)는 지문에 언급되지 않은 내용이다. 따라서 (B) Items are nonrefundable이 정답이다. (C)는 'Scribble Ballpoint Pen, Box of 12'(영수증 3번째 구매 물품 2번째 줄)에서 Scribble 볼펜의 판매 단위가 12자루들이 상자라고 했으므로 지문의 내용과 일치한다. (D)는 '03/01 7:00 P.M.'(상점 정보 아래)에서 구매일자가 3월 1일 오후 7시라고 했으므로 지문의 내용과 일치한다.

어휘 **permissible** adj. 허용되는 **nonrefundable** adj. 환불이 안 되는
dozen n. 12개, 1다스 **transaction** n. 거래

03-06은 다음 일정에 관한 문제입니다.

Bella Vista 아파트 단지의 곧 있을 수리에 대한 ^{03-A}작업 일정표
^{03-A}8월 1일-8월 19일

^{03-B}로비, 복도 및 현관의 ^{03-C}모든 벽 재페인트칠
8월 1일-7일
^{03-C}팀장: Dan Parsons

^{03-B/03-D}메인 로비의 ^{03-D}카펫과 나무 바닥재 교체
8월 8일-19일
팀장: Doris Schmidt

^{03-B}스포츠 시설 내 샤워실과 탈의실 타일 교체
8월 7일-11일
팀장: Harry Seymour

---

^{03-B/04}지하 주차장 ⁰⁴(지하 1층) 재포장
8월 5일-18일
팀장: Larry Smithers

프로젝트와 관련된 세부 사항에 대해서는 여러분의 팀장에게 연락하시기 바랍니다. ⁰⁵주민들에게 최소한의 방해만 되도록, 작업은 오직 오전 8시 30분부터 오후 6시 30분까지만 이루어질 것입니다. 상기 일정은 작업의 진행에 따라 변경의 여지가 있습니다. 팀원들은 팀장으로부터 어떠한 변경 사항에 대해서라도 통지받을 것입니다. ⁰⁶장비와 물품을 건물 안팎으로 옮기기 위해서는 G-3 입구만 이용해주시기 바랍니다.

renovation n. 수리, 수선 **complex** n. (건물) 단지 **hall** n. 복도
crew n. (특정한 기술을 가지고 함께 일을 하는) 팀 **wooden** adj. 나무의, 목재의
flooring n. 바닥재 **retile** v. 타일을 다시 깔다 **repave** v. 다시 포장하다
underground adj. 지하의 **minimal** adj. 최소한의
disturbance n. 방해, 소란 **be open to** ~의 여지가 있다
notify v. 통지하다 **equipment** n. 장비

03 Not/True 문제

문제 일정에서 언급되지 않은 것은?
(A) 작업은 8월 동안 시행될 것이다.
(B) 시설의 몇몇 구역이 수리를 받을 것이다.
(C) Dan Parsons는 페인트공 팀을 이끌 것이다.
(D) 로비 바닥은 타일이 다시 깔릴 것이다.

해설 일정에 언급된 내용을 지문에서 찾아 보기와 대조하는 Not/True 문제이다. 이 문제는 질문에 핵심 어구가 없으므로 각 보기의 핵심 어구와 관련된 내용을 지문에서 찾아 대조한다. (A)는 'Work Schedule', 'August 1-August 19'(제목)에서 작업 일정이 8월 1일부터 8월 19일까지라고 했으므로 지문의 내용과 일치한다. (B)는 'the lobby, halls, and entrances'(표 1행 1번째 줄), 'main lobby'(표 2행 1번째 줄), 'shower and changing rooms at sports facility'(표 3행 1번째 줄), 'underground parking facility'(표 4행 1번째 줄)에서 수리되는 구역으로 로비, 복도, 현관, 메인 로비, 스포츠 시설 내 샤워실과 탈의실, 지하 주차장을 언급했으므로 지문의 내용과 일치한다. (C)는 'Repainting of all walls'(표 1행 1번째 줄), 'Crew manager: Dan Parsons'(표 1행 3번째 줄)에서 벽 재페인트칠 작업의 팀장이 Dan Parsons라고 했으므로 지문의 내용과 일치한다. (D)는 'Carpet and wooden flooring replacement in main lobby'(표 2행 1번째 줄)에서 메인 로비의 카펫과 나무 바닥재 교체가 진행될 것이라고 했으므로 지문의 내용과 일치하지 않는다. 따라서 (D) The lobby floors will be retiled가 정답이다.

어휘 **undergo** v. 받다

04 추론 문제

문제 8월 15일에 무엇이 일어날 것 같은가?
(A) Bella Vista의 수리가 완료될 것이다.
(B) Larry Smithers가 주차장에서 인부들을 감독할 것이다.
(C) 로비의 일부 벽은 페인트칠 될 것이다.
(D) 타일이 샤워실에 깔릴 것이다.

해설 8월 15일에 무엇이 일어날 것 같은지를 추론하는 문제이다. 질문의 핵심 어구인 August 15와 관련하여, 'Repaving of underground parking facility (B1), August 5-18, Crew manager: Larry Smithers'(표 4행)에서 8월 5일부터 18일까지 지하 주차장 재포장이 진행되며, 팀장은 Larry Smithers라고 했으므로 8월 15일에는 Larry Smithers가 주차장에서 인부들을 감독할 것이라는 사실을 추론할 수 있다. 따라서 (B) Larry Smithers will supervise workers in the parking area가 정답이다.

paraphrasing
parking facility 주차장 → parking area 주차장

어휘 **reception area** 로비, 응접실

05 육하원칙 문제

문제 직원들은 왜 특정한 시간 동안만 일하도록 허용되는가?
(A) 회사가 초과 근무 수당을 지급하기를 원치 않는다.
(B) 그 시간 전에 건물이 문을 닫는다.
(C) 시설의 주민들을 신경 쓰이게 할 수 있다.

(D) 팀장들이 다른 작업을 하기로 되어 있다.

해설 직원들이 왜(Why) 특정한 시간 동안만 일하도록 허용되는지를 묻는 육하원칙 문제이다. 질문의 핵심 어구인 work during certain hours와 관련하여, 'So that there will be minimal disturbance for residents, work will only take place between 8:30 A.M. to 6:30 P.M.'(표 하단 1번째 줄)에서 주민들에게 최소한의 방해만 되도록 작업은 오직 오전 8시 30분부터 오후 6시 30분까지만 이루어질 것이라고 했으므로 (C) The residents of the facility may be bothered가 정답이다.

어휘 **bother** v. 신경 쓰이다, 귀찮게 하다
be booked for ~하기로 되어 있다, ~의 약속이 있다

06 추론 문제

문제 Bella Vista 아파트 단지에 대해 암시되는 것은?
(A) 현재 비어 있는 가구가 없다.
(B) 수년 전에 건설되었다.
(C) 하나 이상의 입구를 가지고 있다.
(D) 공사 중이다.

해설 질문의 핵심 어구인 the Bella Vista Apartment Complex에 대해 추론하는 문제이다. 'Please use only entrance G-3 to move equipment and supplies in and out of the building.'(표 하단 4번째 줄)에서 장비와 물품을 건물 안팎으로 옮기기 위해서는 G-3 입구만을 이용하라고 했으므로 건물에는 한 개 이상의 입구가 있다는 사실을 추론할 수 있다. 따라서 (C) It has more than one entrance가 정답이다.

어휘 **under construction** 공사 중인

07-10은 다음 양식에 관한 문제입니다.

스프링데일 예술 축제

연례 07/09-B스프링데일 예술 축제가 올해에는 6월 1일부터 4일까지 개최될 것입니다. 09-C장소는 Donovan가 156번지에 있는 스프링데일 시민 문화 회관이 될 것입니다. 오전 10시에 개방하여 오후 7시에 닫을 예정입니다.

공간이 제한되어 있으므로 10참가에 관심 있는 예술가들은 가능한 한 신속히 부스를 예약하시도록 권고됩니다. 10예약은 재판매업자나 대행인이 아닌 예술가 본인이 직접 하셔야 합니다. 부스는 조명, 탁자, 작품을 걸어 둘 칸막이 및 의자 두 개를 포함합니다. 08결제는 5월 15일까지 이루어져야 하며 그렇지 않으면 예약을 잃을 것입니다. 취소에 대해 환불을 제공해 드리지 못해 유감스럽게 생각합니다. 이 양식을 작성하셔서 Larch거리 5998번지 스프링데일 예술 협회의 Leona Helms에게 제출해 주십시오. 현금, 신용카드, 우편환에 의한 결제 모두 받습니다. 문의 사항이 있으시면, 555-0967로 전화 주십시오.

10성명	10Terry Clark	주소	18번지 Rose가, 스프링데일
전화번호	555-4453	이메일	terryc@speedmail.com
10예술품 종류	10회화		

부스 선택:
□10/8 피트 □10/20 피트 □12/24 피트 ☒14/28 피트

결제 수단: ☒현금 □우편환 □신용카드 번호: _____

서명: _Terry Clark_

venue n. 장소 **urge** v. 권고하다 **agent** n. 대행인
partition n. 칸막이 **forfeit** v. 잃다, 박탈당하다 **fill in** 작성하다
money order 우편환

07 주제/목적 찾기 문제

문제 양식의 목적은 무엇인가?
(A) 미술 강좌에 등록하기 위해
(B) 축제에 등록하기 위해
(C) 멤버십을 신청하기 위해
(D) 대회에 참가하기 위해

해설 양식의 목적을 묻는 목적 찾기 문제이다. 'Springdale Art Festival will be held this year from June 1-4'(1문단 1번째 줄)에서 스프링데일 예술 축제가 6월 1일부터 4일까지 개최될 것이라고 한 후, 관심 있는 예술가들이 부스를 예약할 수 있는 양식을 제공하고 있으므로 (B) To register for a festival이 정답이다.

어휘 **enroll** v. 등록하다 **competition** n. 대회, 경쟁

08 육하원칙 문제

문제 5월 15일에 일어날 일은 무엇인가?
(A) 전시를 위한 선택이 이루어질 것이다.
(B) 예술 축제의 행사 장소가 개장할 것이다.
(C) 결제되지 않은 예약은 취소될 것이다.
(D) 환불이 더 이상 제공되지 않을 것이다.

해설 5월 15일에 일어날 일이 무엇인지(What)를 묻는 육하원칙 문제이다. 질문의 핵심 어구인 May 15와 관련하여, 'Payment must be made before May 15 or reservations will be forfeited.'(2문단 3번째 줄)에서 5월 15일까지 결제가 이루어지지 않으면 예약을 잃게 될 것이라고 했으므로 (C) Unpaid reservations will be canceled가 정답이다.

paraphrasing
reservations will be forfeited 예약을 잃게 될 것이다 → reservations will be canceled 예약이 취소될 것이다

09 Not/True 문제

문제 행사에 대해 언급된 것은?
(A) Leona Helms에 의해 준비되고 있다.
(B) 4일 동안 계속될 예정이다.
(C) 지역 미술관에서 열린다.
(D) 일반 대중에게 무료이다.

해설 질문의 핵심 어구인 the event와 관련된 내용을 지문에서 찾아 보기와 대조하는 Not/True 문제이다. (A)는 지문에 언급되지 않은 내용이다. (B)는 'Springdale Art Festival will be held this year from June 1-4'(1문단 1번째 줄)에서 스프링데일 예술 축제가 6월 1일부터 4일까지 열린다고 했으므로 (B) It is scheduled to last for four days가 정답이다. (C)는 'The venue will be the Springdale Community Center'(1문단 1번째 줄)에서 장소는 스프링데일 시민 문화 회관이라고 했으므로 지문의 내용과 일치하지 않는다. (D)는 지문에 언급되지 않은 내용이다.

어휘 **last** v. (특정한 시간 동안) 계속되다 **gallery** n. 미술관, 화랑

10 추론 문제

문제 Mr. Clark에 대해 암시되는 것은?
(A) 행사 중에 이틀만 참가할 것이다.
(B) 미술 협회의 회원이다.
(C) 이전에 행사에 참여한 적이 있다.
(D) 그 자신의 예술 작품 중 일부를 전시할 것이다.

해설 질문의 핵심 어구인 Mr. Clark에 대해 추론하는 문제이다. 'Artists interested in participating are urged to reserve a booth'(2문단 1번째 줄)와 'Reservations must be made by the artists themselves'(2문단 2번째 줄)에서 참가에 관심 있는 예술가들은 본인이 직접 부스를 예약하라고 했고, 표의 'Name, Terry Clark'(표 1행)와 'Type of Art, Paintings'(표 3행)에서 Terry Clark가 회화를 전시한다고 했으므로 Terry Clark는 예술 축제에 자신의 회화를 전시하기 위해 부스를 예약하는 양식을 작성했다는 사실을 추론할 수 있다. 따라서 (D) He will display some of his own artwork가 정답이다.

Chapter 10 기사(Article & Report)

예제 해석   p.419

기사

[1]세계의 국가들 유례없는 여름 기온을 기록하다

9월 30일 - 세계날씨기구(WWO)의 연구원 Dr. Christian Mulligan이 [1]올해 4개의 국가가 극적인 기온 상승을 기록했다고 발표했다. [3]어제 있었던

WWO의 언론 발표에서, Dr. Mulligan은 지난해 동안 몇몇 국가들이 심한 혹서를 견뎠다고 말했고, 이는 해당 기관에서 수집된 통계에 따르면, 적어도 부분적으로는 기후 변화로 인한 환경이라고 한다.

1월에, 콜롬비아는 최근 몇십 년만에 최고치인 기온 섭씨 42도를 기록했다. 4개월 후인 5월에, 파키스탄은 기온 섭씨 53도로, 아시아 대륙 전체에서 최고 기록을 세웠다. 7월에 44도로, 러시아가 뒤를 이었는데, 이것은 이 나라에서 130년 만에 가장 더운 여름이었다. 자국 사상 최고치를 넘은 곳은 핀란드였는데, 한 세기 전의 35도에서 상승하여, 올해 37도를 기록했다.

WWO는 이러한 기온 변화가 여러 가지 요인에 의해 야기된 것이라고 말한다. 지구 온난화는 북극 빙원이 녹는 속도를 증가시켰고, 이는 기온을 상승시켰다. 오염 물질 또한 한 가지 요인인데, 오염 물질이 지구를 태양으로부터 보호하는 오존층에 영향을 미치기 때문이다. 대기로 들어오는 자외선의 증가가 지구의 온도를 높이고 있다.

---

heat wave 혹서, 열기 **statistics** n. 통계 **Celsius degree** 섭씨(온도)
decade n. 10년 **surpass** v. 넘어서다, 경신하다
register v. 기록하다, 나타내다 **factor** n. 요인, 원인
global warming 지구 온난화 **arctic** adj. 북극의 **icecap** n. 빙원, 만년설
melt v. 녹다 **pollution** n. 오염 물질, 오염 **ozone layer** 오존층
UV adj. 자외선의 (ultraviolet) **atmosphere** n. 대기, 공기

Q1.
문제 기사의 목적은 무엇인가?
(A) 날씨 패턴에 대한 예측을 제공하기 위해
(B) 기후 변화와 관련된 관측 내용을 보도하기 위해
(C) 한 기관의 활동에 대해 독자들에게 알리기 위해
(D) 국가들이 특정 조치를 취해야 함을 제안하기 위해

어휘 **forecast** n. 예측, 예보 **observation** n. 관측, 관찰 **measure** n. 조치

Q2.
문제 가장 높은 기온은 언제 기록되었는가?
(A) 1월에
(B) 5월에
(C) 7월에
(D) 9월에

Q3.
문제 세계날씨기구에 대해 암시된 것은?
(A) 최근 Dr. Mulligan을 고용했다.
(B) 핀란드에 지사가 있다.
(C) 세계 기온에 대한 자료를 수집한다.
(D) 대중에게 연간 보고서를 발표한다.

어휘 **branch** n. 지점, 지부 **release** v. 발표하다

Hackers Practice
p.422

유형 연습
01 (B)   02 (C)   03 (A)

01 기사

이번 주 Columbus 외곽에서, Kepler 제약회사의 2억 달러 규모의 다목적 개발에 대한 공사가 시작되었다. 현재 의약품 판매 세계 2위인 이 회사는, 본사에 900명의 직원이 있는데, 이는 작년부터 12퍼센트 증가하고, 10년에 47퍼센트 증가한 것을 나타낸다. 새로운 복합 건물은 추가적인 사무 공간, 연구 실험실, 검사 센터, 그리고 강당을 제공할 것이다. 회사의 빠른 성장은 18년 전에 건축된 현재의 건물에 인구 과밀을 야기했다.

---

mixed-use 다목적 이용의 **represent** v. 나타내다, 해당하다
house v. (장소를) 제공하다 **overcrowding** n. 인구 과밀

문제 이 기사가 어디에서 출판되었을 것 같은가?
(A) 부동산 안내 책자에서
(B) 경제 잡지에서
(C) 보건 간행물에서

해설 **추론 문제** 기사를 볼 수 있는 곳을 추론하는 문제이다. 'construction began on a $200 million mixed-use development for Kepler Pharmaceuticals'에서 제약회사의 다목적 개발에 대한 공사가 시작되었다고 한 후, 지문 전체에 걸쳐 회사의 의약품 판매 순위 및 성장 규모에 대해 설명하고 있으므로 경제 잡지에 실린 기사임을 추론할 수 있다. 따라서 (B) In a business journal이 정답이다.

어휘 **real estate** 부동산

02 기사

일류 창고형 매장들의 판매 보고서는 보풀 제거기가 올해의 최대 판매 제품 중 하나라는 것을 보여준다. Cleaners사에 의해 제조된, Clean-Well 보풀 제거기는 미국에서 4월 이래로 백만 대 이상이 팔렸다. 이것은 매달 평균 약 15만 대가 팔린 셈이다. 이 제품의 인기는 지난 몇 달 사이에 상승했는데 이것이 세탁기, 의류, 융단 및 다른 물건들에서의 보풀을 제거하는 데 효과적이기 때문이다.

---

warehouse club 창고형 매장 **lint** n. 보풀

문제 기사는 주로 무엇에 대한 것인가?
(A) 일류 창고형 매장
(B) 제조 회사
(C) 가장 잘 팔리는 청소 용품

해설 **주제/목적 찾기 문제** 기사가 주로 무엇에 대한 것인지를 묻는 주제 찾기 문제이다. 'Sales reports in leading warehouse clubs show that a lint remover is one of the top-selling products of the year.'에서 일류 창고형 매장들의 판매 보고서는 보풀 제거기가 올해의 최대 판매 제품 중 하나라는 것을 보여준다고 한 후, 판매 대수 및 인기 요인에 대해 설명하고 있으므로 (C) A best-selling cleaning product가 정답이다.

Paraphrasing
lint remover 보풀 제거기 → cleaning product 청소 용품

03 기사

Nelly Stadlin의 *All Gather Round*가 Rosebud 영화사에 의해 제작되기로 선택되었다는 것이 금요일에 밝혀졌다. Stadlin의 3부작 중 마지막인, 이 베스트셀러 소설은 대공황 시대의 오클라호마에 살았던 허구적인 한 가족의 분투를 묘사한다. 촬영은 주인공 Beth Abney역을 연기할 배우 Kelly Rader와 함께 6개월 후에 시작될 것으로 예상된다. 다른 배역 선정은 현재 시점에서는 미정이다.

---

reveal v. 밝히다, 드러내다 **depict** v. 묘사하다, 그리다
fictional adj. 허구의, 소설의 **struggle** n. 분투 **shooting** n. (영화) 촬영

문제 Nelly Stadlin은 누구인가?
(A) 소설 작가
(B) 영화 제작자
(C) 은퇴한 역사가

해설 **육하원칙 문제** Nelly Stadlin이 누구인지(Who)를 묻는 육하원칙 문제이다. 질문의 핵심 어구인 Nelly Stadlin과 관련하여, 'Nelly Stadlin's *All Gather Round*'와 'The best-selling novel, Stadlin's last in a three-part series'에서 Nelly Stadlin의 *All Gather Round*는 그녀의 3부작 중 마지막인 베스트셀러 소설이라고 했으므로 Nelly Stadlin은 소설 작가임을 알 수 있다. (A) A fiction author가 정답이다.

Hackers Test
p.423

01 (D)	02 (C)	03 (A)	04 (D)	05 (C)
06 (B)	07 (D)	08 (C)	09 (B)	10 (B)
11 (A)	12 (B)			

01-04는 다음 기사에 관한 문제입니다.

Randolph 건물을 개조할 Douglas 박물관

Douglas 박물관은 오늘 01Lauderhill 재단으로부터 500만 달러의 보조금 ○

을 받았다고 발표했는데, 이 재단은 중요한 건축물을 보존하기 위해 기금을 모금한다. ⁰¹이 자금은 Douglas 박물관의 넓게 뻗은 부지 위에 있는 역사적으로 중요한 건물인 Randolph 건물의 외관을 복원하기 위해 사용될 것이다.

^{02-B}Randolph 건물은 110년 전에 지어졌으며, ^{02-A}이것은 나라에서 가장 희귀하고 귀중한 책, 음악 악보, 미술품, 그리고 골동품들의 일부를 가지고 있다. ^{02-D}그것의 내부는 골동품 가구의 복원뿐만 아니라, 건물 전체에 걸친 새 조명 및 전시장의 설치도 포함하여, 10년 전에 대규모의 보수 공사를 겪었다.

4월 15일에, 그것을 원래 상태로 되돌려 놓겠다는 목표로, 건물 외관에 대한 공사가 시작될 것이다. 이를 달성하기 위해, ⁰³두 전문가의 용역이 확보되었다. 20세기 초기 건축물의 전문가인 ⁰⁴Martin Walker가 이 프로젝트를 주도할 것이다. 그와 긴밀하게 협력하는 것은 예술품 복원을 전문으로 하는 Beth Anders가 될 것이다. 그녀는 조각품 및 건물을 꾸미는 다른 장식적인 요소들에 집중할 것이다. 이 프로젝트는 최소 3개월이 걸릴 것으로 예상되며, 이 기간 동안 그 건물은 방문객들에게 폐쇄될 것이다.

award v. 주다, 수여하다: n. 상　**grant** n. 보조금　**preserve** v. 보존하다
notable adj. 중요한, 눈에 띄는　**restore** v. 복원하다　**exterior** n. 외관
significant adj. 중요한　**construct** v. 짓다, 건축하다
rare adj. 희귀한　**antique** n. 골동품; adj. 골동품의, 고풍스러운
interior n. 내부　**undergo** v. 겪다, 받다　**restoration** v. 복원
furnishing n. 가구　**condition** n. 상태　**secure** v. 확보하다
adorn v. 꾸미다

01 육하원칙 문제

문제　Douglas 박물관은 어떻게 보수 공사를 위한 자금을 얻었는가?
(A) 정부로부터 상을 받았다.
(B) 소장품 중 몇몇 미술품을 팔았다.
(C) 방문객들로부터 많은 기부금을 모았다.
(D) 한 단체로부터 보조금을 받았다.

해설　Douglas 박물관이 어떻게(How) 보수 공사를 위한 자금을 얻었는지를 묻는 육하원칙 문제이다. 질문의 핵심 어구인 Douglas Museum get the funds for the renovation work와 관련하여, 'it has been awarded a $5 million grant from the Lauderhill Foundation'(1문단 2번째 줄)에서 Douglas 박물관이 Lauderhill 재단으로부터 보조금을 받았고, 'The money will be used to restore the exterior of the Randolph Building'(1문단 4번째 줄)에서 이 자금은 Randolph 건물의 외관을 복원하기 위해 사용될 것이라고 했으므로 (D) It accepted a grant from an organization이 정답이다.

Paraphrasing
has been awarded a ~ grant 보조금을 받았다 → accepted a grant 보조금을 받았다

어휘　**collection** n. 소장품　**donation** n. 기부금　**organization** n. 단체

02 Not/True 문제

문제　Randolph 건물에 대해 언급되지 않은 것은?
(A) 귀한 물품들을 소장하고 있다.
(B) 한 세기가 넘었다.
(C) 10년 동안 닫혀 있었다.
(D) 복원된 내부를 가지고 있다.

해설　질문의 핵심 어구인 the Randolph Building과 관련된 내용을 지문에서 찾아 보기와 대조하는 Not/True 문제이다. (A)는 'it contains some of the nation's rarest and most valuable books, music manuscripts, artworks, and antiques'(2문단 2번째 줄)에서 그것, 즉 Randolph 건물이 나라에서 가장 희귀하고 귀중한 물품들을 포함한다고 했으므로 지문의 내용과 일치한다. (B)는 'The Randolph Building was constructed 110 years ago'(2문단 1번째 줄)에서 Randolph 건물이 110년 전에 지어졌다고 했으므로 지문의 내용과 일치한다. (C)는 지문에 언급되지 않은 내용이다. 따라서 (C) It was closed for a decade가 정답이다. (D)는 'Its interior underwent extensive renovations'(2문단 5번째 줄)에서 그것, 즉 Randolph 건물의 내부가 대규모의 보수 공사를 겪었다고 했으므로 지문의 내용과 일치한다.

Paraphrasing
valuable 귀중한 → precious 귀한
110 years 110년 → over a century 한 세기가 넘는

어휘　**house** v. 소장하다　**decade** n. 10년

03 동의어 찾기 문제

문제　3문단 다섯 번째 줄의 단어 "secured"는 의미상 –와 가장 가깝다.
(A) 확보된
(B) 보류된
(C) 보호된
(D) 첨부된

해설　secured를 포함하고 있는 구절 'the services of two specialists have been secured'(3문단 3번째 줄)에서 secured가 '확보된'이라는 뜻으로 사용되었다. 따라서 '확보된'이라는 뜻을 가진 (A) obtained가 정답이다.

어휘　**withhold** v. 보류하다　**protect** v. 보호하다　**attach** v. 첨부하다, 붙이다

04 추론 문제

문제　Ms. Anders에 대해 추론될 수 있는 것은?
(A) Douglas 박물관의 직원이다.
(B) 대학생일 때 건축학을 전공했다.
(C) Randolph 건물을 위한 새 미술품을 구입했다.
(D) Mr. Walker의 지휘 아래에서 일할 것이다.

해설　질문의 핵심 어구인 Ms. Anders에 대해 추론하는 문제이다. 'Martin Walker ~ will take the lead on the project. Working closely with him will be Beth Anders'(3문단 5번째 줄)에서 Martin Walker가 프로젝트를 주도할 것이며 Beth Anders가 그와 긴밀하게 협력할 것이라고 했으므로 Ms. Anders가 Mr. Walker의 지휘 아래에서 일할 것이라는 사실을 추론할 수 있다. 따라서 (D) She will work under the supervision of Mr. Walker가 정답이다.

어휘　**purchase** v. 구입하다　**supervision** n. 지휘, 감독

05-08은 다음 기사에 관한 문제입니다.

6월 6일. ⁰⁵많은 학생들, 교직원들 및 의료 전문가들이 객원 연구원 Dr. Steve Manning에 의해 진행된 연구 발표에 참석하기 위해 화요일에 뉴저지 주에 있는 Logan 대학교에 모였다. ^{06-A/06-B}Dr. Manning은 캘리포니아 주의 De Anda 대학교에 있는 아동 건강 관리 연구 부장으로, ^{06-B}식단과 운동이 학교에서 아동의 성취도에 미치는 영향에 대한 연구에서 얻은 그의 조사 결과를 발표했다.

^{06-C}5년이 넘는 기간 동안, 그는 각기 다른 학년 학생들의 다양한 실태를 관찰했고, 건강한 생활습관을 가진 아동들이 그들의 친구들보다 학교에서 더 잘 수행한다는 것을 알아냈다. "한 예로, 가정과 학교에서 적절한 영양분을 섭취한 아이들은 더 높은 인지 능력을 보여주는 경향이 있었습니다. 이 조건에 정기적인 운동이 병행되었을 때, 동일 학생들은 또한 수업에 더 몰두할 가능성이 높아졌습니다"라고 그는 설명했다. 그는 또한 식이와 운동의 알맞은 조합은 학교에서 더 주의 깊고 이에 따라 지식을 더 잘 받아들이는 경향이 있는 아이들을 만드는 것 같다고 덧붙였다. ─ [1] ─.

^{07-D}이러한 결과들은 왜 어떤 학생들이 학습 장애를 보이는지를 설명해 준다. ─ [2] ─. Dr. Manning은 16퍼센트의 조사 참가자들이 분명히 가정에서 충분한 음식을 섭취하지 못했다는 것을 발견했다. ⁰⁸그 중에, 30퍼센트는 정기적으로 지방이나 당분 함량이 높은 음식을 섭취했다. ─ [3] ─. ^{06-D}Dr. Manning은 특정한 음식들과 운동 프로그램들을 추천함으로써 그의 보고서를 보충했다. 그는 또한 학교가 학부모들과 협력해서 아이들이 각 요소의 적절한 양을 섭취할 수 있도록 보장해줄 것을 권장했다. ─ [4] ─.

이 행사는 Logan 대학교에 의한 정규 프로젝트의 일부로, 건강, 학문, 문화 그리고 사회의 발전과 관련해 대중을 교육시키고자 한다. Dr. Manning의 발표에 대한 필기록은 www.loganedu.com에서 다운로드가 가능하다. Dr. Manning의 연구의 전체 내용을 알아보는 것에 관심 있는 사람은 그의 온라인 데이터베이스 www.deanda.edu/manning으로 가면 된다.

a crowd of 많은　**faculty** n. (대학·고교의) 교직원
visiting scholar 객원 연구원　**cross section** 다양한 실태, 대표적 단면(실례)
peer n. 친구, 동기　**nutrition** n. 영양분　**cognitive** adj. 인지의
engage v. 몰두하다　**attentive** adj. 주의 깊은
be disposed to ~의 경향이 있다　**absorb** v. 받아들이다, 흡수하다
shed light on 설명하다　**undertaking** n. (중요한) 프로젝트, 일, 사업
transcript n. (연설 등의) 필기록

05 육하원칙 문제

문제 Dr. Manning은 어디에서 그의 연구 결과를 발표했는가?

(A) 지역 시민 문화 회관에서
(B) 조직의 본사에서
(C) 교육 기관에서
(D) 법인 연구 시설에서

해설 Dr. Manning이 어디에서(Where) 그의 연구 결과를 발표했는지를 묻는 육하원칙 문제이다. 질문의 핵심 어구인 release his study results와 관련하여, 'A crowd of students, faculty, and medical professionals gathered Tuesday at New Jersey's Logan University to attend the release of a study by visiting scholar Dr. Steve Manning.'(1문단 1번째 줄)에서 많은 학생들, 교직원들 및 의료 전문가들이 Dr. Steve Manning의 연구 발표에 참석하기 위해 뉴저지 주의 Logan 대학교에 모였다고 했으므로 (C) At an educational institution이 정답이다.

Paraphrasing
University 대학교 → an educational institution 교육 기관

어휘 community center 시민 문화 회관 corporate adj. 법인의, 공동의

06 Not/True 문제

문제 Dr. Manning에 대해 언급되지 않은 것은?

(A) 평소에 그의 연구를 캘리포니아에서 수행한다.
(B) 아동의 지능에 대한 전문가이다.
(C) 행사에서 운동과 식이 요법에 대한 제안을 했다.
(D) 여러 해에 걸쳐 조사 자료를 수집했다.

해설 질문의 핵심 어구인 Dr. Manning과 관련된 내용을 지문에서 찾아 보기와 대조하는 Not/True 문제이다. (A)는 'Dr. Manning, director of child healthcare research at California's De Anda University'(1문단 2번째 줄)에서 Dr. Manning은 캘리포니아 주의 De Anda 대학교에 있는 아동 건강 관리 연구 부장이라고 했으므로 지문의 내용과 일치한다. (B)는 'Dr. Manning, director of child healthcare research at California's De Anda University, presented his findings from a study on the influence of diet and exercise on children's performance in school.'(1문단 2번째 줄)에서 Dr. Manning은 아동 건강 관리 연구 부장으로, 식단과 운동이 학교에서 아동의 성취도에 미치는 영향에 대한 연구에서 얻은 그의 조사 결과를 발표했다고 했으므로 지문의 내용과 일치하지 않는다. 따라서 (B) He is an expert on intelligence in children이 정답이다. (C)는 'Dr. Manning supplemented his report by recommending specific foods and exercise routines.'(3문단 4번째 줄)에서 Dr. Manning은 특정한 음식들과 운동 프로그램들을 추천함으로써 그의 보고서를 보충했다고 했으므로 지문의 내용과 일치한다. (D)는 'Over a period of five years, he observed a cross section of students from different grade levels'(2문단 1번째 줄)에서 5년이 넘는 기간 동안, Dr. Manning은 각기 다른 학년 학생들의 다양한 실태를 관찰하였다고 했으므로 지문의 내용과 일치한다.

Paraphrasing
exercise routines 운동 프로그램 → fitness 운동
recommending specific foods 특정 음식 추천 →
diet suggestions 식이 요법 제안

07 Not/True 문제

문제 연구에 대해 언급된 것은?

(A) 초등학생들로 제한된 연구였다.
(B) 오직 학업 성취를 높이기 위한 조건에 관해서만 초점을 두었다.
(C) 아이들의 식단에 비타민제를 보충할 것을 제안했다.
(D) 일부 아동들이 왜 학습 장애를 겪는지를 밝혀냈다.

해설 질문의 핵심 어구인 the study와 관련된 내용을 지문에서 찾아 보기와 대조하는 Not/True 문제이다. (A), (B), (C)는 지문에 언급되지 않은 내용이다. (D)는 'The results shed light on why some students might be having academic problems.'(3문단 1번째 줄)에서 이러한 연구 결과들은 왜 어떤 학생들이 학습 장애를 보이는지를 설명해 준다고 했으므로 지문의 내용과 일치한다. 따라서 (D) It revealed why some children may have learning difficulties가 정답이다.

Paraphrasing
academic problems 학습 장애 → learning difficulties 학습 장애

어휘 solely adv. 오직 reveal v. 밝히다, 드러내다

08 문장 위치 찾기 문제

문제 [1], [2], [3], [4]로 표시된 위치 중, 다음 문장이 들어갈 곳으로 가장 적절한 것은?

"설상가상으로, 실험 참가자들 중 절반이 하루에 20분 미만으로 운동했다."

(A) [1]
(B) [2]
(C) [3]
(D) [4]

해설 지문의 흐름상 주어진 문장이 들어가기에 가장 적절한 곳을 고르는 문제이다. Making matters worse, half of the tested participants exercised for less than 20 minutes a day에서 설상가상으로 실험 참가자들 중 절반이 하루에 20분 미만으로 운동했다고 했으므로, 주어진 문장 앞에 실험 참가자들과 관련된 내용이 나올 것을 예상할 수 있다. [3]의 앞부분에서 16퍼센트의 연구 참가자들이 가정에서 충분한 음식을 섭취하지 못한다고 했고, [3]의 앞 문장인 'Of those that were, 30 percent regularly consumed foods that were high in fat or sugar'(3문단 3번째 줄)에서 그 중에 30퍼센트는 정기적으로 지방이나 당분 함량이 높은 음식을 섭취했다고 했으므로, [3]에 주어진 문장이 들어가면 실험 참가자들에 대한 조사 결과를 설명하는 자연스러운 문맥이 된다는 것을 알 수 있다. 따라서 (C) [3]이 정답이다.

Paraphrasing
study participant 연구 참가자 → tested participant 실험 참가자

09-12는 다음 기사에 관한 문제입니다.

시장이 시의 상징을 발표하다
Donna Wood 작성

월요일 오전 시청에서, [09]시장 Joel Weeks는 일리노이주, Riverbend의 새 로고를 소개하기 위한 기자회견을 개최했다. 로고 채택은 Riverbend의 인구가 2,500명을 넘어 공식적으로 도시로 공표된 후 단 2년 만에 나온 것이다.

디자인은 작년에 열린 대회 동안 예술가 Ralph McCord에 의해 제출된 수상작을 기반으로 한 것이다. [10-D]디자인은 떠오르는 태양을 향해 두 언덕 사이로 흐르는 Candle강의 묘사를 특징으로 삼고 있다. 강의 왼쪽 둑에는 가지 하나가 물 위에 뻗어있는 나무 한 그루가 서 있다. 반대편에는, [10-B]검은 황소가 강의 가장자리 옆에 앉아 있다. [10-B]목련꽃은 나중에 나무에 추가되었다.

[11]기준 및 선정 위원회 의장인 Sylvia Morris에 따르면, "Mr. McCord의 디자인은 우리가 준비한 지침을 충족시켰으며 우리는 그의 최종 이미지가 고결함, 근면, 그리고 농업 도시로서의 전통과 같은 우리 도시의 가치를 상징한다고 생각합니다." [10-C]이미지는 파란색 띠를 배경으로 하여 금색 별들로 테를 두른 원반에 둘러싸여 있다. 그에 더하여, 이 지역의 작가인 Kyle Holmes에 의해 창안된 표어는 "대지로부터 생명이 나오다"라고 읽히며 새 로고 아래에 나온다.

[12]로고는 이번 달 후반을 시작으로 모든 공문에 사용될 것이다. 게다가, 이 이미지의 형태는 돌에 새겨져 시청으로 들어가는 입구 위에 놓여질 것이다. 로고는 Riverbend의 웹사이트인 www.riverbend.il.gov의 홈페이지에도 추가되었다.

press conference 기자회견 adoption n. 채택, 선택
surpass v. 넘다, 초월하다 declare v. 공표하다, 선언하다
winning entry 수상작 feature v. 특징으로 삼다
representation n. 묘사, 표현 bank n. 둑, 제방
extend v. (팔·손 등을) 뻗다, 내밀다 edge n. 가장자리 chair n. 의장
fulfill v. 충족시키다, 완료하다 symbolize v. 상징하다
nobility n. 고결함, 숭고함 heritage n. 전통, 유산 agricultural adj. 농업의
enclose v. 둘러싸다 disc n. 원반 bordered adj. 테를 두른
against prep. ~을 배경으로 slogan n. 표어, 슬로건
official correspondence 공문

09 주제/목적 찾기 문제

문제 기사는 주로 무엇에 대한 것인가?

(A) 공공 기념물의 제막식
(B) 도시의 로고 채택

(C) 대회에 필요한 요건
(D) 시장의 캠페인 공표

해설　기사가 주로 무엇에 대한 것인지를 묻는 주제 찾기 문제이다. 'Mayor Joel Weeks held a press conference to present the new logo for Riverbend, Illinois'(1문단 1번째 줄)에서 시장인 Joel Weeks가 일리노이 주, Riverbend의 새 로고를 소개하기 위한 기자회견을 개최했다고 한 후, 로고 채택이 Riverbend가 도시로 공표됨에 따른 것임을 언급하고 로고 디자인에 대한 세부 내용을 설명하고 있으므로 (B) The adoption of a city logo가 정답이다.

어휘　unveiling n. (기념비 등의) 제막식, 초연　monument n. 기념물 requirement n. 요건, 필요조건　competition n. 대회

10 Not/True 문제

문제　Mr. McCord의 원래 디자인의 특징이 아닌 것은?
(A) 앉아 있는 동물
(B) 한 종류의 꽃
(C) 장식된 테두리
(D) 강 이미지

해설　질문의 핵심 어구인 Mr. McCord's original design과 관련된 내용을 지문에서 찾아 보기와 대조하는 Not/True 문제이다. (A)는 'a black bull sits beside the river's edge'(2문단 3번째 줄)에서 검은 황소가 강의 가장자리 옆에 앉아있다고 했으므로 지문의 내용과 일치한다. (B)는 'Magnolia flowers were later added to the tree.'(2문단 4번째 줄)에서 목련꽃은 나중에 나무에 추가되었다고 했으므로 지문의 내용과 일치하지 않는다. 따라서 (B) A type of flower가 정답이다. (C)는 'The image is enclosed within a disc bordered by gold stars'(3문단 3번째 줄)에서 이미지는 금색 별들로 테를 두른 원반에 둘러싸여 있다고 했으므로 지문의 내용과 일치한다. (D)는 'It features a representation of the Candle River flowing between two hills'(2문단 1번째 줄)에서 디자인은 두 언덕 사이로 흐르는 Candle강의 묘사를 특징으로 삼고 있다고 했으므로 지문의 내용과 일치한다.

어휘　seated adj. 앉아 있는　decorative adj. 장식이 된 border n. 테두리, 가장자리

11 추론 문제

문제　Sylvia Morris에 대해 암시되는 것은?
(A) 가장 좋은 디자인을 선정하는 데 참여했다.
(B) 공문을 담당하고 있다.
(C) 예술가로서의 교육을 받았다.
(D) 이 지역의 시청을 설계했다.

해설　질문의 핵심 어구인 Sylvia Morris에 대해 추론하는 문제이다. 'standards and selection committee chair Sylvia Morris'(3문단 1번째 줄)에서 Sylvia Morris가 기준 및 선정 위원회 의장이라고 했으므로 Sylvia Morris가 로고 디자인 선정 위원회 의장으로서 디자인 선정에 참여했다는 사실을 추론할 수 있다. 따라서 (A) She participated in choosing the best design이 정답이다.

어휘　participate in ~에 참여하다　be in charge of ~을 담당하다

12 육하원칙 문제

문제　Mr. McCord의 디자인은 무엇에 사용될 것인가?
(A) 모든 정부 청사
(B) 시청의 문서
(C) 도로 표지판
(D) 관광 안내 책자

해설　Mr. McCord의 디자인이 무엇에(What) 사용될 것인지를 묻는 육하원칙 문제이다. 질문의 핵심 어구인 Mr. McCord's design be used on과 관련하여, 'The logo will be used in all official correspondence'(4문단 1번째 줄)에서 로고가 모든 공문에 사용될 것이라고 했으므로 (B) City hall letters가 정답이다.

Paraphrasing
official correspondence 공문 → City hall letters 시청의 문서

어휘　government building 정부 청사　letter n. 문서, 편지 street sign 도로 표지판

예제 해석 p.427

메시지 대화문

Jeff Simmons	8:12

안녕하세요 Ms. Gotti. ¹방금 회의장에 도착했어요. ²저는 21번 배달 구역에 있어요.

Miriam Gotti	8:15

알겠어요, Jeff. 지금 제 팀원 중 몇 명과 함께 가고 있어요. 그곳에 20분 안에 도착할 거예요.

Jeff Simmons	8:17

알겠어요. ¹제가 행사를 위한 비품을 내려놓을까요?

Miriam Gotti	8:21

네. Mr. Cooper와 방금 통화를 했어요. 그는 2층의 로비에 있어요. ²그에게 내려가서 당신을 만나라고 부탁했어요.

Jeff Simmons	8:22

좋네요! ³그때 준비를 시작해도 괜찮을까요?

Miriam Gotti	8:23

물론이죠! Mr. Cooper가 경비를 통과하는 데 필요할 서식을 가지고 있어요.

Miriam Gotti	8:24

그건 그렇고, 저희는 D홀에 있어요.

Jeff Simmons	8:25

알겠어요! 이따가 거기서 만나요, Ms. Gotti.

conference n. 회의　bay n. 구역　unload v. (짐을) 내리다 security n. 경비, 보안

Q1.
문제　Mr. Simmons는 왜 Ms. Gotti에게 연락했는가?
(A) 추가 지시를 요청하기 위해
(B) 배송에 대해 알리기 위해
(C) 행사 참석을 확인하기 위해
(D) 몇몇 서류에 대해 묻기 위해

어휘　instruction n. 지시　attendance n. 참석

Q2.
문제　Mr. Cooper는 어디에서 Mr. Simmons를 만날 것인가?
(A) D홀에서
(B) 로비에서
(C) 21번 배달 구역에서
(D) 경비실에서

Q3.
문제　8시 23분에, Ms. Gotti가 "By all means"라고 썼을 때, 그녀가 의도한 것은?
(A) 가능한 한 빨리 장소에 도착하려고 할 것이다.
(B) Mr. Simmons가 그의 계획을 이행하기를 바란다.
(C) 일이 기간 내에 완료되기를 기대한다.
(D) Mr. Simmons가 그를 도울 수 있는 사람들을 찾기 바란다.

어휘　venue n. 장소　follow through with ~을 이행하다　time frame 기간

Hackers Practice p.430

유형 연습
01 (B)　　02 (C)

01 메시지 대화문

Betsy Lindhof	8:52

지난 금요일에 제 이메일 받으셨나요? Ms. Farrow에 대해서요?

Daniel Sung	8:55

아뇨, 그녀가 왜요? 문제가 있나요?

Betsy Lindhof	8:56

아, 그저 그녀가 오늘 업무를 시작할 수 없다는 거예요. 개인적으로 급한 일이 있대요. 그래도, 내일은 올 수 있어요.

Daniel Sung	8:57

알겠어요, 문제 없어요. 오늘은 그저 예비 교육을 주로 할 거예요. 그녀가 따라잡을 수 있어요.

Betsy Lindhof	8:58

그럴 것 같았어요. 그냥 알아 두셨으면 했어요.

Daniel Sung	8:59

고마워요. 나머지 신입 사원들이 교육장에서 기다리고 있어요. 금방 그곳으로 갈게요.

orientation n. 예비 교육 **catch up** 따라잡다

문제 8시 58분에, Ms. Lindhof가 "That's what I thought"이라고 썼을 때, 그녀가 의도한 것은?

(A) Mr. Sung이 그녀를 대신할 수 있다고 확신했다.
(B) Ms. Farrow의 불참이 문제가 될 것이라고 생각하지 않았다.
(C) 추가 수업이 실시되어야 할 것이라고 추측했다.

해설 **의도 파악 문제** Ms. Lindhof가 의도한 것을 묻는 문제이므로, 질문의 인용 어구(That's what I thought)가 언급된 주변 문맥을 확인한다. 'she won't be able to start work today'(8:56)에서 Ms. Lindhof가 Ms. Farrow는 오늘 업무를 시작할 수 없다고 하자 Daniel Sung이 'She can catch up.(8:57)'에서 그녀가 따라잡을 수 있다고 한 후, Ms. Lindhof가 'That's what I thought'(그럴 것 같았어요)이라고 한 것을 통해, Ms. Lindhof는 Ms. Farrow의 불참이 문제가 될 것이라고 생각하지 않았음을 알 수 있다. 따라서 (B) She did not believe Ms. Farrow's absence would be an issue가 정답이다.

02 메시지 대화문

Emma Browning	15:39

안녕하세요 Sarah. 오늘 오후에는 사무실로 돌아갈 수 없을 것 같아요. ^A^회의가 길어지고 있어요. 이메일로 대신 프레젠테이션을 보내줄 수 있나요?

Sarah Clapp	15:41

안녕하세요 Emma. 그럼요. 하지만 내일 전까지 이것을 살펴볼 시간이 있을 것 같나요?

Emma Browning	15:46

물론이죠. ^B^집으로 가는 기차에서 읽고 오후 7시쯤에 제 메모를 보내드릴 수 있어요.

Sarah Clapp	15:47

정말 감사드려요, 하지만 당신께 폐를 끼치는 게 아니었으면 좋겠어요. 분명히 당신은 해야 할 일이 산더미처럼 있을 거예요.

Emma Browning	15:48

네, 하지만 괜찮아요. 이번이 당신의 첫 고객 미팅이고 제가 도와드리겠다고 약속했어요... ^C^당신이 잘하지 못할 거라고 생각한다는 말은 아니에요. 당신은 분명히 잘할 거예요.

Sarah Clapp	15:51

감사해요, Emma! 지금 당신께 문서를 보내고 있어요.

make back 돌아가다 **look over** ~을 살펴보다 **put out** ~에게 폐를 끼치다
have a lot on one's plate 해야 할 일이 산더미처럼 있다 **as we speak** 지금

문제 Ms. Browning에 대해 언급되지 않은 것은?

(A) 회의가 아마 늦게 끝날 것이다.
(B) 기차로 직장까지 통근한다.
(C) Ms. Clapp의 능력에 대해 확신이 없다.

해설 **Not/True 문제** 질문의 핵심 어구인 Ms. Browning과 관련된 내용을 지문에서 찾아 보기와 대조하는 Not/True 문제이다. (A)는 'My meeting is running long.'(15:39)에서 회의가 길어지고 있다고 했으므로 지

문의 내용과 일치한다. (B)는 'I can read it on my way home on the train'(15:46)에서 집으로 가는 기차에서 읽을 수 있다고 했으므로 지문의 내용과 일치한다. (C)는 'which is not to say I don't think you'll do well. I'm sure you will.'(15:48)에서 Sarah Clapp이 잘하지 못할 것이라고 생각한다는 말이 아니라고 하며 분명히 잘할 거라고 했으므로 지문의 내용과 일치하지 않는다. 따라서 (C) She is uncertain about Ms. Clapp's abilities가 정답이다.

어휘 **commute** v. 통근하다 **ability** n. 능력

Hackers Test p.431

01 (C)	02 (B)	03 (D)	04 (C)	05 (C)
06 (B)	07 (A)	08 (B)	09 (B)	10 (C)

01-02는 다음 메시지 대화문에 관한 문제입니다.

Claire Fontaine	오전 9:38

방해해서 미안해요. 인쇄소에 벌써 들렀나요?

Joe Greyson	오전 9:39

아뇨. 아직 우체국이에요. 왜요?

Claire Fontaine	오전 9:43

사보의 복사본을 추가로 20부 가져다줄 수 있나요? 제 새로운 수습 직원들을 위한 거예요.

Joe Greyson	오전 9:46

문제 없어요. ^01^그들에게 줄 회사 안내서는 충분히 있나요?

Claire Fontaine	오전 9:48

그럴 거예요. ^01^비품실에 그것들이 한 상자 있어요. 뒤쪽 근처예요. 저번 달에 그곳에서 봤어요.

Joe Greyson	오전 9:51

Mr. Jennings가 지난주에 그것들을 모두 사용했어요. 제가 그들에게 더 인쇄해달라고 요청할게요.

Claire Fontaine	오전 9:55

^02^20부만 구해주세요. 안내서를 곧 바꿀 계획이라, 그것보다 더 필요하지는 않을 거예요.

Joe Greyson	오전 9:57

그럴게요. ^02^제가 찾아온 다음에 당신의 사무실로 가져다 드릴게요.

print shop 인쇄소 **company newsletter** 사보 **trainee** n. 수습 직원
handbook n. 안내서 **supply room** 비품실

01 의도 파악 문제

문제 오전 9시 48분에, Ms. Fontaine이 "I believe so"라고 썼을 때, 그녀가 의도한 것은?

(A) 추가로 사보가 인쇄되어야 한다는 것에 동의한다.
(B) 인쇄소에 잠깐 들를 수 있다고 생각한다.
(C) 충분한 수의 안내서가 있다고 생각한다.
(D) 사보가 배포되었다는 것을 알고 있다.

해설 Ms. Fontaine이 의도한 것을 묻는 문제이므로, 질문의 인용어구(I believe so)가 언급된 주변 문맥을 확인한다. 'Do you have enough company handbooks to give them?'(9:46 A.M.)에서 Joe Greyson이 새로운 수습 직원들에게 줄 회사 안내서가 충분히 있는지 묻자, Ms. Fontaine이 'I believe so'(그럴 거예요)라고 한 후, 'There's a box of them in the supply room.'(9:48 A.M.)에서 비품실에 그것들이 한 상자 있다고 한 것을 통해, Ms. Fontaine이 충분한 수의 안내서가 있다고 생각한다는 것을 알 수 있다. 따라서 (C) She thinks there are a sufficient number of handbooks가 정답이다.

Paraphrasing
enough 충분한 → a sufficient number of 충분한 수의

어휘 **drop by** 잠깐 들르다 **distribute** v. 배포하다

02 육하원칙 문제

문제   Mr. Greyson은 무엇을 하겠다고 제안하는가?

(A) 회사 안내서를 일부 수정하는 것

(B) Ms. Fontaine의 직장에 추가 복사본을 가져다 주는 것

(C) 더 많은 상품을 주문하기 위해 상점에 전화하는 것

(D) 비품실에서 일부 상자를 가지고 가는 것

해설   Mr. Greyson이 무엇(What)을 하겠다고 제안하는지를 묻는 육하원칙 문제이다. 질문의 핵심 어구인 Mr. Greyson offer to do와 관련하여 'Just get 20. We plan to make changes to the handbook soon, so we won't need more than that.'(9:55 A.M.)에서 Ms. Fontaine이 안내서를 곧 바꿀 계획이므로 20부만 구매해 달라고 부탁하자, 'I can bring them to your office after I pick them up.'(9:57 A.M.)에서 Mr. Greyson이 그것들을 찾아온 다음에 Ms. Fontaine의 사무실로 가져다 주겠다고 했으므로 (B) Drop off some extra copies at Ms. Fontaine's workplace가 정답이다.

어휘   modification n. 수정   workplace n. 직장, 일터

03-06은 다음 온라인 채팅 대화문에 관한 문제입니다.

Steve Williams   오전 9:10
Laura, ⁰³우리가 Winston 법률 사무소의 사무실을 위해 주문한 커튼에 문제가 있어요. ^{03/04}우리의 공급업체에 우리가 원래 선택했던 천이 다 떨어졌대요.

Laura Davis   오전 9:13
그렇군요. 우리는 이달 말까지 그 프로젝트를 완료하기로 되어 있어요. 우리는 어쩌면 좋죠?

Michael Smith   오전 9:15
⁰⁴제가 어젯밤에 새로운 천 샘플들을 찾을 수 있었어요, Steve. 몇 시간 걸리긴 했지만 ⁰⁵제 생각엔 저희가 쓸 만한 것들을 제가 찾은 것 같아요. 당신에게 그것들의 사진을 이메일로 보냈어요.

Steve Williams   오전 9:18
고마워요, Michael! 만약 우리가 적합한 것을 찾을 수 있다면, 우리는 여전히 마감을 맞출 수 있을지도 몰라요.

Laura Davis   오전 9:20
그러길 바라요. 그 고객에게 그들의 프로젝트가 또 연기되었다고 알리는 것은 피하고 싶어요.

Steve Williams   오전 9:22
Michael, 이것들 중 몇몇은 괜찮을 것 같아요. ⁰⁵제가 지금 그것들을 고객에게 보여줄게요.

Laura Davis   오전 9:24
제게도 진행 상황을 계속 알려 주세요, Steve. ⁰⁶이 프로젝트를 위한 일정을 제가 다시 조정해야 할지 알아야 해요.

run out of ~이 다 떨어지다, ~을 다 쓰다   fabric n. 천, 직물
originally adv. 원래, 본래   locate v. 찾다   suitable adj. 적합한
make the deadline 마감을 맞추다   avoid v. 피하다   delay v. 연기시키다
keep ~ posted ~에게 (진행 상황을) 계속 알려 주다
readjust v. 다시 조정하다

---

03 추론 문제

문제   필자들은 어느 분야에서 일할 것 같은가?

(A) 회계

(B) 법

(C) 섬유 제조

(D) 인테리어 디자인

해설   필자들이 일하는 분야를 추론하는 문제이다. 'there is a problem with the curtains we ordered for the offices of Winston Legal Services. Our supplier has run out of the fabric that we originally chose.'(9:10 A.M.)에서 Mr. Williams가 자신들이 Winston 법률 사무소의 사무실을 위해 주문한 커튼에 문제가 있고, 자신들이 원래 선택했던 천이 공급업체에 다 떨어졌다고 한 것을 통해 필자들은 고객을 위해 커튼을 선택하고 주문하는 업무와 관련 있는 인테리어 디자인 분야에 일한다는 사실을 추론할 수 있다. 따라서 (D) Interior design이 정답이다.

04 육하원칙 문제

문제   Mr. Smith는 어제 무엇을 했는가?

(A) 고객과 문제에 대해 논의했다

(B) 새 사무실 공간의 개관식에 참석했다

(C) 제품의 대체재를 찾으려고 했다

(D) 긴급 프로젝트 보고서를 작성했다

해설   Mr. Smith가 어제 무엇(What)을 했는지를 묻는 육하원칙 문제이다. 질문의 핵심 어구인 Mr. Smith do yesterday와 관련하여, 'Our supplier has run out of the fabric that we originally chose.'(9:10 A.M.)에서 Steve Williams가 자신들이 원래 선택했던 천이 공급업체에 다 떨어졌다고 하자, 'I was able to locate some new fabric samples last night'(9:15 A.M.)에서 Mr. Smith가 어젯밤에 새로운 천 샘플을 찾았다고 했으므로 (C) Attempted to find out substitutes for a product가 정답이다.

Paraphrasing
locate 찾다 → find out 찾다

어휘   attempt v. ~하려고 하다   substitute n. 대체재   complete v. 작성하다   urgent adj. 긴급한

05 의도 파악 문제

문제   오전 9시 22분에, Mr. Williams가 "some of these could work"라고 썼을 때, 그가 의도한 것은?

(A) 일부 이메일 주소가 정확하다.

(B) 그가 직물의 품질을 확인할 것이다.

(C) 고객은 아마 선택된 것을 승인할 것이다.

(D) 그는 사업 계획에 몇 가지 변경을 해야 한다.

해설   Mr. Williams가 의도한 것을 묻는 문제이므로, 질문의 인용어구(some of these could work)가 언급된 주변 문맥을 확인한다. 'I think I found some that we can use. I e-mailed photographs of them to you'(9:15 A.M.)에서 Michael Smith가 '우리가 쓸 수 있는 것, 즉 쓸 수 있는 천을 찾은 것 같다며 그것들의 사진을 당신, 즉 Mr. Williams에게 이메일로 보냈다고 하자, Mr. Williams가 'some of these could work'(이것들 중 몇몇은 괜찮을 것 같아요)라고 한 후, 'I'll show them to the client now.'(9:22 A.M.)에서 지금 그것들을 고객들에게 보여주겠다고 한 것을 통해, Mr. Williams는 고객이 선택된 천을 사용하는 것을 아마 승인할 것이라고 생각한다는 것을 알 수 있다. 따라서 (C) A client will probably approve of a selection이 정답이다.

어휘   correct adj. 정확한, 옳은   material n. 직물, 천   approve of ~을 승인하다, 동의하다   selection n. 선택(된 것)

06 Not/True 문제

문제   Ms. Davis에 대해 사실인 것은?

(A) 마감일을 바꾸고 싶어 한다.

(B) 한 프로젝트의 일정을 담당하고 있다.

(C) 고객 발표를 준비한다.

(D) 부재 중일 것이다.

해설   질문의 핵심 어구인 Ms. Davis와 관련된 내용을 지문에서 찾아 보기와 대조하는 Not/True 문제이다. (A)는 지문에 언급되지 않은 내용이다. (B)는 'I need to know if I have to readjust the schedule for this project.'(9:24 A.M.)에서 Ms. Davis가 자신이 이 프로젝트의 일정을 다시 조정해야 할지 알아야 한다고 했으므로, Ms. Davis가 프로젝트 일정을 담당한다는 사실을 알 수 있다. 따라서 (B) She is in charge of a project timeline이 정답이다. (C)와 (D)는 지문에 언급되지 않은 내용이다.

Paraphrasing
schedule for ~ project 프로젝트를 위한 일정 → project timeline 프로젝트 일정

어휘   be eager to ~을 하고 싶어 하다   deadline n. 마감일   be away 부재 중이다

Hank Warden	(오전 11:26)

안녕하세요. ⁰⁷저는 Bene-Connect Wireless사에서 일하고 있습니다. 당신의 아파트에 라우터를 설치하러 왔는데, 아무도 집에 안 계시네요. 근처에 있으신 가요?

Michaela Howe	(오전 11:28)

아. 완전히 깜빡 잊었네요. 사실은 제가 지금 공항에 있어요. 이제 막 비행기를 타려던 참이에요.

Hank Warden	(오전 11:29)

네. 괜찮아요. 우린 꽤 쉽게 일정을 변경할 수 있어요.

Michaela Howe	(오전 11:35)

하지만 ⁰⁸작년에 당신의 회사에서 설치해 준 라우터가 더 이상 작동하지 않아서 새로운 것이 꼭 설치되었으면 해요. 건물 관리인에게 연락해서 그녀가 당신에게 제 아파트 출입을 허가해줄 수 있는지 확인해 볼게요.

Michaela Howe	(오전 11:40)

방금 관리인 Susan Lewis와 이야기했고, 그녀가 당신을 들여보내 줄 거라고 했어요. 2층에 있는 사무실로 가서 그녀를 만나세요.

Hank Warden	(오전 11:42)

알겠어요. 그리고 ⁰⁹그녀가 작업 지시서에 서명해도 괜찮으신가요? 회사에서 제가 모든 일을 시작하기 전에 허가를 요구해요.

Michaela Howe	(오전 11:43)

<u>문제가 되지 않을 거예요.</u>

Hank Warden	(오전 11:44)

좋아요. 새로운 라우터는 당신이 여행에서 돌아오면 모두 설치되어 있을 거예요. ^{10-C}그것이 무슨 문제를 일으킨다면, 저희에게 알려주시면 여전히 보증 기간 내인 경우 무료로 교체해드릴 거예요.

router n. 라우터(네트워크에서 데이터의 전달을 촉진하는 중계 장치)
nearby adj. 근처의, 가까운   **slip one's mind** 깜빡 잊다
reschedule v. 일정을 변경하다   **building manager** 건물 관리인
work order form 작업 지시서   **authorization** n. 허가(증)
under warranty 보증 기간 중인

---

07 추론 문제

문제   Mr. Warden은 누구일 것 같은가?
(A) 기술자
(B) 판매원
(C) 집주인
(D) 배관공

해설   질문의 핵심 어구인 Mr. Warden에 대해 추론하는 문제이다. 'I'm with Bene-Connect Wireless. I've come to your apartment to install a router'(11:26 A.M.)에서 Mr. Warden이 자신이 Bene-Connect Wireless사에서 일하고 있고 라우터를 설치하기 위해 아파트에 방문했다고 했으므로 Mr. Warden이 기술자라는 사실을 추론할 수 있다. 따라서 (A) A technician이 정답이다.

어휘   **technician** n. 기술자   **landlord** n. 집주인   **plumber** n. 배관공

---

08 추론 문제

문제   Ms. Howe에 대해 무엇이 암시되는가?
(A) 그날 나중에 Ms. Lewis를 만날 것이다.
(B) Bene-Connect사의 기존 고객이다.
(C) 인터넷 공급업체에 고용되어 있다.
(D) 출장을 막 돌아왔다.

해설   질문의 핵심 어구인 Ms. Howe에 대해 추론하는 문제이다. 'I really need the new router set up because the one your company installed last year isn't working anymore'(11:35 A.M.)에서 Ms. Howe가 작년에 상대방의 회사, 즉 Bene-Connect Wireless사에서 설치해 준 라우터가 더 이상 작동하지 않아서 새로운 것이 꼭 설치되었으면 한다고 했으므로 Ms. Howe가 Bene-Connect사의 기존 고객이라는 사실을 추론할 수 있다. 따라서 (B) She is an existing customer of Bene-Connect가 정답이다.

어휘   **employ** v. 고용하다, 근무하다   **business trip** 출장

---

09 의도 파악 문제

문제   오전 11시 43분에, Ms. Howe가 "That shouldn't be a problem"이라고 썼을 때, 그녀가 의도한 것은?
(A) 기꺼이 기기를 스스로 수리할 것이다.
(B) 다른 사람이 그녀 대신에 서명하는 것을 신경 쓰지 않는다.
(C) 기술자를 만나기 위해 로비로 내려갈 수 있다.
(D) 소프트웨어 설치 과정에 익숙하다.

해설   Ms. Howe가 의도한 것을 묻는 문제이므로, 질문의 인용어구(That shouldn't be a problem)가 언급된 주변 문맥을 확인한다. 'Is it OK if she sign the work order form?'(11:42 A.M.)에서 Mr. Warden이 그녀, 즉 건물 관리인이 작업 지시서에 서명해도 괜찮은지 묻자, Ms. Howe가 'That shouldn't be a problem'(문제가 되지 않을 거예요)이라고 한 것을 통해, Ms. Howe가 다른 사람이 그녀 대신에 서명하는 것에 대해 신경 쓰지 않는다는 것을 알 수 있다. 따라서 (B) She does not mind if someone else signs for her가 정답이다.

어휘   **be willing to** 기꺼이 ~하다   **device** n. 기기, 장치
be familiar with ~에 익숙하다   **installation** n. 설치

---

10 Not/True 문제

문제   Bene-Connect Wireless사에 대해 언급된 것은?
(A) 일주일 내내 서비스를 제공한다.
(B) 새로운 제품을 출시할 계획이다.
(C) 보증 기간 중에는 제품 교체에 비용을 청구하지 않는다.
(D) 자사의 고객들 사이에서 설문조사를 실시하고 있다.

해설   질문의 핵심 어구인 Bene-Connect Wireless와 관련된 내용을 지문에서 찾아 보기와 대조하는 Not/True 문제이다. (A)와 (B)는 지문에 언급되지 않은 내용이다. (C)는 'If it gives you any trouble, just let us know and we will change it for free as long as it's still under warranty.'(11:44 A.M.)에서 그것, 즉 새로운 제품이 문제를 일으키면 보증 기간 내에는 무료로 교체해 줄 것이라고 했으므로 지문의 내용과 일치한다. 따라서 (C) It does not charge to replace items under warranty가 정답이다. (D)는 지문에 언급되지 않은 내용이다.

Paraphrasing
for free 무료로 → does not charge 비용을 청구하지 않다

어휘   **release** v. 출시하다, 풀어주다   **conduct** v. (특정한 활동을) 하다

Chapter 12 광고(Advertisement)

예제 해석   p.435

일반 광고

> ¹Pinewood Towers
> 사업을 운영하기 위한 최적의 장소!
>
> 포틀랜드의 금융 지구 내에 위치한, Pinewood Towers는 여러분의 회사를 수용할 최적의 장소입니다. 널찍한 공간에 더하여, 건물은 제공합니다:
>
> - 24시간 경비 서비스
> - 주차를 위한 세 개의 지하층
> - 커피숍과 구내 식당
> - 충분한 관리 직원
>
> 대중교통 수단에서 불과 몇 분 거리인, Pinewood Towers는 Poplar가 776번지에 매우 편리하게 위치해 있습니다. 우리는 현재 10명에서 40명을 수월하게 수용할 수 있는 공간들을 보유하고 있습니다. 각 공간은 독자적인 로비, 화장실 및 창고를 포함합니다. ^{2-C}모든 공간은 인터넷 및 전화 연결을 갖추고 있으며 추가 요금을 내시면 가구 또한 비치될 수 있습니다.
>
> Pinewood Towers의 빈 공간들을 안내원과 함께 둘러보길 원하시면, 월요일부터 금요일까지 오전 9시에서 오후 6시 사이에 555-8877번으로 전화하셔서 저희 중개인들 중 한 명에게 말씀해 주십시오. 그리고 이 달에만, ^{2-B/3}한 공간 ○

을 1년 혹은 그 이상 임대하는 모든 세입자들은 ³15퍼센트 공제를 받을 자격이 주어집니다. 이 드문 기회를 이용하시려면 오늘 전화하세요!

house v. 수용하다, 거처할 곳을 주다　situate v. 위치시키다, 짓다
vacancy n. 공간, 공석　be equipped with ~을 갖추고 있다
furnish v. (가구를) 비치하다　tenant n. 임차인　be eligible to ~할 자격이 있다
deduction n. 공제, 유추　take advantage of ~을 이용하다

Q1.
문제　광고되고 있는 것은?
(A) 기업 이사 서비스
(B) 부동산 투자 회사
(C) 사무 공간을 포함하고 있는 건물
(D) 저장 시설

어휘　corporate n. 기업　real estate 부동산, 토지　investment n. 투자

Q2.
문제　Pinewood Towers에 대해 언급된 것은?
(A) 건설이 완성에 가까워지고 있다.
(B) 단기 임대 계약만 제공한다.
(C) 세입자들에게 가구를 제공할 수 있다.
(D) 추가 직원 40명을 고용할 것이다.

어휘　completion n. 완성　short-term adj. 단기의　lease n. 임대차 계약
contain v. 포함하다　facility n. 시설

Q3.
문제　광고에 따르면, 누가 할인 요금을 받을 자격이 있는가?
(A) 시설의 현재 임차인
(B) 넓은 사무 공간을 임대하는 사람들
(C) 소기업 소유주들
(D) 12개월 이상 임대하는 사람들

어휘　reduced adj. 할인한, 감소한

Hackers Practice
p.438

유형 연습
01 (B)　　02 (B)　　03 (C)

01 일반 광고

Riverdale 골동품 경매!
이번 일요일 오후 1시 30분에 Riverdale 도심 Dalecourt가 354번지의 Henderson's Antiques 연례 골동품 경매에 오십시오. 이 특별한 행사는 지역 소아병원을 위한 기금을 모으기 위해 개최됩니다. 경매에 나온 물품들은 지역 내 주민들과 사업체들에 의해 기증된 것이며, 가구, 가정용품, 수공예품 및 수집품을 포함합니다! www.hendersonantiques.com을 방문하셔서 경매에 나온 물품들 목록을 살펴 보십시오.

antique n. 골동품, 고미술품　auction n. 경매　local adj. 지역의
region n. 지역, 분야　houseware n. 가정용품　artwork n. 수공예품
collectible n. 수집품　take a look 훑어보다　up for ~을 위해 내놓은

문제　행사의 목적은 무엇인가?
(A) 새 재고품을 위한 공간을 만들기 위해
(B) 자선 목적의 기금을 모으기 위해
(C) 지역 주민들로부터 기부를 간청하기 위해

해설　주제/목적 찾기 문제 행사의 목적을 묻는 목적 찾기 문제이다. 'This special event is held to raise funds for the local children's hospital.'에서 이 특별 행사는 지역 소아병원을 위한 기금을 모으기 위해 개최된다고 했으므로 (B) To collect money for a charitable cause가 정답이다.

Paraphrasing
raise funds 기금을 모으다 → collect money 기금을 모으다

어휘　make room for ~을 위해 공간을 만들다　charitable adj. 자선의, 관대한
cause n. 목적, 대의명분　solicit v. 간청하다

02 구인 광고

구인: 아침 식사 교대조 주방장

직무: Hal's Diner에서 월요일부터 금요일까지 오전 5시 30분부터 오전 11시까지 아침 식사 교대조를 담당할 주방장을 구합니다. 선발된 지원자는 달걀, 팬케이크 및 육류를 포함한 아침 식사용 석쇠에 구운 요리 준비를 책임질 것입니다. 주방장은 또한 다른 두 명의 요리사들을 감독하고 다음 교대조에 필요한 일일 물품 목록을 작성하는 것을 담당할 것입니다.

자격: 최소 6년간 주방 직원으로 일한 요리사를 찾고 있습니다. 관리자 경험 역시 유리합니다.

shift n. 교대조　head cook 주방장　duty n. 직무, 의무
be in charge of ~을 담당하다　oversee v. 감독하다
supply n. (준비) 물품, 필수품　qualification n. 자격　asset n. 유리한 것, 자산

문제　광고되는 직위에 요구되는 직무는 무엇인가?
(A) 식품 구매
(B) 팀 관리
(C) 주말 근무

해설　육하원칙 문제 광고되는 직위에 요구되는 직무가 무엇인지(What)를 묻는 육하원칙 문제이다. 질문의 핵심 어구인 a required task와 관련하여, 'He or she will also be in charge of overseeing the other two cooks'에서 다른 두 명의 요리사들을 감독해야 한다고 했으므로 (B) Managing a team이 정답이다.

Paraphrasing
overseeing 감독하기 → Managing 관리하기

어휘　task n. 직무, 과제

03 일반 광고

이동하실 경제적인 방법을 찾고 계십니까? 도시 거주자들을 위해 특별히 제작된 자전거 Yorktown Cycle을 이용해보세요.
• 편안하고, 똑바로 선 좌석 위치
• 접을 수 있고, 가벼운 구조
• 튼튼하고, 어떤 날씨에도 견딜 수 있는 타이어
대부분의 주요 소매 상점에서 기본적인 장비 세트를 마련하시고 부속품을 가지고 원하는 대로 바꿔보세요. www.yorktowncycle.com에서 우리의 카탈로그를 보십시오.

economical adj. 경제적인　get around 이동하다, 돌아다니다
dweller n. 거주자　upright adj. 똑바로 선, 수직의
foldable adj. 접을 수 있는　durable adj. 튼튼한, 내구성 있는
all-weather 어떤 날씨에도 견딜 수 있는

문제　광고는 누구를 대상으로 할 것 같은가?
(A) 신체 단련 열광자들
(B) 비즈니스 여행객들
(C) 도시 통근자들

해설　추론 문제 광고의 대상을 추론하는 문제이다. 'a bike made specifically for city dwellers'에서 도시 거주자들을 위해 특별히 제작된 자전거라고 했으므로 (C) Urban commuters를 대상으로 하는 광고임을 추론할 수 있다. 따라서 (C) Urban commuters가 정답이다.

Paraphrasing
city dwellers 도시 거주자들 → Urban commuters 도시 통근자들

어휘　enthusiast n. 열광자, 팬　commuter n. 통근자

Hackers Test
p.439

01 (C)	02 (D)	03 (C)	04 (C)	05 (B)
06 (D)	07 (B)	08 (D)	09 (C)	10 (D)
11 (B)	12 (B)			

01-04는 다음 광고에 관한 문제입니다.

관리직 기회

Dilly Dogs N' Fries 체인점은 [03-A]정규 지역 관리자직에 대해 지원서를 받고 있습니다. [01]우리는 이 기회를 사내 직원들에게 제공하기를 원합니다. [04-C]이 직위의 책무는 식당의 뉴저지주 동부 12개 지점 운영의 모든 면을 감독하는 것을 포함하며, 각 지점이 회사의 음식 및 서비스 품질 기준을 확실히 충족하게 하는 것입니다. [02-B]지역 관리자의 직무는 새로운 직원 고용 및 교육, 판매합계액 분석 및 보고, 그리고 주 식품 및 노동 안전 규정 준수를 보장하는 것을 포함할 것입니다. [02-A]지역 관리자는 사업 성장에 대한 논의를 목적으로 경영진과 자주 연락하게 될 것입니다. [02-C]국내 출장이 요구됩니다. 지원자는 경영학 석사 학위를 소지해야 하며 기본 회계 업무에 다소 정통해야 합니다. [03-C]강한 통솔력과 지도 기술은 필수입니다. 이 직책에 지원하고 싶은 현 직원들은 자기소개서와 이력서를 총무부의 Blake Carlton에게 blacarl@dilly.com으로 보내주시기 바랍니다.

---

franchise n. 체인점, 가맹점 영업권 aspect n. 면, 양상 operation n. 경영
ensure v. 확실하게 하다, 보증하다 compliance n. 준수, 순응
executive n. 경영진, 임원; adj. 경영의, 행정상의 master's degree 석사 학위
business management 경영학 familiarity n. 정통함, 친함
accounting n. 회계 (업무), 회계학 mandatory adj. 필수의, 강제의

01 추론 문제

문제 광고는 누구를 대상으로 하는가?

(A) 새로운 훈련생들
(B) 경영학 전문가들
(C) 현 직원들
(D) 판매 부장들

해설 광고의 대상을 추론하는 문제이다. 'We would prefer to offer the opportunity to staff within the company.'(2번째 줄)에서 회사는 이 기회를 사내 직원들에게 제공하기를 원한다고 했으므로 회사에 근무하는 현 직원들을 대상으로 하는 광고임을 추론할 수 있다. 따라서 (C) Existing employees가 정답이다.

Paraphrasing
staff within the company 사내 직원들 → Existing employees 현 직원들

어휘 trainee n. 훈련생 specialist n. 전문가, 전공자

02 Not/True 문제

문제 광고에 따르면, 직책의 책무가 아닌 것은?

(A) 상급 관리자와의 회의
(B) 판매 자료 파악
(C) 여러 장소 여행
(D) 시장 조사 수행

해설 질문의 핵심 어구인 a responsibility of the job과 관련된 내용을 지문에서 찾아 보기와 대조하는 Not/True 문제이다. (A)는 'He or she will communicate often with the executive for the purpose of discussing the business's growth.'(9번째 줄)에서 지역 관리자는 사업 성장에 대한 논의를 목적으로 경영진과 자주 연락하게 될 것이라고 했으므로 지문의 내용과 일치한다. (B)는 'The duties of the district manager will include ~ analyzing and reporting sales figures'(6번째 줄)에서 지역 관리자의 직무는 판매합계액 분석 및 보고를 포함할 것이라고 했으므로 지문의 내용과 일치하며, (C)는 'Local travel is required.'(10번째 줄)에서 국내 출장이 요구된다고 했으므로 지문의 내용과 일치한다. (D)는 지문에 언급되지 않은 내용이다. 따라서 (D) Conducting market research가 정답이다.

Paraphrasing
the executive 경영진 → upper management 상급 관리자

어휘 upper adj. 상급의 keep track of ~에 대해 계속 파악하고 있다
conduct v. 수행하다 market research 시장 조사

03 Not/True 문제

문제 광고되는 자리에 대해 언급된 것은?

(A) 임시직이다.
(B) 완전한 복리 후생 제도를 제공한다.
(C) 지휘 기량을 필요로 한다.
(D) 교육의 수료를 요구한다.

해설 질문의 핵심 어구인 the advertised position과 관련된 내용을 지문에서 찾아 보기와 대조하는 Not/True 문제이다. (A)는 'a full-time district manager position'(1번째 줄)에서 정규 지역 관리자직이라고 했으므로 지문의 내용과 일치하지 않는다. (B)는 지문에 언급되지 않은 내용이다. (C)는 'Strong leadership and coaching skills are mandatory.'(13번째 줄)에서 강한 통솔력과 지도 기술은 필수라고 했으므로 (C) It will require some leading skills가 정답이다. (D)는 지문에 언급되지 않은 내용이다.

Paraphrasing
leadership 통솔력 → leading skills 지도 기술

어휘 temporary adj. 임시의, 일시적인 benefits package 복리 후생 제도

04 Not/True 문제

문제 Dilly Dogs N' Fries에 대해 언급된 것은?

(A) 직원들을 위한 교육 시설을 유지한다.
(B) 주 식품 안전 지침을 준수하지 않았다.
(C) 뉴저지주 근방에 십여 개의 지점을 경영한다.
(D) 모든 신입 직원들에 대해 추천서를 요구한다.

해설 질문의 핵심 어구인 Dilly Dogs N' Fries와 관련된 내용을 지문에서 찾아 보기와 대조하는 Not/True 문제이다. (A)와 (B)는 지문에 언급되지 않은 내용이다. (C)는 'The responsibilities of the position include overseeing ~ operations for the restaurant's 12 locations in eastern New Jersey'(3번째 줄)에서 이 직위의 책무는 식당의 뉴저지주 동부 12개 지점 운영을 감독하는 것을 포함한다고 했으므로 (C) It operates a dozen branches around New Jersey가 정답이다. (D)는 지문에 언급되지 않은 내용이다.

어휘 comply v. 따르다 dozen n. 십여 개, 다스(12개짜리 한 묶음)
letter of reference 추천서 incoming adj. 신입의, 들어오는

05-08은 다음 광고에 관한 문제입니다.

Alladin 쇼핑몰 – 쇼핑하기에 훌륭한 새로운 장소!

모든 쇼핑을 하기 위한 최적의 장소를 찾고 계십니까? 최근 완공 이후, Alladin 쇼핑몰은 이제 모든 주민들과 방문객들에게 열려 있으며 여러분의 모든 쇼핑 요구를 확실히 만족시킵니다. 두바이의 중심부에 위치한, [05/06]쇼핑몰은 Mercato 백화점을 수용하고 있는데, [05]이 백화점은 6개 층에 있는 소매점들이 특징입니다. [06-A/06-B]이 유명한 쇼핑 목적지는 [06-B]남성복과 여성복, 아동복, 스포츠 용품과 가정 용품, 그리고 화장품과 향수 매장을 제공합니다. 여성 매장은 다양한 액세서리와 [06-C]방대한 제화 매장을 자랑합니다.

그리고, 가벼운 식사가 필요하시다면, 고급 정찬 식사뿐만 아니라 아랍식, 이탈리아식, 중국식, 일본식, 그리고 미국식 패스트푸드까지 갖춘 저희의 6층 식당가로 오세요. 이후에 저녁 식사를 위한 무언가가 필요하십니까? [05]지하층에 있는 저희의 슈퍼마켓은 폭넓게 선택할 수 있는 양질의 수입 식료품과 현지 식료품을 특징으로 합니다.

또한, Priority Shopper 카드 소지자에게 제공되는 많은 혜택을 이용하십시오. 우리의 서비스 카운터 중 어느 곳에서든 [07]카드를 신청하시고, 쇼핑몰 내 선정된 상점들에서 연중 계속되는 할인과 절약을 누려보세요. 무료 선물을 받을 자격을 갖추기 위해 여러분의 카드에 포인트를 쌓으십시오. 구매 대금을 결제하실 때마다 여러분의 카드를 그냥 제시하시면 됩니다!

Alladin 쇼핑몰의 상점, 제품, 행사 및 [08]판촉 상품에 대한 더 많은 정보를 위해서는, 간단히 www.alladinmall.com을 방문해 주십시오. [06-D]Alladin 쇼핑몰은 매일 오전 10시부터 오후 9시까지 영업합니다.

Alladin 쇼핑몰... 여러분이 만족할 때까지 쇼핑하십시오!

---

located adj. ~에 위치한 heart n. 중심 house v. 수용하다; n. 집, 주택
feature v. 특징을 이루다 retail space 소매점 famed adj. 유명한
bite n. 가벼운 식사 fare n. 식사 take advantage of ~을 이용하다
year-round 연중 계속되는 to one's heart's desire 만족할 때까지, 흡족하도록

05 추론 문제

문제 Alladin 쇼핑몰에 대해 암시되는 것은?

(A) 외국 회사에 의해 운영된다.
(B) 7개 층의 쇼핑 구역을 갖고 있다.
(C) 방문하는 관광객을 위한 정기 왕복 버스를 제공한다.
(D) 호텔 옆에 위치한다.

해설 질문의 핵심 어구인 Alladin Shopping Mall에 대해 추론하는 문제이다. 'the mall houses the Mercato Department Store, which features six floors of retail space'(1문단 4번째 줄)에서 쇼핑몰은 Mercato 백화점을 수용하고 있는데 이 백화점은 6개 층에 있는 소매점이 특징이라고 했고, 'Our supermarket on the basement floor'(2문단 3번째 줄)에서 지하 층에 있는 슈퍼마켓을 언급했으므로 Alladin Shopping Mall은 Mercato 백화점 내 지상 6개 층의 소매점과 지하층 슈퍼마켓까지 총 7개 층의 쇼핑 구역을 갖고 있다는 사실을 추론할 수 있다. 따라서 (B) It has seven floors of shopping area가 정답이다.

Paraphrasing
retail space 소매점 → shopping area 쇼핑 구역

어휘 **foreign** adj. 외국의, 해외의   **shuttle** n. 정기 왕복 버스

06 Not/True 문제

문제 Mercato에 대해 언급되지 않은 것은?
(A) 유명한 백화점이다.
(B) 남녀 의류를 제공한다.
(C) 상당한 구두 컬렉션을 보유하고 있다.
(D) 주말에는 더 늦게 폐장한다.

해설 질문의 핵심 어구인 Mercato와 관련된 내용을 지문에서 찾아 보기와 대조하는 Not/True 문제이다. (A)는 'the mall houses the Mercato Department Store'(1문단 4번째 줄)에서 쇼핑몰은 Mercato 백화점을 수용하고 있다고 한 후, 'This famed shopping destination'(1문단 5번째 줄)에서 Mercato 백화점이 유명한 쇼핑 목적지라고 했으므로 지문의 내용과 일치한다. (B)는 'This famed shopping destination offers men's and women's wear'(1문단 5번째 줄)에서 이 유명한 쇼핑 목적지가 남성 복과 여성복을 제공한다고 했으므로 지문의 내용과 일치한다. (C)는 'a vast footwear department'(1문단 7번째 줄)에서 방대한 제화 매장이 있다고 했으므로 지문의 내용과 일치한다. (D)는 'Alladin Mall is open every day from 10 A.M. to 9 P.M.'(4문단 2번째 줄)에서 Mercato 백화점이 있는 Alladin 쇼핑몰이 매일 오전 10시부터 9시까지 영업한다고 했으므로 지문의 내용과 일치하지 않는다. 따라서 (D) It closes later on the weekends가 정답이다.

Paraphrasing
famed 유명한 → well-known 유명한
wear 복, 의류 → clothing 의류
a vast footwear department 방대한 제화 매장 → a large shoe collection 상당한 구두 컬렉션

07 육하원칙 문제

문제 쇼핑몰은 무엇을 카드 소지자들에게 제공할 것인가?
(A) 전용 라운지 입장
(B) 일부 제품들에 대한 할인가
(C) 특별 행사 초대장
(D) 무료 제품 샘플

해설 쇼핑몰이 무엇을(What) 카드 소지자들에게 제공할 것인지를 묻는 육하 원칙 문제이다. 질문의 핵심 어구인 provide to cardholders와 관련하여 'Register for the card ~, and enjoy year-round discounts and savings'(3문단 2번째 줄)에서 카드를 신청하고 연중 계속되는 할인과 절약을 누려보라고 했으므로 (B) Reduced prices on some products가 정답이다.

Paraphrasing
discounts 할인 → Reduced prices 할인가

어휘 **cardholder** n. 카드 소지자   **access** n. 입장, 이용
private adj. 전용의, 개인의   **lounge** n. 라운지, 대합실
complimentary adj. 무료의

08 육하원칙 문제

문제 독자들은 어떻게 판촉 상품에 대해 알 수 있는가?

(A) 전화함으로써
(B) 행정실을 방문함으로써
(C) 이메일을 보냄으로써
(D) 웹사이트를 살펴봄으로써

해설 독자들이 판촉 상품에 대해 어떻게(How) 알 수 있는지를 묻는 육하원 칙 문제이다. 질문의 핵심 어구인 promotions와 관련하여 'For more information on ~ promotions, simply visit www.alladinmall.com.'(4문단 1번째 줄)에서 판촉 상품에 대한 더 많은 정보를 위해서는 간단히 웹 사이트를 방문해 달라고 했으므로 (D) By looking at a Web site가 정답이다.

어휘 **look through** 살펴보다, 검토하다

09-12는 다음 광고에 관한 문제입니다.

[09]2Storage는 플로리다 최대의 보관소 제공업체 체인입니다. 임시로 여러분의 물품들을 보관할 수 있는 네 가지의 편리한 선택 사항들을 제공합니다.

주니어	디럭스
30달러부터	100달러부터
6.75평방미터	13.5평방미터
소형 가전제품, 운동 장비, 다른 개인 소지품들에 적합함	소형 주택 및 사무실의 물품들에 적 합함
프리미엄	[10]프리퍼드
200달러부터	[10]가격과 크기가 다양함
18평방미터	문서 보관함, 덮개를 씌운 자동차 주 차, 온도 조절 장치가 있는 기기를 포 함함
대형 주택 및 사무실의 물품들에 적 합함	

* 더 많은 정보를 위해서는, 555-5044로 전화 주세요. [11-A/C/D]무료 손수레, 포장 재료, 보안 잠금장치들이 제공됩니다. [11-B]추가 비용을 내시면, 고객님들은 수거 와 배송 일정을 잡으실 수 있습니다. 또한, 신규 고객이시면, [12-B]무료 2Storage 모바일 애플리케이션에서 할인 쿠폰을 받으세요.

storage n. 보관소, 저장   **temporarily** adv. 임시로, 잠정적으로
appliance n. 가전제품, 기기   **vary** v. 다양하다, 다르다
control n. 조절 장치, 제어   **handcart** n. 손수레   **pickup** n. 수거, 수집

09 추론 문제

문제 2Storage에 대해 암시되는 것은?
(A) 최근에 서비스를 추가했다.
(B) 가장 큰 단위의 크기는 200평방미터이다.
(C) 한 군데보다 많은 지점이 있다.
(D) 시설들이 24시간 내내 운영된다.

해설 질문의 핵심 어구인 2Storage에 대해 추론하는 문제이다. '2Storage is Florida's largest chain of storage providers.'(1문단 1번째 줄)에 서 2Storage가 플로리다 최대의 보관소 제공업체 체인이라고 했으므로, 2Storage의 지점이 여러 개가 있다는 사실을 추론할 수 있다. 따라서 (C) It has more than one location이 정답이다.

10 육하원칙 문제

문제 어느 선택 사항이 다양한 크기로 나오는가?
(A) 주니어
(B) 디럭스
(C) 프리미엄
(D) 프리퍼드

해설 어느(Which) 선택 사항이 다양한 크기로 나오는지를 묻는 육하원칙 문제 이다. 질문의 핵심 어구인 option comes in different sizes와 관련하여, 'PREFERRED', 'Prices and sizes vary'(표 2행 2열 1, 2번째 줄)에서 프리 퍼드 선택 사항의 경우 가격과 크기가 다양하다고 했으므로 (D) Preferred 가 정답이다.

Paraphrasing
different sizes 다양한 크기 → sizes vary 크기가 다양하다

11 Not/True 문제

문제 2Storage에 의해 무료로 제공되지 않는 것은?

(A) 손수레
(B) 수거 서비스
(C) 포장 재료
(D) 보안 잠금장치

해설 질문의 핵심 어구인 offered for free by 2Storage와 관련된 내용을 지문에서 찾아 보기와 대조하는 Not/True 문제이다. (A), (C), (D)는 'Complimentary handcarts, packing materials, and security locks are provided.'(2문단 1번째 줄)에서 무료 손수레, 포장 재료, 보안 잠금장치들이 제공된다고 했으므로 지문의 내용과 일치한다. (B)는 'For an extra charge, customers may arrange for pickup'(2문단 2번째 줄)에서 추가 비용을 내면 고객들은 수거 일정을 잡을 수 있다고 했으므로 지문의 내용과 일치하지 않는다. 따라서 (B) Pickup services가 정답이다.

Paraphrasing
for free 무료로 → Complimentary 무료의

12 Not/True 문제

문제 모바일 애플리케이션에 대해 사실인 것은?

(A) 고객들이 특별 요청을 제출할 수 있도록 한다.
(B) 사용자들이 무료로 이용 가능하다.
(C) 등록을 요구하지 않는다.
(D) 한 달의 시험 기간을 제공한다.

해설 질문의 핵심 어구인 the mobile application과 관련된 내용을 지문에서 찾아 보기와 대조하는 Not/True 문제이다. (A)는 지문에 언급되지 않은 내용이다. (B)는 'our free 2Storage mobile application'(2문단 3번째 줄)에서 무료 2Storage 모바일 애플리케이션이라고 했으므로 지문의 내용과 일치한다. 따라서 (B) It is available at no cost to users가 정답이다. (C)와 (D)는 지문에 언급되지 않은 내용이다.

Paraphrasing
free 무료의 → at no cost 무료로

어휘 registration n. 등록 trial period 시험 기간, 수습 기간

Chapter 13 공고(Notice & Announcement)

예제 해석   p.443

공고

공지:
모든 Grosvenor 전자 회사 고객님들께

[1]4월 1일을 시작으로, 제품 교환에 대한 수정된 방침이 시행될 예정임을 고객님들께 알리고자 합니다. 구매한 물품에 결함이 있거나 제대로 작동하지 않는다면, 오직 같은 물품으로만 교환될 수 있습니다. 자사는 반품된 상품에 대해 [2-B]현금 환불은 제공하지 않을 것입니다.

교환을 요청하시려면, 원래 포장에 담긴 상품을 구매 영수증과 함께 상품이 구매되었던 소매점의 서비스 카운터로 가져오시기 바랍니다. 고객님들께서는 문제에 대한 간략한 설명을 포함하는 양식을 기입하시도록 요청될 것입니다. 양식을 제출하신 후, 제품이 수리될 수 있는지 알아내기 위해 [2-D]자사 기술자들 중 한 명이 제품을 검사할 것입니다. 수리가 가능하다면, 영업일 5일 이내에 무료로 수리해 드릴 것입니다. 만약 상품을 수리할 수 없다면, 물품이 더 이상 재고에 없지 않는 한 새로운 것으로 교체해 드릴 것입니다. 이러한 경우에, 고객들은 교환 대신 상품 교환권을 받으실 수 있는 선택권이 있습니다.

이해해 주셔서 감사드립니다. 질문이 있으시다면, 고객 서비스 상담원에게 연락하시기 바랍니다. [3]저희 웹사이트 www.grosvenorelectronics.com은 이러한 방침 변경 사항을 반영하기 위해 곧 업데이트될 것입니다.

take effect 시행하다, 효력을 발휘하다 defective adj. 결함이 있는
merchandise n. 상품, 제품 irreparable adj. 수리할 수 없는

---

in stock 재고의, 비축되어 store credit 상품 교환권
in lieu of ~ 대신에 reflect v. 반영하다

Q1.
문제 공고의 목적은 무엇인가?

(A) 구매자들에게 새로운 가게 정책을 알리기 위해
(B) 가게 서비스에 대한 의견을 요청하기 위해
(C) 수리부의 신설을 알리기 위해
(D) 상품 교환권에 대한 세부 사항을 제공하기 위해

어휘 guideline n. 정책, 지침 feedback n. 의견

Q2.
문제 Grosvenor 전자회사에 대해 언급된 것은?

(A) 새로운 지역으로 이전할 것이다.
(B) 몇몇 경우에는 현금 환불을 제공한다.
(C) 일주일에 5일 영업한다.
(D) 기술 직원들을 두고 있다.

어휘 rebate n. 환불

Q3.
문제 공고에 따르면, 곧 무슨 일이 일어날 것인가?

(A) 신제품들이 가게에 도착할 것이다.
(B) 가게의 웹 페이지가 변경될 것이다.
(C) 상품의 가격이 조정될 것이다.
(D) 직원들이 추가 교육을 받을 것이다.

어휘 adjust v. 조정하다 undergo v. 받다, 겪다

Hackers Practice   p.446

유형 연습
01 (C)   02 (B)   03 (A)

01 공고

모든 승객들은 출입국 관리 지역에서의 사진 촬영이 허용되지 않는다는 것을 알아두시기 바랍니다. 또한, 담당 직원을 위해 여권, 완성된 세관 양식이 준비되었는지 확인하십시오. 앞으로 나오라는 지시를 받을 때에만 출입국 심사대로 나아가십시오. 10세 이하의 아동과 함께 여행하는 가족들 외에는, 한 번에 한 분만 다뤄질 것입니다.

permit v. 허용하다 customs n. 세관, 관세 proceed v. 나아가다, 계속하다
apart from ~ 이외에

문제 공고는 왜 쓰였는가?

(A) 양식을 작성하는 것에 대한 지시를 주기 위해
(B) 출발 규정의 변화를 알리기 위해
(C) 출입국 확인을 위한 지침을 제공하기 위해

해설 주제/목적 찾기 문제 공고가 쓰인 목적을 묻는 목적 찾기 문제이다. 'All passengers are informed that photography in the immigration area is not permitted.'에서 모든 승객들은 출입국 관리 지역에서의 사진 촬영이 허용되지 않는다는 것을 알아두라고 한 후, 출입국 관리 지역에서의 주의점과 출입국 접수 관련 내용을 안내하고 있으므로 (C) To provide guidelines for an immigration check가 정답이다.

02 공고

참가 등록 양식, 귀하의 조각품 사진 5매 및 작품에 대한 간략한 설명을 전국예술협회 (NAA) 사무실로 제출해 주십시오. 대회에 참가하도록 선정된 지원자들은 저희 직원 중 한 명의 전화 연락을 받게 될 것입니다. 참가비 38달러는 1월 26일 전에 납부되어야 합니다.

entry n. 참가, 입장 description n. 설명 prior to ~ 전에, ~에 앞서

문제 선정된 참가자들은 어떻게 통지받을 것인가?

(A) 편지를 받을 것이다.
(B) 전화로 연락받을 것이다.
(C) 직원이 방문할 것이다.

해설 **육하원칙 문제** 선정된 지원자들이 어떻게(How) 통지받을 것인지를 묻는 육하원칙 문제이다. 질문의 핵심 어구인 selected participants be notified와 관련하여, 'Those applicants selected to compete in the competition.'에서 대회에 참가하도록 선정된 지원자들은 직원 중 한 명의 전화 연락을 받을 것이라고 했으므로 (B) They will be contacted by phone이 정답이다.

Paraphrasing
be called 전화 연락을 받다 → be contacted by phone 전화로 연락받다

03 공고

> 통근자들은 33번 버스가 도로 건설로 인해 4월 9일부터 4월 22일까지 Rainforest가를 지나지 않을 것임을 알아두십시오. 그 대신에, 노선이 변경될 것이고, 버스는 Ogden가를 지나게 될 것입니다. Rainforest가에 있는 목적지로 가시는 분들은 지하철 2호선을 타서 Waterford 역에 내리시기 바랍니다.
>
> route n. 노선 destination n. 목적지 urge v. 권고하다, 충고하다

문제 공고는 어디서 볼 수 있을 것 같은가?
(A) 버스 정류장에서
(B) 온라인 지도에서
(C) 공사 현장에서

해설 **추론 문제** 공고를 볼 수 있는 곳을 추론하는 문제이다. 'Commuters are informed that Bus #33 will not be passing on Rainforest Avenue'에서 통근자들은 33번 버스가 Rainforest가를 지나지 않을 것임을 알아두라고 했다. 따라서 버스를 타는 통근자들에게 버스 노선이 변경될 것임을 알리는 공고라는 것을 알 수 있으며, 이 공고는 버스 정류장에서 볼 수 있다는 사실을 추론할 수 있다. 따라서 (A) At a bus stop이 정답이다.

Hackers Test
p.447

01 (C)	02 (B)	03 (D)	04 (A)	05 (D)
06 (C)	07 (C)	08 (A)	09 (A)	10 (D)
11 (D)	12 (B)			

01-04는 다음 공고에 관한 문제입니다.

> 공고
>
> [01]Rushmore 빌딩의 관리진은 여러분들의 불만 사항을 전해 들어 건물의 현재 엘리베이터를 새것으로 교체하기로 합의했습니다. 새 엘리베이터는 더 적은 유지보수를 필요로 하고 또한 더 빠른 이용을 제공할 것입니다. 개선 비용을 충당하기 위해, [02]저희는 5월 1일부터 각 거주자들에게서 걷어지는 월간 요금을 10달러 인상할 것입니다. 작업이 진행되는 동안 엘리베이터 이용의 지연을 예상하시기 바랍니다. 불편을 최소화하기 위해, 작업은 다음과 같이 단계적으로 진행될 것입니다:
> • 서쪽 로비: 4월 1-4일
> • 동쪽 로비: 4월 8-10일
> • 남쪽 로비: 4월 18-22일
> • [03-D]북쪽 로비: 5월 1-4일
>
> 이 기간 동안, [03-B/04]동쪽 로비와 북쪽 로비의 엘리베이터는 1-15층 거주자들에게 지정될 것이고 [04]다른 두 곳은 16-32층 거주자들에게 지정될 것입니다. 모든 엘리베이터는 지하 주차장 출입을 제공합니다.
>
> 문의나 우려 사항은 555-0418로 건물 관리자에게 연락하십시오.
>
> management n. 관리자, 경영진 maintenance n. 유지보수, 관리
> improvement n. 개선, 발전 due n. 요금, 세금 tenant n. 거주자, 세입자
> effective adj. 시행되는, 효과적인 underway adj. 진행 중인, 움직이고 있는

01 주제/목적 찾기 문제

문제 공고는 주로 무엇에 대한 것인가?
(A) 보안 절차에 대한 변경 사항

(B) 세입자들의 최근 불만 사항
(C) 건물의 개선
(D) 일부 아파트를 임대할 기회

해설 공고가 주로 무엇에 대한 것인지를 묻는 주제 찾기 문제이다. 'The Rushmore Building's management ~ agreed to replace the building's current elevators with new ones.'(1문단 1번째 줄)에서 Rushmore 빌딩의 관리진이 건물의 현재 엘리베이터를 새것으로 교체하기로 합의했다고 한 후, 엘리베이터 교체 작업에 대해 설명하고 있으므로 (C) An improvement to a building이 정답이다.

어휘 security n. 보안, 경비 procedure n. 절차

02 육하원칙 문제

문제 5월에 무슨 일이 일어날 것인가?
(A) 특별 행사가 열릴 것이다.
(B) 일부 요금이 인상될 것이다.
(C) 관리사무실이 문을 닫을 것이다.
(D) 몇몇 주차 공간이 이용 가능해질 것이다.

해설 5월에 무슨(What) 일이 일어날 것인지를 묻는 육하원칙 문제이다. 질문의 핵심 어구인 May와 관련하여, 'we will be raising the monthly dues ~ effective May 1'(1문단 3번째 줄)에서 5월 1일부터 월간 요금을 인상할 것이라고 했으므로 (B) Some charges will be increased가 정답이다.

Paraphrasing
will be raising the ~ dues 요금을 인상할 것이다 → charges will be increased 요금이 인상될 것이다

어휘 charge n. 요금; v. 부과하다

03 Not/True 문제

문제 북쪽 로비에 대해 언급된 것은?
(A) 추가적인 유지보수를 필요로 할 것이다.
(B) 건물 관리진에게 지정된다.
(C) 가장 많은 수의 엘리베이터가 있다.
(D) 개선이 되는 마지막 순서일 것이다.

해설 질문의 핵심 어구인 the north lobby와 관련된 내용을 지문에서 찾아 보기와 대조하는 Not/True 문제이다. (A)는 지문에 언급되지 않은 내용이다. (B)는 'the elevators in the ~ north lobby will be reserved for residents of floors 1 through 15'(2문단 1번째 줄)에서 북쪽 로비의 엘리베이터는 1-15층 거주자들에게 지정될 것이라고 했으므로 지문의 내용과 일치하지 않는다. (C)는 지문에 언급되지 않은 내용이다. (D)는 'North lobby: May 1 to 4'(1문단 아래 4번째 줄)에서 북쪽 로비가 작업 기간 중 가장 나중인 5월 1-4일에 작업된다고 했으므로 지문의 내용과 일치한다. 따라서 (D) It will be the last to receive an upgrade가 정답이다.

04 추론 문제

문제 Rushmore 빌딩에 대해 추론될 수 있는 것은?
(A) 지상 32층이다.
(B) 상업 목적의 세입자들에게 장소를 임대한다.
(C) 거주자들을 위한 4층짜리 주차 공간이 있다.
(D) 외부 회사에 의해 관리된다.

해설 질문의 핵심 어구인 Rushmore Building에 대해 추론하는 문제이다. 'the elevators in the east lobby and north lobby will be reserved for residents of floors 1 through 15, while the other two will be for residents of floors 16 through 32'(2문단 1번째 줄)에서 동쪽 로비와 북쪽 로비의 엘리베이터는 1-15층 거주자들에게 지정될 것이고 다른 두 곳은 16-32층 거주자들에게 지정될 것이라고 했으므로 Rushmore Building이 32층짜리 건물이라는 사실을 추론할 수 있다. 따라서 (A) It is 32 floors above the ground가 정답이다.

어휘 lease v. 임대하다, 대여하다 commercial adj. 상업적인, 상업용의

22회 금융 및 경제 관련 연례 회담

⁰⁶경제 관계 관련 국제 협의회(ICER)는 *Capital*지와 협력하여, 9월 18일과 19일에 뉴욕 맨해튼에 있는 Palace 호텔의 대연회장에서 열리는 "미래 경제 정세 예측" 회담에 참석하시도록 귀하를 초대합니다. ⁰⁵저희는 오늘날 세계 경제에서 금융 업계의 변화하는 역할을 살펴보고 그 분야의 전문가가 앞으로 나아갈 방향을 구상할 것이므로 저희와 함께하시기 바랍니다.

이 회담에서, 여러분은 최근의 사건들이 금융 업계에 끼친 영향과 앞으로 금융 업계를 형성할 정책 동향에 대해 알게 되실 겁니다. 논의 주제는 세계 은행 산업이 맡은 역할에 영향을 미치는 요소들, 점점 더 연결되는 세계 속에서의 국제 금융 규정, 그리고 기업의 투자 결정이 개발 도상국 발전에 미치는 영향을 포함합니다. 초청된 기조 연설자는 Liberty America 은행장인 Mr. Arthur Lowenstein과 독일의 Wachstum 투자 은행의 현 은행장인 Ms. Bettina Kaufmann입니다.

행사 등록이 반드시 필요하며 현장에서는 등록하실 수 없습니다. ⁰⁷등록을 하기 위해 저희 웹사이트 www.icer.com/eventreg를 방문해주시기 바랍니다. 참가비는 ICER 회원 단체 소속일 경우 60달러이고 아닌 경우에는 120달러입니다. ⁰⁸*Capital*지 구독자들은 호텔 숙박에 대한 특가 제공도 이용하실 수 있습니다. 회담 개최 장소 근처에 있는 호텔 객실을 예약하시려면 s.garnier@icer.org로 Susan Garnier에게 연락하십시오.

---

finance n. 금융 **in cooperation with** ~와 협력하여 **forecast** n. 예측
climate n. 정세, 분위기, 기후 **plot** v. 구상하다 **professional** n. 전문가
emerging economies 개발 도상국 **keynote speaker** 기조 연설가
subscriber n. 구독자 **take advantage of** 이용하다
special offer 특가 제공 **lodging** n. 숙박

---

05 추론 문제

문제　공고는 누구를 대상으로 할 것 같은가?

(A) 행사 주최자들
(B) 출판업계 임원들
(C) 공무원들
(D) 은행업 종사자들

해설　공고의 대상을 추론하는 문제이다. 'we examine the changing role of the financial industry in today's global economy and plot the way forward for professionals in the field'(1문단 4번째 줄)에서 오늘날 세계 경제에서 금융 업계의 변화하는 역할을 살펴보고 그 분야의 전문가가 앞으로 나아갈 방향을 구상할 것이라고 했으므로 금융 업계에 종사하는 사람을 대상으로 하는 공고임을 추론할 수 있다. 따라서 (D) Banking professionals가 정답이다.

06 육하원칙 문제

문제　회담은 어디에서 열리는가?

(A) 출판사의 사무실에서
(B) 주최 단체의 본사에서
(C) 숙박 시설에서
(D) 투자 은행에서

해설　회담이 어디에서(Where) 열릴 것인지를 묻는 육하원칙 문제이다. 질문의 핵심 어구인 conference being held와 관련하여, 'The International Council on Economic Relations (ICER), ~ invites you to attend its conference, ~ at the Grand Ballroom of the Palace Hotel in Manhattan, New York.'(1문단 1번째 줄)에서 경제 관계 관련 국제 협의회(ICER)가 뉴욕 맨해튼에 있는 Palace 호텔의 대연회장에서 열릴 회담에 관계자들을 초대하고 있으므로 (C) At an accommodation facility가 정답이다.

　　Paraphrasing
　　Hotel 호텔 → accommodation facility 숙박 시설

07 육하원칙 문제

문제　관심 있는 참가자들은 무엇을 하도록 요청되는가?

(A) 비용을 우편으로 보낸다
(B) 회원 카드를 가져온다
(C) 웹사이트에서 등록한다
(D) 행사장에서 등록한다

해설　관심 있는 참가자들은 무엇(What)을 하도록 요청되는지를 묻는 육하원칙 문제이다. 질문의 핵심 어구인 interested participants와 관련하여, 'Please visit our Web site at www.icer.com/eventreg to sign up.'(3문단 1번째 줄)에서 등록을 하기 위해 웹사이트를 방문해 달라고 했으므로 관심 있는 참가자들은 웹사이트에서 등록하도록 요청된다는 것을 알 수 있다. 따라서 (C) Sign up on a Web site가 정답이다.

08 육하원칙 문제

문제　참가자들은 어떻게 숙박 할인을 받을 수 있는가?

(A) 간행물을 구독함으로써
(B) 명시된 날짜 전에 예약함으로써
(C) Ms. Garnier에게 이메일을 보냄으로써
(D) 쿠폰을 다운받음으로써

해설　참가자들이 어떻게(How) 숙박 할인을 받을 수 있는지를 묻는 육하원칙 문제이다. 질문의 핵심 어구인 a discount on accommodations와 관련하여, 'Subscribers to *Capital Magazine* may also take advantage of a special offer on hotel lodgings.'(3문단 3번째 줄)에서 *Capital*지 구독자들은 호텔 숙박에 대한 특가 제공을 이용할 수 있다고 했으므로 간행물을 구독하면 숙박에 대한 할인을 받을 수 있음을 알 수 있다. 따라서 (A) By subscribing to a publication이 정답이다.

어휘　**publication** n. 간행물 **specified** adj. 명시된

09-12는 다음의 공고에 관한 문제입니다.

모든 직원에게 공지

자사 제품의 유용성에 관한 고객 불만사항에 대한 대응으로, King Industries 사는 회사에서 개발한 모든 제품을 테스트하고 평가하는 데 책임을 지게 될 품질 보증부를 신설했습니다. — [1] —. 이와 관련해, ⁰⁹자사 최신 네트워킹 제품인 QX2B 라우터의 테스트에 참여할 지원자를 찾고 있으며, 이 제품은 6개월 후에 출시 예정입니다.

¹²참여자들은 제품에 첨부된 소프트웨어를 이용하여 제품을 설치하는 것이 어느 정도로 어려운지를 알아내기 위한 일련의 과제들을 수행해야 할 것입니다. — [2] —. ^{11-A}이러한 작업들에서 얻은 피드백은 어떤 기능성 오류라도 수정하고 완벽한 사용 설명서를 만드는 데 이용될 것입니다. ^{10-D}이 제품은 제한된 기술적 지식을 가진 소비자를 위한 제품이므로, 뛰어난 컴퓨터 사용능력은 요구되지 않습니다. — [3] —. 자세한 테스트 관련 지침들은 공학 기술부의 Tim Jenkins가 준비한 문서로 제공될 것입니다.

^{11-B/D}테스트는 5월 14일 목요일 오후에 4층 회의실로 잠정 예정되어 있습니다. ^{11-C}참여에 관심이 있으시다면, 상사에게 허가를 받고 3시간짜리 테스트를 진행하는 동안 방해받지 않도록 해주십시오. — [4] —. 신청을 하시려면, 회사의 온라인 게시판에서 "QX2B 검사"라는 제목의 게시물을 찾으십시오. 추가 공고는 선택된 참가자 명단과 함께 다음 주 수요일에 공고될 것입니다.

---

usability n. 유용성 **quality assurance** 품질 보증
accompanying adj. 첨부된, 동반된 **functionality** n. 기능성
tentatively adv. 잠정적으로, 시험적으로

---

09 주제/목적 찾기 문제

문제　공고는 무엇에 대한 것인가?

(A) 회사 행사에 참여하는 것
(B) 소비자 의견을 다루는 것
(C) 직업 훈련 세미나에 참여하는 것
(D) 부서 회의에 참석하는 것

해설　공고가 무엇에 대한 것인지를 묻는 주제 찾기 문제이다. 'we are looking for volunteers to participate in testing of our latest networking product, the QX2B router'(1문단 3번째 줄)에서 자사 최신 네트워킹 제품인 QX2B 라우터의 테스트에 참여할 지원자를 찾고 있다고 했으므로 (A) Taking part in a company event가 정답이다.

10 Not/True 문제

문제 King Industries사에 대해 언급된 것은?

(A) 새로운 직원을 채용하고 있다.
(B) 결함이 있는 제품을 제조한다.
(C) 인적 네트워크 형성 행사를 주최하고 있다.
(D) 소비자용 제품을 판매한다.

해설 질문의 핵심 어구인 King Industries와 관련된 내용을 지문에서 찾아 보기와 대조하는 Not/True 문제이다. (A), (B), (C)는 지문에 언급되지 않은 내용이다. (D)는 'the product is intended for consumers with limited technical knowledge'(2문단 3번째 줄)에서 King Industries사에서 만든 이 제품은 제한된 기술적 지식을 가진 소비자들을 위한 제품이라고 했으므로 지문의 내용과 일치한다. 따라서 (D) It sells consumer devices가 정답이다.

어휘 **faulty** adj. 결함이 있는 **networking** n. 인적 네트워크 형성

11 Not/True 문제

문제 테스트에 대해 언급되지 않은 것은?

(A) 제품의 사용을 용이하게 해줄 것이다.
(B) 오후 시간의 일부가 소요될 것이다.
(C) 참가자를 위한 승인이 필요할 것이다.
(D) 온라인으로 실시될 것이다.

해설 질문의 핵심 어구인 testing과 관련된 내용을 지문에서 찾아 보기와 대조하는 Not/True 문제이다. (A)는 'Feedback from the exercise will be used to correct any mistakes with functionality and develop a complete user manual.'(2문단 2번째 줄)에서 이러한 작업들에서 얻은 피드백은 어떤 기능성 오류라도 수정하고 완벽한 사용 설명서를 만드는 데 이용된다고 했으므로 지문의 내용과 일치한다. (B)는 'Testing has been ~ scheduled for the afternoon of Thursday, May 14'(3문단 1번째 줄)에서 테스트는 5월 14일 오후에 예정되어 있다고 했으므로 지문의 내용과 일치한다. (C)는 'If you are interested in joining, please make sure that you have your supervisor's permission'(3문단 2번째 줄)에서 참여에 관심이 있으면 상사에게 허가를 받으라고 했으므로 지문의 내용과 일치한다. (D)는 'Testing has been ~ scheduled ~ in the meeting room on the fourth floor.'(3문단 1번째 줄)에서 테스트는 4층 회의실에 예정되어 있다고 했으므로 지문의 내용과 일치하지 않는다. 따라서 (D) It will be conducted online이 정답이다.

어휘 **facilitate** v. 용이하게 하다 **portion** n. 일부

12 문장 위치 찾기 문제

문제 [1], [2], [3], [4]로 표시된 위치 중, 다음 문장이 들어갈 곳으로 가장 적절한 것은?

"지원자들은 이 절차와 관련하여 제품 엔지니어들이 놓쳤던 아직 처리되지 않은 오류를 발견할 수도 있습니다."

(A) [1]
(B) [2]
(C) [3]
(D) [4]

해설 지문의 흐름상 주어진 문장이 들어가기에 가장 적절한 곳을 고르는 문제이다. The volunteers might encounter outstanding problems that our product engineers missed regarding this process에서 지원자들이 이 절차와 관련하여 제품 엔지니어들이 놓쳤던 아직 처리되지 않은 오류를 발견할 수도 있다고 했으므로 주어진 문장 앞에 지원자들이 수행할 절차와 관련된 내용이 있을 것임을 예상할 수 있다. [2]의 앞 문장인 'Participants will need to perform a series of tasks to determine how difficult it is to set up the product using the accompanying software.'(2문단 1번째 줄)에서 참여자들은 제품에 첨부된 소프트웨어를 이용하여 제품을 설치하는 것이 어느 정도로 어려운지를 알아내기 위한 일련의 과제를 수행해야 한다고 했으므로 [2]에 주어진 문장이 들어가면 제품을 설치하는 일련의 과제 수행 절차를 통해 오류를 발견할 수 있다는 내용을 설명하는 자연스러운 문맥이 된다는 것을 알 수 있다. 따라서 (B) [2]가 정답이다.

어휘 **outstanding** adj. 아직 처리되지 않은, 뛰어난

Chapter 14 회람(Memo)

예제 해석   p.451

회람

Sauriol 철도 회사 (SRC)

수신: 역 관리자들
발신: Antoine Bellefeuille, 운영부장
날짜: 4월 19일
제목: 공사 작업

4월 25일에, [2B]유럽 전역의 Sauriol 철도 회사 역에서 [1]새로운 신속 매표 구역의 공사가 시작될 것입니다. [1]이 구역은 승객들이 편리하게 사용할 수 있는 새로운 발권 기계들을 포함할 것임을 역 관리자들에게 알립니다. 관리자들은 또한 진행 중인 작업이 어떤 탑승객에게도 안전상의 위험을 일으키지 않도록 보장하기 위해 주기적으로 공사를 확인하도록 요청됩니다.

Sauriol 철도 회사는 빠르고 효율적인 운송을 제공하는 데 헌신합니다. 여러분께서 아시다시피, 많은 사람들은 어느 목적지로든 그들의 여행을 위해 우리의 열차에 의존합니다. [2A]매년 승객 수가 늘어남에 따라, 고객들을 불편하게 하지 않으면서 증가하는 이용량을 처리하는 것이 어느 때보다도 더 중요해졌습니다. 그러므로, 우리는 이러한 문제들을 처리하기 위한 노력의 일환으로, [2C]최근에 구입한 기계들을 놓을 신속 매표 창구를 추가할 것입니다.

각 공사 작업은 일주일 이상 걸리지 않을 것이지만, 이는 물론 역의 규모와 설치될 기계의 수에 따라 좌우될 것입니다. 그것과는 상관없이, [3]모든 작업은 7월 중순쯤에는 완료될 것입니다.

ticketing n. 매표 **periodically** adv. 주기적으로
pose v. 일으키다, 제기하다 **risk** n. 위험 **dedicated** adj. 헌신하는
rely on 의존하다 **address** v. 처리하다

Q1.

문제 회람의 목적은 무엇인가?

(A) 직원들에게 열차 운행 일정 변경을 알리기 위해
(B) **직원들에게 기계의 설치에 대해 알리기 위해**
(C) 업무 실적에 대한 의견을 요청하기 위해
(D) 장비 사용에 대한 지시를 하기 위해

어휘 **notify** v. 알리다 **performance** n. 실적, 성과 **instruction** n. 지시

Q2.

문제 Sauriol 철도 회사에 대해 언급되지 않은 것은?

(A) 고객층이 증가해 오고 있다.
(B) 유럽에서 운송 서비스를 제공한다.
(C) 최근에 새 장비를 구입했다.
(D) **추가 열차를 구입하려고 계획하고 있다.**

Q3.

문제 7월 중순에 일어날 일은 무엇인가?

(A) 매표 구역의 공사가 시작될 것이다.
(B) 관리자들이 안전 점검을 시행할 것이다.
(C) 신속 매표 창구가 이전될 것이다.
(D) **역에서의 공사가 완료될 것이다.**

어휘 **relocate** v. 이전하다, 이동시키다

Hackers Practice   p.454

유형 연습
01 (C)   02 (C)   03 (A)

01 회람

9월 20일 금요일에, 영업 부서와 마케팅 부서 전체가 새크라멘토에서의 행사에 필요할 것입니다. 그 결과, 그날로 예정되었던 회사 야유회는 다음 주로 변경 ◐

되었습니다. 뿐만 아니라, 장소도 Wright 박물관에서 Chimney 공원으로 바뀌었습니다. Chimney 공원으로 가는 교통편을 마련하시려면, 내선 번호 44번으로 Ethel Grey에게 연락 주시기 바랍니다.

furthermore adv. 뿐만 아니라 **venue** n. (콘서트·스포츠 경기·회담 등의) 장소

문제 Chimney 공원에서 어떤 행사가 열릴 것인가?

    (A) 영업 회의

    (B) 제품 출시

    (C) 회사 야유회

해설 **육하원칙 문제** Chimney 공원에서 어떤(What) 행사가 열릴 것인지를 묻는 육하원칙 문제이다. 질문의 핵심 어구인 Chimney Park와 관련하여, 'the company picnic ~ has been moved to the following week. Furthermore, the venue has been changed from the Wright Museum to Chimney Park.'에서 회사 야유회가 다음 주로 변경되었고, 장소도 Wright 박물관에서 Chimney 공원으로 바뀌었다고 했으므로 (C) A company outing이 정답이다.

    Paraphrasing

    the company picnic 회사 야유회 → A company outing 회사 야유회

어휘 **convention** n. 회의, 집회 **launch** n. 출시

02 회람

전 직원분들께 안전 검사관 팀이 목요일 오전 9시 30분부터 오후 5시 30분까지 공장을 방문할 것임을 알려 드리고자 합니다. 모든 작업 공간이 잘 정돈되고 안전장비가 점검되었는지 확인하시기 바랍니다. 검사관이 묻는 모든 질문에 대답해 주시기 바랍니다. 문의 사항이 있으시면, 귀하의 관리자에게 이야기해 주십시오.

inspector n. 검사관 **make certain** 확인하다, 확실히 하다
tidy adj. 잘 정돈된

문제 이 회람은 누구에게 보내졌을 것 같은가?

    (A) 검사 팀 구성원들

    (B) 장비 공급 회사 관리자들

    (C) 제조 공장 직원들

해설 **추론 문제** 회람의 대상을 추론하는 문제이다. 'We would like to inform all staff that a team of safety inspectors will be visiting the factory'에서 전 직원에게 안전 검사관 팀이 공장을 방문할 것임을 알린다고 했으므로 제조 공장의 직원들을 대상으로 하는 회람임을 추론할 수 있다. 따라서 (C) Workers at a manufacturing plant가 정답이다.

    Paraphrasing

    the factory 공장 → a manufacturing plant 제조 공장

어휘 **supplier** n. 공급 회사, 공급자 **manufacturing** adj. 제조의

03 회람

자사는 5월 3일부터 5일까지 시애틀에서 다가오는 유기농업 무역 박람회에 참가할 것입니다. 우리는 직원들이 전시장에서의 여러 교대 근무에 지원하는 것을 권장합니다. 여러분은 정상 시급에 더하여 4시간의 교대 근무 당 50달러의 추가 장려금을 지급받을 것입니다. 관심이 있으신 분들은 홍보부 사무실의 Martine Kotter에게 말씀해 주십시오.

booth n. 전시장 **shift** n. 교대 근무 (시간) **hourly rate** 시급
public relations 홍보 (활동)

문제 회사에 대해 언급된 것은 무엇인가?

    (A) 다가오는 행사를 위한 참가자를 찾고 있다.

    (B) 현재 회사의 급여 체계를 개혁하고 있다.

    (C) 최근에 회사의 근무 교대 방침을 수정했다.

해설 **Not/True 문제** 질문의 핵심 어구인 the company와 관련된 내용을 지문에서 찾아 보기와 대조하는 Not/True 문제이다. (A)는 'We encourage our employees to volunteer at the booth for different shifts.'에서 직원들이 전시장에서의 여러 교대 근무에 지원하는 것을 권장한다고 했으므로 지문의 내용과 일치한다. 따라서 (A) It is looking for participants for

---

an upcoming event가 정답이다. (B)와 (C)는 지문에 언급되지 않은 내용이다.

어휘 **restructure** v. 개혁하다, 구조를 조정하다 **pay scale** 급여 체계

Hackers Test
p.455

01 (A)	02 (D)	03 (B)	04 (C)	05 (B)
06 (C)	07 (D)	08 (B)	09 (C)	10 (B)
11 (C)	12 (D)			

01-04는 다음 회람에 관한 문제입니다.

수신: XT Radio 직원
발신: Samantha Garrison
제목: 최신 소식
[03]날짜: 7월 28일

우리가 최근에 더 많은 청취자들을 끌어모으고 있기 때문에, [01]우리 방송국에서 제공하고 있는 프로그램의 범위를 확대하기로 결정했습니다. 설문 조사를 진행한 이후에, 우리는 많은 청취자들이 스포츠를 주제로 하는 종류의 쇼를 즐기곤 했다는 것을 알게 되었습니다. 따라서, [02-B/C]우리는 밀워키 지방의 지역 팀에 중점을 둔 한 시간짜리 스포츠 토크쇼를 시작할 것입니다.

이 쇼는 축구, 농구, 하키, 야구 등과 관련된 뉴스와 기사들을 다룰 것입니다. [02-A]우리는 거기에 최소 세 명의 각기 다른 진행자들이 있기를 바랍니다. [03]다음 달에, 우리는 웹사이트에 라디오 진행자에 대한 구인 공고를 게시할 것입니다. 지역 스포츠에 대한 광범위한 지식이 있는 재능 있는 방송 진행자를 알고 있다면, 반드시 그들을 우리에게 추천해 주십시오. 그들은 jobs@xtradio.com으로 이메일을 보내서 우리에게 연락할 수 있습니다. [04]우리는 라디오나 다른 방송 매체에서의 이전 경험이 있는 사람들을 고용하기를 선호합니다. Mitch Bergman과 같은 사람이 이상적인 후보일 것입니다. 하지만, 그는 아직 다른 곳에 계약되어 있습니다.

station n. 방송국, 정류장 **launch** v. 시작하다, 착수하다
presenter n. 진행자, 발표자 **broadcaster** n. 방송 진행자, 방송인
by all means 반드시, 무슨 수를 써서라도

01 주제/목적 찾기 문제

문제 회람의 목적 중 하나는 무엇인가?

    (A) 새로운 계획을 논의하기 위해

    (B) 새로운 스포츠 리그를 알리기 위해

    (C) 프로그램의 성공에 대해 알리기 위해

    (D) 작품명에 대한 의견을 요청하기 위해

해설 회람의 목적 중 하나를 묻는 목적 찾기 문제이다. 'we've decided to expand the range of programs that we offer on our station'(1문단 1번째 줄)에서 방송국에서 제공하고 있는 프로그램의 범위를 확대하기로 결정했다고 한 후, 새로운 프로그램에 대한 계획을 설명하고 있으므로 (A) To discuss a new initiative가 정답이다.

어휘 **initiative** n. 계획, 진취성 **league** n. 리그, 모임

02 Not/True 문제

문제 스포츠 라디오 쇼에 대해 언급되지 않은 것은?

    (A) 여러 진행자들을 출연시킬 것이다.

    (B) 지역 팀에 중점을 둘 것이다.

    (C) 60분 동안 진행될 것이다.

    (D) 운동선수들을 인터뷰할 것이다.

해설 질문의 핵심 어구인 the sports radio show와 관련된 내용을 지문에서 찾아 보기와 대조하는 Not/True 문제이다. (A)는 'We would like it to have at least three different presenters.'(2문단 2번째 줄)에서 프로그램에 최소 세 명의 각기 다른 진행자들이 있기를 바란다고 했으므로 지문의 내용과 일치한다. (B)와 (C)는 'we're going to launch a one-hour sports talk show that will focus on local teams'(1문단 3번째 줄)에서 지역 팀에 중점을 둔 한 시간짜리 스포츠 토크쇼를 시작할 것이라고 했으므로 지문의 내용과 일치한다. (D)는 지문에 언급되지 않은 내용이다. 따라서 (D) It will interview athletes가 정답이다.

Paraphrasing
three different presenters 세 명의 각기 다른 진행자들 → multiple hosts 여러 진행자들
one-hour 한 시간 → 60 minutes 60분

어휘 **feature** v. 출연시키다 **athlete** n. 운동선수

03 육하원칙 문제

문제 방송국은 8월에 무엇을 할 것인가?
(A) 새로운 토크쇼 진행자를 소개한다
(B) 사람들이 직책에 지원할 것을 요청한다
(C) 청취자들을 위한 특별 대회를 연다
(D) 경기를 실시간으로 방송한다

해설 방송국이 8월에 무엇(What)을 할 것인지를 묻는 육하원칙 문제이다. 질문의 핵심 어구인 station ~ in August와 관련하여, 'DATE: July 28'(상단 4번째 줄)에서 회람이 7월 28일에 보내졌다고 했고, 'Next month, we're going to post job advertisements for radio hosts on our Web site.'(2문단 2번째 줄)에서 다음 달에 웹사이트에 라디오 진행자에 대한 구인 공고를 게시할 것이라고 했으므로 방송국이 8월에 라디오 진행자 자리에 지원해줄 것을 사람들에게 요청할 것임을 알 수 있다. 따라서 (B) Invite people to apply for a job이 정답이다.

Paraphrasing
radio hosts 라디오 진행자 → job 직책

어휘 **broadcast** v. 방송하다; n. 방송

04 추론 문제

문제 Mitch Bergman에 대해 암시되는 것은?
(A) 전문 운동선수였다.
(B) 쇼에 대한 몇 가지 의견을 제시했다.
(C) 방송에서의 경험이 있다.
(D) 높은 임금을 요구했다.

해설 질문의 핵심 어구인 Mitch Bergman에 대해 추론하는 문제이다. 'We would prefer to hire people who have some previous experience in radio or another broadcast media. Someone like Mitch Bergman would be our ideal candidate.'(2문단 5번째 줄)에서 라디오나 다른 방송 매체에서의 이전 경험이 있는 사람들을 고용하기를 선호하고 Mitch Bergman과 같은 사람이 이상적인 후보일 것이라고 했으므로, Mitch Bergman이 라디오나 다른 방송 매체에서의 이전 경험이 있다는 사실을 추론할 수 있다. 따라서 (C) He has experience in broadcasting이 정답이다.

Paraphrasing
radio or another broadcast media 라디오나 다른 방송 매체 → broadcasting 방송

05-08은 다음 회람에 관한 문제입니다.

날짜: 5월 11일
수신: 모든 부서
발신: Meredith Glover, 인사부장
제목: 주차 관련 공고

신입 사원들이 Penumbra사의 직원으로 추가되면서, ⁰⁵회사 주차장 이용에 관련된 규칙을 검토하는 것이 필요하게 되었습니다. 아시다시피, 이제 직원들이 더 적은 공간만 이용할 수 있기 때문에, ⁰⁵우리 모두는 몇 가지 조정을 해야 할 것입니다.

⁰⁶다음 달을 시작으로, 선착순으로 주차를 허용하는 자사의 현 정책은 폐지될 것입니다. 대신에, 번호가 붙은 공간들이 특정 집단이나 부서에 할당될 예정입니다. 입구에 가장 가까운 다섯 개 공간은 오로지 장애인들을 위해 지정된 채로 있을 것입니다. — [1] —. 그 다음 10개 공간은 고위 경영진을 위한 자리입니다. 그 다음의 매 20 공간씩, 다음과 같은 순서로, 재정회계부, 인사부, 그리고 영업 마케팅부에 할당될 것입니다. ⁰⁸주차 공간을 찾지 못한 분은 Anderson가에 있는 주차장에 그들의 차량을 주차해야 할 수도 있습니다. — [2] —.

회사 부지에 주차를 하실 때에는, 허가증이 필요함을 상기하시기 바랍니다. 🔃

그것을 차량의 계기판에 올려 놓으시거나 백미러에 매달아서 차량의 앞 유리를 통해 반드시 보이도록 해주시기 바랍니다. — [3] —. ⁰⁷만약 차를 주차장에 48시간 이상 주차해 두어야 한다면, 허가증을 인사부로부터 받으셔야 합니다. 이 규정을 위반한 차량은 견인될 것입니다. — [4] —. 여러분의 협조에 감사드립니다. 문의 사항이나 용건은 각 부서 관리자에게 말씀해 주시기 바랍니다.

addition n. 추가 **adjustment** n. 조정
on a first-come-first-served 선착순으로
scrap v. (행사·제도 등을) 폐지하다 **designate** v. 지정하다
disabled adj. 장애를 가진 **lot** n. (특정 용도용) 부지, 지역 **permit** n. 허가(증)
visible adj. 보이는, 알아 볼 수 있는 **windshield** n. (자동차 등의) 앞 유리
dashboard n. (자동차·비행기의) 계기판 **rear-view mirror** (자동차의) 백미러
violation n. 위반 **tow** v. 견인하다 **cooperation** n. 협조
address v. (요구·의견 등을 ~에게) 말하다 **respective** adj. 각자의, 각각의

05 주제/목적 찾기 문제

문제 주로 논의되는 것은 무엇인가?
(A) 곧 있을 업무 할당 일정
(B) 시설 이용을 위한 설명
(C) 회사에 의해 고용된 신입 사원
(D) 주차장 건설에 대한 정보

해설 지문에서 주로 논의되는 것을 묻는 주제 찾기 문제이다. 'it has become necessary to review the rules regarding the usage of the company parking lot'(1문단 1번째 줄)에서 회사 주차장 이용을 다루는 규칙을 검토하는 것이 필요하다고 했고 'we will all need to make some adjustments'(1문단 3번째 줄)에서 이에 대해 몇 가지 조정을 해야 한다고 한 후, 변경된 주차장 이용 방법에 대해 설명하고 있으므로 (B) Instructions for the use of a facility가 정답이다.

Paraphrasing
the company parking lot 회사 주차장 → a facility 시설

06 육하원칙 문제

문제 다음 달에 일어날 일은 무엇인가?
(A) 주차 허가증이 발행될 것이다.
(B) 건설 작업이 시작될 것이다.
(C) 수정된 규정이 시행될 것이다.
(D) 여행 비용이 지급될 것이다.

해설 다음 달에 일어날 일이 무엇인지(What)를 묻는 육하원칙 문제이다. 질문의 핵심 어구인 next month와 관련하여, 'Beginning next month, our current policy of permitting parking ~ will be scrapped. Instead, numbered spaces will be assigned to specific groups or departments.'(2문단 1번째 줄)에서 다음 달을 시작으로, 주차를 허용하는 회사의 현 정책은 폐지될 것이며, 대신에 번호가 붙은 공간들이 특정 집단이나 부서에 할당될 예정이라고 했으므로 주차와 관련해 수정된 규정이 시행될 것임을 알 수 있다. 따라서 (C) A revised regulation will take effect가 정답이다.

Paraphrasing
policy 정책 → regulation 규정

어휘 **issue** v. 발행하다 **take effect** 시행되다 **allowance** n. 비용, 수당

07 육하원칙 문제

문제 사원들은 어떻게 장기 주차 허가를 얻을 수 있는가?
(A) 직속 상사에게 이야기해서
(B) 기존의 허가증을 교체해서
(C) 특별 허가증에 대한 비용을 지불해서
(D) 특정 부서에 연락해서

해설 사원들이 어떻게(How) 장기 주차 허가증을 얻을 수 있는지를 묻는 육하원칙 문제이다. 질문의 핵심 어구인 permission for long-term parking과 관련하여, 'If you must leave your car parked in the lot for more than 48 hours, permission must be obtained from the human resources department.'(3문단 3번째 줄)에서 차를 주차장에 48시간 이상 주차해 두어야 한다면, 허가증을 인사부로부터 받아야 한다고 했으므로 (D) By contacting a particular department가 정답이다.

Paraphrasing

long-term parking 장기 주차 → parked ~ more than 48 hours
48시간 이상 주차하다

어휘 **permission** n. 허가 **immediate** adj. 즉속의, 직접적인
existing adj. 기존의 **license** n. 허가증, 면허증

08 문장 위치 찾기 문제

문제 [1], [2], [3], [4]로 표시된 위치 중, 다음 문장이 들어갈 곳으로 가장 적절한 것은?

"회의를 위해 사무실을 방문하시는 고객들 또한 그 장소로 가도록 안내되어야 합니다."

(A) [1]
(B) [2]
(C) [3]
(D) [4]

해설 지문의 흐름상 주어진 문장이 들어가기에 가장 적절한 곳을 고르는 문제이다. Clients visiting the office for meetings must also be directed to that location에서 회의를 위해 사무실을 방문하는 고객들 또한 그 장소로 가도록 안내되어야 한다고 했으므로 주어진 문장 앞에 장소와 관련된 내용이 있을 것임을 예상할 수 있다. [2]의 앞 문장인 'Anyone unable to find a space may park their vehicles at the garage on Anderson Avenue.'(2문단 6번째 줄)에서 주차 공간을 찾지 못한 사람은 Anderson 가의 주차장에 주차할 수 있다고 했으므로 [2]에 주어진 문장이 들어가면 주차 공간을 찾지 못한 사람뿐 아니라 회의를 위해 사무실을 방문하는 고객들도 Anderson가의 주차장에 주차하도록 안내되어야 한다는 자연스러운 문맥이 된다는 것을 알 수 있다. 따라서 (B) [2]가 정답이다.

어휘 **direct** v. (길을) 안내하다

09-12는 다음 회람에 관한 문제입니다.

수신: 전 직원
발신: George Andrews, 최고 운영 책임자
날짜: 2월 1일
제목: 다가오는 운영 계획

Longwave Instruments사는 일정표 짜기, 생산 및 채용 과정을 포함하는 현재 운영 시스템에 변화를 시행할 것입니다. 자사는 이런 특정 분야의 연구들을 수행하기 위해 Maxwell 컨설팅 회사의 서비스를 계약했습니다. 그들의 연구와 제안을 바탕으로, 자사의 현재 정책과 절차에 변화가 생길 것입니다.

⁰⁹Maxwell 컨설팅 회사의 팀은 우려되는 분야를 발견하기 위해 자사의 기존 운영 과정을 분석하기 시작할 것입니다. 전 직원이 가능한 한 협조하고 그들이 가진 어떤 질문에도 대답하는 것이 필수적입니다. ⁰⁹/¹⁰두 달간의 평가 단계 후에, 자사는 권고 사항 목록을 받게 될 것입니다. ¹⁰이 목록은 경영진과 부서장들 간의 토론을 통해 한 달의 기간을 거쳐 다듬어질 것입니다. 동시에, 선택된 직원 그룹은 이 과정의 다음 단계인 운영상의 변경 시행을 위해 훈련을 받게 될 것입니다.

시행은 ¹¹ᴬ자사 운영 부장 Wendy Fansler에 의해 지휘될 것입니다. ¹¹ᶜ그녀와 그녀의 팀은 권고 사항을 채택하고 자사의 정책 및 운영 과정이 종합적인 운영 안내서에 상세히 기록되도록 하는 것을 책임질 예정입니다. 이 9달짜리 과정이 시작되면, Maxwell 컨설팅 회사는 더 이상 자사의 일상 업무를 조사하지 않을 것입니다. 하지만, 그들은 계속해서 석 달마다 조사할 것입니다.

¹²열두 달의 기간이 끝날 때쯤, 자사는 변경 사항이 유익했는지 아니었는지 밝히기 위한 평가를 시행할 것입니다. 직원들은 의견을 제공할 것이고, ¹²시스템에 대한 필수적인 변경이 그때 이루어질 것입니다.

recruitment n. 채용 **carry out** ~을 수행하다 **analyze** v. 분석하다
identify v. 발견하다 **vital** adj. 필수적인 **cooperative** adj. 협조적인
assessment n. 평가 **phase** n. 단계 **refine** v. 다듬다, 개선하다
undergo v. ~을 받다, 경험하다 **adopt** v. 채택하다
comprehensive adj. 종합적인, 포괄적인 **look into** ~을 조사하다
day-to-day 일상의, 나날의 **modification** n. 변경

09 육하원칙 문제

문제 Maxwell 컨설팅 회사에서 온 팀은 무엇을 할 것인가?

(A) 잠재적 고객을 찾는다
(B) 직원들의 우려를 검토한다
(C) 변화에 대한 제안을 한다
(D) 직원을 위한 세미나를 실시한다

해설 Maxwell 컨설팅 회사에서 온 팀이 무엇을(What) 할 것인지를 묻는 육하원칙 문제이다. 질문의 핵심 어구인 the team from Maxwell Consulting과 관련하여, 'The team from Maxwell Consulting will start analyzing our existing procedures'(2문단 1번째 줄)에서 Maxwell 컨설팅 회사의 팀은 기존 운영 과정을 분석할 것이라고 했고 'After a two-month assessment phase, we will be presented with a list of recommendations.'(2문단 3번째 줄)에서 두 달간의 평가 단계 후에 자사가 권고 사항 목록을 받게 될 것이라는 내용을 통해 Maxwell 컨설팅 회사에서 온 팀이 변화에 대해 제안할 것임을 알 수 있다. 따라서 (C) Make suggestions for changes가 정답이다.

Paraphrasing

a list of recommendations 권고 사항 목록 → suggestions for changes 변화에 대한 제안

어휘 **potential** adj. 잠재적인 **conduct** v. 실시하다

10 육하원칙 문제

문제 시행 단계는 언제 시작될 것인가?

(A) 한 달 후
(B) 세 달 후
(C) 아홉 달 후
(D) 열두 달 후

해설 시행 단계가 언제(When) 시작될 것인지를 묻는 육하원칙 문제이다. 질문의 핵심 어구인 the implementation phase begin과 관련하여, 'After a two-month assessment phase, we will be presented with a list of recommendations. This list will be refined over a one-month period ~. At the same time, a chosen group of employees will undergo training for the next phase of this process – implementation of operational changes.'(2문단 3번째 줄)에서 두 달간의 평가 단계 후에, 권고 사항 목록을 받게 될 것이고, 이 목록은 한 달의 기간을 거쳐 다듬어질 것이며, 동시에 선택된 직원 그룹이 다음 단계인 운영 상의 변경 시행을 위해 훈련을 받게 될 것이라고 했으므로 두 달간의 평가 단계와 한 달간의 권고 사항 검토 단계 이후인 세 달 후에 시행 단계가 시작될 것임을 알 수 있다. 따라서 (B) After three months가 정답이다.

11 Not/True 문제

문제 Wendy Fansler에 대해 언급된 것은?

(A) Maxwell 컨설팅 회사의 최고 간부이다.
(B) 설문 조사를 시행할 것이다.
(C) 일련의 활동들을 기록할 것이다.
(D) 신입 사원 그룹을 훈련시켜야 한다.

해설 질문의 핵심 어구인 Wendy Fansler와 관련된 내용을 지문에서 찾아 보기와 대조하는 Not/True 문제이다. (A)는 'our operations manager Wendy Fansler'(3문단 1번째 줄)에서 자사의 운영 부장 Wendy Fansler라고 했으므로 지문의 내용과 일치 하지 않는다. (B)는 지문에 언급되지 않은 내용이다. (C)는 'She and her team will be responsible for ~ ensuring that our policies and procedures are documented'(3문단 1번째 줄)에서 그녀와 그녀의 팀은 자사의 정책 및 운영 과정이 상세히 기록되도록 하는 것을 책임질 예정이라고 했으므로 (C) She will be documenting a set of activities가 정답이다. (D)는 지문에 언급되지 않은 내용이다.

Paraphrasing

policies and procedures 정책 및 운영 과정 → a set of activities 일련의 활동들

12 추론 문제

문제 Longwave Instruments사에 대해 암시되는 것은?

(A) 제조 공장을 이전하려고 계획하고 있다.
(B) Maxwell 컨설팅 회사가 실시한 시험에 통과했다.
(C) 다른 기업과 합병하려고 준비하고 있다.
(D) 일 년 후에 추가적인 시스템 변경을 할 수도 있다.

해설 질문의 핵심 어구인 Longwave Instruments에 대해 추론하는 문제이다. 'At the end of the 12-month period'(4문단 1번째 줄), 'any necessary modifications to the systems will be made at that time.'(4문단 2번째 줄)에서 열두 달의 기간이 끝날 때쯤 시스템에 대한 필수적인 변경이 진행될 것이라고 했으므로 일 년 후에 Longwave Instruments사가 추가적인 시스템 변경을 할 수도 있다는 사실을 추론할 수 있다. 따라서 (D) It may make further system changes after a year가 정답이다.

Paraphrasing
At the end of the 12-month period 열두 달의 기간이 끝날 때쯤
→ after a year 일 년 후에
modifications to the systems 시스템에 대한 변경 → system changes 시스템 변경

어휘 administer v. (시험·계획 등을) 실시하다 merge v. 합병하다

Chapter 15 안내문(Information)

예제 해석 p.459

안내문

AirConnect 수송 서비스

[1]여러분이 공항으로, 또는 공항으로부터 이동해야 할 때, 운에 맡기지 마십시오 – 신속하고 편리하며 가격도 알맞은 공항 이동 서비스를 위해 AirConnect사에 의지하십시오. 자사는 전국적으로 인정받는 업체로 국내의 여러 국제공항에서 영업하고 있습니다.

[1]정기 왕복 승합차
혼자 여행하십니까? 다른 승객들과 동승함으로써 돈을 절약해 보십시오. [2-D]각 정기 왕복 승합차는 최대 8명의 승객과 그들의 수하물을 아무 문제없이 수용할 수 있습니다. [2-A]자사의 승합차는 24시간 내내 운행하며 대부분의 주요 공항에서 매 시간 출발합니다. 승객 수와 그들의 행선지에 따라 이동 시간은 달라질 수 있음을 알아두시기 바랍니다.

[1]고급 리무진
[2-C]시간이 아주 중요할 때, 여러분의 집 또는 사무실에서의 빠르고 효율적인 왕복 이동을 위해 자사의 고급 리무진 서비스를 예약하십시오. 유명한 방문객을 위해 공항으로 마중 나가도록 조치할 수도 있습니다. 자사 소유의 고급 대형 승용차와 스포츠 범용 차 중에서 차량을 선택하실 수 있으며, 각 차량은 정중하고 전문적인 직원이 운전합니다.

[1]신규! VIP 서비스
방문 내내 자사의 VIP 수송 서비스를 이용해 보십시오. 여러분이 가시고 싶은 곳 어디로든 모시기 위해 대기하는 차량과 운전사가 준비된 편리함을 누리실 수 있습니다. [2-B]개인적인 관광 역시 준비될 수 있습니다.

AirConnect사는 일년 내내 영업합니다. 555-9989로 전화하셔서 예약하시기 바랍니다. 특별 할인을 받으시려면 저희 웹사이트 www.airconnect.com을 통해 예약하십시오.

---

transport n. 수송, 운송 leave ~ to chance ~를 운에 맡기다
affordable adj. (가격 등이) 알맞은 transfer n. 이동, 환승
seat v. 수용하다, ~만큼의 좌석을 갖다
around the clock 24시간 내내, 밤낮으로 vary v. 달라지다, 바뀌다
of the essence 아주 중요한, 없어서는 안 될
executive adj. 고급의, 중요 인물을 위한 round-trip adj. 왕복의, 왕복 여행의
distinguished adj. 유명한, 뚜렷한
fleet n. 동일 회사 소유의 전 선박, 항공기, 차량 courteous adj. 정중한, 친절한
24/7 일년 내내, 하루 24시간 1주 7일 동안 (24 hours a day, 7 days a week)

Q1.
문제 안내문은 어디에서 찾을 수 있을 것 같은가?
(A) 항공사 웹사이트에서
(B) 기차역에서
(C) 회사 브로슈어에서
(D) 신문의 자동차면에서

어휘 automotive adj. 자동차의

Q2.
문제 정기 왕복 승합차에 대해 언급된 것은?
(A) 끊임없이 운행한다.
(B) 관광을 위해 임대될 수 있다.
(C) 서두르는 사람들에게 가장 알맞다.
(D) 10명을 수용할 수 있다.

어휘 continuously adv. 끊임없이 accommodate v. 수용하다, 숙박시키다

Hackers Practice p.462

유형 연습
01 (C)   02 (B)   03 (B)

01 안내문

Ray Block은 직사광선에 노출되기에 앞서 피부에 발라져야 합니다. 손가락 끝을 사용해서 제품을 고르게 바르십시오. Ray Block을 눈가나 입가와 같이 민감한 부위에는 바르지 마십시오. 베인 곳, 긁힌 곳, 또는 벌어진 상처 근처에는 사용을 피하십시오. 제품이 어떠한 피부 자극이라도 유발시키는 경우, 즉시 비누와 물로 씻어 내십시오. Ray Block을 다른 피부 제품이나 화장품과 함께 사용하지 마십시오. 이 제품은 유해한 자외선으로부터 최대 6시간까지 피부를 보호합니다.

---

prior to ~에 앞서, 먼저 evenly adv. 고르게 sensitive adj. 민감한
irritation n. 자극, 과민증 UV adj. 자외선의(ultraviolet) ray n. 선, 광선

문제 안내문은 무엇에 대한 것인가?
(A) 보디용 비누
(B) 약물
(C) 피부 제품

해설 **주제/목적 찾기 문제** 안내문이 무엇에 대한 것인지를 묻는 주제 찾기 문제이다. 'Ray Block should be applied on the skin'에서 Ray Block은 피부에 바르는 것이라고 했고, 'The product protects the skin from harmful UV rays for up to six hours.'에서 이 제품은 유해한 자외선으로부터 최대 6시간까지 피부를 보호한다고 했으므로 (C) A skin product가 정답이다.

02 안내문

Electro-Lite사 제품을 구매해 주셔서 감사합니다. 모든 자사 제품들은 구매한 날부터 유효한 1년짜리 보증서와 함께 판매됩니다. 보증서를 활성화시키려면, 동봉된 카드가 작성되어 구매일로부터 7일 이내에 영수증 사본과 함께 자사로 보내져야 합니다. 제품과 관련해 어떠한 문제라도 경험하시는 경우에는, 24시간 상담 서비스 전화인 1-800-555-7436으로 연락해 주시면 자사 직원들 중 한 명이 기꺼이 도와 드릴 것입니다.

---

warranty n. 보증서, 보증 activate v. 활성화하다 gladly adv. 기꺼이, 기쁘게

문제 고객들은 언제 보증서 카드를 제출해야 하는가?
(A) 구매일로부터 하루 이내에
(B) 구매일로부터 일주일 이내에
(C) 구매일로부터 한 달 이내에

해설 **육하원칙 문제** 고객들이 언제(When) 보증서 카드를 제출해야 하는지를 묻는 육하원칙 문제이다. 질문의 핵심 어구인 the warranty card와 관련하여, 'To activate your warranty, the enclosed card must be ~ sent to us within seven days of purchase'에서 보증서를 활성화시키려면 구매일로부터 7일 이내에 동봉된 카드가 보내져야 한다고 했으므로 (B) Within a week of purchase가 정답이다.

Paraphrasing
must ~ submit 제출해야 → must be ~ sent 보내져야
within seven days 7일 이내에 → within a week 일주일 이내에

간단히 등록 카드를 작성하고 승무원에게 건네줌으로써 Club Cumulus 상용 고객 우대 제도에 오늘 등록하십시오! ^A/C^귀하의 현재 여행에 대한 마일리지를 청구하시려면, 자사 서비스 창구들 중 한 곳을 방문하시고 귀하의 탑승권, 사진이 있는 신분증 및 회원 번호를 준비해 주십시오. 적립된 마일리지에 대한 내역서는 매월 귀하의 지정 이메일 주소로 전송됩니다.

frequent flyer program (항공사) 상용 고객 우대 제도 **claim** v. 청구하다
accumulate v. 적립하다, 축적하다, 모으다 **specified** adj. 지정된

문제 현재 비행의 마일리지를 청구하기 위해 필요하지 않은 것은?

(A) 탑승권
(B) 등록 양식
(C) 신분증

해설 **Not/True 문제** 질문의 핵심 어구인 claim mileage for the current flight와 관련된 내용을 지문에서 찾아 보기와 대조하는 Not/True 문제이다. (A)와 (C)는 'To claim mileage for your current trip, ~ have your boarding pass, a photo ID, and your membership number ready.'에서 현재 여행에 대한 마일리지를 청구하려면 탑승권, 사진이 있는 신분증 및 회원 번호를 준비하라고 했으므로 지문의 내용과 일치한다. (B)는 지문에 언급되지 않은 내용이다. 따라서 (B) A registration form이 정답이다.

Paraphrasing
current flight 현재 비행 → current trip 현재 여행
a photo ID 사진이 있는 신분증 → A piece of identification 신분증

Hackers Test
p.463

01 (C)	02 (D)	03 (A)	04 (B)	05 (C)
06 (B)	07 (C)	08 (D)	09 (C)	10 (A)
11 (D)	12 (B)			

01-04는 다음 안내문에 관한 문제입니다.

Nomadica H2OXP®

^01^Nomadica H2OXP®를 선택해 주셔서 감사합니다. 이 제품은 특별히 디자인된 휴대용 수분 공급 기구로 무미 무취한 내구성 있는 고급 플라스틱으로 만들어졌습니다. 빠르고 쉬운 사용을 위해 귀하의 가방 혹은 허리에 물병을 휴대하십시오. ^02-D^이 물병은 잡기 편한 손잡이가 있는 누수 방지 뚜껑과 구부리기 쉬운 빨대를 특징으로 하며, 둘 다 세척과 교체를 위해 쉽게 해체할 수 있습니다. 뿐만 아니라, 식수의 깨끗함을 보장하기 위해 제품에 특허받은 정수 시스템이 딸려 있습니다.

이 제품은 매 사용 후에 닦아야 합니다. 깨끗한 물과 순한 세제만 사용해 손으로 설거지하십시오. 수납하기 전에 자연 건조되도록 두십시오. ^02-C^식기세척기에 제품을 넣지 마십시오.

한정된 기간만 제공!
^03^자사 제품, 판촉 행사 및 향후 제품 출시에 대한 정보를 받는 것에 등록하신 후 무료 ThermaCool 단열 운반 케이스를 받아 보십시오. 이 운반 케이스는 음료를 하루 종일 차갑게 유지해 주며 벨트 고리 부착 장치와 가방 잠금장치를 포함합니다. custreg@nomadica.com으로 이메일을 보내시거나 ^03^자사의 무료 상담 전화인 1-888-555-0770으로 연락해 주십시오.

30년 이상, Nomadica는 평생 가도록 제작된 고품질의 여행 액세서리를 만드는 것으로 알려져 왔습니다. 자사 제품들은 경험 많은 여행자들과 야외 활동의 열렬한 지지자들에 의해 어디에서나 이용되고 추천됩니다. ^04^교환 부품과 수리점 목록을 위해서는, www.nomadica.com에 접속해 주십시오.

portable adj. 휴대용의 **hydration** n. 수분 공급, 수화
durable adj. 내구성이 있는, 오래가는 **tasteless** adj. 무미의, 아무런 맛이 없는
odorless adj. 무취의 **waist** n. 허리 **leak-proof** 누수 방지의
flexible adj. 구부리기 쉬운, 유연한 **patent** v. 특허를 받다
detergent n. 세제 **air-dry** 자연 건조하다 **storing** n. 수납, 저장
insulate v. 단열 처리를 하다 **fastener** n. 잠금장치 **toll-free** 무료의
hotline n. 상담 전화 **enthusiast** n. 열렬한 지지자, 열광적인 팬

문제 안내문의 목적은 무엇인가?

(A) 웹사이트에서 구매하도록 사람들을 장려하기 위해
(B) 고객들에게 품질 보증서를 갱신할 것을 상기시키기 위해
(C) 제품 사용법에 대해 최근 구매자들에게 가르쳐 주기 위해
(D) 새로운 서비스에 대해 매장 직원들에게 알려 주기 위해

해설 안내문의 목적을 묻는 목적 찾기 문제이다. 'Thanks for choosing the Nomadica H2OXP®.'(1문단 1번째 줄)에서 Nomadica H2OXP®를 선택해 주셔서 고맙다고 한 후, 제품의 특징 및 제품 세척 방법에 대해 설명하고 있으므로 (C) To instruct recent buyers on the use of a product가 정답이다.

어휘 **instruct** v. 가르치다, 알려 주다

02 Not/True 문제

문제 H2OXP®에 대해 언급된 것은?

(A) 여러 가지 색이 구입 가능하다.
(B) 뜨거운 액체로 채워지면 안 된다.
(C) 식기세척기에 사용하기에 안전하다.
(D) 세척을 위해 해체될 수 있다.

해설 질문의 핵심 어구인 H2OXP®와 관련된 내용을 지문에서 찾아 보기와 대조하는 Not/True 문제이다. (A)와 (B)는 지문에 언급되지 않은 내용이다. (C)는 'Do not place the product in the dishwasher.'(2문단 2번째 줄)에서 식기세척기에 제품을 넣지 말라고 했으므로 지문의 내용과 일치하지 않는다. (D)는 'It features a leak-proof cap with an easy-grip handle and a flexible drinking tube, both of which you can easily take apart for cleaning'(1문단 3번째 줄)에서 이 물병은 잡기 편한 손잡이가 있는 누수 방지 뚜껑과 구부리기 쉬운 빨대를 특징으로 하며, 둘 다 세척을 위해 쉽게 해체할 수 있다고 했으므로 (D) It may be disassembled for cleaning이 정답이다.

Paraphrasing
take apart 해체하다 → be disassembled 해체되다

어휘 **disassemble** v. 해체하다, 분해하다

03 육하원칙 문제

문제 독자들은 왜 Nomadica에 전화해야 하는가?

(A) 정보를 받으려고 등록하기 위해
(B) 제품 사용 설명서를 요청하기 위해
(C) 간단한 설문 조사를 완료하기 위해
(D) 할인 제공을 이용하기 위해

해설 독자들이 왜(Why) Nomadica에 전화해야 하는지를 묻는 육하원칙 문제이다. 질문의 핵심 어구인 call Nomadica와 관련하여, 'Get a free ThermaCool insulated carrying case when you register to receive details about our products, promotions, and future releases.'(3문단 1번째 줄)에서 제품, 판촉 행사 및 향후 제품 출시에 대한 정보를 받는 것에 등록하면 무료 ThermaCool 단열 운반 케이스를 받을 수 있다고 한 후, 'call our toll-free hotline at 1-888-555-0770'(3문단 3번째 줄)에서 무료 상담 전화로 연락하라고 했으므로, 이 회사에 대한 정보를 받는 것에 등록하기 위해서는 전화를 해야 함을 알 수 있다. 따라서 (A) To register to receive information이 정답이다.

Paraphrasing
details about our products, promotions, and future releases 제품, 판촉 행사 및 향후 제품 출시에 대한 정보 → information 정보

어휘 **brief** adj. 간단한, 짧은

04 육하원칙 문제

문제 웹사이트에서 이용 가능한 정보는 무엇인가?

(A) Nomadica 지점들의 목록
(B) 수리와 교체 부품에 대한 정보
(C) 야외 활동의 열렬한 지지자들을 위한 여행 제안
(D) 무료 가방을 얻기 위한 쿠폰

해설 웹사이트에서 이용 가능한 정보가 무엇인지(What)를 묻는 육하원칙 문제

이다. 질문의 핵심 어구인 available on the Web site와 관련하여, 'For replacement parts and a list of repair centers, please go to www. nomadica.com.'(4문단 3번째 줄)에서 교환 부품과 수리점 목록을 위해서는, www.nomadica.com에 접속하라고 했으므로 (B) Details about repairs and replacements가 정답이다.

Paraphrasing
replacement parts and ~ repair centers 교환 부품과 수리점 목록 → Details about repairs and replacements 수리와 교체 부품에 대한 정보

어휘 **directory** n. 목록, 주소 성명록 **obtain** v. 얻다, 구하다

05-08은 다음 안내문에 관한 문제입니다.

> ⁰⁵Blount Memorial 도서관의 본관에 오신 것을 환영하며, 이곳은 Victoria, Kimball 및 New Hope에 있는 세 곳의 다른 분관들과 더불어 Marion 자치군 전역에 서비스를 제공합니다.
>
> ⁰⁶⁻ᴰ/⁰⁷이 3층짜리 건물은 ⁰⁶⁻ᴰAlfred Blount 재단의 보조금을 사용해서 1985년에 완공되었습니다. ⁰⁶⁻ᴬ/ᶜMarion 자치군 토박이인 Mr. Blount는 ⁰⁶⁻ᶜ테네시주의 예전 주지사이기도 합니다. 본 시설의 일상적인 운영은 Jasper시와 Marion 자치군으로부터 자금을 제공받아 이루어집니다. 추가적인 지원은 테네시주에서 나옵니다.
>
> 건물의 1층은 행정실, 회의실, 복사 센터 및 지역 탁아소를 수용합니다. 2층에는 주요 소장 읽을거리들이 있으며, 아동용 책, 다양한 장르의 베스트셀러 책들, 그리고 최신 잡지와 신문 구독물을 포함합니다. ⁰⁷꼭대기 층은 신문 기록 보관소와 역사학, 계보학 및 지구 과학에 특별히 초점을 맞춘 연구 도서관을 포함합니다. 도서관 전 구역에 책상들, 컴퓨터 자리 및 독서 휴게실이 흩어져 있습니다. 구내에는 전적으로 휠체어가 들어갈 수 있습니다.
>
> 본관 도서관은 월요일부터 금요일까지 오전 8시부터 오후 8시까지, 토요일에는 오전 9시부터 오후 6시까지, 그리고 일요일에는 오후 1시부터 오후 5시까지 개방합니다. 모든 주요 공휴일에는 휴관합니다. 다른 분관들에서는 개방 시간이 다를 수 있으므로, 안내 데스크에서 문의하시기 바랍니다. ⁰⁸회의실들 중 하나를 예약하시려면, 방문객들은 도서관 행정실에 555-2120, 내선 14번으로 연락하시는 것이 요구됩니다.
>
> **story** n. (건물의) 층 **grant** n. (정부나 단체에서 주는) 보조금
> **former** adj. 예전의, 과거의 **governor** n. (미국의) 주지사, (한 기관의) 장, 관리자
> **house** v. 수용하다, 거처를 제공하다 **administrative office** 행정실, 관리 사무실
> **archive** n. 기록 보관소 **genealogy** n. 계보학
> **scatter** v. 흩어지다, 흩뿌리다 **premises** n. 구내, 부지
> **wheelchair-accessible** 휠체어가 들어갈 수 있는 **inquire** v. 문의하다, 묻다

05 추론 문제

문제 안내문은 어디에서 볼 수 있을 것 같은가?
(A) 지역 신문에서
(B) 사서 매뉴얼에서
(C) 도서관 안내 책자에서
(D) 문학 잡지에서

해설 안내문을 볼 수 있는 곳을 추론하는 문제이다. 'Welcome to the main branch of the Blount Memorial Library'(1문단 1번째 줄)에서 Blount Memorial 도서관의 본관에 온 것을 환영한다고 한 후, 도서관의 설립과 운영, 시설, 이용 시간 등에 대해 설명하고 있으므로 도서관에 대해 안내하는 안내문임을 추론할 수 있다. 따라서 (C) In a brochure of a library가 정답이다.

06 Not/True 문제

문제 Alfred Blount에 대해 언급되지 않은 것은?
(A) Marion 자치군에서 태어났다.
(B) 방대한 양의 책을 소장했다.
(C) 한때 공무원이었다.
(D) 그의 재단이 재정적 지원을 제공했다.

해설 질문의 핵심 어구인 Alfred Blount와 관련된 내용을 지문에서 찾아 보기와 대조하는 Not/True 문제이다. (A)는 'Mr. Blount, a Marion County native'(2문단 2번째 줄)에서 Mr. Blount는 Marion 자치군의 토박이라고 했으므로 지문의 내용과 일치한다. (B)는 지문에 언급되지 않은 내용이다.

따라서 (B) He owned a large collection of books가 정답이다. (C)는 'Mr. Blount, ~ a former governor of the state of Tennessee.'(2문단 2번째 줄)에서 Mr. Blount는 테네시주의 예전 주지사라고 했으므로 지문의 내용과 일치한다. (D)는 'This three-story structure was completed in 1985 with a grant from the Alfred Blount Foundation.'(2문단 1번째 줄)에서 이 3층짜리 건물은 Alfred Blount 재단의 보조금을 사용해서 1985년에 완공되었다고 했으므로 지문의 내용과 일치한다.

Paraphrasing
a former governor 예전 주지사 → once a public official 한때 공무원

07 추론 문제

문제 방문자들이 건물의 3층에서 무엇을 할 수 있을 것 같은가?
(A) 잡지들을 훑어본다
(B) 인기 있는 소설을 찾아본다
(C) 오래된 출판물을 자세히 본다
(D) 회의에 참여한다

해설 방문자들이 건물의 3층에서 무엇을 할 수 있을 것 같은지를 추론하는 문제이다. 질문의 핵심 어구인 the building's third floor와 관련하여, 'This three-story structure'(2문단 1번째 줄)에서 이 건물은 3층짜리라고 한 후, 'The top floor includes our newspaper archives'(3문단 4번째 줄)에서 꼭대기 층은 신문 기록 보관소를 포함한다고 했으므로 방문자들이 3층에서 오래된 신문을 볼 수 있다는 사실을 추론할 수 있다. 따라서 (C) Study old publications가 정답이다.

어휘 **browse** v. 훑어보다, 둘러보다

08 육하원칙 문제

문제 회의 시설은 어떻게 예약될 수 있는가?
(A) 행정실을 방문해서
(B) 양식을 작성해서
(C) 지점으로 가서
(D) 전화를 걸어서

해설 회의 시설이 어떻게(How) 예약될 수 있는지를 묻는 육하원칙 문제이다. 질문의 핵심 어구인 a meeting facility be booked와 관련하여, 'To reserve one of the meeting rooms, ~ contact ~ at 555-2120, extension 14.'(4문단 3번째 줄)에서 회의실들 중 하나를 예약하려면 555-2120, 내선 14번으로 연락하라고 했으므로 (D) By dialing a number가 정답이다.

Paraphrasing
a meeting facility be booked 회의 시설이 예약되다 → reserve ~ the meeting rooms 회의실을 예약하다

09-12는 다음 안내문에 관한 문제입니다.

> Baron 영화사의 ¹¹⁻ᶜ감독 Michelle Devries와 제작자 Dario Mantovani를 대표해서, 모든 배우와 제작진에게 이번 영화 제작 동안의 노고에 대한 감사의 말을 전하고자 합니다. ¹¹⁻ᴮ다음 주는 촬영 마지막 주이며, 그 후에 우리는 파티를 개최하고, 영화 최종판을 상영하며, 영화 개봉을 할 계획입니다. 아래에서 다가올 행사들에 대한 정보를 확인하시기 바랍니다.
>
> 마무리 파티:
> ⁰⁹촬영 마지막 날인 8월 5일에, Baron 영화사는 Melrose가 6654번지에 있는 Orange Grove 호텔에서 오후 7시에 마무리 파티를 개최할 것입니다. 저녁 뷔페가 음료와 함께 제공될 것입니다. 이후의 댄스파티를 위해 라이브 밴드가 있을 것입니다. 모든 배우와 제작진에게 이번 주에 초대장이 발송될 것입니다. 이 초대장은 여러분이 손님 한 명을 데려오는 것을 허용합니다. 그렇지만, 귀하의 참석 여부를 7월 30일까지 내선 443번의 Preethi Samraj에게 확인해 주어서 그녀가 최대한 빨리 예약을 할 수 있도록 해 주십시오.
>
> ¹⁰영화 상영회:
> 영화 편집 작업의 최종일이 9월 2일로 예정되어 있습니다. 9월 5일에 영화사에서 배우와 제작진 전체를 대상으로 한 영화 상영회를 개최할 것입니다. 상영회 중 간식과 다과가 제공될 것이며, 가족 또는 친구들을 최대 네 명까지 데려오실 수 있습니다. 그러나, ¹⁰여러분이 참석할지와 몇 장의 입장권이 필요할지 홍보팀의 Colin Huntington에게 알려 주시기 바랍니다. 입장권이 없는 분은 영화사 구내에 있는 것이 허용되지 않을 것입니다.

¹²개봉:
¹¹⁻ᴬ *Trade Winds*는 다음 날 저녁에 Hollywood대로 334번지의 Oakland 영화관에서 오후 8시에 대중에게 개봉될 것입니다. ¹²이 행사는 초청객에 한할 것인데, 좌석 수가 제한되어 있고 ¹¹⁻ᴬ/¹²오로지 영화사의 경영진과 언론 관계자들만 초대할 것이기 때문입니다. 이 개봉은 정장 차림을 요하는 행사이므로, 초대된 분들은 알맞게 복장을 갖춰 주시기 바랍니다. 초대장 없이는 입장이 허락되지 않을 것이므로 초대장을 지참해 주시기 바랍니다.

on behalf of ~을 대표해서 **cast and crew** 배우와 제작진
premiere n. 개봉, 초연; v. 처음 공개되다 **executive** n. 경영진, 임원
press n. 언론 **black-tie** 정장 차림을 요하는

---

09 육하원칙 문제

문제 안내문에 따르면, 8월에 무엇이 일어날 것인가?

(A) 배우와 제작진은 새 프로젝트를 시작하기 위해 모일 것이다.
(B) 영화가 영화관에서 처음 공개될 것이다.
(C) 제작 영화의 촬영이 완료될 것이다.
(D) 호텔에서의 행사를 위한 예약이 이루어질 것이다.

해설 8월에 일어날 일이 무엇인지(what)를 묻는 육하원칙 문제이다. 질문의 핵심 어구인 in August와 관련하여, 'On the final day of filming on August 5'(2문단 1번째 줄)에서 촬영 마지막 날이 8월 5일이라고 했으므로 (C) Filming of a production will be completed가 정답이다.

Paraphrasing
the final day of filming 촬영 마지막 날 → Filming of a production will be completed 제작 영화의 촬영이 완료될 것이다

어휘 **assemble** v. 모이다

---

10 육하원칙 문제

문제 영화 상영회 입장권을 요청하려면 연락되어야 하는 사람은 누구인가?

(A) Colin Huntington
(B) Dario Mantovani
(C) Preethi Samraj
(D) Michelle Devries

해설 영화 상영회 입장권을 요청하려면 연락되어야 하는 사람이 누구인지(Who)를 묻는 육하원칙 문제이다. 질문의 핵심 어구인 request passes to a movie screening과 관련하여, 'Film Screening:'(3문단 제목)과 'please notify Colin Huntington in public relations ~ how many passes you will need'(3문단 3번째 줄)에서 영화 상영회 참석을 위해 몇 장의 입장권이 필요할지 홍보팀의 Colin Huntington에게 알려 주라고 했으므로 영화 상영회 입장권을 요청하려면 Colin Huntington에게 연락해야 함을 알 수 있다. 따라서 (A) Colin Huntington이 정답이다.

Paraphrasing
movie screening 영화 상영회 → Film Screening 영화 상영회

---

11 Not/True 문제

문제 *Trade Winds*에 대해 언급되지 않은 것은?

(A) Baron 영화사의 경영진을 위해 상영될 것이다.
(B) 아직 대중에게 공개되지 않았다.
(C) Michelle Devries에 의해 감독되었다.
(D) 언론 관계자들로부터 긍정적인 평가를 받았다.

해설 질문의 핵심 어구인 *Trade Winds*와 관련된 내용을 지문에서 찾아 보기와 대조하는 Not/True 문제이다. (A)는 '*Trade Winds* will have its public premiere'(4문단 1번째 줄)에서 *Trade Winds*가 대중에게 개봉될 것이라고 한 후, 'we will be exclusively inviting studio executives'(4문단 2번째 줄)에서 오로지 영화사의 경영진만 초대할 것이라고 했으므로 지문의 내용과 일치한다. (B)는 'Next week is our final week of shooting, after which we plan to ~ hold a movie premiere.'(1문단 2번째 줄)에서 다음 주가 촬영 마지막 주이고 그 이후에 영화 개봉을 할 계획이라고 했으므로 지문의 내용과 일치한다. (C)는 'director Michelle Devries'(1문단 1번째 줄)에서 감독이 Michelle Devries라고 했으므로 지문의 내용과 일치한다. (D)는 지문에 언급되지 않은 내용이다. 따라서 (D) It received positive reviews from members of the press가 정답이다.

---

12 추론 문제

문제 개봉에 대해 암시되는 것은?

(A) 언론과의 질의응답 시간을 포함할 것이다.
(B) 모든 배우와 제작진을 위한 것은 아니다.
(C) 영화사 구내에서 개최될 것이다.
(D) 복장 규정 요건이 없다.

해설 질문의 핵심 어구인 the premiere에 대해 추론하는 문제이다. 'Premiere:'(4문단 제목)와 'The event will be by invitation only, ~ and we will be exclusively inviting studio executives and members of the press.'(4문단 2번째 줄)에서 개봉은 초청객에 한할 것이고 오로지 영화사의 경영진과 언론 관계자들만 초대할 것이라고 했으므로 개봉이 모든 배우와 제작진을 위한 것은 아니라는 사실을 추론할 수 있다. 따라서 (B) It is not for all members of the cast and crew가 정답이다.

Paraphrasing
by invitation only 초청객에 한하는 → not for all members of the cast and crew 모든 배우와 제작진을 위한 것은 아닌

어휘 **question period** 질의 응답 시간

Section 3 지문 유형별 공략 – Multiple Passages

Chapter 16 이메일(편지) 연계 지문

예제 해석·해설   p.468

이메일 & 이메일

수신: Emmanuel Turner <emmanuel.turner@rocketmail.com>
발신: Pauline Buenaventura <pauline.buenaventura@atlantahikers.com>

Atlanta Hikers Club에 가입해 주셔서 감사드립니다. 요청하신 대로, 3월에 예정된 행사 목록이 여기 있습니다:

• 3월 4일, Stone 산에서의 하이킹
• 3월 12일, Pele 공원에서의 장거리 달리기 대회
• 3월 21일, 자선 행사
• 3월 28일, 시상식

fun run (자선기금 모금을 위한) 장거리 달리기 대회 **charity** n. 자선, 자비
gala n. 행사, 축제 **awards ceremony** 시상식

수신: Pauline Buenaventura <pauline.buenaventura@atlantahikers.com>
발신: Emmanuel Turner <emmanuel.turner@rocketmail.com>

3월 4일에 귀하께서 주최하신 훌륭한 행사에 대해 감사드리고 싶습니다. 저는 장거리 달리기 대회에 참가하기 위해 등록했지만, 유감스럽게도 참석할 수 없을 것 같습니다. 하지만, 21일에 있을 모금 행사에서 귀하를 뵙겠습니다!

participate v. 참가하다 **make it** 참석하다, 출석하다 **fundraising** n. 모금

문제 Mr. Turner는 최근에 어떤 행사에 참석했는가?

(A) 산 하이킹
(B) 장거리 달리기 대회
(C) 모금 행사
(D) 시상식

해설 **육하원칙 문제** 두 지문의 내용을 종합해서 풀어야 하는 연계 문제이다. 질문의 핵심 어구인 Mr. Turner ~ attend에서 Mr. Turner가 어떤(Which) 행사에 참석했는지를 묻고 있으므로 Mr. Turner가 작성한 이메일을 먼저 확인한다.

두 번째 이메일의 'thank you for the wonderful event you held on March 4'에서 3월 4일에 주최한 훌륭한 행사에 감사하다고 했으므로 Mr. Turner가 3월 4일의 행사에 참석했다는 첫 번째 단서를 확인할 수 있다. 그런데 3월 4일의 행사가 무엇인지 제시되지 않았으므로 첫 번째 이메일에서 3월 4일의 행사를 확인한다. 첫 번째 이메일의 'March 4, hike at Stone Mountain'에서 3월 4일의 행사는 Stone 산에서의 하이킹이라는 두 번째 단서를 확인할 수 있다.

Mr. Turner가 3월 4일의 행사에 참석했다는 첫 번째 단서와 3월 4일의 행사는 Stone 산에서의 하이킹이라는 두 번째 단서를 종합할 때, Mr. Turner는 Stone 산에서의 하이킹에 참석했음을 알 수 있다. 따라서 (A) A mountain hike가 정답이다.

Hackers Practice
p.469

유형 연습			
01 (C)	02 (B)	03 (B)	04 (A)

01-02 편지 & 편지

Ms. Kimmel께,

01-A본 대학은 새로운 과학관을 세우기 위해 캠퍼스 부근의 땅을 매입할 계획이기 때문에 모금 캠페인을 열고 있습니다. 그 결과, 01-C우리는 동창회 회원들에게 기부해 주실 것을 간청하고 있습니다. 어떠한 액수의 기부금이든 매우 환영받을 것입니다. 02아낌없는 후원에 대한 감사의 뜻으로, 귀하의 이름이 로비 벽에 위치하게 될 후원자 명판에 새겨질 것입니다.

Alan Blanche, 동창회, Buckeye 대학

adjacent adj. 부근의, 인접한　**appeal** v. 간청하다, 호소하다
alumni n. 동창회　**make a contribution** ~에 기부하다
appreciate v. 환영하다, 고마워하다　**engrave** v. 새기다
plaque n. (사건·인물을 기념하는 금속·석제의) 명판

Mr. Blanche께,

제가 도움을 드리게 되어 기쁩니다. 그 대학의 화학과 졸업생으로서, 새로운 과학관이 설계 중임을 듣게 되어 아주 기쁩니다. 그곳이 장차 입학할 학생들에게 도움이 될 것이라 확신합니다. 02동봉된 1,000달러짜리 수표를 확인하실 수 있습니다. 이것이 조금이나마 도움이 되길 바랍니다.

Diane Kimmel

delighted adj. 아주 기뻐하는　**benefit** v. 도움이 되다, 이익이 되다
enclosed adj. 동봉된　**check** n. 수표

01 Not/True 문제

문제　캠페인에 대해 언급된 것은?
(A) 학생 회관을 짓기 위한 돈을 마련할 것이다.
(B) 장학금 제도에 자금을 제공할 것이다.
(C) 그 대학교의 예전 학생들을 대상으로 하고 있다.

해설　질문의 핵심 어구인 the campaign에 대해 묻는 Not/True 문제이므로 캠페인이 언급된 첫 번째 편지에서 관련 내용을 확인한다. (A)는 'The college is holding a fundraising campaign ~ in order to construct a new science building.'(1번째 줄)에서 대학이 새로운 과학관을 세우기 위해 모금 캠페인을 열고 있다고 했으므로 지문의 내용과 일치하지 않는다. (B)는 지문에 언급되지 않은 내용이다. (C)는 'we are appealing to alumni members to make a contribution'(2번째 줄)에서 동창회 회원들에게 기부해 줄 것을 간청하고 있다고 했으므로 (C) It is targeting former students of the college가 정답이다.

Paraphrasing
alumni members 동창회 회원들 → former students 예전 학생들

어휘　**fund** v. 자금을 제공하다　**scholarship** n. 장학금
former adj. 예전의, 이전의

02 육하원칙 문제　연계

문제　Ms. Kimmel은 무엇에 대한 자격을 가지게 될 것인가?

(A) 명예 학위
(B) 명판에 그녀의 이름이 새겨지는 것
(C) 세금 우대

해설　두 지문의 내용을 종합해서 풀어야 하는 연계 문제이다. 질문의 핵심 어구인 Ms. Kimmel be eligible for에서 Ms. Kimmel이 무엇(What)에 대한 자격을 가지게 될 것인지를 묻고 있으므로 Ms. Kimmel이 작성한 편지를 먼저 확인한다.

두 번째 편지의 'Enclosed you will find a check in the amount of $1,000.'(3번째 줄)에서 동봉된 1,000달러짜리 수표를 확인해 보라고 했으므로 Ms. Kimmel이 기부를 했다는 첫 번째 단서를 확인할 수 있다. 그런데 기부를 하면 무엇에 대한 자격이 주어지는지 제시되지 않았으므로 첫 번째 편지에서 기부자들에게 주어지는 자격을 확인한다. 첫 번째 편지의 'In gratitude for your generous support, your name will be engraved on a sponsors' plaque'(3번째 줄)에서 아낌없는 후원에 대한 감사의 뜻으로 이름이 후원자 명판에 새겨질 것이라는 두 번째 단서를 확인할 수 있다.

Ms. Kimmel이 기부를 했다는 첫 번째 단서와 기부를 하면 이름이 후원자 명판에 새겨질 것이라는 두 번째 단서를 종합할 때, Ms. Kimmel의 이름이 후원자 명판에 새겨질 것임을 알 수 있다. 따라서 (B) Her name on a plaque가 정답이다.

어휘　**eligible** adj. 자격이 있는　**honorary** adj. 명예직의

03-04 이메일 & 공고

수신　<service@mayberrylibrary.com>
발신　Dan Hastings <hasty@zoomail.com>

담당자께,

저는 Mayberry 도서관의 회원이며 제안 사항이 있습니다. 정기 간행물 코너에 젊은 사람들을 위한 출판물이 많지 않습니다. 03제 또래 사람들은 영화, 오락, 또는 대중문화에 관한 잡지를 더 많이 보고 싶어 합니다. 이러한 출판물들을 추후에 추가하는 것을 고려해 주시기 바랍니다.

Dan Hastings

publication n. 출판물　**periodical** n. 정기 간행물　**pop culture** 대중문화

MAYBERRY 공립 도서관

여러분의 제안들은 우리 시설을 발전시키고 대중에게 더 좋은 서비스를 제공하는 데 도움이 됩니다. 여러분의 읽는 즐거움을 위해 우리 도서관의 정기 간행물 코너에 다음 제목의 잡지들을 제공하게 되어 기쁘게 생각합니다.

• *Sensational Seniors*지: 활동적인 고령자들을 위한 월간 잡지
• 03*Silver Screen*지: 젊은 영화팬들을 위한 주간 출판물
• 04*Pets and Play*지: 반려동물을 키우는 사람들을 위한 연 4회 발행 잡지

도서관에서 보고 싶은 출판물에 대한 추천이 있으시면, service@mayberrylibrary.com으로 메일을 보내 주십시오.

serve v. (상품·서비스를) 제공하다　**senior citizen** 고령자
quarterly adj. 연 4회 발행의, 계절마다의　**title** n. 출판물, 책

03 추론 문제　연계

문제　Mr. Hastings는 어떤 출판물을 즐겨 읽는 것 같은가?

(A) *Sensational Seniors*지
(B) *Silver Screen*지
(C) *Pets and Play*지

해설　두 지문의 내용을 종합적으로 확인한 후 추론해서 풀어야 하는 연계 문제이다. 질문의 핵심 어구인 Mr. Hastings ~ enjoy reading에서 Mr. Hastings가 즐겨 읽을 것 같은 출판물을 묻고 있으므로 Mr. Hastings가 작성한 이메일을 먼저 확인한다.

첫 번째 지문인 이메일의 'People my age would like to see more magazines about movies, entertainment, or pop culture.'(2번째 줄)에서 Mr. Hastings 또래 사람들은 영화, 오락, 또는 대중문화에 관한 잡지를 더 많이 보고 싶어 한다 또래 사람들은 첫 번째 단서를 확인할 수 있다. 그런데 Mr. Hastings가 즐겨 읽을 만한 출판물의 제목이 제시되지 않았으므로 공고에서 출판물의 제목을 확인한다. 두 번째 지문인 공고의 '*Silver Screen Journal*: ~ for young movie lovers'(4번째 줄)에서 *Silver Screen*지는 젊은 영화팬들을 대상으로 한다는 두 번째 단서를 확인할 수 있다.

Mr. Hastings가 영화에 대한 잡지를 보고 싶어 한다는 첫 번째 단서와 *Silver Screen*지는 젊은 영화팬들을 대상으로 한다는 두 번째 단서를 종합할 때, Mr. Hastings는 *Silver Screen*지를 즐겨 읽을 것이라는 사실을 추론할 수 있다. 따라서 (B) *Silver Screen Journal*이 정답이다.

04 육하원칙 문제

문제 *Pets and Play*지는 얼마나 자주 발행되는가?

(A) 1년에 4번
(B) 매 3주마다
(C) 한 달에 두 번

해설 *Pets and Play*지가 얼마나 자주(How often) 발행되는지를 묻는 육하원칙 문제이므로 질문의 핵심 어구인 *Pets and Play*가 언급된 공고에서 관련 내용을 확인한다. 두 번째 지문인 공고의 '*Pets and Play*: A quarterly magazine'(5번째 줄)에서 *Pets and Play*지가 연 4회 발행 잡지라고 했으므로 (A) Four times a year가 정답이다.

Paraphrasing
quarterly 연 4회의 → Four times a year 1년에 4번

Hackers Test
p.470

01 (B)	02 (D)	03 (A)	04 (C)	05 (B)
06 (B)	07 (A)	08 (D)	09 (C)	10 (D)
11 (D)	12 (B)	13 (A)	14 (A)	15 (B)
16 (B)	17 (D)	18 (C)	19 (C)	20 (C)

01-05는 다음 두 이메일에 관한 문제입니다.

수신 John Walton <jwalton@mountainpromotions.com>
발신 Mary Allen <mallen@mountainpromotions.com>
제목 장비 설치 workschedule.word
날짜 5월 5일

Mr. Walton께,

우리 기술자들은 5월 7일 수요일에 당신의 부서에 컴퓨터 장비를 설치하기로 예정되어 있었습니다. 유감스럽게도, ⁰¹작업을 연기해야 할 것 같은데, 그날에 ⁰⁴회계부의 컴퓨터 시스템 개선 작업을 요청받았기 때문입니다. 이 작업은 긴급하므로, 우리는 다른 선택 사항이 없습니다. 대신에 우리 기술자들이 목요일 오전에 설치 작업을 하는 것이 가능하겠습니까? 이것이 곤란하시다면, 우리가 가능한 시간을 보여 주는 ⁰²첨부된 작업 일정표를 참고해 주시기 바랍니다. 보시다시피, 5월 12일 월요일 전까지는 작업을 할 다른 시간이 없을 것입니다. 설치 작업은 몇 시간 걸리지 않을 것입니다.

또한, 당신의 직원들 일부는 새로운 데스크톱 컴퓨터를 받을 것입니다. ⁰⁵그들의 컴퓨터에서 필요한 파일들을 모두 저장하도록 지시해 주시기 바랍니다. 그들은 파일들을 회사의 웹 게시판에 업로드하거나, USB 플래시 드라이브에 저장할 수 있습니다.

당신의 인내와 협조에 감사드립니다.

Mary Allen
기술지원부 이사
Mountain Promotions사

equipment n. 장비 installation n. 설치
accounting department 회계부 urgent adj. 긴급한
inconvenient adj. 곤란한, 불편한 attach v. 첨부하다, 붙이다
instruct v. 지시하다, 가르치다 flash drive 플래시 드라이브
patience n. 인내 cooperation n. 협조

수신: Mary Allen <mallen@mountainpromotions.com>
발신: John Walton <jwalton@mountainpromotions.com>
제목: 회신: 장비 설치
날짜: 5월 5일

안녕하세요 Mary,

메시지에 감사드립니다. 사실, 우리는 목요일에 중요한 마감이 있어서, 그날은 아마도 우리에게 최적의 시간이 아닌 듯 합니다. ⁰³·⁰⁴당신의 기술자들이 하게

될 작업 중 일부는 웹 카메라 설치인데, 우리는 이 웹 카메라들이 금요일에 있을 우리 회사 다른 지부 마케팅부서와의 온라인 회의에 필요합니다. 따라서, 설치 작업은 우리 부서 역시도 다소 긴급한 사안이며, 이는 그 회의에 때맞춰 장비를 사용할 수 있어야 하기 때문입니다. ⁰⁴제가 관리자인 Tina Ryder와 이야기해 보니, 그녀의 부서는 시스템 개선 작업을 위해 아마 목요일 아침까지 기다릴 수 있을 것이라고 합니다. 그러니, 설치 작업을 수요일로 다시 한번 일정을 잡아 주시면, 매우 감사하겠습니다.

혼란을 드려 죄송하지만, 모든 일이 잘 진행되리라 생각합니다. 당신은 Tina와 일정을 확인하실 수 있습니다. ⁰⁵당신의 지시 사항에 대해서도 직원들에게 알려 주겠습니다. 당신의 도움에 감사드리며, 수요일에 뵙겠습니다.

John Walton
마케팅부 부이사
Mountain Promotions사

operational adj. 사용할 수 있는 in time 때맞추어, 제시간에
grateful adj. 감사하는 confusion n. 혼란 work out (일이) 잘 진행되다

01 주제/목적 찾기 문제

문제 Ms. Allen은 왜 Mr. Walton에게 이메일을 썼는가?

(A) 전화 회의를 계획하기 위해
(B) 작업 일정을 변경하기 위해
(C) 컴퓨터 몇 대를 주문하기 위해
(D) 시스템 업그레이드를 요청하기 위해

해설 Ms. Allen이 Mr. Walton에게 이메일을 쓴 목적을 묻는 목적 찾기 문제이므로 Ms. Allen이 작성한 이메일을 확인한다. 첫 번째 이메일의 'I will have to delay the work'(1문단 2번째 줄)에서 작업을 연기해야 할 것 같다고 한 후, 가능한 다른 날짜에 대해 언급하고 있으므로 (B) To change a work schedule이 정답이다.

Paraphrasing
delay the work 작업을 연기하다 → change a work schedule 작업 일정을 변경하다

02 육하원칙 문제

문제 Ms. Allen이 Mr. Walton에게 무엇을 발송했는가?

(A) 곧 있을 발표에 대한 메모
(B) 추후 회의 일정
(C) 프로그램 설치를 위한 지시 사항
(D) 작업 시간표 한 부

해설 Ms. Allen이 Mr. Walton에게 무엇(What)을 발송했는지를 묻는 육하원칙 문제이므로 Ms. Allen이 작성한 이메일에서 질문의 핵심 어구인 forward와 관련된 내용을 확인한다. 첫 번째 이메일의 'please refer to the attached work schedule'(1문단 5번째 줄)에서 첨부된 작업 일정표를 참고하라고 했으므로 Ms. Allen이 작업 일정표를 발송했음을 알 수 있다. 따라서 (D) A copy of a work timetable이 정답이다.

Paraphrasing
work schedule 작업 일정표 → a work timetable 작업 시간표

어휘 forward v. 발송하다; adv. 앞으로 upcoming adj. 곧 있을, 다가오는

03 Not/True 문제

문제 회의에 대해 언급된 것은?

(A) 몇몇 장비가 설치되는 것을 필요로 한다.
(B) 후일로 미뤄졌다.
(C) 사무실 외부에서 열릴 것이다.
(D) Mary Allen에 의해 준비되었다.

해설 질문의 핵심 어구인 the conference에 대해 묻는 Not/True 문제이므로 회의가 언급된 두 번째 이메일에서 관련 내용을 확인한다. (A)는 'Part of the work your technicians will be doing is the installation of Web cameras, which we need for an online conference'(1문단 2번째 줄)에서 기술자들이 할 작업의 일부는 웹 카메라 설치이며 웹 카메라가 온라인 회의에 필요하다고 했으므로 지문의 내용과 일치한다. 따라서 (A) It requires that some devices be installed가 정답이다. (B), (C), (D)는 지문에 언급되지 않은 내용이다.

Paraphrasing
Web cameras 웹 카메라 → some devices 몇몇 장비

어휘   **device** n. 장비   **organize** v. 준비하다, 조직하다

04 추론 문제 연계

문제   Tina Ryder는 누구일 것 같은가?

(A) 컴퓨터 기술자
(B) 마케팅 직원
(C) 회계부 관리자
(D) Mr. Walton의 개인 비서

해설   두 지문의 내용을 종합적으로 확인한 후 추론해서 풀어야 하는 연계 문제이다. 질문의 핵심 어구인 Tina Ryder가 언급된 두 번째 이메일을 먼저 확인한다.
두 번째 이메일의 'I spoke to the supervisor, Tina Ryder, and she said her department could probably wait until Thursday morning to have their system upgraded.'(1문단 5번째 줄)에서 자신, 즉 Tina Ryder가 관리자로 있는 부서의 시스템 개선 작업은 목요일 아침까지 기다릴 수 있다고 했으므로 Tina Ryder는 시스템 개선 작업을 진행될 부서의 관리자라는 첫 번째 단서를 확인할 수 있다. 그런데 어떤 부서에서 시스템 개선 작업이 진행될 것인지 제시되지 않았으므로 첫 번째 이메일에서 관련 내용을 확인한다. 첫 번째 이메일의 'we've been asked to do a computer system upgrade in the accounting department'(1문단 2번째 줄)에서 컴퓨터 시스템 개선 작업을 요청한 것은 회계부라는 두 번째 단서를 확인할 수 있다. Tina Ryder는 시스템 개선 작업이 진행될 부서의 관리자라는 첫 번째 단서와 회계부에서 컴퓨터 시스템 개선 작업을 요청했다는 두 번째 단서를 종합할 때, Tina Ryder는 회계부 관리자라는 사실을 추론할 수 있다. 따라서 (C) A manager of the accounting department가 정답이다.

Paraphrasing
the supervisor 관리자 → A manager 관리자

05 육하원칙 문제 연계

문제   Mr. Walton이 무엇을 할 것이라고 말하는가?

(A) 전화 회의를 다른 날짜로 연기한다
(B) 그의 직원들에게 몇몇 파일을 저장하라고 상기시킨다
(C) Ms. Ryder와 일정에 대해 이야기한다
(D) 다른 지부의 이사와 연락한다

해설   두 지문의 내용을 종합해서 풀어야 하는 연계 문제이다. 질문의 핵심 어구인 Mr. Walton ~ will do에서 Mr. Walton이 무엇(What)을 할 것이라고 말하는지를 묻고 있으므로 Mr. Walton이 작성한 두 번째 이메일을 먼저 확인한다.
두 번째 이메일의 'I will inform my staff about your instructions as well.'(2문단 1번째 줄)에서 Mr. Walton이 Ms. Allen의 지시 사항을 직원들에게 알려 줄 것이라는 첫 번째 단서를 확인할 수 있다. 그런데 직원들에게 알려 줄 Ms. Allen의 지시 사항이 무엇인지 제시되지 않았으므로 Ms. Allen이 작성한 첫 번째 이메일에서 Ms. Allen이 전달한 지시 사항을 확인한다. 첫 번째 이메일의 'Please instruct them to save all needed files from their computers.'(2문단 1번째 줄)에서 Ms. Allen은 Mr. Walton의 직원들이 컴퓨터에서 필요한 파일을 모두 저장하도록 지시해 달라고 Mr. Walton에게 요청했다는 두 번째 단서를 확인할 수 있다.
Mr. Walton이 Ms. Allen의 지시 사항을 직원들에게 알려 줄 것이라는 첫 번째 단서와 Ms. Allen은 Mr. Walton의 직원들이 파일을 모두 저장하도록 지시해 달라고 Mr. Walton에게 요청했다는 두 번째 단서를 종합할 때, Mr. Walton은 그의 직원들에게 파일을 저장하라고 상기시킬 것임을 알 수 있다. 따라서 (B) Remind his staff to save some files가 정답이다.

06-10은 다음 편지와 이메일에 관한 문제입니다.

10월 15일

[07-A]Lourdes Finch
구매 책임자
[07-A]Serendipity 리조트

Ms. Finch께,

[06]저는 귀사가 12월에 태국에서 개장 예정인 리조트 두 곳의 식료품 공급 ⟳

회사를 찾고 있다는 광고를 최근에 *Hospitality Asia*지에서 우연히 발견했습니다. [07-C]Singha 식품 회사는 싱가포르에 위치한 회사이며 방대한 종류의 신선 식품, 정육 및 유제품을 동남아시아 전역에 판매합니다. [06/08]우리는 귀사와 제휴를 시작하는 것에 매우 관심이 있습니다.

[07-A]Singha 식품 회사는 훌륭한 명성을 지니고 있으며 이미 귀사와 비슷한 다수의 고객과 함께 일하고 있습니다. 우리는 귀사의 리조트에 다양한 수입 식품 및 음료뿐만 아니라 가장 신선한 지역 특산품도 공급할 수 있습니다. 현재 우리가 공급하는 모든 상품들을 포함한 카탈로그를 동봉했습니다. 목록에 포함되지 않은 품목을 원하신다면, 기꺼이 찾아드릴 것입니다.

저는 3일 후에 방콕을 방문할 예정이므로 귀하와 만나 가능성 있는 제휴에 대해 논의할 수 있다면 기쁘겠습니다. [09]10월 18일부터 21일 사이에 시간이 되시는지 알려주시기 바랍니다. alchan@singhafoods.com으로 저에게 연락하시면 됩니다.

빠른 시일 내에 소식을 들을 수 있기를 기대합니다.

Alexis Chan 드림
영업부 사원
Singha 식품 회사

come across 우연히 발견하다, ~와 마주치다   **supplier** n. 공급 회사
vast adj. 방대한   **dairy products** 유제품   **reputation** n. 명성
numerous adj. 다수의, 수많은   **import** v. 수입하다

수신   Alexis Chan <alchan@singhafoods.com>
발신   Lourdes Finch <lourdesf@serendipityresorts.com>
제목   귀하의 문의 사항
날짜   10월 17일

Ms. Chan께,

공급업체를 찾는 자사 광고에 응답해주셔서 감사합니다. 저와 자사 직원들은 귀사의 카탈로그를 보고 귀사가 공급하는 식품의 다양성과 품질에 깊은 인상을 받았습니다. [10-A]자사는 신선한 과일, 야채, 생선과 정육, 그리고 유제품을 포함하는 현지 제품들의 공급업체는 이미 찾았습니다. 하지만, [10-D]수입 식품 및 음료를 귀사에서 공급해 주는 것에 대해서 귀하와 만나 논의하는 데 관심이 있습니다.

[09]귀하께서 방문하시는 첫날은 제가 선약이 꽉 차 있기에, 둘째 날에 만날 수 있다면 기쁘겠습니다. 귀하를 Gautama로 446-D번지에 있는 자사 본사에서 12시 30분에 만나는 것으로 임시 약속을 정하겠습니다. 이때가 귀하께 괜찮으신지 알려주시기 바랍니다.

귀하와 이야기하기를 고대하며, 이것이 장기적이고 유익한 사업 제휴의 시작이기를 기대합니다.

Lourdes Finch 드림
구매 책임자
Serendipity 리조트

impressed adj. 깊은 인상을 받은   **tentative** adj. 임시의, 잠정적인
headquarters n. 본사

06 주제/목적 찾기 문제

문제   편지는 왜 쓰였는가?

(A) 호텔 체인의 일자리에 지원하기 위해
(B) 출판물에 게재된 광고에 응답하기 위해
(C) 물품 배달의 상태에 대해 문의하기 위해
(D) 이용 가능한 상품에 대한 정보를 요청하기 위해

해설   편지가 쓰인 목적을 묻는 목적 찾기 문제이므로 편지의 내용을 확인한다. 첫 번째 지문인 편지의 'I recently came across an advertisement in *Hospitality Asia* which indicated that your company is looking for food suppliers'(1문단 1번째 줄)에서 식료품 공급 회사를 찾고 있다는 광고를 *Hospitality Asia*지에서 우연히 발견했다고 한 후, 'We would be very interested in entering a partnership with you.'(1문단 4번째 줄)에서 Serendipity 리조트와 제휴를 시작하는 것에 매우 관심이 있다고 했으므로 (B) To respond to an advertisement in a publication이 정답이다.

Paraphrasing
Hospitality Asia *Hospitality Asia*지 → publication 출판물

07 Not/True 문제

문제 Singha 식품 회사에 대해 언급된 것은?

(A) 여러 숙박 시설과 함께 일한다.
(B) 접대 시설에서의 특별한 행사에 음식을 제공한다.
(C) 본사는 방콕에 위치해 있다.
(D) 아시아 외부 지역으로 사업을 확장하고 있다.

해설 질문의 핵심 어구인 Singha Foods Incorporated에 대해 묻는 Not/True 문제이므로 첫 번째 지문인 Singha 식품 회사 직원이 작성한 편지에서 관련 내용을 확인한다. (A)는 'Singha Foods ~ already have numerous clients similar to your company that we work with.'(2문단 1번째 줄)에서 Singha 식품 회사는 이미 귀사와 비슷한 고객과 함께 일하고 있다고 했고 'Lourdes Finch', 'Serendipity Resorts'(편지 상단)에서 편지 수신자인 Lourdes Finch가 Serendipity 리조트 소속이라고 했으므로 Singha 식품 회사는 Serendipity 리조트와 비슷한 시설들과 함께 일하고 있음을 알 수 있다. 따라서 (A) It works with several accommodation facilities가 정답이다. (B)는 지문에 언급되지 않은 내용이다. (C)는 'Singha Foods Incorporated is a company located in Singapore'(1문단 2번째 줄)에서 Singha 식품 회사는 싱가포르에 위치한 회사라고 했으므로 지문의 내용과 일치하지 않는다. (D)는 지문에 언급되지 않은 내용이다.

Paraphrasing
numerous 다수의 → several 여러 가지의
Resorts 리조트 → accommodation facilities 숙박 시설

어휘 cater v. (행사에) 음식을 제공하다   hospitality adj. 접대용의, 응접용의; n. 환대

08 동의어 찾기 문제

문제 편지에서, 1문단 다섯 번째 줄의 단어 "entering"은 의미상 –와 가장 가깝다.

(A) 끝내는
(B) 가는
(C) 되돌아가는
(D) 시작하는

해설 첫 번째 지문인 편지의 entering을 포함하고 있는 문장 'We would be very interested in entering a partnership with you.'(1문단 4번째 줄)에서 entering이 '(활동·상황 등을) 시작하는'이라는 뜻으로 사용되었다. 따라서 '시작하는'이라는 뜻을 가진 (D) starting이 정답이다.

09 추론 문제   연계

문제 Ms. Finch와 Ms. Chan은 어느 날짜에 만날 것 같은가?

(A) 10월 16일
(B) 10월 18일
(C) 10월 19일
(D) 10월 21일

해설 두 지문의 내용을 종합적으로 확인한 후 추론해서 풀어야 하는 연계 문제이다. 질문의 핵심 어구인 Ms. Finch and Ms. Chan ~ meet에서 Ms. Finch와 Ms. Chan이 만날 것 같은 날짜를 묻고 있으므로 Ms. Chan이 작성한 편지를 먼저 확인한다.
첫 번째 지문인 편지의 'Please let me know if you are free at any time between October 18-21.'(3문단 2번째 줄)에서 10월 18일부터 21일 사이에 시간이 되는지 알려달라고 했으므로 Ms. Chan은 10월 18일부터 21일 사이에 방콕에서 Ms. Finch를 만날 것이라는 첫 번째 단서를 확인할 수 있다. 그런데 Ms. Finch가 Ms. Chan을 만날 날짜가 정확히 제시되지 않았으므로 이메일에서 Ms. Finch가 Ms. Chan을 만날 날짜를 확인한다. 두 번째 지문인 이메일의 'I ~ would be happy to meet with you on the second day.'(2문단 1번째 줄)에서 Ms. Finch가 Ms. Chan의 방콕 방문 두 번째 날에 만나기를 원한다는 두 번째 단서를 확인할 수 있다.
Ms. Chan이 10월 18일부터 21일까지 방콕을 방문할 것이라는 첫 번째 단서와 Ms. Finch는 Ms. Chan이 방콕을 방문한 두 번째 날에 만나기를 원한다는 두 번째 단서를 종합할 때, Ms. Finch와 Ms. Chan은 10월 19일에 만날 것이라는 사실을 추론할 수 있다. 따라서 (C) October 19가 정답이다.

10 Not/True 문제

문제 이메일에서 Serendipity 리조트에 대해 언급된 것은?

(A) 유제품 공급자를 찾고 있다.

(B) 본사에 추가 인력을 채용하고 있다.
(C) 운영 비용을 줄일 방법을 찾고 있다.
(D) 수입품을 구매하려고 계획하고 있다.

해설 질문의 핵심 어구인 Serendipity Resorts에 대해 묻는 Not/True 문제이므로 두 번째 지문인 Serendipity 리조트 직원이 작성한 이메일에서 관련 내용을 확인한다. (A)는 'We have already found suppliers for local items including ~ dairy products.'(1문단 2번째 줄)에서 리조트는 유제품을 포함한 현지 제품의 공급업체를 이미 찾았다고 했으므로 지문의 내용과 일치하지 않는다. (B)와 (C)는 지문에 언급되지 않은 내용이다. (D)는 'we would be interested in meeting with you to discuss your company supplying us with imported foods and beverages'(1문단 4번째 줄)에서 수입 식품 및 음료를 공급받는 것에 대해 논의하는 데 관심이 있다고 했으므로 수입품을 구매하려는 계획을 갖고 있음을 알 수 있다. 따라서 (D) It is planning to purchase imported items가 정답이다.

Paraphrasing
imported foods and beverages 수입 식품 및 음료 → imported items 수입품

11-15는 다음 두 이메일과 일정표에 관한 문제입니다.

수신 Julia Richmond <julr@templetontour.co.nz>
발신 June Perry <jupe@templetontour.co.nz>
제목 새로운 가이드
날짜 11월 1일

안녕하세요 Julia,

[11]저는 방금 Vincent Peale로부터 메시지를 받았고, 오늘 그는 두 달 후에 그만둔다는 통지를 했습니다. 듣기로는 그는 오클랜드에 있는 여행사로부터 일자리 제의를 받았습니다. 그는 자사를 위해 일하는 데 보낸 시간에 매우 만족스러워했지만, 오클랜드가 그의 가족이 사는 곳이기 때문에, 그 제의를 수락했습니다.

우리는 모두 Vincent가 떠나는 것을 보는 것이 슬프겠지만, 우리는 1월과 2월의 관광 성수기를 위해 후임자를 찾아야 합니다. 이 직책을 위해 Robert Phong을 어떻게 생각하십니까? 제가 제대로 기억한다면,[12-B]그는 여러 언어를 구사하는데, 그것은 우리의 몇몇 외국인 고객들에게 큰 도움이 되었습니다. 또한, 그 역할을 맡을 후보자에 대한 다른 제안이 있다면 저에게 알려주시기 바랍니다.

감사합니다!

June Perry

notice n. 계약 해지의 통고, 예고   apparently adv. 듣기로는, 명백히
replacement n. 후임자, 대체   candidate n. 후보자
fill the role 역할을 맡다, 임무를 다하다

수신 June Perry <jupe@templetontour.co.nz>
발신 Julia Richmond <julr@templetontour.co.nz>
제목 회신: 새로운 가이드
날짜 11월 2일

안녕하세요 June,

Vincent가 우리를 떠날 것이라니 유감입니다. 그는 우리 여행사에 있었던 최고의 여행 가이드 중 한 명이며, 저는 그와 함께 일하는 것이 매우 즐거웠습니다.

[13]후임자와 관련하여, Robert는 그 자리에 아주 좋을 것입니다.[12-B]그는 여기 여행사의 인턴이었던 기간 동안 많은 훌륭한 의사소통 및 대인 관계 능력을 보여주었습니다.[13]하지만, 인턴 기간 동안 그는 저에게 대학원에 다닐 생각이라고 말했으며, 그래서 그는 시간이 나지 않을 수도 있습니다. 만일 그렇다면,[13/14]저는 Veronica Santini를 추천하고자 합니다. 그녀는 인턴으로서 한결같이 업무를 잘 수행했으며, 유적지에 대해 아는 것이 많고, 친절한 성품을 지니고 있습니다. 그리고 저는 [14]그녀가 그녀의 현 직책이 요구하는 것보다 더 많은 것을 할 수 있는 능력이 있다고 생각합니다.

Julia

exhibit v. 보이다, 나타내다   interpersonal adj. 대인 관계의
graduate school 대학원   unavailable adj. 시간이 나지 않는, 이용할 수 없는
knowledgeable adj. 아는 것이 많은   site n. 유적지, 장소

	¹⁵⁻ᴬ월요일	화요일	수요일	목요일	금요일	¹⁵⁻ᴬ토요일	¹⁵⁻ᴬ일요일
¹⁴/¹⁵⁻ᴮ반나절 시내 관광	¹⁴Veronica Santini, 오후 2시	¹⁴Veronica Santini, 오후 2시	¹⁵⁻ᴮHarry Dennis, 오전 9시	¹⁴Veronica Santini, 오후 2시	¹⁴Veronica Santini, 오전 9시	¹⁵⁻ᴮ⁄ᴰHarry Dennis, 오전 9시	¹⁴Veronica Santini, 오후 2시
¹⁵⁻ᶜ종일 시내 관광	Harry Dennis, ¹⁵⁻ᶜ오전 10시	Kenneth Albright, 오전 10시	Kenneth Albright, 오전 10시	Harry Dennis, 오전 10시	Kenneth Albright, 오전 10시	¹⁵⁻ᴰVeronica Santini, Kenneth Albright, ¹⁵⁻ᶜ⁄ᴰ오전 10시	Harry Dennis, ¹⁵⁻ᶜ오전 10시

일정에 관해 질문이 있으시다면, 관광 여행 책임자인 Julia Richmond에게 말하세요. 또한, 여러분이 일을 할 수 없는 날짜에 대해서는 예약 담당 사원인 Brenda Lane에게 알려주시기 바랍니다. 직원들은 관광이 시작되기 30분 전에 출발 지점에 도착해야 합니다.

associate n. 사원, (사업·직장) 동료 **departure** n. 출발

11 육하원칙 문제

문제 Ms. Perry는 무엇을 받았다고 말하는가?

(A) 외국인 고객으로부터의 메시지
(B) 견습 프로그램에 관한 문의
(C) 구직자의 이력서
(D) 직원의 사직 통지

해설 Ms. Perry가 무엇(What)을 받았다고 말하는지를 묻는 육하원칙 문제이므로 Ms. Perry가 받은 이메일에서 질문의 핵심 어구인 Ms. Perry say she received와 관련된 내용을 확인한다. 첫 번째 지문인 이메일의 'I ~ got a message from Vincent Peale, and he gave his two months notice'(1문단 1번째 줄)에서 Vincent Peale로부터 메시지를 받았고 그가 두 달 후에 그만둔다는 통지를 했다고 했으므로 (D) An employee's notice of resignation이 정답이다.

어휘 **apprentice** n. 견습, 견습생 **resignation** n. 사직

12 Not/True 문제 연계

문제 Robert Phong에 대해 언급된 것은?

(A) Templeton 여행사의 예약 담당자로 일한다.
(B) Templeton 여행사에서 인턴 기간 동안 외국인 고객들을 상대했다.
(C) 공식적으로 인증받은 여행 가이드가 되기 위해 교육을 받았다.
(D) 오클랜드에 위치한 다른 여행사의 일자리를 수락했다.

해설 두 지문의 내용을 종합해서 풀어야 하는 연계 문제이다. 질문의 핵심 어구인 Robert Phong이 언급된 첫 번째 이메일을 먼저 확인한다.
첫 번째 지문인 이메일의 'he ~ was very helpful for some of our foreign clients'(2문단 3번째 줄)에서 그, 즉 Robert Phong이 우리, 즉 Templeton 여행사의 외국인 고객들에게 큰 도움이 되었다는 첫 번째 단서를 확인할 수 있다. 그런데 어떤 일을 하며 외국인 고객들에게 도움이 되었는지 제시되지 않았으므로 Robert가 언급된 또 다른 이메일에서 관련된 내용을 확인한다. 두 번째 지문인 이메일의 'he was an intern here at the agency'(2문단 2번째 줄)에서 그가 이 여행사, 즉 Templeton 여행사의 인턴이었다는 두 번째 단서를 확인할 수 있다.
Robert Phong이 Templeton 여행사의 외국인 고객들에게 큰 도움이 되었다는 첫 번째 단서와 그가 Templeton 여행사의 인턴이었다는 두 번째 단서를 종합할 때, 그가 Templeton 여행사 인턴 기간 동안 외국인 고객들을 상대했음을 알 수 있다. 따라서 (B) He handled foreign clients during his internship at Templeton Tour Agency가 정답이다. (A), (C), (D)는 지문에 언급되지 않은 내용이다.

13 주제/목적 찾기 문제

문제 두 번째 이메일은 왜 쓰였는가?

(A) 직원 채용 결정에 관한 의견을 제공하기 위해
(B) 인턴직 지원자에 대한 의견을 요청하기 위해
(C) 학업 조건에 대한 질의에 답변하기 위해
(D) 승진 제의에 응답하기 위해

해설 두 번째 이메일이 쓰인 목적을 묻는 목적 찾기 문제이므로 두 번째 이메일의 내용을 확인한다. 두 번째 지문인 이메일의 'Regarding a replacement, Robert would be great in the position.'(2문단 1번째 줄)과 'However,

~ he may be unavailable. If that is the case, I would recommend Veronica Santini.'(2문단 2번째 줄)에서 후임자와 관련하여 Robert가 그 자리에 아주 좋을 것이지만 시간이 나지 않을 수도 있다고 하며, 만일 그렇다면 Veronica Santini를 추천하고자 한다고 했으므로 직원 채용 결정에 관한 의견을 제공하는 이메일임을 알 수 있다. 따라서 (A) To provide opinions on a staffing decision이 정답이다.

어휘 **staffing** n. 직원 채용 **qualification** n. 조건, 자격

14 추론 문제 연계

문제 Veronica Santini에 대해 추론될 수 있는 것은?

(A) 여행 가이드직으로 승진되었다.
(B) 최근에 여행사의 일자리에 지원했다.
(C) 대학원에 다니고 있으므로 시간이 나지 않는다.
(D) Julia Richmond의 개인 비서로 고용되었다.

해설 두 지문의 내용을 종합적으로 확인한 후 추론해서 풀어야 하는 연계 문제이다. 질문의 핵심 어구인 Veronica Santini가 언급된 이메일을 먼저 확인한다.
두 번째 지문인 이메일에서 'I would recommend Veronica Santini'(2문단 4번째 줄)와 'she's capable of doing more than her current position requires'(2문단 5번째 줄)에서 Veronica Santini를 추천하고, 그녀는 그녀의 현 직책이 요구하는 것보다 더 많은 능력이 있다고 생각한다는 첫 번째 단서를 확인할 수 있다. 그런데 Veronica Santini가 어떤 자리에 추천되었는지 제시되지 않았으므로 일정표에서 관련 내용을 확인한다. 세 번째 지문인 일정표의 'Tour Guide Work Schedule'(제목)과 '1/2 day city tour, Veronica Santini'(표 2행)에서 Veronica Santini가 여행 가이드로서 반나절 시내 관광을 담당하고 있다는 두 번째 단서를 확인할 수 있다.
Veronica Santini를 추천하고, 그녀는 그녀의 현 직책이 요구하는 것보다 더 많은 능력이 있다고 생각한다는 첫 번째 단서와 Veronica Santini가 여행 가이드로서 반나절 시내 관광을 담당하고 있다는 두 번째 단서를 종합할 때, Veronica Santini가 여행 가이드직으로 승진되었다는 사실을 추론할 수 있다. 따라서 (A) She was promoted to a tour guide position이 정답이다.

어휘 **promote** v. 승진하다 **assistant** n. 비서, 조수

15 Not/True 문제

문제 Templeton 여행사에 대해 사실이 아닌 것은?

(A) 일주일 내내 관광 여행 프로그램을 운영한다.
(B) Harry Dennis에게 종일 관광만을 배정했다.
(C) 오전 10시에 관광객들을 위한 일일 여행을 제공한다.
(D) 토요일에 가장 많은 시내 관광 여행을 운영할 것이다.

해설 질문의 핵심 어구인 Templeton Tour Agency에 대해 묻는 Not/True 문제이므로 Templeton 여행사가 언급된 일정표에서 관련 내용을 확인한다. (A)는 세 번째 지문인 일정표의 'Monday ~ Sunday'(표 1행)에서 일주일 내내 관광 여행 프로그램을 운영한다는 것을 알 수 있으므로 지문의 내용과 일치한다. (B)는 '1/2 day city tour'(표 2행 1열)와 'Harry Dennis, 9 a.m.'(표 2행 4열, 표 2행 7열)에서 Harry Dennis가 반나절 시내 관광도 담당하고 있다는 것을 알 수 있으므로 지문의 내용과 일치하지 않는다. 따라서 (B) It has assigned only full-day tours to Harry Dennis가 정답이다. (C)는 'Full day city tour'(표 3행 1열)와 '10 a.m.'(표 3행 2열 - 8열)에서 종일 시내 관광이 매일 오전 10시에 시작한다고 했으므로 지문의 내용과 일치한다. (D)는 'Saturday'(표 1행 7열)와 'Harry Dennis, 9 a.m., Veronica Santini, Kenneth Albright, 10 a.m.'(표 3행 7열)에서 다른 요일과 달리 세 번의 관광 여행이 있다는 것을 알 수 있으므로 지문의 내용과 일치한다.

어휘 **assign** v. 배정하다, 부여하다 **excursion** n. 여행

16-20은 다음 두 이메일과 영수증에 관한 문제입니다.

¹⁶저는 반품하는 것과 관련하여 몇 가지 질문이 있습니다. ¹⁷/¹⁸ᴬ저는 지난 토요일 귀사의 연말 할인 행사 때 Trenton 지점에서 스웨터를 구입했으며, 이곳 Cherry Hill에 있는 동네 Glitter N' Gloss 매장에서 그것을 반품하고 싶습니다.

저는 또한 제가 환불을 받을 수 있는지, 아니면 물품을 다른 것으로 교환해야만 하는지 궁금했습니다. ¹⁷저는 그것을 신용카드로 결제했으며 원본 영수증을 가지고 있습니다. 저에게 주어진 선택지가 무엇인지 알려주시기 바랍니다. 감사합니다.

Macy Plummer 드림

branch n. 지점 **year-end sale** 연말 할인 행사 **return** v. 반품하다, 환불하다
local adj. 동네의, 지역의 **wonder** v. 궁금해하다 **refund** n. 환불
exchange v. 교환하다 **option** n. 선택지, 선택

수신: Macy Plummer <m.plummer@flexmail.com>
발신: 고객 서비스 <help@glitterngloss.com>
제목: 회신: 저의 구매
날짜: 1월 5일

Ms. Plummer께,

이메일을 보내주셔서 감사합니다. 귀하의 질문에 답변드리자면, 물품이 어디에서 처음 구매되었는지와 상관없이, 심지어 온라인에서 구매되었더라도 ¹⁷저희는 고객들이 어느 매장에서든지 물품을 반품할 수 있게 허용합니다. 귀하께서는 구입 후 30일 이내에 원본 영수증을 제시하시기만 하면 됩니다. 귀하의 편의를 위해, 아래에 몇 가지 다른 주요 정책을 게시하였습니다.

- ²⁰수영복, 화장품, 그리고 상품권은 반품될 수 없다.
- ¹⁷모든 환불은 원래의 결제 형태로 이뤄질 것이다.
- 온라인 구매의 경우, ¹⁸ᴮ물품에 결함이 있다고 판명되는 경우를 제외하고, 환불에 배송비가 포함되지 않을 것이다.

제가 귀하의 모든 질문에 답변했기를 바랍니다. ¹⁹저희는 귀하의 고객 서비스 경험에 관한 몇 가지 질문들을 이메일로 보낼 수도 있습니다. 이 설문지를 받으시면, 작성하시고 저희에게 돌려보내 주십시오. 감사합니다.

Keith Nance 드림
Glitter N' Gloss 고객 서비스 담당자

allow v. 허용하다 **regardless of** ~과 상관없이 **originally** adv. 처음에, 원래
present v. 제시하다, 보여주다 **post** v. 게시하다, 올리다; n. 게시물
guideline n. 정책, 지침 **cosmetics** n. 화장품 **payment** n. 결제
faulty adj. 결함이 있는 **questionnaire** n. 설문지 **fill out** 작성하다

	Glitter N' Gloss		
	구매해주셔서 감사합니다!		
	Trenton, 뉴저지주		

| 날짜: 12월 30일 | | 시간: 오후 4시 16분 | |
| 회원 번호: (해당 없음) | | | |

²⁰품목	수량	가격
해변용 샌들	1	6.40달러
스웨터	1	14.99달러
헤어밴드	3	2.49달러
²⁰립스틱	1	4.90달러
수건 세트	1	12.00달러
지불: xxxxxxxxxxxx5437		
소계		40.78달러
세금		2.38달러
총계		43.16달러

¹⁸ᴰ저희는 모든 Glitter N' Gloss 회원들에게 특별한 할인과 독점적인 혜택을 제공합니다! 관심이 있으시다면, www.glitterngloss.com을 방문하세요.

applicable adj. 해당되는, 적용되는 **exclusive** adj. 독점적인 **benefit** n. 혜택

16 육하원칙 문제

문제   Ms. Plummer는 무엇과 관련하여 도움이 필요한가?

(A) 특정 가게 찾기
(B) 반품 정책 알기
(C) 매장의 할인 판매 날짜 알기
(D) 다른 사이즈의 물품 찾기

해설   Ms. Plummer가 무엇(What)과 관련하여 도움이 필요한지를 묻는 육하원칙 문제이므로 Ms. Plummer가 작성한 이메일에서 질문의 핵심 어구인 Ms. Plummer need assistance with와 관련된 내용을 확인한다. 첫 번째 지문인 이메일의 'I have a couple of questions about making a return.' (1문단 1번째 줄)에서 자신, 즉 Ms. Plummer가 반품하는 것과 관련하여 몇 가지 질문이 있다고 했으므로 (B) Understanding a return policy가 정답이다.

어휘   **assistance** n. 도움 **locate** v. 찾다 **particular** adj. 특정한
understand v. 알다, 이해하다 **learn** v. 알다, 배우다

17 추론 문제 연계

문제   Ms. Plummer에 대해 암시되는 것은?

(A) 주로 주말에 쇼핑한다.
(B) Glitter N' Gloss의 단골손님이다.
(C) 최근에 다른 도시로부터 이사했다.
(D) 그녀의 신용카드로 환불 받을 자격이 있다.

해설   두 지문의 내용을 종합적으로 확인한 후 추론해서 풀어야 하는 연계 문제이다. 질문의 핵심 어구인 Ms. Plummer가 작성한 첫 번째 이메일을 먼저 확인한다.
첫 번째 지문인 이메일의 'I bought a sweater ~ last Saturday'(1문단 1번째 줄)와 'I paid for it with a credit card and have the original receipt.'(2문단 2번째 줄)에서 자신, 즉 Ms. Plummer가 지난 토요일에 스웨터를 구입했고, 그것을 신용카드로 결제했으며 관련 원본 영수증을 가지고 있다는 첫 번째 단서를 확인할 수 있다. 그런데 지난 토요일에 스웨터를 신용카드로 결제했으며 원본 영수증을 가지고 있다는 것이 무엇을 받을 자격을 의미하는지가 제시되지 않았으므로 두 번째 이메일에서 관련 내용을 확인한다. 두 번째 지문인 이메일의 'we do allow customers to return items to any store ~. You only need to present the original receipt within 30 days of a purchase'(1문단 1번째 줄)에서 저희, 즉 Glitter N' Gloss는 고객들이 어느 매장에서든지 물품을 반품할 수 있게 허용하고, 환불을 위해서는 구입 후 30일 이내에 원본 영수증을 제시하기만 하면 되며, 'All refunds will be in the original form of payment'(2문단 2번째 줄)에서 모든 환불은 원래의 결제 형태로 이뤄질 것이라는 두 번째 단서를 확인할 수 있다.
Ms. Plummer가 스웨터를 지난 토요일에 신용카드로 구입했으며 원본 영수증을 가지고 있다는 첫 번째 단서와 환불을 위해서는 구입 후 30일 이내에 원본 영수증을 제시해야 하며 환불은 원래 결제 형태로 이뤄질 것이라는 두 번째 단서를 종합할 때, Ms. Plummer는 그녀의 신용카드로 환불 받을 자격이 있음을 확인할 수 있다. 따라서 (D) She is entitled to a refund on her credit card가 정답이다.

어휘   **frequent customer** 단골손님 **be entitled to** ~할 자격이 있다

18 Not/True 문제

문제   Glitter N' Gloss에 대해 사실이 아닌 것은?

(A) 한 개보다 많은 매장을 가지고 있다.
(B) 때때로 배송비를 환불해준다.
(C) 최근에 온라인 매장을 열었다.
(D) 멤버십 프로그램을 운영한다.

해설   질문의 핵심 어구인 Glitter N' Gloss에 대해 묻는 Not/True 문제이므로 Glitter N' Gloss가 언급된 이메일들과 영수증 모두에서 관련된 내용을 확인한다. (A)는 첫 번째 지문인 이메일의 'I bought a sweater at your Trenton branch ~, and I'd like to return it to ~ Glitter N' Gloss store here in Cherry Hill.'(1문단 1번째 줄)에서 Glitter N' Gloss가 Trenton 지점과 Cherry Hill 지점을 포함하여 1개보다 많은 매장을 가지고 있다는 것을 알 수 있으므로 지문의 내용과 일치한다. (B)는 두 번째 지문인 이메일의 'refunds will not include the cost of shipping, except when items are found to be faulty'(2문단 3번째 줄)에서 물품에 결함이 있다고 판명되는 경우에는, 환불에 배송비가 포함될 수 있다는 것을 알 수 있으므로 지문의 내용과 일치한다. (C)는 지문에 언급되지 않은 내용이다. 따라서 (C) It recently launched an online store가 정답이다. (D)는 세 번째 지문

인 영수증의 'We offer special discounts and exclusive benefits to all Glitter N' Gloss members!'(영수증 하단 1번째 줄)에서 Glitter N' Gloss가 회원들에게 특별한 할인과 독점적인 혜택을 제공한다는 것을 알 수 있으므로 지문의 내용과 일치한다.

어휘 on occasion 때때로 operate v. 운영하다

19 육하원칙 문제

문제 Mr. Nance에 따르면, Ms. Plummer는 무엇을 받을 것이라고 예상할 수 있는가?
(A) 상품권
(B) 제품 카탈로그
(C) 설문조사 요청
(D) 무료 선물

해설 Mr. Nance에 따르면 Ms. Plummer가 무엇을(What) 받을 것이라고 예상할 수 있는지를 묻는 육하원칙 문제이므로 Mr. Nance가 작성한 두 번째 이메일에서 관련 내용을 확인한다. 두 번째 지문인 이메일의 'We may e-mail you some questions about your customer service experience. If you receive this questionnaire, please fill it out and return it to us.'(3문단 1번째 줄)에서 귀하, 즉 Ms. Plummer의 고객 서비스 경험에 관한 몇 가지 질문들을 이메일로 보낼 수 있으며, 이 설문지를 받으면, 작성하여 돌려달라고 했으므로 (C) A survey request가 정답이다.

Paraphrasing
questionnaire 설문지 → survey 설문조사

어휘 request n. 요청; v. 요청하다

20 육하원칙 문제 연계

문제 영수증의 어느 품목이 Glitter N' Gloss로 반품될 수 없는가?
(A) 스웨터
(B) 헤어밴드
(C) 립스틱
(D) 수건 세트

해설 두 지문의 내용을 종합해서 풀어야 하는 연계 문제이다. 질문의 핵심 어구인 item on the receipt cannot be returned to Glitter N' Gloss에서 영수증의 어느(Which) 품목이 Glitter N' Gloss로 반품될 수 없는지를 묻고 있으므로 반품 정책이 언급된 두 번째 이메일을 먼저 확인한다.
두 번째 지문인 이메일의 'Swimwear, cosmetics, and gift cards may not be returned'(2문단 1번째 줄)에서 수영복, 화장품, 그리고 상품권은 반품될 수 없다는 첫 번째 단서를 확인할 수 있다. 그런데 영수증에 어느 품목이 있는지 제시되지 않았으므로 영수증에서 관련 내용을 확인한다. 세 번째 지문인 영수증의 'Item'(영수증 6번째 줄), 'Lipstick'(영수증 10번째 줄)에서 립스틱이 구매되었다는 두 번째 단서를 확인할 수 있다.
수영복, 화장품, 그리고 상품권은 반품될 수 없다는 첫 번째 단서와 립스틱이 구매되었다는 두 번째 단서를 종합할 때, 화장품인 립스틱은 반품될 수 없다는 것을 알 수 있다. 따라서 (C) The lipstick이 정답이다.

Paraphrasing
lipstick 립스틱 → cosmetics 화장품

Chapter 17 양식 연계 지문

예제 해석·해설 p.478

메뉴 & 리뷰 & 이메일

CHEVEUX SOYEUX의 최신 모발 관리!
* 윤기 강화 (15달러)   * 집중 컨디셔닝 (20달러)
* 두피 관리 (60달러)   * 중화 컨디셔닝 (40달러)

treatment n. 관리 shine n. 윤(기), 빛 enhance v. 강화하다
scalp n. 두피 corrective adj. (약 등이) 중화하는

후기   Cheryl Aiden(chai@everymail.com) 작성 ○

Cheveux에서의 최근 방문에서, 저는 모발 관리에 20달러만을 썼고 그 결과가 꽤 우수하다는 것을 알게 되었습니다. 미용실의 다른 모발 관리도 도움이 되며 품질이 좋다는 것 역시 알게 되었습니다. 이것들을 매우 추천합니다.

remarkable adj. 우수한, 놀라운 good value 품질이 좋은

수신: Cheryl Aiden <chai@everymail.com>
발신: <clientservices@cheveuxsoyeux.com>

저희 웹사이트에 Cheveux Soyeux에 대한 리뷰를 써주셔서 감사합니다. 그렇게 함으로써, 귀하께서는 150달러의 상품권을 받는 것에 자동으로 응모되었으며, 귀하께서 타게 되었습니다. 저희가 우편으로 이것을 보내드릴 수 있도록 주소를 알려주시길 바랍니다.

draw n. 추첨 gift card 상품권

문제 필자는 어떤 종류의 서비스에 대해 비용을 지불했는가?
(A) 윤기 강화
(B) 집중 컨디셔닝
(C) 두피 관리
(D) 중화 컨디셔닝

해설 **육하원칙 문제** 두 지문의 내용을 종합해서 풀어야 하는 연계 문제이다. 질문의 핵심 어구인 the writer pay for에서 필자가 어떤(What) 종류의 서비스에 대해 비용을 지불했는지를 묻고 있으므로 필자가 작성한 리뷰를 먼저 확인한다.
두 번째 지문인 리뷰의 'I spent ~ $20 on my hair treatment'에서 필자가 모발 관리에 20달러를 썼다는 첫 번째 단서를 확인할 수 있다. 그런데 20달러짜리 모발 관리가 무엇인지 제시되지 않았으므로 첫 번째 지문인 메뉴에서 20달러인 서비스를 확인한다. 메뉴의 'Deep conditioning ($20)'에서 집중 컨디셔닝이 20달러라는 두 번째 단서를 확인할 수 있다.
리뷰를 작성한 필자가 모발 관리에 20달러를 썼다는 첫 번째 단서와 집중 컨디셔닝이 20달러라는 두 번째 단서를 종합할 때, 필자가 비용을 지불한 서비스는 집중 컨디셔닝임을 알 수 있다. 따라서 (B) Deep conditioning이 정답이다.

Hackers Practice p.479

유형 연습
01 (C)   02 (B)   03 (B)   04 (A)

01-02 전단지 & 이메일

Code Sources 인터넷 서비스, 1776번지 Olsen가 (전화번호) 555-9978
빠르고, 효과적이며, 믿을 수 있습니다!
늘 고장 난 것처럼 형편 없는 인터넷 연결에 지치십니까? 그렇다면 Code Sources 인터넷 서비스보다 멀리서 찾지 마십시오! 우리는 직장과 가정 모두에 초고속 인터넷 연결을 제공해 드립니다. 다운로드는 빠르고 쉬우며, 보안 시스템은 귀하의 컴퓨터를 보호할 수 있도록 도와 드립니다. [01]일반, 기업 및 프리미엄 패키지에 대한 모든 정보를 원하시면 www.codesourcesinternet.com을 방문하십시오. [02]6월 중에 프리미엄 서비스를 신청하실 때 이 전단지를 제시하시고, 첫 달 요금에서 50퍼센트를 할인받으십시오!

dependable adj. 믿을 수 있는 security n. 보안
sign up for ~을 신청하다, 가입하다

수신 <customerservice@codesourceinternet.com>
발신 Ellen Delain <edelain@shopsmart.com>

담당자께,

저는 지난달 제 가게에 인터넷 서비스를 신청했고 인터넷 연결의 속도와 신뢰성에 매우 만족해 왔습니다. 그런데, 어제 첫 청구서를 받아보니 전액이 청구되었습니다. [02]귀사의 전단지는 제가 첫 달에는 요금의 반값만 지불하면 된다고 명시했습니다. 따라서, 저는 8월까지 정상 요금을 지불하지 않아야 하는데, [02]제 패키지가 할인을 받을 수 있는 자격을 주기 때문입니다. 오류가 있었다면 제게 알려주시기 바랍니다.

Ellen Delain

dependability n. 신뢰성 qualify v. ~에게 자격을 주다, 권한을 주다

---

01 육하원칙 문제

문제 웹사이트에서 찾을 수 있는 것은 무엇인가?

(A) 가입 신청서
(B) 판매 대리점 목록
(C) 패키지에 대한 설명

해설 웹사이트에서 찾을 수 있는 것이 무엇인지(What)를 묻는 육하원칙 문제이므로 질문의 핵심 어구인 the Web site가 언급된 전단지를 확인한다. 첫 번째 지문인 전단지의 'Visit www.codesourcesinternet.com for full details on our ~ packages.'(3번째 줄)에서 패키지에 대한 모든 정보를 원하면 www.codesourcesinternet.com을 방문하라고 했으므로 (C) A description of packages가 정답이다.

Paraphrasing
full details on ~ packages 패키지에 대한 모든 정보
→ A description of packages 패키지에 대한 설명

어휘 subscription n. 가입, 구독 outlet n. 판매 대리점, 계열 판매점

02 추론 문제 연계

문제 Ms. Delain에 대해 암시되는 것은?

(A) 가입을 취소하고 싶어 한다.
(B) 프리미엄 서비스에 가입했다.
(C) 대금 청구서를 받지 않았다.

해설 두 지문의 내용을 종합적으로 확인한 후 추론해서 풀어야 하는 연계 문제이다. 질문의 핵심 어구인 Ms. Delain이 작성한 이메일을 먼저 확인한다.
두 번째 지문인 이메일의 'Your flyer indicated that I would only pay half the fee for the first month.'(3번째 줄)에서 첫 달에는 요금의 반값만 지불하면 된다고 전단지에 명시되어 있었다고 한 후, 'my package qualifies me for a discount'(4번째 줄)에서 자신의 패키지가 할인을 받을 수 있는 자격을 준다고 했으므로 자신, 즉 Ms. Delain이 신청한 패키지는 첫 달에 요금에서 반값을 할인받을 수 있다고 전단지에 명시되어 있다는 첫 번째 단서를 확인할 수 있다. 그런데 Ms. Delain이 신청한 패키지가 제시되지 않았으므로 전단지에서 할인이 적용되는 패키지를 확인한다. 첫 번째 지문인 전단지의 'Present this flyer when you sign up for our premium service during the month of June, and receive 50 percent off your first bill!'(4번째 줄)에서 6월 중에 프리미엄 서비스를 신청할 때 전단지를 제시하면 첫 달 요금에서 50퍼센트를 할인받을 수 있다는 두 번째 단서를 확인할 수 있다.
Ms. Delain이 신청한 패키지는 첫 달 요금에서 반값을 할인받을 수 있다고 전단지에 나와 있다는 첫 번째 단서와 6월 중에 프리미엄 서비스를 신청할 때 전단지를 제시하면 첫 달 요금에서 50퍼센트를 할인받을 수 있다는 두 번째 단서를 종합할 때, Ms. Delain은 프리미엄 서비스에 가입했다는 사실을 추론할 수 있다. 따라서 (B) She subscribed for the premium service가 정답이다.

Paraphrasing
sign up for 신청하다 → subscribed for ~에 가입했다

어휘 subscribe v. 가입하다, 구독하다 billing statement 대금 청구서

03-04 일정표 & 기사

Fountainview 영화제
9월 12-15일에 Powerhouse 극장에서

영화 상영:
A Time of Passion, 9월 12일, 오후 8시*
04*The Summer Queen*, 9월 13일, 오후 7시*
Danger Dolls, 9월 14일, 오후 8시
Over the Hill, 9월 15일, 오후 9시*

*영화 상영 이후에 영화 감독과 함께 하는 질의 응답 시간이 이어질 것입니다.

screening n. (영화) 상영 **question and answer period** 질의 응답 시간

유망한 영화감독인 03-B Melanie Hayes는 San Pedro 영화사의 최신작인 *Bridge to Heaven*을 감독하도록 선발되었다. 그 감독은 Fountainview 영화제의 토론 시간에 그녀의 새로운 프로젝트에 대해 이야기했다. "저는 이 영화에 대해 매우 신이 나 있습니다. 우리는 2주 내로 작업에 착수할 예정입니다."라고 그녀는 말했다. 04 Hayes는 그녀의 영화인 *The Summer Queen*을 상영

하기 위해 영화제에 참석했는데, 이 작품은 비평적 그리고 경제적 성공을 모두 이루었다.

up-and-coming adj. 유망한 **slate** v. (일자리 등에) 선발하다 **work on** 착수하다

03 Not/True 문제

문제 Ms. Hayes에 대해 언급된 것은?

(A) 이전에도 영화제에서 그녀의 영화를 상영한 적이 있다.
(B) 새로운 영화를 감독할 예정이다.
(C) 영화 상 수상자였다.

해설 질문의 핵심 어구인 Ms. Hayes에 대해 묻는 Not/True 문제이므로 두 번째 지문인 Ms. Hayes가 언급된 기사에서 관련 내용을 확인한다. (A)는 지문에 언급되지 않은 내용이다. (B)는 'Melanie Hayes has been slated to direct San Pedro Studio's newest production'(1번째 줄)에서 Melanie Hayes는 San Pedro 영화사의 최신작을 감독하도록 선발되었다고 했으므로 지문의 내용과 일치한다. 따라서 (B) She is scheduled to direct a new film이 정답이다. (C)는 지문에 언급되지 않은 내용이다.

Paraphrasing
been slated to ~ ~하기로 선발되었다 → is scheduled to~ ~하기로 예정되다
newest production 최신 작품 → new film 새로운 영화

04 육하원칙 문제 연계

문제 영화제 동안 Ms. Hayes의 영화는 몇 시에 상영되었는가?

(A) 7시에
(B) 8시에
(C) 9시에

해설 두 지문의 내용을 종합해서 풀어야 하는 연계 문제이다. 질문의 핵심 어구인 Ms. Hayes' film에서 Ms. Hayes의 영화가 몇 시(what time)에 상영되었는지를 묻고 있으므로 Ms. Hayes의 영화가 언급된 기사를 먼저 확인한다.
두 번째 지문인 기사의 'Hayes was at the festival showing her film *The Summer Queen*'(4번째 줄)에서 Hayes는 그녀의 영화인 *The Summer Queen*을 상영하기 위해 영화제에 참석했다고 했으므로 Fountainview 영화제에서 상영된 Ms. Hayes의 영화가 *The Summer Queen*이라는 첫 번째 단서를 확인할 수 있다. 그런데 *The Summer Queen*이 몇 시에 상영되었는지 제시되지 않았으므로 일정표에서 상영 시간을 확인한다. 첫 번째 지문인 일정표의 '*The Summer Queen* ~ 7 P.M.'(4번째 줄)에서 *The Summer Queen*이 오후 7시에 상영되었다는 두 번째 단서를 확인할 수 있다.
Fountainview 영화제에서 상영된 Ms. Hayes의 영화는 *The Summer Queen*이라는 첫 번째 단서와 *The Summer Queen*은 오후 7시에 상영되었다는 두 번째 단서를 종합할 때, 영화제 동안 Ms. Hayes의 영화는 오후 7시에 상영되었다는 것을 알 수 있다. 따라서 (A) At 7 o'clock이 정답이다.

Hackers Test p.480

01 (B)	02 (D)	03 (C)	04 (B)	05 (A)
06 (B)	07 (B)	08 (D)	09 (A)	10 (C)
11 (C)	12 (B)	13 (D)	14 (B)	15 (B)
16 (C)	17 (B)	18 (C)	19 (D)	20 (C)

01-05는 다음 송장과 이메일에 관한 문제입니다.

Big Wheels
928번지 Grandview가
피츠버그, 펜실베이니아주 15122

거래 번호: 78954
날짜: 6월 5일
이름: Vince Morgan

04품목	04품목 코드	수량	가격
02-D자전거타기용 셔츠	ST3110	3	49.98달러
물병	QK1932	2	11.98달러
03선글라스	OJ3821	1	0369.99달러
헬멧	SJ0503	1	89.99달러
02-D/04자전거타기용 반바지	04HW1027	1	20.10달러
자전거 자물쇠	YB1991	1	15.25달러
		02-A합계:	257.29달러

한 곳에서 자전거 액세서리와 의류를 모두 살 수 있는 상점인 Big Wheels에서 구매해 주셔서 감사합니다. 상자에 들어 있는 송장과 비교하여 모든 상품을 확인해 주시기 바랍니다. 또한, ^{01-C}운송 중에 어떠한 것이라도 손상되었다면, 저희 직원 중 한 명에게 555-7273으로 바로 전화하시거나 service@bigwheels.net으로 메시지를 보내 주시기 바랍니다. 전화하실 때 거래 번호를 갖고 계시거나 귀하의 이메일에 거래 번호를 포함해 주시기 바랍니다.

Big Wheels는 모든 상품의 품질을 보증합니다. ^{01-A/01-B}만약 어떤 이유에서든 구매품에 만족하지 않으신다면, 30일 이내로 반품하실 수 있습니다. ^{01-B}상점 포인트나 교환이 제공될 것입니다. ^{01-D}반드시 모든 구매품들을 본래 포장에 넣어 돌려 보내 주시기 바랍니다.

transaction n. 거래 one-stop 한 곳에서 다 살 수 있는
apparel n. 의류, 의복 merchandise n. 상품
guarantee v. 품질 보증을 하다, 보장하다; n. 애프터서비스, (제품의) 보증서
original adj. 본래의 packaging n. 포장

수신: 고객 서비스, Big Wheels <cservice@bigwheels.com>
발신: Vince Morgan <v.morgan@znet.com>
제목: 최근 배송 주문서.word
날짜: 6월 5일

신속한 서비스에 감사드립니다. 저는 오늘 아침에 ^{02-C}저의 주문품(78954번)을 받았는데, 저의 구매품과 관련해서 몇 가지 문제가 있습니다. 첫 번째로, ⁰³선글라스에 대해 금액이 청구되었다는 사실을 알아 차렸습니다. 사실, 그 물품은 배송 중에 손상되었던 이전 구매품에 대한 교체품이었으므로, 저는 이것에 대해 청구되어야 한다고 생각하지 않습니다. 게다가, 저는 노란 헬멧을 요청했는데, 그것은 도착하지 않았습니다. ⁰⁴또한, 자전거타기용 반바지가 잘못된 사이즈로 왔습니다. 저는 스몰을 주문했는데, 라지를 받았습니다. 올바른 상품들을 가능한 한 빨리 보내 주신다면 감사하겠습니다. 귀사의 편의를 위해 제 주문서 사본을 첨부합니다. ⁰⁵이전에는 귀사와 이런 문제가 있었던 적이 없었으며, 이 오류들을 즉시 바로잡아 주신다면 감사하겠습니다. 빨리 응답해 주시기 바랍니다.

Vince Morgan 드림

speedy adj. 신속한, 빠른 replacement n. 교체품, 대체품
bill v. (대금을) 청구하다 fix v. 바로잡다

01 Not/True 문제

문제 송장에 언급되지 않은 것은?
(A) 어떤 물품이라도 구매 한 달 이내에 반품될 수 있다.
(B) 구매품에 만족하지 않는 고객은 현금 환불을 받을 수 있다.
(C) 물품 손상을 알리기 위해서 직원에게 연락할 수 있다.
(D) 반품되는 구매품들은 본래 상자에 넣어 보내져야 한다.

해설 송장에 대해 묻는 Not/True 문제이다. 이 문제는 질문에 핵심 어구가 없으므로 각 보기와 관련된 내용을 첫 번째 지문인 송장에서 확인한다. (A)는 'If for any reason you are not pleased with your purchase, you may return it within 30 days.'(2문단 1번째 줄)에서 구매품에 만족하지 않는다면 30일 이내로 반품할 수 있다고 했으므로 지문의 내용과 일치한다. (B)는 'If for any reason you are not pleased with your purchase, you may return it within 30 days. A store credit or exchange will be provided.'(2문단 1번째 줄)에서 구매품에 만족하지 않는다면 반품할 수 있고, 상점 포인트 또는 교환이 제공될 것이라고 했으므로 지문의 내용과 일치하지 않는다. 따라서 (B) Customers unsatisfied with a purchase can get a cash refund가 정답이다. (C)는 'if anything was damaged during shipment, call one of our representatives ~ or send us a message'(1문단 2번째 줄)에서 운송 중에 어떠한 것이라도 손상되었다면 직원 중 한 명에게 전화하거나 메시지를 보내라고 했으므로 지문의 내용과 일치한다. (D)는 'Be certain to send back all purchases in their original packaging.'(2문단 2번째 줄)에서 반드시 모든 구매품들을 본래 포장에 넣어 돌려 보내달라고 했으므로 지문의 내용과 일치한다.

Paraphrasing
within 30 days 30일 이내에 → within a month 한 달 이내에

02 Not/True 문제

문제 Mr. Morgan에 대해 언급된 것은?
(A) 구매품에 대해 200달러 미만으로 청구되었다.

(B) 손상된 물품에 대해 상점 포인트를 요구했다.
(C) 주문 번호를 알려 주는 것을 잊었다.
(D) 최근 몇 벌의 운동복을 주문했다.

해설 질문의 핵심 어구인 Mr. Morgan에 대해 묻는 Not/True 문제이므로 Mr. Morgan이 언급된 송장과 Mr. Morgan이 작성한 이메일 모두에서 관련 내용을 확인한다. (A)는 첫 번째 지문인 송장의 'TOTAL: $257.29'(표 8행)에서 주문 합계 총액이 257.29달러라고 했으므로 지문의 내용과 일치하지 않는다. (B)는 지문에 언급되지 않은 내용이다. (C)는 두 번째 지문인 이메일의 'my order (#78954)'(1번째 줄)에서 Mr. Morgan이 자신의 주문 번호가 78954번이라고 했으므로 지문의 내용과 일치하지 않는다. (D)는 첫 번째 지문인 송장의 'Biking shirts'(표 2행 1열)와 'Biking shorts'(표 6행 1열)에서 Mr. Morgan이 자전거타기용 셔츠와 자전거타기용 반바지를 주문했다는 것을 알 수 있으므로 지문의 내용과 일치한다. 따라서 (D) He recently ordered some athletic clothing이 정답이다.

어휘 athletic adj. 운동용의

03 육하원칙 문제 연계

문제 Mr. Morgan에게 얼마가 잘못 청구되었는가?
(A) 49.98달러
(B) 11.98달러
(C) 69.99달러
(D) 89.99달러

해설 두 지문의 내용을 종합해서 풀어야 하는 연계 문제이다. 질문의 핵심 어구인 Mr. Morgan incorrectly charged에서 Mr. Morgan에게 얼마(How much)가 잘못 청구되었는지를 묻고 있으므로, Mr. Morgan이 작성한 이메일을 먼저 확인한다.
두 번째 지문인 이메일의 'I noticed that I was charged for the sunglasses. Actually, this item was a replacement for a previous purchase which was damaged during shipment, so I don't believe I should be billed for it.'(2번째 줄)에서 선글라스에 대해 금액이 청구되었는데, 사실 그 물품은 배송 중에 손상되었던 이전 구매품에 대한 교체품이었기 때문에 이에 대해 청구되어야 한다고 생각하지 않는다고 했으므로 선글라스 가격이 잘못 청구되었다는 첫 번째 단서를 확인할 수 있다. 그런데 선글라스 가격이 제시되지 않았으므로 송장에서 선글라스 가격을 확인한다. 첫 번째 지문인 송장의 'Sunglasses, $69.99'(표 4행)에서 선글라스의 가격이 69.99달러라는 두 번째 단서를 확인할 수 있다.
Mr. Morgan에게 선글라스 가격이 잘못 청구되었다는 첫 번째 단서와 선글라스 가격이 69.99달러라는 두 번째 단서를 종합할 때, Mr. Morgan에게 69.99달러가 잘못 청구되었음을 알 수 있다. 따라서 (C) $69.99가 정답이다.

04 육하원칙 문제 연계

문제 품목 HW1027에 대한 선택 사항으로 무엇이 제공되는가?
(A) 색상
(B) 사이즈
(C) 재질
(D) 브랜드

해설 두 지문의 내용을 종합해서 풀어야 하는 연계 문제이다. 질문의 핵심 어구인 an option for item HW1027에서 품목 HW1027의 선택 사항으로 무엇(What)이 제공되는지를 묻고 있으므로 HW1027이 언급된 송장을 먼저 확인한다.
첫 번째 지문인 송장의 'ITEM, ITEM CODE'(표 1행), 'Biking shorts, HW1027'(표 6행)에서 HW1027이 자전거타기용 반바지 품목에 대한 품목 코드라는 첫 번째 단서를 확인할 수 있다. 그런데 자전거타기용 반바지에 대한 선택 사항으로 무엇이 제공되는지 제시되지 않았으므로 이메일에서 관련 내용을 확인한다. 두 번째 지문인 이메일의 'Also, the biking shorts came in the wrong size. I ordered a small, but I got a large.'(4번째 줄)에서 자전거타기용 반바지가 잘못된 사이즈로 왔으며, 스몰을 주문했는데, 라지를 받았다는 두 번째 단서를 확인할 수 있다.
품목 HW1027이 자전거타기용 반바지라는 첫 번째 단서와 자전거타기용 반바지를 주문할 때 사이즈를 선택할 수 있다는 두 번째 단서를 종합할 때, 품목 HW1027에 대한 선택 사항으로 사이즈가 제공된다는 것을 알 수 있다. 따라서 (B) Size가 정답이다.

어휘 option n. 선택 사항, 선택권 material n. 재질, 직물

05 추론 문제

문제 Big Wheels에 대해 암시되는 것은?

(A) 이전에 Mr. Morgan과 거래를 한 적이 있다.
(B) 오직 웹사이트에서만 물건을 판매한다.
(C) 배송에 대한 요금을 청구한다.
(D) 최근에 신상품 라인을 출시했다.

해설 질문의 핵심 어구인 Big Wheels에 대해 추론하는 문제이므로 Mr. Morgan이 Big Wheels로 보낸 이메일에서 관련 내용을 확인한다. 두 번째 지문인 이메일의 'I've never had problems like this with your company before'(6번째 줄)에서 Mr. Morgan이 이전에 Big Wheels와 이러한 문제가 있었던 적이 없었다고 한 내용을 통해 Big Wheels가 이전에 Mr. Morgan과 거래를 한 적이 있다는 사실을 추론할 수 있다. 따라서 (A) It has done business with Mr. Morgan before가 정답이다.

어휘 **do business with** ~와 거래하다

06-10은 다음 초대장과 기사에 관한 문제입니다.

귀하께서는 공식적으로 제15회 연례 특별 행사 박람회에 초대되었습니다

이는 음식 공급자들, 공급업체들, 행사 계획자들 그리고 다른 파티 관련 산업 전문가들의 제품과 서비스를 소개하기 위한 시의 가장 큰 행사입니다.

07-이 특별 행사 박람회는 이 산업에 특별한 관심을 가진 초대장이 있는 손님들만 올 수 있습니다. 06/07-A/C이 행사는 Daisyland 컨벤션 센터에서 8월 11일 목요일에 시작하여 8월 14일 일요일까지, 매일 오전 11시부터 오후 6시까지 개최될 것입니다.

09첨부된 책자는 A홀에서의 케이크 장식 기술 시연, B홀에서의 쿠키 제빵 도구, C홀에서의 한정된 예산에 따른 파티 기획, 그리고 D홀에서의 독특한 행사 주제 창작을 포함한 모든 계획된 행사에 대한 세부 사항을 제공합니다.

행사에 참석하시려면, 단순히 이 초대장을 입구에서 제시해 주십시오.

모든 분들을 박람회에서 뵙기를 기대합니다.

occasion n. 행사, 특별한 일 **showcase** v. 소개하다, 전시하다; n. 전시, 진열
on a budget 한정된 예산으로

지역 제빵업자 박람회에서 돋보이다
8월 20일

08-D/09Stafford 시내에 있는 Berlin 제과점의 Beth Spellman은 지난 금요일 Daisyland 컨벤션 센터에서 열린 특별 행사 박람회에서 그녀의 우수한 음식 전시품으로 인해 표창을 받았다. 09전국에서 온 업계 전문가들은 09/10-BMs. Spellman의 재미있고 독특한 케이크 시연과 10-B꽃을 주제로 한 로맨틱한 결혼 케이크 디자인을 칭찬했다.

Ms. Spellman의 가게인 Berlin 제과점은 오랫동안 박람회의 공동 후원자였으며 올해 이렇게 놀랄 만한 참가자의 수를 갖게 되어 자랑스러워 했다. 10-AStafford 현지인이자 10-A/C전문 제빵업자 Elinor Spellman의 딸인 10-C/DBeth Spellman은 그녀의 20대에 10-D제빵과 음식 장식을 공부하기 위해 독일과 프랑스로 유학을 갔다. 그녀는 유럽에서 돌아오자마자 배운 것을 이용했고 제빵과 관련한 모친의 유산을 이어 나갔다. 그때부터, 그녀는 시의 매우 다양한 파티와 축하 행사의 음식 공급자가 되었다.

Ms. Spellman은 다음 달에 뉴욕 시의 요리를 배우는 학생들을 위해 열리는 국제 케이크 장식 세미나에서 다시 그녀의 특별한 시연을 제공할 계획이라고 말했다. 그때까지, 시내 Stafford 광장에 있는 Berlin 제과점(www.berlinbakes.com)에서 Ms. Spellman의 맛있는 작품 몇몇을 반드시 골라 보도록 하자.

shine v. 돋보이다, 빛을 내다 **outstanding** adj. 우수한, 뛰어난
commend v. 칭찬하다 **turnout** n. 참가자의 수, 집합
put to use 이용하다, 사용하다 **legacy** n. 유산, 물려준 것
caterer n. 음식 공급자 **culinary** adj. 요리의, 음식의 **creation** n. 작품, 창작

---

06 육하원칙 문제

문제 8월 14일에 무슨 일이 일어날 것인가?

(A) 특별 행사가 시작될 것이다.
(B) 박람회가 끝날 것이다.
(C) 손님 명단이 완성될 것이다.

(D) 센터가 일시적으로 닫을 것이다.

해설 8월 14일에 무슨(What) 일이 일어날 것인지를 묻는 육하원칙 문제이므로 질문의 핵심 어구인 August 14이 언급된 초대장을 확인한다. 첫 번째 지문인 초대장의 'The event will be held ~ beginning Thursday, August 11 through Sunday, August 14'(2문단 2번째 줄)에서 행사는 8월 11일 목요일에 시작하여 8월 14일 일요일까지 개최될 것이라고 했으므로 (B) The expo will come to an end가 정답이다.

어휘 **come to an end** 끝나다 **temporarily** adv. 일시적으로, 임시적으로

07 Not/True 문제

문제 초대장에 포함되지 않은 것은?

(A) 박람회 날짜
(B) 발표자들의 이름
(C) 행사 장소
(D) 참석자들의 유형

해설 초대장에 대해 묻는 Not/True 문제이다. 이 문제는 질문에 핵심 어구가 없으므로 각 보기의 핵심 어구와 관련된 내용을 첫 번째 지문인 초대장에서 확인한다. (A)는 'The event will be held ~ beginning Thursday, August 11 through Sunday, August 14'(2문단 2번째 줄)에서 행사는 8월 11일 목요일에 시작하여 8월 14일 일요일까지 개최될 것이라고 했으므로 지문의 내용과 일치한다. (B)는 지문에 언급되지 않은 내용이다. 따라서 (B) The names of presenters가 정답이다. (C)는 'The event will be held at the Daisyland Convention Center'(2문단 2번째 줄)에서 행사는 Daisyland 컨벤션 센터에서 개최될 것이라고 했으므로 지문의 내용과 일치한다. (D)는 'The Special Events Expo is by invitation only for guests who have a special interest in the industry.'(2문단 1번째 줄)에서 이 특별 행사 박람회는 이 산업에 특별한 관심을 가진 초대장이 있는 손님들만 올 수 있다고 했으므로 지문의 내용과 일치한다.

어휘 **presenter** n. 발표자 **attendee** n. 참석자

08 Not/True 문제

문제 특별 행사 박람회에서 무슨 일이 있었는가?

(A) Berlin 제과점이 장기 후원자로서 영예를 받았다.
(B) 유학생들이 세미나를 개최했다.
(C) Stafford의 시장이 환영 연설을 했다.
(D) Ms. Spellman이 특별한 인정을 받았다.

해설 질문의 핵심 어구인 Special Events Expo에 대해 묻는 Not/True 문제이므로 두 번째 지문인 Special Events Expo가 언급된 기사에서 관련 내용을 확인한다. (A), (B), (C)는 지문에 언급되지 않은 내용이다. (D)는 'Beth Spellman ~ was recognized for her outstanding food displays at the Special Events Expo'(1문단 1번째 줄)에서 Beth Spellman은 이 특별 행사 박람회에서 그녀의 우수한 음식 전시품으로 인해 표창을 받았다고 했으므로 지문의 내용과 일치한다. 따라서 (D) Ms. Spellman received some special recognition이 정답이다.

어휘 **honor** v. 영예를 주다 **host** v. 개최하다 **mayor** n. 시장
recognition n. 인정

09 추론 문제 연계

문제 Ms. Spellman의 시연은 어디에서 일어났을 것 같은가?

(A) A홀
(B) B홀
(C) C홀
(D) D홀

해설 두 지문의 내용을 종합해서 풀어야 하는 연계 문제이다. 질문의 핵심 어구인 Ms. Spellman's demonstration이 언급된 기사를 먼저 확인한다.
두 번째 지문인 기사의 'Beth Spellman ~ was recognized for her outstanding food displays at the Special Events Expo last Friday at the Daisyland Convention Center.'(1문단 1번째 줄)에서 Beth Spellman이 지난 금요일 Daisyland 컨벤션 센터에서 열린 특별 행사 박람회에서 그녀의 우수한 음식 전시품으로 인해 표창을 받았다고 한 후, 'Industry experts from around the country commended Ms. Spellman's ~ cake presentations'(1문단 4번째 줄)에서 전국에서 온

업계 전문가들이 Ms. Spellman의 케이크 시연을 칭찬했다는 첫 번째 단서를 확인할 수 있다. 그런데 그녀의 시연이 어디에서 일어났는지 제시되지 않았으므로 초대장에서 관련 내용을 확인한다. 첫 번째 지문인 초대장의 'The attached brochure gives details on all planned events, including demonstrations on cake decoration techniques in Hall A'(3문단 1번째 줄)에서 첨부된 책자는 A홀에서의 케이크 장식 기술 시연을 포함한 모든 계획된 행사에 대한 세부 사항을 제공한다는 두 번째 단서를 확인할 수 있다. Ms. Spellman이 지난 금요일 Daisyland 컨벤션 센터에서 열린 특별 행사 박람회에서 우수한 음식 전시품으로 인해 표창을 받았고, 업계 전문가들이 그녀의 케이크 시연을 칭찬했다는 첫 번째 단서와 A홀에서 케이크 장식 기술 시연이 일어난다는 두 번째 단서를 종합할 때, 그녀의 케이크 장식 시연은 Hall A에서 일어났다는 사실을 알 수 있다. 따라서 (A) Hall A가 정답이다.

10 Not/True 문제

문제 Ms. Spellman에 대해 언급된 것은?

(A) 원래 독일 출신이다.
(B) 케이크는 생일 파티를 위한 것이다.
(C) 어머니 또한 제빵업자였다.
(D) Stafford에서 음식 장식을 배웠다.

해설 질문의 핵심 어구인 Ms. Spellman에 대해 묻는 Not/True 문제이므로 두 번째 지문인 Ms. Spellman이 언급된 기사에서 관련 내용을 확인한다. (A)는 'A stafford local ~ Beth Spellman'(2문단 3번째 줄)에서 Stafford 현지인 Beth Spellman이라고 했으므로, 지문의 내용과 일치하지 않는다. (B)는 'Ms. Spellman's ~ romantic, flower-themed wedding cake designs'(1문단 5번째 줄)에서 Ms. Spellman의 꽃을 주제로 한 로맨틱한 결혼 케이크 디자인이라고 했으므로 지문의 내용과 일치하지 않는다. (C)는 'daughter of professional baker Elinor Spellman, Beth Spellman'(2문단 4번째 줄)에서 전문 제빵업자 Elinor Spellman의 딸인 Beth Spellman이라고 했으므로 지문의 내용과 일치한다. 따라서 (C) Her mother was a baker as well이 정답이다. (D)는 'Beth Spellman went overseas to Germany and France to study baking and food decorating'(2문단 5번째 줄)에서 제빵과 음식 장식을 공부하기 위해 독일과 프랑스로 유학을 갔다고 했으므로 지문의 내용과 일치하지 않는다.

11-15는 다음 주문 양식, 이메일, 온라인 후기에 관한 문제입니다.

---

www.meadowcrestfurniture.com
MEADOWCREST FURNITURE사

홈	상품	주문	고객 추천글	연락

주문 번호: PQ413957L
주문 날짜: 4월 25일

15-B배송지: Clair Walker
Walk Tall 마케팅사
11126번지 Hayslip로
휴스턴, 텍사스주 77041

제품 설명	수량	가격	총액
제품 번호 LV29116B – Blaine Taylor사 "Oasis" 2인용 15-B소파 – 치수: 180 x 86 x 61 cm	1	440.00달러	440.00달러
11-B맞춤 천 덮개 – 패턴 Z810(파란색 면 폴리에스테르 혼방) – 11-B야드 당 1.20달러	10 야드	1.20달러	12.00달러
메모: 11-C텍사스주 내에서의 배송은 15달러이며 국내 다른 지역으로는 25달러입니다. 11-A모든 배송은 지불 확인 후 10일 이내에 이뤄집니다. 11-D교환, 반품, 환불을 요청하거나 다른 문제가 있으면 cs@meadowcrestfurniture.com으로 이메일을 보내주십시오. 이제 저희는 품목당 60달러의 비용으로 가구를 치워주는 서비스도 제공합니다. 13총 500달러 이상의 주문에는 이 서비스가 무료입니다.	소계 할인 세금 배송 총계		452.00달러 (0.00달러) 27.12달러 15.00달러 494.12달러

출력

---

description n. 설명 dimension n. 치수, 크기 custom adj. 맞춤의
fabric n. 천, 직물 upholstery n. 덮개 shipping n. 배송
elsewhere adv. 다른 지역에 payment n. 지불, 납부

removal n. 제거, 철거
total v. 총 ~이 되다

수신: Meadowcrest Furniture사 <cs@meadowcrestfurniture.com>
발신: Clair Walker <c.walker@mailranch.com>
제목: 주문 PQ413957L
날짜: 4월 26일

담당자분께,

저는 어제 소파를 주문했습니다. 유감스럽게도, 12저는 그것을 위해 예정된 공간을 부정확하게 측정해서 그것을 더 큰 것으로 교체하고 싶습니다. 귀사의 온라인 카탈로그를 살펴보았고 제품 번호 LV68423A로 정했습니다. 이것은 같은 제조사에 의해 만들어졌지만, 2인용이 아닌 3인용입니다. 저는 또한 Lerner Home사에서 나온 황갈색의 장식용 쿠션 세 개도 추가하고 싶습니다(제품 번호 PW14692K).

13요청 드린 변경 사항으로 인해, 제가 무료로 가구를 치워주는 서비스를 받을 자격이 된다는 것을 알게 되었으니, 제 오래된 소파가 확실하게 처분되었으면 합니다. 14제 문제를 처리해주시는 것에 감사드립니다.

Clair Walker 드림

incorrectly adv. 부정확하게 look through 살펴보다
settle on (생각 끝에) ~을 정하다 tan-colored adj. 황갈색의
throw pillow 장식용 쿠션 dispose of ~을 처리하다, 없애다
responsibly adv. 확실하게, 책임감 있게

---

www.meadowcrestfurniture.com

MEADOWCREST FURNITURE사

홈	상품	주문	고객 추천글	연락

www.meadowcrestfurniture.com에서 구매가 조회되는 고객들만 후기를 제출할 수 있습니다.

제품명: Blaine Taylor "Oasis" 3인용 소파
이 제품에 관한 모든 후기 보기

이 제품을 좋아합니다! ★★★★★
15-BClair Walker에 의해 작성됨, 5월 12일

제 사무실 주변의 실내 장식을 조금 새로 할 때라고 결정해서, 새 커피 테이블과 의자 몇 개를 구입한 후에 15-B저희 로비에 있는 오래된 소파를 위의 제품으로 교체하였습니다. 거의 즉시, 고객들로부터 이것에 관해 칭찬을 들었습니다. 이 소파는 잘 만들어졌고, 공간을 멋지게 채우고, 매우 편안합니다. 그리고 비록 이 제품이 저렴하진 않지만, 제 고객들이 이것 때문에 환영 받는 기분임을 아는 것은 그 소파가 그 비용만큼의 가치가 있도록 해줍니다.

verify v. 조회하다, 확인하다 submit v. 제출하다
redecorate v. 실내 장식을 새로 하다 reception area 로비, 안내실
compliment n. 칭찬 v. 칭찬하다 worth adj. ~의 가치가 있는
expense n. 비용, 지출

11 Not/True 문제

문제 Meadowcrest Furniture사에 대해 사실이 아닌 것은?

(A) 주문품을 배송하는 데 1주일 넘게 걸릴 수 있다.
(B) 직물을 야드 단위로 판매한다.
(C) 배송에 단일 요금을 청구한다.
(D) 상품의 반품을 허용할 것이다.

해설 질문의 핵심 어구인 Meadowcrest Furniture에 대해 묻는 Not/True 문제이므로 Meadowcrest Furniture가 언급된 첫 번째 지문인 주문 양식에서 관련 내용을 확인한다. (A)는 'All deliveries are made within 10 days of payment confirmation.'(표 4행 1열)에서 모든 배송이 지불 확인 후 10일 이내에 이뤄진다고 했으므로 지문의 내용과 일치한다. (B)는 'Custom fabric upholstery', '$1.20 per yard'(표 3행 1열)에서 맞춤 천 덮개가 야드 당 1.20달러라고 했으므로 지문의 내용과 일치한다. (C)는 'Shipping is $15 within the state of Texas and $25 for elsewhere in the country.'(표 4행 1열)에서 텍사스주 내에서의 배송은 15달러이며 국내 다른 지역으로는 25달러라고 했으므로 지문의 내용과 일치하지 않는다. 따라서 (C) It charges a single rate for shipping이 정답이다. (D)는 'To request changes, returns, and refunds, or for other concerns, send an e-mail'(표 4행 1열)에서 교환, 반품, 환불을 요청하거나 다른 문제가 있으면 이메일을 보내달라고 했으므로 지문의 내용과 일치한다.

어휘 textile n. 직물 charge v. (요금 등을) 청구하다 rate n. 요금, 속도

12 주제/목적 찾기 문제

문제 Ms. Walker는 왜 이메일을 보냈는가?
(A) 다른 천을 요청하기 위해
(B) 제품 크기를 변경하기 위해
(C) 납부 지연을 알리기 위해
(D) 배송지 주소를 정정하기 위해

해설 Ms. Walker가 이메일을 보낸 이유를 묻는 목적 찾기 문제이므로 이메일의 내용을 확인한다. 두 번째 지문인 이메일의 'I incorrectly measured the space it is intended for and would like to replace it with a larger one'(1문단 1번째 줄)에서 그것, 즉 소파를 놓기로 예정된 공간을 부정확하게 측정해서 소파를 더 큰 것으로 교체하고 싶다고 하였으므로 (B) To change an item size가 정답이다.

Paraphrasing
replace ~ with a larger one 더 큰 것으로 교체하다 → change ~ size 크기를 변경하다

어휘 delay n. 지연

13 추론 문제 연계

문제 Ms. Walker에 대해 암시되는 것은?
(A) 우편으로 카탈로그를 받았다.
(B) 그녀의 쿠션은 Blaine Taylor사에 의해 제작되었다.
(C) 신속한 배송을 위해 요금을 지불했다.
(D) 그녀의 새 주문은 적어도 500달러였다.

해설 두 지문의 내용을 종합적으로 확인한 후 추론해서 풀어야 하는 연계 문제이다. 질문의 핵심 어구인 Ms. Walker가 작성한 이메일을 먼저 확인한다. 두 번째 지문인 이메일의 'With the changes I've requested, I see that I qualify for the free furniture removal service'(2문단 1번째 줄)에서 자신이 요청한 변경 사항으로 인해 무료로 가구를 치워주는 서비스를 받을 자격이 된다는 것을 알게 되었다고 했으므로 Ms. Walker가 요청한 변경 사항이 무료로 가구를 치워주는 서비스를 받을 자격을 주었다는 첫 번째 단서를 확인할 수 있다. 그런데 무료로 가구를 치워주는 서비스를 받는 자격이 무엇인지 제시되지 않았으므로 Ms. Walker가 작성한 주문 양식에서 관련 내용을 확인한다. 첫 번째 지문인 주문 양식의 'For orders totaling $500 or more, the service is free.'(표 4행 1열)에서 총 500달러 이상 주문하면 그 서비스, 즉 가구를 치워주는 서비스가 무료라는 두 번째 단서를 확인할 수 있다. Ms. Walker가 요청한 변경 사항으로 인해 무료로 가구를 치워주는 서비스를 받을 자격이 주어졌다는 첫 번째 단서와 그 서비스를 무료로 받으려면 500달러 이상을 주문해야 한다는 두 번째 단서를 종합할 때, Ms. Walker의 변경 사항이 적용된 새로운 주문이 적어도 500달러였다는 사실을 추론할 수 있다. 따라서 (D) Her updated order cost at least $500가 정답이다.

어휘 expedite v. 신속히 처리하다

14 동의어 찾기 문제

문제 이메일에서, 2문단 두 번째 줄의 표현 "attending to"는 의미상 ~와 가장 가깝다.
(A) ~로 가는 것
(B) ~을 처리하는 것
(C) ~을 돕는 것
(D) ~을 차려주는 것

해설 두 번째 지문인 이메일의 attending to를 포함하고 있는 문장 'Thank you for attending to my concern.'(2문단 2번째 줄)에서 attending to는 '~을 처리하는 것'이라는 뜻으로 사용되었다. 따라서 '~을 처리하는 것'이라는 뜻을 가진 (B) dealing with가 정답이다.

15 Not/True 문제 연계

문제 Walk Tall 마케팅사에 대해 언급된 것은?
(A) 새로운 장소가 훨씬 더 크다.

(B) 로비에 새로운 가구가 비치되었다.
(C) 매출액 증가를 겪었다.
(D) 새로운 보조원을 채용했다.

해설 두 지문의 내용을 종합해서 풀어야 하는 연계 문제이다. 질문의 핵심 어구인 Walk Tall Marketing이 언급된 주문 양식을 먼저 확인한다.
첫 번째 지문인 주문 양식의 'Ship to: Clair Walker, Walk Tall Marketing'(양식 상단 1번째 줄 오른쪽), 'sofa'(표 1행 2열)에서 Walk Tall 마케팅사의 Clair Walker에게 소파가 배송될 것이라는 첫 번째 단서를 확인할 수 있다. 그런데 소파가 배송되는 이유가 무엇인지 제시되지 않았으므로, Clair Walker가 작성한 온라인 후기에서 관련 내용을 확인한다. 세 번째 지문인 온라인 후기의 'Posted by Clair Walker'(6번째 줄), 'I replaced an old sofa in my reception area with the item above.'(8번째 줄)에서 Clair Walker가 자신의 사무실 로비에 있는 오래된 소파를 온라인 후기에 언급한 제품으로 교체하였다는 두 번째 단서를 확인할 수 있다.
Walk Tall 마케팅사의 Clair Walker에게 소파가 배송될 것이라는 첫 번째 단서와 Clair Walker가 자신의 사무실 로비에 있는 오래된 소파를 교체하였다는 두 번째 단서를 종합할 때, Clair Walker의 사무실인 Walk Tall 마케팅사 로비에 소파, 즉 새로운 가구가 비치되었다는 것을 알 수 있다. 따라서 (B) Its reception area has been refurnished가 정답이다. (A), (C), (D)는 지문에 언급되지 않은 내용이다.

어휘 refurnish v. ~에 새로운 가구·비품을 설치하다 growth n. 증가, 성장 receptionist n. 접수 담당자

16-20은 다음 인사 기록, 회람, 급여 명세서에 관한 문제입니다.

Pittsburgh Express사
50년이 넘는 동안 [16]피츠버그 전역에서 승객들에게 서비스 제공

직원 인사 기록 6-425번
이 파일에 있는 정보는 기밀입니다. 처리하거나 타인에게 공개할 때 신중해 주십시오.

[19]이름: Harold White
전체 주소: 1730번지 Fallowfield로, 피츠버그 펜실베이니아주, 15216
전화: 555-6364   이메일: h.white@writeme.com
비상시 연락: Rebecca Simpson   관계: 여동생
비상시 전화번호: 555-9027

부서: 운행   [16]직무: 도시 버스 운전기사
[19]계약 만료일: 6월 15일   근속 연수: 10
[19]시급: 15달러
[18-C]혜택: 의료 보험, 연금 기금, 병가, 휴일 휴가

고충 사항: 없음
징계 조치: 없음
사고 기록: 1

confidential adj. 기밀의, 비밀의 discretion n. 신중함, 재량
medical insurance 의료 보험 pension n. 연금 sick leave 병가
grievance n. 고충 (사항), 불만 disciplinary action 징계 조치

Pittsburgh Express사
회람

수신: 전 직원
발신: Michael O'Rourke, 인사부장
제목: 고용 조건
[18-D]날짜: 3월 16일

여러분이 아시다시피, [17]Pittsburgh Express사는 Felton Capital사에 인수되었고, 이 회사가 올해 6월 1일에 소유권을 가질 것입니다. 새로운 소유주는 남기로 결정한 모든 기존 직원들을 유지하는 것에 동의했습니다. 남기로 결정한 사람들에게 [18-C]Felton Capital사는 만료일까지 여러분의 현재 계약을 이행할 것입니다. 하지만, 혜택은 이제 의료 보험, 연금, 병가, 휴일 휴가, 야간 근무 수당을 포함할 것입니다. 여러분 각자의 계약이 종료된 후에, 여러분은 추가적인 조건을 포함할 수도 있는 새로운 계약을 협상하도록 요청받을 것입니다.

그 대신에, 여러분은 새로운 소유주가 인계받기 전에 고용을 종료하는 것을 선택할 수도 있습니다. 이 경우, 여러분은 근속 연수에 따라 퇴직금을 받을 것입니다. [18-D]여러분의 결정은 5월 15일까지 요구되며 다른 고용 정보와 함께 Felton ⊙

Capital사와 공유될 것입니다. 감사합니다.

assume v. (권력을) 쥐다, 맡다 **retain** v. 유지하다, 보유하다
honor v. 이행하다, 지키다 **allowance** n. 수당, 허용
alternatively adv. 그 대신에, 그렇지 않으면 **terminate** v. 종료하다, 끝내다
take over 인계받다, 장악하다 **severance package** 퇴직금, 퇴직 수당

직원 급여 명세서

회사 자회사: Pittsburgh Express사

¹⁹직원 이름: Harold White   ¹⁹급여 기간: 7월 1일부터 7월 31일
²⁰⁻ᴰ지급 수단: X 회사 수표
               ___ 은행 계좌 이체

급여 개요	공제
²⁰ᴬ근무 시간: 80	²⁰ᴮ국세: 111.60달러
¹⁹시급: 20.00달러	²⁰ᴮ주세: 13.39달러
기본급: 900.00달러	의료 보험: 15.00달러
초과 근무: 216.00달러	연금 기금: 12.50달러
야간 근무 수당: 135.00달러	기타 공제: 0.00달러
상여금: 0.00달러	

실수령액: 1,098.51달러	지급 만기: 8월 10일
병가: 0	휴일 휴가: 0
사용 일수: 0	사용 일수: 0
남은 일수: 5	남은 일수: 10

subsidiary n. 자회사, 계열사 **bank transfer** 은행 계좌 이체
deduction n. 공제, 추론 **overtime** n. 초과 근무, 야근 **net pay** 실수령액
payable adj. 지급 만기의, 지급해야 할

16 추론 문제

문제 Pittsburgh Express사는 무엇일 것 같은가?
(A) 해운 회사
(B) 시 신문사
(C) 버스 회사
(D) 의료 서비스 제공업체

해설 질문의 핵심 어구인 Pittsburgh Express에 대해 추론하는 문제이므로 Pittsburgh Express사의 인사 기록을 확인한다. 첫 번째 지문인 인사 기록의 'Serving passengers throughout Pittsburgh'(제목 2번째 줄)에서 Pittsburgh Express사가 피츠버그 전역에서 승객들에게 서비스를 제공한다고 했고 'Position: City bus driver'(3문단 1번째 줄)에서 직원의 직무가 도시 버스 운전기사라고 했으므로, Pittsburgh Express사가 버스를 운행하는 회사라는 사실을 추론할 수 있다. 따라서 (C) A bus company가 정답이다.

어휘 **shipping firm** 해운 회사

17 주제/목적 찾기 문제

문제 회람의 목적은 무엇인가?
(A) 새로운 징계 방침을 공지하기 위해
(B) 직원들에게 소유권 변경에 대해 알리기 위해
(C) 새로운 직원을 채용하기 위한 계획을 알리기 위해
(D) 직원들에게 평가에 대해 상기시키기 위해

해설 회람의 목적을 묻는 목적 찾기 문제이므로 회람의 내용을 확인한다. 두 번째 지문인 회람의 'Pittsburgh Express has been acquired by Felton Capital, which will assume ownership on June 1 of this year'(1문단 1번째 줄)에서 Pittsburgh Express사가 Felton Capital사에 인수되었고 이 회사가 올해 6월 1일에 소유권을 가질 것이라고 한 후, 소유권 변경과 관련된 세부 사항을 설명하고 있으므로 (B) To notify staff about a change of ownership이 정답이다.

어휘 **evaluation** n. 평가, 사정

18 Not/True 문제 연계

문제 Felton Capital사에 대해 사실인 것은?
(A) 잔류를 선택하는 직원들에게 보너스를 줄 것이다.
(B) 회사의 이름을 바꿀 계획을 가지고 있다.
(C) 야간 근무 수당을 새로운 혜택으로 추가했다.
(D) 직원들에게 결정을 내리는 데에 일주일의 시간을 주었다.

해설 두 지문의 내용을 종합해서 풀어야 하는 연계 문제이다. 질문의 핵심 어구인 Felton Capital에 대해 묻는 Not/True 문제이므로 Felton Capital이 언급된 두 번째 지문인 회람에서 관련 내용을 먼저 확인한다. (A)와 (B)는 지문에 언급되지 않은 내용이다. (C)는 'Felton Capital will honor your current contracts ~. However, benefits will now include medical insurance, pensions, sick leave, holiday leave, and a night-shift allowance.'(1문단 3번째 줄)에서 Felton Capital사는 현재 계약을 이행할 것이지만 이제 의료 보험, 연금, 병가, 휴일 휴가, 야간 근무 수당을 포함할 것이라고 했고 첫 번째 지문인 인사 기록의 'Benefits: Medical insurance, pension fund, sick leave, holiday leave'(3문단 4번째 줄)에서 기존의 혜택이 의료 보험, 연금 기금, 병가, 휴일 휴가라고 했으므로 Felton Capital사가 야간 근무 수당을 새로운 혜택으로 추가했음을 알 수 있다. 따라서 (C) It added a night-shift allowance as a new benefit이 정답이다. (D)는 회람의 'Date: March 16'(상단 4번째 줄)에서 회람이 3월 16일이 보내졌다고 했고 'Your decisions are needed by May 15'(2문단 2번째 줄)에서 직원들의 결정이 5월 15일까지 요구된다고 했으므로 지문의 내용과 일치하지 않는다.

19 추론 문제 연계

문제 Mr. White에 대해 암시되는 것은?
(A) 다른 회사의 일자리를 제안받았다.
(B) 다른 부서로 옮길 것을 요청받았다.
(C) 보통 일주일에 50시간을 일한다.
(D) 시급 인상을 받았다.

해설 두 지문의 내용을 종합적으로 확인한 후 추론해서 풀어야 하는 연계 문제이다. 질문의 핵심 어구인 Mr. White가 언급된 인사 기록에서 관련 내용을 먼저 확인한다.
첫 번째 지문인 인사 기록의 'Name: Harold White'(2문단 1번째 줄), 'Contract valid until: June 15', 'Hourly rate: $15'(3문단 2, 3번째 줄)에서 Harold White의 계약 만료일이 6월 15일이고 시급이 15달러라는 첫 번째 단서를 확인할 수 있다. 그런데 계약 만료일 이후의 시급이 얼마인지 제시되지 않았으므로 급여 명세서에서 관련 내용을 확인한다. 세 번째 지문인 급여 명세서의 'Employee name: Harold White', 'Pay period: July 1 to July 31'(1문단 2번째 줄), 'Hourly rate: $20.00'(표 2행 1열 2번째 줄)에서 7월 1일부터 7월 31일의 급여 기간 동안 Harold White의 시급이 20달러라는 두 번째 단서를 확인할 수 있다.
Harold White의 계약 만료일이 6월 15일이고 시급이 15달러라는 첫 번째 단서와 7월 1일부터 7월 31일의 급여 기간 동안 Harold White의 시급이 20달러라는 두 번째 단서를 종합할 때, Mr. White가 시급 인상을 받았다는 사실을 추론할 수 있다. 따라서 (D) He received an increase in his hourly rate가 정답이다.

어휘 **normally** adv. 보통, 정상적으로

20 Not/True 문제

문제 급여 명세서에 포함되지 않은 것은?
(A) 근무한 시간 수
(B) 납부된 세금의 종류
(C) 고용 시작일
(D) 선호하는 지급 방식

해설 급여 명세서에 포함된 내용을 지문에서 찾아 보기와 대조하는 Not/True 문제이다. 이 문제는 질문에 핵심 어구가 없으므로 각 보기의 핵심 어구와 관련된 내용을 세 번째 지문인 급여 명세서에서 확인한다. (A)는 'Hours worked: 80'(표 2행 1열 1번째 줄)에서 근무 시간이 80시간이라고 했으므로 지문에 언급된 내용이다. (B)는 'National tax: $111.60', 'State tax: $13.39'(표 2행 2열 1, 2번째 줄)에서 국세가 111.60달러, 주세가 13.39달러라고 했으므로 지문에 언급된 내용이다. (C)는 지문에 언급되지 않은 내용이다. 따라서 (C) The start date of employment가 정답이다. (D)는 'Payment by: X Company check', '___ Bank transfer'(1문단 3, 4번째 줄)에서 지급 수단인 회사 수표와 은행 계좌 이체 중에 회사 수표에 표시되어 있으므로 지문에 언급된 내용이다.

어휘 **method** n. 방식, 수단

Chapter 18 기사 연계 지문

예제 해석·해설   p.488

기사 & 이메일

달러스에 본사를 둔 텔레비전 채널 KVBS가 곧 Peak Media 그룹(PMC)과 합병할 것이라고 발표했다. 9월 6일부터, KVBS는 PMC의 프로그램 편성 방송을 시작할 것이다. 게다가, PMC는 채널의 텔레비전 프로그램 일정에 내년 1월에 방송을 시작할 아침 뉴스 프로그램을 추가할 계획을 가지고 있다고 말했다.

conglomeration n. 그룹, 복합 기업   programming n. 프로그램 편성
viewing n. 텔레비전 프로그램   broadcast v. 방송하다

수신: Erik Wade <erikwade@PMC.com>
발신: Iris Svenson <irissvenson@KVBS.com>
우리의 새로운 프로그램의 진행자를 고용하는 것에 대해 논의하기 위해 이번 주 중에 귀하와 만나고 싶습니다. 저는 몇몇 가능성 있는 후보들에게 연락했으며 그들은 모두 그 자리에 대해 관심을 표했습니다. 인터뷰를 위해 누구에게 연락할 것인지 결정하기 위해 귀하와 함께 후보들을 검토하고 싶습니다. 귀하께서 언제 한가하신지 알려 주십시오.

potential adj. 가능성 있는, 잠재적인   candidate n. 후보

문제   Iris Svenson에 대해 암시되는 것은?

   (A) 텔레비전 진행직에 지원하고 싶어 한다.
   (B) 뉴스 프로그램의 진행자를 모집하려 하고 있다.
   (C) 최근에 몇몇 인터뷰를 실시했다.
   (D) 합병을 위한 조건을 종합하고 있다.

해설   추론 문제 두 지문의 내용을 종합적으로 확인한 후 추론해서 풀어야 하는 연계 문제이다. 질문의 핵심 어구인 Iris Svenson이 작성한 이메일을 먼저 확인한다.
두 번째 지문인 이메일의 'irissvenson@KVBS.com'에서 Iris Svenson은 KVBS 직원이고, 'I would like ~ to discuss hiring a host for our new program.'에서 그녀가 새로운 프로그램의 진행자를 고용하려고 한다는 첫 번째 단서를 확인할 수 있다. 그런데 새로운 프로그램이 어떤 종류인지 제시되지 않았으므로 기사에서 새로운 프로그램의 종류를 확인한다. 첫 번째 지문인 기사의 'KVBS ~ will soon be merging with the Peak Media Conglomeration (PMC)'에서 KVBS가 PMC와 합병한다는 것과, 'PMC ~ has plans to add a morning news program'에서 PMC에서 아침 뉴스 프로그램을 추가할 것이라는 두 번째 단서를 확인할 수 있다.
KVBS 직원인 Iris Svenson이 새로운 프로그램의 진행자를 고용하려고 한다는 첫 번째 단서와 KVBS와 합병할 PMC에서 아침 뉴스 프로그램을 추가할 것이라는 두 번째 단서를 종합할 때, Iris Svenson이 뉴스 프로그램의 진행자를 모집하려 하고 있다는 사실을 추론할 수 있다. 따라서 (B) She is trying to recruit a host for a news program이 정답이다.

어휘   presenter n. 진행자, 발표자   terms n. 조건

Hackers Practice   p.489

유형 연습

| 01 (C) | 02 (A) | 03 (B) | 04 (C) |

01-02 기사 & 기사

젊은 예술가들을 위한 새로운 장학금 프로그램
문화예술부의 보도 자료에 따르면, 새로운 장학금 프로그램이 곧 시작될 것이라고 한다. 해당 부서는 주 전역에서 10명의 지원자가 선발될 젊은 예술가 장학금 프로그램을 창설했다. [02]당선자들은 서스캐처원주 내에 있는 어떤 학교에 대해서든 전액 장학금을 제공받게 된다. 부서 대변인 Gary Brown은 "그 프로그램은 지역 내 미술 성장을 촉진시키기 위한 당국의 계속되는 노력의 일부입니다."라고 밝혔다.

press release 보도 자료   ministry n. (정부의 각) 부서   ○

---

launch v. (계획 등을) 시작하다   province n. (행정 구역으로서의) 주(州), 지방
funding n. 자금 제공, 자금   spokesperson n. 대변인
ongoing adj. 계속하고 있는, 진행 중의   fine art 미술 (회화, 조각 등)

장학금을 받은 지역 예술가
[01/02]지역 화가 Brenda Kahn은 지난주에 문화예술부로부터 전액 장학금을 받았으며, [02]그녀는 Royal Victoria 미술 학교에서 공부를 할 계획이라고 말했다. 이 장학금은 매년 주 내 예술가들에게 지급되는 10건의 장학금 중 하나이다. Kahn은 가을에 장학금에 지원하였으며, 젊은 예술가들을 지원하기 위해 그 부서가 이런 노력을 기울이고 있다는 것이 감격스럽다고 말했다.

grant v. 수여하다, 주다   award v. (사람에게 상·장학금 등을) 수여하다
give out 지급하다, ~을 나눠주다   apply for ~에 지원하다
thrilled adj. 감격한, 아주 신이 난   put forth an effort 노력하다

---

01 육하원칙 문제

문제   Brenda Kahn은 누구인가?

   (A) 학교 교사
   (B) 문화예술부 대변인
   (C) 장학금 수령인

해설   Brenda Kahn이 누구인지(Who)를 묻는 육하원칙 문제이므로 질문의 핵심 어구인 Brenda Kahn이 언급된 두 번째 기사에서 관련 내용을 확인한다. 두 번째 기사의 'Local painter Brenda Kahn was awarded a full scholarship from the Ministry of the Arts last week'(1번째 줄)에서 지역 화가 Brenda Kahn은 지난주에 문화예술부로부터 전액 장학금을 받았다고 했으므로 (C) The recipient of a scholarship이 정답이다.

   Paraphrasing
   was awarded a full scholarship 전액 장학금을 받았다 → The recipient of a scholarship 장학금 수령인

어휘   instructor n. 교사   recipient n. 수령인, (어떤 것을) 받는 사람

02 추론 문제 연계

문제   Royal Victoria 미술 학교에 대해 암시되는 것은?

   (A) 서스캐처원주에 위치해 있다.
   (B) 문화예술부에 의해 운영된다.
   (C) 지역 내 학생들에게 장학금을 제공한다.

해설   두 지문의 내용을 종합적으로 확인한 후 추론해서 풀어야 하는 연계 문제이다. 질문의 핵심 어구인 Royal Victoria Art Academy가 언급된 두 번째 기사를 먼저 확인한다.
두 번째 기사의 'Local painter Brenda Kahn was awarded a full scholarship ~ and said she plans to study at the Royal Victoria Art Academy.'(1번째 줄)에서 지역 화가 Brenda Kahn은 전액 장학금을 받았으며, Royal Victoria 미술 학교에서 공부를 할 계획이라는 첫 번째 단서를 확인할 수 있다. 그런데 Royal Victoria 미술 학교가 어떤 주에 있는지 제시되지 않았으므로 첫 번째 기사에서 Royal Victoria 미술 학교가 어떤 주에 있는지 확인한다. 첫 번째 기사의 'Winners will receive full funding for any school located within the province of Saskatchewan.'(3번째 줄)에서 당선자는 서스캐처원주 내에 있는 어떤 학교에 대해서든 전액 장학금을 제공받게 된다는 두 번째 단서를 확인할 수 있다.
Brenda Kahn이 전액 장학금을 받았으며, Royal Victoria 미술 학교에서 공부를 할 계획이라는 첫 번째 단서와 당선자는 서스캐처원주 내에 있는 어떤 학교에 대해서든 전액 장학금을 제공받게 된다는 두 번째 단서를 종합할 때, Royal Victoria 미술 학교는 서스캐처원주에 위치해 있다는 사실을 추론할 수 있다. 따라서 (A) It is located in Saskatchewan이 정답이다.

어휘   operate v. 운영하다, 관리하다

03-04 기사 & 도표

증가하는 것으로 보이는 온라인 마케팅
온라인 마케팅에 대한 추세가 늘어남에 따라, 기업들은 어떻게 온라인 마케팅이 다른 형태의 광고와 맞서서 기대에 부합할 수 있는지를 알고 싶어 한다. 이 문제를 다루기 위해서는, 하나의 광고 비용 대 광고가 도달하게 되는 인원수와 같은 비교할 수 있는 자료를 이용하는 것이 필요하다. 예를 들어, [03/04]회사는 1,000명의 목표 고객에 도달하기 위해 온라인으로는 평균 7달러를 지불해야 한다.   ○

^{04-C}이 수치는 그 다음으로 가장 가격이 알맞은 선택에 비해 4배 낮고, 가장 비싼 것에 대해서는 대략 60배 정도 싼 가격이다. 이처럼 극명한 차이의 주요 원인은 온라인 광고는 주로 클릭 수에 따라 비용이 지불되는 반면에, 다른 형태의 광고의 경우에는, 기업이 막대한 비용을 선불로 지불해야 하기 때문이다.

be eager to ~을 하고 싶어 하다 **measure up** (기대에) 부합하다, 미치다
address v. (어려운 문제 등을) 다루다 **comparable** adj. 비교할 수 있는
versus prep. ~대, ~에 비해 **figure** n. 수치, 숫자
affordable adj. (가격이) 알맞은 **stark** adj. (차이가) 극명한
up front 선불로

광고 수단의 비용 비교
^{04-C}수치들은 1,000명의 고객에 도달하는 데 드는 평균 비용을 나타낸다.

*수단들은 증가하는 비용 순으로 등급을 매겼다.

represent v. 나타내다, 의미하다 **in order of** ~ 순으로

---

03 육하원칙 문제

문제 온라인으로 1,000명의 고객에 도달하기 위해 평균적으로 얼마가 드는가?
(A) 1달러
(B) 7달러
(C) 60달러

해설 온라인으로 1,000명의 고객에 도달하기 위해 평균적으로 드는 비용이 얼마인지(How much)를 묻는 육하원칙 문제이다. 질문의 핵심 어구인 reach 1,000 customers online이 언급된 기사에서 관련 내용을 확인한다. 첫 번째 지문인 기사의 'a company must spend an average of $7 online to reach 1,000 of its target consumers'(3번째 줄)에서 회사는 1,000명의 목표 고객에 도달하기 위해 온라인으로는 평균 7달러를 지불해야 한다고 했으므로 (B) $7가 정답이다.

Paraphrasing
customers 고객 → target consumers 목표 고객

어휘 **on average** 평균적으로

04 Not/True 문제 연계

문제 우편을 통한 광고에 대해 언급된 것은?
(A) 라디오 광고보다 두 배 많은 사람들에게 도달한다.
(B) 다른 모든 광고 수단의 절반 정도로 효과적이다.
(C) 온라인 광고보다 거의 60배 더 비싸다.

해설 두 지문의 내용을 종합해서 풀어야 하는 연계 문제이다. 질문의 핵심 어구인 advertising by mail이 언급된 도표를 먼저 확인한다.
두 번째 지문인 도표의 'Figures represent the average cost in dollars of reaching 1,000 customers.'(1번째 줄)에서 수치들은 1,000명의 고객에 도달하는 데 드는 평균 비용을 나타낸다고 했고, 'Mail'의 그래프 막대를 통해 우편은 가장 비용이 많이 드는 수단이라는 첫 번째 단서를 확인할 수 있다. 그런데 다른 수단과 비교했을 때 어느 정도인지 정확히 제시되지 않았으므로 기사에서 관련 내용을 확인한다. 첫 번째 지문인 기사의 'a company must spend an average of $7 online to reach 1,000 of its target consumers. This figure is ~ nearly 60 times cheaper than the most expensive one.'(3번째 줄)에서 1,000명의 목표 고객에 도달하기 위해 온라인으로는 평균 7달러를 지불해야 하고, 이 수치는 가장 비싼 것에 비해서는 대략 60배 정도 싼 가격이라는 두 번째 단서를 확인할 수 있다.
우편은 1,000명 고객에 도달하는 데 드는 평균 비용이 가장 많이 드는 수단이라는 첫 번째 단서와 1,000명의 목표고객에 도달하기 위해 평균 7달러의 비용을 지불해야 하는 온라인은 가장 비싼 것에 비해 대략 60배 정도 싼 가격이라는 두 번째 단서를 종합할 때, 우편은 온라인에 비해 60배 정도 비용이 더 든다는 것을 알 수 있다. 따라서 (C) It is almost 60 times more costly than online advertising이 정답이다. (A)는 지문에 언급되지 않은 내용이며, (B)는 두 번째 지문인 도표에서 보여지듯이 'Mail'의 그래프 막대를 통해

우편이 가장 비용이 많이 드는 수단임을 알 수 있으므로 지문의 내용과 일치하지 않는다.

Hackers Test
p.490

01 (B)	02 (C)	03 (C)	04 (C)	05 (B)
06 (B)	07 (A)	08 (A)	09 (C)	10 (B)
11 (A)	12 (B)	13 (B)	14 (B)	15 (A)
16 (D)	17 (C)	18 (C)	19 (A)	20 (B)

01-05는 다음 기사와 편지에 관한 문제입니다.

작가 Wendy Armstrong 헬레나를 방문할 예정

^{01/02}수상 작가인 Wendy Armstrong은 다음 주 목요일인 9월 22일, 그녀의 최신작 홍보를 위한 북아메리카 책 투어 여정 중에 헬레나에 들를 것이다.

Armstrong은 그녀의 연작소설 Pioneer로 잘 알려져 있으며, 이 소설은 Warren 가족과 1800년대 중반 골드러시 때 미 서부지역에서 삶을 만들어 나가려는 그들의 투쟁에 관한 이야기이다. 현재 그녀는 1920년대 뉴욕의 이민자 가족에 기반을 둔 새로운 연작소설로도 같은 성공을 이루기 위해 시도하고 있다. ^{03-C}Arrivals라는 제목의 그녀의 최신 소설은 독자들에게 나폴리 출신의 Pucci 가족과 그들이 미국으로 온 이야기를 소개할 것이다. 겨우 2주 전에 출간되었지만, Arrivals는 이미 문학 부문 베스트셀러 목록에 있으며, ^{03-C}평론가들은 몇 년 사이 Armstrong의 최고 작품이라며 극찬하고 있다.

Armstrong은 그녀의 작가 활동 기간 동안 14편의 소설을 집필했으며, 작가로서 수많은 상을 받았다. 그녀는 그녀의 남편 Nathan과 함께 아이다호주의 보이시에서 소규모 농장을 운영하며 살고 있다. 한가한 시간에, ⁰⁵Armstrong은 장차 작가가 되려는 사람들에게 강연을 하기 위해 종종 대학을 방문하고, 그들에게 값진 충고와 제안을 해준다.

⁰²Armstrong은 오전 11시 30분에 Spencer & Chang 서점에서 짧은 소설 낭독과 강연을 할 예정이다. 그 이후에, 그녀는 판매 중인 그녀의 신작 소설에 사인을 해 줄 것이다. 시민들은 행사에 참여하도록 초대되며 좌석이 한정되어 있기 때문에 일찍 도착하도록 권고된다. 더 자세한 내용을 위해서는, 555-3876으로 Spencer & Chang 서점에 연락하면 된다.

leg n. (여행의) 여정, 구간 **publicize** v. 홍보하다
tale n. 이야기 **struggle** n. 투쟁 **gold rush** 골드러시, 새 금광지로의 쇄도
attempt to ~하려고 시도하다 **immigrant** n. 이민자
entitled adj. ~라는 제목의 **rave** v. 극찬하다, 열변을 토하다
run v. 운영하다, 관리하다 **ranch** n. 농장 **aspiring** adj. 장차 ~가 되려는

9월 17일

Wendy Armstrong
87번지 Upland Heights로
보이시, 아이다호주 86701

Ms. Armstrong께,

작가님께서 신작 소설을 홍보하기 위해 곧 헬레나를 방문하실 예정이라는 기사를 지역 신문에서 우연히 발견했습니다. 저는 Northwestern 문과대학의 현대문학 교수이며, 본교 역시 헬레나에 있습니다. ⁰⁵기사에 작가님께서 가끔 대학에서 강연을 하신다고 언급되어 있었는데, 혹시 이번 방문 중에 본교의 학부에 그와 비슷한 강연을 해 줄 여유 시간이 있으신지에 관해 문의 드리고자 이렇게 편지를 씁니다. 촉박한 통보라는 것을 알고 있지만, 본교의 학생들 중 열정적인 독자들은 성공한 작가의 강연을 들을 수 있는 기회를 감사히 여길 것이라고 생각하기 때문에 작가님께 연락드리기로 결정했습니다. ⁰⁴작가님께서 오실 수 없다 하더라도 충분히 이해하지만, 초청을 고려해주시기 바랍니다. 필요하시다면 작가님께 기꺼이 강연료를 드리도록 하겠습니다.

감사합니다. 그리고 저에게 leodaniels@nua.edu 또는 전화 (406) 555-9907로 연락해 주시기 바랍니다.

⁰⁵Leo Daniels 드림
현대문학 교수
Northwestern 문과대학

come across 우연히 발견하다, 마주치다 **occasionally** adv. 가끔
inquire v. 문의하다, 질문을 하다 **short notice** 촉박한 통보
avid adj. 열성적인, 열렬한

01 주제/목적 찾기 문제

문제 기사의 주 목적은 무엇인가?

(A) 서점 확장을 독자들에게 알리기 위해
(B) 저명한 손님의 곧 있을 방문을 홍보하기 위해
(C) 새로이 출간된 출판물을 대중에게 알리기 위해
(D) 작가에 관한 배경 정보를 제공하기 위해

해설 기사의 목적을 묻는 목적 찾기 문제이므로 기사의 내용을 확인한다. 첫 번째 지문인 기사의 'Award-winning author Wendy Armstrong will make a stop in Helena ~ during the North American leg of her book tour to publicize her newest work.'(1문단 1번째 줄)에서 수상 작가인 Wendy Armstrong이 최신작 홍보를 위한 북아메리카 북투어의 여정 중에 헬레나에 들를 것이라고 한 후, Wendy Armstrong의 이력과 그녀의 방문 일정에 대해 설명하고 있으므로 (B) To promote a famous guest's upcoming visit이 정답이다.

Paraphrasing
Award-wining author 수상 작가 → a famous guest 저명한 손님
make a stop 들르다 → visit 방문

어휘 newly adv. 새로이 publication n. 출판(물), 발표

02 추론 문제

문제 Spencer & Chang에 대해 암시되는 것은?

(A) 대학 캠퍼스 내에 위치해 있다.
(B) Armstrong의 소설을 위한 특별 구역이 있다.
(C) 9월 22일에 문학 행사를 개최할 것이다.
(D) 특별 행사를 위한 사전 예약을 받는다.

해설 질문의 핵심 어구인 Spencer & Chang에 대해 추론하는 문제이므로 Spencer & Chang이 언급된 기사에서 관련 내용을 확인한다. 첫 번째 지문인 기사의 'Award-winning author Wendy Armstrong will make a stop in Helena next week on Thursday, September 22 ~ to publicize her newest work.'(1문단 1번째 줄)에서 수상 작가 Wendy Armstrong이 다음 주 목요일인 9월 22일에 자신의 최신작 홍보를 위해 헬레나에 들를 것이라고 했고, 'Armstrong will give a short reading and presentation at Spencer & Chang Bookstore at 11:30 A.M.'(4문단 1번째 줄)에서 Armstrong이 Spencer & Chang 서점에서 짧은 소설 낭독과 강연을 할 예정이라고 했으므로 Spencer & Chang 서점이 9월 22일에 문학 행사를 개최할 것이라는 사실을 추론할 수 있다. 따라서 (C) It will be hosting a literary event on September 22가 정답이다.

Paraphrasing
a short reading and presentation 짧은 소설 낭독과 강연 →
a literary event 문학 행사

어휘 advance adj. 사전의

03 Not/True 문제

문제 Wendy Armstrong에 대해 언급된 것은?

(A) Northwestern 대학에서 현대문학을 전공했다.
(B) 그녀의 가족 이야기를 바탕으로 한 일련의 소설을 쓸 것이다.
(C) 그녀의 최신 소설에 대해 비평가들의 호평을 받았다.
(D) 교육기관에서 강연하는 비용을 청구한다.

해설 질문의 핵심 어구인 Wendy Armstrong에 대해 묻는 Not/True 문제이므로 Wendy Armstrong이 언급된 기사에서 관련 내용을 확인한다. (A)와 (B)는 지문에 언급되지 않은 내용이다. (C)는 'Entitled *Arrivals*, her newest novel'(2문단 4번째 줄)과 'critics are raving about the work, saying it is Armstrong's best writing in years'(2문단 6번째 줄)에서 그녀의 최신 소설인 *Arrivals*에 대해 평론가들이 몇 년 사이 Armstrong의 최고 작품이라며 극찬하고 있다고 했으므로 지문의 내용과 일치한다. 따라서 (C) She received critical acclaim for her latest novel이 정답이다. (D)는 지문에 언급되지 않은 내용이다.

Paraphrasing
critics are raving 평론가들은 극찬하고 있다 → critical acclaim 비평가들의 호평
newest novel 최신 소설 → latest novel 최신 소설

어휘 critical adj. 비평가의 acclaim n. 호평, 격찬 institution n. 기관

04 동의어 찾기 문제

문제 편지의 1문단 일곱 번째 줄의 단어 "consider"는 의미상 ~와 가장 가깝다.

(A) ~을 믿다
(B) 일정을 잡다
(C) ~에 대해 고려하다
(D) 받아들이다

해설 두 번째 지문인 편지의 consider를 포함하고 있는 문장 'I completely understand if you are unable to come, but hope you will consider our invitation.'(1문단 7번째 줄)에서 consider가 '고려하다'라는 뜻으로 사용되었으므로 (C) think about이 정답이다.

어휘 believe in ~을 믿다 schedule v. 일정을 잡다 accept v. 받아들이다

05 추론 문제 연계

문제 누가 Ms. Armstrong이 Northwestern 대학교에서 하는 강연에 참석할 것 같은가?

(A) 문학 교수들
(B) 작가가 되고자 하는 젊은 사람들
(C) 백일장 참가자들
(D) 작가 협회의 회원들

해설 두 지문의 내용을 종합적으로 확인한 후 추론해서 풀어야 하는 연계 문제이다. 질문의 핵심 어구인 a talk given by Ms. Armstrong at the Northwestern University에서 누가 Ms. Armstrong이 Northwestern 대학교에서 하는 강연에 참석할 것 같은지를 묻고 있으므로 Ms. Armstrong에게 보내는 편지를 먼저 확인한다.
두 번째 지문인 편지의 'The article mentioned that you occasionally speak at universities, and I am writing to inquire whether you might have some free time during your visit to give a similar presentation to our departments.'(1문단 3번째 줄)와 'Leo Daniels, Professor of Modern Literature, Northwestern University of the Arts'(편지 하단)를 통해 Northwestern 문과대학 현대문학 교수인 Leo Daniels가 Ms. Armstrong에게 기사에서 언급된 것과 비슷한 강연을 학부에 해줄 것을 요청하고 있다는 첫 번째 단서를 확인할 수 있다. 그런데 기사에서 언급된 강연이 어떤 것인지 제시되지 않았으므로 기사에서 강연과 관련된 내용을 확인한다. 첫 번째 지문인 기사의 'Armstrong often visits universities to give talks to aspiring writers'(3문단 2번째 줄)에서 Armstrong은 장차 작가가 되려는 사람들에게 강연을 하기 위해 종종 대학들을 방문한다는 두 번째 단서를 확인할 수 있다.
Northwestern 문과대학 교수인 Leo Daniels가 Ms. Armstrong에게 기사에서 언급된 것과 비슷한 강연을 학부 학생들에게 해줄 것을 요청하고 있다는 첫 번째 단서와 Armstrong은 작가가 되려는 사람들에게 강연을 하기 위해 종종 대학들을 방문한다는 두 번째 단서를 종합할 때, Ms. Armstrong이 Northwestern 대학교에서 하는 강연에 참석할 사람은 작가가 되고자 하는 학생들이라는 사실을 추론할 수 있다. 따라서 (B) Young people who want to be authors가 정답이다.

Paraphrasing
aspiring writers 장차 작가가 되려는 사람들 → people who want to be authors 작가가 되고자 하는 사람들

06-10은 다음 보고서와 기사에 관한 문제입니다.

06Canalvia시 대중 교통 당국의 연례 보고서 요약

Canalvia시의 대중 교통 이용이 전년에 비해 6.4 퍼센트 하락했다. 이 감소는 지난 3년간 계속되는 경향이다. 09버스와 전철은 승객 정원의 72퍼센트로만 운영되어오고 있다.

버스와 전철 체계 운영의 원가는 연간 5천2백만 달러였다. 그러나, 승객들은 승차권의 4천3백만 달러 어치만을 구매했다. 올해로 연속 3년째 이 체계는 결국 시가 손해를 보게 했다.

많은 버스 정류장과 전철역들이 매우 낡았고 긴급하게 개조가 필요하다. 또한, 대중 교통의 안전이 많은 지역 거주민들 사이에서 문제가 되었다. 안전 문제에 대해 400건 이상의 항의가 작년에 제출되었다. 많은 승객들은 또한 올해 운임 인상에 대해 항의했고, 연간 승차권의 판매가 7 퍼센트 하락했다.

083월에 다가오는 두 새로운 전철역의 개관이 승차권 판매 증가를 도울 것이 ➡

지만, 다른 변화들이 손해를 막기 위해 필수적이다.

summary n. 요약, 개요 transit authority 대중 교통 당국
annual adj. 연례의, 매년의 public transportation 대중 교통
compare v. 비교하다 previous adj. 이전의
continuing adj. 계속되는, 연속적인 trend n. 경향, 추세 run v. 운영하다
passenger n. 승객 capacity n. 정원, 용량, 수용력 in a row 연속적으로
end up 결국 ~이 되다 outdated adj. 낡은 urgently adv. 긴급하게, 급히
renovation n. 개조, 수리 security n. 안전 complaint n. 항의, 불만
file v. 제출하다 fare n. 운임, 요금 pass n. 승차권, 정기권
upcoming adj. 다가오는, 곧 있을

Canalvia시 대중 교통 당국이 전철역들을 개관하고 변화를 공표하다
Sheldon Drake 작성

Ellen Carrington시장은 Canalvia시의 [08]Lakeland와 Harbor 지구에 있는 두 개의 새로운 전철역을 어제 공식적으로 개관했다. [08]전철역들은 오늘 운영되기 시작할 것이고 대개 주택 지역을 상업 지구 및 금융 지구와 연결할 것이다. 이 새로운 역들은 주차 시설, 매표소, 소매 판매점과 식당을 포함한다.

Lakeland에서의 기념 행사에 이어, Canalvia시 대중 교통 당국의 이사, Melvin Banks는 올해의 몇 가지 변화를 알리는 짧은 연설을 했다. [09]4월부터, 버스와 전철 체계의 안전 요원이 14퍼센트 늘어날 것이다. 게다가, 시 의회는 오래된 역과 버스 정류장의 개조를 시작하기 위한 계획을 승인했다. 이 사업은 6월에 시작되고, 8천2백만 달러의 비용으로 2년간 계속될 것이다. 자금은 지방세와 기업 후원으로 마련될 것이다.

Mr. Banks는 이 변화들이 거주자들의 요구에 응한 것이고, 교통 당국의 연간 보고의 결과라고 말했다. 이 운송 체계는 작년에 9백만 달러를 잃었다. [10]Mr. Banks는 개선들이 더 많은 승객들을 유치하고 손해를 줄일 수 있기를 바란다.

announce v. 공표하다, 알리다 district n. 지구, 지역
operational adj. 운영상의, 사용할 수 있는 link v. 연결하다
residential area 주택 지역 downtown n. 상업 지구
ceremony n. 기념 행사 security n. 안전 city council 시 의회
approve v. 승인하다 renovate v. 개조하다 last v. 계속되다
fund n. 자금 local tax 지방세 corporate adj. 기업의
sponsorship n. 후원 in response to ~에 응하여
decrease v. 줄이다 loss n. 손해

06 주제/목적 찾기 문제

문제 보고서는 주로 무엇에 관한 것인가?

(A) Canalvia시의 연간 예산
(B) 도시의 대중 교통 체계
(C) 버스 노선 확장 계획
(D) 승객 요금의 인상

해설 보고서가 주로 무엇에 관한 것인지를 묻는 주제 찾기 문제이므로 보고서의 내용을 확인한다. 첫 번째 지문인 보고서의 'Summary of Canalvia Transit Authority Annual Report'(제목)에서 Canalvia시 대중 교통 당국의 연례 보고라고 한 후, 도시의 대중 교통 체계 운영 현황에 대해서 설명하고 있으므로 (B) A city's public transportation systems가 정답이다.

어휘 budget n. 예산 expansion n. 확장

07 추론 문제

문제 Canalvia시에 대해 암시되는 것은 무엇인가?

(A) 시의 버스 노선이 정원을 채워 운영되지 못하고 있다.
(B) 인구의 감소를 경험하고 있다.
(C) 승객 요금을 인상하려고 계획하고 있다.
(D) 주민들이 추가 안전을 필요로 한다.

해설 질문의 핵심 어구인 Canalvia시에 대해 추론하는 문제이므로 Canalvia시에 대한 정보가 언급된 보고서에서 관련 내용을 확인한다. 첫 번째 지문인 보고서에서 'Buses ~ have been running at only 72 percent passenger capacity.'(1문단 2번째 줄)에서 버스가 승객 정원의 72퍼센트로만 운영되어오고 있다고 했으므로 시의 버스 노선이 정원을 채워 운영되지 못하고 있다는 사실을 추론할 수 있다. 따라서 (A) Its bus line isn't running at full capacity가 정답이다.

Paraphrasing
running at only 72 percent passenger capacity 승객 정원의 72퍼센트로만 운영되다 → isn't running at full capacity 정원을 채워 운영되지 못하고 있다

어휘 population n. 인구 fare n. 운임, 요금 neighborhood n. 주민, 이웃 additional adj. 추가의

08 육하원칙 문제 연계

문제 Harbor 전철역은 언제 운영되기 시작했는가?

(A) 3월에
(B) 4월에
(C) 5월에
(D) 6월에

해설 두 지문의 내용을 종합해서 풀어야 하는 연계 문제이다. Harbor 전철역이 언제(When) 운영되기 시작했는지를 묻고 있으므로 Harbor 전철역이 언급된 기사를 먼저 확인한다.
두 번째 지문인 기사의 'two new train stations in the Lakeland and Harbor'(1문단 1번째 줄)와 'The stations become operational today'(1문단 2번째 줄)에서 Harbor 전철역이 새롭게 운영되기 시작했다는 첫 번째 단서를 확인할 수 있다. 그런데 몇 월에 운영되기 시작했는지 제시되지 않았으므로 보고서에서 관련 정보를 확인한다. 첫 번째 지문인 보고서의 'The upcoming opening of two new train stations this March'(4문단 1번째 줄)에서 두 개의 새로운 전철역이 3월에 개관할 예정이었다는 두 번째 단서를 확인할 수 있다.
Harbor 전철역이 새롭게 운영되기 시작했다는 첫 번째 단서와 새로운 전철역이 3월에 개관할 예정이었다는 두 번째 단서를 종합할 때, 3월에 Harbor 전철역이 운영되기 시작했음을 알 수 있다. 따라서 (A) In March가 정답이다.

09 육하원칙 문제

문제 4월에 일어날 일은 무엇인가?

(A) 역들이 임시로 폐쇄될 것이다.
(B) 새로운 예산안이 시행될 것이다.
(C) 안전 요원들이 늘어날 것이다.
(D) 버스정류장들이 건설될 것이다.

해설 4월에 일어날 일이 무엇인지(What)를 묻는 육하원칙 문제이므로 질문의 핵심 어구인 April이 언급된 기사에서 관련 내용을 확인한다. 두 번째 지문인 기사의 'Starting in April, security personnel ~ will be increased'(2문단 2번째 줄)에서 4월부터 안전 요원이 늘어날 것이라고 했으므로 (C) Security staff will be increased가 정답이다.

Paraphrasing
personnel 요원 → staff 요원

어휘 temporarily adv. 임시로 implement v. 시행하다 construct v. 건설하다

10 육하원칙 문제

문제 왜 교통 당국이 변화를 주고 있는가?

(A) 운영 비용을 줄이기 위해
(B) 승차권 판매를 증가시키기 위해
(C) 증가하는 인구에 대응하기 위해
(D) 사업을 유치하기 위해

해설 왜(Why) 교통 당국이 변화를 주고 있는지를 묻는 육하원칙 문제이므로 질문의 핵심 어구인 changes가 언급된 기사에서 관련 내용을 확인한다. 두 번째 지문인 기사의 'Mr. Banks hopes the improvements will help attract more passengers and decrease losses.'(3문단 2번째 줄)에서 Mr. Banks, 즉 대중 교통 당국의 이사가 개선들이 더 많은 승객들을 유치하고 손해를 줄일 수 있기를 바란다고 했으므로 변화들은 승차권 판매를 증가시키기 위한 것임을 알 수 있다. 따라서 (B) To increase ticket sales가 정답이다.

Paraphrasing
changes 변화 → improvements 개선
attract more passengers and decrease losses 더 많은 승객들을 유치하고 손해를 줄이다 → increase ticket sales 승차권 판매를 증가시키다

어휘 **cut down** 줄이다, 삭감하다 **operation** n. 운영, 작업
respond v. 대응하다, 반응하다 **growing** adj. 증가하는, 성장하고 있는

11-15는 다음 기사, 웹페이지, 이메일에 관한 문제입니다.

이제 싱가포르로 매일 항공편을 운행하는 Oz-Air사

Oz-Air사는 시드니와 동남아시아의 중심지인 싱가포르 사이를 매일 운행한다는 것을 발표했다. ¹³ᴮ8시간의 직항 항공편이 오전 9시 40분에 시드니에서 매일 출발할 것이다. 또한, 돌아오는 항공편은 매일 오후 6시 20분에 시드니로 다시 향할 것이다.

"사업을 위해 여행하든 혹은 관광차 여행하든, 승객들은 직원들로부터 동일한 특별 서비스를 기대할 수 있습니다."라고 Oz-Air사의 마케팅 부장 Jennifer Hogan은 말한다. "저희는 고급 식사와 친절한 서비스로 여행 중에 여러분을 소중히 보살필 것입니다." 싱가포르는 다문화적인 환경에서 관광지, 쇼핑, 요리, 그리고 독특한 경험들을 제공하며 점점 인기 여행지가 되었다.

¹¹새 경로를 기념하기 위해, Oz-Air사는 싱가포르행 왕복 항공권을 단 569달러에 제공하고 있다. 추가적인 정보는 항공사의 웹사이트 www.oz-air.co.au/singaporepromotion에서 찾을 수 있다.

hub n. 중심지 **nonstop** adj. 직행의, 도중에 정거하지 않는
exceptional adj. 특별한, 예외의 **gourmet meal** 고급 식사
attentive adj. 친절한, 세심한 **increasingly** adv. 점점, 더욱더
sight n. 관광지, 명소 **setting** n. 환경

---

www.oz-air.co.au/flights/ticketing/confirmation

승객 성명: Edmund Chang	
주소: 3098번지 42번가, 시드니 뉴사우스웨일스주, 호주	
이메일: chang@nswenterprises.com	전화: (902)555-9388
¹³ᴮ/ᴰ항공편: ZA 909	¹³ᴮ/ᶜ출발: 3월 15일, 오전 9시 40분, ¹³ᴮ시드니
¹³ᴰ/¹⁵돌아오는 항공편: ZA 908	¹⁵출발: 3월 18일, 오후 6시 20분, 싱가포르
등급: 이코노미 플러스	¹²상용 고객 번호: 없음

주의 사항: 항공사에 의해 제공된 모든 판촉 운임은 취소가 불가능합니다. 하지만, 예정된 출발일자의 최소 10일 전에 통지를 주시면, 다른 변경들은 가능합니다. 그러한 경우 100달러의 수수료가 적용됩니다.

제출

flight number 항공편 **frequent flyer** (항공사의) 상용 고객, 특정 항공사의 비행기를 이용하여 항공 여행을 자주 하는 단골 고객 **promotional** adj. 판촉의, 홍보의
applicable adj. 적용되는, 해당되는

수신 <bookings@ozair.co.au>
발신 Edmund Chang <chang@nswenterprises.com>
제목 항공편
날짜 1월 14일

담당자분께,

저는 최근에 3월 15일자 싱가포르행 항공권을 구매했습니다. ¹⁴저는 그곳에서 **생물학 연구 학회에 참석할 것입니다.** 저는 NSW Enterprises사에 있는 동료 Fred Banks와 학회에 대해 논의하고 있었고, 그에게 귀사의 판촉 할인에 대해 말해주었습니다. ¹⁴저희 연구가 학회의 주제로 직접적으로 연관이 있기 때문에, 그는 저와 동행하고 싶어 합니다. 하지만, 제가 돌아오기로 계획하고 있던 날짜에 그가 이용 가능한 좌석이 없습니다. 그런데 ¹⁵그 다음 날에는 이용 가능한 좌석이 많이 있습니다. 제 동료와 제가 함께 이동할 수 있도록 저의 표를 바꿀 수 있을까요? 저희는 돌아오는 항공편의 자리가 아직 비어 있는 동안 빨리 예약하고 싶으므로 가능한 한 빨리 제게 알려주시기 바랍니다.

Edmund Chang 드림

biological adj. 생물학의 **conference** n. 학회, 회담
associate n. 동료 **promotional offer** 판촉 할인
directly related to ~와 직접적으로 연관이 있다
subject n. (논의 등의) 주제, 대상 **accompany** v. 동행하다, 동반하다
vacant adj. 비어 있는

---

11 육하원칙 문제

문제 Oz-Air사는 왜 특별가를 제공하는가?

(A) 새 항로를 홍보하기 위해
(B) 창립일을 기념하기 위해
(C) 상용 고객 프로그램을 알리기 위해
(D) 경쟁 항공사보다 많이 판매하기 위해

해설 Oz-Air사가 왜(Why) 특가를 제공하는지를 묻는 육하원칙 문제이므로 질문의 핵심 어구인 Oz-Air offering the special과 관련된 내용이 언급된 첫 번째 지문인 기사를 확인한다. 기사의 'To celebrate the new route, Oz-Air is offering return tickets to Singapore for only $569.'(3문단 1번째 줄)에서 새 경로를 기념하기 위해 Oz-Air사가 싱가포르행 왕복 항공권을 단 569달러에 제공하고 있다고 했으므로 (A) To promote its new route가 정답이다.

어휘 **special** n. 특별가; adj. 특별한 **commemorate** v. 기념하다
establishment n. 창립, 설립 **publicize** v. 알리다, 광고하다
outsell v. ~보다 많이 판매하다

12 추론 문제

문제 Mr. Chang에 대해 암시되는 것은?

(A) 비즈니스석으로 업그레이드를 요청했다.
(B) Oz-Air사의 상용 고객 프로그램 회원이 아니다.
(C) 일 때문에 시드니 시외로 자주 여행한다.
(D) 모든 필요한 연락처를 제공하지 않았다.

해설 질문의 핵심 어구인 Mr. Chang에 대해 추론하는 문제이므로 Mr. Chang을 언급한 웹페이지에서 관련 내용을 확인한다. 두 번째 지문인 웹페이지의 'FREQUENT FLYER NUMBER: None'(2번째 표 3행 2열)에서 상용 고객 번호가 없다고 했으므로 Mr. Chang은 Oz-Air사의 상용 고객 프로그램 회원이 아니라는 사실을 추론할 수 있다. 따라서 (B) He is not a member of Oz-Air's frequent flyer program이 정답이다.

어휘 **business class** (비행기의) 비즈니스석 **necessary** adj. 필요한

13 Not/True 문제 연계

문제 Mr. Chang의 다가오는 비행에 대해 언급한 것은?

(A) 다른 특별 할인과 결합할 수 없다.
(B) 약 8시간 동안 계속될 것이다.
(C) 저녁에 출발하기로 예정되어 있다.
(D) 단지 편도 여행일 것이다.

해설 두 지문의 내용을 종합해서 풀어야 하는 연계 문제이다. 질문의 핵심 어구인 Mr. Chang's upcoming flight에 대한 내용이 언급된 기사와 웹페이지 모두에서 관련 내용을 확인한다.
두 번째 지문인 웹페이지의 'FLIGHT NUMBER: ZA 909, DEPARTURE: March 15, 9:40 A.M., Sydney'(2번째 표 1행)에서 Mr. Chang의 항공편이 3월 15일 오전 9시 40분에 시드니에서 출발한다는 첫 번째 단서를 확인할 수 있다. 그런데 이 항공편에 대한 다른 정보가 제시되지 않았으므로 기사에서 관련 내용을 확인한다. 첫 번째 지문인 기사의 'Nonstop eight-hour flights will depart daily from Sydney at 9:40 A.M.'(1문단 2번째 줄)에서 8시간의 직항 항공편이 시드니에서 오전 9시 40분에 매일 출발한다는 두 번째 단서를 확인할 수 있다.
Mr. Chang의 항공편이 3월 15일 오전 9시 40분에 시드니에서 출발한다는 첫 번째 단서와 8시간의 직항 항공편이 시드니에서 매일 오전 9시 40분에 출발한다는 두 번째 단서를 종합할 때, Mr. Chang의 다가오는 비행은 약 8시간이 소요될 것임을 알 수 있다. 따라서 (B) It will last for approximately eight hours가 정답이다. (A)는 지문에 언급되지 않은 내용이다. (C)는 'DEPARTURE: ~ 9:40 A.M.'(2번째 표 1행)에서 오전 9시 40분에 출발한다고 했으므로 지문의 내용과 일치하지 않는다. (D)는 'FLIGHT NUMBER: ZA 909'(2번째 표 1행 1열)와 'RETURN FLIGHT NUMBER: ZA 908'(2번째 표 2행 1열)에서 왕복 여행임을 알 수 있으므로 지문의 내용과 일치하지 않는다.

어휘 **combine** v. 결합하다, 겸하다 **one-way** adj. 편도의

14 추론 문제

문제 이메일에 근거하여, Mr. Chang은 어느 분야에서 일하는 것 같은가?

(A) 여행 및 관광
(B) 과학 연구
(C) 경제 연구
(D) 광고 및 홍보

해설 이메일에 근거하여 질문의 핵심 어구인 Mr. Chang에 대해 추론하는 문제이므로 Mr. Chang이 작성한 이메일을 확인한다. 세 번째 지문인 이메일의 'I am attending the Biological Studies Conference'(1번째 줄)와 'our work is directly related to the subject of the conference'(3번째 줄)에서 Mr. Chang은 생물학 연구 학회에 참석할 것이며, 연구가 학회의 주제와 직접적으로 연관이 있다고 했으므로 Mr. Chang이 과학 연구 분야에서 일한다는 사실을 추론할 수 있다. 따라서 (B) Scientific research가 정답이다.

Paraphrasing
Biological Studies 생물학 연구 → Scientific research 과학 연구

어휘 economic adj. 경제의

15 육하원칙 문제 연계

문제 Mr. Chang은 무엇을 하기를 원하는가?

(A) 3월 19일 항공편으로 두 좌석을 예약한다
(B) 동료의 도착일자를 변경한다
(C) 취소 비용을 환불 받는다
(D) 동료를 학회에 등록한다

해설 두 지문의 내용을 종합해서 풀어야 하는 연계 문제이다. 질문의 핵심 어구인 Mr. Chang want to do에서 Mr. Chang이 할 원하는 것이 무엇인지(What)를 묻고 있으므로 Mr. Chang이 보낸 이메일을 먼저 확인한다.
세 번째 지문인 이메일의 'there are many seats available the next day. Would it be possible to change my ticket so that my colleague and I can travel together?'(5번째 줄)에서 Mr. Chang이 다음 날에는 이용 가능한 좌석이 많이 있으므로, 동료와 함께 이동할 수 있도록 자신의 표를 바꿀 수 있는지 문의하고 있다는 첫 번째 단서를 확인할 수 있다. 그런데 Mr. Chang이 바꾸고 싶은 다음 날의 날짜가 언제인지 제시되지 않았으므로 웹페이지에서 관련 내용을 확인한다. 두 번째 지문인 웹페이지의 'RETURN FLIGHT NUMBER: ZA 908, DEPARTURE: March 18'(2번째 표 2행)에서 돌아오는 항공편이 3월 18일에 출발한다는 두 번째 단서를 확인할 수 있다.
Mr. Chang이 다음 날에는 이용 가능한 좌석이 많이 있으므로 동료와 함께 이동할 수 있도록 표를 바꾸고 싶어 한다는 첫 번째 단서와 원래 Mr. Chang의 돌아오는 항공편은 3월 18일에 출발한다는 두 번째 단서를 종합할 때, Mr. Chang이 3월 19일 항공편으로 자신과 동료의 좌석을 예약하고 싶어 함을 알 수 있다. 따라서 (A) Book two seats for a flight on March 19가 정답이다.

16-20은 다음 기사, 편지, 이메일에 관한 문제입니다.

SCOPE 방송국이 AWPS에 막대한 돈을 기부하다

[16]호주 야생 동물 보호 협회(AWPS)는 월요일 특별 행사에서 Scope 방송국(SBC)이 그들의 활동에 120만 달러를 기부했다고 발표했다. AWPS의 회장인 Cindy Stubbs는 SBC사의 지사장인 Audrey McKay로부터 수표를 받기 위해 참석했다. McKay는 [16]기금의 절반이 채널의 시청자들로부터 온 것이며 한 달간의 모금 캠페인 동안 모인 것이라고 설명했다. 시청자들이 온라인 기부를 하도록 설득하는 짧은 광고가 SBC사에서 방송되었다. 나머지 기금은 SBC사의 회사 보조금이었다. Stubbs는 짧은 연설에서 기부에 대해 McKay에게 정중히 감사를 표했으며 기금이 전국의 여러 야생 동물 보호 구역의 운영에 사용될 것이라고 말했다.

SBC사는 내년의 모금 기간까지는 추가 기부금을 보조하지 않을 것이지만, 기부는 www.sbc.co.au/donate에서 여전히 받고 있다. 뿐만 아니라, [18]SBC사는 우수 후원자로 등록하는 사람들의 기부금에 추가 100달러를 더할 것이다.

effort n. 활동, 노력 on hand 참석한, 출석한 month-long adj. 한 달간의
fundraising n. 모금 broadcast v. 방송하다
urge v. 설득하다, 권하다 match n. 보조금; v. 자금을 보조하다
graciously adv. 정중하게 reserve n. 보호 구역, 비축; v. 예약하다, 남겨두다
contribution n. 기부금, 기부

2월 2일

Miriam Smythe
987번지 Eucalyptus가
멜버른, 빅토리아주 3001

Ms. Smythe께,

[17/18]Scope 방송국 모금 프로그램의 우수 후원자로 등록해 주셔서 정말 감사합니다! 귀하의 기금은 다양한 프로그램과 기관을 통해 전국의 야생 동물 보호에 쓰일 것입니다. [18]귀하의 신용카드에 400달러의 기부금이 청구되었으며, 귀하의 개인 기록을 위한 영수증이 귀하께 이메일로 발송되었습니다.

전 세계적으로 저희가 기부하는 모든 단체의 목록을 포함한, [17/19-B]SBC사의 후원 네트워크에 관한 정보 책자를 동봉했습니다. 그리고 [19-B]귀하가 선택하신 대로, AWPS 로고가 새겨진 중간 크기의 티셔츠가 사은품으로 포함되었습니다!

귀하의 지속적인 시청에 감사드리며, 이러한 중요한 단체에 대한 귀하의 후원에 감사드립니다. 우리의 노력이 지구의 생물들을 보호하는 데 변화를 가져올 수 있습니다. 질문이나 우려되는 점이 있으시다면, charbell@sbc.co.au로 언제든 자유롭게 저에게 연락해 주시기 바랍니다.

Charmaine Bell 드림
모금 부서
Scope 방송국

go towards (돈이) ~에 쓰이다 a range of 다양한 brochure n. 책자
viewership n. 시청, 시청자, 시청률 patronage n. 후원, 보호

수신: Charmaine Bell <charbell@sbc.co.au>
발신: Miriam Smythe <smire@victoriamail.com>
제목: 후원자 소포
날짜: [19-C]2월 7일

Ms. Bell께,

[19-C]저는 어제 SBC사로부터 소포를 받았고 [19-B]책자와 편지에 대해 감사드립니다. 유감스럽게도, [19-A]소포에 포함된 선물은 요청했던 것과 같이 중간 크기가 아니었습니다. 분명 누군가가 어쩌면 큰 크기의 것을 동봉한 것이 틀림없습니다. 올바른 크기를 받을 수 있을까요? 필요하다면 제가 가지고 있는 것을 다시 돌려보낼 수 있습니다.

또한, [20]저는 영수증을 포함한 이메일을 아직 받지 못했습니다. 그것을 저에게 보내주실 수 있나요? 기부금은 세금 공제가 되기 때문에, 제 회계사가 그것의 사본을 필요로 할 것입니다.

이러한 문제들에 대한 귀하의 도움에 감사드립니다.

Miriam Smythe 드림

by accident 어쩌다, 우연히 deductible adj. 세금 공제가 되는
accountant n. 회계사

16 주제/목적 찾기 문제

문제 기사는 주로 무엇에 대한 것인가?

(A) 회사 경영진의 임명
(B) 자선 단체의 운영
(C) 온라인 광고 출시
(D) 모금 캠페인의 성공

해설 기사가 주로 무엇에 대한 것인지를 묻는 주제 찾기 문제이므로 기사의 내용을 확인한다. 첫 번째 지문인 기사의 'The Australia Wildlife Protection Society (AWPS) announced ~ that Scope Broadcasting Corporation (SBC) had donated $1.2 million to its efforts.'(1문단 1번째 줄)에서 호주 야생 동물 보호 협회(AWPS)가 Scope 방송국(SBC)이 그들의 활동에 120만 달러를 기부했다고 발표했다고 한 후, 'half the funds ~ were gathered during a month-long fundraising campaign'(1문단 5번째 줄)에서 기금의 절반이 한 달간의 모금 캠페인 동안 모인 것이라고 하며 성공적으로 이루어진 모금 캠페인에 대해 설명하고 있으므로 (D) The success of a fund-raising campaign이 정답이다.

어휘 appointment n. 임명 executive n. 경영진, 간부 charitable adj. 자선의
fund-raising adj. 모금의, 모금 활동의

17 추론 문제

문제 Ms. Smythe에 대해 추론될 수 있는 것은?

(A) 최근에 특별 행사에 참석했다.
(B) SBC사의 텔레비전 프로그램을 드물게 시청한다.
(C) 후원 네트워크의 회원 자격을 보유한다.
(D) 정기적으로 AWPS의 계획을 후원한다.

해설 질문의 핵심 어구인 Ms. Smythe에 대해 추론하는 문제이므로 Ms. Smythe에게 보내진 편지에서 관련 내용을 확인한다. 두 번째 지문인 편지의 'Thank you so much for signing up as a premium sponsor of Scope Broadcasting Corporation's fundraising program!'(1문단 1번째 줄)에서 Ms. Smythe에게 Scope 방송국 모금 프로그램의 우수 후원자로 등록해 주어 감사하다고 한 후, 'Enclosed you will find an informational brochure about SBC's support network'(2문단 1번째 줄)에서 SBC사의 후원 네트워크에 관한 정보 책자를 동봉했다고 했으므로 Ms. Smythe가 후원 네트워크의 회원 자격을 보유하게 되었다는 사실을 추론할 수 있다. 따라서 (C) She holds membership in a support network가 정답이다.

어휘 hold v. 보유하다 membership n. 회원 (자격·신분) initiative n. 계획

18 추론 문제 연계

문제 Scope 방송국에 대해 암시되는 것은?

(A) Ms. Smythe의 재정 기부금을 보조했다.
(B) 모금된 모든 기금을 AWPS에 제공한다.
(C) Ms. Smythe의 이름으로 추가 100달러를 기부할 것이다.
(D) 모든 후원자들에게 사은품을 보낼 것이다.

해설 두 지문의 내용을 종합적으로 확인한 후 추론해서 풀어야 하는 연계 문제이다. 질문의 핵심 어구인 Scope Broadcasting Corporation이 언급된 기사를 먼저 확인한다.
첫 번째 지문인 기사의 'SBC will add an extra $100 to the contributions of those signing up as premium supporters'(2문단 3번째 줄)에서 Scope 방송국이 우수 후원자로 등록하는 사람들의 기부금에 추가 100달러를 더할 것이라는 첫 번째 단서를 확인할 수 있다. 그런데 우수 후원자의 기부금에 대한 정보가 제시되지 않았으므로 편지에서 관련 내용을 확인한다. 두 번째 지문인 편지의 'Thank you so much for signing up as a premium sponsor of Scope Broadcasting Corporation's fundraising program!'(1문단 1번째 줄)과 'Your credit card has been charged the donation amount of $400'(1문단 3번째 줄)에서 Ms. Smythe가 Scope 방송국 모금 프로그램의 우수 후원자로 등록했으며, 400달러의 기부금이 Ms. Smythe의 신용카드에 청구되었다는 두 번째 단서를 확인할 수 있다.
Scope 방송국이 우수 후원자로 등록하는 사람들의 기부금에 추가로 100달러를 더할 것이라는 첫 번째 단서와 Ms. Smythe가 Scope 방송국 모금 프로그램의 우수 후원자로 등록했으며, 400달러의 기부금이 청구되었다는 두 번째 단서를 종합할 때, Scope 방송국이 Ms. Smythe의 이름으로 추가 100달러를 기부할 것이라는 사실을 추론할 수 있다. 따라서 (C) It will donate an extra $100 in the name of Ms. Smythe가 정답이다.

어휘 raise v. 모금하다, 조달하다

19 Not/True 문제 연계

문제 Ms. Smythe에게 보내진 소포에 대해 언급된 것은?

(A) 크기가 맞지 않는 홍보용 티셔츠를 포함했다.
(B) AWPS에 관한 정보 책자가 빠져 있었다.
(C) 거주지에 2월 7일에 도착했다.
(D) 잘못하여 손상된 상품을 포함했다.

해설 두 지문의 내용을 종합해서 풀어야 하는 연계 문제이다. 질문의 핵심 어구인 package sent to Ms. Smythe와 관련된 내용이 언급된 이메일을 먼저 확인한다.
세 번째 지문인 이메일의 'the gift contained in the package was not medium as requested'(1문단 1번째 줄)에서 Ms. Smythe가 요청했던 중간 크기가 아닌 다른 크기의 물건을 소포로 받았다는 첫 번째 단서를 확인할 수 있다. 그런데 Ms. Smythe가 받은 물건이 무엇인지 제시되지 않았으므로 편지에서 관련 내용을 확인한다. 두 번째 지문인 편지의 'as you selected, a medium T-shirt ~ has been included as a free gift'(2문단 2번째 줄)에

서 Ms. Smythe가 선택한 대로 중간 크기의 티셔츠가 사은품으로 포함되어 보내졌다는 두 번째 단서를 확인할 수 있다.
Ms. Smythe가 요청한 것과 다른 크기의 물건을 소포로 받았다는 첫 번째 단서와 Ms. Smythe에게 중간 크기의 티셔츠가 사은품으로 포함되어 보내졌다는 두 번째 단서를 종합할 때, Ms. Smythe에게 보내진 소포가 그녀가 요청한 크기와 맞지 않는 홍보용 티셔츠였다는 것을 알 수 있다. 따라서 (A) It included a promotional T-shirt that does not fit이 정답이다. (B)는 편지의 'Enclosed you will find an informational brochure'(2문단 1번째 줄)와 이메일의 'appreciate the brochure'(1문단 1번째 줄)에서 정보 책자가 동봉되었고, 책자에 대해 감사하다고 했으므로 지문의 내용과 일치하지 않는다. (C)는 이메일의 'February 7'(이메일 상단)과 'I received the package yesterday'(1문단 1번째 줄)에서 소포를 어제 받았다고 했고 이는 이메일 발신 날짜의 하루 전인 2월 6일이므로 지문의 내용과 일치하지 않는다. (D)는 지문에 언급되지 않은 내용이다.

어휘 fit v. (치수가) 꼭 맞다, 알맞다 residence n. 거주지, 집 accidentally adv. 잘못하여, 우연히

20 추론 문제

문제 Charmaine Bell은 무엇을 할 것 같은가?

(A) Ms. Smythe의 후원자 자격을 갱신한다
(B) 재정 문서 한 부를 전송한다
(C) Ms. Smythe의 개인 회계사에게 연락한다
(D) 더 큰 크기의 물품을 보낸다

해설 질문의 핵심 어구인 Charmaine Bell에 대해 추론하는 문제이므로 Charmaine Bell에게 보내는 이메일에서 관련 내용을 확인한다. 세 번째 지문인 이메일의 'I have not yet received an e-mail containing a receipt. Could you please send it to me?'(2문단 1번째 줄)에서 이메일의 발신자인 Ms. Smythe가 Charmaine Bell에게 영수증이 포함된 이메일을 아직 받지 못했으며 그것을 보내줄 수 있냐고 했으므로 Charmaine Bell이 재정 문서 한 부를 전송할 것이라는 사실을 추론할 수 있다. 따라서 (B) Forward a copy of a financial document가 정답이다.

어휘 forward v. 전송하다, 전달하다

Chapter 19 광고 연계 지문

예제 해석·해설 p.498

광고 & 광고 & 이메일

Clockwork사의 최신 시계인 Chrono-Watch 3000은 운동을 좋아하는 남성을 염두에 두고 디자인되었습니다. 2,200달러로 가격이 책정된, Clockwork사의 Chrono-Watch 3000은 전국의 Bullion Fine Jewelry 직판점에서 구매 가능합니다.

timepiece n. 시계 **outlet** n. 직판점

만일 여러분 인생의 활동적인 남성을 위한 완벽한 선물을 찾고 계시다면, 멀리서 찾지 마십시오. Genevex사의 Metrowatch는 어떠한 경우에도 완벽한 선물이 됩니다. Metrowatch는 태양 에너지로 작동되고 2캐럿짜리 다이아몬드가 박힌 시계 표면을 가지고 있습니다.

occasion n. 경우, 일 **set** v. (보석 등을) 박아 넣다

수신: Charlotte Becker <c.becker@mailroom.com>
발신: Brent Oldwood <b.oldwood@monomail.com>
혹시 Allan의 생일을 위해 줄 선물을 아직 고르지 못했다면, 제가 아마 도와드릴 수 있을 것 같습니다. 저는 지난주에 온라인으로 둘러보던 중에 모든 종류의 시계를 판매하는 상점을 찾았습니다. 이 링크를 확인해보세요: www.watchfinder.com.

browse v. 둘러보다 **check out** 확인하다

문제 Chrono-Watch 3000에 대해 암시되는 것은?

(A) Metrowatch보다 비싸다.
(B) 보석과 금속으로 장식되어 있다.
(C) Metrowatch와 같은 유형의 사용자를 위한 것이다.
(D) 웹사이트에서 구매 가능하다.

해설 **추론 문제** 두 지문의 내용을 종합적으로 확인한 후 추론해서 풀어야 하는 연계 문제이다. 질문의 핵심 어구인 the Chrono-Watch 3000가 언급된 첫 번째 광고를 먼저 확인한다.

첫 번째 광고의 'the Chrono-Watch 3000, was designed with the athletic man in mind'에서 Chrono-Watch 3000는 운동을 좋아하는 남성을 위해 디자인되었다는 첫 번째 단서를 확인할 수 있다. 그리고 두 번째 광고의 'the perfect gift for the active man'과 'Metrowatch makes an ideal gift'에서 Metrowatch가 활동적인 남성에게 적합하다는 두 번째 단서를 확인할 수 있다.

Chrono-Watch 3000이 운동을 좋아하는 남성을 위한 시계라는 첫 번째 단서와 Metrowatch가 활동적인 남성에게 적합한 시계라는 두 번째 단서를 종합할 때, Chrono-Watch 3000은 Metrowatch와 같은 유형의 사용자를 위한 제품이라는 사실을 추론할 수 있다. 따라서 (C) It is for the same type of user as the Metrowatch가 정답이다.

어휘 **precious stone** 보석

Hackers Practice

p.499

유형 연습
01 (C)　　02 (B)　　03 (C)　　04 (B)

01-02 광고 & 안내문

Interlingua 장난감과 게임

Interlingua사는 신뢰받는 어린이용 장난감 및 게임 제작사입니다. 재미있고 교육적인 수백 개의 제품들을 온라인상에서 선택해 보십시오. 01아래에 있는 링크를 클릭하셔서 판매 중인 특정 제품에 대한 완전한 정보를 살펴보십시오.

• 02미취학 아동용 장난감 (3세 이상)　　• 퍼즐 게임 (5세 이상)
• 조립식 장난감 (4세 이상)　　• 보드 게임 (6세 이상)

웹사이트에 게재된 가격들은 배송비와 세금을 포함하지 않는다는 점을 유의해 주십시오.

specific adj. 특정한　**preschool** adj. 취학 전의　**tax** n. 세금

동물원에서의 하루

아이들에게 동물들과 그들이 내는 소리를 어떻게 식별할 수 있는지 가르쳐 줍니다. 03세 이상 아이들에게 적합합니다.

• 배송비 불포함 가격: 44.95달러　　• 중량: 2.4파운드
• 제품 크기: 5.1×4.2×10.8인치　　• 제품은 3일 내에 배송됩니다.

identify v. 식별하다, 분간하다　**dimension** n. 크기, 규모

---

01 육하원칙 문제

문제 웹사이트에서 볼 수 있는 것은 어떤 정보인가?

(A) 가게 영업 시간
(B) 배송비
(C) 제품 설명

해설 웹사이트에서 볼 수 있는 것이 어떤(What) 정보인지를 묻는 육하원칙 문제이므로 질문의 핵심 어구인 the Web site가 언급된 광고에서 관련 내용을 확인한다. 첫 번째 지문인 광고의 'Click on the links ~ to view ~ information about ~ items for sale.'(2번째 줄)에서 링크를 클릭해서 판매 중인 제품에 대한 정보를 살펴보라고 했으므로 (C) Item descriptions가 정답이다.

Paraphrasing
information about ~ items 제품에 대한 정보 → Item descriptions 제품 설명

02 추론 문제 연계

문제 동물원에서의 하루는 무엇일 것 같은가?

(A) 아동용 도서
(B) 미취학 아동용 장난감
(C) 퍼즐 게임

해설 두 지문의 내용을 종합적으로 확인한 후 추론해서 풀어야 하는 연계 문제이다. 질문의 핵심 어구인 A Day at the Zoo가 언급된 안내문을 먼저 확인한다.

두 번째 지문인 안내문의 'Suitable for children 3 years of age and older.'(1번째 줄)에서 A Day at the Zoo가 3세 이상 아이들에게 적합하다는 첫 번째 단서를 확인할 수 있다. 그런데 3세 이상 아이들에게 적합한 제품이 어떤 종류로 분류되는지 제시되지 않았으므로 광고에서 관련 내용을 확인한다. 첫 번째 지문인 광고의 'Preschool toys (ages 3 and up)'(4번째 줄)에서 3세 이상 아이들을 위한 제품은 미취학 아동용 장난감으로 분류된다는 두 번째 단서를 알 수 있다.

A Day at the Zoo가 3세 이상 아이들에게 적합하다는 첫 번째 단서와 미취학 아동용 장난감이 3세 이상 아이들을 위한 것이라는 두 번째 단서를 종합할 때, A Day at the Zoo는 미취학 아동용 장난감이라는 사실을 추론할 수 있다. 따라서 (B) A preschool toy가 정답이다.

03-04 광고 & 이메일

카피라이터 구인: Harlequin 광고 회사

Harlequin 광고 회사는 로스앤젤레스에 있는 팀에 합류할 카피라이터를 구하고 있습니다. 04지원자는 반드시 전문적인 집필 경력을 가지고 있어야 하며 광고업에 정통해야 합니다. 뿐만 아니라, 우선권은 제2외국어에 유창함을 보이는 사람에게 주어질 것입니다. 또한, 지원자는 현재 로스앤젤레스 거주자이거나 8월 15일 전까지 이전할 수 있는 사람이어야 합니다. 03지원하기 위해서는 전체 업무 경력과 본인이 집필한 작품의 사본을 Arlene Sorkin에게 a.sorkin@harlequinads.com으로 보내 주시기 바랍니다.

copywriter n. 카피라이터　**background** n. 경력　**advertising** adj. 광고의
preference n. 우선권, 선호　**fluency** n. (말·문체의) 유창(함)

수신: Pamela Lopez <pamlo@mmail.com>
발신: Jane Duvall <j.duvall@starmail.com>
제목: 직업 전망

안녕하세요 Pam,

당신이 막 로스앤젤레스로 이사를 왔고 일을 구하고 있다고 들었어요. 실은, 04제가 아는 한 광고 대행 회사가 카피라이터를 구하고 있어요. 당신이 익숙한 분야와는 다른 분야지만 2개 국어로 쓰인 Linguesa지에서 일했던 당신의 경험은 강점이 될 거예요. 좀 더 자세한 내용은 첨부 파일을 읽어 보세요.

prospect n. 전망　**be used to** ~에 익숙해지다
bilingual adj. 두 개 언어로 쓰인　**advantage** n. 강점, 유리한 점

---

03 육하원칙 문제

문제 Harlequin 광고 회사는 지원자들에게 무엇을 준비하라고 요청하는가?

(A) 추천서
(B) 졸업장 사본
(C) 집필 문서 샘플

해설 Harlequin 광고 회사가 지원자들에게 무엇을(What) 준비하라고 요청하는지를 묻는 육하원칙 문제이므로 질문의 핵심 어구인 ask applicants to provide가 언급된 광고를 확인한다. 첫 번째 지문인 광고의 'To apply, please send a complete work history and copies of your written work'(5번째 줄)에서 지원하기 위해서는 전체 업무 경력과 본인이 집필한 작품의 사본을 보내라고 했으므로 (C) Writing samples가 정답이다.

Paraphrasing
copies of ~ written work 집필한 작품의 사본 → Writing samples 집필 문서 샘플

어휘 **reference** n. 추천서, 증명서, 참조　**diploma** n. 졸업장

04 육하원칙 문제 연계

문제 Ms. Lopez는 직업에 필요한 어떤 자격 요건을 가지고 있지 않은가?

(A) 도시 내 거주
(B) 광고업에 대한 지식

(C) 제2외국어에 대한 전문적 지식

해설 두 지문의 내용을 종합해서 풀어야 하는 연계 문제이다. 질문의 핵심 어구인 qualifications ~ Ms. Lopez not have에서 Ms. Lopez가 직업에 필요한 어떤(Which) 자격 요건을 가지고 있지 않은지를 묻고 있으므로 Ms. Lopez 에게 보내는 이메일을 먼저 확인한다.

두 번째 지문인 이메일의 'an advertising agency ~ is looking for a copywriter. It's a different field than you're used to'(1번째 줄)에서 광고 대행 회사가 찾고 있는 카피라이터라는 직업은 Ms. Lopez가 익숙한 분야 와는 다르다는 첫 번째 단서를 확인할 수 있다. 그런데 카피라이터라는 직업 과 관련하여 Ms. Lopez가 익숙하지 않은 분야가 어떤 분야인지 제시되지 않 았으므로 광고에서 광고 대행 회사가 카피라이터에 대해 어떤 자격을 요구하 는지를 확인한다. 첫 번째 지문인 광고의 'Applicants must ~ be familiar with the advertising industry.'(1번째 줄)에서 지원자는 반드시 광고업에 정통해야 한다는 두 번째 단서를 확인할 수 있다.

카피라이터는 Ms. Lopez가 익숙하지 않은 분야의 직업이라는 첫 번째 단서 와 카피라이터에 대한 지원자는 광고업에 정통해야 한다는 두 번째 단서를 종 합할 때, Ms. Lopez는 보기에 제시된 자격 요건 중에 광고업에 대한 정통함 을 갖고 있지 않음을 알 수 있다. 따라서 (B) Knowledge of advertising 이 정답이다.

어휘 residency n. (특정 장소에서의) 거주   expertise n. 전문적 지식

Hackers Test
p.500

p.500

01 (D)	02 (B)	03 (C)	04 (A)	05 (D)
06 (C)	07 (C)	08 (D)	09 (A)	10 (D)
11 (D)	12 (C)	13 (B)	14 (A)	15 (A)

01-05는 다음 광고와 이메일에 관한 문제입니다.

TRIPOD PHOTO AND VIDEO SERVICES

01Tripod Photo and Video Services사는 어떤 행사든 훌륭한 사진과 비디 오 촬영을 제공한다는 것을 자랑스럽게 생각합니다. 03-B자사는 생일 파티, 기념 일, 결혼 등과 같은 여러 종류의 행사를 다룹니다. 전문 편집 소프트웨어뿐 만 아니라 고해상도와 고화질의 카메라를 사용하여, 최고 품질의 결과물을 보장합 니다. 또한, 자사는 전문 사진 작가, 비디오 제작자 그리고 그래픽 아티스트들로 이루어진 팀으로 구성되어 있으며 이들은 고객의 모든 요구 사항을 충족시키기 위해 촬영일 이전, 당일, 이후에 걸쳐 일합니다.

03-ATripod Photo and Video Services사는 다루어야 할 행사와 요구되는 결 과물에 따라 다양한 패키지를 제공하는데, 02/03-A이것은 사진 앨범 또는 CD, 액 자에 담긴 사진, 원본 비디오와 편집된 비디오의 DVD 02또는 이 품목들의 조합 으로 이루어져 있습니다.

그리고 오직 이번 달 동안에만, 04800달러 이상의 촬영 패키지 상품을 주문하 시면 50달러의 상품권을 받으실 수 있습니다!* 이번 달이 지나기 전에 예약을 하시려면, customersupport@tripodvideo.com으로 간단히 이메일을 보 내 주시면 되고, 추후 자사의 어떠한 서비스에도 사용하실 수 있는 상품권을 보 내 드리겠습니다.

Tripod Photo and Video Services사나, 특별 판매 상품 및 패키지 상품에 대해 좀 더 알고 싶으시면, 자사 웹사이트 www.tripodvideo.com을 확인하 시기 바랍니다.

*반드시 5월 31일까지 예약이 이루어져야 특별 상품권 제공을 받으실 자격이 주어집니다.

take (a) pride in ~를 자랑하다   high-resolution 고해상도의
high-definition 고화질의   output n. 결과물, 출력물
be made up of ~로 구성되다   videographer n. 비디오 제작자
consist of ~로 이루어지다, 구성되다   raw adj. 편집되지 않은, 날 것의
combination n. 조합, 결합   package deal 패키지 상품
reservation n. 예약   promotion n. 판촉 상품, 판촉 활동

수신 Adrian Winston <a.winston@giantredmail.com>
발신 Deanna Lloyd <customersupport@tripodvideo.com>
날짜 5월 28일
제목 문의 사항

Mr. Winston께,

6월 22일에 있을 귀사의 20주년 창립 기념일 촬영을 위해 어제 보내 주신 자사 서비스 예약에 대한 메시지에 감사드립니다. 04귀하께서 600달러의 예산 내에 서 기념식 전체가 비디오로 녹화되기를 바라신다는 것을 잘 알았습니다. 저희 도 기쁜 마음으로 그렇게 해 드리겠습니다만, 우선 몇 가지 추가적인 정보가 필 요합니다.

첫째로, 귀하께서 기념식이 오후 7시에 Breckinridge 호텔에서 시작된다고 말 씀하셨는데, 기념식이 얼마 동안 계속될지 알려 주시겠습니까? 또한, 촬영 파일 이 어떻게 전해지는 것을 선호하시는지요? 03-D저희는 파일을 디스크로 복사해 드릴 수도 있고 이메일을 통해 보내 드릴 수도 있습니다. 귀하께서 디스크를 원 하신다면, 몇 개의 사본이 필요한지 알려 주시기 바랍니다. 마지막으로, 저희는 행사가 얼마나 크게 이루어질 것인지를 알아야 합니다. 이는 몇 명의 촬영 스태 프를 파견해야 하는지에 대한 정보를 저희에게 제공해 줄 것입니다.

05일단 이와 같은 세부 사항을 알게 되면, 제가 귀하께 비용 견적서를 보내 드 릴 수 있습니다. 저와 이야기를 나눌 필요가 있으시다면, 제 번호는 555-9004 입니다.

Deanna Lloyd 드림

book v. 예약하다   document v. 기록하다   camera operator 촬영 스태프
estimate n. 견적서, 견적

01 주제/목적 찾기 문제

문제 광고는 주로 무엇에 대한 것인가?
  (A) 전문 사진사를 위한 편집 소프트웨어
  (B) 사진 촬영 스튜디오에서 대여 가능한 장비
  (C) 무료 제품에 대한 곧 있을 홍보 활동
  (D) 회사에 의해 제공되는 미디어 관련 서비스

해설 광고가 주로 무엇에 대한 것인지를 묻는 주제 찾기 문제이므로 광고의 내용 을 확인한다. 첫 번째 지문인 광고의 'Tripod Photo and Video Services takes pride in providing quality photography and video coverage of any occasion.'(1문단 1번째 줄)에서 Tripod Photo and Video Services사는 어떤 행사든 훌륭한 사진과 비디오 촬영을 제공한다고 한 후, Tripod Photo and Video Services사가 제공하는 서비스에 대한 세 부 정보를 언급하고 있으므로 (D) Media-related services offered by a company가 정답이다.

Paraphrasing
photography and video coverage 사진과 비디오 촬영 →
Media-related services 미디어 관련 서비스

어휘 complimentary adj. 무료의

02 동의어 찾기 문제

문제 광고에서, 2문단 두 번째 줄의 표현 "consist of"는 의미상 -와 가장 가깝다.
  (A) ~로 만들어지다
  (B) 포함하다
  (C) ~을 목적으로 만들어지다
  (D) 개발하다

해설 광고의 consist of를 포함한 구절 'which can consist of photo albums or CDs, framed pictures, DVDs of raw and edited videos, or combinations of these items'(2문단 2번째 줄)에서 consist of는 '~으로 이루어지다'라는 뜻으로 사용되었다. 따라서 '포함하다'라는 뜻을 가진 (B) include가 정답이다.

03 Not/True 문제

문제 Tripod Photo and Video Services사에 의해 제공되는 서비스로 언급되지 않은 것은?
  (A) DVD 형태의 원본 출력물
  (B) 사교 모임 촬영
  (C) 사진 확대
  (D) 영상의 온라인 전송

해설 질문의 핵심 어구인 a service provided by Tripod Photo and Video Services에 대해 언급되지 않은 바를 묻는 Not/True 문제이므로 Tripod Photo and Video Services사의 서비스가 언급된 광고와 이메일 모두에

서 관련 내용을 확인한다. (A)는 첫 번째 지문인 광고의 'Tripod Photo and Video Services provides ~ DVDs of raw ~ videos'(2문단 1번째 줄)에서 Tripod Photo and Video Services사는 원본 비디오의 DVD를 제공한다고 했으므로 지문의 내용과 일치한다. (B)는 첫 번째 지문인 광고의 'The company covers different kinds of events, including birthday parties, anniversaries, weddings, and more.'(1문단 2번째 줄)에서 생일 파티, 기념일, 결혼 등과 같은 여러 종류의 행사를 다룬다고 했으므로 지문의 내용과 일치한다. (C)는 지문에 언급되지 않은 내용이다. 따라서 (C) Photograph enlargement가 정답이다. (D)는 두 번째 지문인 이메일의 'We can copy them onto discs or send them via e-mail.'(2문단 3번째 줄)에서 파일을 디스크로 복사해 줄 수도 있고 이메일을 통해 보내 줄 수도 있다고 했으므로 지문의 내용과 일치한다.

Paraphrasing
DVDs of raw ~ videos 원본 비디오의 DVD → Raw output to DVD
DVD 형태의 원본 출력물

어휘 **social event** 사교 모임 **enlargement** n. 확대

04 육하원칙 문제 연계

문제 왜 Mr. Winston은 특별 판촉 행사에 대한 자격이 없는가?
(A) 그의 예산이 최소 구매 요건 이하이다.
(B) 지정일 전에 요청하지 않았다.
(C) 비디오 영상이 아닌 사진을 요구하고 있다.
(D) 패키지 상품을 요청하지 않았다.

해설 두 지문의 내용을 종합적으로 확인해서 풀어야 하는 연계 문제이다. 질문의 핵심 어구인 Mr. Winston ineligible for the special promotion에서 Mr. Winston은 왜(Why) 특별 판촉 행사에 대한 자격이 없는지를 묻고 있으므로 Mr. Winston에게 보내진 이메일을 먼저 확인한다.
두 번째 지문인 이메일의 'you want the entire celebration to be documented on video within a budget of $600'(1문단 2번째 줄)에서 Mr. Winston이 600달러의 예산 내에서 기념식 전체가 비디오에 녹화되기를 바란다는 첫 번째 단서를 확인할 수 있다. 그런데 Mr. Winston의 예산이 특별 판촉 행사에 대한 자격 조건에 적합한지 제시되지 않았으므로 광고에서 특별 판촉 행사에 대한 조건을 확인한다. 첫 번째 지문인 광고의 'get a $50 gift certificate when ordering a video package deal of $800 or more'(3문단 1번째 줄)에서 800달러 이상의 촬영 패키지 상품을 주문하면 50달러의 상품권을 받을 수 있다고 했으므로 특별 상품권 제공 행사는 800달러 이상의 촬영 패키지 상품을 주문하는 경우에만 적용된다는 두 번째 단서를 확인할 수 있다.
Mr. Winston이 600달러의 예산 내에서 기념식에 대한 비디오 녹화를 원한다는 첫 번째 단서와 특별 상품권 제공 행사는 800달러 이상의 촬영 패키지 상품을 주문하는 경우에만 적용된다는 두 번째 단서를 종합할 때, Mr. Winston의 예산은 특별 상품권 제공 행사가 적용되는 상품의 가격보다 적음을 알 수 있다. 따라서 (A) His budget is under the minimum purchase requirement가 정답이다.

05 추론 문제

문제 Ms. Lloyd에 대해 암시되는 것은?
(A) 비디오 제작팀의 일원이다.
(B) 기념 행사 장소가 어디인지 모른다.
(C) 기념 행사를 위한 서비스를 제공하지 못한다.
(D) Tripod Photo and Video Services사를 위해 비용 견적서를 작성한다.

해설 질문의 핵심 어구인 Ms. Lloyd에 대해 추론하는 문제이므로 Ms. Lloyd가 작성한 이메일에서 관련 내용을 확인한다. 두 번째 지문인 이메일의 'Once I have these details, I can send you a cost estimate.'(3문단 1번째 줄)에서 세부 사항을 알게 되면, 비용 견적서를 보내 줄 수 있다고 했으므로 Ms. Lloyd가 비용 견적서를 작성한다는 사실을 추론할 수 있다. 따라서 (D) She compiles price estimates for Tripod Photo and Video Services가 정답이다.

어휘 **compile** v. (자료·표를) 작성하다, 편집하다

06-10은 다음 광고와 편지에 대한 문제입니다.

자원봉사자 구인
[10]Walton 노인 센터, 3324번지 29번가 윌리엄즈버그, 버지니아주

[06]Walton 노인 센터에서 행사와 활동을 계획하고 촉진시켜 줄 자원봉사자를 긴급히 필요로 합니다. [08]700명 이상의 회원들과 함께, 센터는 지역 노령 주민을 위해 교육적이고 재미있는 활동들을 제공하는 것을 목표로 합니다.

직무:
다양한 활동들을 계획하고 수행하기 위해 자원봉사자들은 우리의 활동 진행자 Evelyn Parsons와 함께 일할 것입니다. [08]이러한 활동들은 미술과 공예 그리고 음악, 요리, 언어에 대한 간단한 수업을 포함할 것입니다. 선발된 지원자들은 또한 현지 식당이나, 여흥을 즐길 수 있는 장소나 공원으로의 소풍의 소풍을 돕게 될 것입니다. 또한, 자원봉사자들은 1년에 두 번 회원들이 개최하는 음악과 연극 공연을 준비하는 것도 돕게 될 것입니다.

[07-C]자격 요건:
지원자들은 반드시 최소 19세여야 하며 유효한 운전면허증을 소지하고 있어야 합니다. [07-B]노인들과 함께 일한 이전 경험 또한 선호됩니다. 모든 지원자들은 또한 지난 2년 내에 응급 치료 과정을 통과한 사람이어야 합니다.

자원봉사자가 되기 위해 지원하시려면, 월요일부터 토요일, 오전 9시에서 오후 6시 사이에 센터 행정실을 방문해 주시기 바랍니다. 간단히 양식을 작성해 주시고, 저희 직원 중 한 명에게 제출해 주십시오. 자원봉사자로 선발되었는지 여부는 모든 지원자들에게 서신을 통해 연락을 드릴 것입니다. 추가 질문이 있으시면, 555-7982로 센터에 연락해 주시기 바랍니다.

be in urgent need of 긴급히 필요하다 **facilitate** v. 촉진하다, 용이하게 하다 **aim to do** ~하는 것을 목표로 하다 **entertaining** adj. 재미있는 **population** n. 주민, 인구 **coordinator** n. 진행자 **carry out** ~을 수행하다 **craft** n. 공예 **outing** n. 소풍 **site** n. 유적지, 현장, 부지 **theatrical** adj. 연극의 **put on** (쇼·음악회 등을) 개최하다 **in possession of** ~을 소유하여 **first aid** 응급 치료

6월 16일
[10]Gianni Forno
18-B번지 Westchester가
윌리엄즈버그, 버지니아주

Mr. Forno께,

Walton 노인 센터의 자원봉사자가 되는 것에 관심을 가져 주셔서 대단히 감사합니다. 우리의 회원들을 위해 특별 활동이나 행사를 준비하는 것을 귀하께서 기꺼이 도와주시려는 점을 고맙게 생각합니다.

우리는 귀하의 지원과 귀하께서 이전에 찰스턴에 있는 비슷한 기관에서 봉사 활동을 했던 경력에 깊은 인상을 받았습니다. 안타깝게도, 지금으로서는 귀하를 자원봉사자로 받아들일 수 없을 것 같습니다. [09]귀하께서 가까운 시일 내에 응급 치료 과정을 재이수하신다면 우리는 귀하를 우리의 자원봉사자 일원으로서 기쁘게 맞이할 수 있을 것입니다. 유감스럽게도, 이 자격 요건은 주의 법이기 때문에 귀하의 경우만 특별히 예외를 둘 수가 없습니다.

다시 한번, 자원봉사자가 되기 위해 지원해 주신 것에 대해 감사합니다. 문의 사항이 있으시거나 제가 도움이 될만한 일이 있으면 거리낌 없이 555-7982로 전화 주시기 바랍니다.

Evelyn Parsons 드림
활동 진행자
Walton 노인 센터

regretfully adv. 유감스럽게도 **make an exception** 예외로 하다

06 주제/목적 찾기 문제

문제 광고는 왜 쓰였는가?
(A) 노인 편의 시설을 홍보하기 위해
(B) 간호인직의 빈 자리가 있음을 알리기 위해
(C) 사람들에게 활동들을 돕도록 요청하기 위해
(D) 연구 참여자를 모집하기 위해

해설 광고가 쓰인 목적을 묻는 목적 찾기 문제이므로 광고의 내용을 확인한다. 첫

번째 지문인 광고의 'The Walton Senior Citizens Center is in urgent need of volunteers to plan and facilitate events and activities.'(1문단 1번째 줄)에서 Walton 노인 센터에서 행사와 활동을 계획하고 촉진시켜 줄 자원봉사자를 긴급히 필요로 한다고 했으므로 (C) To request people to assist with activities가 정답이다.

어휘 job opening (직장의) 빈 자리   caretaker n. 간호인, 돌보는 사람

07 육하원칙 문제

문제 지원자들에게 요구되는 자격이 무엇인가?

(A) 간호 학사 학위
(B) 노인과 일해 본 이전 경험
(C) 통용되는 운전면허증
(D) 다른 언어를 말할 수 있는 능력

해설 지원자들에게 요구되는 자격이 무엇인지(What)를 묻는 육하원칙 문제이므로 질문의 핵심 어구인 a required qualification for applicants가 언급된 광고를 확인한다. 첫 번째 지문인 광고의 'Requirements: Applicants must be ~ in possession of a valid driver's license.'(3문단 1번째 줄)에서 지원자들은 자격 요건으로 유효한 운전면허증을 소지하고 있어야 한다고 했으므로 (C) A current license to drive가 정답이다. (B)는 'Previous experience working with senior citizens is also preferred.'(3문단 1번째 줄)에서 노인들과 함께 일한 이전 경험 또한 선호된다고 했지만, 이것이 자원봉사자가 되기 위해 요구되는 자격 요건은 아니므로 답이 될 수 없다.

Paraphrasing
a valid driver's license 유효한 운전면허증 → A current license to drive 통용되는 운전면허증

08 추론 문제

문제 센터의 회원들에 대해 암시되는 것은?

(A) 센터 내에 거주한다.
(B) 연간 회비를 지불해야 한다.
(C) 지속적인 치료를 필요로 한다.
(D) 취미 활동을 추구하도록 장려된다.

해설 질문의 핵심 어구인 the members of the center에 대해 추론하는 문제이므로 센터 회원들을 언급한 광고에서 관련 내용을 확인한다. 첫 번째 지문인 광고의 'With over 700 members, the center aims to provide educational and entertaining activities for the local senior citizen population.'(1문단 2번째 줄)에서 700명 이상의 회원들과 함께, 센터는 지역 노령 주민을 위해 교육적이고 재미있는 활동들을 제공하는 것을 목표로 한다고 했고, 'These will include arts and crafts, and simple classes in music, cooking, and languages.'(2문단 2번째 줄)에서 이러한 활동들은 미술과 공예 그리고 음악, 요리, 언어에 대한 간단한 수업을 포함한다고 했으므로 센터의 회원들은 다양한 분야에서의 취미 활동을 추구하도록 장려된다는 사실을 추론할 수 있다. 따라서 (D) They are encouraged to pursue hobbies가 정답이다.

어휘 reside v. 거주하다   annual adj. 연간의, 1년의, 해마다의
constant adj. 지속적인, 불변의   medical attention 치료

09 육하원칙 문제

문제 Mr. Forno는 센터의 자원봉사자가 되기 위해 무엇을 반드시 해야 하는가?

(A) 의료 수련 과정을 통과한다
(B) 최신 운전면허증을 취득한다
(C) 추천서를 제출한다
(D) 나이 자격 요건을 충족하기 위해 1년을 기다린다

해설 Mr. Forno가 센터의 자원봉사자가 되기 위해 무엇(What)을 반드시 해야 하는지를 묻는 육하원칙 문제이므로 질문의 핵심 어구인 in order to become a volunteer at the center가 언급된 편지를 확인한다. 두 번째 지문인 편지의 'Should you take a first aid course again in the near future, we would be happy to welcome you as one of our volunteer staff.'(2문단 3번째 줄)에서 Mr. Forno가 가까운 시일 내에 응급 치료 과정을 재이수한다면 자원봉사자 일원으로서 맞이할 수 있을 것이라고 했으므로 (A) Pass a medical training course가 정답이다.

Paraphrasing
take a first aid course 응급 치료 과정을 이수하다 → Pass a medical training course 의료 수련 과정을 통과하다

어휘 character reference 추천서

10 추론 문제 연계

문제 Mr. Forno에 대해 암시되는 것은?

(A) 이전에 노인과 함께 일한 적이 없다.
(B) 의료 과정 이수를 계획하고 있다.
(C) 이전에 Ms. Parsons에 의해 고용된 적이 있다.
(D) Walton 노인 센터가 위치해 있는 도시에 살고 있다.

해설 두 지문의 내용을 종합적으로 확인한 후 추론해서 풀어야 하는 연계 문제이다. 질문의 핵심 어구인 Mr. Forno가 언급된 편지를 먼저 확인한다.

두 번째 지문인 편지의 'Gianni Forno, ~ Williamsburg, VA'(편지 상단)에서 Mr. Forno는 버지니아주 윌리엄즈버그에 거주하고 있다는 첫 번째 단서를 확인할 수 있다. 그런데 Walton 노인 센터가 어디에 있는지 제시되지 않았으므로 광고에서 Walton 노인 센터의 위치와 관련된 사항을 확인한다. 첫 번째 지문인 광고의 'Walton Senior Citizens Center, ~ Williamsburg, VA'(광고 상단 부분)에서 Walton 노인 센터도 역시 버지니아주 윌리엄즈버그에 있다는 두 번째 단서를 확인할 수 있다.

Mr. Forno가 버지니아주 윌리엄즈버그에 거주하고 있다는 첫 번째 단서와 Walton 노인 센터가 버지니아주 윌리엄즈버그에 있다는 두 번째 단서를 종합할 때, Mr. Forno는 Walton 노인 센터가 있는 도시에 살고 있다는 사실을 추론할 수 있다. 따라서 (D) He lives in the city the Walton Senior Citizens Center is located in이 정답이다.

11-15는 다음 광고, 송장, 이메일에 관한 문제입니다.

MOORELAND 출판사

귀하의 제품과 서비스를 저희 잡지에서 홍보하세요. 11-D10년 전에 설립되어, 11-B저희 회사의 출판물들은 미국 전역의 다양한 독자들을 끌어 모으고 있고, 저희는 지난 4년간 Media Publisher 상을 수상하였습니다. 11-C다음은 저희가 가지고 있는 출판물들의 일부 견본입니다:

· Tech Today지는 컴퓨터 사용과 관련된 최신 첨단 기기들을 특별히 다룹니다.
· Fan World지는 당신이 가장 좋아하는 스포츠 팀과 운동 선수들에 대해 알도록 해줍니다.
· Modern Living지는 패션, 여행, 집 디자인 등의 동향을 강조합니다.
· Political Summit지는 현대의 세계적인 이슈에 대한 심층적인 분석을 제공합니다.

11-A1/4면, 1/2면, 전면 광고 중에서 선택하세요. 가격은 각각의 잡지에 따라 다릅니다. 저희의 다른 이용 가능한 출판물들에 대한 정보를 얻으시려면, www.moorelandpub.com을 방문하세요. 동일한 잡지에 3개월 동안 광고를 내도록 등록하시고 15퍼센트 할인을 받으세요. 12Mooreland 비즈니스 협회 회원들은 10퍼센트의 추가 할인을 받을 자격이 주어집니다.

promote v. 홍보하다, 촉진하다   establish v. 설립하다, 수립하다
diverse adj. 다양한   title n. 출판물, 서적, 제목   carry v. ~을 가지고 있다, 다루다
high-tech adj. 첨단 기술의   computing n. 컴퓨터 사용
keep up with ~에 대해 알다, 알게 되다   highlight v. 강조하다, 돋보이게 하다
in-depth adj. 심층의   contemporary adj. 현대의, 동시대의

Mooreland 출판사   송장 번호: 4547

고객 이름: Cassandra Harding
12단체: Active Life
이메일: c.harding@activelife.com
전화번호: 555-0913

잡지	광고가 나올 월	금액
14Political Summit지	143월	350.00달러
Fan World지	4월	150.00달러
Modern Living지	5월	200.00달러
Tech Today지	6월-7월	270.00달러
	소계	970.00달러
	1210% 할인	(97.00)달러

총계	873.00달러
납부 기한	2월 10일

* 광고들은 고화질 이미지 파일로 advertising@moorelandpub.com으로 보내시면 됩니다. 변경을 요청하거나 파일의 정보를 수정하려면, 출판물이 발행되기로 예정된 2주 전에 저희에게 연락해주십시오.

invoice n. 송장, 청구서 **subtotal** n. 소계 **high-resolution** adj. 고화질의
revise v. 수정하다, 변경하다 **due** adj. ~하기로 예정된

수신: Oscar Lawrence <advertising@moorelandpub.com>
발신: Cassandra Harding <c.harding@activelife.com>
제목: 오류
날짜: ¹⁴3월 3일

Mr. Lawrence께,

¹³저는 귀사가 저희의 지난번 테니스 경기를 위해 제공한 광고에 매우 만족해서, 올해 저희의 가장 큰 행사들 중 하나를 홍보하기 위해 귀사에 연락드렸습니다. 그러나 ¹⁴저는 이번 달 귀사의 잡지들 중 하나에 실린 저희 단체에 관해 게재된 광고에 있는 오류를 알리게 되어 실망스럽습니다. 그 광고는 데이턴에서 열릴 저희의 여름 마라톤 등록이 7월 10일 이전에 완료되어야 한다고 쓰여 있습니다. 제가 2월 7일에 보낸 광고의 수정 버전에 명시된 바와 같이, 등록은 실제로 7월 20일에 마감됩니다. 귀사에서 실수로 잘못된 날짜가 포함된 기존의 버전을 참고하신 것이 틀림없다고 생각됩니다. ¹⁵귀사의 웹사이트에 수정 안내문을 올려주시고 구독자들에게 알림 이메일을 보내 주시기 바랍니다.

Cassandra Harding 드림

registration n. 등록 **mistakenly** adv. 실수로 **refer** v. 참고하다, 인용하다
notification n. 알림, 통지 **subscriber** n. 구독자

11 Not/True 문제

문제 Mooreland 출판사에 대해 언급되지 않은 것은?
(A) 세 가지 크기로 광고를 인쇄한다.
(B) 전국적으로 잡지를 배포한다.
(C) 네 종류보다 많은 종류의 잡지를 발행한다.
(D) 4년 전에 설립되었다.

해설 질문의 핵심 어구인 Mooreland Publishing에 대해 언급되지 않은 바를 묻는 Not/True문제이므로 Mooreland 출판사의 광고인 첫 번째 지문에서 관련 내용을 확인한다. (A)는 'Choose from quarter-, half-, and full-page ads.'(3문단 1번째 줄)에서 1/4면, 1/2면, 전면 광고 중에서 선택하라고 했으므로 지문의 내용과 일치한다. (B)는 'our company's publications attract a diverse audience of readers across the US'(1문단 2번째 줄)에서 자신들의 출판물, 즉 잡지가 미국 전역의 다양한 독자를 끌어 모으고 있다고 했으므로 지문의 내용과 일치한다. (C)는 'Below is just a small sample of the titles that we carry'(1문단 3번째 줄)에서 다음, 즉 네 가지 목록은 자사 출판물들의 일부 견본이라고 했으므로 지문의 내용과 일치한다. (D)는 'Established a decade ago'(1문단 1번째 줄)에서 10년 전에 설립되었다고 했으므로 지문의 내용과 일치하지 않는다. 따라서 (D) It was founded four years ago가 정답이다.

어휘 **distribute** v. 배포하다, 나눠주다 **nationwide** adv. 전국적으로
found v. 설립하다

12 추론 문제 연계

문제 Active Life에 대해 추론할 수 있는 것은?
(A) 정치인을 위한 행사를 주최했다.
(B) 특별 프로젝트를 위한 기금을 조성하고 있다.
(C) 비즈니스 협회의 회원이다.
(D) 선정된 고객들에게 할인을 제공한다.

해설 두 지문의 내용을 종합적으로 확인한 후 추론해서 풀어야 하는 연계 문제이다. 질문의 핵심 어구인 Active Life가 언급된 송장을 먼저 확인한다.
두 번째 지문인 송장의 'Organization: Active Life'(2번째 줄), '10% discount'(표 7행)에서 Active Life의 주문에 10퍼센트 할인이 적용되었다는 첫 번째 단서를 확인할 수 있다. 그런데 10퍼센트 할인이 어떤 경우에 적용되는지 제시되지 않았으므로 광고에서 관련 내용을 확인한다. 첫 번째 지문인 광고의 'Members of the Mooreland Business Association are

---

eligible to receive an additional 10 percent discount.'(3문단 4번째 줄)에서 Mooreland 비즈니스 협회 회원들은 10퍼센트의 추가 할인을 받을 자격이 주어진다는 두 번째 단서를 확인할 수 있다.
Active Life의 주문에 10퍼센트 할인이 적용되었다는 첫 번째 단서와 Mooreland 비즈니스 협회 회원들은 10퍼센트의 추가 할인을 받을 자격이 주어진다는 두 번째 단서를 종합할 때, Active Life가 Mooreland 비즈니스 협회의 회원이라는 사실을 추론할 수 있다. 따라서 (C) It is a member of a business association이 정답이다.

어휘 **politician** n. 정치인 **raise** v. 조성하다, 들어올리다
select adj. 선정된, 엄선한; v. 고르다

13 추론 문제

문제 Ms. Harding에 대해 암시되는 것은?
(A) 광고 회사의 소유주이다.
(B) 이전에 Mooreland 출판사의 서비스를 이용한 적이 있다.
(C) 일부 출판물들의 무료 사본을 받을 것이다.
(D) 마라톤에 등록할 것이다.

해설 질문의 핵심 어구인 Ms. Harding에 대해 추론하는 문제이므로 Ms. Harding이 작성한 이메일에서 관련 내용을 확인한다. 세 번째 지문인 이메일의 'I was very satisfied with the advertising your company provided for our last ~ tournament'(1문단 1번째 줄)에서 자신, 즉 Ms. Harding은 자신들의 지난번 테니스 경기를 위해 Mooreland 출판사가 제공했던 광고에 매우 만족했었다고 했으므로 Ms. Harding이 이전에 Mooreland 출판사의 서비스를 이용한 적이 있다는 사실을 추론할 수 있다. 따라서 (B) She has used Mooreland Publishing's services before가 정답이다.

14 육하원칙 문제 연계

문제 어느 잡지에 오류가 있는 광고가 포함되어 있는가?
(A) *Political Summit*지
(B) *Fan World*지
(C) *Modern Living*지
(D) *Tech Today*지

해설 두 지문의 내용을 종합해서 풀어야 하는 연계 문제이다. 어느(Which) 잡지에 오류가 있는 광고가 포함되어 있는지 묻고 있으므로 질문의 핵심 어구인 magazine includes an advertisement with an error와 관련된 내용이 언급된 이메일을 확인한다.
세 번째 지문인 이메일의 'Date: March 3'(상단 박스)에서 이메일이 3월 3일에 쓰인 것을 알 수 있고, 'I am disappointed to report an error in the advertisement published for my organization in one of your magazines this month'(2번째 줄)에서 이번 달 잡지들 중 하나에 실린 저희 단체, 즉 Active Life에 관해 게재된 광고의 오류를 알리게 되어 실망스럽다는 첫 번째 단서를 확인할 수 있다. 그런데 이번 달, 즉 3월에 Active Life에 관한 광고가 실리는 잡지가 무엇인지 제시되지 않았으므로 Active Life로 발행된 송장에서 관련 내용을 확인한다. 두 번째 지문인 송장의 'Political Summit, March'(표 2행)에서 3월에 광고가 실리는 잡지는 *Political Summit*지라는 두 번째 단서를 확인할 수 있다.
3월 잡지에 오류가 있는 광고가 실렸다는 첫 번째 단서와 3월에 광고가 실리는 잡지는 *Political Summit*지라는 두 번째 단서를 종합할 때, 오류가 있는 광고가 실린 잡지는 *Political Summit*지임을 알 수 있다. 따라서 (A) *Political Summit*지가 정답이다.

15 육하원칙 문제

문제 Ms. Harding은 Mr. Lawrence에게 무엇을 하라고 요청하는가?
(A) 정정 사항을 게재한다
(B) 두 번째 송장을 발송한다
(C) 지불을 확인한다
(D) 행사에 참석한다

해설 Ms. Harding이 Mr. Lawrence에게 무엇(What)을 하라고 요청하는지를 묻는 육하원칙 문제이므로 Ms. Harding이 작성한 이메일에서 질문의 핵심 어구인 ask ~ to do와 관련된 내용을 확인한다. 세 번째 지문인 이메일의 'Please put a correction notice on your Web site'(7번째 줄)에서 Ms. Harding이 Mr. Lawrence에게 웹사이트에 수정 안내문을 올려달라고 했으므로 (A) Post a revision이 정답이다.

Paraphrasing
put a correction notice on ~ Web site 웹사이트에 수정 안내문을 올리다
→ Post a revision 정정 사항을 게재하다

Chapter 20 공고 연계 지문

예제 해석·해설   p.506

공고 & 이메일

> Wallingford 주민센터가 5월에 육아 세미나를 주최합니다
> Wallingford 주민센터는 어린 자녀가 있는 부모들을 위한 두 차례의 세미나를 주최할 예정입니다. 첫 번째는 5월 12일에 있을 것이고 *유아 교육*이라는 제목이며, 두 번째는 유아를 위한 주거 안전이며 5월 14일에 개최됩니다. 관심 있으신 참가자들은 등록을 위해 5월 9일부터 11일까지 Glenda Ingram에게 (709) 555-8249로 연락해 주시면 됩니다.

host v. 주최하다 **entitle** v. (~라고) 제목을 붙이다, 표제를 붙이다
toddler n. 유아 **take place** 개최되다, 일어나다

> 수신: Anna Grimes <annagrimes@filter.com>
> 발신: Donna Wilson <donnawilson@tonomail.com>
> 저는 Wallingford 주민센터가 개최하는 몇 개의 세미나에 대한 공지를 봤으며 특히 한 개가 당신의 흥미를 끌 것 같다고 느꼈습니다. 우리는 일전에 우리 아이들을 가르치는 방법에 대해 이야기를 나눈 적이 있었으므로, 우리가 세미나에 함께 참석할 수 있겠다고 생각했습니다. 알려 주시면, 제가 등록하겠습니다.

a couple of 몇 개의, 두서너 개의 **in particular** 특히, 그 중에도
the other day 일전에, 며칠 전에 **attend** v. 참석하다 **sign up** 등록하다

문제 어떤 날짜에 Ms. Wilson이 세미나 시간에 참석할 것 같은가?
(A) 5월 9일
(B) 5월 11일
(C) 5월 12일
(D) 5월 14일

해설 **추론 문제** 두 지문의 내용을 종합적으로 확인한 후 추론해서 풀어야 하는 연계 문제이다. 질문의 핵심 어구인 Ms. Wilson ~ attend a seminar session에서 Ms. Wilson이 어떤 날짜에 세미나에 참석할 것인지를 묻고 있으므로 Ms. Wilson이 작성한 이메일을 먼저 확인한다.
두 번째 지문인 이메일의 'We were talking the other day about methods for teaching our kids, so I thought we could attend the seminar together.'에서 Ms. Wilson이 이메일 수신자와 자녀 교육에 대해 이야기했고, 함께 세미나에 참석할 것을 제안하고 있다는 첫 번째 단서를 확인할 수 있다. 그런데 자녀 교육에 대한 세미나가 열리는 날짜가 제시되지 않았으므로 공고에서 해당 세미나의 날짜를 확인한다. 첫 번째 지문인 공고의 'The first is on May 12 and entitled *Early Childhood Education*'에서 유아 교육에 대한 세미나가 5월 12일에 열릴 것이라는 두 번째 단서를 확인할 수 있다.
Ms. Wilson이 자녀 교육에 대한 세미나 참석을 제안했다는 첫 번째 단서와 유아 교육에 대한 세미나가 5월 12일에 열릴 것이라는 두 번째 단서를 종합할 때, Ms. Wilson이 5월 12일에 세미나에 참석할 것이라는 사실을 추론할 수 있다. 따라서 (C) May 12가 정답이다.

어휘 **session** n. (특정한 활동을 위한) 시간

Hackers Practice   p.507

유형 연습
01 (A)   02 (C)   03 (A)   04 (B)

01-02 공고 & 양식

> 어려움에 처한 아이들에게 헌신하세요
> Caroline Becker 재단은 전 세계의 가난한 어린이들에게 음식, 깨끗한 물, 의료 서비스 및 교육에 대한 원조를 제공합니다. 어린이를 후원함으로써, 우리의 사명에 도움을 주실 수 있습니다. 후원자들은 ^{01-A}우리의 연간 소식지뿐만 아니라, 그들이 돕고 있는 어린이에 대한 최신 정보를 연 4회 받아 보게 됩니다.
> ^{01-C}우리는 현재 다음의 지역들에 후원자가 필요합니다:
>
> 리마, ^{01-C}페루   취학 연령 아이들에게 교과서를 제공할 수 있도록 100달러를 기부해 주세요.
> ⁰²캄팔라, ^{01-C/02}우간다   ⁰²한 어린이에게 한 달 동안 학교 급식을 제공할 수 있도록 50달러를 기부해 주세요.
>
> 기부를 하시려면, 첨부된 양식을 잘라서 보내 주세요.

make a commitment to ~에 헌신하다 **in need** 어려움에 처한
assistance n. 원조, 도움, 조력 **needy** adj. 가난한
health care 의료 서비스 **sponsor** v. 후원하다; n. 후원자
mission n. 사명, 임무 **annual** adj. 연간의, 한 해의
quarterly adv. 연 4회의 **donate** v. 기부하다 **school lunch** 학교 급식
contribution n. 기부, 기여 **clip** v. 잘라내다

> Caroline Becker 재단
> 후원 양식
> 이름: *Mary Martin* 전화번호 *555-9382* 휴대 전화번호 *003-555-7898*
> 주소: *1485번지 Oakwood가, 롤리, 노스캐롤라이나주*
> ⁰²기부할 지역: □ 리마, 페루 ⁰²■ 캄팔라, 우간다
> 기부 금액: *50달러*
> 지불 방법: □ 신용카드 ■ 현금 □ 개인 수표

01 Not/True 문제

문제 재단에 대해 언급된 것은?
(A) 소식지를 1년에 한 번 발행한다.
(B) 가난한 아이들을 위한 집을 제공한다.
(C) 두 나라에 자원봉사자를 필요로 한다.

해설 재단에 대해 묻는 Not/True 문제이므로 질문의 핵심 어구인 the foundation이 언급된 첫 번째 지문인 공고에서 관련 내용을 확인한다. (A)는 'our annual newsletter'(3번째 줄)에서 우리, 즉 재단의 연간 소식지라고 했으므로 지문의 내용과 일치한다. 따라서 (A) It publishes a newsletter once a year가 정답이다. (B)는 지문에 언급되지 않은 내용이다. (C)는 'We are currently in need of sponsors in the following areas'(4번째 줄), 'Peru'(5번째 줄), 'Uganda'(6번째 줄)에서 재단은 현재 페루와 우간다 두 지역에 대한 후원자가 필요하다고 했으므로 지문의 내용과 일치하지 않는다.

Paraphrasing
annul 연간의 → once a year 1년에 한 번

어휘 **volunteer** n. 자원봉사자

02 육하원칙 문제 연계

문제 Ms. Martin은 무엇에 도움을 제공할 것인가?
(A) 의료
(B) 교육
(C) 음식

해설 두 지문의 내용을 종합해서 풀어야 하는 연계 문제이다. 질문의 핵심 어구인 Ms. Martin providing assistance with에서 Ms. Martin이 무엇(What)에 도움을 제공할 것인지를 묻고 있으므로 Ms. Martin이 작성한 양식을 먼저 확인한다.
두 번째 지문인 양식의 'Send my donation to'(양식 기입란 3번째 줄)와 'Kampala, Uganda'(양식 기입란 3번째 줄)에서 Ms. Martin은 우간다의 캄팔라에 기부할 것이라는 첫 번째 단서를 확인할 수 있다. 그런데 캄팔라에 어떤 도움이 제공되고 있는지 제시되지 않았으므로 공고에서 캄팔라에 제공되는 도움이 무엇인지 확인한다. 첫 번째 지문인 공고의 'Kampala, Uganda, Donate $50 to provide one child with a month of school lunches.'(6번째 줄)에서 우간다의 캄팔라에 기부하는 50달러로 한 명의 아이에게 한 달 동안 학교 급식을 제공할 수 있다는 두 번째 단서를 확인할 수 있다.

Ms. Martin이 우간다의 캄팔라에 기부를 할 것이라는 첫 번째 단서와 그곳에 기부하는 돈으로 아이들에게 학교 급식을 제공할 수 있다는 두 번째 단서를 종합할 때, Ms. Martin은 음식에 대한 도움을 제공할 것임을 알 수 있다. 따라서 (C) Food가 정답이다.

Paraphrasing
school lunches 학교 급식 → Food 음식

03-04 공고 & 이메일

Evergreen 출판사 워크숍 일정
[03]인사과에서는 편집 기술에 대한 3개의 워크숍을 준비할 것입니다. 직원 분들은 관심 있는 어떤 강의라도 등록하실 수 있습니다. 예정되어 있는 강습은 다음과 같습니다:

워크숍	진행자	날짜
언어의 흐름을 원활하게 하기	Rosalind Beatty	5월 2일
[04]현대 영어에서 언어의 변화	Elizabeth Lim	6월 3일
편집 소프트웨어 사용하기	George Thomas	7월 1일

더 많은 정보가 필요하시거나 등록을 하시려면, personnel@evergreen.com으로 이메일을 보내 주십시오.

editorial adj. 편집(상)의, 편집자의
facilitator n. 진행자, (교육 과정·워크숍 시행에 있어) 촉진자, 협력자
linguistic adj. 언어의 **register** v. 등록하다

수신: 인사과 <personnel@evergreen.com>
발신: Colm Meaney <colmmeaney@evergreen.com>
제목: 워크숍
날짜: 5월 1일
지난주에, 저는 귀하의 부서에서 준비한 워크숍 중 하나에 등록했습니다. 그런데, 제 선택을 변경하고 싶습니다. [04]편집 소프트웨어 워크숍이 열리는 날에 저는 휴가 중일 것입니다. 대신에 Ms. Lim의 강의에 등록할 수 있겠습니까? 알려주시기 바랍니다.

arrange v. 준비하다, 정리하다

03 주제/목적 찾기 문제

문제 공고는 왜 쓰였는가?
(A) 직원들이 몇몇 행사에 참여하도록 초대하기 위해
(B) 일정 변경을 직원들에게 알리기 위해
(C) 진행자들에 대한 정보를 제공하기 위해

해설 공고가 쓰인 목적을 묻는 목적 찾기 문제이므로 첫 번째 지문인 공고의 내용을 확인한다. 'The personnel department will be arranging three workshops on editorial techniques. Staff may sign up for any class they are interested in.'(1번째 줄)에서 인사과에서 편집 기술에 대한 3개의 워크숍을 준비할 것이고 직원들은 관심 있는 강의에 등록할 수 있다고 했으므로 (A) To invite employees to attend some events가 정답이다.

04 추론 문제 연계

문제 어떤 워크숍에 Mr. Meaney가 참석할 것 같은가?
(A) 언어의 흐름을 원활하게 하기
(B) 현대 영어에서 언어의 변화
(C) 편집 소프트웨어 사용하기

해설 두 지문의 내용을 종합적으로 확인한 후 추론해서 풀어야 하는 연계 문제이다. 질문의 핵심 어구인 Mr. Meaney ~ participate in에서 Mr. Meaney가 어떤 워크숍에 참석할 것 같은지를 묻고 있으므로 Mr. Meaney가 작성한 이메일을 먼저 확인한다.
두 번째 지문인 이메일의 'I will be on vacation on the day the editorial software workshop will be held. Could I sign up for Ms. Lim's class instead?'(2번째 줄)에서 이메일의 발신자, Mr. Meaney가 편집 소프트웨어 워크숍이 열리는 날에 휴가 중일 것이므로 대신에 Ms. Lim의 강의에 등록할 수 있을지를 묻고 있으므로 Mr. Meaney가 Ms. Lim의 강의에 참가하고 싶어 한다는 첫 번째 단서를 확인할 수 있다. 그런데 Ms. Lim이 어떤 워크숍을 진행하는지 제시되지 않았으므로 공고에서 관련 내용을 확인한다. 첫 번째

지문인 공고의 'Linguistic Changes in Modern English, Elizabeth Lim'(표 3번째 줄)에서 Elizabeth Lim이 현대 영어에서 언어의 변화에 대한 워크숍을 진행한다는 두 번째 단서를 확인할 수 있다.
Mr. Meaney가 Ms. Lim의 워크숍에 참석하고 싶어 한다는 첫 번째 단서와 Ms. Lim이 현대 영어에서 언어의 변화에 대한 워크숍을 진행한다는 두 번째 단서를 종합할 때, Mr. Meaney가 현대 영어에서 언어의 변화에 대한 워크숍에 참가할 것이라는 사실을 추론할 수 있다. 따라서 (B) Linguistic Changes in Modern English가 정답이다.

Hackers Test   p.508

01 (C)	02 (C)	03 (B)	04 (C)	05 (B)
06 (A)	07 (B)	08 (B)	09 (D)	10 (A)
11 (B)	12 (B)	13 (D)	14 (C)	15 (A)

01-05는 다음 공고와 회원 양식에 관한 문제입니다.

METROPOLITAN 역사 박물관 (MMH)
중기 왕국의 보물 전시회

일시: 2월 28일, 오전 10시
장소: MMH 전시회장 D

[01]Metropolitan 역사 박물관은 고대 이집트의 중기 왕국 보물들의 최신 전시를 보여 드리게 되어 기쁩니다. 무기, 보석, 조각품, 그림 및 그 외 이 시기의 물건들을 포함한 300개가 넘는 물품들이 전시될 것입니다.

물품들의 일부는 MMH의 소장품이며, 다른 물품들은 카이로, 토리노, 베를린 및 런던의 박물관으로부터 대여해 온 것들입니다. 전시는 5월 31일까지 계속될 것입니다.

이에 더하여, [02]이집트의 고대 유물부 차관인 [02/04]Mustafa Khalil이 2월 27일 오후 7시에 전시를 방문할 것입니다. [02/04]그는 현대 시대에서의 고고학의 중요성에 대해 강연할 것이며, 중기 왕국의 역사에 관한 짧은 영상물이 상영될 것입니다. 이 행사들 다음에는 다과와 전채 요리가 제공될 것입니다. [04]이 행사에 대한 예약은 필수입니다. 입장료는 1인당 75달러지만, MMH의 골드 후원자들은 무료로 입장이 가능합니다. [04]예약을 하시려면 홍보 담당자에게 전화 주십시오. 아직 MMH의 후원자가 아니시라면, 주저 마시고 [03]동봉된 양식을 작성해 주십시오. 귀하의 후원을 감사하게 생각합니다.

Middle Kingdom (고대 이집트의) 중기 왕국 **newest** adj. 최신의
on display 전시된 **article** n. 물건 **partly** adv. 일부, 부분적으로
loan n. 대여, 빌린 것 **antiquity** n. 고대의 유물, 골동품
archaeology n. 고고학 **refreshment** n. 다과 **appetizer** n. 전채 요리
public relations 홍보

Metropolitan 역사 박물관 (MMH)
후원 신청서:

혜택	회원
1년간 박물관 무료 입장	골드, 실버
연 4회 발행되는 *Contemporary Archaeologist*지	
연례 대연회 티켓	
모든 특별 행사, 연설, 강의 시리즈에 대한 입장권	오직 골드에만 해당
예약된 특별 초대전	

[05]회비는 실버 후원자의 경우 120달러, 골드 후원자의 경우 200달러입니다. 다음의 정보를 기입하여 홍보부에 귀하의 납입액과 함께 돌려주시면 됩니다.

이름: ____Rachel Conrad____
주소: ____6522번지 Lark Crescent가____
가족 구성원: ____David Conrad (남편)____
전화번호: ____(309) 555-9905____
이메일: ____racon@tmail.com____
[05]희망 후원 종류: [05]■ 골드 □ 실버
지불 방법:■ 수표 □ 신용카드 □ 우편환

[04]행사 예약을 원하시는 모든 후원자들께서는 홍보 담당자인 Mark Lee에게 555-4323으로 전화하시면 됩니다. 추가 정보를 위해서는, 웹사이트 www.mmh.org를 방문해 주십시오. ❍

entry n. 입장, 출입   **quarterly** adj. 연 4회의   **admission** n. 입장, 입학
reserved adj. 예약된, 따로 둔
private viewing (전시회 일반 공개 전의) 특별 초대전

01 주제/목적 찾기 문제

문제   공고는 주로 무엇에 대한 것인가?
(A) 박물관이 후원하는 짧은 여행
(B) 교육 기관 견학
(C) 박물관이 주최하는 행사
(D) 유적 보존을 위한 기금 모금 행사

해설   공고가 주로 무엇에 대한 것인지를 묻는 주제 찾기 문제이므로 공고의 내용을 확인한다. 첫 번째 지문인 공고의 'The Metropolitan Museum of History is pleased to present its newest exhibit of treasures from the Middle Kingdom of ancient Egypt.'(1문단 1번째 줄)에서 Metropolitan 역사 박물관은 고대 이집트 중기 왕국 보물들의 최신 전시를 보이게 되어 기쁘다고 한 후, 전시할 물품 및 예정된 강연에 대해 설명하고 있으므로 (C) An event hosted by the museum이 정답이다.

어휘   **excursion** n. 짧은 여행, 유람   **fundraiser** n. 모금 행사

02 추론 문제

문제   Mustafa Khalil에 대해 암시되는 것은?
(A) MMH의 박물관장이다.
(B) 전시회를 위해 일부 물품을 빌려줬다.
(C) 고고학 전문가이다.
(D) 그의 다큐멘터리들 중 하나를 보여줄 것이다.

해설   Mustafa Khalil에 대해 추론하는 문제이므로 질문의 핵심 어구인 Mustafa Khalil을 언급한 공고에서 관련 내용을 확인한다. 첫 번째 지문인 공고의 'Associate Minister of Antiquities for the nation of Egypt, Mustafa Khalil'(3문단 1번째 줄)에서 Mustafa Khalil이 이집트의 고대 유물부 차관이라고 한 후, 'He will speak about the importance of archaeology in the modern age'(3문단 2번째 줄)에서 그가 현대 시대에서의 고고학의 중요성에 대해 강연할 것이라고 했으므로 Mustafa Khalil은 고고학에 대해 강연할 능력이 있는 전문가라는 사실을 추론할 수 있다. 따라서 (C) He is an expert on archaeology가 정답이다.

03 동의어 찾기 문제

문제   공고에서, 4문단 첫 번째 줄의 표현 "fill out"은 의미상 -와 가장 가깝다.
(A) 돌려주다
(B) 작성하다
(C) 참석하다
(D) 검사하다

해설   첫 번째 지문인 공고의 fill out을 포함하고 있는 구절 'fill out the enclosed form'(4문단 1번째 줄)에서 fill out이 '작성하다'라는 뜻으로 사용되었다. 따라서 '작성하다, 기입하다'라는 뜻을 가진 (B) complete가 정답이다.

04 육하원칙 문제   연계

문제   후원자들은 Mr. Khalil의 강연을 듣기 위해 무엇을 해야 하는가?
(A) 티켓을 구매한다
(B) 사무실을 방문한다
(C) Mark Lee에게 연락한다
(D) 양식에 기입한다

해설   두 지문의 내용을 종합해서 풀어야 하는 연계 문제이다. 질문의 핵심 어구인 sponsors do to hear Mr. Khalil's talk에서 후원자들이 Mr. Khalil의 강연을 듣기 위해 무엇(What)을 해야 하는지를 묻고 있으므로 Mr. Khalil이 언급된 공고를 먼저 확인한다.
첫 번째 지문인 공고의 'Mustafa Khalil'(3문단 1번째 줄), 'He will speak about the importance of archaeology in the modern age'(3문단 2번째 줄)에서 Mustafa Khalil이 현대 시대에서의 고고학의 중요성에 대해 강연할 것이라고 했고, 'Reservations for this event are necessary.'(3문단 5번째 줄)와 'Call our public relations manager to make a booking.'(3문단 6번째 줄)에서 이 행사를 위한 예약은 필수이며 예약을 하기 위해서는 홍보 담당자에게 전화해야 한다고 했으므로 Mr. Khalil이 강연을

할 것이고 강연을 듣기 위해서는 홍보 담당자에게 전화해서 예약을 해야 한다는 첫 번째 단서를 확인할 수 있다. 그런데 홍보 담당자가 누구인지 제시되지 않았으므로 양식에서 홍보 담당자를 확인한다. 두 번째 지문인 양식의 'All sponsors who wish to make reservations for the events can call our public relations manager, Mark Lee'(양식 하단 1번째 줄)에서 행사 예약을 원하는 모든 후원자들은 홍보 담당인 Mark Lee에게 전화해야 한다는 두 번째 단서를 확인할 수 있다.
Mr. Khalil의 강연을 듣기 위해서는 홍보 담당자에게 전화해서 예약해야 한다는 첫 번째 단서와 홍보 담당자가 Mark Lee라는 두 번째 단서를 종합할 때, Mr. Khalil의 강연을 듣기 위해서는 Mark Lee에게 연락해야 함을 알 수 있다. 따라서 (C) Contact Mark Lee가 정답이다.

05 추론 문제

문제   Ms. Conrad에 대해 암시되는 것은?
(A) 기관의 과거 후원자였다.
(B) 200달러의 후원금을 청구받을 것이다.
(C) 이전에 이 박물관의 행사에 참석한 적이 있다.
(D) 영상물 상영에 참석할 계획이다.

해설   질문의 핵심 어구인 Ms. Conrad에 대해 추론하는 문제이므로 Ms. Conrad가 작성한 양식에서 관련 내용을 확인한다. 두 번째 지문인 양식의 'Fees are $120 for a silver sponsor and $200 for a gold sponsor.'(표 하단 1번째 줄)에서 회비는 실버 후원자의 경우 120달러이고 골드 후원자의 경우 200달러라고 했고, 'Type of sponsorship requested: gold'(양식 기입란 6번째 줄)에서 Ms. Conrad의 희망 후원 종류가 골드라고 했으므로 Ms. Conrad는 골드 후원 자격을 신청하고 있으며 200달러가 청구될 것이라는 사실을 추론할 수 있다. 따라서 (B) She will be charged a $200 sponsorship fee가 정답이다.

06-10은 다음 공고와 기사에 관한 문제입니다.

Webdeals 경매 및 소매 웹사이트

공고:

Webdeals는 세계적으로 유명한 경매 및 소매 웹사이트이며, 이제 30퍼센트의 주식이 공식적으로 거래됨을 발표하게 되어 기쁩니다. 투자자들은 회사의 주식을 구입할 수 있으며, 주식은 작년 한 해 동안 6.4퍼센트의 주가 상승을 기록하였습니다. ⁰⁶주식은 5월 19일인 어제 주당 43.82달러의 시작 가격으로 상장되었습니다.

⁰⁹Webdeals는 곧 중국, 인도, 인도네시아, 러시아 및 일본의 고객들을 대상으로 하는 다섯 개의 새로운 온라인 사이트들을 포함하도록 시장을 확장할 것입니다. ^{07-C}이 사이트들은 해당 국가의 언어로 이용이 가능하도록 만들어질 것이며 해당 국가 고객들의 동향과 취향을 고려할 것입니다. ^{07-B}이러한 확장은 Webdeals의 순이익을 최소 12퍼센트 증가시킬 것으로 기대됩니다. ^{07-A}새로운 사이트들은 10월 1일부터 운영될 것입니다. 지금이야말로 엄청난 투자 기회를 이용할 수 있는 절호의 기회입니다.

투자자들은 Webdeals 전체에 대한 일반 주식, 혹은 특정 지역 사이트에 해당하는 개별적인 주식을 매입할 수 있습니다. 위에 언급된 국가들의 주가는 지금 더 낮은 주당 28달러의 매입 가격이었지만, 미국과 같이 안정적인 시장은 주당 49달러로 더 높습니다. 투자 기회에 대한 추가적인 정보는 www.webdeals.com/investmentrelations에서 이용하실 수 있습니다. 또는, 간단히 여러분의 재정 고문 담당자나 금융 기관에서 세부사항을 얻으실 수 있습니다.

auction n. 경매   **retail** n. 소매   **world-famous** adj. 세계적으로 유명한
share n. 주식   **publicly** adv. 공식적으로   **investor** n. 투자자
stock value 주가   **make public** (주식을) 상장하다, 공표하다
net profit 순이익   **incredible** adj. 엄청난, 놀라운   **particular** adj. 특정한
purchase price 매입 가격   **stable** adj. 안정적인
access v. 이용하다, 접근하다   **institution** n. 기관

벌써 Webdeals 주식으로부터 이익을 얻는 투자자들

지분 중 30퍼센트가 공식적으로 거래될 것이라고 공표한 지 불과 일주일 만에, 투자자들은 이미 그들의 Webdeals 주식 가치가 오르는 것을 보고 있다. 주식의 시가는 43.82달러였으며, 영업일 5일만에 증권거래소는 현재 가격을 44.12달러로 보고했다. ⁰⁸이 기업이 최근 몇 년 동안 수익성에서 어떤 증가도 보이지 않았기 때문에 상승세는 투자자들로부터의 이와 같은 관심을 예측하지 못했던 ➡

금융 전문가들을 놀라게 했다.

[10]Webdeals는 새로운 시장으로의 확장을 위한 자본금을 모으기 위한 노력으로 대중에게 주식을 공개했다. 이 회사는 일반 주식을 사거나 특정 나라들을 위해 계획된 웹사이트들 중 어떤 개별 주식에라도 투자할 수 있도록 선택권을 제공했다. 비록 일반 주식의 주가 인상에 비해 크지는 않았지만, 모든 주식의 가치가 올랐다.

지역	5월 22일 시가	5월 26일 종가
[09]중국	30.32달러	30.78달러
[09]인도	29.74달러	29.97달러
[09]인도네시아	32.87달러	33.02달러
[09]러시아	28.34달러	28.44달러

아직 이 사이트들이 운영되고 있지 않음에도 불구하고, [07-D]대부분의 투자자들이 사이트들의 잠재력에 대한 신뢰를 갖고 있었기 때문에 전반적으로 열 것으로 인상이 보고되었다. 초기에, Webdeals는 다섯 곳의 새로운 시장에 사이트를 열 계획을 했으며, 사이트들은 각 나라의 언어를 사용할 것이다. 그러나, [09]이 소매 업체는 이전에 계획되었던 곳들 중 한 곳에 충분한 관심이 없다는 것을 발견했고, 지금은 네 개의 사이트만 열 계획이다.

earn v. 얻다, 획득하다 **stock exchange** 증권거래소
profitability n. 수익성 **capital** n. 자본, 자금 **individual** adj. 개별의, 개인의
significant adj. 커다란, 현저한, 의미 있는 **particular** adj. 특정한
across the board 전반적으로, 전면적인 **confidence** n. 신뢰, 신임
potential n. 잠재력, 가능성; adj. 잠재적인 **initially** adv. 초기에는

06 육하원칙 문제

문제 Webdeals의 주식은 언제 처음 대중에게 공개되었는가?
(A) 5월 19일
(B) 5월 20일
(C) 5월 22일
(D) 5월 26일

해설 Webdeals의 주식이 언제(When) 처음 대중에게 공개되었는지를 묻는 육하원칙 문제이므로 질문의 핵심 어구인 stock shares first offered to the public이 언급된 공고에서 관련 내용을 확인한다. 첫 번째 지문인 공고의 'The shares were made public yesterday, May 19'(1문단 3번째 줄)에서 주식은 5월 19일인 어제 상장되었다고 했으므로 (A) May 19가 정답이다.

Paraphrasing
were ~ offered to the public 대중에게 공개되었다 → were made public 상장되었다

07 Not/True 문제

문제 Webdeals의 새로운 온라인 사이트에 대해 언급되지 않은 것은?
(A) 10월에 이용 가능할 것이다.
(B) 가치가 12퍼센트 증가할 것이다.
(C) 현지 언어로 이루어질 것이다.
(D) 투자자들의 신뢰를 얻었다.

해설 Webdeals의 새로운 온라인 사이트에 대해 언급되지 않은 바를 묻는 Not/True 문제이므로 질문의 핵심 어구인 Webdeals' new online sites가 언급된 공고와 기사 모두에서 관련 내용을 확인한다. (A)는 첫 번째 지문인 공고의 'The new sites should be operational by October 1.'(2문단 4번째 줄)에서 새로운 사이트들은 10월 1일부터 운영될 것이라고 했으므로 지문의 내용과 일치한다. (B)는 첫 번째 지문인 공고의 'These expansions are expected to increase net profits for Webdeals by a minimum of 12 percent.'(2문단 3번째 줄)에서 이러한 확장은 Webdeals의 순이익을 최소 12퍼센트 증가시킬 것으로 기대된다고 했으므로 지문의 내용과 일치하지 않는다. 따라서 (B) They will increase in value by 12 percent가 정답이다. (C)는 첫 번째 지문인 공고의 'These sites will be made available in the local languages'(2문단 2번째 줄)에서 이 사이트들은 해당 국가의 언어로 이용 가능하도록 만들어질 것이라고 했으므로 지문의 내용과 일치한다. (D)는 두 번째 지문인 기사의 'most investors had confidence in the potential of the sites'(3문단 1번째 줄)에서 대부분의 투자자들은 이 사이트들의 잠재력에 대한 신뢰를 갖고 있었다고 했으므로 지문의 내용과 일치한다.

Paraphrasing
should be operational 운영될 것이다 → going to be available 이용

가능할 것이다

어휘 **value** n. 가치 **local** adj. 현지의

08 육하원칙 문제

문제 기사에 따르면, 왜 일부 전문가들이 주식 가치 상승에 놀랐는가?
(A) 사이트들 중 다수가 아직 운영 전이다.
(B) Webdeals의 수익이 성장을 멈췄다.
(C) 주식 공개가 짧은 기간 동안만 이루어졌다.
(D) 회사가 몇 개의 사이트들을 폐쇄해야 했다.

해설 왜(why) 일부 전문가들이 주식 가치 상승에 놀랐는지를 묻는 육하원칙 문제이므로 질문의 핵심 어구인 experts surprised가 언급된 기사에서 관련 내용을 확인한다. 두 번째 지문인 기사의 'The increase surprised financial experts, ~ because the company had not shown any increase in profitability in recent years.'(1문단 3번째 줄)에서 이 기업이 최근 몇 년 동안 수익성에서 어떤 증가도 보이지 않았기 때문에 상승세가 금융 전문가들을 놀라게 했다고 했다. 따라서 (B) Webdeals' earnings had stopped growing이 정답이다.

Paraphrasing
profitability 수익성 → earnings 수익
had not shown any increase 어떤 증가도 보이지 않다 → stopped growing 성장을 멈추다

어휘 **operational** adj. 운영상의 **earning** n. 수익, 소득
make public 공개하다, 공표하다 **shut down** 폐쇄하다

09 육하원칙 문제 연계

문제 Webdeals는 어떤 국가에 웹사이트를 출시하지 않기로 결정했는가?
(A) 미국
(B) 중국
(C) 인도네시아
(D) 일본

해설 두 지문의 내용을 종합해서 풀어야 하는 연계 문제이다. 질문의 핵심 어구인 not to launch a Web site에서 Webdeals가 어떤(Which) 국가에 웹사이트를 출시하지 않기로 결정했는지를 묻고 있으므로 Webdeals의 웹사이트가 출시될 국가를 언급한 공고를 먼저 확인한다.
첫 번째 지문인 공고의 'Webdeals will soon be expanding its market to include five new online sites targeted towards customers in China, India, Indonesia, Russia, and Japan.'(2문단 1번째 줄)에서 Webdeals는 곧 중국, 인도, 인도네시아, 러시아 및 일본의 고객들을 대상으로 하는 다섯 개의 온라인 사이트를 열 것이라는 첫 번째 단서를 확인할 수 있다. 그런데 첫 번째 단서에서 언급된 국가들 중 어떤 국가에 사이트를 열지 않을 것인지 제시되지 않았으므로 기사에서 사이트가 출시되지 않을 국가를 확인한다. 두 번째 지문인 기사의 'China'(표 2번째 줄), 'India'(표 3번째 줄), 'Indonesia'(표 4번째 줄) 및 'Russia'(표 5번째 줄)에서 중국, 인도, 인도네시아, 러시아의 주식 가격을 언급한 후, 'the retailer ~ now plans to launch only four sites'(3문단 3번째 줄)에서 지금은 4개의 사이트만 열 계획이라고 했으므로 중국, 인도, 인도네시아, 러시아에만 웹사이트를 열 계획이라는 두 번째 단서를 확인할 수 있다. 웹사이트를 중국, 인도, 인도네시아, 러시아, 일본에 열 계획이었다는 첫 번째 단서와 현재 계획은 중국, 인도, 인도네시아, 러시아에만 웹사이트를 여는 것이라는 두 번째 단서를 종합할 때, Webdeals는 일본에 웹사이트를 열지 않기로 했음을 알 수 있다. 따라서 (D) Japan이 정답이다.

10 육하원칙 문제

문제 Webdeals는 왜 주식 중 일부를 상장했는가?
(A) 몇몇 새로운 시장에 진입하기 위해
(B) 대출금 전액을 갚기 위한 돈을 얻기 위해
(C) 대중의 압력에 응하기 위해
(D) 기업 이미지를 개선하기 위해

해설 Webdeals가 왜(Why) 주식 중 일부를 상장했는지를 묻는 육하원칙 문제이므로 질문의 핵심 어구인 make ~ company shares public에 대해 언급된 기사에서 관련 내용을 확인한다. 두 번째 지문인 기사의 'Webdeals opened the shares to the public in an effort to raise capital for expansions into new markets.'(2문단 1번째 줄)에서 Webdeals는 새로운 시장으로의 확장을 위한 자본금을 모으기 위한 노력으로 대중에게 주식을 공개했다고 했

으로 (A) To enter into several new markets가 정답이다.

Paraphrasing
for expansions into new markets 새로운 시장으로의 확장을 위해 →
To enter into ~ new markets 새로운 시장에 진입하기 위해

어휘 **pay off** (빚 따위를) 전액 갚다 **loan** n. 대출금, 대여
corporate adj. 기업의, 법인의

11-15는 다음 공고, 일정표, 이메일에 관한 문제입니다.

공고: 모든 Tech-Train 피트니스 센터 강사들

아시다시피, [11]우리의 교육 시설 증축이 거의 완료되었습니다. 이것은 몇몇 예정된 수업 장소에 영향을 미칠 것입니다. 10월 1일부터, 우리는 에어로빅과 호신술 수업을 위해 새로운 대형 체조실을 사용하기 시작할 것입니다. 또한, [12-A]모든 요가 수업은 실내 수영장 옆에 위치한 전문 교실에서 열릴 것입니다. [12-B]요가실은 이제 강사와 조교들의 사용을 위한 개인 탈의 공간과 샤워실을 갖추고 있습니다. 이곳 또한 10월부터 이용 가능할 것입니다. 마지막으로, 중간 크기의 운동실 두 곳이 2층에 증축되었습니다. 이곳들은 모든 소그룹 댄스 피트니스 운동을 위해 사용될 것입니다. 여러분의 수업이 어디에서 실시될 것인지 확인하시려면 추후 업무 일정을 살펴보시기 바랍니다. 지난 두 달 간의 공사 동안 여러분의 인내에 감사드리며, 우리는 우리 직원들이 변화와 증축이 유익하다고 생각하기를 바랍니다.

addition n. 증축, 추가 **instructional** adj. 교육의 **self-defense** n. 호신술
specialized adj. 전문의 **workout** n. 운동 **beneficial** adj. 유익한, 이로운

Tech-Train 피트니스 센터: [12-D]가을 수업 일정(10월-12월)

수업	[13-C/D]날짜/시간	강사/장소
[12-B]초급 요가	월/목 오전 9시-10시	Bev Peabody, 요가실
중급 요가	화/금 오전 9시-10시 30분	Raine Lewis, 요가실
[12-B/D]고급 요가	수/토 오전 10시-11시 30분	Bev Peabody, [12-B]요가실
초급 댄스 피트니스	화/금 오전 8시 30분-10시	Jay Ang, A 운동실 (2층)
중급 댄스 피트니스	수/토 오전 9시-10시 30분	Jay Ang, A 운동실 (2층)
고급 댄스 피트니스	목/금 오후 6시 30분-8시	Jay Ang, B 운동실 (2층)
초보자 호신술	월/목 오전 8시-9시 30분	Helen Boyd, 체조실
중급자 호신술	화/금 오전 8시-9시 30분	Jay Ang, 체조실
상급자 호신술	수/토 오후 2시-3시 30분	Helen Boyd, 체조실
[13-B]에어로빅	화/수 오전 8시-9시30분	Raine Lewis, 체조실

[14]일정과 관련한 문의 사항이나 용건이 있으시면 센터 부원장에게 이메일로 연락하십시오.

수신 Serena Cruz <scru@techtrainfitness.com>
발신 Jay Ang <jang@techtrainfitness.com>
제목 [14]일정 문제
날짜 9월 28일

안녕하세요 Serena,

저는 방금 다가오는 올 가을의 수업 일정을 보았습니다. 유감스럽게도, 저는 겹치는 것을 우연히 발견했습니다. 당신은 저를 화요일과 금요일에 제가 가르치는 다른 수업과 겹치는 호신술 수업 일정을 잡았습니다. 저는 그것이 단지 실수였음을 확신하지만, 우리는 조정을 해야 할 것입니다.

제게 한 가지 해결책이 있을 것 같습니다. [15]제가 Helen Boyd와 이야기했는데, 그녀는 기꺼이 저와 시간 및 수업을 바꾸어 주려고 합니다. 이것이 괜찮은지 저에게 알려주십시오. 그렇다면, 제가 고급 수업을 맡고 그녀가 중급 수업을 맡을 수 있을 것입니다.

감사합니다!

Jay

happen v. 우연히 ~하다, 발생하다 **conflict** n. 겹치는 것, 상충, 충돌
overlap v. 겹치다, 겹쳐지다 **oversight** n. 실수, 간과 **adjustment** n. 조정

---

11 주제/목적 찾기 문제

문제 공고는 주로 무엇에 대한 것인가?
(A) 업무 일정 관리 시스템의 변화
(B) 피트니스 센터의 증축 시설

(C) 강사에 의해 제공되는 새로운 수업
(D) 일부 운동실의 임시 폐쇄

해설 공고가 주로 무엇에 대한 것인지를 묻는 주제 찾기 문제이므로 공고의 내용을 확인한다. 첫 번째 지문인 공고의 'the additions to our instructional facilities are nearly complete'(1번째 줄)에서 교육 시설 증축이 거의 완료되었다고 한 후, Tech-Train 피트니스 센터의 증축으로 인한 변화의 세부 사항을 제공하고 있으므로 (B) Added facilities at a fitness center가 정답이다.

어휘 **scheduling** n. 일정 관리 **temporary** adj. 임시의 **closure** n. 폐쇄, 폐지

12 Not/True 문제 연계

문제 Bev Peabody에 대해 언급된 것은?
(A) 2층에 위치한 교실에서 가르칠 것이다.
(B) 지정된 탈의실과 샤워실에 출입할 수 있을 것이다.
(C) 수업 중에 보조 강사를 교육할 것이다.
(D) 이번 가을에는 평일에만 수업을 진행할 것이다.

해설 두 지문의 내용을 종합해서 풀어야 하는 연계 문제이다. 질문의 핵심 어구인 Bev Peabody가 언급된 일정표를 먼저 확인한다. 두 번째 지문인 일정표의 'Introduction to Yoga, ~ Bev Peabody, Yoga Room'(표 2번째 줄)과 'Advanced Yoga, ~ Bev Peabody, Yoga Room'(표 4번째 줄)에서 Bev Peabody가 요가실에서 초급 요가와 고급 요가를 가르친다는 첫 번째 단서를 확인할 수 있다. 그런데 요가실에 대한 다른 정보가 제시되지 않았으므로 요가실이 언급된 공고에서 관련 내용을 확인한다. 첫 번째 지문인 공고의 'The yoga room now has its own private changing area and shower for the use of instructors and their assistants.'(4번째 줄)에서 요가실이 이제 강사와 조교들의 사용을 위한 개인 탈의 공간과 샤워실을 갖추고 있다는 두 번째 단서를 확인할 수 있다. Bev Peabody가 요가실에서 초급 요가와 고급 요가를 가르친다는 첫 번째 단서와 요가실이 이제 강사와 조교들의 사용을 위한 개인 탈의 공간과 샤워실을 갖추고 있다는 두 번째 단서를 종합할 때, 강사인 Bev Peabody가 지정된 탈의실과 샤워실에 출입할 수 있을 것임을 알 수 있다. 따라서 (B) She will have access to a reserved dressing room and shower가 정답이다. (A)는 첫 번째 지문인 공고의 'all yoga courses will be held in a specialized room located next to the indoor swimming pool'(3번째 줄)에서 모든 요가 수업은 실내 수영장 옆에 위치한 전문 교실에서 열릴 것이라고 했으므로 지문의 내용과 일치하지 않는다. (C)는 지문에 언급되지 않은 내용이다. (D)는 두 번째 지문인 일정표의 'Fall Class Schedule'(제목)과 'Advanced Yoga, Wed./Sat, ~, Bev Peabody'(표 4번째 줄)에서 가을 수업 일정에 Bev Peabody는 수요일과 토요일에 고급 요가를 가르친다고 했으므로 지문의 내용과 일치하지 않는다.

Paraphrasing
changing area 탈의 공간 → dressing room 탈의실

어휘 **have access to** ~에 출입할 수 있다 **reserved** adj. 지정된, 예약된

13 Not/True 문제

문제 Tech-Train 피트니스 센터에 대해 사실인 것은?
(A) 단기간 동안 평소보다 적은 수업을 할 것이다.
(B) 서로 다른 수준의 에어로빅 수업을 제공한다.
(C) 수업들은 매 주 한 번 이루어진다.
(D) 일요일에는 수업을 진행하지 않을 것이다.

해설 질문의 핵심 어구인 Tech-Train Fitness Center에 대해 묻는 Not/True 문제이므로 두 번째 지문인 Tech-Train 피트니스 센터에 대한 정보가 언급된 일정표에서 관련 내용을 확인한다. (A)는 지문에 언급되지 않은 내용이다. (B)는 'Aerobics'(표 11번째 줄)에서 에어로빅은 한 개의 수업만 진행된다는 것을 알 수 있으므로 지문의 내용과 일치하지 않는다. (C)는 'Day/Time'(표 2열)에서 모든 수업들이 매주 두 번 진행된다는 것을 알 수 있으므로 지문의 내용과 일치하지 않는다. (D)는 'Day/Time'(표 2열)에서 일요일에는 수업이 진행되지 않음을 알 수 있으므로 지문의 내용과 일치한다. 따라서 (D) It will not conduct classes on Sundays가 정답이다.

14 추론 문제 연계

문제 Serena Cruz는 누구일 것 같은가?
(A) 피트니스 센터의 호신술 강사

(B) 춤에 중점을 둔 수업의 참가자
(C) 피트니스 클럽의 부원장
(D) 개인 운동강사 자리의 지원자

해설　두 지문의 내용을 종합해서 풀어야 하는 연계 문제이다. 질문의 핵심 어구인 Serena Cruz에게 보내진 이메일을 먼저 확인한다.

세 번째 지문인 이메일의 'Schedule problem'(이메일 제목)에서 이메일 수신자인 Serena Cruz에게 일정 문제에 대한 이메일이 보내졌다는 첫 번째 단서를 확인할 수 있다. 그런데 왜 Serena Cruz에게 이 이메일이 보내졌는지에 대한 정보가 제시되지 않았으므로 일정과 관련된 이메일에서 관련 내용을 확인한다. 두 번째 지문인 일정표의 'Contact the center's assistant director by e-mail if you have any questions or concerns regarding the schedule.'(표 하단 1번째 줄)에서 일정과 관련한 문의 사항이나 용건이 있다면 센터 부원장, 즉 Tech-Train 피트니스 센터 부원장에게 이메일로 연락하라는 두 번째 단서를 확인할 수 있다.

Serena Cruz에게 일정 문제에 대한 이메일이 보내졌다는 첫 번째 단서와 일정과 관련한 문의 사항이나 용건이 있다면 센터 부원장에게 이메일로 연락하라는 두 번째 단서를 종합할 때, Serena Cruz는 피트니스 센터의 부원장이라는 사실을 추론할 수 있다. 따라서 (C) An assistant director at a fitness club이 정답이다.

15 육하원칙 문제

문제　Helen Boyd는 무엇을 하는 것에 동의했는가?

(A) 동료와 예정된 수업을 교환한다
(B) 일정 변경에 대해 학생들에게 알린다
(C) 동료와 교실을 바꾼다
(D) 고급보다 덜 어려운 수업에 등록한다

해설　Helen Boyd가 무엇(What)을 하는 것에 동의했는지를 묻는 육하원칙 문제이므로 질문의 핵심 어구인 Helen Boyd agreed to do와 관련된 내용이 언급된 이메일을 확인한다. 세 번째 지문인 이메일의 'I spoke to Helen Boyd, and she is happy to switch times and classes with me.'(2문단 1번째 줄)에서 이메일의 발신자인 Jay Ang은 Helen Boyd와 이야기했고, 그녀가 기꺼이 시간 및 수업을 바꾸어 주려고 한다고 했으므로 (A) Trade a scheduled class with a colleague가 정답이다.

Paraphrasing
switch ~ class 수업을 바꾸다 → Trade ~ class 수업을 교환하다

어휘　trade　v. 교환하다, 맞바꾸다　enroll　v. 등록하다

Part 5				p.516
101 (D)	102 (B)	103 (D)	104 (B)	105 (D)
106 (B)	107 (C)	108 (D)	109 (C)	110 (A)
111 (B)	112 (D)	113 (A)	114 (C)	115 (A)
116 (A)	117 (C)	118 (D)	119 (C)	120 (C)
121 (A)	122 (C)	123 (D)	124 (D)	125 (B)
126 (A)	127 (C)	128 (B)	129 (A)	130 (D)

Part 6				p.519
131 (B)	132 (C)	133 (D)	134 (C)	135 (D)
136 (C)	137 (D)	138 (A)	139 (B)	140 (D)
141 (A)	142 (C)	143 (D)	144 (A)	145 (D)
146 (B)				

Part 7				p.523
147 (C)	148 (A)	149 (D)	150 (D)	151 (A)
152 (A)	153 (B)	154 (B)	155 (C)	156 (D)
157 (D)	158 (A)	159 (D)	160 (B)	161 (A)
162 (D)	163 (C)	164 (A)	165 (D)	166 (B)
167 (C)	168 (A)	169 (B)	170 (A)	171 (C)
172 (A)	173 (B)	174 (C)	175 (D)	176 (B)
177 (D)	178 (A)	179 (C)	180 (B)	181 (D)
182 (A)	183 (B)	184 (B)	185 (D)	186 (A)
187 (D)	188 (C)	189 (D)	190 (A)	191 (A)
192 (D)	193 (A)	194 (B)	195 (D)	196 (A)
197 (C)	198 (A)	199 (D)	200 (C)	

101 동사 어휘 고르기

해설 'Opreme Gym에 가입하려면 일시불 요금을 내야 한다'라는 문맥이므로 동사 (D) join(가입하다, 합류하다)이 정답이다. (A) train은 '교육시키다, 훈련시키다', (B) fit은 '맞다, 일치시키다', (C) add는 '추가하다, 첨가하다'라는 의미이다.

해석 Opreme Gym에 가입하려면, 사람들은 200달러의 일시불 요금을 내야 한다.

어휘 one-time adj. 일시불의, 한 반만의

102 부정형용사 채우기

해설 '어떤 이상한 온라인 활동이라도 감지할 때마다 상사에게 알린다'라는 의미가 되어야 하므로 (B) any(어떤 ~라도, 몇몇의)가 정답이다. (A) several과 (C) these는 복수 명사 앞에 쓰이므로 단수 명사 activity 앞에 올 수 없다.

해석 Inslee Solutions사의 직원들은 어떤 이상한 온라인 활동이라도 감지할 때마다 상사에게 알릴 것이 요구된다.

어휘 alert v. 알리다, 경고하다 detect v. 감지하다, 발견하다 unusual adj. 이상한

103 수식어 거품을 이끄는 것 채우기

해설 이 문장은 주어(The bonus)와 동사(will be paid)를 갖춘 완전한 절이므로 ___ the team ~ quarter는 수식어 거품으로 보아야 한다. 이 수식어 거품은 동사(meets)가 있는 거품절이므로, 거품절을 이끌 수 있는 부사절 접속사 (D) only if(~해야만)가 정답이다.

해석 그 팀이 3분기의 매출 목표를 달성해야만 상여금이 지급될 것이다.

어휘 meet v. 달성하다, 채우다 sales goal 매출 목표 even so 그렇기는 하지만

104 태에 맞는 동사 채우기

해설 주절(bouquets ~ usual)에 동사가 없으므로 동사 (B), (C), (D)가 정답의 후보이다. '꽃다발이 가격이 더 높게 매겨진다'라는 수동의 의미이고 빈칸 뒤에 목적어가 없으므로 수동태 동사 (B) are priced가 정답이다.

해석 꽃이 수요가 높은 대중적인 휴일 동안에는 꽃다발이 평소보다 가격이 더 높게 매겨진다.

어휘 be in great demand 수요가 많다, 잘 팔리다 price v. 가격을 매기다; n. 가격

105 부사 어휘 고르기

해설 '배터리가 충분히 충전되다'라는 문맥이므로 부사 (D) sufficiently(충분히)가 정답이다. (A) locally는 '국지적으로, 장소적으로', (B) formally는 '공식적으로, 형식적으로', (C) accurately는 '정확하게, 틀림없이'라는 의미이다.

해석 Tenglide 면도기는 배터리가 충분히 충전되는 경우에 한 시간 넘게 작동할 수 있다.

어휘 razor n. 면도기, 면도칼

106 전치사 채우기

해설 '구매의 30일 이내에 반품 또는 교환할 수 있다'라는 의미가 되어야 하므로 (B) of(~의)가 정답이다.

해석 상점에서 구입하신 물품은 구매의 30일 이내에 반품 또는 교환하실 수 있습니다.

107 형용사 어휘 고르기

해설 '새로 출시된 전기 자동차는 많은 개선된 특징들을 지닌다'라는 문맥이므로 형용사 (C) improved(개선된, 향상된)가 정답이다. (A) obsolete는 '진부한, 시대에 뒤진', (B) permissible은 '허용되는, 허가할 수 있는', (D) probable은 '있음 직한, 유망한'이라는 의미이다.

해석 새로 출시된 전기 자동차는 더 효율적인 배터리를 포함한, 많은 개선된 특징들을 지닌다.

어휘 electric car 전기 자동차 feature n. 특징, 기능

108 부사절 접속사 채우기

해설 이 문장은 필수성분(Job candidates ~ portfolio)을 갖춘 완전한 절이므로 ___ they ~ interview는 수식어 거품으로 보아야 한다. 이 수식어 거품은 동사(can be invited)가 있는 거품절이므로, 거품절을 이끌 수 있는 부사절 접속사 (A), (B), (D)가 정답의 후보이다. '면접에 초청될 수 있기 전에 포트폴리오를 제출해야 한다'라는 의미가 되어야 하므로 (D) before(~하기 전에)가 정답이다. 전치사 (C) by는 거품절이 아니라 거품구를 이끈다.

해석 입사 지원자들은 면접에 초청될 수 있기 전에 포트폴리오를 제출하고 적성 검사를 통과해야 한다.

어휘 job candidate 입사 지원자 portfolio n. 포트폴리오, 작품집 aptitude test 적성 검사

109 명사 어휘 고르기

해설 '등록은 7월 6일에서 8일까지 있을 것이다'라는 문맥이므로 명사 (C) Registration(등록, 신고)이 정답이다. (A) Content는 '내용, 주제', (B) Requirement는 '필요, 요건', (D) Procedure는 '절차, 방법'이라는 의미이다.

해석 새로운 학년의 첫 학기 등록은 7월 6일에서 8일까지 있을 것이다.

어휘 school year 학년

110 전치사 채우기

해설 '기술적 오류 때문에 리허설을 할 수 없었다'라는 의미가 되어야 하므로 (A) due to(~ 때문에)가 정답이다.

해석 밴드 Tiers는 기술적 오류 때문에 Harrison 극장에서 공연을 위한 리허설을 할 수 없었다.

어휘 performance n. 공연, 성과　but for ~이 없(었)다면

111 주어와 수일치하는 동사 채우기

해설 문장에 동사가 없으므로, 동사 (A)와 (B)가 정답의 후보이다. 주어(The promise)가 단수이므로 단수 동사 (B) has created가 정답이다. 주어와 동사 사이에 있는 수식어 거품(of higher pay in urban areas)은 동사의 수 결정에 영향을 주지 않는다.

해석 도시 지역에서의 더 높은 급여에 대한 가능성은 그 국가의 지방 지역에서의 노동력 부족을 야기했다.

어휘 promise n. 가능성, 약속　urban adj. 도시의, 도시에 사는
rural adj. 지방의, 시골의

112 부사 어휘 고르기

해설 '갑작스러운 고지 후에 많은 항공편들이 예기치 않게 연착되었다'라는 문맥이므로 부사 (D) unexpectedly(예기치 않게, 뜻밖에)가 정답이다. (A) alertly는 '기민하게, 조심성 있게', (B) expertly는 '전문적으로, 훌륭하게', (C) carefully는 '주의하여, 신중히'라는 의미이다.

해석 다가오고 있는 폭풍에 대한 갑작스러운 고지 후에 애틀랜타 국제공항에서의 많은 항공편들이 예기치 않게 연착되었다.

어휘 announcement n. 고지, 발표

113 병치 구문 채우기

해설 '더 적은 시간을 일하지만 같은 양을 해내기를 바란다'라는 의미로 보아 등위 접속사 yet(그러나)이 연결해야 하는 것은 to 부정사 두 개이다. yet 앞에 to 부정사(to work)가 왔으므로 yet 뒤의 빈칸에도 to 부정사가 와야 한다. 이때, yet 뒤에 온 to 부정사의 to는 생략이 가능하므로 to produce를 대신하는 (A) produce가 정답이다.

해석 경영진은 직원들이 더 적은 시간을 일하지만 그들이 지금 하고 있는 것과 같은 양을 해내기를 바란다.

어휘 management n. 경영진, 경영

114 동명사 채우기

해설 전치사(instead of)의 목적어 자리에 올 수 있는 것은 명사 (A)와 (D), 또는 동명사 (C)이다. '미리 주문하는 것 대신에 매일 아침에 재료를 구입한다'라는 의미가 되어야 하므로 동명사 (C) ordering이 정답이다. order가 '주문'이라는 의미일 경우에는 가산 명사인데 빈칸 앞에 관사가 없으므로 단수 명사 (A)는 빈칸에 올 수 없고, 복수 명사 (D)는 '미리 주문들 대신에 매일 아침에 재료를 구입한다'라는 어색한 의미를 만들기 때문에 답이 될 수 없다.

해석 최대한의 신선함을 보장하기 위해, Gebita Catering의 요리사는 미리 주문하는 것 대신에 매일 아침에 지역 시장에서 재료를 구입한다.

어휘 ensure v. 보장하다, 반드시 ~하게 하다　maximum adj. 최대의, 최고의
in advance 미리, 사전에

115 부사 자리 채우기

해설 동사(is known)를 꾸미기 위해서는 부사가 와야 하므로 부사 (A) widely(널리, 폭넓게)가 정답이다.

해석 Verra 백화점은 이전 계절의 할인된 디자이너 브랜드 의류를 판매하는 것으로 널리 알려져 있다.

어휘 designer adj. 디자이너 브랜드의, 고급의

116 형용사 자리 채우기

해설 복합 명사(net worth)를 꾸미기 위해서는 형용사 (A) 또는 분사 (D)가 올 수 있다. '대략적인 순자산'이라는 의미를 만드는 형용사 (A) approximate(대략적인, 근사한)가 정답이다. 빈칸에 분사 (D) approximating을 쓰면 '가까워지는 순자산'이라는 어색한 의미가 된다.

해석 Hayes 호텔의 최고 경영자는 5억 달러의 대략적인 순자산을 보유한 것으로 전해진다.

어휘 net worth 순자산　approximation n. 근사치

117 to 부정사 채우기

해설 이 문장은 주어(one), 동사(must undergo), 목적어(an eye test)를 갖춘 완전한 절이므로 ____ a driver's license ~ Massachusetts는 부사 역할을 하는 수식어 거품으로 보아야 한다. 따라서 수식어 거품이 될 수 있는 to 부정사 (C) To maintain이 정답이다. 이 경우 To maintain은 목적(유지하기 위해)을 나타내는 to 부정사이다.

해석 매사추세츠주의 운전 면허증을 유지하기 위해, 10년마다 한 번씩 시력 검사를 받아야 한다.

어휘 driver's license 운전 면허증　undergo v. 받다, 겪다
maintain v. 유지하다, 주장하다

118 전치사 채우기

해설 이 문장은 주어(Mr. Kramer), 동사(does not have), 목적어(much)를 갖춘 완전한 절이므로 ____ packing up ~ equipment는 수식어 거품으로 보아야 한다. 따라서 수식어 거품을 이끌 수 있는 전치사 (B), (C), (D)가 정답의 후보이다. '모든 장비를 챙기는 것을 제외하고는 할 일이 많지 않다'라는 의미가 되어야 하므로 (D) Except for(~을 제외하고는, ~ 외에는)가 정답이다. 부사절 접속사 (A) As though는 거품구가 아니라 거품절을 이끈다.

해석 모든 장비를 챙기는 것을 제외하고는, Mr. Kramer는 무역 박람회의 마지막 날에 할 일이 많지 않다.

어휘 equipment n. 장비, 설비　trade fair 무역 박람회　as though 마치 ~처럼
regarding prep. ~에 관하여　along with ~과 함께, ~에 덧붙여

119 형용사 어휘 고르기

해설 '장학금 지원자들은 추가 서류를 제출할 것이 요구된다'라는 문맥이므로 형용사 (C) supplemental(추가의, 보충의)이 정답이다. (A) agreeable은 '받아들여질 만한, 알맞은', (B) cooperative는 '협력하는, 협조하는', (D) respectable은 '존경할 만한, 훌륭한'이라는 의미이다.

해석 Hartford 대학교 장학금 지원자들은 담당하는 위원회가 그들의 지원을 제대로 검토할 수 있도록 추가 서류를 제출할 것이 요구된다.

어휘 properly adv. 제대로, 올바르게　evaluate v. 검토하다, 평가하다
application n. 지원, 적용

120 현재분사와 과거분사 구별하여 채우기

해설 빈칸이 복합 명사(beauty trends) 뒤에 있으므로 명사를 꾸밀 수 있는 분사 (A)와 (C)가 정답의 후보이다. 명사와 분사가 '미용 유행들이 강조되다'라는 의미의 수동 관계이므로 과거분사 (C) highlighted가 정답이다.

해석 매주마다, Brushla의 웹사이트는 소비자들을 위해 요즘의 주요 패션 잡지들에서 강조되는 최신 미용 유행들을 간추린다.

어휘 summarize v. 간추리다, 요약하다　trend n. 유행, 추세
highlight v. 강조하다, 하이라이트 표시를 하다

121 형용사 어휘 고르기

해설 'Ms. Brunson이 자리를 비우는 동안 임시 관리자직은 Mr. Hart에게 주어질 것이다'라는 문맥이므로 형용사 (A) acting(임시의, 대리의)이 정답이다. (B) complete는 '완전한, 완성된', (C) timely는 '적시의, 시기적절한', (D) highest는 '최고의'라는 의미이다.

해석 Ms. Brunson이 휴가로 자리를 비우는 동안, 임시 관리자직은 Mr. Hart에게 주어질 것이다.

어휘 on leave 휴가로

122 가정법 표현 채우기

해설 If절에 had p.p.(had been found)가 왔으므로 주절에는 이와 짝을 이루는 would have p.p.가 와야 한다. 따라서 (C) would not have spread가 정답이다. 주절에는 would와 같은 조동사가 꼭 와야 하므로 would가 없는 나머지 보기들은 답이 될 수 없다.

해석 만약 그 바이러스가 더 일찍 발견되었다면, 전국에 퍼지지 않았을 것이다.

어휘 spread v. 퍼지다, 펴다

123 부사 채우기

해설 '2호점을 여는 것의 정당한 이유가 될 만큼 충분히 수익성이 있게 되었다'라는 의미가 되어야 하므로 (D) enough(충분히)가 정답이다. 참고로, enough는 형용사나 부사를 뒤에서 꾸며주는 부사임을 알아둔다.

해석 Ms. Martin의 가게는 2호점을 여는 것의 정당한 이유가 될 만큼 충분히 수익성이 있게 되었다.

어휘 profitable adj. 수익성이 있는, 유익한
justify v. ~의 정당한 이유가 되다, 옳다고 하다
somehow adv. 어떻게든지 해서, 어쩐지

124 명사 관련 어구 완성하기

해설 빈칸 앞의 conference와 함께 쓰여 '회의 참석자'라는 의미의 어구를 이루는 (D) participants가 정답이다. (conference participant: 회의 참석자) (A)의 respondent는 '응답자', (B)의 commuter는 '통근자', (C)의 recipient는 '수령인'이라는 의미이다.

해석 컨벤션 센터의 웹사이트에 따르면, 회의 참석자들은 각 발표 후에 질문을 할 기회가 있을 것이다.

어휘 opportunity n. 기회

125 원급/비교급/최상급 표현 채우기

해설 '직원 수를 줄이기보다는 모두의 급여를 줄이다'라는 의미가 되어야 하므로 (B) rather than(~보다)이 정답이다.

해석 재정 문제를 해결하기 위해서, Gerber & Partners사는 직원 수를 줄이기보다는 모두의 급여를 줄이기로 결정했다.

어휘 resolve v. 해결하다, 결심하다 financial adj. 재정의, 금융의
issue n. 문제, 쟁점 by all means 기어코, 반드시

126 관계대명사 채우기

해설 빈칸 뒤에 주어가 없는 불완전한 절(saved ~ money)이 와서 빈칸 앞의 명사(recycling program)를 꾸며 주고 있으므로, 불완전한 절을 이끌 수 있는 관계대명사 (A)와 (C)가 정답의 후보이다. 선행사(recycling program)가 사람이 아닌 사물이므로, 사물 관계대명사 (A) which가 정답이다. 명사 자리에 와서 명사절을 이끄는 명사절 접속사 (B) what과 완전한 절을 이끄는 관계부사 (D) where는 답이 될 수 없다.

해석 Francis Woods는 재활용 프로그램을 높이 평가했는데, 그 프로그램은 회사가 많은 금액의 돈을 절약하게 했다.

어휘 praise v. 높이 평가하다, 칭찬하다

127 사람명사 추상명사 구별하여 채우기

해설 주어 자리에 올 수 있는 것은 명사이므로 명사 (B)와 (C)가 정답의 후보이다. 'Sacramento Film Prize의 최종 후보자들이 초청될 것이다'라는 의미가 되어야 하므로 사람명사 (C) Finalists(최종 후보자)가 정답이다. 추상명사 (B) Finale(마지막 부분, 피날레)를 쓰면 'Sacramento Film Prize의 마지막 부분이 초청될 것이다'라는 어색한 의미가 된다.

해석 Sacramento Film Prize의 최종 후보자들은 축제의 마지막 날에 그들의 영화를 상영하도록 초청될 것이다.

어휘 screen v. 상영하다, 심사하다

128 동사 어휘 고르기

해설 '주주 회의에서 확장 계획에 대한 세부 사항들을 설명할 것이다'라는 문맥이므로 동사 (B) reveal(설명하다, 밝히다)이 정답이다. (A) conduct는 '하다, 행동하다', (C) prompt는 '일으키다, 자극하다', (D) apply는 '적용하다, 활용하다'라는 의미이다.

해석 다음 달의 주주 회의에서 Jackson Solutions사의 최고 경영자 Doug Stevenson이 그의 확장 계획에 대한 세부 사항들을 설명할 것이다.

어휘 shareholder n. 주주

129 형용사 자리 채우기

해설 복합 명사(sales techniques)를 꾸미기 위해서는 형용사가 필요하므로 형용

사 (A) different(색다른, 다른)가 정답이다.

해설 Sarah Vasquez는 직원들이 항상 고객들에 대한 새로운 접근 방식을 지니도록 주기적으로 색다른 판매 기술들을 적용할 것을 지시한다.

어휘 periodically adv. 주기적으로, 때때로 adopt v. 적용하다, 채택하다
differentiate v. 구별하다, 구분 짓다 differentiation n. 구별, 차별

130 부사 어휘 고르기

해설 '어젯밤의 축제에서 환경 운동에 대한 기여로 감사히 상을 받았다'라는 문맥이므로 부사 (D) gratefully(감사하여, 기꺼이)가 정답이다. (A) frequently는 '자주, 흔히', (B) routinely는 '일상적으로, 관례대로', (C) closely는 '밀접하게, 면밀히'라는 의미이다.

해석 어젯밤의 Leadership in Philanthropy 축제에서, Connor Michaels가 환경 운동에 대한 그의 기여로 감사히 상을 받았다.

어휘 gala n. 축제, 경축 행사 cause n. 운동, 이유

131-134는 다음 웹페이지에 관한 문제입니다.

www.mandyashtonfashions.com/new

Mandy Ashton의 여름 컬렉션은 아직 온라인에서 구매 가능합니다. 그러나, 수량이 제한되어 있습니다. [131]그러므로, 만약 고객님들이 남아있는 물품을 구매하고 싶으시다면 서두르셔야 합니다.

[132]이 컬렉션과 관련하여, Mandy Ashton은 남태평양의 바다에서 보이는 청명한 색 조합에서 영감을 받았습니다. [133]각 작품은 진정시키는 녹색과 파란색 톤을 특징으로 합니다. Mandy Ashton은 항상 남태평양의 바다 및 섬과의 유대감을 느꼈지만 오염의 위험에 대해 염려합니다. [134]그녀는 쉽게 영향을 받는 환경을 보호하는 것이 중요하다고 생각합니다. 그것이 바로 Mandy Ashton Fashions가 모든 수익금의 10퍼센트를 정화 활동에 계속해서 기부하려는 이유입니다. 여러분은 Mandy Ashton Fashions에서 쇼핑함으로써 이러한 활동을 지지할 수 있습니다.

quantity n. 수량, 다량 pick up 구매하다, 찾아오다 serene adj. 청명한, 고요한
combination n. 조합, 결합 concerned adj. 염려하는, 관련된
sensitive adj. 영향받기 쉬운, 섬세한 proceeds n. 수익금, 돈
effort n. 활동, 노력

131 접속부사 채우기 주변 문맥 파악

해설 빈칸이 콤마와 함께 문장의 맨 앞에 온 접속부사 자리이므로, 앞 문장과 빈칸이 있는 문장의 의미 관계를 파악하여 접속부사인 네 개의 보기 중 하나를 정답으로 골라야 한다. 앞 문장에서 수량이 제한되어 있다고 했고, 빈칸이 있는 문장에서는 고객들이 남아있는 물품을 구매하고 싶다면 서둘러야 한다고 했으므로, 원인과 결과를 나타내는 문장에서 사용되는 (B) Accordingly(그러므로)가 정답이다.

어휘 likewise adv. 마찬가지로, 또한 besides adv. 게다가
occasionally adv. 가끔, 때때로

132 관계사 자리 채우기

해설 이 문장은 주어(Mandy Ashton)와 동사(was inspired)를 갖춘 완전한 절이므로 ___ found ~ South Pacific은 수식어 거품으로 보아야 한다. 따라서 수식어 거품인 관계절을 만드는 (C)와 (D)가 정답의 후보이다. 관계절이 남태평양의 바다에서 청명한 색 조합이 보인다는 현재의 상태를 나타내는 문맥이므로 현재 시제 (C) that are가 정답이다.

133 알맞은 문장 고르기

해설 (A) 재활용된 재료로 만들어진 물품들은 가격이 인하됩니다.
(B) 일부 제품들은 저희가 예상했던 것보다 더 빠르게 판매되고 있습니다.
(C) Mandy Ashton Fashions는 자선 단체와 제휴합니다.
(D) 각 작품은 진정시키는 녹색과 파란색 톤을 특징으로 합니다.

해설 빈칸에 들어갈 알맞은 문장을 고르는 문제이므로 빈칸의 주변 문맥이나 전체 문맥을 파악한다. 앞 문장 'For this collection, Mandy Ashton was inspired by the serene color combinations (that are) found in the waters of the South Pacific.'에서 이 컬렉션과 관련하여 Mandy Ashton은 남태평양의 바다에서 보이는 청명한 색 조합에서 영감을 받았다고 했으므

로 빈칸에는 작품의 색상과 관련된 내용이 들어가야 함을 알 수 있다. 따라서 (D) Each piece features calming green and blue tones가 정답이다.

어휘 **mark down** 가격을 인하하다 **anticipate** v. 예상하다, 기대하다
charitable group 자선 단체 **calm** v. 진정시키다, 침착해지다

134 명사 어휘 고르기 주변 문맥 파악

해설 '그녀는 쉽게 영향을 받는 ___을 보호하는 것이 중요하다고 생각한다'라는 문맥이므로 모든 보기가 정답의 후보이다. 빈칸이 있는 문장만으로 정답을 고를 수 없으므로 주변 문맥이나 전체 문맥을 파악한다. 앞 문장에서 'Mandy Ashton이 오염의 위협에 대해 염려한다(Mandy Ashton ~ is concerned about the threat of pollution.)'고 했으므로 환경이 쉽게 영향을 받아 오염될 수 있으므로 보호해야 한다는 것임을 알 수 있다. 따라서 명사 (C) environments(환경)가 정답이다.

어휘 **investment** n. 투자 **detail** n. 세부, 항목 **textile** n. 직물, 옷감

135-138은 다음 안내문에 관한 문제입니다.

다음은 Ormevivi 화장품의 가정용 필링 방법에 대한 설명입니다. 최상의 결과를 위해, 지성 피부에는 일주일에 두 번, 건성 피부에는 일주일에 한 번 이 방법을 실행하세요. 135Agepro 마사지 크림을 얼굴에 충분히 바르는 것으로 시작합니다. 씻어내지 않고, ReViVi 마스크를 붙이고 3분 동안 그대로 둡니다. 약간 얼얼한 느낌은 정상입니다. 136하지만, 아주 큰 통증이 느껴진다면 즉시 제거하세요. 137다음으로, 화장솜을 이용해서 닦아내고, 그러고 나서 꼼꼼히 건조시키세요. 이것이 끝나면 수분 크림을 바르고 싶을 수도 있습니다. 138저희는 수분 기초 제품을 추천합니다. 가능하면, 별도로 판매되는 ReViVi 데이 크림을 사용해보세요.

procedure n. 방법, 절차 **apply** v. 바르다, 적용하다 **rinse** v. 씻다, 헹구다
stinging adj. 얼얼한, 찌르는 듯이 아픈 **cotton pad** 화장솜
moisturizer n. 수분 크림, 피부 로션 **ideally** adv. 가능하면, 이상적으로
separately adv. 별도로, 따로따로

135 부사 자리 채우기

해설 동명사구(applying Agepro Massage Cream)를 꾸미기 위해서는 부사가 와야 하므로 부사 (B) generously(충분히, 후하게)가 정답이다.

어휘 **generosity** n. 관대, 아량 **generousness** n. 관대함, 후함

136 알맞은 문장 고르기

해석 (A) 그러므로, 당신은 저희에게 가능한 한 빨리 알려주셔야 합니다.
(B) 햇빛은 피부 표층을 영구적으로 손상시킬 수 있습니다.
(C) 하지만, 아주 큰 통증이 느껴진다면 즉시 제거하세요.
(D) 그것들을 함께 섞는 것은 마스크의 효과를 제한할 것입니다.

해설 빈칸에 들어갈 알맞은 문장을 고르는 문제이므로 빈칸의 주변 문맥이나 전체 문맥을 파악한다. 앞 문장 'A slight stinging sensation is normal.'에서 약간 얼얼한 느낌은 정상이라고 했으므로 빈칸에는 통증과 관련된 내용이 들어가야 함을 알 수 있다. 따라서 (C) However, remove it immediately if you feel any significant pain이 정답이다.

어휘 **top layer** 표층, 최상층 **permanently** adv. 영구적으로, 불변으로
significant adj. 아주 큰, 상당한 **effectiveness** n. 효과, 유효

137 병치 구문 채우기

해설 '닦아내고 건조시키다'라는 문맥으로 보아, 등위접속사(and)에 연결되는 것은 동사 wash와 또 다른 동사이다. 앞의 동사가 동사원형(wash)이므로 동사원형 (D) dry가 정답이다.

138 동사 어휘 고르기 주변 문맥 파악

해설 '수분 기초 제품을 ___한다'라는 문맥이므로 모든 보기가 정답의 후보이다. 빈칸이 있는 문장만으로 정답을 고를 수 없으므로 주변 문맥이나 전체 문맥을 파악한다. 앞 문장에서 '수분 크림을 바르고 싶을 수도 있다(you may want to apply moisturizer)'고 한 후, 뒤 문장에서 '별도로 판매되는 ReViVi 데이 크림을 사용해보라(you should try ReViVi Day Cream, which is sold separately)'고 했으므로 수분 기초 제품을 추천한다는 것임을 알 수 있다. 따라서 동사 (A) recommend(추천하다)가 정답이다.

어휘 **include** v. 포함하다 **demonstrate** v. 설명하다, 보여주다
direct v. (편지·소포 등을) 보내다, 지시하다

139-142는 다음 이메일에 관한 문제입니다.

발신: Taylor Lim, 부사장 <t.lim@corefinance.com>
수신: 전 직원 <staff@corefinance.com>
날짜: 11월 2일
제목: 사이버 보안 문제
첨부 파일: 공식 성명서

직원분들께,

139우리 시스템이 다수의 의심스러운 거래를 감지했습니다. 더 조사해보니, 고객들이 이러한 송금에 대해서 인지하지도 못했다는 것을 알게 되었습니다. 140더욱이, 우리 보안 팀은 여러 계정에서 잠재적인 보안 문제를 발견했습니다. 우선, 제가 공식적인 공개 성명서의 초안을 작성할 것입니다. 141그것은 이 상황과 회사가 취하고 있는 조치에 대해 설명할 것입니다. 결국, 우리는 또한 모든 고객에게 문자 메시지와 이메일을 통해 알려야 할 것입니다. 142안내문은 우리 웹사이트에도 게시될 예정입니다. 마지막으로, 만약 이상한 무언가를 발견하신다면 주저하지 말고 보안팀에게 연락해주십시오. 협조해 주셔서 감사드립니다.

Taylor Lim 드림

cybersecurity n. 사이버 보안 **detect** v. 감지하다, 발견하다
transaction n. 거래, 매매 **wire transfer** 송금
potential adj. 잠재적인, 가능성이 있는 **draft** v. 초안을 작성하다; n. 초안
measure n. 조치, 측정 **cooperation** n. 협조, 협력

139 형용사 어휘 고르기 전체 문맥 파악

해설 '시스템이 다수의 ___한 거래를 감지했다'는 문맥이므로 모든 보기가 정답의 후보이다. 빈칸이 있는 문장만으로 정답을 고를 수 없으므로 주변 문맥이나 전체 문맥을 파악한다. 뒷부분에서 '이상한 무언가를 발견한다면 주저하지 말고 보안팀에게 연락해달라(do not hesitate to contact security if you see anything unusual yourself)'고 했으므로 시스템이 의심스러운 거래를 감지했다는 것임을 알 수 있다. 따라서 형용사 (B) suspicious(의심스러운)가 정답이다.

어휘 **personal** adj. 개인적인, 개인의 **international** adj. 국제적인
identical adj. 동일한, 똑같은

140 접속부사 채우기 전체 문맥 파악

해설 빈칸이 콤마와 함께 문장의 맨 앞에 온 접속부사 자리이므로, 앞 문장과 빈칸이 있는 문장의 의미 관계를 파악하여 접속부사인 (A), (B), (D) 중 하나를 정답으로 골라야 한다. 앞부분에서 시스템이 다수의 의심스러운 거래를 감지했다고 했고, 빈칸이 있는 문장에서는 보안 팀이 여러 계정에서 잠재적인 보안 문제를 발견했다고 했으므로, 앞에서 언급된 내용에 추가 정보를 덧붙이는 내용의 문장에서 사용되는 (A) Moreover(더욱이)가 정답이다.

어휘 **except** prep. ~을 제외하고; conj. ~을 제외하고
otherwise adv. 그렇지 않으면

141 인칭대명사 채우기 주변 문맥 파악

해설 '___은 이 상황과 조치에 대해 설명할 것이다'라는 문맥에서 빈칸이 문장의 주어 자리이므로, 대명사인 모든 보기가 정답의 후보이다. 빈칸이 있는 문장만으로 정답을 고를 수 없으므로 주변 문맥이나 전체 문맥을 파악한다. 앞 문장에서 이메일 발신자가 공식적인 공개 성명서(an official public statement)의 초안을 작성했다고 했으므로 상황과 조치에 대해 설명하는 것은 공개 성명서임을 알 수 있다. 따라서 3인칭 단수 대명사 (A) It이 정답이다.

142 알맞은 문장 고르기

해석 (A) 이것은 우리 고객들 중 일부에게서 지적을 받았습니다.
(B) 일부 액수는 심지어 100만 달러를 넘었습니다.
(C) 안내문은 우리 웹사이트에도 게시될 예정입니다.
(D) 그 팀은 적시에 이 문제를 완전히 해결했습니다.

해설 빈칸에 들어갈 알맞은 문장을 고르는 문제이므로 빈칸의 주변 문맥이나 전체 문맥을 파악한다. 앞 문장 'we will also have to notify all of our clients via text message and e-mail'에서 또한 모든 고객에게 문자 메시지와 이메일을

통해 알려야 할 것이라고 했으므로 빈칸에는 알림 방법에 관한 내용이 들어가야 함을 알 수 있다. 따라서 (C) Information will be posted on our Web site as well이 정답이다.

어휘 **point out** 지적하다, 가리키다 **resolve** v. 해결하다, 결심하다
in a timely fashion 적시에

143-146은 다음 기사에 관한 문제입니다.

> **건축 역사의 일부를 소유하라**
>
> [143]존경받는 건축가 Chan-mi Gwon의 초기 작품 중 하나가 막 경매에 부쳐졌다. 그녀의 유명한 정육면체 스타일의 완벽한 예인 이 나무로 된 침실 5개짜리 건축물은 Silverton 교외에 있는 2에이커 크기의 토지에 자리 잡고 있다. [144]이 경매 소식은 큰 관심을 끌어모았다. Ms. Gwon의 주거용 건물의 대부분은 역사적 위상과 건축적 우수성 때문에 공식적인 랜드마크가 되었고 더 이상 개인 소유하에 있지 않다. 경매는 8월 27일에 열릴 예정이다. [145]입찰하고 싶은 사람들은 그 날짜 이전에 등록할 것이 권해진다. [146]시작가는 1,200만 달러이지만, 전문가들은 최종가가 훨씬 더 올라갈 것으로 예상한다.
>
> **put up for sale** 경매에 부치다, 팔려고 내놓다 **celebrated** adj. 유명한
> **cubic** adj. 정육면체의, 3차원의 **structure** n. 건축물, 구조
> **property** n. 토지, 부동산 **outskirt** n. 교외, 변두리 **ownership** n. 소유, 소유권
> **on account of** ~ 때문에 **status** n. 위상, 지위 **excellence** n. 우수성, 탁월함
> **auction** n. 경매

143 형용사 어휘 고르기 전체 문맥 파악

해설 '___한 건축가의 초기 작품 중 하나가 막 경매에 부쳐졌다'라는 문맥이므로 모든 보기가 정답의 후보이다. 빈칸이 있는 문장만으로 정답을 고를 수 없으므로 주변 문맥이나 전체 문맥을 파악한다. 뒤 문장에서 '그녀의 유명한 정육면체 스타일(her celebrated cubic style)'이라고 했고, 뒷부분에 'Ms. Gwon의 주거용 건물의 대부분은 역사적 위상과 건축적 우수성 때문에 공식적인 랜드마크가 되었다(Most of Ms. Gwon's residential buildings have become official landmarks ~ on account of their historical status and architectural excellence.)'고 했으므로 존경받는 건축가의 작품이 경매에 부쳐진 것임을 알 수 있다. 따라서 형용사 (D) admired(존경받는)가 정답이다.

어휘 **new** adj. 새로운 **unknown** adj. 무명의, 알려지지 않은
amateur adj. 아마추어의, 비전문가의

144 알맞은 문장 고르기

해석 (A) 이 경매 소식은 큰 관심을 끌어모았다.
(B) 이것들은 최근에 박물관으로 개조되었다.
(C) 그것은 시내 지역의 중심부에 위치해 있다.
(D) 그 액수는 아마도 가격 제시를 막지 않을 것이다.

해설 빈칸에 들어갈 알맞은 문장을 고르는 문제이므로 빈칸의 주변 문맥이나 전체 문맥을 파악한다. 앞부분 'One of (admired) architect ~ early works has just been put up for sale.'에서 존경받는 건축가의 초기 작품 중 하나가 막 경매에 부쳐졌다고 한 후, 경매에 부쳐진 건축물에 대해 설명하고 있으므로 빈칸에는 이 경매 소식과 관련된 내용이 들어가야 함을 알 수 있다. 따라서 (A) News of the sale has attracted great interest가 정답이다.

어휘 **convert** v. 개조하다, 전환하다 **figure** n. 액수, 수치
discourage v. 막다, 방해하다 **offer** n. 가격 제시, 호가

145 동명사 채우기 주변 문맥 파악

해설 전치사(in)의 목적어 자리에 올 수 있는 것은 명사 (A)와 (B), 또는 동명사 (D)이다. 뒤 문장에서 입찰하는 사람이 내게 될 금액으로 1,200만 달러($12 million)가 언급되었고 '입찰하고 싶은 사람들은 등록할 것이 권해진다'라는 의미가 되어야 하므로 동명사 (D) bidding이 정답이다. 단수 명사 (A)는 bid가 가산 명사이므로 관사와 함께 쓰여야 하고, 복수 명사 (B)는 입찰 자체, 즉 호가가 얼마에 제시되는지 관심 있는 사람들이 등록해야 한다는 어색한 의미를 만들기 때문에 답이 될 수 없다.

어휘 **bid** v. 입찰하다; n. 입찰

146 올바른 시제의 동사 채우기

해설 but 뒤의 절이 전문가들은 최종가가 훨씬 더 올라갈 것으로 예상한다는 현재

의 상황을 나타내는 문맥이므로 현재 시제 (B) expect가 정답이다.

어휘 **expect** v. 예상하다, 기대하다

147-148은 다음 광고에 관한 문제입니다.

> 건조하고 먼지가 많은 공기로 괴로우신가요? 알레르기나 천식으로 고생하시나요?
> EasyBreathe Cool Mist 가습기로 당신의 집이나 사무실을 쾌적하게 유지하세요!
>
> 특징:
> - [147-A]시끄러운 모터나 팬이 없음
> - 교체할 값비싼 필터가 없음
> - [147-C]열이나 증기가 없음
> - 관리하고 세척하기가 쉬움
> - [147-B]가볍고 소형임—어디를 가든지 휴대 가능
> - [147-D]전기 요금을 낮게 유지시키는 절전 모드
> - 집안 어느 방에나 어울리는 날렵하고 멋진 디자인
>
> EasyBreathe Cool Mist 가습기를 구입하여 항상 상쾌하고 깨끗한 공기를 마시는 느낌을 만끽하세요. [148]www.easybreathe.com에서 온라인으로 주문할 수 있습니다.
>
> **bother** v. 괴롭히다, 성가시게 하다 **trouble** v. 고생시키다, 난처하게 하다
> **asthma** n. 천식 **comfortable** adj. 쾌적한, 편안한 **humidifier** n. 가습기
> **power-saving** adj. 절전의 **sleek** adj. 날렵한, 매끈한
> **stylish** adj. 멋진, 유행을 따르는

147 Not/True 문제

문제 제품의 특징으로 열거되지 않은 것은?
(A) 조용한 작동
(B) 휴대성
(C) 증기 방출
(D) 에너지 효율

해설 질문의 핵심 어구인 a feature of the product와 관련된 내용을 지문에서 찾아 보기와 대조하는 Not/True 문제이다. (A)는 'No noisy motors or fans'(2문단 2번째 줄)에서 시끄러운 모터나 팬이 없다고 했으므로 지문의 내용과 일치한다. (B)는 'Lightweight and compact—bring it everywhere you go'(2문단 6번째 줄)에서 가볍고 소형이라 어디를 가든지 휴대 가능하다고 했으므로 지문의 내용과 일치한다. (C)는 'No heat or steam'(2문단 4번째 줄)에서 열이나 증기가 없다고 했으므로 지문의 내용과 일치하지 않는다. 따라서 (C) Steam emission이 정답이다. (D)는 'Power-saving mode to keep your electricity bill low'(2문단 7번째 줄)에서 전기 요금을 낮게 유지시키는 절전 모드가 있다고 했으므로 지문의 내용과 일치한다.

Paraphrasing
No noisy motors or fans 시끄러운 모터나 팬이 없음 → Silent operation 조용한 작동
Power-saving 절전의 → Energy efficiency 에너지 효율

어휘 **silent** adj. 조용한, 소리 없는 **portability** n. 휴대성, 휴대할 수 있음
emission n. 방출, 배출 **efficiency** n. 효율, 능률

148 육하원칙 문제

문제 고객들은 어떻게 제품을 구입할 수 있는가?
(A) 웹사이트를 방문함으로써
(B) 매장에 감으로써
(C) 전화번호로 전화함으로써
(D) 행사에 참석함으로써

해설 고객들이 어떻게(How) 제품을 구입할 수 있는지를 묻는 육하원칙 문제이다. 질문의 핵심 어구인 customers buy the product와 관련하여, 'You can order it ~ at www.easybreathe.com.'(3문단 2번째 줄)에서 www. easybreathe.com에서 제품을 주문할 수 있다고 했으므로 (A) By visiting a Web site가 정답이다.

Paraphrasing
buy 구입하다 → order 주문하다

어휘 **attend** v. 참석하다, 다니다

149-150은 다음 공고에 관한 문제입니다.

모든 Doveport 아파트 단지 입주민들께 드리는 공고

고령 주민들의 우려에 대응하여, ¹⁴⁹오후 11시부터 오전 6시 사이에 로비를 제외한 모든 공동 시설에서 야간 경보 시스템이 가동될 예정입니다. 여기에는 세탁실, 체육관, 수영장이 포함됩니다.

이 시간 동안, 입주민 여러분의 개인 키 코드로는 이 장소들의 문을 열지 못할 것입니다. 억지로 그것들을 열려고 하는 것은 자동으로 보안 알람을 가동시킬 것입니다. ¹⁴⁹개인 창고 공간을 포함한 다른 모든 곳에는 여전히 출입하실 수 있으실 것입니다. 제한 구역 어디에든 예외적인 출입이 필요한 경우, ^{150-D}24시간 내내 도움을 드릴 저희 경비 직원에게 연락하십시오. 다시 말씀드리자면, 수리가 진행되는 동안 추후 공지가 있을 때까지 대주차장은 폐쇄될 예정입니다.

complex n. 단지, 복합 건물 in response to ~에 대응하여, 답하여
overnight adj. 야간의, 하룻밤 동안의 activate v. 가동하다, 활성화시키다
force v. 억지로 ~하다, 강요하다 trigger v. 가동하다, 유발하다
storage n. 창고, 저장 restricted adj. 제한된, 한정된
around the clock 24시간 내내

---

149 육하원칙 문제

문제 공고에 따르면, 어느 시설이 오후 11시부터 오전 6시 사이에 계속 출입 가능할 것인가?
(A) 피트니스 센터
(B) 대주차장
(C) 수영장
(D) 창고 공간

해설 어느(which) 시설이 오후 11시부터 오전 6시 사이에 계속 출입 가능할 것인지를 묻는 육하원칙 문제이다. 질문의 핵심 어구인 facility ~ accessible between 11 P.M. and 6 A.M.과 관련하여, 'overnight alarm systems will now be activated in all common facilities ~ between 11 P.M. and 6 A.M.'(1문단 1번째 줄)에서 오후 11시부터 오전 6시 사이에 모든 공동 시설에서 야간 경보 시스템이 가동될 예정이라고 했고, 'You will still have access to everywhere else, including your personal storage space.'(2문단 2번째 줄)에서 개인 창고 공간을 포함한 다른 모든 곳에는 여전히 출입할 수 있을 것이라고 했으므로 (D) The storage area가 정답이다.

Paraphrasing
remain accessible 계속 출입 가능하다 → still have access 여전히 출입할 수 있다

150 Not/True 문제

문제 Doveport 아파트 단지에 대해 언급된 것은?
(A) 최근에 문을 열었다.
(B) 주민들은 대부분 고령자이다.
(C) 반려동물을 허용하지 않는다.
(D) 24시간 경비를 제공한다.

해설 질문의 핵심 어구인 Doveport Apartment Complex와 관련된 내용을 지문에서 찾아 보기와 대조하는 Not/True 문제이다. (A), (B), (C)는 지문에 언급되지 않은 내용이다. (D)는 'our security staff who will remain available around the clock'(2문단 4번째 줄)에서 경비 직원이 24시간 내내 도움을 줄 것이라고 했으므로 지문의 내용과 일치한다. 따라서 (D) It offers 24-hour security가 정답이다.

Paraphrasing
around the clock 24시간 내내 → 24-hour 24시간

어휘 senior n. 고령자; adj. 상위의

151-152는 다음 메시지 대화문에 관한 문제입니다.

Jason Baker [오후 2:37]
^{151/152-A}집에서는 인터넷에 연결할 수 없어서 휴대폰으로 메시지를 보냅니다. ¹⁵¹제가 사는 지역에 정전이 되었나요?

Noel Richards [오후 2:38]
Timbercomms사에 연락해 주셔서 감사합니다. 고객님만 그런 것이 아닙니다. 주소를 알려주시겠습니까?

Jason Baker [오후 2:40]
캘리포니아주, Red Hawk, Easthaven로 34번지예요.

Noel Richards [오후 2:43]
알겠습니다. 폭풍이 약간의 피해를 일으켰지만, 저희가 수리하는 중입니다.

Jason Baker [오후 2:44]
연결이 언제 다시 되는지 아시나요? ^{152-A}저는 사실 일하는 중이었거든요.

Noel Richards [오후 2:45]
죄송하지만, 저희 수리 직원들은 오늘 오후 4시 정도가 되어서야 문제가 해결될 것으로 예상합니다.

Jason Baker [오후 2:47]
그럼 괜찮겠네요. 감사합니다.

---

outage n. 정전, 단수 windstorm n. 폭풍 make repairs 수리하다
personnel n. 직원, 인사과 estimate v. 예상하다, 추산하다
resolve v. 해결하다, 결심하다

151 의도 파악 문제

문제 오후 2시 38분에, Mr. Richards가 "You're not the only one"이라고 썼을 때, 그가 의도한 것은?
(A) 비슷한 문제들이 보고되었다.
(B) 등록하는 데에 시간이 조금 걸린다.
(C) 많은 사람들이 홍보 활동에 참여하기를 원한다.
(D) 많은 집들이 파손되었다.

해설 Mr. Richards가 의도한 것을 묻는 문제이므로, 질문의 인용어구(You're not the only one)가 언급된 주변 문맥을 확인한다. 'I'm sending a message from my phone because I can't connect to the Internet at home. Is there an outage in my area?'(2:37 P.M.)에서 Jason Baker가 집에서는 인터넷에 연결할 수 없어서 휴대폰으로 메시지를 보낸다고 하면서 자신이 사는 지역에 정전이 되었는지를 묻자, Mr. Richards가 'You're not the only one(고객님만 그런 것이 아닙니다)'이라고 한 것을 통해, Jason Baker 외의 다른 사람들도 인터넷에 연결할 수 없다는 문제를 보고했음을 알 수 있다. 따라서 (A) Similar issues have been reported가 정답이다.

어휘 take part in ~에 참여하다, 참가하다 promotion n. 홍보 (활동), 승진

152 Not/True 문제

문제 Mr. Baker에 대해 사실인 것은?
(A) 집에서 일하고 있었다.
(B) 종종 접속 문제를 겪는다.
(C) 인터넷 요금제를 업그레이드하기로 결정했다.
(D) 최근에 새로운 곳으로 이사했다.

해설 질문의 핵심 어구인 Mr. Baker와 관련된 내용을 지문에서 찾아 보기와 대조하는 Not/True 문제이다. (A)는 'I'm sending a message from my phone because I can't connect to the Internet at home.'(2:37 P.M.)에서 Mr. Baker가 집에서는 인터넷에 연결할 수 없어서 휴대폰으로 메시지를 보낸다고 했고 'I was actually in the middle of work.'(2:44 P.M.)에서 사실 일하는 중이었다고 했으므로 지문의 내용과 일치한다. 따라서 (A) He was working from home이 정답이다. (B), (C), (D)는 지문에 언급되지 않은 내용이다.

어휘 plan n. (약정) 제도, 계획

153-154는 다음 광고지에 관한 문제입니다.

Oak Grove 농장은 여러분이 사과 따기 행사에 저희와 함께하시도록 초대합니다
¹⁵⁴10월 21일 일요일

입장료는 3달러입니다. 12세 미만의 어린이는 무료로 입장합니다. 사과를 직접 따시면 되고, 저희가 바구니를 제공해 드립니다. 사과는 파운드당 1달러이니, 원하시는 만큼 많이 따세요! 모든 방문객에게 무료 주차가 가능합니다.

¹⁵³사과 따기를 마치신 후, 저희 식당인 Red Kettle 카페에서 점심을 함께하세요. 카페는 오전 11시부터 오후 3시까지 운영하며 다양한 수프, 샌드위치,

---

갓 딴 사과로 만든 파이를 제공합니다. 오후 2시부터 3시까지 카페에서 파이 만들기 대회가 열릴 예정입니다.

Oak Grove 농장은 해가 진 뒤에도 재미있습니다! [154]연례 모닥불 행사는 오후 6시 30분에 시작합니다. 모닥불 주변에서 따뜻한 사과 사이다가 제공될 것입니다.

Oak Grove 농장으로 오시려면, 서쪽으로 76번 주간 고속도로를 타시다가 Kenmar로로 나오세요.

---

bonfire n. 모닥불   **interstate highway** 주간 고속도로

153 추론 문제

문제   Oak Grove 농장에 대해 추론되는 것은?
(A) 상품 중 일부를 웹사이트에서 판매한다.
(B) 식당에서 자체 상품을 이용한다.
(C) 일 년 내내 다양한 과일을 재배한다.
(D) 어린이들에게 할인된 입장료를 청구한다.

해설   질문의 핵심 어구인 Oak Grove Farms에 대해 추론하는 문제이다. 'After you've finished picking your apples, join us for lunch at our restaurant, the Red Kettle Café. The café ~ serves ~ pies made from fresh-picked apples.'(2문단 1번째 줄)에서 사과 따기를 마친 후에 Oak Grove 농장의 식당인 Red Kettle 카페에서 점심을 함께하라고 하면서 카페가 갓 딴 사과로 만든 파이를 제공한다고 했으므로 식당이 파이를 만드는 데 농장에서 갓 딴 사과를 이용한다는 사실을 추론할 수 있다. 따라서 (B) It uses its own products in its restaurant가 정답이다.

Paraphrasing
apples 사과 → products 상품

어휘   **entry fee** 입장료

154 육하원칙 문제

문제   10월 21일 저녁에 일어날 일은 무엇인가?
(A) 뷔페 저녁 식사
(B) 야외 모닥불 피우기
(C) 사과 따기
(D) 파이 만들기

해설   10월 21일 저녁에 일어날 일이 무엇인지(What)를 묻는 육하원칙 문제이다. 질문의 핵심 어구인 on the evening of October 21와 관련하여, 'Sunday, October 21'(제목 2번째 줄), 'Our annual bonfire begins at 6:30 P.M.'(3문단 1번째 줄)에서 10월 21일 일요일에 연례 모닥불 행사가 오후 6시 30분에 시작한다고 했으므로 (B) An outdoor fire가 정답이다.

Paraphrasing
on the evening 저녁에 → at 6:30 P.M. 오후 6시 30분에
bonfire 모닥불 → fire 모닥불

어휘   **fire** n. 모닥불, 불

155-157은 다음 브로슈어에 관한 문제입니다.

Unity 네일 숍
단골 고객 프로그램

저희는 많은 고객님들이 뷰티 숍 서비스를 위해 정기적으로 Unity 네일 숍에 방문하시기를 즐긴다는 것을 알고 있습니다. 그래서 [156-D]저희는 대부분의 단골 고객님들을 위한 할인 프로그램을 제공하게 되어 자랑스럽습니다.

[155]프로그램은 다음의 혜택들을 포함합니다:
- 매니큐어나 페디큐어를 10회 지불하시고 11번째는 무료로 받으세요. 저희의 할인 카드를 이용하여 결제 내역을 기록하세요.
- [156-B/D]단체로 어떤 뷰티 숍 서비스라도 이용하실 때 총 요금에서 10퍼센트를 할인받으세요. 이 할인은 4인 이상 단체에 가능합니다.
- 한 달에 세 개가 넘는 서비스를 이용하실 때 5달러 할인 쿠폰을 받으세요. [156-B]이 쿠폰들은 어떤 뷰티 숍 서비스나 상품에도 사용될 수 있습니다.

* 서비스 요금을 낼 때마다 [157]할인 카드에 도장을 찍는 것을 잊지 마세요. 쿠폰과 할인은 중복될 수 없으며, 고객님들은 서비스당 하나의 할인 제공만 이용하실 수 있습니다.

---

salon n. 뷰티 숍, 가게   **frequent customer** 단골 고객
regularly adv. 정기적으로, 자주   **keep track of** ~을 기록하다, 놓치지 않다

155 동의어 찾기 문제

문제   2문단 첫 번째 줄의 단어 "benefits"는 의미상 –와 가장 가깝다.
(A) 지불금
(B) 계정
(C) 이점
(D) 행사

해설   benefits를 포함하고 있는 구절 'The program includes the following benefits:'(2문단 1번째 줄)에서 benefits가 '혜택'이라는 뜻으로 사용되었다. 따라서 '이점'이라는 뜻을 가진 (C) advantages가 정답이다.

156 Not/True 문제

문제   Unity 네일 숍의 고객 프로그램에 대해 사실인 것은?
(A) 한 곳이 넘는 장소에서 제공된다.
(B) 특정 서비스 세트에 제한된다.
(C) 월말에 만료될 것이다.
(D) 개인과 단체 모두에게 제시된다.

해설   질문의 핵심 어구인 Unity Nail Salon's customer program과 관련된 내용을 지문에서 찾아 보기와 대조하는 Not/True 문제이다. (A)와 (C)는 지문에 언급되지 않은 내용이다. (B)는 'Get 10 percent off your total bill when you use any salon service as a group.'(2문단 4번째 줄)에서 단체로 어떤 뷰티 숍 서비스라도 이용할 때 총 요금에서 10퍼센트를 할인받으라고 했고, 'These coupons can be used for any salon service or product.'(2문단 6번째 줄)에서 이 쿠폰들은 어떤 뷰티 숍 서비스나 상품에도 사용될 수 있다고 했으므로 지문의 내용과 일치하지 않는다. (D)는 'we're ~ offer a discount program for our most frequent customers'(1문단 2번째 줄)에서 Unity 네일 숍이 대부분의 단골 고객들을 위한 할인 프로그램을 제공한다고 했고, 'Get 10 percent off your total bill when you use any salon service as a group.'(2문단 4번째 줄)에서 단체로 어떤 뷰티 숍 서비스라도 이용할 때 총 요금에서 10퍼센트를 할인받으라고 했으므로 고객 프로그램이 개인과 단체 모두에게 제공되는 것을 알 수 있다. 따라서 (D) It is packaged for both individuals and groups가 정답이다.

어휘   **expire** v. 만료되다, 만기가 되다   **package** v. 제시하다, 포장하다

157 육하원칙 문제

문제   고객들은 무엇을 하도록 상기되는가?
(A) 미리 예약한다
(B) 주간 서비스의 일정을 잡는다
(C) 여러 할인을 중복시킨다
(D) 할인 카드에 도장을 찍는다

해설   고객들이 무엇(What)을 하도록 상기되는지를 묻는 육하원칙 문제이다. 질문의 핵심 어구인 customers reminded to do와 관련하여, 'Remember to have your discount card stamped'(3문단 1번째 줄)에서 할인 카드에 도장을 찍는 것을 잊지 말라고 했으므로 (D) Get a discount card stamped가 정답이다.

Paraphrasing
have ~ discount card stamped 할인 카드에 도장을 찍다 → Get a discount card stamped 할인 카드에 도장을 찍다

어휘   **appointment** n. 예약, 약속

158-160은 다음 공고에 관한 문제입니다.

Wickford 공립 도서관
운영 시간 변경

[158-C]Wickford 공립 도서관은 대중들의 방문 경향의 변화에 맞추기 위해 일일 운영 시간을 변경할 것입니다. 이러한 변경은 도서관이 운영 비용을 줄이고 출판물 컬렉션 관리에 더 많은 자원을 들이게 할 것입니다.

11월 3일부터 다음과 같은 일정이 적용될 것입니다:
[158-A]월요일부터 수요일, 오전 9시부터 오후 7시까지

목요일과 금요일, 오전 9시부터 오후 6시까지
토요일과 일요일, 오전 9시부터 오후 4시까지

¹⁵⁹주말에는 메인 데스크가 오후 2시에 닫고 따라서 해당 시간부터 폐관 때까지 사서 서비스를 이용할 수 없다는 점을 유의하시기 바랍니다. 이용객들은 다른 건물 시설을 계속 이용할 수 있지만, ¹⁵⁹어떠한 책도 대출할 수 없을 것입니다. 또한, 모든 도서관 이용객들은 오후 4시까지 건물에서 나가야 합니다. 일부 도서관 직원들은 이용객들에게 폐관 시간을 상기시키고 다른 방식의 도움을 제공하기 위해 현장에 남아있을 것입니다.

¹⁶⁰추가 도서관 서비스가 필요한 이용객들을 위해 *Bridgestead 도서관이 매일 오전 8시부터 오후 8시까지 문을 엽니다.*

accommodate v. 맞추다, 수용하다   habit n. 경향, 습관
operating cost 운영 비용, 영업 경비   devote v. 충당하다, 전념하다
maintenance n. 관리, 유지   librarian n. 사서   patron n. 이용객, 고객
check out 대출하다, 확인하다   on-site adj. 현장의, 현지의

158 Not/True 문제

문제 Wickford 공립 도서관에 대해 사실인 것은?
(A) 주말에 더 일찍 문을 닫을 것이다.
(B) 건물의 일부분을 보수하고 있다.
(C) 이용객들의 제안으로 운영 시간을 변경했다.
(D) 컴퓨터 시스템을 교체할 것이다.

해설 질문의 핵심 어구인 the Wickford Public Library와 관련된 내용을 지문에서 찾아 보기와 대조하는 Not/True 문제이다. (A)는 'Monday to Wednesday, 9 A.M. to 7 P.M.', 'Thursday and Friday, 9 A.M. to 6 P.M.', 'Saturdays and Sundays, 9 A.M. to 4 P.M.'(2문단 2~4번째 줄)에서 월요일부터 수요일은 오전 9시부터 오후 7시까지, 목요일과 금요일은 오전 9시부터 오후 6시까지, 토요일과 일요일은 오전 9시부터 오후 4시까지 운영한다고 했으므로 지문의 내용과 일치한다. 따라서 (A) It will close earlier on the weekends가 정답이다. (B)와 (D)는 지문에 언급되지 않은 내용이다. (C)는 'The Wickford Public Library is changing its daily hours of operation to accommodate changes in the public's visiting habits.'(1문단 1번째 줄)에서 Wickford 공립 도서관이 대중들의 방문 경향의 변화에 맞추기 위해 일일 운영 시간을 변경할 것이라고는 했지만 이용객들의 제안이 있었는지는 지문에 언급되지 않은 내용이다.

Paraphrasing
Saturdays and Sundays 토요일과 일요일 → weekends 주말

어휘 renovate v. 보수하다, 개조하다

159 육하원칙 문제

문제 주말 오후 2시에 일어날 일은 무엇인가?
(A) 사서 서비스가 오후에 재개된다.
(B) 이용객들이 건물에서 나가도록 요구된다.
(C) 반납된 도서가 연체된 것으로 간주된다.
(D) 그날의 대출 서비스가 중단된다.

해설 주말 오후 2시에 일어날 일이 무엇인지(What)를 묻는 육하원칙 문제이다. 질문의 핵심 어구인 at 2 P.M. on the weekends와 관련하여, 'on weekends, the main desk closes at 2 P.M., and so librarian services will not be available from that time until closing'(3문단 1번째 줄)에서 주말에는 메인 데스크가 오후 2시에 닫고 따라서 해당 시간부터 폐관 때까지 사서 서비스를 이용할 수 없다고 했고, 'they will not be able to check out any books'(3문단 3번째 줄)에서 어떠한 책도 대출할 수 없을 것이라고 했으므로 (D) Checkout services are halted for the day가 정답이다.

Paraphrasing
not be able to check out any books 어떠한 책도 대출할 수 없다 → Checkout services are halted 대출 서비스가 중단되다

어휘 resume v. 재개되다, 되찾다   halt v. 중단하다, 멈추다

160 육하원칙 문제

문제 만약 이용객들이 추가 서비스가 필요하다면 무엇을 해야 하는가?
(A) 수석 사서에게 연락한다
(B) 다른 도서관을 방문한다
(C) 특별 예약을 한다

(D) 도서관의 웹사이트를 방문한다

해설 만약 이용객들이 추가 서비스가 필요하다면 무엇(What)을 해야 하는지를 묻는 육하원칙 문제이다. 질문의 핵심 어구인 patrons do if they need additional services와 관련하여, 'For patrons who need additional library services, Bridgestead Library is open from 8 A.M. to 8 P.M. daily.'(4문단 1번째 줄)에서 추가 도서관 서비스가 필요한 이용객들을 위해 Bridgestead 도서관이 매일 오전 8시부터 오후 8시까지 문을 연다고 했으므로 (B) Visit a different library가 정답이다.

어휘 head adj. 수석의, 중요한

161-163은 다음 광고에 관한 문제입니다.

Sky-High Hot-air Balloons는 인생 최고의 놀이기구 탑승을 제공합니다

재미있는 열기구를 타고 구름 사이를 떠다니는 것을 꿈꿔본 적이 있나요? — [1] —. Sky-High Hot-air Balloons와 함께 여러분의 꿈을 실현하세요!

· 가족 또는 친구와 추억을 만들어보세요
· 배우자 또는 동반자와 함께 낭만적인 탑승을 즐기세요
· 가장 소중한 고객에게 특별한 감사를 표현하세요

여러분이 무엇을 축하하든, Sky-High Hot-air Balloons는 신나고 잊지 못할 탑승을 제공합니다. ¹⁶¹저희는 기념일, 청혼 등을 위한 특별한 식사와 사진 패키지를 제공합니다. — [2] —. 구름 속에서 특별한 소풍을 함께하거나 전문적인 탑승 사진을 찍고 싶으신가요? 저희가 모든 것을 해드립니다!

여러분은 Sky-High사가 신뢰할 수 있는 명성을 가진 안정된 기업임을 확신할 수 있습니다. ^{162-B}East Metro Weekly는 최근에 10년 연속으로 Sky-High Hot-air Balloons를 Somerville 지역의 5대 오락 활동 제공업체 중 하나로 선정했습니다. ^{162-A/163}저희는 15년 넘게 영업해왔고 ¹⁶³모든 안전 규정을 따릅니다. — [3] —.

^{162-C}가격에 대해 더 알아보거나 탑승을 예약하려면, 555-3928로 예약 담당자에게 전화 주세요. — [4] —. 단체에는 특별 요금이 가능합니다.

ride n. 놀이기구 타기, 승차   float v. 떠다니다, 떠오르다   hot-air balloon 열기구
unforgettable adj. 잊지 못할   anniversary n. 기념일
professional adj. 전문적인, 전문의   established adj. 안정된, 확립된
protocol n. 의례, 협정   coordinator n. 담당자, 조정자   rate n. 요금, 비율

161 육하원칙 문제

문제 Sky-High Hot-air Balloons에 의해 무엇이 제공되는가?
(A) 특별 행사를 위한 패키지
(B) 제휴 식당에서의 할인
(C) 무료 기념 영상
(D) 기업들을 위한 단체 요금

해설 Sky-High Hot-air Balloons에 의해 무엇이(What) 제공되는지를 묻는 육하원칙 문제이다. 질문의 핵심 어구인 offered by Sky-High Hot-air Balloons와 관련하여, 'We offer special dining-and-photography packages for anniversaries, marriage proposals, and more.'(3문단 2번째 줄)에서 Sky-High Hot-air Balloons가 기념일, 청혼 등을 위한 특별한 식사와 사진 패키지를 제공한다고 했으므로 (A) Packages for special events가 정답이다.

Paraphrasing
anniversaries, marriage proposals, and more 기념일, 청혼 등 → special events 특별 행사

어휘 commemorative adj. 기념의

162 Not/True 문제

문제 Sky-High Hot-air Balloons에 대해 사실이 아닌 것은?
(A) 15년 넘게 영업해왔다.
(B) 지역 사회에서 좋게 평가받는다.
(C) 전화상으로 예약을 받는다.
(D) 고객들을 위한 소식지를 발행한다.

해설 질문의 핵심 어구인 Sky-High Hot-air Balloons와 관련된 내용을 지문에서 찾아 보기와 대조하는 Not/True 문제이다. (A)는 'We've been in business for more than 15 years'(4문단 3번째 줄)에서 Sky-High

Hot-air Balloons가 15년 넘게 영업해왔다고 했으므로 지문의 내용과 일치한다. (B)는 'East Metro Weekly recently listed Sky-High Hot-air Balloons as one of the top five providers of recreational activities in the Somerville area for the 10th year in a row.'(4문단 1번째 줄)에서 East Metro Weekly는 최근에 10년 연속으로 Sky-High Hot-air Balloons를 Somerville 지역의 5대 오락 활동 제공업체 중 하나로 선정했다고 했으므로 지문의 내용과 일치한다. (C)는 'To ~ book a ride, ~ at 555-3928.'(5문단 1번째 줄)에서 탑승을 예약하려면 555-3928로 전화 달라고 했으므로 지문의 내용과 일치한다. (D)는 지문에 언급되지 않은 내용이다. 따라서 (D) It publishes a newsletter for its customers가 정답이다.

Paraphrasing
in business 영업하는 → open 영업하는
Somerville area Somerville 지역 → community 지역 사회

어휘 take reservations 예약을 받다

163 문장 위치 찾기 문제

문제 [1], [2], [3], [4]로 표시된 위치 중, 다음 문장이 들어갈 곳으로 가장 적절한 것은?
"결과적으로, Sky-High사는 전체 역사상 사고가 난 적이 전혀 없습니다."
(A) [1]
(B) [2]
(C) [3]
(D) [4]

해설 지문의 흐름상 주어진 문장이 들어가기에 가장 적절한 곳을 고르는 문제이다. As a result, Sky-High has never had an accident in its entire history에서 결과적으로 Sky-High사는 전체 역사상 사고가 난 적이 전혀 없다고 했으므로, 주어진 문장 앞에 Sky-High사의 사고 방지에 대한 내용이 있을 것임을 예상할 수 있다. [3]의 앞 문장인 'We've been in business for more than 15 years and follow all safety protocols.'(4문단 3번째 줄)에서 Sky-High사는 15년 넘게 영업해왔고 모든 안전 규정을 따른다고 했으므로, [3]에 주어진 문장이 들어가면 Sky-High사가 안전 규정을 따르므로 15년 동안 사고가 난 적이 전혀 없다는 것을 강조하는 자연스러운 문맥이 된다는 것을 알 수 있다. 따라서 (C) [3]이 정답이다.

164-167은 다음 기사에 관한 문제입니다.

5월 15일—최근 몇 년 동안, 사람들은 그들이 무엇을 섭취하는지에 대해 점점 더 의식해오고 있다. 시카고 주에서만, 유기농과 건강에 좋은 음식을 특별히 제공하는 수십 개의 식당들이 문을 열었고, 다른 수천 개의 식당들은 건강에 신경을 쓰는 손님들을 만족시키기 위해 메뉴를 확장했다.

이러한 추세의 결과로, ¹⁶⁴많은 건강에 좋은 식품들은 구매하기가 더 어려워졌다. 특정 과일과 야채의 평균 가격은 지난 10년 동안 두 배 이상이 되었다. 게다가, ¹⁶⁵건강에 좋은 농산물의 이용은 주로 부유한 도시 지역이나 사람들이 정원을 가꾸는 시골 지역에서나 가능한 호사가 되었다. 이 두 곳 사이에는 식품 불모지가 있는데, 그곳에서는 대부분의 집에서 걸어서 갈 수 있는 거리 내에 식료품점이나 농산물 시장이 없다. 이러한 지역에서, 사람들은 어쩔 수 없이 편의점에서 포장된 음식을 구매하게 된다.

다행히도, 시카고 지역에서의 상황은 변하고 있다. 시의회는 지난달에 편의점이 신선한 과일과 야채를 취급하도록 요구하는 법안을 통과시켰다. 이러한 재료들은 매장 재고의 최소 20퍼센트를 차지해야 한다. 게다가, Ellison 시장은 접근성을 높이기 위해 도시 주변에 추가로 30개의 농산물 시장을 만들겠다고 약속했다. ¹⁶⁶슈퍼마켓 체인인 Lovell Stores도 제 역할을 하고 있다. ¹⁶⁷그것은 현지에서 더 많은 농산물을 입수함으로써 비용을 절감했고 현재 매장에서 판촉 활동을 하고 있다. 이러한 조치들이 모두 합쳐져서, 건강에 좋은 식품을 더 저렴하고 소비자층이 더 이용하기 쉽게 만들 것이다.

consume v. 섭취하다, 소비하다 specifically adv. 특별히, 명확하게
health-conscious adj. 건강에 신경 쓰는 trend n. 추세, 경향
double v. 두 배로 되다; n. 두 배 luxury n. 호사, 사치(품)
upscale adj. 부자의, 평균 이상의 walking distance 걸어서 갈 수 있는 거리
convenience store 편의점 bill n. 법안, 청구서 inventory n. 재고, 물품 목록
pledge v. 약속하다; n. 약속 accessibility n. 접근성, 이용 가능함
do one's part 제 역할을 하다 measure n. 조치, 측정
the buying public 소비자층

164 주제/목적 찾기 문제

문제 기사는 주로 무엇에 대한 것인가?
(A) 건강에 좋은 식품 선택지의 이용 가능성
(B) 지역 사업체들을 위한 세금 혜택
(C) 지역 학생들의 음식 섭취
(D) 새로 제정된 인근 토지 이용 제한법

해설 기사가 주로 무엇에 대한 것인지를 묻는 주제 찾기 문제이다. 'many healthy food products have become more difficult to buy'(2문단 1번째 줄)에서 많은 건강에 좋은 식품들이 구매하기가 더 어려워졌다고 한 후, 구매가 어려워진 현재의 상황과 조치에 대한 세부 내용을 설명하고 있으므로 (A) The availability of healthy food choices가 정답이다.

어휘 tax incentive 세금 혜택, 감세 조치 intake n. 섭취, 흡입
zoning law 토지 이용 제한법

165 Not/True 문제

문제 부유한 도시 지역에 대해 언급된 것은?
(A) 중대한 환경적 우려 대상이다.
(B) 증가하는 범죄율을 겪는다.
(C) 농산물을 이용하는 기회를 제공한다.
(D) 최고의 식당들을 끌어들인다.

해설 질문의 핵심 어구인 upscale urban neighborhoods와 관련된 내용을 지문에서 찾아 보기와 대조하는 Not/True 문제이다. (A), (B), (D)는 지문에 언급되지 않은 내용이다. (C)는 'access to healthy produce has become a luxury available mostly in upscale urban areas'(2문단 2번째 줄)에서 건강에 좋은 농산물의 이용은 주로 부유한 도시 지역에서나 가능한 호사가 되었다고 했으므로 지문의 내용과 일치한다. 따라서 (C) They provide access to produce가 정답이다.

Paraphrasing
neighborhoods 지역 → areas 지역

어휘 crime rate 범죄율 access n. 이용하는 기회, 접근
attract v. 끌어들이다, 유인하다

166 동의어 찾기 문제

문제 3문단 네 번째 줄의 단어 "chain"은 의미상 ~와 가장 가깝다.
(A) 전선
(B) 기업 그룹
(C) 구조
(D) 순서

해설 chain을 포함하고 있는 구절 'Even supermarket chain Lovell Stores is doing its part.'(3문단 4번째 줄)에서 chain이 '(사업체) 체인'이라는 뜻으로 사용되었다. 따라서 '기업 그룹'이라는 뜻을 가진 (B) group이 정답이다.

167 추론 문제

문제 Lovell Stores에 대해 추론될 수 있는 것은?
(A) 더 큰 회사에 인수되었다.
(B) 시카고에 신규 매장을 열 것이다.
(C) 생산물을 더 저렴하게 만들었다.
(D) 주간 농산물 시장을 후원할 계획이다.

해설 질문의 핵심 어구인 Lovell Stores에 대해 추론하는 문제이다. 'It has reduced costs by obtaining more produce locally and now offers promotions in its stores.'(3문단 5번째 줄)에서 Lovell Stores가 현지에서 더 많은 농산물을 입수함으로써 비용을 절감했고 현재 매장에서 판촉 활동을 하고 있다고 했으므로 Lovell Stores가 현지에서 더 많은 농산물을 입수하여 저렴하게 판매하고 있다는 사실을 추론할 수 있다. 따라서 (C) It made its products more affordable이 정답이다.

Paraphrasing
produce 농산물 → products 생산물

어휘 acquire v. 인수하다, 얻다 affordable adj. 저렴한, (가격이) 알맞은

---

[168]수신: Cordelia Bryant <cordeliabryant@bernstein.com>
발신: Madison Stanley <maddiestanley@mymail.com>
제목: 상품
날짜: 4월 3일
첨부 파일: 사진 2장

안녕하세요, Ms. Bryant. [168]Bernstein 가구점에서의 제 최근 주문과 관련된 문제로 인해 연락드립니다. — [1] —.

저는 3월 17일에 소파 하나와 의자 두 개를 주문했습니다. [169-A]상품들은 예정대로 4월 2일에 도착했습니다. 아쉽게도, 제가 집에 없어서 그것들을 살펴볼 수 없었습니다. — [2] —. 제 남편이 배송을 받았고 상품들을 집 안으로 들였습니다.

제가 집에 왔을 때, [169-B]바로 소파 왼쪽에 있는 큰 얼룩을 발견했습니다. 의자 중 하나에도 물에 의한 손상 흔적이 보였습니다. [171]아마도 운송 중에 상품들이 습기 같은 것에 노출되었던 것 같습니다. — [3] —.

저는 이 상품들이 최대한 빨리 교환되도록 처리하고 싶습니다. 검토하실 수 있도록 상품 사진을 이 이메일에 첨부했습니다. — [4] —. [170]저희는 5월 1일과 6월 15일 사이에 여행을 갈 예정이므로, 출발 전에 손상된 상품들이 수거되고 새 상품이 배송되는 것이 매우 중요합니다.

언제쯤 새로운 배송을 받을 수 있는지 저에게 알려주세요.

Madison Stanley 드림

reach out 연락을 취하다, 손을 뻗다 **as scheduled** 예정대로, 계획대로
inspect v. 살피다, 점검하다 **accept** v. 받다, 받아들이다
immediately adv. 바로, 즉시 **stain** n. 얼룩; v. 얼룩지게 하다
expose v. 노출시키다, 드러내다 **moisture** n. 습기, 수분 **transit** n. 운송, 환승
arrange v. 처리하다, 마련하다 **essential** adj. 매우 중요한, 필수의
damaged adj. 손상된, 피해를 입은

---

168 추론 문제

문제 Ms. Bryant는 어떤 종류의 사업체에서 일할 것 같은가?

(A) 가구 소매점
(B) 창고 시설
(C) 이사업체
(D) 청소 대행사

해설 Ms. Bryant가 일하는 사업체를 추론하는 문제이다. 'To: Cordelia Bryant' (상단 1번째 줄)에서 이메일의 수신자가 Cordelia Bryant라고 했고, 'I'm reaching out because of a problem with my recent order from Bernstein Furniture.'(1문단 1번째 줄)에서 이메일 발신자가 Bernstein 가구점에서의 최근 주문과 관련된 문제로 인해 연락한다고 했으므로 이메일 수신자인 Cordelia Bryant가 Bernstein 가구 소매점에서 일한다는 사실을 추론할 수 있다. 따라서 (A) A furniture retailer가 정답이다.

어휘 **storage** n. 창고, 저장

169 Not/True 문제

문제 Ms. Stanley의 상품들에 대해 언급된 것은?

(A) 늦게 배달되었다.
(B) 손상된 채 도착했다.
(C) 잘못된 색상이다.
(D) 사용 흔적이 보였다.

해설 질문의 핵심 어구인 Ms. Stanley's items와 관련된 내용을 지문에서 찾아 보기와 대조하는 Not/True 문제이다. (A)는 'The items arrived as scheduled on April 2.'(2문단 1번째 줄)에서 상품들이 예정대로 4월 2일에 도착했다고 했으므로 지문의 내용과 일치하지 않는다. (B)는 'I immediately noticed a large stain on the left side of the sofa. One of the chairs also showed signs of water damage.'(3문단 1번째 줄)에서 바로 소파 왼쪽에 있는 얼룩을 발견했고 의자 중 하나에도 물에 의한 손상 흔적이 보였다고 했으므로 지문의 내용과 일치한다. 따라서 (B) They arrived damaged가 정답이다. (C)와 (D)는 지문에 언급되지 않은 내용이다.

170 육하원칙 문제

문제 Ms. Stanley는 Ms. Bryant에게 무엇을 하라고 요청하는가?

(A) 몇몇 사진의 수령을 알린다
(B) 일부 상품들을 5월 1일 전에 가져간다
(C) 회사 수표로 환불을 지급한다
(D) 수리 일정을 최대한 빨리 잡는다

해설 Ms. Stanley가 Ms. Bryant에게 무엇(What)을 하라고 요청하는지를 묻는 육하원칙 문제이다. 질문의 핵심 어구인 Ms. Stanley request that Ms. Bryant do와 관련하여, 'We'll be traveling between May 1 and June 15, so it's essential that the damaged items are removed ~ before our departure.'(4문단 2번째 줄)에서 Ms. Stanley가 5월 1일과 6월 15일 사이에 여행을 갈 예정이므로 출발 전에 손상된 상품이 수거되는 것이 매우 중요하다고 했으므로 (B) Pick up some items before May 1가 정답이다.

Paraphrasing
are removed 수거되다 → Pick up 가져가다
damaged items 손상된 상품들 → some items 일부 상품

어휘 **acknowledge** v. 받았음을 알리다, 인정하다 **check** n. 수표, 계산서

171 문장 위치 찾기 문제

문제 [1], [2], [3], [4]로 표시된 위치 중, 다음 문장이 들어갈 곳으로 가장 적절한 것은?

"아시다시피, 4월 1일에 폭우가 내렸습니다."

(A) [1]
(B) [2]
(C) [3]
(D) [4]

해설 지문의 흐름상 주어진 문장이 들어가기에 가장 적절한 곳을 고르는 문제이다. As you may know, there was heavy rain on April 1에서 알다시피 4월 1일에 폭우가 내렸다고 했으므로, 주어진 문장 앞에 비로 인한 문제에 관한 내용이 있을 것임을 예상할 수 있다. [3]의 앞 문장인 'I think perhaps the items were exposed to some sort of moisture during transit.'(3문단 2번째 줄)에서 아마도 운송 중에 상품들이 습기 같은 것에 노출되었던 것 같다고 했으므로, [3]에 주어진 문장이 들어가면 상품이 습기에 노출된 이유를 언급하는 자연스러운 문맥이 된다는 것을 알 수 있다. 따라서 (C) [3]이 정답이다.

어휘 **heavy rain** 폭우

172-175는 다음 온라인 채팅 대화문에 관한 문제입니다.

Gilbert Cassidy   [오전 8:47]
안녕하세요, Catherine, Marc! Greenville의 Landmax 프로젝트와 관련하여 우리가 지금까지 해온 진행 상황을 확인하고 싶어서요.

Catherine Sherrill   [오전 8:49]
안녕하세요, Gilbert! 우리는 계획한 대로 진행하고 있어요. [172]시의회에서 우리의 청사진을 검토했고 우리가 매입할 토지에 타운하우스를 짓겠다는 제안서를 승인했어요.

Gilbert Cassidy   [오전 8:50]
좋은 소식이네요! 당신은 어떤가요, Marc? 당신의 첫 번째 프로젝트를 감독할 준비가 되었나요?

Marc Hernandez   [오전 8:51]
네, 물론입니다. 저는 도급업자와 공사 일정을 검토하고 있어요. 그는 언제든지 우리가 준비되면 작업을 시작할 준비가 되어 있다고 합니다.

Gilbert Cassidy   [오전 8:53]
훌륭해요. 그러면 [173]공사가 정확히 언제 시작될 수 있을 것 같나요?

Catherine Sherrill   [오전 8:55]
그건 Marc 담당으로 알고 있어요, 하지만 [173]제가 먼저 한 말씀 드리자면 [174]우리는 부동산 매매가 마무리되고 나서야 시작할 수 있어요. 제가 월요일에 소유주와 이야기했고, 2월 28일까지 마무리될 것으로 예상한다고 했어요.

Gilbert Cassidy   [오전 8:58]
그렇군요. 공사 예상 기간이 어떻게 되는지 다시 알려주시겠어요?

Marc Hernandez [오전 9:00]
도급자와 저는 프로젝트가 완료되기까지 9개월에서 10개월이 걸릴 것이라는 데 동의했고, 이는 ¹⁷⁵내년 1월까지 모든 타운하우스가 입주를 위한 준비가 될 것을 의미해요.

Gilbert Cassidy [오전 9:03]
좋습니다. 제게 계속 최신 정보를 알려주세요. 공사가 시작되어야 판매팀이 각 타운하우스를 구매자들에게 분양할 수 있어요.

town council 시의회 blueprint n. 청사진, 계획
supervise v. 감독하다, 관리하다 go over 검토하다, 복습하다
contractor n. 도급업자, 계약자 occupancy n. 입주, (건물, 방, 토지 등의) 사용

172 추론 문제

문제 필자들은 어느 업계에서 일할 것 같은가?

(A) 건설
(B) 광고
(C) 소매
(D) 회계

해설 필자들이 일하는 업계를 추론하는 문제이다. 'The town council has reviewed our blueprints and approved our proposal to build townhouses on the property we're buying.'(8:49 A.M.)에서 Catherine Sherrill이 시의회에서 자신들의 청사진을 검토했고 자신들이 매입할 토지에 타운하우스를 짓겠다는 제안서를 승인했다고 한 것을 통해 필자들은 청사진을 만들고 토지를 매입하여 타운하우스를 짓는 업무와 관련 있는 건설업계에서 일한다는 사실을 추론할 수 있다. 따라서 (A) Construction이 정답이다.

173 의도 파악 문제

문제 오전 8시 55분에, Ms. Sherrill이 "I know that is Marc's area"라고 썼을 때, 그녀가 의도한 것은?

(A) Marc에게 업무를 주었다.
(B) 일정을 담당하고 있지 않다.
(C) Marc가 질문에 답변하기를 바란다.
(D) 업무를 완료하는 데에 Marc의 승인이 필요하다.

해설 Ms. Sherrill이 의도한 것을 묻는 문제이므로, 질문의 인용어구(I know that is Marc's area)가 언급된 주변 문맥을 확인한다. 'when exactly do you think construction can begin?'(8:53 A.M.)에서 Gilbert Cassidy가 공사가 정확히 언제 시작될 수 있을 것 같은지를 묻자, Ms. Sherrill이 'I know that is Marc's area(그건 Marc 담당으로 알고 있어요)'라고 한 후, 'I may say something first'(8:55 A.M.)에서 자신이 먼저 말해주겠다고 한 것을 통해, Ms. Sherrill이 공사 일정을 담당하지 않음을 알 수 있다. 따라서 (B) She is not in charge of a schedule이 정답이다.

어휘 be in charge of ~을 담당하다 permission n. 승인, 허가

174 육하원칙 문제

문제 Ms. Sherrill은 프로젝트에 대해 누구와 이야기했는가?

(A) 고객
(B) 의회장
(C) 부동산 소유주
(D) 주 계약자

해설 Ms. Sherrill이 프로젝트에 대해 누구(Who)와 이야기했는지를 묻는 육하원칙 문제이다. 질문의 핵심 어구인 Ms. Sherrill speak to about a project와 관련하여, 'we can't begin until after the sale of the property has been finalized. I spoke to the owner on Monday'(8:55 A.M.)에서 Ms. Sherrill이 부동산 매매가 마무리되고 나서야 공사를 시작할 수 있고 자신이 월요일에 소유주와 이야기했다고 했으므로 Ms. Sherrill이 공사를 시작할 곳의 부동산 소유주와 이야기했음을 알 수 있다. 따라서 (C) A property owner가 정답이다.

175 육하원칙 문제

문제 다음 해에 일어날 일은 무엇으로 예상되는가?

(A) 새로운 프로젝트의 계획이 제안될 것이다.
(B) 영업팀이 부동산 분양을 시작할 것이다.

(C) 주택이 입주 가능할 것이다.
(D) 은행으로의 월납이 끝날 것이다.

해설 다음 해에 일어날 일이 무엇(What)으로 예상되는지를 묻는 육하원칙 문제이다. 질문의 핵심 어구인 expected ~ in the following year와 관련하여, 'all of the townhouses should be ready for occupancy by January of next year'(9:00 A.M.)에서 Marc Hernandez가 내년 1월까지 모든 타운하우스가 입주를 위한 준비가 될 것이라고 했으므로 (C) Residences will be available to move into가 정답이다.

Paraphrasing
townhouses 타운하우스 → Residences 주택
be ready for occupancy 입주를 위한 준비가 되다 → be available to move into 입주 가능하다

어휘 residence n. 주택, 거주지

176-180은 다음 광고와 영수증에 관한 문제입니다.

Harmony World에서 선율과 어우러지세요.

밴드를 시작하시나요? 학교에 악기가 필요하신가요? 아니면 항상 음악을 연주하는 법을 배우고 싶으셨나요? 오늘 Harmony World에 오셔서, 당신의 음악적 측면과 조화되어 보세요.

Harmony World는 워싱턴 카운티에서 가장 큰 악기 상점입니다. 저희는 다양한 악기를 취급합니다. 세계 최고 브랜드의 새로운 악기를 구입하거나, ¹⁷⁸새로운 구매품에 대한 포인트를 얻기 위해 구형 악기를 보상 판매하세요. ¹⁷⁶저희는 저렴한 장비 대여 및 수리 서비스도 제공합니다. 오늘 www.harmonyworld.com을 방문하여 전체 제품 및 서비스를 살펴보세요.

^{177-B}평일에는, 세 곳의 사설 현장 스튜디오 중 한 곳에서 기타, 피아노, 드럼의 일대일 강습을 진행합니다. ^{177-D}저희 강사들은 모두 전문적으로 연주했던 교육받은 음악가들입니다. ^{177-A}그들은 초보자부터 고급자까지 모든 실력 수준에 맞춰 드립니다. 강습에 등록하려면 저희 웹사이트의 '강습' 페이지를 방문하세요.

¹⁷⁹만약 저희 상점 제품에서 50달러 이상을 구매하시면, 무료 Music Master 한 부를 받으실 것입니다. 이 책은 분명히 당신이 유능한 음악가가 되도록 돕는 다양한 강습을 포함하고 있습니다.

in tune (가락이) 조화되어, 장단이 맞아서 instrument n. 악기, 기구
trade in 보상 판매하다 affordable adj. 저렴한, 알맞은
professionally adv. 전문적으로 cater v. 맞추다, 만족시키다
sign up for ~을 신청하다 merchandise n. 제품, 재고품

¹⁷⁸Harmony World
102 Conner 가
페이엇빌, 알래스카주 72701
전화: 555-1091

	상품	가격
1	¹⁷⁸Harding 전자 기타	239.99달러
2	기타 피크	2.99달러
3	메트로놈	17.99달러
4	Harding 소형 앰프	32.99달러
	소계	293.96달러
	¹⁷⁸상점 포인트	44.10달러
	판매세 (6.5%)	16.24달러
	¹⁷⁹합계	266.10달러

^{180-C}결제: SHARP 신용 카드
¹⁷⁸고객 이름: Kelsey Usher
XXXX-XXXX-XXXX-1241

모든 판매는 최종으로 간주됩니다. ^{180-D}환불 요청은 받아들여지지 않을 것입니다. 하지만, 고객들은 상품을 동일하거나 더 저렴한 가격의 것과 교환할 수 있습니다. 더 많은 도움이 필요하시면 ^{180-A}월요일부터 금요일까지 정상 업무 시간에 ^{180-B}555-2109로 전화 주십시오.

amplifier n. 앰프, 증폭기 normal adj. 정상의, 보통의

176 육하원칙 문제

문제 사람들은 Harmony World 웹사이트에서 무엇을 할 수 있는가?

(A) 소식지를 신청한다
(B) 대여 장비를 찾아본다
(C) 음악 모음집을 다운로드한다
(D) 고객 서비스 센터와 채팅한다

해설 사람들이 Harmony World 웹사이트에서 무엇(What)을 할 수 있는지를 묻는 육하원칙 문제이므로 질문의 핵심 어구인 people do on Harmony World's Web site와 관련된 내용이 언급된 광고를 확인한다. 첫 번째 지문인 광고의 'We also offer affordable equipment rentals and repair services. Go to www.harmonyworld.com today to browse our complete line of products and services.'(2문단 3번째 줄)에서 Harmony World가 저렴한 장비 대여 및 수리 서비스도 제공하므로 오늘 www.harmonyworld.com을 방문하여 전체 제품 및 서비스를 살펴보라고 했으므로 (B) Find rental equipment가 정답이다.

Paraphrasing
browse 살펴보다 → Find 찾다

177 Not/True 문제

문제 강습에 대해 언급된 것은?
(A) 고급 실력을 가진 사람들만을 위한 것이다.
(B) 주말에 열린다.
(C) 단체를 위해 계획된다.
(D) 숙련된 전문가들에 의해 진행된다.

해설 질문의 핵심 어구인 lessons와 관련된 내용을 지문에서 찾아 보기와 대조하는 Not/True 문제이므로 첫 번째 지문인 강습에 대해 언급된 광고에서 관련 내용을 확인한다. (A)는 'They cater to every skill level from beginner to advanced.'(3문단 2번째 줄)에서 그들, 즉 강사들은 초보자부터 고급자까지 모든 실력 수준에 맞춰준다고 했으므로 지문의 내용과 일치하지 않는다. (B)는 'On weekdays, we hold one-on-one lessons'(3문단 1번째 줄)에서 평일에 일대일 강습을 진행한다고 했으므로 지문의 내용과 일치하지 않는다. (C)는 지문에 언급되지 않은 내용이다. (D)는 'Our instructors are trained musicians who have all played professionally.'(3문단 2번째 줄)에서 강사들이 모두 전문적으로 연주했던 교육받은 음악가들이라고 했으므로 지문의 내용과 일치한다. 따라서 (D) They are given by experienced professionals가 정답이다.

어휘 design v. 계획하다, 기획하다 experienced adj. 숙련된, 경험이 있는

178 추론 문제 연계

문제 Harmony World에 대해 사실일 것 같은 것은?
(A) 기타를 수리할 수 없었다.
(B) Ms. Usher의 보상 판매 신청을 받아들였다.
(C) 대여료를 환불했다.
(D) Ms. Usher에게 할인을 제공했다.

해설 두 지문의 내용을 종합적으로 확인한 후 추론해서 풀어야 하는 연계 문제이다. 질문의 핵심 어구인 Harmony World의 광고를 먼저 확인한다.
첫 번째 지문인 광고의 'trade in your old gear for credit toward your new purchase'(2문단 2번째 줄)에서 새로운 구매품에 대한 포인트를 얻기 위해 구형 악기를 보상 판매할 수 있다는 첫 번째 단서를 확인할 수 있다. 그런데 Ms. Usher가 보상 판매를 했는지가 제시되지 않았으므로 영수증에서 관련 내용을 확인한다. 두 번째 지문인 영수증의 'Harmony World'(표 위 1번째 줄), 'Harding Electric Guitar'(표 2행 2열), 'Store credit $44.10'(표 7행), 'CUSTOMER NAME: Kelsey Usher'(표 아래 2번째 줄)에서 Kelsey Usher가 Harmony World에서 Harding 전자 기타를 사는 데에 상점 포인트를 사용했다는 두 번째 단서를 확인할 수 있다.
새로운 구매품에 대한 포인트를 얻기 위해 구형 악기를 보상 판매할 수 있다는 첫 번째 단서와 Kelsey Usher가 Harmony World에서 Harding 전자 기타를 사고 상점 포인트를 사용했다는 두 번째 단서를 종합할 때, Kelsey Usher가 Harmony World에서 새 전자 기타를 살 때 Harmony World가 Kelsey Usher의 구형 기타 보상 판매 신청을 받아들였다는 사실을 추론할 수 있다. 따라서 (B) It accepted Ms. Usher's trade-in offer가 정답이다.

179 육하원칙 문제 연계

문제 Ms. Usher는 무엇을 받을 것인가?
(A) 무료 부대용품

(B) 향후 구매를 위한 상품권
(C) 교육용 출판물
(D) 연장된 품질보증서

해설 두 지문의 내용을 종합해서 풀어야 하는 연계 문제이다. 질문의 핵심 어구인 Ms. Usher receive에서 Ms. Usher가 무엇(What)을 받을 것인지를 묻고 있으므로 Ms. Usher가 받은 영수증을 먼저 확인한다.
두 번째 지문인 영수증의 'TOTAL $266.10'(표 9행)에서 Ms. Usher가 제품 구매에 266.10달러를 지불했다는 첫 번째 단서를 확인할 수 있다. 그런데 구매 혜택이 무엇인지 제시되지 않았으므로 광고에서 관련 내용을 확인한다. 첫 번째 지문인 광고의 'If you buy over $50 in merchandise ~, you will receive a free copy of *Music Master*. This book contains a variety of lessons'(4문단 1번째 줄)에서 제품에서 50달러 이상을 구매하면 무료 *Music Master* 한 부를 받을 것이고 그 책이 다양한 강습을 포함한다는 두 번째 단서를 확인할 수 있다.
Ms. Usher가 제품 구매에 266.10달러를 지불했다는 첫 번째 단서와 제품에서 50달러 이상을 구매하면 다양한 강습을 포함하고 있는 무료 *Music Master* 한 부를 받을 것이라는 두 번째 단서를 종합할 때, Ms. Usher가 강습이 포함된 책을 받을 것임을 알 수 있다. 따라서 (C) An instructional publication이 정답이다.

Paraphrasing
book 책 → publication 출판물

어휘 complimentary adj. 무료의, 칭찬하는 instructional adj. 교육용의 warranty n. 품질보증서

180 Not/True 문제

문제 어떤 정보가 영수증에 포함되어 있지 않은가?
(A) 상점의 휴일 영업시간
(B) 상점의 연락 정보
(C) 이용객의 결제 방법
(D) 공식적인 반품 규정

해설 영수증에 언급되지 않은 내용을 지문에서 찾아 보기와 대조하는 Not/True 문제이다. 이 문제는 질문에 핵심 어구가 없으므로 각 보기의 핵심 어구와 관련된 내용을 두 번째 지문인 영수증에서 확인한다. (A)는 'normal work hours, Monday to Friday'(표 아래 7번째 줄)에서 정상 업무 시간이 월요일부터 금요일까지라고 했지만 휴일 업무 시간은 지문에 언급되지 않은 내용이다. 따라서 (A) The business hours during holidays가 정답이다. (B)는 'please call us at 555-2109'(표 아래 6번째 줄)에서 555-2109로 전화하라고 했으므로 지문의 내용과 일치한다. (C)는 'PAYMENT: SHARP CREDIT CARD'(표 아래 1번째 줄)에서 고객이 결제를 SHARP 신용 카드로 했다고 했으므로 지문의 내용과 일치한다. (D)는 'Requests for refunds will not be accepted. However, customers may exchange items for something of equal or lesser value.'(표 아래 4번째 줄)에서 환불 요청이 받아들여지지 않을 것이지만 고객들은 상품을 동일하거나 더 저렴한 가격의 것과 교환할 수 있다고 했으므로 지문의 내용과 일치한다.

Paraphrasing
work hours 업무 시간 → business hours 영업시간
call 전화하다 → contact 연락

어휘 business hours 영업시간, 업무 시간

181-185는 다음 편지와 이메일에 관한 문제입니다.

RADCLIFFE 호텔

Sam Cohen
120 Millville로
런던, N1 3LJ

8월 4일

Mr. Cohen께,

181옥스퍼드에 있는 Radcliffe 호텔의 객실을 예약해주셔서 감사합니다. 이 편지는 9월 9일부터 11일까지의 3박 숙박을 확정합니다. 귀하께서 저희와 함께 하시게 되어 기쁩니다.

객실에는 소형 냉장고, 텔레비전, 무료 와이파이가 갖춰져 있습니다. 텔레비전에는 호텔에 대한 정보뿐만 아니라, 다양한 뉴스와 엔터테인먼트 선택 사항을

제공하는 500개 이상의 채널이 있습니다.

귀하의 편의를 위해, 호텔에는 매일 무료 조식을 즐길 수 있는 카페뿐만 아니라 현대식 세계 요리를 제공하는 식당이 1층에 있습니다. 조식은 매일 오전 6시부터 10시까지 제공됩니다. 귀하께서는 또한 언제라도 룸서비스를 주문하실 수 있습니다. ¹⁸³수영장은 2층에, 체육관은 3층에 위치해 있습니다. 객실 키 카드로 둘 다를 이용하실 수 있습니다. 그곳들은 오전 6시부터 오후 8시까지 운영됩니다.

고객 서비스팀 드림
Radcliffe 호텔
영국, 옥스퍼드

confirm v. 확정하다, 확인하다   equipped adj. (장비를) 갖춘
entertainment n. 엔터테인먼트, 오락
contemporary adj. 현대의, 동시대의   cuisine n. 요리, 요리법

수신: 직원 <staff@radcliffehotel.com>
발신: Sam Cohen <s.cohen@unimail.com>
제목: 문제
날짜: 9월 12일

담당자분께,

제 이름은 Sam Cohen이고, ¹⁸²저는 호텔에서 최근에 묵었던 손님이었습니다. 저는 4층에서 열린 도시 계획 협의회에 참석했습니다. ¹⁸³정확한 객실 호수는 기억할 수 없지만, 저는 수영장 바로 옆에 있었습니다.

¹⁸⁴제가 운동화를 체육관에 두고 와서 이메일을 보냅니다. ¹⁸⁵제가 체크아웃하기 전에 그것을 가져오려고 했지만, 공항 셔틀에 늦었다는 것을 알게 되었습니다. 버스에 있는 직원에게 알리려고 했으나, 그는 제가 이메일로 담당자에게 연락할 것을 조언해주었습니다.

만약 신발을 찾으신다면, 등록된 제 집 주소로 다시 보내 주시기 바랍니다. 최대한 빨리 받기 위해서 제가 기꺼이 긴급 배송비를 지불하겠습니다. 감사드리며, 향후 그곳 호텔에서 다시 묵기를 기대합니다!

Sam Cohen 드림

urban adj. 도시의, 도회지의   recall v. 기억하다, 상기하다
athletic shoe 운동화   retrieve v. 가져오다, 회수하다
expedite v. 급히 보내다, 신속히 처리하다

---

181 주제/목적 찾기 문제

문제 편지는 왜 쓰였는가?
  (A) 할인을 제공하기 위해
  (B) 거래를 요청하기 위해
  (C) 요청에 답하기 위해
  (D) 예약을 확정하기 위해

해설 편지가 쓰인 목적을 묻는 목적 찾기 문제이므로 편지의 내용을 확인한다. 첫 번째 지문인 편지의 'Thank you for booking a room at the Radcliffe Hotel ~. This confirms your three-night stay from September 9 to 11.'(1문단 1번째 줄)에서 Radcliffe 호텔의 객실을 예약한 것에 대한 감사를 표하며 이 편지가 9월 9일부터 11일까지의 3박 숙박을 확정한다고 했으므로 (D) To confirm a booking이 정답이다.

어휘 extend v. 제공하다, 연장하다   solicit v. 요청하다, 간청하다

182 육하원칙 문제

문제 Mr. Cohen은 왜 호텔에 묵고 있었는가?
  (A) 협의회에 참석하고 있었다.
  (B) 사교 행사에 초대받았다.
  (C) 지사를 방문하고 있었다.
  (D) 휴가 중이었다.

해설 Mr. Cohen이 왜(Why) 호텔에 묵고 있었는지를 묻는 육하원칙 문제이므로 Mr. Cohen이 작성한 이메일에서 질문의 핵심 어구인 staying at the hotel과 관련된 내용을 확인한다. 두 번째 지문인 이메일의 'I was a recent guest at your hotel. I attended an urban planning conference that took place on the fourth floor.'(1문단 1번째 줄)에서 Mr. Cohen이 호텔에서 최근에 묵었던 손님이었고 4층에서 열린 도시 계획 협의회에 참석했다고 했

으므로 (A) He was taking part in a convention이 정답이다.

Paraphrasing
attended ~ conference 협의회에 참석했다 → was taking part in a convention 협의회에 참석하고 있었다

어휘 take part in ~에 참석하다, 참가하다   branch office 지사, 지점

183 육하원칙 문제 연계

문제 Mr. Cohen의 방은 몇 층에 위치해 있었는가?
  (A) 1층
  (B) 2층
  (C) 3층
  (D) 4층

해설 두 지문의 내용을 종합해서 풀어야 하는 연계 문제이다. 질문의 핵심 어구인 Mr. Cohen's room located에서 Mr. Cohen의 방이 몇 층(which floor)에 위치해 있었는지를 묻고 있으므로 Mr. Cohen이 작성한 이메일을 먼저 확인한다.
두 번째 지문인 이메일의 'I can't recall my exact room number, but I was right next to the pool.'(1문단 2번째 줄)에서 정확한 객실 호수는 기억할 수 없지만 Mr. Cohen이 수영장 바로 옆에 있었다고 했으므로 Mr. Cohen이 수영장 옆에 있는 객실에서 묵었다는 첫 번째 단서를 확인할 수 있다. 그런데 수영장이 어디에 있는지 제시되지 않았으므로 편지에서 관련 내용을 확인한다. 첫 번째 지문인 편지의 'A pool is located on the second floor'(3문단 3번째 줄)에서 수영장이 2층에 위치해 있다는 두 번째 단서를 확인할 수 있다.
Mr. Cohen이 수영장 옆에 있는 객실에서 묵었다는 첫 번째 단서와 수영장이 2층에 위치해 있다는 두 번째 단서를 종합할 때, Mr. Cohen의 방이 수영장이 있는 2층에 있었음을 알 수 있다. 따라서 (B) The second floor가 정답이다.

184 육하원칙 문제

문제 Mr. Cohen은 무엇을 두고 왔는가?
  (A) 수영복
  (B) 신발
  (C) 필기구
  (D) 파일

해설 Mr. Cohen이 무엇을(What) 두고 왔는지를 묻는 육하원칙 문제이므로 Mr. Cohen이 작성한 이메일에서 질문의 핵심 어구인 leave behind와 관련된 내용을 확인한다. 두 번째 지문인 이메일의 'I left my athletic shoes at the gym'(2문단 1번째 줄)에서 Mr. Cohen이 운동화를 체육관에 두고 왔다고 했으므로 (B) Footwear가 정답이다.

Paraphrasing
athletic shoes 운동화 → Footwear 신발

어휘 writing material 필기구

185 추론 문제

문제 Radcliffe 호텔에 대해 추론될 수 있는 것은?
  (A) 3박 숙박에 특별 가격을 제공한다.
  (B) 공공장소에 보안 카메라가 있다.
  (C) 분실물 보관소가 있다.
  (D) 손님들에게 공항으로의 교통편을 제공한다.

해설 질문의 핵심 어구인 Radcliffe Hotel에 대해 추론하는 문제이므로 Radcliffe 호텔에 보내는 이메일에서 관련 내용을 확인한다. 두 번째 지문인 이메일의 'I planned to retrieve them before checking out, but ~ running late for the airport shuttle. ~ your employee on the bus, ~ advised me to contact you by e-mail.'(2문단 1번째 줄)에서 Mr. Cohen이 체크아웃하기 전에 그것, 즉 운동화를 가져오려고 했지만 공항 셔틀에 늦었고 버스에 있는 직원이 이메일로 담당자에게 연락할 것을 조언했다고 했으므로 Radcliffe 호텔이 공항 셔틀을 제공한다는 사실을 추론할 수 있다. 따라서 (D) It provides guests with airport transportation이 정답이다.

Paraphrasing
airport shuttle 공항 셔틀 → airport transportation 공항으로의 교통편

어휘 security n. 보안, 안전

186-190은 다음 웹페이지, 고객 후기, 이메일에 관한 문제입니다.

Brownwood Vineyards
www.brownwoodvineyardsnapa.com/groups

[186-A]단체 패키지
화요일부터 일요일까지 이용 가능

Brownwood Vineyards는 내퍼에서 와인 시음을 위한 최적의 장소입니다. Malbec, Merlot, Cabernet Sauvignon과 같은 최고의 와인을 즐겨보세요. [186-D/190]또한 상을 받은 화이트 와인인 저희의 Chardonnay도 있고, [190]그것은 시음에서 유일한 화이트 와인입니다. 다음의 단체 패키지 중 하나로 저희의 와인 제조 작업을 구경하고, 아름다운 경치를 즐겨보세요.

– 스탠더드
[186-C]3가지 와인과 간식, [186-B]인당 60달러

– 엑스트라
[186-C]5가지 와인과 3가지 코스 식사, [186-B]인당 120달러

– 프리미엄
[186-C]5가지 와인과 5가지 코스 식사, [186-B]인당 170달러

– [187]플래티넘
[186-C]무제한 시음과 7가지 코스 식사 및 [187]포도 압착 체험, [186-B]인당 300달러

이용 가능 여부 및 예약은 groups@brownwoodvineyardsnapa.com으로 문의하십시오.

---

prime adj. 최적의, 가장 좋은 exquisite adj. 최고의, 정교한

내퍼 포도주 양조장 후기
www.napawineryreviews.com/brownwoodvineyards

이름: Kenichi Yamamoto
방문일: 6월 2일
평점: ★★★★★

후기: 저는 팀 야유회를 위해 단체 패키지를 예약했습니다. 포도주 양조장 직원이 호텔에서 저희를 태워 그들의 아름다운 구내로 데려갔고, 그곳에서 저희는 요리사가 준비한 맛있는 식사와 정선된 와인을 즐겼습니다. [187]가장 좋았던 부분 중 하나는 단연코 포도 압착 활동이었습니다. 모두가 그것을 하면서 아주 재미있어했습니다. [188]한 가지 불만이 있다면, 저희가 탔던 승합차가 불편했다는 점일 것입니다. 그래도 저는 전반적인 경험에 별 5개 만점에 5개를 주겠습니다.

---

winery n. 포도주 양조장 outing n. 야유회, 여행 property n. 구내, 부동산
selection n. 정선, 선택 definitely adv. 단연코, 분명히

수신: Kenichi Yamamoto <k.yamamoto@stansonlink.com>
발신: Brenda Meyers <b.meyers@stansonlink.com>
날짜: 6월 3일
제목: 고맙습니다

Kenichi께,

저희의 여행을 준비해주셔서 다시 한번 감사드립니다. [189]제가 이렇게 빨리 시카고에 있는 본사로 돌아가야 한다는 것이 아쉽습니다. 저는 처리할 급한 업무가 있습니다. 어쨌든, [189]당신을 만나서 Stanson Link사의 샌프란시스코 사무소의 다른 팀원들과 체험을 같이 하게 되어 즐거웠습니다. 저는 당신의 준비 능력에 깊은 인상을 받았고, 제가 여행에 대해 경영진에게 제출하는 보고서에 그 점을 기록할 것입니다.

혹시 작은 부탁 하나를 드려도 될까요? [190]저희가 시음했던 화이트 와인을 몇 상자 주문하고 싶습니다. 제 생각에 그것은 저희 고객들에게 훌륭한 선물이 될 것 같습니다.

고맙습니다,

Brenda Meyers 드림
Stanson Link사

---

arrange v. 준비하다, 주선하다 shame n. 아쉬운 일, 부끄러움
attend to 처리하다, 돌보다 organization n. 준비, 조직
make a note of ~을 기록하다, 필기하다

---

186 Not/True 문제

문제 Brownwood Vineyards에 대해 사실이 아닌 것은?

(A) 투어를 위해 매일 운영된다.
(B) 개인별로 패키지 요금을 청구한다.
(C) 모든 시음에 음식을 제공한다.
(D) 그곳의 와인 중 하나로 상을 받았다.

해설 질문의 핵심 어구인 Brownwood Vineyards와 관련된 내용을 지문에서 찾아 보기와 대조하는 Not/True 문제이므로 첫 번째 지문인 Brownwood Vineyards의 웹페이지에서 관련 내용을 확인한다. (A)는 'Group packages', 'Available Tuesday through Sunday'(제목 1, 2번째 줄)에서 단체 패키지가 화요일부터 일요일까지 이용 가능하다고 했으므로 지문의 내용과 일치하지 않는다. 따라서 (A) It is open every day for tours가 정답이다. (B)는 '$60 per person', '$120 per person', '$170 per person', '$300 per person'(2문단 2, 4, 6, 8번째 줄)에서 각 패키지의 가격이 인당 60달러, 120달러, 170달러, 300달러라고 했으므로 지문의 내용과 일치한다. (C)는 'Three wines paired with snacks', 'Five wines paired with three-course meal', 'Five wines paired with five-course meal', 'Unlimited tastings paired with seven-course meal'(2문단 2, 4, 6, 8번째 줄)에서 각 패키지에 3가지 와인과 간식, 5가지 와인과 3가지 코스 식사, 5가지 와인과 5가지 코스 식사, 무제한 시음과 7가지 코스 식사가 포함된다고 했으므로 지문의 내용과 일치한다. (D)는 'We also have an award-winning white wine, our Chardonnay'(1문단 2번째 줄)에서 상을 받은 Brownwood Vineyards의 Chardonnay도 있다고 했으므로 지문의 내용과 일치한다.

Paraphrasing
Available 이용가능한 → opened 운영되는
per person 인당 → by the person 개인별로
award-winning 상을 받은 → won an award 상을 받았다

어휘 charge v. 요금을 청구하다

187 추론 문제 연계

문제 Mr. Yamamoto는 어느 패키지를 예약했을 것 같은가?

(A) 스탠더드
(B) 엑스트라
(C) 프리미엄
(D) 플래티넘

해설 두 지문의 내용을 종합적으로 확인한 후 추론해서 풀어야 하는 연계 문제이다. 질문의 핵심 어구인 package ~ Mr. Yamamoto ~ book에서 Mr. Yamamoto가 어느 패키지를 예약했을 것 같은지를 묻고 있으므로 Mr. Yamamoto가 작성한 고객 후기를 먼저 확인한다.
두 번째 지문인 고객 후기의 'One of the highlights was definitely the grape-pressing activity.'(3번째 줄)에서 가장 좋았던 부분 중 하나는 단연코 포도 압착 활동이었다고 했으므로 Mr. Yamamoto가 포도 압착 활동을 포함하는 패키지를 예약했다는 첫 번째 단서를 확인할 수 있다. 그런데 포도 압착 활동이 어느 패키지에 포함되는지 제시되지 않았으므로 웹페이지에서 관련 내용을 확인한다. 첫 번째 지문인 웹페이지의 'Platinum', 'grape-pressing experience'(2문단 7, 8번째 줄)에서 플래티넘 패키지에 포도 압착 체험이 포함된다는 두 번째 단서를 확인할 수 있다.
Mr. Yamamoto가 포도 압착 활동을 포함하는 패키지를 예약했다는 첫 번째 단서와 플래티넘 패키지에 포도 압착 체험이 포함된다는 두 번째 단서를 종합할 때, Mr. Yamamoto가 포도 압착 활동을 포함하는 플래티넘 패키지를 예약했다는 사실을 추론할 수 있다. 따라서 (D) Platinum이 정답이다.

188 육하원칙 문제

문제 Mr. Yamamoto가 그의 Brownwood Vineyards 방문에 대해 무엇을 가장 좋아하지 않는가?

(A) 가이드의 친절함
(B) 일부 식사의 맛
(C) 이동 수단 서비스
(D) 패키지 투어의 가격

해설 Mr. Yamamoto가 그의 Brownwood Vineyards 방문에 대해 무엇(What)을 가장 좋아하지 않았는지를 묻는 육하원칙 문제이므로 Mr. Yamamoto가 작성한 고객 후기에서 질문의 핵심 어구인 like least about his visit to

Brownwood Vineyards와 관련된 내용을 확인한다. 두 번째 지문인 고객 후기의 'If I had one complaint, it would be that the van we took was uncomfortable.'(4번째 줄)에서 한 가지 불만이 있다면 Mr. Yamamoto가 탔던 승합차가 불편했다는 점일 것이라고 했으므로 (C) The transportation service가 정답이다.

Paraphrasing
van 승합차 → transportation 이동 수단

어휘 **value** n. 가격, 가치

189 추론 문제

문제 Ms. Meyers가 Stanson Link사에 대해 암시하는 것은?
(A) 임원을 승진시킬 것이다.
(B) 곧 재조직될 것이다.
(C) 두 도시에 사무실이 있다.
(D) 화상 회의 일정을 잡았다.

해설 질문의 핵심 어구인 Stanson Link에 대해 Ms. Meyers가 암시하는 것을 추론하는 문제이므로 Ms. Meyers가 작성한 이메일에서 관련 내용을 확인한다. 세 번째 지문인 이메일의 'I have to return to the head office in Chicago so soon'(1문단 1번째 줄)에서 Ms. Meyers가 빨리 시카고에 있는 본사로 돌아가야 한다고 했고, 'it was delightful to ~ share the experience with the rest of the team at Stanson Link's San Francisco office'(1문단 2번째 줄)에서 Stanson Link사의 샌프란시스코 사무소의 다른 팀원들과 체험을 같이 하게 되어 즐거웠다고 했으므로 Stanson Link사는 시카고와 샌프란시스코에 사무실이 있다는 사실을 추론할 수 있다. 따라서 (C) It has offices in two cities가 정답이다.

어휘 **reorganize** v. 재조직하다, 재편성하다

190 추론 문제 연계

문제 Ms. Meyers에 대해 추론될 수 있는 것은?
(A) Chardonnay를 선물로 주고 싶어 한다.
(B) 원래 계획된 것보다 더 많은 손님을 데려갔다.
(C) 포도주 양조장으로 곧 돌아갈 것이다.
(D) 와인에 대한 전문적인 지식을 가지고 있다.

해설 두 지문의 내용을 종합적으로 확인한 후 추론해서 풀어야 하는 연계 문제이다. 질문의 핵심 어구인 Ms. Meyers가 작성한 이메일을 먼저 확인한다.
세 번째 지문인 이메일의 'I'd like to order a few cases of the white wine we tasted. I think it would make an excellent gift for our clients.'(2문단 1번째 줄)에서 Ms. Meyers가 시음했던 화이트 와인을 몇 상자 주문하고 싶고 그것이 고객들에게 훌륭한 선물이 될 것 같다고 생각한다고 했으므로 Ms. Meyers가 시음했던 화이트 와인을 선물로 주고 싶어 한다는 첫 번째 단서를 확인할 수 있다. 그런데 시음했던 화이트 와인이 무엇인지 제시되지 않았으므로 웹페이지에서 관련 내용을 확인한다. 첫 번째 지문인 웹페이지의 'We also have ~ our Chardonnay, that is the only white wine in our tastings.'(1문단 2번째 줄)에서 시음에서 유일하게 화이트 와인인 Chardonnay가 있다는 두 번째 단서를 확인할 수 있다.
Ms. Meyers가 시음했던 화이트 와인을 선물로 주고 싶어 한다는 첫 번째 단서와 시음에서 유일하게 화이트 와인인 Chardonnay가 있다는 두 번째 단서를 종합할 때, Ms. Meyers가 시음했던 화이트 와인인 Chardonnay를 선물로 주고 싶어 한다는 사실을 추론할 수 있다. 따라서 (A) She wants to give the Chardonnay as a gift가 정답이다.

어휘 **expert** adj. 전문적인; n. 전문가

191-195는 다음 두 이메일과 주문 확인서에 관한 문제입니다.

수신: Jeffrey Bolton <jeffrey@cholawservices.com>
발신: Office Market <info@officemarketstore.net>
날짜: 5월 3일
제목: 판촉

Mr. Bolton께,

고객님은 저희 로열티 프로그램의 회원이시기 때문에, [191]특별 판촉을 제공해드리고자 합니다. 고객님은 사무용품을 30퍼센트 할인된 가격에 구매하실 수 있습니다. 이것은 기간 한정 거래이므로, 물량이 남아 있는 동안 혜택을 누리세요. [193]저희가 새로운 재고품을 위한 공간을 마련해야 하기 때문에 현재 전 품목 ⟳

이 할인 중입니다.

지금 www.officemarketstore.net에 가셔서 재고에 있는 상품을 구매하실 수 있습니다. [194]웹사이트는 계속해서 업데이트되므로, 상품이 목록에 없다면 그것은 품절되었다는 의미입니다. 5월 7일에 상품을 구매하는 고객에게는 메모장 한 상자도 무료로 제공될 것입니다.

언제나 그렇듯, [195]일반 배송은 무료이며 영업일 5~7일 이내 배송을 예상하실 수 있습니다. 거리에 따른 [195]추가 요금으로 2일 내 신속 배송이 가능합니다.

거래에 감사합니다.

Office Market 팀 드림

promotion n. 판촉, 홍보 **office supply** 사무용품
take advantage 혜택을 취하다 **merchandise** n. 재고품, 상품
in stock 재고가 있는 **sold out** 품절된 **memo pad** 메모장
business day 영업일, 평일

수신: Jeffrey Bolton <jeffrey@cholawservices.com>
발신: Angela Mercer <angela@cholawservices.com>
날짜: 5월 7일
제목: 주문

Jeffrey께,

Office Market 할인에 대해 알려주셔서 감사합니다. 저희 부서에 필요한 물품 목록입니다. [193A]제가 다른 모든 것들은 올해 초에 Office Barn에서 다시 채웠습니다. [193B]종이만 급하다는 점을 참고해주세요. 나머지는 급하지 않지만 세일로 할인된 가격에 구매하면 좋을 것 같습니다. [194]제가 프린터 잉크도 찾아보려고 했지만 웹사이트에서 찾을 수 없어서 다른 곳에서 사야 할 것 같습니다. 내일 Office Market에서 아래에 있는 물품들을 주문해주세요. 다시 한번 감사합니다!

· 일반 종이 20박스
· 고급 종이 10박스
· 대형 봉투 1,000장
· 펜 10자루

Angela Mercer 드림
Cho Law Services사

restock v. 다시 채우다, 보충하다 **urgent** adj. 급한, 시급한
critical adj. 위급한, 중요한 **envelope** n. 봉투

주문해주셔서 감사합니다
www.officemarketstore.net

고객 이름: Jeffrey Bolton
회원 계정 번호: 3774-2201
주문 번호: F838-32
주문 날짜: 5월 8일
결제 수단: 신용카드

상품	상품 번호	가격	수량	합계
일반 종이	88291	박스당 30달러	20	600달러
고급 종이	88242	박스당 50달러	10	500달러
봉투 대형	83210	장당 0.03달러	1,000	30달러
펜	72919	팩당 1달러	10	10달러
* 상기 가격은 30퍼센트 할인을 포함합니다			소계	1,140달러
			[195]배송	50달러
			합계	1,190달러

만약 상품이 주문에서 누락되었다면, 즉시 orders@officemarketstore.net 또는 24시간 고객 서비스 상담 전화를 통해 555-3083으로 저희에게 연락 바랍니다.

account n. 계정, 계좌 **missing** adj. 빠진, 없어진
immediately adv. 즉시, 즉각 **hotline** n. 상담 전화, 직통 전화

191 주제/목적 찾기 문제

문제 첫 번째 이메일의 목적은 무엇인가?
(A) 온라인 상점을 소개하기 위해

(B) 고객에게 할인을 설명하기 위해
(C) 새로운 개점 시간을 공지하기 위해
(D) 공급업체에 대한 변경을 알리기 위해

해설 첫 번째 이메일의 목적을 묻는 목적 찾기 문제이므로 첫 번째 이메일의 내용을 확인한다. 첫 번째 이메일의 'we would like to offer you a special promotion. You can get your office supplies at a 30 percent discount.'(1문단 1번째 줄)에서 특별 판촉을 제공해준다고 하면서 이메일 수신인인 고객이 사무용품을 30퍼센트 할인된 가격에 구매할 수 있다고 했으므로 (B) To explain an offer to a customer가 정답이다.

Paraphrasing
discount 할인 → offer 할인

어휘 opening time 개점 시간, 영업 시작 시간

192 육하원칙 문제

문제 Office Market은 무엇을 하는 중인가?
(A) 가게 장소를 개조하는 것
(B) 결제 시스템을 교체하는 것
(C) 경쟁사와 합병하는 것
(D) 오래된 재고품을 처리하는 것

해설 Office Market이 무엇(What)을 하는 중인지를 묻는 육하원칙 문제이므로 Office Market에서 보내는 첫 번째 이메일에서 질문의 핵심 어구인 in the process of doing과 관련된 내용을 확인한다. 첫 번째 이메일의 'All items are currently on sale because we need to make room for new merchandise.'(1문단 3번째 줄)에서 Office Market이 새로운 재고품을 위한 공간을 마련해야 하기 때문에 현재 전 품목이 할인 중이라고 했으므로 Office Market이 기존 재고품을 처리하고 있는 중임을 알 수 있다. 따라서 (D) Disposing of old stock이 정답이다.

Paraphrasing
merchandise 재고품 → stock 재고품

어휘 merge v. 합병하다, 합치다 dispose v. 처리하다, 배치하다

193 Not/True 문제

문제 Ms. Mercer에 대해 언급된 것은?
(A) 이전에 몇 가지 물건을 구매했다.
(B) 영업 부서를 담당한다.
(C) 급하게 봉투가 필요하다.
(D) Office Barn에서 쇼핑하는 것을 선호한다.

해설 질문의 핵심 어구인 Ms. Mercer와 관련된 내용을 지문에서 찾아 보기와 대조하는 Not/True 문제이므로 Ms. Mercer가 보내는 두 번째 이메일에서 관련 내용을 확인한다. (A)는 'I restocked everything else earlier this year from Office Barn.'(1문단 2번째 줄)에서 Ms. Mercer가 다른 물건들을 올해 초에 Office Barn에서 다시 채웠다고 했으므로 지문의 내용과 일치한다. 따라서 (A) She purchased some items earlier가 정답이다. (B)와 (D)는 지문에 언급되지 않은 내용이다. (C)는 'only the paper is urgent'(1문단 2번째 줄)에서 종이만 급하다고 했으므로 지문의 내용과 일치하지 않는다.

Paraphrasing
restocked 다시 채웠다 → purchased 구매했다

194 추론 문제 연계

문제 Ms. Mercer는 왜 프린터 잉크를 찾을 수 없었던 것 같은가?
(A) 다른 매장에서 판매된다.
(B) 웹사이트에서 품절되었다.
(C) 할인에 포함되지 않았다.
(D) 더 이상 제조되지 않는다.

해설 두 지문의 내용을 종합적으로 확인한 후 추론해서 풀어야 하는 연계 문제이다. 질문의 핵심 어구인 Ms. Mercer unable to find printer ink에서 Ms. Mercer가 왜 프린터 잉크를 찾을 수 없었던 것 같은지를 묻고 있으므로 Ms. Mercer가 작성한 두 번째 이메일을 먼저 확인한다. 두 번째 이메일의 'I tried to look for printer ink too, but I couldn't find it on the Web site'(1문단 3번째 줄)에서 Ms. Mercer가 프린터 잉크도 찾아보려고 했지만 웹사이트에서 찾을 수 없었다는 첫 번째 단서를 확인할 수 있다. 그런데 웹사이트에서 찾을 수 없는 이유가 무엇인지 제시되지 않으므

로 첫 번째 이메일에서 관련 내용을 확인한다. 첫 번째 이메일의 'The Web site is continuously updated, so if an item is not listed, that means it has sold out.'(2문단 1번째 줄)에서 웹사이트가 계속해서 업데이트되므로 상품이 목록에 없다면 그것은 품절되었다는 의미라고 했으므로 품절된 상품은 웹사이트에서 목록에 없다는 두 번째 단서를 확인할 수 있다. Ms. Mercer가 프린터 잉크도 찾아보려고 했지만 웹사이트에서 찾을 수 없었다는 첫 번째 단서와 품절된 상품은 웹사이트에서 목록에 없다는 두 번째 단서를 종합할 때, 프린터 잉크가 품절되어 Ms. Mercer가 웹사이트에서 찾을 수 없었다는 사실을 추론할 수 있다. 따라서 (B) It was sold out on a Web site가 정답이다.

Paraphrasing
was ~ unable to find 찾을 수 없었다 → wouldn't find 찾을 수 없었다

어휘 handle v. 판매하다, 다루다

195 추론 문제 연계

문제 Mr. Bolton의 주문에 대해 암시되는 것은?
(A) 해외에서 운송될 것이다.
(B) 더 이상 재고에 없는 상품을 포함한다.
(C) 경품에 대한 매장의 마감일을 맞췄다.
(D) 이틀 내로 배송될 것이다.

해설 두 지문의 내용을 종합적으로 확인한 후 추론해서 풀어야 하는 연계 문제이다. 질문의 핵심 어구인 Mr. Bolton의 주문 확인서를 먼저 확인한다. 세 번째 지문인 주문 확인서의 'Shipping', '$50'(표 7행 4, 5열)에서 Mr. Bolton이 배송에 50달러를 지불했다는 첫 번째 단서를 확인할 수 있다. 그런데 무엇에 대한 배송비인지 제시되지 않았으므로 첫 번째 이메일에서 관련 내용을 확인한다. 첫 번째 이메일의 'standard shipping is free'(3문단 1번째 줄), 'Expedited, two-day shipping is available for an extra fee'(3문단 2번째 줄)에서 일반 배송은 무료이지만 추가 요금으로 2일 내 신속 배송이 가능하다는 두 번째 단서를 확인할 수 있다. Mr. Bolton이 배송에 50달러를 지불했다는 첫 번째 단서와 일반 배송은 무료이지만 추가 요금을 내면 2일 내 신속 배송이 가능하다는 두 번째 단서를 종합할 때, Mr. Bolton이 2일 내에 배송되는 신속 배송을 위해 50달러의 추가 요금을 냈다는 사실을 추론할 수 있다. 따라서 (D) It will be delivered in two days가 정답이다.

Paraphrasing
shipping 배송 → be delivered 배송되다

어휘 overseas n. 해외; adv. 해외에서

196-200은 다음 안내문, 이메일, 기사에 관한 문제입니다.

저서 목록
196-C/D아래는 작가 Martha Nelson의 도서 목록입니다. 196-C모두 www.victarpublishing.com에서 오디오 형식으로 다운로드할 수 있습니다.

196-B Telling Stories
196-B작가의 자서전에서, 그녀는 고향인 보스턴으로 연애편지를 씁니다.

Boston Guards
보스턴의 형사 Dolores Sanchez는 이 긴장감 넘치는 스릴러 소설에서 범죄를 해결하기 위해 수색 중입니다.

Sanchez Strong
Boston Guards의 속편으로, Sanchez 형사는 스페인에서 국제 임무를 맡습니다.

Before the Sun Sets
이 로맨스 소설은 마지막 소원을 가진 채 죽어가는 여성 Maria가 중심이 됩니다.

196-D Victar 출판사에서 곧 나올 소설들

198 Dolores Rising
Boston Guards에서 시작된 198시리즈의 세 번째 책이자 최종 편입니다. 고향으로 돌아온 Dolores는 오래된 적을 맞닥뜨립니다.

Short Stories
이전에 출판되지 않았던 소설들이 하나의 모음집에 모아졌습니다.

bibliography n. 저서 목록, 문헌학 autobiography n. 자서전
detective n. 형사; adj. 탐색하는 quest n. 수색, 원정
suspenseful adj. 긴장감 넘치는 sequel n. 속편, 결과

assignment n. 임무, 과제 center on ~이 중심이 되다, ~에 초점을 맞추다
confront v. 맞닥뜨리다, 맞서다

수신: Jackie Dennett <j.dennet@bookscafe.com>
발신: Ming Oh <ming@ohliteraryagency.com>
날짜: 8월 14일
제목: 도서 출간

안녕하세요 Jackie,

[197]Books Café에서의 행사를 위한 준비를 재확인하고자 합니다. 당신이 행사를 계속해서 잘 진행되게 하실 수 있다는 것을 조건으로 Ms. Nelson은 도서 사인회 시간에 참석하는 것에 동의했습니다. 그녀의 인기로 인해, 그녀는 많은 인파를 모으는 경향이 있어서 저희는 좁은 장소에서 열렸던 지난 행사들에서 몇몇 안타까운 사고들이 있었습니다. [199]적어도 천 명의 방문객들을 수용할 수 있는지를 확인하셔야 할 것입니다. 만약 그것이 불가능하다면, 저희는 다른 장소를 빌려야 할 것입니다.

[197]현재 제가 그녀의 모든 홍보 활동을 마무리하고 있으므로, 제게 알려주시기 바랍니다.

Ming Oh 드림

double-check v. 재확인하다, 재점검하다
provided conj. ~을 조건으로 하여, 만일 ~이라면 tend to ~하는 경향이 있다
make sure 확인하다, 반드시 ~하다
accommodate v. 수용하다, 공간을 제공하다

보스턴 중앙 신문

Martha Nelson의 귀향

9월 9일—국제적으로 찬사를 받는 작가 [198/200]Martha Nelson이 그녀의 유명한 추리 시리즈의 세 번째 책 출간을 축하하기 위해 어제 귀향했고, 비평가들은 그 책에 극찬했다. [200]첫 주 판매 예상치는 이미 이전 작품을 능가하는 궤도에 올랐다. Ms. Nelson의 인기는 [199]어제 Boston Star 극장에서 열린 도서 사인회에서 확연히 드러났다. [198/199]그녀의 최신 도서 사인회가 거의 5,000명의 사람들을 끌어모았다. 몇몇 방문객은 또한 큰 박수갈채로 끝났던 저자의 즉흥 낭독을 볼 만큼 운이 좋았다.

homecoming n. 귀향, 귀국 acclaimed adj. 칭찬을 받는, 호평을 받는
rave review 극찬, 호평 projection n. 예상, 추정
on track 궤도에 올라, 순조롭게 나아가서 surpass v. 능가하다, 초과하다
predecessor n. 이전 것, 전임자 witness v. 보다, 목격하다
spontaneous adj. 즉흥의, 자발적인 applause n. 박수(갈채), 성원

196 Not/True 문제

문제 Ms. Nelson의 작품에 대해 언급되지 않은 것은?

(A) 상으로 인정받았다.
(B) 그중 하나는 Ms. Nelson의 삶에 관한 것이다.
(C) 오디오 버전으로 출시되었다.
(D) 일부는 아직 발행되지 않았다.

해설 질문의 핵심 어구인 Ms. Nelson's works와 관련된 내용을 지문에서 찾아보기와 대조하는 Not/True 문제이므로 첫 번째 지문인 Ms. Nelson의 저서가 나열된 안내문에서 관련 내용을 확인한다. (A)는 지문에 언급되지 않은 내용이다. 따라서 (A) They have been recognized with awards가 정답이다. (B)는 'Telling Stories', 'the author's autobiography'(2문단 1, 2번째 줄)에서 Telling Stories가 작가의 자서전이라고 했으므로 지문의 내용과 일치한다. (C)는 'Below is a list of books by author Martha Nelson. All are available to download in audio format'(1문단 1번째 줄)에서 아래는 작가 Martha Nelson의 도서 목록이고 모두 오디오 형식으로 다운로드할 수 있다고 했으므로 지문의 내용과 일치한다. (D)는 'Below is a list of books by author Martha Nelson.'(1문단 1번째 줄), 'Upcoming novels from Victar Publishing'(3문단 제목)에서 작가 Martha Nelson의 도서 목록에는 없지만 곧 나올 소설들이 있다는 것을 알 수 있으므로 지문의 내용과 일치한다.

Paraphrasing
audio format 오디오 형식 → audio versions 오디오 버전
Upcoming 곧 나올 → have not been printed yet 아직 발행되지 않았다

어휘 recognize v. 인정하다, 공인하다

197 추론 문제

문제 Mr. Oh는 무엇을 담당하는 것 같은가?

(A) 문학 작품을 교정하는 것
(B) 법률 상담을 제공하는 것
(C) 홍보 행사를 준비하는 것
(D) 작가의 수입을 관리하는 것

해설 질문의 핵심 어구인 Mr. Oh responsible for에 대해 추론하는 문제이므로 Mr. Oh가 작성한 이메일에서 관련 내용을 확인한다. 두 번째 지문인 이메일의 'I just want to double-check on preparations for the event at Books Café.'(1문단 1번째 줄)에서 Mr. Oh가 Books Café에서의 행사를 위한 준비를 재확인하고자 한다고 했고, 'I am currently wrapping up all of her promotional activities'(2문단 1번째 줄)에서 현재 자신이 Ms. Nelson의 모든 홍보 활동을 마무리하고 있다고 했으므로 Mr. Oh가 홍보 행사 준비를 담당한다는 사실을 추론할 수 있다. 따라서 (C) Organizing promotional events가 정답이다.

Paraphrasing
preparations 준비 → Organizing 준비하는 것
promotional activities 홍보 활동 → promotional events 홍보 행사

어휘 proofread v. 교정하다 legal advice 법률 상담 finance n. 재정, 금융

198 추론 문제 연계

문제 Ms. Nelson에 대해 추론될 수 있는 것은?

(A) Dolores Rising 책에 사인했다.
(B) 보스턴으로 다시 이주할 것이다.
(C) Victar 출판사와 10권짜리 계약을 했다.
(D) 어떤 작품도 국제적으로 출간하지 않았다.

해설 두 지문의 내용을 종합적으로 확인한 후 추론해서 풀어야 하는 연계 문제이다. 질문의 핵심 어구인 Ms. Nelson과 관련된 내용이 언급된 기사를 먼저 확인한다.
세 번째 지문인 기사의 'Martha Nelson ~ celebrate the release of the third book in her famous detective series'(1번째 줄)에서 Martha Nelson이 그녀의 유명한 추리 시리즈의 세 번째 책의 출간을 축하할 것이라고 했고, 'The signing of her newest book attracted almost 5,000 people.'(4번째 줄)에서 그녀의 최신 도서 사인회가 거의 5,000명의 사람들을 끌어모았다고 했으므로 Ms. Nelson의 추리 시리즈의 세 번째 책을 위한 사인회가 열렸다는 첫 번째 단서를 확인할 수 있다. 그런데 추리 시리즈의 세 번째 책 제목이 무엇인지 제시되지 않았으므로 안내문에서 관련 내용을 확인한다. 첫 번째 지문인 안내문의 'Dolores Rising', 'The third ~ book of the series'(3문단 1, 2번째 줄)에서 Dolores Rising이 시리즈의 세 번째 책이라는 두 번째 단서를 확인할 수 있다.
Ms. Nelson의 추리 시리즈의 세 번째 책을 위한 사인회가 열렸다는 첫 번째 단서와 Dolores Rising이 시리즈의 세 번째 책이라는 두 번째 단서를 종합할 때, Ms. Nelson이 사인회에서 Dolores Rising 책에 사인했다는 사실을 추론할 수 있다. 따라서 (A) She signed copies of Dolores Rising이 정답이다.

199 추론 문제 연계

문제 Ms. Nelson은 왜 Boston Star 극장에서 행사를 열었던 것 같은가?

(A) 그녀의 호텔에서 가장 가까운 장소였다.
(B) 그녀의 책이 영화로 만들어지고 있다.
(C) 그녀의 소설 중 하나에 등장했다.
(D) Books Café가 너무 좁았을 것이다.

해설 두 지문의 내용을 종합적으로 확인한 후 추론해서 풀어야 하는 연계 문제이다. 질문의 핵심 어구인 Ms. Nelson hold an event at the Boston Star Theater에서 Ms. Nelson이 왜 Boston Star 극장에서 행사를 열었던 것 같은지를 묻고 있으므로 Boston Star Theater가 언급된 기사를 먼저 확인한다.
세 번째 지문인 기사의 'her book signing event, held yesterday at the Boston Star Theater. The signing ~ attracted almost 5,000 people.'(4번째 줄)에서 Ms. Nelson의 사인회가 어제 Boston Star 극장에서 열렸고 거의 5,000명의 사람들을 끌어모았다는 첫 번째 단서를 확인할 수 있다. 그런데 사인회가 왜 Boston Star 극장에서 열렸는지 정확하게 제시되지 않았으므로 이메일에서 관련 내용을 확인한다. 두 번째 지문인 이

메일의 'You will need to make sure that you can accommodate at least a thousand visitors. If that isn't possible, we will have to rent a different location.'(1문단 4번째 줄)에서 Books Café가 적어도 천 명의 방문객들을 수용할 수 있는지를 확인해야 하고 만약 그것이 불가능하다면 다른 장소를 빌려야 할 것이라는 두 번째 단서를 확인할 수 있다.

Ms. Nelson의 사인회가 어제 Boston Star 극장에서 열렸고 거의 5,000명의 사람들을 끌어모았다는 첫 번째 단서와 Books Café가 적어도 천 명의 방문객들을 수용할 수 있는지를 확인해야 하고 만약 그것이 불가능하다면 다른 장소를 빌려야 할 것이라는 두 번째 단서를 종합할 때, Books Café가 적어도 천 명의 방문객들을 수용할 수 없어서 Boston Star 극장에서 사인회가 열렸다는 사실을 추론할 수 있다. 따라서 (D) Books Café would have been too small이 정답이다.

어휘 **venue** n. 장소 **feature** v. 특별히 포함하다, 특징으로 삼다

200 육하원칙 문제

문제 기사에 따르면, Ms. Nelson의 추리 시리즈 중 최신 도서에 대해 무엇이 예상되는가?

(A) 장편 영화로 만들어질 것이다.

(B) 첫 주에 5,000부가 팔릴 것이다.

(C) 적어도 그녀의 이전 책만큼 인기가 있을 것이다.

(D) 아마도 네 번째 책으로 이어질 것이다.

해설 Ms. Nelson의 추리 시리즈 중 최신 도서에 대해 무엇이(what) 예상되는지를 묻는 육하원칙 문제이므로 기사에서 질문의 핵심 어구인 Ms. Nelson's latest book in her detective series와 관련된 내용을 확인한다. 세 번째 지문인 기사의 Martha Nelson ~ celebrate the release of the third book in her famous detective series'(1번째 줄)에서 Martha Nelson이 그녀의 유명한 추리 시리즈의 세 번째 책의 출간을 축하할 것이라고 했고, 'First-week sales projections are already on track to surpass its predecessor.'(3번째 줄)에서 Ms. Nelson의 최신 도서의 첫 주 판매 예상치가 이미 이전 작품을 능가하는 궤도에 올랐다고 했으므로 (C) It will be at least as popular as her previous book이 정답이다.

Paraphrasing
predecessor 이전 작품 → **previous book** 이전 책

어휘 **turn into** ~로 만들다, ~으로 변하다 **feature film** 장편 영화

Part 5   p.544

101 (D)	102 (C)	103 (A)	104 (B)	105 (C)
106 (B)	107 (C)	108 (A)	109 (D)	110 (D)
111 (A)	112 (A)	113 (D)	114 (A)	115 (C)
116 (C)	117 (C)	118 (B)	119 (B)	120 (D)
121 (C)	122 (C)	123 (A)	124 (C)	125 (C)
126 (B)	127 (B)	128 (C)	129 (D)	130 (C)

Part 6   p.547

131 (A)	132 (D)	133 (D)	134 (B)	135 (A)
136 (B)	137 (A)	138 (A)	139 (B)	140 (B)
141 (D)	142 (A)	143 (B)	144 (B)	145 (C)
146 (A)				

Part 7   p.551

147 (D)	148 (B)	149 (D)	150 (A)	151 (D)
152 (A)	153 (A)	154 (B)	155 (A)	156 (D)
157 (A)	158 (C)	159 (C)	160 (B)	161 (C)
162 (D)	163 (D)	164 (C)	165 (B)	166 (B)
167 (C)	168 (D)	169 (A)	170 (A)	171 (C)
172 (C)	173 (B)	174 (A)	175 (D)	176 (A)
177 (D)	178 (D)	179 (A)	180 (B)	181 (D)
182 (C)	183 (B)	184 (A)	185 (D)	186 (A)
187 (B)	188 (C)	189 (B)	190 (D)	191 (C)
192 (A)	193 (B)	194 (D)	195 (B)	196 (B)
197 (A)	198 (A)	199 (D)	200 (B)	

101 전치사 채우기

해설 동사 base와 함께 쓰여 '~에 기초하다'라는 의미를 만드는 (D) on이 정답이다.

해석 팀원들 다수가 전체 프로젝트가 기초하고 있는 디자인 컨셉에 대해 의견 차이를 보였다.

어휘 disagreement n. 의견 차이, 불일치 entire adj. 전체의

102 태에 맞는 동사 채우기

해설 '그 회사는 관련되어 왔다'라는 의미가 되어야 하므로 has been과 함께 수동태 동사를 만드는 p.p.형 (C) involved가 정답이다. 현재 시제 (A), 동사원형 또는 현재 시제 (D)는 has been 다음에 올 수 없다.

해석 새로운 회사임에도 불구하고, 그 회사는 모든 고객 프로젝트에 밀접하게 관련되어 왔고, 훌륭한 평판을 얻었다.

어휘 business n. 회사, 사업 reputation n. 평판, 명성

103 전치사 채우기

해설 '해외 투자 계획에 관한 회사의 의도'라는 의미가 되어야 하므로 (A) with respect to(~에 관하여)가 정답이다.

해석 회의 중에, 이사회 임원들 중 한 명이 해외 투자 계획에 관한 회사의 의도에 이의를 제기했다.

어휘 intention n. 의도, 의향 initiative n. 계획 across from ~의 맞은편에
by means of ~의 도움으로

104 등위접속사 채우기

해설 '몇몇 연사들이 교통 체증을 겪었지만 모두 제시간에 왔다'라는 의미가 되어야 하므로 (B) but(그러나)이 정답이다.

해석 몇몇 연사들이 회의장으로 오는 도중에 교통 체증을 겪었지만, 모두 개회 발표

105 동사 관련 어구 채우기

해설 '원인을 진단할 수 있기 전에 엔진이 분해되어야 할 것이다'라는 문맥이므로 '분해하다'라는 의미를 갖는 동사 어구 (C) taken apart가 정답이다. (A)의 inaugurate는 '개시하다, 취임시키다', (B)의 lessen은 '줄이다', (D)의 turn up은 '(소리·온도 등을) 올리다'라는 의미이다.

해석 정비사들이 문제의 원인을 정확히 진단할 수 있기 전에 그 차의 엔진이 분해되어야 할 것이다.

어휘 mechanic n. 정비사, 수리공 diagnose v. 진단하다 source n. 원인, 근원

106 보어 자리 채우기

해설 동사(remain)의 주격 보어 자리를 채우는 문제이다. 보어가 될 수 있는 것은 명사나 형용사이므로 모든 보기가 정답의 후보이다. 이 중 주어의 상태를 설명해 주는 형용사 (B) local(지역의, 현지의)이 정답이다. 명사 (A) locality(부근), (C) locals(주민, 현지인), (D) location(장소)은 주어(Herdigen)와 동격 관계를 이루지 못하므로 답이 될 수 없다.

해석 비록 다른 회사들이 제조를 해외로 외주 제작하기 시작했지만, Herdigen사는 지역에 남았고, 그들의 모든 제품을 국내에서 만들었다.

어휘 outsource v. 외주 제작하다 manufacturing n. 제조, 제조업
domestically adv. 국내에서 locality n. 부근, 장소

107 올바른 시제의 동사 채우기

해설 '성공적인 거래가 체결되다'라는 수동의 의미이므로 수동태 동사 (C)와 (D)가 정답의 후보이다. 주절 동사(were)가 과거이므로 that절(종속절)에도 과거 동사가 와야 한다. 따라서 (C) were concluded가 정답이다.

해석 무역 전시회의 주최자들은 몇몇 성공적인 거래가 행사 참가자들에 의해 체결되었다는 것을 듣고 기뻐했다.

어휘 organizer n. 주최자 deal n. 거래, 계약 conclude v. 체결하다, 끝내다

108 가정법 동사 채우기

해설 If가 생략되어 주어(anything)와 조동사(Should)가 도치된 절에는 동사원형이 와야 하므로 동사원형 (A) happen이 정답이다. 현재 시제 (B), 과거 또는 과거분사 (C), 동명사 또는 현재분사 (D)는 조동사 다음에 올 수 없다.

해석 만약 사무실 시설 내에서 보통과 다른 어떤 일이 생기면, 직원들은 즉시 건물 경비 회사에 전화를 걸어야 한다.

어휘 out of the ordinary 보통과 다른, 이상한 immediately adj. 즉시
dial v. 전화를 걸다

109 전치사 채우기

해설 '연말쯤에 출시될 것이다'라는 의미가 되어야 하므로 시점을 나타내는 (D) around(~쯤에)가 정답이다. (B) on과 (C) through도 시간을 나타낼 수 있지만, on은 날짜·요일·특정일 앞에 오고 through는 기간을 나타내는 표현 앞에 온다.

해석 새 모델은 연말쯤에 출시될 것이다.

어휘 launch v. 출시하다, 개시하다

110 동사 어휘 고르기

해설 '작은 상자에 담겨 운송하기 쉽게 하기 위해 특수하게 만들어진다'라는 문맥이므로 (D) crafted((공들여) 만들다)가 정답이다. (A)의 diminish는 '줄이다, 약화시키다', (B)의 commit은 '저지르다, 약속하다', (C)의 redeem은 '보완하다, 만회하다'라는 의미이다.

| 해석 | 그 가구 제품들은 작은 상자에 담겨 운송하기 쉽게 하기 위해 특수하게 만들어진다. |
| 어휘 | **specially** adv. 특수하게, 명확하게 **compact** adj. 작은, 조밀한 |

111 to 부정사 채우기

해설	동사 compel(was compelled) 다음에는 to 부정사가 와야 하므로, (A) to call이 정답이다. 동명사 (B), 동사원형 (C), 단수 동사 (D)는 동사 compel 다음에 올 수 없다.
해석	Mr. Jenkins는 그의 직원들이 수많은 부주의한 회계 실수를 했다는 것을 알아차린 후, 어쩔 수 없이 전 직원 회의를 소집해야만 했다.
어휘	**be compelled to** 어쩔 수 없이 ~하다 **careless** adj. 부주의한 **accounting** n. 회계

112 형용사 어휘 고르기

해설	'빈자리는 다음 주에 채워질 것이다'라는 문맥이므로 (A) vacant(빈, 비어 있는)가 정답이다. (B) enhanced는 '증대한, 강화한', (C) agreeable은 '기분 좋은, 기꺼이 동의하는', (D) selective는 '선택하는'이라는 의미이다.
해석	빈자리는 여름에 정보 기술 부서에 합류하는 인턴에 의해 다음 주에 채워질 것이다.
어휘	**position** n. 자리, 직위 **fill** v. 채우다, 메우다

113 다른 명사를 수식하는 명사 채우기

해설	명사 gas(가스)와 함께 '가스 누출'이라는 복합 명사를 만드는 (D) leak(누출)가 정답이다. (A) damage는 '손상', (B) repair는 '수선, 수리', (C) barrier는 '장벽'이라는 의미이다.
해석	소방국은 잠재적으로 유해한 가스 누출이 신고된 직후에 Pillar Towers의 거주자들에게 건물을 비우도록 명령했다.
어휘	**tenant** n. 거주자, 임차인 **evacuate** v. 비우다, 대피시키다 **potentially** adv. 잠재적으로 **report** v. 신고하다, 보도하다

114 형용사 자리 채우기

해설	명사(results)를 꾸밀 수 있는 것은 형용사이므로 형용사 (A) contradictory(모순된)가 정답이다. 동사 (B), (C)는 명사를 꾸밀 수 없고, 명사 (D) contradiction은 명사 results와 복합 명사를 이룰 수 없다.
해석	만약 두 개의 서로 다른 연구실에 의해 진행된 초기 실험들이 모순된 결과를 가져온다면, 연구원들은 세 번째 제공업체를 찾아내야 할 것이다.
어휘	**initial** adj. 초기의, 처음의 **separate** adj. 서로 다른, 분리된 **seek out** ~을 찾아내다

115 상관접속사 채우기

해설	상관접속사 and와 맞는 짝인 (C) both가 정답이다. (A) either와 (D) whether는 or와 맞는 짝이다. (B) each는 단수 명사 앞에 와야 하는데 뒤에 복수 명사(risks)가 왔으므로 답이 될 수 없다.
해석	정부 공무원들은 그러한 대규모 주택 개발 사업과 관련된 범위와 위험들에 대해 불안해했다.
어휘	**official** n. 공무원 **unsure** adj. 불안한, 의심스러워하는 **scope** n. 범위 **residential** adj. 주택의, 주거의

116 현재분사와 과거분사 구별하여 채우기

해설	명사(passengers)를 꾸미기 위해서는 분사 (B) 또는 (C)가 와야 한다. 수식 받는 명사(passengers)와 분사가 '탑승객들이 도착하다'라는 의미의 능동 관계이므로 현재분사 (C) arriving(도착하다)이 정답이다. 복합 명사(명사 + 명사)가 아닌 경우, 명사(arrival)는 명사(passengers)를 꾸밀 수 없으므로 명사 (D) arrival은 답이 될 수 없다. 참고로, 동사 arrive는 자동사이므로 수동 관계를 의미하는 과거분사로 쓰일 수 없다.
해석	Carson 국제공항에 도착하는 승객들을 위해 최근에 건설된 터미널은 5월 31일에 대중에게 개방될 것으로 예상된다.
어휘	**construct** v. 건설하다, 짓다 **public** n. 대중, 일반 사람들

117 전치사 채우기

해설	'주 전체에 걸쳐서'라는 의미를 만드는 (C) throughout(~ 전체에 걸쳐서)이 정답이다. (A) upon은 on 대신 사용되는 전치사이다. (B) inside는 '~ 안쪽에', (D) above는 '~ 위에'라는 의미이다.
해석	지역 뉴스는 주 전체에 걸쳐서 심각한 기상 경보를 내렸고 도로 이용을 삼가라고 권고했다.
어휘	**issue** v. (선언·명령·경보 등을) 내리다, 발행하다 **severe** adj. 심각한, 엄중한 **stay off** 삼가다, ~에서 떨어져 있다

118 단수 명사와 복수 명사 구별하여 채우기

해설	빈칸은 전치사 of의 목적어 자리이므로 명사 (A)와 (B)가 정답의 후보이다. part는 '부품, 부분'을 의미하는 가산 명사이므로 앞에 관사가 오거나 복수형이어야 하는데, 빈칸 앞에 관사가 없으므로 복수형 (B) parts가 정답이다.
해석	기계 관리 부서장은 엔진이 제대로 기능하기 위해서는 핵심적인 부품들의 교체가 필요하다는 것을 알아챘다.
어휘	**maintenance** n. 관리, 유지 **replacement** n. 교체 **vital** adj. 핵심적인, 필수적인 **function** v. 기능하다 **properly** adv. 제대로

119 부사 어휘 고르기

해설	'직원들을 객관적으로 대하고 개인적인 의견이 결정에 간섭하지 않도록 하다'라는 문맥이므로 (B) objectively(객관적으로)가 정답이다. (A) conditionally는 '조건부로', (C) compassionately는 '동정적으로', (D) approvingly는 '찬성하여'라는 의미이다.
해석	그 교수는 많은 사장들이 직원들을 객관적으로 대하고 개인적인 의견이 결정에 간섭하지 않도록 하는 것을 어려워한다고 말했다.
어휘	**interfere** v. 간섭하다

120 의미 구별하여 명사 채우기

해설	동사(increase)의 목적어 자리에 올 수 있는 것은 명사나 동명사이므로 명사 (A), (B), (D)가 정답의 후보이다. '새로운 공장이 완공되자마자 생산을 늘릴 수 있을 것이다'라는 의미가 되어야 하므로 (D) production(생산, 제작)이 정답이다. (A) product(생산품)는 가산 명사이므로 앞에 관사가 오거나 복수형이어야 하고, (B) produce(농산물)는 '새로운 공장이 완공되자마자 농산물을 늘릴 수 있을 것이다'라는 어색한 의미가 되므로 답이 될 수 없다.
해석	그 회사는 새로운 공장이 완공되자마자 생산을 50퍼센트 정도 늘릴 수 있을 것이다.
어휘	**increase** v. 늘리다, 높이다 **complete** v. 완성하다, 완료하다

121 형용사 어휘 고르기

해설	'새롭게 재디자인된 용기가 상점 선반에서 제품들을 쉽게 알아볼 수 있게 하다'라는 문맥이므로 (C) recognizable(알아볼 수 있는)이 정답이다. (A) fashionable은 '최신 유행의, 유행하는', (B) compatible은 '양립할 수 있는, 모순이 없는', (D) preferable은 '오히려 나은, 보다 바람직한'이라는 의미이다.
해석	Derry Milk사는 그들의 새롭게 재디자인된 용기가 상점 선반에서 그들의 제품을 더 쉽게 알아볼 수 있게 하기를 바란다.
어휘	**packaging** n. 용기, 포장 **shelf** n. 선반

122 부사 자리 채우기

해설	동사(allocate)를 꾸밀 수 있는 것은 부사이므로 부사 (C) reasonably(합리적으로)가 정답이다. 동사 또는 명사 (A), 명사 또는 형용사 (B), 형용사 (D)는 동사를 꾸밀 수 없다.
해석	예산 위원회는 적절한 인재를 합리적으로 배치할 충분한 시간을 감안하여 사업 제안서를 승인했다.
어휘	**budget** n. 예산 **proposal** n. 제안서 **allocate** v. 배치하다, 배분하다 **human resources** 인재, 노동력 **reasoning** n. 추리, 추론; adj. 추리하는 **reasonable** adj. 도리에 맞는, 정당한

123 전치사 채우기

해설 이 문장은 주어(Many customers), 동사(have been), 보어(unwilling to switch)를 갖춘 완전한 절이므로 ___ some ~ offers는 수식어 거품으로 보아야 한다. 보기 중 수식어 거품을 이끌 수 있는 전치사 (A) despite가 정답이다. 부사 (B), (C), (D)는 수식어 거품을 이끌 수 없다.

해석 몇몇 매력적인 판촉 할인에도 불구하고 많은 고객들이 Beat Cellular사로 바꾸는 것을 마음 내켜하지 않았다.

어휘 unwilling adj. 마음 내키지 않는 switch v. 바꾸다
attractive adj. 매력적인 offer n. 할인

124 명사 어휘 고르기

해설 '객실과 시설의 상태를 점검하는 검사관 팀을 고용한다'라는 문맥이므로 (C) condition(상태)이 정답이다. (A) relevance는 '적절, 타당성', (B) elimination은 '제거', (D) concentration은 '집중'이라는 의미이다.

해석 Signal 호텔은 호텔 체인점들의 모든 객실과 시설의 상태를 점검하는 검사관 팀을 고용한다.

어휘 employ v. 고용하다, 쓰다 inspector n. 검사관, 시찰자
facility n. 시설

125 부사 자리 채우기

해설 동사(was aligned)를 꾸미기 위해서는 부사가 필요하므로 부사 (C) more closely가 정답이다. 참고로, 부사 more가 부사 closely를 강조하여 '보다 밀접하게'라는 의미를 나타낸다. 형용사 (A), (B), (D)는 동사를 꾸밀 수 없다.

해석 Mr. Anderson은 KPI사를 떠나 Thornwoode사로 갔는데 그는 그의 가치관과 포부에 보다 밀접하게 결합되는 회사에서 일하고 싶었기 때문이다.

어휘 align v. 결합하다, 정렬하다 value n. 가치관, 가치 aspiration n. 포부

126 부사 어휘 고르기

해설 '몹시 바쁜 스케줄은 깊이 있는 일대일 대화를 할 수 있는 시간을 좀처럼 허락하지 않는다'라는 문맥이므로 (B) rarely(좀처럼 ~하지 않는)가 정답이다. (A) frequently는 '자주', (C) consistently는 '일관되게, 모순이 없게', (D) typically는 '전형적으로, 일반적으로'라는 의미이다.

해석 Mr. Bloom의 몹시 바쁜 스케줄은 그가 팀원들과 깊이 있는 일대일 대화를 할 수 있는 시간을 좀처럼 허락하지 않는다.

어휘 hectic adj. 몹시 바쁜 in-depth adj. 깊이 있는, 면밀한
one-on-one adj. 일대일의, 단 두 사람 사이의

127 동사 어휘 고르기

해설 '다가오는 몇 주 이내에 추가적인 최신 정보를 공개하다'라는 문맥이므로 (B) release(공개하다, 발표하다)가 정답이다. (A) inform(알려주다)도 답이 될 수 있을 것 같지만 inform 뒤의 목적어 자리에는 정보를 전달받는 대상이 나와야 하므로 답이 될 수 없다. (C) exhibit은 '전시하다', (D) propose는 '제의하다, 제안하다'라는 의미이다.

해석 GMT사의 고위 간부들은 다가오는 몇 주 이내에 Hawkland Electric사와의 합병에 관한 추가적인 최신 정보를 공개할 것으로 예상된다.

어휘 further adj. 추가적인 update n. 최신 정보 merger n. 합병
coming adj. 다가오는, 다음의

128 명사 어휘 고르기

해설 '휠체어를 탄 사람들을 위해 공공건물들에 대한 접근성을 향상시키다'라는 문맥이므로 (D) accessibility(접근성)가 정답이다. (A) operation은 '작동', (B) capability는 '능력, 재능', (C) evaluation은 '평가'라는 의미이다.

해석 시의회는 휠체어를 탄 사람들을 위해 공공건물들에 대한 접근성을 향상시킬 법률을 신속히 승인했다.

어휘 approve v. 승인하다 legislation n. 법률 improve v. 향상시키다

129 지시대명사 채우기

해설 뒤에 분사(wishing)를 수식어로 받아 '원하는 사람들'을 의미하므로 (D) those가 정답이다. 관계대명사 (A)는 선행사가 있어야 하므로 답이 될 수 없다.

해석 Moda-Lita사는 산업에 새로운 전망을 가져오길 희망하는 헌신적이고 열정적인 디자이너들로 구성된 팀에서 일하길 원하는 사람들을 위한 몇몇 공석을 가지고 있다.

어휘 opening n. 공석, 빈자리 dedicated adj. 헌신적인
passionate adj. 열정적인 perspective n. 전망, 관점

130 부사 어휘 고르기

해설 '연회는 엄격히 회원들을 위한 것이므로 입장하기 전에 초대장이 제시되어야 한다'라는 문맥이므로 (C) strictly(엄격하게)가 정답이다. (A) supremely는 '극도로, 지극히', (B) debatably는 '논쟁의 여지가 있게', (D) widely는 '넓게, 크게'라는 의미이다.

해석 내일 저녁 연회는 엄격히 Ravenport Country 클럽의 회원들을 위한 것이므로, 입장이 허가되기 전에 초대장이 반드시 제시되어야 한다.

어휘 banquet n. 연회, 성찬 invitation n. 초대장
present v. 제시하다, 보여주다 entry n. 입장
permit v. 허가하다; n. 허가증

131-134는 다음 광고에 관한 문제입니다.

당신은 열정적인 독서가인가요? 그렇다면 새로운 ShockRead 모바일 전자책 단말기를 써 보세요! 끊임없이 움직이는 독서가들에게 더할 나위 없이 좋은, 이것은 거의 모든 곳에 가져갈 수 있고 한 번의 충전으로 20시간 동안 작동합니다. [131]이것은 진실로 엄청난 편리함을 제공합니다.

더구나, ShockRead는 20기가바이트의 많은 저장 공간을 가지고 있습니다. [132]따라서, 당신의 디지털 서재가 광대할지라도 걱정할 필요가 없습니다. 그리고 만약 당신이 책을 읽고 싶지 않다면, ShockRead는 버튼 터치 한 번으로 그 어떤 책도 오디오북으로 바꿀 수 있습니다. [133]당신은 여러 가지의 자연스러운 목소리와 속도 중에서 선택할 수 있습니다.

온라인에서 7월 10일부터 ShockRead를 구매하세요. [134]www.shockread.com을 방문하시고 일주일 전에 미리 주문하시면 10퍼센트 할인을 누릴 수 있습니다.

avid adj. 열정적인 e-reader n. 전자책 단말기
on the go 끊임없이 움직이는, 정신없이 바쁜 incredible adj. 엄청난, 대단한
substantial adj. 많은, 상당한 storage n. 저장 공간

131 부사 어휘 고르기 주변 문맥 파악

해설 '이것은 ___ 엄청난 편리함을 제공한다'라는 문맥이므로 모든 보기가 정답의 후보이다. 빈칸이 있는 문장만으로는 정답을 고를 수 없으므로 주변 문맥이나 전체 문맥을 파악한다. 앞 문장에서 '끊임없이 움직이는 독서가들에게 더할 나위 없이 좋은 이것은 거의 모든 곳에 가져갈 수 있고 한 번의 충전으로 20시간 동안 작동한다(Perfect for readers on the go, it can be taken almost anywhere and runs for 20 hours on a single charge.)'고 했으므로 강조의 의미를 나타내는 (A) truly(진실로)가 정답이다.

어휘 lastly adv. 마지막으로, 끝으로 originally adv. 원래, 처음에는
rarely adv. 드물게

132 형용사 어휘 고르기 주변 문맥 파악

해설 '당신의 디지털 서재가 ___일지라도 걱정할 필요가 없다'라는 문맥이므로 모든 보기가 정답의 후보이다. 빈칸이 있는 문장만으로는 정답을 고를 수 없으므로 주변 문맥이나 전체 문맥을 파악한다. 앞 문장에서 'ShockRead는 20기가바이트의 많은 저장 공간을 가지고 있다(ShockRead has a substantial 20 gigabytes of storage)'고 했으므로 ShockRead는 광대한 디지털 서재가 있을지라도 걱정할 필요가 없음을 알 수 있다. 따라서 형용사 (D) extensive(광대한)가 정답이다.

어휘 affordable adj. (가격 등이) 알맞은 adjustable adj. 조정할 수 있는
simplistic adj. 지나치게 단순화한

133 알맞은 문장 고르기

해석 (A) 그 공간은 수천 권의 책을 다운로드할 수 있도록 할 것입니다.
(B) 일부 독서가들은 그들의 컬렉션에 어떤 책이 있는지 모릅니다.
(C) 쇼핑 서비스는 선택된 지역에서만 이용 가능합니다.
(D) 당신은 여러 가지의 자연스러운 목소리와 속도 중에서 선택할 수 있습니다.

해설 빈칸에 들어갈 알맞은 문장을 고르는 문제이므로 빈칸의 주변 문맥이나 전체 문맥을 파악한다. 앞 문장 'ShockRead can turn any book into an audio book'에서 ShockRead는 그 어떤 책도 오디오북으로 바꿀 수 있다고 했으므로 빈칸에는 오디오북과 관련된 내용이 들어가야 함을 알 수 있다. 따라서 (D) You can select from several natural voices and speeds가 정답이다.

어휘 **select** adj. 선택된 **location** n. 지역, 장소

134 부사 어휘 고르기

해설 '일주일 전에 미리 주문하면 10퍼센트 할인을 누릴 수 있다'라는 문맥이므로 부사 (B) beforehand(~ 전에 미리)가 정답이다.

어휘 **anytime** adv. 언제든 **lately** adv. 최근에 **instantly** adv. 즉시

135-138은 다음 편지에 관한 문제입니다.

> Brad Warren
> 6809번지 Harvest로
> 볼더, 콜로라도주 80301
>
> Mr. Warren께,
>
> 저희가 전화로 이야기했을 때, 당신은 볼더 도심지에 식당을 열 계획이라고 말씀하셨습니다. ¹³⁵제가 당신의 새로운 가게를 위한 이상적인 장소를 찾았습니다. ¹³⁶이것은 귀하의 크기 요건을 충족시킬 뿐만 아니라, 귀하의 가격 범위 내에도 있습니다.
>
> 하지만 한 가지 조건을 아셔야 합니다. ¹³⁷소유주는 적어도 5년간 머무를 수 있는 세입자를 찾고 있습니다. 이러한 종류의 장기 임대차 계약과 관련된 위험 요소가 있다는 것을 알지만, 그는 그 장소를 꽤 저렴하게 임대할 의향이 있습니다. 그는 제가 예상했던 것보다 약 15퍼센트 더 적게 요구하고 있습니다.
>
> ¹³⁸이번 주에 이 건물을 둘러보는 것에 관심이 있으시다면 알려주세요. 만약 그렇지 않다면, 그 대신에 제가 당신과 공유할 수 있는 몇 가지 다른 대안들을 생각해 두었습니다. 제게 (303) 555-9276으로 전화 주세요.
>
> Hillary Evans 드림
> City 부동산업자

ideal adj. 이상적인 **location** n. 장소 **requirement** n. 요건, 요구 **within** prep. 내에 **range** n. 범위 **condition** n. 조건, 상태 **risk** n. 위험 (요소) **involve** v. 관련시키다, 내포하다 **lease** n. 임대차 계약 **be willing to** ~할 의향이 있다 **rent** v. 임대하다 **rather** adv. 꽤, 상당히 **cheaply** adv. 저렴하게 **property** n. 건물, 부동산 **alternative** n. 대안 **share** v. 공유하다, 나누다

135 올바른 시제의 동사 채우기 주변 문맥 파악

해설 문장에 동사가 없으므로 동사 (A), (B), (C)가 정답의 후보이다. '새로운 가게를 위한 이상적인 장소를 찾다'라는 문맥인데, 이 경우 빈칸이 있는 문장만으로는 정답을 고를 수 없으므로 주변 문맥이나 전체 문맥을 파악한다. 뒤 문장에서 '이것은 귀하의 크기 요건을 충족시킬 뿐만 아니라, 귀하의 가격 범위 내에도 있다(Not only does it meet your size requirements, but it's also within your price range)'고 했으므로 새로운 가게를 위한 이상적인 장소를 찾는 것이 방금 완료되었음을 알 수 있다. 따라서 과거에 발생한 일이 현재까지 영향을 미치거나 방금 완료된 것을 표현할 때 사용되는 현재완료 시제 (A) have found가 정답이다.

136 도치 구문 채우기

해설 부정어(Not)가 문장 맨 앞에 왔으므로 주어와 동사가 도치된 구조가 나와야 한다. 보기에 있는 동사 meet이 일반동사이므로 do 조동사(does)가 앞으로 나가고 주어(it)와 동사원형(meet)이 사용된 (B) does it meet이 정답이다. 참고로, not only A but also B가 절(does it meet ~ requirements)과 절(it's ~ range)을 연결하고 있다.

137 알맞은 문장 고르기

해석 (A) 소유주는 적어도 5년간 머무를 수 있는 세입자를 찾고 있습니다.
(B) 건설 공사가 특정 구역에서 이미 진행 중입니다.
(C) 그 건물은 가장 최근의 안전 점검을 통과하지 못했습니다.
(D) 이것이 당신이 희망했던 것보다 약간 더 작아서 유감입니다.

해설 빈칸에 들어갈 알맞은 문장을 고르는 문제이므로 빈칸의 주변 문맥이나 전체 문맥을 파악한다. 앞 문장 'You should be aware of one condition, however.'에서 알아야 할 한 가지 조건이 있다고 한 후, 뒤 문장 'I know that there is risk involved with these kinds of long-term leases'에서 이러한 종류의 장기 임대차 계약과 관련된 위험 요소가 있는 것을 안다고 했으므로 빈칸에는 장기 임대차 계약에 관한 요구 조건이 들어가야 함을 알 수 있다. 따라서 (A) The owner is looking for a tenant who can stay at least five years가 정답이다.

어휘 **owner** n. 소유주, 주인 **tenant** n. 세입자 **construction** n. 건설 공사 **underway** adj. 진행 중인 **pass** v. 통과하다 **recent** adj. 최근의 **inspection** n. 점검 **somewhat** adv. 약간, 다소

138 유사의미 동사 중에서 고르기 전체 문맥 파악

해설 '이 건물을 ___ 것에 관심이 있으면 알려달라'라는 문맥이므로 모든 보기가 정답의 후보이다. 빈칸이 있는 문장만으로 정답을 고를 수 없으므로 주변 문맥이나 전체 문맥을 파악한다. 지문 앞부분에서 발신자가 상대방의 새로운 가게를 열만한 적합한 장소를 찾았다고 한 후, 뒤 문장에서 '만약 그렇지 않다면 그 대신에 상대방과 공유할 수 있는 몇 가지 다른 대안들을 생각해 두었다(If not, I've come up with a few other alternatives that I can share with you instead.)'고 했으므로 그 장소를 둘러보는 것에 관심이 있으면 알려주고, 만약 관심이 없다면 다른 대안을 논의하자고 제안하고 있음을 알 수 있다. 따라서 '둘러보다, 살펴보다'를 의미하는 동사 view의 -ing형 (A) viewing이 정답이다. (B)의 design은 '디자인하다, 설계하다', (C)의 show는 '보여주다', (D)의 sell은 '팔다'라는 의미이므로 문맥에 어울리지 않는다.

139-142는 다음 공고에 관한 문제입니다.

> 모든 Cheswick 타워 주민들께 드리는 공고
>
> ¹³⁹많은 분들께서 평소와 다르게 높은 가스 요금에 관해 관리 사무소로 연락하셨습니다. ¹⁴⁰철저한 검사를 한 후에, 저희는 많은 계량기들이 결함이 있음을 발견했습니다. 그것들은 노후되어서 매달 사용되는 가스량을 정확하게 측정하지 못하고 있습니다. 그러므로, 저희는 각 아파트의 계량기가 교체되도록 계획했습니다. ¹⁴¹이 작업은 다음 주 중에 실시될 것입니다. 이는 문제를 해결하고, 여러분이 추후에 정확한 청구서를 받도록 보장할 것입니다.
>
> 또한, 초과 지불하셨던 분들은 배상을 받으실 것입니다. 여러분이 돌려받으실 정확한 금액은 다음 달 청구서에서 보여질 것입니다.
>
> ¹⁴²이것이 초래한 불편에 대해 사과 드립니다.

notice n. 공고 **resident** n. 주민 **a number of** 많은 **management office** 관리 사무소 **conduct** v. 하다, 처리하다 **thorough** adj. 철저한 **meter** n. 계량기 **arrange** v. 계획하다, 배치하다 **replace** v. 교체하다 **ensure** v. 보장하다 **bill** v. 청구서를 보내다; n. 청구서 **overpay** v. 초과 지불하다 **reimburse** v. 배상하다 **cause** v. 초래하다, 야기하다

139 전치사 고르기

해설 '평소와 다르게 높은 가스 요금에 관해 관리 사무소로 연락했다'는 의미가 되어야 하므로 (B) concerning(~에 관해)이 정답이다.

어휘 **between** prep. ~ 사이에 **except** prep. ~을 제외하고는

140 형용사 어휘 고르기 주변 문맥 파악

해설 '많은 계량기들이 ___ 하다'라는 문맥이므로 모든 보기가 정답의 후보이다. 빈칸이 있는 문장만으로 정답을 고를 수 없으므로 주변 문맥이나 전체 문맥을 파악한다. 뒤 문장에서 '그것들은 노후되어서 매달 사용되는 가스량을 정확하게 측정하지 못한다(They are not accurately measuring the amount of gas used each month because they are getting old.)'고 했으므로 많은 계량기가 결함이 있음을 알 수 있다. 따라서 (B) defective가 정답이다.

어휘 **absent** adj. 없는, 부재의 **hazardous** adj. 위험한 **complex** adj. 복잡한

141 알맞은 문장 고르기

해석 (A) 더 적은 에너지를 사용하기 위해 당신이 할 수 있는 일들이 있습니다.
(B) 최근에 전기 요금이 낮아지고 있습니다.
(C) 여러분은 더 이상 종이로 된 청구서를 받지 않을 것입니다.

(D) 이 작업은 다음 주 중에 실시될 것입니다.

해설   빈칸에 들어갈 알맞은 문장을 고르는 문제이므로 빈칸의 주변 문맥이나 전체 문맥을 파악한다. 앞 문장 'we have arranged for the meter in each apartment to be replaced'에서 각 아파트의 계량기가 교체되도록 계획했다고 한 후, 뒤 문장 'This should solve the problem and ensure that you are billed correctly in the future.'에서 이는 문제를 해결하고 추후 정확한 청구서를 받도록 보장할 것이라고 했으므로 빈칸에는 아파트 계량기 교체와 관련된 세부 사항이 들어가야 함을 알 수 있다. 따라서 (D) The work will be carried out sometime next week이 정답이다.

어휘   lately adv. 최근에   no longer 더 이상 ~아닌   carry out 실시하다, 수행하다

142 명사 자리 채우기

해설   전치사(for)의 목적어 자리에 올 수 있는 것은 명사이므로 한정사(any)로 수식된 명사 (A) any inconveniences가 정답이다. 형용사 (B)와 (D), 부사 (C)는 명사 자리에 올 수 없다. 참고로, 빈칸 뒤의 this has caused you는 앞의 목적어(any inconveniences)를 꾸미는 수식어 거품이며, 목적격 관계대명사 which 또는 that이 생략된 관계절이다.

143-146은 다음 기사에 관한 문제입니다.

> 음료의 새로운 선도자
>
> [143]목요일에 발표된 Regalia사 연구 보고서에 따르면, Fizz Devil사가 음료 제조업 분야에서 선두에 섰다.
>
> Regalia사의 연구원들은 Fizz Devil사가 성공적으로 스스로를 경쟁사들과 차별화시켰다고 말한다. [144]음료업계의 경향에 대응해, Fizz Devil사는 그들의 제품들을 변경했다. 마케팅 책임자 Andrea Thompson은 "저희는 사람들의 음료 선호에서 새로운 패턴을 발견했습니다. [145]그들은 설탕이 든 청량음료보다 더 나은 대안을 찾고 있었습니다. 그래서 저희는 이것을 활용하여 건강에 좋은 병 음료 제품을 개발했습니다."라고 말했다.
>
> 제품들은 전국의 상점들에서 찾을 수 있다. [146]그 제품 라인은 Homerun Thirst와 Yoga Refresh와 같은 이름의 음료들을 포함한다.

take the lead in ~에서 선두에 서다   manufacturing n. 제조업, 제조
remark v. 말하다, 언급하다   modify v. 변경하다, 수정하다
state v. 말하다, 진술하다   identify v. 발견하다   preference n. 선호(도)

143 전치사 채우기

해설   '목요일에 발표된 Regalia사 연구 보고서에 따르면'이라는 의미가 되어야 하므로 (B) according to(~에 따르면, 의하면)가 정답이다.

144 명사 어휘 고르기 주변 문맥 파악

해설   '음료업계의 ___에 대응해, 그들의 제품들을 변경했다'라는 의미가 되어야 하므로 (B) trend(경향)와 (C) decline(하락)이 정답의 후보이다. 빈칸이 있는 문장만으로 정답을 고를 수 없으므로 주변 문맥이나 전체 문맥을 파악한다. 뒤 문장에서 '사람들의 음료 선호에서 새로운 패턴을 발견했다(We identified a new pattern in people's drink preferences.)'고 했으므로 음료 시장의 경향이 바뀌고 있음을 알 수 있다. 따라서 명사 (B) trend가 정답이다.

어휘   source n. 원천, 근원   control n. 통제

145 알맞은 문장 고르기

해석   (A) 그들은 수돗물보다 깨끗한 병에 든 생수를 구매하기를 원했습니다.
     (B) 그들은 과일주스보다 탄산음료를 선호했습니다.
     (C) 그들은 설탕이 든 청량음료보다 더 나은 대안을 찾고 있었습니다.
     (D) 그들은 제조업체들이 더 작은 병에 담긴 음료를 생산하기를 원했습니다.

해설   빈칸에 들어갈 알맞은 문장을 고르는 문제이므로 빈칸의 주변 문맥이나 전체 문맥을 파악한다. 앞 문장 'We identified a new pattern in people's drink preferences.'에서 사람들의 음료 선호에서 새로운 패턴을 발견했다고 했고, 뒤 문장에서 이것을 활용하여 건강에 좋은 병 음료 제품을 개발했다(We then used this to develop a line of healthy bottled drinks.)고 했으므로 빈칸에는 사람들이 건강에 좋은 음료를 선호한다는 내용이 들어가야 함을 알 수 있다. 따라서 (C) They were seeking better alternatives to

sugary soft drinks가 정답이다.

어휘   tap water 수돗물   carbonated drink 탄산음료
alternative n. 대안, 대체물   soft drink 청량음료

146 올바른 시제의 동사 채우기

해설   문장에 동사가 없으므로 동사 (A), (B), (D)가 정답의 후보이다. '그 제품 라인은 음료들을 포함한다'라는 일반적인 특징을 표현하고 있으므로 현재 시제 (A) features가 정답이다. 과거 시제 (B)는 이미 끝난 과거의 동작이나 상태를 표현하므로 답이 될 수 없다. 분사 (C)는 동사 자리에 올 수 없다.

어휘   feature v. ~을 특별히 포함하다, 특징으로 삼다

147-148은 다음 광고지에 관한 문제입니다.

> Carbury 배관
> *배관 공사 & 배수 서비스*
>
> [148-A]이 업계에서 20년 이상의 경력을 가진 저희 배관 공사 전문가들은 진정으로 최고입니다!
>
> [147]저희는 고객님의 모든 배관 공사 문제를 처리하기 위해 다음을 포함한 많은 전문적인 서비스들을 제공합니다:
>
> ✓ 막힌 곳과 누수 보수
> ✓ 싱크대 수리
> ✓ 물 여과 장치 설치
> ✓ [148-B]보일러 교체
> ✓ 양수기 수리
> ✓ ...그리고 더 많은 것들!
>
> 이 전단지를 가지고 오셔서 무료 상담과 저희의 전문가들 중 한 명으로부터 고객님의 첫 방문으로 인한 10퍼센트 할인을 받으세요.
> 이 판촉 활동은 다른 할인과 병행될 수 없다는 것을 유의해 주세요.
>
> Carbury 배관
> 22 Pewter로
> 앨버커키, 뉴멕시코주 87111
> 555-8829

plumbing n. 배관, 배관 공사   specialized adj. 전문적인, 전문화된
address v. 처리하다   renovation n. 수리   combine v. 병행하다, 결합하다
offer n. 할인, 제공

147 주제/목적 찾기 문제

문제   광고지의 목적은 무엇인가?
     (A) 한정된 기간 동안의 할인을 홍보하기 위해
     (B) 사무실 배관 공사 작업을 알리기 위해
     (C) 새로운 배관공들을 모집하기 위해
     (D) 다양한 서비스들을 광고하기 위해

해설   광고지의 목적을 묻는 목적 찾기 문제이다. 특별히 이 문제는 지문의 중반에 목적 관련 내용이 언급되었음에 유의한다. 'We offer a number of specialized services'(2문단 1번째 줄)에서 우리는 많은 전문적인 서비스를 제공한다고 했으므로 (D) To advertise various services가 정답이다.

어휘   recruit v. 모집하다   plumber n. 배관공

148 Not/True 문제

문제   Carbury 배관의 전문가들에 대해 언급된 것은?
     (A) 30년의 경력을 갖고 있다.
     (B) 고장난 온수기를 고칠 수 있다.
     (C) 욕실 개보수를 전문으로 한다.
     (D) 그들의 웹사이트에서 판촉 행사를 하고 있다.

해설   질문의 핵심 어구인 Carbury Plumbing's specialists와 관련된 내용을 지문에서 찾아 보기와 대조하는 Not/True 문제이다. (A)는 'With more than 20 years of experience in the business, our plumbing specialists are truly the best!'(1문단 1번째 줄)에서 이 업계에서 20년 이상의 경력을 가진 우리 배관 전문가들이 진정으로 최고라고 했으므로 지문의 내용과 일치하지 않는다. (B)는 'Boiler replacements'(3문단 4번째 줄)에서 보일러

교체를 한다고 했으므로 지문의 내용과 일치한다. 따라서 (B) They can fix broken water heaters가 정답이다. (C)와 (D)는 지문에 언급되지 않은 내용이다.

Paraphrasing
Boiler 보일러 → water heaters 온수기

어휘 decade n. 10년

149-150은 다음 송장에 관한 문제입니다.

Arbinton 조경 회사 　　　　　　　　　　　　송장

37번지 Cauliflower로
댈러스, 텍사스주 75201　　　　^{150-D}오늘 날짜　　7월 6일
전화: 555-9273　　　　　　　송장 번호　　347528
팩스: 555-9274　　　　　　　고객 ID　　　893A
www.arbintonland.com　　　　¹⁴⁹지급 만기일　7월 31일

청구 대상

Mr. Cameron Reynolds
Poindexter 제약
500번지 Emory가
댈러스, 텍사스주 75221
555-6723

설명	총액
서비스 요금: 정원 설계	230.00달러
인건비: 시간당 $20달러씩 18시간	360.00달러
소계	590.00달러

의견		
1. 고객님의 수표에 송장 번호를 포함시켜주십시오.	^{150-B}4.5%의 세금	26.55달러
	*기타	75.50달러
2. ^{150-D}6월 6일 송장에서의 한 물품에 대한 가격 오류를 바로잡기 위해 요금이 추가되었습니다.	합계	692.05달러
	모든 수표는 Arbinton 조경 회사로 지불되게 해주십시오.	

^{150-C}만약 문의 사항이 있으시다면, 이곳으로 연락해주십시오:
Mark Devers, 555-2268, m_devers@arbintonland.com
고객님의 거래에 감사드립니다!

due date 만기일　labor charge 인건비　correct v. 바로잡다, 정정하다

149 육하원칙 문제

문제 Mr. Reynolds는 7월 31일까지 무엇을 해야 하는가?
(A) 그의 고객 신원 확인 번호를 확인한다.
(B) 새로운 송장을 위해 Arbinton사에 연락한다.
(C) 추가 요금에 대해 문의한다.
(D) 전체 송장 금액을 지불한다.

해설 Mr. Reynolds가 7월 31일까지 무엇(What)을 해야 하는지를 묻는 육하원칙 문제이다. 질문의 핵심 어구인 July 31과 관련하여, 'Due Date, July 31'(INVOICE 하단 4번째 줄)에서 지급 만기일이 7월 31일이라고 했으므로 (D) Pay the total invoice amount가 정답이다.

어휘 identification n. 신원 확인, 신분증　additional adj. 추가의

150 Not/True 문제

문제 송장에서 언급되지 않은 것은?
(A) 설계 요금은 시간제로 청구되었다.
(B) 세금이 총액에 추가되었다.
(C) Mr. Devers는 문의 전화를 받을 수도 있다.
(D) 지난달의 송장에 착오가 있었다.

해설 질문의 핵심 어구인 invoice와 관련된 내용을 지문에서 찾아 보기와 대조하는 Not/True 문제이다. (A)는 지문에 언급되지 않은 내용이다. 따라서 (A) Design fees were charged by the hour가 정답이다. (B)는 'Tax at 4.5%'(comments 옆 표 1번째 줄)에서 세금이 총액에 추가되었으므로 지문의 내용과 일치한다. (C)는 'If you have any questions, please contact: Mark Devers, 555-2268'(청구서 하단 1번째 줄)에서 문의 사항이 있다면,

Mark Devers에게 555-2268로 연락해 달라고 했으므로 지문의 내용과 일치한다. (D)는 'Today's Date, July 6'(INVOICE 하단 1번째 줄)에서 오늘 날짜가 7월 6일이라고 했고, 'Charge was added to correct a pricing error for an item on the June 6 invoice.'(Comments 하단 2번째 줄)에서 6월 6일 송장에서의 가격 오류를 바로잡기 위해 요금이 추가되었다고 했으므로 지문의 내용과 일치한다.

Paraphrasing
error 오류 → mistake 착오

어휘 charge v. 청구하다　by the hour 시간제로　inquiry n. 문의, 질문

151-152는 다음 메시지 대화문에 관한 문제입니다.

Emily Jones　　　　　　　　　　　　[오후 2:20]
^{151-A}연례 안전 워크숍이 곧 있을 예정인데, 저는 그것에 대해 별로 들은 것이 없어요. 어디에서 열릴 예정인지 아시나요?

Chris Cochran　　　　　　　　　　　[오후 2:21]
Greenwood 사무실이요. ^{151-B}사실 모든 정보가 방금 회사 웹사이트에 게시되었어요.

Emily Jones　　　　　　　　　　　　[오후 2:25]
아, 그렇군요. ¹⁵²Greenwood가 차로 3시간 정도 떨어진 데 있다고 나와 있어요. 상당한 주행 거리네요.

Chris Cochran　　　　　　　　　　　[오후 2:27]
전적으로 동의해요. 작년에는 장소가 훨씬 더 가까웠어요. 어쨌든, Mr. Tate가 우리가 함께 갈 수 있도록 두 대의 큰 SUV를 빌릴 거라고 했어요.

Emily Jones　　　　　　　　　　　　[오후 2:28]
괜찮은 것 같네요. 우리는 언제 떠나나요?

Chris Cochran　　　　　　　　　　　[오후 2:30]
^{151-C}수요일 오후에 출발해서, 이틀 내내 연수를 하고, 워크숍이 끝나면 금요일 밤에 돌아올 거예요.

Emily Jones　　　　　　　　　　　　[오후 2:31]
알겠어요. 그럼 수요일에 봐요. 정보 고마워요, Chris.

annual adj. 연례의, 매년의　post v. 게시하다, 공고하다; n. 우편물
quite adv. 상당히, 꽤　totally adv. 전적으로, 완전히　venue n. 장소

151 Not/True 문제

문제 안전 워크숍에 대해 언급되지 않은 것은?
(A) 매년 열린다.
(B) 세부 사항은 온라인에서 찾을 수 있다.
(C) 이틀간의 연수를 포함한다
(D) 참석하는 것이 의무적이지 않다.

해설 질문의 핵심 어구인 safety workshops와 관련된 내용을 지문에서 찾아 보기와 대조하는 Not/True 문제이다. (A)는 'The annual safety workshops are coming up soon'(2:20 P.M.)에서 연례 안전 워크숍이 곧 있을 예정이라고 했으므로 지문의 내용과 일치한다. (B)는 'All the information was actually just posted on the company Web site.'(2:21 P.M.)에서 사실 모든 정보가 방금 회사 웹사이트에 게시되었다고 했으므로 지문의 내용과 일치한다. (C)는 'We'll leave on Wednesday afternoon, do two full days of training, and head back Friday night once the workshops are done.'(2:30 P.M.)에서 수요일 오후에 출발해서 이틀 내내 연수를 하고 워크숍이 끝나면 금요일 밤에 돌아올 것이라고 했으므로 지문의 내용과 일치한다. (D)는 지문에서 언급되지 않은 내용이다. 따라서 (D) It is not mandatory to attend them이 정답이다.

어휘 detail n. 세부 사항, 정보　mandatory adj. 의무적인, 필수의

152 의도 파악 문제

문제 오후 2시 27분에, Mr. Cochran이 "I totally agree"라고 썼을 때, 그가 의도한 것은?
(A) 장소까지의 거리에 대해 걱정하고 있다.
(B) 차량의 크기에 대해 걱정하고 있다.
(C) 추가적인 수업이 제공되어야 한다고 생각한다.
(D) 자신들이 목요일에 돌아와야 한다고 생각한다.

해설 Mr. Cochran이 의도한 것을 묻는 문제이므로, 질문의 인용어구(I totally agree)가 언급된 주변 문맥을 확인한다. 'Greenwood is about three hours away by car. That's quite a drive.'(2:25 P.M.)에서 Emily Jones가 Greenwood, 즉 워크숍이 열릴 장소가 차로 3시간 정도 떨어진 데 있다고 하면서 상당한 주행 거리라고 하자, Mr. Cochran이 'I totally agree'(전적으로 동의해요)라고 한 것을 통해, Mr. Cochran이 워크숍 장소까지의 거리에 대해 걱정하고 있다는 것을 알 수 있다. 따라서 (A) He is concerned about the distance to a venue가 정답이다.

어휘 **vehicle** n. 차량

153-154는 다음 편지에 관한 문제입니다.

Vanter 은행
790번지 West 32번가, 뉴욕, 뉴욕주 10105

6월 10일

Mr. Oscar Morrison
63번지 Packerston로
포킵시, 뉴욕주 12601

Mr. Morrison께,

저희 콜센터는 고객님의 계좌와 관련해 저희가 갖고 있는 문제에 대해 고객님께 연락하려고 몇 차례 시도했으나 실패했습니다. [154-C]만약 7월 11일 금요일까지 고객님으로부터 연락이 없다면, 고객님의 소기업 저축 계좌가 닫힐 것임을 숙지해 주십시오. 그날, [154-A/D]저희는 또한 고객님의 남아 있는 잔액 350달러를 외부적으로 연결된 고객님의 Fulton 은행의 당좌 예금 계좌로 이체할 것입니다.

가능한 한 빨리 1-800-555-2996으로 저희에게 전화주십시오. 저희는 월요일부터 금요일까지, 오전 8시부터 오후 9시까지 고객님을 돕기 위해 이곳에 있습니다. [153]저희에게 연락하실 때 문제 조회 번호인 100076965를 이용해 주십시오.

Vanter 은행을 선택해 주셔서 감사합니다.

Louise Robertson 드림
Vanter 은행 예금 사원

---

account n. 계좌 **savings** n. 저축, 저금 **transfer** v. 이체하다, 이전하다
balance n. 잔액, 잔고 **externally** adj. 외부적으로, 외부에서
issue n. 문제, 발행 **reference number** 조회 번호

---

153 추론 문제

문제 Mr. Morrison에 대해 암시되는 것은?
(A) 직원에게 조회 암호를 제공할 것이다.
(B) Vanter사에 그의 기업 계좌를 닫아 달라고 요청했다.
(C) 전화로 연락 받기를 바라고 있다.
(D) Ms. Robertson에게 이메일 주소를 주는 것을 잊어버렸다.

해설 질문의 핵심 어구인 Mr. Morrison에 대해 추론하는 문제이다. 'Please use issue reference number 100076965 when you contact us.'(2문단 2번째 줄)에서 은행으로 연락할 때 문제 조회 번호인 100076965를 이용해 달라고 한 내용을 통해 Mr. Morrison이 직원에게 조회 암호를 제공할 것이라는 사실을 추론할 수 있다. 따라서 (A) He will provide a reference code to a representative가 정답이다.

어휘 **representative** n. 직원, 대리인

---

154 Not/True 문제

문제 예금 계좌에 대해 언급되지 않은 것은?
(A) 인출 가능한 자금이 아직 있다.
(B) 월간 이체 한도에 이르렀다.
(C) 조치가 취해지지 않는다면 닫힐 수도 있다.
(D) 다른 기관의 계좌에 연결되어 있다.

해설 질문의 핵심 어구인 savings account와 관련된 내용을 지문에서 찾아 보기와 대조하는 Not/True 문제이다. (A)는 'we will also transfer your remaining balance of $350.00'(1문단 3번째 줄)에서 남아 있는 잔액 350달러를 이체할 것이라고 했으므로 지문의 내용과 일치한다. (B)는 지문에 언급되지 않은 내용이다. 따라서 (B) It has reached the monthly

---

transfer limit이 정답이다. (C)는 'if we do not hear from you ~ your small business savings account will be closed'(1문단 2번째 줄)에서 연락이 없다면 소기업 저축 계좌가 닫힐 것이라고 했으므로 지문의 내용과 일치한다. (D)는 'we will also transfer your remaining balance of $350.00 to your externally linked checking account at the Bank of Fulton'(1문단 3번째 줄)에서 남아 있는 잔액을 외부적으로 연결된 Fulton 은행의 당좌 예금 계좌로 이체할 것이라고 했으므로 지문의 내용과 일치한다.

어휘 **fund** n. 자금 **withdrawal** n. 인출 **reach** v. ~에 이르다, 달하다
limit n. 한도, 제한 **institution** n. 기관, 단체

155-157은 다음 안내문에 관한 문제입니다.

---

[155]기밀 유지 협약

이 협약의 모든 의도와 목적에 따라, "기밀 정보"는 Viridian International사에서의 고용 기간 동안 피고용인들에게 노출된 모든 기업 자료에 적용될 것입니다. 이러한 정보는 오로지 회사의 소유물로 간주될 것이며 개인적이고 사적인 용도를 위한 것이 아닙니다. [156-B]기밀 유지 협약은 회사와 그것의 사업에 대한 모든 다른 관련 세부 사항에 더해 모든 서류, 보고서, 제안서, 디자인, 기술, 모형 및 연구 자료에 적용됩니다. [156-A]모든 구두 및 서면 의사소통 또한 기밀 정보로 간주되어야 합니다.

이 협약서에 서명하면서, 피고용인은 다음에 동의합니다:

1. 기밀 정보는 회사의 사전 허가 없이는 어떤 방법으로든 타인에게 이전될 수 없습니다.
2. [156-D]기밀 정보는 어떤 이유로든 복제될 수 없습니다.
3. [156-C]피고용인의 회사 근무 기간 동안 회사와 관련된 자료로 이루어진 모든 산물 역시 기밀 정보로 간주될 것입니다.
4. [157]고용 계약의 종료에 따라, 피고용인들은 기밀 정보로의 접근을 포함한 모든 특권을 잃을 것입니다.

---

non-disclosure agreement 기밀 유지 협약
confidential adj. 기밀의, 비밀의 **refer** v. 적용되다, 관련되다
solely adv. 오로지, 다만 **property** n. 소유물, 재산 **verbal** adj. 구두의
duplicate v. 복제하다, 베끼다 **termination** n. 종료, 종결
privilege n. 특권, 특전

---

155 주제/목적 찾기 문제

문제 안내문의 목적은 무엇인가?
(A) 직원들에게 회사 정책에 대해 교육하기 위해
(B) 정책 변화를 강조하기 위해
(C) 피고용인 권리를 보호하기 위해
(D) 일자리를 제의하기 위해

해설 안내문의 목적을 묻는 목적 찾기 문제이다. 특별히 이 문제는 전체 지문을 요약하여 목적을 찾아야 한다. 'Non-Disclosure Agreement'(제목)에서 안내문이 기밀 유지 협약에 관한 것임을 알 수 있고 'For all intentions and purposes of this agreement, "confidential information" will refer to any corporate data revealed to employees of Viridian International throughout their employment with the company.'(1문단 1번째 줄)에서 이 협약의 모든 의도와 목적에 따라, 기밀 정보는 Viridian International사에서의 고용 기간 동안 피고용인들에게 노출된 모든 기업 자료에 적용될 것이라고 한 후, 기밀 정보를 노출시키지 않기 위한 회사 규정을 나열했으므로 (A) To educate staff on company policy가 정답이다.

---

156 Not/True 문제

문제 기밀 정보에 대해 언급되지 않은 것은?
(A) 두 사람 사이에서 말해질 수 있다.
(B) 다양한 다른 문서들을 포함한다.
(C) 피고용인들이 회사를 위해 만드는 자료들을 포함한다.
(D) 관리자의 허가가 있으면 복제될 수 있다.

해설 질문의 핵심 어구인 confidential information과 관련된 내용을 지문에서 찾아 보기와 대조하는 Not/True 문제이다. (A)는 'All verbal ~ communication should also be considered confidential information.'(1문단 6번째 줄)에서 모든 구두 의사소통 또한 기밀 정보로 간주되어야 한다고 했으므로 지문의 내용과 일치한다. (B)는 'The non-disclosure agreement applies to all forms, reports, proposals, designs, techniques, models, and research data, along with any other related details of the company and its business.'(1문단 4번째 줄)에서 기밀 유지 협약은 회사와 그것의 사업에 대한 모든 다른 관련 세부 사항에 더해 모든 서류, 보고서, 제안서, 디자인, 기술, 모형 및 연구 자료에 적용된다고 했으므로 지문의 내용과 일치한다. (C)는 'Any creation of company-related material ~ will also be considered confidential information.'(2문단 5번째 줄)에서 회사와 관련된 자료로 이루어진 모든 산물 역시 기밀 정보로 간주될 것이라고 했으므로 지문의 내용과 일치한다. (D)는 'No confidential information will be duplicated for any reason.'(2문단 4번째 줄)에서 기밀 정보는 어떤 이유로든 복제될 수 없다고 했으므로 지문의 내용과 일치하지 않는다. 따라서 (D) It can be copied with managerial consent가 정답이다.

어휘 **managerial** adj. 관리자의, 관리상의 **consent** n. 허가, 동의

157 육하원칙 문제

문제 직원들은 계약이 끝나면 무엇을 해야 하는가?

(A) 회사 자료에 대한 접근을 그만둔다
(B) 개별적인 협약에 서명한다
(C) 퇴직자 면접에 참여한다
(D) 관련 없는 산업에서 일자리를 구한다

해설 직원들이 계약이 끝나면 무엇(What)을 해야 하는지를 묻는 육하원칙 문제이다. 질문의 핵심 어구인 at the end of their contracts와 관련하여, 'Upon termination of an employment contract, employees will lose all privileges, including access to confidential information.'(2문단 7번째 줄)에서 고용 계약의 종료에 따라, 피고용인들은 기밀 정보로의 접근을 포함한 모든 특권을 잃을 것이라고 했으므로 (A) Give up access to company data가 정답이다.

Paraphrasing
at the end of their contracts 계약이 끝나면 → Upon termination of an employment contract 고용 계약의 종료에 따라

어휘 **give up** 그만두다, 포기하다 **separate** adj. 개별적인
exit interview 퇴직자 면접 **unrelated** adj. 관련 없는, 언급되지 않은

158-160은 다음 공고에 관한 문제입니다.

Mount Victory 리프트 시간 변경

지역 내 최고의 관광 명소 중 하나인 Mount Victory 리프트는 하절기 영업 시간을 연장합니다. — [1] —. 겨울에, 리프트는 스키 타는 사람들을 산 정상까지 나르고 그들이 정상의 많은 코스들 중 하나를 내려오는 것을 즐길 수 있도록 합니다. 158-B여름 동안, 158-C/160방문객들은 리프트를 타고 정상까지 가서, Mountaineer 레스토랑에서 경치를 즐길 수 있습니다. — [2] —.

길어진 여름을 이용하기 위해, 158-DMount Victory 리프트는 이제 오전 8시부터 오후 10시까지 운행합니다. — [3] —. 158-DMountaineer 레스토랑 또한 손님들의 편의를 위해 이용 시간을 오전 8시부터 오후 9시까지 연장합니다. — [4] —.

보도를 하이킹하고 싶으신 분들을 위해. 공원 경비원들은 159길은 하루 중 아무 때나 개방되지만, 밤 시간은 피하는 것이 제일 좋다는 점을 모든 분들께 상기시켜 드립니다. 159야생 동물들에 의해 제기되는 위험뿐만 아니라, 그 시간은 잘 보기가 어렵고, 하이커들이 길을 잃거나 다칠 수 있습니다. 또한, "출입 금지"라고 표시된 모든 길들은 항상 피하셔야 합니다.

tourist attraction 관광 명소 **region** n. 지역 **extend** v. 연장하다, 늘리다
trail n. 코스, 산길 **take advantage of** ~을 이용하다
convenience n. 편의 **park ranger** 공원 경비원
pose v. 제기하다, 자세를 취하다 **wild animal** 야생 동물 **off limits** 출입 금지의

158 Not/True 문제

문제 리프트에 대해 언급된 것은?

(A) 하이커들의 이용을 위해 예약되어 있다.
(B) 겨울에 해당하는 달에만 작동된다.
(C) 산의 정상에서 끝난다.
(D) 식당과 영업시간이 같다.

해설 질문의 핵심 어구인 chairlift와 관련된 내용을 지문에서 찾아 보기와 대조

하는 Not/True 문제이다. (A)는 지문에 언급되지 않은 내용이다. (B)는 'During the summer, visitors can ride'(1문단 3번째 줄)에서 여름 동안 방문객들이 리프트를 탈 수 있다고 했으므로 지문의 내용과 일치하지 않는다. (C)는 'visitors can ride up to the top'(1문단 4번째 줄)에서 방문객들은 정상까지 타고 간다고 했으므로 (C) It ends at the top of the mountain이 정답이다. (D)는 'chairlift is now running from 8 A.M. to 10 P.M.'(2문단 1번째 줄)에서 리프트는 이제 오전 8시부터 오후 10시까지 운행한다고 했고, 'Restaurant is ~ extending its service hours from 8 A.M. through 9 P.M.'(2문단 2번째 줄)에서 레스토랑은 운영 시간을 오전 8시부터 오후 9시까지로 연장한다고 했으므로 지문의 내용과 일치하지 않는다.

어휘 **reserve** v. 예약하다, 남겨 두다 **establishment** n. 시설, 설립

159 추론 문제

문제 산길에 대해 암시되는 것은?

(A) 종종 나무들에 의해 막혀 있다.
(B) 여름에는 들어갈 수 없다.
(C) 낮에 더 안전하다.
(D) 야생 동물들을 보기 위해 만들어졌다.

해설 질문의 핵심 어구인 mountain paths에 대해 추론하는 문제이다. 'tracks are ~ best to avoid ~ at night'(3문단 2번째 줄)에서 길은 밤 시간에 피하는 것이 좋다고 한 후, 'In addition to the danger posed by wild animals, it can be difficult to see, and hikers can get lost or injured.'(3문단 2번째 줄)에서 야생 동물들에 의해 제기되는 위험뿐만 아니라, 잘 보기가 어렵고 하이커들이 길을 잃거나 다칠 수 있다고 했으므로 산길이 낮에 더 안전하다는 사실을 추론할 수 있다. 따라서 (C) They are safer during the day가 정답이다.

어휘 **inaccessible** adj. 들어갈 수 없는, 접근하기 어려운
intended adj. ~을 위해 만들어진

160 문장 위치 찾기 문제

문제 [1], [2], [3], [4]로 표시된 위치 중, 다음 문장이 들어갈 곳으로 가장 적절한 것은?

"그들은 그 다음에 리프트를 타거나 하이킹하여 산을 내려올 수 있습니다."

(A) [1]
(B) [2]
(C) [3]
(D) [4]

해설 지문의 흐름상 주어진 문장이 들어가기에 가장 적절한 곳을 고르는 문제이다. They can then either take the lift or hike back down the mountain에서 그들은 그 다음에 리프트를 타거나 하이킹하여 산을 내려올 수 있다고 했으므로, 주어진 문장 앞에 산을 오르는 것에 관한 내용이 있을 것임을 예상할 수 있다. [2]의 앞 문장이 'visitors can ride up to the top'(1문단 4번째 줄)에서 방문객들은 리프트를 타고 정상까지 간다고 했으므로, [2]에 주어진 문장이 들어가면 리프트를 타고 정상에 오른 다음에 리프트를 타거나 하이킹하여 산을 내려올 수 있다는 자연스러운 문맥이 된다는 것을 알 수 있다. 따라서 (B) [2]가 정답이다.

161-163은 다음 웹페이지에 관한 문제입니다.

Redfield시
Redfield 시청의 공식 웹사이트

홈 | 온라인 서비스 | 공고 | 자주 묻는 질문

161자주 묻는 질문

1. Redfield 시청의 근무 시간은 어떻게 되나요?
Redfield 시청의 모든 부서들은 월요일부터 금요일, 오전 8시부터 오후 5시까지 열려 있습니다. 본 관청은 또한 주말에도 오전 8시부터 오후 2시까지 열려 있습니다. Redfield 시청은 모든 국경일에는 닫는다는 것을 유념해 주십시오.

2. 부서 명부는 어디에서 찾을 수 있나요?
162부서들과 각 부서장들은 상단의 주요 내비게이션 바의 온라인 서비스를 클릭함으로써 찾을 수 있습니다. 각 부서의 연락 정보는 그 페이지의 시청 부서 하단에 열거되어 있을 것입니다. 부서 위원회 회원들의 이메일 주소 역시 각

부서장 아래에 열거되어 있을 것입니다.

3. Redfield 시청의 ^{163-C}주간 이메일 공고를 신청하려면 어떻게 해야 하나요? 고객님의 이메일 주소를 저희에게 신청하시려면, 메인 툴바의 공고에 가시면 됩니다. 그러고 나서 왼쪽에 E-mail 공고라고 표시된 링크를 클릭하고 구독을 위한 단계를 따라가시면 됩니다. ^{163-B}특정 이메일 공급업체들은 Redfield 시청으로부터의 이메일 공고를 인지하지 못한다는 것을 유념해 주십시오. ^{163-D}정확한 수신을 위해, 이메일 공고가 스팸으로 표시된 것은 반드시 체크를 해제해 주십시오.

official adj. 공식의, 공인된 **department** n. 부서, 부처
note v. 유념하다, 주목하다 **national holiday** 국경일
respective adj. 각각의, 각자의 **division** n. 부서, 부
notification n. 공고, 통지 **subscribe** v. 구독하다, 가입하다
transmission n. 수신, 전송

161 주제/목적 찾기 문제

문제 웹페이지는 왜 만들어졌는가?
(A) 시민들이 투표를 위해 등록하는 것을 장려하기 위해
(B) 주민들에게 시청의 위치를 알리기 위해
(C) 흔히 하는 질문에 대한 답변을 제공하기 위해
(D) 방문객들에게 도시의 역사를 설명하기 위해

해설 웹페이지가 만들어진 목적을 묻는 목적 찾기 문제이다. 'Frequently Asked Questions'(상단 제목)에서 자주 묻는 질문이라고 한 후, Redfield 시청에 대한 질문들에 대해 답변을 제공하고 있으므로 (C) To provide answers to common questions가 정답이다.

Paraphrasing
Frequently Asked Questions 자주 묻는 질문 → common questions
흔히 하는 질문들

어휘 **register** v. 등록하다 **vote** v. 투표하다 **direction** n. 위치

162 육하원칙 문제

문제 방문객들은 어떻게 부서장들의 연락처 정보를 찾을 수 있는가?
(A) 위원회 회원들에게 이메일을 보냄으로써
(B) 본청에 직접 전화함으로써
(C) 웹사이트에서 계정을 만듦으로써
(D) 상단의 링크를 클릭함으로써

해설 방문객들이 부서장들의 연락처 정보를 어떻게(How) 찾을 수 있는지를 묻는 육하원칙 문제이다. 질문의 핵심 어구인 contact information for department heads와 관련하여, 'Departments and respective division heads can be found by clicking on Online Services on the main navigation bar above.'(2문단 2번째 줄)에서 부서들과 각 부서장들은 상단의 주요 내비게이션 바의 온라인 서비스를 클릭함으로써 찾을 수 있다고 했고, 'Contact information for each department will be listed ~ on that page.'(2문단 3번째 줄)에서 각 부서의 연락 정보는 그 페이지에 열거될 것이라고 했으므로 (D) By clicking on a link at the top이 정답이다.

163 Not/True 문제

문제 이메일 공고에 대해 언급된 것은?
(A) 양식을 기입함으로써 요청될 수 있다.
(B) 모든 이메일 공급업체들에 의해 인지된다.
(C) 매주 두 번 발송된다.
(D) 스팸 메시지로 오인될 수 있다.

해설 질문의 핵심 어구인 e-mail notifications와 관련된 내용을 지문에서 찾아 보기와 대조하는 Not/True 문제이다. (A)는 지문에 언급되지 않은 내용이다. (B)는 'certain e-mail providers may not recognize e-mail notifications from Redfield Town Hall'(3문단 3번째 줄)에서 특정 이메일 공급업체들은 Redfield 시청으로부터의 이메일 공고를 인지하지 못한다고 했으므로 지문의 내용과 일치하지 않는다. (C)는 'weekly e-mail notifications'(3문단 1번째 줄)에서 주간 이메일 공고라고 했으므로 지문의 내용과 일치하지 않는다. (D)는 'Be sure to uncheck e-mail notifications labeled as spam to allow for proper transmission.'(3문단 4번째 줄)에서 정확한 수신을 위해, 이메일 공고가 스팸으로 표시된 것은 반드시 체크를 해제해달라고 했으므로 지문의 내용과 일치한다. 따라서 (D)

They may be mistaken for spam messages가 정답이다.

어휘 **fill out** 기입하다 **mistake for** ~으로 오인하다

164-167은 다음 온라인 채팅 대화문에 관한 문제입니다.

Wendy Tran 오후 3:32
안녕하세요. Hogan's Fish and Chips의 유리잔에 관해 이야기할 수 있을까요?

Vincent Chou 오후 3:33
주문 번호 272480이죠, 맞나요?

Wendy Tran 오후 3:35
네, 바로 그거예요. ¹⁶⁴소유주인 Ms. Lin이 그녀의 로고 디자인을 변경하고 싶어 하는데, 저는 그녀가 수정된 이미지를 보내주기를 아직도 기다리고 있어요.

Vincent Chou 오후 3:36
아. 우리는 그녀의 견본품을 마무리하려던 참이었어요.

Wendy Tran 오후 3:37
성가시다는 것을 이해하지만, ¹⁶⁴우리는 그녀의 요구를 충족시켜야 해요. 도움이 될지 모르겠지만, 그녀가 새로운 디자인을 7월 8일까지 이메일로 보내줄 수 있다고 했어요.

Vincent Chou 오후 3:38
하지만 우리는 곧 시작될 또 다른 프로젝트가 있어요. 우리는 목요일에 Kerala Curry House의 디자인 작업을 시작해야 해요. ¹⁶⁶유감이지만 Ms. Lin이 마감기한을 연장해야 할 것 같네요.

Wendy Tran 오후 3:40
그건 가능하지 않을 것 같아요. ¹⁶⁶Hogan's는 8월 1일에 문을 열기로 되어 있어서, 2주 내에 모든 것이 준비되어야 해요. 제가 Ms. Lin과 이야기해볼게요.

Wendy Tran 오후 3:46
좋아요, ¹⁶⁵그녀가 7월 6일 오전 8시까지 새로운 디자인을 보내는 것에 동의하도록 했어요. 그건 충분한 시간이죠, 그렇죠?

Vincent Chou 오후 3:47
좋은 것 같네요. ¹⁶⁵우리는 같은 날 오후에 견본품을 보내서 그녀가 그다음 날 아침에 받도록 할 수 있어요. 그녀에게 완전한 주문품을 위해서는 확정 후에 2주를 기다려야 할 것이라고 상기시켜 주세요. ¹⁶⁷1주 신속 작업 방식을 위해 비용을 지불하는 경우 외에는, 그것이 모든 고객들에 대한 우리의 방침이에요.

Wendy Tran 오후 3:48
그러고 보니 생각나네요—¹⁶⁷Abelardo's의 관리자가 그의 커피잔에 관해 전화했어요. 그는 그것들이 가능한 한 빨리 필요하다고 그 옵션을 구매했어요.

owner n. 소유주, 주인 **revised** adj. 수정된, 변경된
satisfy v. 충족시키다, 만족시키다 **request** n. 요구, 요청 **extend** v. 연장하다
deadline n. 마감 기한 **remind** v. 상기시키다 **confirmation** n. 확정, 확인
policy n. 방침, 정책

164 주제/목적 찾기 문제

문제 주로 논의되고 있는 것은 무엇인가?
(A) 견본 이미지를 제작하는 것
(B) 생산 시설을 방문하는 것
(C) 고객의 요청을 받아들이는 것
(D) 제품 출시 행사에 참석하는 것

해설 주로 논의되는 것이 무엇인지를 묻는 주제 찾기 문제이므로 지문의 앞부분을 주의 깊게 확인한다. 'Ms. Lin, the owner, wants to change her logo design'(3:35 P.M.)에서 Wendy Tran이 소유주인 Ms. Lin이 로고 디자인을 변경하고 싶어 한다고 한 후, 'we need to satisfy her request'(3:37 P.M.)에서 그녀, 즉 고객의 요구를 충족시켜야 한다고 하며 충족시킬 방법에 대해 이야기하고 있으므로 (C) Accommodating a client's request가 정답이다.

Paraphrasing
satisfy ~ request 요구를 충족시키다 → Accommodating ~ request
요청을 받아들이는 것

어휘 **accommodate** v. 받아들이다, 수용하다 **attend** v. 참석하다
launch n. 출시 (행사)

165 육하원칙 문제

문제 Ms. Lin은 언제 견본품을 받을 것인가?

(A) 7월 6일
(B) 7월 7일
(C) 7월 8일
(D) 8월 1일

해설 Ms. Lin이 언제(When) 견본품을 받을 것인지를 묻는 육하원칙 문제이다. 질문의 핵심 어구인 Ms. Lin receive the sample product와 관련하여, 'I got her to agree to send the new design by 8 A.M. on July 6'(3:46 P.M.)에서 Wendy Tran이 7월 6일 오전 8시까지 새로운 디자인을 보내는 것에 그녀, 즉 Ms. Lin이 동의하도록 했다고 했고, 'We can ship out the sample product the same afternoon so she receives it the following morning.'(3:47 P.M.)에서 Vincent Chou가 자신들이 같은 날 오후에 견본품을 보내서 Ms. Lin이 그 다음 날 아침에 받도록 할 수 있을 것이라고 했으므로 7월 6일 다음 날인 7월 7일에 Ms. Lin이 견본품을 받을 것임을 알 수 있다. 따라서 (B) July 7가 정답이다.

166 의도 파악 문제

문제 오후 3시 40분에, Ms. Tran이 "I don't think that's possible"이라고 썼을 때, 그녀가 의도한 것은?

(A) 디자인이 승인될 수 없다.
(B) 마감 기한이 연장될 수 없다.
(C) 고객이 연락될 수 없다.
(D) 주문품이 배송될 수 없다.

해설 Ms. Tran이 의도한 것을 묻는 문제이므로, 질문의 인용어구(I don't think that's possible)가 언급된 주변 문맥을 확인한다. 'I'm afraid Ms. Lin will need to extend the deadline.'(3:38 P.M.)에서 Vincent Chou가 유감이지만 Ms. Lin이 마감 기한을 연장해야 할 것 같다고 하자, Ms. Tran이 'I don't think that's possible'(그건 가능하지 않을 것 같아요)'이라고 한 후, 'Hogan's is supposed to open on August 1, and everything has to be ready within two weeks.'(3:40 P.M.)에서 Hogan's가 8월 1일에 문을 열기로 되어 있어서 2주 내에 모든 것이 준비되어야 한다고 한 것을 통해, Ms. Tran은 마감 기한이 연장될 수 없다고 생각한다는 것을 알 수 있다. 따라서 (B) A deadline cannot be extended가 정답이다.

어휘 approve v. 승인하다, 찬성하다

167 추론 문제

문제 Abelardo's에 대해 암시되는 것은?

(A) 8월 1일에 문을 열 것이다.
(B) 새로운 음료 종류를 출시하였다.
(C) 그곳의 주문품은 일주일 내에 준비될 것이다.
(D) 그곳의 경영진이 최근에 바뀌었다.

해설 질문의 핵심 어구인 Abelardo's에 대해 추론하는 문제이다. 'That is our policy for all clients unless they pay for our one-week expedited work plan.'(3:47 P.M.)에서 Mr. Chou가 1주 신속 작업 방식을 위해 비용을 지불하는 경우 외에는 그것, 즉 완전한 주문을 위해 2주를 기다리는 것이 모든 고객에 대한 방침이라고 하자, 'the manager of Abelardo's called about his coffee cups. He needs them as soon as possible and purchased that option.'(3:48 P.M.)에서 Ms. Tran이 Abelardo's의 관리자가 그의 커피잔들이 가능한 한 빨리 필요하다고 그 옵션, 즉 1주 신속 작업 방식을 구매했다고 했으므로 Abelardo's의 주문품이 일주일 내에 준비될 것이라는 사실을 추론할 수 있다. 따라서 (C) Its order will be ready in a week가 정답이다.

어휘 management n. 경영(진)

168-171은 다음 이메일에 관한 문제입니다.

수신: Robert Kane <r_kane@robkanedesigns.com>
발신: Victoria Lim <v_lim@nowtrendingmag.com>
[169]날짜: 10월 25일
제목: 고맙습니다!
첨부 파일: 입장권

Robert께,

[169]저희가 지난달 귀하를 인터뷰한 사설이 이제 Now trending지의 11월호로 출간된다는 것을 알려드리게 되어 매우 기쁩니다.

업계의 전설로서, 저희 Now trending지는 귀하의 브랜드와 가을 패션에 대한 비전에 대해 이야기하게 되어 기뻤습니다. 사진 촬영 또한 Ashley가 사진들이 굉장히 아름답게 나왔다고 공언할 만큼, 놀라운 성공임이 판명되었습니다.

[168]첨부된 것에서 최종판 두 권을 인터뷰와 사진 촬영에 대한 보수인 수표와 함께 확인해 주시기를 바랍니다. 덧붙여, 저의 비서 [170]Gina가 말하기를 귀하께 다음 주 금요일, 11월 2일에 Salinger 센터에서 곧 있을 저희 축제에 대해 알려드렸을 때 아주 흥미로워하셨다고 했습니다. 그러므로, 오후 7시 30분에 시작하는 행사 입장을 위한 귀하와 한 명의 손님에 대한 입장권도 확인해 주시기 바랍니다. [171]귀하께서 오실 수 있는지 없는지 여부를 저에게 최대한 빨리 이메일로 알려주시길 요청드립니다. 귀하와 동행하는 손님이 있다면, 그 분의 이름도 필요합니다.

Victoria Lim 드림
편집장
Now Trending지

attachment n. 첨부 파일, 부착물 editorial n. 사설
marvelous adj. 놀라운 profess v. 공언하다, 주장하다
gala n. 축제, 경축 행사 intrigued adj. 아주 흥미로워 하는 pass n. 입장권
notify v. 알리다, 통지하다 accompany v. 동행하다, 수반하다

168 주제/목적 찾기 문제

문제 이메일은 왜 쓰였는가?

(A) 사업 상담을 준비하기 위해
(B) 사진 촬영 이미지의 승인을 요청하기 위해
(C) 고객을 연례 축제에 초대하기 위해
(D) 제공된 서비스에 대한 보수를 제공하기 위해

해설 이메일이 쓰인 목적을 묻는 목적 찾기 문제이다. 'Attached please find two finalized copies of the edition along with a check as payment for the interview and photo shoot.'(3문단 1번째 줄)에서 첨부된 것에서 최종판 두 권을 인터뷰와 사진 촬영에 대한 보수인 수표와 함께 확인해 달라고 했으므로 (D) To provide payment for services rendered가 정답이다.

Paraphrasing
the interview and photo shoot 인터뷰와 사진 촬영 → services rendered 제공된 서비스

어휘 arrange v. 준비하다 approval n. 승인, 동의 render v. 제공하다

169 육하원칙 문제

문제 인터뷰는 언제 일어났는가?

(A) 9월
(B) 10월
(C) 11월
(D) 12월

해설 인터뷰가 언제(When) 일어났는지를 묻는 육하원칙 문제이다. 질문의 핵심 어구인 interview와 관련하여, 'the editorial we interviewed you for last month'(1문단 1번째 줄)에서 지난달에 인터뷰한 사실이라고 했고, 'Date: October 25'(상단 3번째 줄)에서 이메일을 보낸 날짜가 10월 25일이라고 했으므로 (A) September가 정답이다.

170 육하원칙 문제

문제 누가 Robert에게 축제에 대해 이야기했는가?

(A) Victoria
(B) Ashley
(C) Gina
(D) Leo

해설 Robert에게 누가(Who) 축제에 대해 이야기했는지를 묻는 육하원칙 문제이다. 질문의 핵심 어구인 gala와 관련하여, 'Gina mentioned that when she informed you of our upcoming gala ~ you were very intrigued'(3문단 2번째 줄)에서 Gina가 축제에 대해 당신, 즉 Robert에게

알려주었을 때 Robert는 아주 흥미로워했다고 했으므로 Gina가 Robert에게 축제에 대해 이야기했음을 알 수 있다. 따라서 (C) Gina가 정답이다.

171 추론 문제

문제 Mr. Kane에 대해 암시되는 것은?

(A) 다음 주 금요일 행사에 혼자 참석할 것이다.
(B) 전에 *Now Trending*을 위해 유급 작업을 한 적이 없다.
(C) 손님을 데려올 것이라면 Ms. Lim에게 연락해야 한다.
(D) 내년 봄에 그 잡지로부터 다시 인터뷰를 받을 것이다.

해설 질문의 핵심 어구 Mr. Kane에 대해 추론하는 문제이다. 'I do ask that you notify me as soon as possible by e-mail about whether or not you can come. I will also need the name of your guest, should anyone be accompanying you.'(3문단 5번째 줄)에서 올 수 있는지 없는지 여부를 최대한 빨리 이메일로 알려달라고 한 후, 동행하는 손님이 있다면, 그 분의 이름도 필요하다고 했으므로 손님을 데려올 경우 Ms. Lim에게 연락해야 한다는 사실을 추론할 수 있다. 따라서 (C) He will have to contact Ms. Lim if he brings a guest가 정답이다.

172-175는 다음 기사에 관한 문제입니다.

Tech Speculation 주간지
신종 스마트 착용물

Joshua Hutchins 작성
3월 20일

¹⁷²⁻ᶜ대형 기술업체인 BurTex사에 의해 곧 공개될 새 스마트 시계 라인에 대해 요즘 많은 말이 있었습니다. 이 회사는 이들의 새로운 스마트 시계 디자인을 건강과 신체 단련에서 미래 유행의 선구자로 만들기를 바라고 있습니다.

최근 발행된 보고서는 거의 75퍼센트의 소비자들이 BurTex사의 스마트 시계 제품과 같은 착용 가능한 장비 때문에 건강 관리 분야를 가장 장래성 있는 산업으로 언급했음을 발견하였습니다. — [1] —. 사람들은 자신들의 건강에 대해서는 1차 진료 의사들에게 가장 많은 신뢰를 둡니다. 그러므로, ¹⁷³더 많은 이러한 의사들이 스마트 시계의 유용성을 인정해준다면, 소비자들은 매일 운동 일과에 이 기기를 결합하도록 장려될 것입니다.

¹⁷⁵하지만, 보고서는 BurTex사의 스마트 시계에 대한 전반적인 소비자의 관심이 제품 출시 발표부터 명백히 감소한 것 또한 언급했습니다. — [2] —. 그러한 기기는 특수 품목으로 여겨지는데, 아마도 현재 시장에서의 희소성 때문일 것입니다. ¹⁷⁴지난 2년간 스마트 시계를 구매한 소비자들의 4분의 1이 일상생활에서 얼마나 매우 드물게 이 장비를 사용하는지 언급했습니다. 이 소비자들은 착용 가능한 장비에 대한 불신의 첫 번째 이유로 부정확하고 정밀하지 않은 데이터를 언급했습니다. — [3] —.

게다가, BurTex사의 새로운 시계 라인에 호기심을 느끼는 사람들의 무려 85퍼센트가 사생활에 대한 우려를 나타냈습니다. 스마트 시계는 건강 정보를 친구 및 가족과 공유하는 기능을 포함합니다. — [4] —. 하지만, 많은 사람들이 이러한 정보가 매우 민감하고, 공유가 되었을 때, 많은 사회적 문제를 일으킬 수 있다고 느낍니다.

---

a great deal of 많은, 다량의 **forerunner** n. 선구자
cite v. 언급하다, 인용하다 **promising** adj. 장래성 있는
when it comes to ~에 대해서는 **incorporate** v. 결합하다
device n. 기기 **launch** n. 출시 **scarcity** n. 희소성, 부족
intrigued adj. 호기심을 느끼는

172 Not/True 문제

문제 BurTex사에 대해 언급된 것은?

(A) 그들의 경쟁사들에 비해 크지 않다.
(B) 건강 산업 시장에서 기회를 발견하지 않는다.
(C) 새로운 제품을 곧 출시한다.
(D) 최근 정책 변경을 발표했다.

해설 질문의 핵심 어구인 BurTex Corporation과 관련된 내용을 지문에서 찾아보기와 대조하는 Not/True 문제이다. (A), (B), (D)는 지문에 언급되지 않은 내용이다. (C)는 'There has been a great deal of talk lately about the new line of smart watches soon to be released by technology giant, BurTex. Co.'(1문단 1번째 줄)에서 대형 기술업체인 BurTex사에 의

해 곧 공개될 새 스마트 시계 라인에 대해 요즘 많은 말이 있었다고 했으므로 (C) They are about to launch some new merchandise가 정답이다.

Paraphrasing
soon to be released 곧 공개될 → about to launch 곧 출시하는

어휘 relative to ~에 비하여

173 추론 문제

문제 Mr. Hutchins에 따르면, 1차 진료 의사들에 대해 사실인 것 같은 것은?

(A) 일부는 착용 가능한 장비가 위험하다고 생각한다.
(B) 일부는 스마트 시계의 실용성을 인정한다.
(C) 지금은 대다수가 운동할 때 착용 가능한 기기를 사용한다.
(D) 대다수는 환자의 건강 정보를 추적하는 더욱 정확한 방법을 요구하고 있다.

해설 질문의 핵심 어구인 primary care physicians에 대해 추론하는 문제이다. 'if more of these doctors approve the usefulness of smart watches'(2문단 6번째 줄)에서 더 많은 의사들, 즉 1차 진료 의사들이 스마트 시계의 유용성을 인정해준다면이라고 한 내용을 통해 일부 의사들은 이미 스마트 시계의 유용성을 인정했다는 사실을 추론할 수 있다. 따라서 (B) Some see practicality in smart watches가 정답이다.

Paraphrasing
usefulness 유용성 → practicality 실용성

어휘 track v. 추적하다

174 육하원칙 문제

문제 몇 퍼센트의 소비자들이 그들의 스마트 시계를 거의 사용하지 않는다고 말했는가?

(A) 25퍼센트
(B) 50퍼센트
(C) 75퍼센트
(D) 85퍼센트

해설 자신들의 스마트 시계를 거의 사용하지 않는다고 말한 소비자들이 몇 퍼센트(What percentage)인지를 묻는 육하원칙 문제이다. 질문의 핵심 어구인 consumers said they rarely use their smart watches와 관련하여, 'One quarter of consumers who purchased a smart watch ~ noted how they used the technology very infrequently in their daily lives.'(3문단 6번째 줄)에서 스마트 시계를 구매한 소비자의 4분의 1이 일상생활에서 얼마나 매우 드물게 이 장비를 사용하는지 언급했다고 했으므로 (A) 25 percent가 정답이다.

175 문장 위치 찾기 문제

문제 [1], [2], [3], [4]로 표시된 위치 중, 다음 문장이 들어갈 곳으로 가장 적절한 것은?

"이것은 몇몇 소비자들이 아직 착용 가능한 건강 장비에 확신이 없다는 사실에 기인합니다."

(A) [1]
(B) [2]
(C) [3]
(D) [4]

해설 지문의 흐름상 주어진 문장이 들어가기에 가장 적절한 곳을 고르는 문제이다. This is due to the fact that some consumers are still unsure of wearable health technology에서 이것을 몇몇 소비자들이 아직 착용 가능한 건강 장비에 확신이 없다는 사실에 기인한다고 했으므로, 주어진 문장 앞에 착용 가능한 건강 장비에 대한 소비자의 의견과 관련된 내용이 있을 것임을 예상할 수 있다. [2]의 앞 문장인 'The report ~ stated ~ that overall consumer interest in BurTex's smart watches has apparently declined since the product launch announcement.'(3문단 1번째 줄)에서 보고서가 BurTex사의 스마트 시계에 대한 전반적인 소비자의 관심이 제품 출시 발표부터 명백히 감소한 것을 언급했다고 했으므로, [2]에 주어진 문장이 들어가면 이것, 즉 스마트 시계에 대한 관심이 감소한 것이 아직 착용 가능한 건강 장비에 대한 소비자의 확신이 없다는 사실에 기인한다는 자연스러운 문맥이 된다는 것을 알 수 있다. 따라서 (B) [2]가 정답이다.

어휘 due to ~에 기인하는, ~ 때문에 **wearable** adj. 착용 가능한

176-180은 다음 두 이메일에 관한 문제입니다.

수신: David Marsh <davemarsh@careconstruction.com>
발신: Gary Brent <gbrent@placidpaints.com>
날짜: 9월 2일
제목: 페인트 주문
첨부: 카탈로그

Mr. Marsh께,

최근 페인트 주문에 대해 감사드립니다. 저희는 현재 요청된 색들을 섞고 있는데, 추가의 설명이 필요한 일부 품목에 대해 몇 가지 질문이 있습니다.

¹⁸⁰B227 하늘색 페인트에 대한 두 개의 개별적인 기재 사항이 있었고, 각각은 4리터 한 통씩을 요구하고 있습니다. ¹⁷⁶이것이 오류가 아니고 고객님께서 실제로 두 개를 모두 주문하고 싶으신 것이란 것을 확인해 주시겠습니까?

또한, ¹⁷⁸⁻ᴰ귀하께서 요청하신 색들 중 두 개가 작년 카탈로그의 옛날 색상 코드에 해당합니다. 저희에게 똑같은 상품이 있는데, 지금 선황색은 Y866이고 보라색은 P306입니다. 저는 올해 카탈로그 한 부를 첨부했고 귀하께서 고르신 색들은 강조 표시를 했습니다. 만약 이것들이 사실과 다르다면, 오류를 정정하기 위해 가급적 빨리 저희에게 연락주시기 바랍니다.

귀하의 지속적인 애용에 감사드리며 다른 페인트들은 이미 준비되고 있다는 것을 알려 드립니다. 제시간에 주문품이 배송될 수 있도록 앞으로 24시간 안에 이 세부 사항에 대한 확인을 보내주십시오.

Gary Brent 드림
고객 상담원, Placid Paints사

catalog n. 카탈로그, 목록 further adj. 추가의 clarification n. 설명
entry n. 기재 사항, 입장 pail n. 들통 correspond v. 해당하다, 일치하다
canary yellow 선황색 highlight v. 강조 표시를 하다, 눈에 띄게 하다
patronage n. 애용, 후원

수신: Gary Brent <gbrent@placidpaints.com>
발신: David Marsh <davemarsh@careconstruction.com>
날짜: 9월 10일
주제: 완료된 페인트 주문

Gary께,

저희는 오늘 페인트를 받았습니다. 정보를 주는 데 늦어져 다시 한번 사과드립니다. 하지만 ¹⁷⁹저희 인테리어 디자이너가 자리에 없어서, 세부 정보를 즉시 얻을 수 없었습니다. 아무튼, 페인트가 도착했고, ¹⁷⁸⁻ᴬ이는 저희 일정을 유지하기에 여전히 충분한 시간을 줍니다.

또한, 양식에 있었던 모든 문제점에 대해 다시 한 번 사과드리고 싶습니다. 몇몇 여러 사람들이 주문서에 품목을 추가하였고, 그중 일부가 몇몇 변경이 있었다는 것을 파악하지 못한 것 같습니다. 안타깝게도, 그들은 또한 ¹⁷⁷/¹⁸⁰같은 페인트 색조를 두 번 주문했음을 알아채지 못했습니다. 귀하가 저희에게 이메일을 써서 저희가 그 문제를 여기 저희 사무실에서 해결할 수 있었던 것은 다행입니다. 저희 모든 직원들이 이 변화에 대한 최신 정보를 받았으니 안심하십시오, 이제 이런 일은 다시 일어나지 않을 것입니다.

David Marsh 드림
관리자, Care Construction사

immediately adv. 즉시 in any event 아무튼 shade n. 색조, 명암
resolve v. 해결하다, 풀다 rest assured 안심하다, 믿어도 된다

176 육하원칙 문제

문제 첫 번째 이메일에 의하면, Mr. Brent는 왜 카탈로그를 보냈는가?

(A) 주문의 정확성을 확인하기 위해
(B) 새로운 페인트 색조를 광고하기 위해
(C) 다른 색을 추천하기 위해
(D) 계산 오류를 설명하기 위해

해설 Mr. Brent가 왜(why) 카탈로그를 보냈는지를 묻는 육하원칙 문제이므로 첫 번째 이메일에서 질문의 핵심 어구인 catalog와 관련된 내용을 확인한다. 첫 번째 지문인 이메일의 'Could you please confirm that this was not an error and that you would actually like to place both orders?'(2문단 2번째 줄)에서 이것이 오류가 아니고 두 개를 모두 주문하고 싶은 것인지를

확인해 달라고 했으므로 (A) To check order accuracy가 정답이다.

어휘 accuracy n. 정확성 calculation n. 계산, 셈

177 동의어 찾기 문제

문제 두 번째 이메일에서, 2문단 세 번째 줄의 단어 "shade"는 의미상 -와 가장 가깝다.

(A) 반영
(B) 색조
(C) 표현
(D) 피난처

해설 두 번째 지문인 이메일의 shade를 포함하고 있는 구절 'one order had been made twice for the same paint shade'(2문단 3번째 줄)에서 shade는 '색조'라는 뜻으로 사용되었다. 따라서 '색조'라는 뜻을 가진 (B) tone이 정답이다.

어휘 reflection n. 반영 expression n. 표현 shelter n. 피난처, 은신처

178 Not/True 문제 연계

문제 Care Construction사에 대해 언급된 것은?

(A) 스케줄이 바뀌어야 했다.
(B) Mr. Marsh를 위한 프로젝트를 최근 완료했다.
(C) 몇몇의 새로운 디자인 직원을 이제 막 고용했다.
(D) 주문이 구식의 정보를 참고했다.

해설 질문의 핵심 어구인 Care Construction에 대해 묻는 Not/True 문제이므로 Care Construction사가 언급된 첫 번째와 두 번째 이메일 모두에서 관련 내용을 확인한다. (A)는 두 번째 이메일의 'which still gives us enough time to stay within our schedule'(1문단 3번째 줄)에서 일정을 유지하기에 충분한 시간이 있다고 했으므로 지문의 내용과 일치하지 않는다. (B)와 (C)는 지문에 언급되지 않은 내용이다. (D)는 첫 번째 이메일의 'I am afraid that two of the colors you requested correspond to old color codes from last year's catalog'(3문단 1번째 줄)에서 요청한 색들 중 두 개가 작년 카탈로그의 옛날 색상 코드에 해당한다고 했으므로 지문의 내용과 일치한다. 따라서 (D) Its order referred to outdated information이 정답이다.

어휘 alter v. 바꾸다 refer v. 참고하다 outdated adj. 구식의
Paraphrasing
old color codes 옛날 색상 코드 → outdated information 구식의 정보

179 육하원칙 문제

문제 Mr. Marsh에 따르면, 정보를 보내는 것이 왜 지연되었는가?

(A) 인테리어 디자이너가 자리에 없었다.
(B) 관리자는 아무런 문제를 찾을 수 없었다.
(C) 페인트 색상에 대한 번호가 바뀌었다.
(D) 디자이너는 결정을 하는 데 힘들었다.

해설 정보를 보내는 것이 왜(why) 지연되었는지를 묻는 육하원칙 문제이므로 질문의 핵심 어구인 a delay sending information이 언급된 두 번째 이메일에서 관련 내용을 확인한다. 두 번째 이메일의 'our interior designer was away, so we couldn't get the details immediately'(1문단 1번째 줄)에서 저희 인테리어 디자이너가 자리에 없어서, 세부 정보를 즉시 얻을 수 없었다고 했으므로 (A) The interior designer was not present가 정답이다.

어휘 present adj. 사람이 특정 장소에 있는 decision n. 결정

180 추론 문제 연계

문제 Mr. Marsh의 주문에 대해 암시되는 것은?

(A) 부정확한 주소로 보내졌다.
(B) 색상 B227의 수량 오류를 포함했다.
(C) 해외 공급업체로부터 배송되었다.
(D) 예상보다 더 많은 비용이 들었다.

해설 두 지문의 내용을 종합적으로 확인한 후 추론해서 풀어야 하는 연계 문제이다. 질문의 핵심 어구인 Mr. Marsh가 작성한 두 번째 이메일을 먼저 확인한다. 두 번째 이메일에서 'one order had been made twice for the same paint shade'(2문단 3번째 줄)에서 같은 페인트 색조를 두 번 주문했다는 첫 번째 단서를 확인할 수 있다. 그런데 어떤 페인트 색조를 두 번 주문했는지 제

시되지 않았으므로 첫 번째 이메일에서 관련 내용을 확인한다. 첫 번째 이메일의 'There were two separate entries for the color B227 sky blue paint'(2문단 1번째 줄)에서 B227 하늘색 페인트에 대한 두 개의 개별적인 기재 사항이 있었다는 두 번째 단서를 확인할 수 있다.

같은 페인트 색조를 두 번 주문했다는 첫 번째 단서와 B227 하늘색 페인트에 대한 두 개의 개별적인 기재 사항이 있었다는 두 번째 단서를 종합할 때, B227 하늘색 페인트를 두 번 주문했다는 사실을 추론할 수 있다. 따라서 (B) It contained a quantity error for color B227이 정답이다.

어휘 incorrect adj. 부정확한 foreign adj. 해외의, 외국의

181-185는 다음 광고와 이메일에 관한 문제입니다.

Dover 지역 봉사 활동

Dover 지역 봉사 활동(DCO)은 50년이 넘는 기간 동안 Dover시의 저소득 가정들에게 도움을 제공해 왔습니다. [181]DCO는 지역의 정부 지원을 받는 사회 복지 기관들과 협력하고 있습니다. [182]어려움에 처한 가정들은 다음 단체들을 통해 소정의 보조금을 제공받습니다:

주거 및 의료 관리
• 임대료 보조
• 임대 보증금 지원
• 의료 관리 지원

교육 및 직업 훈련
• [182]구직자를 위한 특정 분야 훈련 프로그램
• 기술력을 향상시키기 위한 기술 개발 수업

당신이 도울 수 있는 방법
DCO로의 당신의 자비로운 기부는 우리가 더 많이 활동하도록 도울 수 있습니다. [184]Dover 지역 봉사 활동에 기부하기 위해, 저희 기부금 페이지 www.doveroutreach.org/donation을 방문해 주십시오. DCO와 관련된 어떤 질문들이 있다면, 행정 부장 Ms. Laura Kingsley에게 555-2338로 연락하거나 l_kingsley@doveroutreach.org로 이메일을 보내주십시오.

outreach n. 봉사 활동 low-income adj. 저소득의, 저수입의
social service 사회 복지 in need 어려움에 처한, 궁핍한
security deposit 임대 보증금 job-seeker n. 구직자
charitable adj. 자비로운 administrative adj. 행정의, 사무의

수신 Douglas Porter <dporter@wvdp.com>
발신 Laura Kingsley <l_kingsley@doveroutreach.org>
제목 월례 단체 회의
날짜 6월 1일

Dr. Porter께,

[183]늘 그렇듯이, Dover 지역 봉사 활동의 회원들을 위한 월례 단체 회의는 매달 두 번째 월요일(6월 10일)에 열릴 것입니다. 당신의 치과 병원인 West Victoria 치과는 지난 10년간 Dover 지역 봉사 활동의 헌신적인 회원이자 후원자였기 때문에, 저희는 이번 월례 회의에서 당신이 발표를 하는 것에 대해 아주 기쁩니다. 저는 당신이 영사기와 마이크 시스템이 필요할 것이라는 것을 알고 있기에 당신을 위해 그 물품들을 꼭 준비해 놓을 것입니다.

[184/185]이번 달의 회의 안건을 확인해 주십시오:

• [184]들어오는 기부금의 부족에 대한 우려; 기부금 페이지를 제외한 다른 방법들에 대한 제안
• 새로운 프로그램을 위한 강사 모집
• 주택 가격 인상; 경제 자료에 대한 논의
• [185]노인 치아 관리에 대한 Dr. Douglas Porter의 특별 발표

항상 그렇듯이, DCO와 관련된 모든 주제에 대한 귀하의 의견과 문의도 환영합니다.

Laura Kingsley 드림
행정 부장, Dover 지역 봉사 활동

practice n. 병원, 의원 delighted adj. 아주 기쁜 agenda n. 안건
incoming adj. 들어오는 senior citizen 노인, 어르신

---

181 육하원칙 문제

문제 누가 Dover 지역 봉사 활동과 함께 일하는가?
(A) 제약 회사들
(B) 인터넷 서비스 제공업체들
(C) 국제적으로 운영되는 회사들
(D) 주 복지 단체들

해설 Dover 지역 봉사 활동과 함께 일하는 것이 누구(Who)인지를 묻는 육하원칙 문제이므로 질문의 핵심 어구인 Dover Community Outreach가 언급된 광고에서 관련 내용을 확인한다. 첫 번째 지문인 광고에서 'DCO works in partnership with local government-funded social service agencies.'(1문단 2번째 줄)에서 DCO는 지역의 정부 지원을 받는 사회 복지 기관들과 협력하고 있다고 했으므로 (D) State welfare groups가 정답이다.

Paraphrasing
social service agencies 사회 복지 기관들 → welfare groups 복지 단체들

어휘 pharmaceutical adj. 제약의, 약학의

182 육하원칙 문제

문제 Dover 지역 봉사 활동은 어떻게 가정들에게 지원을 제공하는가?
(A) 주택 소유권과 관련된 모든 비용을 지불한다.
(B) 70세 이상의 사람들에 대한 건강 비용을 완전히 보장한다.
(C) 직장을 찾는 사람들을 위한 강좌를 제공한다.
(D) 집에서 일하는 사람들을 위해 컴퓨터를 설치해 준다.

해설 가정들에게 어떻게(How) 지원을 제공하는지를 묻는 육하원칙 문제이므로 질문의 핵심 어구인 provide support to families가 언급된 광고에서 관련 내용을 확인한다. 첫 번째 지문인 광고에서 'Families in need are offered small grants through these groups for the following'(1문단 3번째 줄)에서 어려움에 처한 가정들은 다음 단체들을 통해 소정의 보조금을 제공받는다고 한 후, 'Field-specific training programs for job-seekers'(3문단 1번째 줄)에서 구직자를 위한 특정 분야 훈련 프로그램이 있다고 했으므로 (C) They offer classes for people looking for employment가 정답이다.

Paraphrasing
job-seekers 구직자들 → people looking for employment 직장을 찾는 사람들

어휘 ownership n. 소유권, 소유 cover v. 보장하다 expense n. 비용
employment n. 직장, 고용

183 추론 문제

문제 Dr. Porter에 대해 암시되는 것은?
(A) 출판을 위해 연구 자료를 모으고 있다.
(B) 매달 두 번째 월요일에 있는 DCO 회의에 초대된다.
(C) DCO의 설립 이래로 후원자였다.
(D) Dover시에 많은 치과 병원을 소유하고 있다.

해설 질문의 핵심 어구인 Dr. Porter에 대해 추론하는 문제이므로 Dr. Porter에게 보내는 이메일에서 관련 내용을 확인한다. 두 번째 지문인 이메일의 'As usual, the monthly group meeting for Dover Community Outreach members will take place on the second Monday of the month'(1문단 1번째 줄)에서 늘 그렇듯이, Dover 지역 봉사 활동의 회원들을 위한 월례 단체 회의는 매달 두 번째 월요일에 열린다고 했고, 'As your dental practice ~ has been a dedicated member and supporter of Dover Community Outreach for the past 10 years'(1문단 2번째 줄)에서 Dr. Porter의 치과 병원은 지난 10년간 Dover 지역 봉사 활동의 헌신적인 회원이자 후원자였다고 했으므로, Dover 지역 봉사 활동의 후원자인 Dr. Porter가 매달 두 번째 월요일에 열리는 월례 단체 회의에 초대된다는 사실을 알 수 있다. 따라서 (B) He is invited to a DCO meeting every second Monday of the month가 정답이다.

어휘 gather v. 모으다 publication n. 출판, 출간 establishment n. 설립

184 추론 문제 연계

문제 Dover 지역 봉사 활동에 대해 암시되는 것은?
(A) 그들의 웹사이트를 통해 충분한 자금을 모으고 있지 않다.
(B) 제공된 어떤 서비스들을 줄이는 것을 고려하고 있다.

(C) 행정직에 새로운 직원들을 모집하고 있다.
(D) 최근의 주택 비용 증가에 대해 잘 모르고 있다.

해설 두 지문의 내용을 종합적으로 확인한 후 추론해서 풀어야 하는 연계 문제이다. 질문의 핵심 어구인 Dover Community Outreach가 언급된 광고를 먼저 확인한다.
첫 번째 지문인 광고의 'To make a donation to Dover Community Outreach, visit our Contributions Page at www.doveroutreach.org/donation.'(4문단 1번째 줄)에서 Dover 지역 봉사 활동에 기부하기 위해서는 기부금 페이지에 방문해 달라고 했으므로 기부금은 웹페이지에서 낼 수 있다는 첫 번째 단서를 확인할 수 있다. 그런데 기부금에 대한 다른 정보가 제시되지 않았으므로 이메일에서 관련 내용을 확인한다. 두 번째 지문인 이메일의 'this month's meeting agenda:', 'Concerns regarding lack of incoming donations'(2문단 1번째 줄)에서 이번 월례 회의의 안건으로 들어오는 기부금의 부족에 대한 우려가 있다는 두 번째 단서를 확인할 수 있다. 기부금은 웹페이지에서 낼 수 있다는 첫 번째 단서와 이번 달 회의 안건에 들어오는 기부금의 부족에 대한 우려가 있다는 두 번째 단서를 종합할 때, 웹페이지를 통해 들어오는 기부금이 부족하다는 사실을 추론할 수 있다. 따라서 (A) They are not raising enough funds through their Web site가 정답이다.

Paraphrasing
lack of incoming donations 들어오는 기부금의 부족 → not raising enough funds 충분한 자금을 모으고 있지 않다
Contributions page 기부금 페이지 → Web site 웹사이트

어휘 raise v. (자금을) 모으다, 얻어 내다 cut back 줄이다, 삭감하다

185 육하원칙 문제

문제 이메일에 따르면, 월례 회의에서 무엇이 논의될 것인가?
(A) 조직이 기부금을 제공해야 하는 곳
(B) DCO의 새로운 기술 프로그램들
(C) 개인 주택의 가치를 높이는 방법
(D) 중장년층을 위한 치아 관리 제공

해설 월례 회의에서 무엇(what)이 논의될 것인지를 묻는 육하원칙 문제이므로 질문의 핵심 어구인 monthly meeting이 언급된 이메일에서 관련 내용을 확인한다. 두 번째 지문인 이메일의 'this month's meeting agenda:'(2문단 1번째 줄)와 'Special presentation by Dr. Douglas Porter on senior citizen dental care'(2문단 6번째 줄)에서 이번 월례 회의에서 Dr. Douglas가 노인 치아 관리에 대한 특별 발표를 한다고 했으므로 (D) Providing dental care for the elderly가 정답이다.

Paraphrasing
senior citizen 노인 → the elderly 중장년층

186-190은 다음 편지, 송장, 이메일에 관한 문제입니다.

5월 1일

Mr. Borden께,

이 편지는 5월 9일에 임대 계약이 만료되면 저희 회사가 그것을 갱신하지 않을 것임을 알려드리기 위함입니다. 시설, 서비스, 혹은 건물 소유주인 귀하에 대해서는 아무 문제가 없습니다. 186제 사업체가 그저 너무 크게 성장해서, 저희는 더 많은 공간을 필요로 합니다. 저는 지난 5년간의 귀하의 모든 도움에 감사드립니다. 186저희는 5월 10일과 11일에 Facade Towers에 있는 새 사무실로 이전할 것입니다.

187저희가 처음 이사 왔을 때와 같은 상태로 사무실을 되돌려 놓기 위해 저희는 청소업체를 고용했습니다. 계약서에 합의되어 있듯이, 그 서비스에 대해서는 제가 비용을 지불할 것입니다. 분명히 해야 할 사항이 더 있으시다면 emoses@emstranslation.com으로 언제든 제게 연락하시면 됩니다.

Elizabeth Moses 드림
소유주, EMS Translation Services사

renew v. 갱신하다 lease n. 임대 계약; v. 임대하다 owner n. 소유주
relocate v. 이전하다, 이동하다 clarification n. 분명하게 하기, 설명

190OFFICINA SERVICES사   송장: #DTS-3987
4204번지 Grandville 대로, 190내슈빌, 테네시주 37207

전화. 555-2350

187이름: Elizabeth Moses		날짜: 5월 11일
187/188-D주소: EMS Translation Services사 56호, 4층, 188-DStembridge Commercial 빌딩 내슈빌, 테네시주 37207		이메일: emoses@emstranslation.com
188-C제공되는 서비스		비용
188-C카펫 스팀 청소		230달러
바닥 닦기		170달러
화장실과 직원 사무실 청소		120달러
모든 창문 청소		200달러
두 곳의 개인 사무실 청소		150달러
회의실 청소		75달러
	소계	945달러
	세금	90달러
	지불 금액	1,035달러

이 송장에 대한 지불은 서비스 마지막 날로부터 5일 이내에 되어야 합니다. 지불 연체는 위약금을 발생시킬 수 있습니다.

invoice n. 송장 polish v. 닦다, 윤기를 내다
owe v. 지불할 의무가 있다, 빚지고 있다 incur v. (비용을) 발생시키다, 초래하다
penalty n. 위약금, 벌금

수신 Elizabeth Moses <emoses@emstranslation.com>
발신 Harris Lloyd <h.lloyd@officinaservices.com>
제목 긴급
188-B날짜 5월 17일

Ms. Moses께,

189/190저희 업체가 귀하를 위해 수행한 서비스에 대해 이메일을 보냅니다. 서비스 마지막 날은 5월 11일이었으며, 송장은 귀하께서 요청하신 대로 건물 관리인에게 맡겨졌습니다. 귀하께서 청구서를 받으셨는지 모르겠지만, 189저는 아직 보수를 받지 못했습니다. 서비스가 제공된 이후로 6일이 되었습니다.

188-B/189저는 내일까지 귀하께서 지불 금액을 보내주시기를 정중히 요청드립니다. 그 후에는, 귀하께서 서명하신 서비스 계약서에 명시되어 있듯이 190Officina Services사가 귀하께 50달러의 연체료를 청구할 것입니다. 용건이 있으시다면, 이 이메일로 답장하시거나 555-2350으로 제게 연락주시기 바랍니다.

Harris Lloyd 드림

render v. 제공하다, ~이 되게 하다 indicate v. 명시하다, 나타내다

186 육하원칙 문제

문제 EMS사는 왜 사무실에서 나가는가?
(A) 더 많은 공간이 필요하다.
(B) 불만 사항이 너무 많다.
(C) 더 나은 서비스를 찾고 있다.
(D) 다른 회사에 의해 인수되었다.

해설 EMS사가 왜(Why) 사무실에서 나가는지를 묻는 육하원칙 문제이므로 질문의 핵심 어구인 EMS moving out of its office와 관련된 내용이 언급된 편지를 확인한다. 첫 번째 지문인 편지의 'My business has simply grown too large, and we need more room.'(1문단 2번째 줄)에서 EMS사가 그저 너무 크게 성장해서 더 많은 공간을 필요로 한다고 했고 'We will be relocating to our new offices in Facade Towers'(1문단 4번째 줄)에서 Facade Towers에 있는 새 사무실로 이전할 것이라고 했으므로 (A) It needs more space가 정답이다.

Paraphrasing
moving out of ~ office 사무실에서 나가다 → relocating 이전하다
room 공간 → space 공간

어휘 complaint n. 불만 사항 acquire v. 인수하다

187 육하원칙 문제 연계

문제 Ms. Moses는 무엇을 하는 것에 동의했는가?
(A) 같은 건물에 있는 다른 곳을 임대한다

(B) 4층 사무실의 청소 비용을 부담한다
(C) 그녀가 회사를 이전하는 것을 돕도록 Mr. Borden을 고용한다
(D) 이전 사무실 공간에서 바닥을 교체한다

해설 두 지문의 내용을 종합해서 풀어야 하는 연계 문제이다. 질문의 핵심 어구인 Ms. Moses agreed to do에서 Ms. Moses가 무엇을(What) 하는 것에 동의했는지를 묻고 있으므로 Ms. Moses가 작성한 편지를 먼저 확인한다.

첫 번째 지문인 편지의 'We have hired a cleaning company to return the office to the same condition as it was when we first moved in. As agreed in our contract, I will pay for those services.'(2문단 1번째 줄)에서 Ms. Moses가 처음 이사 왔을 때와 같은 상태로 사무실을 되돌려 놓기 위해 청소업체를 고용했고 계약서에 합의되어 있듯이 그 서비스에 대해서는 Ms. Moses가 비용을 지불할 것이라고 했으므로 Ms. Moses가 사무실 청소 비용을 지불할 것이라는 첫 번째 단서를 확인할 수 있다. 그런데 청소할 사무실이 어디에 위치하는지가 제시되지 않았으므로 송장에서 관련 내용을 확인한다. 두 번째 지문인 송장의 'NAME: Elizabeth Moses', 'ADDRESS: EMS Translation Services ~, 4th floor'(표 1, 2행 1열)에서 Ms. Moses의 회사인 EMS Translation Services사가 4층에 있다는 두 번째 단서를 확인할 수 있다.

Ms. Moses가 사무실 청소 비용을 지불할 것이라는 첫 번째 단서와 Ms. Moses의 회사인 EMS Translation Services사가 4층에 있다는 두 번째 단서를 종합할 때, Ms. Moses가 4층에 있는 사무실의 청소 비용을 부담하는 것에 동의했음을 알 수 있다. 따라서 (B) Cover the cost of cleaning a fourth-floor office가 정답이다.

Paraphrasing
pay 지불하다 → **Cover the cost** 비용을 부담하다

어휘 **cover** v. (비용 등을) 부담하다, 덮다, 다루다

---

188 Not/True 문제

문제 Officina Services사에 대해 사실인 것은?
(A) 이사 서비스 제공 업체이다.
(B) 5월 12일까지 완납하도록 요구한다.
(C) 카펫 청소 서비스를 제공한다.
(D) Stembridge Commercial 빌딩에 있다.

해설 질문의 핵심 어구인 Officina Services에 대해 묻는 Not/True 문제이므로 Officina Services사에서 보낸 송장과 이메일에서 관련 내용을 확인한다. (A)는 지문에 언급되지 않은 내용이다. (B)는 세 번째 지문인 이메일의 'DATE May 17'(상단 4번째 줄)와 'I kindly ask that you send payment by tomorrow.'(2문단 1번째 줄)에서 이메일을 보낸 5월 17일 다음 날까지 지불 금액을 보내주기를 정중히 요청한다고 했으므로 지문의 내용과 일치하지 않는다. (C)는 두 번째 지문인 송장의 'SERVICES PROVIDED', 'Steam clean carpets'(표 3, 4행 1열)에서 제공되는 서비스에 카펫 스팀 청소가 있다고 했으므로 지문의 내용과 일치한다. 따라서 (C) It offers a carpet cleaning service가 정답이다. (D)는 두 번째 지문인 송장의 'ADDRESS: EMS Translation Services ~, Stembridge Commercial Building'(표 2행 1열)에서 EMS Translation Services사가 Stembridge Commercial 빌딩에 있다고 했으나 Officina Services사도 Stembridge Commercial 빌딩에 있는지는 언급되지 않았다.

Paraphrasing
Steam clean carpets 카펫 스팀 청소 → carpet cleaning 카펫 청소

어휘 **provider** n. 제공자, 공급자

---

189 주제/목적 찾기 문제

문제 이메일의 주 목적은 무엇인가?
(A) 청소 서비스 날짜를 확인하기 위해
(B) 고객에게 미지불된 청구서에 대해 알리기 위해
(C) 재무제표의 오류를 보고하기 위해
(D) 관리자에게 호실의 문제를 알려주기 위해

해설 이메일의 목적을 묻는 목적 찾기 문제이므로 이메일의 내용을 확인한다. 세 번째 지문인 이메일의 'I am writing about the services my business performed for you.'(1문단 1번째 줄)에서 이메일 발신자의 업체가 이메일 수신자를 위해 수행한 서비스에 대해 이메일을 보낸다고 했고, 'I have yet to receive payment'(1문단 3번째 줄)와 'I kindly ask that you send payment by tomorrow.'(2문단 1번째 줄)에서 이메일 발신자가 아직 보

수를 받지 못했으며 내일까지 지불 금액을 보내주기를 요청한다고 했으므로 (B) To notify a client of an outstanding bill이 정답이다.

어휘 **outstanding** adj. 미지불된, 뛰어난 **financial statement** 재무제표

---

190 추론 문제 연계

문제 Harris Lloyd에 대해 암시되는 것은?
(A) 잘못된 장소로 문서를 발송했다.
(B) 내슈빌에 위치한 사업체를 소유하고 있다.
(C) 송장에 계산 오류를 범했다.
(D) 실수로 Mr. Borden의 비서에게 청구서를 맡겼다.

해설 두 지문의 내용을 종합적으로 확인한 후 추론해서 풀어야 하는 연계 문제이다. 질문의 핵심 어구인 Harris Lloyd가 작성한 이메일을 먼저 확인한다.

세 번째 지문인 이메일의 'I am writing about the services my business performed for you.'(1문단 1번째 줄)와 'Officina Services will charge you a $50 late fee'(2문단 1번째 줄)에서 Harris Lloyd의 업체가 수행한 서비스에 대해 이메일을 보냈다고 하면서 Officina Services사가 50달러의 연체료를 청구할 것이라고 했으므로 Harris Lloyd의 사업체가 Officina Services사라는 첫 번째 단서를 확인할 수 있다. 그런데 Officina Services사가 어디에 위치하는지 제시되지 않았으므로 송장에서 관련 내용을 확인한다. 두 번째 지문인 송장의 'OFFICINA SERVICES INC.', 'Nashville'(송장 상단)에서 Officina Services사가 내슈빌에 있다는 두 번째 단서를 확인할 수 있다.

Harris Lloyd의 사업체가 Officina Services사라는 첫 번째 단서와 Officina Services사가 내슈빌에 있다는 두 번째 단서를 종합할 때, Harris Lloyd의 사업체가 내슈빌에 있다는 사실을 추론할 수 있다. 따라서 (B) He owns a business located in Nashville이 정답이다.

어휘 **calculation** n. 계산 **mistakenly** adv. 실수로

191-195는 다음 기사, 회람, 이메일에 관한 문제입니다.

> **Brayden 부동산이 리노에 지점을 개업하다**
>
> [192-A]지난해 초 라스베이거스에서 개점한 최초의 네바다 지점의 성공에 이어, [191-C/192-A]Brayden 부동산이 리노에 두 번째 사무소를 개업할 것이라고 발표했다. "두 도시의 시장은 유사합니다"라고 [191-B]Brayden 부동산 최고경영자인 Marjorie Olsen은 말한다. "그것이 저희가 이 새로운 사업이 수익성이 있을 것이라고 확신하는 이유입니다." Olsen은 또한 [192-D/194]회사가 리노 지점의 모든 일자리를 위해서 현지에서 고용을 할 것이라고 설명했다. [192-D]이 지점은 총 18명의 관리자와 직원들을 뽑을 것이다.
>
> [191-D]Brayden 부동산은 주로 호텔과 쇼핑센터를 포함하는 상업용 건물들을 취급한다. 콜로라도주 덴버에 본사를 두고 있는 이 회사는 미국 서부의 12개 주에서 운영한다. [194]리노 지점이 2월 14일에 개업하면 회사의 28번째 지점이 될 것이다. 리노 지점이 개점되는 것 이후로 [191-A]Brayden사는 애리조나 주를 겨냥하고 있으며, 피닉스와 투손에서 사무소를 시작할 계획이다.
>
> ---
>
> **realty** n. 부동산 **branch** n. 지점 **venture** n. 사업
> **profitable** adj. 수익성이 있는 **locally** adv. 현지에서
> **recruit** v. (신입 사원 등을) 뽑다, 모집하다 **primarily** adv. 주로, 처음으로
> **deal in** ~을 취급하다 **property** n. 건물, 부동산
> **headquarter** v. ~에 본부를 두다 **operate** v. 운영하다
> **have one's sights set on** ~을 겨냥하다 **envision** v. 계획하다, 구상하다

> 회람:
> 날짜: 2월 3일
>
> 수신: 중개 교육생들
> 발신: Michelle Larsen
>
> 다음 주 교육 일정에 변경 사항이 있습니다. 우선, 저는 몇 가지 채용 문제와 관련하여 도움을 주기 위하여 본사로 오라는 요청을 받았습니다. 그러므로 저는 다음 주에 여러분의 오전 교육을 진행할 수 없을 것입니다. 저를 대신할 사람은 [193-B]Adrian Gist인데, 그는 이번 주 화요일에 여러분의 사무소 시스템 교육을 진행했습니다. 그는 리노에서의 모든 남은 교육 시간을 진행할 것입니다.
>
> 또한, [195]다음 주 금요일에 우리는 Paolo's Grill에서의 만찬으로 교육 수료를 축하할 것입니다. agist@braydenrealestate.com으로 이메일을 보내 Adrian에게 여러분이 오시는지 알려주시기 바랍니다. 각자 한 명의 손님을 데려오 ▶

는 것이 허용됩니다.

substitute for ~을 대신하다 remaining adj. 남은, 남아 있는
completion n. 수료, 완성

수신: Adrian Gist <agist@braydenrealestate.com>
발신: Sofia Suarez <ssuar@braydenrealestate.com>
제목: 축하 만찬
날짜: 2월 4일

안녕하세요 Adrian,

¹⁹⁵저는 다음 주 2월 11일에 있을 식사에 참석하고 싶습니다. 제 남편이 출장으로 부재중일 것이기 때문에 저는 손님은 데려가지 않을 것입니다.

또한, 저는 사무소 교육 시간 마지막에 당신이 모든 신입 중개인들에게 배부했던 명함에 대해 질문이 있습니다. 제 이메일 주소가 잘못 인쇄되어 있었습니다. 저는 이것과 관련해서 누구에게 연락을 해야 할지 몰랐습니다. ¹⁹⁴14일에 사무소가 개업할 때 명함을 나누어 주어야 할 것이므로 제게 알려주시기 바랍니다.

도움에 감사드리며, 다음 주의 교육 시간을 고대하겠습니다.

Sofia Suarez 드림

attend v. 참석하다 business card 명함 distribute v. 배부하다
misprint v. 잘못 인쇄하다 hand out (사람들에게 물건을) 나누어 주다

---

191 Not/True 문제

문제 Brayden 부동산에 대해 언급되지 않은 것은?
(A) 피닉스에서 사업에 착수할 계획이다.
(B) 현재 Marjorie Olsen의 지도하에 있다.
(C) 라스베이거스에서 리노로 사무소를 이전할 것이다.
(D) 상업용 시설과 건물을 전문으로 한다.

해설 질문의 핵심 어구인 Brayden Realty와 관련된 내용을 지문에서 찾아 보기와 대조하는 Not/True 문제이므로 Brayden Realty가 언급된 첫 번째 지문인 기사에서 관련 내용을 확인한다. (A)는 'Brayden ~ envisions offices in Phoenix'(2문단 4번째 줄)에서 Brayden사가 피닉스에서 사무소를 시작할 계획이라고 했으므로 지문의 내용과 일치한다. (B)는 'Marjorie Olsen, CEO of Brayden Realty'(1문단 3번째 줄)에서 Brayden 부동산 최고경영자인 Marjorie Olsen이라고 했으므로 지문의 내용과 일치한다. (C)는 'Brayden Realty has announced it will be opening a second office in Reno' (1문단 2번째 줄)에서 Brayden 부동산이 리노에 두 번째 사무소를 개업할 것이라고 발표했다고 했으므로 지문의 내용과 일치하지 않는다. 따라서 (C) It will move its offices from Las Vegas to Reno가 정답이다. (D)는 'Brayden Realty primarily deals in commercial properties'(2문단 1번째 줄)에서 Brayden 부동산은 주로 상업용 건물들을 취급한다고 했으므로 지문의 내용과 일치한다.

Paraphrasing
envisions 계획하다 → plans 계획하다
primarily deals in commercial properties 주로 상업용 건물들을 취급하다 → specializes in commercial facilities and structures 상업용 시설과 건물을 전문으로 하다

어휘 launch v. 착수하다 under the leadership of ~의 지도하에
specialize in ~을 전문으로 하다 structure n. 건물, 건축물

192 Not/True 문제

문제 리노의 부동산 시장에 대해 언급된 것은?
(A) 라스베이거스의 시장과 유사하다.
(B) 현재의 공급자들에 의해서 수요가 충족되지 못하고 있다.
(C) 미국 서부에서 가장 빠르게 성장하는 시장이다.
(D) 리노 주민들에게 많은 일자리를 제공한다.

해설 질문의 핵심 어구인 the real estate market in Reno에 대해 묻는 Not/True 문제이므로 첫 번째 지문인 부동산 시장에 대해 언급된 기사에서 관련 내용을 확인한다. (A)는 'Following the success of its first Nevada branch, ~ in Las Vegas, ~ it will be opening a second office in Reno. "The market in both cities is similar,"'(1문단 1번째 줄)에서 라스베이거스의 최초의 네바다 지점의 성공에 이어 리노에 두 번째 사무소를 개업할 것이고 두 도시의 시장은 유사하다고 했으므로 지문의 내용과 일치

한다. 따라서 (A) It is comparable to the market in Las Vegas가 정답이다. (B)와 (C)는 지문에 언급되지 않은 내용이다. (D)는 'the firm would be hiring locally for all of the positions in Reno', 'The branch will be recruiting a total of 18 managers and staff.'(1문단 5번째 줄)에서 회사, 즉 Brayden 부동산이 리노 지점의 모든 일자리를 위해 현지에서 고용을 할 것이고 총 18명의 관리자와 직원들을 뽑을 것이라고 했으나, 이는 리노의 부동산 시장에 대한 설명이 아닌 Brayden 부동산의 리노 지점에 대한 설명이므로 지문에 언급되지 않은 내용이다.

Paraphrasing
similar 유사한 → comparable 유사한

어휘 comparable adj. 유사한, 흡사한 substantial adj. 많은, 상당한

193 Not/True 문제

문제 Michelle Larsen이 Adrian Gist에 대해 언급한 것은?
(A) 본사에서 교육생들에게 소개되었다.
(B) 이번 주에 사무소 시스템에 관한 교육을 진행했다.
(C) 최근에 채용 관리자로 고용되었다.
(D) 중개 교육생들을 여러 번 만났다.

해설 질문의 핵심 어구인 Adrian Gist에 대해 Michelle Larsen이 언급한 내용을 지문에서 찾아 보기와 대조하는 Not/True 문제이므로 Michelle Larsen이 Adrian Gist를 언급한 두 번째 지문인 회람에서 관련 내용을 확인한다. (A)는 지문에 언급되지 않은 내용이다. (B)는 'Adrian Gist, who led your office system training session ~ this week'(1문단 3번째 줄)에서 Adrian Gist가 이번 주에 사무소 시스템 교육을 진행했다고 했으므로 지문의 내용과 일치한다. 따라서 (B) He facilitated a session on office systems this week가 정답이다. (C)와 (D)는 지문에 언급되지 않은 내용이다.

Paraphrasing
led ~ training session 교육을 진행했다 → facilitated a session 교육을 진행했다

어휘 facilitate v. 진행하다, 용이하게 하다

194 추론 문제 연계

문제 Sofia Suarez에 대해 암시되는 것은?
(A) 관리자로서 교육을 할 것이다.
(B) 출장을 갈 것이다.
(C) 연례 회의에 참석할 수 없다.
(D) 리노의 주민이다.

해설 두 지문의 내용을 종합적으로 확인한 후 추론해서 풀어야 하는 연계 문제이다. 질문의 핵심 어구인 Sofia Suarez가 작성한 이메일을 먼저 확인한다. 세 번째 지문인 이메일의 'I will ~ hand out business cards when the office opens to the public on the 14th'(2문단 3번째 줄)에서 Sofia Suarez가 14일에 사무소가 개업할 때 명함을 나누어 줄 것이라고 했으므로 Sofia Suarez가 14일에 개업할 사무소에서 일하게 될 사람이라는 첫 번째 단서를 확인할 수 있다. 그런데 14일에 개업하는 사무소 직원에 대한 정보가 제시되지 않았으므로 기사에서 관련 내용을 확인한다. 첫 번째 지문인 기사의 'the firm would be hiring locally for all of the positions in Reno'(1문단 5번째 줄)와 'Reno ~ opens on February 14.'(2문단 3번째 줄)에서 회사가 2월 14일에 개업하는 리노 지점에서의 모든 일자리를 위해서 현지에서 고용을 할 것이라는 두 번째 단서를 확인할 수 있다.
Sofia Suarez가 14일에 개업할 사무소에서 일하게 될 사람이라는 첫 번째 단서와 회사가 2월 14일에 개업하는 리노 지점에서의 모든 일자리를 위해서 현지에서 고용을 할 것이라는 두 번째 단서를 종합할 때, Sofia Suarez는 리노의 주민이라는 사실을 추론할 수 있다. 따라서 (D) She is a resident of Reno가 정답이다.

어휘 annual adj. 연간의

195 육하원칙 문제 연계

문제 Ms. Suarez는 다음 주에 무엇을 할 것인가?
(A) 관리직 교육 프로그램을 위해 리노 사무소에 도착한다
(B) Paolo's Grill에서 다른 교육생들과 함께 축하 행사에 참석한다
(C) 교육 시간 마지막에 새 명함을 찾아간다
(D) 팔려고 내놓은 건물 방문에서 사람들을 인솔한다

해설 두 지문의 내용을 종합해서 풀어야 하는 연계 문제이다. 질문의 핵심 어구인 Ms. Suarez do next week에서 Ms. Suarez가 다음 주에 무엇(What)을 할 것인지를 묻고 있으므로 Ms. Suarez가 작성한 이메일을 먼저 확인한다. 세 번째 지문인 이메일의 'I'd like to attend the meal next week'(1문단 1번째 줄)에서 Ms. Suarez가 다음 주에 있을 식사에 참석하고 싶어 한다는 첫 번째 단서를 확인할 수 있다. 그런데 식사를 어디에서 하는지 제시되지 않았으므로 회람에서 관련 내용을 확인한다. 두 번째 지문인 회람의 'next Friday, we will be celebrating the completion of training with dinner at Paolo's Grill'(2문단 1번째 줄)에서 다음 주 금요일에 Paolo's Grill에서의 만찬으로 교육 수료를 축하할 것이라는 두 번째 단서를 확인할 수 있다.

Ms. Suarez가 다음 주에 있을 식사에 참석하고 싶어 한다는 첫 번째 단서와 다음 주 금요일에 Paolo's Grill에서의 만찬으로 교육 수료를 축하할 것이라는 두 번째 단서를 종합할 때, Ms. Suarez가 다음 주에 교육을 수료한 다른 교육생들과 Paolo's Grill에서의 만찬에 참석할 것임을 알 수 있다. 따라서 (B) Attend a celebratory event with other trainees at Paolo's Grill이 정답이다.

Paraphrasing
celebrating ~ with dinner 만찬으로 축하하다 → celebratory event 축하 행사

어휘 **managerial** adj. 관리직의, 관리의 **for sale** 팔려고 내놓은

196-200번은 다음 이메일, 양식, 기사에 관한 문제입니다.

수신 Harvey Lee <h.lee@deltadawn.com>
발신 Sarah Holland <s.holland@deltadawn.com>
제목 등록
날짜 10월 20일

Harvey께,

어제 주간 회의에 참석하지 못해서 유감입니다, 그런데 연례 여행 박람회에 대한 준비는 어떻게 되어가고 있나요? 저희가 박람회에 등록하기 전에, 제가 확인해야 할 것이 있다는 것을 알려드리고 싶었습니다. 제가 정확하게 기억한다면, Ms. Tucker가 196우리의 홍보용 현수막의 크기는 우리가 얻을 부스의 종류에 맞아야만 한다고 말했습니다. 196그러나 저는 현수막의 치수를 받아보지 못해서, 어떤 종류의 부스를 선택해야 하는지 알 방법이 없습니다. 196치수가 어떤지 저에게 알려주시기 바랍니다. 제가 이 정보를 받으면 바로 등록을 진행할 수 있습니다.

또한 198모든 등록 비용은 회사 법인 카드로 지불될 것임을 알아두십시오. 감사합니다!

Sarah Holland 드림

come along 되어가다 **exposition** n. 박람회, 전시회 **register** v. 등록하다 **confirm** v. 확인하다 **promotional** adj. 홍보의 **measurement** n. 치수 **proceed** v. 진행하다

197/199-C등록 양식: 197/199-C/D제5회 연례 여행 박람회, Penner 전시관, 199-D11월 11-13일

이름	Sarah Holland	부서	마케팅
199-C회사	199-CDelta Dawn 여행사	전화	555-8376
주소	345번지 Union 빌딩, 23호, 뉴올리언스, 루이지애나주		

다음 선택 사항 중 하나를 선택하시기 바랍니다. 나열된 가격들은 오전 10시부터 오후 8시까지 3일간의 모든 행사에 대한 것입니다. 199-D참가자들은 박람회 시작 24시간 전에 각자의 부스를 설치해야 합니다.

대형 부스, 가로 6미터 세로 4미터 ·········· 967달러 ■
중형 부스, 가로 5미터 세로 3미터 ·········· 838달러 □
소형 부스, 가로 4미터 세로 2미터 ·········· 767달러 □

Penner 전시관은 모든 주요 신용카드와 온라인 결제를 받습니다. 198모든 신용카드 결제에는 5달러의 수수료가 적용됩니다. 결제가 확인되면, 네 장의 입장권, 행사 일정표, 그리고 참석하는 모든 업체의 목록을 포함하는 자료집을 받으실 것입니다.

be subject to ~의 대상이다, ~을 받다 **processing fee** 수수료

---

packet n. 자료집, 묶음

제5회 연례 여행 박람회가 또 한 번의 굉장한 성공을 누리다!

Penner 전시관의 제5회 연례 여행 박람회는 역사상 최대의 박람회였으며, 이는 지난 주말의 행사 동안 182개의 업체와 3만 명이 넘는 참가자들을 끌어들였다. 199-C/D여행사인 Broad Horizons사의 대표 Karen Moore는 "행사에 대한 반응은 대단했습니다."라고 말했다. 그녀는 199-A행사에서 그녀의 여행사가 상대적으로 작은 존재였음에도 불구하고 199-B아직도 그녀의 회사는 박람회 참석자들로부터 전화와 이메일이 쇄도하고 있다고 말했다.

행사 주최자인 Barbara Romano는 행사의 성공을 온라인 홍보와 소셜 미디어의 활용 덕분으로 여긴다. "199-A저희는 참여하는 모든 회사와 업체들이 온라인으로 광고하고 소셜 미디어에 박람회를 알릴 것을 강력히 권고했습니다." 200내년 여행 박람회 계획에 대해 질문을 받았을 때, Romano는 25개의 추가 부스가 이용 가능하게 될 것이라고 전했다.

resounding adj. 굉장한 **tremendous** adj. 대단한 **comparatively** adv. 상대적으로 **presence** n. 존재, 참석 **inundate with** ~이 쇄도하다, 밀려들다 **attribute** v. ~의 덕분으로 여기다 **urge** v. 강력히 권고하다, 촉구하다 **publicize** v. 알리다, 광고하다

196 육하원칙 문제

문제 이메일에 따르면, Ms. Holland는 Mr. Lee에게 무엇을 제공할 것을 요청하는가?
(A) 하루 대여 비용
(B) 광고물의 크기
(C) 장소의 위치
(D) 부스의 규모

해설 Ms. Holland가 Mr. Lee에게 무엇(what)을 제공할 것을 요청하는지를 묻는 육하원칙 문제이므로 질문의 핵심 어구인 Ms. Holland가 작성한 이메일에서 관련 내용을 확인한다. 첫 번째 지문인 이메일의 'the size of our promotional banners should be appropriate for the type of booth ~. But I haven't received the measurements for them'(1문단 4번째 줄)과 'Please let me know what they are.'(1문단 6번째 줄)에서 홍보용 현수막의 크기는 부스의 종류에 맞아야만 하는데 Ms. Holland가 현수막의 치수를 받아보지 못했다고 한 후, 이메일 수신인인 Mr. Lee에게 치수를 알려 달라고 했으므로 (B) The size of advertising materials가 정답이다.

Paraphrasing
measurements 치수 → size 크기
promotional banners 홍보용 현수막 → advertising materials 광고물

어휘 **dimension** n. 규모, 크기

197 주제/목적 찾기 문제

문제 양식의 목적은 무엇인가?
(A) 여행업계 모임에 등록하기 위해
(B) 광고 계약의 조건들을 명시하기 위해
(C) 창고 공간의 대여료를 지불하기 위해
(D) 무역 박람회 3일 입장권을 구매하기 위해

해설 양식의 목적을 묻는 목적 찾기 문제이므로 양식의 내용을 확인한다. 두 번째 지문인 양식의 'REGISTRATION FORM: Fifth Annual Travel Exposition'(제목)에서 제5회 연례 여행 박람회 등록 양식이라고 했고, 이름 및 회사와 같은 개인 정보가 기재되어 있으므로 (A) To register for a travel industry conference가 정답이다.

Paraphrasing
REGISTRATION 등록 → register for 등록하다
Travel Exposition 여행 박람회 → travel industry conference 여행업계 모임

어휘 **specify** v. 명시하다 **storage** n. 창고, 보관소

198 추론 문제 연계

문제 Delta Dawn 여행사는 무엇을 해야 할 것 같은가?
(A) 처리를 위한 추가 요금을 지불한다
(B) 추가 전시 부스를 예약한다
(C) 홍보용 현수막의 크기를 줄인다

해설 두 지문의 내용을 종합적으로 확인한 후 추론해서 풀어야 하는 연계 문제이다. 질문의 핵심 어구인 Delta Dawn Travel Agency에서 작성한 이메일을 먼저 확인한다.

첫 번째 지문인 이메일의 'all registration costs will be paid for with the company credit card'(2문단 1번째 줄)에서 Delta Dawn 여행사의 모든 등록 비용은 회사 법인 카드로 지불될 것이라는 첫 번째 단서를 확인할 수 있다. 그런데 회사 법인 카드로 지불하는 경우의 조건이 무엇인지 제시되지 않았으므로 양식에서 관련 내용을 확인한다. 두 번째 지문인 양식의 'All credit card payments are subject to a $5 processing fee.'(2문단 1번째 줄)에서 모든 신용카드 결제에는 5달러의 수수료가 적용된다는 두 번째 단서를 확인할 수 있다.

Delta Dawn 여행사의 모든 등록 비용은 회사 법인 카드로 지불될 것이라는 첫 번째 단서와 모든 신용카드 결제에는 5달러의 수수료가 적용된다는 두 번째 단서를 종합할 때, Delta Dawn 여행사가 법인 카드 결제에 대해 수수료를 내야 한다는 사실을 추론할 수 있다. 따라서 (A) Pay a surcharge for processing이 정답이다.

Paraphrasing
processing fee 수수료 → surcharge for processing 처리를 위한 추가 요금

어휘 surcharge n. 추가 요금

199 Not/True 문제 연계

문제 Ms. Moore에 대해 사실이 아닌 것은?
(A) 소셜 미디어에서 홍보할 것을 요청받았다.
(B) 그녀의 회사는 행사 참석자들로부터 많은 문의를 받았다.
(C) Delta Dawn 여행사의 것과 비슷한 사업체를 운영한다.
(D) 그녀의 부스가 11월 11일에 현장에서 조립되고 있었다.

해설 두 지문의 내용을 종합해서 풀어야 하는 연계 문제이다. 질문의 핵심 어구인 Ms. Moore에 대해 묻는 Not/True 문제이므로 Ms. Moore가 언급된 세 번째 지문인 기사를 먼저 확인한다.
(A)는 'her agency's comparatively small presence at the event'(1문단 3번째 줄)에서 행사에서 Ms. Moore의 여행사가 상대적으로 작은 존재였다고 했고 'We urged all participating companies and businesses to ~ publicize the expo on social media.'(2문단 2번째 줄)에서 참여하는 모든 회사와 업체들이 소셜 미디어에서 박람회를 알릴 것을 강력히 권고했다고 한 것을 통해, 행사에 참여한 Ms. Moore가 소셜 미디어에서 박람회를 알릴 것이 권고되었음을 알 수 있으므로 지문의 내용과 일치한다. (B)는 'her business is still being inundated with calls and e-mails from expo attendees'(1문단 4번째 줄)에서 아직도 Ms. Moore의 회사는 박람회 참석자들로부터 전화와 이메일이 쇄도하고 있다고 했으므로 지문의 내용과 일치한다. (C)는 세 번째 지문인 기사의 'Karen Moore, a representative from travel agency ~ said, "The response to the event was tremendous."'(1문단 2번째 줄)에서 여행사 대표 Karen Moore가 "행사에 대한 반응은 대단했습니다."라고 말했다고 했고 두 번째 지문인 양식의 'REGISTRATION FORM: Fifth Annual Travel Exposition'(제목), 'COMPANY', 'Delta Dawn Travel Agency'(표 2행 1, 2열)에서 Delta Dawn 여행사가 제5회 연례 여행 박람회를 위해 등록 양식을 작성했다는 것을 통해, Ms. Moore의 여행사와 Delta Dawn 여행사 모두 제5회 연례 여행 박람회에 참여했고 Ms. Moore가 Delta Dawn 여행사와 비슷한 사업체를 운영한다는 것을 알 수 있으므로 지문의 내용과 일치한다. (D)는 세 번째 지문인 기사의 'Karen Moore, a representative from travel agency Broad Horizons, said, "The response to the event was tremendous."'(1문단 2번째 줄)에서 여행사 대표 Karen Moore가 "행사에 대한 반응은 대단했습니다."라고 말했다고 했고 두 번째 지문인 양식의 'Fifth Annual Travel Exposition', 'Nov. 11–13'(제목), 'Participants are required to set up their booths 24 hours prior to the start of the fair.'(1문단 2번째 줄)에서 제5회 연례 여행 박람회가 11월 11–13일에 열리고 참가자들은 박람회 시작 24시간 전에 각자의 부스를 설치해야 한다고 했으므로 박람회에 참여한 Ms. Moore는 11월 11일의 24시간 전에 부스를 설치했음을 알 수 있다. 따라서 (D) Her booth was being assembled at a venue on November 11가 정답이다.

Paraphrasing
publicize 알리다 → do promotions 홍보하다

set up 설치하다 → assembled 조립되다

어휘 inquiry n. 문의, 질문

200 육하원칙 문제

문제 Barbara Romano는 무엇을 할 계획인가?
(A) 추후 행사에 판매자로 참여한다
(B) 내년 박람회에서 추가 공간을 제공한다
(C) Penner 전시관의 시설을 확장한다
(D) 온라인 광고 캠페인을 시작한다

해설 Barbara Romano가 무엇(What)을 할 계획인지를 묻는 육하원칙 문제이므로 질문의 핵심 어구인 Barbara Romano가 언급된 기사를 확인한다. 세 번째 지문인 기사의 'When asked about plans for next year's travel exposition, Romano reported that an additional 25 booths would be made available.'(2문단 3번째 줄)에서 내년 여행 박람회 계획에 대해 질문을 받았을 때 Romano가 25개의 추가 부스가 이용 가능하게 될 것이라고 전했다고 했으므로 (B) Offer additional spaces at next year's exposition이 정답이다.

Paraphrasing
booths 부스 → spaces 공간

어휘 vendor n. 판매자, 상인   enlarge v. 확장하다, 확대하다

Hackers
TOEIC
Reading

해커스토익 Hackers.co.kr

 무료 문법&
어휘 인강

 무료 매월
적중예상특강

무료 실시간 토익시험
정답확인&해설강의

무료 온라인
실전모의고사

무료 연습문제
해설 PDF

무료 매일
실전 RC 문제

해커스인강 HackersIngang.com

 본 교재
인강

 무료 진단고사
해설강의

 무료 실전문제
해설강의

 무료 단어암기
MP3

5천 개가 넘는
해커스토익 무료 자료!

대한민국에서 공짜로 토익 공부하고 싶으면

RC 정수진 · RC 이상길

토익 강의 `무료`

베스트셀러 1위 토익 강의 150강 무료 서비스,
누적 시청 1,900만 돌파!

토익 실전 문제 `무료`

토익 RC/LC 풀기, 모의토익 등
실전토익 대비 문제 제공!

LC 한승태 · RC 김동영

최신 특강 `무료`

2,400만뷰 스타강사의
압도적 적중예상특강 매달 업데이트!

고득점 달성 비법 `무료`

토익 고득점 달성팁, 파트별 비법,
점수대별 공부법 무료 확인

*미션 달성 시

전원
무료

가장 빠른 정답까지!

615만이 선택한 해커스 토익 정답!
시험 직후 가장 빠른 정답 확인

더 많은
토익 무료자료 보기 ▶